Scandinavian Europe

Andrew Stone

Tom Masters, Becky Ohlsen, Fran Parnell, John Spelman,
Andy Symington, Carolyn Bain, Simon Richmond

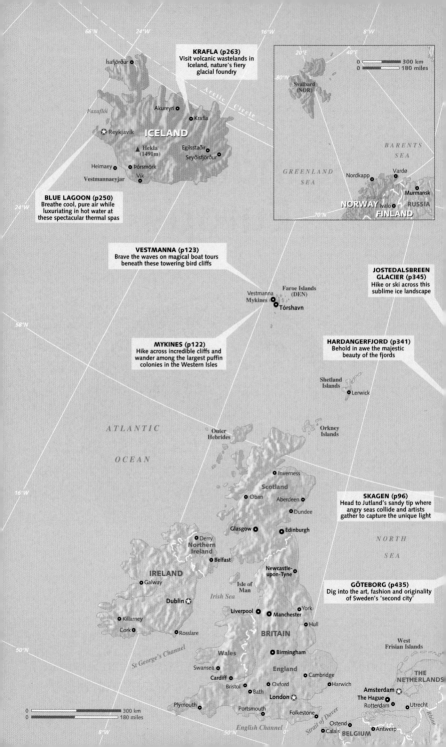

KRAFLA (p263)
Visit volcanic wastelands in Iceland, nature's fiery glacial foundry

BLUE LAGOON (p250)
Breathe cool, pure air while luxuriating in hot water at these spectacular thermal spas

VESTMANNA (p123)
Brave the waves on magical boat tours beneath these towering bird cliffs

JOSTEDALSBREEN GLACIER (p345)
Hike or ski across this sublime ice landscape

MYKINES (p122)
Hike across incredible cliffs and wander among the largest puffin colonies in the Western Isles

HARDANGERFJORD (p341)
Behold in awe the majestic beauty of the fjords

SKAGEN (p96)
Head to Jutland's sandy tip where angry seas collide and artists gather to capture the unique light

GÖTEBORG (p435)
Dig into the art, fashion and originality of Sweden's 'second city'

0   300 km
0   180 miles

Ísafjörður
Akureyri
Krafla
Reykjavík
ICELAND
Hekla (1491m)
Egilsstaðir
Seyðisfjörður
Heimaey
Þórsmörk
Vík
Vestmannaeyjar

Faxaflói

Arctic Circle

20°E
40°E
80°N
Svalbard (NOR)

BARENTS SEA

GREENLAND SEA

Nordkapp
Vardø
Murmansk
NORWAY
Ivalo
RUSSIA
FINLAND
70°N

Faroe Islands (DEN)
Vestmanna
Mykines
Tórshavn

Shetland Islands
Lerwick

ATLANTIC

OCEAN

Outer Hebrides
Orkney Islands

Inverness
Scotland
Oban
Aberdeen
Dundee
Glasgow
Edinburgh

NORTH SEA

Derry
Northern Ireland
Belfast
Newcastle-upon-Tyne

IRELAND
Galway
Dublin
Isle of Man
Irish Sea
Liverpool
Manchester
York
Killarney
Hull
Cork
Rosslare
BRITAIN

St George's Channel

Wales
Birmingham
Swansea
England
Cambridge
Cardiff
Harwich
Bristol
Oxford
Bath
London
Plymouth
Portsmouth
Folkestone
Ostend
Calais
BELGIUM

West Frisian Islands

THE NETHERLANDS
Amsterdam
The Hague
Utrecht
Rotterdam
Antwerp

English Channel

Strait of Dover

0   300 km
0   180 miles

68°N
24°W
16°W
8°W
58°N
24°W
16°W
50°N
8°W
50°N

ROVANIEMI (p195)
Cross the Arctic Circle, hit the awesome Arktikum museum, visit Santa in his official grotto and take a reindeer-sleigh or husky ride in Lapland

ST PETERSBURG (p220)
Tour the Hermitage and ornate Orthodox churches in Europe's fourth-largest city

LAKE SILJAN (p424)
Celebrate Midsummer in the heartland villages surrounding this watery paradise

HELSINKI (p143)
Explore this scenic harbour city for the latest in Finnish design, and home to hard-partying nightowls

TALLINN (p213)
Make a detour to party in this striking medieval town's long summer nights

COPENHAGEN (p38)
Visit Scandinavia's centre of cool and culture for first-rate food, great bars and easy living

To Svalbard (see Inset)

BARENTS SEA

NORWEGIAN SEA

Nordkapp
Vardø
Murmansk
Tromsø
Kandalaksha
RUSSIA
Lofoten Islands
Narvik
Ivalo
Lapland
Kiruna
Sodankylä
Bodø
Kebnekaise (2111m)
Gällivare
Rovaniemi
Mo i Rana
Kemi
Boden
Luleå
Oulu
Oulujärvi
Storuman
Skellefteå
Kajaani
Kokkola
FINLAND
Trondheim
Umeå
Ålesund
Östersund
Örnsköldsvik
Vaasa
Kuopio
Pyhäselkä
Dombås
Sundsvall
Seinäjoki
Keitele
Kallavesi
Galdhøpiggen (2469m)
Gulf of Bothnia
Jyväskylä
Mikkeli
Lake Ladoga
Balestrand
Glåma
SWEDEN
Päijänne
Saimaa
Lillehammer
Siljan
Tampere
Lappeenranta
Bergen
Bollnäs
Pori
Hämeenlinna
Kotka
Vyborg
Oslo
Borlänge
Gävle
Rauma
Turku
Kongsberg
Helsinki
Porvoo
St Petersburg
Stavanger
Moss
Västerås
Mälaren
Gulf of Finland
Skien
Eskilstuna
Uppsala
Kohtla-Järve
Narva
Karlstad
Örebro
Åland
Tallinn
Lake Peipsi
RUSSIA
Kristiansand
Vänern
Norrköping
Hiiumaa
Haapsalu
Skagerrak
Uddevalla
Linköping
ESTONIA
Skagen
Vättern
Saaremaa
Pärnu
Tartu
Pskov
Hirtshals
Huskvarna
Otepää
Frederikshavn
Göteborg
Jönköping
Aalborg
Borås
Gotland
Gulf of Riga
Sigulda
LATVIA
Jutland
Halmstad
Växjö
Kalmar
Ventspils
Århus
Öland
Riga
North Frisian Islands
Helsingør
Helsingborg
BALTIC SEA
Liepāja
HELSINKI (p143)
Esbjerg
Karlskrona
DENMARK
Lund
Malmö
Šiauliai
LITHUANIA
Odense
Copenhagen
Fyn
Zealand
Trelleborg
Klaipėda
Helgoland
Schleswig
Næstved
Bornholm
Gulf of Gdańsk
Svetlogorsk
RUSSIA
Minsk
East Frisian Islands
Kiel
Rødbyhavn
Rügen
Uznam
Łeba
Kaliningrad
Bremerhaven
Wismar
Rostock
Stralsund
Pomeranian Bay
Gdynia
Gdańsk
Hamburg
Świnoujście
BELARUS
Bremen
Elbe
Hrodna
Białystok
Baranavichy
GERMANY
POLAND
Bug
Pripet
Warsaw
Brest

To Svalbard (see Inset)

Scandinavia Highlights

Dramatic fjords, geothermal pools, light-dappled forests and snowcapped mountains – Scandinavia's landscapes alone offer enough highlights to fill an entire book; add to that a heritage rich in legends, vibrant cities that are home to the latest in modern cuisine, buzzing bars and innovative art and design and you're still barely scratching the surface. Here you'll find a choice selection of highlights by residents, travellers and Lonely Planet staff.

CHRISTIAN ASLUND

① MIDNIGHT SUN, NORWAY

Experience the midnight sun. In July most places above the polar circle are blessed with 24 hours of sunshine – if the weather is good of course. The Lofoten islands (p363) are spectacular at this time of year.

timeticktick, Traveller

MIDSUMMER'S DAY, SWEDEN

Midsommardag (p472) is *the* festival of the year and there's much revelry to be found all over Sweden – singing, dancing, beer drinking, strawberries and cream, schnapps, pickled herring and of course folk costumes and the traditional midsummer pole.

Sally Schafer, Lonely Planet Staff

ANDERS BLOMQVIST

PUFFINS, FAROE ISLANDS

If you're lucky enough to enjoy good weather on your trip then you really must visit the island of Mykines (p122). We'd heard that the island had some of the best opportunities for puffin-spotting but it was still a surprise to come across so many during our hike to the Mykinesholmur Lighthouse. We fell completely in love with these characterful birds – it was all we could do to resist the urge to pop a couple in our bag!

Joanna Potts, Lonely Planet Staff

RALPH HOPKINS

4 LONGYEARBYEN, SVALBARD, NORWAY

At 78°N this is the closest most travellers can get to the North Pole. This old mining town is bathed in 24-hour sunlight throughout summer. Polar bears outnumber residents and it's forbidden to leave the settlement without a rifle. The town (p379) boasts many 'most northerly' records.

Jolyon Philcox, Lonely Planet Staff

5 ICE & WHITE WATER, ICELAND

Rafting (p280) on the Austari Jökulsá is an exhilarating way to engage with Iceland's cool, aloof scenery. Green glacial water surges through mossy canyons, creating a roar of white water and setting the blood thumping in your temples. It's such a buzz to leap into a raft and shoot these narrow rapids; but just as wonderful are the wider stretches, where you can abandon ship and be swept along like a cork in the churning current.

Fran Parnell, Lonely Planet Author

CHRISTIANSHAVN (CHRISTIANIA), COPENHAGEN, DENMARK

Christiania (p43) serves as a sanctuary for anyone who is tired of the consumerism and routine of everyday life: with its many activities, shops, music venues, restaurants, parties and social gatherings, it is the true centre of Copenhagen. During the summer there are many parties and mini festivals, with music and just about any other kind of entertainment. During December there is the annual Christmas sale in Grå Hal (Grey Hall), which showcases just about everything Christiania has to offer.

Tue Rasmussen, SpottedbyLocals.com

KULTURHUSET, STOCKHOLM, SWEDEN

You feel like doing something, seeing something, feel a bit cultural? Kulturhuset (p403) is the place to get inspired or just to wander around. There's always something going on for everyone! This place really makes me happy, the exhibitions are cheap or for free and it always has interesting activities going on. It has several exhibitions, theatres, a cinema, cafes, music performances, an impressive library with lots of art books and newspapers from all over the world, a unique library for comics, an imaginative place for children and a creative place for teenagers called LAVA. It also arranges meetings with writers and much more.

Natalia Urbanska, SpottedbyLocals.com

CHARLOTTE HINDL

8 HURTIGRUTEN COASTAL STEAMER, NORWAY

This combination cruise ship and cargo hauler (p343) provides an amazing survey of Norway's coast-line, taking in fjords, fishing villages and craggy island chains. While most passengers are grey-haired tourists who embark on the six-day voyage as part of a package tour, independent travellers making shorter port-to-port journeys find it a first-rate way to explore the country, particularly when standing on deck under the aurora borealis.

John Spelman, Lonely Planet Author

ANDY ROUS

9 WILD FORESTS, FINLAND

When walking the forests of eastern Finland (p174), you know that bears are lurking somewhere out there, but seeing one is another matter. On this trip I decided to track the elusive creatures on a bear-watching trip. Venturing deep into the pinewoods to a purpose-built hide near the Russian border, we waited as the sun lowered in the evening sky, tense with anticipation. First, a fox loped across the clearing, then a golden eagle perched on a dead tree, but finally the king of northern beasts emerged, sniffing the air, and waving its shaggy head from side to side. A magical moment, to see this awesome creature on its home turf.

Andy Symington, Lonely Planet Author

INSPIRATIONAL SKAGEN, DENMARK

It's no accident that Skagen (p96) became an artists colony as its appeal is both ephemeral and constant. The lure of the light has drawn many packing paintbrushes or pens from far beyond its coastline; at times the blending colours of sky, sea and sand can simply inspire awe. Moving sands redefine this landscape – witness the buried church. For a more animated spectacle venture out to the shape-shifting headland of Grenen and watch the waters clash at the point where two seas meet.

Debra Herrmann, Lonely Planet Staff

© INSADCO PHOTOGRAPHY / ALAMY

HELICOPTER ISLAND HOPPING, FAROE ISLANDS

Purists may say that a nation of fishermen should be seen by boat, but I couldn't agree less. The real way to appreciate the Faroes is from the air (p135), as you get to see the islands' extraordinary geography from on high. Heavily subsidised, these trips are very affordable and run like buses between the islands three times a week, getting you long distances in minutes as well as amazing you with the views (get tactical when you board and grab a window seat!).

Tom Masters, Lonely Planet Author

RICHARD CUMMINS

FRANS LEMMER

12 SPECTACULAR LANDSCAPES, ICELAND

From the moonlike lava fields to the snow-covered mountains, there are really no words to describe the jaw-dropping, awe-inspiring beauty of Iceland (p229). Magnificent waterfalls too numerous to count. The contrasting white sea foam washing up on the windswept black sand beach at Vik. The gentle and comically stout Viking horses that must outnumber the people on this island. Watching mischievous seals frolic among black-streaked blue-tinted icebergs floating in a lagoon at Jökulsárlón (p268). I could go on and on but my words would never do it justice. We have already decided we will visit this astonishingly amazing place again.

ladyderinger, Traveller

JOHN ELK

13 BOG BODIES, DENMARK

Ever since reading Seamus Heaney's 'bog people' poems, about amazingly preserved, millennia-old bodies exhumed from Denmark's peat bogs, I've wanted to see them for myself. They didn't disappoint when I got to Denmark years later. The Grauballe Man (p83) near Århus is a compelling Bronze Age whodunnit, but the Tollund Man (p88), serene in his seeming slumber, really takes the breath away.

Andrew Stone, Lonely Planet Author

BERGEN, NORWAY

In Norway, do not miss Bergen (p331). It's about the most beautifully placed town in Scandinavia, surrounded by seven mountains that can all be viewed from the city centre.

srasmus, Traveller

14

CRAIG PERSHOUSE

SLOTTSSKOGSPARKEN, SWEDEN

There is so much to see and do in and around Göteborg, Sweden. One of my favourite places to visit is a park called Slottsskogsparken (p438). Situated in the middle of a thriving town, the park instantly transports you to the countryside. There are animals to look at, and penguins to laugh at, as well as lots of greenery and fresh, crisp Swedish air.

Clare Portman, Traveller

CHRISTER FREDRIKSSON

15

JONATHAN SMI

16 SOFO DISTRICT, SÖDERMALM, STOCKHOLM, SWEDEN

Södermalm (p403) remains Stockholm's hippest 'hood and the streets south of Folkungagatan (dubbed 'SoFo') are its heart and soul. Domain of the retro-chic brigade, it's the place for emerging local fashion, trippy op-shop finds, buzzing bars and restaurants. The last Thursday of every month is SoFo Nights, when many shops open till late and in-store gigs range from DJ sets to fashion shows.

Cristian Bonetto, Lonely Planet Author, Australia

ANDERS BLOMQV

17 BLUE LAGOON, ICELAND

Everybody says it, but for good reason – the Blue Lagoon (p250) is a must! I went twice in my four-day trip to Reykjavík, as it is perfectly located only 20 minutes from Keflavík airport. The Blue lagoon is perfect for a little postarrival and/or predeparture relaxation; just laze around and enjoy the warm thermal water and ethereal atmosphere. Just don't get your hair wet or take a bucket of conditioner as the briny water causes havoc with your hair.

Louise Vicente, Lonely Planet Staff

13

Contents

14 CONTENTS

Regional Map Contents

Iceland p230

Faroe Islands p112

Finland p141

Norway p292

Sweden p390

St Petersburg pp222-3

Tallinn pp214-15

Denmark p34

Destination Scandinavia

Describing Scandinavia as a region of stunning beauty is hard not to do but it's about as helpful as labelling Asia 'exotic'. Epic and spectacular it surely is, but these words do not begin to describe its northern European diversity.

Its visual signifiers for the uninitiated may include Nordic good looks, clean air, healthy outdoor fun and sparse populations, but they hardly do justice to this expanse of extremes.

True, the visitor will find some common features in the languages, culture and environment, in the inhabitants' bewildering dedication to preserved herring and their sinister partiality to bitter, salty liquorice.

And yes, the entire region knows winter's frigid, implacable dark as well as summer's short but spectacular lease, when the place bursts into life in a fevered celebration of nature, food culture and music.

But it's not all statuesque blondes and rugged fjords. Scandinavia spans the vast, Siberian north where polar bears roam; it includes in its grand dimensions the mighty peaks of Sweden and Norway and the gentle rural idyll of the Danish countryside. It encompasses elemental Iceland – nature's volcanic, glacial foundry – as well as the urbane and the cosmopolitan in vibrant Copenhagen and historic Helsinki.

In a single trip you can explore Stockholm's almost Venetian splendour and also acquaint yourself with the ancient ways of migrating reindeer and their herders through great swathes of virgin Lapland forest and lake.

Given all this geographic variety, to fully explore the region you may find yourself using more means of transport than Phileas Fogg, from plane, car and sleek modern train to bicycle, husky sled, parachute, snowmobile, Arctic icebreaker and canoe.

In fact getting around can be half the fun. The train and road networks just, well, work. They also offer great romance – the mountainous Oslo–Bergen train trip is one of the world's most scenic. This watery region also rewards maritime adventurers. Cruise on a ferry between Helsinki and Stockholm or Tallinn, sail all the way from Bergen in Norway to Seyðisfjörður in Iceland via the Faroe Islands, or catch Norway's famous *Hurtigruten* coastal steamer beyond the Arctic Circle.

Getting Started

Scandinavia is an easy destination to like. Efficient and approachable, it ingratiates itself to the traveller. The modern, plentiful and sleek transport infrastructure generally runs with the precision of an atomic clock, standards of living are high and other European languages (English in particular) are widely spoken. What's more, you'll never have to fight for elbowroom or decent hotel beds in the way you might elsewhere during Europe's summer.

What may surprise (and catch out) first time visitors is Scandinavia's diversity. This is a big region containing starkly different terrain, from the severe Arctic north to the expansive forests and mellow farmland further south.

Depending on the season even the same country can feel like a different place; midsummer has little in common with midwinter anywhere in Scandinavia, so it's worth being mindful of this fact when planning your trip.

The weather can be fickle much of the year, so you may well need to pack winter and summer clothes. A little forward planning will also help you squeeze the most out of your trip and make your budget go as far as possible in what can be a costly region to explore. It also pays to prepare for some long journeys as distances can be great, especially in the wilds of Arctic Lapland or the Icelandic interior.

It's worth noting too that the global financial slump is playing havoc with prices, and in some cases the existence of some businesses, particularly in Iceland so plan and travel with this in mind.

See Climate Charts (p486) for more information.

WHEN TO GO

Scandinavia has very distinct summer and winter seasons and extremely different climates, especially when comparing the north and the south. For most travellers, the best time to visit is undoubtedly summer – the brief window from June to August – when you can usually be guaranteed some fine weather

---

DON'T LEAVE HOME WITHOUT...

Sleeping bag or sleeping sheet – even if you're not camping you'll sleep cheaper in hostels with your own sheets, and a sleeping bag is a must in Iceland.

Insect repellent – for keeping mosquitoes and biting insects at bay in summer, especially in Finland and Iceland.

Hat and gloves – for those inevitable cold snaps.

Swiss army knife – essential multipurpose tool.

Watch – everything in Scandinavia runs on time!

Mobile phone – it's easy and inexpensive to get hooked up to local prepaid networks in Scandinavia and handy for making bookings or keeping in touch with other travellers.

Swimsuit and towel – for soaking in 'hot pots' or thermal springs in Iceland, post-sauna swims and spas in Finland, or for the beaches of southern Sweden and Denmark.

Credit card – Scandinavians love to pay with the plastic so it's handy to have a credit card for general use or emergencies; essential for car hire.

Eye mask, earplugs and torch – useful for sleeping on long summer nights; rowdy hostels; and finding your way in the dark.

Small padlock – For securing bags.

Sense of adventure and humour – vital for when those fjords and glaciers are lost in fog, when you just missed the last bus by 30 seconds, when you get the bill for that fancy restaurant 'splurge', and for making new discoveries away from the beaten track.

and long, long hours of daylight. This is the time when camping grounds and hostels are all open, summer festivals are in full swing and there's a buzz of excitement on the streets with lots of shiny, happy Scandinavians. The holiday season begins after Midsummer's Day (usually the third weekend in June). No matter what time of year, Scandinavia rarely feels overcrowded and hotels actually drop their rates in summer. The exceptions are camping grounds and family attractions, which are often packed.

Throughout the region, especially in the south, summer can be surprisingly warm. Spring and autumn – May, June and September – are also good times to visit. You can still expect fine, sunny days and fewer tourists. Beware though, temperature changes can be swift at this latitude – above the Arctic Circle you might find yourself wrapped in layers one day, but wearing only a T-shirt the next. Iceland and the western coast of Norway remain mild thanks to the Gulf Stream, but this also brings rain – hikers and campers should always carry waterproof gear.

Winter (and early spring in the far north) brings its own tourist season, where snowbound activities such as skiing and snowboarding, dogsledding, ice-fishing and snowmobiling are all the rage. Peak ski season in Lapland and the north is generally February to April, when the snow is deep and the gloomy depths of winter are fading away. True winter (November to January) is the time to view the aurora borealis, but otherwise travel in Scandinavia is a pretty cold, dark and miserable option, when the sauna becomes a sanctuary from the snow and much of the tourist infrastructure outside the main cities shuts down completely. Autumn (late August to September) when the forests briefly blaze with colour is the perfect time for hiking and cycling.

See the Climate & When to Go section of the country chapters for more information.

> The northern lights, or aurora borealis appear above the Arctic Circle (latitude 66°), are visible around the equinoxes (late September and March), and during the dark winter.

COSTS & MONEY

By any standards Scandinavia can be expensive, especially for accommodation, eating out and nightlife, but overall the daily costs of travel are comparable to northern Europe and in some cases cheaper than London or Paris. And there are plenty of free things for travellers to do: hiking, visiting churches, parks and gardens, national parks, fjords, glaciers and beaches which all cost nothing more than the effort to get there. Travel costs vary slightly from country to country – Denmark is probably cheapest, followed by Finland, Sweden, Norway and Iceland. Tallinn and St Petersburg are considerably cheaper than anywhere in Scandinavia.

Once you're in the region, your biggest unavoidable expense is finding a bed, but camping (you can pitch a tent in many places for free) and Scandinavia's excellent network of hostels can keep costs down. A night on the town can easily require a small bank loan, but shopping at markets, filling up on lunch buffets and buying alcohol from supermarkets or state-run liquor stores is relatively cheap. Little things like a cup of coffee, doing your laundry or storing your bag in a locker cost about €2 to €3.

> With a shattered economy thanks to a broke banking system, at the time of writing Iceland was considering adopting the euro. Check before you go.

Sightseeing costs can add up (museum admissions range from €3 to €12) but most capital cities offer good-value discount cards that give free admission to sights for a limited period. An ISIC student card or youth card can cut costs in half.

On a rock-bottom budget – camping or staying in hostels, self-catering, using a rail pass or bus transport – you can squeak by on €35 to €60 a day, which is pretty tight and doesn't allow for much amusement. Staying in private hostel rooms, guesthouses or two people sharing in a cheap hotel, eating at least one sit-down meal a day and seeing a few sights, expect to budget €75 to €90 per person per day. Add to that the 'nonessentials' –

shopping, drinking, activities such as cruises, tours and skiing – to come up with your own budget. Travel is a personal thing and everyone spends differently. With around €100 a day and some common sense you can travel pretty comfortably.

Norway, Sweden, Denmark, the Faroes and Iceland each have their own kroner, while Finland uses the euro. The easiest way to carry or obtain money in Scandinavia is with debit and credit cards – ATMs linked to international networks (Cirrus, Maestro, Eurocard, Plus, Visa and MasterCard) are common.

READING UP

There are lots of ways to pique your interest, pick up ideas and fuel the dream before your trip. Reading travel books, studying maps and surfing the internet will all help drive that wanderlust.

Books

Frost on My Moustache: The Arctic Exploits of a Lord and a Loafer by Tim Moore. In this contemporary account following 19th-century traveller Lord Dufferin, British writer Moore hauls himself across the North Atlantic, enduring chronic seasickness, cycling through Iceland's interior, taking a Viking longboat to Norway via the Faroes and finally landing in Spitzbergen. A great read.

The Scandinavian Cookbook by Trina Hahnemann. This Danish cook and caterer to the stars will have you drooling before you've booked your flight, with her 'rødgrød med fløde' (red berry pudding with cream) and other Nordic recipes.

Pole to Pole by Michael Palin. The former Monty Python star and his BBC crew travel from the North to South Pole along the 30° line of longitude. The early part of the trip conveniently includes the far north of Norway, Finnish Lapland, Helsinki, Tallinn and St Petersburg. Palin's casual journal-style narrative is typically funny and engaging.

To the Top of the World: Norway's Coastal Voyage by PE Johnson. The author takes the stunning coastal route from Bergen to Kirkenes, stopping in villages along the way. This is a must-read if you're planning this awesome sea journey.

A Year in Lapland: Guest of the Reindeer Herders by Hugh Beach. This is a unique peek into the lives of the Sami reindeer herders, written by an anthropologist who spent a year living among the Sami in the Jokkmokk district of Swedish Lapland.

In Forkbeard's Wake: Coasting Around Scandinavia by Ben Nimmo. With his sailing boat and a quest to retrace the steps of a Norse warrior, British writer Nimmo comes up with a quirky and funny collection of experiences that reveal a lot about Scandinavia and its people.

Just As Well I'm Leaving by Michael Booth. Not strictly about travel in Scandinavia, but this funny travelogue follows the 19th century travels of Denmark's favourite writer, Hans Christian Anderson.

Walpurgis night, an old pagan springtime ritual adopted by Christianity is celebrated with bonfires, carnivals, partying and drinking on the night of 30th April in Sweden, Finland and Estonia.

Websites

Go Scandinavia (www.goscandinavia.com) Site of the Scandinavian Tourist Board in North America; links to country sites, tour ideas.

Lonely Planet (www.lonelyplanet.com) This site has destination summaries on all Scandinavian countries, plus the Thorn Tree bulletin board for travellers.

Scandinavia News (www.scandinavianews.com) World News network site with English-language news and views from Scandinavia.

CLIMATE CHANGE & TRAVEL

Climate change is a serious threat to the ecosystems that humans rely upon, and air travel is the fastest-growing contributor to the problem. Lonely Planet regards travel, overall, as a global benefit, but believes we all have a responsibility to limit our personal impact on global warming.

FLYING & CLIMATE CHANGE

Pretty much every form of motorised travel generates CO_2 (the main cause of human-induced climate change) but planes are far and away the worst offenders, not just because of the sheer distances they allow us to travel, but because they release greenhouse gases high into the atmosphere. The statistics are frightening: two people taking a return flight between Europe and the US will contribute as much to climate change as an average household's gas and electricity consumption over a whole year.

CARBON OFFSET SCHEMES

Climatecare.org and other websites use 'carbon calculators' that allow travellers to offset the level of greenhouse gases they are responsible for with financial contributions to sustainable travel schemes that reduce global warming – including projects in India, Honduras, Kazakhstan and Uganda.

Lonely Planet, together with Rough Guides and other concerned partners in the travel industry, support the carbon offset scheme run by climatecare.org. Lonely Planet offsets all of its staff and author travel.

For more information check out our website: www.lonelyplanet.com.

TRAVELLING RESPONSIBLY

If you do want to limit the environmental impact of your journey here and you're coming from Europe, overland options by road or rail are a realistic possibility (with the exception perhaps of travel from the UK). Sea links are also plentiful. Travelling overland rather than air travel within the region is certainly going to be more pleasurable and immersive.

Travellers can have a potentially negative impact, particularly when hiking in forests or national parks. The Right of Common Access (Everyman's Right) is a code that applies in Norway, Sweden, Finland and Iceland, meaning you can walk virtually anywhere, provided you respect private land and behave responsibly. Stick to marked trails, leave flora and fauna alone, and always carry rubbish out with you – don't leave it on trails, at camp sites or around huts. Don't use soap or detergent when washing in streams (use a bucket).

If you're using wilderness huts that require paying a fee on an honesty system (as in Iceland), make sure you pay, and leave the huts as you found them. Don't make campfires on private land, and check local regulations before making a fire anywhere. Never cut down wood for a fire, use only dead wood.

When taking an organised tour, check the credentials and philosophy of the tour company. Are they using knowledgeable local guides? Do they have a responsible attitude to the environment and ecosystem?

Accommodation & Food

There's growing number of eco-minded places to stay and eat right across the region, minimising waste, energy consumption and focusing on ethical and healthy products. In many cases eco-accreditation schemes are making this easier, as with Denmark's Green Key mark (p37).

In many cities and towns, recycling bins are provided for plastics and paper etc, so use them. In Sweden and Finland there are collection points (at Alko stores in Finland, for instance) for glass and plastic bottles.

As polar ice retreats each year the fight to lay claim to the oil, gas and other resources locked under the north pole hots up. Norway, Denmark, Russia and Canada all lay claims.

For more on Scandinavian summer festivals, see www.efa-aef.org.

TOP 10

FAROE ISLANDS (DENMARK)   **SWEDEN**   **FINLAND**

TOP 10 MOVIES

Some of Scandinavia's most famous filmmakers in recent years have included Denmark's Lars von Trier, Finland's Aki Kaurismäki and Sweden's Lasse Hallström.

1 *101 Reykjavík* (2000; director Baltasar Kormákur)

2 *Before the Storm* (2000; writer and director Reza Parsa)

3 *The Seventh Seal* (1957; director Ingmar Bergman)

4 *Children of Nature* (1991; director Friðrik Thór Friðriksson)

5 *Leningrad Cowboys Go America* (1989; director Aki Kaurismäki)

6 *My Life as a Dog* (1987; director Lasse Hallström)

7 *Songs From the Second Floor* (2000; director Roy Andersson)

8 *The Dudesons Movie* (2006; directors Jukka Hilden and Jarno Laasala)

9 *The Man Without a Past* (2002; director Aki Kaurismäki)

10 *Under the Sun* (1998; director Colin Nutley)

TOP 10 FESTIVALS

1 **Tromsø International Film Festival** (mid-January) One of Norway's most exciting cultural festivals (p370).

2 **by:Larm** (mid-February) There are more than 350 gigs across the burgeoning music hub of Oslo (p382)

3 **May Day & Eve** (1 May) This is the Labour Day holiday everywhere except Denmark; 30 April is Valborgsmässoafton (p472) in Sweden and Vappu (p149) in Finland, with some of the biggest liquid-fuelled student celebrations imaginable.

4 **Midsummer** (around 23 June) Celebrated throughout Scandinavia in late June, this a national holiday; Midsummer Eve is usually a big party with bonfires and dancing.

5 **Roskilde Rock Festival** (late June/early July) The Roskilde is one of Europe's biggest and best rock-music festivals (p58) celebrated in Denmark.

6 **Copenhagen Cooking** (Denmark, July) Scandinavia's largest food festival with dozens of events taking place over one week at the end of August (p45).

7 **Copenhagen Jazz Festival** (July) Ten-day jazz fest (p44) held in Denmark's capital.

8 **Savonlinna Opera Festival** (July) A month of high culture in the stunning Olavinlinna Castle (p177) in Finland.

9 **Stockholm Pride** (late July/early August) Scandinavia's biggest gay and lesbian festival (p472) held in the Swedish capital.

10 **Þjóðhátíð** (early August) This crazy festival celebrating Iceland's independence is held on Vestmannaeyjar island a month after the rest of the country (p282).

Slow Travel

Yes, you can fly quickly around the region on low cost carriers but trust us, the journey really is half the fun in Scandinavia. The bus and rail (p31) transport works, it's relatively inexpensive and in most cases it is simply a pleasure, not least on some wonderfully scenic train journeys. Oh, and it also happens to be far greener.

If you're driving, particularly in the far north, keep your speed down. Domesticated reindeer herds frequently wander onto the road, and quite apart from your own safety, a dead reindeer is a financial loss to its owner.

Events Calendar

Throughout the region certain seasons and months are celebrated with festivals, events and general wassailing including midsummer and May Day. The summer months with warmer days and short nights are the busiest for festivities of all types but the colder months have their share of events too, centred often around Christmas, New Year and to a lesser extent Easter. See the Directory section in individual country chapters for additional details.

JANUARY

KIRUNA SNOW FESTIVALT　　last week in Jan
Based around a snow-sculpting competition, this annual Swedish event (www.kiruna.com/snow festival) draws artists from all over.

FEBRUARY

ÞORRABLÓT
This midwinter feast for the fearless includes delicacies such as putrid shark.

MARCH

VASALOPPET　　1st Sun in Mar
This ski race (www.vasaloppet.se) between Sälen and Mora, started in 1922, salutes Gustav Vasa's history-making flight on skis in 1521; it has grown into a week-long ski fest and celebration with different races, short, gruelling or just for fun.

EASTER FESTIVAL　　Easter
Thousands of Sami participate in reindeer racing, theatre and cultural events (www.saami-easterfes tival.org) in Norway's Karasjok and Kautokeino.

BEER DAY　　1 Mar
Dating back to the glorious day in 1989 when beer was legalised in Iceland. As you'd expect, Reykjavík's clubs and bars get particularly wild.

APRIL

SUMARDAGURINN FYRSTI　　1st day of summer
Optimistic Icelanders celebrate summer's advent on the first Thursday after April 19, with Reykjavík holding the biggest carnival-style bash.

JAZZKAAR　　mid-Apr
Jazz greats from all around the world converge on the picturesque Estonian city of Tallinn (www .jazzkaar.ee).

REYKJAVÍK ARTS FESTIVAL　　two weeks in Apr
The city is taken over by local and international theatre performances, films, lectures and music (www.artfest.is).

VALBORGSMÄSSOAFTON　　30 Apr
(WALPURGIS NIGHT)
This public holiday, a pagan holdover that's partly to celebrate the arrival of spring, involves lighting huge bonfires, singing songs and forming parades.

MAY

COPENHAGEN MARATHON　　mid-May
Scandinavia's largest marathon (www.sparta.dk) is on a Sunday in mid-May and draws around 5000 participants and tens of thousands of spectators.

JUNE

OLD TOWN DAYS　　early Jun
Week-long fest (www.vanalinnapaevad.ee) featuring dancing, concerts, costumed performers and plenty of medieval merrymaking.

SKAGEN FESTIVAL　　late Jun
Held over four days this festival (www.skagen festival.dk) in Skagen features folk and world music performed by Danish and international artists.

ROUND ZEALAND BOAT RACE　　late Jun
Held over three days this substantial yacht race circles the island of Zealand, starting and ending in Helsingør.

ROSKILDE FESTIVAL　　late Jun
Northern Europe's largest music festival (www .roskilde-festival.dk) rocks Roskilde for four consecutive days each summer. Advance ticket sales are on offer in December, and the festival usually sells out.

JULY

FREDERIKSSUND VIKING FESTIVAL
late Jun–early Jul

Held in Frederikssund over a two-week period. Costumed 'Vikings' present an open-air drama, followed by a banquet with Viking food and entertainment (www.vikingespil.dk).

COPENHAGEN JAZZ FESTIVAL
early Jul

This is the biggest entertainment event of the year in the capital, with 10 days of music. The festival (www.jazzfestival.dk) features a range of Danish and international jazz, blues and fusion music, with 500 indoor and outdoor concerts.

VARMAKELDA BONFIRE
1st weekend of Jul

Bonfires and hot-spring fun at Fuglafjørður on Eysturoy on Faroe

ÓLAVSØKA
28-29 Jul

Norway's largest and most exciting traditional festival, celebrating the 10th-century Norwegian king Olav the Holy, who spread Christian faith on the isles.

G!FESTIVAL
mid- to late Jul

The Islands' original and biggest music festival (www.gfestival.com) features local and international artists on Syðrugøta beach in Gøta.

STOCKHOLM JAZZ FESTIVAL
19-23 Jul

Held on the island of Skeppsholmen, this internationally known jazz fest (www.stockholmjazz.com) brings artists from all over, including big names like Van Morrison and Mary J Blige.

WORLD WIFE-CARRYING CHAMPIONSHIPS
early Jul

Finland's, nay, the world's premier wife-carrying event held in Sonkajärvi. Don't forget to bring the wife.

AUGUST

MEDIEVAL WEEK
early Aug

Find yourself an actual knight in shining armour at this immensely popular annual Swedish fest (www.medeltidsveckan.se) in Visby, Gotland's medieval jewel.

HAMLET SUMMER PLAYS
1st half of Aug

Theatre performances of Shakespeare's Hamlet take place at Kronborg Slot in Helsingør (www.hamletsommer.dk).

ÅRHUS FESTIVAL WEEK
last Fri in Aug

The 10-day Århus Festuge bills itself as Denmark's largest annual multicultural festival (www.aarhusfestuge.dk) and features scores of music performances, theatre, ballet, modern dance, opera, films and sports events at indoor and outdoor venues.

AIR GUITAR WORLD CHAMPIONSHIPS
early Aug

Finnish town Oulu's annual 15 minutes of fame.

OSLO INTERNATIONAL JAZZ FESTIVAL
Aug

Six days of amazing gigs (www.oslojazz.no).

NOTODDEN BLUES FESTIVAL
early Aug

Another seminal Norwegian music fest (www.bluesfest.no), featuring dozens of bands, such as the Fabulous Thunderbirds and Koko Taylor.

SEPTEMBER

COPENHAGEN COOKING
end Aug–early Sep

Scandinavia's largest food festival (www.copenhagencooking.dk) focuses on the gourmet end of the food spectrum.

REYKJAVÍK INTERNATIONAL FILM FESTIVAL

This annual occurrence sees blockbusters make way for international art films in cinemas across the city, and talks from film directors from home and abroad (http://isl.riff.is).

REYKJAVÍK JAZZ FESTIVAL

A fun yearly cultural event is the Jazz Festival (www.jazz.is) with jazz concerts around the city.

OCTOBER

ICELAND AIRWAVES
3rd week of Oct

This five-day event (www.icelandairwaves.com), in Reykjavík, is one of the world's most cutting-edge music festivals: don't expect to sleep.

NOVEMBER

STOCKHOLM INTERNATIONAL FILM FESTIVAL
mid- to late Nov

Screenings of new international and independent films, director talks, and discussion panels draw cinephiles to this important annual festival (www.stockholmfilmfestival.se); tickets go quickly, so book early if you're interested.

Itineraries
CLASSIC ROUTES

SCANDI IN A NUTSHELL
10 Days / Copenhagen to Copenhagen

The obvious place to start is well-connected **Copenhagen** (p38). Spend a couple of days here before catching a train to **Stockholm** (p395) for two days, then take the overnight ferry to **Helsinki** (p143). If you're in a hurry you could spend just the day in Helsinki and get the ferry back to Stockholm, especially if you book a cabin and get some sleep, or take in some Helsinki nightlife and a day trip to charming **Porvoo** (p155), Finland's second-oldest town, or even **Tallinn** (p213). If you're keen to experience some midnight sun (or northern lights in winter or early spring), jump on the overnight train to **Rovaniemi** (p195), on the Arctic Circle. Returning to Helsinki, and then Stockholm, take the overnight train to **Oslo** (p295) for the day, then the rail trip to **Flåm** (p343) and the combination boat/bus trip along the Sognefjord to **Bergen** (p331). From here, go to **Kristiansand** (p323) and take the ferry to **Hirtshals** (p98) in Denmark then return to Copenhagen via **Århus** (p80).

With three weeks or longer spend more time in Sweden, at **Malmö** (p426), **Göteborg** (p435) or **Kalmar** (p451), more time in Norway, with three days in **Fjærland** (p345) and **Geiranger** (p347), or more time in Denmark at **Odense** (p70) on the way back to Copenhagen.

A quick city-hop using the train or bus and ferries. If time is very short, you'll be limited to the capitals or you may have to skip Helsinki. Iceland is out of the question!

BALTICS & THE EAST
Three Weeks / Stockholm to Stockholm

Wild, expansive Finland, sharing a border and a fair slice of history with Russia, is quite unlike the Scandinavian ideal presented by Sweden, Norway and Denmark. This itinerary combines a brief tour of the Baltics with southern Finland.

Start in Stockholm so you can take advantage of the fantastic overnight **ferries** (p477) to **Helsinki** (p143), with their smorgasbord meals and all-night partying. After a couple of days in the Finnish capital take the ferry (1½ to three hours) to medieval **Tallinn** (p213) in Estonia. Returning to Helsinki (Tallinn can be done as a day trip if time is short), take the overnight sleeper train to **St Petersburg** (p220). You must have a visa, which can be obtained in Helsinki through specialist agents or at the Russian embassy (allow at least a week). After a few days in this enchanting, imperial city, return to Helsinki.

If it's summertime, take the train to the shimmering lakescapes of **Savonlinna** (p177), with its awesome medieval castle and opera festival, or **Kuopio** (p182), home of the world's biggest smoke sauna, or northwest to the dynamic, cultural city of **Tampere** (p167). At any time of year you could also take the overnight train to **Rovaniemi** (p195), for a reindeer-sleigh or husky ride cross the Arctic Circle and then visit Santa in his official grotto.

Finally, you can return to Sweden by taking the train to **Turku** (p157) then the ferry to Stockholm through the southern archipelago via the **Åland islands** (p162) – stop off at the islands for as long as you wish and maybe take a cycle touring holiday.

The Finnish capital Helsinki offers easy access to the charming and splendidly preserved old town of Tallinn as well as the cultural treasures of St Petersburg. Finland's own attractions include Father Christmas himself and the beautiful Lakeland.

ROADS LESS TRAVELLED

THE VIKING TRAIL
Four to Six Weeks / Copenhagen to Reykjavík

From **Copenhagen** (p38) head to the fascinating **Viking Ship Museum** (p59) in Roskilde, then on to Jutland and on to **Jelling** (p87) the Viking burial ground at **Lindholm Høje** (p93) before taking the ferry from **Hirtshals** (p384) to **Kristiansand** (p323) in Norway. Spend a few days in **Bergen** (p331) before taking the train to **Flåm** (p343) and the boat/bus trip along the **Sognefjord** (p343) to see the Viking ruins at **Balestrand** (p344). From Bergen, there is one summer ferry a week to Iceland. You can stop at the **Faroe Islands** (p110) and wait for the following week's ferry, visiting **Vestmanna Bird Cliffs** (p123 and **Mykines** (p122).

The ferry continues to Iceland, arriving at **Seyðisfjörður** (p266). From here the best route to Reykjavík is along the south coast past **Skaftafell Glacier** (p269). In Reykjavík, visit the **Saga Museum** (p240) and the Viking village of **Hafnarfjörður** (p251), take a trip to the **Blue Lagoon** (p250), then fly out. If you plan to return by ferry, take a bus trip through the interior to **Akureyri** (p257) then bus back to Seyðisfjörður on the Ring Rd. Remember there's only one ferry a week, so plan for either one or two weeks in Iceland.

Alternatively, fly direct from Copenhagen or Oslo to Reykjavík, and spend a week or more travelling around the Ring Rd.

The Viking Age had its beginnings in Denmark, Norway and Sweden in the 9th century AD, and it was a Viking who settled Iceland. You can still see the remains of Viking fortresses, burial grounds, longboats and churches, while exploring their ancient route.

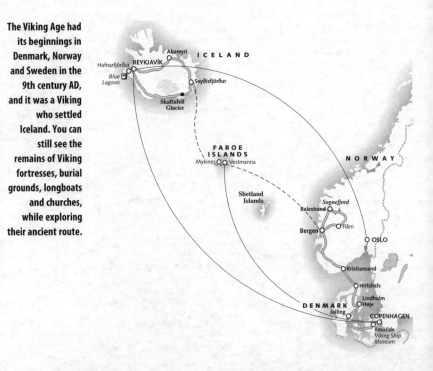

BEYOND THE ARCTIC CIRCLE   Three Weeks / Helsinki Return or Stockholm

There's something magical and foreboding about the Arctic Circle, the imaginary line at 66°33′N latitude where the sun never truly sets in midsummer
and never peeps above the horizon in winter. The remarkable clarity of light,
eerie remoteness, Sami culture and reindeer herds add to the mystique. A
trip to Nordkapp (the North Cape), the most northerly point in Europe,
is something of a spiritual pilgrimage for many travellers. This trip is best
tackled in summer (July and August), when the midnight sun shines and all
public transport is running, but September to March is the time to see the
northern lights and experience dogsledding and other activities.

Start at **Helsinki** (p143). Take the overnight train to **Rovaniemi** (p195),
visit the **Santa Claus Village** (p199) then take a bus up to the Sami village of
Inari (p201) to learn about the Sami way of life. From here there are direct
buses all the way to **Nordkapp** (p375) via Karasjok in Norway. After standing at the top of Europe with a glass of bubbly, catch the coastal steamer
Hurtigruten to the stunning **Lofoten Islands** (p363) with a possible stop in
Tromsø (p369). From here you can continue on the steamer all the way to
Bergen (p331), or get back to the mainland at **Narvik** (p361) and take the
train to **Kiruna** (p466) in Sweden. Unfortunately, the famous Ice Hotel
will have melted away by summer but you can still visit the Ice Hotel Art
Centre in a giant freezer!

From Kiruna head south to Haparanda where you can cross back into
Finland at the border town of **Tornio** (p200) – and have a round of midnight
golf before returning to Helsinki. Or go to Boden, perhaps via the Sami village
and museum of **Jokkmokk** (p465), and catch the train to Stockholm.

Go to the top of
Europe, visit a Sami
village, play golf
through two
countries – all
possible above
66°33′N.

TAILORED TRIPS

THE GREAT OUTDOORS

Scandinavia's pristine environment begs to be explored at close range – on foot, a bicycle, canoe, skis, skates or dogsled! This itinerary is not a point-to-point tour, but suggestions on where you can enjoy some of Scandinavia's best activities.

Spring/Summer

Flat, rural and not too big, Denmark is a haven for cycling. Popular areas include **Bornholm** (p65), **Funen** (p70) and the **Lake District** (p87) of Jutland. The

Finns are also avid cyclists. The best region for pedalling are the **Åland islands** (p162), but rides anywhere in the eastern Lakeland area and around **Turku** (p157) or **Oulu** (p191) are rewarding. In Sweden head for **Skåne** (p426) or **Gotland** (p455).

Hiking in national parks and forests is sensational in Scandinavia – Iceland and Lapland in particular have some of Europe's last great wilderness areas, and trails, huts and camping grounds are set up for walkers. In Iceland, the **Landmannalaugar-Þórsmörk trek** (p276) is an awesome walk through lava flows and lunar landscapes. In Finland, try **Oulanka National Park** (p195) and treks in **Karelia** (p188). In Sweden, the 450km **Kungsleden** (King's Trail, p468) is a major marked hiking route.

Other summer activities include canoeing, white-water rafting and fishing; see the Activities section of each chapter for information.

Winter/Spring

Skiing – both downhill and cross-country – is a national obsession in Finland, Sweden and Norway, and December to April is the time to go. The best resorts include **Lillehammer** (p329) in Norway, **Åre** (p462) in Sweden, and **Levi** (p203) and **Ruka** (p194) in Finland.

Think of Arctic Lapland and it's not hard to imagine mushing through the snow behind a team of huskies or a reindeer sleigh. While you'll have to budget big for these activities, Scandinavia is one of the best places in the world to do it. In Norway, try **Tromsø** (p369) or **Karasjok** (p377) and in Sweden head to **Kiruna** (p466). In Finland, **Rovaniemi** (p195) is a magnet for winter activities and there are husky farms organising safaris at **Muonio** (p203) and **Ivalo** (p201).

Other winter highlights to add to your itinerary should include the **Ice Hotel** (p466) at Jukkasjärvi near Kiruna in Sweden and the **Arctic Icebreaker cruise** (p199) at Kemi in Finland.

ON THE RAILS

With a Eurail or InterRail Pass (see p509) you can take to the rails and cover
a lot of ground in Scandinavia economically, including discounts on ferries.
To get the most out of your pass, long (possibly overnight) trips work well,
but you can always pay for shorter trips to reach more places. Consider
this megacircuit.

Start in **Copenhagen** (p38) and take the train via **Malmö** (p426) to **Stockholm**
(p395). Cruise on the overnight ferry (50% discount) to **Helsinki** (p143), then the
overnight train to **Oulu** (p191) or **Rovaniemi** (p195), almost at the Arctic Circle –
if you have time, consider stops in **Kuopio** (p182) or **Tampere** (p167). Rail down
the Gulf of Bothnia coast to **Vaasa** (p173), where you can catch a ferry across
to **Umeå** (p462) in Sweden. From here catch a train south to lakeside **Östersund**
(p461), then west to **Trondheim** (p353) in Norway.
You're now heading toward the spectacular fjords
of Norway, where you'll have to combine bus and
boat travel with the train. The rail line heads south
to **Dombås** (p330) and on to Oslo: detour on the
spectacular journey to **Åndalsnes** (p348). Take the
bus to **Geiranger** (p347) for the unmissable cruise
on **Geirangerfjorden** (p347).

From here you can return to the main train line
and Oslo, or make your way through the western
fjords to **Bergen** (p331) and take the spectacularly
scenic train to **Oslo** (p295) from there. Finally,
board the train for **Göteborg** (p435), Sweden, and
back to Copenhagen.

ISLAND-HOPPING BY BIKE

Southern Scandi is great for cycling and there
are some lovely islands and beaches waiting to be discovered. Grab a set of
wheels in **Copenhagen** (p38) and spend a couple of days exploring around
the Danish capital. Take the ferry out to **Bornholm** (p65) and spend a few
days cycling, stopping at island beaches and its wonderful, inexpensive
smokehouses. Back on the mainland (it's possible to take a ferry direct
to Sweden), head up to Kalmar, the jumping off point for the windmill-
crammed island of **Öland** (p453), a natural beauty with lots of good camping. Next stop is a ferry from Oskarshamn to
the large island of **Gotland** (p455), great for
cycling through prehistoric sites. Continue up
to **Stockholm** (p395), which has its own amazing archipelago of some 24,000 islands. About
70km north, the port of Grisslehamn is the
place for the short ferry hop across to **Eckerö**
(p166) in Finland's Åland islands, though a
much easier option is to take the ferry direct
from Stockholm to **Mariehamn** (p163), the island
capital. You could spend a week or more cycling and camping on this beautiful island archipelago, before taking the ferry across to **Turku**
(p157) in Finland. Explore Finland's beautiful
southeast coast and beaches before taking the
train to **Helsinki** (p143) and selling your bike!

Denmark

Denmark is the bridge between Scandinavia and northern Europe. To the rest of Scandinavia, the Danes are fun loving, frivolous, party animals, with relatively liberal, progressive attitudes. Their culture, food, architecture and appetite for conspicuous consumption owes as much, if not more, to their German neighbours to the south, than their former colonies – Sweden, Norway and Iceland to the north.

Denmark's capital, Copenhagen, is one of the most charming and accessible cities in northern Europe, with excellent museums, shops, bars, nightlife and, in particular, restaurants. Elsewhere, though there are other cities of interest such as Odense and Århus, Denmark's chief appeal lies in its gently idyllic countryside, coastline and historic sights such as Neolithic burial chambers; the bodies of well-preserved Iron Age people exhumed from their slumber in peat bogs; and atmospheric Viking ruins and treasures.

FAST FACTS

- **Area** 43,075 sq km
- **Capital** Copenhagen
- **Currency** Danish krone (Dkr): €1 = Dkr7.44; US$1 = Dkr5.61, UK£1 = Dkr8.29, $A1 = Dkr4.06, CA$1 = Dkr4.66, NZ$1 = Dkr3.16, ¥100 = Dkr5.76
- **Famous for** Hans Christian Andersen, the *Little Mermaid*, bacon, Carlsberg beer, marauding Vikings
- **Official Language** Danish
- **Phrases** *jah/nie* (yes/no), tak *(thanks)*, farvel (goodbye), *skål* (cheers)
- **Population** 5.45 million
- **Telephone Codes** country code ☎ 45; international access code ☎ 00
- **Visa** not required for citizens of the EU, USA, Canada, Australia and New Zealand (see p106)

HIGHLIGHTS

- Soak up the dynamic city life of **Copenhagen** (p38), packed with historical interest, cool cafes, cutting-edge design, cosy bars and lively clubs.
- Taste the best of the modern Scandinavian culinary revolution in Copenhagen's excellent **restaurants** (p47), or elsewhere in the country's historic and atmospheric inns.
- Soak up the history in outstanding Renaissance castles, such as Hamlet's **Helsingør** (p55).
- Escape to empty beaches and extensive forests, and relax beside picture-postcard harbours on the idyllic island of **Bornholm** (p65).
- Watch angry seas collide above luminous **Skagen** (p96), on Denmark's slender northern tip.

ITINERARIES

- **One week** You could comfortably spend five days in Copenhagen seeing the museums and enjoying the nightlife and excellent restaurants. A trip north along the coast to the magnificent modern art museum, Louisiana, and then further north still to Helsinborg Slot, before returning south via Frederiksborg Slot would be a great way to spend the other two days. If the weather is nice, head for the north coast of Zealand for historic fishing villages and gorgeous sandy beaches.
- **Two weeks** After time in Copenhagen, a quick catamaran ride will take you to the Baltic island of Bornholm, said to be the sunniest part of Denmark, and great for cycling and beaches. Alternatively head east, stopping off on the island of Fyn to see Hans Christian Andersen's birthplace in Odense. Continue east to the Jutland peninsula for magnificent seascapes and the bustling, cosmopolitan city of Århus.

CLIMATE & WHEN TO GO

Denmark has a relatively mild climate. May and June can be a delightful time to visit: the countryside is a rich green (although rain and chilly winds can never be ruled out). July to August is peak tourist season with many open-air concerts, plenty of street activity and beach basking and potential savings on accommodation, as some business-oriented hotels drop their rates. Autumn is pleasant. October can be a visual feast of golden colours in wooded areas and still relatively mild. Winter is cold, dark, wet, or freezing, and often all four.

HISTORY

Denmark has a wealth of sites for people interested in the Neolithic past. First settled around 4000BC, most probably by prehistoric hunter-gatherers from the south, it has been at the centre of Scandinavian civilisation ever since, and there are plenty of reminders of that past in the shape of the ancient burial chambers which pepper the countryside and the traces of fortifications at, for example, Trelleborg (see p61).

The Danes themselves are thought to have migrated south from Sweden in around AD 500 but it was the descendants of what were, initially, a peaceful, farming people, that are better known today. What we think of as modern Denmark was an important trading centre within the Viking empire and, again, the physical evidence of this part of the country's history is to be found throughout the country today. In the late 9th century, warriors led by the Viking chieftain, Hardegon, conquered the Jutland peninsula. The Danish monarchy, Europe's oldest, dates back to Hardegon's son, Gorm the Old, who reigned in the early 10th century. Gorm's son, Harald Bluetooth, completed the conquest of Denmark and spearheaded the conversion of the Danes to Christianity; his story and his legacy is well showcased in the tiny, historical hamlet of Jelling (p87). Successive Danish kings sent their subjects to row their longboats to England and conquer most of the Baltic region. They were accomplished fighters, swordsmiths, shipbuilders and sailors, qualities well-illustrated at the excellent Viking Ship Museum in Roskilde (p58).

In 1397 Margrethe I of Denmark established a union between Denmark, Norway and Sweden to counter the influence of the powerful Hanseatic League that had come to dominate the region's trade. Sweden withdrew from the union in 1523 and over the next few hundred years Denmark and Sweden fought numerous border skirmishes and a few fully fledged wars, largely over control of the Baltic Sea. Norway remained under Danish rule until 1814.

In the 16th century the Reformation swept through the country, accompanied by church burnings and civil warfare. The fighting ended

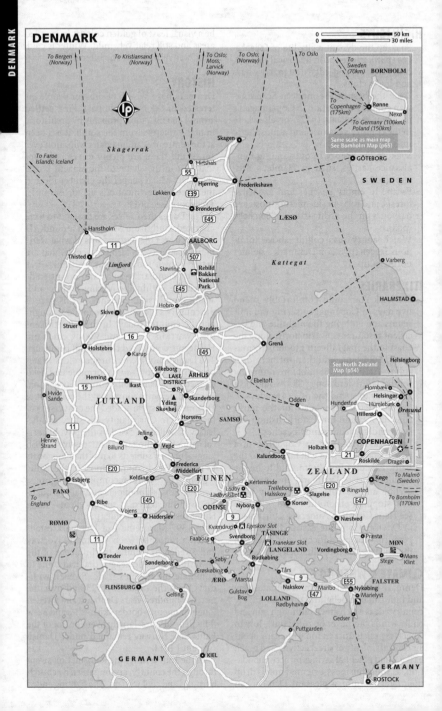

in 1536, the Catholic Church was ousted and the Danish Lutheran Church headed by the monarchy established.

Denmark's Golden Age was under Christian IV (1588–1648), with Renaissance cities, castles and fortresses flourishing throughout his kingdom. A superb example is Egeskov (p75) on Funen. In 1625 Christian IV, hoping to neutralise Swedish expansion, entered an extremely ill-advised and protracted struggle known as the Thirty Years' War. The Swedes triumphed and won large chunks of Danish territory. Centuries worth of Danish kings and queens are laid to rest in sarcophagi on dramatic display at Roskilde Cathedral (p58).

Literature, the arts, philosophy and populist ideas flourished in the 1830s, and Europe's Year of Revolutions in 1848 helped inspire a democratic movement in Denmark, which overnight, and in typically orderly Danish fashion, adopted male suffrage and a constitution on 5 June 1849, forcing King Frederik VII to relinquish most of his power and become Denmark's first constitutional monarch. Denmark lost the Schleswig and Holstein regions to Germany in 1864.

Denmark remained neutral throughout WWI and also declared its neutrality at the outbreak of WWII. Nevertheless, on 9 April 1940, the Germans invaded, albeit allowing the Danes a degree of autonomy. For three years the Danes managed to walk a thin line, running their own internal affairs under Nazi supervision, until in August 1943 the Germans took outright control. The Danish Resistance movement mushroomed and 7000 Jewish Danes were smuggled into neutral Sweden.

Although Soviet forces heavily bombarded the island of Bornholm, the rest of Denmark emerged from WWII relatively unscathed. Postwar Social Democrat governments introduced a comprehensive social welfare state in the postwar period, and still today Denmark provides its citizens with extensive cradle-to-grave social security.

Denmark joined NATO in 1949, and the European Community, now the EU, in 1973. The Danes offer tepid support for an expanding EU. In 1993 they narrowly voted to accept the Maastricht Treaty, which established the terms of a European economic and political union, only after being granted exemptions from common-defence and single-currency provisions. They also voted not to adopt the euro in 2000.

In 2004 the country's most eligible bachelor Crown Prince Frederik married Australian Mary Donaldson in a hugely popular and exhaustively covered fairytale wedding. They now have two children.

It has not all been fairytales though. Accustomed to being a blameless paragon of international virtue, Denmark has experienced harsh criticism from some unusual quarters. Critics say its increasingly tough immigration laws are proof of creeping xenophobia and racism, earning it a rebuke from the European Council.

This seemed to have little impact on the popularity of their long serving prime minister, Anders Fogh Rasmussen, who was returned to power (most likely for the last time in 2007, not least because the economy tanked and Denmark's housing bubble popped as the world entered a slump).

PEOPLE

Denmark's 5.45 million people are a generally relaxed bunch. It takes a lot to shock a Dane, and even if they are, they probably won't show it. This was the first country in the world to legalise same sex marriages, and became (in)famous during the 1960s for its relaxed attitudes to pornography.

They are an outwardly serious people, yet with an ironic sense of humour. They have a strong sense of family and an admirable environmental sensitivity. Above all, they are the most egalitarian of people – they officially have the smallest gap between rich and poor in the world – proud of their social equality in which none have too much or too little.

RELIGION

The vast majority of Danes are members of the National Church of Denmark, an Evangelical Lutheran denomination (a proportion of each Dane's income tax goes directly to the church), but less than 5% of the population are regular churchgoers.

ARTS
Literature

By far the most famous Danish author is Hans Christian Andersen. Other prominent Danish writers include religious philosopher Søren Kierkegaard, whose writings were a forerunner of existentialism, and Karen Blixen, who penned Out of Africa and Babette's Feast, both made into acclaimed movies in the 1980s. One of Denmark's foremost contemporary authors is Ib Michael, a magic realist who has seen many of his novels and poems translated into English.

Architecture & Design

For a small country Denmark has had a massive global impact in the fields of architecture and design. Arne Jacobsen, Verner Panton, the recently deceased Jørn Utzon and Hans J Wegner are now considered among the foremost designers of the 20th century, and the tradition of great furniture and interior design remains strong in the country's design schools, museums and independent artisanal workshops. Copenhagen is the country's architectural and design shop window with museums such as the Danish Design Center (p42) and Opera House (p44), maintaining the country's enviable international reputation.

Cinema & TV

As with its design prowess, Denmark's success and influence in the realm of cinema has far exceeded what you might expect from a country of this size. Denmark has scored regular Oscar success with films such as Babette's Feast, Gabriel Axel's adaptation of a Karen Blixen novel; Bille August's Pelle the Conqueror; and more recently a trio of statues for short films.

The last decade or so has seen director Lars von Trier stir up repeated controversy – and win numerous international film prizes – with his challenging films such as Breaking the Waves, Dancer in the Dark and Dogville, starring Nicole Kidman. Von Trier was a leading member of the Dogme95 film movement with its famous list of cinematic dos and don'ts. The movement scored notable international hits such as Thomas Vinterberg's Festen (The Party) and Lone Scherfig's Italian for Beginners. Another influential artistic figure is film director and experimental documentary maker Jørgen Leth.

Visual Arts

Before the 19th century, Danish art consisted mainly of formal portraiture, exemplified by the works of Jens Juel (1745–1802). A Golden Age ushered in the 19th century with such fine painters as Wilhelm Eckersberg (1783–1853) and major sculptors such as Bertel Thorvaldsen (1770–1844), although he chose to spend most of his life in Rome.

Later in the century the Skagen School evolved from the movement towards outdoor painting of scenes from working life, especially of fishing communities on the northern coasts of Jutland and Zealand. Much of it is exhibited at the Skagens Museum (p96). Leading exponents of the Skagen School were PS Krøyer and Michael and Anna Ancher. In the mid-20th century, a vigorous modernist school of Danish painting emerged, of which Asger Jorn (1914–73) was a leading exponent. Many of his works are on display at the art museum in Silkeborg (p87).

Denmark's towns and cities contain a vibrant selection of home-grown and international contemporary art; even the smallest towns can surprise. Two of the best, small art museums and galleries outside the capital are Faaborg's Art Museum (p76) and the Aros (p81) gallery in Århus. And then, of course, there is the magnificent Louisiana Museum of Modern Art (p53), on the coast north of Copenhagen.

Theatre & Dance

The Royal Danish Ballet, which performs in Copenhagen's **Royal Theatre** (☎ 3369 6969; Kongens Nytorv) from autumn to spring, is regarded as northern Europe's finest. Copenhagen is also home to several contemporary dance troupes and festivals.

ENVIRONMENT

If you want to travel sustainably Denmark is the place to do it. Creating a modest carbon footprint and minimising your environmental impact have been made very easy indeed. For starters there's the excellent public transport network and the fact that it's easy to cycle almost everywhere.

Arrive in Denmark by plane at Copenhagen airport you will see the country's major contribution to improving the global environment: a row of wind turbines, technology the country has made its own. Danes also lead the way in their consumption of organic produce, recycling and environmentally friendly transport: more Danes commute by bicycle than any other European nationality.

The Land

The Danish government has initiated an ambitious plan to restore the wetlands and re-establish marshes and streams throughout the country. In November 2009 the eyes of the world were on Copenhagen as world leaders gathered to formulate a new, global climate agreement to replace the one reached in Kyoto.

Wildlife

Still commonly seen in Denmark are wild hare, deer and many species of birds, including magpies, coots, swans and ducks. Returning the wetlands should help endangered species such as the freshwater otter make a comeback. The Danes are particularly proud of their eagles – they have two pairs

THE KEY TO TRAVELLING GREEN

Denmark's hospitality industry is also trying to help you limit your impact on the environment. More than 80 properties have so far earned Green Key certification from the larger hotels, to summer cottages, camping sites and even the odd restaurant. There are 56 separate criteria for certification, including use of chemicals, water and energy consumption, waste recycling and food preparation (with points for local sources).

A useful website for visitors interested in ecological farm stays is www.ecoholiday.dk, which lists 12 farms throughout Denmark that don't use pesticides or chemical fertilisers and which often allow guests to get involved in farm life including feeding the animals. They can make excellent family destinations.

of golden eagles who live in Lille Vildemose, close to Aalborg on Jutland, and are national celebrities. Twitchers may also spot kingfishers *(isfugl)*, black storks (sort stork) and European honey buzzards *(hvepsevåge)*.

FOOD & DRINK

Staples & Specialities

Proud of it though they are, even the Danes would concede that their traditional cuisine is rather heavy and unhealthy. They eat a great deal of meat, mostly pork and usually accompanied by something starchy and a gravy-like sauce. However, one Danish speciality has conquered the world: smørrebrød, or the Danish open sandwich.

Other commonly encountered dishes include *frikadeller* (meatballs), *flæskesteg* (roast pork with crackling, actually it's mostly crackling), *hvid labskovs* (beef and potato stew) and *hakkebøf* (beefburger with fried onions). The Danes are great smokers too; you'll find smoke houses preserving herring, eel, cod livers, shrimp and other seafood all around the coast of the country. The most renowned are on Bornholm.

Where to Eat & Drink

More brutal honesty regarding the Danish food scene: the modern Danish food revolution pretty much begins and ends in

Copenhagen. Beyond the capital most restaurant food is limited to pizza and kebabs, and perhaps the odd second-rate Italian, Chinese or Thai place.

That said, outside of Copenhagen you can still find great Danish home cooking in the country's traditional *kroer* or 'inns' and Århus and Odense do also have one or two notable, international-standard restaurants. Eating out here is not cheap, however. You can expect to pay Dkr250 for a decent three-course meal in the capital, rising easily to Dkr900 in the best places.

Drinks

The Danes are enthusiastic drinkers, and not just of their world famous domestic beers. The most popular spirit in Denmark is caraway-spiced Aalborg aquavit; it's drunk straight down as a shot, followed by a chaser of beer. Øl (beer), vin (wine) and spirits are reasonably cheap and easily bought compared to other Scandinavian countries.

COPENHAGEN

pop 1.5 million

Stockholm might be more grandiose and Oslo more spectacularly located, but there is no more charming, exciting and stimulating city in Scandinavia than Copenhagen.

This thousand-year-old harbour town has managed to retain much of its historic charm – with its copper spires, cobbled squares and pastel-coloured gabled town houses – while at the same time being everything a modern metropolis should be, home to cutting-edge designers, a super efficient transport system and an impressive environmental conscience. It has intriguing, independent shops galore; excellent restaurants and bars; world-class museums and art collections; and brave new architecture. This is also a royal city, home to the beloved Queen Margrethe II and her family.

And just when you think you've got to know the city's urban delights, you discover beautiful sandy beaches, wooded parks and elegant lakes just minutes away.

HISTORY

For more millennia than anyone can be sure of, Copenhagen was a fisherman's settlement on the shores of what we now call the Øresund Straits, the narrow belt of water between Denmark and Sweden.

Wendish pirates, who marauded the coast in the 12th century, prompted the locals, led by Bishop Absalon, to build a fort on a small island in the harbour – where the modern day Danish parliament stands on Slotsholmen; you can still see the foundations of the original fort in the cellar museum.

The city of København ('købe' means 'to buy', 'havn' is 'harbour') gradually grew to the north of Slotsholmen, where the restaurants of Gammel Strand now stand, founded on the wealth that came from the herring caught by the local fishermen. But it wasn't until the 15th century that Copenhagen took over as the capital of Denmark from Roskilde.

Denmark's great Renaissance king, Christian IV (1588–1648), transformed Copenhagen into an impressive capital. From there he controlled much of Scandinavia – with numerous ambitious buildings including Rosenborg Slot and the Rundetårn. Eventually Christian IV brought the country to its knees with overspending and reckless foreign forays.

By the early 19th century the once mighty Danish empire was greatly diminished. Twice in the early 19th century the British navy bombarded the city but its people bounced back with a cultural Golden Age, led by the likes of Hans Christian Andersen and Søren Kierkegaard.

ORIENTATION

Copenhagen airport is just 12 minutes away from the city centre by trains that terminate at Central Station (Hovedbanegården). Just across the street, to the east of the station's main entrance, is Denmark's number one tourist attraction, Tivoli Gardens; beyond that is the town hall square (Rådhuspladsen), from where the city's main shopping street, Strøget (actually several connecting streets and squares), leads to the city's other main square, Kongens Nytorv. From here the ever-bustling quayside of Nyhavn, with its countless cafes, bars and restaurants, leads to the harbour.

Meanwhile, if you exit the station to the west you arrive in one of the city's more lively nightlife and shopping quarters, Vesterbro. North, across the shallow city lakes (originally planned as a fire break), is another lively shopping and nightlife district, Nørrebro.

INFORMATION
Bookshops
Foreign newspapers are available at the Central Station, in the Illum and Magasin du Nord departments stores and a few newsstands on Strøget.

Nordisk Korthandel (www.scanmaps.dk; Studiestræde 26-30; 10.30am-5.30pm Mon-Fri, 9.30am-3pm Sat) Offers a superb but pricey collection of travel guides and maps.

Discount Cards
Copenhagen Card (24hr card adult/child Dkr199/129, 72hr card Dkr429/249, adult card covers 2 children under 10yr) Secures unlimited travel on buses and trains around Copenhagen and North Zealand, and on the city's waterbuses. It also gives free or discounted admission to 60 of the region's museums and attractions. Cards are sold at the Wonderful Copenhagen tourist office, Central Station, major Danske Statsbaner (DSB) stations and at many hotels, camping grounds and hostels. Be aware though that several of the city's attractions are either free or at least free one day of the week. Visit www.visitcopenhagen.dk for more information.

Internet Access
Boomtown (33 32 10 32; www.boomtown.net; Axeltorv 1-3; per hr Dkr35; 24hr;)
Hovedbiblioteket (33 73 60 60; 15 Krystalgade; 10am-7pm Mon-Fri, 10am-2pm Sat) A public library offering free internet access on four computers.

Laundry
Istedgades Møntvask (Istedgade 45; wash & dry 10kg load Dkr40; 7am-9pm)

Left Luggage
Central Station (per 24hr small/large locker Dkr25/35, maximum 72hr; 5.30-1am Mon-Sat, 6-1am Sun) Lockers are in the lower level near the Reventlowsgade exit.

Medical Services
Frederiksberg Hospital (38 16 38 16; Nordre Fasanvej 57) West of the city centre, has a 24-hour emergency ward.
Steno Apotek (Vesterbrogade 6c; 24hr) Pharmacy opposite Central Station.

Money
Banks, all of which charge transaction fees, are found throughout the city centre. Banks in the airport arrival and transit halls are open 6am to 10pm daily.

The **Forex exchange booth** (Central Station; 7am-9pm) has the lowest fees but you will find other exchange shops all along Strøget.

You'll find 24-hour, cash-exchange ATMs that exchange all major foreign currencies for Danish kroner, minus a hefty Dkr25 to Dkr30 fee, at **Den Danske Bank** (Central Station) and **Nordea** (Axeltorv).

Post
Central Station Post Office (8am-9pm Mon-Fri, 10am-4pm Sat & Sun)
Post Office (Købmagergade 33; 10am-5.30pm Mon-Fri, to 2pm Sat) Offers poste-restante services.

Tourist Information
Wonderful Copenhagen (70 22 24 42; www .visitcopenhagen.dk; Vesterbrogade 4a; 9am-4pm Mon-Fri, to 2pm Sat Jan-Apr & Sep-Dec, 9am-6pm Mon-Sat May-Jun, to 8pm Mon-Sat, 10am-6pm Sun Jul & Aug) This tourist office distributes the informative *Tourist in Copenhagen* as well as *Copenhagen This Week*, a free city map, and brochures covering all the regions of Denmark.

Travel Agencies
Kilroy Travels (33 11 00 44; www.kilroytravels.com; Skindergade 28; 10am-5.30pm Mon-Fri, to 2pm Sat)
Wasteels (33 14 46 33; Skoubogade 6; 9am-5pm Mon-Fri, 10am-noon Sat)

SIGHTS
One of the great things about Copenhagen is its accessibility and size. You can walk across the city centre in an hour, and travel further with great ease thanks to the cycle paths, metro, trains and buses, all of which means you can pack in many of the sights in two days.

Tivoli
Copenhagen's historic **amusement park** (33 15 10 01; www.tivoli.dk, in Danish; adult/child Dkr85/45; 11am-11pm Sat-Thu, 11-1am Fri mid-Apr–mid-Jun & mid-Aug–mid-Sep, 11am-midnight Sun-Thu, 11-1am Fri & Sat mid-Jun–mid-Aug) has been Denmark's number one tourist attraction pretty much since the day it opened more than 160 years ago. It's not Disneyland but Tivoli has an innocent, old-fashioned charm, particularly after dark when its wonderful illuminations work their magic. There are flower beds, food pavilions, amusement rides, carnival games and various stage shows. Tivoli has many restaurants of varying quality and price levels, though it might be more cost effective to buy sandwiches from the bakery in the Wonderful Copenhagen tourist information office across the street from the main entrance on Vesterbrogade.

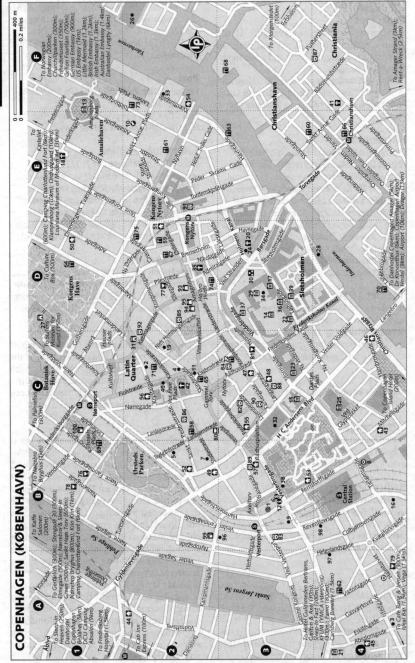

COPENHAGEN (KØBENHAVN)

Nationalmuseet

For a whistle-stop tour through the history of Denmark, nothing can beat the **Nationalmuseet** (National Museum; ☎ 33 13 44 11; www.natmus.dk; Ny Vestergade 10; admission free; ⏱ 10am-5pm Tue-Sun): here you will find the world's most extensive collection of Danish artefacts from the Palaeolithic period to the 19th century. Naturally, the stars of the show are the Vikings, those much maligned, but actually very sophisticated Scandinavian marauders. Highlights include Bronze Age burial remains in oak coffins and various examples of *lur* (musical horns) that were used for ceremony and communication, ancient rune stones, a golden sun chariot, the silver Gundestrip cauldron and Viking weaponry. But the displays don't stop with the Vikings; there are excellent collections covering the Middle Ages and Renaissance period too, plus delightful Egyptian and classical antiquities, as well as frequently changing special exhibitions. There's even an excellent, hands-on Children's Museum.

Rosenborg Slot

This early 17th-century **castle** (☎ 33 15 32 86; www.rosenborgslot.dk; adult/child Dkr70/free; ⏱ 10am-4pm May & Sep, to 5pm Jun-Aug, 11am-3pm Oct, to 2pm Tue-Sun Nov-Apr), built by Christian IV in the Dutch Renaissance style, stands at the edge of **Kongens Have** (King's Gardens; admission free). It is a fairytale castle and one of Copenhagen's great landmarks. Inside you'll find glorious marbled and painted ceilings, gilded mirrors, priceless Dutch tapestries, solid silver lions, and gold- and enamel-ware. The Royal Treasury, in the castle basement, is home to the Danish crown jewels.

Statens Museum for Kunst

Denmark's national **gallery** (☎ 33 74 84 94; www.smk.dk; Sølvgade 48-50; admission free; ⏱ 10am-5pm

DENMARK

FREE THRILLS

Copenhagen is not the cheapest city in the world, so any freebies are most welcome. Following a trial period in early 2006, both the Nationalmuseet (p41) and Statens Museum for Kunst (p41) now have free admission all the time. And there are plenty of other free museums and sights in the city.

- Danish Design Center (free on Wednesday from 5pm to 9pm only; below)
- Ny Carlsberg Glyptotek (free on Wednesday and Sunday; below) – sculpture and painting museum, south of Tivoli Gardens.

Tue & Thu-Sun, to 8pm Wed) houses an impressive collection of works from Danish artists, particularly those of the 19th-century Golden Age such as Hammershøj and Eckersburg, in the original building; while the dramatic glass extension contains more modern works from international names like Picasso and Munch as well as more contemporary Danish artists such as Per Kirkeby, Søren Jensen, Michael Ancher, Richard Mortensen and CW Eckersberg.

Ny Carlsberg Glyptotek

This splendid **museum** (☎ 33 41 81 41; www.glyptoteket.dk; Dantes Plads 7, HC Andersens Blvd; adult/child Dkr50/free; Wed & Sun free; ☽ 10am-4pm Tue-Sun), occupying a grand period building near Tivoli Gardens, has now received a thorough restoration programme. The museum's impressive collection features Etruscan art, 18th- and 19th-century paintings from France and Denmark (the Gauguins are particularly notable) and sculpture spanning five millennia (including more than 30 works by Rodin). At its heart is a beautiful tropical winter garden with a cafe.

Dansk Design Center

Denmark's **temple to design** (☎ 33 69 33 69; www.ddc.dk; HC Andersens Blvd 27; adult/child Dkr50/free; ☽ 10am-5pm Mon, Tue, Thu & Fri, to 9pm Wed, 11am-4pm Sat & Sun) has an excellent permanent exhibition of local design through the decades in the basement and a regularly changing temporary exhibition on the ground floor.

Slotsholmen

An island separated from the city centre by a moat-like canal on three sides and the harbour on the other side, Slotsholmen is the site of **Christiansborg Palace** (☎ 33 92 64 92) home to Denmark's parliament. There are many sites on the island, including a **teatermuseet** (theatre museum), a museum housing the **royal coaches**, and a magnificent **Tøjhusmuseet** (armoury museum), but the grandest is the **Slots-og Ejendomysstyrelsen** (Royal Reception Chambers; ☎ 33 92 64 92; www.ses.dk; adult/child Dkr65/30 ☽ guided tours in English 11am, 1pm & 3pm May-Sep, 3pm Tue-Sun Oct-Apr), the ornate Renaissance hall where the queen entertains heads of state.

The **Ruins of Absalon's Fortress** (adult/child Dkr40/20; ☽ 10am-4pm, closed Mon in winter) are the excavated foundations of Bishop Absalon's original castle of 1167 and of its successor, Copenhagen Slot. They can be visited in the basement of the present palace.

Thorvaldsens Museum (☎ 33 32 15 32; Bertel Thorvaldsens Plads; adult/child Dkr20/free, admission free Wed; ☽ 10am-5pm Tue-Sun) features imposing statues by the famed Danish sculptor Bertel Thorvaldsen, who was heavily influenced by Greek and Roman mythology. Enter from the direction of Vindebrogade.

The **Royal Library** (☎ 33 47 47 47; Søren Kierkegaards Plads; ☽ 10am-7pm Mon-Sat) dates from the 17th century, but the focal point these days is its ultramodern walkway-connected extension dubbed the 'Black Diamond' for its shiny black granite facade. The sleek, seven-storey building houses 21 million books and other literary items such as Hans Christian Andersen's original manuscripts. The building itself is open for visits and guided tours (adult/child Dkr25/10, open 10am to 6pm) and has a cafe and restaurant.

Rundetårn

The **Round Tower** (☎ 33 73 03 73; www.rundetaarn.dk; Købmagergade 52; adult/child Dkr25/5; ☽ 10am-8pm Mon-Sat, noon-8pm Sun Jun-Aug, 10am-5pm Mon-Sat, noon-5pm Sun Sep-May) provides a fine vantage point for viewing the old city. Christian IV built it in 1642 as an astronomical observatory for the famous silver-nosed astronomer Tycho Brahe. Halfway up the 209m-high spiral walkway is a hall with changing exhibits. The tower houses the oldest functioning observatory in Europe and offers evening **astronomy programmes** (☽ 7-10pm Tue & Wed Sep-Dec, 1-4pm Sun Jun-Aug) and by day you may also be lucky enough to see a dramatic, live projection of the sun.

Latin Quarter

Also known as Pisserenden (which needs no translation), the historic university quarter is a grid of narrow streets and, often, half-timbered town houses to the north of Strøget filled with independent shops and Bohemian cafes.

Climb the stairs of the **University Library** (enter from Fiolstræde) to see one quirky remnant of the 1807 British bombardment of Copenhagen – a cannonball in five fragments and the object that it hit, a book titled *Defensor Pacis* (Defender of Peace).

Opposite the university is **Vor Frue Kirke** (8am-5pm, closed to viewing during services & concerts), Copenhagen's neoclassical cathedral. The building dates from 1829, but stands on the site of earlier churches. Inside are imposing neoclassical statues of Christ and the 12 apostles, the most acclaimed works of the Golden Age sculptor, Bertel Thorvaldsen. A couple of blocks east of the cathedral is the pretty square of **Gråbrdre Torv**, which has several medium-priced restaurants with outdoor seating. On the northern side of the Latin Quarter is **Kultorvet**, a lively square where you'll almost certainly find impromptu street entertainment on sunny days, as well as beer gardens, flower stalls and produce stands.

Gardens

The stretch of gardens along Øster Voldgade offers a refuge from the city traffic. **Kongens Have**, the large public park behind Rosenborg Slot, is a popular sunbathing spot.

The **Botanisk Have** (Botanical Gardens; ☎ 35 32 22 22; main entrance Gothersgade 140; 8.30am-6pm May-Sep, to 4pm Tue-Sun Oct-Apr) on the western side of Rosenborg Slot has fragrant trails. Its **Palmehus** (10am-3pm Mon, Tue, Thu & Fri, 1-3pm Wed, Sat, Sun & public hol) is a large, walk-through glasshouse growing a variety of tropical plants.

Christianshavn

A kind of alternative commune, known as the Freetown of Christiania ever since its 1960s heyday, Copenhagen's picturesque canal quarter once did a roaring open trade in soft drugs. A clampdown and police raids have put a stop to that and it's less of a circus these days, although the alternative, hippy ideal lives on. Built on reclaimed land in the 17th

century by Christian IV, it's a great place to wander beside the canals and visit the quarter's pleasant cafes.

To get there, walk over the bridge from the northeastern side of Slotsholmen or you can take the Metro from Kongens Nytorv or Nørreport direct to Christianshavnstorv.

Vor Frelsers Kirke

Close to Freetown of Christiania is the 17th-century **Vor Frelsers Kirke** (☎ 31 57 27 98; www.vor frelserskirke.dk; Sankt Annæ Gade 29; admission free, tower adult/child Dkr20/10; 11am-4.30pm Apr-Aug, to 3.30pm Sep-Mar, closed during services, tower closed Nov-Mar), which has an impressive baroque altar and an elaborately carved pipe organ, propped up by two unhappy looking decorative elephants. For a panoramic view of the city and across to Sweden, climb the 400 steps of the church's 95m-high spiral tower. The last 160 steps run spectacularly along the outside rim, narrowing to the point where they disappear at the top.

Carlsberg Brewery

At the **Carlsberg Brewery Visitor Centre** (☎ 33 27 13 14; www.visitcarlsberg.com; Gamle Carlsberg Vej 11; adult/child incl 1 beer Dkr50/free; 10am-4pm Tue-Sun), you can find out about the history of Danish beer and the modern-day brewing process at the self-proclaimed 'probably best' beer in the world. The experience is capped off with a sampling of the present-day product. It is a little outside of the centre of the city to the west: take bus No 6A westbound or the S-Tog (S-train, whose 10 lines pass through Central Station) to Enghave station.

Waterfront

The home of the royal family since 1794 **Amalienborg Palace** (adult/child Dkr55/free; 10am-4pm) comprises four austere mansions surrounding the central square and guarded by sentries, who are relieved at noon by a ceremonial changing of the guard. You can view the interior of the northwestern mansion, with its royal memorabilia and study rooms of three kings.

Inland along Frederiksgade is the splendid **Frederikskirken** (☎ 33 15 01 44; www.marmorkirken.dk; admission free, guided tour adult/child Dkr25/10; 10am-5pm Mon-Thu, noon-5pm Fri-Sun, dome tour 1pm & 3pm mid-Jun–Aug, 1pm & 3pm Sat & Sun Sep-May). It's known universally as Marmorkirken (Marble Church) and the view from its great dome is spectacular.

DENMARK

Back on Amalienborg Plads, and 500m north along Amaliegade, is Churchillparken, where you'll find **Frihedsmuseet** (admission free; ☺ 10am-4pm Tue-Sat, to 5pm Sun), with moving relics from the history of the Danish Resistance against Nazi occupation.

About 150m north of the Frihedsmuseet you pass the spectacular **Gefion Fountain** that features the goddess Gefion, ploughing the island of Zealand with her four sons yoked as oxen. Another 400m north along the waterfront is the statue of the unjustly famed **Little Mermaid** (Den Lille Havfrue) – a rather forlorn statue that is actually one of the least interesting of all Copenhagen's many sights.

The **Copenhagen Opera House** (☎ 33 69 69 69; www.operahus.dk; admission Dkr100; ☺ guided tours in English are only for groups) on the island of Holmen facing Amalienborg across the harbour is well worth a visit, even if you can't get a ticket (they sell out months in advance). The foyer is open to the public (there are two restaurants) and you can take a guided tour of Henning Larsen's controversial glass-fronted masterpiece with its vast roof, attacked by critics as ungainly and out of proportion in its waterfront setting.

The latest architectural addition to the city's waterfront is the striking new, Dkr900 million, three-stage **Skuespilhuset** (Royal Danish Playhouse; ☎ 33 69 69 69; www.kglteater.dk; Sankt Anne Plads 36; guided tours in English are only for groups Dkr100; ☺ 9.30am Wed-Sat, 10am Sun), the country's new national theatre overlooking the harbour directly across from the new Opera House. Most productions are in Danish. Tickets must be bought in advance from either www.billetnet .dk or at the box office.

ACTIVITIES
Swimming & Sunbathing
Weather permitting, there are reasonably good opportunities to swim and sunbathe on stretches of beach around 5km from the city centre at the spectacularly redeveloped **Amager Strand**; take the Metro to Lergravsparken and then walk east for about 1km, close to Klampenborg train station. Alternatively, come the summer there is a lively 'beach' scene on the city centre harbourfront itself in and around the Islands Brygge open air harbour pool, right in the heart of the city (open only from June to August), although you might want to grease up, cross Channel-swimmer style first. Alternatively there's the heated circular indoor pool at the **DGI-Byen Centre** (☎ 33 29 80 00; www.dgi-byen.dk; Tietgensgade 65, Vesterbro) near the station.

TOURS
Quickshaw Tours
Copenhagen's '**quickshaws**' (☎ 35 43 01 22; www .rickshaw.dk, in Danish; 30-min tour Dkr160) are two-seater, open carriages powered by fit young pedal-pushers. They operate daily and can be found at most main squares. They can also be used as taxis – the price starts at Dkr40 and you pay Dkr4 per minute thereafter. Each quickshaw seats two adults and one child.

Canal Tours
The best way to see Copenhagen is from the water. There are several ways to take a boat tour around the city's canals and harbour from April to mid-October. Multilingual guides give a lively commentary in English. **DFDS Canal Tours** (www.canaltours.dk; adult/child Dkr60/30), leave from the head of Nyhavn or the Marriott Hotel. Tours take 50 minutes, passing the *Little Mermaid*, Christianshavn and Christiansborg Palace, and leave every half hour between 10am and 5pm. **Netto-Boats** (☎ 32 54 41 02; www.netto-baadene.dk; adult/child Dkr30/15) are cheaper, run the same times and depart from Holmens Kirke and from Nyhavn.

Canal boats also make an excellent, traffic-free alternative for getting to some of Copenhagen's waterfront sites. DFDS Canal Tours charges Dkr75 for a one-day 'water-bus' pass (Dkr30 for children) or Dkr35 per trip from mid-May to mid-September. The boats leave Nyhavn every 30 minutes between 10.15am and 4.45pm (to 5.45pm mid-June to mid-August) and make a dozen stops, including at the *Little Mermaid*, Nationalmuseet and Vor Frelsers Kirke (with no commentary), allowing you to get on and off as you like. The **HUR public transport system** (www.hur.dk, in Danish) runs a boat service linking the Royal Library, Nyhavn and Nordre Toldbod, near the *Little Mermaid*, every 20 minutes until 7pm.

Bear in mind that not all tour boats have roofs and the weather is ever-changing in Copenhagen harbour, so be sure to pack for all conditions.

FESTIVALS
The **Copenhagen Jazz Festival** (☎ 33 93 20 13; www .jazzfestival.dk) is the city's largest music event, invigorating the whole city with 10 days of music

in early July. The festival presents a wide range of Danish and international jazz, blues and fusion music in more than 500 indoor and outdoor venues, with music wafting out of practically every public square, park, pub and cafe from Strøget to Tivoli Gardens.

Copenhagen Cooking (www.copenhagencooking.dk) is Scandinavia's largest food festival with dozens of events taking place during one week at the end of August.

SLEEPING

Copenhagen's range of hotels has expanded massively in the last few years, from the likes of Nimb and Skt Petri at the top end, to the cheap (for this part of the world at least) and cheerful Cab Inn chain and the fabulous Danhostel on HC Andersens Blvd. Camping options remain limited, however, not least by the weather.

The city's traditional hotel quarter is centred on the area behind Central Station, on and around Istedgade. Here you will find numerous bland business hotels and medium-range chains. This also happens to be the city's red-light district, with some fruity shop window displays and the occasional group of rowdy winos and glazed addicts lingering in shop doorways.

The tourist office can book rooms in private homes (Dkr300/450 for singles/doubles; there is a Dkr100 booking fee if you do it via the tourist office when you arrive, otherwise it is free over the phone or internet in advance). It also books unfilled hotel rooms, often at discounted rates. You can also visit the website www.bedandbreakfast.dk for B&B accommodation throughout Denmark.

Budget

Camping Charlottenlund Fort (☎ 39 62 36 88; www.campingcopenhagen.dk; Strandvejen 144, Charlottenlund; camp sites per adult/tent Dkr80/25) This is 6km north of the city centre beside a delightful sandy beach overlooking the Øresund sea. Take bus No 14 for a half-hour trip.

Sleep-In Fact (☎ 33 79 67 79; www.sleep-in-fact.dk; Valdemarsgade 14; dm Dkr100-120; ☺ end Jun–end Aug; P ▣) Located in a converted sports hall, this central hostel is basic but cheap. Perhaps it's more suited to younger travellers.

Copenhagen Airport Hostel (☎ 22 45 91 14; www.copenhagenairporthostel.dk; Amagerlandsvej 181, Kastrup; dm Dkr115; P ▣) A cosy house converted into shared accommodation, this is not exactly close to the airport (which is a 25-minute walk away), but it is friendly and clean, and offers laundry and a TV room.

City Public Hostel (☎ 33 31 20 70; www.city-public-hostel.dk; Absalonsgade 8; dm Dkr110-150; ☺ early May–mid-Aug, 24hr reception; ☎) A central, well-run hostel with dorms sleeping six to 23; they are both mixed and separate gender. Breakfast costs Dkr25, or Dkr20 if it's included with the bed price. There is an outdoor barbecue area.

Danhostel Copenhagen Bellahøj (☎ 38 28 97 15; www.danhostel.dk/bellahoej; Herbergvejen 8, Bellahøj; dm/d Dkr140/110; ☺ Feb–early Jan, 24hr reception; P ▣) This is based in a quiet suburban neighbourhood with 250 dorm beds and a limited number of family rooms (doubles). You can take bus No 2A to Brønshøj from Rådhuspladsen or direct from the airport and get off at Fuglsangs Allé. The night bus is No 82N.

Danhostel Copenhagen Amager (☎ 32 52 29 08; www.danhostel.dk/copenhagen; Vejlands Allé 200, Amager; dm/d Dkr110/340; ☺ early Jan–mid-Dec; P ▣) Located in an isolated part of Amager just off the E20 this is one of the largest hostels in Europe, with 528 beds in two-, three-, four- and five-bed rooms. Take bus No 5A from Rådhuspladsen to Sundbyvesterplads and change to bus 77. Until 5pm Monday to Friday, bus No 46 runs from Central Station directly to the hostel.

Danhostel Copenhagen Downtown (☎ 70 23 21 10; www.copenhagendowntown.com; Vandkunsten 5; dm/d Dkr130/549; ☺ year-round). This characterful, buzzing new hostel could not be more centrally located, right beside the main pedestrian shopping street, Strøget, and prides itself on its cultural dynamism, with several artists in residence.

Danhostel Copenhagen City (☎ 33 11 85 85; www.danhostel.dk; HC Andersens Blvd 50; dm Dkr150; ☺ year-round) The best of Copenhagen's hostels occupies a modern high-rise overlooking the harbour a short walk from Central Station. With a reception that resembles a boutique hotel, a great cafe and a 25% discount on the facilities at the DGI-Byen swimming pool and sports centre included in the price, it is a good idea to book well in advance.

Midrange

Cab Inn City (☎ 33 46 16 16; www.cabinn.com; Mitchellsgade 14; s/d/tr Dkr545/675/805; P ✕ ▣ ▣) Cab Inns are modern, rather clinical but boast good facilities (including kettle and TV) and reliable levels of comfort (although the ship's cabin – cab-in, geddit? – style means small rooms and rather narrow bunk-style beds). This is the best located of all Copenhagen's Cab Inns, considering it's a short walk south of Tivoli Gardens. There's free foyer internet access. You do usually have to book well in advance here as it is pretty much unrivalled for price and location.

Cab Inn Scandinavia (☎ 35 36 11 11; www.cabinn .com; Vodroffsvej 57; s/d/tr/q Dkr545/665/785/905; P) This Cab Inn has 201 compact rooms in this chain's familiar spartan style. The rooms are comfortable and have TV and private bathroom. The hotel lies a little further out of town than the Cab Inn City, about a 10-minute walk north across the windy city lakes in a rather uninspiring neighbourhood.

Cab Inn Express (☎ 33 21 04 00; www.cabinn.com; Danasvej 32-34; s/d/tr/q Dkr545/665/785/905; P) A few blocks away from the Scandinavia is the third sister hotel.

our pick Hotel Fox (☎ 33 95 77 55; www.hotelfox.dk; Jarmers Plads 3; min rate per adult Dkr790). This exciting and radical hotel features one-off rooms, each of which is designed by a group of international artists and designers. The hotel reception transforms into a DJ bar by night and is as funky as they come. Located five minutes from the town hall square and Strøget, it's on the fringe of the Latin Quarter.

Hotel Christian IV (☎ 33 32 10 44; www.hotelchris tianiv.dk; Dronningens Tværgade 45; s/d Dkr860/995; ☎) This simple, contemporary hotel located in the city centre close to Kongens Have makes every effort with its light, comfortable rooms and added extras like use of a nearby fitness centre and bikes for rent (Dkr100 per day).

Hotel Rainbow (☎ 33 14 10 20; www.copenhagen -rainbow.dk; Frederiksberggade 25; r with/without bathroom Dkr995/790; X ▣) Hotel Rainbow is a small, friendly and exclusively gay hotel in an excellent location right near the Rådhus end of Strøget, so the city's shopping, drinking and clubbing are at your feet. The hotel is on the top floor and has just a few bright and airy rooms. Use the street-level intercom and book ahead. There is a two-night minimum stay from April to September.

Hotel Guldsmeden Bertrams, Carlton & Axel (☎ 33 25 04 05/33 22 15 00/33 31 32 66; www.hotelgul dsmeden.dk; Vesterbrogade 107 & 66; s/d Dkr945/1145; P X ▣) Sandra and Marc Weinert's excellent Guldsmeden group now has three attractive and welcoming hotels in Copenhagen. The Axel is the latest and boasts a spa and is vaguely Balinese style, while both Bertrams and Carlton are decked out in the chain's characteristic French colonial style. The Bertrams and Axel are four star, the Carlton is a three star. The Axel is the most central, while Bertrams and Carlton are close to the groovy nightlife and shops of Vesterbro.

Hotel Alexandra (☎ 33 74 44 44; www.hotel-alexandra .dk; HC Andersens Blvd 8; s/d Dkr945/1320; P X ▣) The lovely, cosy Alexandra is packed with classic Danish furniture to really get you in the mood for a stay in this great design capital. As well as an excellent restaurant, Bistroen, it also boasts a Green Key environmental award, judged on more than 50 environmental criteria

Hotel Nyhavn 71 (☎ 33 43 62 00; www.71nyhavnhotel .com; Nyhavn 71; s/d Dkr995/1195) Superbly located the harbour end of Nyhavn, this beautiful converted grain house boasts four-star luxury, albeit with sometimes rather small rooms. It's close to the excellent nightlife of the Nyhavn canal.

Hotel 27 (☎ 70 27 56 27; www.hotel27.dk; Løngangstræde 27; s/d Dkr1086/1395; P X ☎) This very centrally located hotel, just 220m from Tivoli Gardens and the town hall square is the epitome of a contemporary Danish design hotel with many extras including cable TV. There is even an ice bar.

Square (☎ 33 38 12 00; www.thesquare.dk; Rådhuspladsen 14; s Dkr1100-1775, d Dkr1250-2360) This relative newcomer on Copenhagen's town hall square could not be better located nor better equipped with attractive, modern, minimalist rooms and breakfast included. There are cheaper hotels in town, but few offer as much style for the money particularly if you are lucky to bag one of the frequent special offers.

Copenhagen Island (☎ 33 38 96 00; www.copen hagenisland.com; Kalvebod Brygge 35; s/d Dkr1600/ 1990; P ▣) The slick interior style and stunning views across the western harbour from the 315 rooms of this thoroughly modern Scandinavian hotel more than make up for its slightly out of the way location (a 15-minute walk from the city centre proper; or one stop on the local S-train from nearby Dybbelsbro station to the Central Station). The rack rates might look high but we've included this in the Midrange selection because the Island often has very special bargain rates (Dkr795/995), and we get the feeling they struggle to reach capacity most of the time.

Top End

Hotel Skt Petri (☎ 33 45 91 00; www.hotelsktpetri
.com; Krystalgade 22; s/d from Dkr1295/1495; P ✗ 🖳)
Whatever you may think of her, Paris Hilton
probably knows a thing or two about hotels,
and this is where she stayed on a recent visit.
Skt Petri is one of Copenhagen's coolest luxury hotels. The rooms are cosseting, and some
have balconies or enchanting city views or
both. There's a gym and a magnificent, bright,
high foyer just made for sipping cocktails and
feeling fabulous in.

Hotel Nimb (☎ 88 70 00 00; www.nimb.dk;
Bernstorffsgade 5; r Dkr1995-7500; P ✗ 🖳) Copenhagen's first, proper boutique hotel
opened in Tivoli Gardens in early 2008 to international acclaim. With a beautiful interior,
two excellent restaurants, and every conceiv-
able luxury – including some not so conceiv-
able, it has its own in-house dairy – it became
the place to overnight in the Danish capital
over night.

Hotel d'Angleterre (☎ 33 12 00 95; www.dangleterre
.dk; Kongens Nytorv 34; s from Dkr2680, d Dkr3060-3920;
P ✗ 🖳) This lavish and, let's be honest,
ever so slightly camp, five-star hotel has long
reigned unchallenged as the city's top overnight spot for celebrities, Eurotrash and minor
royalty. It doesn't skimp on the extras, including a top-notch health club in the basement,
but other newer arrivals on the Copenhagen
hotel scene probably hold greater appeal for
younger guests.

EATING
Around Strøget

La Glace (☎ 33 11 46 46; www.laglace.dk; Skoubougade
3; per slice Dkr42; ☾ 8.30am-5.30pm Mon-Thu, to 6pm Fri,
9am-5pm Sat, 11am-5pm Sun, closed Sun Apr-Sep) The
best and oldest cake shop in Copenhagen
serves sensational gateaux and does a wicked
hot chocolate.

Wokshop Cantina (☎ 33 91 61 21; www.wokshop.dk;
Ny Adelgade 6; soups Dkr60-99; curries Dkr109; ☾ noon-2pm
& 5.30-10pm Mon-Fri, 6-10pm Sat) This basement can-
teen in a street just off Kongens Nytorv (beside
the grand Hotel d'Angleterre) serves excellent
and cheap Thai and Vietnamese staples.

Riz Raz (☎ 33 15 05 75; Kompagnistræde 20; buffet lunch/dinner Dkr79/89, mains Dkr139; ☾ 11.30am-
11pm) Regularly voted one of the city's best
cheap eats in the media, Riz Raz offers a
great-value southern Mediterranean buffet, and plenty of outside seating. There
are good meat mains too. Riz Raz also has

a 2nd branch in the Latin Quarter at Store
Kanikkstræde 19.

Café Victor (☎ 33 13 36 13; Ny Østergade 8; mains
Dkr79-300; ☾ 8-1am Mon-Wed, 8-2am Thu-Sat, 11am-11pm
Sun) An old-school (actually, it was the first
in Denmark) Parisian-style brasserie replete
with zinc bar, cafe and restaurant. Dressy and
expensive, it is still the place to mingle with
the Danish jet set, and the classic French cuisine is super.

Slotskælderen hos Gitte Kik (☎ 33 11 15 37;
Fortunstræde 4; mains Dkr89; ☾ 11.30am-3.30pm Mon-
Fri) Hidden away in a quiet sidestreet off
Amagertorv, this traditional Danish lunch
restaurant is a great place to try classic Danish
staples like *frikadeller*, *sild* (herring) and, of
course, a wide range of smørrebrød all for
under Dkr100.

Nimb (☎ 88 70 00 00; Bernstorffsgade 5; www.nimb.dk;
mains Dkr230; ☾ 11.30am-10pm) Copenhagen's most
exclusive hotel also boasts a fabulous delicatessen, a luxury restaurant (with the unlikely
name of Hermann) and this less pricey, glamorous brasserie-style restaurant with a terrace
overlooking Tivoli Gardens. Lunch is more
simple, more classically Danish food while
dinner brings more lavish French ingredients
such as duck, foie gras and steaks.

Latin Quarter

Atlas Bar (☎ 33 15 03 52; Larsbjørnstræde 18; ☾ noon-
midnight Mon-Sat) Atlas Bar is an enduringly
popular semi-subterranean corner restaurant
in the heart of the Latin Quarter. Its globally
inspired blackboard menu changes regularly
but there is always a good vegetarian option
and the portions are generous. You can eat
very well here for under Dkr100. Upstairs is
the excellent, authentic and reasonably priced
Thai restaurant, Flyvefisken.

Geranium (☎ 33 11 13 04; www.restaurantgeranium
.dk; Kronprinsessegade 13; fixed menu Dkr748; ☾ lunch &
dinner Tue-Fri, dinner Sat) Strictly speaking it's a little
outside of the Latin Quarter, but Geranium is
one of the best restaurants in Copenhagen and
is located in one of the most beautiful dining
rooms (a conservatory in Kongens Have).
Multi-award winning chef Rasmus Kofoed's
thoroughly modern food is made with only
organic or biodynamic ingredients – and that
includes the wine list.

Nørrebro

Nørrebro is a great place to eat with countless cool cafes and bars. Head for Elmegade

for contemporary takeaways (sushi, bagels, sandwiches, coffee, beer), Blågardsgade for healthy snacks, or Sankt Hans Torv for stylish cafes and ice-cream parlours, and there is the nightclub Rust around the corner.

Kiin Kiin (☎ 35 35 75 55; www.kiin.dk; Guldbergsgade 21; theatre menu Dkr450, 11 courses Dkr750; ☯ 5.30pm-midnight Mon-Sat) If frozen green curry with beetroot, plus 10 other similarly molecularly-inspired courses of modern Thai food appeal – and they did to the little man from Michelin who gave it a star recently – this serene, contemporary Thai place in Nørrebro will be right up your 'soi'. The name means 'Time to eat' in Thai.

Nørrebro Bryghus (☎ 35 30 05 30; www.noerrebrobryghus.dk; Ryesgade 3; lunch dishes under Dkr100, evening mains around Dkr189; ☯ 11am-midnight Mon-Wed, 11-2am Thu-Sat, to 10pm Sun) Anders Kissmeyer's celebrated contemporary beer cathedral brews its own lager, stout, ale and weiss beers in-house and serves excellent, refined brasserie food (venison with lingon berry purée, or smoked scallops with lobster cream for instance), to a cool, young clientele.

Vesterbro

our pick Cofoco (☎ 33 13 60 60; Abel Cathrines Gade 7; www.cofoco.dk; ☯ 7.30pm-midnight Mon-Sat; 3 courses Dkr275) One of several excellent value, fixed menu places owned by the same team, Cofoco offers a glamorous setting and refined Franco-Danish food (foie gras, pear and pork terrine, for instance, or duck leg with Jerusalem artichoke and mushrooms), on a budget. **Les Trois Cochons** (☎ 33 31 70 55; Værndemsvej 10) is another great-value restaurant from the same people, which we also heartily recommend.

Famo (☎ 33 23 22 50; Saxogade 3; www.famo.dk; fixed menu Dkr350; ☯ 6pm-midnight Tue-Sun) Not quite as cheap as it used to be, but the four course, authentic, rustic Italian food on offer in the cosy Osteria is still great value, as evidenced by the usually large number of locals packing it out every night.

Around Nyhavn

Produce market (Israels Plads; ☯ 9am-5pm Mon-Fri, to 2pm Sat) This is the main city produce market, just a few minutes' walk north of Nørreport Station.

Custom House (☎ 33 31 01 30; www.customhouse.dk; Havnegade 44; mains Dkr135-255; ☯ 10am-11pm) In the old ferry terminal (from the days before the Øresund Bridge) at the harbour end of

the Nyhavn canal, British design guru and restaurateur, Sir Terence Conran, has created a hugely popular gourmet complex house with Japanese (ebisu), Italian (bacino) and New York steak house (bar and grill) restaurants. As you'd expect, the decor is almost as delicious as the food, and the views across the harbour to the opera house and Christianshavn are equally delectable

Cap Horn (☎ 33 12 85 04; Nyhavn 21; mains Dkr179-199; ☯ 9am-11pm) Amid many a middling canalside restaurant, Cap Horn stands out, serving excellent, fresh Danish seafood including grilled langoustine and aioli for Dkr129.

Salt (☎ 33 74 14 44; www.salt.dk; Toldbodgade 24-28; mains Dkr195-265; ☯ noon-4pm & 5-10pm). The excellent, fresh and often innovative modern Mediterranean/Danish food – poached rabbit filet; baked cod with olives and chorizo, to name two dishes – from the kitchen here is matched by its location in a charming harbourside, 200-year-old converted grain warehouse.

Christianshavn & Christiania

Lagkagehuset (☎ 32 57 36 07; www.lagkagehuset.dk; Torvegade 45; sandwiches & salads Dkr45; ☯ 6am-7pm) One of the best bakeries in town lies right in the heart of Christianshavn and is highly recommended for sandwiches and salads. It has a sister bakery in the Wonderful Copenhagen Tourist office opposite the main entrance to Tivoli.

Morgenstedet (www.morgenstedet.dk; Langgaden; mains Dkr70; ☯ noon-9pm Tue-Sun) This long-established vegetarian and vegan place has a pretty garden in the heart of Christiania. Its dish of the day is usually a curry.

Café Wilder (☎ 32 54 71 83; www.cafewilder.dk; Wildersgade 56; mains Dkr85-145; ☯ 9am-midnight) The archetypal Christianshavn cafe serves good salads and pastas by day and French brasserie food by night to a groovy local crowd.

Restaurant Viva (☎ 27 25 05 05; www.restaurantviv.dk; Langebrogade Kajplads 570, opposite Danisco; mains Dkr125) Housed in a converted ferry moored in Copenhagen harbour just east of Langebro (a continuation of HC Andersens Blvd), this charming place serves modern Mediterranean dishes and, naturally, plenty of excellent seafood. There is an outdoor deck lounge bar on the roof – a lovely place to kick back on a summer's evening.

Noma (☎ 32 96 32 97; www.noma.dk; Strandgade 93; fixed menu Dkr900; ☯ lunch & dinner Tue-Sat, dinner Mon) The undisputed (well, almost) best restaurant in Denmark sources its ingredients exclusively – and often foraged – from the Nordic countries. Chef Rene Redzepi is an innovative genius, not afraid to overturn conventions.

DRINKING

Drinking is one of the Danes' chief pastimes and Copenhagen is packed with a huge ranges of places from cosy, old-school cellar bars or 'bodegas', to the cavernous fleshpots close to Rådhuspladsen, and the many more, quirky, characterful, loungey, grungy, design-ey, boozy, artsy places elsewhere. The line is often blurred between cafe, bar and restaurant, with many places changing role as the day progresses. Nørrebro and Vesterbro (especially along Istedgade, west of the red-light district, and Halmtorvet, closer to the station) are well worth exploring, but Østerbro, too, is starting to acquire a more low-key nightlife scene.

Barbarellah Bar (☎ 33 32 00 61; Nørre Farimagsgade 41; ☼ 4pm-2am Mon-Thu, 4pm-4am Fri & Sat) Close to groovy Nansensgade, where you'll find several more bars, restaurants and boutiques worth visiting, this spacey cafe-cocktail bar is named after owner Barbara (and the Roger Vadim film, of course), who also does a nice line in trendy clothes and furniture. A honey pot for the city's best DJs.

Bibendum (☎ 33 33 07 74; www.vincafeen.dk; Nansensgade 45; ☼ 4pm-midnight Mon-Sat) This cosy little cellar is home to the best wine bar in Copenhagen, run by an exceptionally knowledgeable, and blessedly snobbery-free crowd of wine enthusiasts serving a broad range of, often New World, wines by the glass.

Berlin Bar (☎ 33 12 29 30; Pilestræde 23; ☼ 10am-midnight Mon-Wed & Sun, 10-2am Thu, 10-3am Fri & Sat) This brand new bar in the former premises of flashy-tastic Cafe Ketchup (always popular with reality TV stars and footballers' floosies), promises more of the same late night ogling action with a bar, restaurant and downstairs dancefloor. The decor and lighting remains glitzy-glam, but real improvement is the food: the chef is formerly of London's fusion temple, the Sugar Club.

Karrierebar (☎ 33 21 55 09; www.karrierebar.com; ☼ 6pm-midnight Tue-Wed, 6pm-1am Thu, 4pm-4am Fri, 10am-4am Sat, 10am-5pm Sun) Forget the food, which is middling (as is the service), this cool bar in the heart of the city's old meat-processing quarter remains one of the destination venues

in the city for the late 20s early 30s media and art crowd right now. With lighting by Olafur Eliasson no less.

Ruby (☎ 33 93 12 03; www.rby.dk; Nybrogade 10; ☼ 4pm-1am Mon-Wed, 4pm-2am Tue-Sat) If you are looking for the coolest cocktail bar in Copenhagen, this discrete (from the outside at least) place beside the canal is it. With self-proclaimed cocktail nerds behind the bar, and the city's most dazzling youth in front of it.

Roberts Coffee (☎ 33 32 66 10; www.robertscoffee .dk; Larsbjørnsstræde 17; ☼ 10am-11pm Mon-Thu, 10-1am Fri, 11am-midnight Sat, noon-7pm Sun) Organic, fresh, expertly roasted and brewed coffee with a great view over the busy crossroads in the heart of Pisserendern.

Studenterhuset (☎ 35 32 38 61; www.studenter huset.com; Købmagergade 52; ☼ noon-midnight or later Tue-Sun) There is something happening – live music, DJs, quizzes, table football competitions – most nights at Copenhagen's perennially popular student bar (open to all). This is a relaxed student hang-out with drinks and light eats, including vegetarian or meat sandwiches (Dkr40) during the day.

ENTERTAINMENT

Weekday nights, which can be a little quiet, are when the cafes and cocktail bars come into their own, but Copenhagen really revs into gear from Thursday to Saturday when it turns into a genuine 24-hour party city. Club admission is usually around Dkr60, but you can often get in for free before a certain time in the evening. Major international rock acts often play the national stadium, Parken in Østerbro, at Forum in Frederiksberg or Valbyhallen in Valby, but you can just as easily catch the likes of Rufus Wainwright or Kaiser Chiefs playing at Vega. Visit www .aok.dk or for full listings. The monthly, free magazine *Copenhagen This Week* also lists concerts and entertainment schedules in detail.

Denmark's stunning, new national **DR Koncerthus** (concert hall; ☎ 35 20 30 30; www.1.dr.dk /koncerthus; Emil Holms Kanal 20, Amager; admission varies) designed by French architect Jean Nouvel opened in early 2009 and promises more than 200 concerts a year, predominantly by Danmarks Radio's own symphony orchestra, but also a wide range of classical and contemporary performers. The remarkable blue cube houses four performance spaces, chief among them a 1800-seat concert hall boasting impeccable acoustics. Be warned, concerts sell out well in advance, but returns are available from the box office on the day.

Live Music

Stengade 30 (☎ 35 36 09 38; www.stengade30.dk; Stengade 18, Nørrebro; ⏱ 9pm-5am although varies) Though it is little more rough and ready than some of the slicker offerings on Copenhagen's growing club scene, the music and buzz are consistently good and the bar prices a little lower in Stengade 30. Rub-a-dub Sundays are now legendary.

Culture Box (☎ 33 32 50 50; www.culture-box.com; Kronprinsessegade 54A; ⏱ 11pm-6am Thu-Sat although varies) A genuinely world-class showcase for – mainly – electronica (techno, house, drum n bass etc) with a relaxed, noncommercial, non-up-itself atmosphere.

Copenhagen Opera House (☎ 33 69 69 69; www.operahus.dk) The city's most bombastic building overlooking the waterfront houses world-class opera as well as the odd curve-ball act such as Elvis Costello and Nick Cave. Tickets must be bought in advance from either www.billetnet.dk or at the box office.

Gefärlich (☎ 35 24 13 24; www.gefarlich.dk; Fælledvej 7, Nørrebro; admission usually free; ⏱ 5pm-1am Tue, 5pm-3am Wed & Thu, 5pm-4.30am Fri & Sat) This deeply groovy bar-club-restaurant-lounge-cafe-hairdresser-clothing store-art space (really) has made a major splash on the Nørrebro nightlife scene. It gets packed on weekends, with the incriminating evidence usually posted on MySpace by midweek.

Nord (☎ 33 36 25 00; www.nordlounge.dk; Vesterbrogade 2E; admission free; ⏱ 10pm-5am Fri & Sat) This over 30s nightclub/lounge is a new and welcome arrival on the city's nightlife scene, particularly in this location where the other options tend to involve drinking a lot of beer and falling over. Things are a little more sedate at Nord, but who can fail to fall for classic '80s and '90s pop?

Rust (☎ 35 24 52 00; www.rust.dk; Guldbergsgade 8; admission varies) Rust is a Copenhagen club-scene stalwart and continues to pack a university-age crowd in from Wednesdays through to the weekend with DJs and live music in a multilevel location with two dancefloors, a lounge and cocktail bar. It is located in the heart of groovy Nørrebro, just around the corner from the cafe square Sankt Hans Torv. The music runs the full gamut from disco to hip-hop, although the club was an electronic pioneer in its infancy. Expect to wait in line at weekends.

Studenterhuset (☎ 35 32 38 61; Købmagergade 52; admission varies) The students' house welcomes all with themed nights (Tuesday is Gay Day; Wednesday is International Evening; Thursday is live jazz, Friday is live rock, and Saturday varies). There's a very cheap beer happy hour from noon to 7pm. During the daytime it's a cafe serving cheap sandwiches.

Vega (☎ 33 25 70 11; www.vega.dk; Enghavevej 40) Vega is the daddy of all Copenhagen's live music and club venues with two stages (Store, or 'Big' Vega, and Lille or, you guessed it, 'Little' Vega), plus the luscious Ideal lounge bar and another new bar recently opened, all housed in a fabulous 1950s former trade union HQ by Vilhelm Lauritizen. Admission is free to the Vega Natklub (11pm to 5am Friday and Saturday) if you arrive before 1am, or usually Dkr60 thereafter. Book tickets via www.billetnet.dk or www.billetnet.dk.

Copenhagen Jazz House (☎ 33 15 26 00; www.jazzhouse.dk; Niels Hemmingsensgade 10; admission Dkr100-150) This is one of northern Europe's leading jazz spots with a terrific ambience. Danish musicians and occasional international names feature, and after concerts on Thursday, Friday and Saturday nights, the place becomes a lively disco from 1am to 5am. This is the main hub for the annual Copenhagen Jazz Festival. Tickets are available from the box office half an hour before performances or via www.billetnet.dk.

Mojo (☎ 33 11 64 53; Løngangstræde 21; admission Dkr50; ⏱ 8pm-3am) Small, scruffy and friendly, this is a prime spot for blues. Bands play most nights of the week.

Loppen (☎ 32 57 84 22; Loppebygningen, Christiania; admission Dkr30-180; ⏱ nightclub 2-5am Fri & Sat) This is a celebrated and much-loved veteran of the Copenhagen live-music scene that hosts bands playing everything from soul to punk rock on various nights, and runs a late disco.

Gay & Lesbian Venues

Denmark was the first country to permit same-sex marriage and has had a gay scene for over 30 years – initially centred on Centralhjørnet – so it's not surprising that it remains welcoming to gays and lesbians with numerous bars, cafes and clubs. For more information and listings visit www.copenhagen-gay-life.dk. Meanwhile, the city hosts the World Out Games from 25 July to 2 August 2009.

Code (☎ 33 26 36 26; www.code.dk; Rådhustræde 1; ⏰ 4pm-midnight Wed & Thu, 4pm-5am Fri & Sat) Copenhagen's latest gay venue is this stylish club-bar, which appeals to a more mature crowd with '80s and '90s hits and lively events.

Club Foxy (Mehldahlsgade 4; Dkr60; ⏰ 11pm-6am Thu-Sat) The newest gay club has a decadent yet intimate reputation.

Oscar Bar & Cafe (☎ 33 12 09 99; www.oscarbarcafe.dk; Rådhuspladsen 77; ⏰ noon-2am, kitchen noon-10pm) A popular corner cafe meeting place for gays and lesbians near Rådhuspladsen, this is a good place to get up to speed with what is happening on the gay scene in Copenhagen.

Central Hjørnet (☎ 33 11 85 49; www.centralhjornet.dk; Kattesundet 18; ⏰ noon-2am) The oldest gay bar in the village remains at the heart of the gay scene.

Jailhouse CPH (☎ 33 15 22 55; www.jailhousecph.dk; Studiestræde 12; ⏰ 3pm-2am Mon-Thu, to 5am Fri & Sat, 3pm-2am Sun) This hilarious and popular themed restaurant and bar promises plenty of penal action, with uniformed 'guards' and willing guests.

Cinemas

There are numerous cinemas showing first-release movies, and most of them lie within 200m of Rådhuspladsen. It is customary in Denmark to show foreign-language films in the original language with subtitles.

SHOPPING

Copenhagen is a superb, if expensive, shopping city. Everywhere you go you find small, independent boutiques selling – in particular – unique ceramics, clothing, glassware and homeware, often made by the person manning the till.

Meanwhile, on and around the main pedestrian shopping street, Strøget, big names – both domestic and international – pull out all the stops with lavish window and interior displays. In truth, though, Strøget struggles to compete with other parts of the city, like the area at the western end of Istedgade in Vesterbro for street fashion, shoes, food and second-hand clothing; Elmegade, Blågårdsgade and Ravnsborggade in Nørrebro for antiques, clothing and homeware; and Bredgade, close to Nyhavn, for art and antiques, and it is sadly shabby

at its western end these days. Strøget does still have your one-stop designer shop, Illums Bolighus on Amagertorv. Nearby are the Illum department store and the Royal Copenhagen silver and porcelain stores, which are great for gifts. Copenhagen's high fashion street is Kronprinsensgade, but you will find the cheaper clothing chains on nearby Købmagergade.

For an excellent array of stores catering to outdoor pursuits, head to Frederiksborggade north of Nørreport Station. If the weather drives you indoors, you could head for the city's two malls, Fisketorvet, in Sydhavn and Fields on Amager (the latter is Scandinavia's largest mall). Both have a large range of middling clothing and household stores as well as cafes and restaurants.

Nearly everything closes on Sunday, although some grocers and supermarkets remain open in residential areas, such as Istedgade and Nørrebrogade.

GETTING THERE & AWAY
Air

Copenhagen's modern international airport is in Kastrup, 10km southeast of the city centre. Flights connect frequently with most major Danish and Scandinavian destinations. Many airline offices are north of Central Station near the intersection of Vester Farimagsgade and Vesterbrogade.

Boat

The ferry to Oslo, operated by **DFDS Seaways** (☎ 33 42 30 00/+44 871 522 9955; www.dfdsseaways.co.uk; Dampfærgevej 30), departs from the Nordhavn area north of the city (past Kastellet).

Bus

International buses leave from Central Station; advance reservations on most routes can be made at **Eurolines** (☎ 33 88 70 00; www.eurolines.dk; Reventlowsgade 8).

Car & Motorcycle

The main highways into Copenhagen are the E20, which goes west to Funen and east to Malmö, Sweden; and the E47, which connects to Helsingør. If you're coming into Copenhagen from the north on the E47, exit onto Lyngbyvej (Rte 19) and continue south to get into the heart of the city.

As well as airport booths, the following rental agencies have city branches:

Avis (☎ 70 24 77 07; www.avis.dk; Kampmannsgade 1)
Budget (☎ 33 55 05 00; www.budget.dk; Vester Farimagsgade 7)
Europcar (☎ 89 33 11 33; www.europcar.dk; Gammel Kongevej 13)
Hertz (☎ 33 17 90 20; www.hertz.dk; Ved Vesterport 3)

Close to Copenhagen airport, **Rent A Wreck** (☎ 32 54 00 33; www.rent-a-wreck; Amagerstrandvej 418) hires actually not that old, but usually quite used, cars from as little as Dkr363 per day. Rates are even more competitive on longer hires. The downside is having to drive around with the company name emblazoned on the doors.

Train

Long-distance trains arrive and depart from Central Station (Hovedbanegården). There are three ways of buying a ticket, and the choice can be important depending on how much time you have before your train leaves. *Billetautomats* are coin-operated machines and are the quickest, but only if you've mastered the zone-system prices. They are best for S-train tickets. If you're not rushed, then **DSB Billetsalg** (⏱ 8am-7pm Mon-Fri, 9.30am-4pm Sat) is best for reservations. There's a numbered-ticket queuing system. **DSB Kviksalg** (⏱ 5.45am-11.30pm) is for quick ticket buying, although queues can build up quite a bit at busy times (ie rush hour). Alternatively you can make reservations at www.dsb.dk, which has an English-language option.

GETTING AROUND
To/From the Airport

A train links the airport with Central Station (Dkr30, 17 minutes, three times hourly). The airport is 15 minutes and about Dkr250 from the city centre by taxi. The Metro links the airport to the eastern side of the city, stopping at Christianshavn Torv, Kongens Nytorv and Nørreport stations (www.m.dk; Dkr30, 12 minutes, every five minutes).

Bicycle

At Central Station beneath platform 12, Københavns Cykler rents out bicycles for Dkr75 a day.

If you just want to ride in the city centre, look for a free-use City Bike; they've got solid spokeless wheels painted with sponsors' logos. There are approximately 125 City Bike racks scattered throughout central Copenhagen, although available bikes are often few and far between. If you're lucky enough to find a bike rack with an actual bike in it, all you have to do is deposit a Dkr20 coin in the stand to release the bike. You can return the bicycle into any rack to get your money back. Except during weekday rush hours, you can carry bikes on S-trains for Dkr10.

Bus & Train

Copenhagen has a large public-transport system consisting of a small but excellent new underground and overground driverless Metro system (www.m.dk; trains run a minimum of every three minutes); an extensive metropolitan rail network called S-Tog (S-train; www.dsb.dk), whose 10 lines pass through Central Station (København H); and a vast bus system, whose main terminus is nearby at Rådhuspladsen.

Buses, Metro and trains use a common fare system based on the number of zones you pass through. The basic fare of Dkr20 for up to two zones covers most city runs and allows transfers between buses and trains on a single ticket as long as they're made within an hour. Third and subsequent zones cost Dkr10 more with a maximum fare of Dkr90 for travel throughout North Zealand. Alternatively get a 24-hour pass allowing unlimited travel in all zones for Dk115/58 per adult/child. Two children under 12 travel free when accompanied by an adult.

On buses, fares are paid to the driver when you board, while on S-trains tickets are purchased at the station and then punched in the yellow time clock on the platform (it is not necessary to punch tickets bought from *billetautomats*).

Trains and buses run from about 5am to 12.30am, though buses continue to run through the night (charging double fare) on a few main routes. For schedule information about buses, call ☎ 36 13 14 15; for trains call ☎ 70 13 14 15.

Car & Motorcycle

With the exception of the weekday-morning rush hour, when traffic can bottleneck coming into the city (and going out around 5pm), traffic is usually manageable. Getting around by car is not problematic other than the usual challenges of finding parking spaces. Still, it's far better to explore sights within the city centre on foot or by using public transport.

For kerbside parking, buy a ticket from a streetside *parkomat* and place it inside the windscreen. Parking costs from Dkr10 to Dkr28 depending on how close you are to the city centre. Overnight kerbside parking is generally free and finding a space is not usually too much of a problem.

Taxi

Taxis with signs saying *'fri'* (meaning 'free') can be flagged down or you can phone ☎ 35 35 35 35. The basic fare is Dkr24 (Dkr37 if you book over the phone), plus Dkr11.50 per kilometre between 7am and 4pm, Dkr12.50 between 4pm and 6am, and Dkr15.80 from 11pm to 7am Friday to Saturday. Fares include a service charge, so tipping is not expected. All taxis accept credit cards.

AROUND COPENHAGEN
Klampenborg

Klampenborg is a favourite spot for family outings from Copenhagen. It is only 20 minutes from Central Station on the S-train's line C (Dkr40). **Bellevue Beach**, 400m east of Klampenborg Station, is a sandy strand that gets packed with sunbathers in summer. A large grassy area behind the beach absorbs some of the overflow.

About 10-minute walk west from the station is **Bakken** (☎ 39 63 73 00; Dyrehavevej 62; ☽ noon-midnight Apr–late-Aug), the world's oldest amusement park. A blue-collar version of Tivoli Gardens, it's a pleasantly old-fashioned carnival of bumper cars, slot machines and beer halls.

Bakken is on the southern edge of **Dyrehaven**, an extensive expanse of beech woods and meadows crossed with peaceful walking and cycling trails. Dyrehaven was established in 1669 as a royal hunting

ground and is the capital's most popular picnic area – it's excellent for cycling and running too. At its centre, 2km north of Bakken, is the old manor house **Eremitagen**, a good vantage point for spotting herds of deer.

Louisiana Museum of Modern Art

Denmark's foremost modern **art museum** (☎ 49 19 07 19; www.louisiana.dk; Gl Strandvej 13; adult/child Dkr90/free; ☽ 10am-10pm Tue-Fri, 11am-6pm Sat & Sun) is housed in several low-level galleries atmospherically located beside the Øresund sea. It is surrounded by beautiful grounds full of sculptures by the likes of Henry Moore and Alexander Calder. The museum's permanent collection features works by Giacometti, Picasso, Warhol, Rauschenberg and many more, and there are outstanding changing exhibitions. It's a terrific spot even if you're not passionate about modern art. There's also a diverting **Children's Wing** and a lakeside garden, cafe and restaurant with fantastic views across the water to Sweden.

The Louisiana Museum of Modern Art is situated about a 10-minute walk north on Strandvej from Humlebæk Station, which is 35 minutes on the S-train's line C from Copenhagen (Dkr90).

ZEALAND

Though, naturally, Copenhagen is the centre of gravity for most visitors to Denmark's eastern island, there is plenty to make it worth your while to explore beyond the city limits. This is an island with a rich history, a beautiful coastline and plenty of gentle rolling countryside and of course there's Helsingør Slot, better known as Hamlet's

---

DETOURS: ORDRUPGAARD

This **country manor** (www.ordrupgaard.dk; Vilvordevej 10, Charlottenlund; adult/child Dkr70/free; ☽ 1-5pm Tue, Thu & Fri, 10am-6pm Wed, 11am-5pm Sat & Sun) turned art gallery to the north of Copenhagen has a small but fabulous 19th-century art collection both Danish (Johannes Larsen, Wilhelm Hammershøj and Joakim Skovgaard are well represented, but there are plenty of others) and international (including Gauguins, Corots and Pisarros). The striking extension by Zaha Hadid, the world's most famous female architect, and the house of renowned Danish designer Finn Juhl, which adjoins the grounds add to its charms. The house is a unique example of so-called Gesammtkunstwerk (total art). The house and the interior decoration – the rooms, the furniture, the colours and art – were designed in their entirety by Juhl. To get here, take the S-train to Lyngby and then bus No 388 will drop you within a two-minute walk.

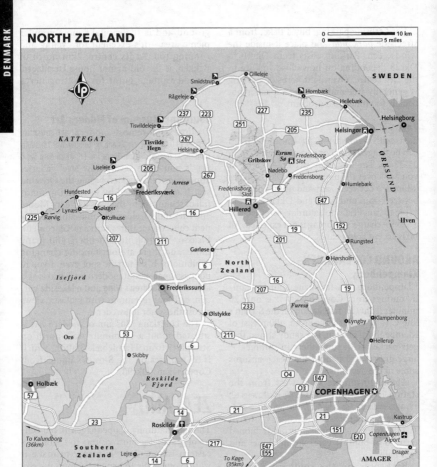

NORTH ZEALAND

castle, Elsinore, and Frederiksborg Slot, a magnificent Renaissance castle. Older still are the remarkable Viking ships of Roskilde, excavated from Roskilde fjord in the 1950s and housed in a purpose-built museum.

NORTH ZEALAND

One of the most popular day trips from Copenhagen is a loop tour taking in Frederiksborg Slot in Hillerød and Kronborg Slot in Helsingør. With an early start you might even have time to reach one of the north-shore beaches before making your way back to the city, although it is more rewarding to allow an extra day for wandering between shoreline towns along this idyllic coastline.

If you're driving between Helsingør and Copenhagen, ignore the motorway and take the coastal road, Strandvej (Rte 152), which is far more scenic, although it can get crowded on summer weekends.

Frederiksborg Slot

Hillerød, 30km northwest of Copenhagen, is the site of **Frederiksborg Slot** (☎ 48 26 04 39; www.frederiksborgmuseet.dk; adult/child Dkr60/15; ⏲ 10am-5pm Apr-Oct, 11am-3pm Nov-Mar), an impressive Dutch Renaissance castle that's spread across three islands. The oldest part of the castle dates from Frederik II's time, though most of the present structure was built by his son Christian IV in the early 17th century. After parts of the castle were ravaged by fire in 1859, Carlsberg beer baron JC Jacobsen spearheaded a drive to restore the castle and make it a national museum.

The sprawling castle has a magnificent interior with gilded ceilings, full wall-sized tapestries, royal paintings and antiques. The richly embellished **Riddershalen** (Knights' Hall) and the **coronation chapel**, where Danish monarchs were crowned between 1671 and 1840, are well worth the admission fee.

The S-train (A and E lines) runs every 10 minutes between Copenhagen and Hillerød (Dkr90), a 45-minute ride. From Hillerød Station follow the signs to Torvet, then continue along Slotsgade to the castle, a 15-minute walk in all. Alternatively, take bus No 701 or 702 which can drop you at the gate.

Helsingør (Elsinore)
pop 34,000

There are, generally, two reasons visitors come to the charming harbour town of Helsingør, at the north eastern tip of Zealand. If they are Swedish, they come to stock up on cheap(er) booze (this is the closest point to Sweden, and ferries shuttle back and forth across the Øresund every half hour). More likely is that they have come to stand in awe of, and soak up the atmosphere of, Denmark's most famous and imposing castle, Elsinore, home of Shakespeare's indecisive anti-hero, Hamlet. The **tourist office** (☎ 49 21 13 33; www.visithelsingor .dk; Havnepladsen 3; ☏ 10am-4pm Mon-Fri, to 1pm Sat Sep–25 May, to 5pm Mon-Fri, to 3pm Sat 26 Jun–31 Aug) is opposite the train station.

SIGHTS

Helsingør's top sight is **Kronborg Slot** (☎ 49 21 30 78; www.kronborg.dk; adult/child Dkr85/25; ☏ 11am-3pm Tue-Sun Jan-Mar, to 4pm Tue-Sun Apr, 10.30am-5pm May-Sep, 11am-4pm Tue-Sun Oct, 11am-3pm Tue-Sun Nov & Dec), made famous as the Elsinore Castle of Shakespeare's Hamlet (it has been, and remains, the venue for summer performances of the play in recent decades during the annual Hamlet festival – often with major English or US stars in the lead role). Kronborg's primary function was not as a royal residence, but rather as a grandiose tollhouse, wresting taxes (the infamous and lucrative 'Sound Dues') for more than 400 years from ships passing through the narrow Øresund. Stand by the cannons facing Sweden and you immediately see what a key strategic military and naval choke point this was. The castle is

on the northern side of the harbour within easy walking distance of the station.

From the tourist office head up Brostræde and along Sankt Anna Gade. This will take you through the **medieval quarter** and past the old cathedral, **Sankt Olai Kirke** (St Anna Gade 12, ☏ 10am-4pm Mon-Sat Apr-Oct, to 2pm Mon-Sat Nov-Mar); the small **City History Museum** (admission free; ☏ noon-4pm Tue-Fri, 10am-2pm Sat, noon-4pm Sun); and **Sct Mariæ Kirke and Karmeliterklostret** (adult/child Dkr20/5; church ☏ 9am-noon Mon-Wed & Fri 4-6pm Thu; guided tours 2pm Mon-Fri May-Sep), one of Scandinavia's best-preserved medieval monasteries. From here Sudergade leads to the tree-lined, cobbled central square of **Axeltorv**, where you will find several cafes and takeaways. Further out of town are **Danmarks Tekniske Museum** (☎ 49 22 26 11; www.tekniskmuseum.dk, in Danish; Fabriksvej 25; adult/child Dkr65/free; ☏ 10am-5pm Tue-Sun) with historic aeroplanes and motor cars among other exhibits, and **Øresundsakvariet** (☎ 35 32 19 70; www.oresundsakvariet.ku.dk, in Danish; Strandpromenaden 5; adult/child Dkr50/30; ☏ 10am-5pm), an aquarium with local sea life.

Meanwhile, a 20 minute train ride south west of Helsingør takes you to a very different kind of royal castle from Kronborg Slot. **Fredensborg Slot** (☎ 48 48 48 00; www.ses .dk; adult/child Dkr50/20; ☏ garden tours 1pm & 4.30pm) evolved during the early 18th century as a royal hunting lodge. Its present day role is as the royal family's summer residence and number one party palace: this is where the wedding reception of Crown Prince Frederik and Tasmanian Mary Donaldson took place. It is a peaceful spot for a stroll or a picnic, with lush rolling lawns, forest and formal gardens beside Esrum Sø (Lake Esrum). The private gardens, herb garden and orangerie most closely surrounding the house are only open during July.

SLEEPING

Helsingør Camping Grønnehave (☎ 49 28 49 50; www.helsingor.dk/campingpladsen; Strandalleen 2; camp sites per adult/child Dkr60/30, cabins Dkr350) A well-spaced beachside camping ground that is east of the hostel and close to one of the area's best beaches.

Danhostel Helsingør (☎ 49 21 16 40; www.helsin gorhostel.dk; Nordre Strandvej 24; dm Dkr175, r Dkr475-850; ☏ Feb-Nov; **P**) The hostel, housed in the imposing red-brick Villa Moltke, 2km northwest of the centre, is right by the water with its own beach. Rooms are simple but clean.

DENMARK

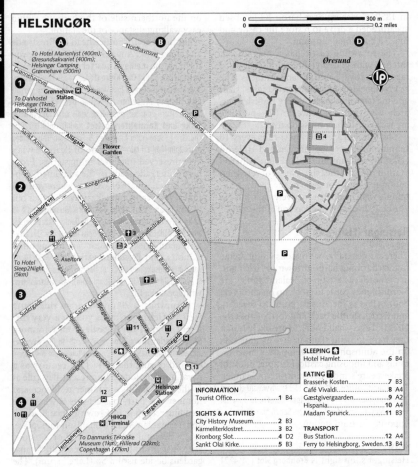

HELSINGØR

INFORMATION	
Tourist Office	1 B4

SIGHTS & ACTIVITIES	
City History Museum	2 B3
Karmeliterklostret	3 B2
Kronborg Slot	4 D2
Sankt Olai Kirke	5 B3

SLEEPING	
Hotel Hamlet	6 B4

EATING	
Brasserie Kosten	7 B3
Café Vivaldi	8 A4
Gæstgivergaarden	9 A2
Hispania	10 A4
Madam Sprunck	11 B3

TRANSPORT	
Bus Station	12 A4
Ferry to Helsingborg, Sweden	13 B4

Hotel Hamlet (☎ 49 21 05 91; fax 49 26 01 30; Bramstræde 5; s/d Dkr725/995) Hamlet has charming, cosy, old-fashioned rooms with lots of stripped pine panelling and green leather upholstery. It's located right by the harbour and station.

Hotel Sleep2Night (☎ 49 27 01 00; www.sleep2night .com; Industrivej 19; s/d Dkr735/825; 🖳) This new, wooden chalet-style accommodation is Denmark's beautifully designed take on the US motel with simple but well-equipped rooms and free internet connections throughout. It's good value but it's a 20-minute journey from the centre of town, to the south of Helsingør. Take bus 805 or 803.

Hotel Marienlyst (☎ 49 21 14 00; www.marienlyst .dk; Ndr Strandvej 2; s/d Dkr1080/1380) This is the clos-

est things get to glamour and luxury in these parts, as this modern conference hotel has a casino, swimming pool and views across the sea to Sweden.

The tourist office also books rooms in private homes for Dkr450 to Dkr800. Singles cost the same as doubles. The tourist office also offers a phone and online booking service (☎ 49 21 13 33; www.visithelsingor.com), although there is a steep Dkr75 service charge.

EATING & DRINKING

Brasserie Kosten (☎ 49 20 00 14; www.kosten.dk; Stengade 81B; mains Dkr99-180; 🕙 noon-10pm Mon-Fri, 11am-10pm Sat & Sun) Sturdy traditional Danish food, such as *frikadeller* (meatballs) and steaks, are the menu staples at this simple but light-filled, unpretentious restaurant – part of a small restaurant complex that also includes Chinese and Mexican places, in a converted harbour building. There's a nice terrace overlooking the harbour, open in the summer.

Hispania (☎ 49 21 23 38; www.hispania-restaurant.com; Stengade 7; mains Dkr145, tapas Dkr55-65) For some reason a finding a real, authentic Spanish tapas bar in Helsingør took us a bit by surprise, but the kitchen staff is Spanish, and this is the real deal, with a charmingly eclectic interior and a good range of Spanish wines. Try the excellent chorizo croquettes.

Gæstgivergaarden (☎ 49 21 19 78; www.gaestgivergaarden.dk, in Danish; Kampergade 11; 3-course lunch Dkr115) This traditional Danish pub offers a good-value lunch menu.

Café Vivaldi (☎ 49 26 00 38; Stengade 9; lunch Dkr57-75, mains Dkr99; ۞ 10am-11pm Mon-Sat, noon-10pm Sun) Part of a small chain, this pleasant French-Italian cafe at the end of the high street serves salads, sandwiches and omelettes.

Madam Sprunck (☎ 49 26 48 49 www.madamsprunck.dk; Stengade 48; mains Dkr198; ۞ 11.30am-midnight) This Helsingør institution, housed in a building dating back to 1781, is situated around a charming courtyard with outdoors seating in summer. As well as serving great evening meals in its restaurant, it also does a lavish brunch (Dkr135) and a two-course lunch menu for Dkr160.

GETTING THERE & AWAY
Trains departing from Hillerød (Dkr60, 30 minutes) run at least once hourly. Trains from Copenhagen run a few times hourly (Dkr90, 50 minutes). **Scandlines** (☎ 33 15 15 15; www.scandlines.dk) and **HH Ferries** (☎ +46 42 198000, hh.net.dynamicweb.se) sail every half hour from Helsingør to Helsingborg, in Sweden. Prices vary, but are roughly Dkr48 return per adult or from Dkr600 if you are taking a car with two passengers.

ZEALAND'S NORTH COAST
The entire stretch of coast from Helsingør west to Liseleje is, in effect, Zealand's holiday zone with literally thousands of traditional Danish summer houses packing the woodlands and beachfronts. The festive atmosphere that takes over the charming, half timbered fishing villages, such as Gilleleje and Hornbæk, and the long, sandy, impeccably clean beaches, more than make it worth visiting.

Hornbæk, the next main town west of Helsingør, has the best and most easily accessible beach on the north coast. The beach is a vast expanse of silky white sand and grassy dunes that run the entire length of the town, and it has a Blue Flag. From the train station, it's just a five-minute walk directly down Havnevej to the harbour where you'll find a great seafood kiosk and the yacht marina. Simply climb the dunes to the left and you're on the beach. The library doubles as the **tourist office** (☎ 49 70 47 47; www.hornbaek.dk; Vestre Stejlebakke 2A; ۞ 1-7pm Mon, closed Tue, 10am-7pm Wed, 1-5pm Thu, 10-5pm Fri, 10-2pm Sat).

Zealand's northernmost town, **Gilleleje**, has the island's largest fishing port. Visitors usually head straight for the harbour and adjacent sandy beach. The harbour has several wonderful seafood kiosks, selling freshly caught crayfish platters, fish and chips and even sushi. The **tourist office** (☎ 48 30 01 74; www.gilleleje.dk; Hovedgade 6; ۞ 10am-6pm Mon-Sat mid-Jun–Aug, to 4pm Mon-Fri, to 3pm Sat Aug–mid-Jun) is in the centre. There are excellent beaches either side of the town and others along the coast to the west, especially at **Rågeleje**, **Dronningmølle** and at **Smidstrup Strand**, where conditions are often good for windsurfing. All have Blue Flags.

Tisvildeleje is a pleasant seaside village known for its bohemian and artistic communities, with a long, straggling main street that leads to an even longer beach. It really transforms in July when the holiday makers arrive. Out of season it can be rather desolate. The **tourist office** (☎ 48 70 74 51; www.helsinge.com; Banevej 8; ۞ noon-5pm Mon-Fri, 10am-3pm Sat mid-Jun-Aug) is at the train station. Behind the beach is Tisvilde Hegn, a windswept forest of twisted trees and heather-covered hills laced with good walking paths.

SLEEPING
Dronningmølle Strandcamping (☎ 49 71 92 90; www.dronningmolle.dk; Strandkorgen 2B, Dronningmølle; camp sites per adult/child Dkr75/50, tent Dkr80-210) This excellent, four-star camp site is on the coast road between Hornbæk and Gilleleje. You have to cross the main road to get to the beach, but it is a beauty and has a Blue Flag. Tent sites come with all amenities – electricity, water and even in some cases, cable TV.

Ewaldsgården Guest House (☎ 49 70 00 82; www.ewaldsgaarden.dk; Johannes Ewalds Vej 5, Hornbæk; s/d Dkr500/765) Though not close to the beach, this cosy and elegant guesthouse is excellent value and has pretty, light-filled rooms.

Helenekilde Badehotel (☎ 48 70 70 01; www .helenekilde.com; Strandvejen 25, Tisvildeleje; s Dkr795-11695, d Dkr895-1795) A beautiful, recently renovated bathing hotel that is built on the cliffs overlooking the beaches at Tisvildeleje; it's about a 10-minute walk from the main street.

Hotel Villa Strand (☎ 49 70 00 88; www.villas trand.dk, in Danish; Kystvej 2; s/d from Dkr895/995) Villa Strand is a pleasant, quiet place to the west of Hornbæk centre and very close to the beach. There are cheaper doubles in garden bungalows and plusher rooms with balconies in the main building.

Hotel Bretagne (☎ 49 70 16 66; www.hotelbretagne .dk; Sauntevej 18, Hornbæk; s/d Dkr995/1195) This is an imposing, whitewashed former clinic with lovely, modern, comfy rooms, and good facilities including wi-fi.

Gilleleje Badehotel (☎ 48 30 13 47; www.gillele jebadehotel.dk; Hulsøvej 15, Gilleleje; d Dkr1190-1390) The grandest of the north coast's bathing hotels is this recently renovated Scandinavian take on a Cape Cod–style place on Gilleleje beach. All rooms have a sea view.

EATING

For eating out along Zealand's northern coast you can't beat the seafood restaurants – usually little more than a few kiosks really – that you find in the harbours.

Fiskehuset Hornbæk (☎ 49 70 04 37; Havenevej 32, Hornbæk; fish & chips Dkr45; ☻ varies) Hornbæk's is the Fiskehuset. Here you can dine like a lord, albeit outdoors with paper serviettes, on smoked cod's roe, cured herring, smoked mackerel, fresh prawns, *fiskfrikadellar* (Danish fish cakes), mussel soup and all manner of wonderful, fresh, local seafood – for under Dkr60.

Adamsen's Fish (Gilleleje Harbour; ☻ 9am-6.30pm Jun-Aug) Adamsen's is the reason why Gilleleje harbour is such a great place to hang out in the summer. Its seafood takeaways – fish cakes Dkr60, sushi Dkr120, shellfish platter Dkr145 – draw the crowds who while away sunny afternoons on the picnic benches here. You can buy fresh fish here too year-round.

Restaurant Hansens Café (☎ 49 70 04 79; www .hansenscafe.dk; Havnevej 19, Hornbæk; ☻ 4-11pm Mon-Sat, noon-10pm Sun) This half-timbered, thatched cottage restaurant, with garden seating serves traditional Danish food and French inspired dishes such as roast beef with horseradish and

pickles, or fried flat fish with mayonnaise and shrimp for under Dkr100.

Restaurant Søstrene Olsen (☎ 49 70 05 50; www .sostreneolsen.dk; Øresundsvej 10, Hornbæk; mains Dkr252, 2-course menu Dkr225; ☻ noon-4pm & 5.30-11pm) Hornbæk is hardly a gourmet mecca, but you will find well-executed, refined, ambitious Franco-Danish food at husband-and-wife team, Thorleif and Minne Aagaard's charming thatched cottage right on the beach.

GETTING THERE & AWAY

The train from Helsingør to Hornbæk takes 25 minutes and costs Dkr30; to Gilleleje, it takes 42 minutes and costs Dkr60. To get to Tisvilde by train you must go via Hillerød. From Helsingør this takes just over an hour and costs Dkr70. The Hillerød train runs to Gilleleje and to Tisvildeleje (Dkr50), but there's no rail link between the two. Trains run twice an hour during the week and once an hour at weekends. There are also buses, which cost the same but take a little longer; from Helsingør station, bus 340 runs to Hornbæk and Gilleleje. Bus 363 runs between Gilleleje and Tisvildeleje (Dkr30, one hour, every two hours).

ROSKILDE
pop 45,000

Most foreigners who have heard of Roskilde know it either as the home of one of northern Europe's best outdoor music festivals, or the sight of several remarkable Viking ship finds, now housed in an excellent, purpose-built museum. To the Danes it is, however, a city of great royal and religious significance as it was the capital city long before Copenhagen, and is still the burial place of 39 monarchs stretching back several hundred years. Located on the southern tip of Roskilde Fjord, the city was a thriving trading port throughout the Middle Ages. It was also the site of Zealand's first Christian church, built by Viking king Harald Bluetooth in AD 980.

The **Roskilde Festival** (www.roskilde-festival.dk; 2009 tickets Dkr1785) takes place over a long weekend in early July in fields just outside the city centre. It attracts the biggest international rock and pop names (175 acts in all – the Pet Shop Boys, Oasis, Coldplay and Kanye West were all scheduled to perform in 2009), along with 75,000 music fans. It is renowned for its relaxed, friendly atmosphere. Most visitors camp on-site, as the accommodation in

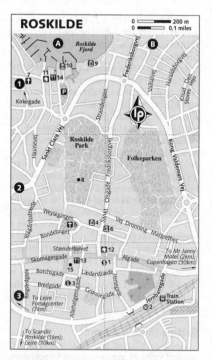

Roskilde itself tends to get booked up well in advance.

Information

Nordea Bank (☎ 46 32 32 33; Algade 4)

Post Office (☎ 70 12 40 00; Jernbanegade 3)

Tourist Office (☎ 46 31 65 65; www.visitroskilde.com; Gullandsstræde 15; ☺ 9am-5pm Mon-Fri, 10am-1pm Sat)

Sights

ROSKILDE DOMKIRKE

Though most of Roskilde's medieval buildings have vanished in fires over the centuries, the imposing twin-spired **cathedral** (☎ 46 35 16 24; www.roskildedomkirke.dk; Domkirkepladsen; adult/child/ under 7 Dkr25/15/free; ☺ 10am-4pm Tue-Sat Oct-Mar, 12.30-4pm Sun Oct-Apr, 9am-5pm Mon-Sat, 12.30-5pm Sun Apr-Sep, guided tours adult/child Dkr20/10, 11am & 2pm Mon-Fri, 11am Sat, 2pm Sun) still dominates the city centre. Started by Bishop Absalon in 1170, Roskilde Domkirke has been rebuilt and added to so many times that this mighty brick edifice represents a millennium of Danish church architectural styles. It's protected under Unesco's World Heritage List.

The cathedral has tall spiky **spires**, eye-catching in their disproportionate slender-ness compared with the solidity of the rest of the building. The cathedral interior is splendid; its **crypts** contain the sarcophagi of 39 Danish kings and queens. Some are lavishly embellished and guarded by marble statues of knights and women in mourning. Others are simple and unadorned. There's something quite affecting about being able to stand so close to the remains of so many of Scandinavia's powerful historical figures. For light relief, take a look at the 15th-century **clock** above the entrance, where a tiny St George on horseback marks the hour by slaying a yelping dragon (a pair of bellows and three out-of-tune organ pipes create its yelp).

OTHER SIGHTS

From the northern side of the cathedral, walk across a field where wildflowers blanket the unexcavated remains of Roskilde's original medieval town, and continue through a green belt all the way to the **Viking Ship Museum** (☎ 46 30 02 53; www.vikingskibsmuseet .dk; Vindeboder 12; adult/child May-Sep Dkr95/free, Oct-Apr Dkr60/free; ☺ 10am-5pm).

This well-presented museum contains five reconstructed Viking ships (c 1000), excavated from Roskilde Fjord in 1962 and brought to shore in thousands of fragments. The five ships – all different – had been filled with stones and scuttled to block the entrance to the fjord to protect the town (at that time, the capital of Denmark) from attack by Norwegian Vikings. The fascinating **waterfront workshops**, a short walk west along the harbour, are a more modern addition to the museum where Viking ship replicas are built using Viking-era techniques. The smells and sounds here are just as they would have been 1000 years ago.

From May to the end of September, you can take a **trip** (adult/child excl museum admission Dkr60/50; daily from 24 Jun–25 Aug, check with the museum for others times) on the waters of Roskilde Fjord in a replica Viking ship. As well as this, the MS *Svendborg* is a veteran cruiser that offers sailing tours (adult/child Dkr95/39) of the fjord from June to August.

Further west is the **Sankt Jørgensbjerg quarter**, where the cobbled Kirkegade walkway leads through a neighbourhood of old straw-roofed houses into the courtyard of the 11th-century **Sankt Jørgensbjerg Kirke**.

Back in the town, a terrific surprise awaits art fans at the **Museum for Samtidskunst** (46 31 65 70; www.mfsk.dk; Stændertorvet 3D; adult/child Dkr30/free; 11am-5pm Tue-Fri, noon-4pm Sat & Sun). Housed in the elegant 18th-century Roskilde Palace, this is a surprisingly cutting-edge contemporary art space, fond of perplexing installations by Danish and international artists.

Roskilde Museum (46 36 60 44; www.roskildemuseum.dk; Sankt Olsgade 18; adult/child Dkr25/free; 10am-4pm) has displays on Roskilde's rich history.

If the Viking Ship Museum has given you a taste for the history of the region, 7km southwest of Roskilde is the fascinating **Lejre Forsøgsenter** (46 48 08 78; www.lejre-center .dk; Slangealleen 2, Lejre; 10am-4pm, to 5pm in summer, closed Mon May, Jun & mid-Aug–Sep), a historic, 43-hectare open-air park – they call it a centre for 'experimental archaeology' – with re-created buildings from the Iron Age, Stone Age, Viking era and the 19th century with variety of activities and special events. You get there by train from Roskilde (Dkr20, six minutes).

Sleeping & Eating
The tourist office books rooms in private homes for Dkr450 for doubles only, plus a Dkr25 booking fee.

Danhostel Roskilde (46 35 21 84; www.danhostel.dk/roskilde; Vindeboder 7; dm Dkr150, r Dkr420-500; P) This harbourside hostel is especially smart and modern, even by Danish hostel standards, with small three-, four-, five-, or six-bed dorms. It's adjacent to the Viking Ship Museum.

Hotel Prindsen (46 30 91 00; Algade 13; www .prindsen.dk; s/d Dkr1396/1495) The town's grandest accommodation, with plenty of chintz and all the trimmings.

Ce Ci (46 38 48 78; Stændertorvet 8; mains Dkr89-178; 11am-11pm) Right on the main square with views to the cathedral is this airy, contemporary Mediterranean cafe serving wraps, sandwiches, burgers and pasta dishes (Dkr78 to Dkr148), as well as evening main courses.

Rådhuskælkderen (46 36 01 00; Fondens Bro 1; www.raadhuskaeldern.dk; 11am-11pm Mon-Sat; mains Dkr200) Right next to the cathedral is this atmospheric, red brick cellar, serving simple modern European and Danish dishes.

Restaurant Snekken (46 35 98 16; Vinderboder 16; www.snekken.dk; 11.30am-11pm; mains Dkr228-285) This modern, glassy restaurants is in a great spot overlooking the fjord and a few metres from the Viking Ship Museum and Roskilde Danhostel. The food perhaps is not worth a trip on its own, but the herring is good for lunch (Dkr78) and there are quite ambitious evening mains such as quail stuffed with foie gras.

Getting There & Around
Trains from Copenhagen to Roskilde are frequent (Dkr70, 25 minutes). From Copenhagen by car, Rte 21 leads to Roskilde; upon approaching the city, exit onto Rte 156, which leads into the centre.

Parking discs are required in Roskilde. There are car parks off Læderstræde, just south of Aldgade, Roskilde Museum and near the Viking Ship Museum.

A bicycle rental shop **Jas Cykler** (46 35 04 20; Gullandsstræde 3; per day Dkr70), just off Skomagergade, rents out distinctive yellow bikes.

KØGE
pop 34,000

Køge is a pretty town which, if not worth a special visit, offers a pleasant diversion if you happen to be passing through on your way by ferry to Bornholm. The one-time medieval trading centre, 42km south of Copenhagen, retains an engaging core of historic buildings that line the narrow streets leading off the broad and busy main square, Torvet.

The **tourist office** (56 67 60 01; www.visitkoege .com; Vestergade 1; 9am-5pm Mon-Fri, 10am-1pm Sat) is just off the square.

You can park in Torvet, but for one hour only during the day, and there are longer-term car parks near the train station. Time discs are required.

A short stroll through the central part of Køge takes you to Denmark's oldest **half-timbered building** (c 1527) at Kirkestræde 20, a marvellous survivor with a fine raked roof. Køge's **historical museum** (☎ 56 63 42 42; Nørregade 4; admission Dkr20; ☼ 11am-5pm Tue-Sun Jun-Aug, 1-5pm Mon-Fri, 11am-3pm Sat, 1-5pm Sun Sep-May) is in a splendid building that dates from 1619. Another gem is **Brogade 23**, decorated with cherubs carved by the famed 17th-century artist Abel Schrøder. Elsewhere best efforts have been made to improve a not very attractive industrial harbour with open air cafes and restaurants. Finally, Køge also has Denmark's only museum dedicated to the artistic process, the tiny **Museum of Sketches** (☎ 56 67 60 01; www.Skitsesamlingen.dk; Vestergade 1; admission free; ☼ 10am-5pm Tue-Sun), which includes the sketches for the statue of the *Little Mermaid* and for the queen's famous tapestries.

Sleeping & Eating

The tourist office can book double rooms in private homes from Dkr450 plus a Dkr25 booking fee.

Danhostel Køge (☎ 56 67 66 50; www.danhostel.dk /koege; Vamdrupvej 1; dm/r Dkr200/380; ☼ Mar-Nov; ℗ 🖳) The hostel is 2km northwest of the centre.

Hotel Niels Juel (☎ 56 63 18 00; www.hotelnielsjuel .dk; Toldbodvej 20; s/d Dkr825/1077) This harbour-front hotel has modern, light rooms and sea views.

Hotel Hvide Hus (☎ 56 65 36 90; www.hotelhvidhus.dk; Strandvejen 111; s/d Dkr825/1275) Well located if a little characterless, this 126 room modern hotel is on the beach with a cafe and restaurant.

StigAnn (☎ 56 63 03 30; www.stigann.dk; Sankt Gertruds Stræd 2; dinner Dkr195-230, 3-course menu Dkr315) Køge's best restaurant by some margin offers refined and ambitious retro-classic dishes such as Tournedos Rossini and Chateaubriand.

Getting There & Away

Køge's train and bus stations are at Jernbanegade 12 on the east side of town. The train station is at the southernmost point of greater Copenhagen's S-train network, at the end of the E line. Trains to Copenhagen run at least three times an hour (Dkr70, 35 minutes). The bus to Copenhagen (Dkr70, one hour) leaves from outside the train station.

Bornholmstrafikken (☎ 56 95 18 66; www.born holmstrafikken.dk; adult Dkr250, car Dkr1350-1435) operates the service from Køge, just south of Copenhagen, to Bornholm. The overnight ferry departs daily at 11.30pm and arrives at 6.30am. It has to be said, it is quicker and almost as cheap take a train via Copenhagen to Ystad in Sweden, and then a catamaran to Rønne from there (total journey time would be around 3½ hours), although it can make sense to sleep while you sail if your itinerary is tight.

TRELLEBORG

In the countryside of southern Zealand **Trelleborg** (☎ 58 54 95 06; Trelleborg Allé; adult/child Dkr55/ free; ☼ 10am-4pm Sat-Thu) is the best preserved of Denmark's four Viking ring fortresses.

There isn't an awful lot to see here, it must be said – there is a reconstructed Viking hall, a small visitor centre and the earthen-walled fortress itself, dating from AD 980. This is made up of various grassy earthworks, hillocks and trenches divided into four symmetrical quadrants. In Viking times, each quadrant contained four long elliptical buildings of wood that surrounded a courtyard. Each of the 16 buildings, which served as barracks, was exactly 100 Roman feet long (29.5m). Concrete blocks mark the outlines of the house foundations. Plaques point out burial mounds and other features.

Trelleborg is 7km west of Slagelse. To get there, take the train to Slagelse (Dkr70, 33 minutes from Roskilde) and then either catch the hourly bus No 312 to Trelleborg (Dkr20, 12 minutes), take a taxi, or rent a bicycle from a shop near the Slagelse tourist office.

SOUTH ISLANDS

The three islands of Møn, Falster and Lolland mark the southernmost part of Denmark. Though they are just a 1½-hour drive from Copenhagen, these three rural oases can seem centuries removed with their gently rolling, unspoiled landscape. Though bridges connect all three islands to each other and Zealand, they often appear disconnected from the modern world, which of course is part of their appeal. Cycling holidays are popular here, as is fishing, sailing, bird-watching and hiking, plus there are several good golf courses. There is also a thriving arts scene on Møn although the island is most celebrated for its striking chalk sea cliffs.

DENMARK

Vordingborg

pop 10,000

Though it isn't actually on the south islands, you will most likely have to pass through the southern Zealand harbour town of Vordingborg, the largest in the region, to reach them. It is worth spending an hour or so in this busy, culturally interesting town, once home to one of the most important defensive fortresses in Denmark, built by Valdemar the Great as a Baltic power base. The remnants of that 14th-century fortress, the 26m **Gåsetårnet** (Goose Tower), is the town's most prominent landmark today and marks the start of the high street. Beside the Goose Tower is **Danmarks Borgcenter** (Slotsruinen 1; adult/child Dkr45/free, incl admission to the Goose Tower; ☉ 10am-5pm Jun-Aug, 10am-4pm Tue-Sun Sep-May) with historically themed exhibitions and, during the summer, a wide range of re-enactment and archaeological activities. It is also now home to Vordingborg tourist office, which shares its opening hours.

Møn

pop 12,000

Ask any Dane, and they will tell you that the white cliffs of eastern Møn (Møns Klint) are one of the great natural 'wonders' of Denmark. That isn't saying much, of course – but the cliffs are rather majestic, and the beaches that ring the island are as good as any in Denmark. Inland you'll find woodland, narrow lanes, medieval churches and prehistoric remains.

One downside is that the island's bus service is sketchy, and to get the best out of Møn, having your own transport helps.

Stege, the main settlement on Møn, is an everyday place, but it is enlivened by its role as the island's gateway town and main commercial centre. **Møn tourist office** (☎ 55 86 04 00; www.visitmoen.com; Storegade 2; ☉ 9.30am-5pm Mon-Fri, 9am-6pm Sat mid-Jun–Aug, 9.30am-4.30pm Mon-Fri, 9am-noon Sat Sep–mid-Jun) is at the entrance to Stege. As well as offering information on the island, you can also book accommodation through the website out of hours.

Stege Kirke (Provstesstræde; admission free; ☉ 9am-5pm Tue-Sun Apr-Sep, to 1pm Oct-Mar) has unique medieval frescoes and a pulpit carved with entertaining visual interpretations of biblical scenes.

MØNS KLINT

The chalk cliffs of Møns Klint, at the eastern tip of the island, were created during the last Ice Age when the calcareous deposits from aeons of compressed seashells were lifted from the ocean floor. The gleaming white cliffs rise sharply for 128m above an azure sea, presenting one of the most striking landscapes in Denmark. The chalk subsoil of the land above the cliffs supports a terrific variety of wildflowers including vivid orchids. There is a strict embargo on picking wildflowers.

The woods of Klinteskoven, behind the cliffs, have a network of paths and tracks. From near the cafeteria you can descend the cliffs by a series of wooden stairways. It's quite a long descent and a strenuous return up the 500-odd stairs. From the base of the steps, turn south along the narrow beach, which leads in about 1km to another stairway at Gråryg Fald. These take you steeply to the top of the cliff, from where a path leads back to the car park. Warning notices and barriers should be heeded. The reasons for this and the history of the cliffs themselves are now explained at a swish new museum here, **Geocenter Møns Klint** (☎ 55 86 36 00; www.moensklint.dk; Stengårdsvej 8, Borre; ☉ 10am-5pm Apr–mid Jun, & Sep-Oct, 10am-6pm mid-Jun–Aug) which also houses a collection of fossils found on the beaches here. The museum is located on the clifftop at Borre and has a lovely cafe/restaurants with views over the sea. Bus 52 stops right outside.

During the summer **boat tours** (☎ 21 40 41 81; www.sejlkutteren-discovery.dk, in Danish) of the coast around the cliffs run with the MS *Discovery* from Klintholm harbour every two hours from 10am to 4pm.

PASSAGE GRAVES

Møn has a wealth of prehistoric remains, although many are vestigial burial mounds. The best preserved sites are the late–Stone Age passage graves of **Kong Asgers Høj** and **Klek-kende Høj**. Both are on the west side of the island within a 2km radius of the village of Røddinge, from where they are signposted. Kong Asgers Høj is close to the narrow road and parking space is limited. The site is extremely well preserved and comprises a grassy mound pierced by a low passageway that leads to a splendid stonelined chamber. Take a torch and mind your head. **Klekkende Høj** is on a hilltop amid fields. From a car park, follow a signposted track to reach the site. The grave has a double chamber and again you need a torch and some agility to creep inside.

CHURCHES OF MØN

Most of the churches on Møn are medieval and many are graced with the best-preserved primitive frescoes in Denmark. The frescoes depict biblical scenes, often interpreted through light-hearted rustic imagery. Post-Reformation Lutherans fearful of what they saw as too much Roman exuberance whitewashed them, ironically preserving the frescoes. The style of Møn fresco painting owes much to the Emelundemestteren (the Elmelunde Master), an accomplished stylist whose name is unknown. Some of his finest work can be seen at **Elmelunde Kirke** (Kirkebakken 41; admission free; ☺ 8am-4pm Oct-May) on the road to Møns Klint.

CYCLING

Although testing at times, cycling on Møn is rewarding given the island's uncharacteristic hilliness. The tourist office has a route map and an excellent printout guide in English to themed bike tours on the island.

SLEEPING & EATING

You can find a list of Møn's many guesthouses and B&Bs at www.visitmoen.com. In Stege, there are bakeries and supermarkets and a handful of cafes.

Camping Møns Klint (☎ 55 81 20 25; www.camping moensklint.dk; camp sites per adult/child/tent Dkr78/54/23; ☺ Apr-Nov) The best located of Møn's camp sites is about 3km from the cliffs. The camping ground is in a pleasant woodland setting with swimming pool and tennis courts as well as horse riding.

Danhostel Møns Klint (☎ 55 81 20 30; www .danhostel.dk/moen; Langebjergvej 1, Borre; dm/d/tr/q Dkr165/330/420/450; ☺ May–mid-Sep; ℗ ✗) This two-star hostel 5km from the beach and cliffs occupies an enchanting lakeside spot opposite the camping ground.

Elmehøj (☎ 55 81 35 35; www.elmehoj.dk; Kirkebakken 38, Elmelunde; s/d/tr/q Dkr315/420/600/800) This large family run guesthouse is in the centre of the island right beside Elmelunde Church. This ivy-covered manor house is imposing and located in pleasant grounds with views over Steve Cove. Rooms are simple and slightly dated. The beach is a short drive away, and there is a riding school nearby.

Præstekilde Klintevej (☎ 55 86 87 88; www .praestekilde.dk; Klintevej, 116, Keldby; s Dkr795-895, d Dkr995-1095, f Dkr1245-1595) This modern, four-star hotel right in the middle of the island is convenient for most of Møn's sights, with an 18-hole golf course nearby, and an indoor pool and restaurant.

Bryguset Møn (☎ 55 81 20 00; www.bryghusetmoen .dk, in Danish; Storegade 18, Stege; burgers, sandwiches & lunch plate Dkr55-125; ☺ noon-9pm Tue & Wed, to 10pm Thu & Fri, 10am-10pm Sat, to 9pm Sun) This new microbrewery is the latest place to eat and drink in the island's capital. It has outdoor seating in summer.

David's (☎ 33 13 80 57; Storegade 11A, Stege; 2-course menu Dkr225; ☺ 10am-5pm Mon-Sat, alternate Fri & Sat evenings during summer) Ambitious modern French-Danish food is on offer here, using locally sourced ingredients for very reasonable prices. Dishes include duck breast with a port wine sauce and Danish summer vegetables.

GETTING THERE & AROUND

From Copenhagen take the train to Vordingborg (Dkr111, 1¼ hours); from there it's a 45-minute ride to Stege on bus 62 (Dkr42). From late June to mid-August, bus 632 makes the 45-minute run (Dkr20) from Stege to Møns Klint a few times a day. The bus stops at the hostel and camping ground en route. During the rest of the year the bus stops within about 3km of Møns Klint.

Falster
pop 43,000

Falster is the middle of the three islands to the south of Zealand and, as with Lolland and Møn the people who live here – most of whom live in the only town of any significance, Nykøbing – are largely concerned with farming and tourism. The east coast of Falster is lined with white sandy beaches that attract huge numbers of German and Danish holidaymakers, many of whom own tree-shrouded cabins along the wooded coastline.

The most glorious stretch of beach is at **Marielyst**, which is 12km from Nykøbing. The beach draws crowds in summer, but it's so long that you can always achieve some sense of escape. The southern tip of the island, Gedser Odde, is the southern most point of Denmark. The **tourist office** (☎ 54 13 62 98; www. visitlolland-falster.com, in Danish; Marielyst Strandpark 3; ☺ 9am-4pm Mon-Sat, 10am-2pm Sun mid-Jun–Aug, to 2pm Mon-Fri, 9am-4pm Sat Sep–mid-Jun) is in a modern complex on the western entrance to the resort as you come in from the E55. Go left at the big roundabout. There is also a tourist office in **Nykøbing** (☎ 54 85 13 03; Østergågade 7; ☺ 10am-5pm Mon-Thu, 10am-6pm Fri, 10am-1pm Sat).

SLEEPING

Marielyst Camping (☎ 54 13 53 07; www.marielyst -camping.dk, in Danish; Marielyst Strandvej 36; camp sites per adult/child Dkr68/34) This central camping ground has a long season and is popular with families. It's 400m from the beach.

Danhostel Nykøbing F (☎ 54 85 66 99; www .danhostel.dk/nykoebingfalster, in Danish; Østre Allé 110; dm Dkr180, r Dkr380-620) This is the nearest hostel to Marielyst, being just 1km east of Nykøbing, Falster's train station. It is a large, institutional-style place about 10km from the beach.

Hotel Nørrevang (☎ 54 13 62 82; www.norrevang.dk; Marielyst Strandvej 32; s/d Dkr870/1105) This thatched, half-timbered house 500m from the beach in Marielyst has 26 rooms, a pool, tennis court and restaurant.

GETTING THERE & AROUND

Trains leave Copenhagen several times each hour for Nykøbing F (Dkr138, two hours) on the western side of the island, from where it's a Dkr26 bus ride to Marielyst on the east (25 minutes), or Gedser (35 minutes) further south. From Gedser there are frequent **Scandlines ferries** (☎ 33 15 15 15; www.scandlines.dk) to Rostock, Germany. The trip takes two hours and costs Dkr45 per person. It's Dkr650 for a car with up to five people.

Lolland

Perhaps conscious of its comparative lack of natural attractions, Lolland offers instead a couple of diverting attractions.

The main town of **Maribo** has an engaging charm, not least because of its lakeside setting. Maribo's **tourist office** (☎ 54 78 04 96; www .visitlolland-falster.com; Torvet; ☺ 10am-5pm Mon-Fri, to 1pm Sat) is on the attractive main square and has masses of information. The town stands amid a scattering of lakes, and its handsome, 15th-century, redbrick **Domkirken** overlooks the gleaming waters of the Søndersø. There are pleasant lakeside **walks** and Maribo has a number of interesting **museums**.

The biggest draw, at least as far as Danes are concerned, is **Knuthenborg Safari Park** (☎ 54 78 80 89; www.knuthenborg; Birketvej 1, Bandholm; adult/ child Dkr155/85; ☺ 10am-5pm). The tigers are the undisputed stars here, although there are plenty of other exotic animals including giraffes, rhinos, gorillas and lions.

Lolland's other town is Nakskov, to the west, dating back to the 13th century. It is a pretty harbour town with a **tourist office** (☎ 54 92 21 72; ☺ 9.30am-5pm Mon-Thu, 9.30am-6pm Fri, 9.30am-1pm Sat) on Axeltorv. You reach Nakskov from Maribo by bus (Dkr42) or from Nykøbing Falster (Dkr70).

SLEEPING & EATING

Maribo Sø Camping (☎ 54 78 00 71; www.maribo -camping.dk; Bangs Havevej 25; adult/child/tent Dkr74/37/20) Just 500m from the town centre, this attractive, well run camping ground has a lovely lakeside location.

Danhostel Maribo (☎ 54 78 33 14; www.danhos tel.dk/maribo; Søndre Boulevarde 82; dm/r Dkr130/350; ☺ May-late-Dec; Ⓟ) Rather a barrack-like hostel but well located close to the beach.

Hotel Maribo Søpark (☎ 54 78 10 11; www.maribo -soepark.dk; Vestergade 29, Maribo; s/d Dkr725/925). This large, modern block is set in attractive parkland beside the town lake. Rooms are a little dowdy but light and spacious. The hotel restaurant, Svanen, serves reasonable modern European food for comparatively good prices (mains, such as pork cheek with wild mushrooms and port wine sauce, Dkr128 to Dkr168).

Lalandia (☎ 54 61 05 05; www.lalandia.dk; Rødby, chalets Dkr890-2220) South of Lolland you will find the massive, 25,000 sq m family holiday park Lalandia, with more than 700 attractive chalets, that sleep from two to eight, as well as cinemas, indoor and outdoor swimming pools, bowling alleys and restaurants.

Vestergade, the main street running west from Torvet in Maribo, has several cafes and restaurants.

Skaanings Gaard Restaurant (☎ 54 78 22 25; Vesterbrogade 55, Maribo; lunch Dkr99; ☺ noon-midnight) Serves a lunch buffet and has plenty of outdoor seating during summer.

Restaurant Bangs Have (☎ 54 78 19 11; www.bang shave.dk; Bangshavevej 23; 2 courses Dkr280) A popular and long established restaurant in a lovely waterfront pavilion with outdoor seating in summer.

GETTING THERE & AWAY

Trains run between Nykøbing F to Maribo (Dkr60, 25 minutes) and on to Nakskov

(Dkr65, 47 minutes) every hour Monday to Friday, and less at weekends. The harbour town of Rødbyhavn is the main ferry link to Germany. Train-ferries (www.scandlines.dk) sail throughout the day to Puttgarden (adult/child/car Dkr40/30/480). The journey takes 45 minutes.

BORNHOLM

pop 44,000

Bornholm is a little Baltic pearl: a Danish island, yet it lies some 200km east of the mainland, north of Poland. It boasts more hours of sunshine than any other part of the country, as well as gorgeous sandy beaches, idyllic fishing villages, numerous historic sights, endless cycle paths and a burgeoning reputation for culinary curiosities and ceramic artists and glass makers.

Unique among Bornholm's attractions are its four 12th-century round churches, splendid buildings whose whitewashed walls, 2m thick, are framed by solid buttresses and crowned with black, conical roofs. Each was designed as both a place of worship and a fortress against enemy attacks, with a gunslot-pierced upper storey. All four churches are still used for Sunday services, but are otherwise open to visitors. The island's tourist website, with information on accommodation, activities, events and transport is at www.bornholm.info.

HISTORY

Bornholm's history reflects its position at the heart of the Baltic and, in its time, Sweden, Germany and Soviet Russia have occupied it. A Danish possession since the Middle Ages, the island fell into Swedish hands in the 17th century, but was won back for Denmark by a fierce local rebellion.

The island suffered cruelly in the chaos at the end of WWII. It was occupied by the Nazis, but when Germany surrendered in May 1945 the commander on Bornholm resisted and Rønne and Nexø suffered heavy damage from Soviet air raids. On 9 May the island was handed over to the Soviets who remained in situ until the following year, when Bornholm was returned to Denmark.

GETTING THERE & AWAY

Assuming you are travelling from the capital, the most cost- and time-effective way to get to Bornholm is to take the train from Copenhagen to Ystad in Sweden, from where you can take the high speed catamaran for one hour across the Baltic to Rønne. The service is operated on a single ticket from **DSB** (☎ 70 13 14 15; www.dsb.dk). This trip goes several times a day, takes just over three hours in total and costs Dkr265 one way with a seat reservation (Dkr530 return). It's also possible to drive to Ystad and cross with a car from there.

Bornholmstrafikken (☎ 56 95 18 66; www.bornholmstrafikken.dk; adult Dkr250, car Dkr1350-1435) operates a ferry service from Køge, just south of Copenhagen, to Bornholm. The overnight ferry departs daily at 11.30pm and arrives at 6am. Køge is, however, around 30 minutes south of Copenhagen by train, which is an additional cost and time if you are travelling from Copenhagen.

The quickest option of all is the 35-minute flight with **Cimber Air** (☎ 74 42 22 77; www.cimber.dk; one way from Dkr500), with several flights a day between Copenhagen and Bornholm. Book ahead for cheaper prices.

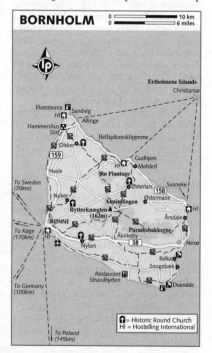

BORNHOLM

0 — 10 km
0 — 6 miles

Ertholmene Islands
Christiansø

Hammeren — Sandvig
HI
Hammershus — Allinge
Slot
Helligdomsklipperne
Olsker
159
Gudhjem
Hasle — Melsted
HI
Rø Plantage
Østerlars — Svaneke
To Sweden — 158
(70km) — Nyker — Almindingen — Østermarie
Rytterknægten — Årsdale
(162m) — HI
RØNNE
To Køge — Paradisbakkerne
(170km) — HI — Akirkeby
Nylars — 38
Balka — Nexø
To Germany — Snogebæk
(100km) — Restaurant
Strandhytten — Dueodde

☐ = Historic Round Church
HI = Hostelling International

To Poland
(145km)

DENMARK

GETTING AROUND
To/From the Airport
The island's airport, Bornholms Lufthavn, is 5km southeast of Rønne, on the road to Dueodde. Bus 7 stops on the main road in front of the airport.

Bicycle
Cycling is a great way to get around. Bornholm is crisscrossed by more than 200km of bike trails, many built over former rail routes. You can start right in Rønne, from where bike routes fan out to Allinge, Gudhjem, Nexø, Dueodde and the central forest. You can download cycle routes across the island for free at www.cykel.bornholm.info.

In Rønne, Bornholms **Cykeludlejning** (☎ 56 95 13 59; www.bornholms-cykeludlejning.dk, in Danish; Nordre Kystvej 5; per day/week Dkr60/250), next to the tourist office, has a large fleet of bikes for hire. Bicycles can usually be rented from hostels and camping grounds around the island for about Dkr60 a day.

Bus
A good, inexpensive bus service around the island is operated by **Bornholms Amts Trafikselskab** (BAT; www.bat.dk; passes per day/week Dkr140/450). Fares are based on a zone system and cost Dkr10 per zone; the maximum fare is for 10 zones. Ask the bus driver about a 'RaBATkort' (10 rides), which can be used by more than one person and saves about 20%. Buses operate all year, but schedules are less frequent from October to April. From May to September, bus 7 leaves from the Rønne ferry terminal every two hours between 8am and 4pm and goes anticlockwise around the island, stopping at Dueodde beach and major coastal villages before terminating at Hammershus. There are more evening buses in the peak season from late June to the end of August. Other buses make direct runs from Rønne to Nexø, Svaneke, Gudhjem and Sandvig.

Car & Scooter
Motor scooters (per day Dkr250), open-topped mini scoot cars (per day Dkr385) or cars (per day Dkr625) can be rented at **Europcar** (☎ 56 95 43 00; Nordre Kystvej 1, Rønne). The office is in the petrol station just along the road from the ferry terminal. **Avis** (☎ 56 95 22 08), further into town, offers similar rates.

RØNNE
pop 15,000
Though not the most charming of the island's harbour towns, virtually everyone who visits Bornholm will end up spending time in Rønne which, as well as having a reasonable-sized shopping area also boasts some engaging museums and an old quarter of cobbled streets flanked by pretty single-storey dwellings. It is the island's largest settlement and is a popular shopping destination for Swedes on day trips.

The **tourist office** (Bornholms Velkomstcenter; ☎ 56 95 95 00; www.bornholm.info; Nordre Kystvej 3; ☉ 9am-5pm Mon-Sat, 10am-3pm Sun mid-Jun–Aug, 9am-4pm Mon-Fri, to noon Sat Feb-May, Sep & Oct, to 4pm Mon-Fri Nov-Jan) is a few minutes' walk from the harbour and has masses of information on all of Bornholm. There's free internet access at the **public library** (Pingels Allé; ☉ 10am-7pm Mon-Tue & Thu, to 3pm Fri, 1-8pm Wed, 10am-2pm Sat) for which you must book a slot first.

Two very pleasant streets with period buildings are the cobblestoned **Laksegade** and **Storegade**.

Bornholms Museum (☎ 56 95 07 35; Sankt Mortensgade 29; adult/child Dkr35/10; ☉ 10am-5pm Mon-Fri, to 2pm Sat) has a surprisingly large collection of local history exhibits, some interesting displays about Christiansø along with many prehistoric finds and a good maritime section decked out like the interior of a ship. **Hjorths Fabrik** (☎ 56 95 01 60; Krystalgade 5; adult/child Dkr35/10; ☉ 10am-5pm Mon-Sat) is a ceramics museum complete with working features.

The handsome round church, **Nylars Rundkirke**, built in 1150 and decorated with 13th-century frescoes, is surrounded by Viking rune stones. It's only a 15-minute ride from Rønne on bus No 6.

Sleeping & Eating
The tourist office books rooms in private homes for singles (Dkr200) and doubles (Dkr290).

Galløkken Camping (☎ 56 95 23 20; www.gallokken. dk; Strandvejen 4; adult/child Dkr69/35; ☉ mid-May–Aug) Just more than 1km south of the town centre. It rents out bikes for Dkr65 per day.

Danhostel Rønne (☎ 56 95 13 40; www.danhostel -roenne.dk; Arsenalvej 12; dm/s/d/tr Dkr150/300/400/ 460; 🅿 ✗) Immaculately kept and close the town. Rooms sleep up to eight, and there is a shared kitchen, laundry, minigolf and bike rental on site.

BB-Hotel (☎ 70 22 55 30; www.bbhotels.dk; Store Torv 17, Rønne; d/tr/q Dkr500/650/800) Accommodation doesn't get much more spartan than this self service place above some shops on the main square, but the rooms are clean and all have baths and toilets en suite, plus breakfast is included in the price. Above all, it's cheap.

Det Little Hotel (☎ 56 90 77 00; www.detlittlehotel .dk; Ellekongstræde 2, Rønne; d/f incl breakfast Dkr750/1200) This recently opened B&B is in a quiet side street close to the town centre and, though the rooms are spartan, they have flat screen TVs, free internet access and mildly funky, modern Danish decor.

Restaurant Fyrtøjet (☎ 56 95 30 12; www.fyrtoejet .dk; Store Torvegade 22, Rønne; mains Dkr160; ☐ 5-11pm) This popular local restaurant in central Rønne serves unadventurous but dependable bistro food for midrange prices.

Gastronomen (☎ 21 48 75 77; www.gastronomen.dk; Laksetorvet, Store Torvegade 29, Rønne; 6 course set menu incl wine Dkr798) Lars Aabech's ambitious cooking has a new venue, having moved from Sandvig to Rønne in 2007. Expect the best local, seasonal ingredients with an Italian twist.

Kvickly supermarket, which is opposite the tourist office, has a good bakery that opens at 6.30am, and a handy bistro that offers sandwiches (Dkr50 to Dkr65) and hearty hot meals (Dkr75 to Dkr90). You'll find numerous fast-food places on Store Torv.

Towards the weekend and in summer, there may be some life in **O'Malley's** (☎ 56 95 00 16; Store Torvegade 2), which caters for an older crowd and has an over-21 age limit for its Friday and Saturday late-night discos.

DUEODDE

Dueodde has a vast stretch of white-sand beach backed by woodlands and dunes. The only 'sight' is the slender lighthouse, which you can climb for views of sea and strand that stretch to the horizon. There's no village, just a bus stop with a single hotel, a restaurant, a cluster of kiosks selling ice cream and hot dogs, and necessary public toilets to cope with the rush from tour coaches in summer. It can be a crowded trek for a couple of hundred metres along boardwalks to reach the superb beach. Once there, head left or right for wide-open spaces.

Sleeping

Dueodde Vandrerhjem (Youth Hostel) & Camping (☎ 56 48 81 19; www.dueodde.dk; Skorkkegårdsvejen 17, Dueodde; s/d/tr/q Dkr225/375/450/530, camp sites adult/child Dkr62/34, tent Dkr25-35; ☐ 1 May–30 Sep) Another lovely, low cost spot to stay on Dueodde beach is this cabin-style, single-storey hostel and camp site with indoor pool, sauna and solarium among other facilities.

Dueodde Camping (☎ 56 48 81 49; Duegårdsvej 2, Dueodde; camp sites adult/child Dkr66/38) A picturesque camping ground right beside the beach, this one boasts an open air pool, tennis court, sauna, solarium and plenty of children's activities, including a fort, trampoline and playground.

Bornholms Familie Camping (☎ 56 48 81 50; www .bornholms-familiecamping.dk; Krogegårdsvejen 2, Dueodde; adult/child/tent Dkr70/40/55, cabins per week Dkr2800-500, luxury 4-person tent Dkr2100-3600; ⓟ ⓰) This must be one of the loveliest camping grounds in Denmark, amid beech and pine trees right beside the wonderful soft, white-sand beach at Dueodde and with facilities including laundry, shared kitchen, minigolf, table tennis, sauna and solarium.

Restaurant Kadeau (☎ 56 97 82 50, Baunevej 18; lunch mains Dkr120-170, dinner mains Dkr170-290; ☐ daily lunch & dinner summer, Fri & Sat evenings low season) A short drive north of Duodde. Restaurant Kadeau occupies a terrific location on the southern coast. Overlooking lapping waves, sand dunes and little else, Kadeau offers contemporary Franco-Nordic food of – for Bornholm – a uniquely high and ambitious standard. It's a champagne and lobster kind of place, although locally raised pork and chicken also often feature and the prices are not unreasonable.

BORNHOLM'S EAST COAST

Bornholm's east coast tends to be fairly built-up and is punctuated by several settlements, all with some interest as stopping-off places.

Snogebæk is a small shoreside fishing village that hangs on to its authenticity because of its small fleet of working boats and its scattering of fishing huts and cabins.

Just north of Snogebæk is the fine beach of **Balka Strand**.

Nexø is Bornholm's second-largest town. It took a hammering from Soviet bombers in WWII and today much of what you see from the harbour outwards is a fairly functional reconstruction. **Nexø-Dueodde Turistinformation** (☎ 56 49 32 00; Åsen 4) is in the centre of town, two blocks inland from the harbour. **Nexø Museum** (☎ 56 49 25 56; Havnen 2; adult/child Dkr25/5; ☐ 10am-4pm Mon-Fri, 9am-2pm Sat mid-May–mid-Oct) is at the harbour and is packed with maritime flotsam and jetsam including an old-fashioned diving suit, cannons, WWII mines and the inner workings of a lighthouse.

The harbour town of **Svaneke** has award-winning historic buildings, especially those near the village church, a few minutes' walk south of the centre. The **tourist office** (☎ 56 49 70 79; Storegade 24; ☒ noon-4.30pm Mon-Fri) is in the post office building, two blocks north of the central square.

Sleeping & Eating

FDM Camping Balka Strand (☎ 56 48 80 74; www .fdmcamping.dk/da-DK/pladser/balka; adult/child Dkr77/42, tents Dkr20-35, cabins Dkr500-550; ☒ 25 Apr–13 Sep) Next to the lovely sandy beach at Balka, this is very convenient for exploring Bornholm's eastern coast.

Danhostel Svaneke (☎ 56 49 62 42; www.danhostel -svaneke.dk; Reberbanevej 9; dm/s/d Dkr160/420/470; ☒ Apr-Oct) This quiet complex of bungalow-style chalet dorms and rooms is 1km south of the centre of Svaneke and close to the water.

Hotel Balka Strand (☎ 56 49 49 49; www.hotelbalkas trand.dk; Boulevarden 9; s/d from Dkr725/895; [P] [X] [Q]) A good base in the Snogebæk-Nexø area is this friendly, smart hotel about 150m from Balka Strand beach.

Hostel Møbelfabrikken (☎ 70 22 08 98; www.mo belfabrikken.dk; Gammel Rønnevej 17A, Nexø; d Dkr495-595, q Dkr625-750) One of the more unusual places to stay on Bornholm is this major glass and ceramic workshop and hostel in Nexø. It hosts various events, courses and exhibitions throughout the year, and you can even rent out the workshop. Rooms are extremely basic, but clean and tidy.

Bryghuset (☎ 56 49 73 21; Torv 5) This friendly microbrewery brews three excellent beers, ideal for washing down all that smoked fish. If you haven't already eaten, it also serves decent pub grub for less than Dkr120.

Rogeriet i Svaneke (☎ 56 49 63 24; Fiskergade 12; counter items Dkr30-60) Perhaps the best smoke-house on the island. It is down by the harbour serving smoked trout, herring, cod's roe and fish *frikadellar*, traditionally washed down with a cool beer while sitting at the outdoor picnic tables.

GUDHJEM

pop 1000

Is this the perfect Danish seaside holiday village? We think it might well be. Gudjhem is just big enough to offer enough for a week's holiday without being too swamped by tourists. There are plenty of places to eat and stay, and excellent beaches within a kilometre or so. Its charming half-timbered houses and sloping streets rolling down to the pleasant harbourfront make it one of the island's most attractive towns.

The **tourist office** (☎ 56 48 52 10; Åbogade 7; ☒ 10am-4pm Jul & Aug, 1-4pm Mon-Sat Sep & Mar-Jun) is a block inland from the harbour alongside the library. Gudhjem has narrow streets and parking is difficult. There's a public car park north-west of the harbour. This is also where you catch the boat to Christiansø (see opposite).

A bike path leads inland 4km south from Gudhjem to the thick-walled, buttressed Østerlars Rundkirke, the most impressive of the island's round churches – bus No 3 goes by the church.

Six kilometres north of Gudhjem along the coast road is the island's leading art museum, **Bornholms Kunst Museum** (☎ 56 48 43 86; www.born holms-kunstmuseum.dk; Helligdommen, Rø; adult/child Dkr70/ free; ☒ 1-5pm Thu & Fri, 10am-5pm Sat & Sun Jan-Mar & Nov-Dec, 10am-5pm Tue-Sun Apr, May, Sep & Oct, 10am-5pm Jun-Aug). This striking modern building overlooking the famously vertiginous Heligdoms cliffs and coastal path contains some of the finest 19th- and early 20th-century art to have been made on the island by Danish artists such as Richard Mortensen and Michael Ancher. There is also an excellent cafe. The coastal bus 7 from Gudhjem to Rønne stops outside the entrance, as does the No 7 coming in the other direction from Rønne.

Sleeping & Eating

Danhostel Gudhjem (☎ 56 48 50 35; www.danhostel -gudhjem.dk; dm/s/d Dkr165/320/410) About 50m from the harbourside bus stop, this hostel is in an attractive spot right by the harbour with small cosy, bright white six-bed dorms.

Therns Hotel (☎ 56 48 50 35; www.therns-hotel.dk; Brøddegade 31; s Dkr500, d Dkr650-850) The management from Danhostel Gudhjem also handles this pleasant place to stay.

Stammershalle Badehotel (☎ 56 48 42 10; www .stammershalle-badehotel.dk; Sdr Strandvej 128, Rø; s Dkr690, d Dkr990-1390) This has to be one of the island's most charismatic places to stay. This imposing 19th century bathing hotel overlooking a rocky part of the coast a few kilometres north of Gudhjem has bags of charm and elegance with Cape Cod–style decor, a superior restaurant and gorgeous views across the sea to Christiansø.

Jantzens Hotel (☎ 56 48 50 17; www.jantzenshotel .dk; Brøddegade 33; s/d from Dkr700/975) The central Jantzens Hotel is a fine old building with stylish, modern rooms and a lovely, light, contemporary conservatory and garden restaurant serving modern European food.

Gudhjem Rogeri (☎ 56 48 57 08; buffet Dkr95) Further along is this waterfront smokehouse, the oldest on the island (dating from 1910) with an all-you-can-eat buffet and some challenging seating, including on the upper floor, which is reached by rope ladder. It has live folk, country and rock music most nights in summer.

SANDVIG & ALLINGE

Sandvig and Allinge have grown together over the years and are generally referred to as Sandvig-Allinge. They are tucked away to the east of Bornholm's rocky northwestern tip and boast an excellent sandy beach to add to their beguiling appeal. Sandvig is a small fishing village, while Allinge has as good a range of restaurants, grand hotels and nightlife as you will find outside of Rønne. Bornholm's best-known sight, Hammershus Slot, is 3km south on the road to Rønne. The impressive, substantial ruins of this 13th-century castle are the largest of their kind in Scandinavia. They are perched dramatically over the sea, flanked by cliffs and a deep valley. One of the best ways of reaching the castle is by following footpaths from Sandvig through the heather-covered hills of Hammeren – a wonderful hour-long hike. The trail begins by the camping ground. If there is a must-see sight on Bornholm, this castle is it.

Sleeping & Eating

Gæstgiveren (☎ 56 44 62 30; Theatrestræde 2; ☯ Jun-Aug) A lively place to stay in the heart of Allinge is this...well, we're not sure how best to describe it really – it's part holiday guest house, part live music venue, part outdoor grill restaurant and bar. If you stay here you can expect to become part of the seasonal, Copenhagen-by-sea community of creative, Bohemian types that spend the summer in Allinge...and not to get much sleep. At the time of writing, prices for 2009 season were yet to be confirmed.

Hotel Sandvig Havn (☎ 56 48 03 01; www.sand vighavn.dk; Strandpromenaden 5, Allinge; s Dkr400-480,

d Dkr600-940; ☯ Apr-Oct) The best of Allinge-Sandvig's grand whitewashed harbour hotels, is this relatively opulent, formal place close to the beach and town. It also has apartments and studios.

Hotel du Nord (☎ 20 95 12 53; www.hotel-du-nord.dk; Storegade 4, Allinge; s Dkr450, d Dkr600-750; ☯ Jul & Aug) This chic little summer hotel is in the centre of Allinge and is highly recommended.

Byskriviergarden (☎ 56 48 08 86; www.byskriver gaarden.dk, in Danish & German; Løsebækegade 3; s/d Dkr650/780; ℗) An enchanting, white-walled, black-beamed converted farmhouse right on the water in Allinge. The rooms are smartly, if sparsely decorated in contemporary style. Try to get the sea-facing ones. There's a pleasant garden and swimmable, kelp-filled rock pools around the corner if you fancy braving the water.

Nordbornholms Rogeri (☎ 56 48 07 30; Kæmpestranden 2, Allinge; mains Dkr95-150) You can't have too many good smoke houses if you ask us, and this is another great one, right on the harbour in Allinge. The Dkr152 all-you-can-eat fish buffet is truly sumptuous.

Restaurant Sommer (☎ 56 48 48 49; Havnegade 19; mains Dkr120-210) Great smørrebrød (four for Dkr120 including tender, pink roast beef with home-made pickles and local salted herring), good seafood and light flavoursome seasonal starters are served on the cosy little harbour-facing terrace.

CHRISTIANSØ
pop 100

Charmingly preserved, tiny Christiansø (it's about 500m long) is a 17th-century fortress-island an hour's sail northeast of Bornholm. It's well worth making time for a day trip, as more than 70,000 visitors do each year (only 3000 spend the night). It has been a seasonal fishing hamlet since the Middle Ages. Christiansø fell briefly into Swedish hands in 1658, after which Christian V decided to turn the island into an invincible naval fortress. Bastions and barracks were built; church, school and prison followed.

By the 1850s the island was no longer needed as a forward base against Sweden and the navy withdrew. Soldiers who wanted to stay on as fishermen were allowed to live as free tenants in the old cottages. Their offspring, and a few latter-day fisherfolk and artists, currently comprise Christiansø's 100 residents. The entire island is an unspoiled

DENMARK

reserve – there are no cats or dogs, no cars and no modern buildings intrude – allowing the rich birdlife, including puffins, to prosper.

There's a small local history museum in Frederickson's tower and a great 360-degree view from Christiansø lighthouse. Otherwise the main activity is walking the footpaths along the fortified walls and batteries that skirt the island. There are skerries with nesting sea birds and a secluded swimming cove on Christiansø's eastern side.

In summer, camping is allowed in a small field at the Duchess Battery (Dkr55 per person). **Christiansø Gæstgiveriet** (☎ 56 46 20 15; r incl breakfast Dkr850), the island's only inn, has a few rooms with shared bathroom and a restaurant. Booking ahead for a room is advised. There's a small food store and a snack shop.

Christiansøfarten (☎ 56 48 51 76) sails daily to Christiansø from Gudhjem and Monday to Saturday from Allinge between mid-May and mid-September. The mailboat from Svaneke sails Monday to Friday year-round. All boats charge Dkr170 per adult and Dkr85 per child for a return journey. Dogs or other pets are forbidden on Christiansø.

FUNEN

pop 476,000

As a stepping stone from Zealand to the Jutland Peninsula, visitors often overlook the rural island of Funen perhaps making a whistlestop visit to Hans Christian Andersen's birthplace and museum in the island's capital, Odense. But there is more to Funen (Fyn in Danish): the towns of Svendborg and Faaborg have a gentle charm, particularly in summer, and there are excellent, clean beaches all around the island.

Close to Faaborg are two of the country's most celebrated gourmet manor house hotels, Steensgaard and Falsled, and there are another 121 manors and castles on the island in all, dating from as far back as the 14th century, most open their grounds to the public.

Funen is connected to Zealand by the Storebælts Forbindlesen (Great Belt's Bridge) and to Jutland by the Lillebælts Bro (Little Belt's Bridge). In all, the impressive span, which runs between the industrial towns of Korsør and Nyborg, covers 18km – even longer than the Øresunds Fixed Link. If you're taking a train, the cost of crossing is included in your fare; however, if you're driving, there's a costly bridge toll each way (under-6m/over-6m vehicles Dkr215/310) and Dkr115 for a motorbike. For more information, go to www.visitfyn.com.

If you are visiting Funen by bike – as many Danish holidaymakers do – a useful guide is the *Cykelguide Fyn* (Dkr119) available from most tourist offices, which shows cycle routes throughout Funen and its neighbouring islands. Virtually all towns on Funen have places renting bicycles by the day or week from around Dkr65 per day.

ODENSE

pop 158,000

There's plenty more to Odense than the legacy of its – and Denmark's – most famous son, the writer and traveller Hans Christian Andersen. Nevertheless, HCA's (as he's known in these parts) birthplace and adjoining museum are the number one draw, even if there is no concrete evidence to show he ever lived in the house in question (the man himself denied it, in fact). Elsewhere in the country's third largest city there are some excellent restaurants; one of the best shopping zones outside of Copenhagen; a thriving cultural and exhibition space, Brandts Klædefabrik; and the largest stage in Scandinavia in Odense Koncerthus. For more information on the city, go to www.visitodense.com.

Information
INTERNET ACCESS

Boomtown Netcafé (☎ 63 11 15 05; Pantheonsgade 4; per hr Dkr30) A plush gamers' place with fast internet connection.

Odense Central Library (Odense Banegård Center; ☯ 10am-7pm Mon-Thu, to 4pm Fri, to 2pm Sat) Offers free use of the internet.

LEFT LUGGAGE

At the train station, left-luggage lockers cost Dkr10 to Dkr20 for 24 hours. Also at the eastern end of Vestergade, close to HC Andersens Hus, is another left-luggage place which charges Dkr3 to Dkr6 per hour.

MONEY

Nordea (Vestergade 64)

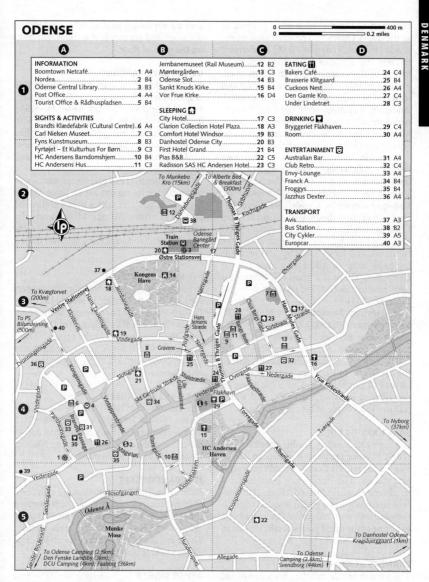

ODENSE

0 —— 400 m
0 —— 0.2 miles

INFORMATION
Boomtown Netcafé.................................**1** A4
Nordea...**2** B4
Odense Central Library........................**3** B3
Post Office..**4** A4
Tourist Office & Rådhuspladsen..........**5** B4

SIGHTS & ACTIVITIES
Brandts Klædefabrik (Cultural Centre)..**6** A4
Carl Nielsen Museet.............................**7** C3
Fyns Kunstmuseum...............................**8** B3
Fyrtøjet – Et Kulturhus For Børn..........**9** C3
HC Andersens Barndomshjem.............**10** B4
HC Andersens Hus...............................**11** C3

Jernbanemuseet (Rail Museum)........**12** B2
Møntergården......................................**13** C3
Odense Slot..**14** B3
Sankt Knuds Kirke................................**15** B4
Vor Frue Kirke......................................**16** D4

SLEEPING
City Hotel...**17** C3
Clarion Collection Hotel Plaza............**18** A3
Comfort Hotel Windsor.......................**19** B3
Danhostel Odense City........................**20** B3
First Hotel Grand.................................**21** B4
Pias B&B...**22** C5
Radisson SAS HC Andersen Hotel.......**23** C3

EATING
Bakers Café..**24** C4
Brasserie Klitgaard..............................**25** B4
Cuckoos Nest.......................................**26** A4
Den Gamle Kro.....................................**27** C4
Under Lindetræt..................................**28** C3

DRINKING
Bryggeriet Flakhaven...........................**29** C4
Room..**30** A4

ENTERTAINMENT
Australian Bar......................................**31** A4
Club Retro..**32** C4
Envy-Lounge..**33** A4
Franck A...**34** B4
Froggys...**35** B4
Jazzhus Dexter.....................................**36** A4

TRANSPORT
Avis..**37** A3
Bus Station...**38** B2
City Cykler..**39** A5
Europcar...**40** A3

POST

Post Office (Brandts Passage; 10am-5.30pm Mon-Fri, to 1pm Sat)

TOURIST INFORMATION

Tourist Office (66 12 75 20; www.visitodense .com; 9.30am-4.30pm Mon-Fri, 10am-3pm Sat & Sun mid-Jun–Aug, 9.30am-4.30pm Mon-Fri, 10am-3pm Sat &

Sun Sep–mid-Jun) At Rådhus, a 15-minute walk from the train station.

Sights

HC Andersens Hus (65 51 46 01; www.museum.odensen .dk; Bangs Boder 29; adult/child Dkr60/free; 10am-4pm Tue-Sun Jan-May & Sep-Dec, 9am-6pm Jun-Aug) lies amid the picturesque houses of the old, working-

DENMARK

class part of Odense, now often referred to as the 'HCA Quarter'. The museum was expanded to mark Andersen's 200th anniversary in 2005 and contains a thorough and lively telling of the amazing life Andersen lived, put into an interesting historical context and leavened by some good audiovisual material. Andersen was supposedly born on the corner room of the building although the author himself denied this in later life and there is no concrete evidence to support this view.

Next door to the museum is the charming **Fyrtøjet – Et Kulturhus for Børn** (Tinderbox – A Cultural Centre for Children; ☎ 66 14 44 11; www.fyretoet.com; Hans Jensens Stræde 21; admission Dkr70; ☽ 9am-6pm Jun-Aug, 10am-4pm Fri-Sun Feb-May & Sep-Dec), where youngsters can explore the magical world of Hans Christian Andersen through storytelling and music (in English as well as Danish during the summer), and by dressing up and pretending to be some of Andersen's most famous characters. There is a good cafe/restaurant here (sandwiches Dkr75 to Dkr85; two-course menu Dkr155).

HC Andersens Barndomshjem (☎ 65 51 46 01; Munkemøllestræde 3-5; adult/child Dkr25/free; ☽ 11am-3pm Tue-Sun Jan-May & Sep-Dec, 10am-4pm Mon-Sun Jun-Aug) has a couple of rooms of exhibits in the small house where Hans Christian lived from the age of two to 14, when he left to seek his fortune in Copenhagen. This is the house he describes in his autobiographies and which features in a couple of his fairy stories.

SANKT KNUDS KIRKE

Odense's 13th-century, Gothic **cathedral** (☎ 66 12 03 92; Flakhaven; admission free; ☽ 9am-5pm Mon-Sat, noon-5pm Sun) reflects Odense's medieval wealth and stature. The stark white interior has a handsome rococo pulpit, a dazzling, 16th-century altarpiece and a gilded wooden triptych crowded with over 300 carved figures and said to be one of the finest pieces of religious art in northern Europe.

BRANDTS KLÆDEFABRIK

The former textile mill has been converted into an impressive **cultural centre** (☎ 65 20 70 00; www.brandts.dk, in Danish; Brandts Passage; combined ticket adult/child Dkr70/free; ☽ 10am-5pm) with a photography museum (Dkr35), a modern art gallery (Dkr40) and a museum of graphics and printing (Dkr35). The superb exhibition spaces often present excellent temporary exhibitions from artists from all over the world. There's

also an appealing roof terrace overlooking the town and an excellent artbook/gift shop on the ground floor.

DEN FYNSKE LANDSBY

This is a delightful **open-air museum** (☎ 65 51 46 01; Sejerskovvej 20; adult/child Dkr60/free; ☽ 10am-7pm mid-Jun–mid-Aug, 10am-5pm Tue-Sun Apr–mid-Jun & mid-Aug–Oct, 11am-3pm Nov-Mar), furnished with period buildings authentically laid out like a small country village, complete with barnyard animals, a duck pond, apple trees and flower gardens.

The museum is in a green zone 4km south of the city centre via bus No 42. From May to September you can take a boat (adult/child Dkr45/35) from Munke Mose down the river to Erik Bøghs Sti, from where it's a 15-minute woodland walk along the river to Den Fynske Landsby.

FYNS KUNSTMUSEUM

In a stately, neoclassical building, this **museum** (☎ 65 51 46 01; Jernbanegade 13; adult/child Dkr40/free; ☽ 10am-4pm Tue-Sun) has a serene atmosphere and contains a quality collection of Danish art from the 18th century to the present. There are small collections of fine sculptures and contemporary art; changing exhibitions are also staged.

CARL NIELSEN MUSEET

This **museum** (☎ 65 51 46 01; Claus Bergs Gade 11; admission free; ☽ 2-6pm Thu & Fri 16 Jun–31 Aug, 4-8pm Thu & Fri 1 Sep–31 May) in Odense's concert hall details the career of the city's native son Carl Nielsen, Denmark's best-known composer.

JERNBANEMUSEET

Railway buffs should not miss the collection of 19th-century locomotives at the **rail museum** (☎ 66 13 66 30; Dannebrogsgade 24; adult/child Dkr60/24; ☽ 10am-4pm) just behind the train station. There are also mini railways for children of all ages to ride on.

OTHER SIGHTS

One of the most attractive parts of Odense is the park beside the river Å (pronounced 'Oh') that runs through the city to the south of the main shopping quarter. It is a popular picnicking and jogging spot. The main shopping action is focussed on the busy pedestrianised street Vestergade and side streets such as Lille Gråbrødstræd. The central square Flakhavn, framed by Odense Rådhuspladsen and Sankt Knuds Kirke, features Svend Wiig Hansen's giant bronze, the reclining *Oceania* in front of the town hall, while the east side of the city centre has some of Odense's oldest buildings, including Andersen's birthplace. You can follow a rewarding walking route from the centre by crossing the busy Torvegade and strolling down Nedergade, a cobblestoned street lined with leaning, half-timbered houses and antique shops, and then returning via Overgade. En route you'll pass the 13th-century **Vor Frue Kirke** (10am-noon Mon-Sat). Finally, **Møntergården** (☎ 66 14 88 14; Overgade 48-50; 10am-4pm Tue-Sun), the modest city museum, has various displays on Odense's history from the Viking Age and a couple of 16th- and 17th-century half-timbered houses. Nightlife is centred on Brandts Passage, a pedestrian corridor lined with restaurants, bars and cafes, many with outdoor seating in summer, leading to Brandts Klædefabrik.

Around the corner, **Møntergården** (☎ 66 14 88 14; Overgade 48-50; 10am-4pm Tue-Sun), the modest city museum, has various displays on Odense's history from the Viking Age and a couple of 16th- and 17th-century half-timbered houses.

Sleeping

DCU Camping (☎ 66 11 47 02; www.camping-odense.dk; Odensevej 102; adult/child/tent Dkr73/45/45) Just under 4km from the city centre, this camping ground is top notch, with an open-air pool, various sports facilities and 12 cabins for rent.

Danhostel Odense City (☎ 63 11 04 25; www .cityhostel.dk; Østre Stationsvej 31; dm/s/d/tr/q incl breakfast Dkr160/465/630/695/760;) An excellent, modern 140-bed place with four- and six-bed dorms, a kitchen and laundry facilities located alongside the train and bus stations.

Alberte Bed & Breakfast (☎ 66 12 30 12; www .albertte.dk; Sophie Breums Vej 10; s/d/tr/q Dkr410/435/525/ 635;) A few minutes' walk north east of the train station is this cosy, clean, tidy suburban house B&B with cooking facilities and TVs in rooms. Breakfast costs Dkr 35 to Dkr50.

Cab Inn (☎ 63 14 57 00; www.cabinn.dk; Østre Stationsvej 7; s Dkr485, d Dkr675-805) The reliably cheap and modern bargain hotel chain has arrived in Odense with a 200-plus room establishment right beside the station.

City Hotel (☎ 66 12 12 58; www.cityhotelodense .dk; Hans Mulesgade 5; s Dkr615-815, d Dkr915-1115) A comfortable modern hotel located in the city centre close to the Hans Christian Andersen museum.

Clarion Collection Hotel Plaza (☎ 66 11 77 45; www .choicehotels.dk; Østre Stationsvej 24; s/d from Dkr795/895;) Overlooking the green spaces of Kongens Have in the centre of the city, this comfortable hotel is one of Odense's best. Its 68 rooms are decorated in a rather chintzy, provincial Old English style but are fairly luxurious. There's also a gym. You get the best rates online.

Comfort Hotel Windsor (☎ 66 12 06 52; www .choicehotels.dk; Vindegade 45; s/d from Dkr795/845) This reasonably priced, if somewhat dowdy hotel is located right in the city centre. Being more business-orientated, it has good off-peak deals, especially if you book online.

First Hotel Grand (☎ 66 11 71 71; www.firsthotels .dk; Jernbanegade 18; s/d incl breakfast from Dkr975/1175) Close to the station, this recently refurbished member of the First Hotels chain is the height of modernity compared to most of Odense's accommodation with a new, slick modern Danish decor and a spacious, glamorous brasserie bar, the Brasserie Grand (open lunch and dinner Monday to Saturday).

Radisson SAS HC Andersen Hotel (☎ 66 14 78 00; www.radissonsas.com; Claus Bergs Gade 7; s/d Dkr1575/1875) As you'd expect of the SAS chain, this is a modern, well run, business-style hotel, close to the HC Andersens Hus and Koncerthus in the centre of town.

Pia's B&B (☎ 66 13 02 38; www.pias-bb.dk; Absalonsgade 14; d/tr/q Dkr6490/675/760) If you are in town for a while, you could consider this cosy apartment in a pretty little cottage close to the main shopping street. It has a fully equipped kitchen, private entrance and is excellent value. Breakfast is Dkr50

Eating

Numerous, mainly fast-food, places line Kongensgade and there's an excellent Bakers at Vestergade 26, the main shopping street.

Odense Banegård Center, which incorporates the train and bus stations, has low-priced options including a **DSB Café** (5am-10pm Mon-Fri, 8am-10pm Sat & Sun), a supermarket and a pub.

Cuckoos Nest (☎ 65 91 57 87; www.cuckoos.dk; Vestergade 73; mains Dkr139-159; 9am-midnight Mon-Wed, 9-1am Thu, 9-2am Fri & Sat, 10am-11pm Sun). A great stalwart of Odense's nightlife scene is this cavernous bar and restaurant on the corner of the main shopping street and Brandts Passage. A lengthy and wide-ranging menu includes everything from nachos and burgers to confit de canard.

Brasserie Klitgaard (☎ 63 13 14 55; www.brasseriek litgaard.dk; Gravene 4; 3 courses Dkr200; ☿ 6pm-midnight Sun-Wed, 6pm-2am Thu-Sat) A good value, stylish evening-only restaurant and cocktail bar serving beautifully presented modern brasserie dishes such as warm smoked salmon rillettes with rye bread and duck with red cabbage, salt baked potatoes, mustard glaze and salted cucumber.

Den Gamle Kro (☎ 66 12 14 33; Overgade 23; 2 courses Dkr325) One of Odense's most atmospheric restaurants is spread throughout several rooms of a half-timbered, 17th-century house serving hefty, traditional Danish and French food. It's mostly meat-based fare, but tasty.

Kvægtorvet (☎ 65 91 50 01; www.kvaegtorvet.com; Rugårdsvej 25; 4/12 courses Dkr325/550; ☿ lunch & dinner Mon-Fri, dinner only Sat) Klavs Styrbæk is one of Funen's leading chefs and his superb restaurant is renowned for its accomplished, ambitious modern Danish food made using locally sourced meat and seafood, such as pheasant with chestnuts and grilled scallops with coconut and lime.

Under Lindetræt (☎ 66 12 92 86; www.underlinde traet.dk; Ramsherred 2; 2 courses Dkr330; ☿ dinner) Right opposite the HC Andersens Hus is one of the city's leading restaurants, housed in a lovely 18th-century cottage. Chef Brian Madsen's food is refined, classic Franco-Danish, with an emphasis on Alsace and Tuscany.

Munkebo Kro (☎ 65 97 40 30; www.munkebo-kro .dk; Fjordvej 56, Munkebo; mains Dkr350, 2-course lunch Dkr280) Fiercely expensive his food may be, but chef Thomas Pasfill's food is renowned throughout Denmark for its refinement and creativity (monkfish and king crab ballontine bisque, is one classic dish). This delightful thatched coaching inn, dating from 1826 and overlooking a small fjord 15km north of Odense, is the perfect setting. There are 22 rooms here too, with prices from Dkr1195/1395 per single/double

Drinking

Room (Brandts Passage 6-8; ☿ 10am-10pm Sun-Wed, 10am-midnight Thu, to 1am Fri, to 3am Sat, to 6pm Sun) One of Odense's trendiest venues is this light, bright modern Mediterranean styled cafe-nightclub in the Brandt's Passage area. DJs play – mostly house – every Thursday, Friday and Saturday.

Bryggeriet Flakhaven (☎ 566 12 02 99; www.bryg geriet.dk/flakhaven; Flakhaven 2; ☿ 11.30am-10pm Mon-Sat, 3-10pm Sun) This colourful microbrewery located close to the town hall brews a decent variety of beers and bitters on site and serves an appetising global menu (mains Dkr170 to Dkr220) of Mexican, Spanish, Texan and Danish classics, such as beer marinated chicken breast.

Entertainment

Franck A (☎ 66 12 27 57; www.francka.dk; Jernbanegade 4; ☿ 11am-late) Everyone knows Franck A's, one of the main nightlife venues in the city, with a large, light, raw brick cafe-bar-restaurant serving steaks, burgers and brunches throughout the day, and DJs playing Thursday to Saturday. It attracts a younger crowd at weekends.

Froggys (☎ 65 90 74 47; www.froggyscafe.dk; Vestergade 68; ☿ 11am-late, to 10pm Sun) Another popular cafe-restaurant-club which has DJs and sometimes live music at weekends, and rough and ready food (burgers Dkr95) throughout the day.

Club Retro (www.retro.dk; Overgade 45; admission varies; ☿ midnight-6am Sat) One of a chain of three clubs in Denmark, the Odense branch hosts local and international DJs on Saturday only. Age restrictions apply most nights (ie over 21s).

Envy-Lounge (Brandts Passage 31; ☿ 9.30am-midnight Mon-Wed, to 2am Thu-Sat, 10.30am-11pm Sun) Odense's most glamorous nightlife venue, the Envy lounge-bar is, by day, a cool, light cafe – the epitome of Scandinavian chic. DJs play in the evening every Saturday starting around 10pm.

Australian Bar (☎ 66 11 83 90; Brandts Passage 10) With either live music or dancing happening most nights; it's in the heart of Odense's buzzing nightlife quarter.

Brandts Klædefabrik (☎ 66 13 78 97; Brandts Passage) Has an outdoor amphitheatre that's a venue for free summer weekend concerts.

Café Biografen (☎ 66 13 16 16; Brandts Klædefabrik; tickets Dkr70-90) Shows first-run movies on three screens. Biocity (Odense Banegård Center) is another multiplex cinema on the 1st floor of the train station.

Jazzhus Dexter (☎ 66 11 27 28; www.dexter.dk; Vindegade 65) Jazzhus Dexter has good live music (mostly of the jazz variety) groups virtually every night of the week starting around 8pm.

Getting There & Away

Odense is on the main railway line between Copenhagen (Dkr214, 1½ hours, every 15 minutes), Århus (Dkr187, 1¾ hours, hourly), Aalborg (Dkr286, three hours, hourly) and Esbjerg (Dkr169, two hours, every 30 minutes). The ticket office is open from about 6am to 8.15pm most days, but closes at 4.35pm on Saturday. Buses leave from the rear of the train station.

Odense is just north of the E20; access from the highway is clearly marked. Rte 43 connects Odense with Faaborg; Rte 9 connects Odense with Svendborg.

Getting Around

Odense is Denmark's number one bicycle city (it's official), with over 60,000 locals getting around on two wheels every day, and 360km of cycle paths. Bicycles can be rented at **City Cykler** (☎ 66 13 97 83; www.citycykler.dk; Vestergade 27; per day Dkr155; ☻ 10am-5.30pm Mon-Fri, to 1pm Sat), west of the city centre.

Driving in Odense is not that difficult outside of rush hour, although many of the central sights are on pedestrian streets, so it's best to park your car and then explore on foot. You can find substantial car parks around Brandts Klædefabrik and the Carl Nielsen Museet. Parking costs around Dkr12 for one hour.

There are several car-rental companies in town:

Avis (☎ 66 14 39 99; Østre Stationsvej 37)
Europcar (☎ 66 14 15 44; Kongensgade 69)
PS Bilundejning (☎ 66 14 00 00; Middelfartvej 1) This is a competitive local option (from around Dkr340 per day) if you are not required to drop the car off in another town or city.

LADBYSKIBET (LADBY SHIP)

This **historical site** (☎ 65 32 16 67; Vikingevej 123; adult/child Dkr40/free; ☻ 10am-5pm Jun-Aug, to 4pm Tue-Sun Sep-Oct & Mar-May, closed Nov-Feb) comprises the remains of a 22m-long Viking ship that once formed the tomb of a 10th century Viking chieftain. All the wooden planks from the Ladby ship decayed long ago, leaving the imprint of the hull moulded into the earth, along with iron nails, an anchor and the partial remains of the dogs and horses that were buried with their master. There's a separate visitor centre at the arrival car park with a 1:10-scale model of the ship and background information about the site.

Getting There & Away

In the little village of Ladby, 4km southwest of Kerteminde via Odensevej, turn north onto Vikingevej, a one-lane road through fields that ends after 1.2km at the Ladbyskibet car park. You enter through the little museum from where it's a few minutes' walk along a field path to the mound.

Local bus 890 (Dkr20, 30 minutes, eight daily Monday to Friday) makes the trip from Kerteminde to the village of Ladby. Check the schedule with the bus driver, as the last return bus is typically around 4pm. Also, you'll have to walk the Vikingevej section to the museum about 20 minutes away.

EGESKOV SLOT

This magnificent **castle** (☎ 62 27 10 16; www.eges kov.com; combined ticket for all sights except castle adult/child Dkr140/75, plus castle interior Dkr185/100; ☻ 10am-6pm May, Jun, Aug & Sep, to 8pm Jul), complete with moat and drawbridge, is an outstanding example of the lavish efforts that sprang up during Denmark's Golden Age, the Renaissance. There are enough sights and activities here to keep anyone happily occupied for a day. The castle exteriors are the best features. The interior is heavily Victorian in its furnishings and hunting trophies of now rare beasts. The grounds include century-old privet hedges, free-roaming peacocks, topiary, aerial woodland walkways, English gardens and a bamboo grass labyrinth.

The castle grounds usually stay open an hour longer than the castle. Admission to the grounds includes entry to a large antique car museum, which also features some vintage aircraft swooping from the rafters.

Egeskov Slot is 2km west of Kvændrup on Rte 8. From Odense take the Svendborg-bound train to Kvændrup Station (Dkr52) and continue on foot or by taxi.

FAABORG & AROUND

pop 7200

Faaborg is a pretty, historic fishing town on the south coast of Funen. Though its small shopping quarter has rather fallen into decline in recent years, its harbour is flourishing once again and the art museum remains justly renowned. In the 17th century it was home to one of Denmark's largest commercial fleets and it retains many vestiges of that earlier era in its picturesque, cobblestone streets

DENMARK

and leaning, half-timbered houses. This is where you take the ferries to the quiet, time-warp southern islands, most notably Ærø. Faaborg's **tourist office** (☎ 62 61 07 07; www.visit faaborg.dk; Banegårdspladsen 2A; ☼ 9am-5pm Mon-Sat Jun-Sep, to 4.30pm Mon-Fri, 10am-3pm Sat Oct-May) is adjacent to the bus station and car park on the harbour front. You can hire bikes here for Dkr60 a day.

Sights & Activities

The main square, **Torvet**, is a pleasant spot to linger. It features the Svendborg sculptor Kai Nielsen's striking bronze fountain group *Ymerbrønd*; depicting a naked giant suckling at the udders of a cow (depicting a Norse fertility myth) – it caused quite a stir after it was unveiled. A handsome, 18th-century merchant's house is now the town museum, **Den Gamle Gaard** (Holkegade 1; adult/child Dkr30/free; ☼ 10.30am-4.30pm mid-May–Oct, 11am-3pm Sat & Sun Apr–mid-May), complete with period furnishings.

The small **Faaborg Museum for Fynsk Malerkunst** (Grønnegade 75; adult/child Dkr50/free; ☼ 10am-4pm Apr-Oct) is a former winery, which contains a fine collection of Funen art, including works by artists such as Peter Hansen, Jens Birkholm, and Anna Syberg. Kai Nielsen's original granite sculpture of the *Ymerbrønd* is also here. The town landmark is the nearby belltower of **St Nikolai**.

There are numerous daily ferries to the nearby islands of Avernakø and Lyø (Dkr100 return, bicycle Dkr25, car Dkr165) and a passenger service that travels to Bjørnø (Dkr40 return).

There's a small watersports centre at the **Quality Hotel Faaborg Fjord** (☎ 62 61 10 10; Svendborgvej 175; activities Dkr60-100), located about 2km out of town, which offers fast water-based excitement such as kneeboarding, high-speed jumping and being towed along behind a weaving speedboat astride a big banana.

Sleeping & Eating

The tourist office can book rooms in private homes for Dkr250 for single travellers and Dkr400 for doubles plus a Dkr25 booking fee. There are a couple of unremarkable cafes and fast-food places in the town square and more upmarket restaurants along the harbourfront.

Danhostel Faaborg (☎ 62 61 12 03; www.dan-hostel.dk/faaborg; Grønnegade 71-72; dm/d Dkr150/300; ☼ Apr–late Oct) This 69-bed, three-star hostel occupies two handsome historic buildings, close to the Faaborg Museum and the town's indoor swimming baths.

Hotel Færgegaarden (☎ 62 61 11 15; www.hotel fg.dk; Christian IX Vej 31; s/d Dkr700/850) Faaborg's oldest hotel was refurbished recently and is located close to the harbour and town centre. Its restaurant is orientated to the tourists who flock here in the summer, featuring dishes such as veal schnitzel and prawn cocktail (two courses Dkr325).

Hotel Faaborg (☎ 62 61 02 45; www.hotelfaaborg .dk; Torvet; s/d Dkr750/850; ⓟ ▣) This very central hotel has good, welcoming rooms. Its restaurant does tasty herring dishes for Dkr85 and Mediterranean brasserie food.

Det Hvide Pakhus (Christian IXs Vej 2; www.dethvidepa khus.dk; Faaborg Harbour; 1-4 courses Dkr225-410; ☼ lunch & dinner daily high season, closed Mon & Sun low season) This light, airy converted warehouse serving classic Franco-Danish food has been central to the rejuvenation of Faaborg's harbour. It's as popular with locals as it is with tourists.

Faaborg Røgeri (☎ 62 61 42 32; Vestkaj; fish dishes Dkr28-65) Situated to the west of the harbour, this place serves cheap, tasty, home-smoked fish – take away only.

Steensgaard Manor (☎ 62 61 94 90; www.her regaardspension.dk; Steensgaard 4, Millinge; 3/4/7 courses Dkr275/530/740, r from Dkr1415) Remarkably there are not one but two atmospheric manor-inns close to Faaborg. Steensgaard is grander still architecturally, with a moat, beautiful gardens and an interior packed with antiques. The food is slightly more classic, but still exceptional quality – dishes include quail pot au feu with gnocchi, well aged local beef and seafood. It is just off the road to Assens.

Falsled Kro (☎ 62 68 11 11; www.falsledkro.dk; Assensvej 513, Millinge; r from Dkr1750-3090; ☼ lunch & dinner Tue-Sun, also Mon May-Oct) This enchanting white, thatched coaching inn dates back to the 15th century and is home to one of the most celebrated chefs in Denmark, Jean Louis Lieffroy. The food (three courses Dkr 660) blends the best local ingredients – game, seafood, wild mushrooms – with classical French techniques and very modern presentation. The 22 individually decorated, modern country house-style rooms are as beautiful. It is 7km north west along the coast road to Assens from Faaborg.

Getting There & Away

Faaborg has no train service. Bus 961 and 962 from Odense (Dkr66, 1¼ hours) run at least hourly to 11pm. Bus 930 and 962 from Svendborg (Dkr47, 40 minutes, at least hourly) are also frequent throughout the day. Getting to Faaborg by car is straightforward; from the north, simply follow Rte 43, which is called Odensevej as it enters town.

SVENDBORG

pop 27,000

This pretty, relaxed 750-year-old harbour town is a major sailing and kayaking centre, with a small but well stocked shopping quarter and several good dining options. There is still enough marine heritage to counter-balance the fairly soulless modern docks that dominate the waterfront.

It really picks up in the summer when tourists flock to nearby Langeland (see p78). The train and bus stations are two blocks northwest of the dock. The **tourist office** (☎ 62 21 09 80; www.visitsydfyn.dk; Centrumpladsen 4; 9.30am-6pm Mon-Fri, to 3pm Sat mid-Jun–Aug, to 5pm Mon-Fri, to 12.30pm Sat Sep–mid-Jun) has lots of information on South Funen as a whole.

You can rent kayaks from **Nicus Nature** (☎ 40 41 89 82; www.nicusnature.com, in Danish; Vindebyoerevej 31B). It also operates kayak tours.

Sights

At the southern end of Havnepladsen's cobbled quayside, opposite where the Ærø ferry docks, is **Sejlskibsbroen**, a jetty lined with splendidly preserved sailing ships and smaller vessels and with an adjoining marina catering for the great number of yachts that sail local waters. Ask at the tourist centre about the various trips that can be arranged on the old sailing ships.

Just over the bridge from Svendborg is the island of **Tåsinge**, with its pretty harbourside village of Troense and the nearby 17th-century castle **Valdemars Slot** (☎ 62 22 61 06; www.valdemarsslot.dk; Slotsalléen 100; adult/child Dkr75/35; 10am-5pm May-Sep). The castle was built in the early 17th century by Denmark's great Renaissance king, Christian IV, for his son, but later awarded to the naval hero Admiral Niels Juel; it remains in his family to this day. Its lavish interior is crammed with paintings and eccentric objects. In the grounds are the **Danish Yachting Museum** and **Denmark's Toy Museum**, packed with vintage playthings. The grounds of the castle and the

nearby white-sand beach have free access. You can get to Valdemars Slot by bus but a better way is by the MS *Helge*, an old-style ferry that carries passengers from Svendborg to Troense and Valdemars Slot every few hours (Dkr100) from May to September. The castle also has a good Franco-Danish **restaurant** (mains from Dkr200; Wed-Sat), which sells picnic baskets for Dkr118 to Dkr165.

Sleeping & Eating

The nearest camping grounds are located on Tåsinge.

Strandbo B&B (☎ 62 23 10 40; www.strandbostudio.dk; Skårupore Strandvej 52, Skårup; s/d Dkr250/600) A little way out of town, this lovely B&B is right on the water with pleasant gardens and an adjacent art gallery.

Danhostel Svendborg (☎ 62 21 66 99; www.danhostel-svendborg.dk; Vestergade 45; dm/r Dkr260/590; P X) Danhostel is in a renovated 19th-century iron foundry in the town centre. Bike hire costs Dkr60.

Hotel Ærø (☎ 62 21 07 60; www.hotel-aeroe.dk, in Danish; Brogade 1; s/d Dkr825/995; P) Right by the water, the Ærø has large, modern chalet-style rooms. There's a good restaurant serving traditional fare, including a range of light lunches and smørrebrød (Dkr60 to Dkr115).

Hotel Svendborg (☎ 62 21 17 00; www.hotel-svendborg.dk; Centrumpladsen 1; s/d Dkr945/1145) A functional business-style hotel with an excellent location in the heart of the shopping district. It has a neighbouring sister hotel, the Hotel Garni, which has slightly cheaper rooms and fewer frills.

Restaurant Number 5 (☎ 72 18 55 55; Havneplads 3a; mains Dkr168-188; 11.30am-3pm & 5.30-10pm Mon-Sat) This top-end restaurant is housed in a converted 19th-century warehouse right on the harbour front by the historic ships. It serves ambitious Scandinavian food with the odd Italian influence for quite reasonable prices.

Restaurant 13 (☎ 62 22 07 95; www.andersgranhoej.dk; Brogade 13; 3 courses Dkr425; 6pm-midnight Mon-Sat) This is perhaps the last place you'd expect to find a chef of the quality and experience of Anders Granhøj, a former *chef de partie* of the esteemed Hotel Meurice in Paris, but we're grateful he's here cooking his sophisticated, modern food from the best local and luxury ingredients. Expect delicious, juicy Funen mussels, local game, langoustine and foie gras to feature on an enticing menu.

DENMARK

Getting There & Away

There are trains from Odense to Svendborg (Dkr60, 45 minutes, hourly). Ferries to Ærøskøbing depart five times a day, the last one goes at 10.30pm in summer.

LANGELAND

pop 14,500

The long, narrow grain producing island of Langeland, connected by bridge to Funen via Tåsinge, is a natural haven and popular holiday destination for Danes. It has some excellent sandy beaches, enjoyable cycling and rewarding bird-watching. A large part of the island around Dovns Klint has been protected as a wildlife reserve. It is also well known in Denmark for its annual **Langeland Festival** (www .langelandfestival.dk, ☉ late Jul–early Aug), a popular family-orientated music festival often referred to as 'Denmark's largest garden party'.

You can pick up information about the island from Langeland's **tourist office** (☎ 62 51 35 05; www .langeland.dk, in Danish; Torvet 5, Rudkøbing; ☉ 9am-5pm Mon-Fri, to 3pm Sat mid-Jun–Aug, 9.30am-4.30pm Mon-Fri, to 12.30pm Sat Sep–mid-Jun).

Sights & Activities

Langeland's top sight is the red stucco **Tranekær Slot**, a handsome medieval castle that has been in the hands of the one family since 1672. The castle is not open to the public, but its grounds are home to the **Tickon** (Tranekær International Centre for Art & Nature; admission to grounds Dkr25), a collection of intriguing art installations created by international artists and sited around the wooded grounds and lake. **Tranekær Slot Museum** and the **Souvenir Museum** are in the castle's old water mill and old theatre respectively.

Situated about 1km north of the castle is the **Castle Mill** (☎ 63 51 10 10; Lejbølleveje; adult/child Dkr20/ free; ☉ 10am-5pm Mon-Fri & 1-5pm Sat & Sun Jun-mid-Sep, 10am-5pm Mon-Fri & 1-5pm Sat & Sun mid-Sep–May), a 19th-century windmill, with its remarkable wooden mechanics still intact.

Langeland's main town of **Rudkøbing** has a fairly desolate harbour area, but the town centre is attractive and there are some fine old buildings around Rudekøbing Kirke, to the north of Brogade, the street leading inland from the harbour to the main square of Torvet. For beaches, head for **Ristinge** about 15km south of Rudkøbing; for **bird-watching** you'll find a sighting tower at **Tryggelev Nor**,

5km south of Ristinge, and a sanctuary at **Gulstav Bog**, the island's southern tip.

Cycling is a good way to explore Langeland. The tourist office has an excellent English-language edition of a brochure and map (Dkr15) that describes six bike routes on the island. Bikes can be hired at **Lapletten** (☎ 62 51 10 98; Engdraget 1; per day Dkr75).

Sleeping

The tourist office maintains a list of rooms for rent in private homes with doubles costing about Dkr350 to Dkr400.

Danhostel Rudkøbing (☎ 62 51 18 30; www.danhostel .dk/rudkobing; Engdraget 11; camp sites/dm/d Dkr60/140/450; ☉ Apr–end Oct) A basic hostel, which is less than ideally located a way back from the centre or the water. There's also space for tents.

Damgården (☎ 62 59 16 45; www.damgaarden.dk; Emmerbøllervej 5, Emmerbølle, Tranekær; per person Dkr250) Denmark's first organic B&B offers bright, spacious rooms in a pretty farm house with a large garden and serves great home-made breakfasts. The owners can organise tours and outings.

Skrøbelevgaard (☎ 62 51 45 31; www.skrobelevgaard .dk; Skrøbelev Hedevej 4; r from Dkr1695) This secluded converted manor farm 3km from Rudkøbing in the centre of the island is based in buildings dating from the 17th century. The decor is wonderfully camp and over the top, with lavish chandeliers and chintzy soft furnishings, and there is a very impressive wine cellar.

Getting There & Away

Buses make the 25-minute run from Svendborg to Rudkøbing (Dkr35) at least hourly; most connect onwards to Tranekær. There are daily ferries from Rudkøbing to Marstal in Ærø (one way per person/car Dkr90/185) and from Spodsbjerg to Tårs in Lolland.

ÆRØ

pop 6800

Just 30km long and 8km wide, Ærø (pronounced 'with difficulty') holds a special place in the hearts of Danes. Mention it and they will sigh wistfully and perhaps recall a long-ago childhood visit to the quaint old town of Ærøskøbing, or cycling holidays amid the beautiful, gentle countryside peppered with crooked, half-timbered houses with traditional hand-blown glass windows and decorative doorways beautified by hollyhocks. Most young residents leave as soon as they can, however, as, though Ærø is one of the most enchanting of all the islands of the south Funen archipelago, there isn't a great deal going on here out of season. There are some good, small beaches, one of the best being Risemark Strand on the southern tip of the island; it's a great place to tour by bicycle not least as this is in keeping with the spirit of an island which is run almost entirely on sustainable energy sources such as wind and solar power.

Ærøhas' three main towns: Ærøskøbing, Marstal and Søby. **Ærøskøbing tourist office** (☎ 62 52 13 00; Vestergade 1; ☼ 9am-6pm Mon-Fri, 10am-3.30pm Sat & Sun Jun-Aug, 9am-4pm Sep-May) is near the waterfront. **Marstal tourist office** (☎ 62 53 19 60; Havnegade 5; ☼ 10am-4pm Jun-Aug) is a few minutes' walk south of the harbour. The island's tourist website is www.visitaeroe.dk.

Ærøskøbing

pop 750

The words 'higgledy' and 'piggledy' could have been invented to describe the idyllic town of Ærøskøbing. A prosperous merchants' town in the late 17th century, its narrow, winding cobblestone streets are lined with 17th- and 18th-century houses. The tourist office hands out an illustrated leaflet, with a separate insert in English, describing the finest buildings in the town, many of them very well preserved.

Apart from Ærøskøbing's overall charm, the main tourist attraction is **Flaske Peters Samling** (☎ 62 52 29 51; Smedegade 22; adult/child Dkr30/15; ☼ 10am-5pm), a museum in the former poorhouse with displays of local folk art. There are also examples of the work of ship's cook, Peter Jacobsen, 'Bottle Peter', who crafted 1700 ships-in-a-bottle during his long life. **Ærø Museum** (☎ 62 52 29 50; www.arremus.dk; Brogade 3-5; admission Dkr25; ☼ 10am-4pm Mon-Fri, 11am-3pm Sat & Sun, closed Sat & Sun low season) charts the local cultural history.

Søby

This quiet little port has a shipyard, which happens to be the island's biggest employer, a sizable fishing fleet and a busy yacht marina. Five kilometres beyond Søby, at Ærø's northern tip, there's a pebble beach with clear water and a stone **lighthouse** with a view.

Marstal

On the southeastern end of the island, Marstal is Ærø's most modern-looking town and has a web of busy shopping streets at its centre. Marstal has an emphatically maritime history; even its street names echo the names of ships and famous sailors. Its **Søfartsmuseum** (☎ 62 53 23 31; Prinsensgade 1; adult/child Dkr50/free; ☼ 9am-8pm Jul, to 5pm Jun & Aug, 10am-4pm Mar & Sep) has an absorbing collection of nautical artefacts including 250 ships' models and full-size boats. There is a reasonably good **beach** on the southern side of town.

Ancient Ærø

Ærø once had more than 100 prehistoric sites and, although many have been lost, the island still has some atmospheric Neolithic remains, especially in its southeast district, to the west of Marstal. At the small village of Store Rise is the site of **Tingstedet**, the remains of a passage grave in a field behind an attractive **12th-century church**.

At **Lindsbjerg** is the superb hilltop site of a long barrow and two passage graves, one of which has a nicely poised capstone. Just over 1km south of here, following signs and right on the coast, is the fascinating medieval relic of **Sankt Albert's Kirke**. It's within a Viking defensive wall from about the 8th century.

Another striking site is at **Kragnæs**, about 4km west of Marstal. Head through the village of Græsvænge and follow the signs for 'Jættestue' along narrow lanes to reach a small car park, from where it's about 600m along field tracks to the restored grave site.

Sleeping

The island's tourist offices have a list of countryside B&Bs around the island for around Dkr230/350 per single/double. There are camping grounds at **Søby** (☎ 62 58 14 70; www.soeby-camping.dk), **Ærøskøbing** (☎ 62 52 18 54; www.aerocamp.dk) and **Marstal** (☎ 63 52 63 69; www.marstalcamping.dk).

Danhostel Marstal (☎ 51 35 77 54; www.danhostel.dk; Færgestræde 29; dm/s/d Dkr150/300/350; ☼ May-Sep) South of the harbour, this modest, but neatly kept, hostel is right by the sea.

Danhostel Ærøskøbing (☎ 62 52 10 44; www.danhostel.dk; dm/r Dkr175/350; ☼ Apr-Sep; P ☒) A solid, modern red-tiled building, this hostel is 1km from town on the road to Marstal.

DENMARK

Vindeballe Kro (☎ 62 52 16 13; Vindeballevej 1, Ærøskøbing; s/d Dkr450/500) A cheap accommodation option 5km from Ærøskøbing is this characterful inn with 10 rooms run by Maria and Steen Larsen.

Pension Vestergade 44 (☎ 62 52 22 98; www .pension-vestergade44.dk; Vestergade 44; s Dkr600-980, d Dkr780-980; P ☒) Next door to the Ærøhus is this delightful 18th-century house with very stylish, yet homely interiors.

Hotel Ærøhus (☎ 62 52 10 03; www.aeroehus.dk; Vestergade 38; s/d Dkr990/1250) In Ærøskøbing, Hotel Ærøhus occupies a large period building close to the harbour. It has comfortable, modern rooms, a smart garden annexe and two tennis courts. There is also an upmarket restaurant (three courses Dkr375) specialising in local seafood, and it rents bikes for Dkr75 per day.

Eating & Drinking

All three towns have bakeries, restaurants and food stores.

Den Grønne Gren (☎ 62 58 20 45; www.dengron negren.dk; Vester Bregninge 17, Ærøskøbing; mains less than Dkr100; ☺ noon-3pm & 6-9pm Wed-Sun May-Jun, 11am-9pm Jul & Aug, noon-3pm & 6-9pm Wed-Sun Sep & Oct) Janni Bidstrup's charming, homely guesthouse and cafe – actually a few kilometres west of Ærøskøbing – serves all organic food and pizzas from the pizza oven are a speciality. Also offers picnic baskets for two for Dkr250.

Ærøskøbing Røgeri (☎ 62 52 40 07; Havnen 15, Ærøskøbing; ☺ 11am-6pm, to 8pm Jun-Aug) This traditional fish smokehouse in Ærøskøbing harbour serves excellent value plates of fresh-smoked salmon, herring and other fish dishes for Dkr30 to Dkr70 – you eat outside on picnic benches.

Cottage Bar (☎ 62 52 21 43; Strandstræde 39) Just along the road from Hotel Marstal is this popular pub with a busy live folk-music programme.

Getting There & Away

There are year-round **car ferries** (☎ 62 52 40 00; www.aeroe-ferry.dk; adult/child/bike/car Dkr114/72/24/247) to Søby from Faaborg, to Ærøskøbing from Svendborg and to Marstal from Rudkøbing. All run about five times a day and take about an hour. If you have a car it's a good idea to make reservations, particularly at weekends and in midsummer. There's also a ferry between Søby and Mommark that runs a few times daily from spring to autumn at comparable prices.

Getting Around

Bus 790 operates from Søby to Marstal via Ærøskøbing hourly from Monday to Friday, and half as frequently on Saturday and Sunday.

You can rent bikes for Dkr250 to Dkr300 per week at the hostel and camping ground in Ærøskøbing and at **Pilebækkens Cykel og Servicestation** (☎ 62 52 11 10; Pilebækken 11), which is opposite the car park on the outskirts of town.

Søby Cykelforretning (☎ 62 58 18 42; Langebro 4; per day Dkr60) rents out bikes in Søby. The tourist office in Marstal sells a Dkr30 cycling map of a round-island route.

JUTLAND

Denmark doesn't have a North–South divide; culturally, spiritually and to a great extent politically, it is divided into Jutland... and all the rest. Jutlanders are different. Sturdy, down to earth, unpretentious, hard working. You will find an old fashioned hospitality here and an engaging frankness; the landscape is the most epic in all of Denmark (that's not saying much, but there are at least some hills, as well as vast and spectacular sandy beaches); and there are several engaging and characterful cities and towns.

ÅRHUS
pop 238,000

Always the bridesmaid, never the bride, Århus (the second-largest city in Denmark) has tended to labour in the shadows of Copenhagen in terms of its cultural draw for visitors, and it is probably also true that few young Danes grow up with dreams of moving here rather than the capital. But – and it's a big 'but' – this is a terrific city in which to spend a day or two.

It is the cultural and commercial heart of Jutland and has one of Denmark's best music and entertainment scenes (there is a very large student population on account of the city's university). There's also a well-preserved historic quarter, and plenty to see and do, ranging from fantastic museums – not least Aros, one of the best art museums in Denmark – and period churches in the centre, to picturesque woodland trails and beaches along the city's outskirts.

Orientation

Århus is fairly compact and easy to get around. The train station is on the southern side of the city centre. The pedestrian shopping streets of Ryesgade, Søndergade and Sankt Clements Torv extend around 1km from the station to the cathedral at the heart of the old city.

Information

BOOKSHOPS

KFM (Store Torv 5) A bookshop with a good range including travel guides.

Newspaper Shop (Store Torv 7) Sells international papers and magazines. International newspapers are also sold at the train station.

EMERGENCY

Århus Kommunehospital (☎ 87 49 44 44; Nørrebrogade) Has a 24-hour emergency ward.

Emergency (☎ 112) Ambulance and police.

INTERNET ACCESS

Boomtown Netcafé (Åboulevarden 21; per 30 min Dkr25; ☿ 10-2am Mon-Thu, to 8am Fri & Sat, 11am-midnight Sun)

LAUNDRY

Mønt Vask (St Paul's Gade 64) A coin launderette. An average wash and dry costs Dkr65.

LEFT LUGGAGE

Lockers are available at the bus and train stations. Both charge Dkr12 for 24 hours.

POST

Post Office (Banegårdspladsen; ☿ 9.30am-6pm Mon-Fri, 10am-1pm Sat) Beside the train station.

TOURIST INFORMATION

The **Tourist Office** (☎ 87 31 50 10; www.visitaarhus .com; Banegårdspladsen; ☿ 9.30am-6pm Mon-Fri, to 1pm Sun mid-Jun–mid-Sep, to 5pm Mon-Fri, 10am-1pm Sat May–mid-Jun, 9am-4pm Mon-Fri, to 1pm Sat mid-Sep–Apr) is well stocked with brochures and leaflets on the city and its surroundings, and on the rest of Jutland and Denmark. You can also buy the Århus Passport here, a two-day or weekly pass that includes public-transport usage and admission to various attractions (24 hours adult/child Dkr139/58, 48 hours Dkr169/69).

TRAVEL AGENCIES

Kilroy Travels (☎ 86 20 11 44; Fredensgade 40) Specialises in discount and student travel and has friendly, helpful staff.

Sights & Activities

AROS

The towering brick walls of Århus's new showpiece **art museum** (☎ 87 30 66 00; www.aros .dk; adult/child Dkr90/free; ☿ 10am-5pm Thu-Sun & Tue, to 10pm Wed) look rather mundane from the outside but inside it's all sweeping curves, soaring spaces and white walls. One of the top three art galleries in Denmark, it is home to a comprehensive collection of 19th- and 20th-century Danish art and a wide range of arresting and vivid contemporary art. There are pieces here from Warhol and Lichtenstein and, in colourfully lit pickling jars, a work by Danish artist Bjørn Nørgaard consisting of parts of a horse he sacrificed in protest at the Vietnam War (long before British artist Damien Hirst started chopping up animals in the name of art). Perhaps the most compelling exhibit is Ron Mueck's startlingly lifelike giant *Boy*. There are pleasing views over town from the terrace and a good cafe and restaurant.

DEN GAMLE BY

The Danes' seemingly limitless enthusiasm for dressing up and recreating history reaches its zenith at **Den Gamle By** (The Old Town; ☎ 86 12 31 88; www.dengamleby.dk; Viborgvej 2; adult/child Dkr100/ free; ☿ 9am-6pm Jul-Aug, 10am-5pm Apr-Jun & Sep-Nov, to 4pm Feb & Mar 10am-5pm, Dec, 11am-3pm Jan). It's an engaging open-air museum of 75 half-timbered houses brought here from around Denmark and reconstructed as a provincial town, complete with a functioning bakery, silversmith and bookbinder. It's on Viborgvej, a 20-minute walk from the city centre. Bus Nos 3, 14, 25 and 55 will take you there.

The **Botanisk Have** (Botanical Gardens), with its thousands of plants and recreated Jutland environments, occupies the high ground above Den Gamle By and can be reached through an exit from the old town or directly from Vesterbrogade.

ÅRHUS DOMKIRKE

This impressive **cathedral** (☎ 86 20 54 00; Bispetorv; admission free; ☿ 9.30am-4pm Mon-Sat May-Sep, 10am-3pm Mon-Sat Oct-Apr) is Denmark's longest, with a lofty nave that spans nearly 100m. The original Romanesque chapel at the eastern-end

ÅRHUS

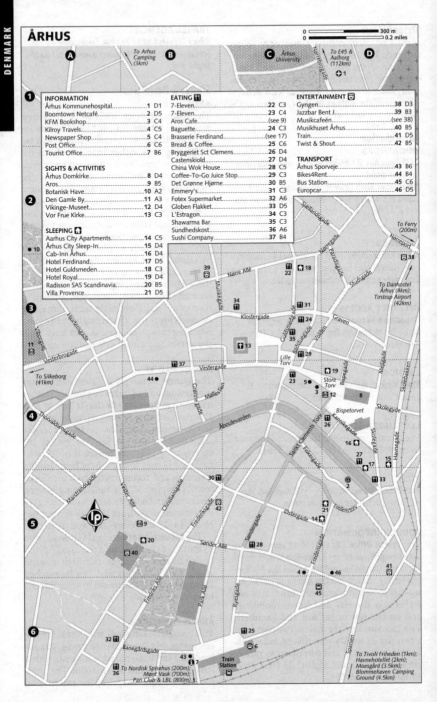

0 _____ 300 m
0 _____ 0.2 miles

INFORMATION
Århus Kommunehospital	**1** D1
Boomtown Netcafé	**2** D5
KFM Bookshop	**3** C4
Kilroy Travels	**4** C5
Newspaper Shop	**5** C4
Post Office	**6** C6
Tourist Office	**7** B6

SIGHTS & ACTIVITIES
Århus Domkirke	**8** D4
Aros	**9** B5
Botanisk Have	**10** A2
Den Gamle By	**11** A3
Vikinge-Museet	**12** D4
Vor Frue Kirke	**13** C3

SLEEPING
Aarhus City Apartments	**14** C5
Århus City Sleep-In	**15** D4
Cab-Inn Århus	**16** D4
Hotel Ferdinand	**17** D5
Hotel Guldsmeden	**18** C3
Hotel Royal	**19** D4
Radisson SAS Scandinavia	**20** B5
Villa Provence	**21** D5

EATING
7-Eleven	**22** C3
7-Eleven	**23** C4
Aros Cafe	(see 9)
Baguette	**24** C3
Brasserie Ferdinand	(see 17)
Bread & Coffee	**25** C6
Bryggeriet Sct Clemens	**26** D4
Castenskiold	**27** D4
China Wok House	**28** C5
Coffee-To-Go Juice Stop	**29** C3
Det Grønne Hjørne	**30** B5
Emmery's	**31** C3
Fotex Supermarket	**32** A6
Globen Flakket	**33** D5
L'Estragon	**34** C3
Shawarma Bar	**35** C3
Sundhedskost	**36** A6
Sushi Company	**37** B4

ENTERTAINMENT
Gyngen	**38** D3
Jazzbar Bent J	**39** B3
Musikcafeén	(see 38)
Musikhuset Århus	**40** B5
Train	**41** D5
Twist & Shout	**42** B5

TRANSPORT
Århus Sporveje	**43** B6
Bikes4Rent	**44** B4
Bus Station	**45** C6
Europcar	**46** D5

dates from the 12th century, while most of the rest of the church is 15th-century Gothic.

Like other Danish churches, the cathedral was once richly decorated with **frescoes** that served to convey biblical parables to unschooled peasants. After the Reformation, church authorities who felt the frescoes smacked too much of Roman Catholicism, had them all whitewashed, but many have now been uncovered and restored. They range from fairy-tale paintings of St George slaying a dragon, to scenes of hellfire. The cathedral's splendid, five-panel, gilt **altarpiece** is a highlight. It was made in Lübeck by the renowned woodcarver Bernt Notke in the 15th century.

VOR FRUE KIRKE

This **church** (☎ 86 12 12 43; Frue Kirkeplads; admission free; ◷ 10am-2pm Mon-Fri, to noon Sat), off Vestergade, has a carved wooden **altarpiece** dating from the 1530s. But far more interesting is what's in its basement: the **crypt** of the city's original cathedral, dating from about 1060. Enter via the stairway beneath the altar. To enter a third chapel, this one with 16th-century frescoes, go through the courtyard and take the left door.

VIKINGE-MUSEET

There's more than the expected vaults in the basement of **Nordea bank** (☎ 89 42 11 00; Sankt Clements Torv 6; admission free; ◷ 10am-4pm Mon-Wed & Fri, to 5.30pm Thu) where there's a small exhibition of artefacts from the Viking Age town that were excavated at this site in 1964 during the bank's construction. The display includes a skeleton, a reconstructed house, 1000-year-old carpentry tools and pottery, and photos of the excavation.

MOESGÅRD

Visit Moesgård, 5km south of the city centre, for its glorious beech woods and the trails threading through them towards sandy beaches. Visit for the well-presented history exhibits from the Stone Age to the Viking Age at **Moesgård Museum of Prehistory** (adult/child Dkr60/free; ◷ 10am-5pm Apr-Sep, to 4pm Tue-Sun Oct-May). But above all else, visit Moesgård for the museum's most dramatic exhibit: the 2000-year-old **Grauballe Man**, or Grauballemanden, whose astonishingly well-preserved body was found in 1952 at the village of Grauballe, 35km west of Århus.

The superb new display on the Grauballe Man is part history lesson, part forensics lesson. Was he a sacrifice to Iron Age fertility gods, an executed prisoner perhaps, or simply a victim of murder? Either way, the broken leg and the gaping neck wound suggests his death, sometime in the last century BC, was a horribly violent one. His body and skin, tanned and preserved by the unique chemical and biological qualities of the peat bogs, are remarkably intact, right down to hair and fingernails.

Away from all this death and violence, there's an enjoyable **trail** dubbed the 'prehistoric trackway' or Oldtidsstien leading from behind the museum across fields of wildflowers, past grazing sheep and through beech woods down to **Moesgård Strand**, Århus' best sandy beach. The trail, marked by red-dotted stones, passes reconstructed historic sights including a dolmen, burial cists and an Iron-Age house. The museum has a brochure with details. You can walk one way and catch a bus back to the city centre, or follow the trail both ways as a 5km round-trip. It's all well worth a half-day or full-day visit, with a picnic perhaps if the weather behaves itself.

Bus 6 from Århus train station terminates at the museum year-round and runs twice an hour.

SWIMMING

There are sandy beaches on the outskirts of Århus. The most popular one to the north is **Bellevue**, about 4km from the city centre (bus 6 or 16), while the favourite to the south is Moesgård Strand.

Tours

A guided 2½-hour bus tour leaves from the **tourist office** (☎ bookings 89 40 67 00) at 10am daily from mid-June to early September, giving a glimpse of the main city sights. The Dkr50 tour is a good deal as it includes entry into Den Gamle By and also leaves you with a 24-hour public bus pass.

Festivals & Events

The 10-day **Århus Festival** (www.aarhusfestuge.dk) in early September turns the city into a stage for nonstop revelry with jazz, rock, classical music, theatre and dance. The festival has hosted such varied bill toppers as the Rolling Stones, Philip Glass, Anne-Sophie Mutter, Ravi Shankar, the City of Birmingham Symphony Orchestra, New York City Ballet, Günter Grass and many more. Each year the festival has a special theme. Events take place all over the city and there is a fringe element also.

Sleeping

BUDGET

The tourist office books rooms in private homes for around Dkr200/300 per single/ double, plus a Dkr25 booking fee.

Århus Camping (☎ 86 23 11 33; www.aarhusnord .dk; Randersvej 400, Lisbjerg; adult/child/tent Dkr77/42/20; ☺ year-round) This large, quite decent, three-star camping ground is about 3km north of Århus.

Danhostel Århus (☎ 86 16 72 98; www.hostel-aarhus .dk; Marienlundsvej 10; dm Dkr160, r Dkr506-620; ☺ late Jan–mid-Dec) It may be 4km north of the city centre but its well worth considering for the lovely parkland setting in a renovated 1850s dance hall. It's at the edge of the Risskov Woods and a few minutes from the beach. Buses 6 and 9 pass nearby.

Århus City Sleep-In (☎ 86 19 20 55; www.citysleep -in.dk; Havnegade 20; dm Dkr130, d with/without bathroom Dkr460/400; ☺ 24hr; ☐ ☒) Run by a youth organisation, the Århus City Sleep-In is in a central former mariners' hotel. It's casual, the rooms are a bit rundown but it's a cheerful place and by far the best budget option in the centre. Sheet hire costs Dkr45 and safety boxes are Dkr20, with Dkr100 deposit. Key deposit is Dkr50. Bike hire costs Dkr60 a day.

Cab Inn Århus (☎ 86 75 70 00; www.cabinn .com; Kannikegade 14; s Dkr485-545, d Dkr615-675; ☐ ☒ ☎) In an ideal central location opposite the Domkirke. The style is standard Cab Inn with small, rather bare but usually clean rooms. Parking costs Dkr60. Free internet and wi-fi access.

MIDRANGE

Havnehotellet (www.havnehotellet.dk; Marselisborg Havnevej 20; d from Dkr495; ☐) A bike or bus ride from the city centre, Havnehotellet offers bright, clean, modern comfort overlooking yachts and the sea. A good midrange bet. Reception hours are short and most guests check in via an electronic reception in the small foyer.

Hotel Guldsmeden (☎ 86 13 45 50; www.hotelgul dsmeden.dk, in Danish; Guldsmedgade 40; s/d Dkr595/845, s/d with bathroom from Dkr1175/1295; ☐ ☎) On the northern side of the city centre, this is our midrange choice in town for friendly staff, delightfully bright French colonial-style rooms with polished wood floors, large four-poster

beds with soft white linen, a small garden terrace and a generally relaxed, stylish ambience. Good (mainly organic) breakfasts.

Aarhus City Apartments (☎ 86 27 51 30; www .hotelaca.dk; Fredensgade 18; s/d Dkr1069/1269; ☐ ☐) A good midrange option especially for self-caterers, these smart, modern one- and two-bedroom apartments right in the city centre have their own kitchen, cable TV and free internet access. There's no reception so you must book ahead.

TOP END

Hotel Ferdinand (☎ 87 32 14 44; www.hotelferdinand.dk; Åboulevarden 28; s/d from Dkr998/1298; ☐ ☒ ☐) At last Århus has a foxy new boutique hotel to rival the best in Copenhagen. Right on the buzzing canalside, the Ferdinand was founded by the people behind the city's top gourmet restaurant, the Prins Ferdinand, which has now closed. Now they have directed their efforts towards this chic, designer hotel, with very reasonable prices. The downstairs brasserie is one of the best value places to eat in the city.

Hotel Royal (☎ 86 12 86 65; www.hotelroyal.dk; Store Torv 4; s/d from Dkr1450/1550; ☐ ☒ ☐) Built in 1838 this is Århus' answer to Copenhagen's d'Angleterre – opulent, ornate, luxurious and characterful, with all modern luxuries.

Radisson SAS Scandinavia (☎ 86 12 86 65; www .radissonsas.dk; Margrethepladsen; from Dkr1615; ☐ ☒ ☐) Right beside Aros and Århus Koncerthus, this massive, modern hotel has every amenity you would expect from this major, international, luxury chain.

Eating & Drinking

The Åboulevarden canal area is the place to head for the most high profile restaurants and cafes – come summer, the canalside throngs with restaurant tables and there is a wonderful party atmosphere at weekends. Nearby Skolegade is packed with popular, studenty pubs and clubs. The narrow streets of the old quarter north of the cathedral are also thick with cafes serving Danish and ethnic foods.

The train station has a DSB cafe, a snack bar and a small **supermarket** (☺ to midnight). Two blocks west is **Føtex supermarket** (Frederiks Allé), with a cheap bakery and deli, and **Sundhedskost** (Frederiks Allé), the city's largest health-food store.

Emmery's (☎ 86 13 04 00; Guldsmedgade 24-26; breakfast/brunch Dkr23/95; ☺ 7.30am-6pm Mon-Fri, 8am-4pm Sat & Sun) A stylish and friendly cafe-cum-delicatessen that serves its own delicious bread, tapas (Dkr95) and sandwiches (Dkr60 to Dkr78), some with vegetarian fillings.

Brasserie Ferdinand (☎ 87 32 14 44; www.hotelfer dinand.dk; Åboulevarden 28; mains Dkr125-165; ☺ lunch & dinner) With a simple yet high-quality menu of French brasserie classics, the chic new hotel brasserie, right on the busy restaurant-packed canalside, is one of the most popular and best value places to eat in Århus right now. Pan fried foie gras (Dkr165) and classic beef tatar (Dkr125) are dependable menu staples.

Aros (☎ 87 30 66 00; mains Dkr140-160; ☺ 10am-5pm Thu-Sun & Tue, to 10pm Wed) A good bet for a snack, the art museum's downstairs cafe serves tasty focaccia sandwiches and lovely sweet treats or go upstairs for good, simple brasserie food.

Castenskiold (☎ 86 55 22 33; Åboulevarden 32; www .castenskiold.net, in Danish; brunch Dkr125, mains Dkr 225, 3 courses Dkr350; ☺ 11am-midnight Mon-Thu, to 2am Fri & Sat, 10am-5pm Sun) One of the best places in the canalside area, this glamorous cafe-restaurant serves basic, all-organic French brasserie classics such as *confit du canard* and tournedos.

Globen Flakket (☎ 87 31 03 33; www.globen-flakket .dk; Åboulevarden 18; mains Dkr168-225; ☺ 10am-10pm daily) The best of the riverside cafe-cum-restaurants, covering all the bases really well. Upstairs you'll find the cosy bar serving very decent wraps, tapas, burgers, brunch and an evening buffet (Dkr79). Downstairs the rather more formal restaurant turns out finer fare such as guinea fowl with smoked white beans and beetroot salsa or beef tournedos with truffled Madeira sauce.

ourpick Nordisk Spisehus (☎ 86 17 70 99; www .nordiskspisehus.dk; MP Brunnsgade 31; mains Dkr150-250, 3 courses Dkr325; ☺ noon-3pm & 5.30-10pm) A kind of budget Noma (see p48), this clean, simple, modern Scandinavian restaurant, a short walk west of the station, serves regional delicacies such as local free range veal, Nordic cheeses and fjord shrimp. We recommend the home-smoked salmon, to which they give an extra last minute hay smoking beneath a glass cloche at your table. It is served with a dazzlingly fresh salad with salt-cured apples, radish and cucumber (Dkr139). Service is friendly and knowledgeable.

Bryggeriet Sct Clemens (☎ 86 13 80 00; www.bryg geriet.dk, in Danish; Kannikegade 10 & 12; mains Dkr170-220; ☺ 11.30am-midnight Mon-Wed, to 2am Thu-Sat) This cosy microbrewery is a short walk from Åboulevarden and serves a range of home-brewed beers, as well as a decent range of cheapish fast food. This is part of the Hereford Beefstouw chain, so the menu is predictably steak-centric (although, less predictably this includes Wagyu beef).

Entertainment

The monthly free publication *What's On in Århus* lists current happenings in detail and is available at the tourist office and other venues around town.

Århus has a vibrant music scene with something for all ages and tastes.

Train (☎ 86 13 47 22; Toldbodgade 6; ☺ to 5am Thu-Sat) One of the biggest venues in Denmark stages concerts by international rock, pop and country stars and there's a late-night disco.

Musikcaféen (☎ 86 76 03 44; Mejlgade 53; ☺ 8.30pm-2am Mon-Sat) This and the adjacent Gyngen are alternative and often vibrant venues with rock, jazz and world music. They are a showcase for hopefuls and up-and-coming acts.

Jazzbar Bent J (☎ 86 12 04 92; Nørre Allé 66; ☺ from 3.30pm Mon-Fri) This is a jazz only, very long-established bar with an impressive guest list. Entry is Dkr80 on guest nights.

Twist & Shout (☎ 86 18 08 55; Frederiksgade 29; ☺ 10am-5am Mon-Thu, from 5pm Fri & 10pm Sat) Lively, small, often packed and friendly, this three-floor disco is the place to head for later in the evening. It's not too precious, there's a mix of music from '60s to house (depending on the floor) and everyone has fun.

Musikhuset Århus (☎ 89 40 40 40; Thomas Jensens Alleé 2) The city concert hall presents dance, opera and concerts by international performers.

The main gay and lesbian social scene is at **Pan Club** (☎ 86 13 43 80; Jaægergårdsgade 42). To find it, head south down MP Bruunsgade on the west side of the train station and then go right down Jaægergårdsgade for 300m and it's on the left-hand side of the road.

Getting There & Away
AIR

SAS flies one way for around Dkr300. The airport, in Tirstrup 44km northeast of Århus, also has direct flights from London. Budget carrier Ryanair flies twice daily between London Stansted and Århus on weekdays and once on Saturday and Sunday. See p106 for details.

BOAT

The ferry operator is **Mols-Linien** (☎ 70 10 14 18). It runs car ferries from Århus to Odden in north west Zealand (adult/child Dkr315/155, car and five passengers Dkr695, 65 minutes).

BUS

The bus station (Fredensgade) has a DSB cafe and a small supermarket. **Abildskou buses** (☎ 70 21 08 88; www.abildskou.dk) run a few times daily between Århus and Copenhagen's Valby Station and the airport, stopping in Odense on the way (adult/child Dkr270/135, three hours). For information on travel to other destinations in Jutland visit www.dsb.dk.

CAR & MOTORCYCLE

The main highways to Århus are the E45 from the north and south and Rte 15 from the west. The E45 curves around the western edge of the city as a ring road. There are a number of turn-offs from the ring road into the city, including Åohavevej from the south and Randersvej from the north.

Cars can be rented from **Europcar** (☎ 89 33 11 11; Sønder Allé 35).

TRAIN

Trains to Århus, via Odense, leave Copenhagen hourly from early morning to 10pm (adult/child Dkr311/156, three hours) and there's a night train at 2am. There are regular trains to Aalborg (Dkr157/79, 1½ hours), and Esbjerg (Dkr216/108, 2½ hours). There's a ticket-queuing system at the station: red for internal; green for international. For local journeys, unless you have mastered use of the quicker ticket machines, be prepared for quite long waits at busy times. Friday trains are always very busy and it's advised to reserve a seat for long journeys.

Getting Around

TO/FROM THE AIRPORT

The airport bus to Århus train station costs Dkr90/65 per adult/child and takes approximately 45 minutes. Check times to the airport at the stands outside the train station; some services start only in August. The taxi fare to the airport is about Dkr750.

BUS

Most in-town buses stop in front of the train station or around the corner on Park Allé. City bus tickets are bought from a machine at the back of the bus for Dkr20 and are good for unlimited rides within the time period stamped on the ticket, which is two hours.

The Århus Card includes both bus travel and entry into many Århus museums. You can buy tickets and passes at **Århus Sporveje** (☎ 89 40 10 10; Banegårdspladsen 20; 10am-6pm Mon-Fri, to 1pm Sat), the city transport service shop across from the train station.

CAR & MOTORCYCLE

A car is convenient for getting to sights such as Moesgårdon on the city outskirts, though the city centre is best explored on foot. There's paid parking along many streets and in municipal car parks, including one on the southern side of Musikhuset Århus. Fees start at Dkr1 for six minutes and Dkr12 for one hour. Overnight (7pm to 8am) is free.

BICYCLE

Bikes4Rent (☎ 87 99 10 20; www.bikes4rent.dk; 8am-7pm; per day Dkr75) offers rental of good quality, new bikes.

TAXI

Taxis congregate outside the Århus mainline station and at Store Torv. Expect to pay around Dkr70 for destinations within the city.

AROUND ÅRHUS

Randers Regnskov

One of the most popular attractions in Jutland is this state-of-the-art indoor rain forest and tropical **zoo** (☎ 87 10 99 99; www.regnskoven.dk; Tørvebryggen 11; Randers; adult/child aged 3-11/under 3 Dkr140/80/free; 10am-4pm Jan-Jun & Sep-Dec, 10am-5pm Jul & Aug, to 6pm early Aug). It is a spectacular space in which you can get close to, and in some cases handle, a wide range of tropical animals from around the world. It is housed in three individual, connected glass domes that artificially recreate the natural tropical environments of South America, Africa, and Asia respectively – there's also an aquarium, and a petting zoo outside.

Within the three climate controlled domes are various raised walkways and tree houses that take you right into the animals' living spaces. They don't seem to mind terribly and many of them have become extremely tame. You can expect to see 250 different animal species including various monkeys, frogs, sloths, reptiles, butterflies, birds and crocodiles (the latter, naturally, do not roam free).

The zoo is 40km north of Århus on the E45 motorway to Aalborg. By train Aalborg is 48 to 56 minutes away (adult/child Dkr94/47); Århus is 36 minutes (Dkr56/34).

JELLING

The tiny, apparently nondescript village of Jelling is a kind of spiritual touchstone for the Danes, and virtually all of them will visit it at some point during their lives. This is the location of one of Denmark's most important historic sites, the **Jelling Kirke**. Inside the small whitewashed church are frescoes dating from the 12th century, and outside the door are two impressive and historically significant rune stones.

The smaller stone was erected in the early 900s by King Gorm the Old, Denmark's first king, in honour of his wife, Queen Thyra. The larger one, raised by Harald Bluetooth and dubbed 'Denmark's baptismal certificate', is adorned with the oldest representation of Christ found in Scandinavia and reads: 'Harald king bade this be ordained for Gorm his father and Thyra his mother, the Harald who won for himself all Denmark and Norway and made the Danes Christians.'

Two huge **burial mounds** flank the church; the one on the northern side is said to be that of King Gorm and the other of Queen Thyra, although excavators in the 19th century found no human remains and few artefacts. This could suggest much earlier grave robbing.

During the 1970s archaeologists excavated below Jelling Kirke and found the remains of three wooden churches. The oldest of these was thought to have been erected by Harald Bluetooth. A burial chamber within this site was also uncovered and revealed human bones and gold jewellery that shared characteristics with artefacts previously discovered within the large northern burial mound. One suggestion is that the bones found beneath the church ruins are those of King Gorm and they were moved there from the old pagan burial mound by Harald Bluetooth out of respect for his recently acquired Christian faith. Queen Thyra remains ephemeral. The Jelling mounds, church and rune stones are designated as a Unesco World Heritage site.

Kongernes Jelling (☎ 75 87 23 50; Gormsgade 23; admission free; ◷ 10am-5pm daily Jun-Aug, 10am-5pm Tue-Sun May & Sep, 1-4pm Tue-Sun Nov-Apr) the information and exhibition centre just across the road from the church, offers a good insight into the history of the Jelling monuments and of early Denmark.

Jelling makes a good two-hour side trip off the Odense–Århus run. Change trains at Vejle for the ride to Jelling (Dkr30, 15 minutes). The church is 100m straight up Stationsvej from the Jelling train station.

THE LAKE DISTRICT

This is a perhaps misleading name for what is more like a gently hilly region with a few medium sized lakes and Denmark's highest point, Yding Skovhøj, but, though it is unlikely to induce nosebleeds, this is a delightful area for rambling. There is also ample opportunity for canoeing, biking and longer distance hiking here. This is also where you'll find Denmark's longest river, the Gudenå, and Mossø, Jutland's largest lake. This area is due south of Silkeborg, slap bang in the centre of Jutland, a half hour's drive west of Århus.

Silkeborg
pop 54,000

Silkeborg overcomes its rather bland modern character with a friendly openness. It is the Lake District's biggest town and is an ideal base for exploring the surrounding forests and waterways. The town has some good restaurants and lively bars and cafes. If you're even slightly interested in Denmark's ancient history, a compelling reason to visit is to see the Tollund Man, the body of a preserved Iron Age 'bog man' who looks for all the world as if he's merely asleep.

The helpful **tourist office** (☎ 86 82 19 11; www .silkeborg.com; Åhavevej 2A; ◷ 9am-5pm Mon-Fri, 10am-2pm Sat, mid-Jun–Aug, 9am-4pm Mon-Fri, 10am-1pm Sat Mar, Apr, Sep & Oct, 10am-3pm Mon-Fri Nov-Mar) is near the harbour and has lots of leaflets including detailed route descriptions of walks and cycle routes. There's a **Jsyke Bank** (☎ 89 22 22 22; Vestergade 16) branch with an ATM. The **Library** (☎ 86 82 02 33; Hostrupsgade 41) is central and well provided with free internet terminals.

SIGHTS

The main (actually virtually the only) attraction at the **Silkeborg Museum** (☎ 86 82 14 99; Hovedgården; adult/child Dkr45/free; ◷ 10am-5pm

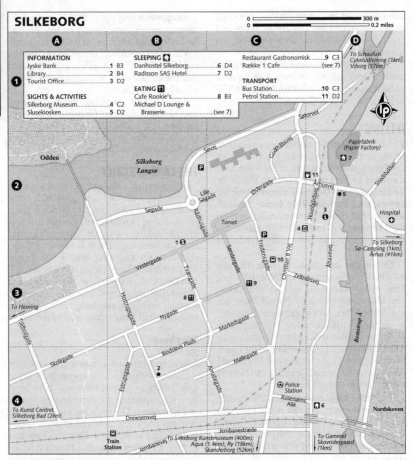

SILKEBORG

0 —————————— 300 m
0 —————————— 0.2 miles

INFORMATION		
Jyske Bank.................................1 B3		
Library......................................2 B4		
Tourist Office...........................3 D2		

SIGHTS & ACTIVITIES		
Silkeborg Museum.....................4 C2		
Sluskekiosken...........................5 D2		

SLEEPING		
Danhostel Silkeborg.................6 D4		
Radisson SAS Hotel..................7 D2		

EATING		
Cafe Rookie's...........................8 B3		
Michael D Lounge &		
Brasserie............................(see 7)		

Restaurant Gastronomisk..........9 C3		
Række 1 Cafe.......................(see 7)		

TRANSPORT		
Bus Station.............................10 C3		
Petrol Station.........................11 D2		

To Schaufuss
Cykeludlejning (1km);
Viborg (37km)

Papirfabrik
(Paper Factory)

Odden

Silkeborg
Langsø

Hospital

To Silkeborg
Sø-Camping (1km);
Århus (41km)

To Herning

To Kunst Centret
Silkeborg Bad (2km)

Police
Station

Rosenørns
Allé

Nordskoven

Train
Station

To Silkeborg Kunstmuseum (400m);
Aqua (1.4km); Ry (18km);
Skanderborg (52km)

To Gammel
Skovridergaard
(1km)

mid-May–Oct, noon-4pm Sat & Sun Nov–mid-May) is the Tollund Man. He is believed to have been executed in 300 BC and his leathery body, complete with the rope still around the neck, was discovered in a bog in 1950. The well-preserved face of the Tollund Man is hypnotic in its detail, right down to the stubble on his chin.

Kunst Centret Silkeborg Bad (☎ 86 81 63 29; www .silkeborgbad.dk; Gjessøvej 40; adult/child Dkr50/free; ☉ 10am-5pm Tue-Sun May-Sep, noon-4pm Tue-Fri, 11am-5pm Sat & Sun Oct-Apr) is a former spa, dating from 1883, and is now a beautiful, modern art space – Art Centre Silkeborg Baths – with permanent works and changing exhibitions of art, sculpture, ceramics, glassware, design and architecture, surrounded by parkland featur-

ing contemporary sculpture. It is about 2km southwest of the town.

The **Silkeborg Kuntsmuseum** (Silkeborg Art Museum; ☎ 86 82 53 88; Gudenåvej 7-9; adult/child Dkr60/free; ☉ 10am-5pm Tue-Sun Apr-Oct, noon-4pm Tue-Fri Nov-Mar) contains some striking work, such as the large ceramic walls by Jean Dubuffet and Pierre Alechinsky that greet visitors at the entrance. It displays many of the works of native son Asger Jorn and other modern artists, including Max Ernst, Le Corbusier and Danish artists from the influential COBRA group. It's 1km south of the town centre.

Situated 2km south of central Silkeborg, **Aqua** (☎ 89 21 21 89; www.aqua-ferskvandsakvarium.dk; Vejsøvej 55; adult/child Dkr100/55; ☉ 10am-6pm Jun-Aug, to 4pm Mon-Fri, to 5pm Sat & Sun Sep-May) is an entertaining aquarium and exhibition centre exploring the ecosystems of the lakes and surrounding area with lots of fishy creatures, otters and fishing birds among the imaginative displays.

ACTIVITIES

Outdoor activities are at the heart of the Lake District's appeal. The track of the old railway from Silkeborg to Horsens is now an excellent **walking** and **cycling** trail of about 50km or so. It passes through the beech forest of **Nordskoven**, itself crisscrossed with hiking and bike trails. To reach Nordskoven simply head south down Åhavevej from the tourist office, then go left over the old railway bridge down by the hostel.

Canoeing is a marvellous way to explore the Lake District and you can plan trips for several days staying at lakeside camping grounds along the way. The canoe-hire places can help plan an itinerary. You can rent canoes for Dkr75/250 per hour/day at **Slusekiosken** (☎ 86 80 08 93) at the harbour.

Bike hire costs Dkr75 per day at **Schaufuss Cykeludlejning** (☎ 86 81 39 38; Nørreskov Bakke 93), which is about 1.5km from Torvet across Silkeborg Langsø and is reached by bus No 5. Silkeborg Sø-camping rents out bikes and canoes from Dkr60 per day.

The world's oldest operating **paddle steamer** (☎ 86 82 07 66; www.hjejlen.com; times & prices vary) offers tours on the lake during the summer.

SLEEPING

Budget and midrange options in town are limited, making B&B accommodation an especially good option. The tourist office publishes a B&B booklet, with singles/doubles costing around Dkr150/300.

Danhostel Silkeborg (☎ 86 82 36 42; www.danhostel -silkeborg.dk; Åhavevej 55; dm Dkr150; ☯ Mar–end Nov; P ☒ ☐) The riverbank location, modern facilities and lack of decent alternatives make this hostel very popular, so book ahead. It's east of the train station. There are only dorms, no private rooms.

Gammel Skovridergaard (☎ 87 22 55 00; www .glskov.dk; Marienlundsvej 36; s/d Dkr1150/1450) This magnificent former manor farm is now a hotel and conference centre with oodles of charm and an idyllic location close to the lakes and forests of Silkeborg, yet only a 15-minute walk from the town centre.

Radisson SAS Hotel (☎ 88 82 22 22; info.silkeborg @radissonsas.com; Papirfabrikken 12; s/d Dkr1325/1625; P ☒ ☐ ⊜) A comfortable, business-class hotel in a converted mill, the Radisson is simply the best place to stay in town. The huge rooms in a simple, appealing modern Scandinavian style, have large beds and all mod cons. There's a bar and restaurant, plus discounted use of a nearby fitness centre.

EATING

Nygade, lined with grill bars and pizza places, is the street to head to for quick inexpensive fast food.

There are a number of cheap food outlets on Søndergade, the pedestrianised main street. The Føtex supermarket (Torvet) has a bakery and an inexpensive cafe.

Much of Silkeborg's cultural and culinary scene is centred on the Papirfabrik (Paper Factory) development on the lakeside. Here, along with the SAS Hotel and the Jysk Musik and Teaterhus (Jutland's Music and Theatre House), is the excellent **Række 1 Cafe** (☎ 88 82 23 13; www.papirfabrikken.nu; Papirfabriksame; ☯ 11am–5pm) and **Michael D Lounge & Brasserie** (☎ 88 82 22 22; Papirfabriksame; 3 courses Dkr398; ☯ lunch & dinner), which serves French brasserie classics and a more refined tasting menu, plus sushi.

Café Rookie's (☎ 86 81 33 44; Nygade 18; sandwiches Dkr45–75; ☯ 11am-11pm) A relaxed place, close to Chaplins, that does chunky ciabatta sandwiches, salads, smoothies and shakes and has several vegetarian options. It stays open until the early hours on Thursday, Friday and Saturday.

Restaurant Gastronomisk (☎ 86 82 40 93; www .gastronomiske.dk; Søndergade 20; lunch Dkr85-135, dinner 5 courses Dkr390; ☯ 11.30am-4pm & 7-11pm Mon-Sat) This cosy brasserie-restaurant in central Silkeborg serves good salads, steaks, sandwiches and soups for lunch and more ambitious French food in the evenings.

GETTING THERE & AWAY

Hourly or half-hourly trains connect Silkeborg with Skanderborg (Dkr45, 30 minutes) and Århus (Dkr65, 49 minutes) via Ry. There are regular daily buses to Århus (Dkr60, 48 minutes).

Skanderborg & Ry

Two smaller, quieter Lake District towns east of Silkeborg are Ry and Skanderborg. Ry, the closer of the two to Silkeborg, is a particularly peaceful place from which to base your exploration of the Lake District. The **tourist office**

(☎ 86 89 34 22; www.visitskanderborg.com; Klostervej 3; ☺ 7am-4pm Mon-Fri, 9am-2pm Sat mid-Jun–Aug, to 4pm Mon-Fri, to noon Sat Sep–mid-Jun) is in the train station. Skanderborg is a rather humdrum town, but with a lovely setting on Skanderborg Lake. It is best known in Denmark for the Skanderborg Festival.

SIGHTS & ACTIVITIES
The Lake District's most visited spot is the whimsically named Himmelbjerget (Sky Mountain), which, at just 147m, is one of Denmark's highest hills. It was formed by water erosion during the final Ice Age as a 'false hill' or *kol*, the sides of which are quite steep. There are a number of interesting memorials surrounding the hilltop's crowning glory, the 25m-tower (admission Dkr5), reached via a marked 6km footpath north east of Ry, or by bus or boat.

If you want to explore the lakes in the district, **Ry Kanofart** (☎ 86 89 11 67; www.kanoferie.dk; Kyhnsvej 20) rents out canoes for Dkr300 per day. For walking and cycling routes ask at the tourist centre for cycling and walking leaflets (Dkr20). **Cykeludlejning** (☎ 86 89 14 91; www.rycykler. dk; Parallelvej 9B) rents out bikes for Dkr75 a day.

The **Skanderborg Festival** (☎ 87 93 44 44; www .smukfest.dk) bills itself as Denmark's most beautiful, and is second only to Roskilde in terms of scale. It takes place during the second weekend in August in Dyrehaven, a parkland a couple of kilometres east of the town, and attracts up to 45,000 people with an entertaining mix of – mostly Danish – rock and pop artists.

SLEEPING & EATING
The tourist office books rooms in homes from Dkr275/350 for singles/doubles.

Knudhule (☎ 86 89 14 07; www.knudhule.dk, in Danish; Randersvej 88; cabins s/d/t Dkr500/600/700, s/d bungalows Dkr400/600) Knudhule is an appealing budget holiday camp on a picturesque lake. There are cabins without bathrooms and bungalows (sleeping up to four) with bathrooms. There's also a small restaurant, minigolf, boat hire and swimming/diving platforms on the lake. To get there from the train station, cross the tracks, turn left and go 2.5km; or take the infrequent bus 311.

The butcher's shop opposite the train station has fried fish and a few other takeaway selections. There's a bakery next door.

Ry Park Hotel (☎ 86 89 19 11; www.ryparkhotel.dk; Kyhnsvej 2, Ry; s/d from Dkr690/1050) Ry's largest hotel

is located right on the lake (you can rent canoes) and boasts an indoor pool and classy, modern midrange French-Italian restaurant, La Saison (mains Dkr178 to Dkr200).

Pizzeria Italia (☎ 86 89 31 33; Skanderbrgvej 3; fish & meat mains Dkr109-147) There are several restaurants and fast-food places on Skanderborgvej including Pizzeria Italia, which offers tasty pastas (Dkr69) and a three-course menu (Dkr179).

GETTING THERE & AWAY
Hourly trains connect Ry and Skanderborg with Silkeborg and Århus. See www.dsb.dk for details.

Viborg
pop 35,000
Quieter and sleepier than Silkeborg, Viborg has a pretty, compact town centre, an important historic and religious heritage and makes another good base for exploring the nearby lakes and surrounding woodland. In 1060 Viborg became one of Denmark's eight bishoprics and grew into a major religious centre. Prior to the Reformation the town had 25 churches and abbeys, though ecclesiastical remnants from that period are few.

ORIENTATION & INFORMATION
The old part of town consists of the streets around Viborg Domkirke. The train station is about 1km southwest of the tourist office.

The **tourist office** (☎ 87 87 88 88; www.visitviborg .dk; Nytorv 9; ☺ 11am-3pm Tue-Sat, noon-3pm Sun Jan-Mar, 11am-4pm Tue-Sat, noon-4pm Apr-Sep, 11am-3pm Tue-Sat, noon-3pm Oct-Dec) is in the centre of town.

There is ample and convenient free parking behind the Sankt Mathias Gade Shopping Centre on the south side of town, but you must use a time disc.

The post office and several banks with ATMs line Sankt Mathias Gade, just south of the main square.

SIGHTS & ACTIVITIES
The tourist office has excellent printouts, including English-language versions, which describe walks around the town with historical and cultural themes.

The multitowered **Viborg Domkirke** (☎ 87 25 52 50; Sankt Mogens Gade 4; admission free; ☺ 10am-5pm Mon-Sat, noon-5pm Sun Jun-Aug, 11am-4pm Mon-Sat, noon-4pm Sun Apr-May & Sep, 11am-3pm Mon-Sat, noon-3pm Sun Jan-Mar) is one of Denmark's largest granite churches and dominates the town. The first church on the site dated from the Viking period. The interior is awash with frescoes painted over five years (1908–13) by artist Joakim Skovgaard and featuring scenes from the Old Testament and the life of Christ.

Skovgaard Museet (☎ 86 62 39 75; Domkirkestræde 2-4; adult/child Dkr35/free; ☻ 11am-4pm Tue-Sun Jan-May, 10am-5pm Tue-Sun Jun-Aug, 11am-4pm Tue-Sun Sep-Dec) lies to the south of Viborg Domkirke. It also features work by Joakim Skovgaard, but here the scenes are more down to earth and include portraits, landscapes and nudes. The museum also features regularly changing exhibitions.

Viborg Stiftsmuseum (☎ 87 87 38 38; Hjultorvet 9; adult/child Dkr25/free; ☻ 11am-5pm Tue-Sun mid-Jun–Aug, 1pm-4pm Tue-Fri, 11am-7pm Sat & Sun Sep–mid-Jun) is a local history museum that tells the story of Viborg's rich religious past.

Sankt Mogens Gade, between the cathedral and the tourist office, has some handsome old houses, including Hauchs Gård at No 7 and the Willesens House at No 9, both dating back to around 1520.

Kunsthallen Brænderigården (☎ 87 25 26 05; www .braenderigaarden.dk; Riddergade 8; ☻ 1-5pm Tue-Sun; adult/ child Dkr40/free) is an interesting contemporary art space showcasing changing exhibitions of architecture, photography, art and sculpture.

During the summer you can take a trip on the Viborg lakes on the *Margrethe I* (adult/ child Dkr40/25). The boat departs from the jetty in the Borgvold car park.

SLEEPING & EATING

Staff at the tourist office can book rooms in private homes with singles/doubles starting at Dkr200/300.

Viborg Sø Camping (☎ 86 67 13 11; www.camp ing-viborg.dk, in Danish; Vinkelvej 36b; camp sites per adult/ child/tent Dkr73/45/20; ☻ late Mar–late Sep) Viborg is a well-ordered, three-star camping ground at a pleasant, leafy location on the east side of Lake Søndersø.

Danhostel Viborg (☎ 86 67 17 81; www.danhostel.dk /viborg; Vinkelvej 36; dm/s/d Dkr150/350/450; P X) This lovely, modern hostel is adjacent to Viborg Sø Camping and also handy for lakeside activities (and very quiet) 2km walk from town. Bike hire is available.

Palads Hotel (☎ 86 62 37 00; www.hotelpalads .dk; Sankt Mathias Gade; s/d from Dkr1095/1195; P X) Straddling four sites, this very grand, beautifully furnished hotel is part of the Best Western chain and has bright, pleasant rooms

(some with kitchenettes). It's just a short walk north of the train station.

Golf Hotel Viborg (☎ 86 61 02 22; www.golf hotelviborg.dk; Randersvej 2; s/d Dkr1140/1275) Best Western also runs this modern place, beside Søndersø Lake a few minutes' walk from the town centre.

The huge Sankt Mathias Gade Centre has cafes, a supermarket, fruit shop and a butcher.

Café Morville (☎ 86 60 22 11; www.cafemorville.d; Hjultorvetk; brunch Dkr110, mains from Dkr95; ☻ 11am-midnight Mon-Fri, 10-1am Sat, noon-11pm Sun) A bustling place on the main square with sleek, modern decor and some good bistro-style dishes.

Kafé Arthur (☎ 86 62 21 26; Vestergade 4; mains Dkr169-218) The bare-brick, stripped floors and candlelight make for a smart, cosy setting.

GETTING THERE & AROUND

Viborg is 66km northwest of Århus on Rte 26 and 41km west of Randers on Rte 16. Trains from Århus (Dk111, 70 minutes) run hourly Monday to Friday, and less frequently at weekends.

The tourist office has 40 bikes for hire for Dkr100 a day.

AALBORG
pop 121,000

Though at the time of going to press they were in the process of tearing half of Aalborg down, we get the feeling things are on the up for what is, at heart, an attractive town. There is a major redevelopment underway on Aalborg's waterfront, and at its centre is a new architecture and design museum, the Utzon Center named after the celebrated, late architect of Sydney Opera House. As well as this, Aalborg has a vibrant nightlife thanks to a large student population, and several other worthwhile sites, not least the remarkable Lindholm Høje, Denmark's largest Viking burial ground. True, there is a fair bit of industrial and commercial development, surrounding the town but the centre contains enough ancient half-timbered buildings to give you an idea of the kind of affluence its Renaissance merchants enjoyed.

Orientation

Aalborg is divided from neighbouring Nørresundby, to the north, by Limfjord a broad stretch of water, which cuts right across northern Jutland. Virtually all of the sights,

AALBORG

eating, drinking and sleeping options lie south of the Limfjord. The town centre, also on this south side of the water, is a 10-minute walk north on Boulevarden from the train and bus stations.

Information

Danish Emigration Archives (☎ 99 31 42 20; Arkivstræde 1) Behind Vor Frue Kirke, helps foreigners of Danish descent trace their roots.

Hovedbiblioteket (City library; Rendsburggade 2; ☽ 10am-8pm Mon-Fri, 10am-3pm Sat) Offers free internet access.

Jyske Bank (Nytorv 1)

Laundrette (cnr Rantzausgade & Christiansgade; ☽ 8am-8pm)

Post Office (Algade 42)

Tourist Office (☎ 99 31 75 00; www.visitaalborg.com; Østerågade 8; ☽ 9am-5.30pm Mon-Fri, 10am-1pm Sat mid-Jun–Aug, to 4.30pm Mon-Fri, 10am-1pm Sat Sep–mid-Jun) Friendly and helpful, with masses of information, including a diary of events, *What's on in Aalborg*.

Sights
OLD TOWN
The whitewashed **Buldolfi Domkirke** marks the centre of the old town, and has colourful frescoes in the foyer. About 75m west of the cathedral is the **Aalborg Historiske Museum** (Algade 48; adult/child Dkr20/free; ☽ 9am-4pm Mon-Fri, to 2pm Sat), with artefacts from prehistory to the present and furnishings and interiors that hint at the wealth Aalborg's merchants enjoyed during the Renaissance.

The alley between the museum and church leads to the rambling **Monastery of the Holy Ghost**, which dates from 1431; the tourist office arranges guided tours in summer (Dkr50). Northeast of the cathedral on Østerågade are three noteworthy historic buildings: the **old town hall** (c 1762), the five-storey **Jens Bangs Stenhus** (built c 1624 by wealthy merchant Jens Bangs) and **Jørgen Olufsens House** (c 1616).

In addition, the half-timbered neighbourhoods around **Vor Frue Kirke** are worth a stroll, particularly the cobbled Hjelmerstald. **Aalborghus Slot**, near the waterfront, is more administrative office than castle, but there's a small **dungeon** (8am-3pm Mon-Fri May-Nov) you can enter for free.

UTZON CENTER

An impressive 700 sq metre design and architecture space the **Utzon Centre** (76 90 50 00; www.utozncenter.dk; Slotspladsen 4; adult/child Dkr60/30; 10am-5pm Tue-Sun), with its distinctive silver roofscape, is right on the harbourfront close to Aalborghus Slot. It bills itself as 'a dynamic and experimental centre of culture and knowledge' and is close to where the celebrated Danish architect, Jørn Utzon (1918–2008), who died shortly after the centre was finished, went to school. It hosts a changing programme of exhibitions on architecture, design, industrial design and art. One of the permanent exhibitions is *Sisu*, a spidsgatter-class yacht designed by Aage Utzon, Utzon's father.

NORDJYLLANDS KUNSTMUSEUM

This **regional art museum** (98 13 80 88; Kong Christian Allé 50; adult/child Dkr40/free; 10am-5pm Tue-Sun), in a stark, modular building designed by Finnish architect Alvar Aalto, has a fine collection of Danish modern art, including work by Asger Jorn and JF Willumsen.

To get to the museum, take the tunnel beneath the train station; it leads to Kildeparken, a green space with statues and water fountains. Go directly through the park, cross Vesterbro and then continue through a wooded area to the museum, a 10-minute walk in all. Alternatively take bus 5, 8, 10 or 11 from the centre of town.

LINDHOLM HØJE

The Limfjorden (chalk fjord) was a kind of Viking motorway providing easy and speedy access to the Atlantic for longboat raiding parties. It's perhaps not surprising then that by far the most important piece of Aalborg's historical heritage is a predominantly Viking one. The hugely atmospheric **Lindholm Høje** (admission free; dawn-dusk) is a Viking burial ground where nearly 700 graves from the Iron Age and Viking Age are strewn around a hilltop pasture ringed by a wall of tall beech trees. Many of the Viking graves are marked by stones placed in the outline of a Viking ship, with two larger end stones as stem and stern. The **museum** (96 31 04 28; admission free; 10am-5pm Apr-Oct), adjacent to the field, depicts the site's history while huge murals behind the exhibits speculate on what the people of Lindholm looked like and how they lived. Lindholm Høje is 15 minutes from Aalborg centre on bus 2.

Sleeping

Accommodation options are pretty good in town, inexpensive compared to other Danish destinations and not generally in massive demand.

Aalborg Camping (98 11 60 44; www.aalborg camping.dk; Skydebanevej 50; adult/child/tent Dkr50/25/22; year-round) In the process of being modernised, this pleasant two-star camping ground is popular with naturists.

Zleep Hotel Aalborg (98 10 97 00; www.zleep.dk; Hadsundvej 182; s/d Dkr449/550) Part of a small chain of no-frills hotels, usually located a little out of town. This one is a 15-minute bus ride (No 182) from Aalborg centre. The rooms are sparse but tidy and have cable TV.

Danhostel Aalborg (98 11 60 44; www.danhostel.dk/aalborg; Skydebanevej 50; dm/s/d Dkr285/478/528;) Handy for boating activities on the fjord but hardly central, the hostel is at the marina 4km west of the centre. It also runs an adjacent camping ground with cabins. Otherwise the facilities are rather basic.

Hotel Hvide Hus (98 98 13 84 00; www.hotel hvidehus.dk; Vesterbro 2; s/d Dkr1070/1275) This large, modern hotel right in the centre of town may not be especially characterful, but its rooms are attractive and modern, the views are superb, and the rates are good for a hotel of this class in Denmark.

Radisson SAS Limfjord (98 16 43 33; www.radis sonsas.com; Ved Stranden 14-16; s/d Dkr1485/1685;) The top-end place in town occupying a grandstand position overlooking the fjord close to all the main attractions, restaurants and shops. Well-furnished, well-equipped, modern rooms with free wi-fi plus a solarium and gym.

EATING

Eating out in Aalborg is very much a never mind the quality, feel the width kind of scenario, and there are precious few genuinely good or original options. A clutch of new places dotted around the town centre caters well enough to all low and midrange budgets and tastes. If it's just ballast you want with your alcohol, then Jomfru Ane Gade, a lively, pedestrian street jammed solid with fast-food style restaurants and bars, is the place to go.

SushiSushi (☎ 98 10 98 40; Ved Stranden 11b; menus Dkr115-250; ☯ noon-10pm Mon-Sat, 4-9pm Sun) Sit and enjoy, or pay and take away terrific, fresh sushi from this small place around the corner from Jomfru Ane Gade.

Pingvin (☎ 98 11 11 66; Brandstrupsgade 11; tapas lunch Dkr138-228, dinner Dkr158-198; ☯ noon-11pm Mon-Sat) This cosy little contemporary wine and tapas bar serves tasty dishes that are perfect for a light meal.

Mundgott Brasserie (☎ 72 11 80 50; www.mundgott.dk; Toldbod Plads 2; mains Dkr175; ☯ 11am-midnight Mon-Sat) One of the more upmarket places to eat in the centre of town, this spacious, well run brasserie has a solid kitchen that turns out mostly classic French brasserie dishes such as coq au vin, made with chickens from Bornholm.

Mortens Kro (☎ 98 12 48 60; Møllea 4-6; mains Dkr189-348; ☯ 5.30-10pm Mon-Sat) Hands down both the best and priciest place to eat in town, Mortens Kro serves lavish, inventive fare such as lobster with a cauliflower crème brûlée or beef with foie gras and truffled croutons.

Penny Lane (Boulevarden 10; cakes from Dkr35; ☯ 10am-6pm Mon-Fri, 10-2pm Sat) This is one of the most charming cafes in Jutland, featuring a well-stocked delicatessen, quirky decor (the owner has a collection of over 5000 English pastry cutters – 'People are strange,' he shrugs, by way of explanation) and terrific cakes and pastries.

DRINKING

Wharf (☎ 98 11 70 10; The Wharf, Borgergade 16) This surprising slice of the UK in deepest Jutland is dedicated to cask ale and serves up to 44 different British, Belgian, Irish and German beers the length of its capacious bar. There's also a good selection of rare single-malt whiskies.

Studenterhuset (Student Union; ☎ 98 11 05 22; Gammeltorv 10) A convivial budget drinking and entertainment option. Lined with bookshelves, it's surprisingly upmarket and, well, studious for a students' union. There's

inexpensive beer, regular live bands and DJ nights.

ENTERTAINMENT

If it's a flirt, a drink or loud repetitive beats in the form of banging techno, Euro-rock or house music you're after, trawl Jomfru Ane Gade, Aalborg's take-no-prisoners party street. The venues themselves are pretty homogenous, so it's best to explore until you hear your kind of music.

Irish House (☎ 98 14 18 17; www.theirishhouse.dk; Østerågade 25; ☯ 1pm-1am Mon-Wed, noon-4am Thu-Sat, 3pm-midnight Sun) A lively Irish pub with live music most nights and a convivial atmosphere.

Getting There & Away

CAR & MOTORCYCLE

The E45 bypasses the city centre, tunnelling under the Limfjord, whereas the connecting Rte 180 leads into the centre. To get to Lindholm Høje or points north from Aalborg centre, take Rte 180 (Vesterbro), which bridges the Limfjord.

Avis (☎ 98 13 30 99) is at the train station. **Europcar** (☎ 98 13 23 55; Jyllandsgade 4) is a short distance to the east.

BUS & TRAIN

Trains run to Århus (Dkr157, 1½ hours, at least hourly) and Frederikshavn (Dkr88, one hour, every two hours). **Abildskov buses** (☎ 70 21 08 88) run to Copenhagen (No 888, Monday to Thursday Dkr170, Friday and Saturday Dkr310, five hours).

Getting Around

City buses leave from the intersection of Østerågade and Nytorv. The bus fare is Dkr16 to any place in greater Aalborg.

Despite a few one-way streets and the often-confusing outer roads that may have you driving in circles, central Aalborg is a fairly easy place to get around by car. There's metered parking in the city centre (Dkr12/80, one/24 hours) and time-limited, free parking along many side streets, but you need to use a parking disc. If you're unable to find a parking space, there's a large parking garage, **Palads Parking** (Ved Stranden 11).

FREDERIKSHAVN

pop 23,500

A transport hub rather than a compelling destination, the bustling port town of

Frederikshavn nevertheless has a certain appeal, a couple of interesting sights and a pleasant enough pedestrianised centre.

An overhead walkway leads from the ferry terminal to the **tourist office** (☎ 98 42 32 66; www .visitfrederikshavn.dk; Skandiatorv 1; 9am-6pm Mon-Sat, to 2pm Sun end-Jun–mid-Aug, 9am-6pm last 2 weeks Jun & Aug, to 4pm Mon-Fri, 11am-2pm Sat Sep–mid-Jun). The train station and adjacent bus terminal are a 10-minute walk to the north.

Sights
BANGSBO

It's well worth exploring this area, about 3km from the centre on the southern edge of town. The main drawcard is **Bangsbo Museum** (☎ 98 42 31 11; Margrethesvej 6; adult/child Dkr40/free; 10am-5pm Jun-Aug, 10.30am-5pm Sep-May, closed Mon Nov-May) an old country estate with an interesting mix of exhibits. The manor house displays antique furnishings and collectibles, while the old farm buildings hold ship figureheads, military paraphernalia and exhibits on Danish Resistance to the German occupation. The most intriguing exhibit is the Ellingå ship, reconstructed remains of a 12th-century Viking-style merchant ship that was dug up from a nearby stream bed. Bus 3 from central Frederikshavn stops near the entrance to the estate, from where it's an enjoyable 500m walk through the woods to the museum. The adjoining **Bangsbo Botanisk Have** (Botanical Gardens) has a deer park and is a pleasant place to stroll or enjoy a picnic.

Bangsbo Fort (☎ 98 42 31 11; Understedvej 21; adult/child Dkr30/free; 10am-5pm Jun-Aug) about 800m over the wooded ridge from the gardens is an atmospheric WWII bunker complex housing some big guns and commanding wonderful views across to Frederikshavn and out to sea.

KRUDTTÅRNET

The whitewashed **Krudttårnet** (☎ 98 42 31 11; Kragholmen 1; adult/child Dkr15/5; 10.30am-5pm Jun-Sep) is a striking old gun tower and powder magazine, that once formed part of the 17th-century citadel that once protected the port. Various pieces of artillery are on display at the top.

Sleeping

Unsurprisingly, given the captive custom of those awaiting onward connections, good-value sleeping options are limited, prices higher and standards lower compared to

other towns in the region. The tourist office books rooms in private homes from Dkr175/200 for singles/doubles, plus a Dkr25 booking fee.

Danhostel Frederikshavn (☎ 98 42 14 75; www.dan hostel.dk/frederikshavn; Buhlsvej 6; dm/s/d Dkr100/250/300; Feb–mid-Dec; P) A pleasant place with chalet-style, six-bed dorms located 2km north of the ferry terminal.

Hotel Herman Bang (☎ 98 42 21 66; www.herman bang.dk, in Danish; Tordenskjoldsgade 3; s/d Dkr595/795, s/d with private bathroom from Dkr795/995; P) The mid-priced rooms here are bright and comfortable, the most expensive are huge, new and luxurious. Avoid the cheapest which are bland, need new carpets and generally offer poor value. There's an upmarket spa next door for beauty and relaxation treatments.

Eating

Frank's (☎ 98 42 22 88; www.franks.dk, in Danish; Silovej 8; mains Dkr160-190; lunch & dinner only) Towering nine stories above the port's gritty industrial heart in a former grain silo, Frank's offers a thrilling bird's-eye view of the dockside loading, unloading and maritime comings and goings. The fine-dining menu doesn't always live up to the views but is strong on fish. Book ahead to bag a window seat.

Damsgaard Supermarked (Havnegade) Next to the tourist office, Damsgaard has a cheap cafeteria with a harbour view and a good buffet breakfast (Dkr48).

Havne Super (Sydhavnesvej 8) If you're catching a ferry, Havne Super is a supermarket at the harbour with a cafeteria and long hours. Consider picking up provisions if you're going on to expensive Norway.

Møllehuset (☎ 98 43 44 00; Skovalleen 45; mains Dkr80-150; 11am-9.30pm Tue-Sat, to 6pm Sun & Mon) An appealing cafe and restaurant in a leafy setting across the roundabout from the botanic gardens serving simple fresh lunches – such as bagels with smoked salmon and asparagus, and good cheese platters – along with more polished dinners.

Getting There & Away
BOAT

From Frederikshavn **Stena Line** (☎ 96 20 02 00) runs ferries six to 10 times daily (Dkr95 to Dkr215, two to 3¼ hours) to Göteborg, Sweden. **Color Line** (☎ 99 56 19 77; www.colorline .com) runs to Oslo once daily (8½ hours). Prices vary by season.

BUS & TRAIN

Frederikshavn is the northern terminus of the DSB train line. Trains run about hourly south to Aalborg (Dkr88) and then onto Copenhagen (Dkr343). **Nordjyske Jernbaner** (☎ 98 45 45 10; www.njba.dk) runs smart new trains every two hours (Dkr48) to Skagen and to Hirtshals at least once a day.

SKAGEN

pop 10,500

Skagen is a magical place, both bracing and beautiful. If you are driving from the south, to get there you pass through kilometre after kilometre of, well, pretty much nothing really, until first pine forests and then an extraordinary landscape of grassy sand dunes heralds this popular vacation region. The town of Skagen (pronounced 'skane') is a busy working harbour and is Denmark's most northerly settlement, just a couple of kilometres from the dramatic sandy spit where the country finally peters out at Grenen, a slender point of wave-washed sand, where seals bask and seagulls soar.

Artists discovered Skagen's luminous light and its colourful, wind-blasted, heath-and-dune landscape in the mid-19th century and fixed eagerly on the romantic imagery of the area's fishing life that had earned the people of Skagen a hard living for centuries. Painters such as Michael and Anna Ancher and Oscar Björck followed the contemporary fashion of painting *en plein air* (out of doors), often regardless of the weather. Their work established a vivid figurative style of painting that became known internationally as the 'Skagen School'.

Today, Skagen is a very popular tourist resort, that is completely packed during high summer. But the sense of a more picturesque Skagen survives and the town's older neighbourhood, Gammel Skagen 5km west, is filled with distinctive, single storey, yellow-walled (they're traditionally painted every Whitsuntide with lime and ochre), red-roofed houses.

The peninsula is lined with fine beaches, including a sandy stretch on the eastern end of Østre Strandvej, a 15-minute walk from the town centre.

The **Skagen music festival** (www.skagenfestival .dk, in Danish) packs the town out with official performers, buskers and appreciative visitors during the last weekend of June.

Orientation & Information

Sankt Laurentii Vej, Skagen's main street, runs almost the entire length of this long thin town, and is never more than five minutes from the waterfront. The **tourist office** (☎ 98 44 13 77; www .skagen-tourist.dk; Sankt Laurentii Vej 22; ☒ 10am-4pm Mon-Fri, 10am-1pm Sat Jan-Mar, 9am-4pm Mon-Fri, 10am-2pm Sat Apr-Jun, late Aug–Oct, 9am-6pm Mon-Sat, 10am-4pm Sun Jul–early Aug) is in the train/bus station.

Sights

GRENEN

Appropriately for such a neatly kept country, Denmark doesn't end untidily at its most northerly point, but on a neat finger of sand just a few metres wide. You can actually paddle at its tip where the waters of the Kattegat and Skagerrak clash and you can put one foot in each sea; but not too far. Bathing is strictly forbidden here because of the ferocious tidal currents and often turbulent seas that collide to create mane-tossing white horses.

The tip is the culmination of a long, curving sweep of sand at Grenen, about 3km northeast of Skagen along Rte 40. Where the road ends there's a car park, cafe and souvenir shops, plus, in high summer, what seems like the entire population of Denmark. Crowds head along the last stretch of beach for the 30-minute walk to the tip. A special tractor-drawn bus, the *Sandormen*, leaves from the car park every half-hour, waits for 15 minutes at the beach end, then returns (adult/child return Dkr20/10). From May to September, buses run from Skagen station to Grenen hourly (Dkr15) until 5pm. Taxis, available at the train station, charge about Dkr75 to Grenen.

SKAGENS MUSEUM

This fine **museum** (☎ 98 44 64 44; Brøndumsvej 4; admission Dkr80; ☒ 10am-5pm or 6pm May-Aug, 11am-4pm Tue-Sun Apr, 1-5pm Wed-Fri, 11am-4pm Sat, to 3pm Sun Nov-Mar) showcases the paintings of Michael and Anna Ancher, PS Krøyer, and of other artists who flocked to Skagen between 1830 and 1930, many of them kitchen-sink portraits of the lives and deaths of the fishing community.

MICHAEL & ANNA ANCHER'S HUS

This poignant domestic **museum** (☎ 98 44 30 09; Markvej 2-4; adult/child Dkr60/free; ☒ 10am-6pm mid-Jun–mid-Aug, 10am-5pm May–mid-Jun, 11am-3pm Sep-Apr) occupies the house that the Anchers bought in 1884 and in which their daughter Helga lived until 1960.

TILSANDEDE KIRKE

This whitewashed medieval **church tower** (☎ 98 44 43 71; adult/child Dkr10/5; ⊙ 11am-5pm Jun-Sep) still rises above the sand dunes that buried the church and surrounding farms in the late 18th century. The tower, in a nature reserve, is 5km south of Skagen and well signposted from Rte 40. By bike, take Gammel Landevej from Skagen.

RÅBJERG MILE

These undulating 40m-high hills comprise Denmark's largest expanse of shifting dunes and are great fun to explore. Råbjerg Mile is 16km south of Skagen, off Rte 40 on the road to Kandestederne. From May to September, bus 99 runs six times a day from Skagen Station (Dkr16, 25 minutes).

Sleeping

Hotel accommodation can be scarce at summer weekends and during the Skagen Festival at the end of June. The tourist office books singles/doubles in private homes for around Dkr300/450, plus a Dkr50 booking fee.

Grenen Camping (☎ 98 44 25 46; adult/child Dkr81/47) A fine seaside location, semiprivate camp sites and pleasant four-bunk huts, 1.5km northeast of Skagen centre. The only downside is the rather tightly bunched sites.

Danhostel Skagen (☎ 98 44 22 00; www.danhostel .dk/skagen; Rolighedsvej 2; dm Dkr150, s/d from Dkr500/600; ⊙ mid-Feb–late Nov; P) Well kept, very popular and 1km from the centre, book ahead in the summer. Rates drop sharply in low season.

Marienlund Badepension (☎ 98 44 13 20; www .marienlund.dk; Fabriciusvej 8; s/d with bathroom Dkr460/800) A modern, comfortable, immaculately kept place that is situated on the quieter western side of town near the open-air museum.

Skagen Sømandshjem (☎ 98 44 25 88; Østre Strandvej 2; s/d with bathroom Dkr620/860, without bathroom Dkr460/800) A harbourside hotel that has bright, pleasant rooms.

Eating & Drinking

Perhaps a dozen seafood shacks line the harbour selling good seafood to eat inside, outside or takeaway. Freshly caught prawns are the favourite fare, costing around Dkr85 for a generous helping.

You'll find a couple of pizzerias, a kebab shop, a burger joint and an ice-cream shop clustered near each other on Havnevej. **Super Brugsen** (Sankt Laurentii Vej 28), a grocery store just west of the tourist office, has a bakery.

Restaurant Pakhuset (☎ 98 44 20 00; Rødspættevej 6; light lunches Dkr65-77, mains Dkr150-230) There's a mix of great fresh fish mains and cheaper light lunches (like fish cakes with remoulade and salad for Dkr72), its long hours and a superb ambience both outdoors (right among the bustle of the harbour) and indoors (a lovely wooden-beamed interior sprinkled with jovial ship mastheads). Its downstairs cafe offers the cheaper dishes.

Ruths Hotel (☎ 98 44 11 24; www.ruths-hotel.dk; Hans Ruths Vej 1; brasserie mains Dkr125-155; gourmet mains Dkr350, 3/6 courses Dkr590/930) This is one of Denmark's grand bathing hotels, beautifully modernised and close to the beach. It also has two excellent restaurants, overseen by the French chef Michel Michaud, formerly of Falsled Kro. The brasserie is lighter and cheaper, with dishes such as home smoked salmon, snails, rib eye and oysters, while Ruths Gourmet is more formal, with titanic dishes such as Cote de boeuf Bordelaise and pigeon cassoulet.

Brøndum's Hotel (☎ 98 44 15 55; Anchersvej 3; mains Dkr150-260) French cuisine is the main influence on the otherwise classic Danish dishes, with lots of fresh seafood such as lobster and turbot as well as tenderloin and chateaubriand. Meals are served in the old-world ambience of the cosy dining room. Rooms cost Dkr850/1350 per single/double, and were fully renovated in 2008.

Jakobs (☎ 98 44 16 90; Havnevej 4; 3 courses Dkr295) Jakobs is a popular restaurant on Skagen's busy main street. It does good homemade brunches (Dkr95), salads and pastas (Dkr79 to Dkr95). By night it's a popular bar staging live music at weekends (usually cover bands).

Buddy Holly's (Havnevej 16) There's nothing cutting edge or elegant about Buddy Holly's, but the predictable sonic menu of dance and disco classics from the '70s, '80s and '90s gets a 30- and 40-something crowd up and dancing.

Getting There & Away

Nordjyske Jernbaner (☎ 98 45 45 10; www.njba.dk, in Danish) runs smart new trains every two hours (Dkr48) to Frederikshavn. A seasonal Skagerakkeren bus (No 99) runs between Hirtshals and Skagen (Dkr37, 1½ hours, six daily mid-June to mid-August). The same bus continues on to Hjørring and Løkken.

Getting Around

Cycling is an excellent way of exploring Skagen and the surrounding area. **Skagen Cykeludlejning** (☎ 98 44 10 70; Banegårdspladsen; per day Dkr75, deposit Dkr200) rents out bicycles and has a stand on the western side of the train station and at the harbour.

Skagen is very busy with traffic in high season. There is free parking for short periods and convenient metered parking (Dkr10 per hour) just by the train station.

HIRTSHALS

pop 6700

A busy, modern little town thanks to a large commercial fishing harbour and ferry terminal, Hirtshals has an easy, friendly character, an excellent aquarium and some fine stretches of beach, although its looks aren't likely to take your breath away. The main street, pedestrianised Nørregade, is lined with a mix of cafes and shops, and with supermarkets that cater to Norwegian shoppers piling off the ferries to load up with relatively cheap Danish meats and groceries. The seaward end of Nørregade opens out into a wide, airy space, Den Grønne Plads (Green Square), which overlooks the fishing harbour and its tiers of blue-hulled boats. There is a **tourist office** (☎ 98 94 22 20; www.visithirtshals.com; Nørregade 40; ⏰ 9.30am-3.30pm Mon-Fri, 9am-2pm Sat mid-Jul–Aug, 10am-3pm Mon-Fri, 9am-2pm Sat Aug-Jun).

Hirtshals' big draw is the **Nordsømuseet** (☎ 98 94 41 88; Willemoesvej 2; adult/child Dkr110/55; ⏰ 10am-6pm mid-Jun–mid-Aug, to 5pm mid-Aug–mid-Jun), an impressive aquarium that re-creates a slice of the North Sea in a massive four-storey tank, containing elegantly balletic schools of thousands of fish. Divers feed the fish at 1pm and the seals at 11am and 3pm.

In the surrounding area there are coastal cliffs and a **lighthouse** on the town's western side. If you want beaches, there's a lovely unspoiled stretch at **Tornby Strand**, 5km south.

Sleeping & Eating

Staff at the tourist office can book rooms in private homes starting at Dkr200 plus a Dkr25 booking fee.

Hirtshals Hostel (☎ 98 94 12 48; www.danhostel nord.dk/hirtshals; Kystvejen 53; dm/s/d Dkr150/370/420; ⏰ Mar-Nov) Occupying a bland building and offering basic facilities about 1km from the centre, the saving grace of this hostel is its location a bucket and spade's throw from the beach.

Hotel Hirtshals (☎ 98 94 20 77; www.hotelhirtshals .dk; Havnegade 2; s/d Dkr795/895) On the main square above the fishing harbour, the Hirtshals has bright, comfortable rooms with high, steepled ceilings and good sea views at the front.

There are cafes and a good bakery at the northern end of Hjørringgade, and there are also a couple of pizza and kebab places on Nørregade.

Hirtshals Kro (☎ 98 94 26 77; Havnegade; mains Dkr149-89) A delightful restaurant in a very old kro that has retained its character. Not surprisingly the menu offers several tasty seafood dishes including a mixed fish plate for Dkr185.

Getting There & Away

BOAT

The ferry company **Color Line** (☎ 99 56 20 00; www.colorline.com) runs year-round ferries to the Norwegian ports of Larvik (6½ hours, twice daily from May to September) and Kristiansand (2½ hours, twice daily). Fares on both routes range from Dkr180/90 per adult/child midweek in the low season to Dkr460/230 on summer weekends for passengers, Dkr720 to Dkr1760 for cars. A new service from **Fjord Line** (☎ 97 96 30 00; www.fjordline .dk) goes to Stavanger and Bergen in Norway (car to Stavanger from Dkr654; to Bergen from Dkr744).

BUS

From May to September a **bus** (☎ 70 13 14 15) from Hirtshals Station to Hjørring (Dkr24) stops en route at Tornby Strand six times a day.

TRAIN

Hirtshals' main train station is 500m south of the ferry harbour but there's also a stop near the Color Line terminal. The railway, which is operated by a private company, connects Hirtshals with Hjørring (Dkr24), 20 minutes to the south. Trains run at least hourly. From Hjørring you can take a DSB train to Aalborg (Dkr72) or Frederikshavn (Dkr48).

ESBJERG
pop 70,000

Let's be honest here, nobody comes to Esbjerg for a holiday, in fact, as with many industrial ports, most visitors rush through as quickly as possible. That said, there are attractive parts to this interesting town, as well as one or two excellent attractions. Esbjerg is the centre of Denmark's extensive North Sea oil activities and in recent years the export of wind turbines has replaced the fishing industry as a major source of income. Although Esbjerg has its fair share of early 20th-century buildings, if period charm is what you're after then head straight to nearby Ribe.

Information

Central Library (☎ 76 16 20 00; Nørregade 19; ☙ 10am-7pm Mon-Thu, to 5pm Fri, to 2pm Sat) Free internet access.

Danske Bank (☎ 79 15 72 00; Torvet 18)

Post Office (☎ 79 12 12 12; Torvet 20)

Tourist Office (☎ 75 12 55 99; www.visitesbjerg.com; Skolegade 33; ☙ 10am-5pm Mon-Fri, 10am-1pm Sat Sep–mid-Jun, 10am-5pm Mon-Fri, 10am-2.30pm mid-Jun–Aug).

Sights & Activities

The single most worthwhile place to visit in town is the **Esbjerg Kunstmuseum** (☎ 75 13 02 11; Havnegade 20; adult/child Dkr50/free; ☙ 10am-4pm), an impressive gallery with an important collection of Danish modern art including work by Asger Jorn.

Also in the town centre, is the small **Esbjerg Museum** (☎ 75 12 78 11; Torvegade 45; adult/child Dkr30/free; ☙ 10am-4pm) containing a few historical artefacts from the area and an amber display. It will offer a short diversion if it's raining.

Sleeping

There's a good range of reasonably priced accommodation in town. The tourist office books rooms in private homes at around Dkr175/300 for singles/doubles.

Ådalens Camping (☎ 75 15 88 22; www.adal.dk; Gudenåvej 20; camp sites adult/child Dkr73/45; ☒) The nearest camping to Esbjerg (5km north of the city via bus 1 or 7) this place has great facilities including a pool, solarium and Jacuzzi.

Danhostel Esbjerg (☎ 75 12 42 58; www.danhostel .dk/esbjerg; Gammel Vardevej 80; dm/s/d Dkr180/350/450; ☙ Feb–mid-Dec) Occupying a handsome former high school 3km northwest of the city centre, this hostel is close to sports facilities including a pool. Take buses 4 and 12.

Cab Inn Esbjerg (☎ 75 18 16 00; www.cabinn.com; Skolegade 14; s/d Dkr545/705; ⓟ ☒ 🖳 📶) This has clean, functional but good-value, cabin-style rooms (so small dimensions and rather narrow bunk beds) right in the centre. The superior rooms are larger and less clinical. There's free internet access.

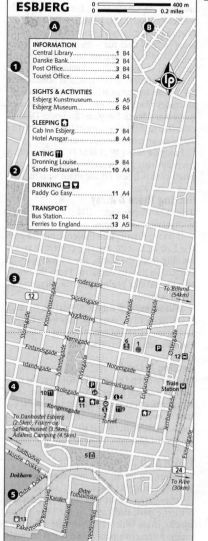

ESBJERG

0   400 m
0   0.2 miles

INFORMATION
Central Library.................1 B4
Danske Bank....................2 B4
Post Office.......................3 B4
Tourist Office...................4 B4

SIGHTS & ACTIVITIES
Esbjerg Kunstmuseum.......5 A5
Esbjerg Museum................6 B4

SLEEPING
Cab Inn Esbjerg................7 B4
Hotel Ansgar....................8 A4

EATING
Dronning Louise...............9 B4
Sands Restaurant.............10 A4

DRINKING
Paddy Go Easy.................11 A4

TRANSPORT
Bus Station......................12 B4
Ferries to England............13 A5

Hotel Ansgar (☎ 75 12 82 44; www.hotelansgar.dk; Skolegade 36; s/d Dkr715/1000) Ansgar is a friendly place with large, comfortable rooms decorated in simple classic Scandinavian style.

Eating & Drinking

Most restaurants and grocery stores are east of Torvet on Kongensgade.

Sand's Restaurant (☎ 75 12 02 07; Skolegade 60; lunch Dkr39-169, mains Dkr89-199) You'll find superb, authentic Danish staples such as smørrebrød, Danish hash, meatballs, smoked eel and *pariserbof* (a fried beef patty on bread with a raw egg yolk, pickles and fresh horseradish) in this cosy, old-fashioned dining room.

Dronning Louise (☎ 75 13 13 44; Torvet 19; mains Dkr135-229; ☺ 10am-late Mon-Sat, to 11.30pm Sun) This jack-of-all-trades place turns out decent sandwiches, burgers and lunch fish plates for under Dkr100, as well as slightly more ambitious brasserie fare and pastries from the cafe counter.

Paddy Go Easy (☎ 75 18 07 72; Skolegade 42) A friendly Irish pub actually run by Irish proprietors that is just off the main square.

Getting There & Away

Trains to Copenhagen (Dkr311, 2¼ hours, hourly) run until 10pm.

If you're driving into Esbjerg from the east, the E20 leads into the city centre. If you're coming from the south, Rte 24 merges with the E20 on the city outskirts. From the north, Rte 12 makes a beeline into the city, ending at the harbour.

DFDS Seaways (☎ in the UK 08705 333 000, in Denmark 33 42 30 00; www.dfdsseaways.co.uk) sails from Esbjerg to Harwich (UK) at least three times a week. For full details see p503.

Getting Around

Most city-bound buses (Dkr16) call at the train station. Parking is free in Esbjerg. There's also a convenient car park on Danmarksgade, but it has a two-hour limit; some unlimited parking is available in the car park on Nørregade, east of the library.

LEGOLAND

Children under 12 will love **Legoland** (☎ 75 33 13 33; www.lego.dk; adult/child 3-13 years Dkr259/229; ☺ 10am-8pm Apr–late Oct, 10am-9pm early Jul–early Aug), a theme park dedicated to the little plastic blocks from which many of the miniature cities, interactive play areas, safari animals, pirates, princesses, astronauts, Vikings and

other displays and attractions are built here. There are some excellent younger children's amusement rides but for wilder rides suited to older children and adults, Legoland compares unfavourably to Copenhagen's Tivoli Gardens. The rides close two hours before the park does.

Legoland is 63km northeast of Esbjerg. There's a frequent bus from Vejle to Legoland (Dkr50, 25 minutes), as well as bus-tour packages from numerous cities, including Esbjerg. Inquire at Esbjerg tourist office.

RIBE
pop 8000

The charming crooked, cobblestone streets of Ribe date from AD 869, making it one of Scandinavia's oldest and Denmark's most attractive towns. It is a delightful chocolate-box confection of half-timbered, 16th-century houses, clear-flowing streams and water meadows. Almost everything, including the hostel and train station, is within a 10-minute walk of Torvet, the town square, which is dominated by the huge Romanesque cathedral.

Information

Danske Bank (☎ 76 88 68 20; Overdammen 4)
Post Office (Sct Nicolaj Gade)
Tourist Office (☎ 75 42 15 00; www.visitribe.dk; Torvet 3; ☺ 9am-6pm Mon-Fri, 10am-5pm Sat, to 2pm Sun Jul & Aug, 9am-5pm Mon-Fri Apr-Jun, Sep & Oct, 10am-1pm Sat Apr-Jun & Sep-Dec)

Sights & Activities

For a pleasant stroll that takes in some of Ribe's handsome half-timbered buildings and winding cobbled lanes, head along any of the streets radiating out from Torvet, in particular Puggårdsgade or Grønnegade from where narrow alleys lead down and across Fiskegarde to Skibbroen and the picturesque old harbour.

Dominating the heart of the town **Ribe Domkirke** (☎ 75 42 06 19; Torvet; adult/child Dkr10/5; ☺ 11am-4pm Apr, 10am-5pm May & Jun, 10am-5.30pm Jul–15 Aug, 10am-5pm 16 Aug–Sep, 11am-4pm Oct, 11am-3pm Nov-Mar) boasts a variety of hugger mugger styles from Romanesque to Gothic. The cathedral's monumental presence is literally sunk into the heart of Ribe. The highlight is the climb up the steeple for breathtaking views.

Ribes Vikinger (☎ 76 88 11 22; Odins Plads 1; adult/child Dkr60/free; ☺ 10am-6pm Jul & Aug, to 4pm Apr-Jun, Sep & Oct, to 4pm Tue-Sun Nov-Mar) is a substantial

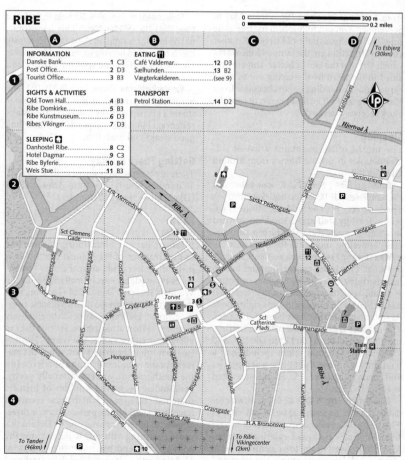

RIBE

INFORMATION	
Danske Bank	1 C3
Post Office	2 D3
Tourist Office	3 B3

SIGHTS & ACTIVITIES	
Old Town Hall	4 B3
Ribe Domkirke	5 B3
Ribe Kunstmuseum	6 D3
Ribes Vikinger	7 D3

SLEEPING	
Danhostel Ribe	8 C2
Hotel Dagmar	9 C3
Ribe Byferie	10 B4
Weis Stue	11 B3

EATING	
Café Valdemar	12 D3
Sælhunden	13 B2
Vægterkælderen	(see 9)

TRANSPORT	
Petrol Station	14 D2

0 --------- 300 m
0 --------- 0.2 miles

To Esbjerg
(30km)

museum opposite the train station; it has archaeological displays of Ribe's Viking past, including a reconstructed marketplace and Viking ship, with lots of hands-on features.

Located 3km south of the centre, is a recreated Viking village called **Ribe Vikingecenter** (☎ 75 41 16 11; Lustrupvej 4; adult/child Dkr75/35; ⏳ 11am-5pm Jul & Aug, 10am-3.30pm May-Jun & Sep), complete with working artisans and interpreters decked out in period costumes. There are hands-on activities to take part in during May and August, such as woodwork and archery, and there are plenty of ponies to pet. Bus 51 (Dkr20) will take you there from Ribe.

Ribe Kunstmuseum (☎ 75 42 03 62; www.ribe-kunstmuseum.dk; Sankt Nicolajgade 10; adult/child Dkr40/free; ⏳ 11am-5pm Thu-Sun Jul-Sep, to 4pm Thu-Sun Oct-Jun) has

a fine collection of 19th-century Golden Age and Silver Age Danish art, including Ludvig Abelin Schou's dramatic *Death of Chione*.

The town also has a couple of interesting local-history museums, including one at the **Old Town Hall** (☎ 75 42 05 34; adult/child Dkr15/5; ⏳ 1-3pm Mon-Fri), the former debtors' prison, displaying a small arsenal of viciously spiked medieval weaponry and the formidable axe of the town executioner. Make sure you look up at the chimney stacks of the building and you might see a stork's nest, and if you're lucky in spring it's possible to see roosting storks with a clutch of chicks.

There isn't any new-fangled CCTV fad in Ribe; instead, a costumed **night watchman** takes care of security, making the rounds from Torvet at 8pm and 10pm from May to September. You can follow him for free as he sings his way through the old streets. Another curious attraction are the famous Ribe storks which arrive at the end of March and are heralded in the town by the laying out of a red carpet and the handing out of chocolate frogs and spring water. The first person to spot the stork receives a reward.

Sleeping

The tourist office maintains a list of singles/doubles in private homes from around Dkr250/350.

Danhostel Ribe (☎ 75 42 06 20; www.danhostel.dk/ ribe; Sankt Pedersgade 16; dm/s Dkr160/325, d Dkr360-560; ☽ Feb–late-Nov; P) The modern, 140-bed hostel has friendly staff and a good, uncrowded location. The new rooms at the top are especially appealing and worth the extra cost.

Weis Stue (☎ 75 42 07 00; www.weisstue.dk; Torvet; s/d Dkr450/600) This is the poorer, quirkier but no less charming sister to the Dagmar opposite. A small, ancient wooden-beamed house, it has rather small, crooked rooms right above its restaurant, but they have bags of character. The restaurant offers lunch plates of herring, meatballs or lobster (Dkr110 to Dkr155) and seasonal specials that might include half a wild duck with fried potatoes, salad pickles and cream sauce (Dkr175). Breakfast is taken at Hotel Dagmar.

Ribe Byferie (☎ 79 88 79 88; Damvej 34; www.ribe -byferie.dk; apt for 2-4 people from Dkr750-1645; P ✗) This unusual development consists of several terraces of new built, self-catering cottages, to the south west of the town centre. It is, in effect, a holiday centre within the town and perfect for families of up to seven. There is a children's club, canoes and bicycles to rent, various other sports facilities and, of course, all the various attractions within Ribe itself.

Hotel Dagmar (☎ 75 42 00 33; www.hoteldagmar.dk, in Danish; Torvet; s/d from Dkr1045/1245; P ✗) The central Hotel Dagmar claims to be the oldest hotel in Denmark, has plush (if mostly rather small) rooms and a great period atmosphere.

Eating

Café Valdemar (☎ 75 42 42 03; www.cafevaldemar.dk; Sct Nicolajgade 6; ☽ 1-11pm Tue-Wed, 1pm-2am Thu, 1pm-5am Fri & Sat) This buzzing cafe and bar offers frequent live music, youthful flirting and most attractive of all, a waterside terrace in the heart of the old town.

Sælhunden (☎ 75 42 09 46; Skibbroen 13; fish & meat mains Dkr65-210; ☽ 10am-10pm) This handsome, old restaurant is right on the quayside. A tasty lunch of smoked herring or smoked ham costs Dkr95, it's also a good spot for a coffee and a slice of cake.

Vægterkælderen (Torvet; lunch Dkr115-135) The basement restaurant in the Hotel Dagmar shares a kitchen with the hotel's classy upstairs restaurant but it has cheaper dishes, including good steaks and fresh fish.

Getting There & Away

There are trains from Esbjerg to Ribe (Dkr60, 40 minutes, hourly) and from Århus to Ribe (Dkr224, two hours 40 minutes).

FANØ

pop 3200

If Esbjerg has one silver lining, it is that one of the treasures of the Danish North Sea is just a short ferry ride away. Fanø is a popular holiday island – technically it lies in the Wadden Sea – for Danes and Germans who throng to its picture postcard villages; stunning, broad, endless sandy beaches; and lively summer season atmosphere. Its two fishing villages, at either end of the island, Nordby (to the north is the main town, where the majority of the islanders live) and Sønderho (on the southern tip), are exceptionally pretty, assiduously preserved jumbles of historic thatched cottages in which time seems to have stood still for the past century or three. Sønderho in particular is one of Denmark's most charming villages. It dates from the 16th century and has more than a hint of Middle Earth to its low level, half-timbered thatched houses.

Fanø, 16km long and only 5km at its widest point, was once home to the largest fleet outside of Copenhagen, and over a period of 150 years was the site for the construction of more than 1000 vessels. In 1741 the Danish king, Christian VI, was forced to sell the island to raise money for the public coffers.

The **tourist office** (☎ 70 26 42 00; www.visitfanoe .dk; Færgevej 1, Nordby; ☽ 10am-5pm Mon-Fri Jan-Mar, Nov & Dec, 10am-5pm Mon-Fri, 10am-1pm Sat Apr-Jun, Sep & Oct, and 10am-4pm Sun Jul & Aug) is close to the harbours in Nordby.

SIGHTS & ACTIVITIES

Families and water-sports fans come to Fanø above all else for the magnificent beaches –

the best of which are around Rindby Strand, Sønderho and Fanø Bad (Denmark's first international seaside resort). All three villages have shops and restaurants. Further north is the vast and breathtaking sand spit, Søren Jessens Sand. The interior of the island features Fanø Klitplantage, a protected nature reserve that is richly rewarding for ornithologists. Amber hunters also flock to the island to hunt along Fanø's beaches.

Fanø Skibsfarts og Dragtsamling (☎ 21 14 00 43; www.fanoskibs-dragt.dk; Hovedgaden 28, Nordby; adult/child Dkr25/5; ☼ 11am-4pm May-Sep) is a small museum that covers the nautical history of this ancient fishing island.

Fanø Museum (☎ 75 16 61 37; www.fanomuseerne.dk; Skolevej 2, Nordby; adult/child Dkr25/5; ☼ 11am-2pm Mon-Sat, to 4pm summer) is housed in a 300-year-old building and is a companion museum to the Skibsfarts og Dragtsamling. It covers the rest of the island's history and boasts a particularly good collection of period furniture.

Fanø Kunstmuseum (☎ 75 16 40 44; www.fanoekunstmuseum.dk; Nordland 5, Sønderho; adult/child Dkr30/15; ☼ 2-5pm Tue-Sun Apr-Oct) features paintings from the 19th and early 20th century by Fanø artists and other Danish artists who have been inspired by the timeless lifestyle and wonderful light of the island.

Fanø Golf Links (☎ 76 66 00 44; www.fanoe-golf-links.dk; Golfvejen 5, Fanø Bad; 18 holes Dkr310) is Denmark's only links course and offers an – often literally – breathtaking 18 holes beside the sea. You can rent equipment, but booking is advised during the summer.

SLEEPING & EATING

There are nine camp sites on Fanø, virtually all within a short walk of the coast. For more information see www.visitfanoe.dk. There are supermarkets in shops in all the main villages on the island.

For rental of holiday homes or apartments, from historic thatched cottages, to modern summer houses, contact **Feriepartner Fanø** (☎ 75 16 26 00; www.feriepartner-fanoe.dk; Hovedgaden 12, Nordby).

Sønderho Kro (☎ 75 16 40 09; www.sonderhokro.dk; Kropladsen 11, Sønderho; r Dkr825-1325) The loveliest place to stay on the island (and renowned around the country) is this thatched inn dating from 1722 whose 14, individually decorated rooms are filled with charming local antiques. The inn also has a notable gourmet restaurant which serves local lamb,

seafood and other seasonal Danish offerings in a refined, French style.

Hotel Fanø Badeland (☎ 75 16 60 00; www.fanoebadeland.dk; Strandvejen 52, Fanø Bad; apt Dkr964-7107) This holiday centre has modern self-catering apartments beside the beach, with an indoor swimming pool, tennis courts, minigolf and restaurant.

Fanø Rogeri (☎ 75 16 34 36; www.fanoeroegeri.dk; Postvejen 16, Rindby; 3 courses Dkr285; ☼ 11am-10pm Tue-Sun) Salmon, shellfish, eel and herring are among the delicacies smoked on the premises and served in the garden during the summer. There is a delicatessen here too, selling a wide range of meats, wine, cheese, *charcuterie* and fish to go. It also claims to serve Denmark's largest ice-cream cone, an insurmountable mound of frozen dairy made up of 45 scoops (Dkr300).

There is a small supermarket, **Merko** (☎ 75 16 35 46; Kirkevejen 32), in Rindby with an in-house bakers and butchers.

GETTING THERE

Fanø Trafikken (☎ 70 23 15 15; www.fanoetrafikken.dk; car summer/winter incl passengers Dkr265/370, adult/child same price year-round Dkr 35/30) ferries depart from Esbjerg for Nordby a couple of times an hour (or more during summer) from 5am to midnight. The trip takes 12 minutes. Once on the island, there is a limited local bus service connecting Nordby and Fanø Bad, Rindby Strand and Sønderho. You can also rent bicycles in Nordby from **Fanø Cykler** (☎ 75 16 25 13; www.fanoecykler.dk; Hovedgaden 96, Nordby & Kirkevejen 67, Rindby; per day Dkr65), **Fanø Bikes** (☎ 28 19 89 50; www.fanobikes.dk) and from **Unika Cykler** (☎ 75 16 24 60; www.unikacykler.dk) which has offices in five locations around the island.

DENMARK DIRECTORY

ACCOMMODATION

Accommodation in this chapter is listed in order of budget from cheapest to most expensive.

Camping & Cabins

Denmark's 516 camping grounds typically charge from Dkr50 to Dkr65 per person to pitch a tent. A camping pass (available at any camping ground) is required (Dkr90) and covers a family group with children under 18 for the season. If you do not have

DENMARK

a seasonal pass you pay an extra Dkr20 a night for a temporary pass. The **Danish Camping Association** (☎ 39 27 88 44; www.campingraa det.dk; Campingrådet, Mosedalvej 15, Valby) inspects and grades Danish camping grounds using a star system and carries a full list on its website.

Hostels

The national Hostelling International office is **Danhostel** (☎ 33 31 36 12; www.danhostel.dk; Vesterbrogade 39, 1620 Copenhagen V).

Most of Denmark's 100 *vandrerhjem* (hostels) in its Danhostel association have private rooms in addition to dorms, making hostels an affordable and popular alternative to hotels (so book ahead from June to August). Dorm beds cost from about Dkr150, while private rooms range from Dkr280 to Dkr400 for singles, and Dkr400 to Dkr500 for doubles. Blankets and pillows are provided, but not sheets; bring your own or hire them for Dkr40 to Dkr60. Sleeping bags are not allowed.

A Danhostel Rabat Card costs Dkr80. Without one you pay Dkr35 extra a night. You can buy them at all Danhostels. Outside Copenhagen, check-in is generally between 4pm and 8pm or 9pm (but a few places close as early as 6pm).

Hotels

Budget hotels start at around Dkr500/650 for singles/doubles. *Kros*, a name that implies country inn but is more often the Danish version of a motel, are generally cheaper, often occupy pleasing period houses and more often than not offer a sense of homeliness that chain hotels cannot hope to compete with. Both hotels and *kros* usually include an all-you-can-eat breakfast. You can find out more about some (though not all – those listed pay to be included) of Denmark's inns and make online bookings at www.krohotel.dk.

Rates listed in this chapter include all taxes and are for rooms with toilet and shower, unless otherwise specified. Some hotels, particularly the large chain or business-orientated ones offer discount schemes at weekends year-round and from May to September when business travel is light.

Other Accommodation

Many tourist offices book rooms in private homes for a small fee, or provide a free list of the rooms so travellers can phone on their own. Rates vary, averaging about Dkr250/350

for singles/doubles. Standards of accommodation may vary widely and some rooms may be very basic. **Dansk Bed & Breakfast** (☎ 39 61 04 05; www.bbdk.dk; PO Box 53, 2900 Hellerup) handles 300 homes throughout Denmark offering private rooms at similar rates.

ACTIVITIES
Cycling

Cycling is a popular holiday activity and there are thousands of kilometres of established cycling routes. Those around Bornholm, Funen and Møn, as well as the 440km Old Military Rd (Hærvejen) through central Jutland, are among the most popular.

Dansk Cyklist Forbund (DCF; ☎ 33 32 31 21; www .dcf.dk; Rømersgade 7, 1362 Copenhagen K) publishes *Cykelferiekort*, a cycling map of the entire country (Dkr60), as well as more detailed regional cycling maps.

DCF also publishes *Overnatning i det fri*, which lists hundreds of farmers who provide cyclists with a place to pitch a tent for Dkr15 a night. Cycling maps can be purchased in advance from DCF or from tourist offices and bookshops upon arrival.

Walking

Even though Denmark does not have substantial forests, many small tracts of woodland are crisscrossed by pleasant walking trails. The Skov og Naturstyrelsen (Forest and Nature Bureau) produces brochures with sketch maps that show trails in nearly 100 such areas.

Water Sports

Canoeing possibilities on Denmark's inland lakes, such as canoe touring between lakeside camping grounds in Jutland's Lake District, are superb. You can hire canoes and equipment at many camping grounds or in main centres such as Silkeborg (p89). The lakes are generally undemanding as far as water conditions go, although some experience is an advantage.

Denmark's remarkable coastline offers terrific windsurfing and kitesurfing possibilities. Good areas are along the northern coast of Zealand at places such as Smidstrup Strand, and in northwest Jutland. The Limfjord area of northwest Jutland is particularly suited to windsurfing and canoeing.

BUSINESS HOURS

Office hours are generally 9am to 5pm Monday to Friday. Most banks are open from 9.30am to 4pm Monday to Friday (to 6pm Thursday), but some still close earlier. Stores are usually open 9.30am to 5.30pm Monday to Thursday, to 7pm on Friday, and to 2pm on Saturday.

DISABLED TRAVELLERS

Overall, Denmark is a user-friendly destination for the disabled traveller. The **Danish Tourist Board** (www.visitdenmark.com) has to date accredited, in association with local disability organisations, 1300 locations as 'accessible to all' throughout the country. It also publishes *Access in Denmark: a Travel Guide for the Disabled*, in English, with helpful information on accommodation, transport and sightseeing options for disabled travellers.

EMBASSIES & CONSULATES

Australia (☎ 70 26 36 76; www.denmark.embassy.gov .au; Dampfærgevej 26, Copenhagen)
Canada (☎ 33 48 32 00; www.canada.dk; Kristen Bernikows Gade1, Copenhagen)
Germany (☎ 35 45 99 00; www.kopenhagen.diplo.de; Stockholmsgade 57, Copenhagen)
Ireland (☎ 35 42 32 33; Østbanegade 21, Copenhagen)
Norway (☎ 33 14 01 24; www.norsk.dk; Amaliegade 39, Copenhagen)
Poland (☎ 39 46 77 00; www.ambpol.dk; Richelius Allé 12, Hellerup)
Sweden (☎ 33 36 03 70; www.sverigesambassad.dk; Sankt Annæ Plads 15A, Copenhagen)
UK (☎ 35 44 52 00; www.britishembassy.dk; Kastelsvej 36-40, Copenhagen)
USA (☎ 33 41 71 00; www.usembassy.dk; Dag Hammarskjölds Allé 24, Copenhagen)

FESTIVALS & EVENTS

Beginning with **Midsummer's Eve** bonfires in late June, Denmark buzzes with outdoor activity throughout the summer. Main attractions are the 180 music festivals that run throughout the country, covering a broad spectrum of music that includes not only jazz, rock and blues but also gospel, folk, classical, country, Cajun and much more.

The highly acclaimed 10-day **Copenhagen Jazz Festival** (http://festival.jazz.dk, in Danish) is celebrated in early July, with outdoor concerts and numerous performances in clubs around the city.

The town of Roskilde hosts an internationally acclaimed **rock festival** (www.roskilde-festival.dk)

on the last weekend of June; a single admission fee includes camping space and entry to all concerts.

There are **folk festivals** in Skagen towards the end of June and in Tønder in late August. The 10-day **Århus Festival** in early September features music and multicultural events. Also don't miss the excellent **Skanderborg Festival** – said to be Denmark's most beautiful (see p90).

GAY & LESBIAN TRAVELLERS

Denmark is a popular destination for gay and lesbian travellers. Copenhagen in particular has an active, open gay community and lots of nightlife options.

Landsforeningen for Bøsser og Lesbiske (LBL; ☎ 33 13 19 48; www.lbl.dk; Teglgårdstræde 13, Copenhagen) is the national organisation for gay men and lesbians. Branch offices in main towns are mentioned in relevant sections. A good English-language website with links to LBL and other gay organisations is www.copenhagen-gay-life.dk.

HOLIDAYS

Summer holidays for schoolchildren begin around 20 June and end around 10 August. Many Danes go on holiday during the first three weeks of July. The following public holidays are observed in Denmark:
New Year's Day (1 January)
Maundy Thursday (Thursday before Easter)
Good Friday to Easter Monday (March/April)
Common Prayer Day (4th Friday after Easter)
Ascension Day (5th Thursday after Easter)
Whit Sunday (5th Sunday after Easter)
Whit Monday (5th Monday after Easter)
Constitution Day (5 June)
Christmas Eve (24 December from noon)
Christmas Day (25 December)

INTERNET ACCESS

Internet cafes charge about Dkr50 an hour. Public libraries also have internet-capable computers and visitors generally have free access to them. Connections are generally fast. Wi-fi hotspots are mushrooming all over the country, many of them free. **TDC** (http://tdc.dk, in Danish) is a network of more than 600 paid-for wi-fi hotspots.

LEGAL MATTERS

Denmark is taking a much harder line on even the 'softest' drugs these days. All forms of cannabis and harder drugs are illegal. If you are arrested for any offence you can be held for up to 24 hours before appearing in court. You have a right to know the charges against you and a right to a lawyer. You are not obliged to answer police questions before speaking to the lawyer.

You can get free legal advice on your rights from the EU legal-aid organisation **EURO-JUS** (☎ 33 14 41 40; ☯ 9am-6pm Mon-Thu, to 4.30pm Fri). Free legal advice clinics can be found in more than 90 places across Denmark. The service is organised by the Danish bar, **Det Danske Advokatsamfund** (☎ 38 38 36 38, 33 96 97 98).

MONEY
ATMs
Major banks have ATMs accepting Visa, MasterCard and the Cirrus and Plus bank cards. All major credit and debit cards are accepted throughout Denmark, although some shops impose a surcharge of up to 5% if you use them, even in the case of debit cards.

Moneychangers
All common travellers cheques are accepted in Denmark. Buy your travellers cheques in higher denominations as bank fees for changing money are a hefty Dkr25 to Dkr30 per cheque, with a Dkr40 minimum. If you're exchanging cash, there's a Dkr25 fee for a transaction. Travellers cheques command a better exchange rate than cash by about 1%.

Post offices will also exchange foreign currency at comparable rates to those at banks.

The Euro
Although Denmark remains outside the Euro zone, acceptance of euros is commonplace. Most hotels and restaurants will take euros, as do many bars, cafes and shops, although you may find reluctance to do so in more remote areas or from very small businesses. Government institutions do not accept euros.

Tipping
Restaurant bills and taxi fares include service charges in the quoted prices, and further tipping is unnecessary.

POST
Denmark has an efficient postal system. Most post offices are open 9am or 10am to 5pm or 5.30pm Monday to Friday and 9am to noon on Saturday. You can receive mail poste restante at any post office in Denmark.

TELEPHONE & FAX
It costs Dkr5 to make a local call at coin phones. You get about twice as much calling time for your money on domestic calls made between 7.30pm and 8am daily and all day on Sunday.

Phonecards (Dkr50 to Dkr100) can be bought at post offices and newspaper kiosks throughout the country.

The country code for calling Denmark from abroad is ☎ 45. To make international calls from Denmark dial ☎ 00 and then the country code for the country you're calling.

TIME
Time in Denmark is normally one hour ahead of GMT/UTC, the same as in neighbouring European countries. Clocks are moved forward one hour for daylight-saving time from the last Sunday in March to the last Sunday in October. Denmark uses the 24-hour clock and all timetables and business hours are posted accordingly.

TOURIST INFORMATION
The tourist board's website is www.visit denmark.com. It also lists the tourist offices throughout the country, plus their opening hours. There are offices in virtually all towns in Denmark.

VISAS
Citizens of the EU, USA, Canada, Australia and New Zealand need a valid passport to enter Denmark, but don't need a visa for stays of less than three months. If you wish to apply for a visa, do so at least three months in advance of your planned arrival.

WOMEN TRAVELLERS
Kvindehuset (☎ 33 14 28 04; Gothersgade 37, Copenhagen) is a help centre and meeting place for women. Dial ☎ 112 for rape crisis or other emergencies.

TRANSPORT IN DENMARK

GETTING THERE & AWAY
Air
The profusion of budget carriers and flights into Denmark from elsewhere on the continent, Ireland and the UK makes flying here affordable. If you're coming from European destinations consider flying into an airport other than Copenhagen, such as

Århus or Billund; airfares are competitive, and the airports are well connected by bus with neighbouring towns and afford fast access to some great parts of northern and central Jutland.

The budget carrier Ryanair, for instance, has regular, cheap flights from Stansted Airport in England to Århus airport and to Malmö, in Sweden (a short hop by rail from Copenhagen). See the following airport websites for full details.

AIRLINES

Scandinavian Airlines (SAS; airline code SK; ☎ 70 10 30 00; www.scandinavian.net) is the largest carrier serving Denmark, connecting it with much of Europe and the rest of the world.

Many other airlines fly into Denmark including the following ones:

Aer Lingus (airline code EI; ☎ +353 818 365000; www.aerlingus.com)

Air France (AF; ☎ 82 33 27 01; www.airfrance.com)

Alitalia (AZ; ☎ 70 27 02 90; www.alitalia.com)

BMI British Midland (BD; ☎ 70 10 20 00; www.flybmi.com)

British Airways (BA; ☎ 70 12 80 22; www.britishairways.com)

Easyjet (U2; ☎ 70 12 43 21; www.easyjet.com)

Finnair (AY; ☎ 33 36 45 45; www.finnair.com)

Icelandair (FI; ☎ 33 70 22 00; www.icelandexpress.com)

KLM Royal Dutch Airlines (KL; ☎ 70 10 07 47; www.klm.com)

Lufthansa (LH; ☎ 70 10 20 00; www.lufthansa.com)

Ryanair (FR; ☎ +353 818 303 030; www.ryanair.com)

Sterling (NB; ☎ 70 10 84 84; www.sterling.dk)

MAIN DANISH AIRPORTS

Århus (☎ 87 75 70 00; www.aar.dk)

Billund (☎ 76 50 50 50; www.bll.dk)

Copenhagen (☎ 32 31 32 31; www.cph.dk)

Land
GERMANY

The E45 is the main motorway running between Germany and Denmark's Jutland Peninsula. There are also three railway lines linking the two countries (2nd-class fares from Copenhagen to Frankfurt are Dkr1307, to Berlin Dkr1010, although be advised fares booked in advance can be substantially cheaper than the prices listed here, see www.dsb.dk for more information). Eurolines operates buses from Copenhagen to Berlin

(Dkr274, seven hours) and Frankfurt via Hamburg (Dkr734, 13 hours), and 17 other German cities (as well as most European countries) several times a week.

NORWAY

Trains operate between Copenhagen and Oslo; the 2nd-class fare (via Sweden; 7½ hours, one or two daily) is Dkr1050. Eurolines offers a daily bus service between Oslo and Copenhagen (Dkr385, nine hours) via Göteborg.

SWEDEN

Trains run many times a day between Denmark and Sweden via a bridge linking Copenhagen with Malmö (Dkr90, 40 minutes), Dkr385 to Göteborg and Dkr965 to Stockholm (five hours). If you're travelling by train, the bridge crossing is included in the fare, but for those travelling by car, there's a Dkr275 toll per vehicle. There are numerous and frequent bus services between Copenhagen and Sweden, including Eurolines buses to Göteborg (Dkr275, 4½ hours) and Stockholm (Dkr385, 9½ hours).

Sea
GERMANY

The frequent Rødbyhavn–Puttgarden ferry takes 45 minutes and is included in train tickets for those travelling by rail; otherwise, the cost per adult is Dkr40 and for a car with up to nine passengers it's Dkr480.

Bornholmstrafikken operates a ferry service at least once a day between Rønne and Sassnitz, Germany (Dkr102 to Dkr203 one way, 3½ hours).

ICELAND & THE FAROE ISLANDS

Smyril Lines (in Denmark ☎ 33 16 40 04, 96 55 03 60, in Faroe Islands 345 900; www.smyril-line.com) operates every week from Esbjerg and Hanstholm to Tórshavn (Faroe Islands) and Seyðisfjörður (Iceland) from mid-May to early September. See the website for pricing and schedule details.

NORWAY

DFDS (☎ 33 42 30 00; www.dfds.dk) operates a daily overnight ferry running between Copenhagen and Oslo. **Colorline** (☎ 99 56 19 77; www.colorline.dk) sails from Hirtshals to Larvik, Kristiansand, Stavanger and Bergen; and from Frederikshavn to Oslo. See the relevant

Getting There & Away sections of the cities for details.

POLAND

Polferries (☎ 33 11 46 45; www.polferries.pl) operates ferries to Świnoujście from both Copenhagen four times a week (from Dkr420, 10 hours) and Rřnne on Saturday (from Dkr260, five hours).

SWEDEN

Scandlines (☎ 33 15 15 15; www.scandlines.dk) and **HH Ferries** (☎ 46 42 198000, http://hh.net.dynam icweb.se) sail every half-hour from Helsingør to Helsingborg, in Sweden. Prices vary, but are roughly Dkr48 return per adult or from Dkr600 if you are taking a car with two passengers.

Other ferries go from Frederikshavn to Göteborg and Oslo, and Rønne to Ystad. See the relevant Getting There & Away sections in this chapter.

UK

DFDS Seaways (in the UK ☎ 08705 333 000; in Denmark ☎ 33 42 30 00; www.dfdsseaways.co.uk) sails from Esbjerg to Harwich at least three times a week at 6pm year-round. It takes 19 hours. The cost for passage in a chair starts from £38 per person, one way.

GETTING AROUND
Air

Most internal flights cost around Dkr500 for a standard ticket and can be much cheaper if you book in advance.

Denmark's domestic air routes are operated by the airlines listed here.
Cimber Air (☎ 70 10 12 18; www.cimber.dk) Services include Copenhagen to Aalborg (50 minutes, three times daily), Rønne (Bornholm, 40 minutes, at least four times daily) and Karup (central Jutland, 50 minutes, 12 times daily weekdays, at least twice on weekends).
SAS (☎ 70 10 30 00; www.scandinavian.net) Links Copenhagen with Aalborg, Århus and Billund about a dozen times a day.

Bicycle

Cycling is a practical way to get around Denmark. There are extensive bike paths linking towns throughout the country and bike lanes through most city centres.

You can rent bikes in most towns for around Dkr70 per day, plus a deposit of about Dkr250. Bikes can be taken on ferries and

most trains for a modest cost; make sure you grab yourself a copy of the DSB pamphlet *Cykler i tog*.

Boat

A network of ferries links virtually all of Denmark's populated islands. Where there's not a bridge, there's usually a ferry, most of which take cars. All vessels meet strict safety requirements and are punctual and reliable. Specific information is given under individual destination sections. **Scandlines** (☎ 33 15 15 15; www.scandlines.com) operates many domestic ferry services. Timetables are widely available in tourist offices and railway stations.

Bus

All large cities and towns have a local and regional bus system, many of them connecting with trains. There are also a few long-distance bus routes, including from Copenhagen to Aalborg or Århus. Travelling by bus on long-distance routes costs about 20% less than travel by train, although it's slower than the train.

The main bus companies operating in Denmark include the following:
Abildskou (☎ 70 21 08 88; www.abildskou.dk) Runs from Copenhagen to Aalborg, Silkeborg and Århus.
Bornholmerbussen (☎ 44 68 44 00; www.bat.dk, in Danish) Operates the bus services on Bornholm.
Graahund Bus (☎ 44 68 44 00; www.graahundbus.dk, in Danish) Operates between Copenhagen and Bornholm, Copenhagen and Randers, Copenhagen and Malmø and Copenhagen and Berlin.
Thinggaard Expressbusser (☎ 70 10 00 10; www .ekspresbus.dk, in Danish) Operates between Copenhagen, Aalborg and Fjerristslev and between Frederikshavn and Esbjerg.

Car & Motorcycle

Denmark is perfect for touring by car. Roads are in good condition and well signposted. Traffic is manageable, even in major cities such as Copenhagen (rush hours excepted). Denmark's extensive network of ferries carries motor vehicles for reasonable rates. It's always a good idea for drivers to call ahead and make reservations.

AUTOMOBILE ASSOCIATIONS

Denmark's main motoring organisation is **Forenede Danske Motorejere** (FDM; ☎ 32 66 01 00/70 13 30 40; www.fdm.dk, in Danish; Firskovvej 32, 2800 Lyngby).

DRIVING LICENCE

A home driving licence, rather than an international one, is sufficient to drive and hire cars in Denmark, although you may also need to supply a passport at hire places.

FUEL

You'll find the best prices for petrol at stations along motorways and at the unstaffed OK Benzin chain, which has self-serve pumps that accept Dkr100 notes as well as major credit cards.

HIRE

You'll generally get the best deal by booking through an international rental agency before you arrive in Denmark. Hire rates for the cheapest cars, including VAT, insurance and unlimited kilometres, begin at about Dkr650 a day, or Dkr450 a day for rentals of two days or more. Most companies offer a special weekend rate that allows you to keep the car from Friday afternoon to Monday morning and include VAT and insurance for around Dkr1200. Europcar offers unlimited kilometres and generally has the cheapest, most flexible weekend deals, but it's wise to call around and compare.

The largest companies, such as **Europcar** (☎ 70 11 66 99; www.europcar.dk), **Avis** (☎ 33 26 80 00; www.avis.dk) and **Hertz** (☎ 0800-1700; www.hertzdk.dk), have offices throughout Denmark.

INSURANCE

Check with your insurance company that your policy is valid for driving in Denmark before you depart.

ROAD RULES

In Denmark you drive on the right-hand side of the road, seat-belt use is mandatory and all drivers are required to carry a warning triangle in case of breakdowns. Speed limits are 50km/h in towns, 80km/h outside built-up areas and either 110km/h or 130km/h on motorways. Motorcycles and cars must use dipped headlights at all times.

It's illegal to drive with a blood-alcohol concentration of 0.05% or greater and driving under the influence is subject to stiff penalties and a possible prison sentence.

Train

With the exception of a few short private lines, the **Danish State Railways** (DSB; www.dsb.dk) runs all Danish train services.

There are two types of long-distance trains: sleek intercity (IC) trains that generally require reservations (Dkr 35) and older, slower interregional (IR) trains that make more stops and don't require reservations. Both cost the same, apart from the InterCity-Lyn, a cushy, pricier express train. Rail passes don't cover reservation fees or surcharges.

Overall, train travel in Denmark is not expensive, in large part because the distances are short. People aged 65 and older are entitled to a 20% discount on Friday and Saturday and a 50% discount on other days. There are also generous discounts for children. InterRail and Eurail passes are valid on DSB ferries and trains.

FAROE ISLANDS

Faroe Islands

Adrift in the foggy North Atlantic Ocean midway between the north of Scotland and Iceland, the stunning Faroe Islands are a largely undiscovered slice of Scandinavia, where the terms 'remote' and 'windswept' usually feel inadequate.

Yet from the first moment you catch sight of these majestic grass-coated rocks that jut vertically out of the water, you'll be glad you made the decision to come. With the scenery dwarfing the colourful villages and turf-roofed churches nestled within it, a dizzying collection of sea cliffs (including the world's highest) and a fascinating old Norse culture to explore, the Faroes won't disappoint anyone looking for accessible adventure.

Made up of 18 islands, each with a personality and identity of its own, the Faroes will appeal to anyone who likes unforgettable scenery, long walks, clean air and watching birdlife on an unprecedented scale. Less expected is the islands' buzzing art and music scene, its raucous taverns and the friendly capital city of Tórshavn. So even if the weather proves uncooperative, this self-assured little demi-nation is likely to surprise and delight even the most cynical traveller.

FAST FACTS

- **Area** 1399 sq km
- **Capital** Tórshavn
- **Currency** Danish krone (Dkr): €1 = Dkr7.44; US$1 = Dkr5.61, UK£1 = Dkr8.29, $A1 = Dkr4.06, CA$1 = Dkr4.66, NZ$1 = Dkr3.16, ¥100 = Dkr5.76
- **Famous for** puffins, wool, whales, Viking sagas
- **Official Languages** Faroese, Danish
- **Phrases** góðan dag (hello), takk (thanks), farvæl (goodbye), orsaka meg (excuse me)
- **Population** 48,668
- **Telephone Codes** country code ☎ 298; international access code ☎ 00
- **Visa** not required for citizens of the EU, USA, Canada, Australia and New Zealand (see p134)

HIGHLIGHTS

- Take to the skies and see the Faroes at their most dramatic on a great value **helicopter trip** (p135) linking the further-flung islands like a bus service.
- Brave the waves beneath the towering bird cliffs on magical boat tours from **Vestmanna** (p123) or **Gjógv** (p124), the Faroes' prettiest village.
- Gasp at the superb panorama of cliffs and headlands viewed from **Kallur lighthouse** (p126), one of the Faroes' most rewarding short hikes.
- Hike across spectacular cliffs and wander among the largest puffin colonies in the country on peaceful **Mykines** (p122).

ITINERARIES

- **Two nights/three days** Head straight for Vestmanna for a boat ride along the spectacular bird cliffs. If driving, continue to charming Gjógv with side trips to Saksun and Eiði outbound, and Funningur, Elduvík and Kirkjubøur on return. Spend the last night in Tórshavn strolling the historical Tinganes district and exploring the lively pubs.
- **Ten days** Fly in on a Friday and take the boat the next morning out to the puffin island of Mykines. Returning on Sunday by helicopter to the capital Tórshavn. Visit the old town, flit up to the Vestmanna Bird Cliffs, explore northern Eysturoy then head for Klaksvík, the launching point for day-trip excursions to Kalsoy and the dramatic boat trip to Fugloy. On Friday buzz by helicopter to Froðba on Suðuroy, explore for a day or two and then return back to Tórshavn by ferry.

CONNECTIONS

The Faroes are well connected to the rest of the region by the Norröna car ferry. For a real Atlantic adventure, pick up the ferry anywhere along its route: it starts out in Hanstholm (Denmark), and stops in Bergen (Norway), Lerwick (Shetland Islands) before arriving at Tórshavn and the heading on to Seyðisfjörður (Iceland).

HOW MUCH?

- **Norðoya toll-tunnel fare** Dkr130
- **Sheepskin jacket** Dkr2600
- **Cuddly toy puffin** Dkr500
- **Medium-sized Faroese flag** Dkr200
- **Faroese sweater** Dkr750-1200

LONELY PLANET INDEX

- **1L of blýfrítt (unleaded petrol)** Dkr9.33
- **1.5L bottle of water** Dkr20
- **330ml bottle of Black Sheep beer (in a pub)** Dkr30
- **Souvenir T-shirt** Dkr150
- **Street snack of fish and chips** Dkr40

CLIMATE & WHEN TO GO

The Faroes joke that they enjoy 'four seasons in one day' – its weather is theatrically unpredictable, but you're usually guaranteed some rain, some sun, some cloud and some wind on any given day. Rainfall is very common (280 days per year on average) but unpredictable and often highly localised.

June to August is by far the best time to visit the Faroe Islands. Days are dreamily long and the weather is comparatively passable, though don't expect anything near Mediterranean heat: July temperatures average only 11°C. In winter, time stands still as daytime darkness, closed hotels and shuttered museums add to the stormy sense of a land forgotten. While never fearfully cold (January average 3°C), it can snow as late as May.

HISTORY

According to Irish missionary Brendan, Celtic monks were already living in eremitic seclusion on the Faroes by the 6th century. Their isolation was ended from around AD 800 when the first Norse farmers arrived. The farmers' independence dwindled with the often forceful imposition of Christianity, and the isles became part of the Kingdom of Norway in 1035. The first bishop's seat was established in Kirkjubøur.

The Faroese parliament (Løgting) lost further influence after Norway fell to Denmark

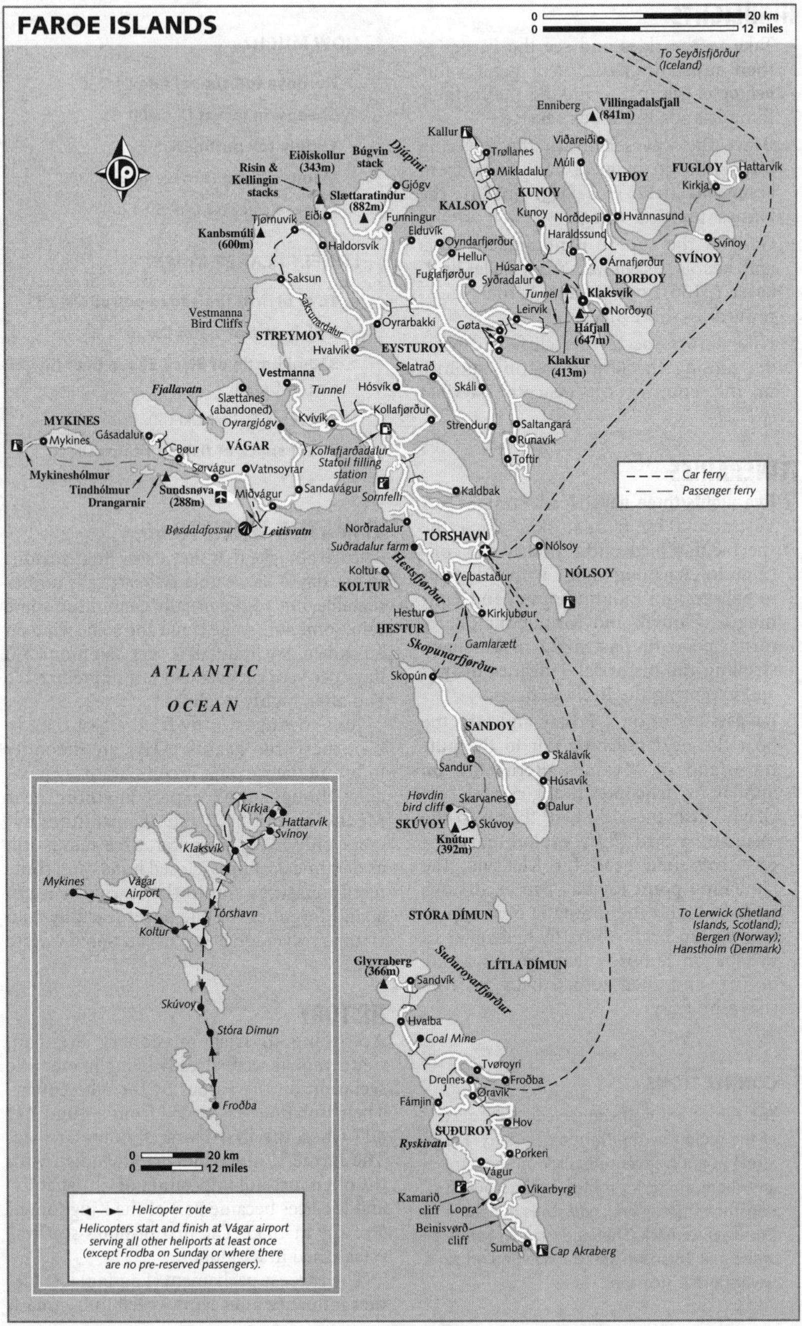
FAROE ISLANDS
0 20 km
0 12 miles
To Seyðisfjörður (Iceland)
Enniberg
Villingadalsfjall (841m)
Kallur
Trøllanes
Viðareiði
Mikladalur
Múli
VIÐOY
FUGLOY
Hattarvík
Kirkja
Eiðiskollur (343m)
Búgvin stack
Djúpini
Risin & Kellingin stacks
Slættaratindur (882m)
Gjógv
KALSOY
KUNOY
Kunoy
Norðdepil
Hvannasund
Tjørnuvík
Eiði
Funningur
Elduvík
Haraldssund
Svínoy
Kanbsmúli (600m)
Haldorsvík
Oyndarfjørður
Hellur
Árnafjørður
SVÍNOY
Fuglafjørður
Húsar
Syðradalur
BORÐOY
Saksun
Tunnel
Klaksvík
Saksunardalur
Leirvík
Norðoyri
Vestmanna Bird Cliffs
Oyrarbakki
Gøta
Hafjall (647m)
STREYMOY
Hvalvík
EYSTUROY
Klakkur (413m)
Selatrað
Vestmanna
Hósvík
Skáli
Fjallavatn
Tunnel
Slættanes (abandoned)
Kollafjørður
MYKINES
Oyrargjógv
Kvívík
Strendur
Saltangará
Mykines
Gásadalur
VÁGAR
Runavík
Bøur
Kollafjarðadalur Statoil filling station
Toftir
Sørvágur
Vatnsoyrar
Car ferry
Passenger ferry
Mykineshólmur
Tindhólmur
Drangarnir
Sundsnøva (288m)
Sandavágur
Sornfelli
Kaldbak
Miðvágur
Bøsdalafossur
Leitisvatn
Norðradalur
TÓRSHAVN
Suðradalur farm
Nólsoy
Koltur
KOLTUR
Hestsfjørður
Velbastaður
NÓLSOY
Hestur
HESTUR
Kirkjubøur
Gamlarætt
Skopunarfjørður
ATLANTIC OCEAN
Skopún
SANDOY
Skálavík
Sandur
Húsavík
Høvdin bird cliff
Skarvanes
Dalur
SKÚVOY
Skúvoy
Knútur (392m)
STÓRA DÍMUN
To Lerwick (Shetland Islands, Scotland); Bergen (Norway); Hanstholm (Denmark)
Glyvraberg (366m)
Sandvík
LÍTLA DÍMUN
Suðuroyarfjørður
Hvalba
Coal Mine
Tvøroyri
Drelnes
Froðba
Fámjin
Øravík
Hov
SUÐUROY
Ryskivatn
Porkeri
Vágur
Kamarið cliff
Lopra
Vikarbyrgi
Beinisvørð cliff
Sumba
Cap Akraberg
Kirkja
Hattarvík
Svínoy
Klaksvík
Mykines
Vágar Airport
Tórshavn
Koltur
Skúvoy
Stóra Dímun
Froðba
0 20 km
0 12 miles
Helicopter route
Helicopters start and finish at Vágar airport serving all other heliports at least once (except Frodba on Sunday or where there are no pre-reserved passengers).

in 1380. Between 1535 and 1856, all trade was governed by the Danish monopoly for which the great stores of Tinganes were developed. The only Faroese to gain temporary trading rights was Magnus Heinason in 1579, who built Skansin Fort in Tórshavn to protect his ships from pirate attacks.

In 1849 the Danish parliament incorporated the islands as a 'county' of Denmark. This provoked strong independence movements, which were re-ignited by the British occupation of the islands during WWII (see boxed text, p131). In 1948 the Danish compromise was to upgrade the Faroes' status to the 'self-governing community within the Kingdom of Denmark', which it remains today. This gave the Faroese legislative power over their own affairs. When Denmark joined the EEC (now EU), the Faroes refused to follow. This smart move protected their fishery-based economy from ruthless EU competition. Following a sharp recession, bank defaults and a population drain in the 1990s, the economy rebounded impressively in the early 21st century, meaning that today the Faroes are a wealthy, modern European country with a very high standard of living.

The Faroe Islands were not suffering during the global economic turndown much at all at the time of writing. The tiny nation even managed to loan its badly-affected neighbour Iceland a very useful 300 million kroner in late 2008.

PEOPLE

The majority of Faroese are of Nordic Viking origin. They share the reserved politeness of their Scandinavian neighbours, but if you spend some time here you'll discover a rich vein of hospitality. Over 35% of the Faroese population live in the capital Tórshavn at least on weekdays. But on summer weekends many return 'home' and suddenly village populations grow up to fivefold. That explains why villages comprising 40 perfectly maintained homesteads have official populations of less than 10.

RELIGION

Christianity is fundamental to Faroese culture; 84% of the population belong to the Evangelical-Lutheran Church with around 10% Plymouth Brethren and a small minority of Roman Catholics.

ARTS

William Heinesen and Heðin Brú are the internationally best-known Faroese writers. However, before written Faroese developed (after 1846) the language had been kept alive through a strong tradition of oral epic poetry *(kvæði)* recited as accompaniment to the classic stomping ringform 'chain dances', which are still a mainstay of summer Ólavsøkan festivities. Today the range of Faroese musical talent is nothing short of astonishing with numerous festivals and a vibrant recording industry. Select and listen to CDs over an espresso at Leikalund (p125) or choose from hundreds on www.tutl.com (Dkr20/38 per CD delivery fee in Europe/rest of the world).

ENVIRONMENT
The Land

Adrift between Iceland and Scotland, these 18 treeless, grassy islands are the remnants of a flat-capped volcanic continent that covered the Atlantic region 100 million years ago. Ice ages have since sculpted characteristic fjords while the sea has etched out numerous sheer cliffs and chasms. The highest peak is Slættaratindur (882m) on Eysturoy.

Wildlife

More than 100 species of birds find summer nesting homes on the Faroe Islands. The coastal cliffs teem with fulmars *(havhestur)*, guillemots *(lomvigi)*, razorbills *(álka)*, various gulls and lovable puffins *(lundi)*. Gannets *(súla)* are easiest to spot on Mykines. Ubiquitous oystercatchers *(tjaldur,*

FAROE ISLANDS

GRINDADRÁP

Hunting long-finned pilot whales *(grind)* is an age-old Faroese tradition called *grindadráp* (see www.whaling.fo).

Pods of these whales are herded by boats into a shallow bay where local people stand waiting on the beach. They insert steel gaffs into the whales' blowholes then cut the jugular and carotid blood vessels with long knives. Loss of blood pressure causes a rapid death. The method is considered the quickest and the least painful way to kill whales.

See the boxed text on p235 for information on the the pros and cons of whaling throughout the region the national bird of the Faroe Islands) nest on clifftop moors amid the alien warbles of longbilled snipe (*mýrisnípa*) and the dive-bombing antics of predatory great skua (*skúgvur*) and Arctic skua (*kjógvi*), best seen on Skúvoy. Nólsoy has a big colony of storm petrels (*drunnhvíti*).

Ubiquitous sheep, the commonest land mammal, have helped shape the islands' distinctively bare, green appearance. Pilot whales are the best-known inhabitants of Faroese waters (see boxed text, p113) along with various other species of whales, plentiful saltwater fish, extensively farmed trout and salmon plus a few seals, considered to be the reincarnations of ancestral spirits.

FOOD & DRINK

Traditional Faroese cuisine is a decidedly hearty affair, built around fish, lamb and potatoes. Wind-drying is a classic method of preservation; *turrur fiskur* (dried fish) and *skerpikjøt* (dried mutton) are Faroese specialities. Traditionally no part of the sheep goes to waste. *Seyðahøvd* (sheep's head) is a delicacy that you might find peering at you from supermarket freezers. Other tourist-frightening staples include baked puffin and *grind og spik* (whale meat and blubber): availability is sporadic and seasonal. Grill-booths and some petrol stations sell hot dogs and burgers. Some offer British-style fish and chips. Vegetarian options are extremely uncommon. Only the capital, Tórshavn has much of a selection of dining options.

Alcohol has only been fully legalised in the Faroe Islands since 1992. It is served at bars, cafes and restaurants and sold (Monday to Friday only) through brewery depots and *rúsdrekkasøla* (state liquor stores), never from grocery shops. The best of several local beers is the rich, dark Black Sheep brew.

TÓRSHAVN

pop 12,352

Tórshavn (Thor's Harbour) is the modern face of the Faroes, an extremely pleasant and laid-back town that is home to around one-quarter of the islands' population. While the town itself only merits one day's exploration, its transport links, good restaurants and hotels make it an excellent base from which to explore the rest of the country.

The capital is centred on the busy harbour and the tiny old-town of Tinganes, behind which lies a compact commercial centre that comes merrily to life on summer weekend nights.

HISTORY

Due to Tórshavn's central location, the Faroes' first Ting (parliament) was set up here in AD 1000, but poor soils meant that the town remained relatively small until 1856. However, once the Danish trading monopoly was replaced by free trade, Tórshavn rapidly evolved into the islands' main trading hub. It has been growing ever since.

ORIENTATION

The Eastern Harbour/ferry terminal is separated from the Western Harbour by the little Tinganes peninsula, home to the charming old town.

You'll find most shops, restaurants and facilities situated directly behind the area surrounding the partly pedestrianised Niels Finsensgøta.

INFORMATION
Bookshops

HN Jacobsens Bókahandil (Map p117; ☎ 311036) Within the same atmospheric 1860s building as the tourist office is the city's top bookshop.

Internet Access

Býarbókasavnið (Town Library; Map p117; ☎ 302030; Niels Finsensgøta 7; ⏰ 10am-6pm Mon-Fri, 10am-1pm Sat)

Føroya Landsbókasavn (National Library; Map p117; ☎ 311626; www.flb.fo; JC Svabosgøta 16; ⏰ 10am-8pm Mon-Wed, to 5pm Thu & Fri)

Tourist Office (Map p117; per hr Dkr40) Two internet computers available.

Left Luggage

Farstødin transport terminal (big/small lockers per 24hr Dkr30/20 per 24hr)

Medical Services

Emergency Dental Service (☎ 314544; ⏰ 1-2pm Sat & Sun) At the hospital.

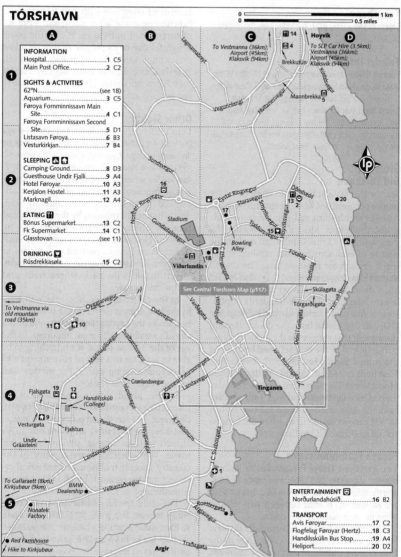

TÓRSHAVN

0 ———————— 1 km
0 ———————— 0.5 miles

INFORMATION
Hospital.................................1 C5
Main Post Office......................2 C2

SIGHTS & ACTIVITIES
62°N.................................(see 18)
Aquarium................................3 C5
Føroya Fornminnissavn Main
  Site..................................4 C1
Føroya Fornminnissavn Second
  Site..................................5 D1
Listasavn Føroya.......................6 B3
Vesturkirkjan..........................7 B4

SLEEPING
Camping Ground.........................8 D3
Guesthouse Undir Fjalli................9 A4
Hotel Føroyar.........................10 A3
Kerjalon Hostel.......................11 A3
Marknagil.............................12 A4

EATING
Bónus Supermarket.....................13 C2
Fk Supermarket........................14 C1
Glasstovan........................(see 11)

DRINKING
Rúsdrekkasøla.........................15 C2

ENTERTAINMENT
Norðurlandahúsið......................16 B2

TRANSPORT
Avis Føroyar..........................17 C2
Flogfelag Føroyar (Hertz).............18 C3
Handilsskúlin Bus Stop................19 A4
Heliport..............................20 D2

To Vestmanna (36km);
Airport (45km);
Klaksvík (94km)

To SLP Car Hire (3.5km);
Vestmanna (36km);
Airport (45km);
Klaksvík (94km)

Hoyvík

Brekkutún

Mannbrekka

Lagmannabreyt

Veugurinlangi

Hvítanesvegur

Sundsvegur

Norðari Ringvegur

Gundadalsvegur

Stadium

Eystari Ringvegur

Staravegur

Smyrilsvegur

Traldursvegur

Hoyvíksvegur

Óðinshædd

Viðarlundin

Bowling
Alley

Fútalág

Storlág

Skúlagøta

Tórgarðsgøta

Oyggjarvegur

Dalavegur

Vardagøta

Hoyðalsvegur

Óðini Geitagøta

Jóans Broncksgøta

Yviri við Strond

See Central Tórshavn Map (p117)

Tinganes

To Vestmanna via
old mountain
road (35km)

Markóagilsvegur

Svabarsvegur

Islandsvegur

Grønlandsvegur

Kannmaí Patursocnarøta

Landavegur

Fjalsgøta

Handilsskúli
(College)

Perskonugøta

Heygsvegur

Á Frælnunum

C. Svabosgøta

Vesturgøta

Fjalstun

Undir
Gráasteini

Landavegur

To Gallaraett (8km);
Kirkjubøur (9km)

BMW
Dealership

Velbastaðvegur

Roettergøta
Argjavegur

Nonatek
Factory

Red Farmhouse
Hike to Kirkjubøur

Argir

Traðagøta

FAROE ISLANDS

Hospital (Map p115; ☎ 313540; JC Svabosgøta) Has a casualty ward.

Money

Outside banking hours, the Hotel Hafnia (Map p117) and the tourist office will exchange cash. ATMs dole out the cash until midnight:

Eik Banki (Map p117; Tinghúsvegur 49)
Føroya Banki (Map p117; Niels Finsensgøta 15)

Post

Central Post Office (Map p117; Posthúsbrekka) The post officce is situated within the new, art-decked City Hall (Snarskivan) building.
Main Post Office (Map p115; Óðinshædd 2)

Telephone

Telecom Shop (Map p117; Telebúðin; Niels Finsensgøta 10) Sells SIM cards.

Tourist Information

Tourist Office (Kunningarstovan; Map p117; ☎ 315788; www.visittorshavn.fo; Mylnugøta; ☼ 7am-5.30pm Mon & Fri, 8am-5.30pm Tue-Thu, 9am-2pm Sat June-Aug, 9am-5.30pm Mon-Fri, 10am-2pm Sat Sept-May) Assists with accommodation and tour bookings, sells maps and transport timetables and offers great free brochures including the handy *Tourist Guide: Faroe Islands*.

SIGHTS
Old Tórshavn

Start with a taste of history in **Tinganes**, a hilly peninsula jumbled with pretty turf-roofed cottages and historic red-painted stone-and-timber buildings. Most date from after the devastating 1673 fire. Guides can explain the history of each structure but random strolling is enough for most visitors. The church **Havnarkirkja** (Bringsnagøta; Map p117; ☼ 10am-2pm Sat) has a distinctive clock tower and a relatively ornate interior by Faroese standards. A photogenic row of colourful old **wharf buildings** (Map p117; Undir Bryggjubakka) lines the docks. Beyond the asphalt that surrounds the modern transport terminal lie the turf-softened bastions of the ruined **Skansin Fort** (Map p117; admission free). First built in 1629 to defend the Royal Trade Monopoly at Tinganes from pirates, it is today topped by a **lighthouse** and four 18th-century cannons. Lower down there are two British WWII canons dating from when the fortress served as British HQ in the Faroes.

Føroya Fornminnissavn

The excellent **Føroya Fornminnissavn** (Historical Museum; Map p115; ☎ 310700; www.natmus.fo; adult/child Dkr30/free; ☼ 10am-5pm Mon-Fri, 2-5pm Sat & Sun mid-May–mid-Sep) is split between two sites in Hoyvík, 3km north of the centre.

The **main site** (Brekkutún 6) beautifully displays Faroese artefacts from the Viking Age to the 19th-century with illustrative photos and notes. In the downstairs section there are five well preserved sloops (open-decked sail boat) from the early 20th century, and the Faroes' greatest artistic treasure, the 15th-century Kirkjubøur church fittings, which include a much photographed carving of the Virgin Mary meeting Elisabeth (mother of John the Baptist).

At a wonderfully peaceful **second site** (Kúrdalsvegur) is a superbly preserved 1920s farmstead complete with bell telephone, a functioning grandfather clock, and a full set of turf-roofed outhouses. It's all the more delightful due to its bucolic setting on a low grassy bluff lush with juicy marsh marigolds. It feels a world away from the city yet it's just 300m off major Hvítanesvegur where red buses 2 and 3 drop you off.

Other Sights

Don't miss the excellent **Listasavn Føroya** (National Art Gallery; Map p115; ☎ 313579; www.art.fo; Gundadalsvegur 9; adult/child/student Dkr60/free/40; ☼ 11am-4pm Mon-Fri, 2-5pm Sat & Sun summer, 2-4pm Tue-Sun winter), a wonderfully light space whose excellent collection of Faroese modern and contemporary art includes moving, death-haunted canvasses by the great Sámal Joensen-Mikines, allegorical cartoons by William Heinesen and quirkier pieces such as Beinta av Reyni's portrait of Eminem as an angel. Beyond the museum is **Viðarlundin**, an attractive wild park where trees and sculptures mingle.

In the centre of town, you may well walk by the low-slung grey warehouse building that is actually the **Løgting** (Tinghúsvegur), one of the world's smallest parliament buildings. In the age of the 'war on terror' it's refreshing to be able to walk up to a seat of government and press your nose up against the window and see the chamber in session.

Further afield, dominating views of the town, is the extraordinary **Vesturkirkja** (Map p115; Landavegur; ☼ 3-5pm Mon-Sat in summer or by arrangement through the tourist office), an enormous 1970s church with an unusual pyramidal copper tower. While hardly representative of the country's deeply traditional ecclesiastical architecture, this eccentric building has become something of an icon for the capital.

The child-friendly **Náttúrugripasavn** (Natural History Museum; Map p117; ☎ 352300; www.ngs.fo; VU Hammershaimbsgøta 13; adult/under 16yr Dkr20/free; ☼ 10am-4pm Tue-Fri & 3-5pm Sat & Sun Jun-Aug, 3-5pm Sun Sep-May) has an informative geological section, a huge selection of taxidermy and a gigantic whale's skull.

A small **aquarium** (Map p115; ☎ 505121; Roettergøta; adult/under 16yr Dkr50/25; ☼ 2-6pm Sat & Sun, weekdays by appointment) that opened in 2007 makes for a fascinating introduction to the marine life of the Faroes, with 40 types of fish on display, including some truly vast catfish, conger eels and lobsters.

Wooden Sailing Boats

Moored right next to each other in the Western Harbour are two beautiful antique wooden sloops, **Westward Ho** and **Norðlýsið** (Map p117; ☎ 218520; www.nordlysid.com). On Tuesday and Thursday in the summer months Norðlýsið organises **fishing trips** (adult/child incl equipment Dkr250/125), leaving at 7pm, and three-hour **cruises** (adult/child Dkr200/100) departing at 9am.

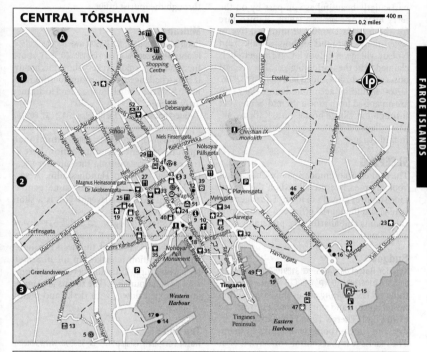

CENTRAL TÓRSHAVN

INFORMATION	
Býarbókasavnið	1 B2
Central Post Office	2 B2
Eik Banki	3 B2
Føroya Banki	4 B2
Føroya Landsbókasavn	5 A3
GreenGate Incoming	6 D3
HN Jacobsens Bókahandil	(see 9)
MB Tours	7 B2
Telecom Shop	8 B2
Tourist Office	9 B2

SIGHTS & ACTIVITIES	
Havnarkirkja	10 B2
Lighthouse	11 D3
Løgting	12 B2
Náttúrugripasavn	13 A3
Norðlýsið	14 B3
Skansin Fort	15 D3
Smyril Line International Tickets	(see 16)
Smyril Line Tours	16 D3
Westward Ho	17 B3
Wharf Buildings	18 B3

SLEEPING	
Bládýpi	19 B2
Guesthouse Skansin	20 D3
Hotel Bólið	21 A1
Hotel Hafnia	22 C2
Hotel Streym	23 D2
Hotel Tórshavn	24 B2

EATING	
Fk Supermarket	25 B2
Food Court	26 B1
Gourmet	(see 35)
Hvonn Brasserie	(see 24)
Merlot	27 B2
Miklagarður	28 B1
Pizza Kjallarin	29 B2
Restaurant Hafnia	(see 22)
Toscana	30 B2

DRINKING	
Café Karlsborg	31 B3
Café Natúr	32 C2
Cippo	33 B2
Gallari Jinx	34 C2
Glitnir	35 B3

Manhattan	36 B2
Patio	37 B1
Tórshøll Pub	38 B2

ENTERTAINMENT	
Eclipse	(see 39)
Havnar Bio	39 B2
Rex	(see 39)

SHOPPING	
Andreas í Vágsbotni	40 B2
Focus	41 B2
Glarsmiðjan	42 B2
HCW Tórgarð	43 B2
Photocare	44 B2
Sirri	45 C2

TRANSPORT	
BVK	46 C2
Farstøðin (Ferries to Suðuroy and Abroad)	47 C3
Farstøðin Transport	48 C3
Ritan Ferry to Nólsoy	49 C3
Steinatún Bus Stop	50 B2
Taxi Rank	51 B2
Taxi Stand 'Auto'	52 B1

Nólsoy Island

The car-free village of Nólsoy (population 258) isn't especially picturesque but makes a strikingly peaceful contrast to bustling Tórshavn, whose Tinganes peninsula looks particularly beautiful as you pass by on the ferry **Ritan** (☎ information 343030). Return fare for the ferry is Dkr40 (20 minutes, five to seven daily). Around an hour's walk from Nólsoy village, a colony of storm petrels is claimed to be the world's biggest. They're best observed at dusk. Guided **bird tours** (☎ 327195, 327064) including accommodation (Dkr450) are organised from June until mid-September through the village hostel-cafe, Kaffistovan. The village celebrates a big **Ovastevnu festival** in mid-August.

SLEEPING

The limited accommodation options can get booked up early especially when the Smyril Line stopover crowd's in town. Tour agencies (p134) and the tourist office can arrange private rooms and apartments, preferably with a day's notice.

Budget

Kerjalon Hostel (Map p115; ☎ 318910; Oyggjarvegur 49; dm/s/d Dkr205/380/410; P X ☐) There's something of *The Shining* about this large hilltop hostel, next to and run by Hotel Føroyar, the town's best. There's a good kitchen and laundry, and simple rooms with bunks in them. The real issue is that central Tórshavn is 3km away by road and 25 minutes on foot using the shortcuts.

Bládýpi (Map p117; ☎ 500600; www.hostel.fo; Dr Jakobsensgøta 14-16; dm/s/tw/tr Dkr200/450/650/850, s/tw/tr/apt with bathroom Dkr600/800/1000/1100; ☺ 8am-6pm Mon-Fri, 10am-11am & 4-8pm Sat & Sun; X ☐) Tórshavn's best budget option, this excellently located and well-run hostel-cum-hotel is spotlessly clean and includes a buffet breakfast in the price. Dorms share spacious sitting areas and an equipped kitchen, although both are usually overrun by Danish school groups during the summer months.

Guesthouse Skansin (Map p117; ☎ 500606; www.hostel.fo; Jekaragøta 8; s/d Dkr450/650, with private bathroom Dkr600/800; ☐) Sister hostel-hotel to Bládýpi, Skanskin is the worst located of the two, but offers up well-kept rooms with fridge and TV. The best are those at the top, notably corner-room No 23, which has extensive harbour views.

Camping ground (Map p115; ☎ 265801, 302425; Yviri við Strond; camp sites per adult Dkr60; ☺ mid-May–mid-Sep) This basic site overlooks a wind-battered but attractive rocky beach and has decent showers and washing machines available. Book through the tourist office.

Midrange

Hotel Bólið (Map p117; ☎ 354900; www.bugv.fo/sida16, in Faroese; Niels Finsensgøta 51; s/d Dkr400/600; X) Above the Smúkkuhjørnið jewellery shop, this handy, if style-challenged, eight-room guesthouse is more B&B than hotel. Phone ahead to arrange arrival times.

Guesthouse Undir Fjalli (Map p115; ☎ 605010; www.undirfjalli.com; Vesturgøta 15-17; s/d incl breakfast Dkr490/645; ☺ Jul–mid-Aug) Functional, en suite student accommodation here is rented to tourists during the summer vacation. Take bus 1 to Handilsskúlin. A second guesthouse run by the same people, Marknagil (Marknagilsvegur 75), is a short distance away.

Hotel Streym (Map p117; ☎ 355500, 533900; www.hotelstreym.com; Yviri við Strond 19; s/d Dkr695/995; ☺ reception 6.30am-10pm) What this well-run hotel lacks in location it makes up for in Scandi style with a funky little dining room and some cool design flourishes. The rooms are simple and stripped down, with desks and plenty of space.

Top End

Hotel Tórshavn (Map p117; ☎ 350000; www.hoteltorshavn.fo; Tórsgøta 4; s/d/ste incl breakfast Dkr1100/1300/3000; ☺ closed Christmas; ☐) The closest Tórshavn has to a boutique hotel, the enviably located Tórshavn feels like the local hub it is, with the busy Brasserie Hvonn on the ground floor. The 43 rooms are sleek and stylish with luxurious white cotton sheets on the large beds, although the superiors are generally not worth the price hike.

Hotel Føroyar (Map p115; ☎ 317500; www.hotelforoyar.com; Oyggjarvegur; s/d Dkr1200/1400, ste Dkr2200-6000; P ☐) The city's top hotel is turf roofed in a nod to tradition, but dark and soothing inside without being overly trendy. Fully renovated in 2008, the hotel now boasts the Clinton Suite, where Bill bedded down during a recent visit. All the rooms are smart, spacious and full of Scandinavian design touches, enjoying great views over the town centre about 3km away. All prices include breakfast.

Hotel Hafnia (Map p117; ☎ 313233; www.hafnia.fo; Áarvegur 4-10; s/d/ste incl breakfast Dkr1250/1450/1900; ◷ closed Christmas; ▣) The Hafnia feels rather dated, yet remains the standard choice for upmarket tour groups. It certainly enjoys a great location, and doubles have flatscreen TVs and are large, although they're not always as bright as they might be for this price.

EATING

Tórshavn has by far the Faroes' best and most varied eating options. Restaurants tend to be relatively expensive, but several pubs and cafes serve cheaper meals. Lunch buffets are great money-savers.

Restaurants

Eating early is a good idea, as many kitchens may have closed well before official closing times.

Hvonn Brasserie (Map p117; ☎ 350035; Tórsgøta 4; mains Dkr75-240; ◷ noon-midnight) Spread over two floors and on warm summer days seeming to attract anyone in town under 30, the trendy bar-restaurant of the Hotel Tórshavn comes highly recommended. Upstairs there's a huge international menu, while downstairs there's bar food and cocktails.

Restaurant Hafnia (Map p117; ☎ 313233; Hotel Hafnia, Áarvegur 4-10; mains Dkr225; ◷ 11.30am-2pm & 6-9.30pm) Huge, mouth-watering seafood buffets (Dkr325; served Tuesday and Thursday evenings in summer) are the greatest drawcard of this upmarket restaurant. Reservations are usually essential. A weekday lunch buffet is a good deal at Dkr128.

Glasstovan (Map p115; ☎ 317500; www.hotelforoyar.com; Oyggjarvegur 45; mains Dkr230; ◷ noon-5pm & 6-10pm) With sweeping views over Tórshavn and sleek design featuring a copper bar, black walls and gleaming white tablecloths, this super-stylish restaurant inside the Hotel Føroyar makes for a real night out with suitably mouth-watering modern Scandinavian cuisine.

our pick Gourmet (Map p117; ☎ 322525; Grímur Kambansgøta 13; mains Dkr240; ◷ 6pm-10pm Mon-Sat) Tórshavn's sleek, cream temple of gastronomy is a great place to splash out. These local pioneers of Nordic Kitchen (blending traditional Scandinavian ingredients with modern cooking styles) offer dishes such as scallop ravioli with foam of dried fish, or thyme salted beef with beets and horseradish.

Merlot (Map p117; ☎ 311121; Magnus Heinasonargøta 20; mains Dkr275; ◷ 5-10pm Mon-Sat) New manage-ment at this old favourite has served the place well and its refined, low-key dining space and friendly staff make for a great meal. The small fish and seafood-based menu ranges from steamed ray in butter sauce, with lobster and almonds, to a simple catch of the day.

Toscana (Map p117; ☎ 311109; Nólsoyar Pállsgøta 13; mains Dkr145-325; ◷ 5-11pm Sun-Thu, 5pm-midnight Fri & Sat) Book ahead for this achingly popular Italian place, which sadly offers no respite from the meat for vegetarians and doesn't include pizza. The food is pretty average and rather overpriced, but the restaurant itself is cosy and romantic.

Quick Eats

For quickly made thin-crust pizzas to go, head for **Pizza Kjallarin** (Map p117; ☎ 353353; Niels Finsensgøta; pizzas Dkr55-80; ◷ 5pm-midnight Sun-Thu, to 5am Fri & Sat).

Three fast-food outlets can be found at **Food Court** (Map p117; SMS Shopping Centre).

Self-Catering

For supermarkets, **Miklagarður** (Map p117; SMS Shopping Centre) is the best stocked, though **Bónus** (Map p115; Óðinshædd) and **Fk** (Map p115; Dr Jakobsensgøta), which has another branch on Brekkutún, are marginally cheaper. Bakery-grocery **Frants Restorff** (Map p117; Tórsgøta; ◷ 7am-11pm) opens helpfully long hours.

DRINKING

The dividing line between a cafe and pub is somewhat blurred in the Faroes but where there's beer and live music, watch how the characteristic Faroese reserve crumbles. The only liquor store in town is called **Rúsdrekkasøla** (Map p115; Smyrílsvegur; ◷ 10am-5.30pm Mon-Fri, to 7pm Thu).

Cafes

Gallari Jinx (Map p117; ☎ 317101; Áarvegur 3; mains Dkr90-160; ◷ 11am-midnight, to 2am Fri & Sat) Airy and arty, this bright and busy cafe attracts a cross section of Tórshavn society. Its Dkr135 brunch is popular, and it's a good place for veggies (relative to the rest of the country!).

Café Karlsborg (Map p117; ☎ 317464; Undir Bryggjubakka; pastries Dkr20-50; ◷ 11am-6pm) Exposed beams, a whitewashed 'rock' wall and plenty of endearingly kitschy knick-knacks make this Tórshavn's most atmospheric harbourside cafe.

FAROE ISLANDS

Bars

Patio (Map p117; ☎ 310400; www.patio.fo; Lucas Debesargøta 3; mains Dkr89-195; ⊙ 11am-midnight Mon-Thu, 11am-2am Fri & Sat) This Danish-run bar-restaurant feels more London or Berlin than Tórshavn, with its stripped-down look and fashion-forward crowd. The cocktails are suitably strong, and there's beer on draft as well as a delicious bar menu.

Café Natúr (Map p117; ☎ 312625; Áarvegur 7; meals Dkr49-69) This atmospheric pub in the heart of Tórshavn is a rowdy place. It serves a good range of brews and great-value bar meals though, so depending on the crowd inside, this can still be a great hang-out.

Glitnir (Map p117; ☎ 321345; Gríms Kambansgøta 13; ⊙ noon-11pm Sun-Thu, to 3am Fri & Sat) Located beneath Tórshavn's poshest restaurant is this thoroughly down-to-earth pub, which makes a nice place to have pint and play darts with the locals.

Manhattan (Map p117; ☎ 319696; Sverrisgøta 15; beers Dkr25; ⊙ 5-11.30pm, to 3.45am Fri & Sat) Gentle acoustic live music (mostly covers) is played here nightly in this cosy British-style pub.

Cippo (Map p117; Tórsgøta 11) In the building adjoining Manhattan is Cippo, a sports bar with pool tables and foosball run by the same management and keeping the same hours.

Tórshøll Pub (Map p117; ☎ 311565; Tróndargøta 24) Drinking in this smoky local dive is a daring social experiment, although it's always busy for its regular Faroese live music evenings.

ENTERTAINMENT

The events-listing pamphlet *Havnartíðindi* is available free from the tourist office.

Norðurlandahúsið (Nordic House; Map p115; ☎ 351351; www.nlh.fo; Norðari Ringvegur 10; ⊙ 10am-6pm Mon-Sat, 2-6pm Sun) This modern, architecturally interesting cultural centre, hosts concerts, plays, exhibitions and conferences. Check the schedule online.

Havnar Bio (Map p117; ☎ 311956; Tinghúsvegur 8; tickets Dkr75) This two-screen cinema shows original films with Danish subtitles.

Upstairs from Havnar Bio are **Eclipse** (Map p117; ⊙ Fri night) and **Rex** (Map p117) the city's slightly sleazy nightclubs.

SHOPPING

Several shops sell souvenirs, from knitwear to cuddly puffin toys. Charming old-world **Andreas í Vágsbotni** (Map p117; ☎ 312040; Grims Kambansgøta) also stocks T-shirts, knitwear and costumed dolls. **Skipshandilin** (Map p117;

☎ 312330; Havnargøta) has fishing tackle, knit-ware, postcards and outdoor clothing. **Sirri** (Map p117; www.sirri.fo; Áarvegur 10) produces elegant designer garments from organic, dye-free wool to local sheepskins. **HCW Tórgarð** (Map p117; Niels Finsensgøta 9) sells CDs of local music.

Intimate private galleries including **Focus** (Map p117; ☎ 315251; Gríms Kambansgøta 20; ⊙ 2-6pm Mon-Fri, 4-6pm Sat) and **Glarsmiðjan** (☎ 216623; Dr Jakobsensgøta; ⊙ 10am-5.30pm Mon-Fri) are great places to peruse and buy Faroese art from.

Photocare (Map p117; Dr Jakobsensgøta 12) down-loads digital photos to disk.

GETTING THERE & AWAY

Ferries to Suðuroy and international destinations plus all long-distance buses depart from the Farstøðin transport terminal. The *Ritan* ferry to Nólsoy uses a different jetty.

Airport

Regular bus 300 from the Farstøðin transport terminal goes via the airport (Dkr90, 55 minutes), see opposite. **Airport Shuttle** (☎ 332473; www.shuttlebuss.com; Dkr150) minibuses pick up from hotels and hostels at around 6.30am, 9am, 1pm and 3pm. Book a day ahead. **Airport Shuttle Express** (☎ 888888; www.taxa.com; Dkr150) offer a similar service.

GETTING AROUND

Car

Parking is free in marked spaces but in the city centre, most are time-limited: look for a 'P' and the number of minutes or hours (*tíma*) of stay permitted. Display your arrival time using a parking disc, available free of charge from tourist offices and banks. For car rental agencies, see p136.

Public Transport

The three main routes of red city buses (Dkr10 per ride) operate half-hourly week-days (hourly weekends and evenings) from the central Steinatún stop. Bus 2 loops anti-clockwise passing close to Hotel Streym, main post office, Føroya Fornminnissavn and Norðurlandahúsið, returning past SMS Shopping Centre before heading south to Argir via the hospital. Bus 3 does the same loop clockwise then west on Landavegur.

The main taxi companies are **Auto** (☎ 311234) and **Bil** (☎ 323232).

THE WESTERN ISLANDS

VÁGAR

If you fly into the Faroes you'll arrive on Vágar (*vow*-whar). While most travellers dash straight off to Tórshavn, Vágar itself has a spectacular cliff-edged western coast that's most entertainingly viewed from the mini-ferry to Mykines (p122), one of the Faroes most lovable, if climatically treacherous, getaways.

Information

The Faroes' only **airport** (☎ 354400; www.floghavn .fo) has a **tourist information desk** (☎ 353300), cafeteria, car hire office and ATM, but no bank. Three minutes' walk west of the terminal, the architecturally dreary **Hotel Vágar** (☎ 332955; www.hotelvagar.fo; s/d Dkr635/855) can exchange cash at mediocre rates. The hotel's rooms are clean, motel-style affairs but its **restaurant** (lunch specials Dkr68, mains Dkr145-185; ◷ 11am-9pm) has fine food, appealing views towards Mykines and Vágar's only bar (beer Dkr25). Consider prebooking meals. The hotel rents low-tech **bicycles** (per half-day Dkr75). These are handy for visiting Bøur but not headlight-equipped for the spooky tunnel to Gásadalur.

Sørvágur

pop 993

Just 1km west of the airport, **Sørvágur** curves somewhat blandly around the eastern end of an attractive fjord. Its main attraction is the twice-daily summer boat service to Mykines (p122) leaving from a harbour at the town's southwestern limit. That's near the petrol station and snack bar, some 150m west of the eccentric **Sørvágs Bygdarsavn** (☎ 333191; 13 Rossatrøðin; admission Dkr30; ◷ by appointment), a tatty little museum in a conspicuous blue house; B&B accommodation can be booked here through most travel agents.

AROUND SØRVÁGUR

Picturesque **Bøur** (population 70) is a bayside huddle of old Faroese homes, several with turf roofs. An intimidatingly tall amphitheatre of *hamrar* (stepped cliffs) stands behind. The 4km trip from Sørvágur is amply justified by spectacular views of **Tindhólmur**, a serrated islet of vertical rock that rises from the frothing waves like a Tolkeinesque fantasy castle. Surreally sliced, Tindhólmur seems to

have had its western half mistakenly erased in post-production. It's one of the Faroes' landscape icons.

Another 4km west of Bøur, **Gásadalur** (*gwa-sa-dal-wur*; population 12) occupies an even grander amphitheatre. The village homes are marginally less photogenic than those of Bøur but beautifully set with Tindhólmur as a delightful backdrop. Road access (no bus) is via a freakily pitch-dark 1.5km tunnel. Alternatively a challenging hike via the former **postman's trail** (2½ hours) starts 700m south of the tunnel's eastern entrance. It passes perilously near the first cliff edge then zigzags very steeply up and over the cairn-marked, 425m **Skarð Pass**. Hiking offers superb views but there are loose sections and the route is dangerous in less-than-perfect visibility.

Miðvágur & Sandavágur

Sandavágur, with its fanciful 1917 church, is 2km from **Miðvágur**, with Vágur's banks, supermarkets and **tourist office** (☎ 333455, 219899; ◷ 1-3pm Mon-Fri). Between the two, **Á Giljanesi** (☎ 333465; www.giljanes.fo; camp sites per adult Dkr60, dm/s/d Dkr160/320/420) is a simple but well-run and spotless hostel. Though almost totally unmanned and with smallish dorms, it's good value with a decent kitchen and lovely bay views from even-numbered rooms facing Koltur's craggy rear-end. The drivers on the airport–Tórshavn route are usually happy to drop you right outside the hostel, even though there's not officially a stop there.

AROUND MIÐVÁGUR

A leisurely but very rewarding 1½-hour hike follows the eastern bank of lake **Leitisvatn**, the country's largest, starting from the main airport road. Look for the small police station (*politi*) and take the road to its side (Hornavegur), turn right on Heiðagøta and go through the gate, where a path runs through often boggy land (rich breeding grounds of oystercatchers, whimbrels and snipes) around the lake shore. The path ends at **Bøsdalafossur**, a unique waterfall where the lake water tumbles over 100m directly into the foaming sea surf below. For particularly inspiring views of the soaring cliff-edged coastline, climb the raised rocks slightly to the east. On your return look out for a spindly rocky spire evocatively nicknamed the **Witch's Finger** (Trøllkonufingur) on the other side of Miðvágur.

FAROE ISLANDS

Another way to enjoy the scenery of Leitisvatn is to book a **lake cruise** (☎ 333123; www.lakeside.fo; tickets Dkr275; ☺ 10am-1pm Mon-Sat, Apr-Sep). Evening cruises that include dinner are also available.

Getting There & Away

For flight details see p134 and p135 for information about buses. Bus 300 runs six to nine times daily between Tórshavn and Sørvágur (Dkr100, one hour) via the airport (Dkr90, 55 minutes) and Miðvágur. One or two daily buses will continue from Sørvágur to Bøur but only by advance request: call ☎ 215610 at least two hours ahead.

Nearly all Faroe Islands car-hire companies offer an airport collection service, which must be prebooked (usually for a Dkr150 airport supplement). None maintain a manned office in the terminal, so it's always best to book ahead.

MYKINES

pop 18

The name of both the Faroes' westernmost island and the sole settlement on it, Mykines (*mitch*-i-ness) is a slice of rock dramatic enough to rival anywhere else in the country, and one of the best bird-watching spots in the Faroes to boot. The eponymous village is an absolute charmer, made up of traditional turf-roofed houses overlooking a precipitous harbour where landing can be a true adventure in inclement weather.

There's no traffic on Mykines and all transport is on foot. The star attraction here is the superb hike to the Mykinesholmur Lighthouse (allow three hours return). The lighthouse, which warns trans-Atlantic traffic of their arrival in Europe, dates from 1909 and is located on the adjacent island of **Mykinesholmur** via a dramatic 35m bridge over a sea-gorge brimming with birdlife. The highlights of the hike are the densely packed puffin burrows you walk past on the Mykines side, as well as the Faroes' only surviving gannet colonies at the very end of Mykinesholmur.

The island's only restaurant and hotel is the charming **Kristianshús** (☎ 312985, 212985; www .mikines.fo; camp sites per adult Dkr50, per person Dkr300; ☺ May-Aug) where up to 30 people can be put up in three different buildings. Decent lunch (Dkr60) and excellent supper (Dkr125) can be had here without pre-ordering, although groups should call ahead. At the time of writ-

ing the management were planning a fourth hotel building, a high-standard 12-room hotel complete with a museum devoted to the work of painter Sámal Joensen-Mikines.

Across the road, the self-catering **Yellow House** (☎ 532614; www.gulahusid.com; dm without/with bed linen Dkr125/200; ☺ Jun-Aug) can sleep up to 25 people. However, you'll need to bring all your food from Vágar.

Helicopters from Vágar (Dkr145) run Sunday, Wednesday and twice on Friday, as well as an extra service from June to August on Monday. Book in advance because if there are no bookings, the Mykines leg of the flight will be cancelled.

From Sørvágur on Vágar, the mostly uncovered mini-ferry **Brynhild** (☎ 343030) should run at 10.20am and 4.30pm in summer (Dkr60, 50 minutes, May to August). However, all transport is highly weather-dependent so it's quite possible to find yourself stranded among the puffins.

STREYMOY

Kirkjubøur

pop 74

Sprinkled along the base of a craggy sea-facing bluff, Kirkjubøur (*cheer*-chi-ba) consists of roughly a dozen tar-blackened chalet homes, some with turf-roofs and whitewashed stone bases. For centuries this was the Faroes' religious and cultural centre. Behind the whitewashed AD 1111 **St Olav's church** lies the never-completed Gothic shell of **Magnus Cathedral**. Today its hefty basalt wall-tops are wrapped with protective black-metal cladding which convert the 13th-century ruins into a unique statement of contemporary art. The structure is open to the public (not to mention the elements) and it's a fascinating place to look around.

Built upon the 900-year-old foundation platform of the long-disappeared bishop's palace is the beautiful turf-roofed farmhouse **Roykstovan** (Smoke Chamber; ☎ 328089; www.paturs son.com; adult/child Dkr30/free; ☺ 9am-5.30pm Mon-Sat, 2-5.30pm Sun Jun-Aug or by appointment). The exterior is colourfully detailed with 19th-century pseudo-Viking carvings. Although a private home (in the Patursson family for 17 generations, no less), two rooms are usually open to public viewing. Their driftwood timbers are scented with history and draped with fascinating artefacts, each telling its own story. By advance arrangement you can even organise a feast at the great banqueting bench fashioned from the life-saving plank of an 1895 shipwreck.

Car is obviously the easiest way to visit, via a dramatic road beyond Gamlarætt. Bus 101 (Dkr20, 30 minutes, several daily) from Tórshavn runs to Gamlarætt port, 2km northwest of Kirkjubøur. If you request in advance (☎ 343030) the 8.10am, 10.30am, 4.30pm and 6.30pm services will continue on to Kirkjubour for you. Alternatively, from Tórshavn you could hike along the classic, very well-trodden mountain trail (two hours) that starts down við Sandá near bus 3's southwestern terminus. **Berg Hestar** (☎ 316896, 216896; www.berghestar.com; ✆ by appointment) will take groups the same way riding Icelandic horses. If coming by car the cliff-clinging side-trip towards Syðradalur farm offers some very appealing views over Koltur.

Vestmanna
pop 1227

This pleasant Streymoy village, curled around a large, dramatic bay is the starting point for the country's most popular tourist excursion, the breathtaking two-hour **boat tour** (adult/child Dkr225/110; ✆ May-Sep) to the soaring **Vestmanna Bird Cliffs**. Boats bob beneath towering cliff faces, past spiky rock pinnacles and through narrow escarpments, sometimes squeezing beneath tight stone arches. You'll spy the breeding areas of guillemots and razorbills as screeching fulmars and kittiwakes soar above like thousands of white dots. Bring a camera and warm clothing.

Two companies **Lamhauge** (☎ 424155; www.sightseeing.fo) and **Skúvadal** (☎ 471600; www.skuvadal.fo) offer essentially identical tours using various-sized boats to fit passenger numbers (minimum five). Each offers up to five departures daily if there's sufficient demand, but there's always a departure at 2pm (the most crowded). Both companies use the tourist harbour (former car-ferry port), 900m east of central Vestmanna's post office, banks and commercial port. The **tourist office** (☎ 471500; www.visit-vestmanna.com; tourist harbour; ✆ 9am-5pm May-Sep) sells Skúvadal tickets and books fishing trips with **Magni Blástein** (☎ 581582).

SLEEPING & EATING
Overlooking the tourist harbour, the super-neat six-room guesthouse **Krákureiðrið** (☎ 424747, 764747; jf.egilsnes@kallnet.fo; Niðarivegur 34; s/tw Dkr350/450; 💻 🛜) has excellent shared showers, a great kitchen and free internet and wi-fi access (with your own computer); its names is pronounced kraka-*rey*-ree. The pleasant **Fjørðurkrógvin Restaurant** (☎ 471505; Tourist Office Bldg; lunch buffet Dkr130, mains Dkr180; ✆ 9am-10pm June 15-Aug 15, 9am-5pm rest of the year) usually caters to groups and is the only restaurant in town. You can buy groceries from the **Shell Filling Station** (tourist harbour; ✆ 7.30am-11pm Mon-Sat, 9am-11pm Sun). Hidden down steps from the post office is the local pub **Bryggjam** (✆ 5pm-midnight).

GETTING THERE & AWAY
Inconveniently timed public buses from Tórshavn (Dkr50, one hour, three to eight daily) require a change from bus 300 (airport service) to bus 100 at the Kollafjarðadalur Statoil (*kotla*-furdla) petrol station. More conveniently, **Øssur Christiansen private buses** (☎ 424254; Dkr140 return; ✆ variable) and **Tora tours** (☎ 315505; www.tora.fo) collect you from Tórshavn hotels, connect with boat trips and add some sightseeing on the way back.

When travelling by car, choose the starkly barren old mountain road (Rte 10) and make brief detours to pretty Norðradalur hamlet and to Kvívík with its 1903 church and minimalist Viking longhouse ruins.

Northern Streymoy
Northern Streymoy's hotel-less villages make delightful detours by car but most visitors find they're not quite stunning enough to justify the awkward access by rare buses from Oyrarbakki.

SAKSUN
pop 28

Over 10km of lonely moorland valley leads from Hvalvík to tiny Saksun. Ignore the scrappy look of the first houses and fork right. After another 1km you'll reach the solitary turf-roofed **church** dramatically perched high above a tidal lake, impressively ringed by crags and waterfalls – one of the Faroes' most photographed sights. From road's end look back at the proud **19th-century farmstead**, which has an almost medieval appearance. It's strictly private property but in midsummer hosts the **Dúvugarður Folk Museum** (☎ 310700; admission Dkr20; ✆ 2-5pm Fri-Wed mid-Jun–mid-Aug).

FAROE ISLANDS

TJØRNUVÍK

pop 70

A gently satisfying 13km drive northwest from Oyrarbakki passes a **'forest' of cairns**, an impressive roadside **waterfall** and Haldlorsvik's unique **octagonal church** before following a cliff ledge into Tjørnuvík. Clasped tightly in a rocky claw of backing mountains, the village is a mostly modern huddle hiding just a few turf-roofed cottages. Great views across a black-sand beach towards the distinctive sea stacks **Risin and Kellingin** (below), are even finer if you scramble northwest up the steep trail marked by white-painted boulders. Serious hikers could trek south across a partially treacherous mountain trail to Saksun (three to four hours).

NORTHERN EYSTUROY

With jaw-dropping scenery everywhere you turn, travelling between the villages of northern Eysturoy makes for one of the most enjoyable experiences in the country. Head here by car to really enjoy it – local bus routes are minimal and poorly timed. The gorgeous village of Gjógv remains a favourite with local and foreign visitors alike.

Eiði

pop 642

The remote village of Eiði (*ay-ee*) rises steeply from a wide green isthmus, affording good views across the sound to Streymoy. Behind a quirky 1881 **church**, the old village core consists of tightly folded alleys hiding the turf-roofed little folk museum **Eiðis Bygdasavn** (☎ 423597; adult/child Dkr30/free; ⌚ 2-4pm Wed & Sun Jun & Jul) that quaintly illustrates traditional Faroese lifestyles. Near the top of the village, the extensively renovated **Hotel Eiði** (☎ 423456; www.hoteleidi.fo; s/d incl breakfast Dkr600/800; ⌚ Jul & Aug) displays the stylish abstract artwork of its charming owner. Eight of the rooms, notably single room No 5, offer pleasant views that are toward the fjord and also shared by its convivial restaurant. Out of season or for cheaper rooms, you can lodge with **Erling Petersen** (☎ 423194; Estur íTúni 8) down in the village centre.

The main reason to visit Eiði is to hike 45 minutes from the village's uppermost road-end to **Eiðiskollur** (cairn-marked once you've climbed a small fence). The rewards are lovely headland panoramas and heart-stoppingly steep views down upon the classic twin sea-stacks **Risin and Kellingin**. Folk legends describe the pair as a giant and hag who turned to stone while attempting to pull the Faroes over to Iceland! Nonwalkers could view Risin and Kellingin using the free binocular stand 3km along the scenic Eiði–Gjógv road or by driving to Tjørnuvík (left).

From Oyrarbakki on the Tórshavn-Klaksvík route, bus 200 (Dkr20, 25 minutes) runs to Eiði seven times every weekday and four times on Saturday.

Gjógv

pop 44

Without doubt one of the Faroes' prettiest villages, Gjógv (*jek*-v) is reached by a long downhill road – any journey here is dramatic, with spectacular views across to Kalsoy. The name Gjógv refers to the picturesque gorge around which the traditional tar-blackened cottages are clustered. One such cottage is the delightful **Debesar Café** (☎ 423523; www.gjogvadventure.fo; coffee & waffles Dkr30; ⌚ 10am-5.30pm May-Sep) that doubles as a souvenir shop and ticket office for highly recommended **boat trips** (Dkr200) around the towering cliffs to spiky **Búgvin Stack**. Once a few customers have assembled, the boat departs from the village harbour, in the eponymous cleft. The Debesar Café also sells village hiking maps (Dkr30). Proceeds supposedly support local environmental projects, though a map isn't really necessary for the Gjógv's most attractive short hike – a very obvious stroll past puffin burrows up the western cliffside. The cafe also rents out houses for visitors.

The village church, while far from being one of the Faroes' most photogenic, is important locally as it was the first church in the country to be consecrated in Faroese rather than Danish.

The only guesthouse in town is **Gjáargarður** (☎ 423171; www.gjaargardur.fo; Viking-style s/d with shared bathroom Dkr300/500, s/d Dkr725/850, s/d/tr with shared bathroom Dkr580/700/900, all incl breakfast; ⌚ closed 15 Dec-15 Jan; P 🔲 🛜), an excellent turf-roofed place with very progressive management who were building a second guesthouse next door when we last visited. The entire place is wheelchair accessible and has charming, simple rooms. The so-called 'Viking style' beds are built cupboard-like into the eaves as they are in traditional Faroese farmhouses. These are great fun for one person but claustrophobically over-cosy for two. Set meals (Dkr120/150 for lunch/dinner) are excellent.

By advance request (☎ 343030) bus 201 connects Gjógv to Oyrarbakki three times each weekday (Dkr40, 40 minutes) via the old village of Funningur, home to the Faroes' most photogenic turf-topped church.

Elduvík
pop 60

Facing Kalsoy's jagged northern tip, Elduvík is a dreamily cute snaggle of tar-blackened traditional cottages divided by the meandering mouth of the pretty Stórá stream. **Home Café** (☎ 444815; ☼ Jun–mid-Aug) offers simple coffee-and-cake to pre-booked groups and has two basic homestay rooms (Dkr200 per person, meals available to overnighters if ordered in advance). The unmarked house is the first red building after you cross the river. There are no scheduled buses to Elduvík in the summer.

KLAKSVÍK & THE NORTHERN ISLES

KLAKSVÍK
pop 4682

Located on a deep fjord with breathtaking vistas to the neighbouring island of Kunoy, Klaksvík presides over its busy harbour full of colourful fishing boats and has the bustling feel of a second city. While far less cosmopolitan than Tórshavn, Klaksvík is a friendly town and a well-connected transport hub that makes a great base for exploring the northern isles.

Information
Alfa Bókahandil (☎ 455533; Nólsoyar Pálsgøta 2) Bookshop that sells postcards.
Føroya Banki (☎ 456377; Klaksvíksvegur 7) Bank with ATM.
Hospital (☎ 455463; Víkavegur 40-44)
Library (☎ 455757; Tingstøðin; ☼ 1-6pm Mon-Fri, 10am-3pm Sat) Two computers with free internet access.
Norðoya Sparikassi (☎ 475000; Ósavegur 1) Bank with ATM.
Photo Care (☎ 457272; Klaksvíksvegur 70) Downloads digital photos to CD.
Post Office (☎ 455008; Klaksvíksvegur 2)
Telecom Shop (Telebúðin; Biskupsstøðgøta 3; ☼ 9am-5.30pm Mon-Fri)

Tourist Office (Norðoya Kunningarstova; ☎ 456939; www.visitnordoy.fo; Nólsoyar Pálsgøta 32; ☼ 10am-noon & 1-4pm Mon-Fri Sep-May) Accommodation and tour bookings. Internet access should be possible from here by 2009.

Sights & Activities
While a large town by Faroese standards, Klaksvík is nonetheless a little short on sights. Photogenic **viewpoints** abound around the harbour but for the best of all, hike for around an hour up the obvious, if occasionally slightly steep, trail to **Klakkur** (413m). The reward is a truly splendid panorama of both the city (especially magnificent as lights come on at dusk) and the fjord-rent drama of the surrounding islands.

Dragin, a 1940s wooden sailing boat, offers inspiring four-hour **sightseeing cruises** (☎ 288611; www.dragin.fo; adult/under 7yr/7-15yr Dkr250/50/100; ☼ cruises 6pm daily Jun-Aug) around the Kallur or Enniberg cliffs, weather and passenger numbers permitting (minimum 10). Coffee and soup are included in the price.

The finest feature of Klaksvík's museum, **Norðoya Fornminnissavn** (☎ 456287; Klaksvíksvegur 84; adult/child Dkr20/free; ☼ 1-4pm mid-May–mid-Sep) is a nostalgic, fully preserved old pharmacy shop room that operated until 1961.

Next door, **Leikalund** (☎ 457151; Klaksvíksvegur 82; ☼ 10am-5.30pm Mon-Fri, 10am-1pm Sat) is a marvellous bookshop and cafe within a restored old wooden-beamed store that dates from the Danish trading monopoly days. There's no better place to listen to (and buy) CDs of Faroese music over a good espresso. Some weekend nights the atmospheric back-room hosts intimate live concerts. Unmissable.

Sleeping
Norðoya Vallaraheim (☎ 223867; Stangavegur 16; dm/ s/d Dkr175/350/450; ☼ Jun-Aug) is the new hostel in town, opened on a trial basis in summer 2008. Check it's open and make bookings via the **tourist office** (☎ 456939; info@klaksvik .fo), which can also arrange B&B rooms, some **self-catering apartments** (from Dkr500) and handles payments/bookings for the out-of-centre **camping ground** (Uti-I-Grov; camp sites per adult Dkr60).

Hotel Klaksvík (☎ 455333; www.hotelklaksvik .fo; Víkavegur 38; s/d incl breakfast Dkr695/895; P ▣) Formerly the Sjómansheim, this large, family-run, alcohol-free hotel commands

FAROE ISLANDS

some great bay views from the best rooms. The rooms themselves are spotless and spacious, many with flatscreen TV. A good breakfast buffet is included.

Eating & Drinking

For a town of its size, Klaksvík has very few eating and drinking options, but those that exist are generally very good.

Hereford (☎ 456434; Klaksvíksvegur 45; mains Dkr175-230; ☯ 6-10pm Tue-Sun) This is the town's best restaurant – an excellent steakhouse that uses rough pine walls and wooden dining booths to create a traditional yet contemporary atmosphere. Popular with tour groups, Hereford is head and shoulders above the competition in terms of food, with excellent pepper steak, coq au vin and sublime desserts.

Víkafé (☎ 454500; Klaksvíksvegur 45; mains Dkr65; ☯ noon-11pm Tue-Thu, noon-1am Fri & Sat, 5-10pm Sun) Beneath Hereford, this lively and inviting cafe serves up salads, sandwiches and nachos as well as a full range of alcoholic drinks to its young clientele. There's live music on Saturday evening.

Hjá Jórun (☎ 455314; Klingrugarður 6; ☯ 11am-11pm) Surprisingly lively considering its location on an industrial estate beside the main road from the subtunnel, this large bakery-cafe offers a wide range of luscious bread, cakes and open-sandwiches. There's also a delicious evening pizza takeaway service (5pm to 10pm; pizzas from Dkr75 to Dkr85).

Hotel Klaksvík Restaurant (mains Dkr95; ☯ noon-2pm & 6-8pm) A bit of a last resort unless you like sterile hotel restaurants where alcohol is forbidden.

Roykstovan (Klaksvíksvegur; ☯ 11am-11pm) An unmarked red door in a graffiti-muralled house leads you into this rough-edged, suffocatingly smoke-fugged pub: ideal for meeting (and hopefully not fighting with) razzed-up seamen.

Maverik (☎ 454570; Gerðagøta; ☯ 6pm-midnight daily, to 4am Fri & Sat) A second slightly less-bacchanalian option that claims to be the only pub in the Faroes to offer outdoor drinking in its small concrete garden.

Supermarkets include **Fk** (Nólsoyar Pálsgøta 12), **Bónus** (Stangavegur 10) and **Inn** (Klaksvíksvegur). Late-night grocery **Kiosk Var** (Klaksvíksvegur; ☯ 7am-11pm Mon-Sat, 8am-11pm Sun) also serves hot dogs.

Buy booze at **Rúsdrekkasøla** (Bøgøta 38; ☯ 2-5.30pm Mon-Thu, 10am-6pm Fri) or from beneath the brewery.

Getting There & Away

If you pick the right day, a helicopter can whiz you virtually anywhere else in the Faroes (see p135). Bus 400 to Tórshavn (Dkr90, 1¾ hours, five to 11 times daily) uses the colourfully illuminated 6.8km Norðoya toll-tunnel via Leirvík. If you're driving from Eysturoy, the toll tunnel costs Dkr130 per car. This is paid directly to the car-hire company, if you're renting a car.

Getting Around

Taxis (☎ 580404, 755555) lurk beside the bus stand. **John W Thomsen bicycle shop** (☎ 455858; Nólsoyar Pálsgøta 26) rents mountain bikes (Dkr200 per day, less if hired for a number of days), although when we visited he claimed no tourists had ever rented bikes from him and was thinking of abandoning the service.

KALSOY

This long, thin succession of abrupt peaks is nicknamed the 'flute' for its many tunnelholes. For a lovely half-day trip from Klaksvík, hire a bike (with bike lights for the tunnels!) and take a Syðradalur-bound car-ferry (Dkr40 return, 20 minutes, up to eight daily) and ride to **Trøllanes**, then hike (45 minutes) to **Kallur lighthouse**. The route is fairly obvious – from the end of the village go through the gate and clamber up the steep hill. Follow the hillside around to the right of the Borgarin peak aiming for a mid-way course, and then cross the snipe-rich depression beyond to the headland – confusingly the lighthouse isn't visible for quite some time, but when you reach it, views are truly spectacular, encompassing six different headlands.

You can do the day trip by bus too, taking connecting bus 506 (Dkr30, 40 minutes, up to five daily – either request the bus from the crew of the ferry, or book the bus in advance on ☎ 505220) from Syðradalur to Trøllanes. However it's a long wait for the next bus back and Trøllanes has neither shop nor accommodation. Bring a torch if you want to walk through the totally unlit 2km tunnel from Trøllanes to **Mikladalur** village. Or better still, hitch a ride with the surprisingly regular traffic.

FAROE ISLANDS

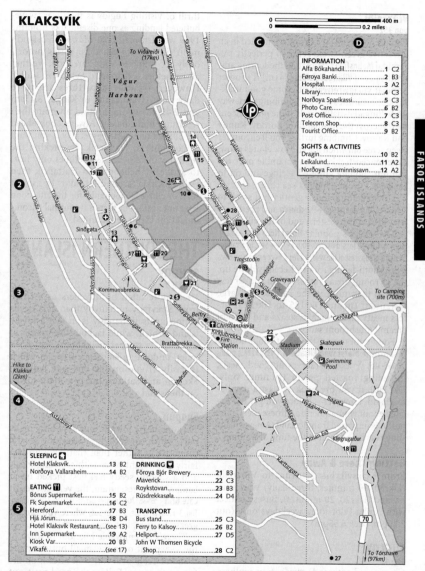

KLAKSVÍK

VIÐOY

Hvannasund
pop 260

The small, nondescript port of **Hvannasund** (*kwana*-sund) guards a cross-fjord causeway. It's the starting point for time-warp mail-boat trips to Fugloy (p128) and for **Alpha Pilot tour-cruises** (☎ 220849; ⏱ 3pm daily, Jul & Aug) that circumnavigate Fugloy (Dkr250) or round Enniberg according to currents and weather. There's nothing to see in the town, save the pretty church, and no facilities either. Buses connect Hvannasund to Klaksvík, timed to meet the incoming Másin ferry from Fugloy, although they need to be booked ahead.

Viðareiði

pop 352

Remote Viðareiði (vee-ar-*oy*-ye), nestled in an attractive green swale between perfectly pyramidal **Malinsfjall** (750m) and the soaring amphitheatre of **Villingadalsfjall** (841m) is another popular village retreat with some good walking opportunities nearby. Climbing part-way up Villingadalsfjall reveals some magnificent views across the headlands of Borðoy, Kunoy and Kalsoy. Climbing further you'll encounter steep scree but when fog and low clouds allow, experienced trekkers can scramble over the summit, along a knife-edge ridge and on to **Enniberg**, Europe's highest sea cliff.

For something much gentler just stroll to Viðareiði's dainty, 1892 **church** and pretty old jetty area at the western end of the village.

The village's popular **Hotel Norð** (☎ 451244; www.hotelnord.fo; s/d Dkr700/900; ✆ Jun-Sep, by arrangement for groups rest of the year) offers sweeping views from south-facing rooms. Recently done up, the 15 rooms are all rather stylish and far less spartan than most in the Faroes. The large restaurant (mains Dkr185 to Dkr225) offers meaty mains such as steaks and lamb in creamy mushroom sauce.

Four doors away the eight-table house-restaurant **Matstovan Elisabeth** (☎ 451275; mains Dkr165-185; ✆ noon-9pm) serves up good meals, including roasted puffin (summer only, Dkr230), if you pre-book at least a day beforehand. However – before you get too excited about your authentic Faroese meal – the puffin is imported from Iceland. A new village shop was being built at the time of writing.

Getting There & Away

From Klaksvík bus 500 runs to Viðareiði (Dkr30, 30 minutes, three daily) via Hvannasund (Dkr20, 20 minutes). Buses connect with Alpha Pilot tours weekdays only (out 2.20pm, back 6.55pm).

FUGLOY

pop 43

Clinging valiantly to Fugloy's steep southern tip, the slopes above **Kirkja** (*cheer*-cha) face a very attractive array of islands. Somewhat gloomier **Hattarvík** is nestled deep in a sweeping valley that rises steeply to the east-coast bird cliffs. Hattarvík's red-roofed 1899 stone church stares wistfully out across the endless Atlantic surf. Neither village has a protected harbour, and for some travellers the real thrill of visiting Fugloy is the dicey, wave-buffeted landing as one disembarks from the 1959 wooden mail-boat *Másin,* the island's main lifeline. Its schedule varies notoriously according to wind direction, weather and whether a detour to Svínoy is added. However, typically departures are twice daily from Hvannasund to Kirkja (8.45am and 2.45pm) taking around an hour then returning immediately. Always book ahead (☎ 505208 or 505218) especially if you want to continue to Hattarvík. By picking the right day there's time (sometimes only just) to arrive by helicopter in Hattarvík then walk to Kirkja (around 1½ hours by asphalt road or cliff-edge footpath) for the afternoon boat out again, but there's no formal accommodation if you get stranded.

THE SOUTHERN ISLANDS

SANDOY

pop 1390

Used more often by travellers as a route from Streymoy to Skúvoy than as a destination in itself, Sandoy is in fact a lovely island, which, while lacking the drama of some of its steeper neighbours, enjoys a quiet, undulating landscape none of which is easily visible on the bus ride between Skopún and Sandur, the two main towns on the island.

Skopún

This one-horse town is only kept busy by its port, which connects it to Streymoy several times a day. Other than that, Skopún is a fairly unpleasant place with scowling locals and a slightly seedy feel best picked up at Sandoy's only restaurant, the very last resort **Café Grill** (☎ 361704; burgers Dkr20-55; ✆ 2-10pm Mon-Thu, 3-11pm Fri & Sat, 3-10pm Sun) where you can get greasy burgers, hot dogs and chips.

There's an enjoyable hike out of town to the viewpoint over the small but dramatic island of Trøllhøvdi (the troll's head) on the far north shore. Follow the road west out of town, which soon becomes a dirt track, climb the steep hill towards Gleðin peak (271m) and you'll soon see the island. The return walk takes about two hours.

Bus 600 runs between Skopún and Sandur (20 minutes, Dkr20, six times a day), connecting to ferries at both ends before continuing to Skálavík on the eastern shore.

Sandur

If you plan to spend the night in Sandoy, do so in Sandur, the more pleasant of the two main towns on the island. Built alongside attractive Sandsvatn Lake on a peninsula jutting out towards Skúvoy, Sandur boasts metropolitan luxuries including a supermarket, a bank with an ATM, a post office and a helpful **tourist office** (☎ 361836; www.visitsandoy.com) that can arrange **accommodation with local families** (s/d incl breakfast Dkr350/450) or can book you in at the local **Ísansgarður Youth Hostel** (s/d Dkr300/420). There's also a **camping ground** (camp sites Dkr60) in Sandur (pay at the tourist office).

The best scenery on the island is east of Sandur. The villages of Húsavík and Dalur both enjoy dramatic settings, with Húsavík boasting a very well preserved Viking farm, and Dalur having a charming church and attractive beach. The tourist office can help with maps for a hike that goes off the Húsavík road and takes you across some superb countryside to Skarvanes and on to Dalur, from where you can take the bus back to Sandur.

Bus 601 connects both Húsavík and Dalur to Sandur (Dkr20, four times a day). You can unofficially rent a car from locals offering B&B, just ask at the tourist office. There are no official car hire outlets on the island. The boat to Skúvoy leaves Sandur between four and five times a day (Dkr40 return, 35 minutes), but you should always call to request the sailing (☎ 505207).

SKÚVOY
pop 49

Named after its large population of great skuas, this small island makes for a great daytrip for ornithologists and hikers alike. The breathtaking cliffs and the rich birdlife mean that tourist numbers are relatively high for a rock of this size, with just one tiny settlement on it.

In July, the powerful great skuas swoop menacingly amid oystercatchers and the clouds of fulmars that soar around the very attractive **Høvdin bird cliffs**. Access is on foot from the island's only village, a mostly tame stroll taking around 45 minutes. Follow the red-painted wooden stakes after the road peters out and make sure you bring a stick to protect your head in case you're dive-bombed!

Skúvoy village (sometimes also called Skúgvoy) is colourful, if not the Faroes' most picturesque. There's a gently photogenic

church beside the heliport and on weekdays the whole place almost has a ghost-town feel. The village lacks a cafe but the owner of the tiny **shop** (☼ 10am-noon & 2-4pm Tue, Thu & Sun) is friendly and very knowledgeable about local ornithology, once you get over his initial tetchiness. Accommodation can be booked through the Sandoy **tourist office** (☎ 361836; www.visitsandoy.com), should you wish to overnight. One comfortable option is the house of **Harry Jot** (☎ 361459, 210028; harryj@post.olivant.fo) just across the stream from the church.

For a satisfying day trip, arrive in Skúvoy by helicopter from almost anywhere else in the country and then return to Tórshavn on the 5.05pm boat-bus-ferry-bus combination (Dkr120, 2¾ hours). Prebook the Skúvoy–Sandur section (☎ 505207) in case you're the only passenger. There's no ferry connection between Skúvoy and Suðuroy.

SUÐUROY

The most southerly of the Faroes, beautiful Suðuroy introduces a more relaxed side to the country. Locals here are famous for their friendliness and (relatively) outgoing nature, and transport hub Tvøroyri makes for an excellent base, boasting two wonderfully atmospheric pubs and an excellent-value guesthouse.

Tvøroyri
pop 1154

Suðuroy's pleasant chief town Tvøroyri (tver-oi-ree) is where most people base themselves. Greater Tvøroyri sprawls gently along the northern slopes of Trongisvágsfjørd from pretty Froðba village (2km east) to junction-settlement Trongisvágur (2km west). The Drelnes ferry port (4km by road) is directly across the fjord. As yet streets remain unnamed. **Suðuroy Kunningarstova** (Tourist Information; ☎ 372490; sout-inf@post.olivant.fo; ☼ 9am-4pm Mon-Fri) is based in Tvøroyri's town hall (kommunia) but also opens a booth at the Drelnes terminal whenever a ferry arrives. Beside the **post office**, the bank **Føroya Banki** has a single ATM.

SIGHTS & ACTIVITIES

The single greatest attraction of the 1852 grass-roofed **museum** (☎ 372480; admission Dkr20; ☼ by appointment) is the curator **Einar Larsen** (☎ 228241), who can usually open the museum up, if given an hour or two's notice, and tell you all about the exhibits on display. A rough

cobble-slope, which was originally used for fish drying, leads down to the functional commercial port past the restored 1836 **Thomsen monopoly-house** containing the brilliant Kgl Handil pub.

Around 1.5km west, **Gallari Oyggin** (☎ 227938; admission Dkr20; 3-8pm Tue-Sun) displays somewhat brutal black metallic sculptures in its garden, but also houses some excellent local paintings inside and has a small cafe.

From quaint **Froðba village**, a gently picturesque stroll past some over-hyped **columnar basalt formations** brings you to the attractive low **Skarvatangi headland**. Or more strenuously follow the clear track up to 325m **Nakkur** for extensive cliff-top views.

SLEEPING & EATING

our pick **Gistingarhúsið Undir Heygnum** (☎ 372046, 223925; guesthouse@kallnet.fo; s/d from Dkr300/450) The 'guesthouse under the hill' is a model of Scandinavian style and cleanliness. Simple but cosy rooms (many with great fjord views) share excellent bathrooms and a fantastic kitchen and lounge. It's just five minutes' stroll east of central Tvøroyri.

Hotel Tvøroyri (☎ 371171; fax 372171; s/d Dkr675/775, with shared bathroom Dkr500/600) Beyond the disconcerting welcome of dead-whale photos, this ultra-central blue cube has fresh, tasteful rooms, a comfy top-floor TV room and a flat roof that might one day make a great cafe. Internet access is promised. With advance notice, the restaurant serves very good set meals (Dkr85 to Dkr125). Lunch (noon to 1.30pm) and dinner (6pm to 8pm) are available. Pizza is available at weekends and there's a rough-edged pub in the basement.

Hot dogs are sold from snack stalls and from the Bónus and Fk supermarkets. **Gaardsbakari** (☎ 371175; 6am-6pm Mon-Fri, to noon Sat, 7-9am Sun) bakes and delivers fresh bread and pastries.

DRINKING

Kgl Handil Pub (☎ 371007; beers Dkr25; 8am-11pm Mon-Thu, 8am-4am Fri & Sat, 3-9pm Sun) Complete with sepia photos, shop-drawers, a 19th-century office room and the original 1882 cash register, this beautifully restored wooden shophouse is the Faroes' most atmospheric cafe pub: a must-see even if you're not

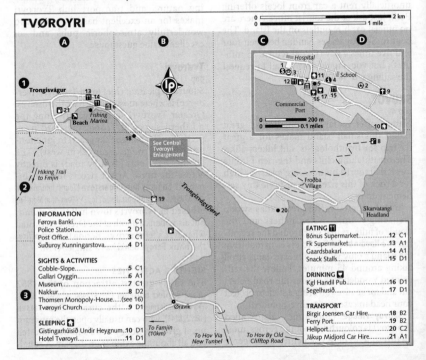

TVØROYRI

0 ——————— 2 km
0 ——————— 1 mile

A   **B**   **C**   **D**

Trongisvágur

Hospital

School

Commercial Port

0 ——— 200 m
0 ——— 0.1 miles

See Central Tvøroyri Enlargement

Fishing Marina

Beach

Hiking Trail to Fámjin

Trongisvøsfjord

Froðba Village

Skarvatangi Headland

Øravik

To Famjin (10km)

To Hov Via New Tunnel

To Hov By Old Clifftop Road

INFORMATION	
Føroya Banki	1 C1
Police Station	2 D1
Post Office	3 C1
Suðuroy Kunningarstova	4 D1

SIGHTS & ACTIVITIES	
Cobble-Slope	5 C1
Gallari Oyggin	6 A1
Museum	7 C1
Nakkur	8 D2
Thomsen Monopoly-House	(see 16)
Tvøroyri Church	9 D1

SLEEPING	
Gistingarhúsið Undir Heygnum	10 D1
Hotel Tvøroyri	11 D1

EATING	
Bónus Supermarket	12 C1
Fk Supermarket	13 A1
Gaardsbakarí	14 A1
Snack Stalls	15 D1

DRINKING	
Kgl Handil Pub	16 D1
Segelhusið	17 D1

TRANSPORT	
Birgir Joensen Car Hire	18 B2
Ferry Port	19 B2
Heliport	20 C2
Jákup Midjord Car Hire	21 A1

thirsty. Sandwiches, mini-pizzas and pies are also available.

Segelhusið (☎ 371007) The next door to the pub is a new venture by the same management; it had only just opened at the time of writing. In an old warehouse, this atmospheric pub hosts dancing and live music, and serves food.

GETTING THERE & AWAY

Tvøroyri's heliport is at Froðba. Twice-weekly (thrice-weekly June to August) helicopters buzz to/from Tórshavn (Dkr215, 30 minutes) via Skúvoy and Stóra Dimun connecting you to the rest of the country.

The impressively comfortable Smyril car-ferry sails between Tórshavn and Drelnes port twice a day (return ticket adult/child & pensioner/student/car DKr 80/40/60/200, two hours) with linking bus services connecting to central Tvøroyri and other Suðuroy villages.

There are two small garages offering car rental on Suðuroy. **Birgir Joensen** (☎ 222352, 571851; Sjógøta 79, Tvøroyri) rents excellent value Hyundais (Dkr400 per day) that can be booked by email via the tourist office in Tvøroryi. **Jákup Midjord** (☎ 371466; sit@post.oli vant.fo; Shell Petrol Station, Trongisvágur) rents a couple of Mazdas (Dkr400 per day).

Northern Suðuroy

An attractive road passing Suðuroy's last **coal mine** descends to unexpectedly sandy beach-bays at **Hvalba** and **Sandvík**. Both villages frame views of the craggy and uninhabited island of **Lítla Dímun**. However, the greatest attraction of a trip is to continue 3km west of Sandvík on a gated, partly unpaved farm track to the bird cliffs of **Glyvraberg**. Hike carefully here as the grassy clifftops are sliced almost invisibly by perilously vertical chasms. One such sphincter-tighteningly deep chasm is crossed by wobbly hidden plank-bridge. Assuming no *Monty Python* character asks your favourite colour (or the flight speed details for unladen swallows), you can cross for magnificent views north to the spiky rock-stack island of Ásmundarstakkur.

Tvøroyri to Hvalba buses (up to five daily) only continue to Sandvík (Dkr30, 30 minutes) by advance reservation. Call ☎ 212324 to book a trip.

Fámjin

A wonderfully photogenic 9km switchback road leads from Øravík to Fámjin. Colourful, if architecturally ordinary, houses are dotted about an emerald-green bowl-valley dripping with waterfalls and backed by an impressive, layered amphitheatre. Fámjin's 1876 **church** (☎ key-holder 371921; donation appropriate) displays the original Mikkelsen **Merkið flag** (see boxed text, above, for more information). The 1880 **Krambúðin á Brúgvaroyri** (☺ 3-10pm Jun-Sep) is a quaint if slightly over-restored harbourfront shop-cafe catering to local tourists who drive in to watch Fámjin's magical sunsets.

Bus 701 (Dkr30, 30 minutes) runs up to five times daily from Tvøroyri. The inspiring **hike** from westernmost Tvøroyri (2½ hours) is cairn-marked but only on the upper sections. Another trail continues south with some steep sections to Ryskivatn lake whence a drivable track links on to Vágur.

Southern Suðuroy

From Øravik a new tunnel through the mountainside takes you to Hov, soon after which the overgrown village of **Porkeri** comes into view with its attractive 1847 turf-roofed **church**. Fjordside **Vágur** is Suðuroy's lacklustre second town. There's an excellent one-room **museum** (☎ 373703, 289003; admission Dkr30; ☺ by appointment) devoted to the work of local artist Ruth Smith, a friendly **tourist office** (☎ 374342; infovag@post.olivant.fo; ☺ 9am-4pm Mon-Fri)

FAROE ISLANDS

and a **wool workshop** (Ullvirkð; ☎ 374006). While overnight tourists are rare, the surprisingly serviceable **Hotel Bakkin** (☎ 373961; s/d Dkr600/700, with shared bathroom Dkr500/600) has good rooms beyond its restaurant-bar. Vágur also boasts a charming little restaurant, **Messan** (☎ 374222; Rte 20; mains Dkr175-195; ☾ noon-2pm & 5-10pm Mon-Thu, noon-11pm Fri & Sat, noon-10pm Sun) at the curve in the bayside road at the tip of the fjord a short distance before the Shell garage. Filling set lunches and a wider choice of à la carte dishes in the evenings are on offer, although it's usually best to pre-order. Hidden in a 1930s Vágur townhouse 700m east, **Pizza Kokkurin** (☎ 373722; Rte 20; ☾ 5pm-10pm Sun-Thu, 5pm-11pm Fri & Sat) bakes good takeaway pizza and will deliver for big orders.

The Vágur area's main attraction is the fine **Kamarið Cliff** viewpoint, 3km southwest which is accessed by a narrow asphalt lane. Even finer is the dizzying **Beinisvørð Cliff** plunging 469m into the sea, just 20m from a bend in the old mountain route to Sumba (just before the conspicuous communications mast). **Cap Akraberg**, the Faroes' southernmost point, has some puffin burrows and a lighthouse with some fantastic views, despite the two vast TV masts.

Visiting southern Suðuroy is best by car. Bus 700 connects Tvøroyri to Vágur (Dkr40, 50 minutes, up to three daily) before going on to Sumba (Dkr50, three daily; by advance request on ☎ 598588) but they bypass the main viewpoints by several kilometres.

FAROE ISLANDS DIRECTORY

ACCOMMODATION

Much of the accommodation on offer in the Faroes is open during the summer months only (typically May to October), although larger hotels and some guesthouses operate year round. As the summer coincides with the vast majority of visitors, it's a good idea to book ahead to ensure you have a bed. Hotels in larger towns typically cost from Dkr600/800 per single/double with private bathroom, although international standard hotels can only be found in Tórshavn.

Cheaper guesthouses (*gistingarhús*) are often better value and typically offer a communal kitchen. However, most have shared bathroom facilities, and as guesthouses are rarely staffed, you'll generally need to pre-arrange arrival times. Youth hostels (*vallaraheim*) charge Dkr120 to Dkr200 for dormitory beds. This assumes you have a sleeping bag without which there's an additional Dkr50 to Dkr65 bed-linen charge.

Tourist offices have useful lists of family B&B options (singles/doubles cost from Dkr350/450) and self-catering house or apartment rentals (two-bed flats from Dkr500), and can book these for you.

Camping (typically Dkr60 per person) is only permitted at recognised camping grounds, which are often attached to youth hostels. The inevitably wet and windy weather can make camping challenging.

ACTIVITIES

Bird-watching (see p113) and hiking are the greatest attractions of the Faroe Islands. Excellent maps are sold and the tourist board publishes brochures describing key trekking routes.

Boat cruises are a wonderful way to see the islands' stunning bird cliffs and remarkable needle-shaped rocky islets known as stacks. Many also offer fishing trips. The national tourist board produces a detailed pamphlet explaining where licences are necessary (Dkr300/500 per day/season), ideal fishing spots and suggested equipment. If bringing your own fishing tackle, it should be disinfected (and certified) before leaving home or on arrival at the airport or harbour (Dkr300). For a multilingual fish-name listing see www.frs.fo/fish.asp?LangId=0.

Scuba diving is possible with PADI-accredited **FaroeDive** (☎ 458939, 218929; www.faroedive.fo) based in Klaksvík.

BOOKS

Liv Kjørsvik Schei's photo-rich book *The Faroe Isles* offers plenty of cultural background. Bradt's *Faroe Islands* travel guide is extremely comprehensive for travellers wanting to visit remote, less obviously interesting areas.

BUSINESS HOURS

Shops generally open from 9.30am to 5.30pm Monday to Friday, later on Thursday and 9am to noon (sometimes 2pm) on Saturday. Banks open from 9.30am to 4pm, and until 6pm on Thursday.

Eateries typically open around noon and close between 9pm and 11pm, though several open evenings only. Pubs and cafes often stay open till 3am at weekends.

CHILDREN

Tórshavn occasionally offers music and theatre shows for kids (ask at the tourist office). Under-14s get bus and ferry discounts of up to 50%, and free entry to many museums.

EMBASSIES & CONSULATES

The Faroes are represented abroad by Danish embassies (see p108) who issue all visas. There are Faroese representative offices in the **UK** (☎ 020 7333 6707; www.faroeislands.org.uk), **Reykjavík** (☎ 511 3200; www.faroes.is) and an **EU Mission** (☎ 02 23 308 55; www.faroes.be) in Brussels.

FESTIVALS & EVENTS

The Faroes boast a large number of summer festivals, many unique to the islands they are held on. For an exhaustive list, see www.faroeislands.com.

Traditional Summer Festivals

Many of these colourful events feature rowing competitions, processions in traditional dress, singing and chain dancing:

Jóansøka Located on Suðuroy the weekend following Midsummer.

Varmakelda Bonfire and hot-spring fun at Fuglafjørður on Eysturoy on the first weekend of July.

Vestanstevna On Vágar in early July.

Ólavsøka Largest and most exciting traditional festival, celebrating the 10th-century Norwegian King Olav the Holy, who spread Christian faith on the isles; held on 28–29 July.

Ovastevnu On Nólsoy in mid-August.

Music Festivals

Asfalt Five stages showcase local bands in central Tórshavn in early July.

G!Festival (www.gfestival.com) The Islands' original and biggest music festival held in mid/late-July features local and international artists on Syðrugøta beach in Gøta.

Summar Festivalur (www.summarfestivalur.fo) At Klaksvík in early August.

GAY & LESBIAN TRAVELLERS

Forget trying to find a local gay scene – there simply isn't one. While gay rights are respected by law here, local conservative attitudes mean that gay travellers should exercise discretion.

HOLIDAYS

Holidays really are holidays in the Faroes: most transport stops running and everything closes down.

New Year's Day 1 January
Easter (Maundy Thursday to Easter Monday) March/April
Flag Day 25 April
Labour Day 1 May
Common Prayers Day April/May
Ascension Day May/June
Whit Sunday, Whit Monday May/June
Constitution Day 5 June
Ólavsøka (Faroese National Days & Festival) 28 and 29 July
Christmas Eve 24 December (some shops open until noon)
Christmas Day 25 December
Boxing Day 26 December
New Year's Eve 31 December

INTERNET ACCESS

There are no internet cafes, but major libraries have free access on their computers. Most hotels have free wireless internet for travellers with their own laptops, although you'll often need to ask for a password.

INTERNET RESOURCES

Faroe Islands Tourist Guide (www.faroeislands.com) Excellent official website giving a comprehensive overview of the islands.

Faroeislands.dk (www.faroeislands.dk) Photos and details of every village.

National Tourist Board (www.visit-faroeislands.com) Very extensive tourist information.

Post Office Philatelic Service (www.faroestamps.fo) Surprisingly detailed thematic site including traditional recipes and bird identification photos.

MAPS

Tourist offices distribute a free 1:200,000 scale *Faroe Islands Map* that includes basic street plans of larger settlements. Bookshops sell 1:20,000 maps (Dkr90), ideal for hikers, and *Føroyar Topografiskt Atlas*, a comprehensive atlas-booklet of 1:100,000 scale maps (Dkr135), perfect for driving tours.

MONEY

The local currency is Faroese króna, worth exactly the same as Danish krone (Dkr), with which it can be used interchangeably. However in mainland Denmark some shops refuse Faroese money, so play safe and swap any remaining Faroese cash to Danish before departure. Likewise, currency exchange offices back home won't be thrilled to see Faroese notes either.

One króna is equal to 100 oyru (spelt krone, øre in Danish). Notes come in Danish and Faroese designs with denominations of Dkr50, Dkr100, Dkr200, Dkr500 and Dkr1000. Coins are in Danish designs only: Dkr0.25 and Dkr0.50, Dkr1, Dkr2, Dkr5, Dkr10 and Dkr20.

Bigger branches of Føroya Banki and Føroya Sparikassi change travellers cheques and major foreign currencies and have multicard **ATMs** (🕐 6am–midnight).

Foreigners spending over Dkr300 in shops marked 'Tax-free' can claim back the 25% VAT (value-added tax): fill in a Tax Refund Cheque in the shop and get it stamped by the sales clerk.

Tipping isn't necessary anywhere in the Faroes.

POST

Tórshavn's **central post office** (FR-100 Tórshavn, Faroe Islands; 🕐 9am–5pm Mon–Fri) offers reliable poste restante. Village post offices often open much shorter hours. Postcards or letters up to 20g cost Dkr7/7.50 by economy/priority airmail to Europe, and Dkr9/10 to the rest of the world.

TELEPHONE

Mobile phone coverage is almost complete. SIM cards are available for unlocked GSM handsets from Telebúðin telecom shops in major towns and can be purchased for Dkr200 including Dkr100 call credit with local calls costing Dkr3/2 per minute during peak/off-peak times. SMS text-messages cost Dkr0.75. Call 🕐 801020 to check your call credit.

TIME

The local time zone (GMT/UTC in winter) is the same as London, five hours ahead of New York and 11 hours behind Sydney.

TOURIST INFORMATION

There are friendly English-speaking tourist offices (kunningarstovan) in each main town. They can help you find accommodation and tours and dole out free copies of the highly recommended 106-page Tourist Guide Faroe Islands, plus a very creditable 1:200,000 scale country map.

EMERGENCY NUMBERS

For police, fire or ambulance call 🕿 112.

TOURS

Tours and bookings are available through local tourist offices and from the following Tórshavn-based organisations:

62°N (Map p115; 🕿 340050; www.62n.fo) Comprehensive services offered across the country, including house rental, canoeing and daily excursions.

GreenGate Incoming (Map p117 🕿 320520; www .greengate.fo; Undir Bryggjubakka 3) Fishing, diving, boat tours and accommodation.

MB Tours (Map p117; 🕿 322121; www.mb.fo; Bryggjubakki 2, Tórshavn) City tours, accommodation, diving and excursions offered.

Smyril Line (Map p117; 🕿 345900; www.smyril-line.fo; Jonas Broncksgøta 37, Tórshavn) Schooner cruises, coach and boat excursions.

Tora Tourist Traffic (🕿 315505; www.tora.fo) Coach tours and accommodation.

VISAS

Citizens of the EU, USA, Canada, Australia and New Zealand need only a valid passport to visit the Faroes for up to three months. Citizens of Nordic countries need only a valid identity card. Those requiring a visa for the Faroes (including South Africans) must have one that specifically identifies the Faroes: ie not a standard Danish or Schengen visa. Apply to the Danish embassy in your country of residence.

TRANSPORT IN THE FAROE ISLANDS

GETTING THERE & AWAY

Air

The Faroe Islands' only airport is near Sørvágur on **Vágar** (code FAE; 🕿 354400; www .floghavn.fo), see p121.

Airlines flying to and from the Faroe Islands:

Air Iceland (airline code NY; 🕿 341000; www.airice land.is)

Atlantic Airways (RC; 🕿 341060; www.atlanticair ways.fo)

Atlantic Airlines, the national airline, flies in twice weekly from London Stansted (April to October only) and once a week from Aberdeen (early June to early July only). Atlantic Airlines also serve the Danish cities of Copenhagen (at least daily), Aalborg (four times a week in summer) and Billund (daily in summer) plus Stockholm in Sweden and Stavanger in Norway (both twice weekly in summer). Both Atlantic Airways and Air Iceland have several weekly summer flights to Reykjavík. Atlantic Airways also has two flights a week to Narssarssuaq in Eastern Greenland (via Reykjavík, twice weekly in summer).

Sea

Many tourists visit the Faroes during a two-day 'forced' stopover when the weekly car-ferry **Norröna** (www.smyril-line.com) arrives in Tórshavn from Hanstholm (Denmark), Bergen (Norway) and Lerwick (Shetland Islands) before continuing to Seyðisfjörður (Iceland). Schedules, fares and the order of stops vary seasonally.

GETTING AROUND

The national transport company **Strandfaraskip Landsins** (☎ 343030; www.ssl.fo) publishes a complete timetable (*Ferðaætlan;* Dkr10) of all ferry, bus and helicopter services available from tourist offices and Tórshavn's Farstøðin transport terminal. The same outlets sell SL Visitor Travelcards giving unlimited travel on all buses and interisland ferries (Dkr400/600 for four/seven days). Certain services offer small discounts to students or for 10-trip multitickets. Note that 'x' on a timetable means 'weekdays'.

Air

At only Dkr85 to Dkr360 per journey, scenic rides in an eight-seater helicopter (*tyrlan*) are the Faroes' greatest travel bargain. Book early by contacting **Atlantic Airways** (☎ 341060; solia@atlantic.fo; ⏱ 8am-4pm Mon-Fri) then pay (cash only) on departure. Beware that bad weather can cause cancellations, and stops are skipped when nobody has pre-booked.

On each operation day (three weekly, or four in summer) helicopters depart from Vágar airport, hopping in quick succession to all other heliports (except on Sunday when Froðba is missed out). The order of stops varies. Detailed timetables can be found at www.atlantic.fo.

Bicycle

Surfaced roads, minimal traffic, light summer nights and stunning scenery all make riding a bicycle (*súkklur*) a tempting proposition. However steep hills, wind, rain and fog argue against it. Road tunnels are cyclists' greatest hazard. Many are freakily dark, others potentially life-threatening due to carbon-monoxide build-up – best avoided.

Good front and rear lighting, extra reflectors, wind- and waterproof-clothing are essential. If things get rough you can pop your bike on certain buses for Dkr30. Mountain bikes can be hired in Klaksvík.

Boat

Almost as visually stunning as helicopter rides are the ferry trips connecting the islands. Particular ones not to be missed are those on the old post boat **Másin** (adult/child & pensioner/student Dkr40/20/30) between Fugloy, Svínoy and Hvannasund; and the **ferry to Mykines** (adult/child & pensioner/student return Dkr120/60/96) from Sørvágur, between May and August. The most important ferry connection is the **Tóshavn–Suðuroy car ferry** (adult/child & pensioner/student/car return DKr80/40/60/200). See www.ssl.fo for full timetables.

Bus

Bygdaleiðir long-distance bus timetables are sensibly coordinated with ferry services, and combined bus-ferry tickets can be purchased once aboard. Read timetable footnotes very carefully: although buses serve virtually every hamlet, rural services might run only on summer weekdays and even then only if you've pre-booked. If you're the only pre-booked passenger you might find that your 'bus' is actually a taxi (albeit charging standard bus-fares).

Car & Motorcycle

On the bigger islands, driving allows you to see vastly more of the Faroes' appealingly remote villages and valleys in a short time. Roads are excellent and destinations are all well signposted.

DRIVING LICENCE

You can drive in the Faroe Islands with a driving licence from EU countries, the US, Canada, Australia and New Zealand. Alternatively an international driving licence is valid.

FAROE ISLANDS

HIRE

Small hire-cars typically start at Dkr300 per day including partial insurance. The minimum age is 20 and you must have held a driving licence for at least one year. Add around Dkr200 for airport or hotel pick-ups or drop offs.

Main Tórshavn rental companies:

62°N (Map p115; ☎ 340050; www.62n.fo; 8am-5pm Mon-Fri) Agents for both Hertz and Europcar.

Avis Føroyar (Map p115; ☎ 313535, outside office hours 217535; www.avis.fo; Staravegur 1-3; 8am-5pm Mon-Fri) Only 100km per day free mileage.

Bilútleigan (☎ 317865; http://heima.olivant. fo/~carrent/) Car delivered to you for free within Tórshavn.

BVK (☎ 283310; www.bvk.fo; Frúroð 6, 8am-5pm Mon-Fri) Also has a second office in Leirvik.

Rentacar (☎ 232121; www.rentacar.fo; Kollafjøður; 8am-5pm Mon-Fri) Low rates and good discounts for longer rents; run by a friendly couple.

ROAD RULES & HAZARDS

Driving is a breeze in the Faroe Islannds: road layout is simple, traffic is thin and drivers are relatively considerate. The extraordinary Vágar–Streymoy and Eysturoy–Borðoy undersea tunnels cost Dkr130 return for small vehicles, paid at designated petrol stations (although not if you drive a rental car, in which case you give the money to the agency).

Driving is on the right-hand side, front and rear seat-belt use is compulsory, and dipped headlights must be kept on at all times. Beware of sheep leaping onto the road; if you hit one, you must call the **police** (☎ 311448) and pay damages.

Speed limits are 80km/h on open highways, 50km/h through villages. Traffic fines are severe and you can lose your licence on the spot for driving over 110km/h or for exceeding the blood alcohol limit (0.05%).

One-lane tunnels and roads have passing bays (marked 'M' in tunnels) every few hundred metres. Priority is always given to one direction – the duty to pull in and let cars coming the other way pass is only yours when the lanes are on your right.

Finland

Remote, forested, cold, sparsely populated Finland has had a hell of a hundred years. It's propelled itself from agricultural backwater of the Russian empire to one of the world's most prosperous and forward-looking nations, with a great standard of living and education, low crime and corruption, and a booming technology industry. Although socially and economically in the vanguard of nations, parts of Finland remain gloriously remote; trendsetting modern Helsinki is counterbalanced by vast forested wildernesses in the north and east.

There's something pure in the Finnish air and spirit that's incredibly vital and exciting. It's an invitation to get out and active year-round. A post-sauna dip in an ice-hole under the majestic aurora borealis, after whooshing across the snow behind a team of huskies isn't a typical winter's day just anywhere. And hiking or canoeing under midnight sun through pine forests populated by wolves and bears isn't your typical tanning-oil summer either.

Finland has seen a growth in tourism and is well placed, with its magnificent wildernesses, healthy tree cover and tradition of cottage culture, to offer a sustainable ecological experience to travellers looking for a new type of lower-impact holiday. It's perhaps Europe's best destination for getting outdoors and revelling in nature's bounty whilst treading but lightly in it.

Nordic peace in a lakeside cottage, summer sunshine on convivial beer terraces, avant-garde Helsinki design, dark melodic music and cafes warm with baking cinnamon aromas are just the beginning of Suomi seduction. And the real bonus? The Finns, who tend to do their own thing and are much the better for it. Independent, loyal, warm and welcoming.

FAST FACTS

- **Area** 338,145 sq km
- **Capital** Helsinki
- **Famous for** saunas, reindeer, racing drivers, heavy metal, Nokia
- **Languages** Finnish, Swedish, Sámi languages
- **Money** euro (€): US$1 = €0.75; UK£1 = €1.11; A$1 = €0.54; CA$1 = €0.62; NZ$1 = €0.42; ¥100 = €0.77
- **Phrases** Kiitos (thank you), moi/hei (hello), anteeksi (excuse me), kippis (cheers)
- **Population** 5.31 million
- **Telephone Codes** country code ☎ 358; international access code ☎ 00
- **Visas** not required for most visitors for stays of up to 90 days (see p208)

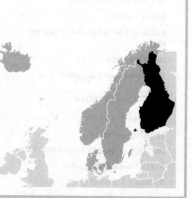

HIGHLIGHTS

- Nose around in Finland's national capital, **Helsinki** (p143), scenic harbour city, creative melting pot for the latest in Finnish design, and home to hard-partying night-owls.
- Cruise Lakeland waterways, gorge on tiny fish, and sweat it in the world's largest smoke sauna at **Kuopio** (p182).
- Enjoy the shimmering lakescapes of the handsome town of **Savonlinna** (p177), as well as fabulous opera in Finland's most spectacular castle.
- Cross the Arctic Circle, hit the awesome Arktikum museum, visit Santa in his official grotto and take a reindeer sleigh or husky ride at **Rovaniemi** (p195) in Lapland.
- Crunch out a shipping lane aboard an ice-breaker and spend a night in the ethereal Snow Castle at **Kemi** (p199).

ITINERARIES

- **One week** Helsinki demands at least a couple of days and is a good base for a day trip to Tallinn (Estonia) or Porvoo. In summer, head to the eastern Lakeland and explore Lappeenranta, Savonlinna and Kuopio (catch a lake ferry between the latter towns). In winter, take an overnight train or budget flight to Lapland (Rovaniemi) for a few days, visiting Santa, exploring Sámi culture and mushing with the huskies. A Helsinki–Savonlinna–

CONNECTIONS

While Finland's road connections with Norway and Sweden are way up in the north of the country, ferries are big business on the Baltic, and an overnight boat can take you to Stockholm (p210) or even as far as Germany (p210). Helsinki's harbour also offers quick and easy boat connections to Tallinn (p210) in Estonia, which sets you up to explore the Baltic states or Eastern Europe in general. Finland's also a springboard for Russia, with bus (p209) and train (p209) services available once you've got a visa sorted out.

Kuopio–Rovaniemi–Helsinki route is a good option.

- **Two weeks** Spend a few days in Helsinki and Porvoo, visit the harbour town of Turku and lively Tampere. Next stop is Savonlinna and Kuopio in the beautiful eastern Lakeland. Head up to Rovaniemi, and perhaps as far north as Inari. You could also fit in a summer festival, some hiking in North Karelia (Ilomantsi or Lake Pielinen) or a quick cycling trip to Åland.

CLIMATE & WHEN TO GO

High season in most of Finland is June to August. This is the time of long, light nights, when no one seems to sleep and numerous festivals (p207) offer everything from chamber music to wife-carrying.

Northern Finland is different. Mosquitoes can be unbearable (literally) in July but better in August, while September is delightful with *ruska* (autumn) colours. October, and February to April are good times to view the northern lights and enjoy winter activities such as skiing and dog-sledding. December is also prime time up north, and charter flights bring thousands of families eager for snow, reindeer and some Christmas spirit.

HISTORY

Finland's story is that of a wrestling mat between two heavyweights, Sweden and Russia, and the nation's eventful emergence from between their grip to become one of the world's most progressive and prosperous nations.

Though evidence of pre-Ice Age habitation exists, it wasn't until around 9000 years ago

---

HOW MUCH?

- **Bus ride** (200km) €33.40
- **Sauna** free–€20
- **Bottle of cheap red in a restaurant** €30
- **Day's bike hire** €10-20
- **Simple log cabin for two** €30-40

LONELY PLANET INDEX

- **1L petrol** €1.50-1.60
- **1L bottle water** €2
- **Half-litre of beer in a bar** €4.50-5.50
- **Snack from a grilli** €2-4
- **Souvenir T-shirt** €15

that settlement re-established after the big chill. The Finns' ancestors moved in to the south and drove the nomadic ancestors of the Sámi north towards Lapland.

The 12th and 13th centuries saw the Swedes begin to move in, Christianising the Finns in the south, and establishing settlements and fortifications. The Russians were never far away, though. There were constant skirmishes with the power of Novgorod, and in the early 18th century Peter the Great attacked and occupied much of Finland. By 1809 Sweden was in no state to resist, and Finland became a duchy of the Russian Empire. The capital was moved to Helsinki, but the communist revolution of October 1917 brought the downfall of the Russian tsar and enabled the Finnish senate to declare independence.

Stalin's aggressive territorial demands in 1939 led to the Winter War between Finland and the Soviet Union, conducted in horribly low temperatures. Little Finland resisted heroically, but was defeated and forced to cede a tenth of its territory. When pressured for more, Finland accepted assistance from Germany. This 'Continuation War' against the Russians cost Finland almost 100,000 lives. Eventually Mannerheim negotiated an armistice with the Russians, ceding more land, and then waged a bitter war in Lapland to oust the Germans. Against the odds, Finland remained independent, but at a heavy price.

Finland managed to take a neutral stance during the Cold War, and once the USSR collapsed, it joined the EU in 1995, and adopted the euro in 2002.

In the new millennium, Finland has boomed, on the back of a strong technology sector, the traditionally important forestry industry, design and manufacturing and, increasingly, tourism. It's a major success story of the new Europe with a strong economy, robust social values and super-low crime and corruption.

For more details on Finnish history, http://virtual.finland.fi has excellent essays on various periods.

PEOPLE

Finland is one of Europe's most sparsely populated countries, with 17 people per sq km, falling to less than one in parts of Lapland. Both Finnish and Swedish are official languages, with some 5.5% of Finns having Swedish as their mother tongue, especially on the west coast and the Åland archipelago. Just over 2% of all Finnish residents are immigrants, one of the lowest percentages of any European country.

Finland's minorities include some 6000 Roma in the south and, in the north, the Sámi, who are divided into various groups.

A capacity for silence and reflection are the traits that best sum up the Finnish character, though this seems odd when weighed against their global gold medal in coffee consumption, their production line of successful heavy bands, and their propensity for a tipple. The image of a log cabin with a sauna by a lake tells much about Finnish culture: independence, endurance (*sisu* or 'guts') and a love of nature.

RELIGION

About 84% of Finns describe themselves as Lutherans, 1.1% are Orthodox and most of the remainder unaffiliated. Only 4% of Finns are weekly churchgoers, one of the world's lowest rates.

ARTS
Architecture & Design

Finland's modern architecture – sleek, functionalist and industrial – has been admired throughout the world ever since Alvar Aalto started making a name for himself during the 1930s. His works can be seen all over Finland today, from the angular Finlandia Talo in Helsinki to the public buildings and street plan of Rovaniemi. Jyväskylä and Seinäjoki are other obligatory stops for Aalto fans.

Earlier architecture in Finland can be seen in medieval churches made from stone or wood – Kerimäki's oversized church is worth seeing, as are the cathedrals at Turku and Tampere. Low-rise Helsinki boasts a patchwork of architectural styles, including the neoclassical buildings of Senate Square, the rich ornamentation of Art Nouveau (Jugendstil), the modern functionalism of Aalto's buildings and the postmodern Kiasma museum.

Finland, like Scandinavia as a whole, is also famous for its design. Aalto again laid a foundation with innovative interior design, furniture and the famous Savoy vase. Finns have created and refined their own design style through craft tradition and using natural materials such as wood, glass and ceramics. Glassware and porcelain such as Iittala and Arabia are world famous.

Cinema

Although around 20 films are produced in Finland annually, few make it onto screens beyond the Nordic countries. The best-known Finnish filmmaker is Aki Kaurismäki, director of the 1989 road film *Leningrad Cowboys Go America*. In 2002 he won the Grand Prix at Cannes for his film *Man Without a Past,* the dark tale of a man who becomes homeless after being mugged and bashed in Helsinki and losing his memory. His brother Mika has made a reputation for insightful documentaries like *Sonic Mirror* (2008), partially looking at Finland's jazz scene

Recent home-grown hits include *Musta jää* (Black Ice, 2007), a characteristically complex Finnish film of infidelity, and *The Home of Dark Butterflies* (2008), a stark look at a Finnish boys' home. For something completely different, check out *Dudesons Movie* (2006), featuring the painful madness of a group of Finnish TV nuts in the style of *Jackass*.

Hollywood's most famous Finn is Renny Harlin, director of action movies such as *Die Hard II, Cliffhanger* and *Deep Blue Sea*. In 2009 he was back home working on the biopic, *Mannerheim,* based on the life of Finland's wartime leader.

Check out the Finnish Film Foundation website at www.kava.fi. Finland hosts some quality film festivals, notably the Midnight Sun Film Festival in Sodankylä and the Tampere International Short Film Festival.

Literature

The *Kalevala,* a collection of folk stories, songs and poems compiled in the 1830s by Elias Lönnrot, is Finland's national epic. Translations and compilations can be found in Finnish bookshops.

Aleksis Kivi's novel *Seven Brothers* is regarded as the founding novel of modern Finnish literature. Its back-to-nature escapism touches something inherent in the forest-loving Finnish character. The theme is echoed in *The Year of the Hare,* written by Arto Paasilinna in the 1970s. Other 20th-century novelists include Mika Waltari who gained fame with *The Egyptian,* and FE Sillanpää, who received the Nobel Prize for literature in 1939. The national bestseller during the postwar period was *The Unknown Soldier* by Väinö Linna. The late Tove Jansson is internationally famous for her Moominland children's stories, and Leena Lander is a contemporary Finnish novelist whose *Tummien perhosten koti* (The Home of the Dark Butterflies) was made into a popular film.

Music

Music is huge in Finland, and in summer numerous festivals all over the country revel in everything from mournful Finnish tango to stirring symphony orchestras to crunchingly potent metal.

Revered composer Jean Sibelius (1865–1957) was at the forefront of the nationalist movement. His stirring tone-poem *Finlandia* has been raised to the status of a national hymn. The Karelian region has its own folk music traditions, typified by the stringed *kantele,* while the Sámi passed down their traditions and beliefs not through the written word but through the song-like chant called the *yoik.*

Finnish bands have made a big impact on the heavier, darker side of the music scale in recent years. The Rasmus, Nightwish, Lordi, HIM, and The 69 Eyes are huge worldwide. But there is lighter music, such as the Von Herzen Brothers, rising indie band Disco Ensemble, emo-punks Poets of the Fall and melodic Husky Rescue. Then there are unstoppable legends like Hanoi Rocks, Flaming Sideburns and the unicorn-quiffed Leningrad Cowboys.

Painting

Finland's Golden Age was the 19th-century National Romantic era, when artists such as Akseli Gallen-Kallela, Albert Edelfelt, Pekka Halonen and the von Wright brothers were inspired by the country's forests and pastoral landscape. Gallen-Kallela is probably Finland's most famous artist. He is known for his *Kalevala*-inspired works – don't miss his frescoes on display in the Kansallismuseo (National Museum) in Helsinki.

The best of Finnish art can be seen at Ateneum (National Gallery) in Helsinki, but there's an art gallery *(taidemuseo)* in just about every Finnish city.

Theatre & Dance

Finns' passion for dance is typified by the tango, which, although borrowed from Latin America, has been refined into a uniquely

FINLAND

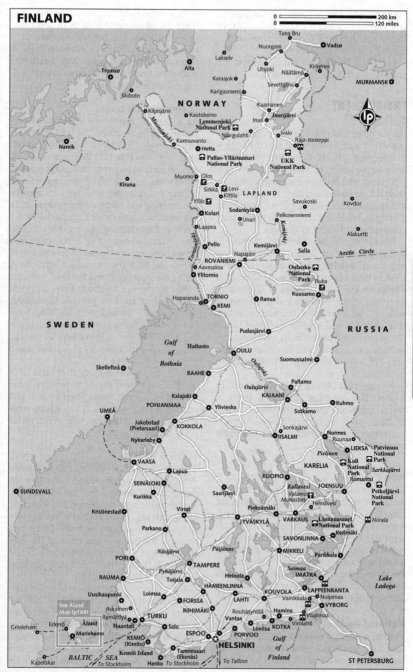

0   200 km
0   120 miles

NORWAY

SWEDEN

RUSSIA

LAPLAND

POHJANMAA

KAJAANI

KARELIA

*Gulf
of
Bothnia*

*Gulf
of
Finland*

*Lake
Ladoga*

BALTIC SEA

Arctic Circle

Tana Bru
Nuorgam
Vadsø
Lakselv
Alta
Karasjok
Utsjoki
Näätämö
Kirkenes
MURMANSK
Karigasniemi
Tromsø
Skibotn
Kaamanen
Kilpisjärvi
Inarijärvi
Kautokeino
Inari
Lemmenjoki
National Park
Ivalo
Raja-Jooseppi
Narvik
Karesuvanto
Njurgulahti
Hetta
Pallas-Yllästunturi
National Park
UKK
National Park
Kiruna
Muonio
Olos
Sirkka
Levi
Savukoski
Kovdor
Ylläs
Kittilä
Kolari
Sodankylä
Pelkosenniemi
Lappea
Unari
Alakurtti
Pello
Kemijärvi
Salla
Napapiiri
ROVANIEMI
Aavasaksa
Oulanko
National
Park
Ylitornio
Ruka
Haparanda
TORNIO
Ranua
Kuusamo
KEMI
Hailuoto
Pudasjärvi
Skellefteå
*Gulf
of
Bothnia*
OULU
Suomussalmi
RAAHE
Oulujoki
Paltamo
Kalajoki
Oulujärvi
UMEÅ
POHJANMAA
Ylivieska
KAJAANI
Kuhmo
Jakobstad
(Pietarsaari)
KOKKOLA
Sotkamo
Nykarleby
Sonkajärvi
Nurmes
Ruunaa
IISALMI
LIEKSA
Patvinsuo
National
Park
VAASA
Lapua
Pielinen
SEINÄJOKI
KUOPIO
Koli
National
Park
Sarkkajärvi
Kurikka
Saarijärvi
JOENSUU
Ilomantsi
Kristinestad
Virrat
Kallavesi
Valamo
Monastery
Petkeljärvi
National
Park
Parkano
Pieksämäki
Heinävesi
Niirala
JYVÄSKYLÄ
VARKAUS
Linnansaari
National Park
Näsijärvi
Päijänne
Kerimäki
SUNDSVALL
PORI
TAMPERE
SAVONLINNA
RAUMA
Pyhäjärvi
Heinola
Saimaa
Parikkala
Toijala
MIKKELI
Uusikaupunki
Loimaa
IMATRA
Askainen
HÄMEENLINNA
KOUVOLA
LAPPEENRANTA
Rymättylä
FORSSA
LAHTI
Nuijamaa
VYBORG
See Åland
Map (p164)
TURKU
RIIHIMÄKI
Vainikkala
Hamina
Vaalimaa
Åland
Salo
Routsinpyhtää
KOTKA
Virolahti
Naantali
Vantaa
Mariehamn
ESPOO
Loviisa
Grissleham
Eckerö
KEMIÖ
(Kimito)
PORVOO
*Gulf
of
Finland*
Kemiö Island
Tammisaari
(Ekenäs)
HELSINKI
ST PETERSBURG
Kapellskar
BALTIC SEA
Hanko
To Stockholm
To Stockholm
To Tallinn

FINLAND

Finnish style. Older Finns are tango-mad and every town has a dance hall or dance restaurant. A similar form of Finnish dancing is the waltz-like *humppa*.

Finland's theatre season is winter; the exceptions are the summer festivals.

ENVIRONMENT

The Land

People often describe Finland offhand as a country of 'forests and lakes', and the truth is that they are spot-on. Some 10% of Suomi is taken up by bodies of water, and nearly 70% is forested with birch, spruce and pine. It's a fairly flat expanse of territory: though the fells of Lapland add a little height to the picture, they are small change compared to the muscular mountainscapes of Norway.

Measuring 338,000 sq km and weighing in as Europe's seventh-largest nation, Finland hits remarkable latitudes: even its southernmost point is comparable with Anchorage in Alaska, or the lower reaches of Greenland. Its watery vital statistics are also impressive, with 187,888 large lakes and numerous further wetlands and smaller bodies of water. Geographers estimate that its total coastline, including riverbanks and lakeshores, measures 315,000km, not far off the distance to the moon.

Forests cover 70% of Finland, the world's highest tree coverage; the main types of forest are pine, spruce and birch. Much of this forest is managed, and timber-harvesting and the associated pulp-milling is an important industry.

Wildlife

Brown bears, lynx, wolverines and wolves are native to Finland, although sightings are rare. You're more likely to see an elk, though hopefully not crashing through your windscreen. In Lapland, the Sámi keep commercial herds of some 230,000 reindeer. Finland is a bird-watcher's paradise, with species like the capercaillie and golden eagle augmented by hundreds of migratory arrivals in spring and summer.

National Parks

Finland's excellent network of national parks and other protected areas is maintained by **Metsähallitus** (www.outdoors.fi), the Finnish Forest & Park Service. In total, over 30,000 sq km, some 9% of the total area, is in some way protected land. The largest and most pristine national parks are in northern Finland, particularly Lapland, where vast swathes of wilderness invite trekking, cross-country skiing, fishing and canoeing.

Environmental Issues

As a general model for environmentally sustainable nationhood, Finland does very well. Though it has a high per-capita carbon-emission rate, this is largely due to its abnormal heating requirements and is offset in many ways. As in much of northern Europe, cycling and recycling were big here decades ago, littering and waste-dumping don't exist, and sensible solutions for keeping the houses warm and minimising heat loss were a question of survival not virtue. Finns in general have a deep respect for and understanding of nature and have always trodden lightly in it, seeing the forest as friend not foe.

But they're not a nation of tree-huggers. Most of the forests are periodically logged, and privately-owned plots are long-term investments for many Finns. Hunting is big here, and animals are kept at an 'optimum' population level by the keen shooting contingent.

And, despite the rushing rivers and clean air, Finland only manages to produce some 16% of its energy needs from hydro- and wind-generated sources. It has a firm commitment to nuclear energy, with a fifth reactor going online in 2010.

FOOD & DRINK

Typically Finnish food is similar to the fare you get elsewhere in Scandinavia and has Swedish and Russian influences – lots of fish, such as Baltic herring, salmon and whitefish, along with heavy food such as potatoes, thick soups, stews and dark rye bread. Finns tend to make lunch the main meal of the day. Breakfast can be anything from coffee and a bun (*pulla*) to a buffet of cold cuts, porridge, eggs, berries and pickled fish.

Beer, wine and spirits are sold by the state network, beautifully named Alko. There are stores in every town and they're generally open from 10am to 6pm Monday to Thursday, till 8pm Friday and 2pm Saturday. The legal age for drinking is 18 for beer and wine, and 20 for spirits. Beer and cider with less than 5%

alcohol can be bought easily at supermarkets, service stations and R-kioskis.

Staples & Specialities

Simple hamburgers, hot dogs and kebabs are a cheap, common snack, served from grilli kiosks. Fish is a mainstay of the Finnish diet. Fresh salmon, herring and Arctic char are common, and the tiny lake fish *muikku* are another treat. In Lappish restaurants, reindeer and elk feature on the menu.

Regional specialities from Karelia include *vety,* a sandwich made with ham, eggs and pickles, and the *karjalanpiirakka,* a savoury rice pasty folded in a thin, open crust. In Tampere, try *mustamakkara,* a thick sausage made from cow's blood. In Savo, especially Kuopio, a highlight is *kalakukko,* fish baked in a rye loaf. Åland is known for its fluffy semolina pancakes. Seasonal berries are a delight in Finland – look out for cloudberries and lingonberries from Lapland, and market stalls selling blueberries, strawberries and raspberries.

Finns drink plenty of beer and among the best local brews are Lapin Kulta and Karhu. Cider is also popular. Uniquely Finnish drinks to sample while here include *salmiakkikossu,* which combines dissolved liquorice sweets with the iconic Koskenkorva vodka (an acquired taste); *sahti,* a sweet, high-alcohol beer; and cloudberry or cranberry liqueurs.

Where to Eat & Drink

Just about every town has a kauppahalli (market hall), the place to head for all sorts of Finnish specialities, breads, cheeses, fresh fish and cheap sandwiches and snacks. The summer kauppatori (market square) also has food stalls and market produce.

Meals in a restaurant *(ravintola)* can be expensive, particularly dinner, but Finns tend to eat their main meal in the middle of the day, so most restaurants and some cafes put on a generous lunch *(lounas)* buffet for between €7 and €10. These include all-you-can-eat salad, bread, coffee and dessert, plus big helpings of hearty fare – sausage and potatoes or fish and pasta are common. Most hotels include a free breakfast buffet.

Finns are big lovers of chain restaurants such as Rosso, Amarillo (steaks and Tex-Mex), Koti Pizza and Hesburger (Finland's answer to McDonald's), which can be found in most towns. At Golden Rax Pizza Buffet you can get all-you-can-eat pizza, pasta, chicken wings, salad, drinks and even dessert for €9 – a cheap refuelling option.

Finns are the world's biggest coffee drinkers, so cafes are everywhere, ranging from 100-year-old Imperial classics to trendy networking joints and simple country caffeine stops.

Vegetarians & Vegans

In terms of specifically vegetarian restaurants, there's not a lot around in Finland, but the big cities have options. It's easy to self-cater at markets, or eat only the salad and vegetables at lunch buffets (which is usually cheaper). Many restaurants also have a salad buffet.

HELSINKI

☎ 09 / pop 568,531

It's fitting that harbourside Helsinki, capital of a country with such a watery geography, melds so graciously into the Baltic Sea. Half the city seems to be liquid, and the tortured writhings of the complex coastline includes any number of bays, inlets and a speckling of islands.

Though Helsinki can seem like a younger sibling to other Scandinavian capitals, it's the one that went to art school, scorns pop music, is working in a cutting-edge design studio and hangs out with friends who like black and plenty of piercings. The city's design shops are legendary, and its music and nightlife scene kicking.

On the other hand, much of what is lovable in Helsinki is older. Its understated yet glorious Art Nouveau buildings, the spacious elegance of its centenarian cafes, the careful preservation of Finnish heritage in its dozens of museums, restaurants that have changed neither menu nor furnishings since the 1930s, they are all part of the city's quirky charm.

Like all of Finland, though, Helsinki has a dual nature. In winter, although it still hums along with skaters, cafe chat and cultural life, you can sometimes wonder where all the people are. In spring and summer they are back again, though, packing green spaces and outdoor tables to get a piece of blessed sun, whirring around on thousands of bicycles, and revving the city's nightlife into overdrive.

FINLAND

HELSINKI IN ONE DAY

Finns are the world's biggest coffee drinkers, so first-up it's Café Strindberg (p152), and then down to the kauppatori (opposite). Grab a picnic and harbour boat to Suomenlinna (p148), the island fortress. Once back, hit Senate Square (opposite) and nearby Uspenski Cathedral (opposite). Then, it's Golden Age art at Ateneum (opposite) or cutting-edge contemporary at nearby Kiasma (opposite). Hit legendary Kotiharjun Sauna (p149) for a sweat, before dinner and at Tavastia (p153) or a bar on Iso-Roobertinkatu (p152).

HISTORY

Helsinki (Swedish: Helsingfors) was founded in 1550 by the Swedish king Gustav Vasa, who hoped to compete with the Hansa trading port of Tallinn across the water. In the 18th century the Swedes built a mammoth fortress on the nearby island of Suomenlinna, but it wasn't enough to keep the Russians out. Once the Russians were in control of Finland, they needed a capital a bit closer to home than the Swedish-influenced west coast. Helsinki was it, and took Turku's mantle in 1812. Helsinki grew rapidly, with German architect CL Engel responsible for many noble central buildings. In the bitter postwar years, the 1952 Olympic Games symbolised the city's gradual revival.

ORIENTATION

Helsinki occupies a peninsula, surrounded by an archipelago of islands. The compact city centre stretches from the harbourside kauppatori, between the international ferry terminals, to Kamppi, the bus station. Airport buses arrive at the nearby train station. The main street axes are the twin shopping avenues of Pohjoisesplanadi and Eteläesplanadi and Mannerheimintie.

INFORMATION
Bookshops

Akateeminen Kirjakauppa (☎ 12141; Pohjois-esplanadi 39; ☼ 9am-9pm Mon-Fri, 9am-6pm Sat, noon-6pm Sun) Finland's biggest bookshop with a huge travel section, maps, Finnish literature and an impressive English section.

Discount Cards

Helsinki Card (☎ 2288 1200; www.helsinkicard.fi; adult 24/48/72hr €33/43/53, child €11/14/17) If you plan to see a lot of sights, the Helsinki Card gives you free travel, entry to more than 50 attractions in and around Helsinki, and discounts on day tours to Porvoo and Tallinn. Buy it at the tourist office, hotels, R-kioskis and transport terminals.

Emergencies

Dial ☎ 112 for all emergencies including ambulance, fire and police and ☎ 10023 for 24-hour medical advice.

Internet Access

Internet access at various public libraries is free. Large parts of the city centre have free wi-fi, as do many bars and cafes – some also have terminals for customers' use.

Library 10 (☎ 3108 5000; Elielinkatu 2; ☼ 10am-10pm Mon-Thu, 10am-6pm Fri, noon-6pm Sat & Sun, shorter hours in summer) On the 1st floor of the main post office. Several half-hour terminals and others bookable by phone.

mbar (☎ 6124 5420; Mannerheimintie 22; per hr €5; ☼ 9am-midnight, later at weekends) In the Lasipalatsi building. Heaps of terminals.

TeleCenter (☎ 670 612; Vuorikatu 8; per hr €2; ☼ 10am-9pm Mon-Fri, 11am-7pm Sat, noon-7pm Sun) Slowish but cheap.

Left Luggage

Small/large lockers cost €3/4 per 24 hours at the bus and train station. There are similar lockers and left-luggage counters at the ferry terminals.

Medical Services

Maria Hospital (☎ 3106 3231; Lapinlahdenkatu 16; ☼ 24hr) For emergency medical assistance.

Töölö Health Station (☎ 310 5015; Sibeliuksenkatu 14; ☼ 8am-6pm Mon, 8am-4pm Tue-Fri) A day-only medical centre.

Yliopiston Apteekki Mannerheimintie (☎ 4178 0300; Mannerheimintie 96; ☼ 24hr); city centre (Mannerheimintie 5; ☼ 7am-midnight) Pharmacies; the branch in the city centre is more convenient.

Money

There are currency-exchange counters at the airport and ferry terminals. ATMs ('Otto') are plentiful in the city.

Forex (☼ 8am-9pm summer, 8am-7pm Mon-Sat autumn-spring) At Pohjoisesplanadi 27, Mannerheimintie 10 and at the train station; the best place to change cash or travellers cheques (flat fee €2).

Post & Telephone

Main post office (☎ 020 451 4400; Mannerheimin-aukio 1; ☼ 7am-9pm Mon-Fri, 10am-6pm Sat & Sun)

Between the bus and train stations. There are almost no phone booths in Finland, but there's a call centre here.

Tourist Information

Helsinki City Tourist Office (☎ 169 3757; www.hel
.fi/tourism; Pohjoisesplanadi 19; ☺ 9am-8pm Mon-
Fri, 9am-6pm Sat & Sun May-Sep, 9am-6pm Mon-Fri,
10am-4pm Sat & Sun Oct-Apr) Busy multilingual office
with booking desk. In summer, they send out uniformed
'Helsinki Helpers' – grab one on the street and ask away.
A cut-down version of the city tourism website can be
delivered to your mobile at www.helsinki.mobi.

SIGHTS
Kauppptori

Finnish cities are traditionally centred around
their market square, and Helsinki's sits right
by the passenger harbour in the old part of
town. Start your exploration of Helsinki here.
It's a forum for selling fish fresh off the boats,
as well as other fresh garden produce and
seasonal berries. Check out the fountain and
mermaid **statue of Havis Amanda**, regarded as a
symbol of Helsinki.

Cathedrals & Churches

Presiding over Senate Square just north
of the kauppatori, chalk-white neoclassical **Tuomiokirkko** (Lutheran Cathedral; ☎ 709 2455;
Unioninkatu 29; ☺ 9am-6pm Mon-Sat, noon-6pm Sun
Sep-May, 9am-midnight Jun-Aug) was designed by
CL Engel but not completed until 1852, 12
years after his death. Its interior is fairly unadorned, unlike that of the red-brick **Uspenski
Cathedral** (☎ 634 267; Kanavakatu 1; ☺ 9.30am-4pm
Mon-Fri, 9.30am-2pm Sat, noon-3pm Sun, closed Mon Oct-
Apr) on nearby Katajanokka island. The two
cathedrals face each other high above the
city like two queens on a theological chess-
board. Built as a Russian Orthodox church in
1868, it features classic onion-topped domes
and now serves the Finnish Orthodox congregation. The high, square interior has a
lavish iconostasis.

Temppeliaukio Church (☎ 494 698; Lutherinkatu 3;
☺ 10am-8pm Mon-Fri, 10am-6pm Sat, noon-1.45pm &
3.30-6pm Sun), designed by Timo and Tuomo
Suomalainen in 1969, remains one of
Helsinki's foremost attractions. Hewn into
solid rock, the church symbolises the modern tendency towards innovation of Finnish
religious architecture and features a stunning
24m-diameter roof covered in 22km of copper
stripping. There are regular concerts, with
great acoustics.

The oldest church in Helsinki is the white
wood **Vanha Kirkko** (Lönnrotinkatu), designed by
CL Engel; its graveyard, where plague victims
were once buried, has been converted into a
public park.

Museums & Galleries
KIASMA

More than a decade on, curvaceous and
quirky metallic **Kiasma** (☎ 1733 6501; www.ki
asma.fi; Mannerheiminaukio 2; adult/under 18yr €7/free;
☺ 10am-8.30pm Wed-Sun, 9am-5pm Tue), designed by
American architect Steven Holl, still stands
testament to modern Helsinki. It exhibits an
eclectic collection of Finnish and international
modern art and still surprises with its striking
contemporary exhibitions.

Kiasma's outstanding success is that it's
been embraced by the people of Helsinki.
Its sleek, glass-sided cafe and terrace are
hugely popular, locals sunbathe on the grassy
fringes and skateboarders perform aerobat-
ics under the stern gaze of Mannerheim's
statue outside.

ATENEUM

Visit Finland's national **gallery** (☎ 1733 6401;
www.ateneum.fi; Kaivokatu 2; adult/student/child €8/6.50/free;
☺ 9am-6pm Tue & Fri, 9am-8pm Wed & Thu, 11am-5pm Sat &
Sun) for a course in the 'who's who' of Finnish
art. It houses Finnish paintings and sculptures
from the 18th century to the 1950s including
works by Albert Edelfelt, the prolific Akseli
Gallen-Kallela, the Von Wright brothers and
Pekka Halonen. Pride of place goes to Gallen-
Kallela's triptych from the Kalevala depicting
Väinämöinen's pursuit of the maiden Aino.
There's also a small but interesting collection
of 19th- and early-20th-century foreign art.
Downstairs is a cafe, a good bookshop and a
reading room with internet terminals.

KANSALLISMUSEO

The impressive **National Museum** (☎ 4050 9544;
www.kansallismuseo.fi; Mannerheimintie 34; adult/child €5.50/
free; ☺ 11am-8pm Tue-Wed, 11am-6pm Thu-Sun), built in
National Romantic style in 1916, looks a bit
like a Gothic church with its heavy stonework
and tall square tower. This is Finland's premier
historical museum and is divided into rooms
covering different periods of Finnish history,
including prehistory and archaeological finds,
church relics, ethnography and changing cultural exhibitions. Look for the imperial throne
of Tsar Alexander I dating from 1809, and the

HELSINKI

FINLAND

To Urho Kekkonen Museum (2km);
Tamminiementien Kahvila (2km);
Seurasaari Island (3km); Seurasaari
Open-Air Museum (3km);
German Embassy (4km)

To Tampere
(190km)

To Hartwall
Arena
(1.5km)

Pohjoinen
Stadiontie

City Winter
Gardens

Talvipuutarha
Botanical
Gardens

INFORMATION
Akateeminen Kirjakauppa........1	E4
Australian Consulate................2	D3
Canadian Embassy....................3	E4
Danish Embassy........................4	E4
Estonian Embassy......................5	F5
Forex..6	E4
Forex..7	E3
Forex..8	E4
French Embassy....................(see 24)	
Helsinki City Tourist Office......9	E4
Irish Embassy..........................10	E4
Japanese Embassy...................11	F4
Latvian Embassy......................12	D6
Library 10...........................(see 14)	
Lithuanian Embassy.................13	F3
Main Post Office.....................14	D3
Maria Hospital........................15	C4
mbar.......................................16	D3
Netherlands Embassy...............17	E4
New Zealand Consulate...........18	E5
Norwegian Embassy.................19	D6
Russian Embassy......................20	F5
Swedish Embassy.....................21	F4
TeleCenter..............................22	E3
Töölö Health Station................23	C2
UK Embassy........................(see 24)	
US Embassy.............................24	F6
Yliopiston Apteekki.................25	C1
Yliopiston Apteekki.................26	E4

SIGHTS & ACTIVITIES
Ateneum.................................27	E3
Design Museum.......................28	E5
Havis Amanda Statue...............29	F4
Kansallismuseo........................30	D3
Kauppatori (Fish Market).........31	F4
Kiasma....................................32	D3
Kotiharjun Sauna.....................33	F1
Mannerheim Museum..............34	D3
Mannerheim Statue.................35	D3
Temppeliaukio Church.............36	C3
Tuomiokirkko..........................37	F3
Uspenski Cathedral..................38	F4
Vanha Kirkko...........................39	E4
Yrjönkadun Uimahalli..............40	D4

SLEEPING
Eurohostel..............................41	G4
Hostel Academica....................42	C4
Hostel Erottajanpuisto............43	E4
Hostel Satakuntatalo...............44	D4
Hostel Stadion........................45	C1
Hotel Arthur...........................46	E3
Hotel Finn...............................47	E4
Hotelli Helka..........................48	C3
Klaus K...................................49	E4
Omenahotelli Eerikinkatu........50	D4
Omenahotelli Lönnrotinkatu....51	D4
Scandic Grand Marina..............52	G4
Stay At Parliament...................53	D3

EATING
Bar Tapasta............................54	E4
Boathouse..............................55	E6
Café Ekberg............................56	D4
Café Engel..............................57	F4
Café Strindberg.......................58	E4
Chez Dominique......................59	E4
Fazer......................................60	E4
Forum Shopping Centre...........61	D4
Hakaniemi Market...................62	E2
Konstan Möljä.........................63	C5
Kosmos..................................64	E4
Koto.......................................65	D4
Lappi......................................66	D4
Namaskaar Bulevardi...............67	D4
Nokka....................................68	F4
Orchid Thai Restaurant............69	D4
Seahorse.................................70	E5
Soppakeittiö........................(see 62)	
Tori..71	F4
vanha Kauppahalli...................72	F4
Zucchini.................................73	E4

Linnankoskenkatu

Humaliistonkatu

Eino Leinonkatu

Sibelius
Park

Sibelius
Monument

Mäntymäent

Helsinginkatu

Töölönlahti

Töölöntori

Töölöntullinkatu

Pohjoinen Hesperiankatu

Eteläinen Hesperiankatu

Apollonkatu

Museokatu

Finlandia
Talo

Hietaniemi
Beach

Töölö

Temppelikatu

Parliament
House

Elielinkatu

Hietaniemi
Cemetery

Arkadiankatu

Pohjoinen

Seurasaarenselkä

Hietaniemenkatu

Kamppi

Leppäsuonkatu

Malminkatu

Lapinlahdenkatu

Länsiväylä

Porkkalankatu

To Kaapelitehdas
(250m)

Ruoholahti

Ruoholahti

Hietalahden
tori

Eira

Merimiehenkatu

Uudenmaankatu

Bulevardi

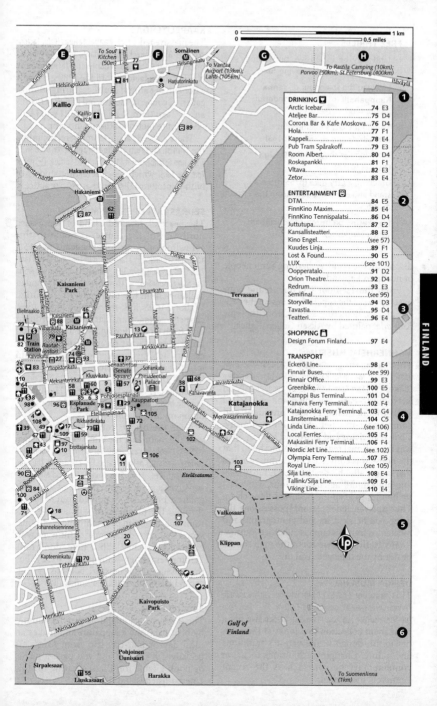

0 — 1 km
0 — 0.5 miles

DRINKING 🍷
Arctic Icebar...............................74 E3
Ateljee Bar..................................75 D4
Corona Bar & Kafe Moskova...76 D4
Hola..77 F1
Kappeli...78 E4
Pub Tram Spårakoff...................79 E3
Room Albert.................................80 D4
Roskapankki.................................81 F1
Vltava...82 E3
Zetor..83 E4

ENTERTAINMENT 🎭
DTM..84 E5
FinnKino Maxim............................85 E4
FinnKino Tennispalatsi.................86 D4
Juttutupa......................................87 E2
Kansallisteatteri...........................88 E3
Kino Engel........................(see 57)
Kuudes Linja................................89 F1
Lost & Found................................90 E5
LUX...................................(see 101)
Oopperatalo.................................91 D2
Orion Theatre...............................92 D4
Redrum...93 E3
Semifinal...........................(see 95)
Storyville......................................94 D3
Tavastia..95 D4
Teatteri...96 E4

SHOPPING 🛍
Design Forum Finland..................97 E4

TRANSPORT
Eckerö Line..................................98 E4
Finnair Buses....................(see 99)
Finnair Office...............................99 E3
Greenbike...................................100 E5
Kamppi Bus Terminal.................101 D4
Kanava Ferry Terminal...............102 F4
Katajanokka Ferry Terminal......103 G4
Länsiterminaali..........................104 C5
Linda Line.........................(see 106)
Local Ferries..............................105 F4
Makasiini Ferry Terminal...........106 F4
Nordic Jet Line.................(see 102)
Olympia Ferry Terminal.............107 F5
Royal Line.........................(see 105)
Silja Line....................................108 E4
Tallink/Silja Line.......................109 E4
Viking Line................................110 E4

FINLAND

display on the reindeer-herding Sámi people of northern Lapland.

From the 1st-floor balcony, crane your head up to see the superb frescoes on the ceiling arches, depicting scenes from the epic *Kalevala*, painted by Akseli Gallen-Kallela.

MANNERHEIM MUSEUM

This fascinating **museum** (☎ 635 443; www.mannerheim-museo.fi; Kalliolinnantie 14; adult/child €8/free; ☒ 11am-4pm Fri-Sun & by appointment), in Kaivopuisto Park, was the home of Marshal CGE Mannerheim, former president and commander-in-chief of the Finnish army, Civil War victor and all-round legend. Such was the national regard for Mannerheim that the house was converted into a museum less than a year after his death in 1951. Entry is by one-hour multilingual guide tour, with plastic booties to keep the hallowed floor clean. The display includes personal possessions, the camp bed he slept in, and photographs and mementos from his famous Silk Road journey. Renny Harlin's movie about the man should be out by the time you read this.

DESIGN MUSEUM

This **museum** (☎ 622 0540; www.designmuseum.fi; Korkeavuorenkatu 23; adult/child €7/free; ☒ 11am-6pm Tue-Sun, also Mon Jun-Aug, 11am-8pm Tue Sep-May) has a permanent collection that looks at the roots of Finnish design in the nation's traditions and nature. Changing exhibitions focus on contemporary design, such as the recent Fennofolk movement.

KAAPELITEHDAS

The massive red-brick **Kaapelitehdas** (Cable Factory; ☎ 4763 8300; www.kaapelitehdas.fi; Tallberginkatu 1C) once manufactured sea cable and later became Nokia's main factory until the 1980s. It's now a bohemian cultural centre featuring studios, galleries, concerts, theatre and dance performances. Take tram 8, bus 15, 20, 21V, 65A or 66A, or the metro to Ruoholahti stop.

There are several museums here, including the **Finnish Museum of Photography** (☎ 6866 3622; www.fmp.fi; Tallberginkatu 1G; adult/child €6/free; ☒ noon-7pm Tue-Sun), which has interesting studies of both photojournalism and artistic practice.

SEURASAARI OPEN-AIR MUSEUM

The peaceful, forested island of Seurasaari, northwest of the centre, is home to this sprawling open-air folk **museum** (☎ 484 511 adult/child €6/free; ☒ 11am-5pm mid-Sep–mid-May, 11am-7pm Wed Jun-Aug, 9am-3pm Mon-Fri, 11am-5pm Sat & Sun late May & early Sep) with more than 80 wooden buildings from the 18th and 19th centuries. Walking trails link the various log houses, chapels, cottages and farmhouses brought here from all over Finland – you'll get a good impression of what rural Finland was like a century ago. In summer, guides dressed in traditional costume demonstrate folk dancing and crafts.

Seurasaari is the best place in Helsinki to see the **Midsummer bonfires**, a popular local tradition on Midsummer's Eve.

Near the bridge connecting Seurasaari with the mainland, the **Urho Kekkonen Museum** (☎ 4050 9650; Seurasaarentie 15, Tamminiemi; adult/child €6/free, free with Helsinki Card; ☒ 11am-5pm Thu-Sun, 11am-7pm Wed, 11am-5pm Mon & Tue mid-May–mid-Aug) gives a glimpse into the life of Finland's greatest president. A guided tour wanders through the magnificent villa and its surrounding park, and peeks into the traditional sauna that hosted diplomatic chinwags with Nikita Khrushchev. While here, don't miss Tamminiementien Kahvila (see p152). For the museum and Seurasaari, take bus 24 from central Helsinki, or tram 4 and walk.

Suomenlinna

The 'fortress of Finland' is just 15 minutes by boat from the kauppatori and makes an ideal day or half-day trip from town, especially if it's sunny and you pack a picnic or book a table for alfresco eating on this Unesco-listed island.

FINLAND

Built in 1748 as Sveaborg to protect against the Russians, the impressive island fortress once held more people than Helsinki but was finally conquered after a prolonged assault in 1808.

At the bridge connecting the two main islands, Iso Mustasaari and Susisaari, is the **Inventory Chamber Visitor Centre** (☎ 668 800; www .suomenlinna.fi; walking tours €6.50, free with Helsinki Card; ⏰ 10am-6pm May-Sep, walking tours depart 11am & 2pm Jun-Aug), which has tourist information, maps and guided walking tours in summer. Here too is **Suomenlinna Museum** (☎ 684 1880; admission €5; ⏰ 10am-6pm May-Sep, 10am-4pm Oct-Apr) featuring a scale model of Suomenlinna as it looked in 1808, and a 30-minute audiovisual display.

Ramble around the various fortifications to your heart's content. There's a blue-sign-posted walking path that takes in many of the main attractions. **Ehrensvärd Museum** (☎ 684 1850; adult/child €3/1; ⏰ 10am-5pm May-Aug, 11am-4pm Sep, 11am-4pm Sat & Sun Apr & Oct) preserves an 18th-century officer's home; opposite is a **shipyard** where sailmakers and other workers have been building ships since the 1750s.

Two museums can be visited with a combination ticket (€6). **Manege** (☎ 1814 5296; admission €4; ⏰ 11am-6pm mid-May–Aug) commemorates WWII and displays heavy artillery. More interesting is **Vesikko** (☎ 1814 6238; admission €4, ⏰ 11am-6pm mid-May–Aug), a claustrophobic WWII-era submarine.

The **church** on Iso Mustasaari was built in 1854 and doubles as a lighthouse; the original gaslight beacon is now electric.

There's an HI hostel on Suomenlinna, as well as a supermarket, several good cafes and a couple of classy restaurants. Locals like to picnic among the fortress ruins with a few drinks – it can get pretty boozy here on summer weekends. At around 5pm it's worth finding a spot to watch the enormous Baltic ferries pass through the narrow gap.

HKL ferries run from the passenger quay at the kauppatori (return €3.80, 15 minutes, three times hourly, 6.20am to 2.20am).

ACTIVITIES

For a sauna and swim, sleek Art Deco **Yrjönkadun Uimahalli** (☎ 3108 7400; Yrjönkatu 21; admission €4-11; ⏰ men 6.30am-9pm Tue, Thu & Sat, women noon-9pm Sun & Mon, 6.30am-9pm Wed & Fri) is a Helsinki institution – a fusion of soaring Nordic elegance and Roman baths. There are separate hours for men and women and, like the saunas, it's compulsory to bathe nude.

In Kallio, **Kotiharjun Sauna** (☎ 753 1535; Harju-torinkatu 1; adult/child €7/4; ⏰ 2-8pm Tue-Fri, 1-7pm Sat, sauna time until 10pm) is a traditional public wood-fired sauna dating back to 1928. These largely disappeared with the advent of shared saunas in apartment buildings, but it's a classic experience, where you can also get a scrub-down and massage. There are separate saunas for men and women.

In summer (or winter, if ice-swimming appeals), hit the beaches at **Hietaniemi**, **Seurasaari**, **Pihlajasaari**, or **Suomenlinna**. Cycling and roll-erblading is popular all around town, and in winter and early spring it's possible to go walking, skating or cross-country skiing on parts of the frozen harbour. Töölönlahti is another particularly popular skating spot, with hire available.

TOURS

There are several cruise companies departing hourly on harbour jaunts from the kauppatori in summer. These cost between €15 and €20, or around €35 with lunch or dinner on board.

Leaving from near the tourist office, **Helsinki Expert** (☎ 2288 1600; www.helsinkiexpert.fi; adult/child €25/15; ⏰ on the hour 10am-2pm summer, 11am winter) runs multilingual 90-minute sightseeing tours in their bright orange bus. The same company offers walking tours.

An excellent budget alternative is to catch the 3T tram and pick up the free *Take the Tram For Helsinki Sightseeing* brochure as your guide around the city centre and out to Kallio.

FESTIVALS & EVENTS

There's something going on in Helsinki year-round. Some of the biggies:

Vappu Held on May Day. The student graduation festival is celebrated by gathering around the Havis Amanda statue, which receives a white 'student cap'.

Helsinki Day (www.hel.fi/helsinkipaiva) Free events celebrating the city's anniversary on June 12.

Ankkarock (www.ankkarock.fi) Rock festival held in nearby Vantaa in early August.

Helsinki Festival (Helsingin Juhlaviikot; ☎ 6126 5100; www.helsinginjuhlaviikot.fi; Mannerheimintie 22-24; tickets €10-50) From late August to early September, this arts festival features chamber music, jazz, theatre, opera and more.

Baltic Herring Market (www.portofhelsinki.fi) In the first week of October fisherfolk and chefs gather at kauppatori to cook the time-honoured fish.

SLEEPING

Bookings are advisable from mid-May to mid-August, although July is often a quiet time for midrange and top-end hotels.

Budget

Rastila Camping (☎ 0310 78517; Karavaanikatu 4; tent sites €13-15, 2-person cabins €38-45, 4-person cabins 53-64, cottages with/without sauna €165/100; P 🖳) Only 20 minutes on the metro from the heart of town, in a pretty waterside location, this camping ground makes sense. As well as tent and van sites, there are wooden cabins and more upmarket log cottages. There are all sorts of facilities including rowboat and canoe hire.

ourpick Hostel Academica (☎ 1311 4334; www .hostelacademica.fi; Hietaniemenkatu 14; dm €18, standard s/d up to €40/60, modern s/d up to €55/75; 🕙 Jun-Aug; P 🖳 🤶 🐾) Finnish students live well, so in summer take advantage of this residence, a super-clean spot packed with features (pool and sauna) and cheery staff. Traditional rooms are older, but still have great additions like bar fridges and own bathrooms. Dorms have only four bunks so even cheapest rooms feel uncrowded. They're also environmentally sound, offsetting all their carbon emissions among other positive steps. HI discounts are available.

Hostel Erottajanpuisto (☎ 642 169; www.erottajan puisto.com; Uudenmaankatu 9; dm €23.50, s/d/tr €49/68/81; 🖳) Helsinki's smallest and most laid-back hostel occupies the top floor of a building in a lively street of bars and restaurants close to the heart of the city. Forget curfews, lockouts, school kids and bringing your own sleeping sheet – this is more like a guesthouse with (crowded) dormitories. Private rooms offer more peace.

Eurohostel (☎ 622 0470; www.eurohostel.fi; Linnankatu 9; dm €22-24, s €38-44, d €43-55; 🖳) On Katajanokka island less than 500m from the Viking Line terminal, this HI-affiliate is busy but a bit soulless and offers both backpacker and 'hotel' rooms. Both share common bathrooms. The small cafe serves a breakfast buffet (€7) and other meals, and there's a morning sauna included.

Also worth recommending:

Hostel Stadion (☎ 477 8480; www.stadionhostel.com; Pohjoinen Stadiontie 3; dm/s/d €19/38/47; 🕙 reception 7-2am, 7-3am in summer; P 🖳) An easy tram ride from town, this HI hostel is actually part of the Olympic Stadium. There are no views though, and it feels old-style with big dorms and shared showers.

Hostel Satakuntatalo (☎ 6958 5233; Lapinrinne 1A; dm €20, s/d €41/60; 🕙 Jun-Aug; P 🖳) Handy for the bus station, this large place includes a good cafe that does a breakfast buffet. All rooms include desk, fridge and student-dorm vibe.

Midrange

Hotelli Finn (☎ 684 4360; www.hotellifinn.fi; Kalevankatu 3B; s/d with toilet €65/75, with toilet & shower €65/80; 🤶) Although not flash, this small, friendly hotel on the top floor of a central city building offers very reasonable rates for the location. Rooms are compact but tidy, with TV.

Omenahotelli (☎ 0600 18018; www.omena.com; r €90) Eerikinkatu (Eerikinkatu 24); Lönnrotinkatu (Lönnrotinkatu 13) This good-value staffless hotel chain has two handy Helsinki locations. As well as a double bed, rooms have a fold-out sofa that can sleep two more, plus there's a microwave and minifridge. Book online or via a terminal in the lobby.

Hotel Arthur (☎ 173 441; www.hotelarthur.fi; Vuorikatu 19; s/d €104/124, weekends €78/94; P 🤶 ♿) Close to the train station, Arthur is small enough to feel you're getting some personal attention but big enough to have all the mod cons, with pleasant decor, spacious rooms, satellite TV and a good restaurant.

Hotelli Helka (☎ 613 580; www.helka.fi; Pohjoinen Rautatiekatu 23A; s/d €136/171, weekends & summer €90/112; P 🖳 🤶 ♿) A substantial renovation has made this a hip hotel with rooms decked out in chocolate browns and wheaty shades. Every room has a print of an autumn forest that hangs over it and is backlit to give rooms a moody glow – daunting but delicious. You can often bag cheap deals here on discount hotel websites. Bikes are for hire at €15 per day.

Stay At Parliament (☎ 251 1050; www.accome.com; Museokatu 18; studio apt from €137/155, summer €79/89; 🕙 reception 8am-8pm Mon-Fri; 🖳 🤶) A step up in style and comfort from many hotels, the apartments here have sleek modern furnishings, kitchenette, internet connections and cable TV. Prices vary seasonally and there are discounts for longer stays. In a great location.

Top End

Helsinki has plenty of big, central business hotels, including the Sokos, Radisson, Scandic and Cumulus chains.

Scandic Grand Marina (☎ 16661; www.scandic -hotels.com; Katajanokanlaituri 7; s/d from €142/181, weekends €95/105, summer r minimum 2 nights €81-91; P 🖳 🤶 ♿) In a converted brick harbour warehouse near the Viking Line terminal on Katajanokka, the Grand Marina is an outstanding hotel with one of Helsinki's best outlooks. Facilities are top notch, with spacious, refurbished rooms, a business centre, a gym and the excellent Makasiini restaurant and bar.

Klaus K (☎ 020 770 4700; www.klauskhotel.com; Bulevardi 2, Helsinki; s/d from €140/180; 🖳 🛜) Easily the slickest of the new generation of design hotels, this snazzy spot has Kalevala quotes woven into the gold walls of the lobby with the thread running a framed verse in every room. It's distinctly Finnish, with luxurious toiletries, space-conscious architecture and sauna-style bathroom ceilings. But there are worldly comforts like high-speed wi-fi and DVDs in all rooms, plus two good restaurants and frostily cool bar.

EATING

Helsinki has by far Finland's best range of Finnish and international cafes and restaurants. Seek out the lunchtime specials if your budget is tight – many restaurants (even the fancy ones) have buffet lunch deals for under €10. In summer, several island restaurants serve lavish plates of seafood.

Restaurants

Zucchini (☎ 622 2907; Fabianinkatu 4; lunch €6-9; 🕑 11am-4pm Mon-Fri) One of the city's few vegetarian eateries, this covers a lot of bases with friendliness and fresh baked quiches and piping hot soups. The sunny terrace out the back is stunning in summer.

Konstan Mölijä (☎ 694 7504; Hietalahdenkatu 14; lunch/dinner buffet €7.50/14; 🕑 11am-10pm Mon-Fri, 2-10pm Sat, dinner buffet from 4pm) You can almost smell the sea in the maritime interior of this old sailor's eatery. It's real working-man's food with a huge buffet that includes soup, salad, bread, meat (always reindeer) and vegetable dishes.

Bar Tapasta (☎ 640 724; Uudenmaankatu 13; tapas €3-5; 🕑 11am-midnight Mon-Thu, 11-2am Fri, 2pm-2am Sat) This is an intimate and welcoming bar with quirky Mediterranean decor, an elegant young crowd and friendly staff. The tapas are cheap and generous; there is also (how did you guess?) pasta, a selection of wines by the glass and popular sangría.

Namaskaar Bulevardi (☎ 6220 1155; Bulevardi 6; lunch €7.50-12, mains €12-18; 🕑 lunch & dinner) There are several branches of this Indian buffet throughout the city, but this is the

best with interesting, stylish decor and an excellent terrace.

Koto (☎ 646 080; www.ravintola-koto.fi; Kalevankatu 21; mains €10-16, lunch €9-15; 🕑 lunch & dinner Mon-Sat) It's blondewood zen at this Japanese joint that does sashimi, yakitori and brilliant sushi. Grab a takeaway pack and head for the park on a sunny summer afternoon.

Orchid Thai Restaurant (☎ 694 5491; Eerikinkatu 20; mains €9-15; 🕑 10.30am-10pm Mon-Fri, noon-10pm, 2-10pm Sun) This cheap and cheerful little spot does tasty Thai with scrumptious stir-fried duck alongside classics such as green curry and cashew-nut chicken.

Tori (☎ 6874 3790; Punavuorenkatu 2; breakfast €6-10, lunch special €8-9, dinner €9-14; 🕑 10am-10pm Mon-Fri, noon-10pm Sat, 2-11pm Sun) Buzzing with a bohemian crowd, this 1950s revival has a menu including beetroot and blue-cheese pasta or a reinvention of meatballs with a brandy sauce. Breakfast is a build-your-own adventure, while lunch sandwiches are good for the cash-strapped.

Seahorse ☎ 628 169; www.seahorse.fi; Kapteeninkatu 11; mains €12-21; 🕑 10.30am-midnight) Seahorse dates back to the '30s and is as traditional a Finnish restaurant as you'll find anywhere. Locals gather in the gloriously unchanged interior to meet and drink over hefty dishes of Baltic herring, Finnish meatballs and cabbage rolls.

our pick Kosmos (☎ 647 255; Kalevankatu 3; mains €15-25, menu €40; 🕑 11.30-1am Mon-Fri, 4pm-1am Sat, closed Jul) Designed by Alvar Aalto, this classical place could qualify as an institution on that fact alone, but the great formal service and reliably excellent food make it a real Helsinki redoubt. A Finnish antipasto plate (including smoked reindeer and Baltic herring) is the ideal start before moving on to meaty mains such as Russian chicken breast served with roe and sauerkraut or lamb kidneys with pilaf.

Lappi (☎ 645 550; Annankatu 22; mains €15-30; 🕑 noon-10.30pm Mon-Fri, 1-10.30pm Sat & Sun) Costumed staff serve up Sámi specialities in this delightfully rustic 'log cabin' restaurant. Try sirloin of elk, as well as various reindeer preparations, vendace (lake fish) and cloudberry desserts.

Nokka (☎ 6128 5600; Kanavaranta 7; mains €24-29, set menus €56-60; 🕑 dinner Mon-Sat, lunch Mon-Fri) Look out for the giant ship's propeller out the front of this distinctively Finnish place. Dishes use local cheeses and game, blended with berry wines to create Suomi sensations. Once a warehouse, the brickwork is warmed by rustic design and its wine cellar remains a highlight.

Boathouse (☎ 6227 1070; Liuskasaari; mains €26-31; ☺ dinner Mon-Sat, May-Sep) The most breezy and welcoming of the upmarket island restaurants, this circular two-deck affair is on Liuskasaari, with ferries from the jetty at Merisatamanranta. The restaurant does great seafood platters and tuna steaks. Instead of a guestbook, visitors pin notes to the lobby's chandelier.

Chez Dominique (☎ 612 7393; www.chezdominique.fi; Rikhardinkatu 4; mains €45-50, set menus €99-139; ☺ lunch & dinner Tue-Fri, dinner Sat, closed Jul) Helsinki's best French restaurant has moved to a larger location but has maintained its pair of Michelin stars. Their menu sticks to French classics such as Dover sole and Anjou pigeon with Finnish flourishes including set menus (from four to nine courses) that include a divine *pulla*.

Cafes

Tamminiementien Kahvila (☎ 481 003; Tamminiementie 8; ☺ noon-10.30pm summer, shorter hours in winter) This memorable cafe is near the Urho Kekkonen Museum in lovely parkland. It's like a cross between a Chekhov play and a flower-loving granny's country cottage and is utterly curious and charming. Catch tram 4 or bus 24 for this beauty.

Café Strindberg (☎ 681 2030; Pohjoisesplanadi 33; ☺ 9am-10pm Mon-Sat, 10am-10pm Sun) This upmarket cafe is a classic place to see and be seen on the Esplanad, with a terrace whose waiter-served seats are much in demand. There's a sumptuous lounge and classy bistro upstairs too.

Fazer (☎ 6159 2959; Kluuvikatu 3; sandwiches & pies €7-10; ☺ 7.30am-10pm Mon-Fri, 9am-10pm Sat) Another historical cafe worth delving into, this is a huge space with plenty of character, classic decor and a small terrace. Founded in 1891 by the Finnish confectionary-making family (you'll see Fazer sweets and chocolate everywhere), it does amazing ice-cream sundaes and also sells cakes and tea to take away.

Café Ekberg (☎ 6811 8660; Bulevardi 9; buffet breakfast & lunch €9; ☺ 7.30am-7pm Mon-Fri, 8.30am-5pm Sat, 10am-5pm Sun) There's been a cafe of this name in Helsinki since 1861 and today it continues to be a family-run place renowned for its pastries such as the Napoleon cake. Their buffet breakfasts and lunches are also popular, plus there's fresh bread to takeaway.

Café Engel (☎ 652 776; Senaatintori; meals €10-18; ☺ 8am-10pm Mon-Fri, 9am-10pm Sat, 10am-10pm Sun) Named for the cathedral's architect, this Senaatintori spot hums with tourists and students alike. There's always a good selection of cakes and enticing meals, often of a vegetarian bent. It's a cultural hub with films shown in the courtyard during summer, irregular piano recitals and a plump English-language magazine selection.

Quick Eats & Self-Catering

In summer there are food stalls, fresh produce and expensive berries at the kauppatori, but the real picnic treats are in the fabulous **Vanha Kauppahalli** (Old Market Hall; Eteläranta 1; ☺ 6.30am-6pm Mon-Fri, 6.30am-4pm Sat, 10am-4pm Sun summer only) nearby, where you can get filled rolls, cheese, breads, fish and an array of Finnish snacks and delicacies (plus there's a small Alko). **Hakaniemi kauppahalli** (☺ 8am-6pm Mon-Fri, 8am-4pm Sat), the traditional market hall by Hakaniemi metro station, is less visited by tourists. Here you'll find **Soppakeittiö** (little soup kitchen; soups €5-8; ☺ 10.30am-4pm Mon-Fri, 10.30am-3pm Sat), a great place to warm the cockles in winter.

For everything from Asian noodles to burgers and kebabs, head to the food court in the basement of the **Forum shopping centre** (Mannerheimintie 20), where you'll also find a supermarket and Alko store.

DRINKING

Helsinki has some of Scandinavia's most diverse nightlife. In winter locals gather in cosy bars, while in summer, early-opening beer terraces sprout all over town.

The centre's full of bars and clubs, with the Punavuori area around Iso-Roobertinkatu one of the most worthwhile for trendy alternative choices. For the cheapest beer in Helsinki (from €2 for a pint during the seemingly perpetual happy hours), hit working-class Kallio (near Sörnäinen metro station), north of the centre. There's a string of earthy local pubs along Helsinginkatu, such as grungy local favourite **Roskapankki** (☎ 735 488; Helsingkatu 20) – whose name means 'trash bank' – and a growing number of trendy bars and cafes.

Ateljee Bar (Sokos Hotel Torni, Yrjönkatu 26; ☺ 2pm-2am Mon-Thu, noon-2am Fri & Sat, 2pm-1am Sun) It's worth the climb up to this tiny perch on the roof of the Sokos Hotel Torni for the city panorama. Taking the lift to the 12th floor is the best option, then there's a narrow winding staircase to the top. Downstairs, the courtyard Tornin Piha is a cute little terrace with good wines by the glass. The rooftop bars of the

Palace and the Sokos Vaakuna hotels are also notable for their great views.

Arctic Icebar (☎ 278 1855; Yliopistonkatu 5, above La Bodega; admission €10; ☽ 10pm-4am Wed-Sat) Not cold enough outside? Then try this bar, which is literally carved out of ice. It's -5°C so you'll need the furry cape they loan you on entry, and the complimentary warming drink included in the price. There's an age minimum of 24. It's above La Bodega.

Corona Bar & Kafe Moskova (☎ 611 200; Eerikinkatu 11-15; ☽ bar 11-2am, cafe 6pm-2am) Those offbeat film-making Kaurismäki brothers are up to their old tricks with this pair of conjoined drinking dens. Corona plays the relative straight man with pool-tables and cheap beer, while Moskova is back in the USSR with a bubbling samovar and Soviet vinyl. At closing they clear the place out by playing Brezhnev speeches. But wait there's more: Dubrovnik, in the same complex, does regular live jazz.

Hola (☎ 694 8983; Helsinginkatu 13; ☽ noon-2am; 🖳) This retro cafe-bar is part of the new look of the once grungy Kallio district. Loungy, worn furniture, retro art on the walls and chilled music make this a popular hang-out with students and a young crowd.

Pub Tram Spårakoff (☎ 123 4800; tickets €8.50, beers €5; ☽ departs hourly 2-3pm and 5-8pm, Tue-Sat mid-May–mid-Aug) Not sure whether to go sightseeing or booze the day away? Do both in this bright-red pub tram, the tipsy alternative to traditional tours around town. There are cheaper places to drink but the trundle of the tram past Helsinki's major landmarks makes for an enjoyable evening. Departs from Mikonkatu, east of train station.

Zetor (☎ 010 766 4450; www.ravintolazetor.fi; Mannerheimintie 3-5; mains €10-22; ☽ 11-4am Sat, 3pm-1am Sun & Mon, 3pm-3am Tue, 3pm-4am Wed & Thu) A fun Finnish restaurant and pub with deeply ironic tractor decor. It's owned by filmmaker Aki Kaurismäki and designed by the Leningrad Cowboys. It's worth going in just for a drink and a ride on a tractor, but the food is decent value too.

Vltava (☎ 766 3650; Elielinaukio 2; bar meals €8-12; ☽ 11-3am or later) Right by the train station, this Czech pub has an excellent terrace, tasty beers, hearty food to soak it up, and classier upstairs bistro seating.

Kappeli (☎ 681 244; Eteläesplanadi 1; ☽ 10am-midnight Mon-Sat, 10am-11pm Sun) In the middle of the park near the kauppatori, this has one of the most popular summer terraces, facing a stage where various bands and musicians regularly play in summer. Inside, there's a vaulted cellar bar, which is fantastic later in the evening or when the sun's not shining. There are also restaurant and cafe sections.

ENTERTAINMENT
Cinemas

Cinemas in Helsinki show original-version films with Finnish and Swedish subtitles.

Kino Engel (☎ 020-155801; www.cinemamondo.fi; Sofiankatu 4; adults €9) This independent theatre shows art-house and Finnish indie film.

Orion Theatre (☎ 6154 0201; www.kava.fi; Eerikinkatu 15; tickets €5; ☽ screenings Tue-Sun) This classic cinema shows classics from the Finnish Film Archive. You need to purchase an annual membership as well as a ticket for the first entry.

FinnKino (☎ 0600 007 007; www.finnkino.fi; adult €9) Operates several Helsinki cinemas with big-name films.

Tennispalatsi (Salomonkatu 15)

Maxim (Kluuvikatu 1)

Gay & Lesbian Venues

Helsinki has a low-key but solid gay scene.

Lost & Found (☎ 680 1010; www.lostandfound.fi; Annankatu 6; ☽ to 4am) This sophisticated gay-hetero bar is still a hugely popular late-night hang-out with people of all persuasions. Head downstairs to the grotto-like dance floor and wait for your favourite chart hits to spin.

Room Albert (☎ 643 626; Kalevankatu 36; www.room bar.fi; ☽ 2pm-2am) A slick bar for gay men, with laid-back tunes.

DTM (☎ 676 315; www.dtm.fi; Iso Roobertinkatu 28; admission €2-10, cafe free; ☽ 9am-4am Mon-Sat, noon-4am Sun; 🖳) Scandinavia's biggest gay club (Don't Tell Mum) is a multilevel complex with an early-opening cafe-bar. There are a couple of dance floors with regular club nights as well as drag shows or women-only sessions.

Live Music

Various bars and clubs around Helsinki host live bands. Big-name rock concerts and international acts often perform at Hartwall Arena (see p154).

Tavastia & Semifinal (☎ 694 8511; www.tavastiak lubi.fi; Urho Kekkosenkatu 4; tickets from €10; ☽ 9pm-late) There's always something happening at Finland's biggest rock-music club. Live bands, including international acts, hit the stage at this hangar-sized venue. Also check out what's on at Semifinal, the smaller venue next door.

Storyville (☎ 408 007; www.storyville.fi; Museokatu 8; 6pm-4am Mon-Sat) Helsinki's number-one jazz club attracts a refined older crowd swinging to boogie-woogie, trad jazz, Dixieland and New Orleans most nights. There's a cool outside-terrace in summer.

Juttutupa (☎ 742 4240; Säästöpankinranta 6) This imposing stone building near Hakaniemi metro is one of Helsinki's top live music bars, focusing on contemporary jazz and rock fusion. The best day is Wednesday, when there's nearly always a high-quality jazz act.

Nightclubs

Helsinki has a dynamic club scene; some nights have age limits (often over 20).

LUX (☎ 020 775 9350; www.luxnightclub.fi; Urho Kekkosen katu 1A; door charge €5-10; 10pm-4am Wed-Sat) Ascend into clubbing heaven at this super-slick club with stellar lighting, Kamppi-top views and high-altitude cocktails. Music runs from sexy lounge to sweaty funk with local DJs and international visitors. Entrance via Kamppi Square.

Redrum (☎ 045 6355 450; www.redrum.fi; Vuorikatu 2; admission €3-10; nightly from 8pm) The wood-panelled interior is drenched in red lighting and a murderous sound system that pushes out house, hip-hop and even spacy disco. Sunday is a chill-down with reggae but most nights have good dancing.

Kuudes Linja (☎ 045 1111 466; www.kuudeslinja .com; Hämeentie 13; tickets €8-12; 9pm-3am Sun & Tue-Thu, 10pm-4am Fri & Sat) A little further out than most, this is the place to find Helsinki's more experimental beats from top visiting DJs playing techno, industrial, post-rock and electro. There are also live gigs.

Teatteri (☎ 681 1130; Pohjoisesplanadi 2) In a stylish former Swedish theatre, this club has three floors of fun, from the sophisticated Long bar, with its modernist paintings and web-spun light fixtures, to the summer-swelling terraces. It's got an older more relaxed crowd and can be packed on weekends.

Sport

If you're around between September and April, take the opportunity to see a major ice hockey game. Big matches are played at the huge **Hartwall Arena** (☎ 0600 10800; www.hartwall -areena.com; Areenakuja 1) in Pasila, north of the centre (tram 7A or 7B). The stadium is home

to Helsinki superleague side Jokerit. Tickets cost €15 to €35.

Theatre & Concerts

For concerts and performances, see *Helsinki This Week*, inquire at the tourist office, or check the website of ticket outlet **Lippupiste** (☎ 0600 900 900; www.lippu.fi). Opera, ballet and classical concerts are held at the **Oopperatalo** (Opera House; ☎ 4030 2211; Helsinginkatu 58; tickets from €15), while performances by the Finnish National Theatre are at the **Kansallis Teatteri** (☎ 1733 1331; www.kansallisteatteri.fi; Läntinen teatterikuja 1), near the train station.

SHOPPING

Known for design and art, Helsinki is an epicentre of Nordic cool from fashion to the latest furniture and homewares. The central but touristy Esplanadi has the chic boutiques of Finnish classics like Marimekko, Stockmann, Aarikka and Artek. The hippest area is definitely Punavuori, which has several good boutiques and art galleries to explore.

For design, you can get some good pointers from **Design Forum Finland** (☎ 6220 810; www.design-forum.fi; Erottajankatu 7 10am-7pm Mon-Fri, 10am-6pm Sat, noon-6pm Sun), which operates a shop that hosts many designers' work. You're often better off price-wise to hunt down your own bargains though. **Design District Helsinki** (www .designdistrict.fi) is a loose confederation of innovative design shops spread through the central area, particularly between Esplanadi and Punavuori. Keep an eye out for the black-and-white sticker in the window of these places.

GETTING THERE & AWAY
Air

There are direct flights to Helsinki from many major European cities and several international ones. See p208 for details. The airport is at Vantaa, 19km north of Helsinki.

Finnair (☎ 0600 140140; www.finnair.fi; Asema-aukio 3; 8am-8pm Mon-Fri, 10am-5pm Sat) and its cheaper partner **Finncomm** (www.fc.fi) fly to 20 Finnish cities, usually at least once per day. **Blue1** (☎ 0600 25831; www.blue1.com) has budget flights to a handful of major Finnish destinations.

Boat

International ferries travel to Stockholm (Sweden), Tallinn (Estonia), Travemünde and

Rostock (Germany). There is also a regular catamaran and hydrofoil service to Tallinn. See p210 for more details.

There are five main terminals, four close to the centre: Kanava and Katajanokka terminals are served by bus 13 and trams 2, 2V and 4, and Olympia and Makasiini terminals by trams 3B and 3T. The last terminal, Länsiterminaali (West Terminal), is served by bus 15.

Ferry tickets may be purchased at the terminal, from a ferry company's office (and often its website) or (in some cases) from the city tourist office. Book in advance during the high season (late June to mid-August).

Bus

Regional and long-distance buses dock at underground **Kamppi Bus Terminal** (www.matka huolto.fi; ⊗ 24hr, tickets 7am-7pm Mon-Fri, 7am-5pm Sat, 9am-6pm Sun), below the Kamppi Centre off Salomonkatu or Frederikinkatu. There are services to Tampere (€28.20, 2½ hours), Turku (€25.70, 2½ hours), Savonlinna (€46.30, 5½ hours) and Kuopio (€50.90, seven hours). You can always buy your ticket on the bus.

Train

Helsinki's **train station** (rautatieasema; ☎ 0600 41902; ⊗ 24hr, tickets 6.30am-9.30pm) is central and easy to find your way around. It's linked by subway to the metro (Rautatientori stop), and is a short walk from the bus station.

The train is the fastest and cheapest way to get from Helsinki to major centres: express trains run daily to Turku, Tampere, Kuopio and Lappeenranta among others, and there's a choice of day and overnight trains to Oulu, Rovaniemi and Joensuu. There are also daily trains (buy tickets from the international counter) to the Russian cities of Vyborg, St Petersburg and Moscow.

GETTING AROUND
To/From the Airport

Bus 615 (€3.40, 40 to 50 minutes, 5am to midnight) shuttles between Vantaa airport and Rautatientori next to the main train station. Bus stops are marked with a blue sign featuring a plane. Faster Finnair buses (€5.90, 30 minutes, every 20 minutes, 5am to midnight) also depart from the railway station, stopping a couple of times en route.

There are also door-to-door **airport taxis** (☎ 0600 555 555; www.airporttaxi.fi), which need to be booked the previous day before 6pm, if you're leaving Helsinki (one to two people €25).

Bicycle

Helsinki is ideal for cycling: the small inner city area is flat, and there are well-marked and high-quality bicycle paths. Pick up a copy of the *Helsinki Cycling Map* from the tourist office.

There are free City Bikes at stands around the centre. Deposit a €2 coin into the stand that locks them, then reclaim it when you return the bike to any stand. For something more sophisticated, **Greenbike** (☎ 8502 2850; www.greenbike.fi; Fredrikinkatu 31; bikes per day/24hr/week from €15/20/60; ⊗ 10am-6pm Mon-Fri, 10am-3pm Sat, 10am-2pm Sun) rents out quality bikes including 24-speed hybrid mountain bikes.

Local Transport

The city's public transport system, **HKL** (☎ 310 1071; www.hkl.fi) operates buses, metro and local trains, trams and a ferry to Suomenlinna. A one-hour flat-fare ticket for any HKL transport costs €2.20 when purchased on board, €2 when purchased in advance. The ticket allows unlimited transfers but must be validated in the stamping machine on board when you first use it. A single tram ticket (take tram 3T for a good sightseeing circuit) is €2 full fare. Tourist tickets (€6 per day, €12/18 per three/five days) are the best option if you're in town for a short period of time. The Helsinki Card gives you free travel anywhere within Helsinki (see p144).

HKL offices (⊗ 7.30am-7pm Mon-Thu, 7.30am-5pm Fri, 10am-3pm Sat) at the Kamppi bus station and the Rautatientori and Hakaniemi metro stations sell tickets and passes, as do many of the city's R-kioskis. The *Helsinki Route Map*, available at HKL offices and the city tourist office, is an easily understood map of the bus, metro and tram routes.

If you're heading to Vantaa or Espoo, you'll need a more expensive regional ticket.

AROUND HELSINKI
Porvoo

☎ 019 / pop 47,832

A great day trip from Helsinki, charming medieval Porvoo is Finland's second-oldest town (founded in 1346). There are three distinct sections to the city: the Old Town, the new town and the 19th-century Empire quarter, built Russian-style under the rule of Tsar Nicholas I of Russia. The **Old Town**, with its tightly clustered wooden houses, cobbled streets and riverfront setting, is one of the most picturesque in Finland. During the day, its craft shops are bustling with visitors; if you can stay the night, you'll have it more or less to yourself. The old painted buildings are spectacular in the setting sun.

The **tourist office** (☎ 520 2316; www.porvoo.fi; Rihkamakatu 4; ☺ 9am-6pm Mon-Fri, 10am-4pm Sat & Sun early Jun-Aug, 9.30am-4.30pm Mon-Fri, 10am-2pm Sat Sep-early Jun), on the southern edge the Old Town, has plenty of information and a free internet terminal.

SIGHTS

The historic stone-and-timber **Tuomiokirkko** (cathedral; ☎ 66111; ☺ 10am-6pm Mon-Fri, 10am-2pm Sat, 2-5pm Sun May-Sep, 10am-2pm Tue-Sat, 2-4pm Sun Oct-Apr) sits atop a hill looking over the quaint Old Town. Vandalised by fire in 2006, it was being gradually renovated at the time of research but had re-opened to visitors. **Porvoo Museum** (☎ 574 7500; www.porvoonmuseo.fi; Vanha Raatihuoneentori; combined admission adult/child €5/1; ☺ 10am-4pm Mon-Sat, 11am-4pm Sun May-Aug, noon-4pm Wed-Sun Sep-Apr) is in two adjacent buildings on the beautiful cobbled Old Town Hall Square. Crossing the old bridge to the west bank of the Porvoonjoki provides a fantastic view of the photogenic, rust-red **shore houses** lining the river bank. These houses were first painted with red ochre to impress the visiting King of Sweden, Gustavus III, in the late 18th century.

On the south side of Porvoo in the Russian-built 19th-century Empire quarter, is **Runeberg House** (☎ 581 330; Aleksanterinkatu 3; admission both museums €6; ☺ 10am-4pm Mon-Sat, 11am-5pm Sun May-Aug, closed Mon & Tue Sep-Apr), the well-preserved, beautiful home of Finland's national poet JL Runeberg. The adjacent **Walter Runeberg Sculpture Museum**, containing 150 sculptures by the poet's son, can be visited on the same ticket.

SLEEPING & EATING

Although there are plenty of places to eat in the new part of town, especially around the kauppatori, Porvoo's most atmospheric cafes, restaurants and bars are in the Old Town and along the riverfront.

Porvoon Retkeilymaja (☎ 523 0012; http://personal .inet.fi/yritys/porvoohostel/; Linnankoskenkatu 1-3; dm/s/d €16/29/38; ☺ check-in 4-7pm; **P**) A 10-minute walk southeast of the Old Town, this historic wooden house holds a well-kept hostel in a grassy garden. It's a bit old school but it's the cheapest bed in town. There's a great indoor pool and sauna complex over the road.

Gasthaus Werneri (☎ 0400 494 876; www.werneri .net, in Finnish; Adlercreutzinkatu 29; s/d/tr €35/50/75) This cosy family-run guesthouse, located about 1km east of the Old Town, is excellent value with just five rooms (with shared bathrooms) and a self-contained apartment.

Hotelli Onni (☎ 050 525 6446; www.hotelonni.fi; Kirkkotori 3; s/d €150/180; ☺) Right opposite the cathedral, this gold-coloured wooden building couldn't be better placed. There's a real range here, from the four-poster bed and slick design of the Funk to the rustic single Peasant. Breakfast is downstairs in the terraced cafe that serves as a popular coffee shop.

Restaurant Timbaali (☎ 523 1020; www.timbaali .com; Välikatu 8; mains €19-26, snails per half-dozen €10.50-13; ☺ 11am-11pm daily May-Aug, 11am-6pm Sun Sep-Apr) In the heart of the Old Town, this rustic restaurant is all about escargot – the speciality is locally farmed snails prepared in a variety of innovative ways. There's also a broad menu of gourmet Finnish cuisine, served in quaint dining rooms or the inner courtyard.

Porvoon Paahtimo (☎ 617 040; Mannerheiminkatu 2; ☺ noon-10pm Mon-Thu, noon-2am Fri, 11-2am Sat, noon-10pm Sun) Right at the main bridge and with a great little terrace hanging over the water, this atmospheric red-brick former storehouse is part cosy bar and part cafe; fresh coffee is roasted here. There's a terrace and boat, which come with blankets on cooler evenings.

GETTING THERE & AWAY

The bus station is on the kauppatori; buses run every half-hour between Porvoo and Helsinki (€10.30, one hour), but the best way to reach Porvoo in summer is by boat.

The historic steamship **JL Runeberg** (☎ 524 3331; www.msjlruneberg.fi) sails daily, except Thursday, from Helsinki (one way/return €22/33) in summer (exact dates vary). The trip takes four hours each way, so you may prefer to return by bus or, on Saturday only, on the vintage diesel train (combined ferry and train ticket €29).

Royal Line (☎ 020 711 8333; www.royalline.fi) is a speedier alternative, zipping through the river and archipelago from Helsinki kauppatori.

SOUTH COAST

The south coast of Finland meanders east and west of Helsinki, revealing harbour towns, marinas, islands and farmland. This is something of a summer playground for Finnish families, with a handful of fading resort towns and the pretty bays, beaches and convoluted islands and waterways of the southern archipelago. Medieval churches, old manors and castles show the strong influence of early Swedish settlers, and Swedish is still a majority language in some of the coastal towns.

TURKU

☎ 02 / pop 175,286

Turku is Finland's oldest town, but today it's a modern maritime city, brimming with museums and boasting a robust harbourside castle and magnificent cathedral. Its heart and soul is the lovely Aurajoki, a broad ribbon spilling into the Baltic Sea harbour and lined with riverboat bars and restaurants.

For travellers, Turku is one of Finland's most visited cities after Helsinki, thanks to the direct ferries from Stockholm, and this is the place to jump out to the Åland islands, head up the west coast, or explore the southwestern archipelago.

Once the capital under the Swedes, Turku (Swedish: Åbo) was founded in 1229, and grew into an important trading centre despite being ravaged by fire many times. In 2011 it's due to shine again as one of the EU's Capitals of Culture (www.turku2011.fi).

Information

Forex (☎ 751 2650; www.forex.fi; Eerikinkatu 23 & 12; 8am-7pm Mon-Fri, 9am-3pm Sat) The best places to change cash and travellers cheques.

Hansa CyberCafé (Hansa Arcade; per hr €2.40; 9am-9pm Mon-Fri, 10am-9pm Sat & Sun) Coin-op internet.

Public Library (☎ 262 3611; Linnankatu 2; 11am-8pm Mon-Thu, 11am-6pm Fri, 11am-4pm Sat) Free internet terminals (15-minute maximum).

Turku Card (24/48hr €21/28) Gives free admission to most museums and attractions in the region, free public transport, and various other discounts. Available from the tourist office or any participating attraction.

Turku City Tourist Office (☎ 262 7444; www.turkutouring.fi; Aurakatu 4; bike hire per day €15, internet per hr €5; 8.30am-6pm Mon-Fri, 9am-4pm Sat & Sun, 10am-3pm winter weekends) Busy, very helpful and with information on the entire region. Rents bikes; has free brief internet access.

Sights & Activities

A great way to soak up Turku's summertime vibe is simply to walk or cycle along the riverbank between the cathedral and the castle, crossing via bridges or the much-loved local pedestrian ferry *(föri)* – pick up a walking-tour brochure from the tourist office.

A visit to lofty **Turku Castle** (Turun Linna; ☎ 262 0300; admission €7, guided tours €2; 10am-6pm daily mid-Apr–mid-Sep, 10am-3pm Tue-Sun mid-Sep–mid-Apr), near the harbour, should be your first stop. Founded in 1280 at the mouth of the Aurajoki, the castle has been rebuilt a number of times since. Notable occupants have included Count Per Brahe, founder of many towns in Finland, and Sweden's King Eric XIV, who was imprisoned in the castle's Round Tower in the late 16th century, having been declared insane. Guided tours of the stronghold area are available in English with advance notice, or daily at midday in June, but do not include the Renaissance rooms on the upper floor, or the extensive museums in the bailey section of the castle, so allow time to explore those yourself.

The open-air **Luostarinmäki Handicrafts Museum** (☎ 262 0350; admission €5; 10am-6pm daily mid-Apr–mid-Sep, 10am-3pm Tue-Sun mid-Sep–mid-Apr), in the only surviving 18th-century area of this medieval town, is one of the best of its kind in Finland and much more intriguing than the name suggests – it's a Turku must-see. In summer artisans work inside its 40 old wooden houses, and musicians stroll its paths.

Forum Marinum (☎ 282 9511; www.forum-marinum.fi; Linnankatu 72; admission €7, with museum ships €12; 11am-7pm daily May-Sep, 10am-6pm Tue-Sun Oct-Apr) is an impressive maritime museum near Turku Castle. As well as a nautically crammed exhibition space devoted to Turku's shipping background, it incorporates a fleet of **museum ships** including the mine layer **Keihässalmi**, the three-masted barque **Sigyn** and the impressive 1902 sailing ship **Suomen Joutsen** (Swan of Finland). The ships can be visited independently of the museum (adult/child €5/3).

Aboa Vetus & Ars Nova (☎ 250 0552; www.aboavetusarsnova.fi; Itäinen Rantakatu 4-6; admission €8; 11am-7pm, closed Mon mid-Sep–Mar, English-language tour 11.30am daily Jul-Aug) are two museums under one roof. Aboa Vetus is an absolutely fascinating museum of live archaeology. You descend

TURKU

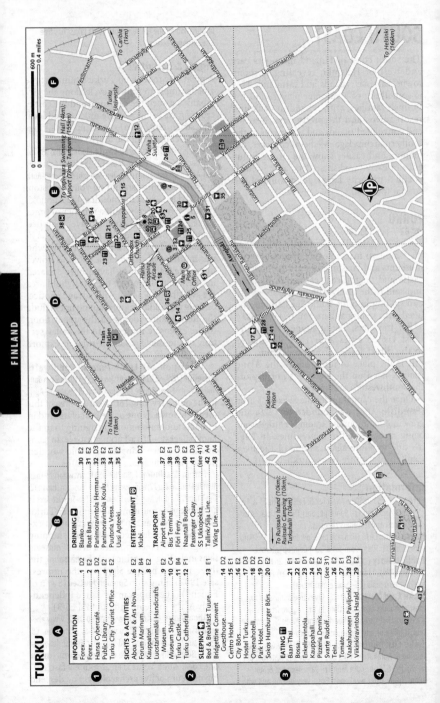

FINLAND

into the comprehensively excavated remains of medieval Turku; these are brought to life by lively commentary, plenty of info and activities for kids, and replica items that make sense of the fragments. Ars Nova is a museum of contemporary art with temporary exhibitions, the highlight of which is the Turku Biennaali, held in summer in odd years.

Commanding **Turku Cathedral** (9am-7pm mid-Sep–mid-Apr, 9am-8pm mid-Apr–mid-Sep), dating from the 13th century, is the national shrine and 'mother church' of the Lutheran Church of Finland. In the south gallery of the cathedral is a small **museum** (adult/child €2/1) containing church relics and artworks.

Archipelago cruises are popular in summer, with daily departures from Martinsilta bridge at the passenger quay. The best option is the two-hour cruise out to Naantali aboard the steamship **SS Ukkopekka** (515 3300; www.ukkopekka.fi; one way/return €20/25, 9.30am, 2pm & 7pm early Jun-late Aug). The same boat also has an evening dinner cruise with buffet meal on Loistokari island from €41 to €48.

Festivals & Events

Big events on the Turku calendar include the **Turku Music Festival** (www.tmj.fi) in the second week in August and **Ruisrock** (www.ruisrock.fi), held on Ruissalo island in early July.

Sleeping

Ruissalo Camping (262 5100; camp sites €10, plus per person €4, 2-/4-person r €35/60; Jun-Aug) On Ruissalo island, 10km west of the city centre, this camping ground has lots of room for tents and a few cabins along with saunas, a cafeteria and nice beaches. It's the bunkhouse for Ruisrock so expect it to be booked out then. Bus 8 runs from the kauppatori to the camping ground.

Hostel Turku (262 7680; www.turku.fi/hostelturku; Linnankatu 39; dm/s/tw €16/36/42; reception 6-10am & 3pm-midnight;) Well located on the river close to the town centre, this is a neat place with good lockers, spacious dorms (no more than four bunks) and a minifridge in each room. There's also bike hire and a speedy internet cafe.

Bed & Breakfast Tuure (233 0230; www.netti.fi/~tuure2; Tuureporinkatu 17C; s/d €37/50;) Very handy for the bus station, and close to the market square, this tidy and friendly guesthouse makes an excellent place to stay. The rooms are bright and thoughtfully decorated, you get your own keys, and there's a microwave, a fridge and free internet use for guests.

Omenahotelli (www.omenahotelli.fi; Humalistonkatu 7; r€63;) This larger hotel, part of a chain that takes internet bookings, is in a refurbished Alvar Aalto–designed building. Still it represents the usual excellent value of the 'apple hotels' with spaces that can sleep up to four (lower digits are closer to the lifts in a warren of rooms). You can also book via the lobby terminal.

Bridgettine Convent Guesthouse (250 1910; birgitta.turku@kolumbus.fi; Ursininkatu 15A; s/d €45/65;) This clean, simple B&B guesthouse, run by the nuns of a Catholic convent, is a haven of peace, without being too officious – silence is expected around the corridors and reception areas after 10pm.

Centro Hotel (469 0469; www.centrohotel.com; Yliopistonkatu 12; s/d €96/106, Sat, Sun & summer €72/85;) Central but far enough from the raucous kauppatori to still be quiet, this place has a good balance. Attentive service always feels friendly, and blondewood rooms are a good compromise between size and price, with superiors that have a more designer feel. The breakfast buffet has fresh pastries and a varied spread that's worth getting out of bed for.

Park Hotel (273 2555; www.parkhotelturku.fi; Rauhankatu 1; s/d €120/150, weekend & summer €95/125;) This Art Nouveau house is a genuine character right down to Jaakko, the parrot that squawks a welcome when you check in. Rooms themselves are lavishly decorated in individual styles and the other facilities, such as a pool table, fireplace-warmed drawing room and breakfast make for a great stay.

Sokos Hamburger Börs (337 381; www.sokoshotels.fi; Kauppiaskatu 6; City Börs s/d €89/104, main hotel s/d €106/146, weekend & summer €71/94;) Towering over the market square, this is the town's biggest hotel. The City Börs option is across the road and has simpler, cheaper rooms. The main hotel comes with the lot: free sauna, flatscreen TVs and tastefully decorated rooms with solid doors that could take a battering ram. The included breakfast is extensive and includes a Japanese option.

Eating

There are plenty of cheap eateries on and around Turku's bustling central kauppatori. The **kauppahalli** (Eerikinkatu 16; 7am-5.30pm Mon-Fri, 7am-3pm Sat) is packed with produce, a sushi bar and a cool cafe in a converted train carriage.

FINLAND

Vaakahuoneen Paviljonki (☎ 515 3324; Linnankatu 38; mains €8-18, fish buffet €9; ⏲ food served 11am-10pm May-Aug) This riverfront jazz restaurant is the place to go for great-value food and entertainment in summer. As well as an à la carte menu there's a daily 'archipelago fish buffet' (June to August), plus a changing ethnic buffet such as Thai, Vietnamese and Indian, all served to foot-tapping live trad-jazz bands.

Enkeliravintola (☎ 231 8088; Kauppiaskatu 16; mains €15-26; ⏲ dinner Tue-Fri, lunch & dinner Sat & Sun) You can't help feeling the celestial presence in the 'angel restaurant', an atmospheric old cafe and dinner restaurant serving thoughtfully prepared Finnish cuisine with the winged wonders omnipresent.

Bossa (☎ 251 5880; www.restaurantebossa.fi; Kauppiaskatu 12; mains €12-19, ⏲ 4pm-10pm Mon-Fri, noon-11pm Sat, 2-9pm Sun) While the sleek, intimate contemporary styling doesn't exactly evoke Rio, the food here is authentically Brazilian. The traditional and hearty *caldo de feijão* is the broth of a black bean stew, while main dishes are large, colourful and tasty. There's live music on most Tuesdays.

Tomate (☎ 4885 5511; Brahenkatu 20; tapas €6.50, mains €12-18; ⏲ 11am-11pm Mon-Fri, noon-midnight Sat, 1-9pm Sun) This ebullient Spanishy restaurant pulls off classics like gazpacho and shrimp-rich paella, washed down with Iberian wines. The selection of three tapas dishes is best with a few *cervezas* on the terrace.

Pizzeria Dennis (☎ 469 1191; Linnankatu 17; dishes €8-15; ⏲ 11am-11.30pm Mon-Thu, 11am-midnight Fri & Sat, 12.30-11pm Sun) With its warren of cosy rooms adorned with Chianti bottles and strings of garlic, this place has genuine Italian flavour, innovative slants on pizza, and food that's a cut above most Finnish pizza and pasta restaurants.

Viikinkiravintola Harald (☎ 276 5050; www.rav intolaharald.fi; Aurakatu 3; menus €27-45, mains €10-22; ⏲ lunch & dinner) Dust off your horned helmet for this Viking restaurant where subtlety is run through with a berserker's broadsword. Food fits the theme and set menus are filling three-course samplers, but picking and mixing means you can indulge in barbarian ribs on a plank, or tar ice-cream with cognac. It's not exactly gourmet, but it is great fun.

Svarte Rudolf (☎ 250 4567; Leirikatu 7; mains €10-18; ⏲ lunch & dinner) The best of the floating restaurants moored on the south side of the Aurajoki, this place does Italian with a leaning towards seafood. While long summer evenings invite top-deck drinking, the downstairs dining room is an elegant alternative.

Also recommended:

Baan Thai (☎ 233 8290; Kauppiaskatu 15; mains €7-12.50, lunch from €6; ⏲ 11am-9pm Mon-Thu, 11am-10pm Fri & Sat, noon-9pm Sun) Authentic spicy Thai food with great-value lunch specials.

Teini (☎ 223 0203; Uudenmaankatu 1; lunch €8.70, mains €13-24; ⏲ lunch & dinner) Local institution for traditional Finnish cuisine.

Drinking & Entertainment

In summer the evening usually begins on the decks of any of half a dozen boats lining the south bank of the river. Although most of these also serve food, they are primarily floating beer terraces with music and lots of shipboard socialising. If the beer prices make you wince, join locals gathering on the grassy riverbank drinking takeaway alcohol. Turku also has some of Finland's most eccentric bars that make for an offbeat pub crawl.

Blanko (☎ 233 3966; Aurakatu 1; ⏲ 11am-midnight Mon-Tue, 11am-2am Wed-Thu, 11am-4am Fri, noon-4am Sat, noon-midnight Sun) This ultrachic cafe by the main bridge is where Turku's hip young things get down to DJs on weekend nights; great sidewalk terrace and excellent tapas and light meals.

Puutorin Vessa (☎ 233 8123; Puutori; ⏲ noon-midnight Mon-Sat, 3pm-midnight Sun) In the middle of a small square near the bus terminal, this novel bar was a public toilet in a former life. Toilet humour and memorabilia adorns the walls and you can even have your drink in a tin potty.

Uusi Apteeki (☎ 250 2595; Kaskenkatu 1; ⏲ 10am-3am) This characterful bar was once a pharmacy; the antique shelving and desks have been retained, but they are filled with hundreds of old beer bottles.

our pick **Panimoravintola Koulu** (☎ 274 5757; Eerikinkatu 18; ⏲ 11am-midnight Mon-Fri, noon-midnight Sat) They've done their homework at this brewery pub, set in a former school, with nine of their own beers and ciders. As well as inkwells and school desks, there's a rowboat on the roof. The restaurant upstairs is good too, and there's a garden with minigolf.

Panimoravintola Herman (☎ 230 3333; Läntinen Rantakatu 37; mains €16-24) Another brewery pub-restaurant with river frontage; its stained glass and large dockside terrace makes for an excellent watering hole. They also do posh pub food and a lunch buffet.

Klubi (☎ 231 2155; www.klubi.net; Humalistonkatu 8A) This massive complex has several speeds from the casual drinking of Kolo ('cave') to the DJ-fuelled nightclub of Ilta, plus regular big Finnish bands at Live. It's part-owned by a local record label, which means it snares its fair share of prominent bands.

Getting There & Away

Finnair and Finncomm fly regularly between Helsinki and Turku airport, 8km north of the city. **Blue1** (☎ 06000 25831; www .blue1.com) has cheap flights to Copenhagen and Stockholm.

From the main **bus terminal** (☎ 0200 4000; Aninkaistenkatu 20) there are hourly express buses to Helsinki (€27.50, 2½ hours), and frequent services to Tampere (€22.40, three hours) and other points in southern Finland.

The train station is a short walk northwest of the centre; trains also stop at the ferry harbour and at Kupittaa train station east of the centre. Bus 32 shuttles between the centre and the main train station. Express trains run frequently to and from Helsinki (€32, two hours), Tampere (€28.70, 1¾ hours) and beyond.

The harbour, southwest of the centre, has terminals for **Tallink/Silja Line** (☎ 0600 15700; www.tallinksilja.com) and **Viking Line** (☎ 333 1331; www.vikingline.fi). Both companies sail to Stockholm (11 hours) and Mariehamn (six hours). Prices vary widely according to season and class, with deck class one-way tickets ranging from €14 to €35.

Getting Around

Bus 1 runs between the kauppatori and the airport (€2.50, 25 minutes). This same bus also goes from the kauppatori to the harbour.

City and regional buses are frequent and you pay €2.50 for a two-hour ticket or €5.50 for a 24-hour ticket.

Bikes can be hired from the city tourist office for €15/60 per day/week.

AROUND TURKU
Naantali
☎ 02 / pop 14,109

The lovely seaside town of Naantali is just 18km from Turku and is set around a pic-turesque horseshoe-shaped harbour. It's a delightfully peaceful, historic sort of spot…or it would be, were it not for the presence of the extraordinarily popular **Muumimaailma** (Moomin World; ☎ 511 1111; www.muumimaailma.fi; 1-/2-day pass 3yr & over €19/28; ☒ 10am-6pm early Jun–late Aug), a sort of Disneyland based on Tove Jansson's Moomintroll books, situated near the centre on Kailo Island. It's one of the country's most popular attractions in summer for young families.

The village itself was developed after the founding of a convent in the 1440s. Today the harbour, lined with cafes and restaurants, the delightful cobbled **Old Town** and the huge **Convent Church** are enough incentive for a day trip here from Turku. Outside the tourist summer season, Naantali is practically deserted. Tourist information is available at **Naantalin Matkailu** (☎ 435 9800; www.naantalinmatkailu.fi; Kaivotori 2; ☒ 9am-6pm Mon-Fri, 10am-3pm Sat & Sun mid-Jun–mid-Aug, 9am-4.30pm Mon-Fri mid-Aug–mid-Jun), near the harbour; it also has internet access and hires bikes.

SLEEPING & EATING

Although an easy day trip from Turku, Naantali has some lovely guesthouses.

Villa Antonius (☎ 0400 820 825; Mannerheiminkatu 9; s/d €85/120) In the heart of the old town, Antonius is a romantic boutique B&B with a variety of rooms decked out with historical memorabilia and furnishings. Downstairs is a charming old-world cafe with light meals, mouth-watering sweets and the house speciality, home-made gingerbread.

Villa Saksa (☎ 040 761 8384; www.villasaksa.doldrums .fi; Rantakatu 6; apt €75-135) With views across to the president's summer palace, this dignified old wooden villa is one of the real finds in Naantali. The apartment is richly decorated in antique pieces with a small kitchen. Prices vary wildly by season and availability, so booking ahead could snag a bargain.

Naantali Spa Hotel (☎ 44550; www.naantalispa.fi; Matkailijantie 2; s/d €129/156; P ⌨ ☏ ⊠ ⚐) The last word in pampering, this spa hotel is ranked one of the best in Finland. Luxurious rooms, exotic restaurants, awesome spa and health facilities – there's even a stationary cruise ship docked outside where you can stay in luxury shipboard cabins. It's like something out of Vegas. If this is too much for the budget, nonguests can use the spa and pool facilities (€10 per two hours).

FINLAND

Merisali (☎ 435 2451; Nunnakatu 1; buffet lunch/dinner €9.70/11.50, Sun breakfast €7.30, lunch/dinner €12/16.50; ☯ breakfast, lunch & dinner) Just below the Convent Church, this iconic restaurant in an old waterfront spa pavilion has a shaded terrace and a mind-blowing smorgasbord for lunch and dinner, including lavish seafood and salads – pack an appetite!

GETTING THERE & AWAY

Buses to Naantali (routes 11 and 110) run every 15 minutes from the kauppatori in Turku (€4.50, 20 minutes). In summer the steamship *Ukkopekka* cruises between Turku and Naantali several times daily (see p159).

HANKO

☎ 019 / pop 9708

With its grand wooden Russian villas, sweep of beach and bustling marina, Hanko (Swedish: Hangö) is easily the pick of Finland's south coast resorts. The town blossomed as a spa in the late 19th and early 20th centuries, when it was a popular and glamorous summer retreat for Russian nobles and artists. These cashed-up holidaymakers built lofty wooden villas on the sandy shore east of the harbour, and with several of them now converted into charming guesthouses, they continue to attract tourists with a taste for the romantic.

The **tourist office** (☎ 220 3411; www.hanko.fi; Raatihuoneentori 5; ☯ 9am-4pm Mon-Fri Sep-May, also 9am-5pm Mon-Fri & 10am-4pm Sat & Sun Jun-Jul) can help with information and the myriad summer activities in town.

Sleeping & Eating

Villa Tellina (☎ 248 6356; www.tellina.com; Appelgrenintie 2; s/d from €50/75, with bathroom from €60/90; ☯ Jun–mid-Aug; **P**) Right by the beach, this rambling place has basic rooms that can be a little tight. The same owners operate Villa Eva (☎ 248 6356; Kaivokatu 2) and Villa Thalatta (☎ 248 6356; Appelgrenintie 1), so it's a good first stop during busy periods.

Villa Maija (☎ 248 2900; www.villamaija.fi; Appelgrenintie 7; d €95-150; ☯ mid-Apr–mid-Oct; **P**) Maija is another outstanding 19th-century timber house with loads of Imperial character. The newer rooms have bathrooms and those with sea views have superb glassed-in verandahs or balconies. Breakfasts feel like a step back to the grandest days of the Russian Empire in a lovely setting with plenty of choices.

Across from the East Harbour is a string of excellent restaurant-bars in converted wooden storehouses, most specialising in seafood, but also pizza and pasta.

Getting There & Away

There are regular daily express buses to/from Helsinki (€22.40, 2¼ hours) via Ekenäs (€7.20, 35 minutes) and a couple of Turku services. The train from Helsinki (€20.20, two hours) requires a change to a local train or bus at Karjaa.

ÅLAND

☎ 018 / pop 27,153

Little known beyond the Baltic, this sweeping archipelago spattered between Finland and Sweden is a curious geopolitical entity that belongs to Finland, speaks Swedish, but has its own parliament, flies its own flag proudly from every pole, and issues its own national stamps.

There are well over 6000 islands, although many of these are merely little mounds of granite rising centimetres above the sea. Indeed, the islands are all remarkably flat: Ålanders are even less thrilled by global warming than most.

This flatness, however, makes the islands ideal for exploration by bike. The main central island (Åland) is connected with those around it by bridge and cable ferry, while, northeast and southeast of here, the archipelago islands are even more rural and remote: on places like Kökar you could be forgiven for believing you have stepped right back in time. Throughout Åland, traditions such as the Midsummer celebration bear a marked local character.

Information

Åland operates on the same time as Finland – that is, one hour ahead of Sweden, and two ahead of GMT. It uses the euro, but most businesses will also accept the Swedish krona.

The main tourist office is in the capital, Mariehamn. The website www.visitaland.com is very helpful, and www.alandsresor.fi lets you book much of the island's accommodation online.

Åland uses the Finnish mobile phone network but service is sketchy. Mail sent in Åland must have Åland postage stamps.

Self-Catering Accommodation

There's a wealth of cottages for rent on Åland. Both Eckerö (below) and Viking (below) ferry lines have a comprehensive list of places that can be booked, as does **Destination Åland** (☎ 040 300 8001; www.destinationaland.com; Elverksgatan 5, Mariehamn).

Getting There & Away

AIR

Air Åland (☎ 17110; Elverksgatan 10; www.airaland.com) has daily flights from Mariehamn to Helsinki and Stockholm. Business airline, **Turku Air** (☎ 02-276 4966; www.turkuair.fi) flies to Turku. The airport is 4km north of Mariehamn and there's a connecting bus service.

BOAT

These are the main companies operating between the Finnish mainland and Åland (and on to Sweden):

Eckerö Linjen (☎ 28000; www.eckerolinjen.fi; Torggatan 2, Mariehamn) Sails to Grisslehamn (€8.90, three hours) from Eckerö.

Tallink/Silja Lines (☎ 0600-15700; www.tallinksilja.com; Torggatan 14) Runs direct services to Mariehamn from Turku (€17, 4½ hours), Helsinki (€39, 11½ hours) and Stockholm (€29, 5½ hours).

Viking Line (☎ 26211; www.vikingline.fi; Storagatan 2) Runs to Helsinki (€34, 11 hours) and Stockholm (€36, nine hours). Also runs to Kapellskär, a quicker crossing with bus connection to Stockholm.

It's also possible to travel using the archipelago ferries to and from mainland Finland via Korpo (southern route, from Galtby passenger harbour) or Kustavi (northern route, from Osnäs passenger harbour), though it's cheaper to break your outward journey in the archipelago.

Getting Around

BICYCLE

Cycling is a great way to tour these flat, rural islands. **Ro-No Rent** (☎ 12820; www.visitaland.com/rono; bicycles per day/week from €8/40, mopeds per day/week €65/210; ⏰ May-Aug) has offices at Mariehamn and Eckerö harbours. Green-and-white signs trace the excellent routes through the islands.

BUS

Five main bus lines depart from Mariehamn's regional bus terminal on Torggatan opposite the library. Bus 1 goes to Hammarland and Eckerö, bus 2 to Godby and Geta, bus 3 to Godby and Saltvik, bus 4 to Godby, Sund and Vårdö (Hummelvik) and bus 5 to Lemland and Lumparland (Långnäs).

BOAT

There are three kinds of interisland ferry. For short trips, free vehicle ferries sail nonstop. For longer routes, ferries run to a schedule taking cars, bicycles and pedestrians. There are also three private bicycle ferries in summer – a ride costs €7 to €9 per bicycle with Hammarland–Geta, Lumparland–Sund and Vårdö–Saltvik routes.

Timetables for all interisland ferries are available at the main tourist office in Mariehamn and online at www.alandstrafiken.ax.

MARIEHAMN

☎ 018 / pop 10,902

Villagey Mariehamn is Åland's main port and capital, a pretty place lined with linden trees and timber houses set between two large harbours. Compared to the rest of the archipelago, it's a metropolis, and gets quite busy in summer with tourists off the ferries, and yachts stocking the marinas. The main pedestrian street, Torggatan, is a colourful and crowded hive of activity, and there are some fine museums – enough to allow a leisurely day's exploration. Outside the season you could safely fire a cannon through the town.

Orientation & Information

Mariehamn lies on a peninsula and has two harbours, Västerhamn (West Harbour), where the ferries pull in, and Österhamn (East Harbour).

The **tourist office** (☎ 24000; www.visitaland.com; Storagatan 8; ⏰ 9am-4pm Mon-Fri Sep-May, plus Sat 10am-3pm Apr-May & Sep, 9am-5pm Mon-Fri, 9am-4pm Sat & Sun Jun-Aug; 💻) has plenty of island info, books tours and has internet access (€1 for 15 minutes). There's also a booth at the ferry terminal. The **library** (☎ 531 441; Strandgatan 8; ⏰ 10am-8pm Mon-Fri, 11am-4pm Sat, noon-4pm Sun) has free internet access.

Sights & Activities

In the centre of town, the **Ålands Museum & Ålands Konstmuseum** (☎ 25426; Stadhusparken;

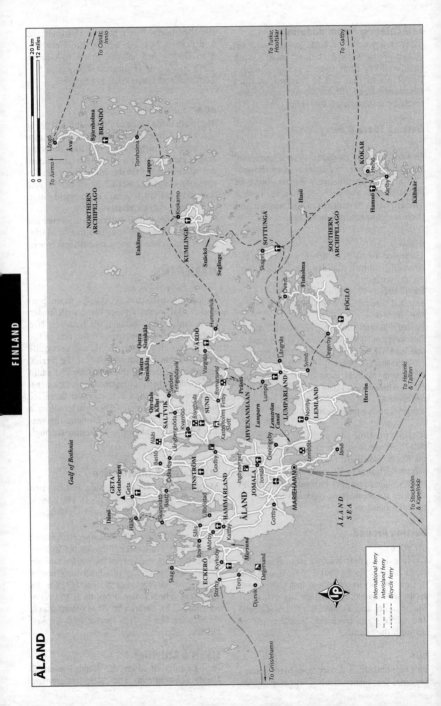

FINLAND

ÅLAND

Gulf of Bothnia

NORTHERN ARCHIPELAGO

SOUTHERN ARCHIPELAGO

ÅLAND SEA

0   20 km
0   12 miles

To Jurmo
To Osnäs; Innö
To Turku; Houtskär
To Gåtby
To Jurmo

Långö
Åva
Björnholma
BRÄNDÖ
Torsholma
Lappo
KÖKAR
Hellsö
Karlby
Källskär
Hamnö
Husö
Krokarno
SOTTUNGA
Skaget
Överö
Finholma
FÖGLÖ
Degerby
Enklinge
KUMLINGE
Snäckö
Seglinge
To Helsinki & Tallinn
Östra Simskäla
VÅRDÖ
Hummelvik
Vargata
Västra Simskäla
Sweden/Tengsödaviik
Överdals
Klint
SALTVIK
Kvarnbo
Bartsboda
Bomarsund
Prästö
Lumparn
Lumpo
Svinö
Herrön
Näs
Bastö
Långbergsöda
Kastelholms Finby
Slott
SUND
ÅHVENANMAA
Lumparland
LUMPARLAND
Norrby
LEMLAND
Degersand
GETA
Getaberget
Geta
Odkalby
Godby
Ingby
Ingbyberget
Önningeby
Lemböte
Jäsö
Danö
Hallo
FINSTRÖM
HAMMARLAND
JOMALA
Jomala
MARIEHAMN
Skarpnåtö
Bästö
ÅLAND
Skag
Sälis
Mörby
Kattby
Gottby
Bovik
ECKERÖ
Kyrkoby
Marsund
Storby
Torp
Djurvik

International ferry
Interisland ferry
Bicycle ferry

To Grisslehamn
To Stockholm & Kapellskär

admission €3; ⓧ 10am-4pm Wed-Mon, 10am-7pm Tue Jun & Aug, 10am-7pm daily Jul, 10am-4pm Wed-Sun, 10am-8pm Tue Sep-May; Ⓖ), housed together in the same building near the market square, give an absorbing account of Åland's history and culture, from prehistory to the present, with displays on local music, seafaring, wildlife and festivals. The art museum features a permanent collection of works by Åland artists as well as changing exhibitions.

The stalwarts of Åland are mariners and the best place to get a feel for their exploits is down at the West Harbour. The **Sjöfartsmuseum** (Maritime Museum; ☎ 19930; Hamngatan 2; admission €5, joint ticket with Pommern €8; ⓧ 9am-5pm May-Aug, 9am-7pm Jul, 10am-4pm Sep-Apr) is a wonderfully kitsch museum of fishing and maritime commerce and ship figureheads. The central feature of the museum is a re-creation of a ship with mast, saloon, galley and cabins. Anchored outside is the real thing – the museum ship **Pommern** (☎ 531 423; separate admission €5), a beautifully preserved four-masted barque built in Glasgow in 1903. The audio-guide (€3.50) can help bring the old ship to life.

Over at the East Harbour, **Sjökvarteret** (Maritime Quarter; ☎ 16033; www.sjokvarteret.com) is a marina, boat-building yard and **museum** (adult/child €4/free; ⓧ 9am-5pm Mon-Fri, 10am-6pm Sat daily mid-Jun–mid-Aug, 9-11am Mon-Fri mid-Aug–mid-Jun) with exhibitions on shipbuilding, craft workshops and a cafe.

There are various options for getting out on the water yourself. Ro-No Rent (p163) also hires kayaks and small boats; for more luxurious seafaring, the **Linden** (☎ 02 421280; www.linden.aland.fi) offers Friday and Saturday lunch and dinner cruises (from €55) in a lovely old schooner.

Sleeping

Rates for Mariehamn's hotels and guesthouses peak in July and August, but expect some hefty discounts outside the summer season.

Gröna Uddens Camping (☎ 21151; www.gronaudden .com; tent site €6 plus per adult €6, 2-/4-person cabins €60/85, r €60; ⓧ mid-May–Aug) A kilometre south of the centre, this camping ground is a family favourite with a safe swimming beach, minigolf course, bike hire and sauna. If the tent plots are a little small, then opt for the spruce red cabins that are fully equipped.

Pensionat Solhem (☎ 16322; fax 16350; Lökskärsvägen; s/d €45/65; Ⓟ) Although it might be 3km south of the centre, it's only 2km from the ferries to this delightful seaside spot that can feel like your very own villa. Rooms are basic with shared bathrooms, but cheerful staff keep the place running like clockwork. Guests also have use of the rowing boats and sauna. The local bus (routes B and D) stops nearby.

Gästhem Kronan (☎ 12617; Neptunigatan 52; s/d €48/69; Ⓟ) Mariehamn has no hostels, but Kronan is a good-value guesthouse with basic but spotless, renovated rooms with shared bathroom. It's in a quiet street a short walk from the ferry terminal. Rooms are discounted outside the June-to-August high season. The welcoming owners also have another summer-only guesthouse, Gästhem Neptun (Neptunigatan 41), which is in the same street, and has more-modern rooms at the same price.

Park Alandia Hotel (☎ 14130; www.parkhotel.vikin gline.fi; Norra Esplanadgatan 3; s/d €87/106; Ⓟ Ⓟ ⓦ Ⓖ) The Park is a modern, comfortable hotel on Mariehamn's main boulevard. A range of smart rooms with TV – some with kitchenette and bathtub – are complemented by a small swimming pool and sauna. Rooms are a bargain on a Sunday, and Viking Lines offers ferry-plus-hotel deals. There's a good restaurant, a cafe and a lively terrace bar at the front.

Eating

Mariehamn's many cafes serve the local speciality, Ålandspannkaka (Åland pancakes), a fluffy square pudding made with semolina and served with stewed prunes.

Café Bönan (☎ 21735; Sjökvarteret; lunch buffet €8; ⓧ 10.30am-2pm daily) This vegetarian place does healthy salad buffets that might throw fresh beans through couscous. You can wash it down with an organic elderflower drink. It's all sourced from ethical producers so it's total guilt-free lunching.

Dino's Bar & Grill (☎ 13939; www.dinosbar.net; Strandgatan 12; mains €13-25; ⓧ lunch & dinner Mon-Sat, dinner Sun) Popular as a meeting spot, this bar does thick burgers and creative pastas and steaks, best eaten on its great outdoor deck. It's a good place to hang around for a few beers, especially when the house band is playing.

Umbra (☎ 51550; www.umbra.ax; Norra Esplanadgatan 2; mains €12-16, lunch €9.90; ⓧ lunch Mon-Fri, dinner daily) This smartly rustic Italian spot is a welcome new Mariehamn arrival. Scrumptious homemade pasta sits alongside stylish antipasti and generously proportioned mains; lunch is a

FINLAND

choice of two great specials that are filling and tasty.

Indigo (☎ 16550; www.indigo.ax; Nygatan 1; mains €19-29; ☺ restaurant 11am-3pm & 5-11pm, bar until 3am weekends) Attractive and upmarket, this stylish restaurant is in a historic brick-and-timber building but the menu is contemporary Scandinavian. It's also a stylish spot for a weekend drink.

FP von Knorring (Östra Hamnen; mains €17-26) This boat restaurant has a great beer terrace for sunny afternoons.

AROUND THE ISLANDS
Sund

Crossing the bridge into the municipality of Sund brings you to Åland's most striking attraction: the medieval 14th-century **Kastelholms Slott** (☎ 432 156; admission €5; ☺ 10am-5pm Mon-Fri May, 10am-5pm daily Jun & Aug, 10am-6pm daily Jul, 10am-4pm Mon-Fri early–mid-Sep, English tours 2pm late Jun-early Aug), a striking and beautifully situated castle. Next to the castle, **Jan Karlsgårdens Friluftsmuseum** (admission free; ☺ 10am-4pm May–mid-Sep, 10am-5pm Jun-Aug) is a typical open-air museum consisting of about 20 wooden buildings, including three windmills, transported here from around the archipelago.

Further east, the ruins of the Russian fortress at **Bomarsund** are accessible all year, as are the cemeteries on Prästö (Priest island). The impressive Russian fortifications date from the 1830s and were destroyed during the Crimean War (1853–56). Near Bomarsund, **Puttes Camping** (☎ 44040; puttes.camping@aland .net; tent sites per person €2.50 plus per tent or vehicle €2, cabins from €29; ☺ May-Aug; Ⓟ ⓖ) is a large, well-equipped site with a beach sauna, a cafe and cabins.

Eckerö

Finland's westernmost municipality, Eckerö is all blonde hair and tanned bodies in summer, packed with holidaying Swedish families making the short ferry-hop across. **Storby** (Big Village), at the ferry terminal, is the main centre, with a **tourist office** (☎ 38095; www.eckero .ax), petrol station and bank. The best beach is at **Degersand** in the south, but away from the coast, Eckerö is typical rural Åland, with winding country lanes and tiny villages.

Storby was once the western extremity of the Russian Empire, and the Bear wanted a show of power to Europe, so CL Engel was commissioned to design a massive, er, post office. The **Post och Tullhuset** (Post & Customs House; ☎ 38689) is enormous and now houses a cafe, post office, exhibition gallery and the small **mailboat museum** (☎ 39000; admission €1.70; ☺ 10am-3pm Jun–mid-Aug, 10am-4pm mid-Jun–Jul), which tells the story of the gruelling archipelago mail route that cost so many lives over 2½ centuries. Bus 1 runs to Mariehamn.

Eckerö is packed with cottage rentals and guesthouses which can be booked through **Ålandsresor** (☎ 28040; www.alandsresor.fi). For camping and cabins, try **Käringsunds** (☎ 38300; www.karingsund.ax; tent sites €6-9, cabins from 5-80, bungalow €90-110; ☺ mid-May–Aug), a family-friendly place with plenty of activities.

Eastern Archipelago Routes

If you have a bit of time on your hands it's possible to island-hop eastwards through the northeast and southeast archipelago routes using ferry transport (free to pedestrians and cyclists). Accommodation options are limited compared with the main islands so it's useful to carry a tent or make advance bookings.

To the north you can travel through Vårdö then take the 1½-hour ferry ride to Kumlinge. Another 1½ hours by ferry via Lappo brings you to Torsholma on the scattered island group of Brändö. It's then possible to hop via Jurmo all the way to Turku. By public transport, take bus 4 from Mariehamn to Hummelvik harbour on Vårdö island. From Turku, take a bus to Kustavi, and on to Vartsala island to reach the harbour of Osnäs (Vuosnainen).

To the south, it's an easier trip to the port of Långnäs, from where you can hop via Föglö and Sottunga to the far-flung but picturesque island of Kökar, with hiking trails, a 14th-century abbey and an 18th-century church. By local transport from Mariehamn, take bus 5 to Långnäs harbour. From Kökar there are ferries to Galtby harbour on Korppoo island (two hours), then it's 75km by bus to Turku.

If taking a car on these ferries, it's cheaper if you spend a night en route between Finland and mainland Åland. Car spots cost €77 if you want to rush it, but are only €20 if you stopover in the southern or northern archipelago.

SOUTHWESTERN FINLAND

TAMPERE

☎ 03 / pop 207,866

For many visitors, Tampere is Finland's number-one city, and it's easy to see why. It combines Nordic sophistication with urban vitality and a most scenic location between two vast lakes. Through its centre churn the Tammerkoski rapids, whose grassy banks contrast with the red brick of the imposing but picturesque chimneys of the fabric mills that once gave the city the moniker 'Manchester of Finland'.

A popular weekend destination from Britain thanks to its budget flight connection, Tampere doesn't disappoint: its students ensure plenty of evening action, and its regenerated industrial buildings house quirky museums, enticing shops, pubs, cinemas and cafes.

Information

Akateeminen Kirjakauppa (☎ 248 0111; Hämeenkatu 6; ⏰ 9am-9pm Mon-Fri, 9am-6pm Sat, noon-6pm Sun) Extensive selection of English-language books.

Forex (☎ 020 751 2620; www.forex.fi; Hämeenkatu 4; ⏰ 9am-9pm Mon-Fri, 9am-6pm Sat, noon-6pm Sun) Moneychangers in the Stockmann building. There's another branch that's by the main square, and open shorter hours.

GoTampere Oy (tourist office) (☎ 5656 6800; www .gotampere.fi; Rautatienkatu 25; ⏰ 9am-5pm Mon-Fri Jan-May, 9am-8pm Mon-Fri, 9.30am-5pm Sat & Sun Jun-Aug, 9am-5pm Mon-Fri, 9.30am-5pm Sat & Sun Sep, 9am-5pm Mon-Fri, 11am-3pm Sat & Sun Oct-Dec) In the railway station. Has free internet terminals and a booking desk.

Internet Café Madi (☎ 050 922 2346; Tuomiokirkonkatu 36; per hr €3; ⏰ 10am-10pm Mon-Fri, 11am-10pm Sat & Sun) Free tea and coffee.

Tampere City library (Metso; ☎ 565 614; Pirkankatu 2; ⏰ 10am-8pm Mon-Fri, 10am-4pm Sat, 11am-5pm Sun, 10am-7pm weekdays only Jun-Aug) Has several internet terminals, some first-come-first-served (15-minute time limit).

Sights

FINLAYSON CENTRE

Tampere's era as industrial city began with the arrival of Scot James Finlayson, who established a small workshop by the Tammerkoski here in 1820. He later erected a huge cotton mill, now sensitively converted into a mall of cafes and shops; you'll also find a cinema here, as well as a great brewery-pub and the offbeat **Vakoilumuseo** (Spy Museum; ☎ 212 3007; www.vakoilumuseo.fi; Satakunnankatu 18; adult/child €7/5.50; ⏰ noon-6pm Mon-Sat, 11am-5pm Sun May-Aug, 11am-5pm daily Sep-Apr). This plays to the budding secret agent in all of us: as well as histories of famous Finnish and foreign spies, it has numerous Bond-style gadgets and some interactive displays. For a little extra, the kids can take a suitability test for KGB cadet school.

LENIN MUSEUM

Admirers of bearded revolutionaries won't want to miss the small **Lenin Museum** (☎ 276-8100; www.lenin.fi; Hämeenpuisto 28; adult/child €5/2; ⏰ 9am-6pm Mon-Fri, 11am-4pm Sat & Sun), housed in the Workers' Hall where Lenin and Stalin first met at a conference in 1905. His life is documented by way of photos and documents; it's a little dry but it's fascinating to see, for example, Vladimir's old school report (a straight-A student). There's a crazy gift shop where you can buy Lenin pens, badges, T-shirts and other souvenirs of the Soviet era.

MUUMILAAKSO

Explore the creation of Tove Jansson's enduringly popular Moomins in this **museum** (Moomin Valley Museum; ☎ 5656 6578; Hämeenpuisto 20; adult/child €4/1; ⏰ 9am-5pm Mon-Fri, 10am-6pm Sat & Sun, closed Mon Sep-May) in the basement of the public library building. It contains original drawings and elaborate models depicting stories from Moomin Valley (English explanations available), computer displays, toys and other memorabilia. Naturally, there's a gift shop.

AMURIN TYÖLÄISMUSEOKORTTELI

An entire block of 19th-century wooden houses, including 32 apartments, a bakery, a shoemaker, two general shops and a cafe is preserved in the **Amuri Museum of Workers' Housing** (☎ 5656 6690; Satakunnankatu 49; adult/child €5/1; ⏰ 10am-6pm Tue-Sun May-mid-Sep). It's one of the most realistic house-museums in Finland – many homes look as if the tenant had left just moments ago to go shopping.

SÄRKÄNNIEMI

On the northern edge of town, this promontory **amusement park** (☎ 0207 130200; www.sarkanniemi.fi; adult/child day pass up to €30/25; ⏰ rides noon-7pm mid-May–Aug) is a large complex with several

TAMPERE

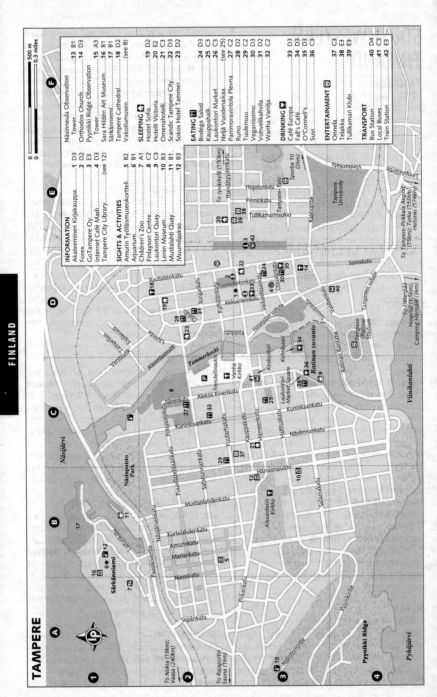

INFORMATION
Akateeminen Kirjakauppa......... 1	D3
Forex.................................... 2	D2
GoTampere Oy........................ 3	E3
Internet Café Madi................... 4	D3
Tampere City Library.............(see 12)	

SIGHTS & ACTIVITIES
Amurin Työläismuseokortteli...... 5	B2
Aquarium............................... 6	B1
Children's Zoo........................ 7	A1
Finlayson Centre..................... 8	C3
Laukontori Quay...................... 9	C3
Lenin Museum....................... 10	B3
Mustalahti Quay..................... 11	B1
Muumilaakso.......................... 12	B3

Näsinneula Observation Tower.... 13	B1
Orthodox Church.................... 14	D3
Pyynikki Ridge Observation Tower. 15	A3
Sara Hildén Art Museum.......... 16	B1
Särkänniemi.......................... 17	B1
Tampere Cathedral................. 18	D2
Vakoilumuseo.....................(see 8)	

SLEEPING 🛏
Hostel Sofia.......................... 19	D2
Hotelli Victoria...................... 20	E2
Omenahotelli........................ 21	C3
Scandic Tampere City............. 22	D3
Sokos Hotel Tammer.............. 23	D2

EATING 🍴
Bodega Salud........................ 24	D3
Kauppahalli.......................... 25	C3
Laukontori Market................. 26	C3
Neljä Vuodenaikaa...........(see 25)	
Panimoravintola Plevna.......... 27	C3
Runo................................... 28	D2
Tuulensuu............................ 29	C3
Veganissimo......................... 30	D3
Vohvelikahvila....................... 31	C3
Wanha Vanilja....................... 32	C2

DRINKING 🍷
Café Europa......................... 33	D3
Fall's Café........................... 34	D3
O'Connell's.......................... 35	D3
Suvi.................................... 36	C3

ENTERTAINMENT 🎭
Onnela................................ 37	C3
Telakka............................... 38	E3
Tullikamari Klubi.................... 39	E3

TRANSPORT
Bus Station........................... 40	D4
Local Buses.......................... 41	C3
Train Station......................... 42	E3

attractions, including a good art gallery and an aquarium. There's a bewildering system of entry tickets and opening times depending on what your interest is; it's cheaper to book online. A day pass is valid for all sights and unlimited rides, while €8 will get you up the observation tower, and into the gallery and farm zoo. To get to Särkänniemi, take bus 4 from the train station.

CHURCHES
Intriguing **Tampere Cathedral** (Tuomiokirkonkatu 3; 9am-6pm May-Aug, 11am-3pm Sep-Apr) is one of the most notable examples of National Romantic architecture in Finland. The famous artist Hugo Simberg was responsible for the frescoes and stained glass; once you've seen them you'll appreciate that they were controversial at the time. A procession of ghostly child-like apostles holds the 'garland of life', the garden of death shows graves and plants tended by skeletal figures, while another image shows a wounded angel being stretchered off by two children.

The small, ornate, onion-domed **Orthodox church** (Tuomiokirkonkatu 3; 11am-5pm Tue-Fri, noon-4pm Sun May-Aug), near the train station, is also worth a visit. During the Civil War, White troops besieged the church, which had been taken over by the Reds.

Activities
Rising between Tampere's two lakes, **Pyynikki Ridge** is a forested area of walking and cycling trails with fine views on both sides. There's a stone **observation tower** (9am-8pm; adult/child €1/0.50) on the ridge, and a cafe at the bottom serving Tampere's best doughnuts. You can easily walk to the tower, or take westbound bus 15 to its terminus and walk back from there along the ridge.

Traditional **Rajaportin Sauna** (222 3823; Pispalan Valtatie 9; adult/child €5/1; 6-10pm Wed, 3-9pm Fri, 2-10pm Sat) is Finland's oldest operating public sauna. It's a great chance to experience the softer steam from a traditionally heated sauna rather than the harsher electric ones. It's a couple of kilometres west of the centre; buses 1, 13, 18, 19 and 26 head out there. There's a cafe on site, and massages can be arranged. Take a towel or rent one there.

The town website (www.tampere.fi) has plenty more ideas for getting active in and around Tampere.

CRUISES
Trips on Tampere's two magnificent lakes are extremely popular in summer and there are plenty of options. Trips on Näsijärvi leave from **Mustalahti quay**, while **Laukontori quay** serves Pyhäjärvi. All cruises can be booked at the tourist office.

From Mustalahti quay, the glorious steamship **SS Tarjanne** (010 422 5600; www.runoilijantie.fi) does evening cruises with optional dinner on Thursday and sometimes Saturday in summer, but is best boarded for the **Poet's Way**, one of the finest lake cruises in Finland. A one-way ticket costs €36 to Ruovesi (4¾ hours) and €47 to Virrat (8¼ hours). For €30 per person, you can sleep in this old boat before or after your trip. Day use of a cabin is also €30. Bicycles can be taken on board for a small fee. You can book a day trip to Virrat or Ruovesi, with one of the legs made by bus (return to Virrat/Ruovesi costs €62/51).

The same company also runs cruises between Tampere and Hämeenlinna.

Festivals & Events
There are events in Tampere almost year-round. Usually held in early March, the **Tampere Film Festival** (www.tamperefilmfestival.fi) is a respected international festival of short films. **Tammerfest** (www.tammerfest.fi) is the city's premier rock-music festival, held over four days in mid-July with concerts at various stages around town. October or early November brings the **Tampere Jazz Happening** (www.tampere .fi), an award-winning event featuring Finnish and international jazz musicians. From mid-October to early January, the **Tampere Illuminations** (www.tampere.fi) brighten the city streets with 40,000 coloured lights.

Sleeping
Camping Härmälä (265 1355; www.fontana.fi; Leirintäkatu 8; tent sites €12 plus per person €4, 2–5-person cabins €42-70; mid-May–Aug; P) Four kilometres south of the centre (take bus 1), this is a spacious camping ground on the Pyhäjärvi lakeshore. There's a cafe, saunas and rowing boats, as well as an adjacent summer hotel with self-contained rooms (singles/doubles €40/54, open June to August).

Hostel Sofia (254 4020; www.hostelsofia.fi; Tuomiokirkonkatu 12A; dm/s/d €25/45/65; P) Tampere's only hostel is right opposite the cathedral and fills up fast. A recent refit has left it looking very spruce, offering rooms with comfortable beds (no bunks), large windows and stepladder shelves, as well as good showers and a kitchenette on every colour-coded floor. YHA members save €2.50, and breakfast and laundry are available. If you're going to arrive late, they'll text you a door code.

Omenahotelli (☎ 020 771 6555; www.omenahotelli .fi; Hämeenkatu 28; r to €65; ☐) At the western end of the main drag, this receptionless hotel offers the usual comfortable rooms with twin beds, a microwave, a kettle and a fold-out couch. Internet is expensive but the rooms are great value for a family of four or two couples. Breakfast is available downstairs for an extra €6.50. Book online or via the terminal at the entrance.

Hotelli Victoria (☎ 242 5111; www.hotellivictoria .fi; Itsenäisyydenkatu 1; s/d €109/142, weekends & summer €79/89; P ☐ 🛜 🏊) Just on the other side of the railway station from the centre, this friendly hotel offers sound summer value with its spruce rooms, free internet and a commendable breakfast spread including waffles, sausage omelette and berry pudding options.

Scandic Tampere City (☎ 244 6111; www.scandic -hotels.com; Rautatienkatu 16; s/d €155/175, summer €102/112; P 🍴 ☐ 🛜 ♿) Right opposite the train station, this hotel has modern Nordic lines and a fistful of facilities including a sauna, a gym, various restaurants and a cocktail bar. The rooms are spacious and spotless with a clean wooden feel. You can borrow bikes or walking poles from reception.

Sokos Hotel Tammer (☎ 020 1234 632; www.soko shotels.fi; Satakunnankatu 13; r €130, weekends & summer r €90-100; P ☐ 🛜) Constructed in 1929, this is one of Finland's oldest hotels and enjoys a fine rapids-side location. After the gloriously old-fashioned elegance of the public areas, the rooms, behind ornate doors, are a little disappointing, though they have the expected facilities and Nordic comfort levels.

Eating

Tampere's speciality, *mustamakkara*, is a mild sausage made with cow's blood, black-pudding style. It's normally eaten with lingonberry jam and is tastier than it sounds. You can get it at the kauppahalli, or a kiosk at Laukontori market.

RESTAURANTS

Neljä Vuodenaikaa (☎ 212 4712; Kauppahalli; dishes €7-15; 🕑 11am-4pm Mon-Fri, 11am-2.30pm Sat) Tucked into a corner of the kauppahalli, this rec-

ommended spot brings a Gallic flair to the Finnish lunch hour with delicious plates such as bouillabaisse and French country salad augmented by excellent daily specials and wines by the glass.

Veganissimo (☎ 213 0323; Otavalankatu 10; 🕑 11am-8pm Mon & Tue, 11am-10pm Wed & Thu, 11am-midnight Fri, 1pm-midnight Sat, 1-7pm Sun) A short stroll from the station brings you to this pleasing new vegan restaurant with smart contemporary decor and a good feeling about the place. Lunch (€7 to €9) is a bargain, with delicious salads; evenings offer a quieter ambience, with dishes such as paella, seitan fillet and big burgers available, as well as various tapa-sized portions and organic wines.

Panimoravintola Plevna (☎ 260 1200, Itäinenkatu 8; mains €9-24; 🕑 food served 11am-10pm) Inside the old Finlayson textile mill, this big barn of a place offers a wide range of delicious beer, cider and perry brewed on the premises, including an excellent strong stout. Meals are large and designed for soaking it all up: massive sausage platters and enormous slabs of pork in classic beerhall style as well as more Finnish fish and steak dishes. 'Vegetables' here means potatoes and onions, preferably fried, but it's all tasty, and service is fast.

Tuulensuu (☎ 214 1553; Hämeenpuisto 23; mains €13-20; 🕑 food 5pm-midnight Sun-Fri, noon-midnight Sat, closed Sun in summer) The best of a range of gastropubs that have recently sprouted, this corner spot has a fine range of beers and wines, as well as a lengthy port and cigar menu. The food is lovingly prepared and features staples such as liver and schnitzel, as well as more elaborate plates like duck confit. Even the bar snacks are gourmet: fresh-roasted almonds.

Bodega Salud (☎ 233 4400; Tuomiokirkonkatu 19; mains €18-30; 🕑 11am-11pm Mon-Fri, noon-midnight Sat, 1-10pm Sun) Enduringly popular for its cosy atmosphere and good salad, fruit and cheese bar, this place blends Spanish and Finnish choices with more offbeat snails, gnu steak and Rocky Mountain oysters. You get a certificate if you eat the latter – shellfish are scarce in Colorado, but rams have been heard bleating in countertenor tones.

QUICK EATS & CAFES

Kauppahalli (Hämeenkatu 19; 🕑 8am-6pm Mon-Fri, 8am-3pm Sat) This intriguing indoor market is one of Finland's best, with picturesque wooden stalls serving a dazzling array of wonderful meat, fruit, baked goodies and fish.

Wanha Vanilja (☎ 214 7141; Kuninkaankatu 15; light meals €3-7; ⊗ 10am-6pm Tue-Fri, 10am-5pm Sat) True to its name, this homelike cafe, a treasure-trove of time-worn furniture, is bursting with the aroma of vanilla, which they add to the coffee.

Runo (☎ 213 3931; Ojakatu 3; sandwiches €3-5; ⊗ 9am-8pm Mon-Sat, 10am-8pm Sun) With an arty crowd and bohemian feel, Runo (meaning 'poem') is an elegant, almost baroque cafe with books, paintings, decent coffee and huge windows that allow you to keep tabs on the weather.

Vohvelikahvila (☎ 214 4225; Ojakatu 2; waffles €3-6; ⊗ 9am-8pm Mon-Sat, 10am-8pm Sun) This cosy and quaint little place does a range of sweet delights, but specialises above all in fresh waffles, which come laden with cream and chocolate.

Drinking & Entertainment

Panimoravintola Plevna (opposite) and Tuulensuu (opposite) are also fine places for a beer or two.

our pick Café Europa (☎ 223 5526; Aleksanterinkatu 29; ⊗ noon-1am Sun-Tue, to 2am Wed-Thu, to 3am Fri-Sat) This is easily Tampere's coolest bar. Furnished with 1930s-style horsehair couches and chairs, it is a romantic old-world European type of place complete with Belgian and German beers, board games, ornate mirrors and chandeliers, and an excellent summer terrace. Upstairs is a small weekend dance club.

O'Connell's (☎ 222 7032; Rautatienkatu 24; ⊗ 4pm-2am) Popular with both Finns and expats, this rambling Irish pub is handy for the train station and has plenty of time-worn, comfortable seating and an air of bonhomie. Its best feature is the range of interesting beers on tap and carefully selected bottled imports. They also do hearty pub meals.

Fall's Café (☎ 223 0061; Kehräsaari; ⊗ noon-midnight Sun-Tue, to 3am Wed-Sat) Set amongst craft shops in a converted brick factory, this bar has a decent range of beers and ciders as well as perhaps Tampere's cutest terrace, a wedge-shaped balcony right by the water where you can watch crazy little fish jumping vertically, in the evening light.

Suvi (☎ 211 0150; Laukontori; ⊗ 10am-late) Moored alongside the Laukontori quay, this is a typical Finnish boat bar offering no-nonsense decktop drinking. Prepare a boarding party and lap up the afternoon sun.

Tullikamari Klubi (☎ 343 9933; www.tullikamari .net; Tullikamarinaukio 2; ⊗ Mon-Sat, to 4am Wed-Sat) This cavernous place, near the train station, is Tampere's main indoor live-music venue; there are usually several bands playing every week, and big Finnish names regularly swing by for concerts.

Telakka (☎ 225 0700; www.telakka.eu; Tullikamarinaukio 3) This is a bohemian bar-theatre-restaurant in another of Tampere's restored red-brick factories. There's live music regularly, theatre performances, art exhibitions and a brilliant summer terrace with colourful blocky wooden seats.

Onnela (☎ 020 775 9470; Puutarhakatu 21; ⊗ Wed-Sun 10pm-4am) This dark building looks like a library from outside but is the town's most popular nightspot, with several different sections playing rock, pop and electronica for a 20s and 30s crowd.

Getting There & Away

Finnair/Finncomm (☎ 383 5333) fly to Helsinki, though it's more convenient on the train really, and serve other major Finnish cities.

Wingo (☎ 0600 95020; www.wingo.fi) also flies to Turku and Oulu.

Ryanair (☎ 0200 39000; www.ryanair.com) from a dedicated terminal, has daily services to London Stansted, 'Frankfurt' Hahn, Bremen, Dublin, Milan Orio al Serio and Riga. You can fly to Tampere direct from Stockholm with **Blue 1** (☎ 06000 25831; www.blue1.com) and from Copenhagen with **SAS** (www.flysas.com). **Air Baltic** (www.airbaltic.com) flies to Riga.

The **bus station** (Hatanpään valtatie 7) is in the south of town. Regular express buses run from Helsinki (€31.70, 2½ hours) and Turku (€28.70, three hours) and most other major towns in Finland are served from here.

The **train station** (www.vr.fi; Rautatienkatu 25) is in the centre at the eastern end of Hämeenkatu. Express trains run hourly to/from Helsinki (€24.60, two hours). There are direct trains to Turku (€22, 1¾ hours), Oulu (€53.10, five hours) and other cities.

Suomen Hopealinja (Finnish Silverline; ☎ 212 3889; www.hopealinja.fi) cruises to Visavuori (single/return €31/47, five hours, 9.30am, Wednesday to Saturday June to mid-August), continuing to Hämeenlinna (single €41, 8½ hours).

Getting Around

Tampere's bus service is extensive and a one-hour ticket costs €2. A 24-hour Traveller's Ticket costs €6. Buses (€2) run between the airport and centre. A separate company serves Ryanair flights (€6).

FINLAND

HÄMEENLINNA

☎ 03 / pop 48,414

Dominated by its namesake, majestic Häme Castle, built in the 13th century, Hämeenlinna (Swedish: Tavastehus) is the oldest inland town in Finland. The town is quiet but picturesque, and its wealth of museums will keep you busy for a day or two. It makes a good stop between Helsinki and Tampere, and you could head on to the latter by lake boat.

The **tourist office** (☎ 621 3373; www.hameenlinna.fi; Raatihuoneenkatu 11; 9am-5pm Mon, 9am-7pm Tue-Fri, also 10am-2pm Sat May-Aug) has plenty of information and free internet.

Hämeenlinna means **Häme Castle** (☎ 675 6820; adult/child €5/3; 10am-6pm May–mid-Aug, 10am-4pm mid-Aug–Apr) so it's no surprise that this bulky twin-towered red-brick fortress is the town's pride and most significant attraction. It never saw serious military action and, after the Russian takeover, was converted into a jail. The interior is a little disappointing, with a modern exhibition annex tacked on to the original building, whose bare rooms don't really evoke its past. The guided tour is recommended.

By the castle are three worthwhile **museums**, which can be visited with the castle on a combined ticket (adult/child €12/6). The most interesting is the Prison Museum, set in a prison block that only closed in 1997.

Finland's most famous composer, Jean Sibelius, was born in Hämeenlinna in 1865 and his childhood home is now an unassuming **museum** (☎ 621 2755, Hallituskatu 11; adult/child €4/1; 10am-4pm May-Aug, noon-4pm Sep-Apr) whose four rooms contain photographs, letters, his upright piano and some family furniture.

Finland loves its house-museums and **Palanderin Talo** (☎ 621 2967; Linnankatu 16; adult/child €4/1; noon-3pm Jun-Aug, noon-3pm Sat & Sun Sep-May) is among the best, as it offers a wonderful insight into well-off 19th-century Finnish life, thanks to excellent English-speaking guided tours.

There are no hostels in town, but there's summer camping and cabins at **Aulangon Lomakylä** (☎ 675 9772; www.aulangonlomakyla.fi; Aulangonheikkiläntie 168; tents & caravan sites €18, d €45, cabins/cottages €50/80; May-Sep; P) on the edge of a nature park, 6km north of the centre.

Hotelli Emilia (☎ 612 2106; www.hotelliemilia.fi; Raatihuoneenkatu 23; s/d €94/114, summer & weekends €79/89; P), on the pedestrian street, is a privately owned hotel and a good deal with further summer discounts.

Hämeenlinna is located on the Helsinki-Tampere motorway and rail line, so trains and express buses to both cities are frequent and fast. In summer you can cruise on a lake ferry to or from Tampere (see p171).

RAUMA

☎ 02 / pop 36,783

Some 600 wooden houses from the 18th and 19th centuries make up Vanha Rauma (Old Rauma), a Unesco site and the main attraction of this seaside town. With its narrow cobbled streets, cafes, **house museums** (combined ticket €6) and 15th-century stone **Church of the Holy Cross**, the Old Town makes modern-day Rauma worthy of a stop along the west coast.

The **tourist office** (☎ 8378 7731; www.rauma.fi; Valtakatu 2; 8am-6pm Mon-Fri, 10am-3pm Sat, 11am-2pm Sun Jun-Aug, 8am-4pm Mon-Fri Sep-May) publishes the helpful pamphlet *A Walking Tour in the Old Town* (free).

Sleeping & Eating

Poroholma Camping & Hostel (☎ 8388 2500; Poroholmantie; tent sites €10 plus per person €4, dm €14, s/d €30/45, cottages €44-54; mid-May–late Aug) On pretty Otanlahti bay about 2km northwest of the town centre, this pleasant camping ground also has a HI hostel in an old villa, as well as summer cottages.

Rauman Kesähotelli (☎ 824 0130; Satamakatu 20; s/d/tr €40/52/72; Jun-Aug; P) About 1km west of the Old Town, this summer hostel is student accommodation most of the year, so it's clean and the facilities are excellent, with a private kitchen and bathrooms shared between two rooms.

Hotelli Vanha Rauma (☎ 8376 2200; www.hotelvanharauma.fi; Vanhankirkonkatu 26; s/d €115/140, weekends & summer €79/89; P) Newly refurbished, this sleek hotel is set in a one-time fish market on the edge of the Old Town. Despite Rauma's creaky wooden feel, rooms here are modern and chic, with flatscreen TV, comfy chairs and views into the park or courtyard.

Wähä Tallbo (☎ 822 6610; Vanhankirkonkatu 3; lunch €7-9, mains €11-20; 10.30am-7pm Mon-Fri, 11am-4pm Sat) This stylish cafe serves up a full menu and does a good-value lunch special. The old-time ambience is the main attraction.

Wanhan Rauman Kellari (☎ 866 6700; Anundilankatu 8; mains €12-18; 11am-11pm Mon-Thu, 11am-midnight Fri & Sat, 1-11pm Sun) On the edge of Vanha Rauma, this stone-and-timber cellar restaurant is a great place to splurge on Finnish specialities,

FINLAND

FINLAND

DETOUR: PORI JAZZ

The biggest claim to fame of historic but workaday port Pori – apart from brewing beer and having a hamburger named after it – is the internationally renowned **Pori Jazz Festival** (☎ 626 2200; www .porijazz.fi; Pohjoisranta 11D; tickets €50-60, 4-day pass €190; ☺ 8.30am-4.30pm Mon-Fri, during festival 8.30am-10pm daily). For around 10 days in mid-July, all roads lead to Pori, so pencil it into your trip.

The festival is known worldwide among jazz and blues performers, and has hosted truckloads of big names over the past four decades. And it's not only jazz these days – big-name rock, hip-hop and country stars have headlined here in recent years. Many scheduled and impromptu performances, jam sessions and street shows are free, creating a nonstop buzz around town.

Accommodation during the festival should be booked way in advance, but the **tourist office** (☎ 621 1273; www.pori.fi; Yrjönkatu 17; ☺ 9am-6pm Mon-Fri, 10am-3pm Sat Jun-Aug, 9am-4.30pm Mon-Fri) can help organise a cheap bed (around €30 to €45) on a first-come, first-served basis, either in a private home or on the floor of a school classroom.

While you're in town, visit **Beerhunters** (☎ 641 5599; Antinkatu 1; ☺ 11am-2am), one of Finland's best brewery pubs.

---

seafood and steak. The rooftop beer terrace is terrific in summer.

Getting There & Away

Rauma is connected by regular buses to Pori, Turku (€18.20, 1½ hours) and Tampere (€25.50, three hours). The nearest main-line train station is Kokemäki (take a connecting bus).

VAASA

☎ 06 / pop 57,998

The Gulf of Bothnia gets wasp-waisted around here, and Sweden's a bare 45 nautical miles away, so it's no surprise that a cultural duality exists in Vaasa (Swedish: Vasa). A quarter of the population is Swedish-speaking, and the city has a feel all of its own. You'll hear conversations between friends and colleagues in restaurants and bars flitting between Finnish and Swedish, often in the same sentence, but, even after the centuries, it still feels a little like a border town, torn between two masters.

The **tourist office** (☎ 325 1145; http://matkailu .vaasa.fi; Raastuvankatu 30; ☺ 9am-6pm Mon-Fri, 10am-6pm Sat & Sun Jun-Aug, 9am-4pm Mon-Fri Sep-May; ⌨), in the town hall building just off Raastuvankatu, books accommodation and rents bikes.

Two-in-one **Pohjanmaan Museo** (☎ 325 3800; http://museo.vaasa.fi; Museokatu 3; admission €4; ☺ 10am-5pm Tue-Fri, 10am-8pm Wed, noon-5pm Sat & Sun) is Vaasa's must-see. The art collection upstairs is extraordinary. There's an excellent range of works from the Golden Age of Finnish painting, with Hugo Simberg, Helene Schjerfbeck, and the characteristic expressionist landscapes of Tyko Sallinen particularly well represented.

More surprisingly, there's also a high-quality selection of European masters, purchased for virtually nothing in the chaos of Russia after the revolution. Downstairs, Terra Nova is devoted to the ecosystem of the local environment. This part of the Gulf of Bothnia is known as the Kvarken; the land is still rising as the crust 'rebounds' after the last Ice Age weighed it down.

On Vaskiluoto island, linked by a bridge to the town centre, is the amusement park, **Wasalandia** (☎ 211 1200; www.wasalandia.fi; adult/child day pass €19/15; ☺ from 11am mid-May–mid-Aug, closing varies 4-7pm) and a 'tropical spa', **Tropiclandia** (☎ 211 1300; www.tropiclandia.fi; adult/child €16/12; ☺ 7am-9pm Mon-Fri, 10am-9pm Sat, 10am-8pm Sun, closed most of Sep), both popular with Finnish families and great for young kids.

Sleeping

There's no shortage of bars, cafes and restaurants around the kauppatori and Hovioikeudenpuistikko.

Kenraali Wasa Hostel (☎ 0400-668 521; www .kenraaliwasahostel.com; Korsholmanpuistikko 6-8; s/d/tr €40/50/55; P) Decorated true to its origins as a former military hospital, this place is more guesthouse than hostel, with cosy rooms, an intimate, peaceful feel, bike hire and a good kitchen.

Omenahotelli (☎ 020 771 6555; www.omenahotelli .fi; Hovioikeudenpuistikko 23; r €55; ☎) This is one of the smaller hotels in this chain that takes internet bookings (you can also book using the terminal in the foyer). Rooms are newish, with a twin bed and fold-out couch that can accommodate a couple for the same price.

Eating & Drinking

Strampen (☎ 320 0355; Rantakatu 6; mains €14-23, lunch buffet €9-10; ⏰ 11am-midnight Mon-Thu, 1pm-late Fri & Sat May-Aug) is a waterfront favourite that manages to do top-end meals inside, and affordable burgers and pastas to drinkers on its harbourside terrace.

Sky Bar (☎ 212 4115; Sokos Hotel Vaakuna, Kauppatori; ⏰ 4pm-late) For a drink with a bird's-eye view over the city, head here to the rooftop of the Sokos Hotel Vakuna.

Getting There & Away

From the combined bus and train station, there are frequent buses up and down the coast and trains connecting via Seinäjoki (€9.50, 50 minutes, up to eight daily) to Tampere (€32.50, 2½ hours) and Helsinki (€50.20, four to five hours).

From May to September there are daily ferries (adults/cars €60/65, four hours) between Vaasa and the Swedish town of Umeå (Finnish: Uumaja) with **RG Lines** (☎ 320 0300; www.rgline.com). The ferry terminal is on the western side of Vaskiluoto (take bus 10).

JAKOBSTAD

☎ 06 / pop 19,569

The quaint town of Jakobstad (Finnish: Pietarsaari), about 100km north of Vaasa, has a Swedish-speaking majority and is one of the most distinctive and enchanting spots on this part of the Finnish west coast known as *parallelsverige* (parallel Sweden).

The **tourist office** (☎ 723 1796; www.jakobstad.fi; Köpmansgatan 12; ⏰ 8am-6pm Mon-Fri, 9am-3pm Sat Jun-Aug, 8am-5pm Mon-Fri Sep-May) is next to the town square. There's free internet access at **After Eight** (Storgatan; ⏰ 10am-3pm Mon-Fri), a music cafe and local youth meeting centre.

Skata, the town's historic area filled with around 300 wonderfully preserved 18th-century wooden houses, is just north of the centre and is Jakobstad's highlight. In the old harbour area at Gamla Hamn is the **Jacobstad Wapen** (☎ 723 3639; €1.60; ⏰ when in dock mid-May–late Aug), a meticulously built replica of a 17th-century galleon.

Sleeping

There are plenty of cheap places to eat and drink along the partly pedestrian Kanalesplanaden, one block north of the market square.

Hostel Lilja (☎ 781 6500; www.aftereight.fi/hostel lilja; Storgatan 6; s/d/tr €40/50/60, ste €80, ⏰ 9am-4pm Mon-Fri; ⓟ ⌨) This stylish, modern hostel in the town centre is attached to the funky After Eight music cafe. Spotless rooms have that Scandinavian style; there's a TV room, wood-fired sauna and bike rental.

Westerlund Resandehem (☎ 723 0440; Norrmalmsgatan 8; s/d/tr €27/41/54; ⓟ) Old-fashioned charm in the heart of the historic Skata part of town makes this lovely family-run B&B the first choice for romantics.

Getting There & Away

There are regular buses to Jakobstad from Vaasa (from €19.20, 1½ to 2½ hours) and other towns along the west coast.

Bennäs (Finnish: Pännäinen), 11km away, is the closest railway station to Jakobstad. A shuttle bus (€4, 10 minutes) meets arriving trains.

LAKELAND, KARELIA & THE EAST

Most of southern Finland could be dubbed 'lakeland', but this spectacular area takes it to extremes. It often seems there's more water than land here, and what water it is: sublime, sparkling, and clean, reflecting sky and forests cleanly as a mirror. It's a land that leaves an indelible impression on every visitor.

The greater Lakeland area encompasses Karelia, once the symbol of Finnish distinctiveness and the totem of the independence movement. Most of Karelia today lies over the other side of the Russian border; much of the gruelling attrition of the Winter and Continuation Wars against the Soviet Union was in this area, and large swathes of territory were lost.

LAPPEENRANTA

☎ 05 / pop 59,286

On the southern shores of vast Lake Saimaa, the South Karelian capital of Lappeenranta is an animated Lakeland town with a visible history, a giant sandcastle and a canal that goes all the way to Russia.

Lappeenranta was a frontier garrison town until the construction of the Saimaa Canal in 1856 made it an important trading centre.

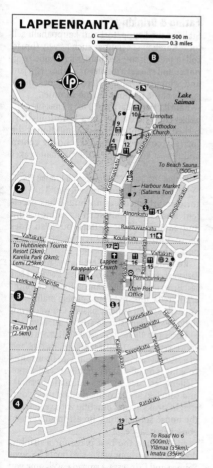

LAPPEENRANTA

These days the canal is a major attraction for tourists, with boats cruising as far as Vyborg, Finland's second-largest city, until it was lost to Russia. Finland's largest lake spreads out from Lappeenranta's harbour, and the town itself is vibrant, with plenty of historical links in its old fortress; it's a good place to sample Karelian food and culture.

Information

The **main tourist office** (☎ 667 788; Kauppakatu 40D, Maakuntagalleria; ⏰ 9am-5pm Mon-Fri Jun-Aug, 10am-4.30pm Mon-Fri Sep-May; 🖳) is on the ground floor of the Maakuntagalleria shopping complex. From June to mid-August there are summer **tourist kiosks** (⏰ 9am-8pm) by the harbour, at the fortress and at the sand castle.

The **public library** (☎ 616 2346; Valtakatu 47; ⏰ 10am-8pm Mon-Fri) has free bookable internet terminals.

Sights & Activities

On a small hill overlooking the harbour, **Linnoitus** is a fortress started by the Swedes and finished by the Russians in the 18th century. Some of the fortress buildings house galleries and craft workshops; others have been turned into fascinating **museums** (☎ 616 226; www3.lappeenranta.fi/linnoitus; adult/child combined ticket €6/free; ⏰ 10am-6pm Mon-Fri, 11am-5pm Sat & Sun Jun-late Aug, 11am-5pm Tue-Sun rest of year). These include the **South Karelia Museum**, with a variety of folk costumes, local history and a scale model of Vyborg as it looked before it fell to the Russians in 1939; the **South Karelia Art Museum**, with a permanent collection of paintings by Finnish and Karelian artists, including a good representation of modern art; and the small **Cavalry Museum**, which exhibits portraits of commanders, uniforms, saddles and guns.

Another daunting fortress sits just below, on the lake side. **Hiekkalinna** (⏰ 10am-9pm 15 Jun-Aug) is a giant sandcastle that uses around three million kilos of sand for its ramparts and themed sculptures. It's great for kids, and has a small village of nearby rides (many free).

There's a public **beach sauna** (admission €4.20; ⊙ women 4-8pm Wed & Fri, men 4-8pm Tue & Thu) at Myllysaari, just east of the harbour area.

Tours

Cruises on Lake Saimaa and the Saimaa Canal are popular, and there are daily departures from late May to mid-September from the passenger quay at the harbour. The day cruise along the Saimaa Canal to Vyborg (Russia) is one of Lappeenranta's biggest drawcards, though you'll need a Russian visa. **Saimaan Matkaverkko** (☎ 0541 0100; fax 541 0140; www.saimaatravel.fi; Valtakatu 49) runs various trips and can also organise a 'cruise visa' for EU citizens (€35), if you can provide them with a copy of your passport at least a week before departure (booking significantly in advance is advisable, as these cruises are heavily subscribed).

Sleeping

Contact the Lappeenranta tourist office for details of some of the many appealing farmhouse stays available in the area.

Huhtiniemi Tourist Resort (☎ 451 5555; www .huhtiniemi.com; Kuusimäenkatu 18; tent sites €10-12 plus per person €4.50, 2-/4-person cottages €35/45, apt €75; ⊙ mid-May–Sep) This large complex 2km west of the centre has a bed for just about everyone. There's the expansive camping ground by the lake (mosquito repellent is a must in summer) as well as tidy cottages with bunks and fridge and self-contained apartments. There are also two HI hostels near here with the same contact details: Huhtiniemi Hostel (dorm beds €10, open June to August), with two simple six-bed dorms, and Finnhostel Lappeenranta (singles/doubles €57/72, open year-round), offering good hotel-style rooms with bathrooms and breakfast, and pool and sauna access in a nearby sport centre. Both have parking Buses 1, 3 and 5 run past; most incoming intercity buses will also stop here.

Guesthouse Kantolankulma (☎ 050 328 7595; www .gasthauslappeenranta.com; Kimpisenkatu 19; s/d €55/80; Ⓟ) Close to the harbour and town centre, this is a spiffing guesthouse with apartment-style rooms ranging from a studio to four-room apartment, but all have full kitchen with utensils, cable TV and bathroom. Call ahead as it is quite often unstaffed.

Eating & Drinking

Stalls at the kauppatori and kauppahalli sell local Karelian specialities such as *vety* (bread roll or pie with smoked ham, sliced boiled egg, mince and spices), rice pie, or waffles with jam and whipped cream. There are more snack stands at the harbour during summer.

Kahvila Majurska (☎ 453 0554; Kristiinankatu 1; pastries €2-5; ⊙ 10am-7pm) In a beautifully furnished 18th-century wooden building at the fortress complex, Majurska oozes charm and does a good range of home-made cakes and quiches.

Kasino (☎ 040 716 8097; Ainonkatu 10 mains €16-26; ⊙ 7am-3pm Mon-Fri, 8am-3pm Sat & Sun) This historic refurbished casino house has excellent Russian options such as salmon blini and *zakuska* (light buffet), but also does more European fare such as steaks and pork schnitzel.

Restaurant Olé (☎ 311 6961; www.ravintolaole.fi; Raatinmiehenkatu 18; ⊙ 11am-midnight Mon-Sat, 1-8pm Sun) Bringing a Mediterranean touch to southern Karelia, this spot does Spanish mains such as paella as well as hefty pastas. On weekends they have live music of variable quality.

Tassos (☎ 010 762 1452; Valtakatu 41; mains €10-31, lunch buffet €12; ⊙ 11am-11pm Mon-Thu, 11am-midnight Fri & Sat, noon-8pm Sun) Excellent Greek-inspired cooking is on offer at this family-friendly spot. Hellenic classics such as dolmades, tsatziki and souvlaki are accompanied by pick-your-weight steaks, pastas bursting with vegies, and the house special, duck breast in sherry and gooseberry sauce.

In summer, the best place for a drink is down at the harbour where two boats, SS Suvi-Saimaa and Prinsessa Armaada, welcome you to their busy beer terraces.

In town, Kauppakatu and Valtakatu each have a lively strip of bars and clubs.

Getting There & Away

Finnair has daily flights between Helsinki and Lappeenranta; take bus 4 to the airport.

All bus and train tickets can be booked at the central office of **Matkahuolto** (⊙ 9am-5pm Mon-Fri), opposite the town park. Regular services include: Joensuu (€38.40, 2½ hours), Helsinki (€35.70, 4¼ hours) and Savonlinna (€25.50, four hours via Parikkala). For Kuopio change at Mikkeli. The bus and train stations are together about 500m south of the centre along Ratakatu, though most buses stop in the centre.

Lappeenranta is on the main rail link between Helsinki (€43.20, 2¼ hours) and Joensuu. For Savonlinna, change at Parikkala.

SAVONLINNA

☎ 015 / pop 26,775

Often considered Finland's prettiest town, Savonlinna shimmers on a sunny day as the water ripples around its centre. Set on two islands between Haapavesi and Pihlajavesi lakes, it's a classic Lakeland settlement with a major attraction: perched on a rocky islet, one of Europe's most visually dramatic castles lords it over the picturesque centre and hosts July's world-famous opera festival in a spectacular setting.

Even if you're no aria-holic, the buzz of the festival makes this the most rewarding time to visit, with animated post-show debriefs over dinner, or bubbly, going deep into the darkless night. But Savonlinna rewards a visit any time of year and has major drawcards like Kerimäki's church and Retretti gallery within easy reach.

Information

Public library (Tottinkatu 6; �---☆ 11am-7pm Mon-Thu, 10am-4pm Fri) Free internet.

Savonlinna Travel (☎ 517 510; www.savonlinna. travel; Puistokatu 1; ☆ 9am-5pm Mon-Fri Aug-Jun, 9am-7pm daily Jul) Tourist information including accommodation reservation, farmstays, festival tickets and tours. Free internet.

Sights & Activities

Standing immense and haughty on a rock in the lake, 15th century **Olavinlinna** (☎ 531 164; www.olavinlinna.fi; adult/child €5/3.50; ☆ 10am-6pm Jun–mid-Aug, 10am-4pm Mon-Fri, 11am-4pm Sat & Sun mid-Aug–May, last tour leaves 1hr before close) is one of the most spectacular castles in northern Europe and as well as being an imposing fortification, is also the spectacular venue for the month-long Savonlinna Opera Festival. The castle's been heavily restored after fire damage, but is still seriously impressive, not least in the way it's built directly on the rock in the middle of the lake. To visit the interior, including original towers, bastions and chambers, you must join a guided tour (around 45 minutes). Tours are multilingual and depart on the hour. Guides are good at bringing the castle to life.

Across from the castle, the **provincial museum** (☎ 571 4712; Riihisaari; adult/child €5/1; ☆ 11am-5pm Tue-Sun, 11am-6pm daily Jul–early Aug), tells of local history and the importance of water transport. Here also is Nestori, a national parks visitor and information centre for the Saimaa region. Moored alongside are four historic ships, all with exhibitions open from May to September during museum hours (same ticket).

Dozens of 1½-hour **scenic cruises** (€11-13) leave from the harbour near the kauppatori daily in summer. **SS Heinävesi** (www.savonlinnan laivat.com) runs daily at 11am to Retretti art gallery in Punkaharju (single/return €22/29, kids €9/14, two hours, mid-June to mid-August), giving you 2½ hours there.

The Savonlinna area is great for **bicycle touring**. Savonlinna Travel rents scooters (three hours €25, day/weekend €50/100) and several places in town rent bikes, including **Savonlinnan Polkupyörähuolto** (☎ 533 977; Olavinkatu 19; ☆ 9am-5pm Mon-Fri), which charges €10 per day. Bikes can be carried on board lakeboats for a small fee. To rent **canoes and rowing boats**, visit Vuohimäki Camping (p178).

Festivals

Savonlinna Opera Festival (☎ 476 750; www.operaf estival.fi; Olavinkatu 27) is Finland's most famous festival, with an enviably dramatic setting; the covered courtyard of Olavinlinna Castle. It offers four weeks of high-class opera performances from early July to early August. The atmosphere in town during the festival is reason enough to come; it's buzzing, with restaurants serving post-show midnight feasts, and animated discussions and impromptu arias on all sides.

The festival's excellent website details the programme. There are tickets in various price bands. The top grades (€105 to €180) are fine, but the penultimate grade (€80 to €98) puts you in untiered seats, so it helps to be tall. The few cheap seats (€38 to €43) have a severely restricted view. Buy tickets up to a year in advance from **Lippupalvelu** (☎ 0600 10800; www.lippupalvelu.fi) or from Savonlinna Travel.

When the opera's done, there's also an important **ballet festival** (☎ 044 500 2176; www .savonlinnaballet.net) running for four days in early August.

Less elegant, but keenly contested in late August, is the **Mobile Phone Throwing World Championships** (www.savonlinnafestivals.com), sometimes held at alternative venues but usually in Savonlinna or nearby Punkaharju.

FINLAND

LOCAL VOICE: JORMA HYNNINEN, BARITONE

As a former artistic director of the event, how is Savonlinna's Opera Festival special? Somehow this Savonlinna festival, this simple architecture, old architecture, is very special. You can't find a castle like this anywhere else. The atmosphere is unique, for the audience and the performers. We singers get something special out of it, and the acoustics are very good.

What else would draw a visitor to Finland to this part of the country? The Savo region is quite special, there's so much water, a lot of lakes, forests, the landscape is more rough than in the south and west of Finland. I was born here in Savo, and I live a third of each year here in my summer cottage. I feel this is the most valuable thing about the area, that in the nature here you can really get away from all the troubles of a normal life, a busy life. The peace of nature in Savo gives a lot. There are many animals, birds, seals and places like Punkaharju with its 'national Finnish landscape'. Then there are many cultural places too: Retretti gallery, at Kerimäki the world's largest wooden church, and, not so far north, around Heinävesi, there's the Valamo monastery and Lintula convent. There are many ship routes in the region, from Savonlinna to Lappeenranta, or to Kuopio. Travelling on the Savo water in an old steamship, that's a very special experience.

Why do other Finns sometimes make fun of the people in this area? People of Savo also have original character. They can be very interested in finding out about where people come from, about their lives. It can even be a little annoying sometimes! But they like to have contact, and are more communicative than other Finns.

Related to Andy Symington

Sleeping

Prices rise sharply during the Opera Festival, when hotel beds are scarce. Fortunately, students are out of town and their residences are converted to summer hotels and hostels. Book accommodation well in advance if you plan to visit during July.

Vuohimäki Camping (☎ 537 353; www.fontana.fi; tents €12 plus per person €4, 4-person r €58-68, 4-/6-person cabins €76/84; ☉ Jun-Aug; Ⓟ) Located 7km southwest of town, this has good facilities but fills quickly in July. Prices for rooms and cabins are cheaper in June and August. It hires canoes, bikes and rowboats.

SS Heinävesi (☎ 533 120; www.savonlinnanlaivat .com; cabins upper/lower deck per person €28/25) During summer this steamer offers cramped but cute two-bunk cabins after the last cruise every afternoon/evening. It's moored right in the centre of things. Nearby, *Lake Star* and *Lake Seal* also offer cabins (☎ 0400-200 117; www.lakestar.info; doubles €40).

Vuorilinna (☎ 73950; www.spahotelcasino.fi; Kylpylaitoksentie; dm/s/d €28/60/74; Ⓟ) Set in several buildings mostly used by students, this friendly complex shares the spa hotel's appealing location across a footbridge from the centre. Rooms are clean and comfortable; the cheaper ones share bathroom and kitchen between two. Dorm rates get you the same deal, and there's an HI discount.

Perhehotelli Hospitz (☎ 515 661; www.hos pitz.com; Linnankatu 20; s/d €85/95; Ⓟ ▯ ⊚) This cosy place near the castle is a Savonlinna classic, built in the 1930s and redolent of that period's elegance, with striped wallpaper, ornate public areas and an orchard garden down to the water. The rooms are also stylish, although beds are narrow and bathrooms small.

Spa Hotel Casino (☎ 73950; www.spahotelcasino .fi; Kasinosaari; s/d €89, large d €111/132; Ⓟ ▯ ⊚ ⊛) Charmingly situated on an island across a footbridge from the kauppatori, this is a good option. Nearly all rooms have a balcony; those that don't, have their own sauna. In 'small' rooms, the beds are arranged toe-to-toe. The rooms aren't luxurious for this price, but guests have unlimited access to the excellent spa facilities, and the location is fantastic.

ourpick Lossiranta Lodge (☎ 511 2323; www .lossiranta.net; Aino Acktén Puistotie; r €100-140, during opera festival €160-210; Ⓟ ⊚ ⅙) This beautifully designed boutique villa boasts a stunning lakeside location and the closest possible view of Olavinlinna. The five unique rooms are impossibly cute, lovingly designed and surprisingly functional. The lodge also operates Tavis, farther along the lakeshore. It's recommended but it's best to book ahead during summer.

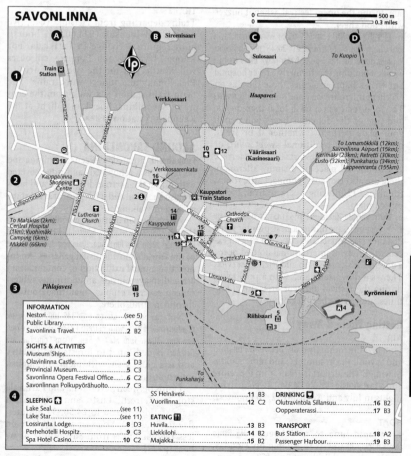

SAVONLINNA

INFORMATION	
Nestori................................(see 5)	
Public Library..............................1 C3	
Savonlinna Travel.........................2 B2	

SIGHTS & ACTIVITIES	
Museum Ships.............................3 C3	
Olavinlinna Castle........................4 D3	
Provincial Museum.......................5 C3	
Savonlinna Opera Festival Office....6 C2	
Savonlinnan Polkupyörähuolto.....7 C3	

SLEEPING	
Lake Seal...............................(see 11)	
Lake Star...............................(see 11)	
Lossiranta Lodge..........................8 D3	
Perhehotelli Hospitz......................9 C3	
Spa Hotel Casino........................10 C2	

SS Heinävesi.............................11 B3	**DRINKING**
Vuorilinna...............................12 C2	Olutravintola Sillansuu...............16 B2
	Oopperaterassi.........................17 B3
EATING	
Huvila....................................13 B3	**TRANSPORT**
Liekkilohi................................14 B2	Bus Station..............................18 A2
Majakka..................................15 B2	Passenger Harbour....................19 B3

Eating & Drinking

The lively lakeside kauppatori is the place for casual snacking. A *lörtsy* (turnover) is typical and comes savoury with meat (lihalörtsy) or sweet with apple (*omenalörtsy*) or cloudberry (*lakkalörtsy*). Savonlinna is also famous for fried muikku (vendace, tiny lake fish); try these at Kalastajan Koju on the kauppatori, or the Muikkubaari on the top floor of the Seurahuone hotel. Also near the kauppatori is Oopperaterassi, a flat wooden deck that's one of Savonlinna's most popular spots for a summertime drink. The opera festival peps up Savonlinna's nightlife, with restaurants open late and pubs thronged with post-performance merriment. Near the castle, on lovely Linnankatu, several handsome cafe-

bars compete for the pre- and post-opera crowd with mini bottles of fizz and traditional, if priced-up, Finnish plates.

Liekkilohi (☎ 050 310 5850; salmon €18; ☽ 11am-2am Jun-Aug) This bright-red pontoon, anchored just off the kauppatori, specialises in 'flamed' salmon, a delicious late-night plate; they also do tasty fried muikku. During the day they put on an excellent fish buffet (€34).

ourpick Majakka (☎ 206 2825; Satamakatu 11; mains €13-24; ☽ 11am-11.30pm Mon-Sat, noon-11.30pm Sun) This restaurant has a deck-like terrace fitting the nautical theme (the name means 'lighthouse'). Local meat and fish specialities are tasty, generously sized and fairly priced and the select-your-own appetiser plate is a nice touch. It's child-friendly too, and opens

FINLAND

late during the opera festival, when it buzzes with good cheer.

our pick **Huvila** (☎ 555 0555; www.panimoravin tolahuvila.fi; Puistokatu 4; mains €14-26; ⏱ noon-midnight Jun-Aug, dinner Tue-Sat Sep-Dec & Mar-May) This noble wooden building was formerly a fever hospital but writes happier stories these days as an excellent microbrewery and smart restaurant. The food focuses on fresh local ingredients, and one of the delicious beers will match your plate perfectly, whether it be fresh, hoppy Joutsen, traditional sweet *sahti*, or the deliciously rich dessert stout. The terrace is a wonderful place on a sunny afternoon; there are also two cosy, compact attic rooms (doubles €120 during opera festival, €65 at other times).

Olutravintola Sillansuu (☎ 531 451; Verkkosaarenkatu 1; ⏱ 2pm-late) Savonlinna's best pub by some distance is compact and cosy, offering an excellent variety of international bottled beers, a decent whisky selection and friendly service. There's a downstairs area with a pool table; during the festival amateur arias are sometimes sung as the beer kegs empty.

Getting There & Away

AIR

Finnair/Finncomm fly daily between Helsinki and Savonlinna in summer, and more seldom in winter. The airport is 15km from the centre and a **taxi shuttle** (☎ 040 536 9545) meets arriving flights in July and August (€12, 20 minutes).

BOAT

From mid-June to mid-August, **MS Puijo** (www.mspuijo.fi) travels to Kuopio on Monday, Wednesday and Friday at 9am (€75 one way, 10½ hours), returning on Tuesday, Thursday and Saturday. You can book a return from Savonlinna with overnight cabin accommodation for €160.

MS Kristina Brahe (www.kristinacruises.com) heads to/from Lappeenranta (€80, 8½ hours) once weekly during summer; the fare includes lunch and return bus transfer to Savonlinna.

BUS

Savonlinna is off major routes, but there are several express buses a day from Helsinki (€52.60, 4½ to 5½ hours), and buses run almost hourly from Mikkeli (€20.90, 1½ hours). There are also services to Joensuu (€28.70, three hours), Kuopio (€28.70, three hours) and Jyväskylä (€35.70, 3½ hours).

TRAIN

Trains departing from Helsinki (€49, five hours) and Joensuu (€24.60, 2½ hours), both require a change in Parikkala. For Kuopio, Jyväskylä and Tampere, rail buses will shuttle you for the two-hour trip to Pieksämäki to connect with trains. The main train station is a walk from the centre of Savonlinna; board and alight at the Kauppatori station instead.

AROUND SAVONLINNA

Punkaharju, situated between Savonlinna and Parikkala, is a renowned sand ridge covered with pines; the surrounding forest and lakes are also beautiful and it is a great area for some cycling or walking.

Worth the trip in itself is wonderful **Retretti** (☎ 775 2200; www.retretti.fi; adult/child €15/5, with Lusto €23/9; ⏱ 10am-5pm Jun & Aug, 10am-6pm Jul; ♿), one of the world's most unusual galleries. An innovative annual exhibition of contemporary art is displayed inside an enormous subterranean cavern complex, man-made but authentic in atmosphere.

Not far away, **Lusto** (☎ 345 100; www.lusto. fi; adult/child €10/5, with Retretti €23/9; ⏱ 10am-7pm Jun-Aug, 10am-5pm May & Sep, 10am-5pm Tue-Sun Oct-Apr) is dedicated to forests and forestry and is a good visit, with plenty of English information.

Trains between Savonlinna and Parikkala stop at Retretti, Lusto and Punkaharju train stations (€3.50 to €4.50, 35 minutes, five to six daily). You can also get here on less regular buses from Savonlinna or by boat (p177).

The world's largest wooden **church** (☎ 578 9111; ⏱ 10am-6pm Jun–mid-Aug, to 7pm Jul, 10am-4pm mid-end Aug) can be found at **Kerimäki**, about 23km east of Savonlinna. It was built in 1847 to seat a (very optimistic) congregation of 5000 people. Regular buses run here from Savonlinna.

JYVÄSKYLÄ

☎ 014 / pop 85,402

Vivacious and young-at-heart, central Lakeland's main town has a wonderful waterside location and an optimistic feel that makes it a real drawcard. Thanks to Alvar Aalto, the city also has a global reputation for its architecture, and petrolheads know it as the legendary venue for the Finnish leg of the World Rally Championships.

FINLAND

Information

The Aalto museum has a free internet terminal.

Avatar (☎ 214 811; Puistokatu 1A; per hr €3; ☽ 10am-10pm) Good internet cafe.

Public library (☎ 624 440; Vapaudenkatu 39-41; ☽ 11am-8pm Mon-Fri, 11am-3pm Sat) Free internet.

Tourist office (☎ 624 903; www.jyvaskylaregion.fi; Asemakatu 6; ☽ 9am-6pm Mon-Fri, 10am-3pm Sat & Sun Jun–mid-Aug, 9am-5pm Mon-Fri, 10am-3pm Sat mid-Aug–Aug) Good info, ticket sales and free internet terminal.

Sights & Activities

Alvar Aalto, a giant of 20th-century architecture, was schooled here, opened his first offices here and spent his summers in nearby Muuratsalo. The city has dozens of Aalto buildings, but stop first at one of his last creations, the **Alvar Aalto Museum** (☎ 624 809; www .alvaraalto.fi; Alvar Aallon katu 7; adult/child €6/free, free on Fri Oct-May; ☽ 11am-6pm Tue-Sun, from 10am Tue-Fri Jul; 🖳 🔖), near the university to the west of the centre. It's very engaging, and you get a real feel for the man and his philosophy; buy a copy of the *Architectural Map Guide* (€2), which plots well over a hundred buildings in and around Jyväskylä, designed by Aalto and other notable figures. They rent simple bikes (€10/15 for one/two days) to help you explore them. Outside town, at Säynätsalo Town Hall, you can sleep in a room that the man himself slept in, and at Muuratsalo you can visit his experimental summer cottage.

Jyväskylä has several other worthwhile museums, all free on Friday, and closed on Monday.

In summer, there are numerous **cruise** options, from short lake trips to longer journeys on the Keitele canal or to Lahti. Check www.jyvaskyla.fi for choices. In winter, the handy **Laajavuori Winter Sports Centre** (☎ 624 885; www.laajavuori.com; Laajavuorentie) has five modest slopes plus a kids' run and 62km of cross-country trails.

Sleeping

Retkeilyhotelli Laajari (☎ 624 885; www.laajavuori.com; Laajavuorentie 15; dm/s/d €26/36/58, weekends €22/32/50; 🅿) Part of Laajavuori sports complex 4km from town, this hostel is often booked out in winter by ski groups. It's easily accessed on bus 25 and has institutional rooms and a burger cafe. HI members get a discount.

Kesähotelli Amis (☎ 443 0100; www.hotelliamis. com; Sepänkatu 3; s/d/tr €48/60/72; ☽ Jun–early Aug;

DETOUR: THE SEAL LAKES

Linnansaari and Kolovesi, two primarily watery national parks in the Savonlinna area, offer fabulous lakescapes dotted with islands; all best explored by hiring a canoe or rowing boat. Several outfitters offer these services, and free camping spots dot the lakes' shores.

This is the habitat of the Saimaa ringed seal, an endangered freshwater species whose population levels have stabilised and are on the increase, although there remain only a precarious 300-odd of the noble greyish beasts.

The parks both have information points, but a good place to start is Nestori centre in the Savonlinna museum. **Saimaaholiday** (www.saimaaholiday.net) and **Kolovesi Retkeily** (☎ 040 558 9163; www.sealtrail.com) are experienced operators for Linnansaari and Kolovesi respectively.

🅿 🖳) Five minutes uphill from the centre, this excellent summer hotel has modern, light and spacious student rooms with kitchenette (no utensils, but there's an equipped kitchen downstairs) and good bathrooms. It's a real bargain, especially given that breakfast and an evening sauna are included.

our pick **Hotel Yöpuu** (☎ 333 900; www.hotelliyopuu .fi; Yliopistonkatu 23; s €99-115, d €146, ste €172-250, weekend s/d €85/110; 🅿 🖳 📶) Among Finland's most enchanting boutique hotels, this exquisite spot has lavishly decorated rooms, all individually designed in markedly different styles (the Africa room is really something to behold).

Eating & Drinking

Katriinan Kasvisravintola (☎ 449 8880; Kauppakatu 11; lunch €6-9; ☽ 11am-2.30pm Mon-Fri) A couple of blocks west of the pedestrian zone, this vegetarian lunch restaurant is an excellent bet. Six euros gets you soup and salad bar, seven buys a hot dish instead of the soup, and nine gets you the lot. It changes daily – you might get pasta, ratatouille or curry – but it's always tasty.

our pick **Figaro** (☎ 212 255; www.figaro-restaurant .com; Asemakatu 4; mains €17-27; ☽ 10.30am-midnight Mon-Sat, noon-10pm Sun) With a warm drawing-room feel and cordial service, this backs up the atmosphere with really excellent food served in generous portions. A delicate pike carpaccio might be followed with aromatic and succulent salmon with coriander and ginger, sizeable steaks on a mountain of fried onion, or reindeer doused in creamy chanterelle sauce.

Ye Old Brick's Inn (☎ 616 233; www.oldbricksinn .fi; Kauppakatu 41; most mains €13-20 11am-2am or 3am, food until 11pm) In the liveliest part of the pedestrian zone, this warm and welcoming pub has several excellent beers on tap, a cosy interior and an outdoor terrace as well as a tasty bar menu.

Sohwi (☎ 615 564; Vaasankatu 21; noon-late Mon-Sat, 2pm-midnight Sun) A short walk from the centre is an excellent bar with a spacious wooden terrace, a good menu of snacks and soak-it-all-up bar meals, and plenty of lively student and academic discussion lubricated by a range of good bottled and draught beers. There's an internet terminal too. A great place.

Getting There & Away

AIR

Finnair/Finncomm operate several flights from Helsinki to Jyväskylä each weekday and fewer on weekends. Jyväskylä airport is 21km north of the centre; shared taxis make the journey for €19.

BUS

The bus terminal shares the Matkakeskus building with the train station and has many daily express buses connecting Jyväskylä to southern Finnish towns, including hourly departures to Helsinki (€43.90, 4½ hours), some requiring a change.

TRAIN

The train station is between the town and the harbour, in the Matkakeskus building. There are regular trains from Helsinki (€41.50, 5½ hours) via Tampere, and some quicker direct trains.

KUOPIO

☎ 017 / pop 91,320

Most things a reasonable person could desire from a summery lakeside town are in Kuopio, with pleasure cruises on the azure water, spruce-forests to stroll in, wooden waterside pubs, and local fish specialities to taste. And what better than a traditional smoke sauna to give necessary impetus to jump into the admittedly chilly waters?

Information

Kuopio Tourist Service (☎ 182 585; www.kuopioinfo .fi; Haapaniemenkatu 17; 9.30am-4.30pm Mon-Fri Sep-May, to 5pm Jun-Aug, also 9.30am-3pm Sat Jul) By the kauppatori. Information on regional attractions and accommodation.

Public library (☎ 182 111; Maaherrankatu 12; 10am-7pm Mon-Fri, 10am-3pm Sat) Free internet.

Sights & Activities

In a country as flat as Finland, **Puijo Hill** is highly regarded. Take the lift to the top of the 75m-high **Puijon Torni** (☎ 255 255; adult/child €4/2.50, free in winter; 9am-10pm) for vast perspectives of (yes, you guessed correctly) lakes and forests. The spruce-forested hill is a popular spot for mountain biking, walking and in winter cross-country skiing, and there's a giant all-season ski jump here where you can often see jumpers in training. There's no public transport but you can walk to the top from the town centre in 30 to 40 minutes.

Time your visit for a Tuesday (or Thursday in summer) so you can sweat in **Jätkänkämppä smoke sauna** (☎ 030-60830; www.rauhalahti.com; adult/ child €11/5.50; 4-10pm Tue, also Thu from Jun-Aug), a memorable and sociable experience that draws locals and visitors. The world's largest *savusauna* (smoke sauna) seats 60; it's mixed, and guests are given towels to wear. Bring a swimsuit for a dip in the lake – devoted locals and brave tourists do so even when it's covered with ice. The restaurant in the adjacent loggers' cabin serves traditional **dinner** (adult/child buffet plus hot plate €18/8.50; 4-8pm) when the sauna's on, with accordion entertainment and a lumberjack show. Bus 7 goes every half-hour from the kauppatori to the Rauhalahti hotel complex, from where it's a 600m walk to the sauna, or take the lake boat from the passenger harbour in summer. Always ring ahead to check the opening days.

If you're going to visit a few Kuopio museums, grab the Museum Card which gives discounted entry. **Kuopion Museo** (☎ 182 603; Kauppakatu 23; adult/child €5/3; 10am-5pm Tue, Thu & Fri, 10am-7pm Wed, 11am-5pm Sat & Sun), in a castle-like Art Nouveau mansion, has a wide scope. The top two floors are devoted to cultural history, but the real highlight is the natural history display, with a wide variety of beautifully presented Finnish wildlife, including a mammoth and an ostrich wearing snowboots. There's little information in English. **Kuopion Korttelimuseo** (☎ 182 625; Kirkkokatu 22; adult/child

€3/free; 10am-5pm Tue-Sun mid-May–Aug, 10am-3pm Tue-Fri, 10am-4pm Sat & Sun Sep–mid-May) is a block of old townhouses and a real delight. Several homes – all with period furniture and decor – are very detailed and thorough, and the level of information (in English) is excellent.

A fascinating, well-presented display, **Suomen Ortodoksinen Kirkkomuseo** (Orthodox Church Museum; ☎ 020 610 0266; Karjalankatu 1; adult/child €5/1; 10am-4pm Tue & Thu-Sun, 10am-6pm Wed May-Aug, noon-3pm Mon-Fri, noon-5pm Sat & Sun Sep-Apr) holds collections brought here from monasteries, churches and *tsasounas* (chapels) in occupied Karelia.

Pikku-Pietarin Torikuja (10am-5pm Mon-Fri, 10am-3pm Sat Jun-Aug) is an atmospheric narrow lane of renovated red wooden houses converted into quirky shops stocking jewellery, clothing, handicrafts and other items. Halfway along is an excellent cafe (open from 8am).

In summer there are regular lake and canal cruises from the harbour. Ninety-minute jaunts cost €11 (half price for children) and depart hourly from 11am to 6pm. There are cruises to Rauhalahti tourist centre (€12 return) Monday to Saturday from early June to mid-August; a good way to get to the smoke sauna. Special theme cruises include dinner and dancing, wine tasting or a trip to a local berry farm. There are also canal cruises and a monastery cruise to Valamo and Lintula, with return bus transport (€60). For short cruises, pay on the boat; for longer ones, book at the tourist office or near the harbour at Kauppakatu 1.

Festivals & Events

Kuopion Tanssii ja Soi is the **Kuopio Dance Festival** (www.kuopiodancefestival.fi) in mid-June, the most international and the most interesting of Kuopio's annual events. There are open-air classical and modern dance performances, comedy and theatre gigs, and the town is generally buzzing at this time.

Sleeping

Camping Rauhalahti (☎ 473 000; www.rauhalahti .com; Kiviniementie; sites €12 plus per person €4, cabins €30-57, cottages €100; late May–Aug; P) Next to the Rauhalahti spa complex, this place has a great location, plenty of facilities and is well set up for families. Bus 7 or 16 will get you here.

Hostelli Hermanni (☎ 040 910 9083; www.hostel lihermanni.net; Hermanninaukio 3E; dm/s/d €20/40/50; P) Tucked away in a quiet area 1.5km south of

the kauppatori, this is a well-run little hostel with comfy wooden bunks and beds, high ceilings and decent shared bathrooms and kitchen. It offers plenty of value; there are rooms suitable for families, and discounts if you stay three nights or more. Check-in is between 2pm and 9pm; if you are going to arrive later, call ahead. Bus 30 from the centre makes occasional appearances nearby.

Matkustajakoti Rautatie (☎ 580 0569; www.kuo pionasemagrilli.com; Asemakatu 1; s/d with bathroom €50/79, without bathroom €40/60; P) This friendly place, run out of the grilli at the railway station, actually offers en suite rooms in the station itself, which are very comfortable, exceedingly spacious and surprisingly peaceful. Across the road, at Vuorikatu 35, they have some cheaper, but also most acceptable rooms, this time with shared bathroom.

Kesähotelli Lokki (☎ 261 4101; www.kesahotel lilokki.fi; Satamakatu 26; s midweek/weekend €39/55, studios €49/70, 2-person apt €69/90; early Jun–early Aug; P) In a perfect harbourside location, this brand-new complex of buildings surrounding a courtyard will arouse your envy of Finland's student population, some of whom normally reside here. The spotless industrial studios have heavy doors, bags of space, comfortable new beds and a kitchenette; the curtains are spangled with the gulls after which the place is named.

Puijon Maja (☎ 255 5250, www.puijo.com; Puijontornintie; s/d/f €56/62/75; P) Right by the tower on top of Puijo Hill, this has neat little rooms with fridge behind sturdy wooden doors. Get one backing onto the forest if you can, to take advantage of the wide windows. Rates include breakfast, sauna and admission to the tower; HI members get a discount.

Spa Hotel Rauhalahti (☎ 030-60830; www.rauhalahti .com; Katiskaniementie 8; s/d €99/130; P) Situated at the Rauhalahti centre, 5km south of town, this place has spa facilities, and there's a restaurant, cafe and popular dance club. In the same complex is the cheaper **Hostelli Rauhalahti** (s/d €72/84), with simple Nordic rooms and full use of the hotel's facilities, as well as an **apartment hotel** (2-/4-person apt from €130/200), with excellent modern pads that have all the trimmings, including, for not much extra dough, a sauna. Take bus 7 from town.

Eating

The **kauppahalli** (8am-5pm Mon-Fri, 8am-3pm Sat) at the southern end of the kauppatori is a

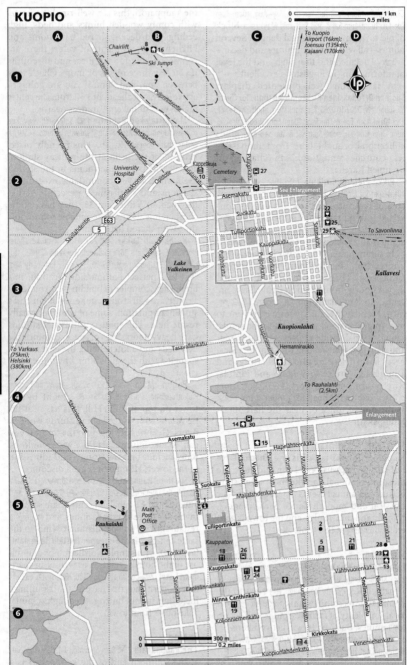

KUOPIO

0 — 1 km
0 — 0.5 miles

To Kuopio
Airport (16km);
Joensuu (135km);
Kajaani (170km)

Chairlift

Ski Jumps

Puijonrinteentie

Suininitie

Tahvanankatu

Rinhtälantie

Sammakkolammentie

University
Hospital

Puijonlaaksontie

Opiotie

Kajaankatu

Kappelikuja

Cemetery

Puijonkatu

See Enlargement

Asemakatu

Suokatu

Tulliportinkatu

Kauppakatu

Savilahdentie

E63

5

Huuhankatu

Lake
Valkeinen

Puistokatu

Vuorikatu

Puijonkatu

Satamakatu

To Savonlinna

Kallavesi

Kuopionlahti

Kuopionlahti

To Varkaus
(75km);
Helsinki
(380km)

Tasavallankatu

Hermanninaukio

Kartanonkatu

Kalliskanniementie

Rauhalahti

To Rauhalahti
(2.5km)

Saaristenkatu

Enlargement

Asemakatu

Hapelahteenkatu

Suokatu

Kasryjokatu

Puijonkatu

Vuorikatu

Puusepankatu

Kuninkaankatu

Muisokatu

Maaherankatu

Haapaniemenkatu

Maijalahdenkatu

Main
Post
Office

Tulliportinkatu

Lukkarinkatu

Kauppatori

Torikatu

Kauppakatu

Satamakatu

Savonkatu

Lapinlinnankatu

Minna Canthinkatu

Koljonniemenkatu

Kuninkaankatu

Vahtivuorenkatu

Stellmankatu

Nementie

Kirkkokatu

Venemiehenkatu

Kuopionlahdenkatu

0 — 300 m
0 — 0.2 miles

FINLAND

INFORMATION		
Kuopio Tourist Service	1	B5
Public Library	2	D5

SIGHTS & ACTIVITIES		
Jätkänkämppä Smoke		
Sauna	3	B5
Kuopion Korttelimuseo	4	C6
Kuopion Museo	5	D5
Pikku-Pietarin		
Torikuja	6	B5
Puijo Hill	7	B1
Puijon Torni	8	B1
Rauhalahti	9	A5
Suomen Ortodoksinen		
Kirkkomuseo	10	B2

SLEEPING 🏠 🏢		
Apartment Hotel		
Rauhalahti	(see 9)	
Camping Rauhalahti	11	A5
Hostelli Hermanni	12	C4
Hostelli Rauhalahti	(see 9)	
Kesähotelli Lokki	13	D6
Matkustajakoti Rautatie	14	C4
Matkustajakoti Rautatie	15	C4
Puijon Maja	16	B1
Spa Hotel Rauhalahti	(see 9)	

EATING 🍴		
Kaneli	17	C6
Kauppahalli	18	C5
Kummisetä	19	C6

Musta Lammas	20	D3
Puijon Torni	(see 8)	
Vapaasatama Sampo	21	D5

DRINKING 🍷		
Albatrossi	22	D2
Helmi	23	D5
Henry's Pub	24	C6
Wanha Satama	25	D2

TRANSPORT		
Airport Buses	26	C5
Bus Station	27	C2
Ferry Booking Office	28	D5
Passenger Harbour	29	D2
Train Station	30	C4

classic Finnish indoor market hall. Here stalls sell local speciality *kalakukko*, a large rye loaf stuffed with whitefish and then baked. It's delicious hot or cold, but you'll probably have to buy a whole one (around €20).

Kaneli (☎ 040-835 8187; Kauppakatu 22; ☒ 10am-7pm Mon-Fri, 10am-5pm Sat, 11am-4pm Sun) This cracking cafe just off the kauppatori evokes a bygone age with much of its decor but offers modern comfort in its shiny espresso machine, as well as many other flavoured coffees to accompany your toothsome and sticky *pulla*.

Vapaasatama Sampo (☎ 581 0458; Kauppakatu 13; muikku dishes €10-14; ☒ 11am-midnight Mon-Sat, noon-midnight Sun) Have it stewed, fried, smoked or in a soup, but it's all about muikku (vendace) here. This is one of Finland's most famous spots to try the small lake fish that drive Savo stomachs. The 70-year-old restaurant is cosy and most typical.

Kummisetä (☎ 369 9880; Minna Canthinkatu 44; most mains €12-19. ☒ food 1-9.30pm Sun-Mon, to 10.30pm Tue-Thu, to 11pm Fri-Sat) The sober brown colours of the 'Godfather' restaurant give it a traditional and romantic feel that's replicated on the menu, with country pâté, pike-perch, chanterelle sauces and berries all making welcome appearances alongside chunky steaks. Food and service are both excellent. There's also a popular back terrace and an attractive bar.

Puijon Torni (☎ 255 5255; mains €19-25; ☒ 11am-10pm Mon-Sat May-Sep, also noon-7pm Sun late Jun-early Aug) Revolving restaurants usually plunge on the culinary altimeter, but the food atop Puijo tower is pretty good, although the decor won't feature in *Finnish Design Yearbook* anytime soon. Choices focus on Suomi specialities, including reindeer, Arctic char and pike-perch, and there are a couple of set menus (€32 and €38).

our pick Musta Lammas (☎ 581 0458; Satamakatu 4; mains €23-29, degustation menu €48; ☒ 5pm-midnight Mon-Sat) One of Finland's best restaurants, the Black Sheep has a golden fleece. Set in an enchantingly romantic brick-vaulted space, it offers delicious gourmet mains with Finnish ingredients and French flair.

Drinking & Entertainment

Kuopio's nightlife area is around Kauppakatu, east of the kauppatori. There are many options in this block, some with summer terraces. Nearby, **Henry's Pub** (☎ 262 2002; www.henryspub.net; Käsityökatu 17; ☒ 9pm-4am) is an atmospheric underworld with bands playing several times a week.

Down by the harbour in massive wooden warehouses, **Wanha Satama** (☎ 197 304; mains €14-18; ☒ 11am-11pm Sun-Tue, 11am-4am Wed-Sat summer) and **Albatrossi** (☎ 368 8000; ☒ 11am-midnight or later May-Sep) have big summer terraces, definitely the place to be on a sunny day, if you're not on the water itself. Nearby **Helmi** (☎ 261 1110; Kauppakatu 2; ☒ 11am-midnight or later) is a downmarket bar with an excellent terrace. It has no frills but does four things, and does them well: pizzas, panini, salads and seriously cheap beer.

Getting There & Away

Several daily flights link Helsinki and Kuopio by **Finnair/Finncomm** (☎ 580 7400; www.finnair.com) and **Blue1** (☎ 06000 25831; www.blue1.com). Kuopio airport is 14km north of town. **Buses** (☎ 020 141 5710) leave from the kauppatori by the Anttila department store 55 minutes before Finnair departures (€5 one way, 30 minutes). A boat service is planned.

The train station is about 300m north of the centre on Asemakatu. There are direct services to Helsinki (€50.40, 4½ to five

FINLAND

SHE AIN'T HEAVY, SHE'S MY WIFE

If the thought of grabbing your wife by the legs, hurling her over your shoulder and running for your life sounds appealing, make sure you're in Sonkajärvi, 100km north of Kuopio near the town of Iisalmi, in early July, for the **Wife-Carrying World Championships** (www.sonkajarvi.fi). What began as a heathenish medieval habit of pillaging neighbouring villages in search of nubile women has become one of Finland's oddest – and most publicised – events.

The championship is a race over a 253.5m obstacle course, where competitors must carry their 'wives' through water traps and over hurdles to achieve the fastest time. Dropping your cargo means a 15-second penalty. The winners get the wife's weight in beer and, of course, the prestigious title of World Wife-Carrying Champions. To enter, you need only €50 and a consenting female. Estonians are particularly proficient; teams from that nation had triumphed in eleven consecutive events to 2008.

There's also a sprint and a team competition; the championship is accompanied by a weekend of drinking, dancing and typical Finnish frivolity, with a big-name band on the Thursday night.

Buses and trains connect Kuopio with Iisalmi, from where buses run to Sonkajärvi, 18km northeast.

hours), Kajaani (€22, 1¾ hours) and Oulu (€41.80, four hours).

The busy bus terminal, just north of the train station, has regular departures to all major towns and villages in the vicinity. Express services to/from Kuopio include: Helsinki (€58.10, 6½ hours), Kajaani (€28.70, 2¾ hours), Jyväskylä (€26.20, 2¼ hours) and Savonlinna (€28.70, three hours).

From mid-June to mid-August, **MS Puijo** (www.mspuijo.fi) travels to Savonlinna (€75 one-way, 10½ hours) on Tuesday, Thursday and Saturday at 9am, returning on Monday, Wednesday and Friday. It passes through scenic waterways, canals and locks, and stops at Heinävesi and Karvio canal among other places. You can book a return with overnight cabin accommodation for €160.

JOENSUU

☎ 013 / pop 57,677

The provincial capital of North Karelia, Joensuu is mainly a jumping-off point for hikes into surrounding wilderness areas. During school term it's a lively university town with students cruising around on bikes, and there are enough bars and restaurants to keep you occupied in the evening. The gentle Pielisjoki rapids divide the town into two parts: most of the town centre is west of the river, but the bus and train stations are to the east.

Karelia Expert (☎ 248 5319; www.kareliaexpert.com, www.jns.fi; Koskikatu 5; 9am-5pm Mon-Fri, also 11am-4pm Sat May-Sep, 11am-4pm Sun Jul; 💻) in the Carelicum, functions as the tourist information office and has free internet.

Carelicum (☎ 267 5222; Koskikatu 5; admission €4; 10am-5pm Mon-Fri, 11am-4pm Sat & Sun) is one of the finest museums to be found in the eastern Lakeland area. The exhibits chart the history, traditions and culture of Karelia, part of which is now in Russia.

Held over a weekend in mid-July, **Ilosaarirock** (☎ 225 550; www.ilosaarirock.fi; tickets per day €10-20) is a highly charged rock festival.

Sleeping

Linnunlahti Camping (☎ 126 272; www.linnunlahticamping.fi; Linnunlahdentie 1; tent sites €12, 4–6-person cabins €35-42) Just south of the centre and right next to the Ilosaari festival stage, this site has a pleasant lakeside location and good-value cottages.

Finnhostel Joensuu (☎ 267 5076; www.islo.fi/accommodation; Kalevankatu 8; s/d from €41/57; P) Under renovation at last visit, this smart HI-affiliated establishment is run by a sports institute and already had great rooms with plenty of space, TVs and mini-balconies.

Kesähotel Elli (☎ 225 927; http://summerhotelelli.fi; Länsikatu 18; s/d/tr €44/60/78, apt €100; mid-May–mid-Aug; P) This student apartment building becomes a summer hotel in a spot that's pleasantly far from the centre of town. The facilities, including sauna, laundry and share kitchens and bathrooms between two rooms, will make you think about enrolling in a Finnish university.

Hotel GreenStar (☎ 010 423 9390; www.greenstar.fi; Torikatu 16; r €55) This brand-spanking new hotel has all the usual facilities without envi-

FINLAND

ronmental guilt: it's designed for low energy consumption. Rooms sleep up to three for the same price with a pullout armchair for a third bed. There's automatic check-in in the foyer as well as internet booking.

Eating & Drinking

As usual the kauppatori is packed with grillis and stalls selling cheap snacks: try the *karjalanpiirakka*, a savoury rice pastry of local origin but eagerly munched all over Finland.

Astoria (☎ 229 766; mains €11-26; 🕑 dinner Mon-Fri, lunch & dinner Sat & Sun, closed Sun Sep-Apr) This rustic but stylish riverfront restaurant specialises in Hungarian cuisine such as goulash, as well as cheaper pizza and pasta dishes. There's a great summer terrace and bar.

Wanha Jokela (☎ 122 891; Torikatu 26, 10am-2am Mon-Thu, 10am-3am Fri & Sat) The oldest pub in town, this bohemian hang-out is well-known locally; it's full of characters and cheap beer.

In summer there's plenty of drinking, socialising and live music at the harbour cafe **Tuulaaki** (Rantakatu; 🕑 11am-3am May-Aug), where the passenger ferries dock.

Getting There & Away

Finnair flies daily to/from Helsinki. Joensuu's airport is 11km from town; the bus service costs €5 one way and departs from Sokos Hotel Kimmel opposite the bus station.

The bus and train stations are side by side across the river on Itäranta. Local buses go to Savonlinna (€28.40, three hours), Kuopio (€26.20, two hours) as well as Helsinki and closer Karelian destinations.

Direct trains run frequently to/from Helsinki (€62.10, 4½ hours) and Jyväskylä (€39.60, 3½ hours), as well as Lieksa (€12, 1¼ hours). For Savonlinna change at Parikkala.

In summer the MS *Vinkeri II* operates twice weekly from Joensuu to Koli (one way/return €30/45, 6½ hours), from where you can connect with another ferry to Lieksa, across Lake Pielinen. Book with **Saimaa Ferries** (☎ 481 244; www.saimaaferries.fi).

ILOMANTSI

☎ 013 / pop 6203

Pushing up against the border that separates Finland from Russia, Ilomantsi is Finland's most Karelian, Orthodox and eastern municipality, and the centre of a charming region

---

DETOURS: VALAMO MONASTERY

Finland's only Orthodox monastery, **Valamo** (☎ 017-570 111; www.valamo.fi; Valamontie 42, Uusi-Valamo) is one of Lakeland's most popular attractions. One of the great, ancient Russian monasteries, old Valamo, after the Revolution and the Winter War, was eventually re-established here. Monks and novices, almost a thousand strong at old Valamo a century ago, now number just five, but the complex in general is thriving.

The first church was made by connecting two sheds; the rustic architecture contrasts curiously with the fine gilded icons. The new church, completed in 1977, has an onion dome and is redolent with incense.

Visitors are free to roam and enter the churches; services take place at 6am and 6pm Monday to Saturday, and 9am and 6pm Sunday, with an extra one daily at 1pm from June to August. A **guided tour** (€4; one hour) is highly recommended for insights into the monastery and Orthodox beliefs.

Valamo makes an excellent place to stay, more peaceful once evening descends. Two **guest-houses** (s/d €30/50; P 🚻) in picturesque wooden buildings provide comfortable, no-frills sleeping with shared bathroom; the **hotel** (s/d/apt €70/100/130; P 🚻) offers a higher standard of accommodation. The complex's eatery, **Trapesa** (🕑 7am-9pm Jun-Aug, 7am-6pm Sun-Thu, 7am-8pm Fri, 7am-9pm Sat Sep-May) has high-quality buffet spreads (€12-15), Russian-style high tea (€7), and evening meals with not a hint of monastic frugality; try the monastery's range of berry wines.

Valamo is clearly signposted 4km north of the main Varkaus–Joensuu road. A couple of daily buses run to Valamo from Joensuu and from Helsinki via Mikkeli and Varkaus. From Heinävesi change at Karvio.

The most pleasant way to get to Valamo (and nearby Lintula Convent, which also has simple accommodation) in summer is on a **Monastery Cruise** (☎ 015 250 250; www.mspuijo.fi; adult/child €65/30) from Kuopio.

FINLAND

where a wealth of wilderness hiking opens up before you.

The excellent tourist centre, **Karelia Expert** (☎ 248 5309; www.kareliaexpert.fi; Kalevalantie 13; 9am-4pm Mon-Fri Sep-May, 9am-5pm Mon-Fri Jun-Aug, also 10am-3pm Sat Jul) can help with just about everything, from cottage reservations to information on trekking routes and hire of camping equipment, snowshoes and cross-country ski gear.

The village centre itself is modern and quite ugly, having been trampled by the Russians, but it's the surrounding region that demands exploration. The **wine tower** (noon-8pm Jun–late Aug) is worth ascending, for views and to sample the locally made berry wine.

Parppeinvaara (☎ 881 248; adult/child €3/2; 10am-6pm Jun-Aug) is the oldest and most interesting of Finland's Karelian theme villages, where you can hear the *kantele* (Karelian stringed instrument) played and try traditional food at the excellent **Parppeinpirtti** (☎ 881 094; lunch €17; noon-3pm).

Ilomantsi celebrates **Petru Praasniekka** on 28 and 29 June and **Ilja Praasniekka** on 19 and 20 July every year.

Contact Karelia Expert about cottages in the surrounding region. The following places to stay are recommended.

B&B Kaksi Karhua (☎ 040 561 0930; www.kaksikarhua.com; Mantsintie 26; s/d €35/60) is set among greenery and a few pecking chickens, lending it a relaxed country house vibe, although it's very handy for the town centre and ski trails in winter. Rooms are freshly painted and smallish, but there's a cheerful welcome and hearty breakfast.

Originally built in 1751, **Anssilan Monola** (☎ 0400 881 181; www.ilomantsi.com/anssila; Anssilantie; s/d €30/60, 4-person cottages €120; P), a former dairy farm, is on a hill 4km south of the village and about 500m off the main road. It's family friendly with rides on horses and sleds for kids; rooms are available in a range of converted farmhouse buildings.

TREKS AROUND KARELIA

Karelia's best trekking routes form the **Karjalan Kierros** (Karelian Circuit; www.karjalankierros.com), a loop of marked trails with a total length of over 1000km between Ilomantsi and Lake Pielinen. For more information on these and other routes contact **Karelia Expert** (www.kareliaexpert.fi) in Ilomantsi or Lieksa, or **Metsähallitus** (☎ 0205 645 500; www.outdoors.fi; Urheilukatu 3A, Lieksa).

Karhunpolku

The **Bear's Trail** (not to be confused with the Bear's Ring in Lapland) is a 133km marked hiking trail of medium difficulty leading north from Patvinsuo National Park near Lieksa, through a string of national parks and nature reserves along the Russian border. The trail ends at Teljo, about 50km south of Kuhmo. You'll need to arrange transport from either end.

Susitaival

The 90km **Wolf's Trail** is a marked trail running south from the marshlands of Patvinsuo National Park to the forests of Petkeljärvi National Park, 21km east of Ilomantsi. This links with the Bear's Trail. It's a three-day trek of medium difficulty (the marshland can be wet underfoot). It passes through some important Winter War battlegrounds near the Russian border. There are wilderness cabins at Sarkkajärvi, Pitkajärvi and Jorho, and farm or camping accommodation in the village of Naarva.

LAKE PIELINEN REGION

In a land full of lakes, Pielinen, Finland's sixth-largest lake, is pretty special. In summer it's the shimmering jewel of North Karelia, surrounded by some of the most beautiful wilderness areas and action-packed countryside in southeast Finland. Here you can hike, raft and fish in summer, and ski, snowmobile and dogsled in winter. Koli National Park rises in the southeast corner, and the main towns around the lake – Lieksa, Nurmes and Koli – are linked by lake ferry in summer.

Lieksa & Ruunaa

☎ 013 / pop 13,181

The small lakeside town of Lieksa is primarily a base and service town, if you're planning any outdoor activities in the region. In winter, husky tours and snowmobile safaris along the Russian border are popular; in summer, hiking, fishing and white-water rafting are all the rage.

Karelia Expert (☎ 248 5312; kareliaexpert.lieksa@kareliaexpert.fi; Pielisentie 2-6; 9am-5pm Mon-Fri, 9am-2pm Sat Jun-Aug, 8am-4pm Mon-Fri Sep-May) is the place to stop at for information on accommodation, fishing, canoeing, smoke saunas and national parks, as well as local hiking maps.

One of Finland's largest open-air museums, the **Pielisen Museo** (☎ 689 4151; www.lieksa.fi/museo;

FINLAND

Pappilantie 2; adult/child €4.50/1.50; 🕙 10am-6pm mid-May–mid-Sep) is a slightly jumbled complex of almost 100 Karelian buildings (many relocated from Russia) and historical exhibits – along with an indoor museum of local war and folk history. The indoor hall is also open (€3, 10am to 3pm Tuesday to Friday) in winter.

Karelia Expert in Lieksa handles information and bookings for all manner of activities around Lieksa and at the **Ruunaa Recreation Area**, 30km east. This is a superb, carefully managed wilderness area perfect for fishing, white-water rafting, wildlife spotting and easy hiking. The drawback is that public transport barely exists, but you should be able to hitch (or go with an organised tour) in summer. **Ruunaa Nature Centre** (☎ 020 564 5757; 🕙 10am-5pm May, 9am-6pm Jun & Jul, 9am-5pm Aug) is near the bridge over the Naarajoki, where most boat trips start. It's a good place to research rafting operators and hiking trails.

SLEEPING

our pick **Kestikievari Herranniemi** (☎ 542 110; www.herranniemi.com; Vuonislahdentie 185; dm €15, cabins €30-68, cottage €120; B&B s/d €52/72; P) It's worth going out of the way and catching a train to Vuonislahti, 28km south of Lieksa, for this brilliant lakeside retreat. The welcoming farm property has a restaurant, a dormitory outbuilding, a range of comfortable rooms and cottages, two lakeside saunas, rowing boats and even massage and herbal therapy.

Ruunaa Hiking Centre (☎ 533 170; www.ruunaa.fi; tent sites €12 plus per person €2, cabins/cottages €35/95) At Ruunaa, in addition to accommodation and services at Naarajoki, the Hiking Centre has a large cafe, camp sites, a kitchen, a sauna and cabins ranging from simple to luxurious. A boardwalk goes a short distance from here to the Neitikoski rapids, a popular fishing and kayaking spot.

In Lieksa itself options include a camping ground and **Hotelli Puustelli** (☎ 511 5500; www.finlandiahotels.fi; Hovileirinkatu 3; s/d €85/110, Sat, Sun & summer €65/80; P 🛜 ♿) by the riverside, with good-sized, if a little musty, rooms with affordable rates that include breakfast and sauna.

GETTING THERE & AWAY

Buses ply the route around Lake Pielinen, and trains run to Lieksa from Joensuu and Nurmes, but the coolest way to arrive here is by lake ferry from Joensuu (via Koli). A big

car ferry (☎ 481 244; www.saimaaferries.fi; adult/child/car/bicycle €15/8/10/2) runs twice daily between Lieksa and Koli from June to mid-August, departing at 9.30am and 3.30pm, returning at 11.30am and 5.30pm.

Koli National Park

Finns consider the views from the heights of Koli, overlooking Lake Pielinen, as the best in the country – the same views inspired several Finnish artists from the National Romantic era. In summer, the national park offers scenic hiking routes, and there's a ferry service between Koli and Lieksa (1½ hours) or Joensuu (seven hours; see p187). In winter, Koli attracts skiers, with two slalom centres and more than 60km of cross-country trails, including 24km of illuminated track.

The hill has road access with a short funicular (free) from the lower car park up to the hotel. From here it's a brief walk to **Ukko-Koli**, the highest point and 200m further is **Akka-Koli**, another peak. On the western slope of Akka-Koli is a 'Temple of Silence', an open space for contemplation with a stone altar and wooden cross mounted in the rock. Also at the car park, **Luontokeskus Ukko** (☎ 010-211 3200; www.metlakoli.net; adult/child €5/2; 🕙 9am-7pm late Jun–early Aug, 10am-5pm Sep-May) is a modern visitor centre with exhibitions on history, nature and the geology of the park, and information on hiking.

In Koli village, **Karelia Expert** (☎ 248 2315; kareliaexpert.koli@kareliaexpert.com; Kolintie 94; 🕙 10am-6pm Mon, 9am-7pm Tue-Fri, 11am-5pm Sat year round, also 11am-5pm Jul) is the tourist office and has a comprehensive range of information and maps. The village also has a post office, supermarket and coin-op internet, but the last stop for banks and fuel is Kollinporti.

The family-run **Koli Retkeilymaja** (☎ 673 131; Niinilahdentie 47; dm €12, d €24; P), on a gravel road 5km from the bus stop, is a basic hostel set in the countryside and offering good-sized twins with a kitchen and smoke sauna, plus a traditional Sámi *kota* (wigwam-like tent).

Nurmes

☎ 013 / pop 8816

On the northern shores of Lake Pielinen, Nurmes is another base for activities such as snowmobiling, ice-fishing, dogsledding and cross-country skiing tours in winter, and canoeing and farmhouse tours in summer. It's a pleasant town in its own

FINLAND

right though, with an 'old town' area (Puu-Nurmes) of historical wooden buildings along Kirkkokatu. A highlight is **Bomba House**, part of a re-created Karelian village 3km east of the centre. Unlike many folk museums in Finland, this one really comes alive with a minivillage featuring a summer market, craft shops and cafes.

Karelia Expert (☎ 050 336 0707; www.nurmes.fi; Raatihuoneenkatu 24; ☺ 10am-6pm Mon, 9am-5pm Tue-Fri, 9am-2pm Sat Jun-Aug) has local information and bookings.

The best places to stay in Nurmes are side by side on the lake shore about 3.5km east of the town centre. **Hyvärilä** (☎ 687 2500; www.hyvarila.com; Lomatie 12; camp sites €13.50, cottages from €38, hostel dm/s €10.50/31, hotel s €42-67, d €52-85; P ⓢ) is a sprawling lakefront holiday resort with a manicured camping ground, two youth hostels, an upmarket hotel, a restaurant and even a golf course.

Bomba Spa Hotel (☎ 687 200; www.bomba.fi; Suojärvenkatu 1; s/d €103/129, apt from €126; P ⊞ ⓢ ⊠), near the Karelian village, is a stylish set-up of rooms and cottages, where you can pamper yourself with the spa and sauna facilities.

Buses run regularly to Joensuu (€25.20, 1¾ hours), Kajaani (€23.70, 1¾ hours), and Lieksa (€10.30, 45 minutes). For Kuhmo, change at Sotkamo. Trains go to Joensuu (€17.20, two hours, two daily) via Lieksa (€7.80, 45 minutes). **Saimaa Ferries** (☎ 481 244; www.saimaaferries.fi; Kirkkokatu 16) operates on Lake Pielinen in summer.

NORTH-CENTRAL FINLAND

KAJAANI
☎ 08 / pop 38,089

Essentially a one-street town, Kajaani makes a handy stopover between Lakeland and the north but has little to keep you beyond the pretty riverside. The city was long an important station on the Kainuu tar transportation route; other claims to fame are that Elias Lönnrot, creator of the *Kalevala*, worked here for a period, using it as a base for his travels, and long-reigning president Urho Kekkonen lived here as a student.

Kajaani Info (☎ 6155 2555; www.kajaani.fi; Kauppakatu 21; ☺ 9am-5.30pm Mon-Fri, 9am-2pm Sat

Jun-Aug, 9am-4.30pm Mon-Fri Sep-May) is the helpful tourist office, just off the tiny town square.

Picturesquely set on a river island, **Kajaani Castle** ruins show all the signs of thorough damage by war, time and more recent mischief. It's a fine spot to bask on the grass on a sunny day. Nearby there's a **tar-boat channel** with a lock built in 1846 to enable the boats laden with tar barrels to pass the Ämmäkoski rapids.

The most interesting sight is at Paltaniemi, 9km northwest of Kajaani. Its enchantingly weathered wooden **church** (☎ 687 5334; Paltaniementie 851; admission free; ☺ 10am-6pm mid-May–mid-Aug) was built in 1726, and has some of Finland's most interesting church paintings, rustic 18th-century works full of life and colour that enliven the roof and walls. Take bus 4 from Kajaani (weekdays only).

Sleeping & Eating
Once you're this far north, eating choice narrows rapidly. The few options that do exist are along the partly pedestrianised Kauppakatu.

our pick Kartanohotelli Karolineburg (☎ 613 1291; www.karolineburg.com; Karoliinantie 4; s/d from €70/80, d with sauna €110, ste €120-250; P) Set in a wooden manor house and outbuildings across the river from town, this makes a refreshing change from sterile business hotels. Run by a friendly family, it offers a wide range of chambers, from suites with their own sauna and terrace, to simpler modern rooms. Elegant furnishings, bosky grounds and classy restaurant fare make it a romantic choice. Prices drop a little in summer.

Pikantti (☎ 628 870; Kauppakatu 10; lunches €6.90-10.90; ☺ 10am-4pm Mon-Fri, 10am-3pm Sat) This unassuming restaurant offers an excellent Finnish lunch buffet of meat, fish, soups and salads in an attractive eating area.

Getting There & Away
Finnair flies to/from Helsinki, and trains run to Helsinki (€62.30, seven hours, four daily) via Kuopio, and northwest to Oulu. Buses serve Kuhmo (€17.70, 1¾ hours) and other towns in the region during the week, with fewer departures at weekends.

KUHMO
☎ 08 / pop 9943

Kuhmo, once a major tar producer, is a good launch pad for the wilderness; it makes a natural base for hiking the UKK (Urho K

Kekkonen) route, Finland's longest marked trek. The vast taiga forest runs from here right across Siberia and harbours 'respect' animals like wolves, bears and lynx. Kuhmo is also un-official capital of Vienan Karjala, the Karelian heartland that is now in Russia. This was the region that artists explored in the Karelian movement, such a crucial part of the develop-ment of Finnish national identity.

The **Kuhmo Chamber Music Festival** (☎ 652 0936; www.kuhmofestival.fi; Torikatu 39) runs for two weeks in late July and has a full programme of about 80 top-quality concerts performed by a variety of Finnish and international musi-cians. Tickets are a steal at around €14 for most events.

Pending restoration of the central tour-ist office, info was available at **Kalevala Spirit** (☎ 0440 755 500; www.kalevalaspirit.fi; Väinämöinen; ⏰ 8am-10pm Jun-Aug, 8am-5pm Mon-Fri Sep-May) at the entrance to the Kalevala Village and at **Petola Luontokeskus** (☎ 0205 646 380; petola@metsa.fi; Lentiirantie 342; ⏰ 10am-5pm Jun-Aug, 10am-4pm Mon-Fri Sep-Dec), an excellent nature centre nearby, focusing on carnivore species.

Four kilometres from the centre of town, **Kalevalakylä (Kalevala Village)** is a theme park about traditional Karelian life, with a number of Karelian wooden buildings including a sauna, craft shops and Pohjolantalo, a large hall that functions as cafe, restaurant and gal-lery. There's also the **Kalevala Spirit Experience** (adult/child €20/10; ⏰ noon & 2pm mid-Jun–mid-Aug), a two-hour tour in Finnish or English that tests your inherent Finnishness with costumed guides, sauna, tar-making, fishing, wood-carving and so on.

If you are interested in the *Kalevala* or Karelian culture, pay a visit to the excel-lent **Juminkeko** (☎ 653 0670; www.juminkeko.fi; Kontionkatu 25; adult/child €4/free; ⏰ noon-6pm Sun-Thu, daily in Jul), which offers everything from audiovisual presentations, to Finland's largest collection of *Kalevala* books and multimedia translations.

Hiking is the big drawcard in Kuhmo, but there are plenty of other ways to get active; the tourist office can help organise things like white-water rafting, while Petola visitor centre has more walking info and can arrange fishing permits. Wildlife safaris and bear-viewing from hides are organised by **Wild Brown Bear** (☎ 040 546 9008; www.wildbrownbear.fi) and **Taiga Spirit** (☎ 040 746 8243; www.taigaspirit.com) for between €130 and €160 a time.

Sleeping

Kalevala Camping (☎ 0440 755 500; www.kalevalaspirit.fi; Väinämöinen 13; camp sites €10, 2-/4-person cabins €35/42, cottages €72/92; ⏰ Jun-Aug) This has basic facilities but a most attractive lakeside location, 4km from town and among tall pines.

Matkakoti Parkki (☎ 655 0271, matkakoti.parkki@elisanet.fi; Vienantie 3; s/d/tr €30/50/60; P) Run in a motherly manner, this quiet and handsome little guesthouse offers excellent value near the centre of town. Rooms are spotless and need to be booked ahead during the festival. They rent bikes for €3 per hour.

Hotelli Kalevala (☎ 655 4100; www.hotellikalevala.fi; Väinämöinen 9; s/d €82/110; P 🖥 🛜 🍴) Four kilometres away, by the Kalevala village, this striking building of wood and concrete is a great place to stay. The pretty rooms in yellow colours mostly have tantalising lake views, with the sound of the lapping water. The restaurant's great too, but it's the facilities that win you over here: they or-ganise anything from snowmobile safaris to spa treatments.

Getting There & Away

Numerous daily buses head to/from Kajaani (€17.70, 1¾ hours), and two Monday to Saturday to Nurmes, changing at Sotkamo. For other destinations, you'll have to go via Kajaani.

OULU

☎ 08 / pop 131,585

Prosperous Oulu is spread across several islands, elegantly connected by pedestrian bridges, and water never seems far away. In summer, the angled sun bathes the kauppatori in light and all seems well with the world. Locals, who appreciate daylight when they get it, crowd the terraces, and stalls groan under the weight of Arctic berries.

Founded in 1605, Oulu grew prosperous in the 18th-century from tar, which was floated down the river from the Kainuu region and shipped to Sweden for shipbuilding. Although pulp factories are a major industry, it's the IT boom that's leading the way in Oulu now and plenty of professional expats live and work here.

Information

Wireless internet is available throughout the city centre on the PanOulu network.

FINLAND

Public library (☎ 558 410; Kaarlenväylä; ☽ 10am-8pm Mon-Fri, 10am-3pm Sat, noon-4pm Sun) On the waterfront opposite the Oulu Theatre. Several internet terminals.

Tourist office (☎ 5584 1330; www.visitoulu.fi; Torikatu 10; ☽ 9am-4pm Mon-Fri) Publishes the useful guide *Look at Oulu*. Should be back at this address by 2009, hopefully with longer hours.

Sights & Activities

The imposing, 19th-century **cathedral** (Kirkkokatu 36; ☽ 11am-8pm Jun & Aug, 11am-9pm Jul, noon-1pm Sep-May) was designed by Carl Engel and has Finland's oldest portrait (dating from 1611) hanging in its vestry. The waterside **kauppatori** is one of the liveliest and most colourful in Finland with its red wooden storehouses (now housing restaurants, bars and craft shops), market stalls, bursting summer terraces and the rotund *Toripolliisi* statue, a humorous representation of the local police.

Tietomaa (☎ 5584 1340; www.tietomaa.com; Nahkatehtaankatu 6; adult/child €13/10; ☽ 10am-6pm mid-Feb–Aug, 10am-8pm Jul, 10am-4pm Mon-Fri, 10am-6pm Sat & Sun Sep–mid-Feb), Scandinavia's largest science

museum can occupy kids for the best part of a day with a giant Imax screen, hands-on interactive exhibits on planets and the human body, and an observation tower. Opposite, **Oulun Taidemuseo** (Oulu Art Museum; ☎ 5584 7450; Kasarmintie 7; adult/child €3/1, free Fri; ☽ 10am-5pm Tue-Sun) is a bright gallery with excellent temporary exhibitions of both international and Finnish contemporary art, and a good permanent collection. The cafe is an exhibit in its own right.

Just north of the town centre and connected by small bridges, **Hupisaaret Park** has bike paths, greenhouses and a summer cafe, as well as a fishway built so that salmon can bypass the hydroelectric dam to get to the spawning grounds.

Oulu's extensive network of wonderful **bicycle paths** is among the best in Finland and nowhere is the Finns' love of two-wheeled transport more obvious than here in summer. Bikes (€2/15 per hour/day) can be hired from Kiikeli **hire shed** (☎ 0440 552 808; ☽ 9am-6pm) near the kauppatori, and from Nallikari Camping. The tourist office have a free cycle-route map.

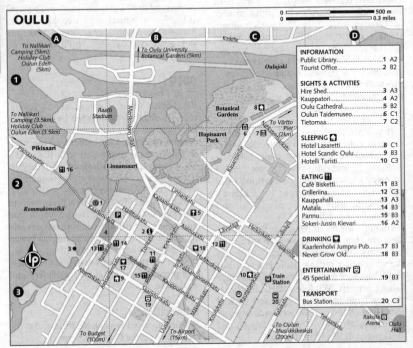

OULU

INFORMATION	
Public Library	1 A2
Tourist Office	2 B2

SIGHTS & ACTIVITIES	
Hire Shed	3 A3
Kauppatori	4 A2
Oulu Cathedral	5 B2
Oulun Taidemuseo	6 C1
Tietomaa	7 C2

SLEEPING	
Hotel Lasaretti	8 C1
Hotel Scandic Oulu	9 B3
Hotelli Turisti	10 C3

EATING	
Café Bisketti	11 B3
Grilleriina	12 C3
Kauppahalli	13 A3
Matala	14 B3
Pannu	15 B3
Sokeri-Jussin Kievari	16 A2

DRINKING	
Kaarlenholvi Jumpru Pub	17 B3
Never Grow Old	18 B3

ENTERTAINMENT	
45 Special	19 B3

TRANSPORT	
Bus Station	20 C3

Festivals & Events

In a country that wrote the book on oddball festivals, Oulu hosts more than its fair share. Take the **Air Guitar World Championships** (www .airguitarworldchampionships.com), which are part of the **Oulu Music Video Festival** (www.omvf.net) in late August. Contestants from all over the world take the stage to show what they can do with their imaginary instruments.

There are two unusual winter events, both the largest of their kind anywhere in the world. The **Oulu Tar Ski Race** (www.oulunhiihtoseura .fi), held in early March, is a 70km skiing race (40km for women) that is entering its 113th year. The **Ice-Angling Marathon** (www.oulutourism .fi) is a 48-hour contest held on the open sea in late March (when the ice is still thick) and draws more than 400 participants.

Pack the breath-mints for the **Garlic Festival** (www.oulunliikekeskus.fi) held over a weekend in mid-July. Eats on offer include everything from garlic potatoes, pizzas and bread to gar-lic-flavoured beer and ice cream – all enhanced by festivities and live entertainment.

Sleeping

There's precious little budget accommodation in Oulu.

Nallikari Camping (☎ 5586 1350; www.nallikari.fi; Hietasaari; camp sites €10-17 plus per adult/child €4/1, cabins €35-40, cottages €80-135; P 🖫 🛜 ⬤) Resembling a small town, this excellent camping ground offers all sorts of options in a location close to the beach on Hietasaari, a 40-minute walk to town via pedestrian bridges. Bus 17 gets you there from the kauppatori (€2.80), as does the tourist train.

Hotelli Turisti (☎ 563 6100; www.hotellituristi.fi; Rautatienkatu 9; s/d €80/95, weekend & summer €55/65; P ⬤) You can't beat this spot for convenience: it's bang opposite the train station. It's a no-nonsense affair with reception doubling as a convenience kiosk, but offers value, with bright modern rooms that have plenty of space. There are rooms sleeping up to five; rates include sauna and breakfast.

our pick **Hotel Lasaretti** (☎ 020 757 4700; www .lasaretti.com; Kasarmintie 13; s/d €115/132, summer €69/79; P 🖫 🛜 ⬤ ⬤) Bright, modern and optimistic, this inviting hotel sits in a group of renovated brick buildings, once a hospital. It's close to town but the parkside location by the bubbling-bright stream makes it feel rural. The artistically modern rooms have floorboards and flatscreens; some have fold-out

sofa-beds for families. Facilities and staff are excellent; there's also a busy restaurant with a sun-kissed terrace.

Holiday Club Oulun Eden (☎ 884 2000; www .holidayclub.fi; Nallikari; s/d €130/150, superior €150/170; P 🎮 🖫 🛜 ⬤ ⬤) This excellent spa hotel by the beach on Hietasaari offers great watery facilities (slides, intricate indoor pools, saunas) and massage treatments. You can also use the whole spa facilities for the day for a pretty reasonable €15 (€9 for kids). You can nearly always get a cheaper room deal online.

Hotel Scandic Oulu (☎ 543 1000; www.scandic -hotels.com; Saaristonkatu 4; s/d €138/158, summer €79/89; P 🎮 🖫 🛜 ⬤) This sleek, recently opened hotel occupies half a city block right in the middle. From the space-opera lights in its spacious foyer to the high-ceilinged rooms with clean Nordic decor and flatscreen, it's a temple to efficiency, hygiene and modern design (art, individuality, look elsewhere).

Eating

Local specialities can be found in and around the lively kauppatori. On the square is the **kauppahalli** (🕓 8am-6pm Mon-Fri, 8am-3pm Sat), with freshly filleted salmon glistening in the market stalls and plenty of spots to snack on anything from cloudberries to sushi.

Café Bisketti (☎ 375 768; Kirkkokatu 8; 🕓 8am-10pm Mon-Thu, 8am-1am Fri & Sat, noon-10pm Sun) This top double-sided spot transforms itself throughout the day. Think twice before getting that pastry with your morning coffee; they're enormous and might not leave room for lunch, when soup, salad, coffee and a pastry are €6.30, and only €7.80 with a tasty hot dish. In the evenings, the terrace is a decent spot for a people-watching beer.

Grilleriina (☎ 370 927; Asemakatu 29; 🕓 6pm-5am) There are grillis, and then there's this – a class above and a step beyond the standard. While it boasts the usual all-possible-permutations menu, it's far tastier than most, and has a spacious, Marimekko-furnished dining room to enjoy the abundant portions at any hour of the night.

Pannu (☎ 0207 928 200; Kauppurienkatu 12; mains €12-29; 🕓 10.30am-10pm Mon-Thu, 10.30am-11pm Fri & Sat, noon-9pm Sun) Secreted away in a brick cellar underneath Stockmann's department store, this spot is famous for its deep-pan pizzas but also does a decent line in salads, steaks, grilled reindeer and Italian-style focaccia and garlic breads.

Sokeri-Jussin Kievari (☎ 376 628; Pikisaarentie 2; mains €13-30; ☒ kitchen 11am-10pm) An Oulu classic, this timbered local on Pikisaari was once a sugar warehouse and has outdoor tables that have good views of the centre. Although the renovated interior has lost a bit of the original character, it's still an attractive spot to eat, with no-frills traditional dishes, including reindeer.

Matala (☎ 333 013; www.matala.fi; Rantakatu 6; mains €19-33; ☒ 4-11pm Mon-Sat) One of a clutch of upmarket restaurants around the kauppatori, this consistently delivers on food, service and, of course, location; outside seating puts you in the middle of things but the awning affords you a little privacy. There are various degustation menus (€48 to €83) using typical northern Finnish ingredients; delicious Arctic char, or veal sweetbreads with globe artichoke are examples from the regularly overhauled à la carte menu.

Drinking & Entertainment

There's plenty going on in Oulu at night. The kauppatori is the spot to start in summer: the terraces lick up every last drop of the evening sun. Keltainen Aitta and Makasiini are the main ones, set in traditional wooden warehouses.

our pick **Never Grow Old** (☎ 311 3936; Hallituskatu 17; ☒ 2pm-2am Sun-Thu, 2pm-3am Fri & Sat) This enduringly popular bar hits its stride after 10pm, with plenty of dancing, DJs and revelry in the tightly packed interior. The goofy decor includes some seriously comfortable and extremely uncomfortable places to sit, and a log-palisade bar that seems designed to get you to wear your drink.

St Michaels (☒ 9am-3am) On the same block is convivial St Michaels, an Irish bar with decent Guinness and whisky selection, and Sarkka, an old-time Finnish bar that charges a €1.50 entrance fee at night but is worth it for the downbeat traditional atmosphere and heroic opening hours.

Kaarlenholvi Jumpru Pub (☎ 562 4500; Kauppurienkatu 6; ☒ 11am-2am Mon-Tue, 11am-4am Wed-Sat, noon-2am Sun) This Oulu institution is a great place for meeting locals and its enclosed outdoor area always seems to be humming with cheerfully sauced-up folk. There's a warren of cosy rooms inside, as well as a nightclub opening from 10pm Wednesday to Saturday.

45 Special (☎ 881 1845; Saaristonkatu 12; ☒ 8pm-4am) This grungy club is Oulu's best rock venue, with wall-to-wall patrons. There's a €5 cover at weekends and regular live gigs.

Getting There & Away

AIR

There are several daily direct flights from Helsinki, operated by Finnair/Finncomm. Blue1 services Helsinki. Bus 19 runs between the centre and the airport (€2.80, 25 minutes, every 20 minutes).

BUS

The bus station, near the train station, has services connecting Oulu with all the main centres. These include Rovaniemi (€38.40, 3½ hours), Tornio (€22, 2½ hours), Kajaani (€31.70, 2½ hours) and Helsinki (€86, 10 to 11 hours).

TRAIN

The station is just east of the centre. Six to 10 trains a day (€63.50, seven to nine hours) run from Helsinki to Oulu; the Pendolino service takes only 6¼ hours (€72). There are also trains via Kajaani, and trains north to Rovaniemi.

KUUSAMO

☎ 08 / pop 16,899

Kuusamo is a remote frontier town 200km northeast of Oulu and close to the Russian border. Wonderful canoeing, hiking and wildlife-watching is available in the surrounding area; nearby Ruka also draws the winter crowds.

There are many possibilities for cross-country skiing, hiking and fishing as well as fast, rugged rapids on the **Kitkajoki** and **Oulankajoki**. The **Karhuntassu centre** (☎ 0306 502 540; www.kuusamo.fi; Torangintaival 2; ☒ 9am-8pm Mon-Fri, 10am-6pm Sat & Sun late Jun–Jul, 9am-6pm Mon-Fri, 10am-4pm Sat & Sun early Aug, 9am-5pm Mon-Fri mid-Aug–late Jun) at the highway junction has comprehensive tourist information, free internet, a national parks info point and a cottage-rental booking desk. There are many tour operators based in Kuusamo and Ruka, offering a full range of winter and summer activities. The Ruka webpage, www.ruka.fi, is a good place to look for active ideas.

Numerous holiday cottages dot the area. Contact the tourist office, **FinFun** (☎ 0203 70021; www.finfun.fi), which has a portfolio of hundreds, or **ProLoma** (☎ 020-792 9700; www.proloma.fi).

Kuusamon Kansanopisto (☎ 050-444 1157; kuusa mon.kansanopisto@koillismaa.fi; Kitkantie 35; s/d €30/50, with shared shower €25/42; **P**) is around the corner from the bus. This folk high school offers great budget accommodation in comfortable spacious rooms with en suites; the bad news is that you have to arrive during office hours (8am to 3.45pm Monday to Friday).

A cordial welcome is guaranteed at sweet main-street **Hotelli Kuusanka** (☎ 852 2240; hotellikuusanka.kuusamo@co.inet.fi; Ouluntie 2; s/d €59/77; **P** **&**), whose blue-shaded rooms are so clean you can smell it.

Finnair flies daily to Helsinki. Buses run daily from Kajaani, Oulu and Rovaniemi.

Oulanka National Park

This is one of the most visited national parks in Finland, thanks mainly to the 80km **Karhunkierros Trail** (Bear's Ring), a spectacular three- or four-day trek through rugged cliffs, gorges and suspension bridges, starting from either the Hautajärvi Visitor Centre or the Ristikallio parking area and ending at the resort village of Ruka, 25km north of Kuusamo.

There are shelters and free overnight huts on the trail. The *Rukatunturi-Oulanka Map* (1:40,000) has trail and hut information. The best online resource is the excellent Metsähallitus website, www.outdoors.fi.

Juuma is another gateway to the region, with accommodation and accessibility to some of the main sights, such as the **Myllykoski** and **Jyrävä** waterfalls. If you don't have the time or resources for the longer walk, you can do the 12km **Little Bear's Ring** from Juuma in around four hours. The trail starts at **Lomakylä Retki-Etappi** (☎ 863 218; www .retkietappi.fi; Juumantie 134; camp sites €10; cabins from €30; ☻ Jun-Sep; **P**), where there are camp sites and cabins.

LAPLAND

Lapland, extending hundreds of kilometres above the Arctic Circle, is Finland's true wilderness and casts a powerful spell. While you won't see polar bears or rocky fjords, there is something intangible here that makes it magical. The midnight sun, the Sámi peoples, the Northern Lights and the wandering reindeer are all components of this magic, as is good old ho-ho-ho himself, who 'officially' resides in this part of the world.

Lapland has awesome wildernesses and is *the* place in Finland to get active. Opportunities to get out and experience this vastness are endless. In winter you can mush with husky-dogs, ski in downhill resorts, cheer for reindeer races on frozen lakes, drill a hole and go ice-fishing or snowmobile through forests. In summer, hike through pristine national parks in endless daylight and raft down white-water rivers. The only limitation here is your budget.

It's important to pick your time in Lapland carefully. In the far north there's no sun for 50 days of the year, and no night for 70-odd days. In June it's very muddy, and in July insects can be hard to deal with. If you're here to walk, August is great and in September the *ruska* colours can be seen. There's thick snow cover from mid-October to May; the best time for skiing and husky safaris is March and April, when you get at least some daylight, and less extreme temperatures.

ROVANIEMI

☎ 016 / pop 58,825

Expanding rapidly on the back of a tourism boom, the 'official' terrestrial residence of Santa Claus is the capital of Finnish Lapland and a more-or-less obligatory northern stop. Its wonderful Arktikum museum is the perfect introduction to the mysteries of these latitudes, and Rovaniemi is a good place to organise activities from.

Thoroughly destroyed by the retreating Wehrmacht in 1944, the town was rebuilt to a plan by Alvar Aalto, with the major streets in the shape of reindeer antlers (no, we couldn't either). Its unattractive buildings are compensated for by its marvellous location on the fast-flowing Kemijoki.

Though the museum is by far the most impressive sight, the tour buses roll north of town, where everyone's favourite beardie-weirdie has an impressive grotto among an array of tourist shops that straddle the Arctic Circle marker. It's free to visit, if not to photograph, the personable chap.

Information

There are lockers (€2 per 24 hours) at both train and bus stations, and a storage counter at the train station.

FINLAND

Etiäinen (☎ 020 564 7820; etiainen@metsa.fi; Koskikatu 44; ☼ 8am-4pm Mon-Fri) Information centre for the national parks, with information on hiking and fishing in Lapland. The office sells maps and fishing permits, and books cottages.

Public library (☎ 322 2463; Hallituskatu 9; ☼ 11am-7pm Mon-Fri, 11am-5pm Sat) Aalto-designed; has free internet.

Tourist Information (☎ 346 270; www.visitrov aniemi.fi; Maakuntakatu 29; ☼ 8am-5pm Mon-Fri Sep-May, 8am-6pm Mon-Fri, 10am-4pm Sat & Sun Jun-Aug, also some weekends Sep & Dec) On the square in the middle of town. Free internet.

Sights & Activities

With its beautifully designed glass tunnel stretching out to the Ounasjoki, **Arktikum** (☎ 322 3260; www.arktikum.fi; Pohjoisranta 4; adult/child/student/family €12/5/8/25; ☼ 9am-7pm mid-Jun–mid-Aug, 10am-6pm daily early Jun, late Aug & Dec, 10am-5pm Tue-Sun Sep-Nov, 10am-6pm Tue-Sun Jan-May) is one of Finland's best museums and well worth the admission fee if you are interested in the north. There are two main exhibitions; one side deals with Lapland, with some information on Sámi culture. The highlight, though, is the other side, with a wide-ranging display on the Arctic itself, with superb static and interactive displays focusing on Arctic flora and fauna, as well as on the peoples of Arctic Europe, Asia and North America.

Across the Ounasjoki and 3km above the town, the **Ounasvaara Ski Centre** (☎ 369 045; www .ounasvaara.fi) has six downhill ski slopes and three ski jumps, plus a summer tobogganing run and the Ounasvaara Sky Hotel. It's a good spot for hiking in summer.

Bicycles can be rented from **Arctic Safaris** (Koskikatu 6) and from **Europcar** (Pohjanpuistikko 2) for €20 a day.

Vesihiisi (☎ 322 2592; Nuortenkatu 11; admission €5.50) has an outdoor and indoor pool as well as saunas, with separate times and sections for men and women. It's cheaper in summer.

Festivals & Events

With the Arctic Circle – and Santa Claus – close by, Christmas is a big time of the year and there are plenty of festive activities in December. In March, Rovaniemi hosts the **Ounasvaara Winter Games**, with skiing and ski-jumping competitions. **Jutajaiset** (www.jutajaiset .fi), in late June, is a celebration of Lapland folklore by various youth ensembles.

Tours

Rovaniemi is Lapland's most popular base for winter and summer activities, offering the convenience of frequent departures and professional trips with multilingual guides.

In summer, things offered by most operators include guided walks, mountain biking (€54 to €60), river cruises (€22), visits to a reindeer farm (€50 to €60) or huskies (€80). Winter activities are snowmobiling (€90 to €115 for a two- to three-hour trip), snowshoe-walking (€70), reindeer-sledding (€100 to €120), husky-sledding (€120 to €180), cross-country skiing (€50 to €60), or a combination. These can include ice-fishing, a sauna, a shot at seeing the Northern Lights, or an overnight trip to a wilderness cottage (€350 to €450). Recommended operators:

Arctic Safaris/Lapland Safaris (☎ 340 0400, 0207 868 700; www.arcticsafaris.fi, www.laplandsafaris.fi; Koskikatu 6) Recent merger of two of the most reliable and well-established outfits.

Eräsetti Safaris (☎ 362 811; www.erasetti.fi; Valtakatu 31). Experienced operator with another office at Santa's village.

Lapland VIP Tour (☎ 0400 542 868; www.laplandvip tour.fi; Valtakatu 33)

Safartica (☎ 311 484; www.safartica.com; Valtakatu 20)

Sleeping

Ounaskoski Camping (☎ 345 304; Jäämerentie 1; camp sites €14 plus per adult/child €4.50/2.50; ☼ late May–mid-Sep) Just across the elegant bridge from the town centre, this camping ground is perfectly situated on the riverbank.

Hostel Rudolf (☎ 321 321; www.rudolf.fi; Koskikatu 41; dm/s/d winter €44/60/88, summer €30/41/52; P ♿) Run by Hotel Santa Claus, where you inconveniently have to go to check in, this staffless hostel is Rovaniemi's only one and can fill up fast. Dorms are comfortable, and the private rooms excellent for the price, with spotless bathrooms, solid desks and bedside lamps; there's also a kitchen available. HI discount.

Guesthouse Borealis (☎ 342 0130; www.guesthouse borealis.com; Asemieskatu 1; s/d/tr €45/56/77; P 🖳 🛜) The cordial hospitality and proximity to the train station make this family-run spot a winner. The rooms have no frills but are bright and clean; some have a balcony. The airy dining room is the venue for breakfast, which features Finnish porridge; there's also a sauna for a small extra charge. Prices rise in winter.

Hotelli Aakenus (☎ 342 2051; www.hotel liaakenus.net; Koskikatu 47; s/d €70/80, summer s/d €55/59;

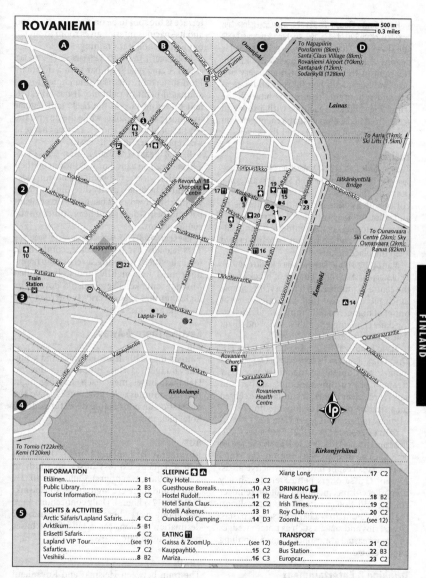

ROVANIEMI

To Näapapiirin;
Porofarmi (8km);
Santa-Claus Village (8km);
Rovaniemi Airport (10km);
Santapark (12km);
Sodankylä (128km)

To Aaria (1km);
Ski Lifts (1.5km)

Lainas

Jätkänkynttilä Bridge

Toripuistikko

To Ounasvaara
Ski Centre (2km); Sky
Ounasvaara (2km);
Ranua (82km)

Kemijoki

Train Station

Lappia-Talo

Rovaniemi Church

Rovaniemi Health Centre

Kirkkolampi

To Tornio (122km);
Kemi (120km)

Kirkonjyrhämä

FINLAND

INFORMATION		
Etiäinen.....................................**1**	B1	
Public Library..........................**2**	B3	
Tourist Information..................**3**	C2	

SIGHTS & ACTIVITIES		
Arctic Safaris/Lapland Safaris.......**4**	C2	
Arktikum..................................**5**	B1	
Eräsetti Safaris........................**6**	C2	
Lapland VIP Tour................(see 19)		
Safartica..................................**7**	C2	
Vesihiisi....................................**8**	B2	

SLEEPING		
City Hotel.................................**9**	C2	
Guesthouse Borealis.................**10**	A3	
Hostel Rudolf...........................**11**	B2	
Hotel Santa Claus....................**12**	C2	
Hotelli Aakenus.......................**13**	B1	
Ounaskoski Camping................**14**	D3	

EATING		
Gaissa & ZoomUp..............(see 12)		
Kauppayhtiö.............................**15**	C2	
Mariza......................................**16**	C3	

Xiang Long..............................**17**	C2	

DRINKING		
Hard & Heavy..........................**18**	B2	
Irish Times...............................**19**	C2	
Roy Club..................................**20**	C2	
ZoomIt...............................(see 12)		

TRANSPORT		
Budget....................................**21**	C2	
Bus Station.............................**22**	B3	
Europcar................................**23**	C2	

(P 🖥 📶) Offering excellent summer value from mid-May right through until the end of August, this friendly, efficient little hotel is a short distance west of the centre of town and only a short stroll from the Arktikum. The bright rooms vary in furnishings and size, but they are all spacious and comfortable.

City Hotel (☎ 330 0111; www.cityhotel.fi; Pekankatu 9; s/d €103/128, Jun-Sep €65/70; P 🖥 📶) There's something pleasing about this place, cheerfully tucked between the convivial ambience of its own restaurant and bar. Although sizeable, it retains an intimate feel, and the stripy sheets, flat TVs and dark panelled furniture add a classy touch to the decent rooms.

Hotel Santa Claus (☎ 321 321; www.hotelsantaclaus .fi; Korkalonkatu 29; s/d €135/162, weekend & summer r €89; P 🖳 📶) Thankfully this excellent hotel is devoid of sleighbells and 'ho-ho-ho' kitsch. It's right in the heart of town and very upbeat and busy, with helpful staff and a great bar and restaurant. The rooms have all the trimmings and are spacious, with a sofa and good-sized beds; a small supplement gets you a superior room, which is slightly bigger.

Eating

Kauppayhtiö (☎ 342 2422; Valtakatu 24; 🕑 10.30am-8pm Mon-Thu, 10.30am-2am Fri & Sat) Rovaniemi's best cafe, this is an oddball collection of retro curios with a coffee-bean and gasoline theme and colourful plastic tables. An espresso machine, bottomless coffee, outdoor seating, salads, sundaes and bohemian Lapland crowd keep the place ticking.

Mariza (☎ 319 616; Ruokasenkatu 2; lunch €6.20-7.20; 🕑 9.30am-3pm Mon-Fri) A couple of blocks from the centre in untouristed territory, this simple lunch place is a real find, and offers a great buffet of home-cooked Finnish food, including daily changing hot dishes, soup and salad. Authentic and excellent.

Xiang Long (☎ 319 331; Koskikatu 21; mains €11-17; 🕑 11am-10pm Mon-Fri, noon-10pm Sat & Sun) This main-street Chinese has friendly service, tasty steamed prawn dim-sum, a salad bar and several reindeer dishes, including one served on a sizzling platter. The lunch buffet (€8.40 Monday to Friday) is great value.

Gaissa & ZoomUp (☎ 321 321; Gaissa mains €19-26, ZoomUp most meals €13-19; 🕑 5.30-11pm Mon-Sat, also Sun Dec & Jan) The upstairs restaurant of the Hotel Santa Claus is split into two attractive areas. Elegant Gaissa offers petite, reindeer-heavy upmarket cuisine, including spot-on reindeer rillettes and slow-roasted lamb that falls off the bone. ZoomUp is a bar with salads, pastas, steaks, ribs and snacks such as potato wedges in a more casual atmosphere aimed at pulling a local crowd.

Drinking & Entertainment

Excluding ski resorts, Rovaniemi is the only place north of Oulu with a half-decent nightlife.

ZoomIt (☎ 321 321; Koskikatu; 🕑 11am-11pm, later on weekends) Large light, modern ZoomIt is a popular, buzzy central bar and cafe, a good place for a drink or coffee while you scope out Rovaniemi. Right in the heart of town, its terrace is the spot to be on a sunny afternoon and its spacious interior gives room to stretch out with a book if it's raining.

Irish Times (☎ 319 925; Valtakatu 33; 🕑 2pm-3am or later) A convivial Irish bar with a distinctly Finnish flavour, this is a fine choice for an animated night of pubbing. It has an excellent heated terrace at the back, and regular live music and karaoke, while the downstairs bar has pool tables. There's a cover charge at weekends, when it's at its best.

Hard & Heavy (☎ 050 447 3543; Koskikatu 25; 🕑 6pm-2am) The band Lordi cashed in on their Eurovision success by opening a 'horror-rock-taurant'. The food's pretty dire, but it's worth visiting the downstairs bar for its extravagant bat-and-belfry decor and heavy tunes on the sound system.

Roy Club (☎ 313 705; Maakuntakatu 24; 🕑 9pm-4am) This friendly bar has a sedate, comfortable top half with cosy seating, a very cheap happy hour until 1am nightly, and well-attended Monday karaoke. There's also a downstairs nightclub that gets cheerily boisterous with students and goes late.

Getting There & Away

AIR

Finnair flies daily from Helsinki and Oulu. The budget carrier Blue1 also flies to Helsinki. Buses meet each arriving flight (€5, 15 minutes). Airport buses leave the bus station an hour before departures, doing hotel pick-ups.

BUS

Rovaniemi is Lapland's main transport hub. Frequent express buses go south to Kemi (€19.20, two hours), Oulu (€38.40, 3½ hours), and there are night buses to Helsinki (€113.80, 12½ hours). Daily connections serve just about everywhere else in Lapland: see destination sections for details. Some buses head on north into Norway.

TRAIN

The train between Helsinki and Rovaniemi (€70 to €75, 10 to 12 hours) is quicker, cheaper and more commodious than the bus. There are three daily direct services (via Oulu), including overnight services (high-season total prices go from €92 in a berth up to €179 in a smart modern cabin with en suite) with car transport and other connections possibilities.

Getting Around

Major car-rental agencies have offices in the centre and at the airport. Helpful **Budget** (☎ 0207 466 620; www.budget.fi; Koskikatu 9) is beside the post office and **Europcar** (☎ 0403 062 870; www.europcar.fi; Pohjanpuistikko 2) is at the Rantasipi Pohjanhovi hotel.

AROUND ROVANIEMI
Napapiiri (Arctic Circle) & Santa Claus Village

The southernmost line at which the sun doesn't set at least one day a year, the Arctic Circle, is called **Napapiiri** in Finland. Though the Arctic Circle can be crossed by road at several points in Lapland, the **Arctic Circle marker** is here, 8km north of Rovaniemi – and built right on top of it is the 'official' **Santa Claus Village** (www.santaclausvillage.info; admission free; ☺ 10am-5pm Sep-May, 9am-6pm early Jun & late Aug, 9am-7pm mid-Jun–mid-Aug), a touristy complex of shops. Here too is **Santa Claus Post Office** (☎ 020 452 3120; www.santaclaus.posti.fi; FIN-96930 Arctic Circle), which receives nearly three-quarters of a million letters each year from children all over the world. Your postcard sent from here will bear an official Santa stamp, and you can arrange to have it delivered at Christmas time.

But the big attraction is, of course **Santa** himself, who sees visitors year-round in a rather impressive new **grotto** (☎ 020 799 999; www.santaclauslive.com; admission free; ☺ 9am-6pm Jun-Aug, 10am-5pm Sep-May), where a huge clock mechanism (it slows the earth's rotation so that Santa can visit the whole world's children on Christmas night) eerily surrounds those queuing for an audience. The portly saint is quite a linguist, and an old hand at chatting with kids and adults alike. A private chat with the man is absolutely free, but you can't photograph the moment… and official photos of your visit start at an outrageous €25.

Napapiiri is 8km north of Rovaniemi on the Sodankylä road. Bus 8 heads there from the train station, passing through the centre (adult/child €6.40/3.60 return).

KEMI
☎ 016 / pop 22,669

Kemi is an industrial town and important deepwater harbour. Although not hugely appealing (in summer only the gem museum and wide waterfront have any sort of siren song), Kemi's home to two of Finland's blockbuster winter attractions: the Arctic ice-breaker *Sampo*, and the Lumilinna (Snow Castle), complete with ice hotel.

Plough through the Gulf of Bothnia pack ice aboard the **Sampo**, a genuine Arctic ice-breaker ship and the only one in the world that regularly accepts tourists. The four-hour cruise includes lunch and ice-swimming in special drysuits – a remarkable experience. The *Sampo* sails at noon on Thursday, Friday and Saturday from late December to mid-April, with several Wednesday departures during busy periods, and costs €225 per person. If you choose to approach and leave the good ship on snowmobiles (with a reindeer visit included), the price is €365. The best time to go is when the ice is thickest, usually in March. Contact **Sampo Tours** (☎ 256 548; www.sampotours.com; Kauppakatu 16), in the same office as tourist information, to book.

Few things conjure the fairy-tale romance of a **snow castle** (☎ 259 502, www.snowcastle.net; adult/child €7/3.50; ☺ 10am-7pm end of Jan–mid-Apr), and few can compete with Kemi's, a favoured destination for weddings, honeymoons, or just general marvelling at the weird light and sumptuously realised decoration of the multistoreyed interior. The design changes every year but always includes an ethereally beautiful chapel (hope the vows last longer than those ice wedding rings), a **snow hotel** and a **restaurant** (3-course menus €34-45).

Kemin Matkailu (☎ 259 690; www.kemi.fi; Kauppakatu 16; ☺ 9am-5pm Mon-Fri) is Kemi's tourist office. The gemstone gallery also has tourist information.

Sleeping

Between late January and early April you can spend the night in the **Snow Hotel** (☎ 259 502; s/d/ste €165/260/310). The interior temperature is -5°C, but a woolly sheepskin and sturdy sleeping bag keep you warm(ish) atop the ice bed. In the morning you can thaw out in the sauna of a nearby hotel.

Hotelli Palomestari (☎ 257 117; www.hotellipalomestari.com; Valtakatu 12; s/d €82/110, weekends & summer €58/79; P ⚟ ☞) This likeable family place is a block south and one west of the train and bus stations and offers friendly service and decent rooms with trademark Finnish furniture including a desk and sofa. There's also a convivial bar.

FINLAND

Getting There & Away

Kemi/Tornio airport is 6km north, and Finnair/Finncomm have regular Helsinki flights. A trip in a shared airport taxi costs €10.

Buses run to Tornio (€5.90, 45 minutes) more than hourly (fewer at weekends), Rovaniemi (€19.20, two hours) and Oulu (€13.50, 1¾ hours) among other places.

There are trains from Helsinki (€70.50, nine hours), Oulu (€15.60, 1¼ hours) and Rovaniemi (€16.70, 1½ hours).

TORNIO

☎ 016 / pop 22,373

Right on the impressive Tornionjoki, the longest free-flowing river in northern Europe, Tornio is joined to its Swedish counterpart Haparanda (Finnish: Haaparanta; p464) by short bridges. Tornio smells not of paper mills but of malt, as the Lapin Kulta brewery drifts its aromas across town. Don't forget that Finland is an hour ahead of Sweden.

Information

Green Line Centre (☎ 432 733; www.visithaparanda-tornio.com; ☽ 8am-8pm Mon-Fri, 10am-6pm Sat & Sun Jun–mid-Aug, 10am-6pm Mon-Fri mid-Aug–May) Acts as the tourist office for both towns. Free internet terminal.
Public library (☎ 432 433; Torikatu 2; ☽ 11am-6pm Tue-Thu, 11am-3pm Fri-Sun) Free internet.

Sights & Activities

Interesting sights near the town centre include the beautiful wooden **Tornio Church** (1686) on Seminaarinkatu, the tiny **Orthodox Church** on Lukiokatuthe, built by order of Tsar Alexander I, the **Lapin Kulta Brewery** (☎ 020 717 5671; Lapinkullantie 1; ☽ free tours 1pm Tue & Thu late Jun-late–Aug) and the **Aineen Taidemuseo** (☎ 432 438; Torikatu 2; adult/child €4/free; ☽ 11am-6pm Tue-Thu, 11am-3pm Fri-Sun), with a big collection of Finnish art from the 19th and 20th centuries.

River-rafting is popular in summer on the Kukkolankoski. Trips are run by **Lapland Connection** (☎ 253 405; www.laplandconnection.com) and **Pohjolan Safarit/Nordic Safaris** (☎ 040 755 1858; www.nordicsafaris.com; Koskitie 130, Kukkola) from between €45 to €75 per person, using inflatable rubber rafts or traditional wooden boats. Safaris Unlimited also has kayaking trips, and both companies offer winter excursions such as snowmobile, reindeer and husky safaris. The tourist office can make bookings for all trips and handles **fishing** permits; there are several excellent spots along the Tornio River.

There's the famous **Green Zone golf course** (☎ 431 711; Näräntie) here straddling Finland and Sweden, allowing you to fire shots into a different country and time zone, or play under the midnight sun. You'll need a Green Card or handicap certificate. There's also a driving range and pitch and putt course here.

Sleeping & Eating

There's a good hostel and upmarket hotel across the bridge in Haparanda (p464).

Camping Tornio (☎ 445 945; www.campingtornio.com; Matkailijantie; tents €6 plus per adult/child €4/1; cabins €42-57; ☽ mid-May–Aug; P) Three kilometres from town, off the road to Kemi. Boat and bike hire, tennis and a beach.

E-City Matkakoti (☎ 480 897; www.ecitybedandbreakfast.com; Saarenpäänkatu 39; s/d €40/60; P ☎) Tornio's best budget option, this is a friendly guesthouse a block north of the brewery, and run by a welcoming young family. Cosy rooms feature comfortable beds and colourful fabrics; the shared bathrooms are clean and have good showers, and breakfast includes traditional Finnish porridge.

Kaupunginhotelli (☎ 43311; www.tornionkaupungin hotelli.fi; Itäranta 4; s/d €112/129, summer & weekends r €94; P ☎ ☎ ☎) Tornio's only real hotel has decent facilities, including a small pool, restaurant, bar, karaoke and nightclub. The rooms are attractive, with colourful bedspreads and plenty of natural light (in summer at least), though closer examination might have you calling for a pot of varnish and a tin of paint to touch things up.

Umpitunneli (☎ 430 360; www.umpitunneli.fi; Hallituskatu 15; mains €12-25; ☽ 11am-2am or later, food served until 9.30pm) The 'Dead-End Tunnel' may be a road to nowhere but it's a most enjoyable one, with a huge terrace, plenty of pissed-up locals adding entertainment value at weekends, and large plates of food, from creamy pastas to steaks and Tex-Mex. There are often live bands, or else the *humppa* (a fast Finnish dance, between a waltz and a foxtrot) music gets going.

Getting There & Away

There are a few daily buses from Rovaniemi (€20.50, two hours), although there are more connections (bus and train) via Kemi (€5.90, 45 minutes, more than hourly, less at weekends, free with rail pass). Many Tornio-bound buses continue to Haparanda, although the distance is so short you can walk.

From Haparanda, there are buses to Luleå, from where trains run to Stockholm, Göteborg and Kiruna.

ROVANIEMI TO INARI

North from Rovaniemi, Hwy 4 (E75) heads up to the vast, flat expanse of northern Lapland and Sápmi, home of the Sámi people and their domesticated reindeer herds wandering the forests and fells. Subtle landscape changes become more severe as you head north, and the feeling of entering one of Europe's last great wildernesses is palpable. The resort town of Saariselkä is the base for hiking or ski-trekking do-it-yourself itineraries in the wonderful UKK National Park, while the Sámi capital of Inari is the place to learn about their traditions and a base for visiting the Lemmenjoki National Park.

Sodankylä
☎ 016 / pop 8982

Likeable Sodankylä is the main service centre for one of Europe's least-populated areas, which has a population density of just 0.8 people per sq km. It makes a decent staging post on the way between Rovaniemi and the north.

The **tourist office** (☎ 618 168; www.sodankyla.fi; Jäämerentie 3; ⏰ 9am-5pm Mon-Fri, 11am-4pm Sat & Sun) is at the intersection of the Kemijärvi and Rovaniemi roads. Next to it, the **old church** (☎ 0400 190 406; ⏰ 9am-6pm Jun–mid-Aug, 9am-5pm Fri-Mon rest of Aug, by request rest of year) is the region's oldest and dates back to 1689.

Sodankylä books out in mid-June for the **Midnight Sun Film Festival** (www.msfilmfestival.fi), which has a comprehensive range of intriguing screenings in three venues.

Camping Sodankylä Nilimella (☎ 612 181; www.naturex-ventures.fi; tents €5 plus per adult/child €4/2, 2-/4-person cabins €36/52, apt €65/95; ⏰ Jun-Aug; P) Across the river from the town, this camping ground has simple but spacious cabins, as well as cottage apartments with their own kitchen and sauna. You can hire bikes for €15 per day.

Majatalo Kolme Veljestä (☎ 0400-539 075; www.majatalokolmeveljesta.fi; Ivalontie 1; s/d/tr €42/58/69; P 💻 🛜) This family-run guesthouse, 500m north of the centre, has small but spotless rooms that share a decent bathroom. Price includes kitchen use, breakfast, a sauna and free tea and coffee.

our pick **Hotelli Karhu** (☎ 613 801; www.hotel-bearinn.com; Lapintie 7; s/d €68/82 May-Oct, €77/100 Nov-Apr; P 🛜 ♿) This central hotel is a great deal, offering buzzy staff, offbeat lobby decor and really inviting chambers, with big fluffy beds, greywood floors and great modern bathrooms.

There are plenty of cafes, supermarkets, takeaways and a couple of bars lined up along the main street, Jäämerentie.

There are regular buses from Rovaniemi, Ivalo and Kemijärvi. The bus terminal is on the main road.

Ivalo
☎ 016 / pop 3500

A small town by most standards, Ivalo (Sámi: Avvil) is a metropolis in these latitudes. With plenty of services and an airport busy with charters around Christmas, it's a useful service centre, but has little to detain the visitor, with Inari's Sámi culture and Saariselkä's plentiful activities so close.

On the main road, **Inarilainen** (☎ 0306 244 120; Ivalontie 7; ⏰ 9am-5pm Mon-Fri) has a tourist information point inside. Across the road, there's a **Metsähallitus centre** (☎ 0205 647 701; Ivalontie 10; ⏰ 9am-4pm Mon-Fri) with national park information.

There are a few daily buses from Rovaniemi (€49.80, 4¾ hours) to Ivalo, continuing north into Norway before returning.

INARI
☎ 016 / pop 550

Though it's Finland's most significant Sámi centre, and one of Lapland's major visitor destinations, you might miss the tiny village of Inari (Sámi: Anár), if you're not paying attention. Don't, for this is the place to begin to learn something of Sámi culture, and has the wonderful Siida museum, as well as excellent handicrafts shops. It's also a great base for heading off to farther-flung locations like Lemmenjoki National Park.

Inari is the seat of the Finnish Sámi parliament, and plans have been finalised for a Sámi cultural centre that will hold it, as well as a library and music archive. The village sits on Lapland's largest lake, Inarijärvi, a spectacular body of water with more than 3000 islands in its 1153 sq km area.

In the centre of the village, **Inari Info** (☎ 661 666; www.inarilapland.org; ⏰ 9am-6pm Jun-Aug, 10am-5pm early Sep, 10am-5pm Mon-Fri mid-Sep–May) is a

FINLAND

goldmine of information and a great place for tips on finding out more about the area and Sámi culture. Here you can rent bikes, kayaks and canoes and there's internet access (€2 per 15 minutes).

Sights & Activities

One of Finland's finest museums, **Siida** (☎ 665 212, www.siida.fi; adult/child/student €8/4/6.50; ☻ 9am-8pm Jun-Sep, 10am-5pm Tue-Sun Oct-May) should not be missed. It's a comprehensive overview of the Sámi and their environment that's actually two museums skilfully interwoven. Outside is the original museum, a complex of **open-air buildings** that reflect post-nomadic Sámi life. There's also a fine craft shop and a top-value cafe, where the €9.50 lunch gets you a hot dish and free use of the salad bar.

Siida's website is itself worth a mention: via the 'services' and 'links' menus you can access a series of excellent pages on the Inari and Skolt Sámi cultures among other treasures.

There's a marked 7.5km walking track (starting from the Siida parking area) to the 18th-century **Pielpajärvi wilderness church**. If you have a vehicle, there's another parking area 3km closer. In winter or spring you'll need snowshoes and a keen attitude to tackle this walk.

Daily cruises run by **Lake & Snow** (☎ 0400 295 731; www.saariselka.fi/lakesnow) sail on Inarijärvi from mid-June (as soon as the ice melts) to mid-August (€15, two hours).

Inarin Porofarmi (☎ 673 912; Kittiläntie 1445; www .reindeerfarm.fi) is a reindeer farm that runs sled-trips in winter and visits in summer with plenty of information on reindeer herding and Sámi culture. The two-hour visit costs €20, or €45 including transport from Inari.

Inari is the main centre for Sámi handicrafts and there are several studios and boutique shops in the village. **Sámi Duodji Ry** (☎ 671 254; Inarintie 51; ☻ 10am-6pm daily Jul & Aug, 10am-5pm Mon-Fri, 10am-3pm Sat Sep-Jun), on the main road, is the main shop of the Finnish association of Sámi craftspeople

The third weekend of January is **Skábmagovat**, a film festival with an indigenous theme. Held over the last weekend of March or first of April, the King's Cup is the grand finale of Lapland's **reindeer-racing** (www.paliskunnat.fi) season and a great spectacle as the de-antlered beasts race around the frozen lake, jockeys sliding like waterskiers behind them.

Sleeping & Eating

Lomakylä Inari (☎ 671 108; www.lomakyla-inari.fi; 2-/4-person cabins €35/45, with bathroom €50/65, cottages with sauna €75-150, camping for 1-2 people €22; ☻ Jun–late Sep; **P** ☐) The closest cabin accommodation to town, this is 500m south of the centre and a good option.

our pick Villa Lanca (☎ 040 748 0984; www.villalanca .com; s/d €43/68, with kitchen €53/78; **P**) Opposite the tourist office, this is Inari's most characterful lodging, with superb boutique rooms decorated with Asian fabrics, feather charms and real artistic flair.

Hotelli Inarin Kultahovi (☎ 511 7100; www.hotelkul tahovi.fi; Saarikoskentie 2; s/d €68/88; **P** ☎ &) Just off the main road towards Lemmenjoki, this cosy family-run place overlooks the rapids and has spruce rooms, some with a great river view. There's a restaurant (mains €15-28, open 11am to 11pm) that serves well-presented, tasty Lappish specialities.

Getting There & Away

Buses run here from Ivalo (€7.20, 30 minutes). Two daily buses hit Inari from Rovaniemi (€52.60, 5¼ hours) and continue to Norway, one to Karasjok, and on to Nordkapp in summer, another to Tana Bru. In summer there's also a bus to Kirkenes.

LEMMENJOKI NATIONAL PARK

Lemmenjoki is Finland's largest national park, covering a remote wilderness area between Inari and Norway. It's prime hiking territory, with desolate wilderness rivers, rough landscapes and the mystique of gold, with solitary prospectors sloshing away with their pans in the middle of nowhere. Boat trips on the river allow more leisurely exploration of the park.

Lemmenjoki Nature Centre (☎ 0205 647 793; ☻ 9am-5pm Jun-Sep) is near the park entrance just before the village of Njurgulahti, about 50km southwest of Inari.

As well as hiking trails and opportunities for gold panning, there's a boat cruise along the Lemmenjoki valley in summer, from Njurgulahti village to the Kultahamina wilderness hut at Gold Harbour. A 20km marked trail also follows the course of the river, so you can take the boat one way, then hike back. There are several places offering camping and/or cabin accommodation, food and boat trips. Inside the park, a dozen wilderness huts provide free accommodation.

There is one taxi-bus on weekdays between Inari and Njurgulahti; check times in advance with the Inari tourist office.

NORTHWESTERN LAPLAND

There's plenty going on above the Arctic Circle in northwestern Lapland, with several ski resorts (Levi, Ylläs, Olos), and a wonderful range of activities in Muonio, including memorable husky-sled treks. The long, lonely journey up Finland's left 'arm' culminates in Kilpisjärvi, tucked in between Sweden and Norway. These are Finland's 'highlands' and, though not especially high altitude, they offer excellent walking and some outstanding views.

Muonio
☎ 016

The village of Muonio is the last significant stop on Rd 21 before Kilpisjärvi and Norway. It sits on the scenic Muonionjoki that forms the border between Finland and Sweden and is a fine base for summer and winter activities. There are plenty of places to stay around here and there's low-key skiing in winter.

The **Kiela Naturium** (☎ 532 280; 10am-6pm) has a giftshop, cafe, free internet, local fish in a tank and a small nature display. There's also a planetarium with an aurora borealis show (adult/child €10/6).

Three kilometres south, the excellent **Harriniva centre** (☎ 530 0300; www.harriniva.fi) has a vast programme of summer and winter activities, ranging from short jaunts to multi-day adventures. In summer these include guided hikes, canoe and boat trips, horse trekking, quad safaris and fishing on the salmon-packed Muonionjoki. You can also rent bikes, boats and rods here and there are various accommodation options. In winter, there are wonderful dog-sledding safaris from 1½ hours (€70) to two days (€530), or trips of a week or longer, perhaps adding reindeer-sledding and snowmobiling to the mix.

Harriniva has the **Arktinen Rekikoirakeskus** (Arctic sled-dog centre) with over 400 lovable dogs, all with names and personalities. A great guided tour of their town (for that is what it is) is €8/5 per adult/child and teaches you plenty about the different breeds of huskies and their characteristics.

Levi
☎ 016

Levi is one of Finland's two most popular ski resorts but it's also a very popular destination for *ruska* season hiking and a cheap base in summer. The **tourist office** (☎ 639 3300; www.levi .fi; Myllyojantie 2; 9am-7pm Mon-Fri, 11am-5.30pm Sat & Sun) should be your first stop for accommodation bookings as well as activities like snowmobile safaris and dogsled treks.

The ski resort (☎ 641 246; www.levi.fi) has 44 downhill slopes, many of which are lit. Opportunities for cross-country skiing are also good, with trails totalling 230km.

Accommodation prices go through the roof in December, and between February and May. Virtually the whole town consists of holiday apartments and cottages, typically sleeping four to six, with sauna, fully equipped kitchen and many other mod cons. In summer, they are a real bargain, costing €45 to €55 per night; in winter €1100 a week is average. Four to five daily buses run between Rovaniemi and Levi (€27.50, 2½ hours).

Hetta & Pallas-Yllästunturi National Park
☎ 016 / pop 1965

One of the easiest long-distance walks in Lapland is the excellent 55km trekking route between the northern village of Hetta (also known as Enontekiö) and **Hotelli Pallas** (☎ 323 355; www.laplandhotels.com; s/d winter €150/180, summer €95/110;). The marked trail passes through Pallas-Yllästunturi National Park, Finland's third-largest, and can easily be completed in four days. There are free wilderness huts, but these can be packed with people in summer so it is wise to carry your own tent. See www.outdoors.fi for details of the route and huts.

The **Skierri** (☎ 0205 647 950; 9am-8pm Mon-Fri, 9am-5pm Sat & Sun Jun-Sep, 9am-4pm Mon-Fri Oct-Feb & May, 9am-5pm Mar & Apr) is the combined local tourist office and a visitor centre for the national park. At the southern end of the trek, the **Pallastunturi Luontokeskus** (☎ 0205 647 930; pallastunturi@metsa.fi; 9am-4pm Mon-Fri Jan–mid-Feb, Oct-Nov & May, 9am-5pm daily other times) at Pallastunturi Fell provides information and can also make hut reservations.

The village of Hetta is the centre of the municipality of Enontekiö, and a good place to start trekking and exploration of the area. It has a large Sámi population, and, though

FARMSTAYS

A growing, and often ecologically sound, accommodation sector in Finland is that of farmstays. Many rural farms, particularly in the south, offer B&B accommodation, a unique opportunity to meet local people and experience their way of life. Plenty of activities are also usually on offer. **ECEAT** (www.eceat.fi) lists a number of organic, sustainable farms in Finland that offer accommodation. Local tourist offices keep lists of farmstay options in the surrounding area; the website www.visitfinland.com links to a few (click on accommodation), and **Lomarengas** (☎ 09-5766 3350; www.lomarengas.fi) also has many listed on its website. In general, prices are good – from around €30 per person per night, country breakfast included. Evening meals are also usually available. Your hosts may not speak much English; if you have difficulties the local tourist office will be happy to help arrange the booking.

a bit spread-out, makes a good stop for a night or two.

ourpick **Hetan Majatalo** (☎ 554 0400; www.hetan -majatalo.fi; hotel s/d €62/84, guesthouse €38/60; P ☐ ☎ &) is in the centre of town, but set back in its own garden away from the road. This welcoming pad offers two types of accommodation in facing buildings: clean and simple guesthouse rooms sharing bathrooms, and very handsome and spacious wood-clad hotel rooms. It's an excellent deal that includes breakfast and sauna.

Buses from Hetta head out to the main road to Rovaniemi (€46.30, five hours) and Kilpisjärvi (€27.20, 3¼ hours) via a swap-over at Palojoensuu. There's a summer service from Rovaniemi to Tromsø in Norway via Hetta, Kautokeino and Alta.

Kilpisjärvi
☎ 016

The remote village of Kilpisjärvi, the northernmost settlement in the 'arm' of Finland, is on the doorstep of both Norway and Sweden. At 480m above sea level, this small border post, wedged between the lake of Kilpisjärvi and the magnificent surrounding fells, is also the highest village in Finland.

The Kilpisjärvi area offers fantastic long and short hikes. The ascent to slate-capped **Saana Fell** (1029m), takes two to three hours return. Also popular is the route through **Malla Nature Park** to the Kolmen Valtakunnan Raja, a concrete block in a lake that marks the **treble border** of Finland, Sweden and Norway. Alternatively, a summer **boat service** (☎ 0400 669 392) drops you a light 3km away (one way/return €15/20, 30 minutes).

Lining the main road are several camping grounds with cabins. Many places are only open during the trekking season, which is from June to September.

Two daily buses connect Rovaniemi and Kilpisjärvi (€63.70, six hours) via Kittilä, Levi and Muonio, with a connection to Hetta. In summer, one heads on to Tromsø in Norway.

FINLAND DIRECTORY

ACCOMMODATION

Sleeping listings in this chapter are divided into three price categories, based on the cost of a standard double room at its most expensive; budget (up to €70), midrange (€70 to €150) and top end (€150 plus).

Camping

Most camping grounds are open only from June to August (ie summer) and popular spots are crowded during July and the Midsummer weekend. Sites usually cost around €10 plus €4 per person. Almost all camping grounds have cabins or cottages for rent, which are usually excellent value from €35 for a basic double cabin to €120 for a cottage with kitchen and bathroom.

If you plan to do a lot of camping, the Camping Card Scandinavia offers useful discounts. Contact the **Finnish Camping Association** (☎ 09-4774 0740; www.camping.fi) for more information.

Finland's *jokamiehenoikeus* (everyman's right) allows access to most land and means you can pitch a tent almost anywhere on public land or at designated free camp sites in national parks.

Hostels & Summer Hotels

If you're travelling alone, hostels generally offer the best-value roof over your head, and can be good value for two people staying in a twin room. Finnish hostels are invariably clean, comfortable and very well-equipped, though most are in somewhat institutional buildings.

Some Finnish hostels are run by the Finnish Youth Hostel Association (SRM), and many more are affiliated. It's worth being a member of **HI** (www.hihostels.com), as members save €2.50 per night at affiliated places. You'll save money with a sleep sheet or your own linen, as hostels tend to charge €4 to €8 for this.

From June to August, many student residences are made over as summer hostels and hotels. These are often great value, as you often get your own room, with kitchen (bring your own utensils though) and bathroom either to yourself or shared between two.

Hotels

Most hotels in Finland cater to business travellers and the majority belong to one of a few major chains, including **Sokos** (www.sokoshotels.fi), **Scandic** (www.scandic-hotels.com) and **Cumulus** (www.cumulus.fi). **Finlandia** (www.finlandiahotels.fi) is an association of independent hotels, while **Omenahotelli** (www.omena.com) offers great-value staffless hotels booked online.

Hotels in Finland are designed with the business traveller in mind and tend to charge them robustly. But at weekends and during the summer holidays, they bring their prices crashing down to try and lure people who aren't on company expense accounts. Prices in three- and four-star hotels tend to drop by 40% or so at these times; so take advantage. Prices listed in this guide are weekday prices unless otherwise specified.

All Finnish hotels have a large, plentiful and delicious buffet breakfast included in the rate and most include a sauna session.

Self-Catering Accommodation

One of Finland's joys is its plethora of cottages for rental, ranging from simple camping cabins to fully equipped bungalows with electric sauna and gleaming modern kitchen. These can be remarkably good value and are perfect for families. There are tens of thousands of cabins and cottages for rent in Finland. By far the biggest national agent for cottage rentals is **Lomarengas** (☎ 0306 502 502; www.lomarengas

.fi; Eteläesplanadi 22, Helsinki). This agency comes highly recommended for reliability. Another good choice is **Villi Pohjola** (☎ 020 344 122; www.wildnorth.net). This arm of the Forests & Parks Service has cottages and cabins for rent all over Finland, but especially in Lapland and the north. Local tourist offices and town websites also have lists.

ACTIVITIES
Canoeing & Rafting

With 10% water coverage, Finland has long been a boating country, and until relatively recently they were an important form of transport on the lakes and rivers. Every waterside town has a place (most frequently the camping ground) where you can rent a canoe, kayak, or rowboat by the hour or day. Rental cottages often have rowboats that you can use free of charge to investigate the local lake and its islands.

Canoe and kayak rentals range in price from €15 to €30 per day, and €80 to €200 per week, more if you need overland transportation to the start or end point of your trip. The website www.canoeinfinland.com has details of several Lakeland routes.

Good places for organised white-water rafting trips include the rapids around Kuhmo (see p190), the Kitkajoki north of Kuusamo (see p194), the rapids of the Tornionjoki and Muonionjoki rivers on the Finland–Sweden border (see p200 and p203), and the Ruunaa Recreation Area in North Karelia (see p189).

Fishing

Finnish waters are teeming with fish, and with people trying to catch them: per capita, Finns must be among the Earth's most enthusiastic anglers. Several permits are required of foreigners (between the ages of 18 and 64) who wish to go fishing in Finland, but they are very easy to arrange. The website www.mmm.fi has all the details. In winter and spring, ice-fishing is popular and requires no licence – just bore a hole in the ice and dangle a line.

Hiking

Hiking is best from June to September, although in July mosquitoes and other biting insects can be a big problem in Lapland. In summer, given the continuous daylight in northern Finland, you can comfortably walk all night if you feel like it, especially in the north. Wilderness huts line the northern trails

---

THE FINNISH SAUNA

Nothing is more traditionally or culturally Finnish than the sauna. For centuries it has been a place to bathe, meditate, warm up during cold winters and even give birth, and most Finns still use the sauna at least once a week. An invitation to bathe in a family's sauna is an honour.

There are three principal types of sauna around these days. The most common is the electric sauna stove, which produces a fairly dry harsh heat compared with the much-loved chimney sauna, which is driven by a log fire and the staple of life at Finnish summer cottages. Even rarer is the true *savusauna* (smoke sauna), which is without a chimney.

Bathing is done in the nude (there are some exceptions in public saunas, which are almost always sex-segregated anyway) and Finns are quite strict about the nonsexual – even sacred – nature of the sauna.

According to sauna etiquette you should wash or shower first. Once inside the sauna (with a temperature of 80° to 100°C), water is thrown onto the stove using a *kauhu* (ladle), producing steam *(löyly)*. A whisk of birch twigs and leaves *(vihta)* is sometimes used to lightly strike the skin, improving circulation. Once you're hot enough, go outside and cool off with a cold shower or preferably by jumping into a lake or pool – enthusiastic Finns do so even in winter by cutting a hole in the ice. Repeat the process.

(they are free and must be shared). According to the law, a principle of common access to nature applies, so you are generally allowed to hike in any forested or wilderness area. The website www.outdoors.fi provides comprehensive information on trekking routes and huts in the system of national parks.

Skiing

Finns love to ski; slopes are generally quite low and so are well-suited to beginners and families. The best resorts are in Lapland, where the fells allow for longer runs. The ski season in Finland runs from late November to early May and slightly longer in the north, where it's possible to ski from October to May. You can rent all skiing or snowboarding equipment at major ski resorts for about €30/110 a day/week. A one-day lift pass costs around €30/160 a day/week. Cross-country skiing is also very popular. The best cross-country skiing is in Lapland, where resorts offer hundreds of kilometres of trails. Cross-country skiing is best during January and February in southern Finland, and from December to April in the north.

Swimming & Saunas

What would Finland be without the physically and mentally cleansing sauna (see above)? Many hotels, hostels and camping grounds have men's and women's saunas that are free with a night's stay.

An *uimahalli* (indoor swimming centre) can be found in most towns and usually has spa and sauna facilities in addition to a pool. A *kylpylä* (spa hotel) is another option for getting hot and wet and they have spectacular facilities. In most places nonguests can use the facilities for a fee.

Winter Activities

Whether you head out for an hour, or on an epic week-long adventure, being whisked across the snow by an enthusiastic team of huskies or reindeer is an experience like no other. Lapland is the best place to do this, but it's also available further south in places like Lieksa. Similar excursions can be made on snowmobiles (skidoos). Operators in the same locations offer these trips. You'll need a valid drivers' licence to use one. You normally share a machine and take turns to drive it: you pay extra if you want one all to yourself.

BUSINESS HOURS

Usual business hours in Finland:

Alko (state alcohol store) 9am to 8pm Monday to Friday, 9am to 6pm Saturday
Banks 9.15am to 4.15pm Monday to Friday
Nightclubs As late as 4am
Pubs 11am to 1am (often later on Friday and Saturday)
Restaurants 11am to 10pm, lunch 11am to 3pm
Shops 9am to 5pm Monday to Friday, to 1pm Saturday

EMBASSIES & CONSULATES

The following is a list of foreign government representatives in Helsinki. Use the Helsinki area telephone code (☎ 09) if calling from elsewhere.

Australia (☎ 4777 6640; australian.consulate
@tradimex.fi; Museokatu 25B) This is the consulate; the
nearest embassy is in Stockholm (p471).

Canada (☎ 228 530; www.canada.fi;
Pohjoisesplanadi 25B)

Denmark (☎ 684 1050; www.denmark.fi;
Mannerheimintie 8)

Estonia (☎ 622 0260; www.estemb.fi; Itäinen
Puistotie 10)

France (☎ 618 780; www.france.fi; Itäinen Puistotie 13)

Germany (☎ 458 580; www.helsinki.diplo.de;
Krogiuksentie 4)

Ireland (☎ 646 006; embassy.ireland@welho.com;
Erottajankatu 7A)

Japan (☎ 686 0200; www.fi.emb-japan.go.jp;
Unioninkatu 20)

Latvia (☎ 4764 720; www.mfa.gov.lv/en/helsinki/;
Armfeltintie 10)

Lithuania (☎ 684 4880; www.lithuania.fi;
Rauhankatu 13A)

Netherlands (☎ 228 920; www.netherlands.fi;
Erottajankatu 19B)

New Zealand (☎ 470 1818; paddais@paddais.net;
Johanneksenrinne 2) This is the consulate-general;
otherwise contact embassy in The Hague, Netherlands.

Norway (☎ 686 0180; www.norge.fi; Rehbinderintie 17)

Russia (☎ 661 877; http://helsinki.rusembassy.org/;
Tehtaankatu 1B)

Sweden (☎ 687 7660; www.sverige.fi;
Pohjoisesplanadi 7B)

UK (☎ 2286 5100; http://ukinfinland.fco.gov.uk; Itäinen
Puistotie 17)

USA (☎ 616 250; www.usembassy.fi; Itäinen
Puistotie 14B)

FESTIVALS & EVENTS

Finland puts on a barrage of music, arts,
cultural, sporting and just plain nutty festivals year-round, but especially between
June and mid-August. Midsummer is a big
deal in any part of Finland, though for most
Finns it's a family time when they disappear to their summer cottages. Pick up the
Finland Festivals booklet in any tourist office
or check out www.festivals.fi.

Air Guitar World Championships (p193) Whacky
festival held in Oulu, late August.

Pori Jazz Festival (p173) Finland's famous jazz festival,
held in mid-July.

Ruisrock (p159) Held in Turku in early July.

Savonlinna Opera Festival (p177) Highbrow festival in
medieval castle in July.

Vappu (May Day) A big day for Finns, especially students,
this holiday is celebrated nationally.

World Wife-Carrying Championships (see p186)
Manic two-day festival held in Sonkajärvi in early July.

HOLIDAYS

Finland grinds to a halt twice a year:
around Christmas and New Year, and during the Midsummer weekend. National
public holidays:

New Year's Day 1 January
Epiphany 6 January
Good Friday
Easter Sunday & Monday
May Day 1 May
Ascension Day May
Whitsunday Late May or early June
Midsummer's Eve & Day Weekend in June closest to
24 June
All Saints Day First Saturday in November
Independence Day 6 December
Christmas Eve 24 December
Christmas Day 25 December
Boxing Day 26 December

INTERNET ACCESS

Every public library in every town has at
least one internet terminal (big libraries
have up to a dozen) that can be used free
of charge. Many tourist offices have an internet terminal that you can use for free
(usually 15 minutes). If you are travelling
with your own computer, things are bright.
Wireless internet access is very widespread;
several cities have extensive networks and
nearly all hotels, as well as many restaurants,
cafes and bars offer free access to customers
and guests.

INTERNET RESOURCES

Almost every town in Finland has a website
chock-full of information, nearly always:
www.[town name].fi.

Aurora Forecast (www.gedds.alaska.edu/
AuroraForecast/) The best predictor of Northern Lights
activity. Based in Alaska, but you can change the view
to Europe.

Finnish Tourist Board (www.visitfinland.com) Official
site full of excellent information from the practical to the
whimsical.

FMI (www.fmi.fi) The Finnish weather forecast.

Forest & Park Service (www.outdoors.fi) Truly excellent resource, with detailed information on all Finland's
national parks and protected areas, as well as activities
listings.

Helsingin Sanomat (www.hs.fi/english/) International
edition of Finland's best daily newspaper.

Virtual Finland (virtual.finland.fi) Maintained by the Ministry of Foreign Affairs, this is an excellent, informative and entertaining website.

MONEY

Finland adopted the euro in 2002, and it remains the only Nordic country to have done so. Euro notes come in five, 10, 20, 50, 100 and 500 denominations and coins in five, 10, 20, 50 cents and €1 and €2.

Cards

Credit cards are widely accepted and Finns are dedicated users of the plastic – buying a beer or cup of coffee with a credit or debit card is not unusual and it's commonplace to pay for accommodation and restaurant meals in this way. Using ATMs with a credit or debit card is by far the easiest way of getting cash in Finland. The ATMs have a name, Otto, and can be found even in small villages.

Moneychangers

Travellers cheques and cash can be exchanged at banks and, in the big cities, independent exchange facilities such as **Forex** (www.forex.fi), which usually offer better rates.

POST

Stamps can be bought at bus or train stations and R-kioski newsstands as well as at the **posti** (post office; www.posti.fi). Airmail postcards and letters weighing up to 20g cost €0.80 to anywhere in the world or €0.70 by slower economy rate.

There are also two main rates for international parcels: a 5kg package to Europe will cost €46 to €49 sent priority, and €31 to €35 sent economy, for example. Post offices sell packing material.

TELEPHONE

Public telephones basically no longer exist on the street in Finland, so if you don't have a mobile you're reduced to making expensive calls from your hotel room, finding a cybercafe and talking over the internet, or tracking down a telecentre, which only really exist in the big cities.

The cheapest and most practical solution for telephoning in Finland is to purchase a Finnish SIM card and pop it in your own phone. Make sure your phone isn't blocked from doing this by your home network first.

If coming from outside Europe, check with your service provider that it will work in Europe's GSM 900/1800 network.

You can buy a prepaid SIM-card at any R-kioski. There are always several deals on offer, and you might be able to pick up a card for as little as €10, including some call credit. You can top the credit up at the same outlets, online, or at ATM machines. At the R-kioski you can also buy cut-rate phone cards that substantially lower the cost of making international calls; there are several varieties, with rates clearly marked.

The country code for Finland is ☎ 358. To dial abroad it's ☎ 00. The number for the international operator is ☎ 020208.

VISAS

A valid passport or EU identity card is required to enter Finland. Most Western nationals don't need a tourist visa for stays of less than three months; South Africans, Indians and Chinese, however, are among those who need a Schengen visa. For more information contact the nearest Finnish embassy or consulate, or the **Directorate of Immigration** (☎ 071 873 0431; www.uvi.fi).

Australian and New Zealand citizens aged between 18 and 30 can apply for a 12-month working holiday visa under a reciprocal agreement – contact the Finnish embassy in your home country.

TRANSPORT IN FINLAND

GETTING THERE & AWAY

Air

Finland is easily reached by air, with a growing number of direct flights to Helsinki from European, American and Asian destinations. It's also served by various budget carriers from several European countries, especially Ryanair and Blue1; check www.whichbudget.com for a complete list. Most other flights are with Finnair or Scandinavian Airlines (SAS). Most flights to Finland land at **Helsinki-Vantaa airport** (HEL; ☎ 0200 14636; www.helsinki-vantaa .fi), situated 19km north of the capital.

Some major airlines flying to and from Finland:

Aer Lingus (☎ 09-6122 0222; www.aerlingus.com)
Aeroflot (☎ 09-659 6552; www.aeroflot.ru)
Air Baltic (☎ 0600 025 831; www.airbaltic.com)
Air Berlin (☎ 0800 913 033; www.airberlin.com)

Air France (☎ 0200 32020; www.airfrance.com)
Austrian Airlines (☎ 020 386 700; www.austrianair
lines.com)
Blue1 (☎ 0600 025 831; www.blue1.com)
British Airways (☎ 09-6937 9538; www.ba.com)
Brussels Airlines (☎ 09-681 1950; www.brusselsair
lines.com)
Easyjet (in UK ☎ 0905 821 0905; www.easyjet.com)
Finnair (☎ 0600 140 140; www.finnair.com)
Iberia (☎ 09-6877 8950; www.iberia.com)
KLM Royal Dutch Airlines (☎ 020 353 355; www
.klm.com)
Lufthansa (☎ 020 358 358; www.lufthansa.com)
Malev Hungarian Airlines (☎ 0600 94484; www
.malev.com)
Ryanair (☎ 0600 16010; www.ryanair.com)
SAS Scandinavian Airlines (☎ 0600 025 831; www
.flysas.com)
Swiss International (☎ 09-6937 9034; www.swiss.com)

Land
BORDER CROSSINGS
There are several border crossings from
northern Sweden to northern Finland and six
road border crossings to Norway. There are
no passport or customs formalities. There are
nine main border crossings between Finland
and Russia including several in the southeast
and two in Lapland. They are more serious
frontiers; you must already have a visa to cross
into Russia.

BUS
Sweden
The only useful bus route between Finland and
Sweden is the walkable trip between the bor-
der towns of Tornio, Finland and Haparanda,
Sweden, from where you can get onward
transport into their respective countries.

Norway
There are five daily routes linking Finnish
Lapland with northern Norway, some run-
ning only in summer. These are operated by
Eskelisen Lapin Linjat (www.eskelisen-lapinlinjat.com),
whose website has detailed maps and time-
tables, as does the Finnish bus website for
Matkahuolto (www.matkahuolto.fi).

All routes originate or pass through
Rovaniemi; the three northeastern routes
continue via Inari to either Kirkenes,
Tanabru/Vadsø or Karasjok. The Karasjok
bus continues in summer to Nordkapp
(North Cape). On the western route, one
Rovaniemi–Kilpisjärvi bus runs on daily to

Tromsø in summer, and a Rovaniemi–Hetta
bus continues to Kautokeino and Alta.

Russia
There are daily express buses to Vyborg and St
Petersburg from Helsinki and Lappeenranta.
These services appear on the website of
Matkahuolto (www.matkahuolto.fi). The one-way fare
from Helsinki to Vyborg is €41.30 (five hours)
and to St Petersburg it's €63.70 (8½ to nine
hours). Book at the bus station in Helsinki
or the Sovavto Central Ticket Office at the
Pulkovskaya Hotel in St Petersburg. **Goldline**
(www.goldline.fi) runs three weekly buses from
Rovaniemi via Ivalo to Murmansk.

CAR & MOTORCYCLE
Vehicles can easily be brought into Finland
on the Baltic ferries from Sweden, Estonia
and Germany, provided you have registration
papers and valid insurance (Green Card).

See p211 for information about driving
in Finland.

TRAIN
The only international train links with Finland
are to/from Moscow and St Petersburg
in Russia.

There are three trains daily from Helsinki
to the Finland Station in St Petersburg, including the sleeper that goes to Moscow. In
2010 new high-speed trains will cut the trip
to 3½ hours. Tickets for these, which travel
via the Finnish towns of Lahti and Kouvola,
are sold at the international ticket counter
at Helsinki station. The rail crossing is at
Vainikkala (Russianside: Luzhayka).

You must have a valid Russian visa, but
border formalities have been fast-tracked so
that passport checks are now carried out on
board the moving train.

The *Sibelius* and *Repin* are Finnish and
Russian trains respectively and run daily
from Helsinki to St Petersburg (€54.80, six
hours) via Vyborg (€39 to €42, four hours).
The *Repin* is a little slower but also offers
first-class sleeping berths.

The *Tolstoi* sleeper runs from Helsinki
via St Petersburg to Moscow (2nd/1st class
€93/139, 13 hours). The fare includes a
sleeper berth. There are a number of more
upmarket sleepers costing up to €350.

Return fares are double, and there are
significant discounts for families and small
groups. See www.vr.fi for details.

FINLAND

Sea

Arriving in Finland by ferry is a memorable way to begin your visit, especially if you dock in Helsinki. Baltic ferries are some of the world's most impressive seagoing craft, especially considering they are passenger ferries rather than cruise ships. The big ferries are floating hotels-cum-shopping plazas, with duty-free shopping, restaurants, bars, karaoke, nightclubs and saunas. Many Scandinavians use them simply for boozy overnight cruises, so they can get pretty rowdy on Friday and Saturday nights, when you may need to book in advance.

Services are year-round between major cities: book ahead in summer and if travelling with a vehicle. The boats are amazingly cheap if you travel deck class (without a cabin): they make their money from duty-free purchases. Many ferry lines offer 50% discounts for holders of Eurail, Scanrail and InterRail passes. Some offer discounts for seniors, and for ISIC and youth-card holders; inquire when purchasing your ticket. There are usually discounts for families and small groups travelling together.

Ferry companies have detailed timetables and fares on their websites. Fares vary according to season. Operators with their Finnish contact numbers:

Eckerö Line (☎ 06000 4300; Tallinn www.eckeroline.fi; Åland www.eckerolinjen.fi)

Finnlines (☎ 010 436 7676; http://passenger.finnlines .com)

Linda Line (☎ 06000 668 970; www.lindaliini.ee)

Nordic Jet Line (☎ 0600 01655; www-eng.njl.fi)

RG Line (☎ 0207 716 810; www.rgline.com)

Tallink/Silja Line (☎ 0600 15700; www.tallinksilja .com)

Viking Line (☎ 0600 41577; www.vikingline.fi)

SWEDEN

The Stockholm–Helsinki, Stockholm–Turku and Kapellskär–Mariehamn (Åland) routes are dominated by Tallink/Silja and Viking Lines, with daily departures. Viking Line is the cheapest of the two operators, with a passenger ticket between Stockholm and Helsinki costing from €34 to €51 (up to €62 on Friday). In summer you can doss down in chairs or the floor, but an extra cabin ticket is obligatory from September to May: the cheapest berths start at €24.

Tallink/Silja Line doesn't offer deck tickets on the Helsinki run: the cheapest cabins start at €122 for the crossing.

It's usually much cheaper to cross to Turku (11 to 12 hours), with tickets starting at €10 on the day ferries. Note that Åbo is Swedish for Turku.

Eckerö Linjen sails from Grisslehamn, north of Stockholm, to Eckerö in Åland. It's by far the quickest, at just two hours, and, with prices starting from €8.90 return, and €11 for a car, it's an amazing bargain. There's a connecting bus from Stockholm and Uppsala.

RG Lines sails from Vaasa in Finland, to Umeå, Sweden (€60 to €80 per person plus €65 per car, 4½ hours) almost daily from March to October. Finnlines runs a simpler cargo ferry, which connects Naantali, near Turku, with Kapellskär three times daily.

ESTONIA

Half a dozen ferry companies ply the Gulf of Finland between Helsinki and Tallinn in Estonia. Car ferries cross in 3½ hours, catamarans and hydrofoils in about 1½ hours, although in winter there are fewer departures and the traffic is also slower due to the ice.

Ferries are cheapest: Eckerö Line has only one departure daily but is the cheapest with a return fare of between €30 and €39 in high season. Tallink, Viking Line and Silja Line have several daily departures (€23 to €28, one way). Vehicle space costs from €20 to €25. Catamarans and hydrofoils cost between €29 and €38 one way depending on the company, time of year, time of day and the day of the week, but online deals, advance purchase specials, and offers can knock this as low as €18. Linda Line, Nordic Jet Line and Tallink offer these routes. Tallink has vehicle space on its fast ferry (€25 to €38 one way for standard-size cars). On the websites you can easily see which departures are offering cheaper rates.

GERMANY

Finnlines runs from Helsinki to Travemünde (from €196 September to May, from €244 June to August one way plus €100 per vehicle) with connecting bus service to Hamburg.

Tallink/Silja also runs a fast ferry from Helsinki to Rostock (27 hours), with seats costing from €72 to €97, and berths starting at €127. Vehicle places are available from €115.

GETTING AROUND

Finland is well served by public transport. A great source to find the best way between

two points is the online route planner at www
.matka.fi, which gives you bus and train options and even walking distances between
stations and town centres.

Air

Finnair runs a fairly comprehensive domestic service mainly out of Helsinki but
also across a few regional centres like Oulu
and Rovaniemi. Standard prices are fairly
expensive, but check the website for offers. Budget carriers Blue1 and FinnComm
offer the cheapest fares for advance
internet bookings.

Airlines flying domestically:

Blue1 (☎ 06000 25831; www.blue1.com) Budget flights
from Helsinki to Kuopio, Oulu, Rovaniemi and Vaasa.

Finnair (☎ 81881; www.finnair.com) Extensive domestic
network.

FinnComm (www.fc.fi) Finnair affiliate offering budget
fares; book via its website or Finnair offices.

Air Åland (☎ 018 17110; www.airaland.com) Flies
between Helsinki and Mariehamn on the Åland islands.

Bicycle

Finland is flat and as bicycle-friendly as any
country you'll find, with many kilometres
of bike paths – also used by inline skaters in summer and cross-country skiers in
winter. Many Finns use the humble bicycle
as their main form of summer transport
around town. The only drawback to an extensive tour is distance, but bikes can be
carried on most trains, buses and ferries.
The best place for cycling is the Åland islands, where a few days or a week of touring is a breeze.

Daily/weekly hire from €15/70 is possible
in most cities. Camping grounds, hotels and
hostels often have cheap bikes available for
local exploration.

Boat

Lake and river passenger services were once
important means of summer transport in
Finland. These services are now largely
kept on as cruises, and make a great, leisurely way to journey between towns. It's a
real Finnish summer experience. The most
popular routes are Tampere–Hämeenlinna,
Savonlinna–Kuopio, Lahti–Jyväskylä and
Joensuu–Koli–Nurmes.

The main coastal sea routes are Turku–
Naantali, Helsinki–Porvoo and the archipelago ferries to the Åland islands.

Bus

All long-distance bus ticketing is handled
by **Matkahuolto** (☎ 0200 4000; www.matkahuolto
.fi), whose excellent website has all timetables. Each town and municipal centre has
a *linja-autoasema* (bus terminal), with local
timetables displayed (*lähtevät* is departures,
saapuvat arrivals). Ticket offices tend to work
normal business hours, but you can always
buy the ticket from the driver.

Buses may be express (*pikavuoro*) or regular (*vakiovuoro*). Fares are based on distance
travelled. The one-way fare for a 100km trip
is €16.30/19.20 for normal/express. On longer
routes, only express services are available.

For student discounts you need to be studying full-time in Finland and buy a student
coach discount card (€6) from any bus station. If booking three or more adult tickets
together, a 25% discount applies, meaning
good news for groups.

Car & Motorcycle

Finland's road network is excellent and well
signposted between centres, although there
are only a few motorways, around major cities. When approaching a town or city, look
for signs saying *keskusta* (town centre). There
are no road tolls.

Finland has some of the world's most
expensive petrol. Many petrol stations are
unstaffed, so you'll need to have bank notes
handy for the machine: they don't accept foreign cards. Change is not given.

HIRE

Car rental in Finland is much more expensive than elsewhere in Europe, but between
a group of three or four it can work out at a
reasonable cost. From the major rental companies a small car costs from €77/320 per
day/week with 300km free per day. As ever,
there are much cheaper deals online.

While the daily rate is high, the weekly rate
offers some respite. Best of all, though, are the
weekend rates. These can cost little more than
the rate for a single day, and you can pick up
the car early afternoon on Friday, and return
it late Sunday or early Monday.

Car-rental franchises with offices in many
Finnish cities include **Budget** (☎ 0207 466 600;
www.budget.fi), **Hertz** (☎ 0800 188 777; www.hertz.com),
Europcar (☎ 0403 062 444; www.europcar.fi; Helsinki) and
Avis (☎ 09-859 8356; www.avis.fi; Helsinki). One of the
cheapest is **Sixt** (☎ 09-350 5590; www.sixt.fi).

ROAD CONDITIONS & HAZARDS

Beware of elk and reindeer, which don't have much respect for car horns and can dash out onto the road unexpectedly. This sounds comical, but elks especially constitute a deadly danger. By law, you must notify the police if there is an accident involving these animals. Reindeer are very common in Lapland during spring and summer when they'll often wander along the roads in herds. Slow right down if you see one, as there will be more nearby.

Snow and ice on the roads, potentially from September to April, and as late as June in Lapland, make driving a serious undertaking. Snow chains are illegal: instead, people use either snow tyres, which have metal studs, or special all-weather tyres. The website www.tiehallinto.fi has webcams on most main roads in Finland, so you can check what condition the roads are in on your prospective route.

ROAD RULES

Finns drive on the right; the speed limit is 50km/h in built-up areas, from 80km/h to 100km/h on highways, and 120km/h on motorways. *All* motor vehicles must use headlights at *all* times, and wearing seat belts is compulsory for *all* passengers. The blood alcohol limit is 0.05%.

A very important difference between Finland and many other countries is that here, cars entering an intersection from the right *always* have right of way. While this doesn't apply to highways, you'll find that in towns, even when you're on fairly major roads cars will nip out from the right without looking: you have to give way, so be careful at every intersection.

Train

Finnish trains are run by the state-owned **Valtion Rautatiet** (VR; ☎ 0600 41900; www.vr.fi) and are an excellent service: they are fast, efficient and cheaper than the bus. They are the best form of transport between major cities.

VR's website is excellent, with comprehensive timetable information and some ticket sales. Major stations have a VR office: this is where to buy your ticket, as the automated machines only accept Finnish bankcards. You can also just hop aboard, find a seat and pay the conductor, but if the ticket office was open where you boarded, you'll be charged a small penalty fee (€3 to €6).

CLASSES

The main classes of trains are the high-speed Pendolino (the fastest and most expensive class), fast Intercity (IC), Express and Regional trains. The first three have both 1st- and 2nd-class sections, while regional trains ('H' on the timetable), are the cheapest and slowest services, and only have 2nd-class carriages.

On longer routes there are two types of sleeping carriage currently in operation. The traditional blue ones offer berths in one-/two-/three-bed cabins, and cost a flat rate of €44 for a single berth (with a 1st-class ticket), and €22/12 per person for double/triple berths, in addition to the cost of an ordinary ticket.

The swish new sleeping cars offer single and double compartments in a double-decker carriage. There are cabins equipped for wheelchair use, and, on the top floor, ones with bathroom. Berths in a single compartment cost €49 to €54 (with a 1st-class ticket), in a two-person compartment €26 to €31.

Some trains transport cars, which is handy if you've brought your own vehicle and are keen on exploring Lapland.

COSTS

Fares vary slightly according to the class of train, with Pendolino the most expensive. A one-way ticket for a 100km express train journey costs approximately €15 in 2nd class. First-class tickets cost 50% more than a 2nd-class ticket. A return fare is about 10% less than two one-way tickets.

Children under 17 pay half fare and children aged under six travel free (but without a seat). A child travels free with every adult on long-distance trips, and there are also discounts for seniors, local students and any group of three or more adults travelling together.

TRAIN PASSES

International rail passes accepted in Finland include the Eurail Scandinavia Pass, Eurail Global Pass and InterRail Global Pass. The Finland Eurail Pass gives you €128/169/230 for three/five/10 days' 2nd-class travel in a one-month period within Finland. The InterRail Finland pass offers travel only in Finland for three/four/six/eight days in a one-month period, costing €109/139/189/229 in 2nd class. The **Finnrail Pass** (www.vr.fi), is available to travellers residing outside Finland and offers a similar deal to the InterRail and Eurail passes though, at the time of writing, it was slightly more expensive.

Tallinn

The 20th century was full of twists and turns for Estonia, but it's now shaken off the dead weight of the Soviet era and turned its focus to the West, and to promises of a richer, shinier future. In recent years it's claimed EU membership and become one of Europe's fastest-growing economies, and the country is now celebrating its return to the world stage – independent, economically robust and tech-savvy, and hell-bent on catching up with its Nordic neighbours in the quality-of-life stakes.

And now the world is tuning in to Estonia's irresistible blend of Eastern European and Nordic charms. Soaking up the long white nights and history of the country's capital, Tallinn, are joys to be savoured. The city fuses medieval and cutting-edge to come up with an energetic new mood all its own – an intoxicating mix of Gothic church spires, glass-and-chrome skyscrapers, wine cellars inside 15th-century basements, lazy afternoons soaking up sun and beer suds on Raekoja plats, and bike paths to beaches and forests – with a few Soviet throwbacks in the mix, for added spice.

Despite its fiercely forward focus and the boom of 21st-century development, Tallinn remains loyal to the fairytale charms of its Old Town, and compact enough to explore on foot. A visit from Helsinki is just too easy to overlook – Tallinn is so much part of the Helsinki experience, it sometimes feels like a distant suburb.

FAST FACTS

- **Population** 400,000
- **Currency** kroon (EEK): €1 = 15.64EEK; US$1 = 11.80EEK; UK£1 = 17.41EEK; A$1 = 8.54EEK; C$1 = 9.80EEK; NZ$1 = 6.65EEK; ¥100 = 12.09EEK
- **Official Language** Estonian
- **Telephone Codes** country code ☎ 372; no area code for Tallinn
- **Visas** not required for travellers from the EU, the USA, Canada and Australia

TALLINN

TALLINN

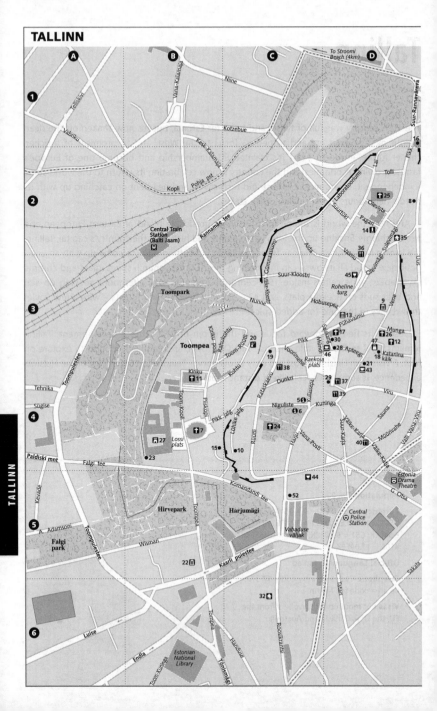

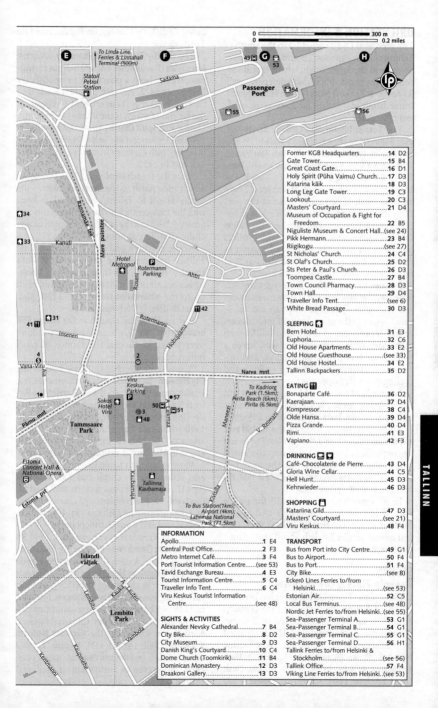

ORIENTATION & INFORMATION

The medieval Old Town, just to the south of Tallinn Bay, comprises Toompea (the upper town) and the lower town, which is still surrounded by much of its 2.5km defensive wall. Its centre is Raekoja plats (Town Hall Square). Immediately east of the Old Town is the modern city centre.

The **Tourist Information Centre** (☎ 645 7777; www.tourism.tallinn.ee; cnr Kullassepa & Niguliste; ☼ 9am-5pm Mon-Fri, 10am-3pm Sat Oct-Apr, 9am-7pm Mon-Fri, 10am-5pm Sat & Sun May & Jun, 9am-8pm Mon-Fri, 10am-6pm Sat & Sun Jul & Aug, 9am-6pm Mon-Fri, 10am-5pm Sat & Sun Sep) offers a full range of services. There are also small information desks at the port (Terminal A), and inside Viru Keskus shopping centre. Here you can purchase the **Tallinn Card** (www.tallinncard.ee; 185-495EEK), which offers free rides on public transport, admission to museums, free excursions and discounts at restaurants, valid from six to 72 hours.

Be sure to stop by the fabulous summertime **Traveller Info Tent** (☎ 5814 0442; www.traveller -info.com; Niguliste; ☼ 9am-9pm or 10pm Jun–mid-Sep), in a tent opposite the official tourist information centre. It produces an invaluable Tallinn map with loads of recommended places, keeps a 'what's on' board (updated daily), and operates entertaining, well-priced walking and cycling tours (see opposite).

For maps of the city and region, check out the bookshop **Apollo** (☎ 683 3400; Viru 23). Change money at nearby **Tavid** (☎ 627 9900; Aia 5; ☼ 24hr).

To keep in touch, head to the **central post office** (Narva maantee 1; ☼ 7.30am-8pm Mon-Fri, 9am-6pm Sat); opposite is Viru Keskus shopping centre, and in the basement here, by the local bus terminal, is **Metro Internet Café** (☎ 610 1519; Viru Keskus; per hr 40EEK; ☼ 9am-11pm).

In an emergency, dial ☎ 110 for police and ☎ 112 for fire, ambulance and urgent medical advice. The **First Aid Hotline** (☎ 697 1145) can advise you in English about the nearest treatment centre.

SIGHTS
Raekoja Plats & Lower Town

Raekoja plats (Town Hall Square) has been the centre of Tallinn life since the 11th century; bathed in sunlight or sprinkled with snow, it's always a photogenic spot. It's dominated by northern Europe's only surviving Gothic **town hall** (☎ 645 7900; adult/student 40/25EEK; ☼ 10am-4pm Mon-Sat Jul & Aug, by appointment Sep-Jun), built from 1371 to 1404. Climb the **tower** (adult/ student 30/15EEK; ☼ 11am-6pm Jun-Aug) for fine Old Town views.

The nearby **Town Council Pharmacy** (Raeapteek; Raekoja plats 11) is another ancient Tallinn institution; there's been a pharmacy or apothecary here since 1422. An arch beside it leads into narrow Saiakang (White Bread Passage), at the far end of which is the lovely 14th-century Gothic **Holy Spirit Church** (☎ 644 1487; adult/student 15/7.50EEK; ☼ 9am-5pm Mon-Sat May-Sep, 10am-2pm Mon-Fri Oct-Apr), with carvings from 1684 and a tower bell cast in 1433.

From the church stroll along Pikk (Long St), which runs north to the **Great Coast Gate** – the medieval exit to Tallinn's port. Pikk is lined with the 15th-century houses of merchants and gentry (check out the fabulous sculpted facade of the art gallery at number 18).

At the northern end of Pikk stands a chief Tallinn landmark, the gargantuan **St Olaf's Church** (Oleviste Kirik; Pikk 48; admission free). Viewseekers unafraid of a bit of sweat should head up to the **observation tower** (☎ 621 2241; adult/ student 30/15EEK; ☼ 10am-6pm Apr-Oct).

Just south of the church is the **former KGB headquarters** (Pikk 59), whose basement windows were sealed to conceal the sounds of cruel interrogations.

A medieval merchant's home houses the **City Museum** (☎ 644 6553; www.linnamuuseum.ee; Vene 17; adult/student 35/10EEK; ☼ 10.30am-6pm Wed-Mon Mar-Oct, to 5pm Wed-Mon Nov-Feb), which traces Tallinn's development from its beginnings through to 1940 with some quirky displays and curious artefacts. The 20th-century section will satisfy any thirst for Soviet propaganda material.

Vene is home to some lovely passageways and courtyards – check out **Katariina käik** (Vene 12), home to artisan studios, and **Masters' Courtyard** (Vene 6), a cobblestoned charmer, some of it dating from the 13th century. It's home to craft stores and a sweet chocolaterie.

Also on Vene is the whitewashed, 1844 **Sts Peter & Paul's Church** (Vene 16), looking like it belongs in Spain. A door in the courtyard leads into the **Dominican Monastery** (☎ 515 5489; www .kloostri.ee; Vene 16; adult/student 90/45EEK; ☼ 10am-6pm mid-May–Aug, visits other times by appointment), founded in 1246 as a base for Scandinavian monks.

The majestic St Nicholas' Church (Niguliste Kirik), now known as the **Niguliste Museum & Concert Hall** (☎ 631 4330; Niguliste 3; adult/ student 35/20EEK; ☼ 10am-5pm Wed-Sun), stages concerts and serves as a museum of medieval church art.

Toompea

A regal approach to Toompea is through the red-roofed 1380 **gate tower** at the western end of Pikk in the lower town, and then uphill along Pikk jalg (Long Leg). The 19th-century Russian Orthodox **Alexander Nevsky Cathedral** (Lossi plats; ☼ 8am-8pm) greets you at the top, planted strategically across from **Toompea Castle**, traditionally Estonia's seat of power. Only a section of the Old Town wall and the **Pikk Herman** bastion, from which the state flag flies, are left from medieval times. The *riigikogu* (parliament) meets in the pink, baroque-style building in front, which is an 18th-century addition. A path leads down from Lossi plats through an opening in the wall to the **Danish King's Courtyard**, where, in summer, artists set up their easels.

The Lutheran **Dome Church** (Toomkirik; ☎ 644 4140; Toom-Kooli 6; ☼ 9am-4pm Tue-Sun), sombre and austere, was founded in 1233, though this edifice dates from the 14th century. From the Dome Church, follow Kohtu to the city's favourite **lookout** over the lower town, cameras at the ready.

The absorbing **Museum of Occupation & Fight for Freedom** (☎ 668 0250; www.okupatsioon.ee; Toompea 8; adult/student 20/10EEK; ☼ 11am-6pm Tue-Sun), just downhill from Toompea, focuses on Estonia's 20th-century occupations (Nazi and Soviet), and the joy of a happy ending.

Kadriorg

To reach **Kadriorg Park**, 2km east of Old Town along Narva maantee, take tram 1 or 3 to the last stop.

The wooded park and its palace were designed for Peter the Great for his wife Catherine I. The park's original centrepiece is Kadriorg Palace, now home to the **Kadriorg Art Museum** (☎ 606 6403; www.ekm.ee; Weizenbergi 37; adult/student 55/30EEK; ☼ 10am-5pm Tue-Sun May-Sep, 10am-5pm Wed-Sun Oct-Apr). The 17th- and 18th-century foreign art is mainly unabashedly romantic, and the palace unashamedly splendid.

The grand new showpiece of Kadriorg (and Tallinn) is KUMU (Kunstimuuseum; ☎ 602 6000; www.ekm.ee; Weizenbergi 34; adult/student 80/45EEK; ☼ 11am-6pm Tue-Sun May-Sep, closed Mon & Tue Oct-Apr), also known as the Art Museum of Estonia. It's a spectacular structure of limestone, glass and copper, and contains the largest repository of Estonian art as well as constantly changing contemporary exhibits.

TOURS

City Bike (☎ 683 6383; www.citybike.ee; Uus 33) rents bikes and has a range of Tallinn tours, as well as tours (cycling or bus) to Lahemaa National Park, the perfect rural retreat from the capital. Two-hour cycling tours (250EEK) of Tallinn run year-round and cover 16km out towards Kadriorg and Pirita.

The guys behind the Traveller Info Tent (opposite) also run walking or cycling city tours. Three-hour bike tours (150EEK to 200EEK) take in the town's well-known eastern attractions (Kadriorg, Pirita etc), or more off-beat areas to the west. There's also an evening pub crawl (200EEK, including drinks). From June to August the tours run daily from the tent itself; the rest of the year they start from Euphoria hostel (below) and need to be booked in advance, via email, phone or through the hostel. Winter tours are weather dependent.

FESTIVALS & EVENTS

For a complete list, visit the events pages of www.tourism.tallinn.ee. Expect an extra-full calendar of events in 2011 as Tallinn celebrates its status as a European City of Culture; check www.tallinn2011.ee.

Jazzkaar (www.jazzkaar.ee) Jazz greats from around the world converge in mid-April.

Old Town Days (www.vanalinnapaevad.ee) Week-long fest in early June featuring dancing, concerts, costumed performers and plenty of medieval merrymaking.

Õllesummer (Beer Summer; www.ollesummer.ee) Popular ale-guzzling, rock-music extravaganza over five days in early July.

Black Nights Film Festival (www.poff.ee) Films and animations from all over the world, bringing life to cold nights from mid-November to mid-December.

SLEEPING

The Tourist Information Centre can help find the right accommodation to fit your budget.

Old House (☎ 641 1464; www.oldhouse.ee; Uus 26) is a good bet, offering an appealing, old-world hostel, guesthouse, and (our favourite) – 17 fantastic Old Town apartments at reasonable prices (from 1200EEK per night).

Euphoria (☎ 5837 3602; www.euphoria.ee; Roosikrantsi 4; dm/d 200/600EEK; ▢ P) So laid-back it's almost horizontal, this new backpackers hostel, just south of Old Town, has adopted some very '60s hippie vibes and given them a modern twist, creating a fun place to stay with a sense of traveller community – especially if you like hookah pipes, bongo drums, jugglers, musos,

TALLINN

TALLINN IN ONE DAY

First, get your bearings by climbing the Town Hall tower on **Raekoja plats** (p216), then explore the cobbled Old Town streets below – museums, shops, churches, courtyards, cafes, whatever takes your fancy. In the afternoon, catch a tram to leafy, lovely **Kadriorg** (p217) and check out its superb museums. Treat yourself to a medieval feast at **Olde Hansa** (opposite), then stop in at a cute cafe or go **bar-hopping** (right) before calling it a day.

---

artists and impromptu late-night jam sessions (pack earplugs if you don't).

Tallinn Backpackers (☎ 644 0298; www.tallinnbackpackers.com; Olevimägi 11; dm 200-225EEK; 🖳 🛜) Staffed by backpackers who are more than happy to go drinking with guests, and in a perfect Old Town location, this place has a global feel and a roll-call of traveller-happy features: free wi-fi and internet, lockers, free sauna, snazzy bathrooms, big-screen movies in the common room, a foosball table and day-trips to nearby attractions.

Bern Hotel (☎ 680 6630; www.bern.ee; Aia 10; s/d from 1173/1330EEK) One of a rash of new hotels on the outskirts of Old Town, Bern is named after the Swiss city to indicate 'hospitality and high quality'. It's nothing special from the outside, but rooms are petite and modern with great attention to detail for the price – nice extras include robes and slippers, air-con, minibar, hairdryer and toiletries. Good internet deals available.

EATING

Bonaparte Café (☎ 646 4444; Pikk 45; pastries 14-20EEK, meals 55-130EEK; 🕑 8am-10pm Mon-Fri, 9am-10pm Sat, 10am-6pm Sun) Flaky croissants and raspberry-mousse cake are a few reasons why Bonaparte ranks as Tallinn's best patisserie. It's also a supremely civilised lunch stop, with the likes of French onion soup and salad Niçoise on the menu. And the quiches – *très magnifique*! A handsome, upmarket restaurant with a decidedly French accent is also on the premises.

Pizza Grande (☎ 641 8718; Väike-Karja 6; small pizzas 39-69EEK; 🕑 11am-11pm) Local students vote this their favourite pizza spot. Enter from the courtyard and check the menu, where some left-of-centre topping combos (chicken, shrimps, blue cheese and peach?) stand alongside the tried-and-true. Salads and pasta dishes all come in under 70EEK.

Kompressor (☎ 646 4210; Rataskaevu 3; pancakes 50-55EEK; 🕑 11-1am) Under an industrial ceiling you can plug any holes in your stomach with cheap pancakes of the sweet or savoury persuasion. The smoked cheese and bacon is a treat, but don't go thinking you'll have room for dessert. By night, this is a decent detour for a drink.

ourpick Vapiano (☎ 682 9010; Hobujaama 10; pizzas & pasta 50-125EEK; 🕑 10am-midnight) Choose your pasta or salad from the appropriate counter and watch as it's prepared in front of you. If it's pizza you're after, you'll receive a pager to notify you when it's ready. This is 'fast food' done healthy, fresh and cheap (without sacrificing quality), and the restaurant is big, bright and buzzing.

Kaerajaan (☎ 615 5400; Raekoja plats 17; mains 135-325EEK; 🕑 11am-midnight) Named after a traditional song and dance, Kaerajaan has quirky decor and an intriguing menu of modern Estonian cuisine, taking traditional dishes and giving them a 21st-century twist – *gravlax* (salmon) with cucumber-lemon sorbet and forest cranberries, pork tenderloin marinated with juniper berries. The jury's out on herring lasagne, however!

For groceries, hit **Rimi supermarket** (Aia 7; 🕑 9am-10pm).

DRINKING

Tallinn without its cafe and bar culture is simply inconceivable. Due to the charm of the surroundings, the Old Town is the obvious place to head to for cellar bars and absurdly cosy cafes.

Kehrwieder (☎ 505 258; Saiakang 1; 🕑 11am-midnight) Sure, there's seating on Raekoja plats, but inside the city's cosiest cafe is where the real ambience is found in spades – stretch out on a couch, read by lamplight and bump your head on the arched ceilings.

FREE THRILLS

- Absorb the medieval magic while wandering **Old Town** (p216)
- Get a breath of fresh air at **Kadriorg Park** (p217)
- Hit the beach at **Pirita** (northeast of the centre; bus 1A, 8, 34A and 38) or retro-Soviet **Stroomi** (4km due west of the centre; bus 40 or 48)
- Browse the artisan studios of **Katariina käik** and **Masters' Courtyard** (p216)

---

ourpick **Café-Chocolaterie de Pierre** (☎ 641 8061; Masters' Courtyard, Vene 6; ☽ 8am-midnight) Nestled inside the picturesque Masters' Courtyard, this snug cafe seems like a hideaway at your granny's place. Filled with antiques, it's renowned for its delectable handmade chocolates – impossible to resist.

Gloria Wine Cellar (☎ 640 6804; Müürivahe 2; ☽ noon-11pm Mon-Sat, to 6pm Sun) This mazelike cellar has a number of nooks and crannies where you can secrete yourself with a date and/or a good bottle of shiraz. Antique furnishings and flickering candles add to the allure.

Hell Hunt (☎ 681 8333; Pikk 39; ☽ noon-late) Try to score a few of the comfy armchairs out the back of this trouper on the pub circuit, beloved by discerning locals of all ages. It boasts an amiable air and reasonable prices for locally brewed beer and cider, plus decent pub grub. Don't let the menacing name put you off – it actually means 'gentle wolf'.

GETTING THERE & AWAY
Air

The national carrier **Estonian Air** (airline code OV; ☎ 640 1163; www.estonian-air.ee; Vabaduse väljak 10, Tallinn) links Tallinn with 20 cities in Europe and Russia. A number of other airlines serve the **Tallinn airport** (www.tallinn-airport.ee).

At the time of research, **Copterline** (www.cop terline.ee) helicopter flights between Helsinki and Tallinn had ceased.

Boat

Tallinn's main sea-passenger terminal is at the end of Sadama, a short, 1km walk northeast of Old Town; most ferries to/from Helsinki dock here.

FINLAND

Oodles of ferries ply the 85km separating Helsinki and Tallinn (ships take two to 3½ hours, hydrofoils approximately 1½ hours). In high winds or bad weather, hydrofoils are often cancelled; they operate only when the sea is ice-free (around late March/April to late December). Larger ferries sail year-round.

All companies provide concessions. Prices are cheaper on weekdays, and outside summer. There's lots of competition, shop around.

Eckerö Line (☎ 664 6000; www.eckeroline.ee; Terminal A, Tallinn) Sails once daily back and forth year-round (300EEK to 390EEK, three to 3½ hours).

Linda Line (☎ 699 9333; www.lindaliini.ee; Linnahall Terminal, Tallinn) Small, passenger-only hydrofoils up to

---

> **SPLURGE**
>
> **Olde Hansa** (☎ 627 9020; www.oldehansa.ee; Vana Turg 1; mains 155-365EEK; ☽ 11am-midnight) One of the few touristy places that's truly worth a visit, this candlelit, medieval-themed restaurant boasts the friendliest service in the country, delicacies like juniper cheese and forest-mushroom soup, and exotic meats such as boar and bear, all impeccably presented.

---

seven times daily late March to late December (295EEK to 455EEK, 1½ hours)

Nordic Jet (☎ 613 7000; www.njl.info; Terminal C, Tallinn) Seven daily crossings with jet catamarans, generally from May to September (from 440EEK, 1¾ hours).

Tallink (☎ 640 9808; www.tallinksilja.com; Terminal D, Tallinn) At least five services daily in each direction; the huge *Baltic Princess* takes 3½ hours, brand-new high-speed ferries take two hours and operate year-round. Prices start at 360EEK.

Viking Line (☎ 666 3966; www.vikingline.ee; Terminal A, Tallinn) Operates a giant car ferry, with two departures daily (from 300EEK, 2½ hours).

SWEDEN

Tallink (☎ 640 9808; www.tallinksilja.com) sails every night year-round between Tallinn's Terminal D and Stockholm's Frihamnen (cabin berth from 2250EEK, 16 hours). Book ahead.

GETTING AROUND

Tallinn has an excellent network of buses, trolleybuses and trams running from 6am to midnight; all three modes of transport use the same ticket system. Buy *piletid* (tickets) from street kiosks (13EEK, or a book of 10 single tickets for 90EEK) or from the driver (20EEK). Validate your ticket using the hole puncher inside the vehicle – watch a local to see how it's done.

The major bus terminal for local buses is at the basement level of Viru Keskus shopping centre or the surrounding streets (just east of Old Town). Public transport timetables are at www.tallinn.ee.

City Bike (☎ 683 6383; www.citybike.ee; Uus 33; per hr/day/week 35/200/765EEK) can help you get around by bike, within Tallinn and around Estonia; see p217 for info on its tours.

Taxis are plentiful, but it's best to order one by phone: **Krooni Takso** (☎ 1212, 638 1111) and **Tulika Takso** (☎ 1200, 612 0000).

St Petersburg

'St Petersburg is Russia, but it is not Russian.' The opinion of Nicholas II, the empire's last tsar, on his one-time capital still resonates. The city is a fascinating hybrid where one moment you can be clapping along to a fun Russian folk music show in a baroque hall or sniffing incense inside a mosaic-covered Orthodox church, the next grooving on the dance floor of an underground club or posing at a contemporary art event in a renovated bakery.

Above all, Europe's fourth-largest city is a visual delight. The Neva River and surrounding canals reflect unbroken facades of handsome 18th- and 19th-century buildings, housing a spellbinding collection of cultural storehouses, culminating in the incomparable Hermitage. It's easy to imagine how such an environment, warts and all, was the inspiration for many of Russia's greatest artists including the writers Pushkin, Gogol and Dostoevsky, and musical maestros such as Rachmaninoff, Tchaikovsky and Shostakovich. This giant warehouse of Russian culture has more to offer the traveller than perhaps anywhere else in the country.

The long summer days of the White Nights season are particularly special; this is when the fountains flow, parks and gardens burst into colour and Peter's citizens hit the streets to party. However with a little preparation, the ice-cold winter also has its own magic and is the perfect time for warming body and soul in all those museums and palaces.

FAST FACTS

- **Population** 4.6 million
- **Currency** rouble (R): €1 = R44.00; US$1 = R33.18; UK£1 = R48.99; A$1 = R24.05; C$1 = R27.57; NZ$1 = R18.71; ¥100 = R34.02
- **Official Language** Russian
- **Telephone Codes** country code ☎ 7; St Petersburg ☎ 812
- **Visa** required by all – begin preparing well in advance of your trip! Try either **Express to Russia** (www.expresstorussia.com) or **Zierer Visa Services** (☎ 1-866 788 1100; www.zvs.com) for assistance.

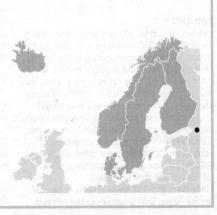

ORIENTATION & INFORMATION

St Petersburg is spread out across many islands, some real and some created through the construction of canals. The central street is Nevsky prospekt (pr), which extends for some 4km from the Alexander Nevsky Monastery to the Hermitage. The vast Neva River empties into the Gulf of Finland, filtered through a number of islands. Most significant of these are Vasilevsky and Petrogradsky islands.

Currency exchange offices and ATMs are available throughout the city.

The English-speaking staff at the **City Tourist Information Centre** (Map p225; ☎ 310 8262; www.visit-petersburg.com; Sadovaya ul 14/52; ☒ 10am-7pm Mon-Sat; Ⓜ Gostiny Dvor) are vague about most things but will do their best to help. There are also branches outside the **Hermitage** (Dvortsovaya pl 12; ☒ 10am-7pm; Ⓜ Nevsky Prospekt) and at the Pulkova 1 and 2 **air terminals** (☒ 10am-7pm Mon-Fri).

Two large, excellent internet cafes are **Café Max** (Map p225; ☎ 273 6655; www.cafemax.ru; Nevsky pr 90/92; per hr R40; ☒ 24hr; Ⓜ Mayakovskaya) and **Quo Vadis** (Map p225; ☎ 333 0708; www.quovadis.ru; Nevsky pr 66; per hr R100; ☒ 24hr; Ⓜ Gostiny Dvor) which is entered from Liteyny pr.

In an emergency call ☎ 01 for fire, ☎ 02 for the police and ☎ 03 for an ambulance. The operator will speak Russian only.

SIGHTS
The Hermitage & Dvortsovaya Ploshchad

Mainly set in the magnificent Winter Palace, the **State Hermitage** (Map p225; ☎ 571 3465; www.hermitagemuseum.org; Dvortsovaya pl 2; adult R350, ISIC cardholders & under 17 free; ☒ 10.30am-6pm Tue-Sat, to 5pm Sun) is stacked with treasures, ranging from Egyptian mummies and Scythian gold to early 20th-century European art by Matisse and Picasso. Avoid queuing for tickets by booking online (US$17.95) through the website.

The museum's main entrance is from **Dvortsovaya ploshchad** (Palace Sq), one of the city's most impressive and historic spaces. Stand back to admire the palace and the central 47.5m **Alexander Column**, named after Alexander I and commemorating the 1812 victory over Napoleon. Enclosing the square's south side is the **General Staff Building** which in its east wing has a much less crowded but just as worthy branch of the **Hermitage** (Map p225; ☎ 314 8260; www.hermitagemuseum.org/html_En/03/hm3_11.html; Dvortsovaya pl 6-8; adult/student R200/free; ☒ 10am-6pm Tue-Sun; Ⓜ Nevsky Pr).

Church of the Saviour on Spilled Blood

This multidomed dazzler of a **church** (Map p225; Spas na Krovi; ☎ 315 1636; http://eng.cathedral.ru/saviour; Konyushennaya pl; adult/student R300/150; ☒ 11am-7pm Thu-Tue Oct-Apr, 10am-8pm Thu-Tue May-Sep; Ⓜ Nevsky Pr), partly modelled on St Basil's in Moscow, was built between 1883 and 1907 on the spot where Alexander II was assassinated in 1881 (hence its gruesome name). The interior's 7000 sq metres of mosaics fully justify the entrance fee.

Russian Museum

The former Mikhailovsky Palace, now the **Russian Museum** (Map p225; Russky Muzey; ☎ 595 4248; www.rusmuseum.ru; Inzhenernaya ul 4; adult/student R350/150; ☒ 10am-5pm Mon, to 6pm Wed-Sun; Ⓜ Gostiny Dvor), houses one of the country's finest collections of Russian art. After the Hermitage you may feel you have had your fill of art, but try your utmost to make some time for this gem of a museum.

St Isaac's Cathedral & Around

The golden dome of this **cathedral** (Map pp222-3; Isaakievsky Sobor; ☎ 315 9732; http://eng.cathedral.ru/isaakievskaya; adult/student R300/150; ☒ 10am-8pm Thu-Mon, closed last Mon of the month; Ⓜ Sadovaya/Sennaya Pl) dominates the city skyline. Its lavish interior is open as a museum, but the real attraction here is the panoramic view from the **colonnade** (adult/student R150/100; ☒ 10am-7pm Thu-Mon, closed last Mon of the month) around the dome's drum and reached by 262 steps.

Behind the cathedral is **ploshchad Dekabristov** (Decembrists' Square; Map pp222–3), named after the Decembrists' Uprising of 14 December 1825, and Falconet's famous statue of Peter the Great, the **Bronze Horseman** (Map pp222–3).

Nevsky Prospekt

You can't leave St Petersburg without having walked at least part of Nevsky Pr (Map p225), Russia's most famous street. Starting at Dvortsovaya pl, notice the gilded spire of the **Admiralty** to your right as you head southeast down Nevsky towards the Moyka River. Across the Moyka, Rastrelli's baroque **Stroganov Palace** houses a branch of the Russian Museum (above).

A block beyond the Moyka, the great arms of the **Kazan Cathedral** (Kazansky Sobor; ☎ 571 4826; Kazanskaya pl 2; admission free; ☒ 10am-7pm, services 10am & 6pm; Ⓜ Nevsky pr) reach out towards the

CENTRAL ST PETERSBURG

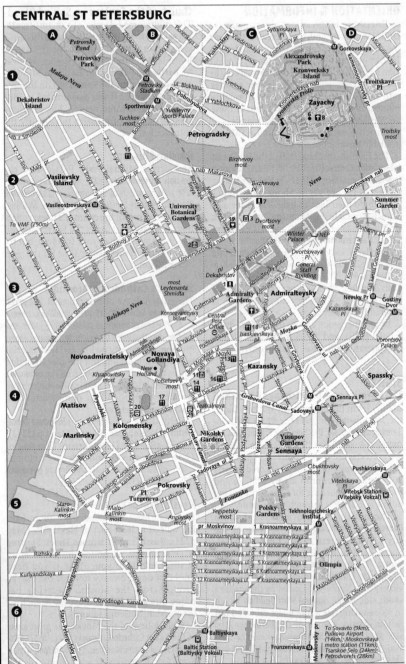

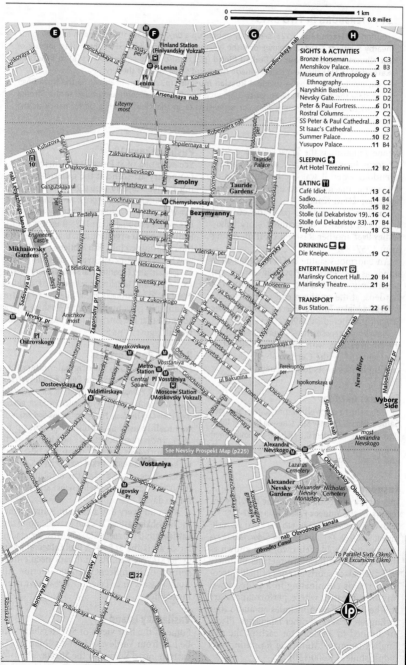

SIGHTS & ACTIVITIES
Bronze Horseman	1 C3
Menshikov Palace	2 B3
Museum of Anthropology & Ethnography	3 C2
Naryshkin Bastion	4 D2
Nevsky Gate	5 D2
Peter & Paul Fortress	6 D1
Rostral Columns	7 C2
SS Peter & Paul Cathedral	8 D1
St Isaac's Cathedral	9 C3
Summer Palace	10 E2
Yusupov Palace	11 B4

SLEEPING
Art Hotel Terezinni	12 B2

EATING
Café Idiot	13 C4
Sadko	14 B4
Stolle	15 B2
Stolle (ul Dekabristov 19)	16 C4
Stolle (ul Dekabristov 33)	17 B4
Teplo	18 C3

DRINKING
Die Kneipe	19 C2

ENTERTAINMENT
Mariinsky Concert Hall	20 B4
Mariinsky Theatre	21 B4

TRANSPORT
Bus Station	22 F6

See Nevsky Prospekt Map (p225)

To Parallel Sixty (3km);
VB Excursions (3km)

ST PETERSBURG

ST PETERSBURG IN TWO DAYS

Touring the **Hermitage** (p221) can easily gobble up a day, but leave the afternoon to stroll in the nearby **Summer Garden** (below), or if the weather is poor, be dazzled by the mosaic interior of the **Church of the Saviour on Spilled Blood** (p221). Also try to squeeze in a visit to **St Isaac's Cathedral** (p221) climbing its colonnade for a bird's-eye view of the city.

On day two start at the splendid **Russian Museum** (p221) then head across the Neva River to explore the **Peter & Paul Fortress** (below). If you have time, continue around to the **Strelka** (below) to see the museums here, or at least take in the view. Catch a performance at the **Mariinsky Theatre** (p227) in the evening.

---

avenue. Opposite is the **Singer Building**, a Style Moderne beauty recently restored to all its splendour when it was the headquarters of the sewing machine company; inside is the bookshop Dom Knigi.

Further along you'll pass the covered arcades of historic department store **Bolsoy Gostiny Dvor** another Rastrelli creation dating from 1757–85.

An enormous statue of **Catherine the Great** stands at the centre of **Ploshchad Ostrovskogo**, commonly referred to as the Catherine Gardens; at the southern end of the gardens is **Aleksandrinksy Theatre** where Chekhov's *The Seagull* premiered in 1896.

Nevsky pr crosses the Fontanka Canal on the **Anichkov most**, with its famous 1840s statues (sculpted by the German Pyotr Klodt) of rearing horses at its four corners.

Summer Garden

St Petersburg's loveliest park, the **Summer Garden** (Map p225; Letny Sad; admission free; 10am-10pm May-Sep, 10am-8pm Oct–mid-Apr; Gostiny Dvor) is a great place to relax beneath leafy trees and beside classical statues.

Yusupov Palace

In a city of glittering palaces, the dazzling interiors of the **Yusupov Palace** (Map pp222-3; 314 9883; www.yusupov-palace.ru; nab reki Moyki 94; adult/student R500/280; 11am-5pm; Sadovaya/Sennaya Pl) more than hold their own. Best known as the place where Rasputin met his untimely end, the palace sports a series of richly decorated rooms culminating in a gilded jewel box of a theatre, where performances are still held. Admission includes an audio tour in English or several other languages. Places are limited to 20 daily for each of the two English-language *Murder of Rasputin* tours (adult/student R300/150).

Pushkinskaya 10

See examples of St Petersburg's thriving contemporary art scene at the galleries occupying **Pushkinskaya 10** (Map p225; 764 5371; www.p10.nonmuseum.ru; Ligovsky pr 53; admission free; 3-7pm Wed-Sun; Pl Vosstaniya). Originally an artists' squat established in 1988 it is now a fully legit nonprofit organization, that also houses the cool music clubs **Fish Fabrique** (164 4857; www.fishfabrique.spb.ru; Ligovsky pr 53; admission R100-150; 3pm-late) and **Experimental Sound Gallery** (GEZ-21; 764 5258; www.tac.spb.ru; Ligovsky pr 53, 3rd fl; admission R100-150; concerts from 9pm). While the art centre commonly goes by the name 'Pushkinskaya 10', note that the entrance is through the archway at Ligovsky pr 53.

Peter & Paul Fortress

Founded in 1703 as the original military fortress for the new city, the **Peter & Paul Fortress** (Map pp222-3; Petropavlovskaya krepost; 238 4550; www.spbmuseum.ru/peterpaul; grounds 6am-10am; exhibitions 11am-6pm Thu-Mon, 11am-5pm Tue; Gorkovskaya). was mainly used as a political prison up to 1917. Individual tickets are needed for each of the fortress's attractions so the best deal is the **combined entry ticket** (adult/student R250/130) which allows access to all the exhibitions on the island (except the bell tower) and is valid for 10 days.

At noon every day a cannon is fired from the **Naryshkin Bastion**. It's fun to walk along the **battlements** (adult/student R100/60). Most spectacular of all is the **St Peter & Paul Cathedral** (adult/student R170/80), with its landmark needle-thin spire and magnificent baroque interior. All Russia's tsars since Peter the Great have been buried here.

Vasilevsky Island

Some of the best views of St Petersburg can be had from Vasilevsky Island's (Map p225) eastern 'nose' known as the **Strelka**. The two

ST PETERSBURG

NEVSKY PROSPEKT

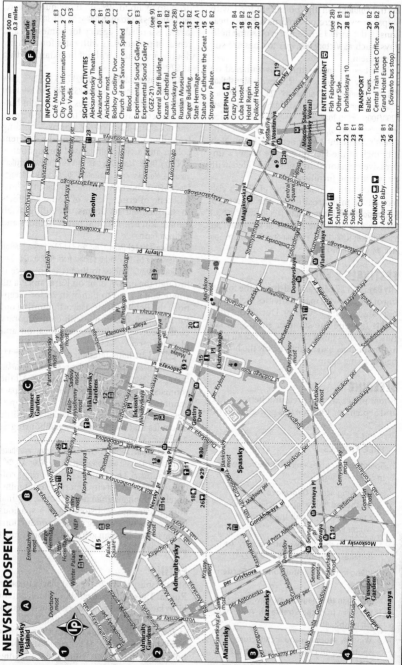

INFORMATION	
Café Max..................................1	E3
City Tourist Information Centre.....2	C2
Quo Vadis...............................3	D3

SIGHTS & ACTIVITIES	
Aleksandrinsky Theatre..............4	C3
Alexander Column.....................5	B1
Anichkov most.........................6	D3
Bolshoy Gostiny Dvor.................7	C2
Church of the Saviour on Spilled	
Blood...................................8	C1
Experimental Sound Gallery..........9	E3
Experimental Sound Gallery.....(see 9)	
General Staff Building................10	B1
Kazan Cathedral.......................11	B2
Pushkinskaya 10...................(see 28)	
Russian Museum........................12	C1
Singer Building........................13	B2
State Hermitage........................14	A1
Statue of Catherine the Great.......15	C2
Stroganov Palace......................16	B2

SLEEPING	
Crazy Duck............................17	B4
Cuba Hostel...........................18	B2
Hotel Repin...........................19	F3
Polikoff Hotel........................20	D2

EATING	
Schaste..............................21	D4
Stolle................................22	B2
Stolle................................23	E1
Zoom Café...........................24	B3

DRINKING	
Achtung Baby........................25	B1
Sochi................................26	B2

ENTERTAINMENT	
Fish Fabrique.....................(see 28)	
Other Side..........................27	B1
Pushkinskaya 10.....................28	E3

TRANSPORT	
Baltic Tours..........................29	B2
Central Train Ticket Office..........30	B2
Grand Hotel Europe..................31	C2
(Sovavto bus stop)..............31	C2

Rostral Columns on the point, studded with ships' prows, were oil-fired navigation beacons in the early 19th century; on some holidays, such as **Victory Day**, gas torches are still lit on them.

The best of many museums gathered on Vasilevsky Island is the riverside **Menshikov Palace** (Menshikovsky Dvorets; ☎ 323 1112; www.hermitagemuseum.org; Universitetskaya nab 15; adult/student R200/100; ⊙ 10.30am-6pm Tue-Sat, 10.30-5pm Sun; Ⓜ Vasileostrovskaya), built in 1707 for Peter the Great's confidant Alexander Menshikov. Now a branch of the Hermitage, the palace's impressively restored interiors are filled with period art and furniture.

Also worth a look are the ghoulish collection of monstrosities in the **Museum of Anthropology & Ethnography** (Kunstkamera; ☎ 328 1412; www.kunstkamera.ru; entrance on Tamozhenny per; adult/student R200/100; ⊙ 11am-6pm Tue-Sat, to 5pm Sun; Ⓜ Vasileostrovskaya).

FESTIVALS & EVENTS

City Day is on 27 May and celebrates the founding of the city with mass festivities including a big parade along Nevsky pr. During the **White Nights** (around the summer solstice in late June) the city comes alive and parties all night as the sun only barely sinks below the horizon before rising again.

SLEEPING

Room prices are at a premium between May and September. Outside this period, rates can

---

FREE THRILLS

Spend zero roubles enjoying the following in St Petersburg:

■ Marching across **Dvortsovaya ploshchad** (Palace Sq), imagining you're a revolutionary about the storm the Winter Palace (p221)

■ Exploring the quirky contemporary art galleries of **Pushkinskaya 10** (p224)

■ Idling in the delightful **Summer Garden** (p224)

■ Taking in the magnificent view across the Neva from the **Strelka** on Vasilevsky Island (p224)

■ Window shopping and architecture spotting along **Nevsky Prospekt** (p221)

---

drop up by up to 30% on those quoted here. **Host Families Association** (HOFA; ☎ 901-305 8874; www.hofa.ru) is a reliable agency for homestays and rental of private flats with rates for a single/double/apartment without breakfast starting at €29/44/118.

Cuba Hostel (Map p225; ☎ 921 7115, 315 1558; www.cubahostel.ru; Kazanskaya ul 5; dm R550; ⬜; Ⓜ Nevsky Pr) This funky hangout presses all the right buttons in terms atmosphere, friendliness, price and location. Each of the dorms – holding from four to 10 beds – is painted a different colour and arty design is used throughout.

Crazy Duck (Map p225; ☎ 310 1304; www.crazyduck.ru; apt 4, Moskovsky pr 4; dm from R750; ⬜; Ⓜ Sadovaya/Sennaya Pl) A cheery newcomer to the city's hostel scene offering plenty of home comforts to supplement its dorms, including a fab lounge, kitchen with top notch facilities and Jacuzzi bath.

Polikoff Hotel (Map p225; ☎ 314 7925; www.polikoff.ru; Nevsky pr 64/11; r incl breakfast from R3000; ⌧ ⬜; Ⓜ Gostiny Dvor) Tricky to find (the entrance is through the brown door on Karavannaya ul, where you'll need to punch in 26 for reception) the Polikoff Hotel is worth hunting out for its rooms brimming with contemporary cool decor, quiet but central location and pleasant service.

ᴏᴜʀᴘɪᴄᴋ Art Hotel Terezinni (Map pp222-3; ☎ 332 1035; www.trezzini-hotel.com; Bolshoy pr 8; s/d with breakfast from R2500/3360; ⌧ ⬜; Ⓜ Vasileostrovskaya) All the rooms are very appealing, even the compact economy singles, at this arty hotel. Standouts are rooms 201 and 214 which have little balconies and overlook the neighbouring St Andrew's Cathedral.

Hotel Repin (Map p225; ☎ 717 9976; www.repin-hotel.ru; Nesky pr 136; s/d with breakfast R2800/3700; ⬜ ⌧; Ⓜ Pl Vosstaniya) The Repin's flower bright colours makes it one of city's more pleasant minihotels with bigger than usual rooms, original antique ceramic wall stoves, and a spacious lounge area where hang some reproductions of the famed Russian artist Ilya Repin's most famous works.

EATING

St Petersburg is one of the best places to eat in Russia. Those on a budget should look out for bliny kiosks throughout the city where a quick snack will not cost you more than R50.

Zoom Café (Map p225; www.cafezoom.ru; Gorokhovaya ul 22; mains R200-400; ⌧ ☎; Ⓜ Nevsky Prospekt) Popular boho/student hangout with regularly changing art exhibitions on its walls. Serves unfussy tasty European and Russian food, has a very relaxed ambience, and a no-smoking zone.

Café Idiot (Map pp222-3; ☎ 315 1675; nab reki Moyki 82; meals R400; ⊗ 11-1am; ☒ ☜; Ⓜ Sennaya Ploshchad) This long-running vegetarian cafe charms with its pre-revolutionary atmosphere. It's an ideal place to visit for a nightcap or late supper. It has free wi-fi.

Schaste (Happiness; Map p225; ☎ 572 2675; www .schaste-est.com; ul Rubinsteyna 15/17; mains R250-400; ⊗ 9am-midnight Mon-Thu, 9-7am Fri, 10-7am Sat, 10am-midnight Sun; Ⓜ Dostoevskaya/Vladimirskaya) Romantic cherubs are the motif of this charming cafe-bar, even on the dot-to-dot puzzles that are printed on the place mats. The vaguely Russian food is tasty and the three-course lunch for R250 is a steal.

Teplo (Map pp222-3; ☎ 570 1974; Bolshaya Morskaya ul 45; mains R260-500; Ⓜ Sadovaya/Sennaya Pl). You'll instantly warm to Teplo's cosy living room atmosphere liberally scattered with cuddly soft toys. The food – roast chicken, salmon in savoy cabbage, sweet and savoury pies and pastries baked daily – is equally comforting.

our pick **Sadko** (Map p225; ☎ 920 8228; www.probka .org; ul Glinki 2; mains R260-650; Ⓜ Sadovaya/Sennaya Pl) Serving all the Russian favourites this impressive restaurant's decor applies traditional floral designs to a slick contemporary style. It has a great children's room and is ideal as a pre- or post-Mariinsky Theatre dining option. The waiters, many music students at the local conservatory, give impromptu vocal performances.

Stolle (www.stolle.ru; pies R60-100; ⊗ 8am-10pm); Konyushennaya per (Map p225; Konyushennaya per 1/6; Ⓜ Nevsky Pr); ul Vosstaniya (Map p225; ul Vosstaniya 32; Ⓜ Cherny-shevskaya) ul Dekabristov 19 & 33 (Map pp222-3; Ⓜ Sadovaya/Sennaya Ploshchad); Vasilyevsky Island (Syezdovskaya & 1-ya linii 50; Ⓜ Vasileostrovskaya) We can't get enough of the traditional Russian savoury and sweet pies at this expanding chain of cafes and we guarantee you'll also be back for more. It's easy to make a meal of it with soups and other dishes that can be ordered at the counter.

DRINKING

our pick **Achtung Baby** (Map p225; Konyushennaya pl 2; entry after 10pm Fri & Sat R300; ⊗ 6pm-6am; Ⓜ Nevsky Pr) The best of several bars and clubs that have taken over the old tsarists-era stables makes great use of the vast, high-ceiling space. We love the furry globes that hang over the bar.

Sochi (Map p225; Kazanskaya ul 7; ⊗ 6pm-6am; Ⓜ Nevsky Pr) Occupying one half of the same building as the microbrewery Tinkoff is this new venture by the woman who launched St Petersburg's DJ-bar scene. Prop yourself at the long bar or groove along with the hipsters to bands and eclectic selections from the DJs.

Other Side (Map p225; www.theotherside.ru; Bolshaya Konyushennaya ul 1; ⊗ noon-last customer, concerts 8pm Sun-Thu, 10pm or 11pm Fri & Sat; Ⓜ Nevsky Pr) There's live music most nights at this fun and funky bar as well as decent food (mains R200 to R500) but most people turn up to enjoy its seven beers on tap.

Die Kneipe (Map pp222-3; Grad Petrov; ☎ 326 0137; www.die-kneipe.ru; Universitetskaya nab 5; ⊗ noon-last customer; Ⓜ Vasileostrovskaya) The refreshing ales and German-style sausage meals are reason enough to stop by this fine microbrewery with a view across the Neva from its outdoor tables.

GETTING THERE & AWAY

Daily express buses run from Turku and Helsinki to Vyborg and St Petersburg (Russian visa required) along highway E18, via the Finnish towns of Porvoo, Kotka and Hamina. Check current timetables and book tickets at the bus station or a travel agency. Note that St Petersburg is Pietari in Finnish, and Vyborg is Viipuri.

A couple of operations in St Petersburg are **Ardis Finnord** (Map p225; ☎ 314 8951; Italiyanskaya ul 37; Ⓜ Gostiny Dvor) which runs two buses daily from its offices to Helsinki (R1400), and **Sovavto** (☎ 740 3985; www.sovavto.ru; Vitebsky pr 3; Ⓜ Moskovskie Vorota) with daily departures from the Park Inn – Pulkovskaya and Grand Hotel Europa to Helsinki (eight hours) and Turku (11 hours).

The latter's buses are timed to arrivals and departures of the Silja Line and Viking Line ferries from Turku to Stockholm.

The train is a more romantic and comfortable way to reach Russia. There are three daily trains from Helsinki to Russia all of which pause at Vyborg before continuing to St Petersburg. You must have a valid Russian visa and passport checks are carried out on board the moving train. For current timetables check www.vr.fi.

The Russian *Tolstoy* sleeper departs Helsinki daily at 6.23pm, arriving in Moscow at 8.25am the next day (one way in 2nd/1st class €101.60/152.60) via St Petersburg (€67.80/102.80); it departs from Moscow daily at 10.50pm and from St Petersburg at 6.07am. The *Sibelius* and *Repin* have daily services between Helsinki and St Petersburg (5½ hours) via Vyborg (3¾ hours). The *Sibelius* (a Finnish train) departs from Helsinki at 7.23am (2nd-/1st-class seats €58.80/92.60). The Russian *Repin* departs at 3.23pm and has 2nd-class seats (€58.80) or 2nd- and 1st-class sleeping berths (€67.80/102.80). From St Petersburg, departures are at 4.34pm (*Sibelius*) and 7.17am (*Repin*).

Buy Russian rail tickets in Helsinki at the special ticket counter in the central station. In St Petersburg tickets can be purchased at the train stations, the **Central Train Ticket Office** (Map p225; ☎ 762 3344; nab kanala Griboedova 24; ☺ 8am-8pm Mon-Sat, 8am-4pm Sun; Ⓜ Nevsky Prospekt) and many travel agencies around town.

GETTING AROUND

The metro (flat fare 17R) is best for covering the large distances across the city. The four lines cross over in the city centre and go out to the suburbs. The most confusing aspect of the system is that all labelling is in Cyrillic. Listen out for the announcements of the station names. A further confusion is that two stations sharing an exit will have different names. For example, Nevsky Pr and Gostiny Dvor are in the same place, but as they are on different lines, they have different names.

Around the centre, *marshrutka* (minibuses) are a very quick alternative to the slow trolleybuses. Costs vary on each route, but the average fare is R20, and fares are displayed prominently inside each van. To stop a *marshrutka*, simply hold out your hand and it will stop. Jump in, sit down, pass cash to the driver (a human chain operates if you are not seated nearby) and then call out '*ostanovityes pozhalusta!*' when you want to get out and the driver will pull over.

Holding your arm out will cause unofficial taxis to stop very quickly. The standard rate for a short distance (1km to 2km) is R100, R200 for a journey roughly between 2km and 5km, and whatever you can negotiate for trips longer than about 5km. As a foreigner, expect to have the price raised – always agree on a price before getting into the taxi. To book a taxi in advance try **Peterburgskoe taksi 068** (Petersburg Taxi; ☎ 068, 324 7777; www.taxi068.spb .ru, in Russian).

Iceland

Iceland is literally a country in the making, a vast volcanic laboratory where mighty forces shape the land and shrink you to an awestruck speck. Here, the very land is alive – geysers gush fountains of steaming water, mud pots gloop and bubble, sulphurous clouds puff from fissures, and slow, grinding glaciers tear great pathways through the mountains. Bathe in turquoise pools, stand behind a toppling cascade, go white-water rafting on chalky-green glacial rivers, kayak under the midnight sun, or crunch across a dazzling-white icecap to experience the full weirdness of Icelandic nature.

Iceland's creatures are larger than life too. There's no better place on earth to come eye-to-eye with sleek, spouting whales – minkes, humpbacks and even blue whales are common visitors to the deeper fjords. Record-breaking numbers of birds nest in the towering sea-cliffs: cutest are the fearless little puffins who flutter and bill in their thousands on the Vestmannaeyjar.

The landscape is infectious: hidden energy and a desire to shape the world are Icelandic traits. Vibrant Reykjavík, that clean, green little capital, must contain the world's highest concentration of dreamers, authors, poets and musicians. Although the recent global recession has hit Iceland particularly hard, the natives are attempting to face it with Scandinavian cool. And for visitors, at least, the crashing króna means a cheaper holiday.

FAST FACTS

- **Area** 103,000 sq km
- **Capital** Reykjavík
- **Currency** króna (Ikr): €1 = Ikr169.17; US$1 = Ikr127.63; UK£1 = Ikr188.37; A$1 = Ikr92.44; CA$1 = Ikr106.05; NZ$1 = Ikr71.91; ¥100 = Ikr130.91
- **Famous for** fishing, sagas, Björk, the Blue Lagoon, a crashing economy
- **Official Language** Icelandic
- **Phrases** halló (hello), gjörðu svo vel (please), takk fyrir (thanks), skál! (cheers!)
- **Population** 313,000
- **Telephone Codes** country code ☎ 354; international access code ☎ 00; reverse-charge operator ☎ 533 5309; telephone area codes don't apply
- **Visa** unnecessary for visitors from Australia, Canada, New Zealand, Scandinavia, EU countries, the UK and the USA staying for under three months (see p285)

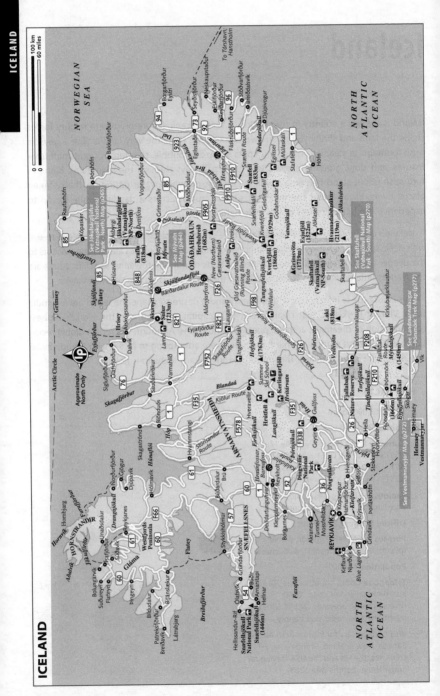

WARNING: POST-CRASH PRICES

Iceland's horrific economic problems (see p233) mean that costs change almost from day to day. In this chapter, we have given prices at the time of research, but a wildly volatile króna and tremendous financial uncertainty mean that nothing is set in stone. Prices may look very different by the time you get here.

HIGHLIGHTS

- Experience Iceland's extremes – inch up a glacier at **Skaftafell** (p269) or tour the smouldering volcanic wastelands of **Krafla** (p263).
- Breathe cool, pure air while luxuriating in hot water at the **Blue Lagoon** (p250), **Mývatn Nature Baths** (p263), or the turquoise pools at **Landmannalaugar** (p275).
- See the ocean giants rolling from the waves on a **whale-watching** (p260) trip in Húsavík.
- Rocket down rapids in a **raft** (p280) or explore the silent beauty of the fjords by **kayak** (p280).
- Cavort with crowds of partygoers on the drunken Reykjavík **runtur** (p247).

ITINERARIES

- **Three Days** Arrive in Reykjavík on Friday to catch the decadent *runtur*. Sober up in Laugadalur geothermal pool, admire the views from Hallgrímskirkja, then absorb some Viking history at the National Museum. On Sunday, visit Gullfoss, Geysir and Þingvellir on a Golden Circle tour. Stop to soak in the Blue Lagoon on the way home.
- **One week** Head for the countryside: chill out on serene Snæfellsnes in the west; the volcanic Vestmannaeyjar with their immense puffin colonies; spot the sea off the southern coast; or drive east to Skaftafell for wonderful hiking and glacier-walking.

CLIMATE & WHEN TO GO

Reykjavík's mildish climate can rapidly degenerate into heavy rain, biting wind or fog; May, June and July are the driest months of the year. In the north and east, the weather is better. Blizzards and fierce sandstorms occur in the interior deserts and on the coastal sand deltas. The **Icelandic Meteorological Office** (☎ 902 0600; www.vedur.is/english) provides a daily weather forecast in English.

Mid-June to August is high season, but most highland tours don't operate until July because of snow. At other times, many tourist facilities outside Reykjavík are closed.

See also p486 for a climate chart.

HISTORY

Irish monks were probably the first people to come to Iceland in around AD 700. Their solitude was rudely shattered by the Age of Settlement (871–930), when a wave of Nordic people descended, driven from the Scandinavian mainland by political clashes. Many raided Ireland and the Scottish islands on the way, bringing Celtic slaves to the new country.

Ingólfur Arnarson, a Norwegian fugitive, became the first official Icelander (AD 871). He settled at Reykjavík (Smoky Bay), which he named after steam he saw rising from geothermal vents. According to 12th-century sources, Ingólfur built his farm on Aðalstræti. Recent archaeological excavations have unearthed a Viking longhouse on that very spot, and the dwelling is now the focus of the city's newest museum, Reykjavík 871+/-2 (p241).

The settlers rejected monarchy and established the world's first democratic parliament at Þingvellir (Parliament Plains; p250), outside Reykjavík. The country converted to Christianity in the year 1000.

Two hundred years of peace ended during the Sturlunga Period (1230–62), when

HOW MUCH?

- **Cuddly troll** Ikr2500
- **Postcard** Ikr100
- **Cinema ticket** Ikr1000
- **Knitted hat** Ikr2000
- **Whale-watching trip** Ikr8000

LONELY PLANET INDEX

- **1L petrol** Ikr140
- **1L bottle of water** Ikr270
- **Pint of Egils beer** Ikr800
- **Souvenir T-shirt** Ikr1800
- **Hot dog** Ikr230

ICELAND

CONNECTIONS

Little Iceland, way out on the edge of nothing, is nevertheless connected by regular flights from Keflavík Airport to Denmark (Copenhagen), Finland (Helsinki), Norway (Bergen, Oslo and Stavanger) and Sweden (Göteborg and Stockholm) – see p285 for details.

For those who like more romance, the ferry from Denmark (p286) along the jaw-dropping fjord to Seyðisfjörður is the most stylish way to arrive.

Iceland's chieftains descended into bloody territorial fighting. The era is epitomised by the life and violent death of historian and political schemer, Snorri Sturluson (p251). Iceland ceded control of the country to Norway in 1262, then was placed under Danish rule in 1397. For the next six centuries, the forgotten country endured a Dark Age of famine, disease and disastrous volcanic eruptions.

In the early 17th century, the Danish king imposed a trade monopoly that was utterly exploited by foreign merchants. In an attempt to bypass the crippling embargo, weaving, tanning and wool-dyeing factories were built, which led to the foundation of the city of Reykjavík.

Iceland's next calamity was volcanic. In 1783 the vast crater row Lakagígar (Laki) erupted for 10 months, devastating southeastern Iceland and creating a lingering poisonous haze. Nearly 75% of Iceland's livestock and 20% of the human population perished in the resulting famine; an evacuation of the country was discussed.

In spite (or perhaps because) of such neglectful foreign rule and miserable living conditions, a sense of Icelandic nationalism slowly began to grow. The Republic of Iceland was established on 17 June 1944 (see p282 for information on Independence Day), symbolically at Þingvellir.

Perversely, while the rest of Europe endured the horrors of WWII, Iceland went from strength to strength. British and then US troops were stationed at Keflavík (right up until September 2006), bringing with them undreamt-of wealth. Subsistence farming gave way to prosperity and a frenzy of new building, funded mainly by American dollars. The Ring Rd, Iceland's main highway which circles the whole country, was finally completed in 1974.

A corresponding boom in the fishing industry saw Iceland extend its fishing limit in the 1970s to 200 miles (322km). This precipitated the worst of the 'cod wars', when the UK initially refused to recognise the new zone and continued fishing within what were now deemed to be Icelandic waters. During the seven-month conflict, Icelandic ships cut the nets of British trawlers, shots were fired, and ships on both sides were rammed.

Iceland's presidency, chiefly ceremonial, is held by Ólafur Ragnar Grímsson. The government's popularity evaporated recently along with the country's wealth, as Iceland's luck turned about again. The world financial crisis hit the country with a sledgehammer blow in September 2008, thanks to massive foreign debt and a severely overvalued currency: see boxed text, opposite. Prime Minister Geir Haarde announced both his own resignation and that of his coalition government at the end of January 2009, following four months of furious protests in the capital. Elections will be held in May 2009, but in the meantime, the Social Democratic Alliance and the Left-Green Movement have formed a new coalition government, headed by Jóhanna Sigurðardóttir, Iceland's first female prime minister.

PEOPLE

Icelanders are reserved but friendly. They value independence, and have a live-and-let-live attitude. However, they are fiercely proud of their seafaring culture and many hold strong pro-whaling views. Icelanders recently discovered that much of their genetic makeup is Celtic, suggesting that far more of the Viking settlers had children by their Celtic slaves than originally thought.

Icelanders' names are constructed from a combination of their first name and their father's (or mother's) first name. Girls add the suffix *dóttir* (daughter) to the patronymic and boys add *son*. Therefore, Jón, the son of Einar, would be Jón Einarsson. Guðrun, the daughter of Halldór, would be Guðrun Halldórsdóttir. Icelanders always call each other by their first names.

The country has one of the world's highest life expectancies: 79.4 years for men and 82.9 years for women. Of a population of 313,000, almost half live in Reykjavík.

ICELAND'S ECONOMIC MELTDOWN

Everything was looking so rosy: in early 2008, Iceland was full of confidence and riding high. However, much of the country's wealth was built over a black hole of debt – its banks' liabilities were more than 10 times its annual GDP. The ripples of the worldwide financial crisis had become a tidal wave by the time they reached Icelandic shores, washing away the country's entire economy.

By October 2008, the Icelandic stock market had crashed; the króna plummeted, losing almost half its value overnight; all three national banks went into receivership; and the country teetered on the brink of bankruptcy.

Relations between Iceland and the UK were strained following the collapse of Icesave (a subsidiary of Iceland's national bank Landsbanki), in which 300,000 British customers had invested their savings. UK prime minister, Gordon Brown invoked terrorist laws to freeze Icelandic assets; this was seen by many Icelanders as unnecessary heavy-handed, and the cause of Kaupþing bank's collapse. At home, protestors rioted in Reykjavík, furious with a government they felt had betrayed them.

Help came in November 2008 with a $2.1 billion IMF loan, and a $3 billion bailout from Scandinavian neighbours; but the immediate future still looks highly uncertain. Spiralling inflation, wage cuts and redundancies mean that Icelanders' incomes have fallen by a quarter in real terms, and national pride has taken a proper kicking. It's possible that the country will vote 'yes' in a referendum on joining the EU in February/March 2009, allowing Iceland to change from a wildly fluctuating króna to a more stable euro economy.

The meltdown is very bad for Icelanders, but current exchange rates make Iceland cheaper for visitors than it has been in years. Every dark cloud...

RELIGION

Iceland officially converted to Christianity around 1000, although followers of the old pagan gods were allowed to worship in private. The Danes imposed Lutheranism in the 1550 Reformation: 84% of Icelanders are Lutheran today.

ARTS
Literature

Bloody, black and powerful, the late 12th- and 13th-century sagas are without doubt Iceland's greatest cultural achievement. Written in terse Old Norse, these epics continue to entertain Icelanders and provide them with a rich sense of heritage. One of the best known, *Egils Saga*, revolves around the complex, devious Egil Skallagrímsson. A renowned poet and skilled lawyer, he's also the grandson of a werewolf and a murderous drunk. You can admire original saga manuscripts in Reykjavík's Þjóðmenningarhúsið (p241).

The best-known modern Icelandic writer is Nobel Prize–winner Halldór Laxness, who lived just outside Reykjavík (p242). His darkly comic work gives a superb insight into Icelandic life. *Independent People*, concerning the fatally proud farmer Bjartur and the birth of the Icelandic nation, is his most famous book and an unmissable read.

Modern Icelandic writers include Einar Kárason, who wrote the outstanding *Devil's Island* (about Reykjavík life in the 1950s); Hallgrímur Helgason, creator of *101 Reykjavík* (about a modern-day city slacker); and Arnaldur Indriðason, whose Reykjavík-based crime fiction, including the award-winning *Silence of the Grave*, regularly tops Iceland's bestseller lists.

Music

Björk is Iceland's most famous musical export, followed by Sigur Rós. The swirling maelstrom of Icelandic popular music constantly throws up new bands. Leaves, Trabant, FM Belfast, Múm, Singapore Sling, Cynic Guru and Benny Crespo's Gang are currently popular at home or abroad or both, several of them brought to a wider audience by the music-documentary *Screaming Masterpiece* (2005).

Bands perform live at venues such as NASA (p248). The major music event of the year is the international-yet-intimate Iceland Airwaves festival (p282).

Visual Arts

Various artists have wrestled with Iceland's enigmatic soul, including the prolific Ásgrímur Jónsson (1876–1958). His work, depicting Icelandic landscapes and folktales, can be seen at the National Gallery in Reykjavík (p242). Pop-art icon Erró (b 1932) is honoured with a permanent collection in Listasafn Reykjavíkur (p242).

Sculptors are well represented: the mystical work of Einar Jónsson (1874–1954; p242) dwells on death and resurrection, and Ásmundur Sveinsson's (1893–1982) sculptures (p242) celebrate Iceland and its stories.

Cinema & TV

Baltasar Kormákur has won international audiences for two of his films. *101 Reykjavík* (2000), based on Hallgrímur Helgason's book of the same name, is the painful, funny tale of a Reykjavík drop-out's fling with his mother's lesbian lover. The thriller *Jar City* (2006), adapted from Arnaldur Indriðason's award-winning novel *Tainted Blood*, follows world-weary Detective Inspector Erlendur as he investigates a brutal murder and some dodgy doings at Iceland's Genetic Research Centre.

For forthcoming films, see the informative www.icelandicfilmcentre.is.

SPORT

Football (soccer) is the most popular sport in Iceland, with large matches played at the Laugardalsvöllur national stadium in Reykjavík. With only a small population to draw from, the league is low-level, although it did produce star midfielder Eidur Gudjohnsen.

Officially, Iceland's national sport is *glíma*, a type of wrestling that dates back to the 12th century. This little-seen activity is most often practised in local sports halls, although the recent foundation of both the **International Glíma Association** (http://internationalglima.com) and a new world-championship competition point to growing interest in the sport.

ENVIRONMENT

The Land

Iceland, a juvenile among the world's land masses, is shaped by desert plateaus (52%), lava fields (11%), *sandur* (sand deltas; 4%) and icecaps (12%). Over half of Iceland lies above 400m and its highest point, Hvannadalshnúkur, rises 2119m above sea level. Only 21% of Iceland is considered habitable.

Iceland's active volcanic zone runs through the middle of the country, from southwest to northeast. Active-zone geological features include lava flows, tubes, geysers, hot springs and volcanoes, and rocks such as basalt, pumice and rhyolite. Geysir (p250), Krýsuvík (p251) and Krafla (p263) are very accessible active areas.

There are very few trees. Most of the native flora consists of grasses, mosses, lichens and wildflowers. *Plöntukort Íslands* (Botanical Map; Ikr1290), available from Reykjavík's bookshops, is a good guide.

Wildlife

The wild-eyed Arctic fox is the only indigenous land mammal; introduced species include reindeer and mice. Polar bears occasionally turn up on the north coast, but their life expectancy in Iceland is short.

The lack of land mammals is compensated for by vast numbers of birds and marine fauna. Kittiwakes, fulmars and gannets form large coastal colonies (best seen at Látrabjarg, p256); there are Arctic terns, golden plovers, ducks, swans, divers and geese at Mývatn (p262); and Vestmannaeyjar (p271) has the largest populations of puffins. The website www.fuglar.is lists what rarities are about. *Fuglakort Íslands* (Bird-watcher's Map; Ikr1290), sold in Reykjavík's bookshops, is a good reference.

Four different seal species and 12 species of cetacean have been spotted: boat trips run from various coastal towns including Reykjavík (p242), although the best sightings are at Húsavík (p260).

National Parks & Nature Reserves

Iceland's national parks (*þjóðgarður*) are Snæfellsjökull (p252); Þingvellir (p250), a Unesco World Heritage Site; and the brand-new Vatnajökull National Park (p268), which combines the former Jökulsárgljúfur (p265) and Skaftafell (p269) parks. There are countless nature reserves (*friðland*), the most significant being Mývatn (p262). Parks and reserves are open to visitors at all times. Wild camping is restricted: for further information, contact the government's environment agency, **Umhverfisstofnun** (☎ 591 2000; www.ust.is). Roughly 5% of the total land area of Iceland is protected, and the government has the ambitious aim of increasing that percentage tenfold over time.

Environmental Issues

Historically, sheep farming and timber extraction caused immense environmental damage. It has been estimated that a mere 1% of Iceland's original woodland remains. Large-

WEIGHING UP THE WHALE DEBATE

After 150 years of hunting, many whale species are now facing extinction. To give populations a chance to recover, the International Whaling Commission (IWC) called for a suspension of commercial whaling in 1986. Most countries complied; however, Iceland continued 'scientific' whaling, a loophole that allows whales to be hunted for DNA samples (although it is possible to take these samples without killing the whale) and then permits the meat to be sold to restaurants.

Following international pressure, there was a lull between 1989 and 2003, after which Icelandic whalers resumed 'scientific' whaling, catching 200 minkes between 2003 and 2007. In 2006, Iceland also began commercial whaling again, with the governmental Icelandic Marine Institute tentatively suggesting that an annual catch of 100 minke and 150 fin whales is sustainable; to date, seven of each have been caught. In response, 25 countries issued a formal protest to the Icelandic government, and conservationists called for a boycott of Iceland and Icelandic goods.

Whaling is an emotional topic. Supporters of the hunt (around 70% of Icelanders) believe minke whales are depleting fish stocks and need culling; whereas antiwhalers fear for the animals and for the flourishing whale-watching industry, which brings in about US$18 million annually.

Whaling in Iceland is regulated by the International Whaling Commission. For more information, see the websites of the **International Whaling Commission** (www.iwcoffice.org), **World Wide Fund for Nature** (www.wwf.org) and **Greenpeace** (www.greenpeace.org).

scale aerial seeding and intensive tree-planting programmes are combatting erosion.

Concerns over declining fish stocks have led the government to invest in other areas, particularly heavy industry (in early 2008, aluminium smelting products accounted for 40% of Iceland's total exports, overtaking fish for the first time). The most controversial project in Icelandic history was the dam built in the Kárahnjúkar peaks in eastern Iceland to power an American aluminium smelting plant. Completed in 2008, it altered the courses of two glacial rivers and flooded a vast area of untouched wilderness.

Iceland is endeavouring to free itself of fossil fuels by 2050, relying instead on geothermal power, hydrogen cells and solar energy.

FOOD & DRINK

Cafes and restaurants in Reykjavík cater to most tastes, but fresh fish, seafood and Icelandic lamb get top billing on most upmarket menus.

The government levies high taxes on alcohol to discourage excessive drinking. Check out Friday-night Reykjavík to see the success of this policy!

Staples & Specialities

Born from centuries of near-starvation, Iceland's traditional dishes reflect a 'waste not, want not' austerity. Specialities include *svið* (singed sheep's head complete with eyeballs),

súrsaðir hrútspungar (pickled rams' testicles) and *hákarl* (putrefied shark meat, buried and rotted for three months to make it digestible). These gruesome dishes are generally only eaten nowadays during the February celebration of Þorri. You can try cubes of shark meat at Kolaportið Flea Market (p249), but be warned that the smell alone makes many foreigners ill! Some restaurants serve whale meat *(hval)*, culled during 'scientific' hunts (see boxed text, above).

Icelanders consume *lundi* (puffin), which looks and tastes like calf liver. Most of the birds are netted on the Vestmannaeyjar (p271). *Harðfiskur* is an everyday snack: these brittle pieces of wind-dried haddock are usually eaten with butter. Delicious yogurtlike *skyr*, made from curdled milk, is a unique treat; sugar, fruit and cream are often added to turn it into a rich dessert. Around Mývatn (p262), look out for a regional pudding: *hverabrauð* (hot-spring bread) is a sweet, dark, sticky loaf, baked in the ground using geothermal heat. *Kleinur* (twisted doughnuts, traditionally deep-fried in lard) are popular snacks to dip in coffee.

Coffee is a national institution, and most cafes offer free refills. The traditional Icelandic alcoholic brew is *brennivín* (burnt wine), a sort of schnapps made from potatoes and caraway seeds with the foreboding nickname *svarti dauði* (black death). Note that if you buy *syrmjolk* from the supermarket, it's sour milk.

Where to Eat & Drink

Reykjavík has no shortage of cosy cafes (commonly open from 11am until 1am, later at weekends) that turn into bars at night. They're great for lingering coffees, light lunches (from about Ikr1500) and late-night beers. Restaurants are more upmarket, often serving gourmet food, with mains from about Ikr2700 to Ikr5000 per person. Some are open for lunch (between 11am and 2pm), and most open nightly (between 6pm and 10pm). In other towns, choice is much reduced and opening times shorter.

Every village has at least one *kaupfélagið* (co-operative supermarket), with Bónus and Netto being the cheapest. Petrol stations and grills sell relatively inexpensive fast-food snacks (a hot dog and chips cost around Ikr800).

Beer, wine and spirits are available to people aged over 20 years from licensed hotels, bars, restaurants and *vín búð* (state monopoly) stores.

Vegetarians & Vegans

Outside Reykjavík, which has three vegan/vegie restaurants, choices are limited. Most places offer one vegie dish, but as this usually involves cheese, vegans may have to self-cater.

REYKJAVÍK

pop 116,992

Iceland's pint-size capital is cute and complex and runs entirely on coffee. It's packed with cosy cafes, top-quality restaurants, fine museums, swirling music and state-of-the-art geothermal pools – all the trappings of a large 21st-century European city, but shrunk down to a minute, manageable size. All these delectable diversions are layered over a foundation of rich Viking history. The froth on top is Reykjavík's eccentric and excessive *runtur*, a wild pub-crawl that starts on Friday night around small, super-stylish clubs and bars, and ends in Sunday brunch and a city-wide hangover.

The world's most northerly capital offers a bewitching combination of small-town innocence and mischievous energy. As if that wasn't enough, Nature herself adds a powerful extra dimension: snow-topped mountains and volcanoes line the horizon; the ocean rolls right up to the very edge of town; and the air is as cold and clean as frozen diamonds.

REYKJAVÍK IN TWO DAYS

Arrive on Friday night to experience the **runtur** (p247). Sober up on Saturday with a quick dip in the **Laugadalur geothermal pool** (p243). Don't miss the panoramic views at **Hallgrímskirkja** (opposite), or the **Perlan & Saga Museum** (p240). Book a **whale-watching trip** (p242) in the morning, then visit the **National Museum** (p241).

ORIENTATION

Reykjavík's old town lies between Tjörnin, Lækjargata, the harbour and the nearby suburb of Seltjarnarnes. Nearly everything in the city – bars, cafes, restaurants, the post office and the tourist office – is within walking distance of the old settlement. The shopping district extends east along Laugavegur from Lækjargata to Hlemmur bus station.

The international airport is an hour's drive away at Keflavík, but getting to the capital is easy peasy. See p249 for details.

INFORMATION

Bookshops

There are three big bookshops offering a superb choice of English-language books, newspapers, magazines and maps.

Eymundsson (Map p240; ☎ 540 2130; Austurstræti 18; ☉ 9am-10pm Mon-Fri, 10am-10pm Sat & Sun)

Iða (Map p240; ☎ 511 5001; Lækjargata 2a; ☉ 9am-10pm)

Mál og Menning (Map p240; ☎ 515 2500; Laugavegur 18; ☉ 9am-10pm Mon-Fri, 10am-10pm Sat & Sun)

Discount Cards

Reykjavík Tourist Card (24/48/72hr Ikr1400/1900/2400) Available at various outlets including the tourist offices; it gives you free entry to galleries, museums, swimming pools and the zoo, and includes a bus pass.

Emergency

Landspítali University Hospital (Map pp238-9; ☎ 543 2000; Fossvogur) Has a 24-hour casualty department.

Internet Access

Libraries have the cheapest internet access (Ikr200 per hour).

Aðalbókasafn (Reykjavík City Library; Map p240; ☎ 563 1717; www.borgarbokasafn.is; Tryggvagata 15;

10am-9pm Mon, 10am-7pm Tue-Thu, 11am-7pm Fri, 1-5pm Sat & Sun)

Ground Zero (Map p240; ☎ 562 7776; Vallarstræti 4; per 15/35/60min Ikr200/350/500; 11am-1am Mon-Fri, noon-1am Sat & Sun) A dedicated internet cafe full of game-playing teenagers.

Medical Services

Dentist on duty (☎ 575 0505)
Health Centre (Map p240; ☎ 585 2600; Vesturgata 7) Doctor's appointment for visitors from Europe costs Ikr2600, for non-Europeans it's Ikr8000.
Læknavaktin (☎ 1770) Doctor on call between 5pm and 11.30pm.
Lyfja Apótek (Map p240; ☎ 552 4045; Laugavegur 16; 9am-6pm Mon-Fri, 11am-4pm Sat) Central pharmacy.
Lyfja Apótek (Map pp238-9; ☎ 533 2300; Lágmúli 5; 8am-midnight) Late-night pharmacy, near the Nordica Hotel. Take bus S2, 15, 17 or 19.

Money

Banks round Austurstræti and Bankastræti offer the best exchange rates. You can exchange foreign currency at hotels, but commission is high. ATMs accept MasterCard, Cirrus, Visa and Electron.

Change Group (Map p240; main tourist office) Also has a branch at the Keflavik airport. Commissions from 2.75% to 8.75%.
Landsbanki Íslands (Map p240; ☎ 410 4000; www .landsbanki.is; Austurstræti; 9.15am-4pm Mon-Fri) No commission charges.

Post

Main post office (Map p240; Pósthússtræti 5; 9am-6pm Mon-Fri)

Telephone

Public phones are elusive in mobile-crazy Reykjavík: try the main tourist office, the street opposite Laugavegur 38, and the Kringlan shopping centre.

Tourist Information

Reykjavík has a helpful main tourist office with a booking service, and satellite desks at the bus terminal and city hall. There are several private offices in the city. Pick up the free booklets *Reykjavík This Month* and *What's On in Reykjavík* for events in the capital. The excellent English-language newspaper *Grapevine*, is widely distributed and has the low-down on what's new in town.

BSÍ bus terminal desk (Map pp238-9; Vatnsmýrar vegur 10)

FREE THRILLS

Reykjavík's attractions are charming, low-key and often costly! But there is some free fun to be had:

- **Nauthólsvík Hot Beach** (Ylströndin; p243) Sunbathe on sand lapped by geothermal seawater.
- **Listasafn Reykjavíkur** (p242) There's at least a day's worth of viewing at Reykjavík Art Museum, made up of three sites across the city.
- **Kólaportið Flea Market** (p249) Atmospheric secondhand market.
- **Perlan** (p240) Gorge on gorgeous views from the top of the city's hot-water tanks.
- **Einar Jónsson Museum garden** (p242) There's a quiet little sculpture garden round the back of the museum.

Main tourist office (Upplýsingamiðstöð Ferðamanna; Map p240; ☎ 580 1550; www.visitreykjavik.is; Aðalstræti 2; 8.30am-7pm Jun–mid-Sep, 9am-6pm Mon-Fri, 9am-4pm Sat, 9am-2pm Sun mid-Sep–May)
Raðhús tourist information desk (Map p240; Tjarnargata 11; 8.30am-4.30pm Mon-Fri, noon-4pm Sat & Sun, closed Sun mid-Sep–mid-May) Inside city hall.

SIGHTS

Hallgrímskirkja

This immense concrete **church** (Map p240; ☎ 510 1000; www.hallgrimskirkja.is; Skólavörðuholt; 9am-5pm mid-Aug–mid-Jun, 9am-7pm mid-Jun–mid-Aug) is Reykjavík's most attention-seeking building, visible from 20km away. Its sweeping frontage represents columns of volcanic basalt, and took a staggering 34 years to build. Rather embarrassingly, it was discovered recently that the original builders skimped on materials, and extensive repair work, scheduled to last until 2010, is underway to replace the defective concrete! Admire the elongated, ultrastark interior; then for an unmissable view of the city, take an elevator trip (restoration work permitting) up the **75m tower** (adult/7-14yr Ikr400/100). Outside, a **statue** of Leifur Eiríksson, the first European to visit America, gazes proudly forth. It was a present from the USA on the 1000th anniversary of the Alþing, Iceland's parliament.

ICELAND

REYKJAVÍK

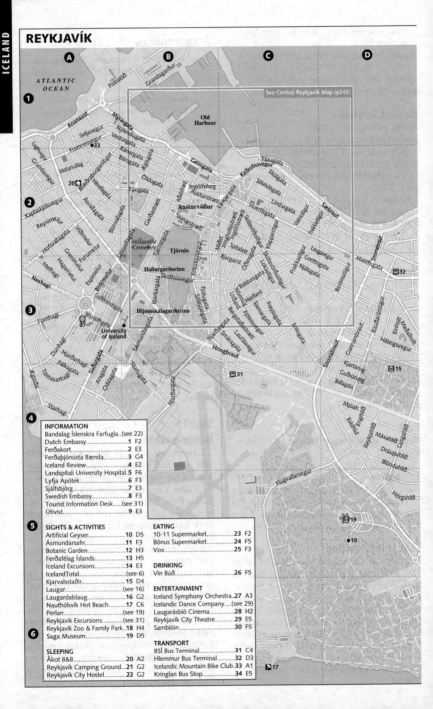

ATLANTIC OCEAN

Old Harbour

See Central Reykjavík Map (p240)

INFORMATION
Bandalag Íslenskra Farfugla..(see 22)
Dutch Embassy.....................1 F2
Ferðakort.............................2 E3
Ferðaþjónusta Bænda............3 G4
Iceland Review.....................4 E2
Landspítali University Hospital.5 F6
Lyfja Apótek.........................6 F3
Sjálfsbjörg............................7 E3
Swedish Embassy...................8 F3
Tourist Information Desk.....(see 31)
Útivist.................................9 E3

SIGHTS & ACTIVITIES
Artificial Geyser...................10 D5
Ásmundarsafn.....................11 F3
Botanic Garden....................12 H3
Ferðafélag Íslands................13 H5
Iceland Excursions................14 E3
IcelandTotal.....................(see 6)
Kjarvalsstaðir.......................15 D4
Laugar............................(see 16)
Laugardalslaug.....................16 G2
Nauthólsvík Hot Beach..........17 C6
Perlan............................(see 19)
Reykjavik Excursions..........(see 31)
Reykjavik Zoo & Family Park..18 H4
Saga Museum......................19 D5

SLEEPING
Ákot B&B............................20 A2
Reykjavík Camping Ground....21 G2
Reykjavík City Hostel............22 G2

EATING
10-11 Supermarket...............23 F2
Bónus Supermarket..............24 F5
Vox....................................25 F3

DRINKING
Vín Búð..............................26 F5

ENTERTAINMENT
Iceland Symphony Orchestra..27 A3
Icelandic Dance Company....(see 29)
Laugarásbíó Cinema.............28 H2
Reykjavík City Theatre..........29 E5
Sambíóin.............................30 F5

TRANSPORT
BSÍ Bus Terminal..................31 C4
Hlemmur Bus Terminal..........32 D3
Icelandic Mountain Bike Club..33 A1
Kringlan Bus Stop.................34 E5

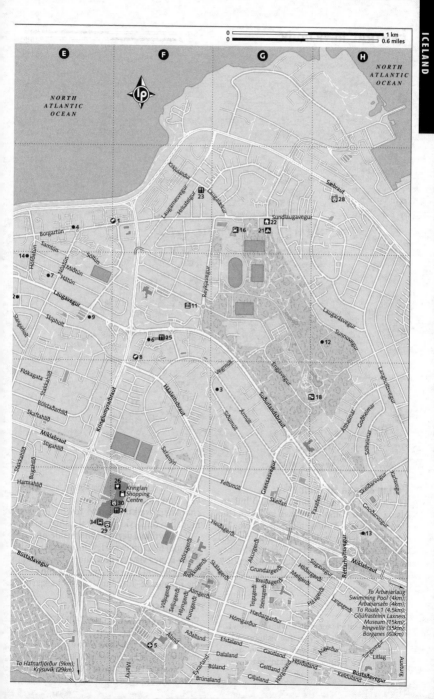

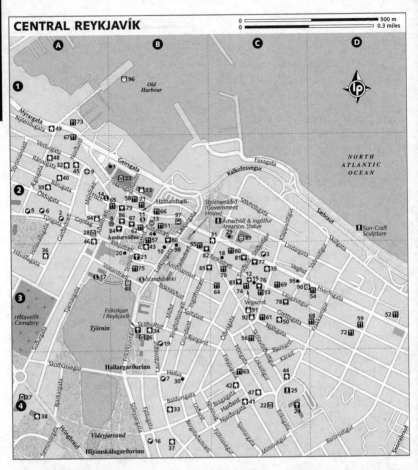

CENTRAL REYKJAVÍK

Perlan & Saga Museum

The huge water tanks on Öskjuhlíð hill are also a tourist complex known as **Perlan** (the Pearl), a popular Sunday afternoon outing for families. Silicon models, thudding axes and bloodcurdling screams bring Iceland's history to life at the excellent **Saga Museum** (Map pp238-9; ☎ 511 1517; www.sagamuseum.is; adult/child/concession

---

Ikr1500/800/1000; ⊙ 10am-6pm Apr-Sep, noon-5pm Oct-Mar). Don't blame the *brennivín* if you see the characters walking round town; they were modelled on Reykjavík inhabitants!

Two **artificial geysers** (one inside and one outside) blast off every few minutes. Upstairs, a **360-degree viewing deck** shares tremendous mountain and city vistas with a cafe and revolving restaurant. Take bus 18 from Lækjartorg.

Volcano Show

Eccentric eruption-chaser Villi Knudsen is the photographer, owner and presenter of this awesome **film-show** (Map p240; ☎ 845 9548; vknudsen2000@yahoo.com; Red Rock Cinema, Hellusund 6a; 1hr show adult/11-16yr/6-10yr Ikr1200/1000/500, 2hr show Ikr1500/1200/600; ⊙ in English 11am, 3pm & 8pm daily, in

---

German 5.30pm daily, in French 1pm Sun Jul & Aug, in English 3pm & 8pm daily Sep-Jun). His explosive footage captures 50 years' worth of Icelandic volcanoes.

Museums

The city's newest museum **Reykjavík 871+/-2** (Settlement Exhibition; Map p240; ☎ 411 6370; www .reykjavik871.is; Aðalstræti 16; adult/12-18yr Ikr600/300; 🕙 10am-5pm; 🚭) is a superb combination of archaeology, technology and imagination. Although the exhibition is compact (it's based around a single Viking longhouse), it's completely absorbing. Best are the tiny wraiths – go and see!

The award-winning **National Museum** (Map p240; ☎ 530 2200; www.natmus.is; Suðurgata 41; adult/under 18yr/concession Ikr600/free/300, admission free Wed; 🕙 10am-5pm daily May–mid-Sep, 11am-5pm Tue-Sun mid-Sep–Apr, to 9pm 1st Thu of month; 🚭) gives a fine overview of Iceland's history and culture. The strongest section shows off swords and silver

hoards from the Settlement Era, but their most treasured artefact is a stunning carved 13th-century church door. Walk or catch bus S1, S3-6, 12 or 14.

The excellent **Þjóðmenningarhúsið** (Culture House; Map p240; ☎ 545 1400; www.thjodmenning.is; Hverfisgata 15; adult/under 16 Ikr300/free, admission free Wed; 🕙 11am-5pm; 🚭) offers intelligent displays about the sagas, and the darkened rooms here contain the actual vellums themselves.

Quaint old buildings have been uprooted from various places, then replanted at **Árbæjarsafn** (Open-Air Museum; off Map pp238-9; ☎ 411 6300; www.arbaejarsafn.is; Kistuhylur 4; adult/under 18yr Ikr600/free; 🕙 10am-5pm daily Jun-Aug, by tour only 1pm Mon, Wed & Fri Sep-May), which is a kind of zoo for houses, 4km from the city centre. Kids love running around the creaky timber homes. Take bus 19.

Out in the suburb of Mosfellsbær, the home of Nobel Prize–winning author Halldór

Laxness (1902–98) is now open to visitors. Highlights of the **Gljúfrasteinn Laxness Museum** (off Map pp238-9; ☎ 586 8066; www.gljufrasteinn.is; Mosfellsbær; adult/6-16yr Ikr500/250; ☑ 9am-5pm Jun-Aug, 10am-5pm Tue-Sun Sep-May) include the study where Laxness wrote his defining works, and his beloved Jaguar parked outside. Buses are an extremely awkward way to get there; you really need a car.

Art Galleries

The **National Gallery** (Map p240; ☎ 515 9600; www .listasafn.is; Fríkirkjuvegur 7; admission free; ☑ 11am-5pm Tue-Sun; ☒) contains works by Iceland's most renowned artists, and provides an interesting glimpse into the nation's psyche: surreal mud-purple landscapes mingle with visions of ogresses, giants and dead men.

The weird symbolist creations of sculptor Einar Jónsson are objects you'll either love or hate: find out which at the cube-shaped **Einar Jónsson Museum** (Map p240; ☎ 551 3797; www.skulptur .is; Njarðargata; adult/under 16yr Ikr400/free; ☑ 2-5pm Tue-Sun Jun–mid-Sep, 2-5pm Sat & Sun mid-Sep–Nov & Feb-May, closed Dec & Jan).

Listasafn Reykjavíkur (Reykjavík Art Museum; www .listasafnreykjavikur.is; admission free) is split over three sites. At the rather wonderful **Ásmundarsafn** (Ásmundur Sveinsson Museum; Map pp238-9; ☎ 553 2155; Sigtún; ☑ 10am-4pm May-Sep, 1-4pm Oct-Apr), you'll find the artist's massive concrete sculptures in the garden, plus there are smaller, spikier works in wood, clay and metals in the igloo-shaped studio he designed. His themes range from folklore to physics. Bus 14 passes close by.

Jóhannes Kjarval (1885–1972) was a fisherman until his crew paid for him to study at the Academy of Fine Arts in Copenhagen. His unearthly Icelandic landscapes can be seen inside the angular glass-and-wood **Kjarvalsstaðir** (Map pp238-9; ☎ 517 1290; Flókagata; ☑ 10am-5pm; ☒). Catch bus 13.

The third Listasafn Reykjavíkur is **Hafnarhús** (Map p240; ☎ 590 1200; Tryggvagata 17; ☑ 10am-5pm; ☒), a severe concrete building containing works by political cartoonist Erró, plus changing modern-art exhibitions.

Parks & Gardens

The only attraction aimed at (youngish) children is **Reykjavík Zoo & Family Park** (Map pp238-9; ☎ 575 7800; www.mu.is; Laugardalur; adult/ 5-12yr Ikr600/500, 1-/10-/20-ride tickets Ikr200/1800/3400; ☑ 10am-6pm mid-May–mid-Aug, 10am-5pm mid-Aug–mid-May; ☒). Don't expect lions and tigers: think

seals, foxes, farm animals and a small aquarium. Nearby are child-size bulldozers, a giant trampoline and mini fairground rides.

Next door, the **Botanic Garden** (Map pp238-9; ☎ 411 8650; botgard@reykjavik.is; Skúlatún 2; admission free; ☑ greenhouse 10am-10pm Apr-Sep, to 5pm Oct-Mar) has sub-Arctic plant species, colourful seasonal flowers, and a cafe from June to August.

Buses 14, 15, 17, 19 and S2 pass within 400m of both attractions.

Other Sights

Old Reykjavík grew up around **Tjörnin** (Map p240), a large lake that echoes with the honks and hootings of thousands of geese, swans, ducks and gulls. The pleasant park at the southern end is laced with walking and cycling paths.

Rising on stilts from the northern shore is the postmodern **Raðhús** (City Hall; Map p240; ☎ 563 2000; Tjarnargata 11; ☑ 8am-7pm Mon-Fri, noon-6pm Sat & Sun; ☒). It contains a tourist information desk, a cafe and a huge, impressive 3-D map of Iceland: a mass of mountains, fjords and volcanoes.

The neat grey basalt building on the southern side of Austurvöllur, the main square, houses the Icelandic parliament, **Alþingi** (Map p240; ☎ 563 0500; www.althingi.is; Túngata; ☒). Next to it is the **Dómkirkja** (Map p240; ☎ 520 9700; Lækjargata 14a; ☑ 10am-5pm Mon-Fri), Iceland's small but perfectly proportioned cathedral.

Available at the tourist office are brochures for themed walks, focused on subjects such as statutory and literary figures, that you can follow around Reykjavík.

ACTIVITIES
Whale- & Puffin-Watching

Iceland is terrific for spotting whales, dolphins and porpoises, with a 97% chance of seeing one (see boxed text, p262). Between April and October, **Elding Whale Watching** (Map p240; ☎ 555 3565; www.elding.is; adult/7-15yr Ikr7600/3300; ☒) runs three-hour trips from the harbour, generally at 9am and 1pm. During breeding season (mid-May to mid-August), they also spin round Lundey to look at the puffins.

Geothermal Pools & Spa

Reykjavík's many outdoor swimming pools, heated by volcanic water, are the social hubs of the city: children play, teenagers flirt, business deals are made, and everyone catches up with the latest gossip.

Don't miss out on a dip: the biggest and best facilities are found at **Laugardalslaug** (Map pp238-9; ☎ 553 4039; Sundlaugavegur 30; adult/child Ikr360/120, swimsuit/towel hire Ikr350/350; ☿ 6.30am-10pm Mon-Fri, 8am-10pm Sat & Sun, to 8pm Oct-Mar; ☒), next door to the camping ground, which has an Olympic-size indoor pool, an outdoor pool, seven Jacuzzi-like 'hot pots', a steam bath, and a curling 86m waterslide for kids big and small. Right next door to Laugardalslaug is a five-star health resort, **Laugar** (☎ 553 0000; www.laugarspa.is; admission Ikr3500; ☿ same hours as pool), with themed saunas, steam rooms and beauty treatments. Catch bus 14 from Lækjartorg.

Bringing a touch of the Riviera to Reykjavík, the Blue-Flag **Nauthólsvík Hot Beach** (Ylströndin; Map pp238-9; ☎ 511 6630; admission free; ☿ 10am-8pm mid-May–mid-Sep) is a dinky crescent of golden sand warmed by 18°C to 20°C geothermal water. There are large crowds in sunny weather. Take bus 19.

SLEEPING

Reykjavík is packed in summer: book accommodation well in advance. Breakfast is usually included in room prices (but not for sleeping-bag accommodation).

Budget

Reykjavík Camping Ground (Map pp238-9; ☎ 568 6944; www.reykjavikcampsite.is; Sundlaugavegur 32; camp sites per person Ikr1000, 2-bed cabins Ikr6000; ☿ mid-May–mid-Sep, reception 3-6pm; ☒ ☒) There's only one camping ground in Reykjavík, and it gets very busy in summer. It holds 650 people, though, so you'd be unlucky not to find a pitch. Laundry and internet facilities. Take bus 14.

Reykjavík City Hostel (Map pp238-9; ☎ 553 8110; www.hostel.is; Sundlaugavegur 34; sleeping bag in 2-/4-/6-bed dm Ikr4300/3000/1200, bed linen Ikr800; ☒ ☒ ☒) Beside the camping ground, the award-winning youth hostel has many commendable points: it's environmentally friendly, and has helpful staff and excellent facilities (24-hour reception, several kitchens, laundry, large-screen TV room, internet access, free wi-fi, bike rental etc). School parties can be noisy – bring ear plugs. Breakfast Ikr1000. The hostel is about 2.5km east of the city centre (take bus 14).

Salvation Army Guesthouse (Map p240; ☎ 561 3203; www.herinn.is; Kirkjustræti 2; sleeping bag in dm Ikr3000, s/d/tr/q Ikr7100/9900/14,000/17,500) This is the nearest thing Reykjavík has to a Japanese capsule hotel! The tiny rooms are highly functional

and frill-free, but it has a wonderfully central location and beats the Downtown hostel effortlessly on price. There's a bustling backpackery atmosphere, guest kitchen and lounging area. Breakfast costs Ikr800.

Reykjavík Central Hostel (Map p240; ☎ 553 8120; www.hostel.is; Vesturgata 17; sleeping bag in 4-/10-bed dm Ikr5200/4400, d with/without bath Ikr13,900/10,900, bed linen Ikr1000; ☒) The most exciting hostelling news in recent times is this, the brand-new 'Downtown' annexe, opened in March 2009 and still with that fresh-paint smell. It has the same fine staff and facilities as its city cousin, but the focus is more on couples and families than young backpackers. This, and its amazing old-town location, mean correspondingly higher prices – the only drawback.

Garður Inn (Map p240; ☎ 562 4000, Jun-Aug 511 5900; www.inns-of-iceland.com; Hringbraut; tw Ikr4900/6500, s/d Ikr15,590/18,900; ☿ Jun-Aug; ☒) The university campus, about 1km from the centre, has utilitarian rooms available once students have left for the summer, all with shared bathrooms. The cheapest sleeping-bag accommodation is in 16-person dorms; the most expensive is in twin rooms.

Midrange

Guesthouse Andrea (Map p240; ☎ 899 1773; www.aurorahouse.is; Njarðargata 43; sleeping bag in dm Ikr4000, s/d Ikr9000/12,000; ☿ mid-May–Sep; ☒) Friendly Siggi runs this hidden place, tucked down a side street in a quiet residential area. Its five private rooms have spruce wooden floors, and are ideal for self-caterers: each has a sink, cooker, fridge and tiny two-seater table. Breakfast not included.

Guesthouse Aurora (Map p240; ☎ 552 5515; Freyjugata 24; ☿ mid-May–Sep; ☒) This is also run by the Guesthouse Andrea people, and is a homely purple town house just round the corner. Room No 33, with a balcony and sea view, is the best.

Áskot B&B (Map pp238-9; ☎ 662 0183; www.askot.is; Ásvallagata 52; s/d/tr with shared bathrooms Ikr9000/12,000/16,000; ☒) This pleasing little family-run place, with more personality than many a Reykjavík guesthouse, is tucked away in a residential district west of the centre. Rooms are decently sized, with an ample number of shared bathrooms and kitchens between them. There are discounts for stays over three days. Breakfast is available in summer.

Gistiheimilið Ísafold (Map p240; ☎ 561 2294; www.isafoldguesthouse.is; Bárugata 11; s/d from Ikr9000/12,000;

P) A rambling old house (a former bakery/rehab centre/bookshop) in peaceful old Reykjavík. Sun-filled bedrooms contain washbasins and rustic beds, there are tea-making facilities in the lounge, and breakfast, served in the attic, is a decent spread. At the nearby annexe (Bárugata 20), all accommodation comes with private bathrooms (around Ikr2000 extra).

Álfhóll Guesthouse (Map p240; ☎ 898 1838; www .islandia.is/alf; Ránargata 8; s/d/tr Ikr9000/12,500/16,000, 2–4-person apt Ikr18,000-23,000; ☺ Jun-Aug) Almost identical in feel and facilities to neighbouring Guesthouse Butterfly, Álfhóll is run by a family of elf enthusiasts.

Baldursbrá Guesthouse (Map p240; ☎ 552 6646; baldursbra@centrum.is; Laufásvegur 41; s/d Ikr8900/14,000) Situated in the genteel 'Embassy District', Baldursbrá is a little oasis within easy walking distance of the city centre. Blessings include a wonderfully friendly welcome, spick little rooms, and a garden with a hot pot. Bathrooms are shared, but all rooms have a washbasin.

Sunna Guesthouse (Map p240; ☎ 511 5570; www .sunna.is; Þórsgata 26; s/d from Ikr10,100/12,800, apt Ikr16,100-32,000; **P** ⌨) Rooms at this guesthouse are simple and sunny with honey-coloured parquet floors. Nine have private bathrooms, and those at the front offer good views of Hallgrímskirkja. Families are made to feel extremely welcome: there are four large family apartments, in addition to the eight neat studio apartments (accommodating one to four people).

Castle House & Embassy Apartments (Map p240; ☎ 511 2166; http://hotelsiceland.net; Skálholtsstígur 2a & Garðastræti 40; 1–6-person apt Ikr11,600-39,900) Turn to these pleasant self-contained apartments for satisfyingly central and commendably quiet accommodation. They are much more personal than a hotel, but come with room service: fresh towels appear daily, and washing-up seems to magically clean itself. Breakfast is not included. The tariff changes depending on demand – cheapest rates are through the website.

Three Sisters (Þrjár Systur; Map p240; ☎ 565 2181; www.threesisters.is; Ránargata 16; 1-/2-person apt Ikr13,500/17,700, family apt Ikr21,800; ☺ Jun-Aug; ⌨) A twinkly-eyed former fisherman runs the Three Sisters, a lovely town house in old Reykjavík, now divided into eight studio apartments. Comfy counterpane beds are flanked by old-fashioned easy chairs and

state-of-the-art flatscreen TVs. Each room comes with a cute fully equipped kitchen. A short stroll seawards is a second building with sleeping-bag accommodation in six-bed dorms (around Ikr3000).

Guesthouse Butterfly (Map p240; ☎ 894 1864; www.kvasir.is/butterfly; Ránargata 8a; s/d/apt Ikr14,600/16,300/24,600; ☺ Jun-Aug; ☜) This is on a quiet residential street within fluttering distance of the centre, and has neat, simply furnished rooms. There's a guest kitchen, and the friendly Icelandic-Norwegian owners make you feel right at home. The top floor has two self-contained apartments with kitchens and balconies.

Galtafell Guesthouse (Map p240; ☎ 551 4344, 699 2525; www.galtafell.com; Laufásvegur 46; s/d/apt from Ikr15,000/17,000/30,500) This guesthouse has a great location, in a quiet, well-to-do suburb within easy walking distance of town. Although the accommodation is nowhere near as grand as the castellated exterior implies, the four spruce apartments each contain a fully equipped kitchen, cosy seating area and separate bedroom, and the three basement doubles are serviceable.

Hótel Leifur Eiríksson (Map p240; ☎ 562 0800; www.hotelleifur.is; Skólavörðustígur 45; s/d/tr Ikr15,200/18,400/21,500) This hotel glories in one of the best locations in Reykjavík: it's slap on the end of arty Skólavörðustígur, and more than half of the small 47 rooms have inspiring views of Hallgrímskirkja. There's no restaurant, but free tea and coffee are available in the lobby, and guests get reduced rates at the Indian Mango restaurant.

Tower Guesthouse (Map p240; ☎ 899 9998; www .tower.is; Grettisgata 22C; 1- & 2-bed apt Ikr16,900-29,900) These central apartments are good value for money, with spotless rooms, private bathrooms and airy shared kitchens.

CenterHotel Klöpp (Map p240; ☎ 595 8520; www .centerhotels.is; Klapparstígur 26; s/d from Ikr22,900/27,000; ☺ closed 18-27 Dec; **P** ⌨) This mellow place has a boutique-hotel spirit. The foyer/breakfast area sets the tone, with gleaming hardwood floors, genial staff, and lots of light pouring in. Rooms are modest in size with minimal furnishings, but warm woody tones, textured mauve bedspreads. Stylish slate-floored bathrooms give them a modern yet cosy feel. All contain a TV, a fridge, a radio, a kettle and an internet connection point, and you can see the sea and mountains from the 5th-floor rooms.

Top End

Hótel Borg (Map p240; ☎ 551 1440; www.hotelborg.is; Pósthússtræti 11; s/d/ste Ikr44,300/56,600/85,300) The city's most historic hotel, Borg is a 1930s Art Deco palace located in prime position on Austurvöllur square. A recent overhaul replaced antiquated charm with super-smart, if somewhat masculine-feeling, beige, black and cream decor. Parquet floors, leather headboards and flatscreen Bang & Olufsen TVs are standard throughout. Bathrooms retain their splendid giant showerheads, and quadruple-glazed windows cut out drunken weekend street noise. The buffet breakfast is an extra Ikr3300.

101 Hotel (Map p240; ☎ 580 0101; www.101hotel.is; Hverfisgata 10; s/d/ste from Ikr45,900/52,900/68,900; 🖥 ⛶) Reykjavík's newest boutique hotel is devilishly divine. Its 38 sensuous rooms – with yielding king- or queen-sized beds, glass-walled showers and rich wooden floors – may mean you boycott the bars and opt for a night in instead. A spa with masseurs, a small gym and a glitterati bar add to the opulence.

EATING

Reykjavík's eateries vary from hot-dog stands to world-class restaurants. Two things are consistent: high quality, and high prices. The best dishes are generally those made from Iceland's outstanding fresh fish, seafood and juicy mountain-reared lamb. For types of eateries, and a guide to and opening hours, see p236.

Reykjavík's dining places are found along Laugavegur, Hverfisgata and Austurstræti. Tips are always included in the bill.

Restaurants

MIDRANGE

Sægreifinn (Map p240; ☎ 553 1500; Geirsgata 9; mains Ikr1000-2300; ⏲ 10am-10pm) Eccentric Sægreifinn serves up fresh seafood in what looks almost like a 1950s English chip shop…except for the barrel seats and stuffed seal. The owner is a sprightly old gent, who buys and cooks all the fish himself; lobster soup and smoked fish are particular specialities. He speaks only Icelandic, so make sure you know what you're asking for! (Whale meat served.)

Grænn Kostur (Map p240; ☎ 552 2028; www.graennkostur.is; Skólavörðustígur 8; daily special Ikr1390; ⏲ 11.30am-9pm Mon-Sat, 1-9pm Sun) This place serves organic, vegetarian set meals that are similar to Á

Næstu Grösum. It's smaller and harder to find, but persevere!

Á Næstu Grösum (First Vegetarian; Map p240; www.anaestugrosum.is; ☎ 552 8410; Laugavegur 20b; daily specials Ikr1490; ⏲ noon-10pm Mon-Sat, 5-10pm Sun) This first-rate, canteen-style vegie restaurant, in a cheerful orange room overlooking Laugavegur, offers several daily specials. It uses seasonal organic veg, with inventive dressings that give lettuce new appeal; and there's extra spice on Indian nights (Friday and Saturday). Organic wine and beer are available.

Hornið (Map p240; ☎ 551 3340; Hafnarstræti 15; 9in pizza Ikr1360-2440, mains Ikr2300-4000; ⏲ 11.30am-11pm) There's an easygoing atmosphere at this bright Art Deco cafe-restaurant, with its warm terracotta tiles, weeping-fig plants and decently spaced tables. Pizzas are freshly made before your eyes, the prettily presented pasta meals will set you up for the day, and you can sample traditional Icelandic fish dishes.

Icelandic Fish & Chips (Map p240; ☎ 511 1118; www.fishandchips.is; Tryggvagata 8; mains around Ikr1500; ⏲ noon-9pm Mon-Fri) A reader-recommended restaurant serving hearty portions of…well, have a guess! It's good value fare (for Iceland, at least), and the owners have put their own singular slant on it with a range of 'Skyronnaises' – skýr-based sauces (eg rosemary and green apple) that add an unusual zing to this most traditional of dishes.

Þrír Frakkar Hjá Úlfari (Map p240; ☎ 552 3939; www.3frakkar.com; Baldursgata 14; mains Ikr2900-4000; ⏲ noon-2.30pm & 6-10pm Mon-Fri, 6-11pm Sat & Sun) Owner-chef Úlfar Eysteinsson has built up an excellent reputation at this snug little restaurant; and it's been given the thumbs-up by Jamie Oliver. Specialities include salted cod, anglerfish and *plokkfiskur* (fish stew) with black bread. (Whale meat served.)

Við Tjörnina (Map p240; ☎ 551 8666; www.vidtjornina.is; Templarasund 3; mains Ikr3400-5500; ⏲ from 6pm) Tucked away on a side street near Tjörn, this famed seafood establishment serves up beautifully presented Icelandic feasts such as guillemot with port, tender lamb fillet and garlic langoustine. The restaurant itself is cosy and wonderfully distinctive; it feels like a quirky upperclass 1930s drawing room.

The northernmost Indian restaurant in the world, **Austur India Félagið** (Map p240; ☎ 552 1630; Hverfisgata 56; mains Ikr2600-4000; ⏲ from 6pm) is an upmarket experience, with minimalist interior and a select choice of sublime dishes.

The atmosphere is relaxed, and the service warm. Apparently this place is a favourite of Harrison Ford's, and who dares argue with Indy? Also recommended is **Indian Mango** (Map p240; ☎ 551 7722; cnr Frakkastígur & Grettisgata; mains Ikr2200-3400; ⏰ from 5pm Mon-Sat), which specialises in Goan-Icelandic fusion food, if you can imagine that. its bestselling creation is *svartfugl* (guillemot) marinaded in Indian spices.

TOP END

Sjávarkjallarinn (Map p240; ☎ 511 1212; www.sjavarkjallarinn.is; Aðalstræti 2; mains Ikr3500-6000; ⏰ 11.30am-2pm & from 6pm daily) Currently *the best* dining experience in Reykjavík, this atmospheric underground restaurant serves up exotic dishes. Shimmering fish and succulent crustaceans are combined with the unexpected (pomegranate, coconut, lychee and chilli) and served up like miniature works of art. It's at the top end of the price scale, but worth every króna – go on, treat yourselves.

Vox (Map pp238-9; ☎ 444 5050; www.voxrestaurant.com; Suðurlandsbraut 2; mains Ikr4000-6000; ⏰ 6.30-10.30pm Tue-Sat) The Hilton's five-star restaurant serves up superb seasonal dishes (think pink-footed goose with caramelised apples), and there's usually a vegie option. The waiters sometimes bring out extra little treats – like their amazing 'invisible gazpacho' – for you to try.

Cafes

The distinction between cafes and bars is vague; see p236 for more information.

Babalú (Map p240; ☎ 552 2278; Skólavörðustígur 22a) More inviting than your own living room, this tiny caff sells only tea, coffee, hot chocolate and the odd crêpe, but it's a fine place to linger. In winter, snuggle down in a cosy corner; and when the sun shines, head for the little rooftop terrace to survey the action in the street below. In summer there's occasional live music.

Kofi Tómasar Frænda (Koffin; Map p240; ☎ 551 1855; Laugavegur 2; snacks around Ikr800; ⏰ 10am-1am Mon-Thu, to 5.30am Fri & Sat, 11am-1am Sun; 📶) Subterranean Koffin has a studenty feel. Relax with magazines and a snack (nachos, lasagne, sandwiches, cakes or chocolate-coated marzipan) and watch disconnected feet scurry along Laugavegur. At night, it turns into a candlelit bar with DJs.

Café Paris (Map p240; ☎ 551 1020; Austurstræti 14; snacks Ikr700-1000; ⏰ 9am-1am Sun-Thu, 9am-5am Fri & Sat) An old favourite, Paris is one of the city's prime people-watching spots, particularly in summer when outdoor seating spills out onto Austurvöllur square, and at night when the leather-upholstered interior fills with tunes and tinkling wine glasses. The selection of light meals, including sandwiches, crêpes, burgers, salads and tacos, is secondary to the socialising.

Kaffi Hljómalind (Map p240; ☎ 517 1980; www.kaffihljomalind.org; Laugavegur 23; snacks Ikr700-1100; ⏰ 9am-11pm Mon-Fri, 11am-11pm Sat & Sun; 📶) This commendable community-run organic and fair-trade cafe is run on a not-for-profit basis. It looks like a 1950s home with 1970s flourishes (prayer flags, patterned chairs, handpainted cups and saucers), and is a meeting-place for Reykjavík's radicals.

Café Garðurinn (Map p240; ☎ 561 2345; Klapparstígur 37; soup/mains Ikr800/1350; ⏰ 11am-6.30pm Mon-Fri, noon-5pm Sat, closed Aug) This tiny but tasteful vegie cafe is based around seven tables and the hum of civilised conversation. Choice is limited, but it's delicious – we can heartily recommend the Catalonian tofu balls! Half portions are available.

Svarta Kaffið (Map p240; ☎ 551 2999; Laugavegur 54; snacks & light meals Ikr900-1500; ⏰ 11am-1am Sun-Thu, to 3am Fri & Sat) Order thick homemade soup (one meat and one veg option daily; Ikr1090) at this cavelike cafe – it's served piping hot in fantastic bread bowls. Svarta Kaffið is also a whimsical nightspot, with African masks and dim lighting adding a certain frisson.

Café Cultura (Map p240; ☎ 530 9314; Hverfisgata 18; snacks & light meals Ikr1000-2900; ⏰ 11.30am-1am Mon-Thu, 11.30am-4am Fri & Sat, 1pm-1am Sun) This arty intercultural cafe has scratched wooden floors and mosaic tables, and offers well-priced Mediterranean- and Arabic-influenced nosh such as felafel, spicy meatballs and couscous cuisine. There's a tolerant attitude to children. It becomes an equally funky bar at weekends.

Vegamót (Map p240; ☎ 511 3040; www.vegamot.is; Vegamótstígur 4; light meals Ikr1300-2200; ⏰ 11am-1am Mon-Thu, 11am-5am Fri & Sat, noon-1am Sun) A long-running cafe-bar-club, but still a voguish place to eat, drink, see and be seen. There's a startling choice on the 'global' menu, including Mexican salad, sesame-fried monkfish, seafood quesadilla and blackened chicken. The attached takeaway charges 10% less.

b5 (Map p240; ☎ 552 9600; www.b5.is; Bankastræti 5; light meals Ikr1500-2000; ⏰ 11am-midnight Sun-Wed, 11-1am Thu, 11-2am Fri & Sat; 📶) With its barely there name and super-sleek interior, this new bistro-bar flirts with pretentiousness but never quite pulls. It's actually a very mellow place, with comfy seating, light Scandinavian-style bistro meals, games consoles for the kids to borrow, and funky tunes on Friday and Saturday nights.

Brons (Map p240; ☎ 578 2020; Pósthússtræti 9; tapas 10 pieces for Ikr3900, light meals Ikr1600-2900) This new bistro focuses on tapas, supplemented by a substantial choice of Mediterranean and Icelandic mains. Unlike some tapas joints, this isn't an excuse to serve minuscule portions – you'll definitely know you've eaten here. It also does a fine brunch (Ikr1390) at the weekend.

Quick Eats

Icelanders swear it's impossible to get a bad hot dog from **Bæjarins Beztu** (Map p240), a van near the harbour, patronised by Bill Clinton! Use the vital sentence *Eina með öllu* ('One with everything') for mustard, ketchup, remoulade and onions.

Late-opening snack bars and kiosks include **Hlölla Bátar** (Map p240; Ingólfstorg; ⏰ 11pm-2am Sun-Thu, 10pm-7am Fri & Sat) and **Emmessís og Pylsar** (Map p240; Ingólfstorg), selling ice cream and hot dogs; and **Nonnabiti** (Map p240; ☎ 551 2312; Hafnarstræti 9; snacks Ikr350-800; ⏰ to 2am).

Wood-fired pizzas at **Eldsmiðjan** (Map p240; ☎ 562 3838; Bragagata 38a; 10in pizza Ikr900-1500; ⏰ 11am-11pm) are reputedly the best in town. No, you weren't hallucinating – the snail topping exists.

Self-Catering

Bónus (⏰ noon-6.30pm Mon-Thu, 10am-7.30pm Fri, 10am-6pm Sat; Laugavegur 59 Map p240; Kringlan Map pp238-9; also ⏰ noon-6pm Sun) is the cheapest supermarket. The more upmarket **10-11** (⏰ 8am-9pm; Austurstræti Map p240; Hverfisgata Map p240; Laugalækur Map pp238-9) has branches all over town.

DRINKING

Reykjavík is renowned for its Friday- and Saturday-night *runtur*, when industrious Icelanders abandon work and party with passion (midweek drinking is not part of Icelandic culture). Beer is expensive. Most people visit a government-owned *vín búð* (the only shops licensed to sell alcohol), tipple at home, then hit the town from midnight to 6am. There's a central *vín búð* (Map p240; Austurstræti 10; ⏰ 11am-6pm Mon-Thu & Sat, to 7pm Fri), and there's another in Kringlan shopping centre (Map pp238–9) that's open the same hours.

Some venues have cover charges (about Ikr1000), and 'in' clubs have long queues at weekends. Things change fast; check *Grapevine* or *Reykjavík This Month* for the latest listings. You should dress up in Reykjavík, although there are pub-style places where you won't feel scruffy in jeans. The minimum drinking age is 20.

Bars & Pubs

Often the only difference between a cafe and a bar is the time of day (see p236).

Kaffibarinn (Map p240; ☎ 551 1588; Bergstaðastræti 1) Damon Albarn from Blur has a stake in this ubertrendy bar, which had a starring role in the cult film *101 Reykjavík*. It's popular with celebs: at weekends you'll need a famous face or a battering ram to get in.

Café Oliver (Map p240; ☎ 552 2300; www.cafeoliver.is; Laugavegur 20a) One of Reykjavík's newest cafebars, Oliver is the most in-vogue place for brunch and for partying late in super style. DJs pump out the tunes on Thursday, Friday and Saturday, with long queues snaking back from the doors.

Kaffi Sólon (Map p240; ☎ 562 3232; www.solon.is; Bankastræti 7a; snacks & light meals Ikr1400-2500; ⏰ 11am-midnight Mon-Wed, to 1am Thu, to 4am Fri, to 5am Sat, noon-midnight Sun; 🛜) Sólon, decked out in white-leather seats and oversized artwork, is a cultivated international bistro during the day and a swish nightclub for a beautiful, martini-drinking set by night. There are long queues, in-demand DJs, moody lighting and (a popular Reykjavík item) a dance floor cramming in around 17 people per square metre.

Hressingarskálinn (Map p240; ☎ 561 2240; Austurstræti 20; mains Ikr1200-1500; 🛜) Known colloquially as Hressó, this large, open-plan cafe-bar serves a diverse menu till 10pm daily (everything from porridge to *plokkfiskur*). At weekends, it loses its civilised veneer and concentrates on beer, bar and dancing; a garden out back provides fresh air. There's usually a DJ or live music on Thursday nights.

Thorvaldsen (Map p240; ☎ 511 1413; Austurstræti 8-10) A super-smart modernist bistro by day, this becomes one of the hottest weekend clubs – dress well or you won't get in, and after midnight be prepared to queue…and queue. There's a tiny dancefloor with weekend DJs. On Thursday the bartenders focus all their creative talents on producing the perfect mojito.

Dillon (Map p240; ☎ 511 2400; Laugavegur 30) Beer, beards and the odd flying bottle…atmospheric Dillon is Reykjavík's RRRRROCK pub. There are occasional live concerts, and an unusual DJ in white-haired white-wine-and-rum-swilling 'rokkmamman' Andrea Jonsdóttir, a kind of female Icelandic John Peel.

Grand Rokk (Map p240; ☎ 551 5522; www.grandrokk.is; Smiðjustígur 6) You'll feel as though you've known this down-to-earth bar all your life. During the day, chess enthusiasts play concentrated matches here; on Friday there's a pub quiz; and at weekends you can sometimes catch one of Reykjavík's more famous bands.

Q-Bar (Map p240; ☎ 578 7868; Ingólfsstræti 3; ⊙ 4pm-1am Sun-Thu, 4pm-5am Fri & Sat) The only bar in Iceland that styles itself as gay, although really it's a pretty mixed crowd. Has frequent gigs.

If Víking beer isn't doing it for you, sup a pint of Guinness at one of Reykjavík's two Irish pubs. **Celtic Cross** (Map p240; ☎ 511 3240; Hverfisgata 26) is actually a very cosy little place, done up like a funeral parlour and with bands in the basement on weekends; and the **Dubliner** (Map p240; ☎ 511 3233; Hafnarstræti 4; ⊙ to 1am Sun-Thu, to 5am Fri & Sat) is popular with foreign tourists.

Nightclubs

Hverfisbarinn (Map p240; ☎ 511 6700; www.hverfisbarinn .is; Hverfisgata 20; ⊙ to 1am Thu, to 5.30am Fri & Sat) This trendy bar and club attracts a young, dressy crowd, and has long queues at weekends. It's done out in a cool modern-Scandinavian style, which adds to the spacious feel. It has live music on Thursday from 9.30pm, and DJs on Friday and Saturday.

Nasa (Map p240; ☎ 511 1313; nasa@nasa.is; Austurvöllur; admission Ikr1500-3500) The biggest nightclub in Reykjavík, Nasa is a stripped-pine affair filled with Prada-clad crowds. It plays chart music and club anthems, and is the city's main live-music venue. Email for upcoming gigs.

ENTERTAINMENT
Live Music
Many of the bars, pubs and clubs listed have live band performances – try Nasa (above), Grand Rokk (above), Hressingarskálinn (p247) and Celtic Cross (above). For gig listings, see the excellent English-language newspaper *Grapevine*, available free from cafes and tourist offices.

The **Iceland Airwaves** (www.icelandairwaves .com) music festival rocks the city during the third week of October, when hordes of visitors descend to sample homegrown and international talent in Reykjavík's small-but-sparky venues.

Theatre & Classical Music
National Theatre (Map p240; ☎ 585 1200; www .leikhusid.is; Lindargata 7; admission adult/under 16 Ikr3400/2800; ⊙ box office 12.30-6pm Mon & Tue, to 8pm Wed-Sun, theatre closed Jul & Aug) Puts on around 12 plays, musicals and operas per year, from modern Icelandic works to Shakespeare.

Reykjavík City Theatre (Map pp238-9; ☎ 568 8000; www.borgarleikhus.is; Listabraut 3, Kringlan; adult/under 12yr Ikr3950/free; ⊙ box office 10am-6pm Mon & Tue, to 8pm Wed-Sun, theatre closed Jul & Aug) The country's second-largest theatre also stages classic and contemporary plays. The Icelandic Dance Company (www.id.is) is in residence here.

For spooky Icelandic folktales, traditional music and glimpses of the city's history, try the English-language performance **Light Nights** (☎ 551 9181; www.lightnights.com; Vonarstræti 3; tickets adult/7-16yr Ikr3000/2000; ⊙ 8.30pm Mon & Tue mid-Jul & Aug) at the **Iðnó Theatre** (Map p240).

The **Iceland Symphony Orchestra** (Map pp238-9; ☎ 545 2500; www.sinfonia.is; Háskólabíó, Hagatorg; tickets Ikr3100-3500) is due to relocate to flashy new premises by the harbour in 2011. For now the orchestra is based at Reykjavík University cinema. There are around 60 classical performances per season, normally on Thursday at 7.30pm.

Cinemas
Films are shown in their original language with Icelandic subtitles; cinemas charge Ikr1000per adult, Ikr550 per child under eight years. The newspaper *Morgunblaðið* lists cinema programmes, or click on the 'Í Bíó' tab at www.kvikmyndir.is.

Reykjavík has seven multiplexes: the closest to the city centre are **Sambíoin** (Map pp238-9; ☎ 575 8900) in Kringlan shopping centre, and **Laugarásbíó** (Map pp238-9; ☎ 553 2075; Laugarás) near the youth hostel. A little further out in the suburb of Kópavogur, five-screen **Smárabíó** (☎ 564 0000; Smáralind) is Iceland's plushest cinema. Central **Regnboginn** (Map p240; ☎ 551 9000; Hverfisgata 54) sometimes shows art-house films.

SHOPPING
Laugavegur is the main shopping street; Austurstræti and Hafnarstræti contain tour-

ist stores selling puffin-decorated trinkets; and Skólavörðustígur sells arty-crafty one-offs.

Handknitting Association of Iceland (Map p240; ☎ 552 1890; www.handknit.is; Skólavörðustígur 19) Traditional handmade hats, socks and sweaters are on sale here…or buy yarn and knitting patterns, and do it yourself!

Kolaportið Flea Market (Map p240; Geirsgata; ☒ 11am-5pm Sat & Sun) Rummage through a pleasing tangle of secondhand goods; or try *hákarl* (rotten shark meat) from the fishmarket if you're brave enough.

Kraum (Map p240; ☎ 517 7797; www.kraum.is; Aðalstræti 10) Contemporary Icelandic design – think fish-skin clothing, silver jewellery, driftwood furniture and ceramic seabirds – fills two storeys of Reykjavík's oldest house.

For cutting-edge Icelandic tunes, try hip record shop **12 Tónar** (Map p240; ☎ 511 5656; 12tonar@12tonar.is; Skólavörðustígur 15), with three floors of music and its own recording label.

Buy bottles of *brennivín* from vín búð (see p247).

GETTING THERE & AWAY
Air

The city airport, Innanlandsflug, serves all domestic destinations, the Faroe Islands and Greenland. Internal flight operator **Flugfélag Íslands** (Air Iceland; ☎ 570 3030; www.airiceland.is) has a desk here, but internet bookings are cheaper.

International flights operate through **Keflavík airport** (www.keflavikairport.com), 48km west of Reykjavík.

Bus

From June to August, there are regular direct services between Reykjavík's **BSÍ bus terminal** (Map pp238-9; ☎ 562 1011; www.bsi.is; Vatnsmýrarvegur 10) and the following places (reduced or no service for rest of the year):

Akureyri (Ikr9000, six hours, daily)
Höfn (Ikr11,200, 8½ hours, daily)
Reykholt (Ikr2900, two hours, Friday and Sunday)
Skaftafell (Ikr8200, seven hours, daily)
Þorlákshöfn (Ikr1400, one hour, two daily)
Þórsmörk (Ikr5200, 3½ hours, daily)

To get from Reykjavík to Egilsstaðir (Ikr15,500) involves an overnight stay in Akureyri or Höfn. In summer, it's possible to get to Húsavík (Ikr11,300) in one day from Monday to Saturday, changing in Akureyri. You'll need to break your journey in Akureyri on the way to Mývatn (Ikr11,800).

For Stykkishólmur (Ikr4500, 2½ hours, daily), change in Vatnaleið.

GETTING AROUND
To/From the Airport

It's a 1km walk into town from the city airport terminal (domestic flights), or there's a taxi rank.

The **Flybus** (☎ 562 1011; www.re.is) to and from Keflavík airport meets all incoming flights. Tickets cost Ikr1500 per adult (Ikr750 for those aged 12 to 15 years) to the main bus station (a journey time of around 50 minutes), or Ikr2000/1000 if you want to be dropped off at your hotel. Buy tickets before you board from the booth just inside the airport doors (credit cards accepted). On the return journey, the bus leaves the BSÍ bus terminal two hours before international departures. Reykjavík City Hostel and the main hotels can arrange transfers to the bus station. Taxis to/from the airport cost between Ikr8700 and Ikr10,500 one way, depending on the time of day.

Bicycle

Cycling is a great way to buzz round the city (although bicycles seem to be invisible to Reykjavík's car drivers). **Borgarhjól SF** (Map p240; ☎ 551 5653; www.borgarhjol.net; Hverfisgata 50; 4hr/half-day/24hr Ikr2000/3000/3600; ☒ 8am-6pm Mon-Fri, 10am-2pm Sat) has bikes for hire, also available from Reykjavík City Hostel and the camping ground (see p243).

Bus

Reykjavík's superb **city bus system** (☎ 540 2700; www.straeto.is/english) runs from 7am to 11pm or midnight (from 10am Sunday). A limited night-bus service runs until 2am on Friday and Saturday. Buses only stop at designated bus stops, marked with the letter 'S'. The two central terminals are Hlemmur (Map pp238–9) and Lækjartorg (Map p240).

The fare is Ikr280 per adult, and Ikr100 for those aged six to 18 years (no change is given). *Skiptimiði* (transfer tickets) are available from the driver if you need to take two buses to reach your destination. The Reykjavík Tourist Card includes a bus pass.

Taxi

Taxi prices are high; flagfall starts at around Ikr500. There are usually taxis outside the bus stations, domestic airport, youth hostel, and pubs and bars on weekend nights.

Alternatively, call **Borgarbíll** (☎ 552 2440), **BSR** (☎ 561 0000) or **Hreyfill-Bæjarleiðir** (☎ 588 5522). Tipping is not expected.

AROUND REYKJAVÍK
Blue Lagoon

As the Eiffel Tower is to Paris, as Disney World is to Florida, so the **Blue Lagoon** (Bláa Lónið; ☎ 420 8800; www.bluelagoon.is; adult/12-15yr Ikr3400/1200, towel/swimsuit/robe hire Ikr650/650/1200, spa treatments from Ikr2000; ☽ 8am-9pm Jun-Aug, 10am-8pm Sep-May; ☒) is to Iceland…with all the positive and negative connotations that implies. Those who say it's too expensive, too clinical, too crowded are kind of right, but ignore them. The Blue Lagoon is a must-see, and you'll be missing something special if you don't go. It was extended in 2007, and now has twice as much space for drifty dreaming.

Set in a vast black lava field, the milky-blue spa is fed by water (at a perfect 38°C, and at Blue Flag standards) from the futuristic Svartsengi geothermal plant, which provides an off-the-planet scene-setter for your swim. Add in steaming silver vents and people coated in silica-mud, and you're in another world.

Be careful on the slippery bridges and bring plenty of conditioner to stop your hair going solid. There's a snack bar, top gourmet restaurant and souvenir shop on site, plus roaming masseurs.

The lagoon is 50km southwest of Reykjavík. Between 10am and 6pm daily, there are six **Reykjavík Excursions** (☎ 562 1011; www.bsi.is) buses from the BSÍ bus terminal (or from your hotel on request). The Ikr4400 cost includes lagoon admission and return fare to Reykjavík (or onward journey to Keflavík airport).

The Golden Circle

Gulp down three of Iceland's most extraordinary natural wonders – Gullfoss, Geysir and Þingvellir – in one day-long circular tour.

Gullfoss (Golden Falls) is a spectacular rainbow-tinged double cascade, which falls 32m before thundering away down a narrow ravine.

Ten kilometres away is **Geysir**, after which all spouting hot springs are named. The **Great Geysir** was plugged in the 1950s, when tourists clogged it with rocks and rubbish, thrown in an attempt to set it off. Since earthquakes in 2000, it has begun erupting again two or three times daily. Nearby, the world's most reliable geyser, **Strokkur** (Butter Churn), spouts every six minutes, when its bulging blue eye bursts into an impressive 15m to 30m plume.

Þingvellir National Park is Iceland's most important historical site: the Vikings established the world's first democratic parliament, the Alþing, here in AD 930. It also has a superb natural setting, on the edge of an immense rift caused by the separating North American and Eurasian tectonic plates. Þingvellir was (finally!) made a Unesco World Heritage Site in 2004.

Interesting features, concentrated in a small area of the park, include: **Lögberg** (marked by a flagpole), the podium for the Alþing; the remains of **búðir** (booths) where attending Vikings camped; a **church** and **farm**, now the President's summer house; **Drekkingarhylur**, where adulterous women were drowned; **Þingvallavatn**, Iceland's largest lake; and several fissures, including **Peningagjá** (wishing spring), **Flosagjá** (named after a slave who jumped his way to freedom) and **Nikulásargjá** (after a drunken sheriff discovered dead in the water).

INFORMATION

Just by the turnoff to Þingvellir, the Park Service Centre contains a cafe and **seasonal tourist desk** (☎ 482 2660; www.thingvellir.is; ☽ 8.30am-8pm Jun-Aug, 9am-5pm daily May & Sep, to 5pm Sat & Sun Oct-Apr).

Above the park, on top of the rift, is an interesting **multimedia centre** (admission free; ☽ 9am-5pm Apr-Oct) exploring the area's nature and history.

SLEEPING & EATING

There is a discreet **cafe** (☽ approximately 9am-5pm winter, 9am-8pm summer) at each of the three sites.

Geysir camping ground (per person Ikr900) Stay at this camping ground, and you'll get to marvel at the spouting springs before the coach parties arrive. Pay at Hótel Geysir, where you're also entitled to use the hot tub and pool for free.

Þingvellir camping grounds (☎ 482 2660; camp sites per adult Ikr800) The Park Service Centre oversees five camping grounds at Þingvellir. The best are those around Leirar (near the centre).

Hótel Geysir (☎ 480 6800; www.geysircenter.is; s/d Ikr12,100/14,750; ☽ Feb-Dec; ☒ ☒) Accommodation is in spick and span and tasteful alpine-style cabins. The hotel can also arrange horse rides, including day trips to Gullfoss (Ikr10,800).

Hótel Valhöll (☎ 480 7100; www.hotelvalholl.is; s/d Ikr16,500/23,500; ☒) Valhöll is a large farmhouse in Þingvellir National Park, tucked down at

---

DETOURS: STOKKSEYRI

If you like screaming, it might be worth detouring to tiny Stokkseyri, 60km east of Reykjavík. Creep round 24 dark, dry ice–filled rooms at the **Ghost Centre** (Draugasetrið; ☎ 483 1202; www .draugasetrid.is; Hafnargata 9; adult/12-16yr Ikr1500/990; ☻ 1-8pm summer, 1-9pm Sat & Sun winter, closed Jan & Feb) while a 40-minute CD-guide (in English, French or German) tells blood-curdling Icelandic ghost stories. Be warned, it's not for the faint-hearted. Suitable for over-12s.

There's fine dining to be had next door at **Við Fjöruborðið** (☎ 483 1550; Eyrarbraut 3a; mains Ikr3000-5000; ☻ Wed & Thu 6-9pm, Fri 6-10pm, Sat & Sun noon-9pm), a seashore restaurant renowned for its lobster dishes.

---

the base of the rift. Some of the rooms are on the small side; positives include peaceful surroundings, a very good restaurant, and the president for your neighbour!

GETTING THERE & AWAY

Golden Circle day tours from Reykjavík cost between Ikr9800 and Ikr13,000 (without lunch). Tour operators include Reykjavík Excursions (p285) and Iceland Excursions (p285); you're usually picked up from your accommodation.

From June to August, scheduled buses run at 8.30am from the BSÍ bus station to Geysir (Ikr3100) and Gullfoss (Ikr3300). In July and August, a service also swings by Þingvellir (Ikr2,600; 11am).

Hafnarfjörður
pop 24,895

The 'Town in the Lava' rests on a 7000-year-old flow and hides a parallel elfin universe, according to locals. It's worth a quick summer jaunt if you've time to spare. The dynamic **tourist office** (☎ 585 5500; www.hafnarfjordur.is; Strandgata 6; ☻ 8am-5pm Mon-Thu, 9am-5pm Fri year round, 10am-3pm Sat & Sun Jun-Aug) is inside the town hall.

SIGHTS & ACTIVITIES

Hafnarfjörður Museum (☎ 585 5780; admission free) is spread across three sites. **Pakkhúsið** (Vesturgata 8; ☻ 11am-5pm daily Jun-Aug, 1-5pm Sat & Sun Sep-May) is the main building, with interesting displays on the town's history. **Sívertsen Hús** (Vesturgata 6; ☻ 11am-5pm Jun-Aug) is an upper-class 19th-century house. At the other end of the social scale is **Siggubær** (Sigga's House; Kirkjuvegur 10; ☻ 11am-5pm Sat & Sun Jun-Aug), a restored fisherman's hut.

The tourist office publishes a smashing sculpture trail map; the highlight is **Hellisgerði** (Reykjavíkurvegur), a peaceful park filled with lava grottoes.

In mid-June, the peace is shattered as Viking hordes invade town for the six-day

Viking Festival, with staged fights and traditional craft demonstrations.

GETTING THERE & AWAY

Hafnarfjörður is a short, easy bus trip from Reykjavík: take bus S1 (Ikr280, 30 minutes, every 20 to 30 minutes) from Hlemmur or Lækjartorg bus stations. The **Flybus** (☎ 562 1011) to/from Keflavík airport also stops for reserved passengers.

Krýsuvík

For a taste of Iceland's weird countryside, Krýsuvík, an abandoned village and volatile geothermal area, makes a fascinating day trip. The area lies about 20km south of Hafnarfjörður; you'll need your own transport. At **Seltún**, boardwalks meander round eggy-smelling, rainbow-coloured steaming vents, mud pots and solfataras, where the ground temperature reaches about 200°C.

Just down the road is **Kleifarvatn**, a creepy 1km-deep lake surrounded by volcanic cinders. It's said to be inhabited by a worm-like monster the size of a whale.

The nearby coast is a bleak stretch of seabird cliffs and black beaches. Dozens of hiking tracks crisscross through this barren territory.

THE WEST

UPPER BORGARFJÖRÐUR

A must for saga fans, the lakes and lava flows of this region feature in *Egils Saga*, and its author, Snorri Sturluson, lived here. Upper Borgarfjörður is 90km north of Reykjavík.

Reykholt & Around

You'd never guess it, but tiny **Reykholt** (www .reykholt.is), 22km east of the Ring Rd and with a population of 42, was once a political and religious power centre. During the blood-thirsty Sturlunga Period (1230–62), it was the home of Snorri Sturluson, Iceland's greatest saga writer, historian and social-climber. Close to the cellar where he was eventually murdered, you can see his circular medieval hot tub **Snorri's Pool** (Snorralaug). The museum **Heimskringla** (☎ 433 8000; www.snorrastofa.is; Reykholt; admission Ikr700; ۞ 10am-6pm daily May-Sep, 10am-6pm Mon-Fri Oct-Apr) explores Snorri's fascinating life, and has recently been augmented by an exhibition focusing on archaeological finds from the settlement.

Deildartunguhver, 4km west of Reykholt, is Europe's most powerful, prolific and pongy hot spring, spouting out at 180L per second. About 18km northeast of Reykholt is **Hraunfossar**, a 1km-long stretch of 'magic waterfalls' mysteriously emerging from beneath a lava flow. Just upstream is **Barnafoss**, where the river Hvítá thunders through a narrow gorge. According to legend, two children drowned here when a natural bridge collapsed.

There's a **camping ground** (☎ 435 1182; Klepp-járnsreykir; per person Ikr700) next to a geothermal swimming pool 6km west of Reykholt. **Hótel Reykholt** (☎ 435 1260; www.fosshotel.is; Reykholt; s/d Jun-Aug Ikr3200/28,900/32,200, Sep-May Ikr16,900/19,500; P 😃) is part of the Fosshótel chain. It's a modern place with boxy but pleasant rooms, sunny staff, a fun Norse-gods theme, and extras including a restaurant and brand-new 'wellness facility' (sauna, massages etc). Cheaper rooms with shared bathrooms are available.

Buses run from Reykjavík to Reykholt (via Deildartunguhver) on Friday and Sunday at 5pm (Ikr2900, two hours). You'll need private transport for Hraunfossar and Barnafoss.

SNÆFELLSNES

[Cue *Twilight Zone* music…] The peninsula is a magnet for UFOs, and for New Age believers who swear that the glacier Snæfellsjökull (1446m) emits a healing aura. It's certainly atmospheric – shadowy mountains, twisting lava flows, tiny fishing villages and scattered farmhouses all sit under the shadow of the glacier. The whole of the peninsula's tip is a national park.

Jules Verne was impressed enough to use Snæfell as the gateway to the underworld in *A Journey to the Centre of the Earth*, and frag-

> ### TROLL TROUBLE
>
> The breathtaking sight of Breiðafjörður's 2700(-ish) islands inspired a legend. Three misanthropic trolls decided to separate the Westfjords from the rest of Iceland. All night, they hacked away huge lumps of earth and hurled the pieces into the nearby fjord. The task was so engrossing that they didn't notice the growing light. As the sun touched them, the two male trolls turned instantly to stone. The trollette almost made it home, when she suddenly remembered that she'd left her cow grazing on Grímsey. Stopping to look at it, both she and Daisy came to a rocky end.

ments of the 2008 Brendan Fraser movie of the same name were filmed here.

Stykkishólmur

pop 1102

Quaint coastal Stykkishólmur is the largest village in Snæfellsnes, overlooked by mighty mountains and a striking church. It makes a serene base for boat trips, horse riding and kayaking or bird-watching. It's also a picturesque shortcut to the Westfjords – car ferries run via Flatey, an island with 19th-century buildings.

The summer-only **tourist office** (☎ 433 8120; travelinfo@stykkisholmur.is; Borgarbraut; ۞ 7am-10pm Mon-Fri, 10am-7pm Sat & Sun Jun-Aug) is inside the swimming pool and sports centre; at other times, consult the knowledgeable staff at the Sæferðir shop-office (opposite) by the harbour.

SIGHTS & ACTIVITIES

There are admirable views of Breiðafjörður (see boxed text, above) from **Súgandisey**, a basalt islet that shelters the picturesque harbour. The shallow waters and myriad islands make the bay a bird-watchers' delight – keep your eyes peeled for Iceland's 'bird king', the powerful-looking white-tailed sea eagle.

Tarry-smelling **Norwegian House** (☎ 438 1640; norskhus@simnet.is; Hafnargata 5; adult/6-16yr Ikr500/300; ۞ 11am-5pm Jun-Aug), the oldest building in town, contains a folk museum, cafe and art gallery.

Ale-lovers may be interested in the new **Mjöður Brewery** (☎ 436 1122; info@mjodurehf.is; Hamraendar 5; admission Ikr1000; ۞ visits by arrangement), where the admission price includes samples of Glacier Beer and your very own tankard.

TOURS

Horse treks, snowmobiling, kayaking, boat tours, even visits to the nearby farm Bjarnarhöfn to see shark meat being cured: **Sæferðir** (Seatours; ☎ 433 2254; www.seatours.is; Smiðjustígur 3; ☉ 9am-8pm Jun-Aug, 8am-4pm Mon-Fri Sep-May) has all the local attractions sewn up. Most activities are June to August only, but some are year-round.

SLEEPING & EATING

Camping ground (☎ 438 1750; camp sites per person Ikr700; ☉ year-round; 🛜) A huge but rather exposed spot on the way into town. Basic facilities include a laundry.

Sjónarhóll HI Hostel (☎ 861 2517; www.hostel.is; Höfðagata 1; sleeping bag in dm Ikr2100, d Ikr5100; ☉ May-Oct; 🅿) The dorm rooms in this charming (if rickety) hostel have fantastic views of the harbour. You can also catch fish on its Breiðafjörður boat tours, then barbecue them on the patio.

Hringhótel Stykkishólmur (☎ 430 2100; www. stykkisholmur.is; Borgarbraut 6; s/d 24,500/28,200; 🅿 🖳) This 79-room hotel was renovated in 2008. It's still fairly ugly from the outside, but rooms are up to a decent standard, and those facing away from town have beautiful mountain views. There's a smart restaurant and bar.

At the time of writing, the cosy old restaurant **Narfeyrarstofa** (☎ 438 1119; Aðalgata 3) was closed due to illness, although it was still opening for late-night drinks on Friday and Saturday. The other restaurant in town, **Fimm Fiskar** (☎ 436 1600; Frúarstígur 1; mains Ikr2500-4000), is a less atmospheric spot but makes up for a plain layout with great food and lovely staff. The speciality is 'seafood candy', a tempting platter of lobster, halibut, shellfish and catfish morsels…and anything else fresh from the fishing boats that day.

Opposite the camping ground is a sit-down **bakery** (Nesvegur 1; ☉ 8.30am-6pm Mon-Fri, 8am-4pm Sat).

GETTING THERE & AWAY

Daily buses ply between Reykjavík and Stykkishólmur (Ikr4500, 2¾ hours), with a change to a connecting bus in Borgarnes. Another change in Vatnaleið is necessary when travelling between Stykkishólmur and Ólafsvík.

See p254 for details of the Stykkishólmur–Brjánslækur ferry.

Snæfellsjökull National Park & Around

The tip of Snæfellsnes peninsula, including the glacier, is a national park. The **visitor centre** (☎ 436 6888; ☉ 10am-6pm mid-May–early Sep) is at Hellnar, an absolutely gorgeous reserve filled with seabirds, 6km outside the main park boundary on the south coast.

The most interesting way up Snæfell is from the western end of the peninsula, along the Móðulækur stream (4WD vehicles can go 4km up the track). This takes you via the red scoria craters of Rauðhólar, the waterfall Klukkufoss and scenic Eysteinsdalur Valley. It takes a couple of days and you may need crampons and ice axes to reach the summit.

ÓLAFSVÍK

As a base, Stykkishólmur has the best facilities, but Ólafsvík (population 1005) is much closer to the park. It has a sheltered **camping ground** (☎ 436 1543; camp sites per adult/tent Ikr300/300; ☉ Jun-Aug) 1km east of the village. Central **Hringhótel Ólafsvík** (☎ 436 1650; www.hotelolafsvik.is; Ólafsbraut 40; s/d Ikr21,000/24,800; ☉ Mar-Oct; 🖳) has comfortable business-class rooms. If you don't mind sharing a bathroom, prices fall by almost 50%. Eating options in Ólafsvík are limited. The hotel has a rather overpriced restaurant; otherwise there's the **bakery** (Ólafsbraut).

HELLNAR

The spirit of the glacier, Bárður, once lived at tiny Hellnar: he couldn't have chosen a more idyllic spot. The park visitor centre and a small cafe overlook a dingley bay, echoing with the shrieks of seabirds, and up the hill stands Iceland's only ecohotel, **Hótel Hellnar** (☎ 435 6820; www.hellnar.is; s/d with sea view Ikr15,950/17,950, with mountain view Ikr14,500/16,500; ☉ mid-May–mid-Sep; 🅿). Its twin-bedded rooms are clean, bright and monastically simple, the restaurant uses local organic produce, and the guest lounge has marvellous sea views. It's quite common to see whales from the window.

THE WESTFJORDS

The remote Westfjords once had a fearsome reputation for witchcraft, and its abandoned villages, crying seabirds and wild Arctic foxes still cast a haunting spell. A dirt road winds down the edge of a lonely peninsula to Látrabjarg, justly famous for its towering cliffs thick with birdlife. Hornstrandir, accessible only in high summer by boat, is a walker's dream – you could lose yourself for days in its craggy mountains. And the sheer tranquillity of end-of-the-earth-town Ísafjörður might make you question ever returning to the hustle of a city.

Getting There & Away

AIR
There are twice-daily flights between Reykjavík and Ísafjörður (Ikr14,000) with **Flugfélag Íslands** (☎ 570 3030; www.airiceland.is).

BOAT
The **Baldur** (☎ 433 2254; www.seatours.is; Smiðjustígur 3, Stykkishólmur) ferry operates between Stykkishólmur and Brjánslækur (one way per car/passenger Ikr3080/3080, 2½ hours). From mid-June to mid-August, it leaves Stykkishólmur at 9am and 3.30pm, and Brjánslækur at 12.15pm and 6.45pm. From mid-August to mid-June, it departs Stykkishólmur at 11am Saturday and 3.30pm Sunday to Friday, and Brjánslækur at 2pm Saturday, 6pm Sunday to Friday.

BUS
Scheduled buses to, from and around the Westfjords are infrequent, headache-inducing and only possible from June to August. The company **Stjörnubílar** (☎ 456 5518; www.stjornubilar.is) runs local buses in this region.

There are two ways of travelling from Reykjavík to Ísafjörður by bus. One service, with changes in Brú/Staðarskáli and Hólmavík, runs on Tuesday, Friday and Sunday. The second service, via the Stykkishólmur–Brjánslækur ferry, runs on Monday, Wednesday and Saturday.

If you're travelling via Brú/Staðarskáli and Hólmavík, you'll need to catch the 8.30am bus from Reykjavík, eventually arriving in Ísafjörður (with luck and a following wind) at 6.15pm. The price for this journey is Ikr12,000, but it makes better sense to buy a West Iceland & Westfjords bus passport (see p287 for details).

If you're travelling via the Stykkishólmur–Brjánslækur ferry, there is a daily bus from Reykjavík to Stykkishólmur (p252), which leaves at 8am from June to August. This doesn't link up well with the ferry service. The bus arrives in Stykkishólmur at 10.30am – too late for the first boat of the day, and around five hours too early for the second.

On the other side of the water, buses meet both ferry services to Brjánslækur on Monday, Wednesday and Saturday. The first bus runs to Ísafjörður (Ikr3000) via Látrabjarg, allowing 1¼ hours at the cliffs; the second bus drives direct to Ísafjörður. In reverse, buses leave Ísafjörður at 9am Monday, Wednesday and Saturday.

If you want to travel between Ísafjörður and Akureyri, you'll also need to change in Holmavík and Brú.

ÍSAFJÖRÐUR
pop 2690

You feel as though you've reached the ends of the earth when you get to Ísafjörður, the Westfjord's largest settlement. Surrounded by vertiginous mountains and deep fjord waters, the town is remote and peaceful, apart from the croaking of ravens.

This tranquility is crumpled up and hurled away in the week after Easter, when the town gears up for two hugely important celebrations: the free two-day **Aldrei Fór Ég Suður** (I Never Went South; www.aldrei.is) music festival, dreamed up by Ísafjörðn-born singer-songwriter Mugison, and **Skíðavikan** (Skiing Week; www.skida vikan.is), the annual skiing festival.

The Westfjords' largest settlement contains a **tourist office** (☎ 450 8060; www.vestfirdir.is; Aðalstræti 7; ☀ 8.30am-6pm Mon-Fri, 10am-3pm Sat & Sun mid-Jun–Aug, 9am-noon & 12.30-4pm Mon-Fri Sep-May), several banks, and a **post office** (Hafnarstræti 9). Internet access is available at the fine **library** (☎ 450 8220; www.isafjordur.is/bokasafn; Eyrartúni; per hr Ikr100; ☀ 1-7pm Mon-Fri, to 4pm Sat), once the town's hospital.

Sights & Activities
The knowledgeable staff at the **Westfjords Maritime Museum** (☎ 456 3291; Neðstíkaupstaður; admission Ikr500; ☀ 10am-5pm daily Jul & Aug, 10am-5pm Mon-Fri, 1-5pm Sat & Sun Jun), based in four 18th-century wooden warehouses, bring the excellent nautical and whaling exhibits to life.

There are some interesting **hikes** round Tungudalur, 2km west of Ísafjörður; ask at the tourist office for detailed walking information. Westfjords Tours (see below) can arrange **kayaking** in the bay, and they also hire out bicycles. In winter, there's **downhill skiing** at Tungudalur.

Tours
Westfjords Tours (Vesturferðir; ☎ 456 5111; www .vesturferdir.is; Aðalstræti 7; ☀ 10am-6pm Mon-Fri) specialises in Hornstrandir visits, including a

ÍSAFJÖRÐUR

INFORMATION
Library..1 C1
Police...2 C2
Post Office.................................3 C2
Tourist Office.............................4 C3

SIGHTS & ACTIVITIES
Westfjords Maritime Museum........5 B4
Westfjords Tours.......................(see 4)

SLEEPING
Camping Ground.........................6 B2
Gamla Gistihúsið........................7 C2
Hotel Edda................................8 B2
Hótel Ísafjörður.........................9 C3

EATING
Gamla Bakaríð...........................10 C3
Kaffi Edinborg.........................(see 4)
Kaffihús Bakarans.....................11 C2
Langi Mangi..............................12 C3

TRANSPORT
Bus Stand.................................13 C2
Bus Stop..................................14 B2
Hornstrandir Boat Departures.....15 C3

four-hour trip to the abandoned village Hesteyri (Ikr9200, Wednesday, Friday and Sunday at 2pm, mid-June to late August).

Sleeping & Eating

Camping ground (☎ 444 4960; Skutulsfjarðarbraut; camp sites per adult plus tent Ikr900; ☷ mid-Jun–mid-Aug) Centrally located behind the secondary school. There's another **camping ground** (☎ 456 5081; camp sites per adult Ikr900) by a pretty waterfall in Tungudalur.

Hotel Edda (☎ 444 4960; www.hoteledda.is; sleeping bag dm from Ikr2100, s/d from Ikr6800/8500; ☷ mid-Jun–mid-Aug) This is a no-frills option in summer, run by Hotel Ísafjörður in the secondary school. Sleeping-bag accommodation is in classrooms, or you can upgrade to a private room.

Gamla Gistihúsið (☎ 456 4146; www.gistihus.is; Mánagata 5; sleeping bag dm Ikr3700, s/d Ikr7600/10,500; ☐) This former hospital and old people's home is a tonic, with sunlight dappling through the windows and homely touches everywhere. The nine neat rooms (with plentiful shared bathrooms) all come with TV, plus there's a guest kitchen and free internet access. Recommended. Breakfast is Ikr1000 for those in sleeping-bag accommodation.

Hótel Ísafjörður (☎ 456 4111; www.hotelisafjordur.is; Silfurtorg 2; s/d from Ikr16,200/19,500) Overlooking Skutulsfjörður and the main square, the town's only hotel is at the hub of things. Rooms are smart and businesslike, with TVs, radios, minibars and shower rooms; deluxe versions also come equipped with bathtubs. The restaurant does good grub, and digestion is aided by a beautiful view over the fjord.

Langi Mangi (☎ 456 3022; Aðalstræti 22; snacks Ikr500-1000; ☷ 11am-11pm Mon-Wed, 11am-1am Thu, 11am-3am Fri, noon-3am Sat, 1-11.30pm Sun) Langi Mangi is an atmospheric little caff-art gallery-bar with a range of coffees, meandering music and homemade soup. There are live performances at weekends.

Kaffi Edinborg (☎ 456 4400; Aðalstræti 7; mains Ikr2400-3000; ☷ 11am-11.30pm) Smoothies come to Ísafjörður with the opening of this blond, open-plan, modern cafe-bar in the town's brand-new cultural centre. The menu covers all bases: sandwiches, burgers, fish and meat mains, several vegie options, and traditional Westfjords dishes such as hashed fish with rye bread.

Two bakeries, **Kaffihús Bakarans** (☎ 456 4770; Hafnarstræti; ☷ 7.30am-6pm Mon-Fri, 9am-4.30pm Sun) and **Gamla Bakarið** (☎ 456 3226; Aðalstræti; ☷ 7am-6pm Mon-Fri, 7am-4pm Sat) are good for bread, buns and chocolate frogs. If you have your own transport, there's a Bónus supermarket about 2km west of town.

HORNSTRANDIR

The wildest corner of the Westfjords has a poignant history: its elderly inhabitants, left behind with no electricity, roads or telephones, made a collective decision to abandon the peninsula in the 1950s. It's now a spectacular nature reserve, which solitary hikers share only with seabirds and Arctic foxes.

The peninsula is accessible by boat from Ísafjörður, with one-way fares around Ikr4600; contact Ísafjörður tourist office for details. There's basic sleeping-bag accommodation at **Hesteyri** (☎ 456 7183; sossa@bolungarvik .is; sleeping bag Ikr3000; ☷ Jul & Aug) in four rooms with kitchen access.

LÁTRABJARG

The world's biggest bird breeding grounds are the towering, 14km-long Látrabjarg cliffs. Fulmars, kittiwakes and fearless puffins fight for nesting space at the westernmost point of the Westfjords. It's a truly impressive sight, but wrap up well; the wind is bitter.

For accommodation, try the beautifully located **Ferðaþjó** (☎ 456 1575; breidavik@patro.is; camp sites per adult Ikr1200, sleeping-bag dm Ikr3000, s/d from Ikr6500/9000; ☷ mid-May–mid-Sep), part of a work- ing farm, on a golden beach at Breiðavík,

12km from the cliffs. Nondorm rooms are in a new minihotel extension; it's functional from the outside, but pleasant inside. You can also pitch tents in a neighbouring field.

THE NORTH

SIGLUFJÖRÐUR

pop 1307

Iceland's northernmost town enjoys a dramatic setting at the very tip of the Tröllskagi peninsula. In the past, herring fishing brought frenzied activity and untold riches; today the town's appeal is its peaceful isolation thrumming with community spirit. The roller-coasting coastal road currently stops at Siglufjörður, although two controversial new tunnels (being built over the next 10 years) will make the town more accessible.

The award-winning **Herring Era Museum of Iceland** (Síldarminjasafn Íslands; ☎ 467 1604; http://herring .siglo.is; Snorragata 15; adult/12-16yr Ikr800/400; ☷ 10am-6pm mid-Jun–mid-Aug, 1-5pm early Jun & mid-Aug–Sep), lovingly created over 16 years, does a stunning job of recreating Siglufjörður's boom days. You can trace the herrings' journey through the museum's three harbourside buildings: from the full-size night-time harbour; to the salting station Roaldsbrakki, looking as though the herring workers have just left; to the huge machinery of the fishmeal- and oil-processing plant. The museum also functions as the **tourist information centre**, and as a theatre and music venue in high summer. Traditional music enthusiasts may be interested in the **Icelandic Folk Music Centre** (Þjóðlagasetur Sr Bjarna Þorsteinssonar; ☎ 467 2300; http://setur.fjallabyggd.is; Norðurgata 1; adult/under 14 Ikr600/free; ☷ 1-5pm Jun & Aug, 10am-6pm Jul), which displays 19th-century instruments and recordings of Icelandic songs and chants.

The area is perfect for hiking, fishing and skiing (although access to the town can be tricky in winter) – ask at the museum for further details. Siglufjörður's biggest shindig takes place on August bank holiday: the lively **Herring Adventure Festival** recreates the gold-rush atmosphere of the town's glory days. Fans of folk music will enjoy **Þjóðlagahátíðin á Siglufirði** (http://festival.fjallaby ggd.is), a delightfully relaxed and low-key affair held over the first weekend in July.

The little **camping ground** (per person Ikr900; ☷ Jun-Aug) is situated right by the town square, and has a toilet block and laundry. In a gilt, cherub-decorated 1930s hotel, whose stately proportions hint at wealthier times, you'll find **Gistihúsið Hvanneyri** (☎ 467 1506; order@hvanneyri .com; Aðalgata 10; sleeping bag in dm/tw Ikr2100/3700, s/d Ikr5500/9500), which has 19 charmingly dated rooms with mountain views. There are a couple of TV lounges, a mighty dining room, and a guest kitchen.

BioCafé (☎ 467 1111; Aðalgata 30; mains Ikr1300-1900, 9in pizza from Ikr1000; ◔ 11.30am-9pm) serves good-value burgers, pizzas, and fish and lamb dishes, and the upstairs bar opens late on Friday and Saturday nights.

The other dining choice in town is friendly **Pizza 67** (☎ 467 2323; Aðalgata; 9in pizza from Ikr1000).

From June to September, you can get from Reykjavík to Siglufjörður by bus, but you'll have to change at Varmahlíð and Sauðarkrókur. The 8.30am service (Ikr10,100) on Monday, Wednesday or Friday will get you to Siglufjörður at 3.30pm on the same day; at other times the journey involves an overnight stop.

AKUREYRI
pop 17,097

Fertile, sheltered Akureyri (www.visitakureyri .is), situated alongside Iceland's greatest fjord, has the warmest weather in a cold country. The best restaurants, cafes and cinemas outside the capital nestle beneath a range of snowcapped peaks. It's a place to linger, admiring the flowery gardens, maple trees, shining sculptures and all the bobbing fishing boats and cruise ships.

Information

The **tourist office** (☎ 462 7733; www.nordurland.is; Hafnarstræti 82; ◔ 7.30am-7pm mid-Jun-Aug, 8am-5pm Mon-Fri & 10am-2pm Sat & Sun May-mid-Jun & Sep, 10am-2pm Mon & Sat, 8am-4pm Tue-Fri Oct-Apr) can organise tours. **Nonni Travel** (☎ 461 1841; www.nonnitravel.is; Brekkugata 5; ◔ 9am-5pm Mon-Fri mid-May-Sep, 10am-3pm Mon-Fri Oct-mid-May) is the main tour agency, specialising in trips to Greenland.

There's a central **post office** (☎ 460 2600; Skipagata 10; ◔ 8.30am-4.30pm Mon-Fri) and the fantastic **municipal library** (☎ 460 1250; Brekkugata 17; ◔ 10am-7pm Mon-Fri Jun-Aug, 10am-6pm Mon-Fri, noon-5pm Sat Sep-May) has an English book section larger than many UK libraries, plus **internet access** (per hr Ikr200) and a cafe. **Akureyri Hospital** (☎ 463 0100; Spítalavegur) is just south of the botanical gardens.

Sights & Activities

Akureyrarkirkja (Eyrarlandsvegur) was designed by Gudjón Samúelsson, the architect of Reykjavík's Hallgrímskirkja. Although the basalt theme connects them, Akureyrarkirkja looks more like a stylised 1920s US skyscraper than its big-town brother. The church admits visitors in summer; check the board outside for opening times, as they change frequently.

Akureyri Museum (Minjasafnið Akureyri; ☎ 462 4162; www.akmus.is; Aðalstræti 58; adult/under 16yr Ikr500/free; ◔ 11am-5pm Jun-mid-Sep, 2-4pm Sun late Sep-Jul) houses local historical items, including an interesting Settlement Era section. The tranquil garden out front set the fashion for Iceland's 19th-century tree-planting craze.

Children's writer Reverend Jón Sveinsson (1857–1944) spent his childhood in Akureyri and his old-fashioned tales of derring-do have a rich Icelandic flavour. Make sure you visit the higgledy-piggledy wooden **Nonnahús** (☎ 462 3555; www.nonni.is; Aðalstræti 54; adult/under 16yr Ikr500/free; ◔ 10am-5pm Jun-Aug), the author's childhood home, and pick up an English translation of his book *At Skipalón*. You can purchase a **joint ticket** (Ikr700) for Nonnahús and Akureyri Museum.

The most northerly botanical garden in the world is **Lystigarður Akureyrar** (Akureyri Botanical Gardens; ☎ 462 7487; Eyrarlandsvegur; ◔ 8am-10pm Mon-Fri, 9am-10pm Sat & Sun Jun-Sep), a delightful picnic spot on sunny days. Opened in 1912, it includes most native Icelandic species, and a further 6600 tough plants from high altitudes and latitudes.

Akureyri has one of the country's best (indoor and outdoor) **swimming pools** (☎ 461 4455; Þingvallastræti 21; adult/6-15yr Ikr370/100, sauna Ikr540; ◔ 7am-9pm Mon-Fri, 8am-6.30pm Sat & Sun) with hot pots, saunas and flumes.

Sleeping

Akureyri often has more visitors than accommodation spaces – bookings are recommended, if you want to stay somewhere central. The tourist office has a list of some very nice farmhouse accommodation (private transport necessary) should everywhere in town be full.

BUDGET

Central camping ground (☎ 462 3379; hamrar@hamrar .is; Þórunnarstræti; camp sites per adult Ikr900; ◔ Jun–mid-Sep) There are ongoing threats to close down this central camping ground, but it's here at least for 2009, with improved security and a fresh splash of paint on the toilet blocks. It's

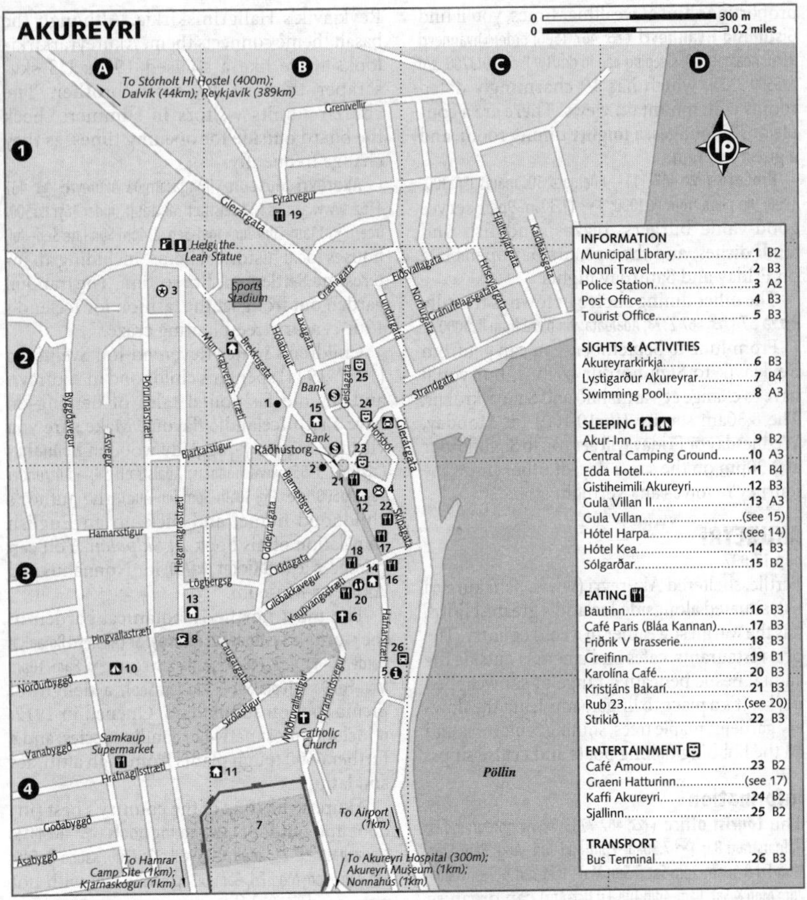
AKUREYRI
0 300 m
0 0.2 miles
A
B
C
D
1
2
3
4
To Stórholt HI Hostel (400m); Dalvík (44km); Reykjavík (389km)
Grenivellir
Eyrarvegur
Glerárgata
Helgi the Lean Statue
Sports Stadium
Hjalteyrargata
Kaldbaksgata
Eiðsvallagata
Hríseyjargata
Norðurgata
Lundargata
Gránufélagsgata
Grænagata
Laxagata
Hólabraut
Brekkugata
Munkaþverárstræti
Þórunnarstræti
Byggðavegur
Ásvegur
Bjarkarstígur
Ráðhústorg
Bank
Geislagata
Hofsbót
Strandgata
Bjarmastígur
Oddeyrargata
Helgamagrastræti
Hamarsstígur
Oddagata
Lögbergsg
Gilsbakkavegur
Kaupvangsstræti
Skipagata
Hafnarstræti
Þingvallastræti
Laugargata
Norðurbyggð
Skólastígur
Möðruvallastræti
Eyrarlandsvegur
Catholic Church
Samkaup Supermarket
Vanabyggð
Hrafnagilsstræti
Goðabyggð
Ásabyggð
Pollin
To Airport (1km)
To Hamrar Camp Site (1km); Kjarnaskógur (1km)
To Akureyri Hospital (300m); Akureyri Museum (1km); Nonnahús (1km)
INFORMATION
Municipal Library 1 B2
Nonni Travel 2 B3
Police Station 3 A2
Post Office 4 B3
Tourist Office 5 B3
SIGHTS & ACTIVITIES
Akureyrarkirkja 6 B3
Lystigarður Akureyrar 7 B4
Swimming Pool 8 A3
SLEEPING
Akur-Inn 9 B2
Central Camping Ground 10 A3
Edda Hotel 11 B4
Gistiheimili Akureyri 12 B3
Gula Villan II 13 A3
Gula Villan (see 15)
Hótel Harpa (see 14)
Hótel Kea 14 B3
Sólgarðar 15 B2
EATING
Bautinn 16 B3
Café Paris (Bláa Kannan) 17 B3
Friðrik V Brasserie 18 B3
Greifinn 19 B1
Karolína Café 20 B3
Kristjáns Bakarí 21 B3
Rub 23 (see 20)
Strikið 22 B3
ENTERTAINMENT
Café Amour 23 B2
Graeni Hatturinn (see 17)
Kaffi Akureyri 24 B2
Sjallinn 25 B2
TRANSPORT
Bus Terminal 26 B3

conveniently located close to the swimming pool, supermarket and town.

Hamrar camp site (☎ 461 2264; hamrar@hamrar.is; camp sites per adult Ikr900; ⌚ mid-May–mid-Sep) This huge camp site, 1.5km south in a leafy setting by the scout camp at Kjarnaskógur, has newer facilities and mountain views. Both places have kitchen and laundry.

Stórholt HI Hostel (☎ 462 3657; www.hostel.is; Stórholt 1; sleeping bag in dm Ikr 2100, s/d Ikr4200/6800; P 🖳) This spotless hostel, 15 minutes' walk from the town centre, has a comfy sitting room and two large kitchens, with a summery decking area outside. There are two attractive summer houses, one holding three people (Ikr8000) and one holding eight (Ikr19,500).

MIDRANGE

Sólgarðar (☎ 461 1133; solgardar@simnet.is; Brekkugata 6; sleeping bag s/d Ikr5000/6000, s/d Ikr5500/7500) The owner works shifts, so don't be surprised if she's bleary eyed! Her three rooms, one with balcony, overlook a quiet residential street and they're gleaming. Breakfast is available (Ikr1000), or there's a kitchen for self-catering, and there are discounts for stays over three days.

Akur-Inn (☎ 461 2500; www.akurinn.is; Brekkugata 27a; sleeping bag s/d Ikr4200/7200, s/d with shared bathroom Ikr5900/8200, d with bathroom Ikr12,600; 🖳) The seven rooms in this lovely old heritage home have a calm atmosphere and lots of 1930s period charm. Crisp white linens and pale neutral colours add to the simple style. There's no kitchen, but breakfast is available (Ikr1200).

Gula Villan (☎ 896 8464; www.gulavillan.is; Brekkugata 8; sleeping bag/s/d Ikr4800/6000/8600) At this family-friendly place, you'll find spotless, snow-white rooms with leafy patterns stencilled on the walls. The owners have another buttercup-yellow building (Þingvallastræti 14) opposite the swimming pool. Both houses have kitchens, or parties of more than four can order breakfast (Ikr1190 per person).

Gistiheimili Akureyri (☎ 462 5588; www.guesthouseakureyri.is; Hafnarstræti 104; s/d Ikr8900/10,400, with shared bathroom Ikr6900/8900) This large-ish place lacks the intimacy of a guesthouse; it's more of a budget hotel with kitchen facilities. The 19 rooms are small but clean, all with TV and washbasins; some have private bathrooms. The sunny, balconied breakfast area (summer only) overlooking bustling Hafnarstræti is the star feature.

Edda Hotel (☎ 444 4000; www.hoteledda.is; Eyrarlandsvegur 28; basic s/d Ikr10,900/13,600, Edda Plus Ikr12,400/15,500; ☷ mid-Jun–late Aug) Around 200 summer rooms are up for grabs in the grammar school: just over half are 'Edda Plus' with TVs and private bathrooms. There's a cafe and large restaurant on site.

TOP END

Hótel Kea (☎ 460 2000; www.keahotels.is; Hafnarstræti 83-5; s/d/tr Ikr28,600/35,000/45,000; ☷) Akureyri's top hotel has been going since 1944. Rooms here are business-class with slightly old-fashioned trimmings; the five nicest have balconies overlooking the fjord. Kea is the only hotel in town with facilities for wheelchair users. Hótel Harpa (singles/doubles/triples Ikr24,300/30,000/39,500) shares Kea's restaurant and reception. In some ways its small rooms are superior; they're recently renovated, with parquet flooring and modern furniture.

Eating

Café Paris (Bláa Kannan; ☎ 461 4600; Hafnarstræti 96; ☷ 9am-10.30pm) This tearoom, with its old wooden interior and swirly-coloured tables, is a peachy place to idle away a morning. In summer, outdoor tables mushroom on the main street, and people flock in for lunch specials (soup, salad and main for Ikr1150), often vegie.

Karolína Café (☎ 461 2755; Kaupvangsstræti 23; ☷ 11.30am-1am Mon-Thu, to 3am Fri & Sat, 2pm-1am Sun) Karolína Café lures a young, crazy-haired crowd with magazines, squashy sofas, alcoholic coffee and monthly art exhibitions.

Greifinn (☎ 460 1600; www.greifinn.is; Glerárgata 20; mains Ikr1700-3000; ☷ 11.30am-10pm) This is a bustling, lively spot popular with families, birthday parties and work outings. The varied menu includes sizzling Tex-Mex, much-praised pizza and big meaty dishes. A bat-phone button on the table summons the waiter in seconds.

Bautinn (☎ 462 1818; Hafnarstræti 92; soups & salads Ikr1390, mains Ikr1600-3400) Open all day, this restaurant is a favourite for its friendly staff, decent prices and loaded salad bar. There's a large glazed conservatory, and a more shadowy interior if you don't enjoy that goldfish-bowl feeling. Dishes include everything from pizzas and salad to puffin and whale.

Strikið (☎ 462 7100; Skipagata 14; mains Ikr2000-4000; ☷ from 11.30am Mon-Sat, from 6pm Sun) Huge windows with panoramic fjord views lend a little magic to this 5th-floor grill and restaurant. It's a tasteful, minimalist affair, with a small but superb-tasting menu of Icelandic seafood and world cuisine: honey-roasted pork, salmon with rocket and basil, lobster tails.

Rub 23 (☎ 462 2223; Kaupvangsstræti 23; mains Ikr3500-4500; ☷ from 6pm Tue-Sat) Above Karolina Café, this super-sleek restaurant is run by Iceland's Chef of the Year 2003. The novelty here is the 'rubs' – 11 different seasoning combinations that you choose to coat your perfectly presented fish or meat main. There's also a separate sushi menu.

Friðrik V Brasserie (☎ 461 5775; Kaupvangsstræti 6; mains Ikr2500-5000; ☷ 6-10pm Tue-Sat) For a gourmet glutton-fest, treat yourself to one of the wonderful creations at Friðrik V. The seasonal menu features Icelandic delicacies cooked with impeccable style, such as pan-fried puffin in red wine, or wild goose in a blueberry and chocolate sauce.

Kristjáns Bakarí (Hafnarstræti 108; ☷ 8am-5.30pm Mon-Fri, 10am-5pm Sat) sells fresh bread, salad and cakes.

Drinking & Entertainment

The British-style **Græni Hatturinn** (☎ 461 4646; Hafnarstræti 96) pub has frequent live music. Karolina Café (left) is a popular weekend hang-out with a more arty crowd.

Inhabitants shake their booties at **Kaffi Akureyri** (☎ 461 3999; Strandgata 7; ☷ 3pm-1am Sun-Thu, to 4am Fri & Sat), a dressy venue good for live music and dancing; **Café Amour** (☎ 461

3030; Raðhústorg 9; 🕑 11am-1am Sun-Thu, to 4am Fri & Sat), a smoky cafe, cocktail lounge and wine bar with an upstairs dance floor and the most garish ceiling you'll ever see; and the very popular **Sjallinn** (🕾 462 2770; Geislagata 14; 🕑 to 3am Fri & Sat), a large nightclub with chart tunes, DJs and bands.

Getting There & Away

AIR

In summer, **Flugfélag Íslands** (🕾 460 7000; www .airiceland.is) has up to seven flights daily between Akureyri and Reykjavík (Ikr14,090). Internationally, **Iceland Express** (www.icelandex press.com) has two flights per week between June and August from Copenhagen (around Ikr 19,900, two hours).

See right for information about flights to Grímsey.

BOAT

See right for information about boats to Grímsey.

BUS

Buses, operated by **Trex** (🕾 553 3737, 461 1106; Hafnarstræti 77), run from the central bus station outside the tourist office.

Buses between Akureyri and Reykjavík depart at least once daily (Ikr9000, six hours) year-round. Buses travelling over the Kjölur route run from 18 June to 4 September, leaving at 8am daily from both Reykjavík and Akureyri (Ikr9900, nine hours).

A bus to Mývatn (Ikr2500, 1½ hours) runs daily from June to August (three per week during the rest of year), continuing to Egilsstaðir (a further Ikr3600, two hours), where you can catch another bus (sometimes a good connection, sometimes not) to Seyðisfjörður. Buses to Húsavík (Ikr2300, 1¼ hours) depart one to four times daily, depending on the time of year. For buses to Dalvík (for the ferry to Grímsey), see right.

AROUND AKUREYRI

South of town is Iceland's most visited 'forest', **Kjarnaskógur**, popular for family outings. A good day walk from Akureyri follows the **Glerárdalur** valley as far as Lambi mountain hut. From Akureyri you can hike up and down **Mt Sulur** (1213m) in about eight hours; if possible, get a lift to the signposted turn-off (it's

a dull walk out of town), from where the summit is a 5km climb.

About 50km east of town is curvy waterfall **Goðafoss**, where Þorgeir Ljósvetningagoði, when asked to decide whether Iceland should adopt Christianity, symbolically threw his statues of the old Norse gods. Buses from Akureyri to Mývatn pass the waterfall.

Grímsey

The main attraction of **Grímsey**, a wind-blown island 40km from the north coast, is that it's the only part of Iceland that lies (partly) inside the Arctic Circle. A large signpost marks the theoretical line; once you've crossed into polar realms, buy a commemorative certificate from the harbourside cafe. Abundant birdlife (puffins, razorbills, guillemots, gulls and psychotic Arctic terns) outnumbers the close-knit community by around one million to 100. The boat ride adds to the mystique of reaching this isolated place.

The **Sæfari** (🕾 458 8970; www.landflutningar.is/ saefari) sails from Dalvík (44km north of Akureyri) to Grímsey island at 9am on Monday, Wednesday and Friday (return Ikr5800, 3½ hours), returning from Grímsey at 4pm. In summer, connecting buses leave Akureyri at 7.30am on Monday, Wednesday and Friday, returning from Dalvík at 7.30pm. The return trip from Akureyri costs Ikr6600.

From mid-June to mid-August on Sunday to Friday, there's one scheduled flight from Akureyri to Grímsey (one way Ikr10,540, 25 minutes) at 1pm. Nonni Travel (p257) can help arrange trips by boat or air.

HÚSAVÍK
pop 2256

Most people visit the 'whale-watching capital of Europe' to do just that; in season, you're almost guaranteed to see these awe-inspiring ocean giants feeding in Skjálfandi bay.

The helpful **tourist information office** (🕾 464 4300; info@husavik.is; Garðarsbraut 7; 🕑 9am-6pm Mon-Fri, 10am-5pm Sat & Sun mid-May–mid-Sep) has internet access (Ikr300 per hour). There's also internet access in the **library** (🕾 464 6165; Stórigarður 17; per hr Ikr250; 🕑 10am-6pm Mon-Thu, to 5pm Fri).

Sights & Activities

The fascinating **Whale Centre** (🕾 464 2520; www .whalemuseum.is; Hafnarstétt; adult/6-14yr Ikr900/450; 🕑 9am-7pm Jun-Aug, 10am-5pm May & Sep) deserves a couple of hours' attention, preferably *before* you go whale-watching. It tells you everything about Icelandic whales and whaling, and the hanging gallery of skeletons allows you truly to appreciate their size.

From May to September (although the main season is June to August), **North Sailing** (Norður Sigling; ☎ 464 7272; www.northsailing.is; Gamli Baukur, Hafnarstétt 9; adult/7-15yr Ikr8200/4000) and **Gentle Giants** (Hvalferðir; ☎ 464 1500; www.gentlegiants .is; Garðarsbraut 6; adult/7-15yr Ikr7900/3400) offer three-hour whale-watching trips on sturdy oaken boats (see boxed text, p262). There's a 97% chance of sightings – mostly minkes and harbour porpoises, although humpback and blue whales also appear. Buy tickets from the 'lighthouse' ticket booths opposite the church.

Once you've recovered your land legs, **Safnahúsið** (Museum; ☎ 464 1860; www.husmus.is; Stórigarður 17; adult/child Ikr500/150; ☉ 10am-6pm Jun-Aug, 9am-4pm Mon-Fri Sep-May), the local museum, has impressive maritime and natural history collections, and admission includes a cup of coffee.

The unique **Icelandic Phallological Museum** (☎ 566 8668; www.phallus.is; Héðinsbraut 3a; Ikr500; ☉ noon-6pm mid-May–early Sep) contains 204 penises – pickled, dried and stuffed – from local mammals ranging in size from a hamster to a blue whale. The only willy missing is that of *Homo sapiens*, although four donors have been lined up.

Sleeping

Camping ground (☎ 845 0705; camp sites per person Ikr850; ☉ summer) This option, located at the northern edge of town, has two brand-new utility buildings, containing a good kitchen, toilets and a washing machine. Possibly the best bargain in Iceland: once you've paid the camping fee, you are allowed to stay for up to 10 nights at no extra cost.

Guesthouse Baldursbrekka (☎ 464 1005; mari am@simnet.is; Baldursbrekka 20; sleeping bag/s/d Ikr2500/3000/6000) The cheapest option, this family home in a quiet cul-de-sac has five dinky rooms, cooking facilities and a garage to hang wet clothes. Breakfast costs Ikr700. If it's full, the pleasant lady at No 17 opposite has four rooms and a guest kitchen; prices are similar. Parking is only admitted on one side of the street – you'll face a fine otherwise.

Vísir Guesthouse (☎ 856 5750; Garðarsbraut 14; dora @visirhf.is; s/d/tr Ikr7500/10,000/15,000; ☉ May-Aug; ☐) An odd little place based in a fish factory. The

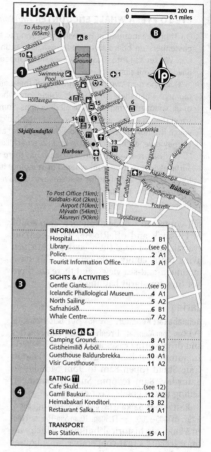

HÚSAVÍK

10 bright, simple rooms (half with sea views, all with shared bathrooms) are set around a rather clattery corridor – noisy guests could spell sleepless nights. There's a good kitchen, a washer and dryer, and internet access.

Gistiheimilið Árból (☎ 464 2220; www.simnet.is /arbol; Ásgarðsvegur 2; s/d/tr Ikr10,400/17,800/25,000) This ex-governor's mansion, on the edge of the park, is the best place to stay in town. It's spacious and welcoming, upper rooms have lovely views of either the harbour or the mountains, and there's interesting ephemera on the walls, including bugles, guns and old photos of Húsavík.

Kaldbaks-Kot (☎ 464 1504; www.cottages.is; 2-/ 4-person house Ikr22,700/32,800) For extraordinarily cosy, well-priced accommodation, try these

ICELAND

EYE TO EYE: A WHALE ENCOUNTER *Fran Parnell*

On Thursday morning in Húsavík, I'm praying to the rain gods to back off. But as I join the other passengers on board the wooden whale-spotting boat, the water is calm and the sun shivers out. We set sail into Skjálfandi bay, snowcapped mountains all around, and within 15 minutes have seen our first minke.

Over the next two hours, sightings of these amazing creatures come thick and fast. It's a rare moment when there *isn't* a whale visible somewhere: shining backs roll from the waves, and blasts of air spout from blowholes in all directions. Some of the whales are so close that you can even smell their breath – a rancid stench of month-old fish. Besides minkes and a solitary dolphin, we watch five humpbacks repeatedly coming up for air. There's ample time to admire their huge flukes as they dive, each patterned with a Rorschachlike blotch as individual as a human fingerprint.

Just before the boat turns for harbour, there's a noise like a steam engine and a humpback surfaces just metres from where I'm standing. Its knobbled head rises from the water, and for long seconds, a prehistoric eye surveys us gravely; then the head submerges, the fluke curves, and the whale is gone.

self-contained wooden cottages, 2km south of Húsavík and off Rte 85. They contain everything you need (fully equipped kitchen, living room, comfy beds, veranda, TV), have mountain-and-sea views, and there are three hot tubs for starlit bathing.

Eating

Heimabakarí Konditori (☎ 464 2901; Garðarsbraut 15; ☼ 8am-5pm Mon-Sat) Fresh bread, sandwiches and droolworthy cakes are sold at the bakery. In summer, it has a harbourside offshoot, Café Skuld (open 8am to 9pm Monday to Saturday, 8am to 6pm Sunday summer), selling baked goods, beer and wine.

Restaurant Salka (☎ 464 2551; Garðarsbraut 6; mains Ikr1400-3200; ☼ 11.30am-10pm Sun-Thu, to 11pm Fri & Sat) This historical building, which was once Iceland's first cooperative, now houses a good restaurant. Salka has a bar and an extensive local menu (with lobster, shrimp, puffin, lamb), plus pizzas and burgers.

Gamli Baukur (☎ 464 2442; www.gamlibaukur.is; Hafnarstétt; mains Ikr1400-3700; ☼ 11.30am-9pm Sun-Wed, to 1am Thu, 11am-3am Fri & Sat summer, restaurant closed winter) Built from driftwood, the Old Tankard is a cosy harbourside restaurant-bar with a nautical theme. Fresh scallops, cod, shrimp and herring are on the menu (hamburgers are here for the fish-disinclined).

Getting There & Away

SBA-Norðurleið (☎ 550 0700; www.sba.is) runs a service between Akureyri and Húsavík (Ikr2300, 1¼ hours), at least once daily in winter and four times daily in summer. From mid-June

to August, there are two services daily to Reynihlíð at Mývatn (Ikr2000, 40 minutes), and one service daily to Ásbyrgi and the waterfall Dettifoss (Ikr3300, 1¾ hours).

MÝVATN

Mývatn is the calm, shallow lake at the heart of a volatile volcanic area. Nature's violent masterpieces are everywhere – crazy-coloured mud pots, huge craters, and still-smouldering eruption debris. Once you've had your fill of geology gone wild, mellow out with cycle rides, birdwatching – geese, Arctic terns, golden plovers, ducks and swans can be seen – and a bathe in the north's version of the Blue Lagoon.

Reykjahlíð (population 193), at the northern end of the lake, is more an assortment of accommodation than a true town, but it makes the best base (Skútustaðir, at the southern end, also has summer facilities). The **tourist office** (☎ 464 4390; www.visitmyvatn.is; Hraunvegur 8; ☼ 9am-7pm Jun-Aug, 10am-5pm Mon-Fri & 10am-4pm Sat & Sun May & Sep, 10am-5pm Mon-Fri Oct-Apr) is in Reykjahlíð, on the main road next to the supermarket, and contains an interesting exhibition on the area's unusual birdlife, geology and volcanic systems.

The down side to Mývatn (Midge Lake) are the dense midge clouds that appear in summer: on the bright side, they don't bite! Also, if hiking, keep a look out for deep fissures, especially if you are travelling with children.

Sights & Activities
AROUND THE LAKE

One of the best ways to experience the 37-sq-km lake is by bicycle or horse; several places in Reykjahlíð rent them. We recommend a ride round the shores, taking in the forested lava headland of **Höfði**; pinnacle formations at **Kálfaströnd**; pseudocraters at **Skútustaðir**, where ponds, bogs and marshlands create havens for nesting birds; the climb up **Vindbelgjarfjall** (529m); and a high-density waterfowl **nesting area** on the northwestern shore (off-road entry is restricted between 15 May and 20 July).

One of the most interesting walks begins at **Stóragjá**, a hot spring near the village. After a few minutes, the path comes to a dead end at a pipeline. Go left and walk a few hundred metres until the track turns south. It crosses a lava field to **Grjótagjá**, a 50°C hot spring in a spooky fissure, then continues to the tephra crater **Hverfell** (sadly scarred by graffiti), and **Dimmuborgir**, a 2000-year-old maze of twisted lava whose highlight is the 'Church', a natural arched cave that looks man-made. Stop for homemade ice cream at the unusual 'Cow-shed Cafe' **Vogafjós** (☎ 464 3800; ⏰ 7.30am-11.30pm May-Oct), nearby on the main road – last time we were there, a sheep came in and peed on the floor!

MÝVATN NATURE BATHS

Ease aching muscles at the **Mývatn Nature Baths** (Jarðböðin við Mývatn; ☎ 464 4411; www.jardbodin.is; Jarðbaðshólar; adult/12-15yr Ikr1400/700, towel/swimsuit rental Ikr350/350; ⏰ 9am-11.30pm Jun-Aug, noon-9.30pm Sep-May), the north's answer to the Blue Lagoon, 5km east of Reykjahlíð. It's much smaller but is nicely landscaped, with a hot pot and saunas.

NÁMAFJALL & HVERIR

Vaporous vents cover the pinky-orange Námafjall ridge. At its foot, fumaroles and solfataras in the Hverir geothermal field scream steam and belch mud. The area rests on the mid-Atlantic rift (hence all the activity), and can be seen from quite a distance. It's just off the Ring Rd 6km east of Reykjahlíð.

KRAFLA

The colourful, sulphurous mud hole **Leirhnjúkur** is Krafla's prime attraction. From there you can meander round the **Krafla Caldera**, where several different lava flows overlie each other; some from the 1984 eruptions are still smoking.

Nearby **Stóra-Viti** is a 320m-wide explosion crater and lake (now inactive…allegedly). The 30-megawatt **Kröflustöð Power Station** sources steam from 17 boreholes around the volcano; step into the **visitor centre** (Gestastofa; ⏰ 12.30-3.30pm Mon-Fri, 1-5pm Sat & Sun Jun-Aug) for an ex-planatory film. One of the power station's preliminary searches produced the whopping crater **Sjálfskapar Viti** (Homemade Hell; near the Krafla car park), when a team drilled into a steam chamber which exploded. Bits of the rig were found 3km away.

Between 18 June and 31 August, a bus runs from Reykjahlíð to Krafla (Ikr1200) at 8am and 11.30am from outside Hótel Reynihlíð.

Tours

From early June to late September (weather permitting), Hótel Reykjahlíð (see p264) runs daily tours to Dettifoss via Krafla (Ikr18,800, seven hours); to Lofthellir, a lava cave with magnificent natural ice sculptures (Ikr14,300, five hours); and to the cratered wasteland of the Askja caldera (Ikr19,400, 12 hours). There's a maximum of eight passengers allowed on each tour, so it's advisable to book tickets in advance.

SBA-Norðurleið (☎ 550 0700; www.sba.is) runs sightseeing tours to the same destinations from mid-June to August, departing from Akureyri, Húsavík and Reykjahlíð. There's also a three-day tour to Askja, Kverkfjöll and the glacier Vatnajökull – see p275 for details.

Mývatn Tours (☎ 464 1920; www.askjatours.is; Ikr14,000) runs a trip to the Askja caldera and Herðubreiðalindir nature reserve from the tourist office at Reykjahlíð at 8am Monday, Wednesday and Friday from 25 June to 31 August (daily from mid-July to mid-August).

Sleeping & Eating

The following options are all in Reykjahlíð (Skútustaðir, at the southern end of the lake, also has seasonal camping, farmhouse and hotel accommodation and a restaurant). Camping at Mývatn is prohibited outside designated areas.

Hlíð Camping Ground (☎ 464 4103; hlid@isholf.is; Hraunbrún; camp sites per tent Ikr900; 🖳) This large stepped camping ground, 300m inland from the church, has internet access, free showers and some decent mountain bikes for hire (Ikr1600 per half-day).

Ferðaþjónustan Bjarg (☎ 464 4240; ferdabjarg @simnet.is; Mývatn; camp sites per tent Ikr1050, sleeping bag from Ikr2500-3900, s/d/tr Ikr7500/11,500/15,500; ⏰ May-Oct; 🖳) This is primarily a large, well-equipped camping ground, perfectly situated on the lakeshore. There's a new shower block with under-floor heating, a laundry service, summer boat (Ikr2000 per hour) and bike (Ikr2000 for 12

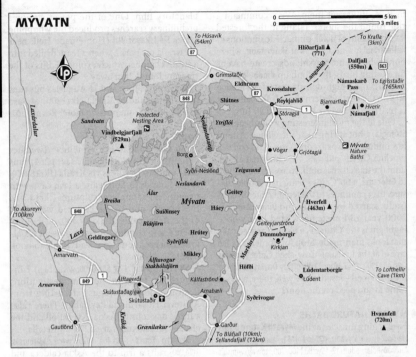

hours) hire, and a nifty kitchen tent. There are also three bright, freshly carpeted rooms in the main building. If you're lucky, you might get to see the owner's smokehouse…quite amazing.

Hraunbrún (☎ 464 4103; sleeping-bag dm Ikr4000; sheet hire Ikr600) For cheap sleeps, try out these four-bed rooms in a Portakabin-style building; just pray your neighbours aren't noisy. There are good kitchen facilities and a shower block; check in at Hlíð camping ground.

Hótel Reykjahlíð (☎ 464 4142; www.reykjahlid.is; s/d/ tr Ikr19,800/25,500/30,900; P 🖵 📶) Owners María and Petur refurbished this lovely lakeside hotel in 2006. Its nine light rooms are now a delicate yellow, with billowing curtains and brand-new beds; all but one have bathtubs. The hotel has a bar and à la carte restaurant (open summer only) with the best views in town.

Hótel Reynihlíð (☎ 464 4170; www.myvatnhotel.is; s/d Ikr27,600/33,800; 🕑 Feb-Oct; P 🖵) The en-suite rooms of this smartish business hotel are modern and decorated in restful shades. British visitors will love the tea-making facilities. Almost half of the rooms have lake views. It has an upmarket restaurant serving Icelandic specialities. It also rents bicycles (Ikr1800 per day).

Eating options in Reykjahlíð are limited to the two hotel restaurants and **Gamli Bærinn** (☎ 464 4270; mains Ikr1700-2300; 🕑 10am-10pm mid-May–mid-Sep, to midnight Jul & Aug). This atmospheric 'country tavern' is a place of two halves. By day, it's a mellow cafe serving coffee, cakes, quiche and baguettes, while at night it becomes an effervescent bar-restaurant offering simple dishes – Arctic charr and chips, *plokkfiskur* and lasagne – and live entertainment.

Look out for dark, sticky *hverabrauð*, baked using geothermal heat. It's sometimes available at the gift shop next to Gamli Bærinn.

Getting There & Away

The main long-distance bus stop is outside Hótel Reynihlíð in Reykjahlíð. Buses between Mývatn and Akureyri also stop at Skútustaðir. From June to August, there's a daily bus (three per week rest of year) between Akureyri and Mývatn (Ikr2500, 1½ hours), continuing to Egilsstaðir (Ikr6100, two hours).

See p262 for information on buses to/from Húsavík.

See p275 for information on buses to/from Reykjavík via Sprengisandur.

JÖKULSÁRGLJÚFUR (VATNAJÖKULL NATIONAL PARK – NORTH)

Sticky-birch forests, orchids and bizarre rock formations fill the rift of **Jökulsárgljúfur** (☎ 465 2359, 465 2195; www.vatnajokulsthjodgardur.is), sometimes called 'Iceland's Grand Canyon'. One highlight is **Ásbyrgi**, a hoof-shaped chasm formed by a flood of biblical proportions from

JÖKULSÁRGLJÚFUR (VATNAJÖKULL NATIONAL PARK - NORTH)

a glacier 200km away. The swirls, spirals and strange acoustics at **Hljóðaklettar** (Echo Rocks) are similarly unearthly, and near the park's southern boundary is **Dettifoss**, Europe's most forcefully flowing waterfall, where around 200 cu metres of water per second thunder over the edge. This whole area was, until recently, called Jökulsárgljúfur National Park, but is now part of the massive Vatnajökull National Park.

Camping is limited to the large camping ground at **Ásbyrgi** (camp sites per adult Ikr900), which have all facilities; and smaller sites at **Vesturdalur** (camp sites per adult Ikr900), which have no showers, and **Dettifoss** (camp sites free), which are for hikers only. The camping grounds are open from June to mid-September. Food is available to purchase at the snack bar, supermarket and petrol station at the **Ásbyrgi farmstead** (Rte 85).

From 18 June to 31 August, daily scheduled buses run from Akureyri (Ikr5400, 3¼ hours) and Húsavík (Ikr3600, 1¾ hours) to major sites in the park.

There's also a daily Mývatn–Dettifoss (Ikr2500, 1½ hours) bus via Krafla (Ikr1200, 15 minutes), leaving at 11.30am from Hótel Reynihlíð in Reykjahlíð and returning from Dettifoss at 2pm.

THE EAST

Iceland's wild reindeer roam the mountains of the empty east, and Iceland's version of the Loch Ness monster calls the area home. The harsh, inhospitable highlands are a complete contrast to the sparkling fjords, which are surrounded by tumbling waterfalls and dotted with tight-knit communities, such as picturesque Seyðisfjörður. The east is also the site of Iceland's controversial aluminium smelter (see p234).

EGILSSTAÐIR

pop 2229

Egilsstaðir is a rather grey service town and the main regional transport hub. Its saving grace is lovely **Lagarfljót** (Lögurinn), Iceland's third-largest lake. Since saga times, tales have been told of a monster, the Lagarfljótsörmurinn, who lives in its depths. All amenities are clustered near the central crossroads, including the regional **tourist office** (☎ 471 2320; www.east.is; 9am-5pm daily year-round;) at the camping ground.

Sleeping & Eating

Camping ground (☎ 471 2320; info@east.is; Kaupvangur 10; camp sites per adult Ikr850, sleeping bag in dm Ikr2300, 5-person huts Ikr10,000; ⊗ year-round; 🖵) Camp sites are lined in utilitarian rows, but the facilities are good (including a kitchen, laundry and internet) and there are some dorm beds available.

Hotel Edda (☎ 444 4000; sleeping bag in dm/tw from Ikr1500/2000, s/d Ikr10,900/13,600; ⊗ Jun–mid-Aug) Based at the school opposite the swimming pool, off Tjarnarbrau, Hotel Edda's rooms have private bathrooms, and there's a restaurant with panoramic views.

Gistiheimilið Egilsstaðir (☎ 471 1114; www.egilsstadir.com; s/d Ikr13,700/18,200; ℗ 🖵) The town was named after this splendid heritage guesthouse and farm, 300m west of the crossroads, on the banks of Lagarfljót. Its sensitively renovated en-suite rooms retain a real sense of character. Breakfast is in the lakeside dining room, which also does a good Icelandic dinner buffet.

Café Nielsen (☎ 471 2626; Tjarnarbraut 1; lunch Ikr1300, dinner mains Ikr2000-3400; ⊗ 11.30am-11.30pm Mon-Thu, to 2am Fri, 1pm-2am Sat, to 11.30pm Sun) Based in Egilsstaðir's oldest house, this top choice straddles the divide between bustling bar and genteel restaurant. There's everything from vegieburgers to scallops with mango and chilli.

The **Shell petrol station** (Fagradalsbraut 13) at the top of town has a popular set lunch.

Getting There & Away

AIR

There are up to five **Flugfélag Íslands** (☎ 471 1210; www.airiceland.is) flights daily between Reykjavík and Egilsstaðir (Ikr15,720).

BUS

The main terminal in Egilsstaðir is at the camping ground. For Akureyri–Mývatn–Egilsstaðir buses, see p260 for Egilsstaðir–Höfn, see p268.

Between June and August, **Ferðaþjónusta Austurlands** (☎ 472 1515, 852 9250) operates two buses per day Monday to Friday, and one bus per day on Saturday and Sunday to Seyðisfjörður (Ikr800, 40 minutes), with three buses on Wednesday and Thursday.

TAXI

Ferry and bus connections are not too hot: if you get stuck, a **taxi** (☎ 892 9247) between Egilsstaðir and Seyðisfjörður costs around Ikr10,000.

SEYÐISFJÖRÐUR

pop 713

Things get lively when the Smyril Line's ferry *Norröna* sails majestically up the 17km-long fjord and docks at pretty little Seyðisfjörður (www.sfk.is). The picturesque multicoloured houses, snowcapped mountains and cascading waterfalls make the perfect welcome to Iceland.

The **tourist office** (☎ 472 1551; ⊗ 9am-noon & 1-5pm Mon, Tue, Wed & Fri, 9am-5pm Thu summer, noon-5pm Tue & Wed rest of year) is inside the ferry terminal.

Sights & Activities

We highly recommend a guided **kayaking trip** (☎ 865 3741; www.iceland-tour.com; 1/2/3hr Ikr2500/4200/5900; ⊗ Jun-Aug) out on the fjord, led by the good-humoured and informative Hlynur. More experienced paddlers can go on six-hour (Ikr10,000) or two-day trips (Ikr28,600) to Austdalur or Skálanes. Hlynur also does **mountain-bike tours** (two-hour trips Ikr3400); or hire a bike and go off on your own (half-/full day Ikr1700/3400).

The Seyðisfjörður to Vestdalur **hike** is a fine taste of the countryside, around Mt Bjólfur to the Seyðisfjörður–Egilsstaðir road.

Seyðisfjörður is full of 19th-century **timber buildings**, brought in kit form from Norway when the herring boom was at its height: read all about them in the brochure *Historic Seyðisfjörður* (Ikr200), available at the tourist office. For an insight into the town's fishing and telecommunications history, there's a worthwhile museum, **Tækniminjasafn Austurlands** (☎ 472 1596; Hafnargata 44; adult/under 18yr Ikr500/free; ⊗ 10am-5pm Jun–mid-Sep, 1-4pm Mon-Fri mid-Sep–May).

On Wednesday evenings in summer, live-music performances are held in the pretty **Blue Church** (Ránargata; tickets Ikr1500-2000; ⊗ 8.30pm Jul–mid-Aug).

Sleeping

Camping ground (☎ 472 1521, 472 1551; ferdamenning @sfk.is; Ránargata; camp sites per adult Ikr600) A pleasant, sheltered grassy camping ground with big hedges and picnic benches.

Hafaldan HI Hostel (☎ 472 1410; seydisfjordur @hostel.is; Ránargata 9; sleeping bag dm Ikr2300, sleeping bag d Ikr6200, d Ikr7200; 🖵) This cheerful arty hostel is split over two sites (facilities are shared). The original building has harbour views, a sunny lounge, newly fitted kitchen, laundry and internet access. The annexe used to

DETOURS: SKÁLENES

You might think Seyðisfjörður is the end of the line, but further retreat is possible. The remote farm **Skálanes** (☎ 690 6966; www.skalanes.com; sleeping bag Ikr5500 incl breakfast; ⌚ mid-May–mid-Sep), 19km east of Seyðisfjörður along the fjord edge, is a beautiful nature and heritage field centre, surrounded by sea cliffs full of abundant birdlife. Accommodation is very simple, although there is running water and a kitchen, and light meals may be provided on request.

Getting there is an adventure in itself. By foot, you could walk the 19km; you can get there on a mountain-bike or canoe hired from Hlynur (see opposite); the 4WD track is accessible for jeeps; or it may be possible for the centre to pick you up from Seyðisfjörður in a boat – contact them to ask.

be the old hospital, but you'd never guess; Indian hangings and funky old furniture make it homely.

Hótel Aldan (☎ 472 1277; www.hotelaldan.com; Oddagata 6) This place is split across three old wooden buildings. Reception and the bar-restaurant (where breakfast is served) are based at Norðurgata 2.

Snæfell (Austurvegur 3; s/d/tr Ikr18,500/24,300/27,700; Ⓟ) Cheaper rooms are here at this creaky, characterful three-storey old post office, with fresh white paintwork, draped muslin curtains and Indian bedspreads to add a splash of colour.

Old Bank (s/d/tr Ikr22,700/29,400/36,000; Ⓟ 💻) Houses a truly gorgeous boutique guesthouse with all mod cons. Its luxury rooms are bright, spacious and furnished with antiques, and beds snuggle under hand-embroidered bedspreads. Triple rooms have wicked alcoves.

Eating

Mini-Ciné (☎ 845 4883; www.thefreedomcouncil.com; Austurvegur 15; ⌚ 11am-6pm Jun-Aug) This cheerfully nutty addition to Seyðisfjörður's eateries combines a cafe and 12-seat 'microcinema' (the smallest in Europe), decorated entirely with 'found' items – fairy lights, vintage posters, old cameras, and tables made from packing cases. Food (soup, toast, waffles and cake) is super simple; mugs of tea and coffee are gigantic. Films start at 9pm daily, with film choice depending on 'favourable alignment of the planets and bribery'.

Skaftfell Café (☎ 472 1633; Austurvegur 42; snacks Ikr450-1100, mains Ikr2000-3500; ⌚ noon-10pm summer; 💻) This recommended, welcoming bistro-bar and internet cafe is a popular place with local artists and musicians. Snacks include omelettes, waffles and toast with caviar, and the freshly caught seafood is great.

Hótel Aldan (☎ 472 1277; Norðurgata 2; mains Ikr2600-3700; ⌚ 7am-9pm mid-May–mid-Sep) Coffee and light meals are served all day. In the evening, damask tablecloths, crystal wine glasses and flickering candles prettify the tables, and the menu features traditional Icelandic ingredients (eg lamb, lobster, reindeer, fish) with contemporary salads and sauces. The bar buzzes when the boat comes in. (Whale meat served.)

There's a **snack bar** (☎ 472 1700; Hafnargata 2) at the Shell petrol station, and a **Samkaup-Strax supermarket** (☎ 472 1201; Vesturvegur 1; ⌚ closed Sun).

Getting There & Away

For bus information, see opposite. Details of the ferry service from mainland Europe are on p286.

THE SOUTH

Containing glittering glaciers, toppling waterfalls, the iceberg-filled Jökulsárlón lagoon, and Iceland's favourite walking area Skaftafell, it's no wonder that the south is the country's most visited region. Various places along the coast offer skiing, ice-climbing, snowmobiling, dog-sledding and hiking opportunities; or head offshore to the charming Vestmannaeyjar (Westman Islands) to view the world's largest puffin colony.

Getting There & Away

Trex (☎ 587 6000; www.trex.is) and **Reykjavík Excursions** (☎ 562 1011; www.re.is) operate bus routes in the south.

Reykjavík–Kirkjubæjarklaustur–Skaftafell–Jökulsárlón–Höfn (Ikr11,200, 8½ hours) June to the end of August; it departs at 8.30am daily from Reykjavík and at 11am from Höfn. Eastbound from Reykjavík the bus passes Kirkjubæjarklaustur at 2.40pm (Ikr6600), Skaftafell at 3.45pm (Ikr8200) and Jökulsárlón at 4.45pm (Ikr9500). Westbound from Höfn it passes Jökulsárlón at noon (Ikr2100), Skaftafell at 1pm (Ikr3600) and Kirkjubæjarklaustur at 1.45pm (Ikr5200).

Skaftafell–Jökulsárlón (Ikr1800, 8.30am & 1pm) Mid-June to 31 August. Stops for two hours at the lagoon before returning.

Höfn-Stafafell–Egilsstaðir (Ikr6300, 3¼ hours) June to mid-September. Departs from Höfn at 8.30am, and from Egilsstaðir at 1.30pm daily. The bus passes Stafafell (eastwards towards Egilsstaðir at around 9am, westwards towards Höfn at around 4.30pm).

Reykjavík–Kirkjubæjarklaustur–Skaftafell, via Landmannalaugar (Ikr9000, 11 hours) Mid-June to 31 August. Departs from Reykjavík at 8.30am and from Skaftafell at 8.15am daily. The bus passes through Kirkjubæjarklaustur at 4.30pm eastbound and 9.15am westbound. Reykjavík Excursions.

STAFAFELL

pop 10

On the southeast coast between nowhere and nowhere, Stafafell is a lovely, lonely hiking area flanked by the **Lón lagoon** and the colourful **Lónsöræfi mountains**.

Wild-haired and welcoming, Bergsveinn is the good-humoured, knowledgable host of the area's only sleeping choice, **Stafafell Hostel** (☎ 478 1717; www.stafafell.com; sleeping bag in dm Ikr2200, s/d from Ikr4500/7000) – when he's not tending to his 500 sheep. The hostel is full of light pine fittings and bright sunshine, and has a peaceful feel. Meals are available in summer if reserved in advance, but bring back-up food. There's also a **camping area** (camp sites per adult Ikr600) and cottages for hire.

Mountain-bus tours (€11,700) to Kollumúli, in the Lónsöræfi mountains, are highly recommended and can be arranged at the hostel from June to August. The hostel can also advise on about a dozen local **walking routes**.

See above for information about scheduled buses.

VATNAJÖKULL

Mighty Vatnajökull is earth's largest icecap outside the poles. It's three times the size of Luxembourg (8300 sq km), reaches a thickness of 1km in places, and if you could find a pair of scales big enough, you'd find it weighed an awesome 3000 billion tonnes! Scores of glaciers flow down from the centre as rivers of crevassed ice.

In June 2008, **Vatnajökoll National Park** (www.vatnajokulsthjodgardur.is) was founded, joining the icecap and Skaftafell and Jökulsárgljúfur National Parks to form one 12,000 sq km megapark, which represents 11% of the entire country. In practice, not much has changed on the ground (although four new visitor centres at Skríðuklaustur, Höfn, Mývatn and Kirkjubæjarklaustur are due to be constructed over the next three years). According to some, the park's creation is mainly a political move to draw attention to the alarming speed at which the ice is melting.

Tours

From June to August, **Vatnajökull Travel** (☎ 894 1616; www.vatnajokull.is) operates a trip from Höfn to Jöklasel (near the edge of the ice), leaving at 8.30am. You arrive around 11am, allowing time for a bone-shaking one-hour skidoo ride. It returns via Jökulsárlón (below), where it's possible to take a boat ride on the lagoon, arriving back in Höfn at 5.15pm. The bus costs Ikr9600. Bus, skidoo and boat ticket combined will set you back Ikr27,000.

If you have your own transport, you can park at the junction of Rte 1 and F985, and then get a **Glacier Jeep** (☎ 478 1000; www.glacierjeeps.is; ☼ 9.30am & 2pm daily May-Oct) ride up the mountain. Jeep and skidoo ride costs Ikr12,500.

Warning

Hiking around the Jöklasel Hut isn't a good idea due to dangerous crevasses.

AROUND VATNAJÖKULL

Jökulsárlón

A ghostly procession of luminous-blue icebergs drifts through the 17-sq-km **Jökulsárlón lagoon**, before floating out to sea. This surreal scene (right next to the Ring Rd between Höfn and Skaftafell) is a natural film set: in fact, you might have seen it in *Batman Begins* (2005) and the James Bond film *Die Another Day* (2002). The ice breaks off from Breiðamerkurjökull glacier, an offshoot of Vatnajökull.

Boat trips (☎ 478 2222; info@jokulsarlon.is; ☼ 9am-7pm Jun-Aug, 9am-5pm late May & early Sep) among the 'bergs are available (Ikr2600).

See left for information about buses.

Höfn

pop 1632

Tiny Höfn makes a handy base for trips to the glacier. The tourist office is inside the **Jöklasýning Glacier Exhibition** (☎ 478 2665; www .joklasyning.is; Hafnarbraut 30; adult/under 16yr Ikr600/ free; ☺ 9am-9pm daily Jun-Aug, 1-6pm daily May & Sep, 1-4pm Mon-Fri Oct-Apr), which has two floors of interesting displays on Vatnajökull and the southeastern corner of Iceland as well as some altogether too-strange glacial mice.

Vatnajökull Travel (see opposite) runs **tours to the glacier**.

There's a **camping ground** (☎ 478 1606; www .campsite.is; Hafnarbraut 52; camp sites per adult Ikr900; ☺ late May–mid-Sep; ▢) that has 16 log cabins sleeping up to six people (Ikr8500 per night); there's a washer/dryer and cooking facilities, but you'll need your own pans.

At the harbour end of town, **Nýibær HI Hostel** (☎ 478 1736; hofn@hostel.is; Hafnarbraut 8; sleeping bag in dm Ikr2200, d Ikr5800; ℗) is a medium-sized place with laundry facilities. In high season, a second building round the corner welcomes in extra guests. Run by the same couple, **Gistiheimiliõ Hvammur** (☎ 478 1503; hvam mur3@simnet.is; Ránarslóõ 2; dm Ikr3000, s/d Ikr7300/9300; ▢), overlooking the boat-filled harbour, is the pick of the guesthouses for its smart rooms and internet connection. There are sinks and satellite TV in every room.

For business-class accommodation, try friendly **Hótel Höfn** (☎ 478 1240; www.hotelhofn.is; Víkurbraut; s/d from Ikr14,990/20,600; ℗ ▢), where many of the rooms look either out to sea or over the glacier. A brand-new extension, opened in 2008, contains larger (and better!) rooms. It also does formal meals, buffets and fast food, including some interesting pizza choices, in its two **dining rooms** (mains Ikr2000-4300; ☺ 9am-9pm).

Kaffi Horniõ (☎ 478 2600; Hafnarbraut; mains Ikr2100-4000; ☺ noon-10pm Mon-Thu, noon-1am Fri & Sat, 3-10pm Sun) is an informal log-cabin cafe-bar decorated with local artwork, and the food comes in stomach-stretching portions. There are a couple of vegie options and a Höfn speciality, garlic-toasted lobster, as well as burgers, pasta, fish mains and salads.

Opened during the 2007 Lobster Festival, rustic-style **Humarhöfnin** (☎ 478 1200; www .humarhofnin.is; Hafnarbraut 4; mains Ikr3000-5000; ☺ 5-10pm) specialises in cooking up pincer-waving little critters.

Buses (see opposite) leave from outside Hótel Höfn.

SKAFTAFELL (VATNAJÖKULL NATIONAL PARK – SOUTH)

Skaftafell, now part of the massive Vatnajökull National Park, encompasses a breathtaking collection of peaks and glaciers. It's the country's favourite wilderness: 160,000 visitors per year come to marvel at thundering waterfalls, twisting birch woods, and the brilliant blue-white Vatnajökull icecap.

The newly renovated **visitor centre** (☎ 478 1627; www.ust.is; ☺ 8am-9pm Jun-Aug, 10am-3pm May & Sep; ▢) contains exhibitions and film screenings about the area, and is staffed by people who really know their stuff.

Walking

Appearing on posters and calendars across the land, Skaftafell's most recognisable feature is **Svartifoss**, a gloomy waterfall that thunders over black basalt columns. Due to immense pressure in this area, rangers are encouraging visitors to explore elsewhere, for example, the easy one-hour return route to **Skaftafellsjökull**. The trail (wheelchair-accessible) begins at the visitor centre and leads to the glacier face, where you can witness the bumps, groans and brilliant blue hues of the ice. The **Icelandic Mountain Guides** (www.mountain guides.is; office ☎ 587 9999; summer base at Skaftafell ☎ 894 2959) lead invigorating glacier walks from April to mid-September (2½ hours costs Ikr4900; minimum age is 10 years).

In fine weather, the circular walk around **Skaftafellsheiõi** is a treat. There are some enjoyable day walks from the camping ground to **Kristínartindar** (1126m), **Kjós** or the glacial lagoon in **Morsárdalur**; plan on about seven hours for each return trip.

Tours

The Laki eruptions of 1783 caused utter devastation to the area. Over 30 billion tonnes of lava spewed from the Laki fissure, the largest recorded flow from a single eruption. The still-volatile **Lakagígar area**, with its spectacular 25km-long crater, is now part of the national park. In July and August, daily 11-hour **Kynnisferõir** (☎ 562 1011; www.re.is) trips from Skaftafell (Ikr10,500, at 8.30am) and Kirkjubæjarklaustur (Ikr7600, at 9.30am) visit the craters.

Sleeping & Eating

Book all accommodation ahead in summer, as Skaftafell is immensely popular.

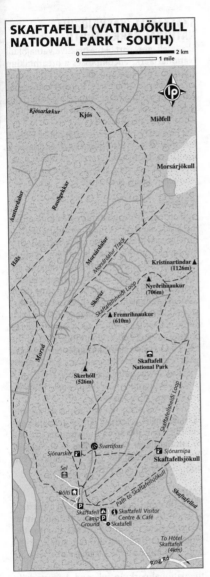

SKAFTAFELL (VATNAJÖKULL NATIONAL PARK - SOUTH)

A CART RIDE TO CAPE INGÓLFSHÖFÐI

The dramatic headland Ingólfshöfði is an isolated nature reserve close to Skaftafell. The only way to access this almost-island, 6km away over treacherous glacial sands, is by **tractor-towed haycart** (☎ 894 0894; www.hofsnes.com; rides lkr4000; ☺ at noon Mon-Sat early May–mid-Aug, plus 9am & 3pm Mon-Sat in Jul) – the departure point is signposted off the Ring Rd. Once there, local guides take you on a fascinating one-hour bird- and nature-walk along the 76m-high cliffs and grassy heath, teeming with puffins, guillemots, razorbills, gulls and great skuas.

---

zying views over the *sandur*. Accommodation is of the simplest kind – sleeping bags either in six-person bunk-bedded wooden huts, or in double rooms – but who needs a five-star hotel with that scenery to gaze at?

Hótel Skaftafell (☎ 478 1945; www.hotelskaftafell .is; Freysnes; s/d May-Sep 32,000/35,300, low season lkr16,800/19,300; ☺ Mar-Oct) At Freysnes, 5km east of the park, Skaftafell's 63 rooms (all with bathroom and TV) are functional rather than luxurious; rooms with glacier views cost a little more. The staff are helpful, and the convivial restaurant is the best place to eat in the area.

The visitor centre shop is the only place to get food inside the park.

Getting There & Away
See p267 for information about buses.

KIRKJUBÆJARKLAUSTUR
pop 114

Kirkjubæjarklaustur (which translates as 'church-farm-cloister') is a tiny settlement lost in the staggeringly vast and empty *sandur*. It's full of sights that hark back to its religious beginnings.

The **tourist information point** has moved around a lot in recent years, and will probably be sprouting up somewhere near the church in 2009. Wherever its location, opening hours will be 9am to 9pm from mid-June to August.

Kirkjugólf's regular basalt columns, cemented with moss, were once mistaken for an old church floor rather than a work of nature, and it's easy to see why. The 'floor' lies in a field about 400m northwest of the petrol station.

Camping ground (camp sites per adult over 16yr lkr900; ☺ Jun–mid-Sep) Camping is permitted only at this large, gravelly location (with laundry facilities), right by the visitor centre.

Bölti (☎ 478 1626; fax 478 2426; Skaftafellsheiði; sleeping bag in 6-person hut lkr3000; sleeping-bag d 7500; ☺ Mar-Oct) This farm, behind the western edge of the camping ground, is superbly located with diz-

Systrastapi (Sisters' Pillar) marks the spot where two nuns were reputedly executed and buried, after sleeping with the devil and other no-nos. **Systrafoss** is the prominent waterfall located near the hotel. The lake **Systravatn**, a short saunter up the cliffs, was once a place where nuns went to bathe.

There's a small **exhibition** (☎ 487 4645; Klausturvegur 2; admission Ikr500; ⊙ 9am-11am Tue-Fri, 2-6pm Sat & Sun Jun-Aug) of archaeological finds from the recently excavated convent. It also includes information on the tub-thumping Reverend Jón Steingrímsson, whose fervent praying stopped the 1783 lava flows.

See p269 for information about tours to the **Lakagígar craters**.

Sleeping & Eating

Kirkjubæ II camping ground (☎ /fax 487 4612; camp sites per adult Ikr750; ⊙ Jun-Aug) Pitch tents on the greensward under a pretty waterfall at this pleasant camping spot above town. Hot showers, kitchen and laundry facilities.

Hótel Klaustur (☎ 487 4900; www.icehotels.is; Klausturvegur 6; s/d from Ikr18,500/21,700) The 57-room Klaustur is run by Icelandair, but is not as sumptuous as other hotels in the chain. Rooms are clean and businesslike, although the walls are rather thin! The restaurant (mains Ikr2300 to Ikr4200) has an à la carte menu with typical Icelandic mains and some unusual starters – snails, anyone?

Systrakaffi (☎ 487 4848; Klausturvegur 13; light meals Ikr900-1700, mains Ikr1900-3500; ⊙ 10am-midnight, to 2am Fri & Sat Jun-Aug, 6-10pm Fri & Sat May & Sep) This ambient little cafe sells a variety of food including chilli-burgers, bacon-burgers, pizzas and reasonably priced fish and meat dishes, including a bouillabaisse-like seafood soup.

For freshly made fast-food snacks, there's the **Skaftárskáli petrol station** (☎ 487 4628).

Getting There & Away

See p267 for information about buses.

ÞÓRSMÖRK

The Woods of Thor is a stunning glacial valley, full of weird rock formations, twisting gorges, a singing cave, mountain flowers and icy streams. Its proximity to Reykjavík (130km) makes it a popular spot in summer, when tents pile up and the camping grounds become partyville. Luckily you don't have to go far to escape the crowds.

Wild camping is prohibited, but the three Þórsmörk huts have **camp sites** (per adult Ikr800) around them. The huts themselves have showers and cooking facilities; reservations are strongly advised, particularly for weekends.

For **Þórsmörk hut** (sleeping bag Ikr3300) make your booking through **Ferðafélag Íslands** (Map pp238-9; ☎ 568 2533; www.fi.is; Mörkin 6, Reykjavík). Bookings for **Básar hut** (sleeping bag Ikr2300) are through **Útivist** (Map pp238-9; ☎ 562 1000; www.utivist .is; Laugavegur 178, Reykjavík). For the **Húsadalur huts** (sleeping bag dm Ikr2800, sleeping bag d Ikr6800) book through bus company **Reykjavík Excursions** (Map pp238-9; ☎ 580 5400; www.thorsmork.is, www.re.is; Vatnsmýrarvegur 10, Reykjavík).

From mid-June to mid-September, buses run between Reykjavík and Húsadalur (over the hill from Þórsmörk) at 8.30am daily (Ikr5200, 3½ hours); from mid-June to August, a second service runs daily at 5pm. They also run a day tour (Ikr14,500) at 9am Monday, Wednesday, Friday and Saturday, with hotel pick-up.

Even though Þórsmörk seems tantalisingly close (only 30km from the Ring Rd), you *cannot* drive there without a 4WD: the gravel road surface eventually turns into boulders.

VESTMANNAEYJAR
pop 4036

Black and brooding, the Vestmannaeyjar islands form 15 eye-catching silhouettes off the southern shore. They were formed by submarine volcanoes around 11,000 years ago, except for sulky-looking Surtsey, the archipelago's newest addition, which rose from the waves in 1963. Ten years later, unforgettable pictures of Heimaey were broadcast across the globe when a huge eruption buried a third of the town under 30 million tonnes of lava. Surtsey was made a Unesco World Heritage Site in 2008, but its unique scientific status means that it is not possible to land there.

Heimaey is the only inhabited island. Its little town and sheltered harbour lie between dramatic *klettur* (escarpments) and two ominous volcanoes – blood-red Eldfell and conical Helgafell. Heimaey's cliffs are a breeding ground for 10 million puffin pairs – see the boxed text, p273.

At the time of writing, the **tourist office** (☎ 481 3322; www.vestmannaeyjar.is; Heiðarvegur; ⊙ 10am-6pm daily mid-May–mid-Sep) had moved to the main street, but was poorly stocked

ICELAND

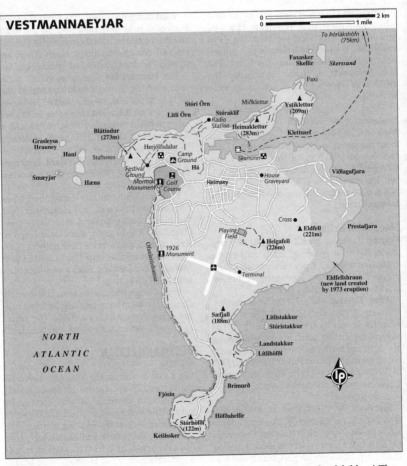

VESTMANNAEYJAR

DETOURS

As you're barrelling along the south coast, be sure to stop at the excellent **Skógar Museum** (☎ 487 8845; www.skogasafn.is; adult/12-15yr Ikr1000/400; ☯ museum 9am-6.30pm Jun-Aug, 10am-5pm May & Sep, 11am-4pm Oct-May), built by 87-year-old Þórður Tómasson. There are various restored buildings (church, turf-roofed farmhouse, school building, cowsheds etc) in the grounds, and a hangar-like building at the back houses an interesting transport museum, plus a cafe and souvenir shop. Nearby is the 62m waterfall **Skógafoss**, shrouded in mist and rainbows.

and being manned by schoolchildren! There are Sparisjóðurinn and Íslandsbanki banks with ATMs the post office. The library has internet access (Ikr200 per hour).

Sights & Activities

The **Aquarium & Natural History Museum** (Fiska-og Náttúrugripasafn; ☎ 481 1997; Heðarvegur 12; adult/child 6-13yr Ikr400/200; ☯ 11am-5pm mid-May–mid-Sep, 3-5pm Sun mid-Sep–mid-May) has fish tanks of hideous-looking Icelandic fish as well as a live video link to a puffin colony. There are fascinating photos of Heimaey's 1973 evacuation in the **folk museum** (Byggðasafn; ☎ 481 1194; Raðhússtræti; adult/child 6-13yr Ikr400/200; ☯ 11am-5pm Mon-Fri, 1-5pm Sat & Sun mid-May–mid-Sep), which was being completely overhauled at the time of

---

LITTLE NORTHERN BROTHERS

Iceland is famous for its puffins (Fratercula arctica). It's hard not to get dewy-eyed over these expressive, sociable little 'clowns of the ocean'; but really they're as tough as old boots, living out on the stormy winter seas and surviving on salt water.

It's easy to spot puffins: they're the clumsiest things in the air. Wings beat frantically 300 to 400 times per minute to keep them aloft, and the birds often crash-land. Underwater, it's a different story – their flight beneath the waves is so graceful that they were once thought to be a bird-fish hybrid.

Every spring, the puffins return to land to breed. They're discerning birds: 60% of the world's population choose to nest in Iceland. From late May to August, the best places to see them include offshore Reykjavík (p242), Látrabjarg (p256), and Heimaey (p271), which has the world's biggest puffin colony. Pufflings start leaving their nests in August. On Heimaey, the young birds are often confused by the town's lights, so every year the town's children stay up late to collect them and point them seawards.

Sadly, a sudden decline in sand eel numbers (the birds' main food source) has led to a corresponding drop in puffin numbers. It remains to be seen whether the populations will recover or continue to fade away. Puffins and their eggs are a traditional part of the Icelandic diet: if you can bring yourself to devour them, you'll often find them on restaurant menus.

---

research. A combined ticket costs Ikr750 per adult, and Ikr350 for children aged six to 13 years.

The explosive hour-long **Volcanic Film Show** (☎ 481 1045; Heiðarvegur; adult/6-12yr Ikr700/400; ☼ 11am, 2pm, 3.30pm & 9pm daily mid-Jun–Aug, 11am & 3.30pm May & Sep, by request at other times) plays at the local cinema, and includes footage on whales and puffin rappelling.

Four hundred buildings lie buried under the 1973 lava; on the edge of the flow is an eerie **House Graveyard** where beloved homes rest in peace. '**Pompei of the North**' (www.pompeinordursins.is) is a modern 'archaeological' excavation, where 10 houses are being dug up. So far, only the crumpled concrete remains of **No 25 Suðurvegur** have been unearthed.

Skansinn, the oldest structure on the island, is a ruinous 15th-century fort built by English marauders; nearby is a picturesque replica **Norse stave church** and an old water tower crushed by the 1973 lava.

Opportunities for **hiking** abound, including walks to Stórhöfði and up the volcanoes Helgafell and Eldfell. It's a treacherous 30-minute climb to the top of **Stóraklif**, 'assisted' by ropes and chains, but worth the terror for the breathtaking views.

Tours

From May to August, **Viking Tours** (☎ 488 4884; www.vikingtours.is; adult/9-14yr Ikr 5000/3400), in the small boats harbour, off Ægisgata, runs daily boat (10.30am and 3.30pm) and bus (1pm)

tours of the island, plus whale-watching and fishing trips on request. If nobody's about, ask in nearby Café Kró.

Sleeping

There are lots of guesthouses to choose from, but they fill up fast after the ferry arrives.

Herjólfsdalur Camp Ground (☎ 692 6952; camp sites per adult Ikr800; ☼ Jun-Aug) Cupped in the bowl of an extinct volcano, this dandelion-dotted camping ground has hot showers, a laundry room and cooking facilities. It's generally sheltered, but if the wind comes from the wrong angle, it can get rough!

Sunnuhöll HI Hostel (☎ 481 2900; www.hotelvestmannaeyjar.is; Vestmannabraut 28b; sleeping bag in dm from Ikr2200, s/d Ikr4200/6200) We have a soft spot for tiny, homely Sunnuhöll hostel, with its seven plain, neat rooms. The cheapest accommodation is in a (mixed) attic dorm. There's a guest kitchen and sitting room, and you can do laundry in Hótel Mamma across the road. Reception is at Hótel Þórshamar.

Gistiheimilið Hreiðrið (☎ 481 1045; http://tourist.eyjar.is; Faxastígur 33; sleeping bag/s/d/tr/q Ikr2500/4800/6900/9000/11,800) Run by the helpful volcano-show people, Ruth and Sigurgeir, this winning guesthouse has a family feel. Features include wall-to-wall puffins, a well-stocked kitchen and cosy TV lounge. There's bike hire, and Ruth also runs bus tours around the island (Ikr3400).

Hotel Þórshamar (☎ 481 2900; www.hotelvestmannaeyjar.is; Bárustígur 2; s/d/ste Ikr11,000/16,100/21,500 May-Sep, discounts at other times; (🖳) Iceland's first cinema is now a hotel, with pale, pleasant rooms and facilities including sauna, hot tubs and snooker room. Of the older rooms, No 209 is the best, tucked in the corner with its own balcony; otherwise go for the three new suites, all with big beds, modern decor and dark wood floors. The same family run several cheaper guesthouses – ask at reception for details.

Eating

Pizza 67 (☎ 481 1567; Heiðarvegur 5; pizza Ikr1100-1700; 🖳) Feathered friends are firmly off the menu: chomp crunchy garlic bread instead in a publike atmosphere.

Café Kró (☎ 488 4884; Harbour) This little harbourside cafe recently underwent an unlikely transformation and turned itself into a Chinese restaurant.

Café Maria (☎ 481 3160; Skólavegur 1; mains Ikr1900-3500; 🕙 11.30-1.30am Mon-Fri, to 1am Sat & Sun) A stuffed raven holds the specials board at this pleasantly down-home cafe-restaurant, which is quiet during the day but busy at night. Pizzas, burgers, savoury crêpes, and fresh fish and meat mains are served, including puffin.

Fjólan (☎ 481 3663; Vestmannabraut 28; mains from Ikr2000; 🕙 7am-11pm year-round) Next door to Hótel Þórshamar, this high-ceiling, gold-column place is the only proper restaurant on the island. The buffet breakfast is open to all; it serves probably the best fish on Heimaey. Staff are friendly and accommodating.

There's a great sit-down **bakery** (Bárustígur 7) and several cheap service-station grills. For self-catering, there's the central igloolike **Vöruval supermarket** (☎ 481 3184; Vesturvegur 18; 🕙 8am-7pm).

Getting There & Away

Air Iceland (☎ 570 3030; www.airiceland.is) flies two or three times daily to and from Reykjavík (Ikr9500, 25 minutes).

The **Herjólfur** (☎ 481 2800; www.herjolfur.is) sails May to August from Þorlákshöfn to the Vestmannaeyjar. It leaves at noon and 7.30pm daily, returning from the island at 8.15am and 4pm. The crossing takes 2¾ hours. The one-way fare per adult/12 to 15 years is Ikr2420/1210.

From Reykjavík, bus No 3/3a (Ikr1400) connects with the ferry, leaving Reykjavík at 10.40am and 5.50pm, returning from Þorlákshöfn at 11.30am and 6.50pm.

THE INTERIOR

The desolate interior is so vast, barren and remote that the Apollo astronauts held training exercises here before the 1969 lunar landings. The highlands are truly one of Europe's greatest remaining wilderness areas. There are practically no services, accommodation, mobile-phone signals and bridges, and no guarantees if things go wrong: careful preparations are essential. Routes are only accessible in July and August.

ROUTES OF CENTRAL ICELAND

Historically, the interior routes were used as summer short-cuts between north and south, places of terror to be traversed as quickly as possible. Some *útilegumenn* (outlaws) fled into these harsh highlands: those who survived gained legendary status, like the superhuman Grettir or Fjalla-Eyvindar, an Icelandic Robin Hood/Butch Cassidy figure.

Routes in this section are summer-only, and are strictly for high-clearance 4WD vehicles. It's recommended that vehicles travel in pairs.

Many mountain huts are run by Ferðafélag Íslands (Map pp238-9; ☎ 568 2533; www.fi.is; Mörkin 6, Reykjavík); accommodation is on a first-come, first-served basis, so book in advance. Facilities tend to be spartan, and if there are kitchens, they generally lack utensils.

Kjölur Route

The Kjölur Rte (35) was once believed to be infested with bloodthirsty outlaws. Nowadays, it's a favourite with visitors: it's greener and more hospitable than the Sprengisandur Rte, and it forms a neat short-cut between Reykjavík and Akureyri. The route's name (Keel) refers to the perceived shape of its topography.

Kjölur's main attraction is **Hveravellir**, a geothermal area of fumaroles and multicoloured hot pools at the northern end of the pass. A camping ground and two mountain huts with kitchens are run by Hveravallafélag (☎ 452 4200; www.hveravellir.is; camp sites per adult Ikr700, sleeping bag in dm/tw Ikr3500/5000, d Ikr14,000).

From 18 June to 4 September, **SBA-Norðurleið** (☎ 550 0770; www.sba.is) buses travel daily over the Kjölur Rte between Reykjavík and Akureyri (Ikr9900, nine hours), departing at 8am from both places. See also p287 for details on Reykjavík Excursions' Highlands Passport.

Sprengisandur Route

The Sprengisandur Rte (F26) may be less interesting than Kjölur, but it does offer some wonderful views of Vatnajökull, Tungnafellsjökull and Hofsjökull, as well as Askja and Herðubreið. The bus passes the photogenic waterfall **Aldeyjarfoss**, which topples over clustered basalt columns.

A good place to break your journey is **Nýidalur**, where there's a **camping ground** (camp sites per adult Ikr900), two Ferðafélag Íslands **huts** (☎ Jul & Aug 854 1194; sleeping bag Ikr3300; ☺ Jul & Aug) and numerous hiking possibilities. A recommended, challenging day hike takes you to the **Vonarskarð Pass** (1000m), a colourful saddle between Vatnajökull, Tungnafellsjökull and the green Ógöngur hills.

From July to August, **Reykjavík Excursions** (☎ 562 1011; www.re.is) buses operate between Landmannalaugar and Mývatn via Sprengisandur. They leave Landmannalaugar at 8.30am on Tuesday, Thursday and Sunday (Ikr10,400, 10 hours), and leave from outside Hótel Reynihlíð (Mývatn) at 8.30am on Monday, Wednesday and Friday.

Daily buses (Ikr6300, four hours) run between Reykjavík (depart 8.30am) and Landmannalaugar (depart 3pm), mid-June to 31 August. See also p287 for details on Reykjavík Excursions' Highlands Passport.

Öskjuleið Route (Askja Way)

Herðubreið and Askja on the Öskjuleið Rte (F88) are the most visited wonders of the Icelandic desert.

HERÐUBREIÐ

Iceland's most distinctive mountain, Herðubreið (1682m), has been described as a birthday cake, a cooking pot and a lampshade, but the tourist industry calls it (more respectfully) the 'Queen of the Desert'. The track around it makes a nice day hike from **Herðubreiðarlindir Nature Reserve**, a grassy oasis created by springs flowing from beneath the lava. There's a **camping ground** (camp sites per adult Ikr900) and **Þorsteinsskáli Hut** (sleeping bag Ikr2800; ☺ Jun-Aug), with basic kitchen, both run by **Ferðafélag Akureyrar** (Akureyri Touring Club; ☎ 462 2720; ffa@ffa.is).

ASKJA

Askja is an immense 50-sq-km caldera, created by a colossal explosion of tephra in 1875. Part of the volcano's collapsed magma chamber contains sapphire-blue **Öskjuvatn**, Iceland's deepest lake at 217m. At its northeastern corner is **Víti**, a hot lake in a tephra crater where the water (around 25°C) is ideal for swimming.

The two **Dreki Huts** (sleeping bag Ikr2800-3300) at **Drekagil** (Dragon Ravine), 8km away, accommodate 50 people, and are run by **Ferðafélag Akureyrar** (Akureyri Touring Club; ☎ 462 2720; ffa@ffa.is).

TOURS

For tours to the Askja caldera, see p263.

Kverkfjöll Route

The 108km-long Kverkfjöll Rte (F905, F910 and F902) connects Möðrudalur with the Ferðafélag Íslands' Sigurðarskáli hut. This is 3km from the impressive lower **Kverkfjöll ice caves**, where a hot river flows beneath the glacier, melting shimmering patterns on the ice walls. There are other (less impressive) ice caves higher up the glacier and a **hot waterfall** (30°C) at Hveragil, about a five-hour return walk from Sigurðarskáli; ask at the hut for directions.

The 85-bed **Sigurðarskáli hut** (sleeping bag Ikr3300) and camping ground can be booked through **Ferðafélag Fljótsdalshéraðs** (☎ 863 5813; ferdafelag@egilsstadir.is).

TOURS

The simplest way to visit Kverkfjöll is with **SBA-Norðurleið** (www.sba.is; 3-day tour Ikr25,000; Akureyri ☎ 550 0700; Reykjavík ☎ 550 0770), with tours departing from Akureyri (8.30am) and the tourist information office at Mývatn (11am) on Monday from early July to late August. Tours are just transport and a guide: you must organise your own accommodation and food. Warm clothing, a thick sleeping bag and strong boots are essential.

FJALLABAK NATURE RESERVE

The Fjallabak Rte (F208) is a spectacular alternative to the coast road between Hella and Kirkjubæjarklaustur. It passes through the scenic nature reserve to **Landmannalaugar**, an area of rainbow-coloured rhyolite peaks, rambling lava flows, blue lakes and hot springs, which can hold you captive for days. Much of the route is along (and in!) rivers and therefore unsuitable for 2WD vehicles.

The star attractions around Landmannalaugar are **Laugahraun**, a convoluted lava field; the soothing **hot springs** 200m west of the Landmannalaugar hut; multicoloured vents at **Brennisteinsalda**; the incredible red crater lake **Ljótipollur**; and the blue lake **Frostastaðavatn**, just over the rhyolite ridge north of Landmannalaugar. **Bláhnúkur**, immediately south of Laugahraun, offers a scree scramble and fine views from the 943m peak.

Ferðafélag Íslands' **hut** (☎ Jul-Sep 854 1192; sleeping bag Ikr3300) at Landmannalaugar accommodates 78 people on a first-come, first-served basis, and books up quickly with tour groups and club members. Others will probably have to use the **camping ground** (camp sites per adult Ikr900), which has toilet and shower facilities.

Getting There & Away

From mid-June to early September, **Reykjavík Excursions** (☎ 562 1011; www.re.is) run a scheduled Reykjavík–Skaftafell (Ikr11,400) bus, which goes by the scenic inland route, weather permitting, departing from Reykjavík and Skaftafell at 8.30am. Also see details for Reykjavík Excursions' Highlights, Highlands and Beautiful South Passports (p288).

LANDMANNALAUGAR TO ÞÓRSMÖRK TREK

The trek from Landmannalaugar to Þórsmörk deserves the same fame as great world walks such as the Inca Trail. The best map is Landmælingar Íslands' *Þórsmörk/ Landmannalaugar* (1:100,000), which you can purchase online through **Ferðakort's** (www.ferdakort.is).

The track is usually passable from mid-July to early September. You shouldn't have any problems if you're in reasonable condition, but don't take the walk at all lightly: it requires substantial river crossings, all-weather gear, sturdy boots and sufficient food and water.

Most people walk from north to south (because of the net altitude loss), taking three to four days. Some continue on to Skógar, making it a six-day trip (which can be difficult if bad weather strikes); huts along this stretch are operated by **Útivist** (Map pp238-9; ☎ 562 1000; www.utivist.is; Laugavegur 178, Reykjavík).

Public huts along the track have wardens, although dates when they're there vary from year to year. They can provide information on trail conditions. Huts may be booked out by tour groups; check with **Ferðafélag Íslands** (Map pp238-9; ☎ 568 2533; www.fi.is; Mörkin 6, Reykjavík) before you set out.

From Landmannalaugar hut, cross the **Laugahraun** lava field and ascend **Brennisteinsalda** (840m). Cross some rhyolite hills, then descend to the steaming vents at **Stórihver** and continue across the moors (covered in obsidian chunks and extensive snowfields) and a mountain pass to the **Hrafntinnusker hut**. From Hrafntinnusker, the track bounces over parallel rhyolite ridges before ascending steeply to a ridge studded with hot springs and fumaroles. Cross more ridges of descending altitude then drop steeply from the **Jökultungur** ridge into the **Álftavatn** valley, where a 4WD track leads to two **huts**.

There are several stream crossings south of Álftavatn; after 5km, you'll pass the privately owned **Hvanngil** hut and camping ground. Cross the footbridge over the Kaldaklofskvísl, follow the route posted 'Emstrur/Fljótshlíð' and ford the knee-deep Bláfjallakvísl. The track enters a lonely and surreal 5km stretch of black sand and pumice desert, skirting the pyramid-shaped peak, **Stórasúla**.

The next barrier is the river **Innri-Emstruá**, which is bridged but may have a knee-deep side channel. After the bridge, continue up to the crest and watch on your left for the 'FÍ Skáli' signpost, which directs you through a desolate desert to the **Botnar** (Emstrur) huts.

Cross a small heath then drop steeply to cross the roiling **Fremri-Emstruá** on a small footbridge. From there, the trail is relatively flat to the Ljósá footbridge.

Over the next hill is the more difficult unbridged river **Þrongá**. The onward route on the opposite bank isn't obvious; look for a V-shaped ravine just west of the marked crossing point. There, the track enters the **Þórsmörk** woodland. When you reach a junction, the right fork leads to Reykjavík Excursions' **Húsadalur hut** and the left fork to the Ferðafélag Íslands' **Þórsmörk hut**. Camping is restricted only to sites near the huts. For more information on Þórsmörk, see p271.

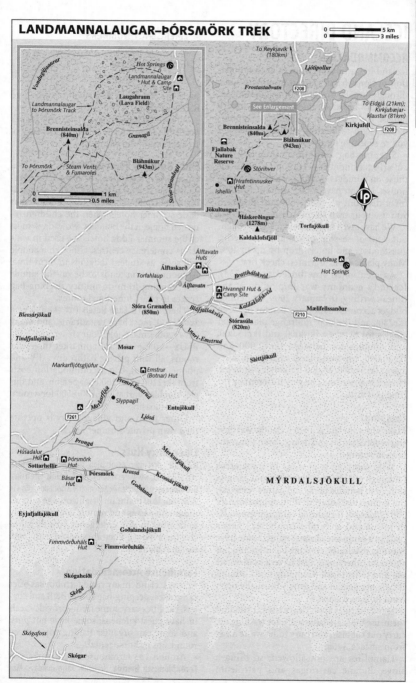

LANDMANNALAUGAR–ÞÓRSMÖRK TREK

ICELAND

ICELAND DIRECTORY

ACCOMMODATION

Iceland has a full spectrum of accommodation options, from spartan mountain huts, through hostels, working farms, guesthouses and school-based summer rooms, to luxury hotels. Walls, even in upmarket accommodation, tend to be thin – bring earplugs if you're sensitive to noise.

Sleeping-bag accommodation is a peculiarly Icelandic concept, and a boon for those on a budget. Many hostels and guesthouses let you have a bed without bedding for a discount on their standard prices, if you use your own sleeping bag.

We have given high-season prices throughout. Out of season, prices at some B&Bs, guesthouses and hotels drop by up to 40%. Many places close in winter; check first.

As mentioned (see boxed text, p233), Iceland's economy was imploding at the time of writing. In January 2009, we defined budget accommodation as a bed for between Ikr2300 and Ikr8000; midrange places offer singles for between Ikr8000 and Ikr15,000, and doubles for between Ikr12,000 and Ikr20,000; top-end places charge an average of Ikr24,000/28,000 for singles/doubles. However, prices may be very different by the time you visit.

Camping

Make sure your tent is up to Icelandic weather: storm-force winds and deluges aren't uncommon in summer.

Wild camping is possible in some areas (although not on fenced land without permission, or in national parks and nature reserves), but is often discouraged. With approximately 130 tjaldsvæði (organised camping grounds) in towns and at rural farmhouses, there's usually a camp site close at hand. Some have washing machines, cooking facilities and hot showers; others may just have a cold-water tap and toilet block. Camping costs around Ikr900 per person and grounds usually open from June to August.

Standard rules apply: leave sites as you find them, use biodegradable soaps for washing up, carry out rubbish, and bury toilet waste away from surface water.

Campfires are not allowed, so bring a stove. Butane cartridges and petroleum

fuels are available in petrol stations and hardware shops.

A free directory Útilega: Tjaldsvæði Íslands (available from tourist offices) lists many of Iceland's camping grounds.

Edda Hotels & Summer Hotels

Once, when Icelandic kids from remote regions were sent away to be educated at boarding schools, the school buildings doubled as basic summer hotels when the children returned home in the holidays. Nowadays, most of the summer Edda hotels are used in winter as conference centres, although a couple still serve as student lodgings in term time. Accommodation tends to be on the simple side, ranging from dormitory sleeping-bag spaces to plain, functional rooms.

There are 13 **Edda Hótels** (☎ 444 4000; www .hoteledda.is); most have restaurants, and many have geothermal pools. Four are termed 'Edda PLUS' – these contain upmarket three-star rooms, all with private bathrooms, TV and phone. Sleeping-bag accommodation costs from Ikr2100 to Ikr2600 per person, and singles/doubles start at Ikr6800/8500 for a room with washbasin.

Other town and village schools operate their own private summer hotels.

Emergency Huts

ICE-SAR (Icelandic Association for Search & Rescue; ☎ 570 5900; www.icesar.com) and **Félag Íslenskra Bifreiðaeigenda** (Icelandic Automobile Association; ☎ 414 9999; www.fib.is) maintain bright-orange huts on mountain passes and remote coastlines, only to be used in dire emergency (it's illegal to stay there if not). They are stocked with food, fuel and blankets.

Farmhouse Accommodation

Across Iceland, many rural farmhouses offer camp sites, sleeping-bag space, B&B and chalets. Facilities vary: some farms provide meals or have guest kitchens; some have hot pots; and some can organise fishing trips, sheep round-ups or horse rental.

Around 133 farmhouses are members of **Ferðaþjónusta Bænda** (Icelandic Farm Holidays; Map pp238-9; ☎ 570 2700; www.farmholidays.is; Síðumúli 2, Reykjavík), which publishes an annual listings guide. Twenty-five are wheelchair-accessible; see the website for details.

Guesthouses

There are various types of *gistiheimilið* (guesthouses), from private homes that let rooms to custom-built motels. Most are comfortable and homey, with kitchens, TV lounges, and buffet-style breakfast (either included in the price, or for around Ikr1000 extra). Some will also offer sleeping-bag accommodation.

As a general guide, sleeping-bag accommodation costs Ikr3000 to Ikr7000 (excluding breakfast); double rooms range from Ikr10,000 to Ikr20,000; self-contained flats cost between Ikr12,000 and Ikr30,000.

A high percentage of places open from June to August only. Students often take over Reykjavík guesthouses from September to May.

Hotels

Every major town has at least one upmarket business-style hotel, usually with somewhat bland but comfortable rooms and all the expected amenities. Prices for singles/doubles start at around Ikr18,000/22,000, usually including a buffet breakfast. Two of the largest home-grown chains are **Fosshótels** (☎ 562 4000; www.fosshotel.is), and **Icelandair Hotels** (☎ 444 4000; www.icehotels.is), which also runs the Edda chain (opposite).

Mountain Huts

Sæluhús (mountain huts) sprout up on popular hiking routes, mostly in wilderness areas. Accommodation is of the rough-and-ready variety: sleeping-bag spaces in communal huts. Some huts have cooking facilities, a warden and camping outside. The huts are open to anyone, but members get a discount. Please do book in advance, as places fill quickly.

The main mountain-hut provider is **Ferðafélag Íslands** (Icelandic Touring Association; Map pp238-9; ☎ 568 2533; www.fi.is; Mörkin 6, Reykjavík), with huts at 13 sites around Iceland. When appropriate, we've given further contact details in this chapter. Sleeping-bag space costs nonmembers from Ikr2000 to Ikr3300; camping (where available) is around Ikr900 per person.

Youth Hostels

Iceland has a network of 25 superb youth hostels, administered by the **Bandalag Íslenskra Farfugla** (Icelandic Youth Hostel Association; Map pp238-9; ☎ 553 8110; www.hostel.is; Sundlaugavegur 34, Reykjavík). All hostels have hot showers, cooking facilities, luggage storage and sleeping-bag accommodation, and almost all have family rooms. If you don't have a sleeping bag, you can hire sheets and blankets (Ikr800 per stay). Most are open summer-only (we strongly advise you to book ahead), so phone before rolling up out-of-season.

Join **Hostelling International** (HI; www.hihostels.com) before you arrive to benefit from HI member discounts. For a dorm bed, HI members pay around Ikr2100 (children aged five to 12 years pay half-price), with a surcharge of Ikr1600, if you want a room to yourself. Breakfast (where available) costs around Ikr1000 extra.

ACTIVITIES
Dogsledding

For exhilarating, summertime glacier-top action, driving your own huskies is hard to beat. **Dog Steam Tours** (☎ 487 7747; www.dogsledding .is) offers sledging on Mýrdalsjökull – contact them for details.

Fishing

Salmon fishing seems like a great idea but a one-day licence may cost anything up to Ikr200,000, making your catch some of the world's most expensive fish! However, you can fish for rainbow trout, sea trout and Arctic char on a more reasonably priced voucher system. Trout fishing runs from April to mid-September, and ice fishing is possible in some areas in winter. For further information, contact the **National Angling Association** (☎ 553 1510; www.angling.is).

Hiking, Trekking & Mountaineering

The best way to see the country is undoubtedly on foot, whether on an afternoon hike or a two-week wilderness trek. However, the weather can leave careful plans in tatters: rain, fog and mist are common, and snow may fall in any season at higher altitudes. The website www.outdoors.is gives very good general information about mountaineering and hiking in Iceland.

In the highlands, straightforward hiking only becomes possible in July, August and early September. At other times, routes are impassable without complete winter gear; and in late spring, melting snow turns many tracks into quagmires where whole vehicles have sunk without trace! Unbridged rivers can be difficult to cross at any time of year.

There are stunning hikes and treks all over the country, including in national parks and nature reserves; only the most well-used trails are marked. The most popular walks are in the deserted Hornstrandir peninsula (p256), in the lake-dominated Mývatn area (p262), around Skaftafell (p269), and the Landmannalaugar to Þórsmörk trek (p276) in the highlands. If you are into mountaineering, there are some serious routes, including Hvannadalshnúkur (2119m), Iceland's highest peak. For information on hiking maps, see p283.

Use caution when walking with children, especially in fissured areas such as Mývatn and Þingvellir, where narrow cracks in the earth can be hundreds of metres deep. Tough boots are needed for negotiating lava fields.

For details on hiking and mountaineering, contact **Ferðafélag Íslands** (Map pp238-9; ☎ 568 2533; www.fi.is; Mörkin 6, Reykjavík), **Íslenski Alpaklúbburinn** (www.isalp.is/english), or the **Icelandic Mountain Guides** (Map pp238-9; ☎ 587 9999; www .mountainguides.is; Vagnhöfði 7b, Reykjavík).

Horse Riding

The Icelandic horse *(Equus scandinavicus)* was brought over by the first settlers, and was prominent in the development of the country. These sweet-natured, small but sturdy animals are perfectly suited to the rough Icelandic terrain and are still used for farm work. They are also ridden recreationally, and are known for their *tölt*, a smooth, distinctive gait that makes riding easy, even for beginners.

You can hire horses through farms and tour agencies throughout the country, with a two-hour/one-day ride costing Ikr 10,000/17,000. In September you can also volunteer for the *réttir* (sheep round-up); contact local tourist offices to arrange this.

Kayaking

Paddling gently along the edges of a fjord is a fantastic way to soak up the silence and feel an intrinsic part of Iceland's wild and lovely landscape. Watch sheep munching seaweed on the shore, look out for seal heads bobbing on the water, and get close to hunting seabirds in Stykkishólmur (p253), Ísafjörður (p254) and Seyðisfjörður (p266).

Rafting

The best option for rafting is with **Activity Tours** (Ævintýraferðir; ☎ 453 8383; www.rafting.is; May-Sep) at the small service town of Varmahlíð in the north of the country. The company runs various day trips on three nearby rivers. The tamest is the three-hour Family Rafting (Ikr6500), suitable for over 12s and oldies; and the most exhilarating is the six-hour trip, for over-18s, which introduces you to Iceland's wildest white water on the Austari Jökulsá (East Glacial River; Ikr9800) with Grades III to IV-plus rapids. If you can't get enough of this entrancing canyon with its surging green-white water, there's also a three-day adventure (Ikr59,800) that speeds you downstream from the Sprengisandur desert and the river's glacial source.

The company's headquarters is just off the Ring Rd (all buses between Reykjavík and Akureyri pass by). They have cottages for rent, or there are two camp sites and a hotel in town, and plenty of farmhouse accommodation in the area – contact the local **tourist office** (☎ 455 6161; www.visitskagafjordur.is; 9am-4pm Mon-Fri, 1-5pm Sat & Sun) for further information.

Scuba Diving & Snorkelling

Visibility of 100m sounds like a crazy dream, but the glacial water in Lake Þingvellir is vision-bendingly clear. The friendly folk at **Dive .is** (☎ 663 2858; www.dive.is; 2 dives at Þingvellir Ikr34,000) run daily tours year-round to the Silfra fissure in the lake, giving you the chance to dive between the North American and European continental plates. Scuba-diving certification is required; nondivers can drift overhead with drysuits and snorkels. The company also runs three- and seven-day diving tours to other sites around the country – see the Tour Calendar on their website for dates and details.

Skiing

Skiers who enjoy out-of-the-way slopes will find some pleasant no-frills skiing in Iceland. In winter, nordic skiing is possible throughout the country, although drawbacks include lack of transport in rural areas, bitterly cold winds and absence of daylight. Both Reykjavík (see www.skidasvaedi.is) and Akureyri (see www .hlidarfjall.is) have winter resorts for downhill skiing, with ski rental and instructors. One-day lift passes cost around Ikr2200 and ski hire Ikr2500. Ísafjörður's annual skiing week (see p254) is good fun, if the weather obliges.

Snowboarding

The Reykjavík and Akureyri ski resorts have facilities for snowboarders, with one-day snowboard rental for around Ikr2500. Bláfjöll has a dedicated snowboarding track.

Swimming

Thanks to an abundance of geothermal heat, every town has at least one *sundlaug* or *sundhöll* (public swimming hall), some with saunas, Jacuzzis and slides. Admission costs around Ikr360/180 per adult/child. And of course there are spa centres such as the Blue Lagoon (p250) and Mývatn Nature Baths (p263).

Whale-Watching

Iceland is one of the best places in the world to see whales and dolphins. Quiet oak-hulled boats minimise disruption to the creatures and can get astonishingly close. Regular sailings depart from Húsavík (p260) and Reykjavík (p242), and on demand in the Vestmannaeyjar (p273). A three-hour trip costs around Ikr8000, and there are sailings from mid-May to September (in winter, the whales migrate south).

BUSINESS HOURS

Most banks are open from 9.15am to 4pm Monday to Friday. Shops are usually open from 9am to 6pm on weekdays, 10am to noon or 4pm on Saturday. Petrol stations stay open until 10pm generally and supermarkets stay open to 9pm daily. Liquor stores open from 11am to 6pm Monday to Thursday, to 7pm Friday and to 2pm on Saturday. Cafes and bars open from 10am to 1am Sunday to Thursday and stay open late until 3am or 6am on Friday and Saturday nights, and restaurants are usually open from 6pm to 10pm. Post offices open from 9am to 4.30pm Monday to Friday.

CHILDREN

Icelanders have a relaxed attitude to kids, but there are not many activities provided especially for them. Frequent bad weather may put you off family camping, but everyone can enjoy a ride on a mild-mannered Icelandic horse (opposite).

Children aged between two and 11 years pay half fare on Flugfélag Íslands (Air Iceland) flights and tours, and are charged half-price for farmhouse and some other accommodation. Bus fares are half price for children aged four to 11. Reykjavík Excursion tours are free for children under 11, and half fare for those aged between 12 and 15. There's a 50% discount at pools, and admission to museums and cinemas varies from full price to free.

Every town has an open-air swimming pool, which will delight water babies. Reykjavík contains some attractions suitable for little kids, such as the family fun park and zoo (p242) and feeding the birds on Tjörnin (p242). The most suitable museums for older children are the open-air Árbæjarsafn (p241) and the dramatic Saga Museum (p240).

CUSTOMS

Visitors are permitted to import up to 3kg worth of food provided it doesn't cost more than Ikr18,500 or include animal products.

Those aged over 18 years may bring in 200 cigarettes or 250g of other tobacco products. Those aged over 20 years may import duty-free 1L of spirits (21% to 79% alcohol) and 1L of wine (less than 21%); or 1L of spirits and 6L of foreign beer; or 1.5L of wine and 6L of beer; or 3L of wine.

To prevent potential contamination, recreational fishing and horse-riding clothes require a veterinarian's certificate stating that they have been disinfected, otherwise officials will charge you for disinfecting clothing when you arrive. It is illegal to bring used horse-riding equipment (saddles, bridles etc) into the country.

Vehicle import duty is waived for students and visitors staying less than one month (extendable up to 12 months), but vehicles cannot be sold without payment of duty.

For a full list of customs regulations, see www.tollur.is.

DANGERS & ANNOYANCES

Iceland has a low crime rate, police don't carry guns, and prisoners go home on public holidays. People aren't the danger here; it's nature that you need to be wary of! In geothermal areas avoid thin crusts of lighter-coloured soil around steaming fissures and mud pots. Snowfields may overlie fissures, sharp lava chunks, or slippery slopes of scoria (volcanic slag). Don't underestimate the weather: only attempt isolated hiking and glacier ascents if you know what you're doing. The super-cautious can read www.safetravel.is for further information.

EMBASSIES & CONSULATES

A full list of Iceland's embassies and consulates is available at www.mfa.is.

The following countries have representation in Reykjavík:

Canada (Map p240; ☎ 575 6500; rkjvk@international.gc.ca; Túngata 14)

Denmark (Map p240; ☎ 575 0300; www.ambreykjavik.um.dk; Hverfisgata 29)

Finland (Map p240; ☎ 510 0100; www.finland.is; Túngata 30)

France (Map p240; ☎ 575 9600; www.ambafrance.is; Túngata 22)

Germany (Map p240; ☎ 530 1100; embager@internet.is; Laufásvegur 31)

Ireland (☎ 554 2355; davidsch@islandia.is; Ásbúð 106, 210 Garðabær)

The Netherlands (Map pp238-9; ☎ 533 1002; holland@holland.is; Borgartún 33)

Norway (Map p240; ☎ 520 0700; www.noregur.is; Fjólugata 17)

Sweden (Map pp238-9; ☎ 520 1230; www.sweden abroad.com; Lágmúli 7)

UK (Map p240; ☎ 550 5100; www.britishembassy.gov.uk; Laufásvegur 31)

USA (Map p240; ☎ 562 9100; www.usa.is; Laufásvegur 21)

FESTIVALS & EVENTS

In addition to the festivals here there are arts festivals and sports tournaments whose dates vary from year to year. For forthcoming live music festivals, see www.musik.is.

February

Þorrablót This midwinter feast is marked with knuckle-whitening meals; see p235 for a sample menu.

Bolludagur (Bun Day; Monday before Lent) Icelanders gorge themselves sick on puff-pastry cream buns. Kids get up early to 'beat' the buns out of their parents with a 'bun wand' (bolluvöndur).

Sprengidagur (Bursting Day; Ash Wednesday) The feast continues. The aim is to stuff yourself with saltkjöt og baunir (salted mutton and split peas) until you burst. Both are Lenten traditions.

March

Beer Day (1 March) Dating back to the glorious day in 1989 when beer was legalised in Iceland. As you'd expect, Reykjavík's clubs and bars get particularly wild.

April

Skíðavíkan/Aldrei Fór Ég Suður (week after Easter) Ísafjörður's combined Skiing Week and free music festival is small but loved by those in the know.

Sumardagurinn Fyrsti (First Day of Summer) Arrives optimistically early on the first Thursday after 19 April, with Reykjavík holding the biggest carnival-style bash. (The First Day of Winter, Fyrsti Vetrardagur, on the third Saturday of October, does not inspire similar merriment.)

May

Reykjavík Arts Festival (www.artfest.is) The city is taken over by local and international theatre performances, films, lectures and music during this two-week event.

June

Sjómannadagurinn The first Sunday is dedicated to seafarers. The Seamen's Union sponsors a party in each coastal town.

Independence Day (17 June) The largest nationwide festival, commemorating the founding of the Republic of Iceland in 1944 with parades and general merriness. Tradition has it that the sun isn't supposed to shine. And it usually doesn't!

Midsummer Celebrated around 24 June in Iceland, but with much less fervour than on the Scandinavian mainland.

August

Þjóðhátíð Vestmannaeyjar This earth-shaking event occurs in Heimaey on the August bank holiday, commemorating the day in 1874 when foul weather prevented the islanders partying when Iceland's constitution was established.

Verslunarmannahelgi Also celebrated on the August bank holiday, the rest of the country celebrates with barbecues, horse competitions, camping and family reunions. Wild boozing takes place in the national parks and at Þórsmörk.

Gay Pride (www.gaypride.is) Thousands of people parade carnival-style through the streets of Reykjavík around the second weekend.

Reykjavík Marathon (www.marathon.is) With shorter distances and fun runs for those who like to grit their teeth less. Held during the daytime before Culture Night.

Culture Night Held on a Saturday in Reykjavík in mid-August, with art, music, dance and a grand fireworks finale.

September

Réttir In the highlands, the autumn sheep roundup is an occasion for rural camaraderie and festivities.

Reykjavík International Film Festival (http://isl.riff.is) This annual occurrence sees blockbusters make way for international art films in cinemas across the city, and talks from film directors from home and abroad.

Reykjavík Jazz Festival (www.jazz.is) Another fun yearly cultural event is the Jazz Festival with jazz concerts around the city.

October

Iceland Airwaves (www.icelandairwaves.com) This five-day event, held in Reykjavík in the third week of October, is one of the world's most cutting-edge music festivals: don't expect to sleep.

GAY & LESBIAN TRAVELLERS

Icelanders have a fairly open attitude towards gays and lesbians. For specific information, contact the gay and lesbian organisation **Samtökin '78** (Map p240; ☎ 552 7878; www.samtokin78.is; 4th fl, Laugavegur 3, Reykjavík), which doubles as an informal community centre and drop-in cafe (8pm to 10.30pm Monday and Thursday). See the website www.gayice .is for news and events.

HOLIDAYS

The following annual holidays are observed in Iceland:

New Year's Day 1 January
Maundy Thursday Thursday before Easter
Good Friday to Easter Monday March/April
First Day of Summer 1st Thursday after 18 April
Labour Day 1 May
Ascension Day May
Whit Sunday & Whit Monday May
Independence Day 17 June
Shop & Office Workers' Holiday First Monday in August
Christmas Eve 24 December (afternoon)
Christmas Day 25 December
Boxing Day 26 December
New Year's Eve 31 December (afternoon)

INTERNET RESOURCES

Iceland Review – What's On guide (www.whatson.is)
Icelandic Tourist Board (www.icetourist.is)
Icelandic Tourist Board – North America (www
.goiceland.org)
Statistics Iceland (www.statice.is)
Visit Reykjavík (www.visitreykjavik.is)

LEGAL MATTERS

Drink-driving laws are very strict in Iceland; one drink can put you over the legal limit of 0.05% blood-alcohol content. The penalty is loss of your licence plus a large fine.

Penalties for possession, use or trafficking of illegal drugs are strict, with long prison sentences and heavy fines.

The legal age for drinking alcohol in Iceland is 20.

MAPS

Ask tourist offices for the free *Map of Reykjavík* and *Around Iceland* booklets (with bags of information plus town plans).

The maps, originally produced by Landmælingar Íslands (National Land Survey of Iceland), are now purchasable from **Ferðakort** (Map pp238-9; ☎ 562 3376; www.ferdakort.is; Brautarholt 8, Reykjavík; ⏰ 10am-5pm Mon-Thu, 10am-4pm Fri), through their website or at their brand-new dedicated map shop in Reykjavík. Most drivers use the general 1:500,000 *Ísland Touring Map*. Also useful are the 1:25,000 and 1:100,000 maps of Skaftafell, the 1:50,000 map of the Vestmannaeyjar, and the 1:100,000 maps of Hornstrandir, Mývatn and the Landmannalaugar-to-Þórsmörk trek.

Maps are also available from tourist offices and bookshops all over Iceland.

MEDIA
Magazines

The free fortnightly **Grapevine** (www.grapevine .is) magazine is an excellent read for Icelandic news and forthright reviews. It's available online, or from tourist offices, hotels, bars and bus stations.

The slicker English-language magazine **Iceland Review** (Map pp238-9; ☎ 512 7575; www .icelandreview.com; Borgartún 23, Reykjavík) is available on subscription for US$40 per year (four issues).

Newspapers

Iceland's main daily newspaper is *Morgunblaðið*. German-, French- and English-language periodicals are available at large bookshops throughout the country.

Radio & TV

The BBC World Service is relayed at FM 94.3 (Reykjavík only). Icelandic TV stations broadcast subtitled British and American programmes during prime time.

MONEY

Icelandic VAT is included in the prices of goods. However, if you spend over Ikr4000 in a shop offering 'Iceland Tax-Free Shopping', you can claim back up to 15%. Shop staff will give you a tax-refund form; hand it in at the tourist office, the airport or the ferry terminal for a rebate. If you spend over Ikr40,000, take your forms and goods to customs before checking in.

ATMs

You can draw cash from any bank using MasterCard or Visa, and from Glitnir using

Diners Club. Exchange rates for ATM cards are usually good.

Credit Cards
MasterCard and Visa are accepted everywhere; Diners Club and American Express are less commonly used. Icelanders use cards for grocery shopping and other small purchases.

Moneychangers
Travellers cheques in foreign denominations, postal cheques and bank notes may be exchanged for Icelandic currency at banks for a small commission (commission-free at Landsbanki Íslands). Beware of using other exchange offices; commissions can reach 8.75% and exchange rates are lower. Any leftover krónur may be exchanged for foreign currency before departure.

Tipping
As service and VAT are always included in prices, tipping isn't required in Iceland.

POST
The **Icelandic postal system** (Pósturinn; www.postur .is) is both reliable and efficient. An airmail letter or postcard to Europe costs Ikr95/105 for economy/priority mail; to places outside Europe it costs Ikr105/140.

Poste restante is available in all cities and villages, but Reykjavík is best set up to handle it. Mail should be addressed with your name to Poste Restante, Central Post Office, Pósthússtræti 5, IS-101 Reykjavík, Iceland.

TELEPHONE
For information about public telephone boxes in Reykjavík, see p237. Elsewhere, there's usually a phone outside the post office or in the petrol station. Many payphones accept credit cards. Be aware that telephone directories are alphabetised by first name, so Guðrun Halldórsdóttir would be listed before Jón Einarsson.

Mobile Phones
Most European phones are compatible with the GSM network used in Iceland in populated areas; for information, contact your phone company. The NMT network covers the interior and other remote regions.

It may be worth buying a pre-paid SIM card (Ikr2500 including Ikr2000 of free call credit), from grocery shops and petrol sta-

tions, which allows you to make calls at local rates. You'll need an unlocked phone for this to work.

Phone Codes
Direct dialling is available to Europe, North America and elsewhere. After dialling the international access code (☎ 00 from Iceland), dial your country code, area/city code and the telephone number.

For dialling into Iceland from abroad, the country code is ☎ 354. There are no area codes: just follow the country code with the seven-digit number.

Within Iceland, just dial the seven-digit number. Most Icelandic mobile phone numbers begin with the digit '8'.

Directory assistance (international) ☎ 1811
Directory assistance (local) ☎ 118
Operator assistance (information) ☎ 114
Operator assistance (to place a call) ☎ 115

TIME
Iceland is always on GMT/UTC, and it has no daylight-saving time. So from late October to late March, Iceland is on the same time as London, five hours ahead of New York and 11 hours behind Sydney. In the northern hemisphere's summer, Iceland is one hour behind London, four hours ahead of New York and 10 hours behind Sydney.

TOURIST INFORMATION
You'll find tourist offices with friendly staff in towns all over the country. Pick up the useful *Around Iceland* (general tourist guide) and *Áning* (accommodation guide); both are annual publications and they're free.

The **Icelandic Tourist Board** (Map p240; ☎ 535 5500; www.icetourist.is; Lækjargata 3, Reykjavík) is the umbrella organisation in charge of tourism. The main tourist office in Reykjavík is **Upplýsingamiðstöð Ferðamála** (Map p240; ☎ 590 1550; www.visitreykjavik.is; Aðalstræti 2, Reykjavík).

TOURS
Iceland's many private tour-bus operators are an excellent option if you're short of time, or want to access beautiful but remote locations without hassle. Most companies run in conjunction with adventure-tour operators, so you can also book snowmobile, horse-riding, whale-watching, rafting, hiking,

bird-watching or Northern Lights tours. You can often do the same trips by Super Jeep or Super Truck (prices are at least double those of a bus tour). The following is a brief list of some of the best tour companies.

Dick Phillips (☎ 01434-381440; www.icelandic-travel .com; Whitehall House, Nenthead, Alston, Cumbria, CA9 3PS) British-based Dick Phillips runs a specialist Icelandic travel service, and has decades of experience leading wild hiking, cycling and skiing trips.

Ferðafélag Íslands (Icelandic Touring Association; Map pp238-9; ☎ 568 2533; www.fi.is; Mörkin 6, Reykjavík) Leads summer treks in Hornstrandir, Landmannalaugar and Þórsmörk, and also has some bus tours and cross-country skiing trips.

Iceland Excursions (Gray Line; Map pp238-9; ☎ 540 1313; www.icelandexcursions.is; Höfðatún 12) Bus-tour operator with comprehensive day trips, plus horse riding, whale-watching, underground explorations, diving, and self-drive holidays.

IcelandTotal (Map pp238-9; ☎ 585 4300; www .icelandtotal.com; Lágmúli 4, Reykjavík) All the standard day trips, plus special-interest tours, eg bird-watching, fishing, cycling.

Nonni Travel (Map p258; ☎ 461 1841; www.nonni travel.is; Brekkugata 5, Akureyri) Specialists in excursions to Greenland.

Reykjavík Excursions (Kynnisferðir; Map pp238-9; ☎ 580 5400; www.re.is; BSÍ Bus Terminal, Vatnsmýrarve-gur 10, Reykjavík) The largest bus-tour operator has summer and winter programmes. Extras include horse riding, snowmobiling, and themed tours tying in with festivals.

Útivist (Map pp238-9; ☎ 562 1000; www.utivist.is; Laugavegur 178, Reykjavík) Day trips and weekend hiking tours.

TRAVELLERS WITH DISABILITIES

Many hotels, restaurants and large shops have facilities for people with disabilities. The airlines can take disabled passengers, as can two of the coastal ferries, the *Baldur* and the *Herjólfur*. Flugfélag Íslands offers discounts to disabled travellers. Facilities aren't available on scheduled bus services, but tours on specially equipped buses can be arranged. For details, contact the tourist information centre in Reykjavík, or the organisation for the disabled, **Sjálfsbjörg** (Map pp238-9; ☎ 550 0360; www .sjalfsbjorg.is; Hátún 12, Reykjavík).

VISAS

The Schengen Agreement means that those from Austria, Belgium, Denmark, Finland, France, Germany, Greece, Italy, Luxembourg, the Netherlands, Norway, Portugal, Spain and Sweden can enter Iceland for up to three months as a tourist with a valid identity card.

Citizens of the European Economic Area (EEA), including Ireland and Great Britain, can visit for up to three months on a passport that is valid for at least three months from their date of arrival.

Citizens from America, Australia, New Zealand, Japan and Canada can travel in Iceland without a visa for up to three months within any six-month period, with the time limit beginning on the first entry to any Schengen Agreement nation.

Other nationalities should check www.utl .is to see whether they require a visa before arriving in Iceland.

VOLUNTEERING

A volunteering holiday is a good (and relatively cheap) way of getting intimately involved with Iceland's people and landscape. The **British Trust for Conservation Volunteers** (BTCV; www.btcv.org) works closely with the Environment Agency of Iceland, placing volunteers at Skaftafell (p269), Jökulsárgljúfur (p265), and Mývatn (p262) and Fjallabak (p275) nature reserves.

WORK

Members of EEA countries have the right to move to Iceland to look for work. Others will have to secure an offer of work and a work permit before moving to the country. See the **Icelandic Directorate of Immigration** (www .utl.is) for residency information.

The economic crash has had disastrous consequences for Icelandic workers, with the unemployment rate trebling between September and November 2008. However, if you're still determined to work in Iceland, your best bet is the employment agency **Nínukot** (☎ 561 2700; www.ninukot.is; PO Box 12015, 132-Reykjavík), which sources au pairs and seasonal workers for the farming and fishing industries.

TRANSPORT IN ICELAND

GETTING THERE & AWAY
Air

Keflavík airport (☎ 425 6000, flight times 425 0777; www.keflavikairport.com), 48km west of Reykjavík, is Iceland's main gateway. Flights to/from Greenland and the Faroe Islands use Reykjavík domestic airport in the city centre.

ICELAND

From June to August, 12 flights per week from Copenhagen land at tiny Akureyri airport, in Iceland's northern 'second city'.

Fares in this section are general indications only, and are for average-priced high-season return tickets. Cheaper deals are generally available if you are flexible, or if you travel in the low season.

AIRLINES FLYING TO & FROM ICELAND

Only a few airlines have scheduled flights to Keflavík, Reykjavík and Akureyri airports. All have great safety records:

Atlantic Airways (airline code RC; ☎ Faroe Islands 34 10 00; www.atlantic.fo)

Eagle Air (FEI; ☎ 562 2640; www.eagleair.is)

Flugfélag Íslands (Air Iceland; NY; ☎ 570 3030; www.airiceland.is)

Icelandair (FI; ☎ 505 0700; www.icelandair.com)

Iceland Express (HW; ☎ 550 0600; www.icelandexpress.com)

SAS (SK; ☎ 588 3600; www.flysas.com)

CONTINENTAL EUROPE

There are regular direct Icelandair flights to Keflavík from Amsterdam (€450), Bergen (Nkr3600), Copenhagen (Dkr2000), Frankfurt (€560), Göteborg (Skr4400), Helsinki (€440), Munich (€560), Oslo (Nkr2800), Paris (€520), Stavanger (Nkr4000) and Stockholm (Skr3000), most of which take approximately 3½ hours. Icelandair also has seasonal flights between Keflavík and Barcelona, Berlin and Milan, taking between six and nine hours.

Iceland Express flies year-round between Keflavík and Copenhagen (Dkr2000, three hours) up to 12 times weekly, and between Keflavík and Berlin (€450, 3½ hours) up to three times weekly. In summer, there are one to three flights weekly between Keflavík and Aalborg, Barcelona, Basel, Billund, Bologna, Eindhoven, Frankfurt Hahn, Friedrichshafen, Göteborg, Genf, Stockholm and Warsaw (all around €450, between three and four hours); and between Akureyri and Copenhagen (Dkr2600, three hours).

SAS runs direct flights from Keflavík to Oslo (Nkr3000, 2¾ hours).

GREENLAND & THE FAROE ISLANDS

In summer, Flugfélag Íslands flies from Reykjavík to Greenland: to Kulusuk (Ikr90,000, two hours) six times a week; and to Narsarsuaq (Ikr90,000, two hours) twice weekly.

Flugfélag Íslands and Atlantic Airways fly between the Faroe Islands and Reykjavík (Ikr90,000, 1½ hours) up to four times weekly from April to October.

UK

Icelandair (☎ 0870 787 4020; www.icelandair.com) has flights to Keflavík from London Heathrow (UK£250, two hours) at least twice daily, and once a day from Manchester (UK£420, 1½ hours). At the time of writing, flights from Glasgow had been temporarily suspended.

Internet-based airline **Iceland Express** (☎ 0870 850 0737; www.icelandexpress.com) flies up to twice daily (less frequently in winter) from London Gatwick to Keflavík (UK£250, three hours).

From Ireland, the cheapest way is to fly with **Ryanair** (www.ryanair.com) from Dublin to London Gatwick, where you can catch the Iceland Express flight to Keflavík.

USA & CANADA

There are daily Icelandair flights between Keflavík and Boston and New York, and several flights a week between Keflavík and Orlando (also Minneapolis from April to October). Online return fares from New York to Keflavík cost about US$1200; the flight takes around six hours.

Summer flights also operate between Keflavík and Halifax and Toronto (around CA$900, six hours).

If you're flying with Icelandair from the US or Canada to Britain or Europe, you can include a free stopover in Iceland as part of your travel itinerary.

Sea

You can travel to Seyðisfjörður in eastern Iceland from Hanstholm or Esbjerg (Denmark) and Tórshavn (Faroe Islands) by the **Smyril Line**'s (www.smyril-line.com) smart car-ferry *Norröna*. See p501 for booking information.

GETTING AROUND
Air

There's an extensive network of domestic flights in Iceland, the fastest way to get from place to place. Flexible travel plans are essential, though, since schedules are dependent on the weather.

Flight prices given in the chapter are for full-fare one-way tickets; however, there are often internet offers, and you may be able to snap up standby tickets for up to half-price. There are significant discounts for senior citizens, students and children.

The main domestic airline, **Flugfélag Íslands** (Air Iceland; ☎ 570 3030; www.airiceland.is), has daily flights in summer (fewer in winter) between Reykjavík and Akureyri (Ikr14,090, 45 minutes), Egilsstaðir (Ikr15,720, one hour), Ísafjörður (Ikr14,090, 40 minutes) and the Vestmannaeyjar (Ikr9510, 25 minutes). Eagle Air has flights to several small domestic airstrips, including Höfn (Ikr11,800, one hour). All prices are inclusive of domestic airport tax.

AIR PASSES

Flugfélag Íslands offers four-/five-/six-sector air passes costing Ikr43,420/50,000/57,780 plus airport tax (Ikr1180). These are valid for one month and must be bought outside Iceland. There's also a Fly As You Please ticket which gives 12 days of unlimited internal flights for Ikr59,220.

Bicycle

Cycling is an interesting if hardcore way to view Iceland's incredible landscape. Gale-force winds, sandstorms, sleet and sudden flurries of snow add to the challenge. Bring the best waterproofing money can buy; and remember, you can always put your bike on a bus if things become intolerable. A mountain bike is probably more practical than a touring rig – you can get off the Ring Rd onto minor roads and unsurfaced tracks. It is wise to bring plenty of spares and several puncture repair kits. The Kjölur Rte through the interior has bridges over all major rivers, so it's accessible to cyclists.

Domestic airline flights charge Ikr3200 per bicycle. You can carry bikes on long-distance buses (Ikr1500), but space may be a problem at busy times.

In areas best suited to cycling, such as Mývatn, Reykjavík and Akureyri, bicycle hire costs around Ikr3500 per day, plus deposit. Children under 15 must wear a helmet by law.

The **Icelandic Mountain Bike Club** (Map pp238-9; ☎ 562 0099; www.fjallahjolaklubburinn.is; Brekkustígur 2) and **Icebike** (www.icebike.net) have lots of information and links about touring in Iceland.

Boat

The main car ferries operating in Iceland are *Herjólfur* (p274), between Þorlákshöfn and Vestmannaeyjar; *Baldur* (p254), between Flatey, Stykkishólmur and Brjánslækur; and *Sæfari* (p260), between Dalvík, Hrísey and Grímsey.

Bus

Iceland's long-distance bus network is divided between several private companies who provide routes in different areas of the country. They're overseen by **BSÍ** (Bifreiðastöð Íslands; ☎ 562 1011; www.bsi.is), based in the BSÍ bus terminal on Vatnsmýrarvegur in Reykjavík. The booking desk sells tickets, and distributes the free *Ísland á Eigin Vegum* (Iceland on Your Own) brochure, which contains timetable information for some southern journeys. From June to August, there are regular buses to most places on the Ring Rd, and to larger towns in the Westfjords. During the rest of the year, the service is limited or nonexistent; check with BSÍ or the following companies for details. The main bus companies include the following:

Reykjavík Excursions (Kynnisferðir; ☎ 580 5400; www.re.is) Reykjanes Peninsula and the Flybus to Keflavík airport, plus tour buses (including summer buses across the interior).

SBA-Norðurleið (☎ 550 0700, 550 0770; www.sba.is) Northeast Iceland.

Stjörnubílar (☎ 456 5518; www.stjornubilar.is) Westfjords.

Trex (Bílar og Fólk; ☎ 587 6000, 553 3737, 551 1166; www.trex.is) South, west and north Iceland.

BUS PASSES

A new, improved set of bus passes are now available, allowing you to pick and choose the routes that serve you best.

Available from Trex:

Full-Circle Passport (Ikr30,000; ☾ Jun-Aug) Valid for one circuit of the Ring Rd in one direction, stopping wherever you like.

Full-Circle Passport/Western Fjords (Ikr44,500; ☾ Jun-Aug) As for the Full-Circle Passport, plus one circuit of the Westfjords, reached only via the ferry *Baldur* (from Stykkishólmur).

Snæfellsnes Passport (Ikr13,800; ☾ mid-Jun–Aug) Valid for one circuit of Snæfellsnes Peninsula, starting and ending in Reykjavík.

West Iceland & Westfjords (Ikr21,000; ☾ Jun-Aug) Valid for one circuit of the Westfjords, to/from Reykjavík via Snæfellsnes Peninsula and Brú.

Available from Reykjavík Excursions:

Highlights Passport (7-/9-/11-/13-/15-day pass Ikr33,500/41,500/47,500/53,000/58,000; ☙ mid-Jun–Aug) Unlimited travel on Reykjavík Excursions' bus routes 6, 9, 11, 112, 14, 15 and 16, and SBA-Norðurleið's bus routes 610, 641 and 661. Will get you to Þingvellir, Gullfoss and Geysir; Landmannalaugar, Þórsmörk, Lakagígar, Jökulsárlón and across the Sprengisandur route.

Highland Circle Passport (Ikr30,500; ☙ Jul-Aug) Valid for one circular route to the north of Iceland via the Sprengisandur and Kjölur routes, on Reykjavík Excursions' bus routes 11, 14 and 112 and SBA-Norðurleið's bus routes SBA1 and 610.

Beautiful South Passport (3-/5-/7-/9-/11-day pass Ikr17,000/25,500/31,000/37,000/42,000; ☙ Jun–Aug). Unlimited travel along the south coast and to Þórsmörk and Lakagígar on Reykjavík Excursions' bus routes 6/6a, 9/9a, 11/11a, 112/112a, 15 and 16.

Beautiful South – Circle Passport (Ikr15,500; ☙ mid-Jun–Aug) A more limited version of the Beautiful South Passport, this will get you as far as Skaftafell, and inland to Landmannalaugar along routes 11/11a and 112/112a.

Car & Motorcycle
AUTOMOBILE ASSOCIATION
The Icelandic national motoring association is **Félag Íslenskra Bifreiðaeigenda** (FÍB; ☎ 414 9999; www.fib.is). Membership is only open to Iceland residents. However, if you already have breakdown cover with an automobile association that's affiliated to ARC Europe, you may be covered by the FÍB – check with your home association.

BRING YOUR OWN VEHICLE
It's relatively easy to bring a vehicle on the ferry from Denmark. Drivers must carry the vehicle's registration documents, proof of valid insurance (a 'green card') and a driving licence (EU, North American and Australian licences are fine; otherwise you may need an international driving permit). After vehicle inspection, an import permit, which lasts for a month, will be issued, after which you must export the vehicle or apply for a permit extension. Contact the **Directorate of Customs** (☎ 560 0300; www.tollur.is) for further information. See also p506.

FUEL & SPARE PARTS
Petrol prices vary: unleaded 95 octane (*blýlaust, 95 okt*) costs around Ikr139.7 per litre, and diesel Ikr164.1. Leaded petrol and LRP (lead replacement petrol) aren't available. Outside Reykjavík, petrol station opening hours vary, but out-of-hours there's usually a self-service pump that will accept Ikr500, Ikr1000 and Ikr2000 bank notes, or Visa/MasterCard. Service stations can be quite widely dispersed; make sure you fill up when you have the chance, and carry a jack, jumpleads, spare tyre etc. Getting stranded on a cold and lonely road is no fun at all.

HIRE
Although rates are expensive by international standards, prices compare favourably against bus or internal air travel. The cheapest vehicles, such as a Toyota Yaris, normally cost around Ikr22,000 per day, with unlimited mileage and VAT included. Rental charges for 4WD vehicles are at least twice that. The Reykjavík tourist office keeps details of special offers. It's often much cheaper to book a car over the internet before you get to Iceland – see p507.

You must be at least 20 years old to hire a car in Iceland, and will need to show a recognised licence (most firms are happy with your home licence, although you could bring an international driving permit to be on the safe side) and pay by credit card.

ROAD CONDITIONS & HAZARDS
Icelandic highways aren't suitable for high speeds – they're two-lane affairs, often narrowing to a single-lane over bridges, and there are sometimes long unsurfaced sections. Headlight and radiator protection from dust and rocks is advisable. Road edges are often steeply cambered, with no shoulders or margins. Beware of oncoming cars driving in the middle of the road.

Four-wheel-drive vehicles are needed on the F-numbered (interior) highway system. If you're planning to drive through the interior, do so with an accompanying vehicle – there are no services, and glacial rivers and drifting sand pose real threats. It goes without saying that you'll need full tool/repair kits (and the expertise to use them) and emergency supplies. It's illegal to drive off-road or off-track: Icelandic soil and vegetation are extremely fragile, and damage caused by vehicles can be irreparable.

Current road conditions can be seen on the website of the **Icelandic Meteorological Office** (www.vedur.is/english), or phone ☎ 1777.

ROAD RULES

Drive on the right and keep your headlights on at all times. The use of seat belts (front and rear) is compulsory. In urban areas, the speed limit is 50km/h or less. On paved/unpaved roads, the speed limit is 90/80km/h. Drink-driving laws are very strict in Iceland and the legal limit is set at 0.05% blood-alcohol content. The penalty for driving over the limit is loss of your licence plus a large fine. Talking on a mobile phone whilst driving is illegal unless using a hands-free kit.

Slow down or give way at blind peaks (marked *blindhæð*) and on single-breadth bridges (marked *einbreið brú*).

Hitching

Lonely Planet does not recommend hitching. Summer hitching is possible but can be inconsistent. The best idea is to find a petrol station, then try to charm drivers who have stopped for a break. At least if waits are long, you can get a coffee! See also p508.

Norway

NORWAY

There's a reason why 19th-century landscape painters continually obsessed over Norway: at almost every corner staggeringly beautiful wilderness lurked to overwhelm their artistic sensibilities. Today that wilderness, various and downright sublime, remains shockingly intact and offers terrain for some of the world's most scenic skiing, hiking and fishing.

Narrow, steep fjords bring dramatic sea valleys deep into rugged farm country topped by blue glaciers. These fjords are easily explored by public ferry and treks along their walls provide some of the most inspiring sights you will experience in life. Along the way you'll encounter dragon-like stave churches from the 13th century.

Much of Norway is above the Arctic Circle, home to the midnight sun, the polar night's gloomy darkness and the aurora borealis. Amid these phenomena are Lofoten's fishing villages and Tromsø, a university town that makes a convenient polar gateway. At the top of mainland Europe is Finnmark, a desolate tundra where you can ride dogsleds into the emptiness. If you still aren't impressed, continue to Svalbard for polar bears and a genuine frontier.

Norway's major cities are picturesque, with districts of old wooden buildings, harbours of fishing boats and plenty of cafes, whose outdoor terraces fill with overeager Norwegians from the very moment the long winter ends. Oslo and Bergen are the biggest cities, and each enjoys esoteric museums (think Viking ships and leprosy), lively nightlife and public transport that takes you straight into the wilderness. Norwegians love festivals (from sheep head feasts to arctic film screenings), though by:Larm and its hundreds of indie bands reigns supreme.

FAST FACTS

- **Area** 385,200 sq km
- **Capital** Oslo
- **Currency** krone (Nkr): €1 = Nkr8.73;
  US$1 = Nkr6.59; UK£1 = Nkr9.72;
  A$1 = Nkr4.77; C$1 = Nkr5.47;
  NZ$1 = Nkr3.71; ¥100 = Nkr6.76
- **Famous for** canned fish, fjords, Vikings
- **Official Language** Bokmål and Nynorsk
- **Phrases** *hei* (hello), *takk* (thanks), *ja* (yes), *nei* (no), *stengt* (closed)
- **Population** 4.7 million
- **Telephone codes** country code ☎ 47; there are no regional codes; international access code ☎ 00
- **Visa** not necessary for most nationalities

CONNECTIONS

Trains and buses link Norway with Russia, Sweden and Finland (p384). Frequent ferries head to Germany and Denmark from several Norwegian ports (p384). Airports in Oslo and Bergen connect Norway to the world, and distant Tromsø, way up in the Arctic Circle, fittingly has direct flights to the warmth of Madrid. Other small international airports can get you to many destinations within Scandinavia (p383).

HIGHLIGHTS

- Sleep in a fisherman's *robu* (shanty) in a remote village on the craggy **Lofoten Islands** (p363).
- Explore lively **Bergen** (p331), whose hilly coastal locale and delightful urban fabric make for excellent strolling and drinking.
- Ruin future attempts to appreciate nature by glimpsing the incomparable beauty of **Hardangerfjord** (p341) or **Sognefjord** (p343).
- Hike or ski across the sublime **Jostedalsbreen glacier** (p345).
- Dogsled (see boxed text, p377) your way across the vast emptiness of Finnmark far past the Arctic Circle.

ITINERARIES

- **One week** Spend a day in Oslo, then catch a train to Bergen. Spend two nights there before taking an unrushed jaunt around Hardangerfjord. Continue to Sognefjord, stay in Balestrand and visit glaciers around Fjærland. Return to Bergen then head to Oslo.
- **Two weeks** After returning to Bergen, take the *Hurtigruten* to medieval Trondheim. Continue to the fishing villages of craggy Lofoten. Explore for a couple days, then take the *Hurtigruten* to Tromsø, where you might catch some midnight sun before returning to Oslo.

CLIMATE & WHEN TO GO

The rainy climate of mainland Norway is surprisingly mild for its latitude; thanks to the Gulf Stream's warming effects, all coastal ports remain ice-free throughout the year, though it can get very cold in mountainous areas away from the coast. Heavy winter snowfalls are common everywhere. See p486 for average temperatures and rainfalls in major cities.

Norway is at its best and brightest from May to September. Peak tourist season is mid-June through August.

HISTORY

Norway's first settlers arrived around 11,000 years ago with the end of the ice age. As the glaciers melted, the earliest hunters and gatherers moved in from Siberia, pursuing migrating reindeer herds. You can see the prehistoric rock drawings of these hunters in the far north on Alta (p373). Shortly afterwards, nomadic European hunters arrived in the south of the country.

Norway greatly impacted Western civilisation during the Viking Age, a period usually dated from the plundering of England's Lindisfarne monastery by Nordic pirates (AD 793). Through the next century, the Vikings conducted raids throughout Europe and established settlements in the Shetland, Orkney and Hebridean islands, the Dublin area (Ireland) and in Normandy (named after the 'North men'). The Viking leader Harald Hårfagre (Fairhair) unified Norway after the decisive naval battle at Hafrsfjord near Stavanger in AD 872; King Olav Haraldsson, adopting the religion of the lands he had conquered, converted the Norwegians to Christianity and founded the Church of Norway in 1024. See Viking artefacts firsthand in Oslo's Vikingskipshuset (p297) and Lofotr Vikingmuseum (p366) in Lofoten.

MIDNIGHT SUN & POLAR NIGHTS

Thanks to Earth's tilt, the polar regions constantly face the sun at their solstices and then turn away during the winter. The Arctic Circle (N66° 33') is the northern limit of constant daylight on the longest day of the year. The northern half of mainland Norway is situated within this circle, but even in southern Norway the sun never sinks far below the horizon. In June and July you won't experience true darkness anywhere. Conversely, winters are dark and long. In Tromsø, for example, the midnight sun lasts from 20 May to 22 July, while the polar night runs from 25 November through to 17 January. Not surprisingly, most northern communities make a ritual of welcoming the sun the first time it peeks above the horizon.

NORWAY

0 — 200 km
0 — 120 miles

SVALBARD

Svalbard
Jan Mayen
NORWAY

Same Scale as Main Map

Nordaustlandet

Ny Ålesund
Spitsbergen
Barentsøya

Longyearbyen
Barentsburg
Sveagruva
Edgeøya

To Jan Mayen

To Norway mainland

ARCTIC
OCEAN

BARENTS
SEA

Nordkapp
Honningsvåg

Hammerfest
Tana Vardø
Bru Vadsø

Kirkenes
E6 Storskog
Alta E6
Finnmark
Karasjok
Finnmarksvidda
Kautokeino

NORWEGIAN
SEA

Mefjordvær
Fjordgard;
Husøy
Skaland
Gryllefjord Tromsø
Andenes Finnsnes
Tromsø

Stokmarknes
Nyksund
Melbu Sortland Harstad E6
Svolvær Narvik
Stamsund Storjord
Skutvik

See Lofoten
Map (p365)

Kjerringøy

BODØ Fauske
Sattstraumen
Nordland

Arctic Circle

Svartisen
IceCap
Mo i Rana

Mosjøen

FINLAND

RUSSIA

ATLANTIC
OCEAN

SWEDEN

Steinkjer

E6 **Nord**
Trøndelag

TRONDHEIM E14
Hell
Sør
Trøndelag

Røros

See Western Fjords &
Central Norway Map (p332)

ÅLESUND **Åndalsnes**
Måløy E136
Nordfjord Geiranger Dombås
Stryn **Rondane**
Galdhøpiggen ▲ E6
(2469m)
Balestrand **Jotunheimen**
Lærdal Lillehammer
Sognefjorden Flåm E16 Hamar
Voss Geilo
Finse
BERGEN
Odda **Hardangervidda**
Rjukan
Haukeligrend Notodden
Buskerud **OSLO**
Telemark Kongsberg
Bø Moss
Haugesund **SKIEN** **FREDRIKSTAD**
Tau Kragerø Larvik Halden
STAVANGER Risør
E39 **Sørlandet**
Lillesand Arendal
Mandal Grimstad *Skagerrak*
KRISTIANSAND

Bottenhavet

HELSINKI

STOCKHOLM

TALLINN

ESTONIA

BALTIC
SEA

E18

E6

NORWAY

The Viking Age declined after 1066, with the defeat of the Norwegian king, Harald Hardråda, at the Battle of Stamford Bridge in England. Norwegian naval power was finished off for good when Alexander III, King of Scots, defeated a Viking naval force at the Battle of Largs (Scotland) in 1263.

In the early 14th century, Oslo emerged as a centre of power and a period of growth followed until 1349, when the bubonic plague swept the country, wiping out two-thirds of the population. In 1380, Norway was absorbed into a union with Denmark that lasted more than 400 years.

Denmark ceded Norway to Sweden in 1814. In 1884 a parliamentary government was introduced in Norway and a growing nationalist movement eventually led to a peaceful secession from Sweden in 1905. In a referendum, Norwegians voted in favour of a monarchy over a republic. Having no royal family of its own, Norway's parliament selected Prince Carl of Denmark to be king. Upon acceptance, he took the title Håkon VII and named his infant son Olav, both prominent names from Norway's Viking past.

Norway stayed neutral during WWI. Despite restating its neutrality at the start of WWII, it was attacked by the Nazis on 9 April 1940, falling to the Germans after a two-month struggle. King Håkon set up a government in exile in England, and placed most of Norway's merchant fleet under the command of the Allies. Although Norway remained occupied until the end of the war, it had an active Resistance movement, which you can ponder in Bergen's Theta Museum (p333) and Narvik's Red Cross War Museum (p361).

The royal family returned to Norway in June 1945. King Håkon died in 1957 and was succeeded by his son, Olav V, a popular king who reigned until his death in January 1991. The current monarch is Harald V, Olav's son, who was crowned in June 1991.

Norway joined the European Free Trade Association (EFTA) in 1960, but has been reluctant to forge closer bonds with other European nations, in part due to concerns about the impact on its fishing and small-scale farming industries. During 1994 a national referendum on joining the EU was held and rejected. Norway has lead many contemporary environmental initiatives, such as the creation of the Svalbard Global Seed Vault (2008), where seeds are stored to protect biodiversity. The government has recently declared a goal of making Norway carbon neutral by 2030, largely by purchasing offsets from developing countries.

PEOPLE

Norway has 4.7 million people and one of Europe's lowest population densities. The majority of modern Norwegians are middle class. Immigration is strictly controlled and only bona fide refugees are admitted. The largest cities are Oslo with 550,000 residents, followed by Bergen, Trondheim and Stavanger.

Most Norwegians are of Nordic origin, and are thought to have descended from central and northern European tribes who migrated northwards around 8000 years ago. In addition, there are about 40,000 Sámi (formerly known as Lapps), the indigenous people of Norway's far north who now make up the country's largest ethnic minority. Some Sámi still live a traditional nomadic life, herding reindeer in Finnmark.

RELIGION

Around 88% of Norwegians belong to the Church of Norway, a Protestant Evangelical Lutheran denomination, but most Norwegians only attend church for Christmas and Easter. Around 1.5% of the population are affiliated with the secular Humanist & Ethical Union and there are a number of smaller Christian denominations. A growing Muslim population exists due to recent immigration.

ARTS

Norway's best-known artists include the moody painter Edvard Munch, responsible for *The Scream*; the landscape painter JC Dahl; classical composer Edvard Grieg; sculptor Gustav Vigeland; and playwright Henrik Ibsen, who penned *A Doll's House*.

Norway's stave churches are some of the oldest wooden buildings on earth. Named for their vertical supporting posts, these structures are often distinguished by dragon-headed gables resembling ornately carved prows of Viking ships. Of the 500 to 600 stave churches originally built, only about 20 of those remaining retain many original components. Other significant architectural contributions include the romantic 'dragon style', found in some historic hotels (p344), occurrences of Art Nouveau, best observed in Ålesund (p349), and some exquisite modern structures, such as Oslo's City Hall (p310) and Den Norske Opera & Ballett (p309).

Norwegian writers Sigrid Undset and Knut Hamsun (a Nazi collaborator) won the Nobel Prize for Literature in 1928 and 1920, respectively. Undset is best known for *Kristin Lavransdottir*, a trilogy portraying the struggles of a 14th-century Norwegian family, and Hamsun for his novel *The Growth of the Soil*. If you're lucky enough to get hold of a copy, Angar Mykle's Lasso *Round the Moon* (1954) might be the best book you've never read. Per Petterson's haunting, straightforward prose in *Out Stealing Horses* (2003) has made him a contemporary bestseller.

Though there aren't many, Norway has produced several good films, including *Elling* (2001), *Buddy* (2003), and *Beautiful Country* (2004). For a Norwegian classic, check out *Ni Liv* (1957), a story concerning the WWII resistance. The Sámi film *Pathfinder* (1987) is a brutal adventure story set in Finnmark 1000 years ago. Information on festivals can be found at www.nfi.no.

Classical music and jazz are very popular in Norway and there are annual music festivals around the country. For details of music festivals, visit www.norway festivals.com or contact the Norwegian Tourist Board. Norway has a thriving rock scene and is largely responsible for black metal (p315).

ENVIRONMENT
The Land

Norway, occupying the western part of the Scandinavian Peninsula shares borders with Sweden, Finland and Russia. The coastline is deeply cut by fjords – long, narrow inlets of the sea bordered by high, steep cliffs. Mountains, some capped with Europe's largest glaciers, cover more than half of the landmass. Only 3% of the country is arable.

With a combination of mountains and a wet climate, it's hardly surprising that Norway has many spectacular waterfalls, including several of the 10 highest in the world.

Wildlife

Norway has wild and semidomesticated reindeer herds, thriving elk populations and a scattering of Arctic foxes, lynxes, musk oxen, bears and wolverines. Lemmings occupy mountain areas through 30% of the country. Polar bears (population 3000 and declining) and walruses are found in Svalbard. Several species of seal, dolphin and whale may be seen around most western and rthern coasts.

Bird life is prolific in coastal areas and puffins, fulmars and kittiwakes are commonly seen. Rarer species include ospreys, golden eagles and white-tailed sea eagles. The islands of Runde (p351), Røst and Værøy (p368) are premier places to watch them.

National Parks

Norway's 37 national parks, covering 15% of the country, don't necessarily attempt to protect any specific landmark, but rather prevent development of remaining wild areas. As a result, park boundaries don't always coincide with the incidence of spectacular natural features, and simply follow contour lines around uninhabited areas.

Norwegian national parks are low profile and lack the traffic and overdeveloped facilities that have turned other countries' parks into seasonal urban areas. Some parks, notably Jotunheimen and Rondane, are increasing suffering from overuse, but in most places pollution and traffic are kept to a minimum. Norwegians sometimes look askance at foreigners' preoccupation with national parks, since fantastic wilderness areas exist everywhere.

Environmental Issues

Industrial waste is highly regulated, recycling is popular and the government seeks to make Norway carbon neutral by 2030. There's little rubbish along the roadsides and general tidiness is a high priority in both urban and rural environments. Plastic bottles and cans may be exchanged for cash at supermarkets.

Loss of habitat has placed around 1000 species of plants and animals on the endangered or threatened species lists, and sport hunting and fishing are more popular here than in most of Europe. Hydroelectric schemes have devastated some mountain landscapes and waterfalls, and over-fishing perpetually haunts the economy.

Whaling in Norway is regulated by the International Whaling Commission. Norway resumed commercial whaling of minke whales in 1993, defying an international ban. The government, which supports the protection of threatened species, contends that minke whales, with an estimated population of 100,000, can sustain a limited harvest.

FOOD & DRINK
Staples & Specialities

Norwegian specialities include grilled or smoked *laks* (salmon), *gravat laks* (marinated salmon), *reker* (boiled shrimp), *torsk* (cod), *fiskesuppe* (fish soup), *hval* (whale) and other seafood. Expect to see sweet brown goat's-milk cheese called *geitost,* and *sild* (pickled herring) with the breads and cereals in breakfast buffets. A fine Norwegian dessert is warm *moltebær syltetøy* (cloudberry jam) with ice cream. Also popular is *eplekake* (apple cake) served with fresh cream. *Lutefisk,* dried cod made almost gelatinous by soaking in lye, is popular at Christmas but it's an acquired taste.

If Norway has a national drink, it's strong black coffee. Most of the beer you'll drink is watery-tasting pilsner. On the other end of the taste spectrum is Norway's bitter aquavit, which does the job at 40% proof.

Where to Eat & Drink

Common throughout all of Norway is the *konditori,* a bakery with tables where you can sit and enjoy pastries and relatively inexpensive sandwiches. Other moderately cheap eats are found at *gatekjøkken* (food wagons and streetside kiosks), which generally have hot dogs for about Nkr15 and hamburgers for Nkr65. Marginally more expensive, but with more nutritionally balanced food, are *kafeterias,* with simple, traditional meals from about Nkr100. In cities, *kafes* almost always function as a hang-out, bar and restaurant. They serve filling 'small dishes' for between Nkr90 and Nkr140. Restaurants vary widely in price, with mains going for Nkr120 to Nkr350.

By international standards, Norwegian restaurant food is bland and heavy, though the cities of Oslo, Bergen, Trondheim and Stavanger have all made vast cuisine improvements.

Urban bars come in three basic forms. The first breed involves well-dressed Norwegians and cool designs. The second is the 'brown bar', so named because of their dusty wooden interiors – these are often accused of being dens for alcoholic men, though bohemians have gentrified many of them. The third type is found in the growing numbers of tourist traps and chain 'Irish' venues.

Vegetarians & Vegans

Being vegetarian in Norway is a challenge and vegan almost impossible. In rural parts of the country, you will live out of a grocery store, though some cafes serve token dishes such as vegetables with pasta. Another easily found option is pizza, though Norwegian pizza is often bland and soggy. You'll find more options in bigger cities, though most menus are entirely based on fish and meat. About half of the kebab stands serve falafel. Norwegian restaurants aim to please, and will often attempt to make you a special order if you ask (don't expect fine results though).

Habits & Customs

When invited to someone's house for a meal, it's polite to bring flowers or a bottle of wine. Guests should take their shoes off in the foyer. Table manners don't differ much from those in most of Europe. Locals tend to eat breakfast at home, lunch between 11.30am and 2pm (often communally with their fellow co-workers) and the evening meal between 6pm and 8pm (often later in larger cities).

OSLO

pop 550,000

Norway's capital is easily the country's most cosmopolitan city, offering diverse nightlife options, an array of cafes and bars, and some excellent museums, not least the Nasjonalgalleriet and Vikingskipshuset.

While Oslo is not as picturesquely stunning as Bergen, its urban fabric does contain the famous Vigeland Park and the city is eminently strollable. For a particularly good urban walk, follow the banks of the Akerselva, where you will encounter several waterfalls and the converted factory buildings that comprise the edge of the trendy Grünerløkka district.

What distinguishes Oslo from many other capitals is its immediate proximity to expansive wilderness areas. Not only is the city at the head of a fjord (not as impressive as those on the west coast, but a fjord all the same), but a large mountainous forest penetrates the city boundary. The pleasant result is that you can take a subway to ski lifts and an extensive network of trails.

HISTORY

Founded by Harald Hardråda in 1048, it's the oldest Scandinavian capital. In 1299, King Håkon V constructed the Akershus Festning here, to counter the Swedish threat from the east. Levelled by fire in 1624, the city was rebuilt in brick and stone on a more easily defended site by King Christian IV, who renamed it Christiania, after his humble self.

In 1814, the framers of Norway's first constitution designated it the official capital of the new realm but their efforts were effectively nullified by Sweden, which had other ideas about Norway's future and unified the two countries under Swedish rule. In 1905, when that union dissolved, Christiania flourished as the capital of modern Norway. The city reverted to its original name, Oslo, in 1925.

ORIENTATION

Oslo's central train station (Oslo Sentralstasjon, or 'Oslo S') is at the eastern end of the city centre. From there the main street, Karl Johans gate, leads through the heart of the city to Det Kongelige Slott. The hip neighbourhood of Grünerløkka is reached by taking Storgata across the Akerselva, while the Grønland immigrant district (also hip) is just east of Oslo S.

Most central city sights are within a 15-minute walk of Karl Johans gate, as are the majority of Oslo's hotels and pensions (guesthouses). Many sights outside Oslo centre, including Vigeland Park and Munchmuseet, are a short tram ride away, and Bygdøy peninsula is a 10-minute ferry ride across the harbour. The trails and lakes of the Nordmarka wilderness are easily reached by T-bane (the underground train system).

OSLO IN TWO DAYS

Stroll down Karl Johans gate, checking out the Nasjonalgalleriet (p300). Head to Bygdøy peninsula (p300) for Viking ships and grab lunch at Tekehtopa (p313). Window-shop along Bogstadveien and lounge around Vigeland Park (p309). Eat dinner at Kampen Bistro (p313) and drink your way back to town along Grønland.

The next day, check out Akershus Festning (p309), explore wilderness and cake at Frognerseteren (p313), and then poke around Grünnerløkka, ending the night at Blå (p314).

INFORMATION

Bookshops

Nomaden (Map ppp298-9; ☎ 221 31 415; Uranienborgveien 4; ☼ closed Sun) Travel guides, maps and gear.
Norli (Map ppp298-9; ☎ 220 04 300; Universitetsgata 24; ☼ closed Sun) Some English-language titles.
Ringstrøms (Map ppp298-9; ☎ 222 00 013; Ullevålsveien 1; ☼ closed Sun) Second-hand and antiquarian.

Discount Cards

Oslo Pass (1/2/3 days Nkr220/320/410) Provides entry to most museums and attractions and free travel on public transport. It's sold at tourist offices and hotels. Students and seniors, who get half-price entry at most sights, usually do better buying a public-transport pass (or walking) and paying separate museum admissions.

Emergency

Ambulance (☎ 113)
Fire (☎ 110)
Police (Map ppp298-9; ☎ 112; Hammersborggatta 10)

Internet Access

Arctic Internet Café (Map ppp298-9; ☎ 221 71 940; Oslo S; per 30/60min Nkr35/60; ☼ 8am-midnight)
Deichmanske Bibliotek (Map ppp298-9; Henrik Ibsens gate 1) Free internet access limited to an hour; unlimited wi-fi.
Use-It See p300; there's free access if younger than 28.

Laundry

Selvebetjent (Map ppp298-9; Ullevålsveien 15; wash Nkr40-90, dry Nkr30; ☼ 8am-9pm)

Medical Services

Jernbanetorget Apotek (Map ppp298-9; ☎ 224 12 483; Fred Olsens gate; ☼ 24hr) Pharmacy opposite Oslo S.

Oslo Kommunale Legevakten (Map ppp298-9; ☎ 229 32 293; Storgata 40) Medical clinic with 24-hour emergency services.

Money

There are banks with ATMs along Karl Johans gate. The tourist office and post office exchange money at a less advantageous rate than banks. **Forex** (Map ppp298-9; ☎ 224 13 060; Fridtjof Nansens plass 6; ⏱ 9am-6pm Mon-Fri) is the largest foreign exchange service in Scandinavia. There's a branch at Oslo S train station.

Post

Main post office (Map ppp298-9; ☎ 231 49 000; Dronningens gate 15; ⏱ 9am-5pm Mon-Fri) To receive mail, have it sent to 'Poste Restante, Oslo Sentrum

Postkontor, Dronningens gate 15, N-0101 Oslo'. There's a convenient branch at Oslo S and on Grensen.

Tourist Information

Den Norske Turistforening (DNT, Norwegian Mountain Touring Club; Map ppp298-9; ☎ 228 22 822; www.dntoslo.no; Storgata 3; ⏱ 10am-4pm Mon-Wed & Fri, 10am-6pm Thu, 10am-2pm Sat, open 1hr earlier in summer) Provides information and maps on hiking in Norway and sells memberships, which include discounted rates on the use of mountain huts along the main hiking routes. You can also book huts and pick up keys (p380).

Oslo Promotion (Map ppp298-9; ☎ 815 30 555; www .visitoslo.com; Fridtjof Nansens plass 5; ⏱ 9am-7pm Jun-Aug, 9am-5pm Mon-Sat Apr, May & Sep, 9am-4pm Mon-Fri Oct-Mar) Pick up the useful *Oslo Guide*.

NORWAY

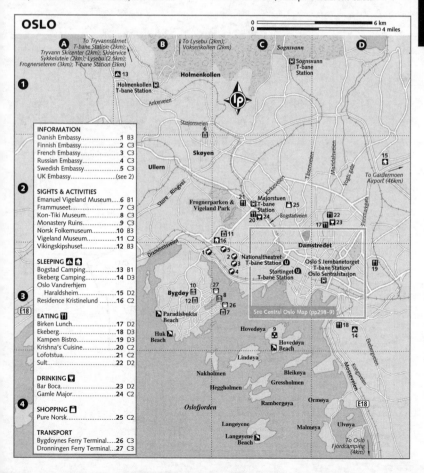

OSLO

0 — 6 km
0 — 4 miles

INFORMATION	
Danish Embassy	1 B3
Finnish Embassy	2 C3
French Embassy	3 C3
Russian Embassy	4 C3
Swedish Embassy	5 C3
UK Embassy	(see 2)

SIGHTS & ACTIVITIES	
Emanuel Vigeland Museum	6 B1
Frammuseet	7 C3
Kon-Tiki Museum	8 C3
Monastery Ruins	9 C3
Norsk Folkemuseum	10 B3
Vigeland Museum	11 C2
Vikingskipshuset	12 B3

SLEEPING	
Bogstad Camping	13 B1
Ekeberg Camping	14 D3
Oslo Vandrerhjem Haraldsheim	15 D2
Residence Kristinelund	16 C2

EATING	
Birken Lunch	17 D2
Ekeberg	18 D3
Kampen Bistro	19 D3
Krishna's Cuisine	20 C2
Lofotstua	21 C2
Sult	22 D2

DRINKING	
Bar Boca	23 D2
Gamle Major	24 C2

SHOPPING	
Pure Norsk	25 C2

TRANSPORT	
Bygdoynes Ferry Terminal	26 C3
Dronningen Ferry Terminal	27 C3

To Tryvannstårnet T-bane Station (2km); Tryvann Skicenter (2km); Skiservice Sykkeluteie (2km); Lysebu (2.5km); Frognerseteren (3km); T-bane Station (3km)

To Lysebu (2km); Voksenkollen (2km)

Sognsvann

Sognsvann T-bane Station

Holmenkollen

Holmenkollen T-bane Station

Ankerveien

Stasjonsveien

Skøyen

Ullern

Store Ringvei

To Gardermoen Airport (46km)

Majorstuen T-bane Station

Frognerparken & Vigeland Park

Bogstadveien

Damstredet

Drammensveien

Nationaltheatret T-bane Station

Oslo S Jernbanetorget T-bane Station/ Oslo Sentralstasjon

Stortinget U T-bane Station

Bygdøy

Paradisbukta Beach

Huk Beach

Hovedøya

Hovedøya Beach

Lindøya

See Central Oslo Map (pp298-9)

Nakholmen

Bleikøya

Gressholmen

Heggholmen

Oslofjorden

Rambergøya

Ormøya

Langøyene

Malmøya

Ulvøya

Langøyene Beach

To Oslo Fjordcamping (4km)

E18

Mossveien

Kongsveien

NORWAY

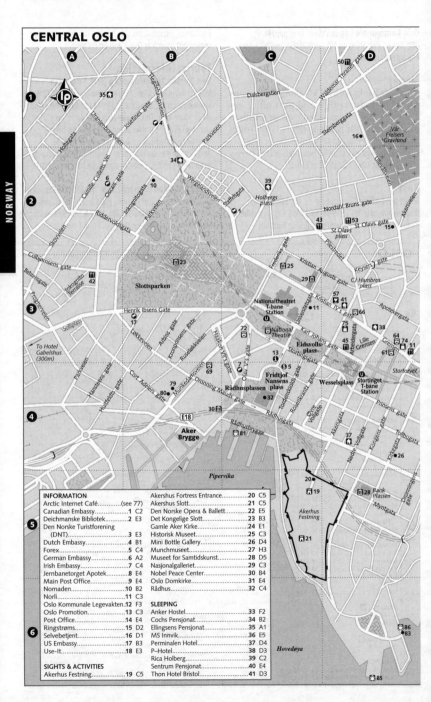

CENTRAL OSLO

Slottsparken

Nationaltheatret T-bane Station

National Theatre

Eidsvolls-plass

Fridtjof Nansens plass

Rådhusplassen

Wesselsplass

Stortinget T-bane Station

Aker Brygge

Piervika

Akerhus Festning

Hovedøya

Vår Frelsers Gravlund

St Olavs plass

C J Hambros plass

Stortorvet

Bank Plassen

To Hotel Gabelshus (300m)

NORWAY

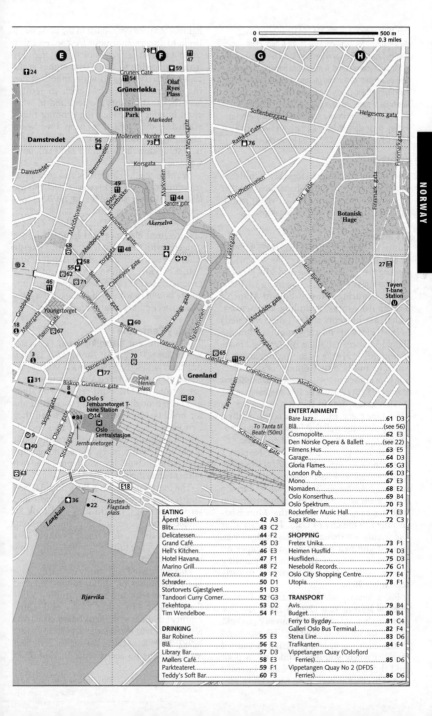

Use-It (Map pp298-9; ☎ 224 15 132; www.use-it.no; Møllergata 3; ⊙ 9am-6pm Mon-Fri Jul & Aug, 11am-5pm Mon-Fri Sep-Jun) This savvy youth information office is aimed at the backpacking crowd. It makes free bookings for inexpensive accommodation and provides advice about anything from finding fishing spots to hitching. Pick up a free copy of *Streetwise* (a comprehensive guide to Oslo on the cheap), use a (free) phone to make a room reservation anywhere in Norway, or tag along on 'off-track tourism' events, where you might take a tour of City Hall, guided by the mayor.

SIGHTS

Many sights are clustered together within easy walking distance of Karl Johans gate. Another important concentration is the Bygdøy peninsula, which contains the Vikingskipshuset.

Art Museums

Come to **Nasjonalgalleriet** (Map pp298-9; ☎ 219 82 000; www.nasjonalmuseet.no; Universitetsgata 13; admission free; ⊙ 10am-6pm Tue, Wed & Fri, 10am-7pm Thu, 11am-5pm Sat & Sun; ⑤) for an impressive collection featuring some of Edvard Munch's best-known works, including *The Scream*, which was brazenly stolen (and recovered) in 1994. Please spend a few minutes admiring Harald Sohlberg's sublime *Winter Night in the Mountains* (1914), a haunting depiction of isolation and beauty. Contemporary collections are housed in their **Museet for Samtidskunst** (Map pp298-9; ☎ 219 82 000; Bankplassen 4; admission free; ⊙ 11am-5pm Tue, Wed & Fri, 11am-7pm Thu, noon-5pm Sat & Sun). One piece, easy to miss, is essentially a small hole in the wall that becomes a claustrophobic duct work. You should go inside.

Dedicated to the life work of Norway's most renowned artist, **Munchmuseet** (Map pp298-9; ☎ 234 93 500; www.munch.museum.no; Tøyengata 53; adult/child/student Nkr65/35/35, free Oct-Mar; ⊙ 10am-6pm Jun-Aug, shorter hours rest of year; ⑤) contains around 5000 drawings and paintings that Munch bequeathed to the city of Oslo. Ten years after *The Scream* was stolen from Nasjonalgalleriet, masked gunmen pulled a similar caper on another version of the famous painting here in 2004; it too was recovered in early September 2006.

For a sensory overload, enter the **Emanuel Vigeland Museum** (Map p297; ☎ 221 45 788; www .emanuelvigeland.museum.no; Grimelundsveien 8; adult Nkr30; ⊙ noon-4pm Sun) containing his life's work and mausoleum – a specially designed vaulted chamber where you duck under a low door (and thus pay tribute to his ashes, interned above) to enter an eerie nave with almost zero

lighting. As your eyes adjust to the dark, you'll begin to discern enormous frescoes reaching up to a distant ceiling, depicting human life from conception to death (sometimes erotically). Entirely surfaced with smooth stone, the bizarre chamber has such incredible acoustics that visitors are required to wear cloth booties to deaden the echoing thuds created by the slightest footstep. Overheard mobile-phone user: 'Sorry mum, I'm in a pornographic church museum. I can't talk now. Call you later, bye!'

Want to see the ridiculous and enormous collection of a wealthy brewer? Check out the **Mini Bottle Gallery** (Map pp298-9; ☎ 233 57 960; www .minibottlegallery.com; Kirkegaten 10; adult/child Nkr85/35; ⊙ noon-4pm Sat & Sun). This 'gallery' crosses architectural elegance and haunted-house gadgetry with the crass overtures of a puerile club. As you admire tens of thousands of tiny bottles of booze set in an environment whose expensive design surpasses many museums, you're bound to wonder if the place is a joke. The answer comes readily in the toilet.

Bygdøy Peninsula

The magnificent **Vikingskipshuset** (Viking Ship Museum; Map p297; ☎ 221 35 280; Huk Aveny 35; adult/child/student Nkr50/30/35; ⊙ 9am-6pm May-Sep, 11am-4pm Oct-Apr; ⑤) houses three Viking ships excavated from the Oslofjord region. The ships had been brought ashore and used as tombs for nobility, who were buried with all they were expected to need in the hereafter, including jewels, furniture, food and servants. Built of oak in the 9th century, these Viking ships were buried in blue clay, which preserved two of them amazingly well.

The impressive **Oseberg**, buried in AD 834 and festooned with elaborate dragon and serpent carvings, is 22m long and took 30 people to row. A second ship, the 24m-long **Gokstad**, is the world's finest example of a long ship. Of the third ship, **Tune**, only a few boards remain.

Dirt paths wind past sturdy old barns, *stabbur* (storehouses on stilts), rough-timbered farmhouses with sod roofs sprouting wildflowers and 140 other 17th- and 18th-century buildings at the **Norsk Folkemuseum** (Map p297; ☎ 221 23 700; Museumsveien 10; adult/child/student Nkr95/25/70; ⊙ 10am-6pm mid-May–mid-Sep, shorter hours rest of year). There's also a reproduction of an

(Continued on page 309)

DIVERSE SCANDINAVIA

This region offers a dazzling array of outdoor adventure, culinary excitement, winter larks and summer fun. It's also a region where getting to the historic and cultural heart is half the adventure, whether it's on one of the world's great rail journeys, cycling or hiking through its epic landscapes, gliding over snow on a husky-drawn sled or skis, or smashing through the ocean pack ice aboard a mighty icebreaker.

Food Fantasies

From inventive fine cuisine, through simple, tasty trencherman's fare to out-there gustatory exotica (some putrid shark with your fermented herring madam?), Scandinavia's food is more than open sandwiches and gravlax.

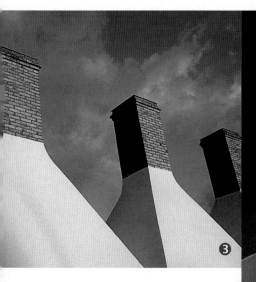

❶ Far-Out Faroe

Down-to-earth staples (p114) and basic preserving methods are the name of the game here, as befits wild, windblown Faroe. Try the excellent air-dried mutton and dried fish, although other delicacies including sheep's head and stuffed puffin may not be for every stomach.

❷ Copenhagen's Gastro Pioneers

Copenhagen is Scandinavia's fine-dining epicentre thanks to the innovative chefs at places like Noma (p48) and Geranium (p47).

❸ Bornholm's Smokehouses

Perhaps not worth the trip to the middle of the Baltic alone, but this delightful and inexpensive Scandinavian cuisine finds its best expression on Bornholm (p65). You'll also find plenty of locally grown food, ice cream and organic goodies on Bornholm.

❹ Stockholm's Everyday Delights

Despite being out-Michelin-starred by flashy Copenhagen, Stockholm can hold its head up thanks to the likes of Mathias Dahlgren (p394). But a major culinary and budget-ary attraction is its good, solid, reasonably priced *husmanskost* (everyman cuisine) such as meatballs and potatoes, *gravlax* (cured salmon) and the ubiquitous *sill* (herring).

❺ Sweet Treats in Iceland

As well as the toothsome pastries found throughout central Scandinavia, Iceland offers the delicious yogurt-like *skyr* dessert, made from curdled milk. Around Mývatn (p262), look out for a regional pudding: *hverabrauð*, a sweet, dark, sticky loaf, baked using hot rocks.

❻ Exotic Iceland

Iceland offers the truly intrepid food adventurer a wild gastronomic ride. Dare you try *svið* (singed sheep's head complete with eyeballs), *súrsaðir hrútspungar* (pickled rams' testicles) and *hákarl* (putrefied shark meat) during the February celebration of Þorri (p235)?

Summer Fun

Scandinavians make the most of the luxuriously long summer days and so can you at a wealth of summer festivals, by taking part in healthy and wholesome outdoor activities, by wildlife watching or by simply pampering yourself in a spa or sauna.

① Cycling

In Sweden head for Skåne (p426) or Gotland (p455). Flat, rural and not too big, Denmark is a haven for cycling. Popular areas include Bornholm (p65), Funen (p70) and the Lake District (p87) of Jutland.

② My Little Pony

Tough little Icelandic horses (slightly bigger than ponies) offer a great way to see Iceland (p280). You can also ride them along the beaches of Skagen (p96) at the tip of Jutland in Denmark.

③ Paddling for It

Mountains plus rivers plus coast mean some excellent ways to get close to the water by canoe, kayak and raft. Many places in Sweden (p470), Denmark's Limfjord (p104) and Iceland's fjords (p280) offer just some of the possible options.

④ Wilderness Hiking

The hiking options in the region's national parks and forests are sensational – Iceland and Lapland in particular have some of Europe's last great wilderness areas. Iceland's Landmannalaugar–Þósmörk trek (p276) promises an awesome walkabout through lava flows and lunar landscapes.

⑤ Pampering

From Finnish smoke saunas at Kuopio (p182) to deep blue Icelandic thermal pools at the Blue Lagoon (p250), Scandinavia is the ideal place to sit and soak.

⑥ Festival Fever

In the glorious, long summer days the whole region comes alive with festivals of every kind from jazz or rock to food fairs (see p24 for a full events calendar) and, well, the downright silly, like Finland's World Wife Carrying Championships (p186).

⑦ Whale-Watching

Iceland (p242) offers great opportunities to spot these leviathans, including minke, sperm and even blue whales, the largest on earth.

⑧ Fjord Cruises

Remember being five and feeling really, really small and full of wonder at the world? Recapture that feeling with a cruise around Norway's Unesco-listed Western Fjords of Geirangerfjorden (p347) and Nærøyfjorden (p331).

Winter Wonders

From winter through to spring, Scandinavia is like a completely new destination from its summer version, offering plenty of indoor and outdoor fun. As well as the obvious such as skiing, consider a ride aboard an icebreaker or a night in an ice hotel. It's also a good time to see the amazing northern lights, one of the world's great natural spectacles.

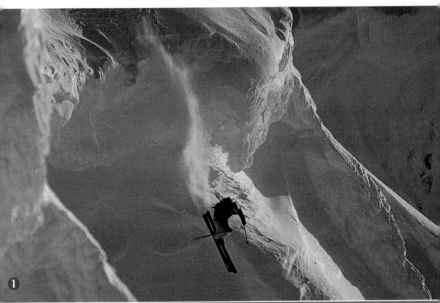

❶ Downhill & Cross-Country

Skiing – both downhill and cross-country – is a national obsession in Finland, Sweden and Norway between December and April. Good options include Lillehammer (p329) in Norway, Åre (p462) in Sweden and Levi (p203) in Finland.

❷ Visit Santa

What are you waiting for? The 'official' terrestrial residence of Santa Claus is the capital of Finnish Lapland, Rovaniemi (p195), which also happens to be reindeer central.

❸ Northern Lights

This mesmerising cosmic storm of solar rays hitting the upper atmosphere is unforgettable if you get lucky. Head to the far north for this one, on the Arctic Circle (p291) or beyond it, then keep your fingers crossed for a clear, starry night.

❹ Stay in an Ice Hotel

Other winter highlights to add to your itinerary should include the Ice Hotel (p466) at Jukkasjärvi near Kiruna in Sweden, complete with bar, ice glasses and reindeer-skin sleeping bags.

❺ Volcanoes

What better way to warm up in winter than to stand near some volcanic vents in Iceland's volcanically active hotspots. Then take a hot bath in the open amidst the snow and ice. Geysir (p250), Krýsuvík (p251) and Krafla (p263) are accessible active areas.

❻ Icebreaker

You simply haven't sailed until you've boarded an Arctic icebreaker and felt it punch through the groaning pack ice at Kemi (p199) in Finland.

❼ Sleighs Away

Imagine mushing through the snow behind a team of huskies or a reindeer-sleigh. Now imagine being able pay for it. If you do have the cash though, Scandinavia is the place to do it. In Norway, try Tromsø (p369), in Sweden head to Kiruna (p466) or in Finland try Rovaniemi (p195).

Historic Journeys

Most famous for its legendary Viking culture, Scandinavia holds plenty of compelling evidence of it, including painstakingly restored longships, rune-stones and burial sites. But it's not just all about the Vikings. The ancient nomadic culture of the Sami still survives along with striking Renaissance and early Christian sites of interest.

① Early Christian to Medieval & Beyond

Modest but ancient Jelling Kirke (p87), burial mounds and runic stones marks the start of the Danish royal family's millennium-long (and counting) story. Also Unesco-listed, Roskilde Domkirke (p59) picks up this story among the tombs of scores of kings and queens.

② Renaissance Splendour

Denmark is groaning with fine Renaissance castles. In many cases with a royal or a count still at home. The finest of them all (minus the aristocracy this time) is dramatic Kronborg Slot (p55), the fictional home of the dilatory Dane Hamlet.

③ Viking Heritage

Discover just what amazing seafarers the Vikings were at Roskilde (p58) in Denmark, and find out more about the culture that these raiders came from at places like Kristiansand (p323) or explore Viking ruins at Balestrand (p344).

④ Timeless Nomads

If you want unique insights into the ancient nomadic culture of the Sami, head to the village and museum of Jokkmokk (p465) for an unforgettable education.

(Continued from page 300)

early-20th-century Norwegian town, including a village shop and an old petrol station. A highlight is a restored **stave church**, built around 1200 in Gol and brought to Bygdøy in 1885. Sunday is a good day to visit, as there's usually folk music and dancing at 2pm (summer only).

Take a look a the *Kon-Tiki* balsa raft at the **Kon-Tiki Museum** (Map p297; ☎ 230 86 767; www .kon-tiki.no; Bygdøynesveien 36; adult/child/student Nkr50/30/35; ☼ 9.30am-5.30pm Jun-Aug, shorter hours rest of year). Norwegian explorer Thor Heyerdahl sailed from Peru to Polynesia in 1947 on the raft to demonstrate that Polynesia's first settlers could have come from South America. Also displayed is the papyrus reed boat *Ra II*, used to cross the Atlantic in 1970.

Check out the durable *Fram* (1892) at the **Frammuseet** (Map p297; ☎ 232 82 950; www.fram .museum.no; Bygdøynesveien 36; adult/child Nkr40/20; ☼ 9am-6.45pm mid-Jun–Aug, shorter hours Sep–mid-Jun), which Roald Amundsen used for the first successful expedition to the South Pole in 1911. You can clamber around inside the boat, go down to the hold where the sled dogs were kept and view fascinating photographic displays of the *Fram* trapped in polar ice.

Ferries make the run to Bygdøy (Nkr20, 15 minutes, every 30 to 40 minutes) from mid-April to early October. The ferry leaves from Rådhusbrygge 3 (opposite Rådhus) and stops first at Dronningen, from where it's a 10-minute walk up to the folk museum. The ferry continues to Bygdøynes, where the *Kon-Tiki*, *Fram* and maritime museums are clustered. You can also take bus 20 to Bygdøy's sights from the National Theatre.

Frognerparken & Vigeland Park

Frognerparken is a wonderful city **park** (Map p297) with expansive green spaces, duck ponds and rows of shady trees – excellent for walks and picnics. Its central walkway, **Vigeland Park**, is lined with life-sized statues by Gustav Vigeland (1869–1943). In nearly 200 highly charged works of granite and bronze, Vigeland presents the naked human form in a range of emotions, from screaming pot-bellied babies to entwined lovers and tranquil elderly couples.

The most impressive piece is the monolith of writhing bodies. The circle of steps beneath the monolith is lined with voluptuous stone

figures, and the form of the complex recalls Egyptian funerary monuments. The park is free and always open.

For a more in-depth look at the development of Gustav Vigeland's work, visit the **Vigeland Museum** (Map p297; ☎ 234 93 700; Nobelsgate 32; adult/child Nkr45/25; ☼ 10am-5pm Tue-Sun Jun-Aug, noon-4pm Tue-Sun rest of year). The museum was built by the city as a home and workshop for Vigeland in exchange for the bulk of his life's work and contains his early statuary, plaster moulds, woodblock prints and sketches.

Nobels Fredssenter

Head inside the brand new **Nobel Peace Centre** (Map pp298-9; ☎ 483 01 000; www.nobelpeacecenter.org; Rådhusplassen 1; adult/child/student Nkr80/free/55; ☼ 10am-6pm Tue-Sun; ⓐ) for hi-tech screens flashily exploring themes of peace and conflict. Aside from presenting the history of the prize and its patron, Alfred Nobel (a dynamite fellow), you can view exhibits on winners from 1901 to present.

Akershus Slott & Festning

King Håkon V began construction of the earthen-walled **Akershus Festning** (Akershus Fortress; Map pp298-9; admission free; ☼ 6am-9pm) in 1299. It's strategically positioned on the eastern side of the harbour; clamber up tree-lined twisting paths to stand precariously above the city and enjoy excellent views over Oslofjord. The grounds are the venue for a host of concerts, dances and theatrical productions during summer. An **information centre** (☎ 230 93 917; ☼ 9am-5pm Mon-Fri, 11am-5pm Sat & Sun mid-Jun–mid-Aug, shorter hours rest of year) recounts the building of the fortress. Changing of the guard occurs at 1.30pm.

In the 17th century, Christian IV renovated **Akershus Slott** (Akershus Castle; Map pp298-9; ☎ 224 12 521; adult/student Nkr65/15/45; ☼ 10am-4pm Mon-Sat, 12.30-4pm Sun May–mid-Sep) into a Renaissance palace, though the front remains decidedly medieval. In its dungeons you'll find dark cubby-holes where outcast nobles were kept under lock and key, while the upper floors have banquet halls and staterooms. The chapel is still used for army events and the crypts of Kings Håkon VII and Olav V lie beneath it.

Den Norske Opera & Ballett

An impressive architectural achievement intended to be Oslo's new face, **Den Norske Opera & Ballett** (pp298-9; ☎ 815 44 488; www.operaen.no;

NORWAY

FREE THRILLS

Easy access to public wilderness within city limits provides many hiking opportunities and, if you brought a tent and determination, a free place to sleep. Specific recommendations:

- **Nordic skiing** (p381) Enjoy stunning views of Oslo from the trails around Frognerseteren.

- **Den Norske Opera & Ballett** (p309) Join the crowds scrambling around this impressive building-cum-public playground.

- **Nasjonalgalleriet** (p300) Look at *The Scream*.

- **Vigeland Park** (p309) Have a picnic amid one of the world's greatest sculpture gardens.

- **Akerselva** (p296) Stoll along the river past waterfalls, factories and pedestrian bridges for an interesting cross-section of Oslo.

Kirsten Flagstads plass 1) features an elegant wooden performance space set dramatically in a translucent cube. The roof, though, might be the best treat. Essentially an urban promenade, its large, sloping plans extend down to the sidewalk. Follow the crowds to scramble around, peer inside and look out over the fjord, as many do at all times of day. It feels kind of like a playground that's for adults and happens to host ballets.

Rådhus

The Nobel Peace Prize is awarded in the **City Hall** (Map pp298-9; ☎ 224 61 900; Fridtjof Nansens plass; adult/child Nkr40/20, admission free Sep-May; ☺ 9am-5pm May-Aug, 9am-4pm Sep-Apr) on 10 December. From the outside, its brick towers add interest to what looks like a staid municipal building. Come inside, though, and you'll be positively transformed by echoing monumental halls covered in colourful murals that depict Norwegian history and mythology. View the main hall for free from the front corridor, walk around yourself, or take a guided tour in English at 10am, noon and 2pm daily (no extra charge).

Det Kongelige Slott

King Harald V sleeps in **Det Kongelige Slott** (Map pp298-9; Henrik Ibsens gate 1), the royal palace, peering from a hill over the Karl Johans axis. Guided tours of 15 rooms are available in English twice daily from June to August. Tickets (Nkr95) are difficult to obtain and are sold at post offices. The rest of the grounds comprise **Slottsparken**, an inviting public park that's free to enter. If you happen to be around at 1.30pm, watch the changing of the guard.

Historisk Museet

The **History Museum** (Map pp298-9; ☎ 228 51 900; www.ukm.uio.no; Frederiks gate 2; admission free; ☺ 10am-5pm Tue-Sun mid-May–mid-Sep, 11am-4pm Tue-Sun rest of year) contains the **National Antiquities Collection**, displaying Viking-era coins, jewellery, weapons and bloodthirsty plunder, as well as medieval church art that includes the dragon-festooned bits of the 13th-century Ål stave church. There's also the **numismatic collection of coins** dating from AD 995, and exhibits on indigenous Arctic cultures.

Churches

Oslo Domkirke (Oslo Cathedral; Map pp298-9; Stortorget 1; admission free; ☺ 10am-4pm) dates from 1697 and is worth seeing for its elaborate stained glass by Emanuel Vigeland, and painted ceiling (completed between 1936 and 1950). The exceptional 1748 altarpiece is a model of the *Last Supper and the Crucifixion* by Michael Rasch. The organ front and pulpit also require your attention.

The medieval **Gamle Aker Kirke** (Map pp298-9; Akersbakken 26; ☺ noon-2pm Mon-Sat) was built in stone around 1100 and is Oslo's oldest building. It's still used for Lutheran services.

ACTIVITIES
Swimming & Sunbathing

Ferries running to Oslofjord's half a dozen islands leave from Vippetangen quay, southeast of Akershus Festning. **Hovedøya** (Map p297), the closest, has a rocky coastline, but its southwestern side is a popular sunbathing area. There are walking paths around the perimeter and the **ruins** (Map p297) of a 12th-century monastery. Boats to Hovedøya leave from Vippetangen once or twice hourly from late May to mid-August, less the rest of the year.

Further south, the undeveloped island of **Langøyene** (Map p297) offers better swimming. It has both sandy and rocky beaches, including one designated for nude bathing. Boats depart late May to mid-August.

The Bygdøy peninsula also has two popular beaches, **Huk** (Map p297) and **Paradisbukta** (Map p297), which can be reached by taking bus 30 from Jernbanetorget to its last stop. While there are some sandy patches, most of Huk comprises grassy lawns and large, smooth rocks ideal for sunbathing. It's separated into two beaches by a small cove; the beach on the northwestern side is open to nude bathing. If Huk seems too crowded, a 10-minute walk through the woods north of the bus stop leads to the more secluded Paradisbukta.

Hiking

An extensive network of trails leads into Nordmarka from Frognerseteren, at the end of T-bane line 1. One good, fairly strenuous walk is from Frognerseteren to Sognsvann lake, where you can take T-bane line 5 back to the city. If you're interested in wilderness hiking, contact DNT (p297).

Cycling

One popular outing is to take the *sykkeltoget* (weekend bike train) to Stryken, 40km north of Oslo, and cycle back through Nordmarka. The train leaves Oslo S in the morning on Saturday and Sunday from May to October. For a shorter ride, take the T-bane to Frognerseteren, where you can zip downhill by road to the centre or enjoy access to off-road action. For a great ride in the city, spin along the Akerselva up to Lake Maridal (11km), passing old factories and waterfalls. See p317 for rental information.

Skiing

Oslo's ski season is roughly from December to March. There are over 1000km of nordic ski trails (free to use) in the Nordmarka area north of Oslo, many of them floodlit; easy-access tracks begin right at the T-bane stations Frognerseteren and Sognsvann. The downhill slopes at **Tryvann Skicenter** (Map p297; ☎ 404 62 700; www.tryvann.no; day lift ticket Nkr310, half-day Nkr225, alpine/nordic rentals Nkr310/200; ⏱ 10am-10pm Mon-Fri, 10am-5pm Sat & Sun) are near Voksenkollen Station.

TOURS

Popular **Norway in a Nutshell** (☎ 815 68 222; www.norwaynutshell.com) day tours cost Nkr2055 – book at tourist offices or at train stations. From Oslo, the typical route includes a rail trip across Hardangervidda to Myrdal, descent to Flåm along the dramatic Flåmbanen, a cruise along Nærøyfjorden to Gudvangen, a bus to Voss, a connecting train to Bergen for a short visit, then an overnight return rail-trip to Oslo (including a sleeper compartment). You can also book one-way tours to Bergen (Nkr1295).

FESTIVALS & EVENTS

Oslo's most festive annual event is the **17 May Constitution Day** celebration, when city residents descend on the royal palace in traditional garb. Other festivals:

Holmenkollen Ski Festival (☎ 229 23 200; www.skiforeningen.no) Attracts ski jumpers from around the world; held in mid-March.

Inferno Metal Festival (www.infernofestival.net) Best to wear black; held in April.

Oslo International Jazz Festival (☎ 224 29 120; www.oslojazz.no) Six days of amazing gigs; held in August.

Øya Festival (www.oyafestivalen.com) In August over 200 bands play everywhere, including medieval ruins.

SLEEPING

When all other options seem unlikely, Use-It (p300) can usually find a place, freely helping travellers book rooms in private homes for between Nkr300 and Nkr500 (excluding breakfast).

The tourist offices book (fee Nkr35) unfilled hotel rooms at discounted rates, which can be worth pursuing during the week but are generally close to the rates that you can book directly from hotels on weekends. Discounts are offered to holders of hotel passes (p381).

Visit www.bbnorway.com, which lists a dozen B&Bs in Oslo.

Budget

HOSTELS

Anker Hostel (Map pp298-9; ☎ 229 97 200; www.ankerhostel.no; Storgata 55; 4-/6-bed dm Nkr215/240, d Nkr560; ☒) You'll find this utilitarian hostel on a cheerless intersection of wide streets. Anker makes up for this by virtue of its excellent location near Grünerløkka. Breakfast costs Nkr85.

Oslo Vandrerhjem Haraldsheim (Map p297; ☎ 222 22 965; www.haraldsheim.no; Haraldsheimveien 4; dm/s/d Nkr245/415/540; ℗ ☒ ☒) Big bright and busy, this modern hostel is surrounded by acres of athletic fields. Though it's 4km from the centre, you can still make out the Oslofjord in the distance. Take tram 13 or 17 to the Sinsenkrysset stop.

NORWAY

NORWAY

Sentrum Pensjonat (Map pp298-9; ☎ 223 35 580; www.sentrumpensjonat.no; Tollbugaten 8; dm/s/d Nkr260/450/650; ⓔ) Dorm rooms contain six beds and cheerfully painted walls. Private rooms can be exceptionally small, but the place is tidy and smack in the heart of Oslo. Shared kitchen.

Perminalen (Map pp298-9; ☎ 230 93 081; www .sentrumpensjonat.no; Øvre Slottsgate 2; dm/s/d Nkr360/ 620/820; ⓔ) This central 55-room pension caters to military personnel, but is open to everyone. All rooms have private bathrooms and less dirt than the vacuum of outer space. Rates include linens and breakfast, served in a pleasant interior court.

CAMPING
Oslo Fjordcamping (Map p297; ☎ 227 52 055; www.oslo fjordcamping.no; Ljansbrukveien 1; camp sites from Nkr140) This family-friendly camping ground by the Oslofjord, about 8km south of the city, has a beach and smaller crowds than its competitors. The facilities could use refurbishment.

Ekeberg Camping (Map p297; ☎ 221 98 568; www .ekebergcamping.no; Ekebergveien 65; camp sites from Nkr170; ⓒ Jun-early Sep; ⓟ) On a scenic hill southeast of the city, Ekeberg provides a great view over Oslo. For this reason, it gets crowded, sometimes unpleasantly. Take bus 34 or 46.

Bogstad Camping (Map p297; ☎ 225 10 800; www .bogstadcamping.no; Ankerveien 117; camp sites Nkr255, cabins from Nkr460; ⓟ) Located at the edge of Nordmarka 9km north of the centre, this large camping ground (which is often crowded) is convenient to Oslo's wilderness, with on-site cafeteria and kitchen (but no cooking implements). Take bus 32 (30 minutes).

To camp in the wild, take T-bane line 1 to Frognerseteren at the edge of Nordmarka or line 5 to Sognsvann. You can't camp at Sognsvann itself, but walk a kilometre or two into the woods and you'll find plenty of natural sites for free.

Midrange
Ellingsen's Pensjonat (Map pp298-9; ☎ 226 00 359; ep@ tiscal.no; Holtegata 25; s Nkr330-460, d Nkr540-650) This homey pension set in a quiet neighbourhood dates from 1890 and many original features (tall ceilings, rose designs, tall thresholds) remain. Rooms are bright and airy. All have a sink and some share bathrooms.

MS Innvik (Map pp298-9; ☎ 224 19 500; www.ms innvik.no; Langkaia; s/d Nkr425/750) Once a car ferry that was used as a travelling theatre, the ves-

sel has been reincarnated as a B&B docked in the harbour overlooking the opera house. It's still a cultural centre, so don't flush your toilet when puppet shows or theatrical events are held below deck.

Cochs Pensjonat (Map pp298-9; ☎ 233 32 400; Parkveien 25; s/d from Nkr460/560) Near the Royal Palace, Cochs' plain pleasant rooms occupy a large turn-of-the-century building with a fine corner location overlooking the beer garden of a cafe across the street.

ourpick Residence Kristinelund (Map p297; ☎ 400 02 411; www.kristinelund.no; s Nkr690-1070, d Nkr890-1180; ⓒ 8am-11pm) Set amid a swanky residential neighbourhood of mansions and embassies, this impressive stately home and its flowering grounds provide a hospitable experience in a quiet corner of Oslo.

Rica Holberg (Map pp298-9; ☎ 231 57 200; www .rica-hotels.com; Holbergs plass 1; s/d from Nkr695/895) Well located near the centre, Rica has rooms that strive for minimalist flair. Some are done in reds, blacks and whites, achieving a sort of neo–De Stijl effect. Others are beige and grey with clean lines. Despite all the simplicity, the building feels old, with twisting staircases and iron balconies in some rooms.

P-Hotel (Map pp298-9; ☎ 233 18 000; www.p-hotels .no; Grensen 19; s/d Nkr795/895; ⓔ) Supremely central and supremely generic, the P-Hotel provides competitively priced private rooms during the business week. No breakfast buffet, instead a food sack is hung on your door.

Top End
Hotel Gabelshus (Map pp298-9; ☎ 232 76 500; www.gabelshus.no; Gabelsgate 16; s/d Sun-Thu Sep-Jun Nkr1495/1695, s/d mid-Jun–Aug & Fri & Sat year-round Nkr995/1195) Elegantly renovated, this place combines two old hotels: a former guesthouse from 1912 and a newer addition designed with genuine flair. The neighbourhood is so quiet that the only noise you're likely to hear is that of squirrels sleeping.

Lysebu (off Map p297; ☎ 215 11 000; www.lysebu.com; Lysebuveien 12; s/d Sun-Thu Sep-Jun Nkr1250/1750, s/d mid-Jun–Aug & Fri & Sat year-round Nkr950/1250; ⓟ 😵) Given to Denmark as an expression of gratitude for WWII food relief, this tranquil, plush hotel sits near the top of a small, forested mountain with expansive views over distant hills. Take T-Bane line 1 to Voksenkollen (25 minutes).

Thon Hotel Bristol (Map pp298-9; ☎ 228 26 000; www.bristol.no; Kristian IV's gate 7; r Nkr1600-2000; ⓟ 😵) The foyer and lounge provide a glimpse into sumptuous days of steamer trunk travel. These arcaded rooms, lit by crystal chandeliers and furnished with stacks of leather chairs, will make you hanker for some tea and club sandwiches (both available). Upstairs, rooms attempt to mirror the elegance below.

EATING

Many of the coolest and cheapest dining options can be found in the neighbourhoods of Grünerløkka, an enclave for Oslo's fashionably dressed, and Grønland, whose population of Asian and Middle Eastern immigrants has established affordable ethnic eating places.

Restaurants

Frognerseteren (off Map p297; ☎ 229 24 040; Holmenkollveien 200; snacks Nkr40-100; ☺10am-10pm Mon-Sat, 11am-9pm Sun) Perched on a mountainside overlooking the city, this 19th-century eatery has big fireplaces, spectacular views and apple cake in an impressive building combining rustic large wooden beams with delicate 'dragon-style' ornamentation. Take T-Bane 1 to the Frognerseteren stop.

Tanta til Beate (off Map pp298-9; ☎ 226 84 613; Schweigaards gate 56; breakfast Nkr55-80, dinner mains Nkr115-170) For hearty egg and bacon breakfasts (served until 4pm), many of Oslo's recovering night owls make their way to this find on the east side of town. At night, eat curries, many of them vegetarian.

Shrøder (Map pp298-9; ☎ 226 05 183; Waldemar Thranes gate 8; soup Nkr59, mains Nkr99-129) Enjoy steaming plates of farm food such as *fårikål* (layers of lamb and cabbage) or dumplings with bacon, in a convivial, sometimes rowdy restaurant typified by cheap tablecloths and free-flowing beer. Definitely haunted by locals, not tourists.

Krishna's Cuisine (Map p297; ☎ 226 92 269; Sørkendalsveien 10B; lunch/dinner Nkr85/125; ☺noon-8pm Mon-Sat) Near Majorstuen T-bane station, Krishna's politely serves a daily vegetarian meal where you might eat corn soup, cucumber salad and a pile of broccoli in yellow curry. Portions are so huge that most just buy a plate of the hot dish.

Mecca (Map pp298-9; ☎ 400 06 555; Østre Elvebakke 7; mains Nkr89-158) Attached to and influenced by the DOGA design centre, Mecca lets you enjoy burgers and produce that come from a local farmers market. The playful interior is done up with harem-like pillows; out-door seating sits on a park. It's a very child friendly place, with even a generous pram parking lot.

Sult (Map p297; ☎ 671 09 970; Thorvald Meyersgate 26; soup Nkr89, mains Nkr189-225) Men in tidy collared shirts and their lady counterparts eat trout and drink beer in a room with a grey slate floor, simple black furniture and large pictures of cows standing in vast fields. A Grünerløkka standout.

Hell's Kitchen (Map pp298-9; Møllergata 23; pizza Nk100-150) Eat pizza in this good-looking bar favoured by the cool kids. Sit in a padded booth dimly lit by designy electric orbs with illuminated bottles of booze beaconing through the dark. It's packed at night.

our pick Kampen Bistro (Map p297; ☎ 221 97 708; Bøgata 21; soup Nkr110, mains Nkr235) Select exactingly prepared dishes (rosemary cod with lentil pureé) from a limited blackboard menu at one of Oslo's finest restaurants, way off the beaten track in a traditionally working-class neighbourhood. High-end, pretty and thoroughly casual, it attracts droves, from the stodgy to the cool. Reservations are needed.

Ekeberg (Map p297; ☎ 232 42 300; Kongsveien 15; mains Nkr118-160; ☺Mon-Sat May-Sep, weather permitting) One of Europe's most beautiful functionalist buildings, Ekeberg fell into ruin until its recent restoration. From its hilltop-forest perch eat fish plates and panini (the sandwiches are mediocre) on a sunny terrace with fabulous views of city and fjord.

Lofotstua (Map p297; ☎ 224 69 396; Kirkeveien 40; mains Nkr180-255; ☺3-10pm Mon-Fri) Run by a family from the Lofoten islands, this restaurant turns out a changing menu of fantastic fish dishes and looks like a dive bar revived as a sea shanty. Nice!

Stortorvets Gjæstgiveri (Map pp298-9; ☎ 233 56 360; Grubbegata 3; mains Nkr189-325) Norway's oldest restaurant's sagging yellow, wooden walls and pretty interior courtyard provide an excellent backdrop for traditional meals. Don't try for a table on 17 May or at Christmas.

Cafes

Tim Wendelboe (Map pp298-9; ☎ 400 04 062; Grunersgate 1; ☺to 5pm) For a fabulous espresso, make certain you head to the tiny cafe at this micro-roaster operated by some geniuses who spend way too much time finding exactly the right beans. If you want Norway's take on the perfect cup, you might well find it here.

NORWAY

Blitx (Map pp298-9; Pilestredet 30C; sandwiches Nkr10-20; ◷ noon-6pm) Inside a barricaded, graffiti-covered building is an activist institution with 30 years of squatting history. Friendly, tattooed punks run a cafe serving unbelievably cheap vegetarian and vegan food. Coffee costs Nkr5.

Delicatessen (Map pp298-9; ☎ 227 14 546; Søndregate 8; small dishes Nkr38-66) A welcoming Grünerløkka institution overlooking a park, this cafe's big windows slide away in summer to catch the breeze. Eat well-seasoned tapas (cheesy risotto, baked chèvre with honey) and drink with locals who seem to sit at the bar for days at a time. Good for vegetarians.

Åpent Bakeri (Map pp298-9; ☎ 224 49 470; Inkognito Terrace 1; sandwiches Nkr55-75) For stellar breads and pastries, stop by this bakery, easily one of Norway's best. An attached cafe makes for an elegant spot to eat giant, grainy rolls that you can load up with berry jam and butter (Nkr15) for one of the cheapest breakfasts around. In nice weather, enjoy pavement seating on a tree-lined street.

Tekehtopa (Map pp298-9; ☎ 222 03 352; St Olav plass 2; mains Nkr85-135) A former pharmacy, Tekehtopa serves espresso, chèvre salads and eclectic fare under a beautifully moulded and painted ceiling. Like every other cafe, it serves Norway's ubiquitous breed of watery pilsner, but you'll feel privileged to drink anything at all in a room this nice.

Grand Café (Map pp298-9; Karl Johans gate 31; lunch Nkr98-165) The cafe at the Grand Hotel has served Oslo's cognoscenti for more than a century. Sink into stuffed leather under a frosted lamps in a room where renovation has stripped away some of the past's aura. Ibsen's top hat lurks dustily by the door.

Quick Eats

Marino Grill (Map pp298-9; ☎ 221 13 018; Torggata 35; sandwiches Nkr35-49) It looks scruffy, but it also turns out delicious kebabs stuffed with flavourful lamb on fresh pita. These guys take pride in their work (most shops in Norway use processed meat and not the real stuff). It's absolutely packed after last call. Falafel are available.

Birken Lunch (Map p297; ☎ 227 16 230; Thorvald Meyersgate 33; mains Nkr40-100) Grab a filling spinach and cheese *bolle* (secret ingredient: a heart-shuddering amount of butter) or some meat and boiled potatoes at this remnant of an eatery that recalls Grünnerløkka's blue-collar roots.

Hotel Havana (Map pp298-9; ☎ 232 30 323; Thorvald Meyersgate 36; dishes Nkr50-100; ◷ 10am-6pm Mon-Sat) A Grünerløkka delicatessen serving great takeaway food. Enjoy substantial fish burgers with homemade aioli, or try cheese sandwiches and fish and chips.

Tandoori Curry Corner (Map pp298-9; ☎ 221 79 906; Grønland 22; mains Nkr55-65) It might look like misery from the street, but you'll find it well worth entering this dive for excellent curries and Indian specialities, many of them vegetarian.

There are numerous cheap pizza, burger and kebab joints along Grønland and Storgata. Fast food abounds in Oslo S.

Self-Catering

One way to save money is to frequent bakeries, many of which sell reasonably priced sandwiches, pastries and hearty wholegrain breads. Along Grønland and Storgata, you'll find many small immigrant groceries selling fresh fruit, some of which open on Sunday.

DRINKING

The line between restaurant, club and bar is blurry. For top-notch boozing, consider Delicatessen (left), Hell's Kitchen (p313), Tekehtopa (p313), Bare Jazz (p316) and Mono (opposite). If you're under 20, places serving anything other than beer and wine can't let you through the door. Use It's *Streetwise* (p300) outlines numerous spots friendly to the young.

our pick Blå (Map pp298-9; ☎ 400 04 277; Brenneriveien 9) Enjoy covered outdoor seating under strings of coloured lights inches from the swirling Ankerselva. Find it amid a beautifully crumbling, graffiti-covered factory complex. There's no sign. From Brenneriveien, turn right to pass under a giant outdoor chandelier. When you get to the bridge the main entry is to your left.

Parkteateret (Map pp298-9; ☎ 223 56 300; Olaf Ryes plass 11) The yellow-and-black foyer of this cool-kid theatre and performance space serves espresso and beer to big crowds that take advantage of excellent outdoor seating overlooking one of Grünnerløkka's English squares.

Teddy's Soft Bar (Map pp298-9; ☎ 221 73 650; Brugata 3A) Established in 1958, Teddy's provides a clear view into the past via its thoroughly unchanged interior. An ancient Wurlitzer sets the tone. While good burgers are served, most come for the suds.

BLACK METAL

Bored of fjords and peace prizes? Perhaps it's time to check out Norway's highly regarded black metal scene, whose notorious, sensational exploits in the mid-1990s raised eyebrows across the globe. At that time, the members of a few big-name bands (Mayhem and Emperor being the most notable) not only committed suicide, but murdered each other, burned stave churches, made trinkets out of fragments of their mates' skulls and beat up bouncers and concert-goers alike. In addition to these and other violent acts, a lot of music was created along the way. Depending on your taste, the goods might sound like a dying Cookie Monster singing through a distortion pedal or liberation from what you perceive to be a Christian-dominated music industry.

While things have calmed down a bit since the gory days, black metal remains popular in Norway. A few of the bands to look out for include Mayhem (much of the previous line-up dead or jailed), Satyricon, Gorgoroth and Dark Throne, and a few of the clubs to view them are Garage (p316) and Rockefeller Music Hall (p316) among other places throughout Norway. If you're lucky enough to spend April in Oslo, you must attend the **Inferno Metal Festival** (www .infernofestival.net). You can buy records and more at Nesebold Records (p316). Don't forget your leather pants!

Bar Boca (Map p297; ☎ 220 41 377; Thorvald Meyersgate 30) This tiny bar shoots for a stylised 1950s Hawaiian surfer look with satisfying results. The place is packed, serves cocktails made with fresh fruit and is home to someone who clearly spent a lot of time compiling obscure period music.

Library Bar (Map pp298–9; ☎ 228 26 000; Kristian IV's gate 7) Wear your finest tweed (not required) and sit among piles of leather-bound tomes in the Hotel Bristol's old-school drinking den. Crystal chandeliers set the tone. It's also a good place for a fancy luncheon sandwich. Overcoats must be checked (Nkr20).

Møllers Café (Map pp298–9; Mariboesgata 9) Come inside for a rough-around-the-edges bar with wooden Art Deco booths, a hard-rock jukebox and a pool table. They only sell beer here (Nkr44), so those aged 18 and 19 especially love it.

Gamle Major (Map pp298–9; ☎ 224 62 904; Bogstadveien 66) Enter to discover an old pub (1921) with wainscotting, a carved wooden bar, brass lamps with frosted covers and a neon sign drolly advertising 'prescriptions'. Look further and you'll realise you've ventured into an illusionist's parlour, one with secret chambers.

Bar Robinet (Map pp298–9; ☎ 222 00 150; Mariboesgata 7) Small, cool and easy to overlook on a back street, this music industry hang-out next to the Rockefeller features understated 1960s decor and very little seating, the best being a pair of red leather benches.

ENTERTAINMENT

The tourist office's monthly *What's on in Oslo* brochure lists concerts, theatre and special events. The best publication for night owls is Use-It's free *Streetwise* (p300). Dress to impress or risk being refused entry to nightspots.

Cinema

Filmens Hus (Map pp298–9; ☎ 224 74 500; Dronningens gate 16) Art-house films.

Saga Kino (Map pp298–9; ☎ 415 19 000; Stortingsgata 28) Mainstream Hollywood.

Gay & Lesbian Venues

There aren't many strictly gay and lesbian clubs in Oslo. Several places attract mixed crowds and some venues offer a weekly gay night. For details on these nights and special events, pick up *Pink Planet* at the tourist office or Use-It's *Streetwise*. **Fire Club Oslo** (www.fireoslo .no) hosts monthly club nights and outrageous masquerades at various spots around town.

London Pub (Map pp298–9; ☎ 227 08 700; CJ Hambros plass 5; ⏰ 3pm-3am) This is Oslo's largest hangout for the studs, where you can shoot stick and dance nightly on a floor. Upstairs tends to attract bigger crowds and younger guys (and to have a cover). Downstairs is mellower.

Live Music

Mono (Map pp298–9; ☎ 224 14 166; www.cafemono.no; Pløensgata 4) For international and Norwegian indie bands, head to this bar where every surface is black. On nights with no performances, you'll hear the bartender play stuff

NORWAY

like Blonde Redhead. An enclosed court-yard draws droves of smokers, since many of Oslo's other bars don't provide space for them.

Garage (Map pp298-9; ☎ 553 21 980; www.ga rage.no; Grønland 18) In addition to Norwegian bands, Garage books international rock acts such as The Presidents of the United States of America. While the sound system is good, the view is not thanks to a too-low stage.

Bare Jazz (Map pp298-9; ☎ 223 32 080; www.bare jazz.no; Grensen 8; ⏳ 10am-6pm Mon-Tue, 10am-11.30pm Wed-Sun) Come inside this record shop and head upstairs to find a lovely bar-cafe with exposed brick walls and voyeuristic opening to the floor below. Owned by Bodil Niska (lady tenor-sax player), it hosts occasional performances.

Also consider the following:

Blå (Map pp298-9; ☎ 400 04 277; Brenneriveien 9) Books amazing rock, jazz and experimental bands to perform in a beautiful compound (see p314).

Cosmopolite (Map pp298-9; ☎ 221 13 308; www .cosmopolite.no; Møllergata 26) Jazz and world music.

Den Norske Opera & Ballett (Map pp298-9; ☎ 815 44 488; www.operaen.no; Kirsten Flagstads plass 1) See p309.

Oslo Konserthus (Map pp298-9; ☎ 231 13 110; www .oslokonserthus.no; Munkedamsveien 14) Emphasises fine jazz and classical music.

Oslo Spektrum (Map pp298-9; ☎ 815 11 211; www .oslospektrum.no; Sonja Henies plass 2) An arena-sized venue for big acts such as Bob Dylan.

Rockefeller Music Hall (Map pp298-9; ☎ 222 03 232; www.rockefeller.no; Torggata 16) Books big-name contemporary rock (eg Bloc Party, Morrissey), jazz and more.

Nightclubs

Blå Map pp298-9; ☎ 400 04 277; Brenneriveien 9) As one DJ put it, Blå is 'always good never bad'. Occasional weekend dance nights will make you nostalgic before you've even had time to leave the city (see p314).

Gloria Flames (Map pp298-9; ☎ 221 71 600; Grønland 18) The King of the Grønland nightclub scene has DJs, such as the highly regarded Alv Gustavsen, playing a heavy mix of rock, indie and esoteric in a room done up with oversized comics.

Nomaden (Map pp298-9; ☎ 908 21 354; www.no madenclub.com; Bernt Ankers gate 17) A diverse crowd overflows into this highly-regarded basement-level club. The floor throbs on account of nearly everyone dancing (far fewer wallflowers than you'll find elsewhere).

SHOPPING

For fashionable men's and women's clothes, independent booksellers, record shops and eyeglass frames, go to Bogstadveien, considered to be Oslo's best shopping street. By doing so, you'll free yourself from the crowds buying ordinary souvenirs off Karl Johans gate. For more cool duds, try the boutiques of the Grünerløkka district, where you'll also find **Fretex Unika** (Map pp298-9; Markveien 53). Oslo's various Salvation Army shops separate their stuff into categories and this branch is where all the trendy clothes go.

Utopia (Map pp298-9; ☎ 213 04 885; Markveien 27) This excellent shop sells well-chosen second-hand chairs, lamps and contemporary home wares of high-end Scandinavian design.

Pure Norsk (Map pp298-9; ☎ 224 64 045; www .purnorsk.no; Theresesgate 14) Come inside for a discerning selection of Norwegian-designed items, such as stylish umbrellas, modern silverware, thick wool blankets or a life-sized luminous moose head of glowing plastic (so realistic you can see veins in its neck).

Neseblod Records (Map pp298-9; ☎ 227 17 822; www.neseblodrecords.com; Rathkesgate 7) A cadaver with a nosebleed greets visitors entering a cramped record shop selling all things metal: a vast collection of 7-inches, CDs, records and rare collectors items. If you ever wanted leather gauntlets made by Arcturus's Sverd and worn by Mayhem's Blasphemer, your luck has finally changed.

If you want a traditional Norwegian sweater, **Husfliden** (Map pp298-9; Møllergata 4) and **Heimen Husflid** (Map pp298-9; Rosenkrantz gate 8) are both large chains selling Norwegian quality clothing and crafts, with items ranging from tacky wooden trolls to folk costumes.

For wine or spirits, there's a Vinmonopolet in the Oslo City (Map pp308–9) shopping complex.

GETTING THERE & AWAY

Air

Most flights land at Oslo's main international airport in Gardermoen, 50km north of the city. Oslo Torp is a secondary airport, 123km south of the city.

Boat

Boats operated by DFDS Seaways provide connection to Denmark and use the docks off Skippergata, near Vippetangen.

Color Line boats run to/from Hirtshals (Denmark) and Kiel (Germany) and dock at Hjortneskaia, west of the central harbour. Connecting buses run to Oslo S, or take tram 10 or 13.

Bus

Long-distance buses arrive and depart from the Galleri Oslo bus station, about a 10-minute walk east from Oslo S.

Car & Motorcycle

The main highways into the city are the E6, from the north and south, and the E18, from the east and west. You'll have to pay a toll of between Nkr15 and Nkr25 each time you enter Oslo.

All major car-rental companies have booths at Gardermoen airport. The following also have offices in the city centre:

Avis (Map pp298–9; ☎ 815 69 044; Munkedamsveien 27)
Budget (Map pp298–9; ☎ 220 17 610; Munkedamsveien 27)

Train

All trains arrive and depart from Oslo S in the city centre. The reservation desks are open from 6.30am to 11pm daily. There's also an **information desk** (☎ 815 00 888) where you can get details on travel schedules throughout Norway. Oslo S has various lockers for between Nkr20 and Nkr50 per 24 hours.

GETTING AROUND

Oslo has an efficient public-transport system with an extensive network of buses, trams, T-bane trains (metro or underground) and ferries. A one-way ticket on any of these services costs Nkr23, if you buy it from a station agent or kerbside machine. You can also buy your ticket from drivers for an Nkr8 surcharge. A *dagskort* (unlimited day ticket) costs Nkr60, but can't be used between 1am and 4am. Weekly/monthly cards cost Nkr160/620 (Nkr80/310 for people under 20 and seniors). Buy them at Trafikanten, staffed T-bane and train stations, and some convenience stores.

While it may seem easy to board the subway and trams without a ticket, if you are confronted by an inspector, you'll be fined Nkr750.

Trafikanten (Map pp298–9; ☎ 815 00 176; Jernbanetorget; ⏰ 7am-8pm Mon-Fri, 8am-6pm Sat & Sun), outside Oslo S station, provides free

schedules and a handy public-transport map, *Sporveiskart Oslo*.

To/From the Airport

FlyToget (☎ 815 00 777; www.flytoget.no) runs high-speed trains between Oslo S and Oslo international airport in Gardermoen (adult/student Nkr160/80, 19 minutes, every 20 minutes) between 4.45am and midnight. Alternatively, you can take a northbound local train (Nkr94, 26 to 40 minutes, hourly but fewer on Saturday). **Flybussen** (☎ 177; www.flybussen.no) sends coaches to Oslo's bus terminal (Nkr120, 40 minutes, three hourly). A taxi costs around Nkr450, though **Oslo Taxi** (☎ 02323) sometimes offers discount rates.

To get to/from Torp Airport, take the **TorpExpressen** (☎ 815 00 176; www.torpekspressen.no; adult/child Nkr150/80) bus from the Galleri Oslo bus terminal (1½ hours). Departures from Oslo leave three hours before Ryanair departures, and leave from Torp after Ryanair flights arrive. At other times, take an hourly Telemarksekspressen bus (or a taxi; from Nkr150, 10 minutes) between Torp and the Sandefjord train station from where there are connections to Oslo.

Bicycle

The best bike rental place is **Skiservice Sykkeluteie** (Map p297; ☎ 221 39 504; www.skiservice .no; Tryvannsveien 2; per day Nkr300) in Nordmarka. Take T-bane 1 towards Frognerseteren and get off at Voksenkollen.

If you don't plan on riding far, **Oslo Citybike** (☎ 220 23 488) provides self-service racks around the city where you can pick up wheels for up to three hours. Purchase 24-hour access cards from the tourist office (Nkr70). Bikes must be exchanged within three hours or you'll lose your deposit (Nkr500).

Boat

Ferries going to Bygdøy leave from Rådhusbrygge every 20 to 40 minutes, while ferries to the islands in Oslofjord leave from Vippetangen.

Bus & Tram

Bus and tram lines extend into the suburbs. There's no central station but most buses and trams converge at Jernbanetorget in front of Oslo S. Most westbound buses, including those to Bygdøy and Vigeland

Park, also stop on the southern side of Nationaltheatret.

Service frequency drops dramatically at night, but on Saturday and Sunday only, Nattlinjer night buses follow the tram routes until 4am (tickets Nkr50; passes not valid).

Car & Motorcycle

Oslo has many one-way streets, but otherwise traffic is not too challenging. Still, the best way to explore central sights is to walk or take local transport.

Metered street parking (Nkr20 to Nk40 per hour), identified by a solid blue sign with a white 'P', can be found throughout the city centre. Hours written under the sign indicate when the meters need to be fed. Unless otherwise posted, parking is free outside that time and on Sunday. There are many multistorey car parks in the city centre, including those at major shopping centres such as Oslo City and Aker Brygge. Fees range from Nkr70 to Nkr200 per 24-hour period. The Oslo Card gives free parking in municipal car parks.

Taxi

Taxis charge from Nkr39 to Nkr90 at flag fall and from Nkr12 to Nkr18 per kilometre. There are taxi stands at Oslo S, shopping centres and city squares. Any taxi with a lit sign is available for hire. Otherwise, phone **Norgestaxi** (☎ 08000) or **Oslo Taxi** (☎ 02323). Meters start running at the point of dispatch, adding to what may become a gigantic bill.

T-bane

The five-line T-bane metro train network, which goes underground in the city centre, is faster and goes further outside the city centre than most bus lines. All lines pass through Nationaltheatret, Stortinget and Jernbanetorget stations.

SOUTHERN NORWAY

The curving south coast exists as a magnet in the summer months for vacationing Norwegian families, who come to the area for its beaches, offshore islands and sailing opportunities. Unless here to pilot masted vessels, first-time foreign travellers generally visit the coast's sleepy wooden towns as a pit stop en route to more exciting locales. The most notable exception is Stavanger, a bustling international city conveniently positioned for exploring surrounding fjords and surfing spots.

STAVANGER & AROUND
pop 120,700

One of Norway's liveliest cities, Stavanger's centre packs in stout hills, a maze of cobbled streets lined with old wooden buildings, and a picturesque harbour (Hågen), which is occasionally dwarfed when massive cruise ships dock. Cute as it is, the place contains numerous cafes and bars, some of which are rowdy even on rainy Sunday nights. Because its Norway's 'Oil Capital', the picturesque city is also extremely cosmopolitan for its size (energy attracts business people from distant lands), thus you'll hear many languages spoken and you'll discover superior international restaurants with superior Norwegian price tags. It's an excellent point from which to begin exploring the stunning Lysefjord and to surf in the cold isolation of the northern Atlantic.

History

Stavanger was once a fishing centre and, in its heyday, had more than 70 sardine canneries. By the 1960s, the depletion of fish stocks had brought an end to the industry. The discovery of North Sea oil spared Stavanger from hard times and created an expat community with nearly 3000 British and US oil people.

Orientation

Adjacent bus and train stations are a 10-minute walk from the harbour, around which most sights cluster.

Information

Library (☎ 515 07 465; Sølverggata 2) In the Sølvberget Stavanger Kulturhus; provides free internet access (but you'll have to wait and there's a time limit).

Tourist Office (☎ 518 59 200; www.visitstavanger.com; Rosenkildetorget 1; ✆ 9am-8pm Jun-Aug, shorter hours & closed Sun Sep-May) Provides details of Stavanger's numerous annual festivals.

Sights

The bizarre **Floro & Fjære** (Flower Island; ☎ 511 10 000; www.florogfjare.no; adult Nkr790-990, child Nkr350; ✆ May-Sep; ♿) blooms brightly with palm trees and exotic plants. Or part of it anyway. The rest is a pile of rocks where grass struggles to grow and sheep struggle to find it. The magical bit is an oasis painstakingly constructed by a horticulturist (and his devoted family) who retired to build this 2.5-hectare garden of lush grass, fig cork and lemon trees, thousands of flowers and a slew of tropical plants. For your tariff, you take a pleasant boat ride (20 minutes) past offshore islands, tour the grounds, and enjoy a stellar four-course meal. Reservations recommended.

Tracing the history of oil formation and extraction in the North Sea, the state-of-the-art **Norsk Oljemuseum** (☎ 519 39 300; www.norskolje .museum.no; Kjeringholmen; adult/child Nkr80/40; ☽ 10am-7pm Jun-Aug, 10am-4pm Mon-Sat, 10am-6pm Sun Sep-May; ☖) nicely balances the technical side of oil exploration with archive footage of significant moments in the history of Norwegian oil. Not least among these are the coverage of the Kielland Tragedy, when 123 workers were killed, and a 1950s commission report concluded that there was no oil in Norwegian waters. There are excellent interactive exhibits for kids.

The following **museums** (☎ 518 42 700; ☽ 11am-4pm mid-Jun–mid-Aug, shorter hours early Jun & late Aug, 11am-4pm Sun Sep-May) have combined same-day admission costs of Nkr60/30 per adult/child. The main **Stavanger Museum** (Muségata 16) has the standard collection of stuffed animals and local history exhibits. More interesting is the **Maritime Museum** (Nedre Strandgate 17), in two restored warehouses, which gives a good glimpse of Stavanger's extensive nautical history. The fascinating **Canning Museum** (Øvre Strandgate 88A) occupies an old sardine cannery, where you'll see ancient machinery in action, learn about various soul-destroying jobs of the past and ogle a large collection of old sardine-can labels. There are also two 19th-century manor houses built by wealthy ship owners: the recently restored **Ledaal** (Eiganesveien 45), which serves as the residence for visiting members of the royal family, and the excellent **Breidablikk** (Eiganesveien 40A), a merchant's opulent villa built in 1881.

A fun quarter for strolling about is Gamle Stavanger, on the west side of the harbour, where cobblestone walkways lead through rows of well-preserved early-18th-century whitewashed wooden houses.

Activities

The area's most popular outing is the two-hour hike to the top of the incredible **Preikestolen** (Pulpit Rock), 25km east of

Stavanger. You can inch up to the edge of its flat top and peer 600m straight down a sheer cliff into the blue water of the Lysefjord for some intense vertigo. The tourist board has details on early-morning public transport to the trailhead.

A good outing, if you have a vehicle, is to take the **car ferry** (☎ 518 68 788; Nkr375, four hrs, one daily mid-May to Aug) from Stavanger to Lysebotn, at the head of the Lysefjord. From there, drive up the mountain pass to Sirdal, along a narrow road that climbs 640m with 27 hairpin turns, for a scenic ride back to Stavanger. Starting at the Øygardsstølen Café car park, near the top of the bends, a strenuous 10km-return hike leads to the second wonder of Lysefjord, the **Kjeragbolten** boulder (chockstone), lodged between two rock faces about 2m apart but with 1000m of empty space underneath.

If you want excellent, unpopulated surf breaks and are willing to brave some cold water, the undeveloped coast around Stavanger attracts purists. For rentals (Nkr350 per day), lessons (Nkr400 gets you gear plus four hours in the water) and advice on where to go, visit **SurfCentrum** (☎ 228 37 873; Breigata 4; ☽ 10am-7pm Mon-Fri, 10am-5pm Sat). The closest surfable spot is 15km to the south.

Tours

If you'd rather look up at Pulpit Rock from the bottom, **Rønde Fjord Cruise** (☎ 518 95 270; www. rodne.no; adult/child Nkr340/175; ☽ tours daily mid-May–Aug, weekend Oct-Apr) has sightseeing boats that cruise the lovely steep-walled Lysefjord, passing fish farms, waterfalls, goats and seals along the way. Discount on internet booking.

Sleeping

Because the local hostel is not open year-round, sleeping cheaply in Stavanger can be a challenge. In summer, rooms at all price levels sell out early.

BUDGET

Stavanger Camping Mosvangen (☎ 515 32 971; www.mosvangencamping.no; Tjensvoll 1B; camp sites with/without car Nkr110/80, dm Nkr120, 2-/4-person huts Nkr350/550; ☽ mid-May–mid-Sep) Situated in a clearing near lake Mosvangen, you'll find a large field with few shade trees and some mass-produced cabins. There's also a dormitory. Nearby walking trails lead to town (3km).

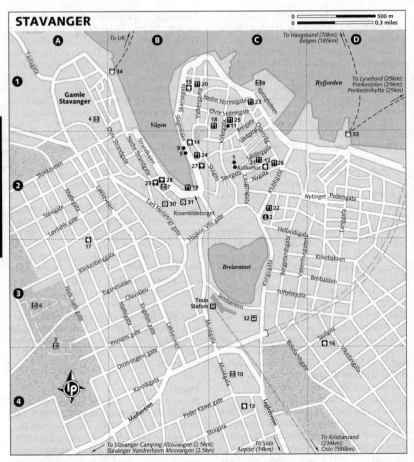

STAVANGER

Preikestolhytta (☎ 971 65 551; www.preikestolhytta. no; dm/d Nkr250/670; ☺ Jun-Aug; ℗) Trees grow from this isolated turf-roof hostel, 25km out of the city and within walking distance of Pulpit Rock and other amazing hikes. The cafeteria works with a culinary school to prepare fine local meals (dinner from Nkr130). Book far in advance. Views are stunning.

Stavanger Vandrerhjem Mosvangen (☎ 515 43 636; www.hihostels.com; Henrik Ibsens gate 19; dm/d Nkr295/650; ☺ Jun-Aug) Lakeside and private, two-bed rooms enjoy access to trails at lake Mosvangen and its ducks in this building that serves as student housing the rest of the year. No breakfast.

Tone's B&B (☎ 515 24 207; www.tones-bb.net; Peder Claussøns gate 22; s/d 350/500) Sleep in one of three comely rooms in this pleasant B&B

on a quiet street up the hill from Gamble. Though shared, the bathroom is attractive and well kept. While sceptics worry that the low price suggests poor quality, Tone would rather charge what she'd like to pay rather than what she'd like to make.

MIDRANGE & TOP END

Rogalandsheimen Gjestgiveri (☎ 515 20 188; www .rogalandsheimen.no; Muségata 18; s/d with shared bathroom Nkr600/725; ℗ ▯) Paintings cover every surface of this charming 19th-century house, which has been an inn for 90 years and wears its age well. None of its 15 homey rooms are alike.

Skansen Hotel (☎ 519 38 500; www.skansenhotel .no; Skansegata 7; s Nkr690-1130, d Nkr775-1190; ▯ ☺) At Skansen, which is small and independent, you'll find modern, uncluttered rooms with clean lines inside an older building near the harbour. A cocktail wizard mans the Broremann Bar, an elegant spot with a good selection of liquor.

Skagen Brygge Hotell (☎ 518 50 000; www.skagenbryggehotell.no; Skagenkaien 30; s/d Fri-Sun & summer Nkr800/975, Mon-Thu rest of year Nkr1410/1520; P ✗ ৬) A modernised former warehouse contains opulent rooms, half of which have stellar views of the harbour – be sure to request one. A delicious breakfast buffet features fresh fruit and French pastry. Less delicious are their outrageous internet fees (200Nkr per day).

Also consider these:

Stavanger Bed & Breakfast (☎ 515 62 500; www.stavangerbedandbreakfast.no; Vikedalsgata 1A; s/d Nkr675/790; P) Plain, linoleum-floored, over-priced rooms with shared bathroom in a quiet neighbourhood.

Myhregaarden Hotel (☎ 515 62 500; www.stavangerbedandbreakfast.no; Vikedalsgata 1A; r Nkr1255-2150; P) Sleep with crystal chandeliers and fireplaces in otherwise minimalist (and extravagant) digs, which opened in 2008.

Eating

The central fish market serves warm, greasy fish cakes (Nkr10) or plates of boiled shrimp and bread (Nkr45) with outdoor tables inches from Hågen's lapping water.

Ostehuset (☎ 518 64 010; Klubbgata 3; mains Nkr77-149; ⏰ 10am-9pm Mon-Fri, 8am-7pm Sat) Popular at lunch, this delicatessen-cafe turns out sandwiches (barbecue bacon), hot dishes (risotto, asparagus and ham) and prepared foods (marinated artichokes) in a chrome and stainless-steel shop. Fine imported cheeses and baked goods.

Kult Kafeen (☎ 518 91 600; Sølvberggata; plates Nkr78-135) This cafe in the Kulturhus does a brisk business with locals retreating from the foreign masses around the Vågen. Enjoy sandwiches, pasta, coffee and beer. Hearty daily meals (Nkr95 to Nkr135), such as a plate of salmon and asparagus, are a relative bargain.

Resept (☎ 515 53 980; Østervåg 43; mains Nkr79-139) This cafe's decor involves leather couches and solid-coloured walls recalling the supergraphics of the '70s. Eat vegetarian pasta with thick slices of bread, or noodles with curry and fried shrimp.

Thai Cuisine (☎ 518 69 788; Kirkegata; Mains Nkr140-185) Well-seasoned and expertly prepared, steaming noodles and large bowls of rice come served in a small room with four tables. Those who enjoy drinking water should try the hot 'Jungle Curry'. The few vegetable options are tasty. Cash only.

Café Sting (☎ 518 93 878; Valberget 3; Nkr148-169) Blessed with a lovely hilltop position and sharing a yard with the Valberg Tower, Sting serves inspired sandwiches (flank steak on garlic bread), salads and burgers (one veggie). The clientele is mostly gay on Friday and Saturday nights when there is often a DJ.

Sjøhuset Skagen (☎ 518 95 180; Skagenkaien 16; mains Nkr199-235) For traditionally prepared seafood (such as blue mussel, trout with peas), this creaky-floored choice is a winner. Find exposed wooden frames, models of ships and pavement seating with views over the harbour.

Tango (☎ 515 01 230; Nedre Strandgate 25; 3-course meals Nkr240-300) For award-winning creative concoctions, locals turn to Chef Kjartan Skjekle, a member of the Norwegian national culinary team. Choose either a three- or five-course seating of meat or fish. There isn't a regular menu, so go with fingers crossed and eat in an elegant wooden and concrete room, softened with linen. Order your table in advance or show up early.

Also recommended:

India Tandoori Restaurant (☎ 518 93 935; Valberggata 14; mains Nkr149-229) Authentic northern Indian dishes (several vegetarian) in a well-decorated room that recalls the subcontinent.

Våland Dampbakeri & Conditori (☎ 518 61 923; Nygaten 24) Turns out flaky pastry, as it has done since 1913.

Drinking

A pile of practically indistinguishable bars on Skagen attract boisterous crowds with outdoor, waterside terraces and cheesy songs playing at top volume ('Dancing Queen'). For more subdued pubs, Skagen, a narrow pedestrian street, is loaded with them.

Cementen (☎ 515 67 800; Nedre Strandgate 25) On the 2nd floor and with views across the quay, friendly bartenders play smart tunes and sometimes host bands. Pick up a used book (Nkr5 to Nkr10) and Sunday beer specials in a room that feels like a private library full of drunk hipsters. It's also favoured by at least one American astronaut.

Gnu (☎ 518 97 345; Nedre Strandgate 25) A super-gaudy and enormous chandelier hangs over bartenders wearing AC/DC T-shirts, some taxidermy and a foosball table.

Beverly Hill's Fun Pub (☎ 518 95 177; Skagenkaien 14A; ⏰ noon-2am) Second home to scads of oil-rig workers and international businessmen is Stavanger's most consistently crowded bar, even on rainy Monday nights. Despite the startling ratio of four men to every woman, it's not even an expressly gay pub.

Entertainment

Checkpoint Charlie (☎ 515 32 245; www.checkpoint.no; Lars Hertervigs gate 5) Friendly dudes tend bar here, where the rock happens on a small stage. Happy-hour beer sells for cheap, and it also screens football matches.

Taket (☎ 518 43 701; Nedre Strandgata 15) Stavanger's biggest disco plays pop hits to a crowded space and decor is lost in blackness. Flashing lights over the dance floor reveal that the place is packed with young bodies. Floors are sticky from various spilled liquids.

For more discerning DJs playing a range from soul to eletronica, head to Cementen.

Getting There & Away
TO/FROM THE AIRPORT

Buses leave frequently for the Sola airport (14km south of town) from the bus station (Nkr70/110 one-way/return, 20 minutes, several times an hour). A taxi costs between Nkr250 and Nkr350.

BOAT

Flaggruten (☎ 518 68 780) runs express passenger catamarans to Bergen (Nkr800, 4¼ hours, one to four daily).

BUS

Nor-Way Bussekspress offers connecting services to Oslo (Nkr650, 10½ hours, one to three daily) and direct to Bergen (Nkr470, 5½ hours, roughly one an hour).

TRAIN

Trains run to Oslo (Nkr871, eight hours, two to four daily) via Kristiansand (Nkr418, 3¼ hours, three to seven daily).

MANDAL
pop 13,800

Norway's southernmost town, is best known for having the country's finest bathing beach (though water temperatures are significantly warmer in the Oslofjord). There are enough cobbled pedestrian laneways in the centre for an hour or two of village exploration.

The 800m-long **Sjøsanden** beach, about 1km from the centre of town, is Norway's sandy Copacabana, with a picturesque forest backdrop.

At the southernmost point in Norway, 36km west of Mandal, you'll find wild coastal scenery and, at times, impressively raging storms and pounding surf. It's picturesquely topped off by the red and white lighthouse, **Lindesnes Fyr** (☎ 382 55 420; www.lindesnesfyr.no; Lindesnes; adult/child Nkr50/free; ⏰ 11am-5pm May–mid-Jun & mid-Aug–Oct, 10am-8pm mid-Jun–mid-Aug), inside which you'll find historical exhibitions and a fine view from the tower.

Mandal Tourist Information (☎ 382 78 300; Bryggegaten 10; ⏰ 9am-7pm Mon-Fri, 10am-4pm Sat & Sun Jun-Aug, 9am-4pm Mon-Fri Sep-May) is a five-minute walk west from the bus station.

Sleeping & Eating

Hald Sommerpensjonat (☎ 382 60 100; www.haldpens jonat.no; Halseveien 37; s with/without bathroom Nkr390/340, d with/without bathroom Nkr660/560) An old white building on an expansive green lawn houses a few dozen rooms done up with sturdy furniture. Most beds are of the bunk variety. Find it 1.5km north of the centre.

Kjøbmandsgaarden Hotel (☎ 382 61 276; www .kjobmandsgaarden.no; Store Elvegaten 57; s/d Nkr890/1085) This former hardware shop dates from 1863 and enjoys a central site surrounded by cute homes and cobbled streets, though rooms themselves don't exhibit much character. Its cafeteria serves traditional Norwegian fare in a wooden room with an upright piano. At night, it becomes a finer restaurant with higher-calibre dishes.

Edgar's Bakeri og Konditori (☎ 382 71 555; Torget) Occupying two floors of a charming white building, this place serves excellent *kaneli svingen* (pastry with vanilla filling) and has fine 2nd-floor views of the *torget* (square).

Provianten (☎ 482 78 888; Torjusheigata 3; mains Nkr295) This elegant delicatessen-restaurant sits right on the water, bakes its own bread and serves high-end culinary concoctions.

On summer nights you'll find a half-dozen water holes on Elvegaten, many of them serving pizzas and burgers.

Getting There & Away

Express buses run two to four times daily between Stavanger (Nkr340, 3¾ hours) and Kristiansand (Nkr90, 45 minutes) via Mandal.

KRISTIANSAND

pop 80,000

The fifth-largest city in the country, summertime Kristiansand offers urban life and a small bathing beach right in the town centre. Strollers will enjoy poking around Posebyen, a district containing a large concentration of white houses from the 17th and 18th centuries. It's a busy seaside holiday resort for Norwegians, but foreign tourists with limited time generally prefer Oslo, Bergen and Stavanger.

Kristiansand is Norway's closest port to Denmark and offers the first glimpse of the country for many ferry goers from the south.

Orientation

The train, bus and ferry terminals are together on the west side of the city centre. Markens gate, a pedestrian street, is the central shopping and restaurant area.

Information

International Internet Café (☎ 380 23 255; Vestre Strandgate 24; per hr Nkr30; ⏰ noon-10pm Mon-Sat, 2-10pm Sun) Skype-enabled internet access.

Kristiansand og Oppland Turistforening (☎ 380 25 263; Kirkegata 15; ⏰ 9am-3.30pm Mon-Wed & Fri, 9am-5pm Thu) Maps and information on wilderness hikes, huts and tours.

Library (☎ 381 24 910; Rådhusgaten 11) Free internet access.

Tourist Office (☎ 381 21 314; www.sorlandet.com; Rådhusgaten 6; ⏰ 8.30am-6pm Mon-Fri, 9am-6pm Sat, noon-6pm Sun mid-Jun–late Aug, 8.30am-3.30pm Mon-Fri rest of year)

Sights & Activities

The most prominent feature to be seen along Strandpromenaden is **Christiansholm Festning** (Christiansholm Fortress; ⏰ 9am-9pm mid-May–mid-Sep), built between 1662 and 1672; there's a fine coastal view from the cannon-ringed wall. From there, walk inland along the tree-lined Festningsgata and turn left onto Gyldenløves gate, passing the **town square** and **Kristiansand Domkirke** (☎ 381 07 750; Kirkegata; admission free, tower Nkr20; ⏰ 10am-4pm Mon-Fri, 10am-2pm Sat mid-Jun–mid-Aug), a huge church that nicely complements the square. Guided tours (adult/child Nkr20/10) of the cathedral, including the tower, run twice daily in summer Monday to Saturday. Organ recitals occur at noon, Tuesday to Saturday.

It's also worth taking a slow stroll around **Posebyen** (Old Town), which takes in most of 14 blocks at the northern end of Kristiansand's characteristic *kvadraturen* (the city's street pattern).

Baneheia and **Ravendalen** (home of Generalen Cafe; see p325) are wooded parks that abut the northwest side of the city centre. Here you'll find a series of hiking trails that lace around some small lakes.

For an intelligent displays of contemporary Norwegian art, the expansive **Galleri Bi-Z** (☎ 380 25 330; Dronningensgate 39) has been delivering high-end goods for more than 40 years and has a national following.

Kristiansand Dyrepark (☎ 380 49 700; www .dyreparken.com; adult Nkr200-230, child Nkr120-270 depending on season; ⏰ 10am-7pm mid-May–early Aug, shorter hours rest of year) has gradually expanded into one of Norway's most popular domestic

NORWAY

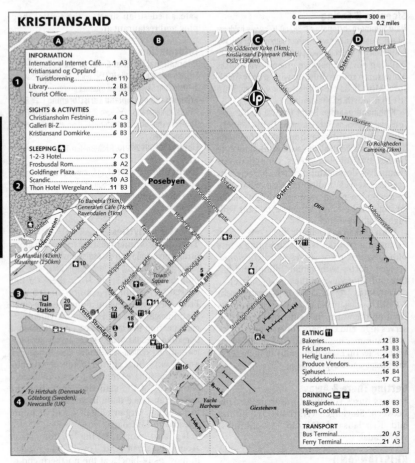

KRISTIANSAND

0 — 300 m
0 — 0.2 miles

INFORMATION
International Internet Café......1 A3
Kristiansand og Oppland
Turistforening................(see 11)
Library.................................2 B3
Tourist Office......................3 A3

SIGHTS & ACTIVITIES
Christiansholm Festning.........4 C3
Galleri Bi-Z..........................5 B3
Kristiansand Domkirke...........6 B3

SLEEPING
1-2-3 Hotel.........................7 C3
Frosbusdal Rom....................8 A2
Goldfinger Plaza...................9 C2
Scandic.............................10 A3
Thon Hotel Wergeland..........11 B3

EATING
Bakeries.............................12 B3
Frk Larsen...........................13 B3
Herlig Land..........................14 B3
Produce Vendors..................15 B3
Sjøhuset............................16 B4
Snadderkiosken....................17 C3

DRINKING
Båksgarden.........................18 B3
Hjem Cocktail......................19 B3

TRANSPORT
Bus Terminal........................20 A3
Ferry Terminal.....................21 A3

To Oddernes Kirke (1km);
Kristiansand Dyrepark (9km);
Oslo (330km)

To Roligheden
Camping (2km)

Posebyen

To Banehia (1km);
Generalen Cafe (1km);
Ravendalen (1km)

To Mandal (42km);
Stavanger (250km)

Town
Square

Train
Station

To Hirtshals (Denmark);
Göteborg (Sweden);
Newcastle (UK)

Yacht
Harbour

Giestehavn

attractions. Mainly catering to families with children, the park includes water rides, a zoo, a 'Nordic wilderness', a cruise on pirate ships and the fantasy village of Kardamomme By. It's off the E18, 9km east of town.

Festivals & Events
Quart Festival (☎ 381 46 969; www.quart.no), a week-long music festival, occurs in June or July. As many as 25 international bands play daily.

Sleeping
Roligheden Camping (☎ 380 96 722; www.roligheden .no; camp sites from Nkr140, 4-person cabins from Nkr750; P) This popular and good city camping ground lies near a small, crowded beach 3km east of town. Take bus 15.

Frosbusdal Rom (☎ 911 29 906; www.gjestehus.no; Frobusdalen 2; s Nkr400-500, d Nkr600-800; P) Loaded with stained glass and period character, this romantic home from 1917 has intimate rooms, some with a balcony. There's no breakfast, but guests have access to a kitchen and splendid dining room.

1-2-3 Hotel (☎ 387 01 566; www.123-hotel.no; Østre Strandgate 25; s/d Nkr590/790; P ▣) Small, independent and located on a quiet street a few blocks from the centre of town, this ideal budget hotel offers prim rooms and a hearty breakfast.

Thon Hotel Wergeland (☎ 381 72 040; www.thon hotels.com/wergeland; Kirkegata 15; s/d Jun-Aug & weekends Nkr850/1050, Sun-Thu & rest of year Nkr1200/1500; P ▣) Rooms inside this old turn-of-the-century masonry building have been newly updated in a contemporary style. It's a short stone's throw from the cobbled town square.

Also recommended:

Scandic (☎ 216 14 200; www.scandichotels.com; Markens gate 39; s/d from Nkr880/1080; P ✕ ▣ ☒) Smartly refurbished rooms with hardwood floors overlook town through big windows (at least those on higher floors).

Goldfinger Plaza (☎ 458 06 886; www.goldfin gereiendom.no, in Norwegian; Tollbodgata 56; s/d Nkr450/550; P ▣) Bargain price for a central location. Rooms have kitchens. Some family apartments available.

Eating

Snadderkiosken (☎ 380 29 029; Østre Strandgate 78A; dishes Nkr20-65) Follow the crowds to this popular takeaway stand. It offers a vast great-value menu, including meatballs, cod with mashed potato, and sausages.

Frk Larsen (☎ 380 71 413; Markens gate 5; mains Nkr85-150) A modish cafe filled with '60s-inspired furniture set over a black-and-white floor, Frk Larsen serves strong coffee, messy salads and big cakes to the cool set.

Herlig Land (☎ 380 90 622; Markensgate 16; mains Nkr139-200) Candlelit and crowded, this over-flowing bar and restaurant spills its guests out onto a heated terrace smack on the town square, where you can eat pizza, salad or filet of lamb.

Sjøhuset (☎ 380 26 260; Østre Strandgate 12A; mains Nkr259-309) This harbourside favourite with stacks of outdoor seating consistently dishes out superb seafood, such as baked monkfish or halibut with cabbage and bacon. The less hungry or the budget-minded should try shellfish soup (Nkr102).

There are bakeries around Rådhus gate and produce vendors on the southeastern side of the cathedral. For a burger in a Victorian-era garden, make your way to Generalen Cafe (below).

Drinking & Entertainment

ourpick Generalen Cafe (☎ 380 90 791; www.ravnedalen .no, in Norwegian; Ravendalen; ☯ May-Aug) Find this red cabin from 1877 hidden in a forest park, next to a floodlit cliff, and on a romantic promenade encircling a swan-filled pond. It's a place you can actually describe as magical without feeling corny. Stop by to enjoy burgers (Nkr150) and beer. On many nights, bands play (rock, blues, folk) to one of the most lively and fun crowds you'll ever find in the woods.

Båksgarden (☎ 380 45 969; Tollbodgaten 5) New, spacious and spotlessly clean, every chair and every booth in this pub comes well-padded for a very comfortable drinking session. Also find a heated outdoor smoking area, a pub menu, and darts.

Hjem Cocktail (☯ 9pm-midnight Tue, 9pm-3am Thu-Sat) This incredibly cool white concrete box is hidden in a small side room of Frk Larsen, where seating consists of a red couch and logs. Dress hip.

Getting There & Away

Trains run to Stavanger (Nkr418, three hours) and Oslo (Nkr619, 4¾ hours) three to seven times daily

Nor-Way Bussekspress runs to Stavanger (Nkr380, four hours) via Mandal (Nkr70, 40 minutes) two to four times daily; to Oslo (Nkr340, 5¼ hours) via Arendal (Nkr120, 1½ hours) seven to nine times daily; and to Bergen (Nkr500, 12 hours, one daily).

For information on ferries to Denmark and Sweden, see p384.

GRIMSTAD
pop 9500

Grimstad is one of the loveliest of the 'white towns' on the Skagerrak coast and has a charming pedestrian centre with narrow streets. It begins to fill in June, as film buffs flock to the Norwegian Short Film Festival. By July, the small town becomes crowded with Norwegians arriving to enjoy their summer holidays. Popular activities include sunbathing on islands, fishing and ice-cream eating.

Today's low-key atmosphere belies Grimstad's past as a major shipbuilding centre – at one point in the 19th century the town had 40 shipyards, and 90 ships were under construction simultaneously.

The **tourist office** (☎ 372 50 168; www.grimstad .net; Storgata 3; ☯ 9am-6pm Mon-Fri, 10am-4pm Sat & Sun Jun-Aug) can suggest various boat trips to the outlying skerries.

Sights

In 1847, Henrik Ibsen started work at Grimstad's Lars Nielsen pharmacy, where he lived in a small room and cultivated his inter-est in writing. By the time he left Grimstad for university studies in Christiania (Oslo), Ibsen had qualified as a pharmacist's assistant and was on his way to future renown as a writer.

Some of his finest works are set in Grimstad's offshore skerries.

The **Grimstad By Museum** (☎ 370 44 653; Henrik Ibsens gate 14; adult/child Nkr40/15; ⊙ 11am-5pm Mon-Sat, 1-5pm Sun May–mid-Sep) includes the virtually untouched Lars Nielsen pharmacy and **Ibsenhuset** (Ibsen House), which contains many of the writer's belongings, such as portraits of mean-looking people.

Sleeping & Eating

Bie Apartment & Feriesenter (☎ 370 40 396; www .bieapart.no; Arendalsveien 85; camp sites Nkr200, cabins Nkr550-1200; P ⛵) This unpicturesque place redeems itself by being the closest option to town, 800m northeast of the centre along Arendalsveien.

Rica Hotel Grimstad Hotel (☎ 372 52 525; www.rica .no; Kirkegata 3; s/d Jun-Aug & weekends Nkr945/1245, Sun-Thu rest of year Nkr1145/1395; P ⛵) In an excellent location smack in the centre, this hotel has an exterior that suggests you'll be sleeping in one of the town's white cuties, but most rooms are part of a bizarre historicist complex.

Apotekergården (☎ 370 45 025; Skolegaten 3; mains from Nkr2000; ⊙ noon-midnight) Inside a former pharmacy dating to 1853, this artful favourite serves swanky tapas and fixed-price menus that run up to Nkr695. It's got some lovely garden seating to better enjoy the sun and breeze of summer.

There are also a handful of restaurants on the water where you can grab an outdoor beer or eat some fish. For unlikely crowds on unexpected nights, **Café Galleri** (☎ 373 20 630; Storgata 28) books DJs and bands in a pleasing wooden bar with a balcony on the 2nd floor.

Getting There & Away

The bus station is on Storgata, at the harbour. Seven to nine express buses run daily to Oslo (Nkr340, 4½ hours) and Kristiansand (Nkr70, 40 minutes). Buses to/from Arendal run once or twice hourly (Nkr45, 30 minutes).

ARENDAL

pop 40,000

Piles of houses smile down from the steep slopes surrounding Pollen, a small bit of flat land that serves as Arendal's centre and harbour. Here you'll find one of the livelier towns on Norway's southern coast with several harbourside cafes whose outdoor seating fills the moment things even begin to resemble warm.

There are many islands (Spornes, in particular) to explore in the archipelago off the coast, some appointed with 19th-century lighthouses. Ask **Arendal Turistkontor** (☎ 370 05 544; www.arendal.com; Sam Eydes plass; ⊙ 9am-7pm Mon-Fri, 11am-6pm Sat & Sun Jul, 9am-7pm Mon-Fri, 11am-2pm Sat Jun & Aug) for details.

Just a few minutes' walk south of the train station brings you into the old harbourside area of **Tyholmen**, with its attractively restored 19th-century wooden buildings. Check out the **Rådhus** (Rådhusgata 10), which was originally a shipowner's home dating from 1815, and later became the town hall in 1844, or the **Aust-Agder Museum** (☎ 370 73 500; Parkveien 16; adult/child Nkr30/15; ⊙ 9am-5pm Mon-Fri, noon-5pm Sun late Jun–mid-Aug, to 3pm mid-Aug–mid-Jun), which displays objects brought home by the town's sailors (from 1832), as well as relics of Arendal's shipbuilding, timber and import-export trades. For an excellent gallery of contemporary art, the **Bomuldsfabriken Art Hall** (☎ 370 13 143; www .bomuldsfabriken.no, in Norwegian; Oddenveien 5) presents exhibitions and a fine permanent collection in a pretty 19th-century textile factory.

Sleeping & Eating

Nidelv Brygge og Camping (☎ 370 11 425; Vesterveien 251, Hisøy; camp sites Nkr110, cabins Nkr300-750) This field, chock-full of caravans staying for months at a time, fronts a calm, swimmable estuary. It's 6km west of Arendal. From town, take any half-hourly bus for Kristiansand or Grimstad (Nkr28).

Ting Hai Hotel (☎ 370 22 201; ting@online.no; Østregate 5; s/d Nkr700/1000) You'll find simple, spacious rooms with little character in this hotel a few blocks from the harbour. You'll also get the impression that the Chinese restaurant downstairs is the place's primary focus.

Clarion Hotel Tyholmen (☎ 370 76 800; www .choice.no; Teaterplassen 2; s/d Sun-Thu Sep-Jun Nkr1120/1320, s/d Fri & Sat Nkr790/990, s/d mid-Jun–Aug Nkr890/1090; P ⛵) Surrounded by boats, this smart harbourside hotel features nice rooms and fine views, close to an enclave of restaurants and cafes.

Café Lind (☎ 370 21 838; Nedre Tyholmsvei 7B; dishes Nkr74-109) Occupying a 200-year-old building, this cafe serves salads, grilled sandwiches (cheddar, salami and avocado), booze, coffee and cakes. Find legitimate art hung on the walls.

For a tasty snack, eat creatures from the waterfront fish market. Plenty of outdoor restaurants and bars, ranging from the high-end Restaurant 1711 to the down-and-dirty Fiskebrygga, line the lively Pollen.

Getting There & Away

Nor-Way Bussekspress runs between Kristiansand (Nkr130, 1¾ hours) and Oslo (Nkr340, four hours) stopping in Arendal seven to nine times daily. Regional buses connect Arendal with Grimstad (Nkr45, 30 minutes, once or twice hourly) and Kristiansand (Nkr130, 1½ hours, hourly).

Arendal is connected with the main rail system by a trunk line from Nelaug.

TELEMARK

Most of the Telemark region is sparsely populated and rural, with steep mountains, deep valleys, high plateaus, and countless lakes. Most visitors come for its incredible stave churches and the Telemark Canal.

Public transport in this region isn't particularly convenient; most buses run infrequently and train lines are largely absent, so sightseeing is best done by car. Telemark's westernmost train station is at Bø; from there, connecting buses lead west to Dalen, Åmot and on to Odda in Hardanger. For tourist information, contact **Telemarkreiser** (☎ 359 00 020; www.visittelemark.com).

Telemark Canal

The Telemark canal system, a marvel completed in 1892, covers 105km of scenic lakes, towns and canals with 18 locks, some impressively narrow and wooden. It runs from the industrialised city of Skien to the small town of Dalen. Between May and September, a couple of century-old **sightseeing boats** (☎ 359 00 030; www.telemarkskanalen.no) make the sluggish, 11-hour journey (adult/child one-way Nkr420/210).

It's common to see elk and beavers at **Buøy Camping Dalen** (☎ 350 77 587; www.dalencamping.com; camp sites Nkr200, s/d/tr Nkr345/395/450, cabins Nkr595-965), 1km from the Dalen dock. The 'dragon-style' **Dalen Hotel** (☎ 350 79 000; www.dalenhotel.no; s/d Jun-Aug Nkr1245/2050, May & Sep Nkr995/1650) is a marvellously intact 19th-century wooden beauty with lots of projecting balconies and gables. The restaurant serves high-end traditional fare. Skien's **hostel** (☎ 355 04 870; www.hihostels .com; Moflatveien 65; dm/s/d Nkr250/450/625; ♿) is a pleasant and tidy modern lodge. To find it, follow signs to 'Skien Fritidspark'.

Trains run every hour or two between Skien and Oslo (Nkr294, 2¾ hours).

Notodden
pop 12,400

Notodden is an industrial town of little note, but the nearby **Heddal stave church** (☎ 350 20 400; www.heddal-stavkirke.no; Heddal; adult/child Nkr40/free, Sun services free; ☉ 9am-7pm late Jun-late Aug, shorter hours May & Sep) rises out of a graveyard like a scaly wooden dragon. The impressive edifice is justifiably one of Telemark's most visited attractions. Of great interest are the 'rose' paintings, a runic inscription, the bishop's chair and the altarpiece. The beast's precise age is unclear, though 1242 is the current best guess. On Sundays from Easter to November, services are held at 11am (visitors are welcome, but to avoid disruption, you must remain for the entire one-hour service); after 1pm, the church is again open to the public.

The town hosts the renowned **Notodden Blues Festival** (☎ 350 27 650; www.bluesfest.no), in early August, featuring dozens of bands, such as the Fabulous Thunderbirds and Koko Taylor.

Buses run once or twice an hour between Kongsberg and Notodden (Nkr95, 35 minutes).

Rjukan
pop 3400

The long, narrow industrial town of Rjukan is squeezed into the deep Vestfjord Valley at the base of the 1883m **Mt Gausta**, Telemark's highest peak. The route to the top starts at lake Heddersvann (1173m), 16km southeast of town (by road Fv651). Lots of outdoor entertainment lies nearby, but the town itself is pretty barren.

Ask the **tourist office** (☎ 350 80 550; www.visit rjukan.no; Torget 2; ☉ 9am-7pm Mon-Fri, 10am-6pm Sat & Sun late Jun-early Aug, 9am-3.30pm Mon-Fri rest of year) about local activities, including alpine skiing, hiking and fun **rail bicycle rides**.

The **Industrial Workers Museum** (☎ 350 99 000; adult/child/student Nkr65/35/50; ☉ 10am-6pm May-Sep, 10am-3pm Tue-Fri Oct-Apr), housed inside a hydroelectric plant dating from 1911, 7km west of Rjukan, details the Norwegian Resistance's daring sabotage of the heavy-water plant used by the Nazis in their atomic efforts.

From the top station of the Krossobanen cable car (Nkr35), above Rjukan, it's an eight-hour walk north to the Kalhovd mountain hut and a network of trails that stretches north and west across the expansive moors of **Hardangervidda**, a bleak and beautiful plateau popular for its wilderness hiking. It also contains Norway's largest wild reindeer herd.

For an incredible experience (unless you are claustrophobic), ride the mind-boggling **Gaustabanen cable railway** (☎ 350 80 550; adult/child return Nkr350/150; ◔ 10am-4pm late Jun–mid-Aug, 10am-4pm Sat or Sun rest of year) deep into a mountain core before climbing more than a kilometre at an improbable 40-degree angle. The thing was built by NATO in 1952 to ensure access to a radio tower in any weather and has recently opened to tourists.

The town itself is thin on places to stay. **Rjukan Gjestegård** (☎ 350 90 527; www.rgg.no; Birkelandsgata 2; dm Nk215, s/d with shared bathroom Nkr350/535) occupies a humdrum post-war building (breakfast costs Nkr70). The underwhelming **Park Hotel** (☎ 350 82 188; www.parkhotell-rjukan.no; Sam Eydes gate 67; s/d from Nkr825/1090) lies right in the town centre but needs an overhaul.

If you're here to ski or hike, you'll find better options near the Gaustablikk ski area, which is accessible by car. **Rjukan Vandrerhjem** (☎ 350 92 040; www.kvitaavatn.no; Kvitåvatn; dm/s/d Nkr200/340/506; ⓟ 🖳) features a cosy pine lodge, six-bunk huts, and incredible wilderness surrounds. **Gaustablikk Høyfjellshotell** (☎ 350 91 422; www.gaustablikk.no; s/d Nkr850/950) overlooks a lake and mountains and is one of Norway's better alpine lodges. Consider paying a bit more for the half-board to enjoy a lavish dinner buffet. It's a skiers haven, so book early in winter.

An express bus runs daily to Oslo (Nkr300, three hours) via Kongsberg (Nkr190, two hours).

BUSKERUD

The forested county of Buskerud stretches northwest from Oslofjord to the central highlands of Norway. Mineral resources, particularly silver, have been thoroughly exploited in Buskerud's hills and mountains.

Kongsberg
pop 24,000

Today's Kongsberg attracts visitors with winter skiing and historic sites left over from its 17th-century glory days. The town was founded in 1624 following the discovery of the world's purest silver deposits in the nearby Numedal Valley. During the resulting silver rush, it briefly became the second-largest town in Norway. The Royal Mint is still here, but the last mine, no longer able to turn a profit, closed in 1957.

ORIENTATION & INFORMATION

Kongsberg is split into old and new by the rushing river. The new eastern section of the area has the main shopping district, a tourist office and transit stations. Find museums, the hostel and Kirkegata on the old side.

The **tourist office** (☎ 322 99 050; www.visitkongs berg.no; Schwabesgate 3; ◔ 9am-7pm Mon-Fri, 10am-2pm Sat & Sun Jul & Aug, shorter hours rest of year) serves as a DNT agent.

SIGHTS

The **Norwegian Mining Museum** (☎ 327 23 200; Hyttegata 3; adult/child Nkr70/20; ◔ 10am-5pm Jul–mid-Aug, noon-4pm rest of year) is just over the bridge on the west side of the Numedalslågen river. Set in an 1844 smelter, it has exhibits on mining and minerals as well as the Royal Mint and the local armaments industry.

The **Lågdal folk museum** (☎ 322 99 050; Tillischbakken 8-10; adult/child Nkr40/10 mid-Jun–mid-Aug, free rest of year; ◔ 11am-5pm mid-Jun–mid-Aug, shorter hours rest of year) has a collection of period farmhouses, WWII exhibits and an indoor museum with re-created 19th-century workshops and a fine optics section. It's a 10-minute walk south of the train station: turn left on Bekkedokk and take the walkway parallel to the tracks, following the signs.

In July and August, there are daily tours of the old **silver mines** (adult/child Nkr140/80) at Saggrenda (8km south of Kongsberg on the road to Notodden), which include a 2.3km train ride through cool subterranean shafts – bring a sweater. Check tour times with the tourist office.

SLEEPING & EATING

Kongsberg HI Hostel (☎ 327 32 024; www.kongsberg-vandrerhjem.no; Vinjesgata 1; dm/s/d Nkr350/690/900; ⓟ 🖳 ♿) The hostel lies near Kongsberg's baroque church. It is set back from a busy road and the grounds contain both a soccer pitch and a children's play area.

Gyldenløve Hotell (☎ 328 65 801; www.gyldenlove .no; Hermann Fossgata. 1; s/d from Nkr850/950; 🖳) The design team did a good job renovating this hotel, whose rooms now come with polished floorboards and clean lines.

Christians Kjeller (☎ 327 64 500; Kirkegata 10; mains Nkr168-400) For excellent fillet of reindeer served in an old wainscoted room with ample fireplace, sit upstairs. Below deck, a pub serves cheaper fare while occupying a cellar from the 1660s (massive stone walls) where folk bands play. Nice beer garden.

GETTING THERE & AWAY

Trains run to Oslo (Nkr165, 1½ hours, roughly hourly). Buses connect Kongsberg with Oslo (Nkr190, 1½ hours) and Notodden (Nkr95, 35 minutes, hourly).

CENTRAL NORWAY

The central region of Norway contains Jotunheimen, a popular wilderness area and national park characterised by dramatic ravines and multiple glaciers. The immensely scenic Oslo–Bergen rail line slices east to west, crossing the stark and white snowscape of the Hardangervidda plateau, a cross-country skiing paradise. For a resort-town feel, try Lillehammer, close to several downhill slopes and host of the 1994 Winter Olympics.

HAMAR
pop 27,500

Do you get jazzed over arenas from Olympics past? If so, you're in luck, winter of '94 style. The unimpressive commercial town sits beside **Mjøsa**, Norway's largest lake, which you can use to escape Hamar by riding **Skibladner** (☎ 611 44 080; www.skibladner.no), the world's oldest operating paddle steamer (1856), to Lillehammer (one-way/return Nkr220/320, three weekly). It's an impressive wooden boat with a restaurant on board.

The **tourist office** (☎ 625 17 503; www.hamarregio nen.no; ✆ 8am-5pm) is inside the **Vikingskipshuset sports arena**, a graceful structure recalling an upturned Viking ship. In July and August, the ice opens to the public for skating (Nkr80).

The extensive open-air **Hedmarksmuseet** (☎ 625 42 700; www.domkirkeodden.no; Strandveien 100; adult/child/student Nkr75/35/60; ✆ 10am-5pm mid-Jun–mid-Aug, shorter hours mid-May–mid-Jun & mid-Aug–mid-Sep) includes 18th- and 19th-century buildings, a local folk history exhibit featuring the creepy Devil's Finger, and the fantastic **Hamardomen** (Glass Cathedral), where the ruins of a medieval cathedral are protected within an elegant glass structure.

Seiersted Pensjonat's (☎ 625 21 244; www.seiersted .no; Holsetgata 64; s/d from Nkr500/700) This pension's 18 centrally located rooms are nicely decorated with painted furniture. Some share bathrooms, and dinner is available from Nkr80.

For an inventive lunch (chicken in kumquat syrup) in the Kustbanken art gallery, try **Valuta** (☎ 625 32 333; Parkgata 21; lunch Nkr99-169; ✆ 11am-4pm Tue-Sat), which occupies a former bank. Otherwise, try to grab an outside table at **Stallgården** (☎ 625 43 100; cnr Bekkegata & Torggata; snacks & mains Nkr80-260), a cafe with broader hours and more pedestrian food.

Drink hooch in **Siste Indre's** (Torggata 53) while relaxing on comfortable leather couches and admiring yellowing pictures of speed skaters. Patrons make liberal use of an upright piano.

Trains run to Oslo (Nkr233, 1½ hours, once or twice hourly), Røros (Nkr484, 3¾ hours, four to eight daily) and to Trondheim (Nkr708, 5½ hours, four to six daily) via Lillehammer.

LILLEHAMMER & AROUND
pop 25,000

Lillehammer, at the northern end of lake Mjøsa, has long been a popular ski resort for Norwegians, and since hosting the 1994 Winter Olympics it has attracted foreign visitors as well.

Lillehammer's centre is small and cute. Storgata, the main pedestrian walkway, is two short blocks east of the adjacent bus and train stations. You'll find more information at the **tourist office** (☎ 612 89 800; www.lillehammerturist.no; Jernebanetorget 2; ✆ 9am-4pm Mon-Fri).

Sights & Activities

Many tour the former Winter Olympic sites, including **Håkons Hall** (the ice-hockey venue) and the **ski jump**; the tourist office brochure lists opening times.

The **Norwegian Olympic Museum** (☎ 612 52 100; www.ol.museum.no; Håkons Hall; adult/child Nkr75/35; ✆ 10am-5pm mid-May–mid-Sep, shorter hours rest of year) provides exhibits on every Olympic Games since 1896.

At Hunderfossen, 15km north of town, speed fanatics can visit the **bobsleigh and luge track** (☎ reservations 610 54 200; www.olympiaparken .no; rides adult/child Nkr190/95) and ride a rubber raft (75km/h) down the actual Olympic run; in summer, when there's no ice, a 'wheeled bob' is used. For Nkr950, a bobsleigh driver can whisk you down at 130km/h. It is possible to poop your snowpants, though you'll only have 70 seconds to do so. Reservations are advised.

Olympics aside, Lillehammer's main attraction is the exceptional **Maihaugen folk museum** (☎ 612 88 900; www.maihaugen.no; Maihaugveien 1; adult/child Nkr120/60; ⏰ 10am-5pm Jun-Aug, shorter hours rest of year), which contains around 180 historic houses, shops, farm buildings and a stave church.

See p329 for details of the *Skibladner* paddle steamer.

Sleeping & Eating

Gjeste Bu (☎ 612 54 321; gjestebu@lillehammer.online.no; Gamlevegen 110; dm Nkr100, s/d from Nkr300/475) Rustic rooms exude loads of character. They are also a real bargain, which is why you must book early. There's a group kitchen, where you'll drink free coffee and meet hikers and skiers. Bathrooms are shared and there's no breakfast.

Lillehammer Hostel (☎ 612 60 024; www.stasjonen.no; dm/s/d Nkr325/695/820; 🖳 🕭) On the 2nd storey of the train station, nicely renovated rooms overlook rail tracks and the lake beyond. Rates include linens. Great for train spotters.

Mølla Hotell (☎ 610 57 080; www.mollahotell.no; Elvegata 12; s/d Nkr1100/1345; 🅿) Built in the shell of an old mill, this interesting hotel combines old machinery with flatscreen TVs to nice effect. There are fine vistas from the rooftop bar.

For winter beer with a roaring fire and a stuffed elk-head, the ski-lodge feel of **Nikkers** (☎ 612 70 556; Elvegata 18; dishes Nkr43-149) will get you in the proper mood. Come to **Svare & Berg** (☎ 610 54 510; Elvegata; dishes Nkr60-145), a cool cafe on a gurgling stream, for beer, soup and locals.

Storgata is lined with shops, bakeries and restaurants.

Getting There & Away

Nor-Way Busekspress runs to Oslo (Nkr310, three hours, three or four times daily). Trains run to Oslo (Nkr332, 2¼ hours, 15 times daily) and to Trondheim (Nkr648, 4½ hours, four times daily).

DOMBÅS

pop 2800

A popular adventure- and winter-sports centre, Dombås makes a convenient break for travellers between the highland national parks and the Western Fjords because it has a few good sleeping options. In town, there isn't much to do except buy fuel and groceries. The **tourist office** (☎ 612 41 444; www.dovrenett.no; ⏰ 9am-8pm mid-Jun–mid-Aug, 9am-4pm Mon-Fri rest of year) is by the central car park and commercial complex.

The **Dovrefjell-Rondane Nasjonalparksenter** (☎ 612 41 444; ⏰ 9am-8pm mid-Jun–mid-Aug, shorter hours rest of year), at the tourist office, has information on all Norwegian national parks. **Dovrefjell National Park**, 30km north of town, protects the 2286m-high Snøhetta massif and provides a habitat for Arctic foxes, reindeer, wolverines and musk oxen.

In a forested spot with mountain views, the excellent family-run **Trolltun Gjestegård & Dombås Vandrerhjem** (☎ 612 40 960; www.trolltun.no; dm/s/d Nkr250/570/850), in an oversized log cabin, lies near nordic trails and alpine lifts. It also offers **hotel rooms** (s/d Nkr850/1090) in a ski lodge where you can find reindeer meals and a pub. It's about 1.5km north of the centre and off the E6.

Dombås lies on the railway line between Oslo (Nkr604, four hours, three to six daily) and Trondheim (Nkr377, 2¾ hours, three to six daily). The spectacular Raumabanen line runs down the Romsdalen valley from Dombås to Åndalsnes (Nkr212, 1¼ hours, two to four times daily).

JOTUNHEIMEN NATIONAL PARK

The Sognefjellet road between Lom and Sogndal passes the northwestern perimeter of Jotunheimen National Park, Norway's most popular wilderness destination. Hiking trails lead to some of the park's 60 glaciers, up to the top of Norway's loftiest peaks, Galdhøpiggen (2469m) and Glittertind (2452m), and along ravines and valleys featuring deep lakes and plunging waterfalls. There are DNT huts and private lodges along many of the routes. For park information, maps and glacier-walk arrangements contact **Lom tourist office** (☎ 612 12 990; www.visitlom.com; ⏰ 9am-8pm mid-Jun–mid-Aug, shorter hours rest of year). Lom contains a **stave church** dating from 1170, lit to fairy-tale effect at night.

Dramatic **Galdhøpiggen**, with its cirques, arêtes and glaciers, is a fairly tough eight-hour day hike from Spiterstulen, with 1470m of ascent, accessible by a toll road (Nkr60 per car). **Krossbu** is in the middle of a network of trails, including a short one to the **Smørstabbreen glacier**. From **Turtagrø**, a rock-climbing and hiking centre midway between Sogndal and Lom, there's a three-hour hike to Fannaråkhytta, Jotunheimen's highest DNT hut (2069m), offering panoramic views.

DNT's fabulous full-service **Spiterstulen lodge** (☎ 612 19 400; www.spiterstulen.no; Lom; camp sites per person Nkr50, dm/s/d Nkr250/330/560), situated at an old *sæter* (summer dairy), lies above the tree-line and makes a great jumping-off point for Galdhøpiggen.

Beautiful Bøverdalen, 18km south of Lom, has the riverside **Bøverdalen Hostel** (☎ 612 12 064; boeverdalen.hostel@hihostels.no; dm/s/d Nkr175/275/400; ◯ Jun-Sep), which arranges summer skiing and glacier-hiking trips. Near the head of Bøverdalen, the lovely **Krossbu Turiststasjon** (☎ 612 12 922; www.krossbu.no, in Norwegian; Krossbu; s Nkr240, d Nkr290-490) has 85 rooms, most of them with shared bathrooms.

OSLO TO BERGEN

The Oslo–Bergen railway line, a seven-hour journey past forests and alpine villages, and across the starkly beautiful **Hardangervidda** plateau, is Norway's most scenic.

Midway between Oslo and Bergen is **Geilo**, a ski centre where you can practically walk off the train and onto a lift. There's also good summer **hiking** in the mountains around Geilo, where you'll find **Geilo Vandrerhjem** (☎ 320 87 060; www.oenturist.no; Lienvegen 137; dm/s/d Nkr275/470/650), a hostel near the train station that doubles as a tourist office.

From Geilo the train climbs 600m through a tundralike landscape of high lakes and snow-capped mountains to the tiny village of **Finse**, near the **Hardangerjøkulen** icecap. Finse has year-round **skiing** and is in the middle of a network of summer **hiking trails**. One of Norway's most frequently trodden trails winds from the Finse train station down to the fjord town of **Aurland**, a four-day trek. There's breathtaking mountain scenery along the way as well as a series of DNT and private mountain huts a day's walk apart – the nearest is Finsehytta, 200m from Finse station. There's also a bicycle route from Finse to Flåm (six hours, downhill) on the century-old **Rallarvegen** railway construction road (see p343).

Myrdal, further west along the railway line, is the connecting point for the spectacularly steep Flåm railway, which twists and turns its way down 20 splendid kilometres to **Flåm** on Aurlandsfjorden, an arm of Sognefjorden.

Many people go down to Flåm, have lunch and take the train back up to Myrdal, where they catch the next Oslo–Bergen train. A better option is to take the ferry from Flåm to Gudvangen (via spectacular Unesco-protected **Nærøyfjorden**, with its thundering waterfalls and lofty peaks), where there's a connecting bus that climbs a steep valley for a dramatically scenic ride to Voss. From there, trains to Bergen run roughly hourly. To include a cruise of the Nærøyfjorden in a day trip from Oslo to Bergen, you'll need to take an early train from Oslo.

BERGEN & THE WESTERN FJORDS

This spectacular region will dazzle your eyeballs with truly indescribable scenery. We'll make a go at it here, but bear in mind that all our superlatives and gushings are actually just understatements. Hardangerfjord, Sognefjord and Geirangerfjord are all variants on the same theme: steep crystalline rock walls dropping with sublime force straight into the sea, often decorated with waterfalls, and small farms harmoniously blending into the natural landscape. Summer hiking opportunities exist along the fjord walls and on the enormous Jostedalsbreen glacier. Bergen, a lively city with a 15th-century waterfront, is exceedingly pleasing to behold, and contains some of Norway's finest nightlife and restaurants.

Information on the entire region is available from **Fjord Norge** (www.fjordnorway.com).

BERGEN
pop 250,000

Norway's second-largest city contends for the honour of being the country's most beautiful. Set on a peninsula surrounded by mountains and the sea, the neatly contained centre offers a tangle of crooked streets, picturesque wooden neighbourhoods and hilltop views. Bergen provides ample opportunities to linger in cafes and bars, while a large university population helps to secure Bergen's claim as western Norway's cultural capital, supporting theatres, a philharmonic orchestra and a notable rock scene. Though big by Norwegian standards, the city retains a charming, almost village-like culture. Drawback: expect rain or showers at least 275 days of the year.

NORWAY

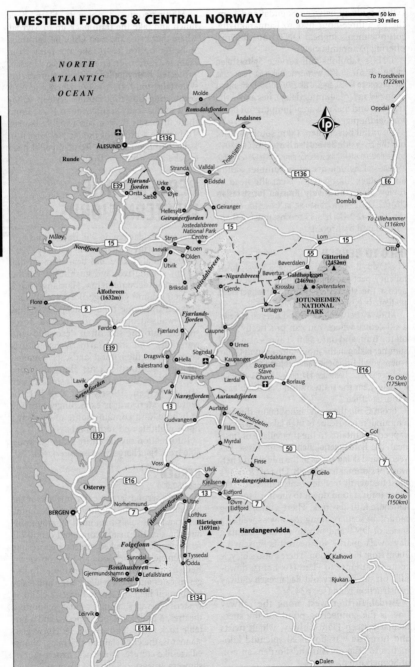

WESTERN FJORDS & CENTRAL NORWAY

Bergen is a terminus of the scenic Bergen–Oslo train line and a convenient place to stay before excursions into fjord country. The *Hurtigruten* coastal steamer begins its six-day journey to Kirkenes from the centre.

History

Bergen was the capital of Norway in the 12th and 13th centuries, and in the early 17th century was Scandinavia's largest city, with a population of 15,000. Bergen's history is tied to the sea, as it was one of the central ports of the Hanseatic League of merchants, which dominated trade in northern Europe during the late Middle Ages. The Hanseatic influence is visible in the sharply gabled row of buildings that lines Bergen's harbourfront.

Orientation

The central area of hilly Bergen remains pleasantly compact and easily manageable on foot. The bus and train stations lie only a block apart on Strømgaten, just a 10-minute walk from the ferry terminals. Most of the restaurants, hotels and museums cluster around Vågen, the inner harbour.

Information

DISCOUNT CARDS

The **Bergen Card** (24/48hr adult Nkr190/250, child Nkr75/100) allows free transport on local buses, free parking and funicular-railway rides as well as admission to most sights. Note that the Schøtstuene and Hanseatic Museum are not covered. It's sold at the tourist office.

INTERNET ACCESS

Cyberhouse (Hollendergaten 9; per hr Nkr60 ⊗ 9am-11pm)

Library (☎ 555 68 500; Strømgaten 6) Free, time-limited access.

LAUNDRY

Jarlens Vaskoteque (☎ 553 25 504; Lille Øvregaten 17; wash/detergent/dry Nkr50/5/15; ⊗ 10am-6pm Mon, Tue & Fri, 10am-8pm Wed & Thu, 10am-3pm Sat)

MEDICAL SERVICES

Legevakt Medical Clinic (☎ 555 68 700; Vestre Strømkai 19; ⊗ emergencies 24hr)

Pharmacy (☎ 552 18 384; Bergen Storsenter; ⊗ 8am-11pm Mon-Sat, 10am-11pm Sun) Near bus station.

POST

Main Post Office (Xhibition Shopping Centre, Småstrandgaten; ⊗ 8am-8pm Mon-Fri, 9am-6pm Sat)

TOURIST INFORMATION

DNT office (☎ 553 35 810; www.bergen-turlag.no; Tverrgaten 4; ⊗ 10am-4pm Mon-Wed & Fri, 10am-6pm Thu, 10am-2pm Sat)

Tourist Office (☎ 555 52 000; www.visitbergen.com; Vågsallmenningen 1; ⊗ 8.30am-10pm Jun-Aug, 9am-8pm May & Sep, 9am-4pm Mon-Sat Oct-Apr)

Sights

The waterfront **fish market** at Torget is a good starting point for exploration of the city's historic district. Bergen has lots of cobblestone streets lined with older homes; one particularly pretty area for strolling is near the funicular station on Øvregaten.

BRYGGEN AREA

Bryggen, the old medieval quarter and Unesco World Heritage site, is home to museums, restaurants and shops. The alleys that run along the less-restored sides of the long timber buildings reveal an intriguing glimpse of the stacked-stone foundations and rough-plank construction of centuries past.

Some of Norway's creakiest floors are in the timber building (1704) housing the **Hanseatisk Museum** (Hanseatic Museum; ☎ 555 44 690; Finnegårdsgaten 1A; adult/child Nkr50/free; ⊗ 9am-5pm mid-May–mid-Sep, 11am-2pm Tue-Sat, 11am-4pm Sun mid-Sep–mid-May). Period character flourishes, while furnishings and odd bedchambers give a glimpse of the austere living conditions of Hanseatic merchants. The entry ticket is also valid for **Schøtstuene** (Øvregaten 50), where the Hanseatic fraternity once met for their business meetings and beer guzzling.

The tiny **Theta Museum** (☎ 553 15 393; Enhjørningsgården; adult/child Nkr20/5; ⊗ 2-4pm Tue, Sat & Sun mid-May–mid-Sep) is a one-room reconstruction of a clandestine Resistance headquarters uncovered by the Nazis in 1942. Find it hidden in an upper storey at the rear of the Bryggen warehouse with the unicorn figurehead.

Rosenkrantztzårnet (Rosenkrantz Tower; ☎ 553 14 380; Bergenhus; adult/child/student Nkr40/free/20; ⊗ 10am-4pm mid-May–Aug, noon-3pm Sun Sep–mid-May) was built in the 1560s by Bergen's governor as a residence and defence post. You can climb down to bedrock and then up to the high-ceilinged bedchambers of a 16th-century tower. Detours along the way allow you to

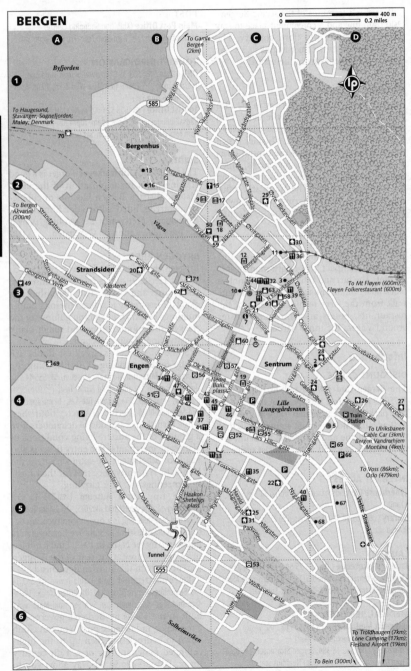

INFORMATION
Cyberhouse....1 C3
DNT Office....2 D4
Jarlens Vaskoteque....3 C3
Legevakten Medical Clinic....4 D5
Library....5 D4
Main Post Office....6 C4
Pharmacy....(see 65)
Tourist Office....7 C3

SIGHTS & ACTIVITIES
Bergen Art Museum....8 C4
Bryggens Museum....9 B2
Fish Market....10 C3
Fløibanen Funicular Station....11 C3
Hanseatisk Museum....12 C3
Håkonshallen....13 B2
Lepramuseet....14 D4
Mariakirken....15 C2
Rosenkrantztztårnet....16 B2
Schøtstuene....17 C2
Theta Museum....18 C2
West Norway Museum of Decorative Art....19 C4

SLEEPING
Augustin....20 B3
Bergen Vandrerhjem YMCA....21 C3
City Box....22 C5
Dormno....23 D3
Hos Inger....24 D4
Hotel Park Pension....25 C5
Hotel Terminus....26 D4
Intermission....27 D4
Marken Gjestehus....28 D4
Skansen Apartments....29 C2
Skansen Pensjonat....30 C3
Steens Hotell....31 C5

EATING
3-Kroneren....32 C3
Brød & Vin....33 C5
Café Opera....34 B4
Chaos Coffee Bar....35 C5
Det Lille Kaffekompaniet....36 C3
Godt Brød....37 B4
Godt Brød....38 C3
Kaffemisjonen....39 C3
Kafé Knøderen....40 C5
Kinsarvik Frukt....41 B4
Naboen....42 B4
Pingvinen....43 B4
Potetkjelleren....44 C3
Pygmallion....(see 21)
Storsenter....(see 65)
Söstrene Hagelin....45 C4
Zupperia....46 C4

DRINKING
Altona Vinbar....(see 20)
Ambrosia Bar....(see 26)
Biskopen....47 B4
Fotballpuben....48 B4
Kafe Kippers....49 A3
Logen Bar....(see 56)
Sjøboden....50 C2

ENTERTAINMENT
Bergen Kino....51 B4
Garage....52 C4
Hulen....53 C6
Kafé Fincken....54 C4
Landmark....55 C4
Logen Teater....56 B4
Metro....57 C4

SHOPPING
Boogaloo....58 C3
Bryggen Husflid....59 C3
Galleriet Shopping Centre....60 C3
Kless Kapet....61 C3
Mint....62 B3
Paraply Reparatøren....63 C3
Robot....(see 58)

TRANSPORT
Avis....64 D5
Bus Terminal....65 D4
ByGarasjen....66 D5
Centrum Bilutleie....67 D5
Hertz....68 D5
Hurtigruten Quay....69 A4
Skoltegrunnskaien (International Ferries)....70 A2
Strandkaiterminal (Express Ferries)....71 B3

suffocate in an actual dungeon or peer into ancient toilet chambers.

Håkonshallen (Håkon's Hall; ☎ 553 16 067; Bergenhus; adult/child/student Nkr40/free/20; 10am-4pm mid-May–Aug, noon-3pm Fri-Wed, 3-6pm Thu Sep–mid-May), completed by King Håkon Håkonsson in 1261 for his son's wedding, had its roof blown off in 1944 when a Dutch munitions boat exploded in the harbour. The hall has since been restored using archaeological artefacts. Be pleasantly disoriented while wandering through Escherian stairways, stopping to squint through blurry antique windows.

The site of Bergen's earliest settlement is now **Bryggens Museum** (☎ 555 88 010; Dregsalmenning 3; adult/child/student Nkr50/free/25; 10am-5pm mid-May–Aug, 11am-3pm Mon-Fri, noon-3pm Sat, noon-4pm Sun Sep–mid-May; ♿). The 800-year-old foundations unearthed during the construction have been incorporated into the exhibits, along with pottery, human skulls and runes.

ART MUSEUMS

Experience the juxtaposition of form and function from the Renaissance to the present at the **West Norway Museum of Decorative Art** (Vestlandske Kunstindustrimuseum; ☎ 553 36 633; www.vk.museum.no; Nordahl Brunsgate 9; adult/child/student Nkr50/free/40; 11am-5pm mid-May–mid-Sep, noon-4pm Tue-Sun mid-Sep–mid-May). The eclectic collection (strong in Jugenstil and modern decorative objects) includes a Lego set, an armchair shaped like a tarantula, Edvard Grieg's table setting, and a quilt made from children's raincoats. Three buildings opposite the lake fountain house the **Bergen Art Museum** (Bergen Kunstmuseum; ☎ 555 68 000; www.bergenartmuseum.no; Rasmus Meyers Allé 3, 7 & 9; adult/child/student Nkr50/free/35; 11am-5pm mid-May–mid-Sep, closed Mon mid-Sep–mid-May; ♿), a superb collection of Norwegian art from the 18th and 19th centuries, including many works by Munch and JC Dahl, as well as works by Picasso, Klee and others.

LEPRAMUSEET

Wash your hands before and after visiting the **Lepramuseet** (Leprosy Museum; ☎ 559 61 155; Kong Oscars gate 59; adult/child/student Nkr40/free/20; 11am-4pm mid-May–Aug), an enclosed wooden complex whose wards, church and kitchen appear tranquil from a cobbled, tree-shaded interior court. Not so inside, which is creepy. Buildings date to 1754.

NORWAY

NORWAY

BERGEN AKVARIET

The **aquarium** (☎ 555 57 171; www.akvariet.no; Nordnesbakken 4; adult/child Nkr150/100; ☼ 9am-8pm May-Sep, 10am-6pm Oct-Apr;) will provide an entire day's entertainment to travellers with small children. Frolic among outdoor pools and tanks, or if it's raining, head inside to check the daily schedule of films and events. Don't miss the collection of confiscated illegal pets on the 1st floor. The entry fee is reduced outside of summer.

MARIAKIRKEN

With its Romanesque entrance and twin towers, **St Mary's church** (☎ 553 15 960; Dreggen 15; adult/child Nkr20/free, admission free Sep–mid-May; ☼ 9.30-11.30am & 1-4pm Mon-Fri mid-Jun–mid-Aug, 11am-12.30pm mid-Aug–mid-Jun), Bergen's oldest building, dates from the 12th century. The interior has 15th-century frescoes and a splendid baroque pulpit.

BERGEN ENVIRONS

The open-air **Gamle Bergen** (☎ 553 94 304; Sandviken; admission free; ☼ 9am-5pm May-early Sep, shorter hours rest of year) presents around 40 buildings from the 18th and 19th centuries, including a dentist's office, bakery and houses. It's 4km north of the city centre and can be reached by city bus.

If you want to tour the former lakeside home and workshop of composer Edvard Grieg, hop on any bus from platform 20, get off at Hosbroen and follow the signs to **Troldhaugen** (☎ 559 22 992; Troldhaugvegen 65; adult/child/student Nkr60/free/20; ☼ 9am-6pm May-Sep, shorter hours Oct-Apr). Although Grieg fans will best appreciate this well-conceived presentation, the main house contains some excellent period furnishings and is generally quite interesting.

Activities

For unbeatable city views, take the **Fløibanen funicular** (☎ 553 36 800; Vetrlidsalmenning 21; adult/child 1-way Nkr35/20; ☼ 8am-midnight May-Aug, 8am-11pm Sep-Apr;) to the top of Mt Fløyen (320m). Trails marked with dilapidated signs lead into the forest from the hilltop station. Trails 1 and 3 are the longest, each making 5km loops through hilly woodlands. For a delightful 40-minute walk back to the city, take trail 4 and connect with trail 6.

The **Ulriksbanen cable car** (☎ 552 02 020; www.ul riken.no; adult/child return Nkr95/50; ☼ 9am-9pm May-Aug,

shorter hours rest of year) to the top of Mt Ulriken (642m) offers a panoramic view of Bergen, fjords and mountains. Many take the cable car one way and walk (about three hours) across a well-beaten trail to the funicular station at Mt Fløyen.

Tours

The train station sells the **Norway in a Nutshell** (☎ 815 68 222; www.fjordtours.com) ticket combining morning trains from Bergen to Flåm, a ferry along the spectacular Aurlandsfjorden and Nærøyfjorden to Gudvangen, a bus to Voss and a train back to Bergen (Nkr935) in time for a late dinner, or you can continue on to Oslo (Nkr1295).

Sleeping

The tourist office books rooms in private homes (single/double from Nkr300/450, plus Nkr50 booking fee); it can also find you last-minute hotel discounts.

BUDGET

Bergen Vandrerhjem YMCA (☎ 556 06 055; www .bergenhostel.com; Nedre Korskirkealmenning 4; budget dm Nkr155, 4-/6-person dm Nkr210/230, d Nkr750; ☼ reception 7am-midnight) Perfectly central. Dorm dwellers reside in plain, linoleum-floor bunk rooms sleeping four to six, or in windowless caverns (noisy) sleeping 15 or 32. Rooftop decks provide views over the water and surrounding garrets. Breakfast costs Nkr50 and bed prices drop after your first night.

Marken Gjestehus (☎ 553 14 404; www.marken -gjestehus.com; Kong Oscars gate 45; 4-/6-/8-person dm Nkr220/195/175, s/d Nkr450/600) Take an old elevator to the 4th floor to find this central hostel. Rooms have wooden floors, spiffy furniture of recent vintage, and big windows. There's a coin laundry and, often, a decent view. Breakfast costs extra.

Intermission (☎ 553 00 400; Kalfarveien 8; dm Nkr180; ☼ mid-Jun–mid-Aug) This old white house has 37 beds, where the hospitable Christian Student Fellowship serves waffles to guests on Monday and Thursday nights. Laundry facilities are available. Breakfast costs Nkr50.

Dorm.no (☎ 982 38 600; www.dm.no; Kong Oscars gate 44; dm Nkr220;) Offers 16 beds with individual reading lamps in an attractive dormitory with linens included. There's a fine rockabilly cafe-pub, a wood terrace with flowers and chairs, and a spotless, good-looking shared kitchen. Breakfast costs extra.

FRYKT OG FRYD

If you've decided to avoid the crowds and visit Bergen in the winter, why not avoid them further and join **Frykt og Fryd** (Fear & Joy), a small group of cold-water enthusiasts who go swimming in the harbour every Sunday at 1pm. Many of the five to 15 people likely to show up will be university students who are very welcoming of anyone brave enough to join their weekly ritual. A Portuguese hymn to the ocean is sung right before the plunge to better fortify the group's collective resolve. To find the informal swim club, head to the USF building (Kafe Clippers). After your dip, you'll be sure to get plenty of stellar advice on where to drink your pain away.

Also recommended:

Bergen Vandrerhjem Montana (☎ 552 08 070; www.montana.no; Johan Blyttsvei 30; 20-/4-person dm Nkr200/265, s/d Nkr650/780; ☺ 3 Jan–20 Dec) A large institutional hostel 5km away by bus 31. Mountain-top with a good view.

Lone Camping (☎ 553 92 960; www.lonecamping.no; Hardangerveien 697, Haukeland; camp sites Nkr150, 2-person cabin Nkr610) Camp sites lie along a grassy lakeshore. It's 19km east of Bergen by bus 900 (30 minutes).

MIDRANGE

City Box (☎ 553 12 500; www.citybox.no; Nygårdsgaten 31; s Nkr400-500, d Nkr500-600) For simple, tasteful rooms with no frills, this place offers great prices by providing no amenities. It's near some of Bergen better cafes and is slightly removed from the tourist zone.

Skansen Pensjonat (☎ 553 19 080; www.skansen-pensjonat.no; Vetrlidsalmenningen 29; s Nkr400-450, d Nkr650-750) Trudge up steep cobbled streets through a pretty neighbourhood to this hilltop house dating from 1918 and with outstanding views. If you're lucky, your period room will have a balcony.

Hos Inger (☎ 553 21 241; inyg@hib.no; Grønnevoler 14m; s/d Nkr500/700) Sleep in a wooden house (110 years old) on a quiet pedestrian street in a residential neighbourhood near the train station. The handful of rooms are comfortable and share a cheerful common kitchen and living room. Breakfast costs Nkr100.

Skansen Apartments (☎ 412 01 780; Nedre Blekvei 6; home.broadpark.no/~ggrin/; 1-/2-person apt Nkr500/800) Beautifully located up a hill in a maze of

pretty, cobbled streets, this small operation lets out a handful of attractive apartments with private kitchens and shared bath. It's in a very quiet location, with views into the harbour below.

TOP END

Hotel Terminus (☎ 552 12 500; www.ght.no; Zander Kaaes gate 6; s/d Nkr750/1150) Thankfully, this classic hotel, long favoured by Norwegian royals, is undergoing renovation. Newly updated rooms restore comfort and grandeur, but at the time of research many awaited badly needed facelifts. Avoid these, but not the fantastic Ambrosia Bar (p339).

Augustin (☎ 553 04 000; www.augustin.no; C Sundtsgata 22; s Nkr750-950, d Nkr1150-1450; 🖳 ♿) A family-run hotel, the Augustin dates to 1919, with age showing nicely in a few parlours. Full of contemporary Norwegian art and design (painting, lamps, furniture), modernised rooms come with beautiful bedspreads and linens. The basement is a 16th-century taverna (p339).

our pick **Steens Hotell** (☎ 553 14 050; www.steenshotel.no; Parkveien 22; s/d Nkr990/1340; P 🖳) Expect Swedish-style rooms with private bathrooms in a 19th-century home; many have pleasant views over a landscaped park. The real treat is the 1890s dining room, where breakfast is served – check out the gilded wallpaper, an odd wooden chandelier and stained glass depicting butchered meat.

Hotel Park Pension (☎ 555 44 400; www.parkhotel.no; Harald Hårfagresgate 35; s/d Nkr1190/1250; P 🖳) This 19th-century charmer is family owned, and stuffed to the rafters with grandma's antiques and unusual tools. Spacious rooms come with private bathrooms and breakfast.

Eating

RESTAURANTS

Fløyen Folkerestaurant (☎ 553 36 999; Bellevuebakken 9; pastries & cakes Nkr15-45; ☺ 11am-8pm May-Sep, 11am-8pm Sat & Sun rest of year) On the summit of Fløyen, this restaurant presides over Bergen with unbeatable views and hot chocolate. In the warmth of summer, the patio fills with sunbathers and beer drinkers.

Brød & Vin (☎ 553 26 704; Christies gate 13; mains Nkr50-100) Eat piles of Asian noodle dishes, such as vegetable chop suey, and drink cheap beer with crowds of Bergen penny-pinchers. The room is comfortable, though the filling fare has a reputation for lacking flavour.

NORWAY

Zupperia (☎ 555 58 144; Nordahl Brunsgate; soup Nkr55-115) Come downstairs to enjoy 11 kinds of soups (with sides of bread), such as *husenottsuppe* (oxtail boiled with vegetables), and reindeer with cream and mushrooms.

Pygmalion (☎ 553 23 360; Nedre Korskirkeallmenningen 4; mains Nkr69-149) Many local vegetarians favour this spot with its fireplace, piped French music and red-checked tableclothes, and respectable selection of meat-free options (stir fry, pasta, veggie burger). Comfortable, but not elegant.

our pick Bein (☎ 555 91 100; Fjøsangerveien 30; sandwiches Nkr75, mains Nkr105-160; ⏰ to 1.30am Sun-Thu, to 2.30am Fri & Sat) For authentic, exactingly prepared Norwegian cuisine, track down this former pharmacy (an Art Deco beauty from 1939) with original labels on drawers (for pregnancy tests, penicillin etc). Eat squash, cod and sausages from the butcher shop around corner in a room that crosses a bar with an informal diner, far from where the tourists roam.

Naboen (☎ 559 06 290; Sigurds gate 4b; mains Nkr98-148) This hidden pub serves local beer (Bayer Ale) with a fine, strong taste. Laid-back regulars quaff it while eating Swedish meatballs and lingonberries from a more-expensive restaurant upstairs of the same name. Enter the fancier room and look for stairs to the basement.

Pingvinen (☎ 556 04 646; Vaskerelven 20; mains Nkr120-149; ⏰ to 3.30am) A casual hang-out with old brick walls and bar-stool seating, this pub has a blackboard that announces the day's few offerings. As a reaction against the trend towards fusion and other international food fads, cooks here embrace traditional Norwegian cuisine and prepare hearty meals (fish with macaroni, meatloaf with leeks, cabbage in a buttery sauce) with finesse.

Potetkjelleren (☎ 553 20 070; Kong Oscargt 1a; mains Nkr280, 3-courses Nkr445; ⏰ 4-10pm Mon-Sat) Eat local specialities, including steinbitt (a kind of ugly catfish) and several kinds of crab, in an old potato cellar with old stones walls covered in thick white-washing. For a celebratory evening with knowledgable and extensive wine-pairings, you'll be hard-pressed to find a better spot.

CAFES

Det Lille Kaffekompaniet (☎ 553 29 272; Nedre Fjellsmug 2) Hidden on a narrow cobbled street behind the funicular station, this intimate coffeeshop brews with skill and serves cakes.

Kafé Knøderen (☎ 416 60 357; Lydeer Sagens gate 22; snacks & light meals Nkr15-78) Enjoy coffee and light pancakes with crystallised sugar, and good sandwiches in this lovely casual cafe filled with light wooden furniture of light greens, blues and greys. There's Murphy's on tap and a turntable playing Janis Joplin.

Café Opera (☎ 552 30 315; Engen 18; light meals Nkr85-140, sandwiches Nkr40-60) A continental vibe permeates through this early-20th-century cafe, serving brown rolls with brie, walnut butter and cherries, salads and daily soups. Big corner windows stare at the opera house and you can lounge on 2nd-floor couches. There are DJs at night.

Chaos Coffee Bar (☎ 553 21 550; Fosswinckels gate 16; light meals Nkr50-80) Bustling at lunch, this neighbourhood cafe, with its thrift-store assortment of colourful tableclothes, lamps and upholstered chairs, serves coffee, beer and peppery vegetable pasta to chatting students.

Kaffemisjonen (☎ 911 90 757; Øvre Korskirkealmenningen 5; sandwiches Nkr55-95) Drink truly superior espresso at its handcrafted best, along with croissants that taste air-lifted from Paris. The room enjoys a beautiful, understated design with a tall ceiling, a worn floor and big windows overlooking a streetscape of buildings from the Middle Ages to the present. Meat sandwiches often come with thick, sweet vinegar.

QUICK EATS

Godt Brød (☎ 553 28 000; Nedre Korskirkealmenningen 12) This bakery does organic breads, pastries and delicious, filling herb-dough pizzas topped with marinated vegetables (Nkr40). There's also a branch at Veste Torggata 2.

Söstrene Hagelin (☎ 553 26 949; Olav Kyrres gate 33; dishes Nkr35-100; ⏰ 9am-6pm Mon-Fri, 10am-3pm Sat) Delicious fish pudding, fish casserole and other such delicacies. Filling takeaway fish balls (Nkr35) come with potatoes.

3-Kroneren (Kong Oscars gate 3; sausages Nkr45) Enjoy a selection of glistening, delicious sausages, including bratwurst reindeer and lamb, from one of Norway's best take-out windows.

SELF-CATERING

Storsenter, at the bus station, has fast-food outlets, a Vinmonopolet and Rimi and Spar supermarkets. Torget's fish market provides fresh fruit and seafood snacks to droves of tourists, including salmon rolls for Nkr20 and a plate of shrimp, crab and fried fish for between Nkr60 and Nkr100.

Kinsarvik Frukt (Olav Kyrres gate 38) is a small grocery store with a health-food section.

Drinking

Bergen loves to drink, and the line between pub, cafe and restaurant is very blurry. Kafé Knøderen (opposite), Café Opera (opposite), Pingvinen (opposite) and Landmark (right) are three stellar options worth considering.

Logen Bar (☎ 552 33 801; Øvre Ole Bulls plass 6) A hangout for artists and journalists, Logan bar has salon-like rooms that benefit from tall ceilings and a balcony. Drink here to feel like you're part of a postimpressionist painting. It's hard to find: enter, go up one set of stairs, turn left and climb a second stairwell. The conversational mood is deliberately set by a lack of music.

Altona Vinbar (☎ 553 04 072; Strandgaten 81; ♥ 6pm-12.30am Mon-Thu, 6pm-1.30am Fri & Sat) A taverna since the 16th-century, this wine bar has small, cell-like rooms that create a subterranean maze connected by incredibly short openings (duck through a hole 1m high). Except for coloured light emited by some incredible lanterns, the place is candle lit.

Biskopen (Sigurds gate 5) Large crowds are attracted to the great beer selection at this dark pub filled with books. Thanks to piles of old furniture, it feels like it's been here forever, though really the goods were imported from an airfield in Evenes.

Ambrosia Bar (☎ 552 12 500; Zander Kaaes gate 6) Here you'll find a grand hotel bar little changed from the time that Roald Amundsen lingered amid its knotty furniture and chandeliers, and plotted polar explorations. Nowadays you can drink from an extensive whiskey menu.

Sjøboden (☎ 553 16 777; Bryggen 29) It's a long, narrow and unpretentious route from entry to this bar in a Hanseatic-era building. Friday nights your odyssey will involve squeezing through crowds, dodging ceiling-suspended barrels and bumping into a bad two-piece passionately playing 'Proud Mary'. Many sing along and few wear cool clothing.

Kafe Kippers (☎ 553 10 060; Georgernes Verft) Enjoy outdoor, harbourside tables, part of a cultural centre, filled with beer drinkers. The view takes in water, rocky hills, islands and boats. There's jazz many nights.

Bein (☎ 555 91 100; Fjøsangerveien 30) Weekend events at this pub-cafe are typified by clas-sic cocktail parties or speciality DJs, such as a masterful 63-year-old bouncer who spins from his encyclopaedic jazz collection from the 1920s and '30s every last Saturday.

Fotballpuben (☎ 559 00 579; Vestre Torggate 9) A long-standing favourite among football enthusiasts, this sports bar provides plenty of scarves, televisions and fans to ensure quality match-watching.

Entertainment

For details and schedules of entertainment events, including classical concerts, contact the tourist office. Atop Mt Fløyen, classical concerts are held nightly at 8pm from mid-June to mid-August.

LIVE MUSIC

Garage (☎ 553 21 980; www.garage.no; Christies gate 14; ♥ from 6pm) Norway's rock headquarters consistently books top bands, including international acts. Concerts are held in a big, black basement space.

Hulen (☎ 553 33 838; www.hulen.no, in Norwegian; Olaf Ryes vei 47) Carved into the bowels of a hill, Hulen occupies a former bomb shelter. The renowned rock club is over 30 years old. Performances occur in a very dark space of the kind that makes everyone look hot. Cheap beer (Nkr32) before 11pm.

Logen Teater (☎ 552 32 015; www.logen-teater.no, in Norwegian; Øvre Ole Bulls plass 6) You'd never know it from the street, but drag yourself inside this place and you'll find a century-old, two-storey, pillared theatre. Concerts are held several times a month; expect to see classical performances, pop and rock.

Also check out Landmark (below).

CINEMA

Bergen Kino (☎ 820 50 005; Neumannsgate 3; tickets Nkr60-80) A 13-screen cinema showing first-run movies.

GAY & LESBIAN

Kafé Fincken (☎ 553 21 316; Nygårdsgaten 2A; ♥ Wed-Sun) Contemporary and stylish, this chrome-and-white bar has a small dance floor. The stuffed stag head covered in flowers is a nice touch.

NIGHTCLUBS

Landmark (☎ 553 17 755; Rasmus Meyers Alle 5; ♥ noon-1am Sun-Thu, noon-2am Fri & Sat) This place, a kind of performative extension of the art museum that owns it, hosts experimental artists, book readings, bands and DJs – care for an explosive hybrid of hardcore and electronic jungle? White carpet, white walls and tall ceilings covered in white cushions create a muted, subtle space of modernist high-design. At night, lighting transforms the room with eerie results. Weekdays, grab a subdued drink and attend an event (often with no cover). On many weekends, dance with Bergen's coolest.

Metro (☎ 555 59 655; Nedre Ole Bullsplass 4; cover Nkr100) Inside the SAS Hotel Norge you'll find a roomful of girls who study economics and the guys who love them dancing to pop songs. There's a dress code, so best not to arrive straight from the mountain.

Shopping

Intimate Skostredet (Shoe Street) provides two blocks of independent boutiques, many of which sell goods made by hip local designers. Stop in **Boogaloo** (☎ 553 28 399; Skostredet 16) for hand-sewn bags, cool duds for both genders, and feminine skirts with strong silhouettes. In the same store, find **Robot** (☎ 916 97 350), selling obscure records and books. Otherwise, browse vintage suits and gowns in **Kless Kapet** (☎ 943 75 885; Skostredet 12).

Elsewhere, the chain **Bryggen Husflid** (☎ 553 28 803; Bugården) offers quality stock of traditional knit sweaters and mittens in a Bryggen environment.

For protection against all that rain, **Paraply Reparatøren** (☎ 553 26 911; 16 Høendergaten) sells designer umbrella, flasks, walking sticks and fancy toilet bits.

Follow a local architecture student's advice and come to **Mint** (☎ 553 15 575; Strandkaien 13) for 'souvenirs I would actually buy'. Find wooden dolls for keeping secret notes plus well-designed pillows, bags, stationery, and jewellery by Norwegian artists (for example, button earrings with tiny words typed on them).

The Galleriet shopping centre, northwest of the post office, has boutiques, camera shops, a grocery store and a good bookshop, Norli.

Getting There & Away

AIR
The airport is in Flesland, 19km southwest of central Bergen. Direct flights connect Bergen with major cities in Norway, plus a handful of international destinations.

BOAT
A daily **Fjord1** (www.fjord1.no) boat runs to Balestrand (Nkr420, four hours) and Flåm (Nkr560, 5½ hours). Northbound express boats go to Måløy (Nkr595, 4½ hours, one daily) and southbound express boats to Stavanger (one-way/return Nkr620/710, four hours, two daily). These leave from Strandkaiterminalen on the western side of Vågen.

The *Hurtigruten* leaves from a newly built terminal east of Nøstegaten.

International ferries dock north of Rosenkrantztårnet at Skoltegunnskaien.

BUS
Express buses run throughout the Western Fjord region, as well as to Stryn (Nkr465, 6½ hours, three daily), Ålesund (Nkr596, 10 hours, two daily), Trondheim (Nkr783, 14¼ hours, one daily) and Stavanger (Nkr470, five hours, eight daily).

TRAIN
Trains run to Oslo (Nkr761, 6½ to 7¾ hours, three to four daily). A local line runs to Voss (Nkr165, 1¼ hours) every hour or two; four of these run to/from Myrdal (Nkr248, two to three hours) for connections to the Flåmsbana railway. Lockers at the train station cost from Nkr15 to Nkr40.

CAR
Avis (☎ 555 53 955; Lars Hilles gate 20A; ⏰ 7.30am-4pm Mon-Fri, 9am-1pm Sat)
Centrum Bilutleie (☎ 552 12 950; Lars Hilles gate 20; ⏰ 8am-4pm Mon-Fri)
Hertz (☎ 559 64 070; Nygaardsgaten 89; ⏰ 8am-4pm Mon-Fri) It has a second office near the airport. Discount with Bergen Card.

Getting Around

TO/FROM THE AIRPORT
Flybussen (www.flybussen.no) operates between the airport and Bergen bus station (Nkr75, 45 minutes, at least twice hourly), stopping at many large hotels. Taxis cost Nkr250 to Nkr300.

BUS
City buses (☎ 177) cost Nkr20 per ride, while fares beyond the centre are based on distance travelled. The free bus 100 runs back and forth between Bryggen and the bus station.

CAR & MOTORCYCLE

It's best to park and explore the city centre on foot. Except where there are meters, street parking is for residents. If you see a 'P' for parking but the sign has 'sone' on it, it's a reserved area. Metered parking has a 30-minute limit in the busiest spots and two hours elsewhere. The parking area at Syndnes allows up to nine hours (free at night). The easiest and cheapest garage is **ByGarasjen** (per 24hr Nkr75; 24hr).

VOSS

pop 6100

Voss is a year-round sports centre with an attractive lakeside location. Conveniently positioned within a short drive of many top-notch athletic experiences and containing a centre that provides most modern amenities, Voss attracts many adventuresome tourists as well as downhill skiers from Bergen. Unfortunately, the town's collection of buildings are pretty drab. The **tourist office** (565 20 800; www.visitvoss .no; Uttrågata; 8am-7pm Mon-Sat, noon-7pm Sun late Jun-early Aug, 9am-2.30pm Mon-Fri rest of year) is a short walk east from the train station.

Voss's second claim to fame is a culinary oddity: deliciously prepared sheep heads (though the whole face lies staring back from your plate, only eat the tongue, cheek and eyes). Hundreds of the things are consumed at an annual sheep festival in late September or early October.

Sights & Activities

For bookings or to get an idea about what's available, the tourist office can advise on white-water rafting (Nkr850), canoeing (Nkr500), waterfall abseiling (Nkr750), riverboarding (Nkr880) and just about any adrenaline-inducing behaviour your loved ones would rather not know about, such as bungee jumping from a parasail (Nkr1800).

The **Mølstertunet Museum** (565 11 511; Mølstervegen 143; adult/child Nkr35/free; 10am-5pm May-Sep, shorter hours rest of year), on the hillside north of town, features 16 farm buildings standing in their original positions, which date from the mid-17th to mid-19th centuries. A **cable car** (rides Nkr50; 11am-5pm mid-May–Aug) whisks you up to the spectacular view from Mt Hangur every 15 minutes. In ski season (December to April) use it to access **Voss Resort** (565 30 220; www.vossresort.com; adult/child lift ticket Nkr325/245) and its 40km of alpine trails, some of which are floodlit at night.

Sleeping & Eating

Voss Camping (565 11 597; www.vosscamping.no; Prestegardsalléen 40; camp sites Nkr140, cabins Nkr500) Small and lakeside, this crowded spot, a convenient 300m from the tourist office, has a few shade trees that break up its grassy field. It attracts caravans.

Voss Vandrerhjem (565 12 017; www.hihostels .com; Evangervegen 68; dm/s/d Nkr295/660/990;) Find modern rooms with private bathrooms and a fine lakeside position about 600m west of the train station. The hostel has bicycles, canoes, kayaks and rowing boats for hire, and there's a sauna.

Fleischer's Hotel (565 20 500; www.fleischers.no; Evangervegen; s/d from Nkr900/1300;) For historic character, check out this classic behemoth from 1864. With its massive dormers and steep roof peaks, it looks like a Swiss fantasy and is very popular in ski season.

In town, most eating comes in the form of bland, busy cafeterias. Among them, **Ringheim Kafe** (565 11 365; Vangsgata 32; mains Nkr49-150) serves cakes, sandwiches, soup and daily meals (chicken with chips, vegetarian stir fry) to people taking advantage of its sunny windows.

Smalahovetunet (565 16 965; meals Nkr300) For hearty traditional fare, visit Ivar Løne's farm. He'll show you around and serve you a sheep head or smoked lamb ribs with homemade beer, cake and coffee. Call four hours ahead so he has enough time to boil your head. The riverside farm is 10km towards Oslo on the E16.

Nightlife options are few. Many enjoy the pub at Hotel Jarl, and on weekends many of the town's younger crew goes to Pentagon, a club at the Park Hotel.

Getting There & Away

Buses stop at the train station. NSB operates the renowned Bergensbanen to/from Bergen (Nkr165, 1¼ hours, eight to 15 daily) and Oslo (Nkr673, six hours, four or five daily). Connect at Myrdal (Nkr101, 45 minutes, eight to 15 daily) with the scenic line down to Flåm.

HARDANGERFJORD

A notch less jagged and steep than Sognefjord, Hardangerfjord's slopes support farms and wildflowers, which picturesquely enhance the green hills as they plunge into the water. The second-longest fjord in Norway, it stretches inland from a cluster of rocky coastal islands

NORWAY

DETOURS: LOFTHUS

In the heart of orchard country, the buildings forming Lofthus' tiny centre are oriented along the water's edge and not the highway, giving the place a yesteryear feel. Many feel it's the prettiest village on Hardangerfjord. In it you'll find the glitzy **Hotel Ullensvang** (☎ 536 70 000; www.hotel -ullensvang.no; s/d Nkr1250/1550; ⓖ), in whose predecessor Edvard Grieg took his holidays, a single cafe that occasionally books live music and a grocery store.

Back in the 12th century, the town's orchards stretched up to the mountain ridge and medieval monks built steps into the mountain to make the hike easier. The steps are still there to make your own hike easier.

To sleep, try **Lofthus Camping** (☎ 536 61 364; www.lofthuscamping.com; camp sites Nkr130, 2-/4-bed cabins Nkr480/590; ⓨ May-Sep; ⓡ). Climb a sliver of a road through 2km of flowering fruit trees before finding this treasure on a grassy bluff with stupendous views over the fjord and the distant glacier Folgefonna. The camping ground lies within an old orchard, and you can pitch your tent under apple, pear and plum trees (and pick and eat freely). Simple cabins cling to the cliff's edge.

---

to the frozen heights of the **Folgefonn** and **Hardangerjøkulen** icecaps. The area is known for its orchards (apples, cherries and plums) and bursts into bloom from mid-May to mid-June. Route 13 between **Brimnes** and **Lofthus** travels through particularly pretty farm country, with bleating goats and stands selling eggs, honey and fruit.

The villages along the east coast of the central part of the fjord (also called Kvinnheradsfjorden) are connected to the national road network by an 11km tunnel under the Folgefonn; **Rosendal** and **Sunndal** are popular destinations, with great mountain and glacier scenery. At Rosendal there's the **Baroniet Rosendal** (☎ 534 82 999; www.baroniet.no; adult/child Nkr75/10, grounds free; ⓨ from 11am May-Sep), Norway's only baronial mansion, an extremely pretty affair dating from 1665 and surrounded by flowering gardens, mountains and little else. From Sunndal, an easy walk leads 3km to lake Bondhusvatnet and the glacier **Bondhusbreen**.

On the other side of Folgefonn, **Odda** is an industrial town with a dramatic location. The town itself isn't pretty, but it's a convenient spot to plot hikes and glacier tours thanks to the **tourist office** (☎ 536 41 297; www.visitodda .com; ⓨ 8am-4pm Mon-Fri). **Tyssedal**, 6km north of Odda, has a **hydroelectric power station museum** (☎ 536 50 050; www.nvim.no; adult/child/student Nkr70/ free/35; ⓨ 10am-5pm May-Aug, shorter hours rest of year) and an impressive **funicular railway**.

At the innermost reaches of Hardangerfjorden you'll find the **Eidfjord** area, with sheer mountains, huge waterfalls, spiral road tunnels and the extraordinary **Kjeåsen**, a deserted farm perched on a mountain ledge about

6km northeast of Eidfjord. For information, contact **Eidfjord tourist office** (☎ 536 73 400; www .visiteidfjord.no; ⓨ 10am-8pm Mon-Fri, 10am-6pm Fri & Sat Jun-Aug, shorter hours rest of year).

At picturesque **Utne**, 55km north of Odda, you'll find an interesting collection of old buildings at the **Hardanger Folk Museum** (☎ 536 70 040; www.hardanger.museum.no; adult/child Nkr50/free; ⓨ 10am-4pm May-Aug, shorter hours rest of year), and the pretty Utne Hotel.

Helpful regional information can be found at www.hardangerfjord.com.

Sleeping & Eating

B&B (☎ 534 82 999; s/d 700/900; ⓟ) In Rosendal, you can stay on the lovely baronial grounds in this B&B, once a 19th-century farmhouse, operated by the museum. A wide-plank dining room serves three-course meals (Nkr400) with herbs from the garden.

Utne Hotel (☎ 536 66 400; www.utnehotel.no; Utne Sentrum; s/d Nkr825/1300; ⓨ Mar-Dec) This historic wooden hotel, known for its fabulous decor, was built in 1722 and has been in romantic business ever since. Meals are available in the dining room (three courses Nkr425). Book ahead for both.

Getting There & Away

While thorough exploration of Hardangerfjord is best accomplished with a car, those with little time and no wheels would do well to book a round-trip **Fjord Tour** (☎ 815 68 222; www.fjord tours.no; adult/child Nkr770/430) from Bergen, which combines bus, ferry and train with stops in Voss, Ulvik and Eidfjord.

Tide (☎ 05505; www.tide.no) operates many of Hardangerfjord's buses and ferries. In summer, there are numerous possibilities for day trips to Hardangerfjord from Bergen using buses and ferries. These last for up to 12 hours with stops of two to six hours allowing brief explorations of towns and surrounds. Destinations include Rosendal (adult/child Nkr400/255), Lofthus (Nkr490/280), Utne (Nkr490/280) and Eidfjord (Nkr770/430). Tickets can be purchased at Bergen's tourist office.

One to three daily Nor-Way Bussekspress buses run from Odda and Utne to Bergen (Nkr520, seven hours) and Oslo (Nkr520, 7¼ hours).

SOGNEFJORDEN

Sognefjorden, Norway's longest (204km) and deepest (1308m) fjord, cuts a deep slash across the map of western Norway. In some places, sheer lofty walls rise more than 1000m above the water, while in others there is a far gentler shoreline with farms, orchards and small towns.

The broad main waterway is impressive, but by cruising into the fjord's narrower arms, such as the deep and lovely Nærøyfjorden (on the Unesco World Heritage List) to Gudvangen, you'll be able to enjoy the idyllic views of sheer cliff faces and cascading waterfalls.

Find regional tourist information at www.sognefjord.no.

Getting There & Away

Fjord1 (☎ 559 07 070; www.fjord1.no) operates express boats between Bergen and Sogndal (Nkr525, 4½ hours, one daily) and a route to Flåm (Nkr605, 5½ hours, one daily), each stopping at towns along the way.

There are local ferries linking the fjord towns and buses. See www.ruteinfo.net and in timetables available in tourist offices.

Flåm
pop 500

A tiny village of orchards and a handful of buildings scenically set at the head of Aurlandsfjorden, Flåm is a jumping-off spot for travellers taking the Gudvangen ferry or the Sognefjorden express boat. It's also the only place on Sognefjorden with rail connections, and is the turnaround point for those doing the Norway in a Nutshell tour, serving as the base station for the dramatic **Flåmsbana** (Flåm railway). Though it sees an amazing 500,000 visitors every summer, walk a few minutes from the centre and you'll experience solitude. Or get up early, watch the first train leave and the town get suddenly empty as horn blasts periodically echo through the valley.

In summer, adventurous visitors arrive from Finse by mountain bike along Rallarvegen, the old road used by workers who built the railroad. It's a five- or six-hour downhill ride, obscenely picturesque, and you

CRUISING THE FJORDS

It can't be overstated: climb aboard a fjord-bound ship in the bloom of summer and you've doomed yourself to the experience of life-changing, metaphysical beauty. Bring an extra layer or two as the wind is bracing even on warm days and you'll want to spend as much time as possible on deck.

Fjord Tours (☎ 815 68 222; www.fjord-tours.com) has mastered the art of making the most of limited time with a series of tours originating in Bergen, in particular **Hardanger in a Nutshell**, **Sognefjord in a Nutshell** and **Norway in a Nutshell**, which are designed to take in the greatest hits of a region and can be accomplished in a single, hurried day. Note that some tours make use of coaches and trains in addition to boats, so carefully look at itineraries, if you want to spend a lot of time on the water. If you'd like to break in a particular town and sleep overnight, you can do so and continue your tour the next day.

Tide (☎ 05505; www.tide.no) operates a network of express passenger boats that travel from Bergen down much of Sognefjord, stopping off in Balestrand and Fjærland among other places. Additional service is offered between Bergen and Hardangerfjord and between Stavanger and Lysefjord.

From mid-April to mid-September, the northbound **Hurtigruten** chugs down the Geirangerfjord en route to Ålesund.

Even those in cars will be cruising the fjords at times, thanks to numerous time-saving (and gorgeous) ferry crossings.

can return your rented bike in the Flåm centre. Contact the **tourist office** (☎ 576 33 313; www .alr.no; ⏰ 8.30am-8pm Jun-Aug, 8.30am-4pm May & Sep), at the train station, for details.

The friendly **Flåm Camping & Hostel** (☎ 576 32 121; www.hihostels.no; dm/s/d Nkr2655/330/570; ⏰ May-Sep) has just 31 beds – book early. It's a few minutes' walk from the station: go up the riverside track and over the bridge. At water level on the fringe of the village, **Heimly Pensjonat** (☎ 576 32 300; www.heimly.no; s/d Nkr650/850) has ordinary rooms with impressive views.

Near the station, there's a **cafeteria** and **Togrestauranten** (☎ 576 32 155; mains Nkr90-165), housed in wooden rail cars, and serving traditional Norwegian dishes. It's either novel or cheesy, depending on your mood and age. For a traditional feast, try the high-end **Fretheim Hotel** (☎ 576 32 300; www.frethheim-hotel.no; mains Nkr270-330), where chefs cure, salt and smoke their own meat and prepare an 'ecological' menu. Want some tasty fish? The informal **Toget Cafe** (mains Nkr100-150) serves up daily specials that are good quality for their price. Want a beer? Enter **Aegir Bryggeri**, a dimly-lit microbrewery with antlers, deer pelts, leather couches and central hearth. If lucky, you'll drink a concoction by David Dudek, a genius guest brewer.

The **Flåmsbana** (☎ 576 32 100; www.flaamsbana .no; adult/child Nkr230/110) runs to Myrdal 10 times daily, some in sync with the Oslo–Bergen service.

Fjord1 ferries and express boats head out to towns around Sognefjorden, with service to Balestrand (Nkr250, two hours, two daily) and Bergen (Nkr605, 5½ hours, one daily), among other places.

Balestrand
pop 800

Quiet Balestrand enjoys a mountain backdrop and fjord views. In the early 19th century, the beauty of its surroundings and the eerie quality of its summer light attracted a community of landscape painters whose work then popularised the area for well-heeled tourists. Today, the low-key farming village remains a favourite destination for travellers, who spend a lot of their time walking and contemplating. The **tourist office** (☎ 576 91 255; www.sognefjord.no; ⏰ 8am-6pm Mon-Sat, 10am-5pm Sun Jun-Aug, 10am-5pm Mon-Sat May & Sep) rents bikes.

The road that runs south along the fjord has little traffic and is a pleasant place to stroll.

It's lined with apple orchards, ornate older homes and gardens, a **19th-century English church** and **Viking burial mounds**. One mound is topped by a statue of the legendary King Bele, erected by Germany's Kaiser Wilhelm II, who spent his holidays here until WWI.

For a longer **hike**, take the small ferry (Nkr15) across the Esefjord to the Dragsvik side, where there is an abandoned country road that forms the first leg of an 8km walk back to Balestrand.

At **Sjøtun Camping** (☎ 576 91 223; www.sjotun .com; camp sites from Nkr35, cabins Nkr250; ⏰ Jun-Sep), a 15-minute walk south along the fjord, you can pitch a tent amid apple trees or rent a rustic four-bunk cabin at great rates. **Balestrand Hostel** (☎ 576 91 303; www.kringsja.no; dm/s/d Nkr255/600/790; ⏰ late Jun–mid-Aug; Ⓟ) is a pleasant lodge-style place perched near the water. **Midtnes Pensjonat** (☎ 576 91 133; www .midtnes.no; s Nkr730, d from Nkr780; Ⓟ), next to the English church, occupies a charming white house where you'll eat breakfast with good views. There's an attractive terrace and a complimentary rowing boat moored steps away. Consider paying a bit more for a room with a fjord-staring balcony.

ourpick Kvikne's Hotel (☎ 576 94 200; www .kviknes.no; d in historic bldg Nkr2210, s/d in modern bldg Nkr1080/1660; ⏰ Apr-Sep; Ⓟ) is a supremely grand and pristinely preserved timber affair from the late 19th century. It boasts a fabulous collection of art and superb craftsmanship in its 'dragon-style' lounges. As you sit in a chair once owned by the landscape painter JC Dahl staring at the summer-lit fjord, you won't be the first to weep. Many rooms have lovely, fjord-oriented balconies – you want one of these. A modern addition is tacked on, which is comfortable, but doesn't compare.

Also at Kvikne's, enjoy a lavish dinner buffet (Nkr445) that would satisfy the most discerning gourmand or head to its bar for some aquavit. Otherwise there's a supermarket and pedestrian restaurant opposite the dock.

Buses run to Sogndal (Nkr113, 1¼ hours, three to five daily). Express boats run to/from Bergen (Nkr420, four hours) and Flåm (Nkr210, 1¾ hours). Between May and September, car ferries run though the narrow Fjærlandsfjorden to Fjærland (Nkr175, 1¼ hours, two daily), gateway to the glacial wonderlands of Jostedalsbreen. For a day tour, Nkr500/250 per adult/child gets a return ferry trip, bus to Fjærland's glacier museum, admission and a visit to the glacier itself. See below for info on the glacier bus to Nigardsbreen.

Sogndal & Around
pop 6700

Sogndal, a modern regional centre, is a starting point for day trips in the area. While it has more amenities than many of the area's smaller towns, it is also far less beautiful. Of most interest is the **Nigardsbreen glacier**, 70km to the north, followed by Norway's oldest **stave church** (dating from 1150 and on the Unesco World Heritage List), in Urnes across the Lustrafjord, and the **Sogn Folkmuseum** near Kaupanger, 11km east of Sogndal. Also in Kaupanger, there's a superb **stave church** dating from 1184. The **tourist office** (☎ 976 00 443; Kulturhus, Gravensteinsgaten; ☼ 9am-6pm Mon-Fri, 10am-4pm Sat mid-Jun–mid-Aug, shorter hours rest of year) is about 500m east of Sogndal bus station.

The tourist office books rooms in private homes (from Nkr200 per person). There's an **HI Hostel** (☎ 576 27 575; www.hihostels.no; dm/s/d Nkr200/280/480; ☼ mid-Jun–mid-Aug), only 15 minutes east of the bus station.

Unless you like Norwegian chain restaurants (Dolly Dimple's), eating here is depressing. The hotel restaurant, **Compagniet** (☎ 576 27 700; Hotel Sogndal, Gravensteinsgaten 5; buffets Nkr295; ☼ 7am-10.30pm), has formal evening buffets, but there's also a cheaper section with some light meals under Nkr100. For an inexpensive meal, try **Kaffir & Co**, a cafeteria in the **Domus** supermarket on Gravensteinsgata.

Buses run to Balestrand (Nkr113, 1¼ hours, three to five daily) and Fjærland (Nkr100, 45 minutes, four to six daily). Twice-daily buses (mid-June to late August) go northeast past Jotunheimen National Park to Lom (Nkr250, 3½ hours) and on to Otta (Nkr315, 4½ hours), on the Oslo–Trondheim railway line.

JOSTEDALSBREEN

With an area of 487 sq km, the many-tongued Jostedalsbreen dominates the highlands between Nordfjord and Sognefjord and is mainland Europe's largest icecap; in some places it is 400m thick. Protected as a national park, the icecap provides extraordinary opportunities for other-worldly glacier hiking.

Nigardsbreen

Among the glacier tongues visible from below, Nigardsbreen ranks among the most dramatic

and easily visited, with guided **hikes** from late May to mid-September across the glacier's rippled blue ice. Small avalanches along distant ice walls sound like gunshots as they fall, and ice chips dropping through crevices sound like tinkling bells.

Outings include easy 1½-hour family walks (adult/child Nkr200/100) and challenging three-hour, blue-ice treks (Nkr475), crossing deep crevasses and requiring hiking boots and warm clothing (instruction and technical equipment included); there's also multiday options. More information on summer glacier walks and kayaking on glacier lakes is available from **Jostedal Breheimsenteret** (☎ 576 83 250; www.jostedal.com; Jostedal; ☼ 9am-7pm late Jun-Aug, 10am-5pm May & Sep), which books trips and operates a cafeteria and an informative **museum** (admission Nkr50).

Friendly **Fimbul Jostedal** (☎ 994 50 921; www.fimbuljostedal.no) offers multiday courses on avalanche survival, ice climbing and Telemark skiing. It also guides experienced skiers along fabulous and remote glacial terrain. A six-day circuit with accommodation in mountain huts costs Nkr4000.

On most days from mid-May through September, return buses leave Sogndal (Nkr305), Balestrand (Nkr541) and Flåm (Nkr754) for Jostedal Breheimsenteret (see the website for schedules). These stop at the Urnes stave church and give you enough time for a short guided hike before coming back. Those who wish to stay longer have **Nigardsbreen Camping** (☎ 576 83 135; Jostedal; tent/caravan sites Nkr100/130, cabins Nkr350; ☼ late May-Sep), whose basic facilities lie 400m from the Breheimsenteret. About 5km away in Gjerde village, **Jostedal Hotell** (☎ 576 83 119; www.jostedal hotel.no; Jostedal; s/d Nkr700/900), an unofficial community centre, has clean rooms and lots of character. Its cafeteria functions as the village pub and has a Friday-night bingo session that attracts people in droves.

Fjærland
pop 300

The location of this quaint farming village at the head of the beautiful Fjærlandsfjorden, near two arms of the **Jostedalsbreen** icecap, makes it one of the most inviting destinations in Norway. The tiny village is Norway's 'Book Town', with a dozen **bookshops** (www.bokbyen.no; ☼ 10am-5pm Mon-Fri May–mid-Sep) selling used stock from an impressive 4km of shelves.

Fjærland's centre is called Mundal. Its annual book fair, held the Saturday nearest 23 June, pulls in booksellers and antiquarians from around the country. The **tourist office** (☎ 576 93 233; www.fjaerland.org) keeps irregular hours.

The **Norwegian Glacier Museum** (☎ 576 93 288; www.bre.museum.no; Fjærland; adult/child Nkr110/50; ☼ 10am-4pm Apr-Oct) offers hands-on exhibits for children. Learn how fjords are formed and wind your way through a tunnel of mock ice. You can drive within 300m of two arms of the glacier: the **Supphellebreen**, where you can walk up to the glacier's edge and touch the ice; and the creaking, blue-iced **Bøyabreen**, where it's not uncommon to witness ice breaks plunging into the lake beneath the glacier tongue.

To avoid crowds, a beautiful three-hour hike leads you from the valley past waterfalls and wildflowers onto a ridge of moss-covered boulders and finally to **Flatbreehytta** (dm Nkr200), a pair of wind-beaten, self-service DNT huts near the summit (1000m), with the glacier expanding immediately behind. Find the trailhead 2km north of the museum on Rv5. Turn at signs for Suppehellebreen and then Flatbreehytta. Park (20Nkr per day) at the marked lot.

Tired? Sleep at **Hotel Mundal** (☎ 576 93 101; www.fjordinfo.no/mundal; Mundal; s/d Nkr1100/1600; ☼ May-Sep), built in 1891. A wooden beauty, it features a welcoming lounge and lovely tower (drop Nkr1950 to sleep in its panoramic guestroom). The place overlooks the village and fjord from a gentle hill. Eat a traditional four-course meal in the fabulous dining room (Nkr540).

Broke? **Bøyum Camping** (☎ 576 93 252; www .fjaerland.org/boyumcamping; camp sites Nkr125, dm/s/d Nkr150/270/340, 6-person cabins Nkr690) offers simple turf-roofed cabins and camp sites on a broad grassy field with mountains rising in the background. Find it near the glacier museum, 2km from the centre. **Brævasshytta Cafeteria** (☎ 576 93 296; snacks Nkr30-50; daily meals Nkr95-125; ☼ May-Sep) is built into the moraine of the glacier's most recent advance. With the glacier right there and in your face, it's like eating in an Imax cinema, but for real (provided the movie reel froze on one image).

Four to six daily buses connect Fjærland to Sogndal (Nkr100, 45 minutes) and Stryn (Nkr190, two hours). Catch them near the glacier museum. If driving, prepare for a heart-stopping toll (Nkr150) along Rv5 between Sogndal and Fjærland.

Between May and September, ferries run to/from Balestrand (Nkr175, 1¼ hours, two daily). The morning departure connects in Balestrand with the boat to Flåm and links with the Bergen-bound ferry.

Briksdalsbreen

From the small town of Olden at the eastern edge of Nordfjord, a scenic road leads 23km up Oldedalen to the Briksdalsbreen glacial tongues, which are extremely accessible and therefore attract hordes of sight-seeing buses.

Glacier-hiking tours are operated by **Briksdal Adventure** (☎ 578 76 800; www.briksdal-adventure .com), near Briksdalsbre Fjellstove, and **Olden Aktiv** (☎ 578 73 888; www.oldenaktiv.no), near the Melkevoll Bretun camping ground. Both organise glacier walks of varying duration that include equipment and don't demand previous experience, such as a seven-hour trek with 2½ hours on the ice (Nkr600).

To behold the glacier, it's a 5km return hike to the face, either up a steep path or a longer and gentle cart track. **Oldedalen Skyss** (☎ 578 76 805; adult/child Nkr170) will be glad to install you in a large golf cart.

To sleep, head to Stryn or stay at **Melkevoll Bretun** (☎ 578 73 864; www.melkevoll.no; camp sites Nkr130, dm Nkr90, basic/fully-equipped cabins Nkr450/750), with gorgeous views of glacier and waterfall, heaps of space between tent pitches, well-furnished cabins and a 'Stone Age cave' for those with sleeping bags. Eat trout and reindeer (mains Nkr110 to Nkr150) in a cafe attached to **Briksdal Fjellstove** (s/d Nkr650/950, cabins Nkr800), a mountain lodge run by Briksdal Adventure.

Between June and August, a bus runs to Stryn (Nkr65, one hour, one to two daily).

Stryn & Loen
pop 2100

Since it lies conveniently on several long-distance routes, many travellers break their journeys here in Stryn. An hour's drive from Briksdalsbreen, it and the neighbouring town of Loen provide a relatively convenient base from which to make glacial excursions, particularly for those who want a restaurant or bar on hand after a day on the ice. Day hikes abound: arm yourself with *Walking in Loen & Lodalen* (1:50,000), which outlines 20 hikes including the strenuous six-hour puff to the summit of Skåla.

The helpful **tourist office** (☎ 578 74 040; www .nordfjord.no; Stryn; ☼ 8.30am-6pm Jun-Aug, shorter hours rest of year) is two blocks south of Tonningsgata, the main drag. Briksdal Adventure (opposite) operates an office out of Sande Camping.

SLEEPING & EATING

Sande Camping (☎ 578 74 590; www.sande-camping.no; Loen; camp sites Nkr120, cabins Nkr315-495; **P**)) Removed from the centre, Sande provides a breathtaking setting on Lovanet (in summer, a lake warm enough for a swim), with step glacier-topped mountains rising dramatically beyond. There's a shop, canoe rentals and a cafeteria. To find it, turn off Rv6 near Hotel Alexander, following signs for Lodalen. You'll find other worthy camping grounds amid the farms on this road.

Stryn Vandrerhjem (☎ 578 71 106; www.hihostels .no; Geilevegen 14, Stryn; dm/s/d Nkr160/390/490; ☼ late May-early Sep) Nicely perched on a hill, with the fjord in the distance, these former German military barracks lie 2km from town.

Vesla Pensjonat (☎ 578 71 006; www.veslapensjon .no; Stryn; s/d Nkr620/800) Boasting a lovely garden, this Victorian place feels like a gingerbread house. There are plenty of cats to scratch and books on the walls. In winter, folk singing is sometimes hosted.

Hotel Alexandra (☎ 578 75 000; www.alexandra.no; s/d Nkr1100/1700) Loen has a few worthwhile beds, including those found at this modern hotel, where many rooms have good views over the fjord. Its pricey dinner buffet provides a top-notch survey of Norwegian cuisine.

For limited food and caffeine, Stryn is the place to go.

GETTING THERE & AWAY

Buses run from Stryn to Bergen (Nkr478, 7¼ hours, one to two daily) and to Ålesund (Nkr261, 3½ hours, two to four daily). The Ålesund route passes Hellesylt (Nkr90, one hour), where there are boat connections to Geiranger.

NORANGSDALEN & SUNNMØRESALPANE

One of the most inspiring parts of the Western Fjords is Norangsdalen, a hidden valley west of Hellesylt. The partially unsealed Rv665 to the villages of Øye and Urke, and the Leknes–Sæbø ferry on beautiful Hjørundfjorden are served by bus from Hellesylt once daily, Monday to Friday mid-June to mid-August.

Hikers and climbers will enjoy the dramatic peaks of the adjacent Sunnmørsalpane, including the incredibly steep scrambling ascent of Slogen (1564m) from Øye and the superb Råna (1586m), a long and tough scramble from Urke.

GEIRANGERFJORDEN

Added to Unesco's World Heritage List in 2005, this archetypal fjord boasts towering, twisting walls that curve inland for 20 narrow kilometres. Along the way abandoned farms cling to the cliffs and breathtakingly high waterfalls, with names such as the Seven Sisters, the Suitor and the Bridal Veil, drop straight into the sea from forests above.

The cruise by public ferry between Geiranger and Hellesylt is almost too nice to view.

Geiranger
pop 250

High mountains with cascading waterfalls and cliff-side farms surround Geiranger, at the head of the crooked Geirangerfjorden. Although the village is quite tiny, it's one of Norway's most-visited spots. Nevertheless, it's reasonably serene during the evening when all the cruise ships and tour buses have departed.

The **tourist office** (☎ 702 63 800; www.visitgei rangerfjorden.com; ☼ 9am-5pm May-Sep) is beside the pier and details hikes.

SIGHTS & ACTIVITIES

At the **Geiranger Fjord Centre** (☎ 702 63 810; www.geirangerfjord.no; adult/child Nkr85/45; ☼ 10am-5pm May-Sep) learn about the essentials that shaped culture in the middle of nowhere: mail packets, avalanches and building roads over impossible terrain.

There's great hiking all around Geiranger to abandoned farmsteads, waterfalls and some beautiful lookout points. One special walk is to **Storseter waterfall**, a 45-minute hike that takes you between the rock face and the cascading falls. You'll get the most spectacular fjord views from **Flydalsjuvet**, about 5km uphill from Geiranger on the Stryn road, and from **Ørnevegen**, about 4km from Geiranger towards Valldal and Åndalsnes.

The highest and most splendid view of the Geiranger valley and fjord is from the **Dalsnibba** lookout (1500m). A bus (Nkr100 return) runs from Geiranger between mid-June and mid-August.

SLEEPING & EATING

Hotels in Geiranger can be quickly booked out by package tours, but cabins and camping spots are plentiful. A dozen camping grounds skirt the fjord and hillsides. Most everything closes from October through April.

You'll see *Rom* signs around the village advertising rooms (around Nkr250/400 per single/double); the tourist office can help book them.

The miniscule town centre has a pair of cafes and a supermarket open even on Sunday.

Grande Fjord Hotel (☎ 702 69 490; www.grande fjordhotel.com; s/d Nkr850/1150; **P**) At a scenic spot on the fjord 2km northwest of the village, this place has many balconies aimed straight at the twisting fjord. Buffet breakfasts (included) and dinners are particularly good.

Naustkroa (☎ 702 63 230; meals Nkr69-145) Head downstairs for a stone terrace overlooking the water where you can eat fish soup, local sausages or chilled poached salmon.

Olebuda (☎ 702 63 005; mains Nkr169-239) Serves fennel salad, trout medallions and reindeer pate amid painted beams and hand-hewn walls. It's got a good bar and pool table.

Stop by Geiranger Galleri a self-designated 'troll-free zone' representing artists from the Western Fjords.

Also recommended:

Geiranger Camping (☎ 702 63 120; www.geiranger camping.no; camp sites from Nkr70; ☺ mid-May–Sep) Right in the centre of Geiranger.

Vinge Camping (☎ 702 63 017; www.vinje-camping.no; cabins Nkr550) Lies 200m past the nature centre uphill. Well landscaped and quiet, except for a booming waterfall.

GETTING THERE & AWAY

From mid-June to late August, buses run to Åndalsnes (Nkr197, three hours). Change at Linge for buses to Ålesund. The Geiranger–Hellesylt ferry (passenger/car Nkr100/210, one hour, four to 10 daily) runs May to late September.

ÅNDALSNES

pop 2500

By Romsdalsfjorden, Åndalsnes is the northern gateway to the Western Fjords. Most travellers arrive on the train from Dombås, a scenic route that descends through a deeply cut val-

ley with dramatic waterfalls. Just before reaching Åndalsnes, the train passes **Trollveggen**, a sheer 1500m-high rock face whose jagged and often cloud-shrouded summit is considered the ultimate challenge among Norwegian mountain climbers. Highway E136 between Dombås and Åndalsnes runs parallel to the railway line and is similarly spectacular.

The town itself is rather nondescript, but the scenery is fabulous and camping grounds are plentiful. The **tourist office** (☎ 712 21 622; www.visitandalsnes.com; ☺ 9am-6pm Mon-Fri, 11am-6pm Sat & Sun mid-Jun–mid-Aug, 8am-2.30pm Mon-Fri rest of year) is at the train station.

Hiking

The mountains and valleys surrounding Åndalsnes offer excellent hiking – contact the tourist office for details of guided trips. One good trail, which goes to the top of Nesaksla (715m), starts right in town 50m north of the roundabout and makes a fine half-day outing. Another is the 1500m-high rock route on Trollveggen.

Sleeping & Eating

Åndalsnes Camping (☎ 712 21 629; www.andalsnes -camping.com; car/caravan sites from Nkr120/145, r Nkr330, 4-/7-person cabins Nkr475/880; ☐) Dramatically situated on the southeastern side of the scenic Rauma river, this camping ground, 2km from the centre, rents canoes and bikes.

Åndalsnes Vandrerhjem (☎ 712 21 382; www .aandalsnesvandrerhjem.no; dm/s/d Nkr260/470/680; ☺ late May-early Sep) This turf-roof place offers rustic accommodation and a pancakes-and-pickled-herring breakfast. It's 2km from the train station (follow the E136 towards Ålesund), just far enough from town to be surrounded by idyllic flowering pastures with fine mountain views.

Grand Hotel Bellevue (☎ 712 27 500; www.grand hotel.no; Åndalgata 5; s/d Nkr850/1050; ☐) Perched on a rise in the town centre, the Bellevue delivers on its name: both sides of the hotel overlook stunning water and mountain scenes. Comfortable rooms are bland and yellow.

The town centre contains a grocery store, bakery, cafeteria and pizza joint.

Getting There & Away

The train from Dombås runs to Åndalsnes (Nkr212, 1½ hours, two to four daily), in sync with Oslo–Trondheim trains. Buses to

Ålesund (Nkr245, 2¼ hours, two to four daily) meet the trains.

ÅNDALSNES TO GEIRANGER

The **Trollstigen** (Troll's Path) winding south from Åndalsnes is a thriller of a road with hairpin bends and a 1:12 gradient, and to add a daredevil element it's practically one lane all the way. On request, the bus makes photo stops at the thundering, 180m-high **Stigfossen waterfall** on its way up to the mountain pass. At the top, the bus usually stops long enough for you to walk to a lookout with a dizzying view back down the valley.

There are waterfalls galore smoking down the mountains as you descend to **Valldal**. You could break your journey here – there are camping grounds, cabins and a hotel – though most travellers continue on, taking the short ferry ride from Linge across to **Eidsdal**. From there, a waiting bus continues along the **Ørnevegen** (Eagle's Hwy), with magnificent bird's-eye views of Geirangerfjorden during the descent into Geiranger village.

ÅLESUND
pop 42,000

Lucky for you, this pretty coastal town burned to the ground in 1904. The amazing rebuilding created a fantastic downtown centre unlike anything else you'll see in Norway – a harmonious collection of pastel buildings almost entirely designed in the Art Nouveau tradition. All the loveliness is well staged on the end of a peninsula, surrounded by islands, water and hills.

The **tourist office** (☎ 701 57 600; www.visit alesund.com; ☒ 8am-7pm Mon-Fri, 8am-6pm Sat & Sun late Jun–mid-Aug, shorter hours rest of year) is near the *Hurtigruten* quay. The post office is on Korsegata. For free internet, visit the **public library** (Kremmergaarden, Korsegata).

Sights & Activities

A popular thing to do is to walk the 418 steps up **Aksla** (189m) for a splendid view of Ålesund and the surrounding islands. Take Lihauggata from Kongensgata, pass the **Rollon statue** and begin the 20-minute jaunt to the top of the hill.

The brilliant **Art Nouveau Centre** (☎ 701 04 970; www.jugendstilsenteret.no; Apotekergata 16; adult/child/student Nkr60/30/30; ☒ 10am-5pm Jun-Aug, shorter hours rest of year) occupies the fabulously restored interior of a former pharmacy.

Exhibits explain the town's rebuilding with a weird time machine and presents the work (furniture, paintings, textiles and glass) of well-known continental Art Nouveau masters alongside their Norwegian counterparts. A tunnel connects you to Kube (wheelchair friendly) whose gleaming white interior exhibits an eclectic range of art from medieval to contemporary.

The town **museum** (☎ 701 23 170; Rasmus Rønnebergs gate 16; adult/child Nkr40/10; ☒ 11am-4pm mid-Jun–mid-Aug, shorter hours rest of year) concentrates on local history, including sealing, fishing, shipping, the fire of 1904 and the German occupation during WWII. A few boats are also shown, including the *Uræd* lifeboat, piloted across the Atlantic in 1904.

The aquarium **Atlanterhavsparken** (☎ 701 07 060; Tueneset; adult/child Nkr120/60; ☒ 10am-7pm Sun-Fri, 10am-4pm Sat mid-Jun–mid-Aug, shorter hours rest of year; ☒), 3km from the centre at the western extreme of the peninsula, introduces visitors to marine life around the Norwegian coast. At 1pm, watch disconcertingly large fish thrash about in the daily feeding frenzy.

Ålesund is a good base for touring the surrounding islands, including the bird island of **Runde** (p351), lighthouses and fjords. The tourist office provides a list of sailing times and itinerary suggestions. Ferries depart from the Skateflukaia ferry terminal.

Weekdays in summer there's a scenic bus-ferry day trip (Nkr410) that includes a cruise down Geirangerfjorden, an hour in Geiranger, and the return to Ålesund via Ørnevegen.

Sleeping

The tourist office keeps lists of a few private rooms that start at around Nkr300 per person.

Ålesund Hostel (☎ 701 15 830; www.hihostels.no; Parkgata 14; dm/s/d Nkr225/550/675; ☒) Tidy and central, the hostel offers clean rooms where touches of old charm show through (dorms sleep 12, however). Enjoy an impressive vaulted common space and a breakfast better than many other Norwegian hostels.

Ålesund Apartment (☎ 915 85 766; www.alesund apartments.no; Kongens gate 32b; 2-/4-person apt Nkr750/1100) Book early to win a fine two-room apartment with a kitchen, a washing machine and an excellent location not far from the *Hurtigruten* quay.

Hotel Brosundet (☎ 701 21 000; www.hotelbrosundet .no; Apotekergata 5; s/d Nkr1090/1290; ☒) A former

NORWAY

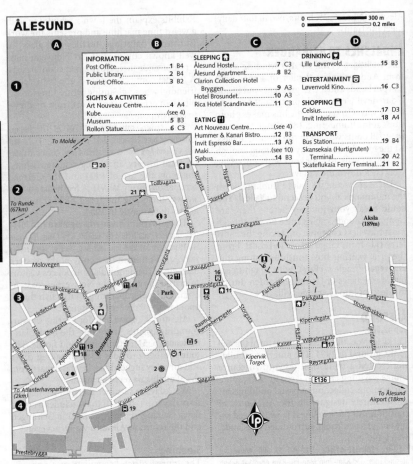

ÅLESUND

INFORMATION	
Post Office	1 B4
Public Library	2 B4
Tourist Office	3 B2

SIGHTS & ACTIVITIES	
Art Nouveau Centre	4 A4
Kube	(see 4)
Museum	5 B3
Rollon Statue	6 C3

SLEEPING	
Ålesund Hostel	7 C3
Ålesund Apartment	8 B2
Clarion Collection Hotel Bryggen	9 A3
Hotel Brosundet	10 A3
Rica Hotel Scandinavie	11 C3

EATING	
Art Nouveau Centre	(see 4)
Hummer & Kanari Bistro	12 B3
Invit Espresso Bar	13 A3
Maki	(see 10)
Sjøbua	14 B3

DRINKING	
Lille Løvenvold	15 B3

ENTERTAINMENT	
Løvenvold Kino	16 C3

SHOPPING	
Celsius	17 D3
Invit Interior	18 A4

TRANSPORT	
Bus Station	19 B4
Skansekaia (Hurtigruten) Terminal	20 A2
Skateflukaia Ferry Terminal	21 B2

warehouse contains rooms interestingly punctured by massive timbers. Large pulleys that were used to haul up fish still exist inside. Sleep inches from the canal amid plush, contemporary stylings. Want privacy? Ask for room 47, a small red lighthouse at the end of a sea break.

Rica Hotel Scandinavie (☎ 701 57 800; www.rica .no; Løvenvoldgata 8; s Nkr895-1295, d Nkr1040-1495; Ⓟ) While its exterior, stairs and hallways retain lavish *Jugendstil* touches, the rooms of this hotel have been stripped and redone with a conventional design.

Clarion Collection Hotel Bryggen (☎ 701 26 400; www.choicehotels.no; Apotekergata 1; s Nkr900-1420, d Nkr1190-1590; Ⓟ ▯ ⑤) This canal-side choice occupies a pastel-yellow warehouse dating

from the town's reconstruction. In addition to breakfast, a basic dinner buffet is included.

Eating & Drinking

Art Nouveau Centre (Apotekergata 16; sandwiches Nkr40-50) Aside from open-faced sandwiches (brie and salami), the museum's stylish cafe serves chocolate-apricot cake (Nkr35) so good that your later travels through Norway's spectacular scenery will be interrupted by wistful memories of your tear-stained and empty plate.

Invit Espresso Bar (☎ 701 56 644; Apotekergata 9; sandwiches Nkr70) This modern espresso bar serves the best steamed drinks in town. Enjoy them with snacks, milkshakes and smoothies on original chairs designed next door, or on a barge on the water.

Hummer & Kanari Bistro (☎ 701 28 008; Kongensgata 19; mains Nk100-275) Downstairs, the bistro serves up ample pizzas and pasta with a well-stocked bar beckoning nearby. The more formal restaurant upstairs turns out a daily menu of fish specialities.

Sjøbua (☎ 701 27 100; Brunholmgata 1a; mains Nkr240-350; ✆ 4-11pm Mon-Sat) A fish restaurant in the belly of an old wharf building. Come inside to find thick masonry walls skewered by huge beams and posts. A large aquarium in the lobby demonstrates what you'll be eating.

Maki (☎ 701 21 000; Apotekergata 5; mains Nkr285-315) The menu changes every three weeks at this experimental fish restaurant. Enjoy new takes on cod mussels, and delicious bottom-feeders you've never heard of in a sleek, modern room on the water. Wait at the nearby bar for a flashy drink under chandeliers encased in glass tubes.

Lille Løvenvold (☎ 701 25 400; Løvenvoldgata 2; ✆ from 11am) Serves beer with b-sides playing in the background. Sit in a few small rooms with velvet chairs and red walls that somehow don't feel like a bordello. There's a good loose-tea selection.

Entertainment

Løvenvold Kino (☎ 701 62 446; Løvenvoldgata 11) A little-changed neobaroque movie house from 1922; come inside for flicks (Nkr80) and original wall paintings.

Shopping

Celsius (☎ 701 00 116; Kaiser Wilhelmsgata 52; ✆ 10am-4pm Tue-Fri, 10am-2pm Sat) The small glass studio blows unconventional pieces with vivid colours. The kiln is at the front of the studio, the shop at the back.

Invit Interior (☎ 701 56 644; Apotekergata 9) For creative modern furniture and the best of Norwegian kitchen appliances, teapots and cool home goods, head to this design firm and shop.

Getting There & Away

Ålesund has daily flights to Oslo and other Norwegian cities. A taxi to/from the airport costs Nkr350, thanks to numerous tolls. Or take the airport bus (Nkr80, 25 minutes). There are buses to Stryn (Nkr261, 3½ hours, one to four daily) via Hellesylt and

to other major coastal and fjord towns. The bus to Åndalsnes (Nkr245, 2¼ hours, two to four daily) is timed to meet arriving and departing trains.

The *Hurtigruten* docks at Skansekaia Terminal.

RUNDE

pop 150

The impressive island of Runde, situated 67km west of Ålesund, plays host to half a million sea birds of 230 to 240 species, including kittiwakes, fulmars, storm petrels and 100,000 pairs of migrating puffins that arrive in May and hang around until late July. You'll see the best bird-watching sites on a two-boat tour (three sailing daily May to August). Buy tickets (adult/child Nkr170/85) at **Goksøyr Camping** (☎ 700 85 905). Ring in advance in high-season.

Runde Camping & HI Vandrerhjem (☎ 907 44 343; www.runde.no; camp sites Nkr100, dm/s/d Nkr200/550/690; ✆ May-Sep), attractively facing the harbour, has cosy rooms with bunk beds; those in the attic are particularly charming. The grassy camp sites are basic and waterside.

Runde is connected to the mainland by bridge. It can be reached by a pleasurable catamaran-bus combination day trip that gives you six hours on the island. It departs from Ålesund's **Skateflukaia ferry terminal** (Nkr590 return, 2½ hours each way, daily) from mid-June to mid-September.

NORTHERN NORWAY

With several great cities and some wondrous natural terrain, you'll be mighty pleased with yourself for undertaking an exploration of this huge territory that stretches on either side of the Arctic Circle. A vast plateau reaches across much of the interior, while small fishing villages cling to the incredibly steep and jagged Lofoten Islands, which erupt vertically out of the ocean. Medieval Trondheim, Norway's third-largest city, provides plenty of culture and charm, while Tromsø, the world's northernmost university town, parties year-round. On some freezing inland mountains you'll find Rorøs, a Unesco-protected copper-mining town, and back on the coast is Narvik, a grotesquely interesting town with incredible downhill skiing.

An alternative to land travel is the *Hurtigruten* coastal steamer, which pulls into every sizeable port, passing some of the best coastal scenery in Scandinavia. A good thing, too, since trains only run as far as Bodø.

RØROS

pop 5600

Røros is a wonderful old copper-mining town with a well-preserved historic district, protected under Unesco's World Heritage List. The little hillside town is dominated by a large wooden church, and contains several galleries. The first mine opened in 1644 but in 1977, after 333 years of operation, the company went bankrupt. The town makes for delightful strolling and everything's within easy walking distance. The **tourist office** (☎ 724 10 000; www.rorosinfo.com; Peder Hiortsgata 2; ☻ 9am-6pm Mon-Sat, 10am-2pm Sun mid-Jun–mid-Aug) can advise on canoeing, fishing, hiking and skiing.

Sights & Activities

Røros' main attractions are the turf-roofed **miners' cottages** and other centuries-old timber buildings; a timber green-and-white **church** (Kjerkgata; tours adult/child Nkr25/free; ☻ 10am-5pm Mon-Sat, 2-4pm Sun mid-Jun–mid-Aug, tours 2pm), built in 1784, and with an excellent baroque interior; its **slag heaps**; and the old smelting works, now part of the **Rørosmuseet** (☎ 724 06 170; Malmplassen; adult/child/student Nkr60/30/50; ☻ 10am-7pm mid-Jun–mid-Aug, shorter hours rest of year). The museum features intricate scale models that brilliantly outline the water- and horse-powered smelting process.

Don't miss the now defunct **Olavsguva mine** (☎ 724 11 165; Kojedalen; tours adult/child/student Nkr60/30/50; ☻ 10am-5pm mid-Jun–mid-Aug), 13km northeast of town. Subterranean tours pass through the historic Nyberget copper mine, dating from the 1650s, into the modern Olavsgruva mine, which operated from 1936 to 1970. The ground can be muddy and the air is a steady 5°C – so bring a sweater and strong footwear. A car or taxi (Nkr450 return) is needed to get there.

Excellent **nordic skiing** tracks lace through the semi-forested Røros plateau, with snow sometimes lingering well into summer. For a modest downhill adventure, two or three hours will allow you to thoroughly explore the six trails (two lifts) at **Hummelfjellet Alpine Centre** (☎ 624 97 100; www.hummelfjell.no, in Norwegian; 2hr lift tickets Nkr220).

Tours

In winter, the tourist office organises excursions by dogsled (adult/child Nkr590/290 for two hours) or horse-drawn sleigh (Nkr600 per hour for four people). You can also join a winter day-trip to the Southern Sámi tent camp in Pinstitjønna, 3km from town and 1km off the road, where you'll dine on reindeer and learn to ice fish and throw axes. The three-hour tour costs Nkr500 per person (minimum 10 people).

Festivals & Events

The biggest winter market is **Rørosmartnan** (Røros Market), begun in 1644 as a meeting place for wandering hunters to sell goods to townspeople. Thanks to a 1853 royal decree, stipulating that a grand market be held annually from the penultimate Tuesday of February to the following Saturday, it continues today with street markets and live entertainment.

Fermund Race (www.femundlopet.no), one of Europe's longest dogsled races starts and ends in Røros in the first week of February.

Sleeping

Erzscheidergården (☎ 724 11 194; www.erzschei dergaarden.no; Spell Olaveien 6; s/d Nkr745/990; ℗) Cosy Erzscheider sits atop a hill, and many of the rooms have fine views across the cathedral's cemetery and the town beyond. It dates from 1780.

Vertshuset Røros (☎ 724 19 350; www.vertshusetroros .no, in Norwegian; Kjerkgata 34; s/d from Nkr790/990, apt from Nkr1060; ℗) Many of the inviting rooms have floors painted in a folk style common in the Røros area and they overlook an enclosed backyard surrounded by 18th-century buildings. The intimate dining room (mains Nkr250 to Nkr300) turns out high-end fare featuring local game, produce and cheeses. There's a cheaper lunch menu.

Quality Hotel Røros (☎ 724 08 000; www.choiceho tels.com; An-Magrittsvei; s/d Nkr1000/1500; ℗ ♿ 🖵) A 15-minute walk uphill from the train station, generic but clean rooms enjoy views over the valley and low, distant mountains. Trailheads lie nearby.

Also recommended:

Idrettsparken Hotell (☎ 724 11 089; www .idrettsparken.no; Øra 25; camp sites Nkr100, cabins from Nkr420, hotel s/d from Nkr665/990; ℗) Simple, tidy and family run.

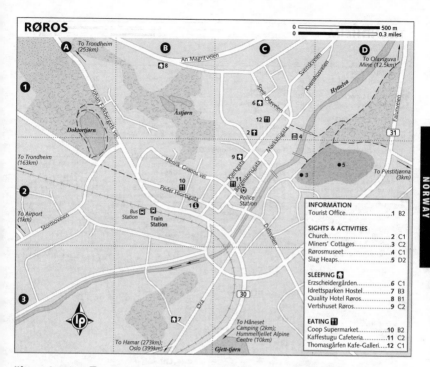

RØROS

INFORMATION
Tourist Office.................................1 B2

SIGHTS & ACTIVITIES
Church..2 C1
Miners' Cottages............................3 C2
Rørosmuseet...................................4 C1
Slag Heaps......................................5 D2

SLEEPING
Erzscheidergården.........................6 C1
Idrettsparken Hostel.....................7 B3
Quality Hotel Røros.......................8 B1
Vertshuset Røros...........................9 C2

EATING
Coop Supermarket.......................10 B2
Kaffestugu Cafeteria...................11 C2
Thomasgården Kafe-Galleri.......12 C1

Håneset Camping (☎ 724 10 600; Osloveien; camp sites Nkr130 plus per person Nkr25, 2-/4-bed cabins Nkr320/420) Find tidy cabins at this pretty camping ground 2km south of town.

Eating

If you need an artful meal that creatively re-interprets traditional mountain cuisine, you can't beat Vershuset Røros.

Thomasgården Kafe-Galleri (☎ 724 12 470; Kjerkgata 48; snacks Nkr35-50) For a nice read in a rustic room filled with ceramics, grab a table and enhance your experience with apple cake and coffee (Nkr35).

Kaffestuggu Cafeteria (☎ 724 11 033; Bergmannsgata 18; mains Nkr80-160) This cafeteria looks like a ski lodge or a Victorian parlour, depending on where you sit. It offers a filling range of bland Norwegian usuals and, if you're lucky, TVs broadcasting ski-jump competitions.

You'll also find a Coop supermarket, a pizza place and a top-notch bakery.

Getting There & Away

Trains run between Oslo (Nkr679, five hours, two to six daily) and Trondheim (Nkr228,

2½ hours, three daily). A late-night bus runs to Oslo (Nkr395, six hours, daily). The Røros airport is served by Widerøe from Oslo (daily except Saturday). It's 1km from town.

TRONDHEIM

pop 145,000

Norway's third-largest city, beautiful Trondheim is a lively university town whose rich medieval history remains prominently visible in the centre. While you can get a feel for the city in a day, there's enough nightlife, food and charm to linger.

Trondheim was founded at the estuary of the winding Nidelva in AD 997 by the Viking king Olav Tryggvason. After a fire razed most of the city in 1681, Trondheim was redesigned with wide streets and Renaissance flair by General Caspar de Cicignon. Today, the steeple of the medieval Nidaros Domkirke is still the highest point in the city centre.

Orientation

The central part of town is on a triangular peninsula that's easy to explore on foot. The

NORWAY

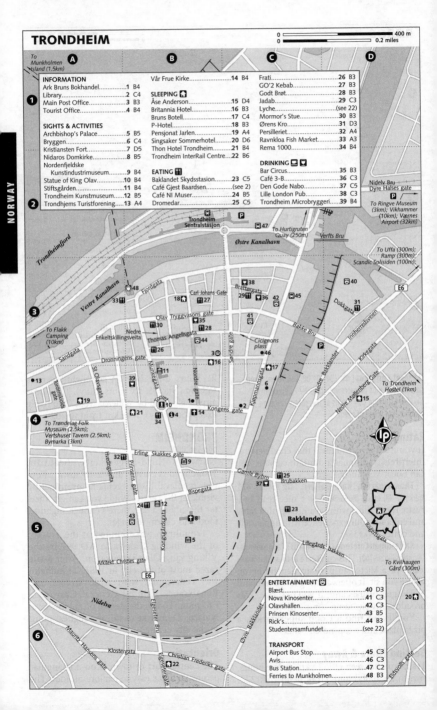

TRONDHEIM

0 — 400 m
0 — 0.2 miles

INFORMATION
Ark Bruns Bokhandel..............1 B4
Library......................................2 C4
Main Post Office......................3 B3
Tourist Office..........................4 B4

SIGHTS & ACTIVITIES
Archbishop's Palace................5 B5
Bryggen..................................6 C4
Kristiansten Fort....................7 D5
Nidaros Domkirke...................8 B5
Nordenfjeldske
   Kunstindustrimuseum.........9 B4
Statue of King Olav...............10 B4
Stiftsgården...........................11 B4
Trondheim Kunstmuseum......12 B5
Trondhjems Turistforening.....13 A4

Vår Frue Kirke.......................14 B4

SLEEPING
Åse Anderson........................15 D4
Britannia Hotel......................16 B3
Bruns Botell..........................17 C4
P-Hotel..................................18 B3
Pensjonat Jarlen....................19 A4
Singsaker Sommerhotel.........20 D6
Thon Hotel Trondheim..........21 B4
Trondheim InterRail Centre....22 B6

EATING
Baklandet Skydsstasion.........23 C5
Café Gjest Baardsen.........(see 2)
Café NI Muser........................24 B5
Dromedar...............................25 C5

Frati.......................................26 B3
GO'2 Kebab...........................27 B3
Godt Brøt...............................28 B3
Jadab.....................................29 C3
Lyche...............................(see 22)
Mormor's Stue......................30 B3
Ørens Kro..............................31 D3
Persilleriet.............................32 A4
Ravnkloa Fish Market............33 A3
Rema 1000.............................34 B4

DRINKING
Bar Circus.............................35 B3
Café 3-B................................36 C3
Den Gode Nabo.....................37 C5
Lille London Pub....................38 C3
Trondheim Microbryggeri.......39 B4

ENTERTAINMENT
Blæst.....................................40 D3
Nova Kinosenter....................41 C3
Olavshallen...........................42 C3
Prinsen Kinosenter................43 B5
Rick's....................................44 B3
Studentersamfundet.........(see 22)

TRANSPORT
Airport Bus Stop....................45 C3
Avis.......................................46 C3
Bus Station............................47 C2
Ferries to Munkholmen..........48 B3

train station, bus station and coastal-steamer quay are across the canal, a few minutes' walk north of the centre.

On and around Torvet, the central square, are a produce market, a statue of King Olav and the 13th-century stone church, Vår Frue Kirke.

Information

Ark Bruns Bokhandel (☎ 735 10 022; Kongens gate 10) Sells English-language books.

Internet (www.tradlosetrondheim.no; per 3/24hr Nkr10/29) A city-sponsored wireless signal covers the central peninsula.

Library (Kongens gate; ⊙ 9am-4pm Mon-Fri, 10am-3pm Sat Jul–mid-Aug, 9am-7pm Mon-Thu, 9am-4pm Fri, 11am-4pm Sat rest of year) Free internet.

Main Post Office (Dronningens gate 10)

Tourist office (☎ 738 07 660; www.trondheim.no; Torvet; ⊙ 8.30am-10pm Mon-Fri, 10am-4pm Sat & Sun Jul & Aug, 9am-6pm Mon-Fri, 10am-4pm Sat & Sun mid-May–Jun, 9am-4pm Mon-Fri, 10am-2pm Sat & Sun Sep–mid-May)

Sights

NIDAROS DOMKIRKE & ARCHBISHOP'S PALACE

The **cathedral** (☎ 735 39 160; www.nidarosdomen.no; Kongsgårdsgata; adult/child Nkr50/25; ⊙ from 9am Mon-Sat, 1-4pm Sun May–mid-Sep, noon-2.30pm Mon-Fri, 11.30am-2pm Sat, 1-3pm Sun mid-Sep–Apr) is Trondheim's most dominant landmark and Scandinavia's largest medieval building. The oldest wing dates to the 12th century, and popular belief holds that the high altar lies precisely over the grave of St Olav, the Viking king who replaced the worship of Nordic gods with Christianity. While you may roam freely, consider attaching yourself to an informative tour (available in German, English and French). Magnificent organ recitals take place from Monday to Saturday at 1pm. From July to August, visitors can climb the cathedral tower for a splendid view of the city.

An interesting feature of the cathedral is its ornately embellished west wall, lined with statues of biblical characters and Norwegian bishops and kings. Destroyed in the 19th century, the rebuilding of this wing lasted into the 20th century with the sculptures made by prominent Norwegian artists.

Admission includes entrance to the courtyard of the adjacent 12th-century **Erkebispegården** (Archbishop's Palace). Commissioned around 1160, it's the oldest

secular building in Scandinavia. Since the palace can only be admired from the outside, the modern **museum** (adult/child Nkr50/25; ⊙ 9am-5pm Mon-Fri, 9am-3pm Sat, noon-5pm Sun mid-Jun–mid-Aug, shorter hours mid-Aug–mid-Jun), in the same compound, provides greater interest. It details the history of the cathedral as it underwent enlargement, modification and multiple conflagrations. Also displayed are archaeological finds from the Archbishop's Palace, which provide a glimpse into everyday medieval life.

Since Nidaros Domkirke serves as the site of coronations, you might take a gander at the Norwegian royal family's **crown jewels** (adult/child Nkr70/25) housed in a vault in the Archbishop's Palace. See three crowns, the sword of the realm and some other jewel-encrusted trinkets.

If you want to see all three sites (cathedral, palace and crown jewels), save money and buy an all-in-one ticket (adult/child Nkr100/50).

ART MUSEUMS

The eclectic **Nordenfjeldske Kunstindustrimuseum** (Museum of Decorative Arts; ☎ 738 08 950; Munkegata 5; adult/student Nkr60/40; ⊙ 10am-5pm Mon-Sat, noon-5pm Sun late Jun-late Aug, 10am-3pm Tue-Sat, noon-4pm Sun Sep–mid-Jun) exhibits a fine collection of contemporary arts and crafts including work by Hannah Ryggen, Norway's highly acclaimed tapestry artist. **Trondheim Kunstmuseum** (☎ 735 38 180; Bispegata 7B; adult/student Nkr50/30; ⊙ 10am-5pm Jun-Aug, 11am-4pm Tue-Sun Sep-May), has a corridor of Munch's lithographs and displays Norwegian and Danish art from 1850 onward.

HISTORIC BUILDINGS & NEIGHBOURHOODS

Scandinavia's largest wooden palace, the late-baroque **Stiftsgården** (☎ 738 08 950; Munkegata 23; adult/child/student Nkr60/30/40; ⊙ 10am-5pm Mon-Sat, noon-5pm Sun, Jun–mid-Aug) was completed in 1778 and is now the official royal residence in Trondheim. Admission is by tour only, on the hour.

The picturesque **Gamle Bybro** (Old Town Bridge) originally dates from 1681, but the current wooden structure was built in 1861. From here, enjoy marvellous views over the **Bryggen**, an amazingly intact collection of tall red, yellow, green and orange 18- and 19th-century warehouses reflected colourfully in the calm river.

On the east side of the bridge lies **Bakklandet**, a neighbourhood of cobblestone streets

NORWAY

containing cafes and plenty of revived working-class residences from the 19th century.

Puff up the hill from this neighbourhood and there's a good view of the city from the top of the 17th-century **Kristiansten Fort** (☎ 739 95 831; Festningsgaten; admission free; ⏲ 10am-3pm Mon-Fri, 11am-4pm Sat & Sun Jun-Aug). Though its buildings open only during the summer, the parklike grounds can be viewed year-round.

The **Trøndelag Folk Museum** (☎ 738 90 100; Sverresborg Allé; adult/child/student Nkr80/30/55; ⏲ 11am-6pm Jun-Aug, 11am-3pm Mon-Fri, noon-4pm Sat & Sun Sep-May), set around the ruins of a medieval castle, is one of Norway's best open-air museums. On a hill with views over town, it displays over 60 period buildings, including a small, 12th-century stave church (visit in winter to understand how cold, dark and miserable services must have been). Catch bus 8 or 9 from Dronningens gate.

RINGVE MUSEUM

The **Ringve Museum** (☎ 738 70 280; www.ringve.no; Lade Allé 60; adult/child/student Nkr75/25/50; ⏲ 11am-3pm, to 5pm mid-May–mid-Sep, 11am-4pm Sun mid-Sep–mid-May) is a fascinating music-history museum set in an 18th-century manor. Music students give tours demonstrating the antique instruments on display. Take bus 3 or 4 from Munkegaten 3km northeast of the city centre.

A lavish **botanical garden** (☎ 735 92 269; Lade Allé 58; admission free; ⏲ 24hr) surrounds the estate, covering 14 hectares near Trondheimfjord. Some sections are strictly geometrical, modelled after Renaissance tastes. Others have sinuous, winding paths.

Activities

A popular place to sunbathe and picnic is **Munkholmen Island**, site of an 11th-century Benedictine monastery and later converted to a prison, a fort and a customs house. From mid-May to early September, ferries (adult/child Nkr50/30 return) leave from the harbour, east of the Ravnkloa fish market.

The western side of Trondheim is bordered by **Bymarka**, a woodland area crossed with good skiing and wilderness trails. To get there, take the tram from St Olavs gate to **Lian**, which has good city views, a bathing lake and hiking paths.

For help with wilderness skiing and hiking, contact the local DNT office, **Trondhjems Turistforening** (☎ 739 24 200; Sand gate 30).

Sleeping

The tourist office books rooms in private homes, mostly on the city outskirts, averaging Nkr300/450 per single/double plus a Nkr30 fee.

Flakk Camping (☎ 728 43 900; www.flakk-camping .no; camp sites from Nkr100, cabins Nkr400-500; ⏲ May-Sep) Situated on a pleasant grassy expanse overlooking the Trondheim Fjord, this small camping ground lies 10km west of the town centre. Local buses stop nearby, or you can ride Flakk's daily shuttle.

Vikhammer (☎ 739 76 164; www.vikhammer.no; camp sites Nkr150, cabins from Nkr400; ♿) Also well-situated on the Trondheim Fjord, this camping ground tends to attract more caravans and bigger crowds. The year-round operation contains a kiosk, several dozen cabins and a playground.

Trondheim InterRail Centre (☎ 738 99 538; www .tirc.no; Elgesetergate 1; dm Nkr150; ⏲ Jul–mid-Aug; 🖥) During summer recess, university students operate this crash pad. Yeah, you'll sleep on an assortment of military cots and other hastily assembled beds with 15 to 40 others, but the place attracts lots of convivial, laid-back people and its cafe-bar offers backpackers filling, tasty dinners for Nkr45.

Singsaker Sommerhotel (☎ 738 93 100; Rogertsgata 1; dm/s/d with shared bathroom Nkr200/410/620) Sleep either privately or in a dark 12-person bunkroom in a building originally built as a club for occupying German officers, set on a hill amid a grassy neighbourhood of beautiful homes. Linen hire is Nkr35.

Trondheim Hostel (☎ 738 74 450; www.trond heim-vandrerhjem.no; Weidemannsvei 41; dm/s/d from Nkr230/490/620; 💷 🖥) On a hillside 2km east of the train station, this hostel has underwhelming rooms that could use a renovation. Internet costs Nkr2 per minute.

Åse Andersen (☎ 735 11 540; Nedre Møllenberg Gate 27; s/d Nkr350/500; ⏲ mid-Jun–Aug) Cosy, wood-panelled rooms and comfortable furniture fill this cheerful ochre-coloured house on a quiet residential street. Linens cost Nkr50 and there's a shared kitchen, bathroom and balcony.

Bruns Botell (☎ 738 07 950; www.bilbrun.no; Kjøpmannsgata 41; s/d Nkr480/630) To check in, find the attendant at the YX gas station. Though you probably won't see any signs indicating this, he runs the Bruns Botell and will give you keys to simple, centrally located rooms at bargain prices. No breakfast is served, though all rooms have a kitchen.

Scandic Solisiden (☎ 216 14 600; www.scandic-hotels .com/solisiden; Beddingen 1; s/d Mon-Fri Sep-Jun Nkr1100/1300, s/d Sat & Sun & mid-Jun–Aug Nkr890/1090; P ᙀ ᙇ) Adjacent to a sunny district of cafes and converted warehouse buildings, this good-looking green cube, with its pleasing wooden interiors has the best disabled rooms in Trondheim.

Britannia Hotel (☎ 738 00 800; www.britannia.no; Dronningens gate 5; s/d Mon-Fri Sep-Jun Nkr1600/1800, s/d Sat & Sun Nkr995/1195, s/d mid-Jun–Aug Nkr900/1100; P ᙀ ᙀ ᙇ) Trondheim's oldest (1897) hotel contains Palmehaven, a magnificent and palm-filled Moorish-revival dining hall, and the Lobby Lounge, which looks like a British men's club. Refurbished rooms upstairs attempt to evoke the aura of age.

Also recommended:

Pensjonat Jarlen (☎ 735 13 218; www.jarlen.no; Kongens gate 40; s/d Nkr490/590) Barren, clean rooms contain private showers and kitchenettes.

P-Hotel (☎ 738 02 350; www.p-hotels.no; Nordre gate 24; s/d Nkr795/895; ᙀ) This chain hotel offers crisp rooms of Scandinavian design. There is no breakfast buffet, but you do get a sack with food.

Thon Hotel Trondheim (☎ 738 84 788; www.thon .no/trondheim; Kongens gate 15; s/d Nkr695/895; ᙀ ᙇ) Modest, modern rooms right in the centre. Breakfast costs Nkr50.

Eating

Lyche (☎ 738 99 500; Elgesetergate 1; dinner Nkr45; ᚚ from 5pm Sun-Fri, from 3pm Sat) One of many fabulous enterprises inside the Studentersamfundet, this cafe (run by students, but emphatically open to all) prepares an amazingly low-priced daily meal, such as a filling heap of pasta with peas and tuna.

Mormor's Stue (☎ 735 22 022; N Enkelts Killingsveile 2; mains Nkr75-99; ᚚ 10am-11.30pm Mon-Sat, 1-11.30pm Sun) Eat sandwiches (Nkr51) and pasta in a cosy house full of lace, parlours and dusty pictures of grandma. On Sundays a calorifically evil cake-and-coffee buffet (Nkr54) fills every seat, as does an evening beer special (from 5pm pay Nkr35) that has long made the joint a popular place to begin the night.

ourpick Ramp (Strandveien at Gregus gate; dishes Nkr80-140) A neighbourhood cafe-bar attracting few tourists, Ramp serves 'ecological' fare (meaning organic and local when possible). Eat bacon and eggs for breakfast, and lamb burgers or vegetarian pie for dinner. Well furnished with vintage furniture, the bohemian joint often books experimental bands and is a good place for booze.

Follow E6 east past the Scandic Hotel and pick up Strandveien on the left side of the roundabout.

Vertshuset Tavern (☎ 738 78 070; Sverresborg Allé 11; mains Nkr100-320) Dating from 1739 and blessed with enormous fireplaces, the menu features traditional, superbly prepared items such as roast elk, herring with beets, and reindeer fillet over mushroom stew. For atmosphere on a budget, try some pancakes with jam and bacon.

Baklandet Skydsstation (☎ 739 21 044; Øvre Baklandet 33; dishes Nkr110-200) A wood-burning stove and hearty fish soup of amazing quality keep people warm in this old wooden home with a sloping floor. There's a daily meal for Nkr150, and lots of folks sipping beer.

Frati (☎ 735 25 733; Munkegata 25; mains Nkr120-210) For a popular Italian spot serving cod primavera, spaghetti with sausage, and lots of garlic, head upstairs to an inviting room with a circular brick fireplace.

Jadab (☎ 735 24 600; Brattørgata 3A; mains Nkr125-220) An Indian place with a large vegetarian menu, Jadab serves so much rice that a side of naan probably won't be needed. The room is clean but shabby and there's a daily buffet (Nkr149) that runs to six.

Ørens Kro (☎ 736 00 635; Dokkgata 8; mains around Nkr200) Hidden in a compound of old brick warehouses, this yellow timbered bar and restaurant (formerly a boat-repair workshop) offers a daily meal (Nkr120) and enjoys pretty surrounds with lots of sunny outdoor seating, some of it stretching over a channel once used to haul ships out of the water. Rusting infrastructure remains.

Also recommended:

Kvilhaugen Gård (☎ 736 00 660; Blussuvollsbakken 40; mains Nkr195-300) Eat traditional food (eg whale, game, fowl) in a lovely farmhouse overlooking the city.

Persilleriet (☎ 736 06 014; Erling Skakkes gate 14; meals Nkt65-79; ᚚ noon-6pm Mon-Fri) Pick up tasty vegetarian fare at this tiny lunch spot.

For cheap vegetarian meals with young activists, see Uffa (p358).

CAFES

Café Gjest Baardsen (☎ 735 14 280; Kongens gate 2; snacks Nkr22-55; ᚚ 10am-6pm Mon-Thu, to 4pm Fri-Sun) Sturdy wooden furniture and tall candles fill this handsome, convivial cafe. It's particularly bustling in the afternoon, as patrons of the adjacent library and occupants of strollers fill the place to eat sandwiches and waffles.

NORWAY

Dromedar (☎ 735 02 502; Nedre Bakklandet 3; sandwiches Nkr65-70) Enjoy steamed coffee and several kinds of tea at this small cafe, whose few sidewalk tables sit upon a pretty cobbled street with lots of cyclists and pedestrians zipping by.

Café Ni Muser (☎ 735 36 311; Bispegata; light dishes Nkr79-109) Sunlit rooms look onto a small plaza (on warm days it's a beer garden) and attract a crowd of artists and architects. It serves tuna sandwiches, quiche and cake.

QUICK EATS & SELF-CATERING

There's an open-air fruit and vegetable market on Torvet each morning, as well as a **Rema 1000** (Torvet). The **Ravnkloa fish market** (☎ 10am-5pm Mon-Fri, 10am-4pm Sat) provides waterside fish cakes (Nkr75) and fishermen (free). For baguette sandwiches and pastries, try **Godt Brøt** (Thomas Angells gate 16). **GO'2 Kebab** (Carl Johans Gate; Nkr55-80) serves substantial (albeit mediocre) kebabs and falafel.

Drinking

Den Gode Nabo (☎ 738 74 240; Øvre Bakklandet; pub fare Nkr59-130) This bar occupies the lower level of an ancient warehouse. Navigating the cavernous space requires beam-dodging and careful foot placement. Inside, admire several centuries of patchwork carpentry and eat pub grub, the day's fish meal (Nkr125) or a pizza buffet (Nkr99).

Trondheim Mikrobryggeri (☎ 735 17 515; Prinsens gate 39) Enjoy brews by the glass or pitcher (pilsner, bitter, pale ale, IPA, amber, porter and stout) amid pleasant brick walls and varnished wooden surfaces. It's bright enough inside to read a book and there's a dart board and decent outside smoking patio.

Café 3B (☎ 735 11 550; Brattørgata 3) Lurch through the door and enter a space that feels like the grimy back stage of an art-house theatre. Everything is black: the walls, the upholstery, the clothes. You'll also find a pool table and a loud, deliberate jukebox.

Bar Circus (☎ 934 61 100; Nordre gate 17; ☎ 8pm-2am Thu-Sun) By 11pm the line out the door becomes formidable. Inside, find a hard-drinking young crowd gazing either blearily or enthusiastically at monitors announcing the next tune the bartender will play. Eager patrons appear to be nostalgic for Halloween and it is not uncommon for some to party in grotesque costume.

Lille London Pub (☎ 400 07 066; Brattøgata 10) This convincing English pub has so much wood glass and brass that it doesn't feel cheesy. It's a good place to watch a match with chips and a lager.

You would also do yourself a favour by drinking at Ramp, Baklandet Skydsstation, Cafe Edgar and, especially, Mormor's Stue (p357).

Entertainment

Studentersamfundet (☎ 738 99 500; Elgeseter-gate 1; ☎ from 5pm) An ideal university student centre that includes a half dozen bars and organises an excellent calendar of film screenings, discos and cool bands. Thousands of students come on weekend nights, with numerous events occurring simultaneously. During summer recess it's quiet.

Rick's (☎ 738 08 750; Nordre gate 11; cover Nkr80-100Nkr; ☎ 10pm-3.30am Thu-Sat) Owners must have stuck a Faustian deal, as there can be no other way to explain how a city the size of Trondheim can fill such a huge club. Multiple bars are distributed over four maze-like floors. Plenty of balconies overlook an expansive dance floor (soundtrack ranges from ultra pop to trance) or you can hang out in a dungeon.

Blæst (☎ 736 00 101; TMV Kaia 17) Incongruously surrounded by yuppie restaurants in a waterfront redevelopment, Blæst occupies an old warehouse and books international and Norwegian rockers, folk bands and black metal (Motorpsycho). Many weekends feature DJs spinning tracks far less mainstream than their counterparts at the bigger clubs.

Olavshallen (Kjøpmannsgata 44) At the Olavskvartalet cultural centre, Olavshallen is the city's main concert hall, hosting performers ranging from the Trondheim Symphony Orchestra to international rock and jazz musicians.

Uffa (www.uffa.no; Innherredsveien 69C) Long ago, the Sex Pistols played at this centre for activists. It organises six to eight punk shows a month in a squat white house with interiors covered in graffiti. Uffa hosts informal political meetings and runs a mostly vegan cafe (open noon to 4pm Tuesday to Thursday and during events; snacks Nkr20). Find it east on E6 opposite a green-steepled church.

For cinema, try **Nova Kinosenter** (☎ 820 54 333; Cicignons plass) or **Prinsen Kinosenter** (☎ 738 08 800; Prinsens gate 2B).

Getting There & Away

AIR
The airport is located in Værnes, 32km east of Trondheim.

BOAT
The *Hurtigruten* docks in Trondheim.

BUS
Nor-Way Bussekspress services run to and from Ålesund (Nkr500, seven hours, one to two daily), Bergen (Nkr783, 14½ hours, one daily), Oslo (Nkr495, nine hours, one to two daily) and Røros (Nkr232, three hours, two to four daily).

CAR & MOTORCYCLE
The E6, the main north–south motorway, passes west of the city centre and tolls total Nkr35, both northbound and southbound (on the Trondheim–Stjørdal section). There's also a Nkr25 toll on vehicles entering the city from 6am to 6pm from Monday to Friday.

For car rentals, there's **Avis** (centre ☎ 738 41 790; Kjøpmannsgata 34; airport ☎ 748 40 100) and **Europcar** (☎ 738 28 850; Thonning Owesens gate 36; airport ☎ 748 26 700).

TRAIN
Trains travel to Oslo (Nkr837, 6½ to 7½ hours, two to six daily), Bodø (Nkr924, 10 hours, two daily) and Røros (Nkr228, 2½ hours, three daily). If you're in a hurry to head north, you should seriously consider taking the overnight train from Oslo, tossing your gear into a locker at the station, and spending the day exploring Trondheim before continuing on an overnight train to Bodø (which, incidentally, goes through Hell).

Getting Around

TO/FROM THE AIRPORT
The airport bus, **Flybussen** (☎ 788 22 500), leaves from the train station (Nkr80, 40 minutes), the Britannia Hotel and other hotels frequently from 5am to 8pm.

BUS
The central transit point for all city buses is the intersection of Munkegata and Dronningens gate. The bus fare is Nkr22 (Nkr55 for a 24-hour ticket). Exact change is required.

CAR & MOTORCYCLE
Parking garages throughout town offer better rates (Nkr150 per day) and greater convenience than the krone-gobbling street-side meters.

BODØ
pop 46,000

Travellers generally use Bodø as a gateway to the Lofoten Islands and elsewhere in Nordland. Most get off their boat or train, poke around for a few hours and then get on the first ferry. Those that linger tend to do so to behold Saltstraumen, one of the world's most impressive maelstroms.

The city's harbour is picturesque and chock-full of small fishing vessels, with steep granite islands rising behind. The town, hurriedly rebuilt after thorough destruction in WWII, is not. Even so, you'll find a passable cafe, a brewery and the closest thing to nightlife for hundreds of kilometres.

Information
Intersport Bodø (☎ 755 49 850; 4th fl, Glassbuset) Holds keys for DNT cabins and sells maps and outdoor gear.
Library (☎ 755 56 100; Rådhuset; ✆ 11am-7.30pm Mon, Tue & Thu, 11am-3pm Wed & Fri, 11am-2pm Sat) Free internet.
Tourist office (☎ 755 48 000; www.visitbodo.com; Sjøgata 3; ✆ 9am-8pm Mon-Fri, 10am-6pm Sat, noon-8pm Sun Jun-Aug, shorter hours Sep-May) Has internet terminals (Nkr60 per hour).

Sights & Activities
The sprawling **Norsk Luftfartsmuseum** (Norwegian Aviation Museum; ☎ 755 07 850; Olav V gate; adult/child/student Nkr90/40/60; ✆ 10am-7pm Sun-Fri, 10am-5pm Sat mid-Jun–mid-Aug, 10am-4pm Mon-Fri, 11am-5pm Sat & Sun mid-Aug–mid-Jun; ☒) features a complete control tower, many esoteric aircraft and a sweat-producing simulator of jet-fighter flying. Kids and brave adults love it. **Nordlandsmuseet** (☎ 755 21 640; Prinsens gate 116; adult/student Nkr35/free; ✆ 9am-4pm Mon-Fri, 11am-4pm Sat & Sun May-Aug, shorter hours Sep-Apr) provides cursory exhibits on Lofoten fishermen, Sámi nomads and Bodø's history, much of it oriented towards the tragic bombing.

Sleeping
Bodøsjøen Camping (☎ 755 63 680; Kvernhusveien; camp sites from Nkr130, cabins Nkr250-500) Three kilometres from town via bus 12, this waterside spot offers a grassy field for

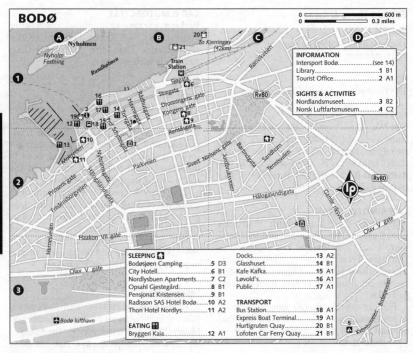

BODØ

0 ————————— 600 m
0 ————————— 0.3 miles

INFORMATION
Intersport Bodø.....................(see 14)
Library...**1** B1
Tourist Office..............................**2** A1

SIGHTS & ACTIVITIES
Nordlandsmuseet.........................**3** B2
Norsk Luftfartsmuseum..............**4** C2

SLEEPING
Bodøsjøen Camping..................**5** D3
City Hotell....................................**6** B1
Nordlysbuen Apartments........**7** C2
Opsahl Gjestegård.....................**8** B1
Pensjonat Kristensen.................**9** B1
Radisson SAS Hotel Bodø......**10** A2
Thon Hotel Nordlys..............**11** A2

EATING
Bryggeri Kaia............................**12** A1
Docks..**13** A2
Glasshuset.................................**14** B1
Kafe Kafka................................**15** A1
Løvold's......................................**16** A1
Public..**17** A1

TRANSPORT
Bus Station................................**18** A1
Express Boat Terminal............**19** A1
Hurtigruten Quay.....................**20** B1
Lofoten Car Ferry Quay..........**21** B1

tenters. The grounds have worthwhile cabins, modern amenities and fine views over sea and mountain.

City Hotell (☎ 755 20 402; Storgata 39; s/d Nkr595/695) You'll find plain rooms with small bathrooms and mediocre decor inside this small yellow hotel a few blocks from the centre of town. A restaurant on the 1st floor serves moderate daily meals (Nkr85).

Pensjonat Kristensen (☎ 755 21 699; Rensåsgata 45; s/d Nkr600/750; ☐) Operated by old-timers, this white clapboard house with its slate grey roof and simple rooms is a only short walk from the centre in a quiet neighbourhood. Modest green plantings emerge when the snow melts.

Nordlysbuen Apartments (☎ 996 35 752; www .nordlysbuen.no; Norlysbuen 19; apt Nkr750-950; ☐) For smart, recently refurbished apartments with modern furniture and full kitchens, this independent joint offers an alterative to the chain hotels.

Opsahl Gjestegård (☎ 754 20 704; Prinsensgata 131; s/d Nkr850/1050; ☐) On a quiet residential street a few blocks from the centre. Some rooms in this homey guesthouse come with wall coverings so brightly floral that you may need to wear sunglasses inside them.

Thon Hotel Nordlys (☎ 755 31 900; www.thonhotels .no/nordlys; Moloveien 14; s/d mid-Jun–Aug Nkr750/850, s/d Sep-Jun Nkr950/1250; ℗ ☒ ☐ ☒) Tall windows and pine floors provide the foundation for the well executed (and somewhat generic) modern design you'd expect from a Scandinavian chain hotel. Half the rooms offer views over the water, the remainder over a parking lot.

Radisson SAS Hotel Bodø (☎ 755 19 000; www radissonsas.com; Storgata 2; s/d Nkr795/1050 mid-Jun–mid-Aug, Nkr1250-1450 Sun-Thu, Nkr975/995 Fri & Sat rest of year; ℗ ☒ ☐) Find trouser presses and a fine rooftop bar with excellent views in this contemporary hotel. Rooms are very comfortable, but beware: you'll have to choose between 'British', 'Chinese', 'Japanese' and 'Scandinavian' design. Unless you want to stare at a tacky wall-mounted fan, consider avoiding the fake trip to Asia.

Eating & Drinking

Kafe Kafka (☎ 755 23 550; Sandgata 5B; meals Nkr92-140; ☒ 11am-1am Mon-Sat, 3pm-midnight Sun) Serving shrimp omelettes, vegetarian lasagne and

other light fare, this cafe-bar with its upholstered couches and numerous references to
Prague makes for a good place to read. On
the radio: Iron & Wine.

Løvold's (☎ 755 20 261; Tollbugata 9; dishes Nkr40-120;
⏰ 9am-6pm Mon-Fri, 9am-3pm Sat) The 2nd-floor
cafeteria above a fisherman's outfitter bus-
tles at lunch time, offering daily specials of
traditional Norwegian grub to a crowd of sea
dogs and hags. Big windows have views over
the water.

Bryggeri Kaia (☎ 755 25 808; Sjøgaten 1; mains Nkr89-
265; ⏰ 11am-3.30am) Eat bacon cheeseburgers,
wine-steamed mussels, and crayfish salad with
asparagus in this stylish brewery (contemporary black furniture and brass vats of beer)
on the water.

Public (☎ 755 58 330; Sjøgata 12; ⏰ 8pm-3.30am
Sun-Thu, 4pm-3.30am Fri & Sat) Super-sized stills
from punk-rock shows line the walls of this
minimalist bar with black leather stools and
a good-sized evening crowd.

For inexpensive food, head to the **docks** for
fresh shrimp or **Glasshuset** (Storgata 12), with a
supermarket and several fast-food choices.

Getting There & Around

The airport is 2km away, with flights to
Svolvær, Trondheim, Tromsø and more. Local
buses (Nkr30) marked 'Sentrumsrunden'
bring you to town.

Bodø is the northern terminus of the
Norwegian train network, with a service to
Trondheim (Nkr924, 10 hours, twice daily). If
you're continuing north by bus, you may need
to get off before Bodø at Fauske. Connections
to Narvik (Nkr467, six hours, twice daily)
connect with the train.

The *Hurtigruten* travels to/from Lofoten,
stopping at Stamsund (Nkr261, 4½ hours)
and Svolvær (Nkr279, six hours). Car ferries
run to Moskenes (Nkr561/155 for car and
driver/passenger, 3¼ hours, five to six daily)
with one sailing stopping at Værøy and Røst
in summer. There's also an express boat to
Svolvær (adult/child Nkr297/149, 3½ hours,
one daily).

AROUND BODØ

The timber-built 19th-century trading station
at sleepy **Kjerringøy**, by luminescent turquoise
seas and soaring granite peaks 42km north of
Bodø, is fantastically preserved as an **open-air
museum** (☎ 755 03 500; www.kjerringoy.no; adult/child/
student Nkr60/free/20; ⏰ 11am-5pm late May-late Aug) set

on a sleepy peninsula. Buses run from Bodø to
Kjerringøy (Nkr86, 1½ hours, one daily). In
summer, it's possible to do a return trip on
the same day.

The spectacular **Saltstraumen Maelstrom**,
claimed to be the world's strongest, suffi-
ciently boggles the mind (except on the rare
off-day when it appears about as powerful as
a flushing toilet). At high tide an immense
volume of water violently churns its whirlpool
way through a 3km-long strait that empties
one fjord into another. The spectacle occurs
four times daily. Consult with the Bodø tourist office (p359) on when to arrive.

NARVIK
pop 18,300

Welcome to what many Norwegians consider
to be the country's ugliest town, a coastal city
whose waterfront is obliterated by a monstrous transhipment facility, where the ore
from the Kiruna mines in Swedish Lapland
is off-loaded from rail cars onto ships bound
for distant smelters.

While some find a kind of grotesque beauty
in this industrial display, most visitors take
pleasure in the ski lift just 500m from the
centre, as well as the excellent hiking and skiing in the surrounding mountain landscape.
Many travellers end up here because it's the
terminus of an impressively picturesque rail
line (the Ofotbanen) running to Riksgränsen
in Sweden.

Orientation & Information

The train station is at the north end of town
while the bus station can be found outside the
bottom level of the AMFI shopping centre.

Ask the helpful Narvik **tourist office** (☎ 769 65
600; www.destinationnarvik.com; Kongens gate 57; ⏰ 9am-
7pm Mon-Fri, 11am-7pm Sat & Sun mid-Jun–mid-Aug, shorter
hours mid-Aug–mid-Jun) about summer tours of the
iron works (Nkr150, two weekly).

Sights & Activities

The gut-wrenching **Red Cross War Museum** (☎ 769
44 426; Kongens gate; adult/child Nkr50/25; ⏰ 10am-10pm
Mon-Sat, 11am-5pm Sun mid-Jun–mid-Sep, 11am-3pm
Mar–mid-Jun) thoroughly documents the many
horrors inflicted upon Narvik, a strategically
important site whose iron works ensured the
small town would be decimated over and
over by its own citizens and by troops from
Poland, Russia, France, Germany and Britain.
The place is stuffed with artefacts: German

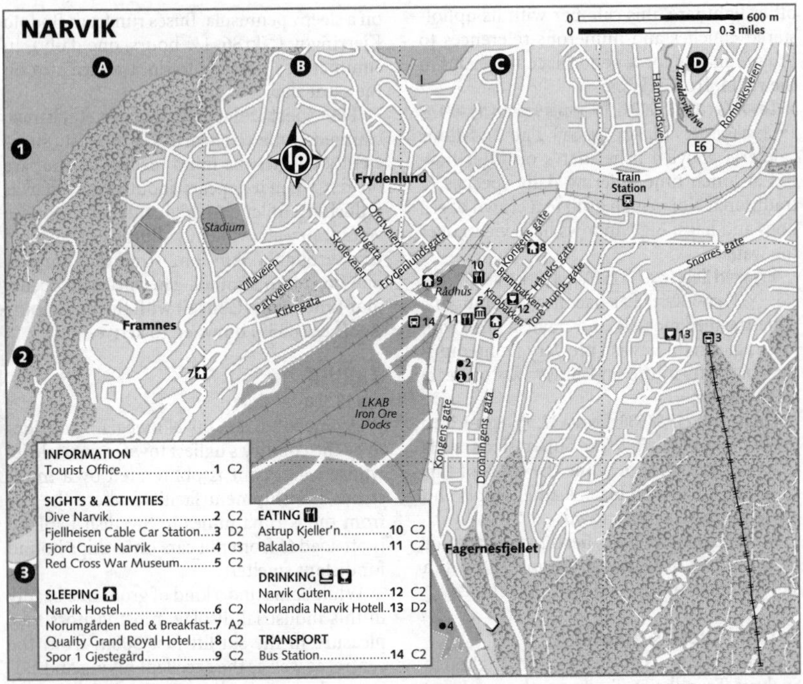

NARVIK
0 600 m
0 0.3 miles
A
B
C
D
1
2
3
Frydenlund
Stadium
Framnes
Hamsundsvei
Taraldsvikelva
Rombaksveien
E6
Train Station
Ofotveien
Brugata
Skoleveien
Frydenlundsgata
Villaveien
Parkveien
Kirkegata
Kongens gate
Brannbakken
Håreks gate
Kinobakken
Tore Hunds gate
Snorres gate
Rådhus
LKAB Iron Ore Docks
Kongens gate
Dronningens gata
Fagernesfjellet
INFORMATION
Tourist Office....1 C2
SIGHTS & ACTIVITIES
Dive Narvik....2 C2
Fjellheisen Cable Car Station....3 D2
Fjord Cruise Narvik....4 C3
Red Cross War Museum....5 C2
SLEEPING
Narvik Hostel....6 C2
Norumgården Bed & Breakfast..7 A2
Quality Grand Royal Hotel....8 C2
Spor 1 Gjestegård....9 C2
EATING
Astrup Kjeller'n....10 C2
Bakalao....11 C2
DRINKING
Narvik Guten....12 C2
Norlandia Narvik Hotell..13 D2
TRANSPORT
Bus Station....14 C2

propaganda, surgical instruments, canons, a ruined plane engine pulled from the fjord, weapons, torpedos and loads of pictures of the town being crushed into nothing.

Weather permitting, the **Fjellheisen cable car** (☎ 916 52 645; Mårveien; adult/child return Nk100/60; ⏲ 10am-1am mid-Jun–Jul, 1-9pm early Jun & Aug) soars 656m for breathtaking views of the midnight sun and the surrounding peaks and fjords.

During ski season, take the cable car to the largest vertical drop in Scandinavia (1000m) and speed back to town enjoying a stupendous view of the sea glistening in the near distance. Contact the tourist office for information, or see www.skiinfo.no/narvik.

Dive Narvik (☎ 995 12 205; www.divenarvik.com) runs multiday dives that explore local waters, chock-a-block with sunken ships from WWII. Dive costs start at Nkr5000 and include room and board.

For a fabulous summertime trek, the old **navvy road** used by those who built the Ofotbanen has been converted into a hiking and biking route that stretches deep into the mountains. Walk one way and ride the train back.

Tours

During the herring runs between October and December, orcas (killer whales) migrate to the fjords near Narvik. In October and November, **Fjord Cruise Narvik** (☎ 913 90 618; www.fcn.no) sends out boats to watch them dine (Nkr950).

Sleeping

Spor 1 Gjestegård (☎ 769 46 020; www.spor1.no; Brugata 2; dm/s/d from Nkr230/450/550) Made for backpackers and in former rail cabins right on the tracks, this place has spare rooms, friendly hosts, a sauna and a well-equipped, clean kitchen. A shed-like bar occupies an outlying building, and is one of the most popular in town.

Narvik Hostel (☎ 769 62 200; www.hihostels.no; Dronningens gate 58; dm/s/d Nkr270/460/660; ♿) Centrally located and sharing space with the modern Victoria Hotel, this hostel has clean and spare rooms with bunks and institutional flooring. It's a friendly place with a cafe on site.

Norumgården Bed & Breakfast (☎ 769 44 857; http.//norumgaarden.narviknett.no; Framnesveien 127; s/d Nkr450/600; ⏲ late Jan-Nov) Used as a German officers' mess in WWII, this atmospheric house brims with oddities and antiques. Reserve early: there's only four rooms. One of them, 'Heidi', has a tiny balcony and was once occupied by King Olav.

Quality Grand Royal Hotel (☎ 769 77 000; www .choice.no; Kongens gate 64; s/d from Nkr890/990; P 🖳 🕹) Narvik's most luxurious hotel provides a sauna, and rooms with butter-coloured walls, good views and ugly ceilings.

Eating & Drinking

There are very few options.

Bakalao (☎ 769 43 660; Kongens gate 42; mains Nkr50-175) A small off-shoot of Narvik's attractive brick fish-hall. Enjoy well-made ready-to-eat dishes such as fish cakes and whale stew.

Astrup Kjeller'n (☎ 769 60 402; Kinobakken 1; mains Nkr150-225) Established in 1903, the heavy stone walls, dim lighting and intimate nooks of this warm place host local specialities and a superb fillet of reindeer.

Narvik Guten (☎ 752 11 887; Dronningens gata 60) A rough-around-the-edges pub entirely filled with locals, its a good place to learn about the city after a few pints under dim lights.

In the winter, the bar at the Norlandia Narvik Hotell attracts skiers thanks to its fine hillside location opposite the cable car.

Getting There & Away

Nearly all flights leave from Hardstad/Narvik airport (Evenes), 1¼ hours away. Narvik's tiny Framneslia airport, 3km west of the centre, serves Bodø and Tromsø.

Buses run to Tromsø (Nkr370, 4¼ hours, three daily), to Bodø (Nkr497, 6½ hours, two daily) via Fauske (Nkr407, 4¾ hours) and to Svolvær (Nkr433, 4½ hours, two daily).

Heading for Sweden along the spectacular Oftbanen railway, there are at least two daily services between Narvik and Riksgränsen (one hour), on the border, and Kiruna (three hours). Trains continue to Lulea (7¼ hours) where you can pick up connections to Stockholm.

LOFOTEN

The spectacular glacier-carved mountains of Lofoten, separated from the mainland by Vestfjorden, soar straight out of the sea – from a distance they appear as an unbroken line, known as the Lofoten Wall.

Lofoten is Norway's prime winter fishing ground. The warming effects of the Gulf Stream draw spawning Arctic cod from the Barents Sea south to the Lofoten waters each winter, followed by migrating north-coast farmer-fishermen, who for centuries have drawn most of their income from seasonal fishing. Although fish stocks have dwindled greatly in recent years, fishing continues to be Lofoten's largest industry and cod is still dried outdoors on ubiquitous wooden racks through early summer.

Many of the fishing community's *rorbuer* (winter shanties) and *sjøhus* (fishermen's bunkhouses) have been converted into luxurious tourist accommodation, providing atmospheric sleeping options.

The main islands of Austvågøy, Vestvågøy, Flakstadøy and Moskenesøy are all ruggedly beautiful. Artists are attracted by Austvågøy's light and there are art galleries in Svolvær, Kabelvåg and the busy fishing village of Henningsvær. Vestvågøy has Lofoten's richest farmland. Flakstadøy and Moskenesøy have sheltered bays and fjords, sheep pastures and sheer coastal mountains looming above strikingly picturesque fishing villages. Cyclists should be sure to try the unbelievable Kaiser Route (p364).

The four main islands are all linked by bridges or tunnels, with buses running the entire length of the Lofoten road (E10) from Fiskebø in the north to Å at road's end in the southwest.

Tourist information is available at www .lofoten-info.no or www.lofoten.info.

Svolvær

pop 4500

A compact towns of old wooden buildings and modern concrete blocks, Lofoten's principle town might be two notches less picturesque than its brothers, but it's still a pretty spot from which to base your explorations, with steep mountains rising sharply in the background and a busy harbour. In Svolvær, more than other places in Lofoten, you'll find modern conveniences and the best of what passes for nightlife.

On the main square, you'll find a couple of banks, a taxi stand, a car-rental agency and the regional **tourist office** (☎ 760 69 800; www.lofoten .info; Torget; 🕑 9am-9.30pm Mon-Fri, 9am-8pm Sat, 10am-9.30pm Sun mid-Jun–mid-Aug, shorter hours rest of year), which can help with bike and kayak rentals. Svolvær's **library** (Vestfjordgata; 🕑 11am-3pm Mon-Fri, to 7pm Wed) provides free internet access.

NORWAY

SIGHTS & ACTIVITIES

Daredevils like to scale **Svolværgeita** (the Svolvær Goat), a distinctive, two-pronged peak visible from the harbour, and then jump the 1.5m from one horn to the other – a grave-yard at the bottom awaits those who miss. For phenomenal views, hikers can ascend the steep path to the base of the Goat and up the slopes behind it. There's also a rough route from the Goat over to the extraordinary **Devil's Gate**; ask the tourist office for details.

For a moving excursion, ride a boat into the **Trollfjord**, so spectacularly steep and narrow that you might just experience the kind of ter-ror and awe associated with the romantic sub-lime. Tours run five times daily in high season and cost Nkr350 per person; the tourist office has details. In summertime, the Northbound *Hurtigruten* also visits and makes a stupefying three-point turn upon departure.

Lofoten Seafari (☎ 479 02 940) at the Rica Hotel, bounces over the waves in inflatable rafts that zoom around some nearby islands in a heart-thumping two-hour trip (Nkr400).

For 83km of breathtaking cycling, head to Holandshamn and make your way back to Svolvær along the **Kaiser Route**. Lonely shore-line, jagged mountains and abandoned farms will be your constant companion. Unlike the west side of Lofoten, this trip takes in parts of the islands that are largely undiscovered by tourists. A long stretch runs parallel to the Trollfjord. The Danish site www.diger mulen.de (no English) outlines the journey (click on Kaiserroute). Do your preplanning at the tourist office, where you can pick up the handy *Sykkel Guide* (Nkr120) containing topographic maps.

SLEEPING & EATING

Svolvær Sjøhuscamping (☎ 760 70 336; www.svolver -sjohuscamp.no; Parkgata 12; r Nkr440-490) On stilts and projecting over the water, this pleasant 100-year-old house has small rooms with bunks and pleasant views. Guests share bathrooms and a kitchen. Turn right on the first road past the library. No breakfast, and linens cost Nkr75.

Lofoten Rorbuer (☎ 915 95 450; www.lofoten-rorbuer .no; r Nkr540) An immaculate private house with a dock and cosy social space. Rooms come with bunks and are set on a small cove. Some have private kitchens, others share facilities. It's about 1km E10 towards the airport on the E10.

Rica Hotel Svolvær (☎ 760 72 222; www.rica -hotels.com; Lamholmen; s/d Nkr795/1045; P ✹ ⚅) Perched on a pier and hovering over the water, this flamboyant place combines mod-ern hotel comforts with nifty *rorbuer* styl-ing. One suite has a hole cut in the floor for indoor fishing.

Bacalao (☎ 760 79 400; Kirkegata; mains Nkr60-130) For a minimalist cafe-bar in a room that feels like a retro-fitted garage, head over to this hang-out for fishermen and students. Bands play some nights; on our visit seven horns and a drummer played 'Hit the Road Jake' to great fanfare. Light food served.

Du Verden (☎ 760 77 099; JE Paulengate 12; dinner mains Nkr175-300) For inventive fish concoctions by an award-winning chef (halibut over cheesy risotto and squash), head to this modern, ro-mantic room with tones of light wood and soft grey, contrasting with bright oil abstracts. There's a cheaper lunch menu.

Kjøkkenet (☎ 760 66 466; Lamholmen; mains Nkr200-265) For excellent traditional fare, this kitchen turns out cod tongues, cured cod with crunchy bits of fat and boiled vegetables, and grilled cod neck. The dining room, with its old fire-place, looks like grandma's house. There's a worthwhile pub next door.

There's a bakery near the square and a **Rimi supermarket** (Torggata) a block inland.

GETTING THERE & AWAY

Svolvær has a small airport (4km from town) where you can catch flights to Bodø.

Buses to/from Vesterålen travel between Svolvær and Sortland (Nkr150, 2¼ hours, three to five daily). Buses to Leknes (Nkr130, two hours, three to six daily) make connec-tions to Å (Nkr215, 3½ hours, two to four daily), stopping at points west. Express buses runs between Svolvær and Narvik (Nkr433, 4½ hours, two daily).

Express boats ply the waters between Svolvær and Bodø (adult/child Nkr297/149, 3½ hours, one daily) and the *Hurtigruten* stops here.

Kabelvåg

If you got off the boat and thought Svolvær's blend of traditional and modern wasn't cute enough, this pleasing village lies only 5km west and is connected by the E10 and a paved walking trail. Narrow channels lined with old warehouses lead to the circular cobbled *torget* (town square), whose pattern of paving recalls

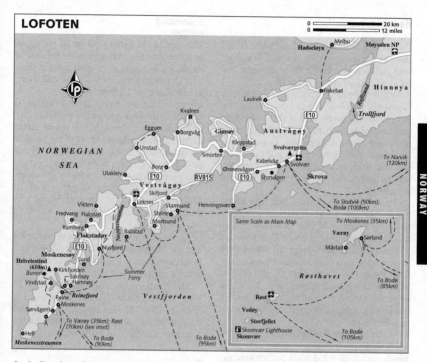

LOFOTEN

NORWEGIAN SEA

Vestvågøy

Austvågøy

Hinnøya

NORWAY

the hulls of small fishing boats, themselves docked nearby.

Behind the old prison, a trail leads uphill to the **statue of King Øystein**, who in 1120 ordered the first *rorbu* to be built to house fishermen who had been sleeping under their overturned rowing boats – not just a kind gesture, as the tax on the exported dried fish was the main source of the king's revenue.

Some of these original *rorbuer* have been excavated as part of the **Lofotmuseet** (☎ 760 69 790; www.lofotmuseet.no; Storvågan; adult/student Nkr50/40; ☼ 9am-6pm mid-Jun–mid-Aug, 9am-3pm Mon-Fri mid-Aug–mid-Jun), a regional history museum on the site of the first town in the polar regions.

Nearby, the seafront **Lofoten Aquarium** (☎ 760 78 665; Storvågan; adult/child/student Nkr80/40/60; ☼ 10am-7pm mid-Jun–mid-Aug, 11am-3pm mid-Aug–Nov & Feb–mid-Jun) shows you some of the personalities that have made Lofoten great, including the heroic cod and some harbour seals in an outdoor tank. You can eat their relatives in the museum cafe (not the seals). Otter feedings occur three times per day.

Sandvika Fjord og Sjøhuscamp (☎ 760 78 145; www.lofotferie.no; camp sites Nkr145, cabins Nkr550-650),

3km and two inlets west of Kabelvåg, sits near the head of a rocky peninsula with good views. Camp sites are few and small, set on grassy patches a bit removed from the RVs. There's a cafeteria on site. The **Kabelvåg Hostel** (☎ 760 69 880; www.hihostels.no; Finnesveien 24; dm/s/d Nkr260/490/660; ☼ Jun–mid-Aug; ⓟ) is at a school 1km north of the village centre. Relatively cheerful dorms (two, four and 10 beds) contain bunks and simple painted furniture. The **Kabelvåg Hotel** (☎ 760 78 800; Kong Østeinsgate 4; s/d Nkr850/1250; ☼ mid-May–mid-Aug) lies in the centre of town. The original wooden beauty was destroyed by fire in 1995 and has since been convincingly rebuilt with an attractive Art Deco bar.

The all-wood **Præstenbrygga** (☎ 760 78 060; Torget; mains Nkr75-140; ☼ from 11am; ▣) lies on the town square and has terraces stretching over the dock. The friendly pub serves bottomless cups of coffee (Nkr20), pizza (whose toppings include cod and smoked whale) and sandwiches. It often books live music.

From Svolvær you can walk the 5km to Kabelvåg or catch one of the roughly hourly buses (Nkr26, 10 minutes).

Henningsvær

pop 470

Picturesque buildings of red and white crowd the narrow channel that bisects this village, with cod racks perched in the background and fishing boats wherever space allows.

While Henningsvær's nickname, the 'Venice of Lofoten', is a tad overblown, few people would disagree that this bohemian enclave and active fishing village is the trendiest place in the archipelago. Especially on weekends, the outdoor seating at the waterside bars and restaurants is ideal for observing the lively scene. There are also a couple of art galleries.

The climbing school's **Den Siste Viking** (☎ 909 54 619; www.nordnorskklatreskole.no, in Norwegian; Misværveien 10; dm/d Nkr180/500) crosses a Lofoten *rorbuer* with an English pub and a Himalayan trekkers' lodge. Its **Klatrekafeen** serves up a small selection of homemade light meals (Nkr75 to Nkr130) and snacks, while booking good musical gigs. They also organise technical climbing expeditions: a guide with equipment costs Nkr2000 for up to four people.

In summer, **Johs Giær Sjøhus og Rorbuer** (☎ 760 74 719; www.giaever-rorbuer.no; Hellandsgata 790; rorbuer Nkr650-1110, r Nkr450-700; ☒) lets out workers' accommodation in a modern house on the harbour belonging to the local fish plant. Spruce wood-panelled rooms share a kitchen and bathrooms. It also has three *rorbuer*.

Henningsvær Bryggehotel (☎ 760 74 750; booking @henningsvaer.dvgl.no; Hjellskjæret; s/d from Nkr1050/1250; ☒) abuts the harbour, with large windows surveying boats puttering up and down the channel. Rooms are stylish and contemporary. There's a rack of rods by the door, if you'd like to catch something.

Buses shuttle between Svolvær (40 minutes), Kabelvåg (35 minutes) and Henningsvær three to five times daily.

Lofotr Vikingmuseum

This 83m-long chieftain's hall, Norway's largest Viking building, has been excavated at Borg, near the centre of Vestvågøy. The **museum** (☎ 760 84 900; www.lofotr.no; adult/child/ student Nkr100/50/75; ☒ 10am-7pm mid-May–Aug, 1-3pm Fri Sep-Apr) offers an insight into Viking life, complete with a scale-model reconstruction of the building, guides in Viking costume and a replica Viking ship, which you can sometimes help row.

Stamsund

pop 1000

The traditional fishing village of Stamsund makes a fine destination largely because of its dockside hostel, a magnet for travellers who sometimes stay for weeks on end. Here, as elsewhere on Lofoten, highlights include hiking and fishing. A popular town activity is to stare at the *Hurtigruten*'s approach.

The wonderful old beach house **Justad Rorbuer og Vandrerhjem** (☎ 760 89 334; fax 760 89 739; dm/s/d Nkr125/300/400, cabins Nkr600-800; ☒ mid-Dec–mid-Oct; ℗), 1.2km from the quay, attracts many repeat customers drawn by the waterside building, friendly manager (ask about hiking routes) and free loans of fishing gear and row boats. Bike rentals cost Nkr80 to Nkr100 per day.

The village centre contains a supermarket and the **Skæbrygga** (fish mains Nkr150-175) bar and restaurant, a cosy, low-ceilinged affair at the water's edge. There's little else.

The *Hurtigruten* coastal steamer stops en route between Bodø (Nkr261, 4½ hours) and Svolvær (Nkr132, 1½ hours). In July and August, buses from Leknes to Stamsund (25 minutes) run three to eight times daily.

Reine

The delightful village of Reine, on the island of Moskenesøy, is on a calm bay backed by ranks of mountain cliffs and pinnacles. It's easy to see the reasons why the village, with its almost fairy-tale setting, has been voted the most scenic place in all of Norway. Aside from eating some fish and taking a hike, the village is incredibly sleepy.

For an exceptional panorama of the lagoon, town and island, hike up the precipitous track to Reinebringen (670m), which starts at the tunnel entrance 1.2km south of the Reine turn-off from the E10 and climbs very steeply to the ridge (448m). Experienced hikers can continue to the peak and then drop steeply down a very exposed route to the col of Navaren and on to Navaren's summit (730m).

In summer, ferries run from Reine to **Vindstad** (Nkr100 return, 15 minutes) through the scenic Reinefjord. From Vindstad, it's a one-hour hike over a ridge to the abandoned settlement of **Bunes**, which is on the other side of the island, with a magnificent beach, vast quantities of driftwood and the 610m-high cliff of **Helvetestind**. Here you'll find some extremely basic camping.

ourpick Hamnøy Mat og Vinbu (☎ 760 92 145; Hamnøy; mains Nkr165-210; ☺ May-Aug) is a family-run place that serves stellar local specialities, including six-fish soup, whale steaks and daily specials caught a few metres away. Enjoy incredible, flaky coal fish in a subtle cream sauce topped with salmon roe. To identify the more esoteric fishes of the day, consult a handy picture book.

All buses from Leknes to Å stop in Reine.

Sakrisøy

Pretty as Reine is, you'll find it hard to suppress the urge to jump out of your bus or car to snap a few pictures of it's rival for visual perfection: in this instance an incredibly charming and quiet village of ochre buildings set on some rocky outcroppings and surrounded by water, mountains and cod drying racks. Here you can gawk at the scenery, grab a dock-side fish cake (Nkr55) from the town's **road-side monger**, and sleep amid the postcard setting in a fine *robuer* at **Sakrisøy Rorbuer** (☎ 760 92 143; www.lofoten-info.no/sakrisoy; rorbuer from Nkr450). Find the reception at Dagmar Gylseth's bizarre **doll museum** and antique shop, where you can also pick up a coffee or waffle.

Sakrisøy is 1km west of Reine towards Hamnøy.

Å

Å is a very special place at what feels like the end of the world on the western tip of Lofoten. A preserved fishing village perched on forbidding rocks connected by wooden footbridges, its shoreline is lined with red-painted *rorbuer*, many of which jut into the sea. Racks of drying cod and picture-postcard scenes occur at almost every turn. Visitors enliven the tiny place in summer, while in winter it's stark, haunting and empty.

SIGHTS & ACTIVITIES

The **Tørrefiskmuseum** (Stockfish Museum; ☎ 911 50 560; adult/student Nkr40/25; ☺ 10am-5pm mid-Jun–mid-Aug, 11am-5pm Mon-Fri early Jun & late Aug, otherwise by appointment), inside a cod plant dating from 1920, details the history of the stockfish industry, taking in every step from catching to cooking. Steinar Larson, the gregarious operator, has long family ties to Å, and explains everything cod (and Å) in enthusiastic, fascinating detail.

Many of Å's 19th-century buildings are set aside as the **Norwegian Fishing Village Museum** (☎ 760 91 488; admission Nkr50; ☺ 10am-5pm late Jun-late Aug, 11am-3pm Mon-Fri Sep–mid-Jun), complete with old boats and boathouses, a bakery from 1844, Europe's oldest cod-liver oil factory and storehouses.

Walk to the camping ground at the end of the village for a good hillside view of Værøy Island, which lies on the other side of **Moskenesstraumen**, the swirling maelstrom that inspired the fictional tales of Jules Verne and Edgar Allen Poe.

SLEEPING & EATING

Moskenesstraumen Camping (☎ 760 91 344; camping for 1/2/3 people Nkr90/110/130, cabins Nkr400-700; Ⓟ) This basic camping ground lies at the south end of Å near an ocean-side cliff. Paths and sites wind around granite boulders that seem to erupt from the ground.

Å HI Hostel (☎ 760 91 121; www.lofoten-rorbu.com; dm Nkr180, rorbuer Nkr850-1550; Ⓟ) The hostel has accommodation in some of the museum's historic seaside buildings that form the picturesque centre of town and offers accommodation in many *rorbuer* of varying sizes, some with fireplace. Breakfast is Nkr60 extra.

Å-Hamna Rorbuer (☎ 760 91 211; www.lofotenferie.com dm/d Nkr110/450, rorbuer Nkr650-1000; Ⓟ) This inviting place is run by a crazy guy who knows way too much about stockfish. Pleasant dorms come with a pretty communal space in a restored 1860s home. Cosy wooden *rorbu*, perched magnificently on the rocks, contain four to eight beds each. In the low season you can get the best for around Nkr400, firewood included.

Brygga restaurant (☎ 760 91 121; mains Nkr150-210; ☺ Jun-Sep) The village's only restaurant cantilevers dramatically over the water and serves primarily fish, though there is a token vegetarian plate. It's a great place to drink beer.

Self-caterers can also buy fresh fish from local fishers, and pick up other supplies at the small food shop behind the hostel office.

GETTING THERE & AWAY

Up to three daily buses from Å to Leknes (Nkr107, 1¾ hours), Svolvær (Nkr200, 3¼ hours) and Sortland (Nkr312 plus Nkr30 for a ferry, 5¼ hours).

Car ferries run from Bodø to Moskenes (Nkr561/155 for car and driver/passenger, 3¼ hours, five to six daily), 5km north of Å. Some of these ferries run via Værøy and Røst.

Værøy & Røst
pop 1400

Lofoten's southern islands of Værøy and Røst have some of the finest **bird-watching** in Norway, with large colonies of fulmars, guillemots, kittiwakes and terns. There are puffins as well, but the population has dropped by more than 50% in the past decade as a result of dwindling stocks of herring, the main food source for puffin chicks.

Craggy, high and rugged, Værøy has a handful of residents hugely outnumbered by 100,000 nesting sea birds. **Hiking trails** take in some of the more spectacular seabird rookeries. The main trail goes along the west coast, beginning about 300m past the island's airstrip, and continues south all the way to the virtually deserted fishing village of Mostad, passing by steep cliffs, sandy beaches and isolated settlements. This 10km hike makes for a full day's outing and is not too strenuous, but it's exposed to the elements, so is best done in fair weather.

In contrast to pointy Værøy, Røst, to the south, is pancake flat. Access to the best bird-watching requires a boat, as the largest rookeries are on offshore islands. Kåroy Rorbucamping (below) can arrange five-hour boat trips (adult/child Nkr300/125) that cruise past major sea-bird colonies (especially puffins) and stop at an 1887 **lighthouse** and a vista point. En route it's common to see seals, and there are occasional sightings of orcas. Other than the boat trip, there's not much to do.

The **tourist office** (☎ 760 95 210; ☻ 10am-3pm Mon-Sat mid-Jun–mid-Aug) is 200m from the ferry landing at Sørland.

SLEEPING & EATING
Kåroy Rorbucamping (☎ 760 96 238; www.karoy .no; per person Nkr150; ☻ May-Aug) Rooms sleep two, four or six at this authentic *rorbu*. Bathrooms are communal and there are self-catering facilities. This fabulous place is situated on the minuscule island of Kåroy; phone from the ferry and a boat will be sent to collect you from Røst.

Preste Gården (☎ 760 95 411; www.prestegaarden.no; Værøy; s/d Nkr475/690, with shared bathroom Nkr400/600) Sleep in the knotty pine attic of an old vic-

arage, next to an onion-domed church, or in a cosy turf-roofed cottage with ocean out front and cliff behind. It's the large house with the flagpole.

Kornelius Kro (☎ 760 95 299; korn-kro@online.no; Værøy; 1-/2-4-bed cabins Nkr550/850/1500) Værøy's only nightlife option also has a restaurant, a pub and a few simple but clean cottages out the back. Check out the wood-fired seawater hot tub.

GETTING THERE & AWAY
Car ferries run from Bodø to Værøy (Nkr139, four to six hours, one daily except Saturday) before continuing to Røst, directly or via Moskenes on Lofoten.

VESTERÅLEN

The islands of Vesterålen aren't quite as dramatic as Lofoten, but they're still very attractive to visitors. For tourist information, consult **Vesterålen Reiseliv** (☎ 761 11 480; www .visitvesteralen.com; Kjøpmannsgata 2, Sortland).

Vesterålen is connected by ferry from Melbu on Hadseløya, to Fiskebøl on Austvågøy (Lofoten). Melbu has a couple of **museums** and a famous **music festival**, featuring classical, jazz and blues, every July. The other main town, **Stokmarknes**, is a quiet market community best known as the birthplace of the *Hurtigruten* coastal steamer.

Nyksund (www.nyksund-info.com), on Langøya, is a former abandoned fishing village that's now re-emerging as an artists' colony. There's a great **walk** over the headland from Nyksund to Stø (three hours return), at the northernmost tip of Langøya. Ask the tourist office for details of **whale-watching tours** from Stø. **Holmvik Brygge** (☎ 761 34 796; www.nyksund .com; Nyksund; s/d Nkr300/500) offers irregular but cosy rooms done up like those in an old fisherman's house. Facilities are shared and there's a pub.

Andenes, on Andøy, seems a long way from anywhere, but there's whale-watching, a whale centre and a lighthouse. Otherwise it's not exciting. **Whale Safari** (☎ 761 15 600; www.whalesafari.no) runs popular three- to five-hour whale-watching cruises from the whale centre between late May and mid-September. Trips depart at least once daily in the morning. Sightings of sperm whales are guaranteed, or your next trip is free.

To sleep, try **Hisnakul Hantural History Centre** (☎ 761 41 203; Hamnegata 1; dm/s/d Nkr150/250/350), which has simple budget rooms above the gallery, or **Den Gamle Fyrmesterbolig** (☎ 761 41 027; Richard Withs gate 11, Andenes; r Nkr500), a charming former lighthouse-keeper's cottage, adjacent to the seaside beacon.

Getting There & Away

Sortland is the main transport hub in Vesterålen. Both Sortland and Stokmarknes are stops for the *Hurtigruten* coastal steamer.

TROMSØ

pop 52,000

At latitude N69°40´, welcome to the world's northernmost university town. In contrast to some of the more sober communities dotting the north coast of Norway, Tromsø is a spirited place with street music, cultural happenings and more pubs per capita than any other Norwegian town – it even has its own brewery.

A backdrop of snowcapped peaks provides spectacular scenery, excellent hiking in summer, and skiing and dogsledding from September to April. Many polar expeditions have departed from Tromsø, earning the city the nickname 'Gateway to the Arctic'. A statue of explorer Roald Amundsen, who headed some of the expeditions, stands in a little square by the harbour.

Orientation

Tromsø's city centre and airport are on the island of Tromsøya, which is linked by bridges to overspill suburbs on both the mainland and the much larger outer island Kvaløya. Storgata is the principal drag.

Information

Library (Grønnegata 94; �%11am-5pm Mon-Fri, 11am-3pm Sat) Free internet in a plush building.

Tourist office (☎ 776 10 000; www.destinasjontromso .no; Kirkegata 2; �%9am-4pm Mon-Fri, 10am-4pm Sat) Free guides and maps.

Troms Turlag DNT (☎ 776 85 175; www.turistforenin gen.no; Grønnegata 32; �%10am-2pm Tue, Wed & Fri, 10am-6pm Thu) Stop by for topographical maps, gear and hiking advice.

Sights & Activities

Tromsø's daringly designed museum of the Arctic, **Polaria** (☎ 777 50 100; Hjalmar Johansens gate 12; adult/child Nkr95/45; �%10am-7pm mid-May–mid-Aug, noon-5pm mid-Aug–mid-May; ☒) presents panoramic films on Svalbard (caution: these inspire spontaneous and expensive trips to the remote icy netherworld), an aquarium with Arctic fish, and a cohort of bearded seals, whose twice-daily feedings delight children.

The **Tromsø Museum** (☎ 776 45 000; www.uit.no; Lars Thøringsvei 10; adult/child Nkr30/15; �%9am-8pm Jun-Aug, shorter hours Sep-May; ☒) simulates the northern lights for visitors currently experiencing the midnight sun. It also presents some well-done displays on Arctic wildlife, Sámi culture and regional history. Take bus 28.

Occupying a restored artillery battery with six big Nazi guns, the **Tromsø War Museum** (☎ 776 55 440; Solstrandveien; adult/child Nkr30/15; �%noon-5pm Wed-Sun Jun-Aug, noon-5pm Sun May & Sep) includes a former ammunition store with an exhibition on the 52,600-tonne German battleship *Tirpitz*, sunk by British air forces at Tromsø in 1944.

Established in 1877, **Mack Brewery** (☎ 776 24 500; Storgata 5; tours Nkr130) produces Mack's Pilsner, Isbjørn, Haakon and several dark beers; the tour fee includes a beer stein, pint and souvenir. You can smell it from a block away. Tours (including pint and souvenir mug) leave from the Ølhallen pub (at 1pm, Monday to Thursday). For more information, see p371.

In addition to exhibits of contemporary paintings, sculpture and applied art, **Nordnorsk Kunstmueum** (Art Museum of Northern Norway; ☎ 776 47 020; Sjøgata 1; admission free; �%10am-5pm Tue-Fri, noon-5pm Sat & Sun; ☒) has a fine collection of 19th-century landscape paintings, which reveal what the far north looked like 150 years ago.

Ever wondered how to skin a polar bear? Want to see a creepy wax figure with dead, zombie eyes whack a baby seal? Such wonders await you inside the low-ceiling warehouse of the **Polarmuseet** (Polar Museum; ☎ 776 84 373; Søndre Tollbugata 11; adult/child/student Nkr50/10/45; �%10am-7pm mid-Jun–mid-Aug, shorter hours rest of year; ☒), as well as artefacts from polar explorations conducted from Tromsø.

Take a midnight-sun stroll through the **botanical gardens** (☎ 776 45 078; Breivika; admission free; �%24hr), which bloom brightly despite its northern locale. Take bus 20.

You can get a fine city view by taking the **Storsteinen Fjellheis** (☎ 776 38 737; Solliveien 12; adult/child return Nkr85/40; �%10am-5pm Apr-Sep), a cable car that runs up Mt Storsteinen (420m), from where a network of trails radiate. Take bus 26 from Stortorget harbour. It's open until

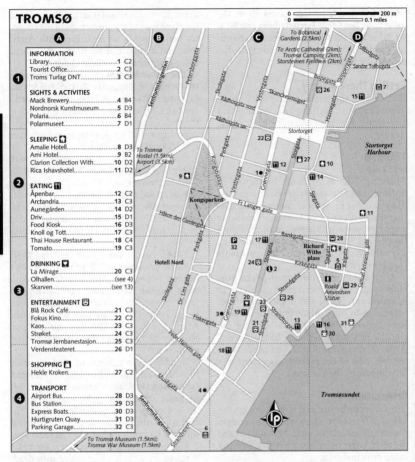

TROMSØ

INFORMATION
Library...**1** C2	
Tourist Office...............................**2** C3	
Troms Turlag DNT......................**3** C3	

SIGHTS & ACTIVITIES
Mack Brewery..............................**4** B4	
Nordnorsk Kunstmuseum..........**5** D3	
Polaria..**6** B4	
Polarmuseet.................................**7** D1	

SLEEPING
Amalie Hotell...............................**8** D3	
Ami Hotel.....................................**9** B2	
Clarion Collection With..........**10** D2	
Rica Ishavshotel.......................**11** D2	

EATING
Åpenbar......................................**12** C2	
Arctandria.................................**13** C3	
Aunegården..............................**14** D2	
Driv...**15** D1	
Food Kiosk................................**16** D3	
Knoll og Tott............................**17** D3	
Thai House Restaurant............**18** C4	
Tomato......................................**19** C3	

DRINKING
La Mirage..................................**20** C3	
Olhallen.................................(see 4)	
Skarven...............................(see 13)	

ENTERTAINMENT
Blå Rock Café............................**21** C3	
Fokus Kino.................................**22** C2	
Kaos...**23** C3	
Strøket......................................**24** C3	
Tromsø Jernbanestasjon..........**25** C3	
Verdensteateret........................**26** D1	

SHOPPING
Hekle Kroken............................**27** C2	

TRANSPORT
Airport Bus................................**28** D3	
Bus Station................................**29** D3	
Express Boats............................**30** D3	
Hurtigruten Quay.....................**31** D3	
Parking Garage..........................**32** C3	

1am on clear nights when the midnight sun is present.

Festivals & Events

Every show at the **Tromsø International Film Festival** (☎ 777 53 090; www.tiff.no), held in mid-January, is packed with both locals and A-list types excited to have major screenings in such an exotic place. Check out movies from northern Norway and the Baltic countries, forgotten classics, weird shorts, American independents and more.

TIL (☎ 776 63 800; www.til.no) services the town's football mania in a small stadium. Team members have received yellow cards for throwing snowballs. Buy tickets at Fokus Kino (p372).

Sleeping

Tromsø Camping (☎ 776 38 037; www.tromsocamping.no; camp sites Nkr150, cabins Nkr450-1000; P) Grounds are so over-crowded with cabins that you might have trouble breathing. It's on the mainland, 2km east of the Arctic Cathedral. Take bus 26.

Tromsø Hostel (☎ 776 57 628; www.hihostels.no; Åsgårdveien 9; dm/s/d Nkr170/300/400; ☽ mid-Jun–mid-Aug; P) Student accommodation for most of the year, this concrete tower has basic bunk-bed rooms, most with splendid views. It's 1.5km west of the city centre. Go west along Fredrik Langes gate and up Kirkegårdsveien, turning into Holtveien where Kirkegårdsveien turns abruptly right, then turn right down Åsgårdveien. Bus 26 runs nearby.

Ami Hotel (☎ 776 82 208; www.amihotel.no; Skolegata 24; s/d Nkr550/650, s/d with shared bathroom Nkr450/590; P 🖥) Ami's plain rooms vary in quality: some are bright and merry, others worn and drab with bathrooms that look like utility closets. Guests share kitchens and the staff are consistently helpful.

Rica Ishavshotel (☎ 776 66 400; www.rica.no; Frederick Langesgate 2; s/d mid-Jun–mid-Aug Nkr950/1200, Sun-Thu Nkr1800/2050, Fri & Sat rest of year Nkr1050/1250; 🖥 ♿) Stylish rooms gaze wonderfully at the large ships that glide in front of this hotel, built right on the quay. Expect slick geometric rugs, plush beds and subtle wood surfaces.

Clarion Collection With (☎ 776 64 200; www.clarion hotel.com; Sjøgata 35-37; s/d Mon-Fri Sep-Jun Nkr1195/1395, s/d mid-Jun–Aug plus Sat & Sun year-round Nkr995/1195; P 🖥 ♿) A modern waterfront building that mirrors the old warehouses on either side; head straight upstairs to the glass-roofed relaxation deck. Rooms are comfy and hallways have pictures of sea captains.

Amalie Hotell (☎ 776 64 800; www.amalie-hotell.no; Sjøgata 5B; s/d Nkr1025/1175) The yellows, reds and wood tones used to decorate this independent hotel won't win any design awards, but its rooms do manage to pull-out a cheerful effect. It's near the water.

Eating

You'll find it hard to tell the difference between a restaurant, cafe and pub in Tromsø, with many spots serving all three roles simultaneously. Be sure to peruse places listed in the Drinking & Entertainment section (right) for more food options.

Åpenbar (☎ 776 84 600; Grønnegata 81; small dishes NKr50-95; 🕒 4pm-1.30am Tue-Thu, 3pm-3am Fri & Sat) Trendy, modern and decked out with the work of local artists, this place doubles as a tapas joint and nightclub. The term tapas is used loosely: yes, they've got bacon-wrapped dates and fine cured meats, but some dishes (mozzarella sticks) taste more like ordinary pub grub.

Knoll og Tott (☎ 776 66 880; Storgata 62; sandwiches Nkr60; 🕒 10am-6pm Mon-Fri, 10am-4pm Sat) Large, filling sandwiches come on warm baguettes. Take your pick from pepperoni and brie, vegetable, roast beef and more in a two-storey place with warm yellow walls.

Aunegården (☎ 776 51 234; Sjøgata 29; dishes Nkr115-155, cakes Nkr65; 🕒 to midnight) Serving amazing cakes (try the chocolate truffle with meringue and syrupy hazelnut crust), this cafe operates

out of a former general store from 1830. It makes salads out of greens that are actually green! There's wine, and intimate spaces.

Driv (☎ 776 00 776; Tollbugata 3; dishes Nkr75-125) This student culture-house occupies an old warehouse and serves pizzas and big burgers with great chips. It also books bands, organises cultural festivals and hosts DJs. There's a harbourside hot tub in winter.

Thai House Restaurant (☎ 776 70 526; Storgata 22; mains Nkr159-209) A notch above causal, this small joint is decked out with white linens candles and modest furniture. An enormous menu offers many vegetarian dishes as well as heaps of squid.

Arctandria Sjømat Resturant (☎ 776 00 725; Strandtorget 1; mains Nkr205-275; 🕒 from 4pm Mon-Sat) Near the harbour and festooned with nautical instruments, this pretty room with white stucco walls and big overhead beams serves high-end seafood, including whale, shellfish and their speciality – smoked and salted seal.

Tromsø's fast-food scene is led by various kebab carts, a food kiosk at the express boat dock and **Tomato** (Stogata 38; meals Nkr60-80), an in-and-out kind of place that stays open past last call to serve falafel, kebabs and fish burgers to rowdy inebriates. You can buy fresh boiled shrimp from fishing boats at Stortorget harbour. There are several bakeries.

Drinking & Entertainment

Tromsø enjoys a thriving nightlife, with many arguing that it's the best scene in Norway. On Friday and Saturday, most nightspots stay open to 4am. Check out Driv (left), an excellent student haunt.

Skarven (☎ 776 00 720; Strandtorget 1; 🕒 Tue-Sat) This well-dressed pub offers an ample wooden room with extensive terrace seating right on the water. Superior bar food is served (it occupies the same building as Arctandria and shares the same owners).

Ølhallen (Storgata 4; 🕒 9am-5pm Mon-Wed, 9am-6pm Fri, 9am-3pm Sat) Try Tromsø's own Mack beer at pubs, cafes or here, next to the brewery. It makes up for its odd hours with old brick walls and decor from the 1920s. Stuffed polar bears greet visitors by the door, as do drunk guys.

Le Mirage (☎ 776 85 234; Storgata 42; mains Nrk85-165) Brown overstuffed faux-leather chairs are the dominant feature in this trendy cafe-bar long

NORWAY

favoured by Tromsø's fashionably dressed. Not loud, it's a good place for conversation. Most use it more for drinks, less for eats.

Kaos (☎ 776 35 999; Strandgata 22) Hidden in a low-ceilinged basement with exposed beams and damaged brick walls, this cool hang-out attracts arthouse DJs and bands. It only lets 90 people inside, so show up early. Frequent beer discounts.

Blå Rock Café (☎ 776 10 020; Strandgata 14) Live bands and DJs (playing rock, naturally) cause hearing damage in a black-coloured club with Elvis pinball and 50 kinds of beer spilling on the floor. Excellent burgers.

Strøket (☎ 776 84 400; Storgata 46) Packed and sweaty on weekends, the three levels of this large disco attract a young crowd (in May, this means every *russ*, see p374, in the city) with pop-dispensing DJs. The 3rd floor allows a view over the masses.

Tromsø Jernbanestasjon (☎ 776 12 348; Strandgata 33) A brown bar whose name means 'Tromsø's Railway Station', this place supports some serious drinking. It's filled with railway artefacts, but the unspoken joke is that this remote city was never close to being connected by rail.

Verdensteateret (☎ 777 53 090; Storgata 93b) This small, stylish cafe occupies part of a lovely Art Noveau movie house from 1915. The bar vends wine, beer and light snacks to people wearing carefully selected eyeglass frames. Small bands (a guy playing a mournful upright bass) and DJs perform most weeks and independent films are intermittently screened in its painted cinema.

For new releases, the six-screen **Fokus Kino** (☎ 777 56 300; Rådhusgata 2) does the job.

Shopping

Hekle Kroken (☎ 776 81 789; Storgata 91; ⏰ from 11am Mon-Sat) A knitting store selling yarn and pattern books, this shop is mostly frequented by locals. It sometimes sells a limited selection of handmade mittens and sweaters a notch cooler (and more expensive) than the mass-produced stuff (also on hand).

Getting There & Away

Tromsø is the main airport hub for northern Norway, with direct flights to Oslo, Bergen, Bodø, Trondheim, Alta, Hammerfest, Kirkenes and Longyearbyen.

Express buses run to Alta (Nkr484, 6½ hours, one daily), and to Narvik (Nkr370,

4¼ hours, three daily), with some timed to continue to Bodø and Svolvær.

The *Hurtigruten* stops here.

Two to four daily express boats run to Harstad (2½ hours) and Finnsness (1¼ hours).

Getting Around

The airport bus (Nkr55) can be picked up at the Radisson SAS Hotel; a taxi (☎ 776 03 000) to the airport costs about Nkr125. City buses 40 and 42 (Nkr23) also run to the airport.

Thoroughly exploring Tromsø can take time, as the city is spread out and many of the sights are outside the centre. Rides on city buses cost Nkr23.

If you have your own car, you'll find it convenient for getting around. Tromsø has numerous parking areas spread around the city, including a huge underground car park off Grønnegata.

FINNMARK

Along the jagged coast, deeply cut by forbidding fjords, you'll find numerous isolated fishing villages: Alta with its Stone Age rock carvings; Kirkenes, a frontier-like town sharing a border with Russia; and Nordkapp, mainland Europe's northernmost point. Or very nearly so; to reach the actual end of the earth, prepare to enjoy an 18km round-trip hike across the eerie peninsula.

Those who head inland will find the vast and empty Finnmarksvidda plateau, a stark expanse with only two major settlements: Karasjok and Kautokeino. They and Finnmarksvidda are part of the heartland of the Sámi people (traditionally know as Lapland), where reindeer herding has occurred for centuries. At either, enjoy a dogsled journey across empty tundra half lit under the bruise-blue winter sky.

There's one drawback: virtually every town in Finnmark was razed to the ground at the end of WWII by retreating Nazis, whose scorched-earth policy was intended to delay the advancing Soviet troops. Unfortunately, the rebuilt towns all look rather grim. Satisfying urban life north of Tromsø does not exist. In the summer, the eerie midnight sun takes over, as do swarms of mosquitoes (at their peak from late June to late July).

You can get information about the entire region from the **Finnmark Tourist Board** (☎ 784 49 060; www.visitnorthcape.com).

ALTA
pop 17,500

Welcome to what some call the nicest gas station in all of Norway. Here you'll find plenty of services and parking, but not all that much to do. Even so, it's easily Finnmark's largest town, and, thanks to the Finnmark Municipal University, home to 2000 students. The biggest attraction in town is a collection of Unesco-protected rock carvings, which date to 4000 BC. If this doesn't grab your fancy, wilderness surrounds the city, as do opportunities to go ice fishing or dogsled riding (inquire at the tourist office).

Orientation & Information

Alta is a sprawling town occupying 15km of coastline. The town's two main centres, Sentrum (it looks like an office park) and Bossekop (hey, at least it's hilly), are 3km apart, and connected by the E6.

Studentbokhandelen (Sentrumsparken 2) Maps and some books in English.

Tourist office (☎ 784 49 554; www.altatours.no; Parksentret Bldg, Sentrum; 8.30am-4pm, Mon-Fri, 10am-2pm Sat)

Tourist office (☎ 784 45 050; www.altatours.no; Sorekskriverveien, Bossekop; 10am-6pm Mon-Fri Jun & Aug, 10am-8pm daily Jun) Has internet access (Nkr15 per 10 minutes).

Sights & Activities

Impressive, World Heritage–protected, **prehistoric rock art** (☎ 784 56 330; www.alta.museum.no; Altaveien 19; adult/child Nkr85/20; 8am-9pm Jun-Aug, 9am-6pm May & Sep, 9am-3pm Mon-Fri, 11am-4pm Sat & Sun Oct-Apr) lies at Hjemmeluft, on the E6, 4km southwest of Bossekop. A 3km-long network of boardwalks leads past many of the 3000 rock carvings of hunting scenes, boats, fertility symbols, bears and reindeer that date back as far as 4000 BC. Wait for the snow to melt before visiting; otherwise the rocks are covered. Admission includes a guide, and entry to the adjacent **Alta Museum**, with regional exhibits.

The Altaelva rushes through the 400m-deep **Sautso**, northern Europe's grandest canyon. The scenic gorge is best seen as part of a tour (Nkr375), which gains you access to the Alta Power Station dam and includes a snack in a traditional Sámi *lavvo* (tent). Contact **Alta Tours** (☎ 784 49 555; www.altatours.no) for bookings.

Alta is also renowned for its **salmon run**; several local companies organise fishing tours.

Sleeping

Solvang Camping (☎ 784 30 477; camp sites Nkr150) Set in a quiet grove of evergreens with views of watery flats where river meets sea, this is a good spot for tenters. Find it 10km east of town along the E6. There's a church on site

Kvenvikmoen Hostel (☎ 900 03 003; www.kvenvikmoen.com; Kvenvikmoen; dm/s/d Nkr250/600/850; May-Aug; P) A new hostel with airy rooms capturing the midnight sun can be found in a quiet spot surrounded by forests and lakes. It's off the E6 at Kvenvik, about 10km west of town.

Baarstua Guesthouse (☎ 784 33 333; www.baarstua.no; Longleveien 2a; s/d Nkr700/900; P) A cheerful red house built in imitation of pre-WWII vernacular dwellings. Enter to find spacious, comfortable rooms each with a private kitchen. Guests have access to a communal sauna.

Thon Hotel Vica (☎ 784 82 222; www.thonhotels.com/vica; Fogdebakken 6; s/d from Nkr1220/1520; P) In a timber-built former farmhouse in Bossekop, Vica offers free sauna, and an outdoor hot-tub overlooking snowcapped peaks. Warm, freshly renovated rooms come wood-panelled, and public spaces are filled with stuffed creatures.

Igloo Hotel (☎ 784 33 378; www.sorrisniva.no; Storelvdalen; per person incl 2-course dinner Nkr2195; mid-Jan–mid-Apr) Entirely made of snow and ice (even the drinking glasses), Igloo lets you enjoy a pleasurable morning sauna and lights that have been embedded in walls, causing them to glow yellow, blue and red. The hotel regularly organises snowmobile excursions into the empty wilderness, with possibilities of ice fishing or sleeping in a Sámi *lavvo*.

Eating

Haldde (lunch Nkr115-175, dinner mains Nkr190-250) The Hotel Vica's kitchen serves huge portions from an Arctic menu that includes reindeer, whale, elk, grouse and a warm bowl of cloudberries served with homemade ice cream. Local ingredients are emphasised.

Alpha-Omega (☎ 784 45 400; Markedsgata 14-16; mains Nkr119-239) On the pedestrian drag in Sentrum, Omega serves inventive dishes and salads. One of these involves a filling piece of salmon baked under a layer of chèvre and accompanied by fried onion, mushrooms and greens (Nkr129). For a casual bar, head across the hall to Alpha.

Self-caterers should head to one of Sentrum's three supermarkets. If you'd like a pasty, **Østlyngens Bakeri & Konditori** (☎ 784 30 555; Park Senteret shopping centre, Sentrum; snacks Nkr8-15) is a bit cheaper than the competition.

Getting There & Away

The **airport** (☎ 784 49 555) is 4km east of Sentrum; follow the E6. Norwegian, SAS and Widerøe service the Alta airport. Many domestic flights arrive each day, often routed through Tromsø.

Taxis (☎ 784 35 353) to town cost about Nkr100. The return trip is often inflated with a pick-up charge.

Nor-Way Bussekspress runs between Tromsø and Alta (Nkr484, 6½ hours, one daily). **FFR** buses run to/from Kautokeino (Nkr220, 2½ hours, four days per week), Karasjok (Nkr395, 4¾ hours, two daily except Saturday) and Honninsvåg (Nkr370, four hours, one to two daily).

For Hammerfest, FFR's ferry (Nkr230, 1½ hours, daily except Saturday) is faster than the bus.

HAMMERFEST

pop 9400

Most visitors to Hammerfest arrive by the *Hurtigruten* and have an hour or two to poke around. Unless you have unusual interests, that's about as much time as you'll need. The fishing town's oddest experience can be found at the Royal & Ancient Polar Bear Society.

Purporting to be Norway's northernmost town (other settlements lie further north, but they are too small to qualify as towns), Hammerfest has suffered as much as that walrus in the polar-bear society: a gale decimated it in 1856, a fire totalled it in 1890 and the Nazis burnt it again in 1944, after which it was rebuilt in the 'Finnmark Ugly' style. Nowadays a newly opened pipeline (the world's longest) sucks in gas from the Barents Sea to a small island in the bay. Though gas-processing bodes well for the town's economy, it remains unclear when it will benefit the depressing townscape. At night, an awe-inspiring fire from the gas plant casts the place in an eerie red glow.

The **tourist office** (☎ 784 12 185; www.hammerfest-turist.no; Havnegata 3; ☉ 10am-5pm mid-Jun–mid-Aug) operates out of the polar-bear society.

Sights & Activities

The **Gjenreisningsmuseet** (Reconstruction Museum; ☎ 784 02 930; Kirkegata 21; adult/child/student Nkr50/free/30; ☉ 9am-4pm mid-Jun–Aug, 11am-2pm rest of year) details the rebuilding of Hammerfest after the German bombings of 1944. As you might guess, such efforts are neither easy nor pleasurable 600km above the Arctic Circle. Nearby, in the town hall, the bizarre **Royal & Ancient Polar Bear Society** (☎ 784 13 100; Rådhuset; adult/child Nkr40/free; ☉ 6am-4pm Mon-Fri, 6am-3pm Sat & Sun late Jun-early Aug, shorter hours rest of year) dedicates itself to preserving northern culture and features exhibits on Arctic hunting and local history. Any visitor can become a member (Nkr225) and waive the admission fee for life, and get a certificate and a champagne toast. The bone they use to 'knight' you – something a male walrus misses dearly – is a real crowd-pleaser.

For lovely views of the town, coast and mountains, climb the 86m-high **Salen Hill**; the 10-minute walking trail begins behind the small park directly up from the town hall. The town keeps some binoculars (free) up top to better enjoy the panorama.

Sleeping & Eating

Storvannet Camping (☎ 784 11 010; storvannet @yahoo.no; Storvannsveien; car sites Nkr150, cabins Nkr380-450; ☉ late May-late Sep; P) Beside a lake and overlooking an apartment complex, this small site fills up early because it's the only decent camping option around. About 2km east of the town centre, it offers cooking facilities.

Hotel Skytterhuset (☎ 784 11 511; www.skytterhuset no; Skytterveien 24; s/d Nkr850/1050; P ☐) The arms of this hotel, up a hill with views over town, originally served as barracks for Finnish fishwives. Despite the utilitarian history, the modern rooms are cheery and sometimes reindeer chew up the garden. Free sauna.

Thon Hotel Hammerfest (☎ 784 29 600; www .thonhotels.no; Strandgata 4; s/d from Nkr1270/1571; P 🖳) Some rooms overlook the fjord and many resemble cabins on ocean liners, albeit an ocean liner with out-of-date decor. The cosy 'library bar' has been nicely dressed with rich wood panelling and leather couches. You can also enjoy a sauna and solarium.

Odd's Mat & Vinhus (☎ 784 13 766; Strandgata 24; mains Nkr225-345) For fantastically prepared Arctic game (such as hare and seal) and fish, the rustic digs of the region's favourite restaurant are accented with rope coils and wooden booths covered in pelts.

Redrum (☎ 784 10 049; Storgata 23) Potent weekend bands (playing rock and folk) pack this excellent find with people of every age. The place rivals and destroys all bars hoping to be Finnmark's coolest.

There's a Coop supermarket east of the town hall, the tasty **Sandberg bakery** (☎ 784 11 808; Strandgata 19), and a chain pizza restaurant and a kebab vendor near the central square.

Getting There & Away

The *Hurtigruten* coastal steamer stops daily. FFR sails an express ferry to Alta (Nkr230, 1½ hours, daily except Saturday), which is quicker than the bus alternative.

Buses run to/from Alta (Nkr230, 2½ hours, two daily), Honningsvåg (Nkr325, 3¼ hours, one to two daily), and Karasjok (Nkr344, 4½ hours, twice daily except Saturday), with one service extending to Kirkenes (Nkr840, 10 to 12 hours).

NORDKAPP

Nordkapp (North Cape), a coastal plateau at N71°10'21" latitude, claims to be the northernmost point in Europe and is the main destination for most visitors to the far north (Knivskjelodden is actually the northernmost point – see right for details). The sun never drops below the horizon from mid-May to the end of July. To many visitors, Nordkapp, with its steep cliffs and stark scenery, emanates a certain spiritual aura – indeed, long before other Europeans took an interest in the area, Nordkapp was considered a power centre by the Sámi people.

It was Richard Chancellor, the English explorer who drifted this way in 1553 on a search for the Northeast Passage, who named North Cape. Following a much-publicised visit by King Oscar II in 1873, Nordkapp became a pilgrimage spot of sorts for tourists.

Nowadays, there's a rip-off Nkr195 entrance fee and a large touristy complex with exhibits, eateries, souvenir shops and a post office to service the 200,000 visitors willing to pay the steep toll. A 180-degree theatre runs a rather repetitious short film, but if you want to really appreciate Nordkapp just take a walk out along the cliffs. If the weather is fair, you can perch yourself on the edge of the continent and watch the polar mist roll in.

The continent's real northernmost point, **Knivskjelodden** (latitude N71°11'8") is, thankfully, inaccessible to vehicles and devoid of tourist fluff. To reach it, head to the marked car park about 7km south of Nordkapp, lace up your boots and hike 9km (18km return) to a lovely promontory. It takes about five hours.

Depending on snow conditions, the toll road to Nordkapp is usually open from May to mid-October; the **Road User Information Centre** (☎ 177) gives opening dates.

The closest town of any size is **Honningsvåg**, 35km from Nordkapp with a population of 3500. Here you'll find a **tourist office** (☎ 784 77 030; www.nordkapp.no; Fiskeriveien 4B; 🕙 8.30am-8pm Mon-Fri, noon-8am Sat & Sun mid-Jun–mid-Aug, 8.30am-4pm Mon-Fri rest of year), the cheery hostel **Northcape Guesthouse** (☎ 472 55 063; www.northcapeguesthouse. com; Elvebakken 5a; dm/s/d Nkr250/300/600), the hotel **Honningsvåg Brygge** (☎ 784 76 464; www.hvg.brygge.no; Vågen 1a; s/d Nkr950/1200), which occupies a nicely converted fishing warehouse, a few restaurants and, unbelievably, a **microbrewery**. Contact the tourist office for area camping options.

Getting There & Away

The *Hurtigruten* stops in Honningsvåg. Northbound ships stop for 3½ hours, long enough for the ship to offer its passengers a Nordkapp tour.

Nor-way Bussekspress runs buses from Alta to/from Honningsvåg (Nkr370, four hours, one to two daily). FFR runs buses to/from Hammerfest (Nkr325, 3¼ hours, one to two daily).

Getting Around

From mid-June to mid-August, local buses run from Honningsvåg (adult/child Nkr90/45, 45 minutes) to Nordkapp departing at 10.45am and 9.30pm, and setting off from the Cape at 1.15pm and 12.15am (observe the midnight sun at midnight). Avoid so-called 'tours', which may charge considerably more for similar services. And get ready to cry: even bus riders get hit with that Nkr195 toll.

You can also rent a bike from the tourist office (Nkr250 per day, Nkr600 for three days). Bring a windbreaker for the bleak, exposed ride and, of course, Nkr195 for the impending tear-duct workout.

KIRKENES

pop 3300

Okay you made it – the end of the line for the *Hurtigruten* and as far east as Cairo. Now what? Kirkenes itself isn't much – after all, it was Norway's most bombed place during WWII, with over a thousand air-raid alarms. A lot of people use it as a jumping-off point into Russia, though be advised that you'd best have your visa in order prior to arrival. If you linger, your best bet is to participate in one of the many excursions offered by the one-stop tourist office. To find the small town centre from the *Hurtigruten* quay, head west (make a right) from the dock and follow the signs. It's about 1.5km. Or just take the waiting shuttle bus.

Information

Library (☎ 789 93 251; Town Sq; ⏲ 11am-5pm Mon, Tue & Thu, 11am-3pm Wed & Fri, 11am-2pm Sat) Has free internet.

Tourist office (☎ 789 92 544; www.kirkenesinfo.no; Presteveien 1; ⏲ 10am-6pm Mon-Fri, 10am-4pm Sat & Sun Jun-Aug, 9am-4pm Mon-Fri rest of year)

Sights & Activities

The **Sør-Varanger Grenselandmuseet** (☎ 789 94 880; Førstevannslia; adult/child/student Nkr30/free/15; ⏲ 10am-6pm mid-Jun–Aug, 10am-3.30pm Sep–mid-Jun) presents the history of the converging cultures in this border region, with displays on WWII history, local geography, religion and Sámi crafts.

Check out the particularly worthwhile **Savio Museum**, which features the work of the Sámi artist Andreas Savio, whose poignant woodcuts and paintings evoke the tension between indigenous life and nature. It's temporarily inside the Sør-Varanger Grenselandmuseet and shares the same hours.

Several tour companies arrange a ton of activities including snowmobile trips along the border (Nkr1150), night-time dogsled rides (Nkr1250), ice-fishing (Nkr790) and scuba diving for gigantic crabs (Nkr850). Main operators:

Arctic Adventure (☎ 951 50 755; www.arctic-adventure.no)

Pasvikturist (☎ 789 95 080; www.pasvikturist.no)

Radius (☎ 789 70 540; www.radius-kirkenes.com)

Sleeping & Eating

Kirkens Barents Hotel (☎ 789 93 299; www.kbhotel.no; Presteveien 3; s/d from Nkr675/825) Reception and many of your fellow guests will probably be Russian at this squat building. It looks tough on the outside, but within, its 14 rooms are clean, comfortable and thoroughly rudimentary.

Sollia Gjestegård (☎ 789 90 820; www.storskog.no; Storskog; d Nkr750, cabins Nkr650-1050) Sleep in six new cabins or a former wooden hospital that survived the war, on a lake a few hundred metres from the Russian border. Husky kennels (dogsledding per adult/child Nkr1200/600) and a restaurant are on the property, which lies 13km southeast from Kirkenes along the E105.

Rica Arctic Hotel (☎ 789 92 929; www.rica.no; Kongensgate 1-3; s/d weekends & mid-Jun–Aug Nkr895/1120, s/d Mon-Fri rest of year Nkr1450/1695; P) This modern block contains decent rooms with generic character (salmon-coloured walls, unimpressive furniture), but wins points with its heated pool and fine restaurant. Don't confuse it with Rica's other property (the Rica Hotel Kirkenes), a grim holding tank for people who didn't book early enough.

Eating & Drinking

There aren't many options for either eating or drinking, but you'll find both performed with fervour.

Vin og Vilt (☎ 789 93 811; Kirkegata 5; mains Nkr200-370) Seasonal Arctic game and fish (reindeer, grouse, crabs) comes in a room that simulates a hunting lodge, although most hunting lodges aren't this elegant.

Ritz (☎ 789 93 481; Dr Wessels gate 17; pizzas Nkr150-199) Kirkenes's main pizza joint offers all-you-can-eat buffets several times a week (avoid the tacos). It also doubles as the biggest weekend nightclub.

Ofelas Pub (Dr Wessels gate 3) Many in town consider this bar to be *the* place to begin an evening, on account of specials on beer served before 11pm. It's the rival weekend disco.

Getting There & Around

From Kirkenes' **airport** (☎ 789 73 520), a 20-minute (15km) drive from town, there are direct flights to Oslo and Tromsø. The airport bus costs Nkr70 and a taxi is about Nkr275. Flying in/out of Ivalo, Finland, some 250km away, may be cheaper. In summer, Lapin Linjat runs a bus to Ivalo's airport (Nkr320, 4½ hours, one daily).

Kirkenes is the terminus of the *Hurtigruten* coastal steamer. A bus meets the boat and runs to town (Nkr25) and on to the airport (Nkr70).

Busses serve Karasjok (Nkr504, 5¼ hours), Hammerfest (Nkr840, 10 to 12 hours) and Alta (Nkr885, 15 hours) three or four times weekly.

Avis (☎ 789 73 705) and **Hertz** (☎ 789 93 973) have offices in Hesseng, but they'll deliver cars to you.

KARASJOK

pop 2900

The most accessible Sámi town and the site of the Sámi Parliament, Karasjok has Finnmark's oldest **church** (1807), the only building left standing in town after WWII. Because of the Nazis' destruction, the centre of today's Karasjok consists of a small strip mall at the junction of the E6 and Rv92. In town, you'll find a worthwhile Sámi museum and the opportunity to take a thrilling ride with Sven and his huskies (see boxed text below).

The **tourist office** (☎ 784 68 800; Porsangerveien; ☼ 9am-7pm Jun–mid-Aug, 9am-4pm Mon-Fri rest of year), in Sámi Park at the junction of the E6 and route Rv92, can arrange salmon fishing, riverboat trips and other activities.

Sami Park (☎ 784 68 800; Porsangerveien; adult/child Nkr100/60; ☼ 9am-7pm Jun–mid-Aug, 9am-4pm Mon-Fri rest of year), a theme park and reindeer farm, feels a bit flashy and plastic, though a 20-minute film by Nils Gaup, a Sámi director once nominated for an academy award, beautifully presents ancient Sámi myths while portraying contemporary Sámi as the normal fellow human beings they are, and not exotic anachronisms. The more staid **Sami National Museum** (☎ 784 69 950; Museumsgata 17; adult/child Nkr25/5; ☼ 9am-6pm Mon-Sat, 10am-6pm Sun early Jun–mid-Aug, shorter hours mid-Aug–May), just 500m northeast of the town centre, covers Sámi history in more depth, though the English guide sheet is hard to follow. you can see traditional clothing, tools and artefacts. Visit the **Sámi Parliament** (Sámediggi; ☎ 784 74 000; Kautokeinoveien 50; admission free), inside a new building with a stunning birch, pine and oak interior. From late June to early August, 30-minute tours take in a tent-shaped assembly hall and the parliamentary library with its tiny starlike lights. At other times of the year, you won't be permitted to see much.

Karasjok Camping (☎ 784 66 135; www.karacamp .no; Kautokeinoveien; camp sites Nkr120, cabins Nkr650-900, with shared bathroom Nkr275-450) Sleep in one of many cabins and kick back on a reindeer skin around the nightly birch fire in the communal *lavvo*, on a wooded hill near the river. The field for camping can be a bit crowded with caravans.

Biepmu Café (☎ 984 66 151; Suomageaidu 2; meals Nkr70-160) Hunters, grandmas and travellers

---

MUSH

Sven Engholm loves dogs and empty wilderness. And over the last 20 years, the 11-time winner of Finnmarksløpet, Europe's longest dogsled race, has hand-built an oasis, **Engholm's Husky** (☎ 784 67 166; www.engholm.no) for similar-minded adventurers. If you ever wanted to learn about mushing – or try your hand at it, Sven is the man to meet. Even if you didn't, you should probably meet him anyway, because if you're sitting on that sled when it jumps forward, you will almost certainly become an addict. Even the most sceptical experience a genuine adrenaline rush thanks to the speed of the sled as it flies up and (more frighteningly) down hills, with you ducking and weaving your head to avoid the whip of evergreen branches. It's a fantastic way to see the landscape, which you can do on tours of varying length ranging from an all-inclusive week (Nkr12,900) to an hour-long jaunt along a river (Nkr600).

Should you want to sleep near the eerie howls produced by pups and dogs, spend a memorable night in a beautifully crafted and rustic **cabin** (dm Nkr250, cabin Nkr300-400 plus per person Nkr200). Each has a wood stove, a kitchen and a bucket to haul up water (no plumbing). There's a sauna, a salmon river and fantastic dinners (Nkr250) featuring stuff like syrupy cakes and reindeer blood sausages. Find it 6km west of Karasjok on the Rv92.

NORWAY

stop in this unpretentious spot for the enormous daily special, which includes coffee (Nkr160). Thus usually means a heaping plate of reindeer (kind of tough and chewy) with carrots, potatoes and a bit of jam.

Karasjok's only pub, behind the gas station at the rotary, isn't the world's prettiest, but Bivdu (the name means 'hunt') is a fun spot with several dart boards. Plus it's fun to stand outside with the smokers in the dead of a dark, cold winter.

FFR buses connect Karasjok with Alta (Nkr395, 4¾ hours, two daily except Saturday), Hammerfest (Nkr344, 4½ hours, twice daily except Saturday) and Kirkenes (Nkr504, 5¼ hours, three or four weekly). A daily Finnish Lapin Linjat bus runs to Rovaniemi (Nkr500, eight hours) via Ivalo (Nkr200, 3½ hours).

KAUTOKEINO
pop 2900

In Kautokeino, around 85% of the townspeople have Sámi as their first language; the town is unlike anywhere else in Norway and it's not uncommon to see locals dressed in traditional garb. Around one-third of the population earns its living working in some aspect of reindeer herding. Because Kautokeino is a small one-road town, there isn't much to do, other than visit the fabulous Juhl's Silver Gallery.

The best time to visit is during the **Easter Festival** (www.saami-easterfestival.org), when thousands of costumed Sámi participate in championship reindeer racing, theatre and cultural events, and the little town bursts at the seams.

The **tourist office** (☎ 784 86 500; ⏰ 10am-4pm Mon-Fri May-Aug) is in a kiosk by the main road.

Inside a rambling building modelled after drifting snow, **Juhls' Silver Gallery** (☎ 784 84 330; www.juhls.no; Galaniitoluodda; admission free; ⏰ 8.30am-9pm mid-Jun–mid-Aug, 9am-6pm rest of year) creates traditional and modern silver jewellery and offers the best of Scandinavian design. Since the Sámi don't have a tradition of metal working – the tools are too heavy for itinerant herders to carry – Juhls' creates much of the jewellery used in Sámi rituals, particularly weddings. The place started 50 years ago, long before anyone dreamed of visiting tourists, and slowly expanded into the present building. Each addition feels like a time warp to a different era. Cake and coffee are served inside.

Arctic Motel & Camping (☎ 784 85 400; Suomalvodda 16; camp sites Nkr130, cabins Nkr650-1200, motel r Nkr600) Operated by a friendly family whose cafe will often cook up some *bidos* (the traditional reindeer stew served at celebrations), the Arctic offers access to a communal kitchen and Sámi *lavvo* with an open fire.

Thon Hotel Kautokeino (☎ 784 87 000; www .thonhotels.com/Kautokeino; Biedjovággeluodda 2; s/d Nkr1300/1600) Newly built, this good-looking wooden hotel features big windows that gaze across expansive steppes. Rooms are cheerful and bright, and the hotel's restaurant serves fine traditional meals, which is lucky, since it's the only real restaurant in town.

Buses connect Kautokeino with Alta (Nkr220, 2½ hours, four days per week).

SVALBARD

The world's most readily accessible piece of the polar north, and one of the most spectacular places imaginable, Svalbard is *the* destination for an unforgettable holiday. This wondrous archipelago is an assault on the senses: vast icebergs and floes choke the seas, and icefields and glaciers frost the lonely heights.

Svalbard also hosts a surprising variety of flora and fauna, including seals, walrus, Arctic foxes and polar bears.

Plan your trip well in advance. When you arrive, you'll almost certainly want to participate in some kind of organised trek or tour, and many need to be booked early. Since travel outside Longyearbyen is both difficult and dangerous, you miss out on a lot if you don't sign up for one. In fact, since polar bears eat humans, it is illegal to leave settlements unless accompanied by someone armed with a rifle.

History

Although known to the Icelanders as early as 1194, the official discovery of Svalbard (then uninhabited) is credited to Dutch voyager Willem Barents in 1596. During the 17th century Dutch, English, French, Norwegian and Danish whalers slaughtered the whale population. They were followed in the 18th century by Russians hunting walrus and seals. The 19th century saw the arrival of

Norwegians, who hunted polar bears and Arctic foxes. In 1906, commercial coal mining began and is continued today by the Russians (at Barentsburg) and the Norwegians (at Longyearbyen and Sveagruva). The 1920 Svalbard Treaty granted Norway sovereignty over the islands.

Orientation & Information

Longyearbyen, the largest settlement on Svalbard, has an airport with flights to/from Tromsø and Oslo. You'll find a post office, bank (with ATM) and library. Barentsburg, the Russian settlement, is about 40km west, while Ny Ålesund, a Norwegian research station with an airstrip, is about 100km northwest. Except in settlements, there are no roads.

The **tourist office** (☎ 790 25 550; www.svalbard.net; ☻ 10am-5pm May-Sep, noon-5pm rest of year) is in central Longyearbyen. For more on travelling in Svalbard, see Andreas Umbreit's *Spitsbergen: Svalbard, Franz Josef, Jan Mayen*, published by Bradt Publications.

The peak time to visit the area is March through May.

Tours

View dozens of exciting options on the tourist office website. Accommodation, transport and meals are usually included in longer tours, but day tours are also available. Popular tour operators:

Basecamp Spitsbergen (☎ 790 24 600; www.basecampexplorer.com) Sleep in pelt-filled rooms on an ice-locked ship with three-days of snowmobile exploration. Summertime thaws prevent this from being a year-round option.

Spitsbergen Tours (☎ 790 21 068; www.terrapolaris.com) Spend a week in the polar night (Nkr10,200), in wintry April (Nkr13,800) or in the summertime high season, when prices range from Nkr7500, if you camp, to Nkr19,000 in single-room accommodation. Prices include dogsledding expeditions, snowmobile tours and boat cruises.

Spitsbergen Travel (☎ 790 26 100; www.spitsbergentravel.no) The giant of the travel scene offers six-day cruises on a former *Hurtigruten* coastal steamer (built 1956), putting in at Barentsburg and Ny Ålesund (from Nkr8,300). They also arrange four-day snowmobile trips (Nkr15,800).

Svalbard Wildlife Service (☎ 790 25 660; www.wildlife.no) Offers varied tours, including a seven-day ski and snowmobile expedition that summits mountains, crosses glaciers and visits an abandoned Russian mining town (Nkr13,900), as well as shorter trips.

Getting There & Away

SAS flies regularly from Tromsø to Longyearbyen. In summer they offer direct flights to/from Oslo.

LONGYEARBYEN

pop 1500

The frontier community of Longyearbyen, strewn with abandoned coal-mining detritus, enjoys a superb backdrop including two glacier tongues, Longyearbreen and Lars Hjertabreen.

The **Svalbard Museum** (☎ 790 26 492; Skjæringa; admission Nkr75; ☻ 10am-5pm May-Sep, noon-5pm rest of year), inside the Svalbard Science Centre, provides insight into the remote experiences of the whalers, trappers, walrus hunters and miners who have impacted Svalbard over the last 400 years.

Tours

Short day trips (Nkr350 to Nkr1300) are commonly offered, including fossil hunting, mine tours, boat trips to Barentsburg and Pyramiden, dogsledding, glacier hiking, ice-caving, kayaking, horse riding and snowmobiling. Contact the tourist office.

Sleeping & Eating

Longyearbyen Camping (☎ 790 21 444; www.longyearbyen-camping.com; camp sites per person Nkr90; ☻ Jun-early Sep) Pitch a tent on some marshy tundra, next to the airport and an hour's walk from town, and enjoy the empty expanse around you. There's a building with a kitchen, and tent and sleeping-bag rentals are available.

Gjestehuset 102 (☎ 790 25 716; www.wildlife.no; dm/s/d Nkr300/495/850) Sleep in a former miners' lodge, a utilitarian structure sarcastically dubbed 'Millionaire's Residence'. There's a shared bathroom, kitchen and lounge. It lies a 20-minute walk to the southern end of town.

Mary-Ann's Polarrigg (☎ 790 23 702; www.polarriggen.com; s/d Nkr595/875) Run by the ebullient Mary-Ann and adorned with hunting memorabilia, the Polarrigg brims with cosiness on the inside. A more forbidding exterior betrays its origins as a workers' billet. Most of the 43 rooms have shared facilities (which includes a lounge with billiards). Linen is Nkr100 extra, and breakfast is Nkr95.

Basecamp Spitsbergen (☎ 790 24 600; www.basecampexplorer.com; s/d Nkr1840/2060) This 16-room hotel provides top accommodation in the centre of town. It shoots for the look of a seal-hunter's cabin (with bunks and rough-hewn boards) grafted with 21st-century plumbing and design flair. A common space has a glass roof for polar-night viewing. Sleeping prices are greatly reduced off-season.

Kroa (☎ 790 21 300; mains around Nkr200) This pub was reconstructed from the remains of a Russian building in Barentsburg. Eat cured seal, Arctic char and salmon beneath the shy gaze of a bust of Lenin.

Huset (☎ 790 22 500; 3-/4-course meals Nkr295/360) For top-notch Arctic and French-style meals, come to Huset to enjoy a menu that prominently features reindeer and grouse. An attached cafe-bar serves fish soup, cod with mushrooms, and burgers for more modest prices (Nkr70 to Nkr165). The place metamorphoses into a nightclub on weekends from 11pm to 4am.

In the central shopping mall, you'll find the Svalbardbutikken supermarket.

Getting Around
Longyearbyen Taxi (☎ 790 21 375) charges Nkr120 between the town and the airport. The airport bus (Nkr40) connects with flights.

AROUND SVALBARD
Independent travel around Svalbard is heavily regulated in order to protect both the virgin landscape and travellers. Travel to the very few settlements is usually done as part of a tour package. One of these settlements is Barentsburg (population 900), a Soviet-era relic. Simultaneously depressing and fascinating, this tiny Russian town still mines and exports coal. A statue of Lenin still stares over the bleak built landscape and the impressive natural landscape that surrounds it.

Tourist cruises might also bring you to **Ny Ålesund**, which, at latitude N79°, is a wild place full of scientists and downright hostile Arctic terns. Remnants of past glories include a **stranded locomotive**, previously used for transporting coal, and an **airship pylon**, used by Amundsen and Nobile on their successful crossing of the North Pole in 1926.

NORWAY DIRECTORY

ACCOMMODATION
During summer, it's wise to reserve all accommodation, particularly at hostels. The cheapest lodging costs less than Nkr400, midrange

accommodation is Nkr400 and Nkr800, while top-end luxury can reach Nkr2000.

Camping & Cabins
Camping grounds are abundant. Tent space costs from Nkr80, at the most basic sites, to Nkr255 in Oslo. Many camping grounds rent simple cabins with basic cooking facilities from about Nkr300. Bedding is rarely provided; bring your own sleeping bag. Visit www.camping.no for extensive listings.

Norway has an *allemannsretten* (right of common access) dating back 1000 years. This allows you to pitch a tent anywhere in the wilderness for two nights, as long as you camp at least 150m from the nearest house or cottage and leave no trace of your stay. From 15 April to 15 September, lighting a fire in the proximity of woodlands is strictly forbidden.

The Norwegian Mountain Touring Association, **Den Norske Turistforening** (DNT; ☎ 228 22 822; www.turistforeningen.no), maintains an extensive network of mountain huts, a day's hike apart, in much of Norway's mountain country, ranging from unstaffed huts with just a few beds to large lodges with superb service.

For unstaffed huts, you must pick up keys (Nkr100 to Nkr150 deposit) in advance from a DNT office or staffed hut. There are two types of unstaffed huts: bare bones and chalets stocked with blankets, pillows, firewood and freeze-dried food for sale (pay by honour system). In these, members/nonmembers pay Nkr165/265 for a bed.

In staffed huts, simply show up – no-one gets turned away, though you might sleep on the floor. Nightly fees for members/nonmembers in a room with one to three beds are Nkr205/270; rooms with four to six beds Nkr165/235; dormitories Nkr105/170; and overflow on the floor Nkr75/140. Breakfast (members/nonmembers Nkr85/110), sandwiches (Nkr10/15), dinner (Nkr125/145) and snacks are served, though members might do better with a full-board option. At all huts, staffed or not, children pay less.

Basic membership for one calendar year is Nkr465/150/265 per adult/child/student.

Many DNT huts are closed between mid-October and mid-February.

Hostels
Norway has 72 *vandrerhjem* (hostels) affiliated with Hostelling International (HI) and several independent operators. Most have two to six

beds per room. Most also have single, double and family rooms at higher prices. Guests must bring their own sleeping sheet and pillowcase, although most hostels hire linen for Nkr60. Nearly all hostels have kitchens where guests can cook their own meals.

The Norwegian Hostelling Association is **Norske Vandrerhjem** (☎ 231 24 310; www.hihostels.no). You can book hostels through the website. HI members get 15% off.

Hotels

Although standard prices are high, most hotels give substantial discounts on Friday and Saturday and in summer (from mid-June until the end of August), which are slow periods for business travel. One important consideration in this land of sky-high food prices is that hotels usually include an all-you-can-eat buffet breakfast, while most pensions do not. The best rates are often found on a hotel's website. Many nationwide chains offer hotel passes, which might entitle you to discounts:

Choice Club (www.choicehotels.no) Offers a free pass and is available at Comfort, Quality and Clarion hotels; entitles you to free nights and discounts.

Fjord Pass (www.fjordpass.no) Costs Nkr120 and is valid year-round at 170 Norwegian hotels. Provides significant discounts on nightly rates.

Rica Loyalty Program (www.rica.no) Stay 10 nights at hotels in Sweden or Norway and get a free weekend night.

Skanplus (www.thonhotels.no) Free membership that qualifies you for discounts.

Private Rooms & Pensions

Private rooms, usually bookable through tourist offices, average Nkr350/450 for singles/doubles and breakfast isn't normally included. Along highways, you may see *'Rom'* signs, indicating informal accommodation for around Nkr300 (without breakfast).

ACTIVITIES
Hiking

Norway has some of northern Europe's best hiking (over 20,000km of trails), ranging from easy routes in the forests around the cities to long treks through mountains. Due to deep winter snows, hiking in many areas is seasonal; in the highlands, it's often limited to the period of late June to September. The most popular wilderness hiking areas are Jotunheimen, Rondane and Hardangervidda,

but no matter where you are a lovely hike will be, too.

There are organised glacier hikes in Briksdal and on Nigardsbreen; Åndalsnes and Lofoten are major centres for mountain climbing. For more information, contact Den Norske Turistforening (see opposite).

Skiing

'Ski' is a Norwegian word and Norway makes a credible claim to having invented the sport. It's no exaggeration to say that it's the national winter pastime and you're seldom far from a ski run. Norway has thousands of kilometres of maintained cross-country (nordic) ski trails and scores of resorts with excellent downhill runs. The Holmenkollen area near Oslo, Geilo (on the Oslo–Bergen railway line), Voss, Narvik and Lillehammer are popular spots. If you're a summer skier, head for the glaciers near Finse, Stryn or Jotunheimen. DNT is a good source of information about skiing.

Fishing

Norway's salmon runs are legendary – in June and July, you can't beat the rivers of Finnmark. No licence is required for saltwater fishing. Regulations vary between rivers, but generally you can't keep fish under 30cm in length. In fresh water, a national licence (available from post offices for Nkr225) is mandatory and often a local licence (available from tourist offices, sports shops, hotels and camping grounds for Nkr60 to Nkr375 per day) will also be required. The lengthy book *Angling in Norway,* available in tourist offices for Nkr185, details fees, regulations and choice spots.

BUSINESS HOURS

Opening hours for tourist offices are listed in each destination section throughout this chapter. Be aware that many museums have short hours (11am to 3pm is quite common), which can make things tight for sightseeing. On Sunday most stores – including bakeries and supermarkets, and some restaurants – are closed.

Banks Open 8.15am to 3pm weekdays.

Libraries Open 10.30am to 5pm Monday to Thursday, 10am to 3.30pm Friday, 10am to 2.30pm Saturday.

Post offices Open 9am to 5pm weekdays, 10am to 2pm on Saturday.

Restaurants Open 8am to 11am, noon to 3pm and 6pm to 11pm.

Shops Open 10am to 5pm weekdays, 10am to 2pm on Saturday.

Supermarkets Open 9am to 9pm weekdays, 9am to 6pm on Saturday.

EMBASSIES & CONSULATES

Australia The nearest Australian embassy is in Copenhagen; contact the Bristish embassy in an emergency.

Canada (Map p298-9; ☎ 229 95 300; www.canada .no; Wergelandsveien 7, Oslo)

Denmark (Map p297; ☎ 225 40 800; www.amboslo .um.dk; Olav Kyrres gate 7, Oslo)

Finland (Map p297; ☎ 221 24 900; www.finland.no; Thomas Heftyes gate 1, Oslo)

France (Map p297; ☎ 232 84 600; www.ambafrance -no.org; Drammensveien 69, Oslo)

Germany (Map pp298-9; ☎ 232 75 400; www.oslo .diplo.de; Oscars gate 45, Oslo)

Ireland (Map pp298-9; ☎ 220 17 200; osloembassy @dfa.ie; Haakon VII's gate 1, Oslo)

Netherlands (Map pp298-9; ☎ 233 33 600; www .netherlands-embassy.no; Oscars gate 29, Oslo)

New Zealand The British embassy handles consular affairs; the nearest New Zealand embassy is in The Hague.

Russia (Map p297; ☎ 225 53 278; www.norway.mid.ru; Drammensveien 74, Oslo)

Sweden (Map p297; ☎ 241 14 200; www.sweden abroad.com; Nobels gate 16, Oslo)

UK (Map p297; ☎ 231 32 700; www.britishembassy.gov .uk; Thomas Heftyes gate 8, Oslo)

USA (Map pp298-9; ☎ 224 48 550; www.usa.no; Henrik Ibsens gate 48, Oslo)

FESTIVALS & EVENTS

Norway is chock-a-block with festivals, which take place in every city, town and village. Most of these are held during the summer. Among the offerings are festivals dealing with rock music, wooden boats, film and cultural spectacles.

Most notable is Norway's Constitution Day (17 May), when people take to the streets in traditional dress and attend celebratory events throughout the country, with the biggest bash in Oslo, where marching bands and thousands of school children parade down Karl Johans gate to be greeted by the royal family. Midsummer's Eve, celebrated by bonfires on the beach, is generally observed on 23 June, St Hans Day. The Sámi (Lapps) hold their most colourful celebrations at Easter in Karasjok and Kautokeino. By:Larm is a huge music festival celebrated in February at a different venue each year.

For information about all of the country's largest festivals, check out www.norway festivals.com.

HOLIDAYS

New Year's Day 1 January

Maundy Thursday Thursday before Easter

Good Friday March/April

Easter Monday March/April

Labour Day 1 May

Constitution Day 17 May

Ascension Day 40 days after Easter

Whit Monday Eighth Monday after Easter

Christmas Day 25 December

Boxing Day 26 December

Norway practically shuts down during the Christmas and Easter weeks, when you'll be lucky to find an open bar or grocery store, even in Oslo.

MONEY
ATMs

These machines are ubiquitous and available in almost every town mentioned in this book.

Currency

The Norwegian krone is most often written NOK in international money markets, Nkr in northern Europe and kr within Norway.

One Norwegian krone equals 100 øre. Coins come in denominations of 50 øre and one, five, 10 and 20 kroner, and bills in denominations of 50, 100, 200, 500 and 1000 kroner.

Exchanging Money

Some post offices and all banks will exchange major foreign currencies and accept all travellers cheques, which command a better exchange rate than cash (by about 2%). Banks open Monday to Friday and close around 3pm, while post offices open later (see p381). You can also change money in kiosks and hotels, but the rate won't be as good.

POST

See p381 for opening hours. Postal rates are high and continue to soar: cards and letters weighing up to 20g cost Nkr7 within Norway, Nkr9 to elsewhere in Europe and Nkr11 to the rest of the world. Mail can be received poste restante at almost all post offices in Norway.

TELEPHONE

All domestic numbers consist of eight digits.

Most payphones accept Nkr1, Nkr5, Nkr10 and Nkr20 coins, and will return unused coins but won't give change so only insert the minimum amount (Nkr5 for all calls) to ensure a connection. **Directory assistance** (☎ 180) costs Nkr9 per minute. A peak-rate national call costs Nkr8 then Nkr0.65 per minute. It is more expensive to call a mobile phone than a landline. Using a hotel room's phone carries prohibitive charges.

Mobile Phones

GSM mobile telephone networks cover over 90% of Norway's populated areas. There are two main service providers: **Telenor Mobil** (☎ 810 70 700; www.telenor.com) and **NetCom** (☎ 238 88 000; www.netcom.no, in Norwegian).

To use your home-county mobile in Norway, contact your carrier about the cost of roaming charges. If you want to use your mobile, but with a Norwegian SIM card, check with your network before leaving home to make sure you won't be blocked from using other carriers. If your phone does accept foreign SIM cards, these can be purchased from any 7-Eleven and from some Narvesen Kiosks. As the connection instructions are entirely in Norwegian, you're better off purchasing the card from a Telehuset outlet, where they'll help you connect on the spot. Cards start at Nkr200, which includes Nkr100 worth of calls.

Mobile-phone rental is currently not possible.

Phone Codes

Norway has no telephone area codes. To make international calls from Norway, dial ☎ 00, then the country code and phone number. The country code for calling Norway from abroad is ☎ 47.

Phonecards

Telekort (phonecards) are sold in Nkr40, Nkr90 and Nkr140 denominations and work out cheaper than using coins. Purchase them at post offices and convenience stores. Credit cards can also be used with many cardphones. For making international calls, your cheapest bet is to forsake Telenor and buy a card issued by a private company. Usually costing Nkr100, these aren't inserted into phones – on the back are local access numbers and a PIN, which you dial after following prompts. The cards can be used from a payphone (Nkr5) or private or hotel line (free). Such cards are hard to find. Look for them at 'ethnic' grocery stores in Oslo and Bergen.

TIME

Time in Norway is one hour ahead of GMT/UTC, the same as Sweden, Denmark and most of Western Europe.

When telling time, note that in Norwegian the use of 'half' means 'half before' rather than 'half past'.

Norway observes daylight-saving time, with clocks set ahead one hour on the last Sunday in March and back an hour on the last Sunday in October. Timetables and business hours are posted according to the 24-hour clock.

TOURIST INFORMATION

There are tourist offices in nearly every town in Norway, usually near the train station, dock or town centre. In smaller towns they may be open only during peak summer months, while in cities they're open year round.

VISAS

Citizens of the USA, Canada, the UK, Ireland, Australia and New Zealand need a valid passport to visit Norway, but do not need a visa for stays of less than three months. The same is true for EU and European Economic Area (EEA; essentially EU and Scandinavia) countries, most of Latin America and most Commonwealth countries.

TRANSPORT IN NORWAY

GETTING THERE & AWAY

Air

The international airport near Oslo is Gardermoen. Torp, 123km to the south, is primarily used by Ryanair. Norwegian international airports:

Bergen (Flesland Airport; code BGO; ☎ 559 98 000; www.avinor.no)

Haugesun (Karmøy Airport; code HAU; ☎ 528 57 900; www.avinor.no)

Kristiansand (Kjevik Airport; code KRS; ☎ 380 65 600; www.avinor.no)

Oslo (Gardermoen Airport; code OSL; ☎ 815 50 250; www.osl.no)

NORWAY

Sandefjord (Torp Airport; code TRF; ☎ 334 27 002; www.torp.no)

Stavanger (Sola Airport; code SVG; ☎ 516 58 000; www.avinor.no)

Tromsø Airport (code TOS; ☎ 776 48 400; www .avinor.no)

Trondheim (Værnes airport; code TRD; ☎ 748 43 000; www.avinor.no)

Scandinavian Airlines Systems (SAS) is the biggest regional carrier. Most of the usual airlines fly into Norway:

Air France (code AF; ☎ 235 02 001; www.airfrance.com)

British Airways (code BA; ☎ 815 33 142; www .britishairways.com)

Finnair (code AY; ☎ 810 01 100; www.finnair.com)

Icelandair (code FI; ☎ 220 34 050; www.icelandair.com)

KLM-Royal Dutch Airlines (code KL; ☎ 226 43 752; www.klm.com)

Lufthansa (code LH; ☎ 223 30 900; www.lufthansa.com)

Norwegian (code DY; ☎ 815 21 815; www.norwegian.no)

Ryanair (code FR; ☎ 820 00 720; www.ryanair.com)

SAS (code SK; ☎ 915 05 400; www.sas.no)

Land

Direct access to Norway by land is possible from Sweden, Finland and Russia. Excepting Russia, border-crossing formalities are nonexistent.

BUS

Eurolines (www.eurolines.com) runs buses to Oslo from hundreds of European cities, including Stockholm, Göteborg (Gothenburg) and Copenhagen.

Denmark

Säfflebussen (☎ 0771-151515; www.safflebussen .se) From Copenhagen to Oslo (Nkr224, eight hours, three daily) runs via Malmö in Sweden.

Swebus Express (☎ 0200-218218; www.swebus express.se) Also runs to/from Copenhagen (Skr357, 8½ hours, three daily).

Finland

Eskelisen Lapin Linjat (☎ in Finland 016-3422 160; www.eskelisen-lapinlinjat.com) Runs daily buses from Rovaniemi (Finland) to Karasjok (€69, 6½ hours, year round), Nordkapp (€127, 11 hours, summer only) and Tromsø (€95, eight hours, summer only).

Sweden

Säfflebussen runs from Stockholm to Oslo (Skr425, 7½ hours, fives times daily) via

Karlstad, and from Göteborg to Oslo (Skr265, four hours, seven daily). Swebus Express has the same routes with similar prices.

In the north, buses run once daily from Umeå to Mo i Rana (eight hours) and from Skellefteå to Bodø (nine hours, daily except Saturday); for details, contact **Länstrafiken i Västerbotten** (☎ 0771-100110; www.tabussen.nu) and **Länstrafiken i Norrbotten** (☎ 0771-100110; www.ltnbd.se), respectively.

TRAIN

Sveriges Järnväg (SJ; ☎ 0771-757575; www.sj.se) operates most major rail lines with daily trains from Stockholm to Oslo (Skr500 to Skr706, six to seven hours) and other points. If you buy tickets seven days in advance, you can usually get better rates. **Connex** (☎ in Sweden 0771-260000; www.connex.se) links Narvik to Stockholm (Skr700 to Skr820, 20 hours, two daily) via Kiruna.

Sea

DENMARK

Color Line (☎ in Norway 810 00 811; www.colorline .com) Runs ferries from Hirtshals to Kristiansand (3¼ hours, one to three daily) and Larvik (four hours, two to five daily). Fares are the same for both routes – depending on day and season, they range from €26 to €62 for passengers and from €101 to €237 for cars.

DFDS Seaways (☎ in Norway 216 21 000, in Denmark 334 23 342; www.dfdsseaways.com) Runs daily overnight ferries between Copenhagen and Oslo, with fares ranging from €53 to €300 depending on cabin class.

Fjord Line (☎ in Norway 815 33 500, in Denmark 979 63 000; www.fjordline.com) Sends three weekly ferries from Hirtshals to Bergen (€44 to €130, 20 hours) via Stavanger (€35 to €128, 12 hours). Cabins and cars cost extra.

Stena Line (☎ in Norway 231 79 100, in Denmark 962 00 200; www.stenaline.com) Operates daily ferries between Frederikshavn and Oslo (Nkr210, 10 hours, six weekly). Cars cost extra.

GERMANY

Color Line runs ferries between Oslo and Kiel (€200 to €350, four weekly). Prices include cabins.

ICELAND & FAROE ISLANDS

For travel to Iceland and the Faroe Islands, see p501, which has information on Smyril Line.

SWEDEN

Color Line (☎ in Sweden 0526-62000) runs between Strömstad (Sweden) and Sandefjord (€22, 2½ hours, two to five daily).

DFDS Seaways (☎ in Sweden 042-26 60 00) Sails daily between Copenhagen and Oslo, via Helsingborg. Passenger fares between Helsingborg and Oslo (14 hours) start at Skr1100, and cars Skr475.

GETTING AROUND

Public transport in Norway is efficient, with trains, buses and ferries often timed to link effectively. The handy *NSB Togruter*, available free at train stations, has rail schedules and information on connecting buses. Boat and bus departures vary with the season and the day, so pick up the latest *ruteplan* (timetables) from regional tourist offices.

When planning your route, particularly if heading into more remote areas, keep in mind that Saturday and Sunday bus services are often greatly reduced, and some are non-existent on Saturday. Nearly every boat, bus and train offers a substantial discount (usually 50%) to students, children and seniors. Always ask when buying a ticket.

Air

Norway has nearly 50 airports, with scheduled commercial flights from Ny Ålesund (Svalbard) in the north to Kristiansand in the south. Air travel is worth considering, even by budget travellers, due to the great distances involved in overland travel.

Norway's main domestic airlines:

Norwegian (code DY; ☎ 815 21 815; www.norwegian .no)

SAS (code SK; ☎ 915 05 400; www.sas.no)

Widerøe (code WF; ☎ 751 11 111; www.wideroe.no)

Bicycle

Given its great distances, hilly terrain and narrow roads, Norway is difficult to extensively tour by bicycle. A big headache for long-distance cyclists will be tunnels, and there are thousands of them.

A number of regions, however, are good for cycling. The *Sykkelguide* series of booklets (Nkr200), with maps and English text, is available from larger tourist offices – routes include Lofoten, Rallarvegen and the North Sea Cycle Route (from the Swedish border at Svinesund to Bergen). Bike rentals are easy to find at many tourist offices, hostels and camping grounds (usually between Nkr200 and Nkr300 per day). For further information visit www.bike-norway.com.

Rural buses, express ferries and nonexpress trains carry bikes for an additional fee (around Nkr100), but express trains don't allow them at all and international trains treat them as excess baggage (Nkr250). Nor-Way Busseskpress charges half the adult fare to transport a bicycle. If you plan to take your bike on long-distance trains, you must make a reservation well in advance.

Boat

An extensive network of ferries and express boats links Norway's offshore islands, coastal towns and fjord districts. See specific destinations for details.

HURTIGRUTEN COASTAL STEAMER

For more than a century Norway's legendary **Hurtigruten** (☎ 810 30 000; www.hurtigruten.no) has been the lifeline for villages scattered along the western and northern coasts. The modern steamers still carry supplies and mail, though the passenger decks now resemble those found on cruise liners.

One ship heads north from Bergen every night, pulling into 35 ports on its 11-day journey to Kirkenes and back. With agreeable weather, expect spectacular scenery.

Many (but not all) ships accommodate deck-class travellers. Those that do have baggage rooms, 24-hour cafeterias and coin laundry. Most passengers prefer cabins (Nkr300 to Nkr1000 per night).

Sample fares for trips from Bergen are Nkr1951 to Trondheim, Nkr3348 to Svolvær, Nkr4300 to Tromsø and Nkr6206 to Kirkenes. At many ports of call, you can leave the ship for several hours. Cars are carried for an extra fee. Students, children, seniors over 67 and accompanying spouses all receive 50% discount.

There are some great low-season deals from September to April.

Bus

Nor-Way Busseskpress (☎ 815 44 444; www.nor-way .no), the main carrier, has routes connecting every main city. There's a host of local bus companies; most of them operate within a single county.

BUS PASSES

In Nordland, several Togbuss (train-bus) routes offer half-price fares to those holding Eurail passes. It operates between Fauske and Bodø, Narvik, Tromsø, Svolvær and Harstad.

NORWAY

NORWAY

RESERVATIONS

Advance reservations are almost never required in Norway, and Nor-Way Bussekspress even has a 'Seat Guarantee – No Reservation' policy. Unless there's more than nine in your party – then you might be stuffed.

Car & Motorcycle

If you plan to drive through mountainous areas in winter or spring, check first to make sure the passes are open, as some are closed until May or June. The **Road User Information Centre** (☎ 175) can tell you about the latest road conditions. Main highways, such as the E16 from Oslo to Bergen and the E6 from Oslo to Kirkenes, are kept open year-round. Cars in snowcovered areas should have studded tyres or carry chains.

If you plan to travel along Norway's west coast, keep in mind that it isn't only mountainous, but deeply cut by fjords. While it's a spectacular route, travelling along the coast requires numerous ferry crossings, which can be time-consuming and costly. For a full list of ferry schedules, fares and reservation phone numbers, consider investing in a copy of *Rutebok for Norge*, the comprehensive transport guide available in larger bookshops. Some counties publish free booklets detailing bus and ferry timetables – tourist offices usually stock copies.

AUTOMOBILE ASSOCIATIONS

The national automobile club is **Norges Automobil-Forbund** (NAF; ☎ 926 08 505; www.naf.no). For 24-hour breakdown assistance call NAF on ☎ 08505.

DRIVING LICENCE

Short-term visitors may hire a car with only their home country's driving licence.

FUEL

Leaded and unleaded petrol is available at most petrol stations. Regular unleaded averages Nkr10.5 per litre in the south, and can exceed Nkr12 per litre in the north. In towns, there are some 24-hour petrol stations, but most close by 10pm or midnight. In rural areas, many stations close in the early evening and don't open on weekends. Many don't take foreign credit cards.

HIRE

Major car-rental companies, such as Hertz, Avis, Rent-a-Wreck and Europcar, have of-

fices at airports and in city centres. Car rentals are expensive: the walk-in rate for a compact car with 200 free kilometres is about Nkr1000 a day, including VAT and insurance. You're likely to get much better deals by booking with an international agency in advance.

Most car-rental companies offer a weekend rate, which allows you to pick up a car after noon on Friday and keep it until 10am on Monday for about Nkr1400 – make sure it includes unlimited kilometres.

To rent a car you must be at least 21 years old and with at least one year's driving experience and hold a valid driver's licence.

INSURANCE

Third-party car insurance (unlimited cover for personal injury and Nkr1 million for property damage) is compulsory, and if you're bringing a vehicle from abroad, you'll have fewer headaches with an insurance company Green Card, which outlines the coverage granted by your home policy. Make sure your vehicle is insured for ferry crossings.

ROAD RULES

In Norway, traffic keeps to the right. All vehicles, including motorcycles, must have their headlights on at all times. The use of seat belts is mandatory and children under the age of four must have their own seat or safety restraint. You're required to carry a red warning triangle in your car for use in the event of breakdown. Motorcycle helmets are mandatory; motorcycles cannot park on the pavement and must follow the same parking regulations as cars. Motorists must always give way to pedestrians at zebra crossings. Vehicles from other countries should bear an oval-shaped nationality sticker.

On motorways, the maximum speed is generally 80km/h (a few roads have segments allowing 90km/h or 100km/h), while speed limits on through roads in built-up areas are generally 50km/h. Mobile police units lurk at roadsides. In particular, watch for signs designating *Automatisk Trafikkontrol*, which means that there's a speed camera ahead. Big, ugly and grey, these boxes will nab you for even 5km/h over the limit. Fines range from Nkr1000 to well over Nkr10,000. Rental-car agencies will automatically add fines to your credit-card bill.

Drink-driving laws are strict in Norway: the maximum permissible blood alcohol concentration is 0.02% and violators are subject to severe fines and/or imprisonment.

The speed limit for caravans (and cars pulling trailers) is usually 10km/h less than for cars. There are a few mountain roads where caravans are forbidden and numerous other roads that are only advisable for experienced drivers, as backing up may be necessary to allow approaching traffic to pass. For a map outlining these roads, and caravan rules, contact **Vegdirektoratet** (www.vegvesen.no).

Hitching

Hitching is legal but uncommon. See p508 for more information.

Train

Norway has an excellent, though somewhat limited, national rail system. **NSB** (Norges Statsbaner, Norwegian State Railways; ☎ 815 00 888; www .nsb.no) operates most lines.

Second-class travel is comfortable. Komfort-class travel, which costs Nkr90 more, isn't worth the extra tariff, unless you really dig free coffee.

Discounted Minipris tickets are often available. It's extremely cheap: you could travel from Oslo to Bergen for Nkr199, or to Stavanger for Nkr299. These tickets may only be purchased online, at least a day in advance. Buy early – these sell out.

The Norway Pass, from **Eurail** (www.eurail .com), allows unlimited train travel for three to eight days within Norway in one month (three/four/five/six/eight days US$265/ 289/319/359/405). Purchase before or after you arrive in Norway. The Flåm line isn't covered (but there's a 30% discount). There's also a 50% discount on some international ferries

Sleeping cars provide high-standard compartments. These cost Nkr850 and have two beds.

Most train stations have luggage lockers for Nkr15 to Nkr40 and many also have a luggage-storage room.

NORWAY

Sweden

Sweden might not seem distinct from its Scandinavian neighbours. But the more time you spend here, the more wonderfully foreign it becomes. One might be tempted to credit its out-there position on the map. But there's more at work here than geographical isolation. Sweden's literature and cinema favour a weighty, gothic sense of drama blended with gallows humour and stark aesthetics – all of which, in some form, at some point, will confront the visitor. For instance, it's hard not to see something faintly hilarious, yet also quite lonesome and sad, in the image of a reindeer wandering crookedly along an all-but-abandoned Lappland highway on a winter afternoon. It's hard not to see as poignant a capital city so far from the middle of anything that is so determined to be the centre of everything. Attentive visitors will notice a tone here that hints at many things: depth of feeling, awareness of doom, absence of sentimentality, strength of principle, avoidance of conflict, a sombre conviction that certain things simply matter. Of course, such intangibles won't likely make it into your post-trip slide show. But the mysterious Swedish sensibility enhances every aspect of a traveller's experience.

It's an exciting time to visit, too – the small country with its long history of consistent moderation happens to be embracing change. Swedish music, fashion, food and art couldn't be more vibrant. Even dull politics is shaking things up. Get in while it's hot.

FAST FACTS

- **Area** 449,964 sq km
- **Capital** Stockholm
- **Currency** krona (Skr): €1 = Skr10.69; US$1 = Skr8.07; UK£1 = Skr11.90; A$1 = Skr5.84; CA$1 = Skr6.70; NZ$1 = Skr4.55; ¥100 = Skr8.27
- **Famous for** Vikings, Volvos, Ericsson, ABBA, meatballs, tennis players, IKEA
- **Official Languages** Swedish, plus the officially protected minority languages Romani, Finnish, Yiddish, Meänkieli (Tornedal) and Sami (actually three languages)
- **Phrases** hej (hello), hej då (goodbye), ja (yes), nej (no), tack (thanks)
- **Population** 9.02 million
- **Telephone Codes** country code ☎ 46; regional codes: Stockholm ☎ 08, Göteborg ☎ 031; international access code ☎ 00
- **Visa** Not needed for most visitors for stays of up to three months

HIGHLIGHTS

- Tour the urban waterways, explore top-notch museums and wander the cobblestone backstreets of Stockholm's **Gamla Stan** (p401).
- Hike through wild landscapes, see herds of reindeer, absorb Sami culture and sleep in the world-famous Ice Hotel in **Lappland** (p466).
- Dig into the art, fashion and originality that give the lie to **Göteborg's** (p435) nickname as Sweden's 'second city'.
- Celebrate Midsummer in the heartland villages surrounding the lovely **Lake Siljan** (p424).
- Admire the picturesque farmsteads and cosmopolitan cities that dot the green fields of **Skåne** (p426).

ITINERARIES

- **One week** Spend three days exploring Stockholm and Uppsala, and two days in and around Göteborg before continuing south to the dynamic cities of Malmö and Lund. Alternatively, explore the Stockholm region more thoroughly, including day trips to Drottningholm and Birka and a couple of days in the archipelago, before heading to Uppsala via Sigtuna.
- **Two weeks** As above, but include a trip northwards to the Lake Siljan region, then further up toward Sundsvall to explore the dramatic cliffs of Höga Kusten. Outdoorsy types may opt to cycle on Gotland or head up to Abisko for great hiking.

CLIMATE & WHEN TO GO

Sweden is at its stunning best from late May to September. Summers are short and intense, and daylight hours are long. Many youth hostels, camping grounds and attractions open only in high summer (late June to early August). This is also when most Swedes holiday, so finding accommodation in areas favoured by the locals (eg Dalarna, Gotland and Öland) may prove difficult. Travel in winter offers some good opportunities for activities such as skiing or dogsled and snowmobile safaris. Big cities are in full swing all year, but smaller towns tend to hibernate when the temperature drops (except for the ski resorts).

For climate charts, see p486.

HISTORY

Written records in Sweden survive only from the late Middle Ages, but the number of ancient fortifications, assembly places, votive sites and graves is impressive.

The Viking Age was under way by the 9th century, and vast repositories of Roman, Byzantine and Arab coins attest to the wealth and power Swedish Vikings accumulated.

Internal squabbles whiled away the bulk of the Middle Ages until Denmark intervened and, together with Norway, joined Sweden in the Union of Kalmar in 1397, resulting in Danish monarchs on the Swedish throne.

A century of Swedish nationalist grumblings erupted in rebellion under the young nobleman Gustav Vasa. Crowned Gustav I in 1523, he introduced the Reformation and a powerful, centralised nation-state. The resulting period of expansion gave Sweden control over much of Finland and the Baltic countries.

King Karl XII's adventures in the early 18th century cost Sweden its Baltic territories. The next 50 years saw greater parliamentary power, but Gustav III led a coup that brought most of the power back to the crown. An aristocratic revolt in 1809 fixed that (and lost Finland to Russia). The constitution produced in that year divided legislative powers between king and Riksdag (parliament).

During a gap in royal succession, Swedish agents chose Napoleon's marshal Jean-Baptiste Bernadotte (renamed Karl Johan) as regent. He became king of Norway and Sweden in 1818, and the Bernadotte dynasty still holds the Swedish monarchy.

Sweden declared itself neutral at the outbreak of WWI, but a British economic blockade caused food shortages and civil unrest. Consensus was no longer possible, and in 1921 a Social Democrat and Liberal coalition government took control for the first time. Reforms followed quickly; the new government introduced the eight-hour work day and suffrage for all adults over age 23.

The Social Democrats dominated politics after 1932. After the hardships caused by the Depression, they reworked the liberal tendencies of the 1920s and combined them with economic intervention policies to introduce Sweden's famed welfare state.

These trends were scarcely interrupted by Sweden's officially neutral (but in practice

SWEDEN

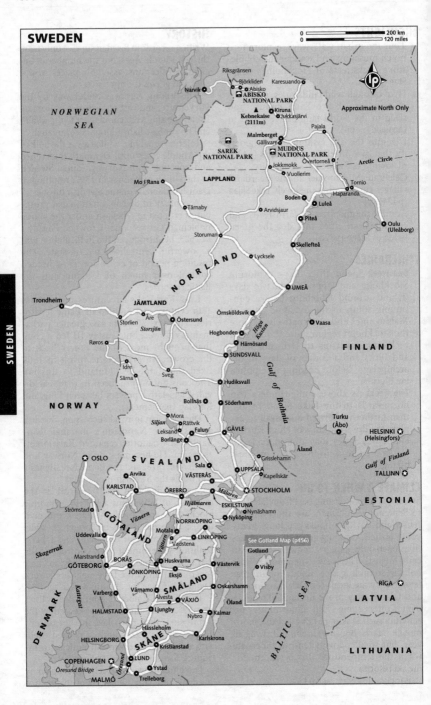

ambiguous) stance in WWII. The Social
Democrats sponsored models for industrial
bargaining and for full employment, which
allowed the economy to blossom. The 1950s
and '60s saw rapidly improved living standards for most Swedes.

Effects of the world recession of the early
1990s provoked frenzied speculation against
the Swedish krona, forcing a massive devalua-
tion of the currency. With both their economy
and national confidence shaken, Swedes voted
narrowly in favour of joining the European
Union (EU), effective 1 January 1995.

Since then, Sweden's welfare state has un-
dergone tough reforms and the economy has
improved considerably, with falling unemployment and inflation. The country has remained outside the single European currency;
a 2003 referendum on whether Sweden should
adopt the euro resulted in a 'no' vote.

In October 2006, the long-entrenched
Social Democrats lost their leadership posi-
tion in parliament. The centre-right Alliance
Party won the election, with new Prime
Minister Fredrik Reinfeldt campaigning on
a 'work first' platform.

The global economic crisis affected Sweden
toward the end of 2008; that year the Swedish
krona dropped to its weakest level since 2002.
As ever, economic tensions fed social anxie-
ties. An annual survey about ethnic diversity,
conducted by Uppsala University researchers, indicated twice as many Swedes had an
'extremely negative' attitude toward racial diversity now than in 2005. (Researchers added,
however, that Sweden is still well ahead of the
rest of Europe in terms of encouraging diversity.) Another 2008 study by a private consult-
ing company showed that one in three Swedes
would like to live in a 'gated community.'

PEOPLE

Sweden's population is relatively small given
the size of the country – it has one of the
lowest population densities in Europe. Most
people are concentrated in the large cities of
Stockholm, Göteborg, Malmö and Uppsala.
Conversely, the interior of Norrland is
sparsely populated.

The majority of Sweden's population is
considered to be of Nordic stock, thought to
have descended from central and northern
European tribes who migrated north after
the end of the last Ice Age, around 10,000
years ago.

HOW MUCH?

- **0.7L bottle of Swedish** *brännvin* **(vodka)** Skr220
- **Coffee with saffron pancake** Skr45-60
- **Souvenir** *Dalahästen* **(wooden horse)** Skr80 & up
- **Movie ticket** Skr85
- **Two-hour tunnelbana (metro) ticket** Skr36-40

LONELY PLANET INDEX

- **1L petrol** Skr10-12
- **1L bottled water** Skr11
- **Pint of lager** Skr52
- **Souvenir T-shirt** Skr200
- **Grillad korv (hot dog)** Skr15-20

About 30,000 Finnish speakers form a
substantial minority in the northeast, near
Torneälven (the Torne River). More than
160,000 citizens of other Nordic countries
live in Sweden.

Circa 17% of Sweden's population are either
foreign born or have at least one non-Swedish
parent. Most immigrants have come from
other European countries, including Russia,
the former Yugoslavia, Poland and Greece.
The largest non-European ethnic group consists of Assyrian/Syriac people. Chile and
Somalia also have a sizeable presence, and
there are around 45,000 Roma.

Swedish music stars José González and
Salem Al Fakir, and film director Josef Fares,
are testament to Sweden's increasingly multicultural make-up. In 2007, the small town
of Södertälje, 30km south of Stockholm, wel-
comed 1268 Iraqi refugees; the US and Canada
combined accepted a paltry 1027. Some 200
languages are now spoken in Sweden.

Sweden first opened its borders to mass
immigration during WWII. At the time it
was a closed society, and new arrivals were
initially expected to assimilate and essentially 'become Swedish'. In 1975 parliament
adopted a new set of policies that emphasised
the freedom to preserve and celebrate traditional native cultures.

Not everyone in Sweden is keen on this idea,
with random acts of hate crimes – including
the burning down of a Malmö mosque in 2004 –

blemishing the country's reputation for tolerance. As hip-hop artist Timbuktu (himself the Swedish-born son of a mixed-race American couple) told the *Washington Post*, 'Sweden still has a very clear picture of what a Swede is. That no longer exists – the blond, blue-eyed physical traits. That's changing. But it still exists in the minds of some people'.

ARTS

Sweden's 19th-century artistic highlights include the warm Art Nouveau oil paintings of Carl Larsson (1853–1919), the nudes and portraits of Anders Zorn (1860–1920), August Strindberg's violently moody seascapes and the nature paintings of Bruno Liljefors (1860–1939). Carl Milles (1875–1955) is Sweden's greatest sculptor, once employed as Rodin's assistant.

Well-known Swedish writers include the poet Carl Michael Bellman (1740–95), playwright August Strindberg (1849–1912) and children's writer Astrid Lindgren (1907–2002). Vilhelm Moberg (1898–1973) won international acclaim with *Utvandrarna* (The Emigrants; 1949) and *Nybyggarna* (The Settlers; 1956).

Swedish cinema is inextricably linked with the name of Ingmar Bergman. His deeply contemplative films (*The Seventh Seal;* *Through a Glass Darkly; Persona*) explore alienation, the absence of god, the meaning of life, the certainty of death and other light-hearted themes. Recently, Trollhättan and Ystad have become filmmaking centres, the former thanks to wunderkind director Lukas Moodysson, whose *Lilja 4-Ever, Fucking Åmål* and *Tillsammans* have all been hits.

Any survey of Swedish music must at least mention ABBA, the iconic, dubiously outfitted winners of the 1974 Eurovision Song Contest (with 'Waterloo'). More current Swedish successes are pop icon Robyn, indie melody-makers Peter Björn & John, and the exquisitely mellow José González, whose cover of The Knife's track 'Heartbeats' catapulted the Göteborg native to international stardom.

Sweden is a living gallery of inspired design, from Jonas Bohlin 'Tutu lamps' to Tom Hedquist milk cartons. While simplicity still defines the Nordic aesthetic, new designers are challenging Scandi functionalism with bold, witty work. A claw-legged 'Bird Table' by Broberg Ridderstråle and a table made entirely of ping pong balls by Don't Feed the Swedes are two playful creations from design collectives like Folkform, DessertDesign, and Defyra.

Aesthetic prowess also fuels Sweden's thriving fashion scene. Since the late 1990s, local

---

THE SAMI IN SWEDEN

Sweden's approximately 15,000 indigenous Sami people (sometimes known by the inappropriate term Lapps) are a significant ethnic minority. These hardy nomadic people have for centuries occupied northern Scandinavia and northwestern Russia, living mainly from their large herds of domestic reindeer. These days, around 10% of Sami live from reindeer husbandry, with many more having migrated to Sweden's urbanised, industrialised south in search of employment. The total population of around 60,000 Sami still forms an ethnic minority in four countries – Norway, Sweden, Finland and Russia. The Sami people refer to their country as Sápmi.

The history of relations between the Sami and Nordic peoples is often dark. Until recently, the Sami religious practice of shamanism was denigrated, and *noaidi* (Sami spiritual leaders) were persecuted. Use of the Sami language was discouraged. Today, despite improved mainstream attitudes, many Sami still encounter prejudice. At an international Sami youth conference held in October 2008, participants demanded that more be done to address the high level of youth suicide in the Sami community.

Nature plays a crucial role in Sami religious traditions, as does the singing of the *yoik* (also spelt *joik*), or 'song of the plains'. Briefly banned, it's now enjoying a resurgence in popularity. Sami education is now available in government-run Sami schools or regular municipal schools. Of the 6000 Sami who still speak their mother tongue, 5000 speak the North Sami dialect.

The booklet *The Saami – People of the Sun & Wind*, published by Ájtte, the Swedish Mountain and Saami Museum in Jokkmokk, describes Sami traditions in all four countries of the Sápmi region and is available at tourist shops around the area.

PEACE, YO

In his will, Alfred Nobel (1833–96), the inventor of dynamite, used his vast fortune to establish the Nobel Institute and the international prizes, in 1901. This idea was reportedly sparked by an erroneous report in a French newspaper, a premature obituary in which the writer condemned Nobel for his explosive invention ('the merchant of death is dead,' it declared). Prizes are awarded annually for physics, chemistry, medicine and literature, as well as the Peace Prize. An awards ceremony is held in Stockholm on 10 December, while the Peace Prize is awarded in Oslo in the presence of the King of Norway.

designers have aroused global admiration: Madonna dons Patrik Söderstam trousers and Acne Jeans sell like hotcakes at LA's hip Fred Segal. In fact, Sweden now exports more fashion than pop.

ENVIRONMENT
The Land
Sweden occupies the eastern side of the Scandinavian peninsula, sharing borders with Norway, Finland and Denmark (the latter a mere 4km to the southwest of Sweden and joined to it by a spectacular bridge and tunnel).

Sweden's surface area (449,964 sq km) is stretched long and thin. Around one-sixth of the country lies within the Arctic Circle, yet Sweden is surprisingly warm thanks to the Gulf Stream: minimum northern temperatures are around -20°C (compared to -45°C in Alaska).

The country has a 7000km-long coastline, with myriad islands – the Stockholm archipelago alone has up to 24,000. The largest and most notable islands are Gotland and Öland on the southeast coast, and the best sandy beaches are down the west coast, south of Göteborg.

Forests take up 57% of Sweden's landscape. The Swedes aren't short of inland lakes, either, with around 100,000 in all. Vänern is the largest lake in Western Europe at 5585 sq km. Kebnekaise (2111m), part of the glaciated Kjölen Mountains along the Norwegian border, is Sweden's highest mountain.

Wildlife
Thanks to Sweden's geographical diversity, it has a great variety of European animals, birds and plants. The big carnivores – bear, wolf, wolverine, lynx and golden eagle – are all endangered species. The elk (moose in the USA), a gentle, knobby-kneed creature that grows up to 2m tall, is the symbol of Sweden. Elk are a serious traffic hazard, particularly at night: they can dart out in front of your car at up to 50km/h. Around 260,000 domesticated reindeer, also no fun to run into on a highway, roam the northern areas, under the watchful eyes of Sami herders. Forests, lakes and rivers support beaver, otter, mink, badger, and pine marten, and hundreds of bird species populate the country.

National Parks
Sweden had the distinction of being the first country in Europe to establish a national park (1909). There are now 28, along with around 2600 smaller nature reserves; together they cover about 9% of the country. The organisation Naturvårdsverket oversees and produces pamphlets about the parks in Swedish and English, along with the excellent book *Nationalparkerna i Sverige* (National Parks in Sweden).

Four of Sweden's large rivers (Kalixälven, Piteälven, Vindelälven and Torneälven) have been declared National Heritage Rivers in order to protect them from hydroelectric development.

Environmental Issues
Ecological consciousness in Sweden is very high and reflected in concern for native animals, clean water and renewable resources. Swedes are fervent believers in sorting and recycling household waste – you'll be expected to do the same in some hotels, hostels and camping grounds. Most plastic bottles and cans can be recycled – supermarket disposal machines give Skr0.50 to Skr1 per item.

FOOD & DRINK
Epicureans around the world are smitten with Sweden's new-generation chefs and their inventive creations. Current luminaries include Bocuse d'Or-recipient Mathias Dahlgren (see the boxed text, p394), TV chef Niklas Ekstedt and New York–based Marcus Samuelsson.

TWO MINUTES WITH MATHIAS DAHLGREN

How does your latest dining venture differ from your last restaurant, Bon Lloc? In my new restaurant I create my cuisine from a Swedish and local platform. While I believe that people and ideas should travel, I think fresh ingredients should travel as little as possible. What remains the same is my own curiosity about, and attitude to, the ingredients and ideas I encounter.

Where does Swedish cuisine stand at the moment? After some years of influences outside our own borders, we're now focussing more on our roots. Swedish chefs are increasingly confident about their own abilities to innovate and impress. I think one of the driving forces in the evolution of modern Swedish cuisine is a longing for our own identity.

Some people argue that Sweden offers either expensive fine dining or lousy budget options, with too few good-quality, midpriced eateries. Your thoughts? We have a relatively short history of restaurant culture in Sweden. For a long time, going to a restaurant was associated with luxury for the common Swede. Here, luxury equates with high taxes, in turn creating a high cost dining experience compared to countries like Spain and Italy. Thankfully, this is changing a bit. Swedish diners have also become more discerning and expectant of good-quality food across the board.

Award-winning chef and owner of Stockholm's Mathias Dahlgren (p409)

Staples & Specialities

While new-school Swedish nosh thrives on experimentation, it retains firm roots in Sweden's culinary heritage. Even the most avant garde chefs admire simple, old-school *husmanskost* (everyman cuisine) like *toast skagen* (toast with bleak roe, créme fraiche and chopped red onion), *köttbullar och potatis* (meatballs and potatoes, usually served with lingonberry jam, or *lingonsylt*), and *pytt i panna* (similar to hash). Seafood staples include caviar, gravlax (cured salmon) and the ubiquitous *sill* (herring), eaten smoked, fried or pickled and often accompanied by capers, mustard and onion. The most contentious traditional food is the pungent *surströmming* (fermented Baltic herring), traditionally eaten in August and September in a slice of *tunnbröd* (thin, unleavened bread) with boiled potato and onions and ample amounts of *snaps*.

Where to Eat & Drink

Most hotels and some hostels provide breakfast buffets laden with cereals and yogurt plus bread, fruit, cold cuts, cheese and the like. Many cafes and restaurants serve a daily lunch special called *dagens rätt* or *dagens lunch* at a fixed price (typically around Skr75) between 11.30am and 2pm. The price includes main course, salad, bread, cold drink and coffee.

To counter the midafternoon slump, Swedes enjoy *fika*, an almost mandatory coffee break. *Konditori* are old-fashioned bakery-cafes where you can get a pastry or a *smörgås* (sandwich) from Skr35, but there are also many stylish, modern cafes where you can enjoy people-watching over pricier Italian coffees, gourmet salads, bagels and muffins.

Pure vegetarian restaurants do exist but they're not common; however, there will usually be at least one vegetarian main-course option on the menu.

Alcoholic Drinks

Lättöl (light beer, less than 2.25% alcohol) and *folköl* (folk beer, 2.25% to 3.5% alcohol) account for about two-thirds of all beer sold in Sweden and can be bought in supermarkets everywhere. *Mellanöl* (medium-strength beer, 3.6% to 4.5% alcohol), *starköl* (strong beer, over 4.5% alcohol) and wines and spirits can only be bought at outlets of the state-owned alcohol store, called Systembolaget, which is open until about 6pm on weekdays and slightly shorter hours on Saturday.

Sweden's trademark spirit, *brännvin,* also called *aquavit* (vodka) and drunk as *snaps,* is a fiery and strongly flavoured drink that's usually distilled from potatoes and spiced with herbs.

The legal drinking age in Sweden is 18 years, although many bars and restaurants impose significantly higher age limits.

Habits & Customs

When invited to someone's house for a meal, it's polite to bring flowers or a bottle of wine. Guests should take their shoes off in the foyer. Table manners don't differ much from those in most of Europe. It's polite to make eye contact with everyone at the table when toasting. Locals tend to eat breakfast at home, lunch between 11.30am and 2pm (taking advantage of the *dagens rätt* bargains) and the evening meal between 6pm and 8pm, often later in larger cities.

STOCKHOLM

☎ 08 / pop 802,600

Sweden's capital is the kind of place other cities love to loathe. Not only is she impossibly beautiful, she's fabulous with fashion, deft with design, and a music meister. And if that's not galling enough, she's clean, green and civil. The old town, Gamla Stan, is one of Europe's most arresting historic hubs, a near-faultless concoction of storybook buildings and thin cobblestone streets.

To the south, lofty Södermalm is the city's creative engine room, sprinkled with experimental art, locally made threads and street-smart bars and clubs. To the north, Norrmalm and Östermalm go glam with A-list designer retail, champagne-sipping Prada slaves and Michelin-star nosh spots.

Only minutes away are pristine forests and, a ferry ride further, the city's enchanting archipelago (skärgård), with its countless string of islands and bucolic bliss.

HISTORY

Rising land sealed Stockholm's destiny, forcing the seat of Swedish Viking power to move from northern Lake Mälaren to the lake's outlet for easier sea-lake trade. Around 1250 Stockholm wrote a town charter and signed a trade treaty with the Hanseatic port of Lübeck. Stockholm's official founder, Birger Jarl, commissioned the Tre Kronor castle in 1252.

After the Black Death of 1350 wiped out around a third of Sweden's population, Danish Queen Margareta Valdemarsdotter added insult to injury by besieging Stockholm from 1391 to 1395. The end result was the Kalmar Union, which linked the crowns of Sweden, Norway and Denmark in 1397. Sweden's discontent under Danish rule peaked with the Stockholm Bloodbath of 1520, when Danish King Christian II tricked, trapped and beheaded 82 Swedish burghers, bishops and nobles on Stortorget in Gamla Stan. One of the 82 victims was the father of Gustav Eriksson Vasa; his quest to retaliate eventually led to widespread rebellion against Danish rule.

Gustav Vasa became King of Sweden on 6 June 1523, now Sweden's national day.

By the end of the 16th century, Stockholm included 9000 people and parts of Norrmalm and Södermalm. Officially proclaimed the capital in 1634, by 1650 the city had a thriving artistic and intellectual culture and a grand new look courtesy of father-and-son architects the Tessins.

When Sweden's northern and southern train lines met at Stockholm's Centralstationen in 1871, an industrial boom kicked in. The city's population reached 245,000 in 1890 (an increase of 77,000 over 10 years).

With the city's postwar economic boom came Eastern Bloc-style suburban expansion and some blemishes on Stockholm's rosy reputation – first the still-unsolved murder of Prime Minister Olof Palme in 1986, then the stabbing death of foreign minister Anna Lindh in 2003.

The worldwide collapse of the IT economy during the 1990s hit tech-dependent Stockholm particularly hard, although the industry has since picked up. These days, the capital is part of a major European biotechnology region, not to mention an ever-rising star on the world fashion and culinary stage.

ORIENTATION

Stockholm is built on 14 islands, with the modern city centre on the main island. The business core is composed of Norrmalm and Vasastan (where they divide is debatable). The historically wealthiest part of town is Östermalm, to the east.

The tourist office is in the eastern part of Norrmalm; the popular park Kungsträdgården is almost next-door. Off the western edge of Norrmalm is the mostly residential island of Kungsholmen.

Smack in the middle of Stockholm is the island housing Gamla Stan (the old town). Two smaller, satellite islands are linked to it by bridges: Riddarholmen to the west and Helgeandsholmen, occupied by the Swedish Parliament building, to the north.

To the east of Gamla Stan is the island of Djurgården, where many of Stockholm's better-known museums are located. The small island of Skeppsholmen sits between Djurgården and Gamla Stan, home to more museums.

SWEDEN

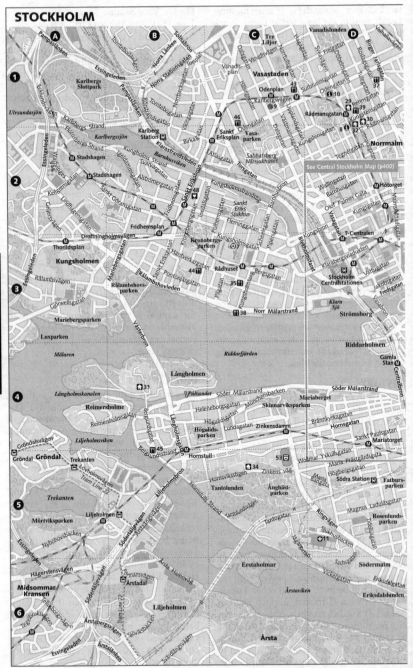

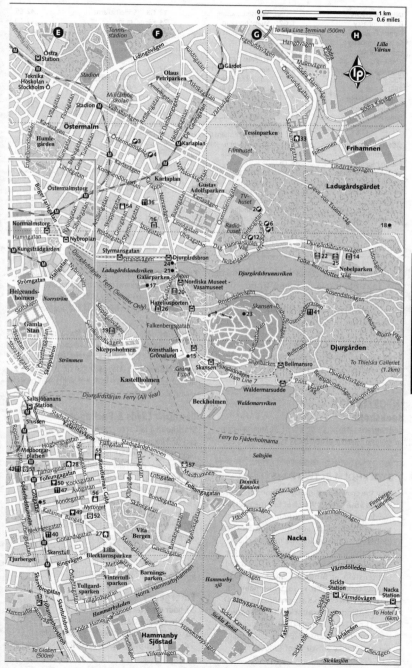

SWEDEN

Södermalm, the city's funky, Bohemian area, inhabits the large island to the south of Gamla Stan. It's linked by the car-and-pedestrian bridge Centralbron as well as by the rather baffling traffic snarl called Slussen.

There are some pleasant picnic and bathing spots around Långholmen, the parklike island to the west of Södermalm.

INFORMATION
Bookshops
Hedengrens (Map p400; ☎ 611 51 28; Sturegallerian) An excellent selection of new books in English.

STOCKHOLM IN TWO DAYS

Beat the crowds to the labyrinthine streets of **Gamla Stan** (p401). Watch St George wrestle the dragon inside **Storkyrkan** (p402), join a tour of the royal palace, **Kungliga Slottet** (p401), or simply watch the midday changing of the guard. From Slussen, catch the ferry across to Skeppsholmen for lunch and Lichtenstein at **Moderna Museet** (p403), before trekking across to Södermalm for dizzying views atop **Katarinahissen** (p404) and partying at **Mosebacke Etablissement** (p411) or **Debaser** (p411). Spend the next day exploring **Skansen** (p402), before dinner and drinks at **Sturehof** (p408).

Kartbutiken (Map p400; ☎ 20 23 03; Kungsgatan 74) The city's widest range of maps and guidebooks.

Konst-ig (Map pp396-7; ☎ 20 45 20; Åsögatan 124) A savvy selection of books on international and Swedish art, architecture and design.

Press Stop (Map p400) Found at a few locations around town – including Centralstationen, Götgatan 31 and Kungsgatan 14 – this is good for international magazines.

Sweden Bookshop (Map p400; ☎ 789 21 31; Slottsbacken 10) A broad selection of high-quality books in English about Sweden.

Discount Cards & Packages
Stockholm a la Carte (☎ 663 0080; www.destination-stockholm.com; from Skr399) Discount hotel-and-sightseeing packages; can be booked online. It's available weekends year-round and throughout the summer.

Stockholm Card (www.stockholmtown.com; adult 24/48/72hr Skr330/460/580, accompanying child Skr165/230/290) Available from tourist offices, camping grounds, hostels, hotels, and Storstockholms Lokaltrafik (SL) public transport centres, the card gives free entry to about 75 attractions (including Skansen), free city parking in metered spaces, free sightseeing by boat and free travel on public transport (including the lift, Katarinahissen, but excluding local ferries and airport buses).

Emergency
24-hour medical advice (☎ 32 01 00)
24-hour police stations Kungsholmen (Map pp396-7; ☎ 401 00 00; Kungsholmsgatan 37, Kungsholmen); Södermalm (Map p400; ☎ 401 03 00; Torkel Knutssonsgatan 20, Södermalm)

Emergency (☎ 112) Toll-free access to the fire service, police and ambulance.

Internet Access
Nearly all hostels have a computer or two with internet access for guests, and most hotels offer wi-fi access in rooms. There are also wi-fi hubs in Centralstationen. Those without their own computer have a number of options around town.

Sidewalk Express (www.sidewalkexpress.se; per hr Skr19) Rows of computer monitors and tall red ticket machines mark out these self-service internet stations, which roam the city. They're found at various locations, including City Bus Terminalen, Kungsgatan 44, Götgatan 25 and Odenplan 22.

Internet Resources
www.stockholmtown.com Excellent tourist information in English (and many other languages).
www.thelocal.se News and features about Sweden, written locally, in English.
www.visit-stockholm.com A newly updated source for travellers, with nearly 500 pages of information on sights, food, accommodation, shopping and getting out of town.

Left Luggage
There are three sizes of **left-luggage boxes** (per 24hr from Skr40-90) at Centralstationen. Similar facilities exist at the neighbouring bus station and at major ferry terminals.

If you have a lost-property inquiry, ask for *tillvaratagna effekter*.

Libraries
Kulturhuset (Map p400; ☎ 50 83 15 08; www .kulturhuset.stockholm.se; Sergels Torg; ☾ Tue-Sun) Has a reading room with international periodicals, newspapers and books, as well as internet access.
Stadsbiblioteket (Map pp396-7; ☎ 50 83 10 60; Sveavägen 73; ☾ 9am-9pm Mon-Thu, 9am-7pm Fri, noon-4pm Sat & Sun, shorter hrs in summer) This is the main city library. It was designed by Erik Gunnar Asplund, and it's the finest example of Stockholm's 1920s neoclassicist style.

Media
The best overall guide for visitors is the monthly *What's On Stockholm*, available free from tourist offices and online at www.stock holmtown.com. Tourist offices also carry two separate accommodation guides in English – one for camping, the other for hotels and hostels – both free.

Medical Services
Apoteket CW Scheele (Map p400; ☎ 454 81 30; Klarabergsgatan 64) 24-hour pharmacy.
CityAkuten (Map p400; ☎ 412 29 00; Apelbergsgatan 48; ☾ 8am-8pm) Emergency health and dental care.
Södersjukhuset (Map pp396-7; ☎ 616 10 00; Ringvägen 52) The most central hospital.

Money
ATMs are plentiful, with a few at Centralstationen; expect queues.

The exchange company Forex has more than a dozen branches in the capital and charges Skr15 per travellers cheque; the following are two handy locations:
Stockholm Arlanda airport (Terminal 2; ☾ 5.30am-10pm Sun-Fri, to 6pm Sat)
Sweden House (Map p400; ☎ 820 03 89; Hamngatan 27; ☾ 10am-6pm Mon-Fri, 10am-5pm Sat, noon-4pm Sun)

Post
You can now buy stamps and send letters at a number of city locations, including newsagents and supermarkets – keep an eye out for the Swedish postal symbol (yellow on a blue background). There's a convenient outlet next to the Hemköp supermarket in the basement of central department store **Åhléns** (Klarabergsgatan 50).

Telephones
Coin-operated phones are virtually nonexistent and payphones are operated with phone cards purchased from any Pressbyrån location (or with a credit card, although this is ludicrously expensive). Ask for a *telefonkort* for Skr50 or Skr120, which roughly equates to 50 minutes and 120 minutes of local talk time respectively. International calls are charged at a higher rate; for calls abroad, you're better off buying a long-distance calling card, available at many Pressbyrån outlets.

Tourist Information
Sweden House (Map p400; ☎ 50 82 85 08; www .stockholmtown.se; Hamngatan 27; ☾ 9am-7pm Mon-Fri, 10am-5pm Sat, 10am-4pm Sun May-Sep, 9am-6pm Mon-Fri, 10am-5pm Sat, 10am-4pm Sun Oct-Apr) The main tourist office is just off Kungsträdgården across from the NK department store. There's a Forex currency-exchange counter in the same building.

SIGHTS
Around 70 museums dot the city, with collections spanning everything from Viking boats

SWEDEN

CENTRAL STOCKHOLM

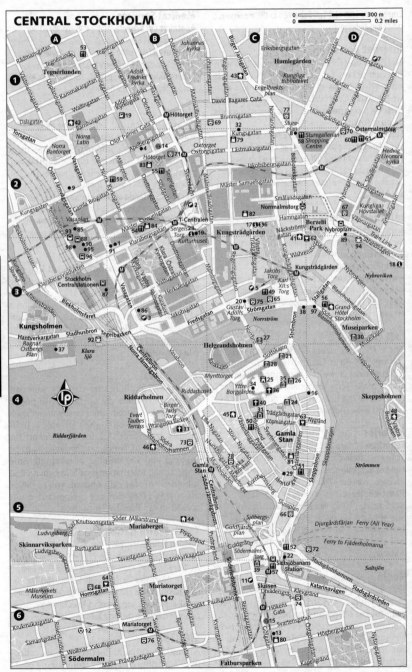

SWEDEN

SWEDEN

to Swedish design. Castle and palace fans are equally spoilt: Stockholm boasts 10 royal pads in and around the city, including the largest palace in the world still in use, and the World Heritage–listed Drottningholm.

Gamla Stan

Once you get over the armies of tourists wielding ice-cream cones and shopping bags, you'll discover that the oldest part of Stockholm is also its most beautiful. The city emerged here in the 13th century and grew with Sweden's power until the 17th century, when the castle of Tre Kronor, symbol of that power, burned to the ground. While ambling along Västerlånggatan, look out for **Mårten Trotzigs Gränd** (Map p400) by No 81: this is Stockholm's narrowest lane, at less than 1m wide.

KUNGLIGA SLOTTET (ROYAL PALACE)

The 'new' **palace** (Map p400; ☎ 402 61 30; www.roy alcourt.se; Slottsbacken; adult/child each attraction Skr90/35, combined ticket Skr130/65; most attractions 🕑 10am-4pm mid–late May & early–mid-Sep, 10am-5pm Jun-Aug, noon-3pm Tue-Sun mid-Sep–mid-May) is built on the ruins of Tre Kronor, which burned to the ground in the 17th century. Its 608 rooms make it the largest royal palace in the world still used for its original purpose. Many visitors find the **Royal Apartments** (Map p400) the most interesting, with two floors of royal pomp and portraits of pale princes.

The Swedish regalia, crowns, sceptres, orbs and keys are displayed at **Skattkammaren** (the Royal Treasury; Map p400), by the southern entrance to the palace near **Slottskyrkan** (the Royal Chapel; Map p400). **Gustav III's Antikmuseum** (Map p400) displays the Mediterranean treasures, particularly sculpture, acquired by the eccentric monarch. Descend into the basement **Museum Tre Kronor** to see the foundations of 13th-century defensive walls and exhibits rescued from the medieval castle during the fire of 1697.

The **Changing of the Guard** takes place in the outer courtyard at 12.15pm Monday to Saturday and 1.15pm Sunday and public holidays June to August, and 12.15pm Wednesday and Saturday and 1.15pm Sunday and public holidays September to May.

OTHER SIGHTS

Near the palace, **Storkyrkan** (Map p400; ☎ 723 30 09; adult/under 17yr Skr25/free; ⊗ 9am-6pm mid-May–Oct, 9am-4pm rest of year) is the Royal Cathedral of Sweden, consecrated in 1306. The most notable feature is the life-sized *St George & the Dragon* sculpture, dating from the late 15th century. On nearby Stortorget is the excellent **Nobelmuseet** (Map p400; ☎ 53 48 18 00; Stortorget; adult/7-18yr Skr60/20; ⊗ 10am-5pm Wed-Mon, to 8pm Tue mid-May–mid-Sep, 11am-5pm Wed-Sun, to 8pm Tue mid-Sep–mid-May, open to 8pm Tue year round), presenting the history of the Nobel Prize and past laureates.

The large collection of royal memorabilia at **Livrustkammaren** (Royal Armoury; Map p400; ☎ 51 95 55 44; www.livrustkammaren.se; Slottsbacken 3; adult/under 19yr Skr60/free; ⊗ 10am-5pm Jun-Aug, 11am-5pm Tue-Sun, to 8pm Thu Sep-May) includes ceremonial costumes and colourful carriages. **Kungliga Myntkabinettet** (Royal Coin Cabinet; Map p400; ☎ 51 95 53 04; Slottsbacken 6; adult/child Skr50, Mon free; ⊗ 10am-4pm) is opposite the palace and covers the history of money and finance.

The island of Riddarholmen has some of the oldest buildings in Stockholm, most prominently **Riddarholmskyrkan** (Map p400; ☎ 402 61 30; adult/child Skr30/10; ⊗ 10am-4pm mid-May–late May & early Sep–mid-Sep, 10am-5pm Jun-Aug), with its striking iron spire, home to the royal necropolis.

Re-opening in early 2010, the atmospheric **Medeltidsmuseet** (Medieval Museum; Map p400; ☎ 50 83 17 90; www.medeltidsmuseet.stockholm.se; Strömparterren) is situated at the other end of the island. While preparing to build a Riksdag car park here in the late 1970s, construction workers unearthed foundations dating from the 1530s. The ancient walls were preserved as found and a museum was built around them. While the main museum remains closed, a temporary (and very modest) outpost has been set up inside **Kulturhuset** (Sergels Torg; admission free; ⊗ 11am-7pm Tue-Fri, 11am-5pm Sat & Sun).

Djurgården

The royal playground, Djurgården is an urban oasis of parkland with some of Stockholm's best attractions. To get here,

take bus 47 from Centralstationen or the regular Djurgården ferry services from Nybroplan or Slussen. Beyond the large tourist haunts are plenty of small gems, including some excellent art collections. You can rent bikes near the bridge, and cycling is the best way to explore the island.

SKANSEN

The world's first open-air museum, **Skansen** (Map pp396-7; ☎ 442 80 00; www.skansen.se; adult Skr60-145, child Skr20-60, depending on the time of year; ⊗ 10am-8pm May–late Jun, 10am-10pm late Jun–Aug, 10am-8pm Sep, 10am-4pm Mar, Apr & Oct, 10am-3pm Nov-Feb) was founded in 1891 by Artur Hazelius to give visitors an insight into how Swedes lived once upon a time. You could easily spend a day here and still not see it all. It's meant to be 'Sweden in miniature', complete with villages, nature, commerce and industry. The glassblowers' cottage is a popular stop; watching the intricate forms emerge from glowing blobs of liquid glass is transfixing. The Nordic Zoo, with moose, reindeer, wolverine and other native wildlife is a particular highlight, especially in spring when baby critters scamper around. Check the website for individual workshop closing times.

VASAMUSEET

A good-humoured glorification of some dodgy calculation, **Vasamuseet** (Map pp396-7; ☎ 51 95 48 00; www.vasamuseet.se; Galärvarvsvägen 14; adult/under 19yr Skr95/free, 5-8pm Wed Sep-May Skr75; ⊗ 8.30am-6pm Jun-Aug, 10am-5pm Thu-Tue, 10am-8pm Wed Sep-May) is the custom-built home of the massive warship *Vasa*. A whopping 69m long and 48.8m tall, the pride of the Swedish crown set off on its maiden voyage on 10 August 1628. Within minutes, the top-heavy vessel and its 100-member crew capsized tragicomically to the bottom of Saltsjön. Tour guides explain the extraordinary and controversial 300-year story of its death and resurrection, which saw the ship painstakingly raised in 1961 and reassembled like a giant 14,000-piece jigsaw. Almost all of what you see today is original. Guided tours are in English every 30 minutes in summer, and at least twice daily the rest of the year.

OTHER SIGHTS

The epic **Nordiska Museet** (National Museum of Cultural History; Map pp396-7; ☎ 51 95 60 00; www

.nordiskamuseet.se; Djurgårdsvägen 6-16; adult/under 19yr Skr60/free, free from 4pm Wed Sep-May; ☺ 10am-5pm Jun-Aug, 10am-4pm Mon-Fri, to 8pm Wed, 11am-5pm Sat & Sun Sep-May) is Sweden's largest cultural history museum, with a sprawling collection of all things Swedish, from sacred Sami objects and Strindberg paintings to fashion, shoes, home interiors and even table settings.

Junibacken (Map pp396-7; ☎ 58 72 30 00; adult/3-15yr Skr110/95; ☺ 9am-6pm Jul, 10am-5pm Jun & Aug, 10am-5pm Tue-Sun Sep-May) whimsically re-creates the fantasy scenes of Astrid Lindgren's children's books. Catch the flying Story Train over Stockholm, shrink to the size of a sugar cube and end up in Villekulla cottage where kids can shout, squeal and dress up like Pippi Longstocking.

More family fun can be had at **Gröna Lund Tivoli** (Map pp396-7; ☎ 58 75 01 00; www.gronalund.com; admission/under 7yr Skr70/free; ☺ noon-10pm Mon-Sat, to 8pm Sun Jun, 11am-10pm Sun-Thu, to 11pm Fri & Sat Jul–early Aug, varies May & early Aug–mid-Sep), a fun park with dozens of rides and amusements – the *Åkband* day pass (Skr280) gives unlimited rides, or individual rides range from Skr20 to Skr60. Big-name concerts are often held here in summer.

Central Stockholm

The fashionable, high-heeled heart of modern-day Stockholm beats in bustling Norrmalm. Near T-Centralen station is **Sergels Torg** (Map p400), a severely modern public square (though it's actually round) bordered on one side by the imposing Kulturhuset. Norrmalm is also home to the beloved public park **Kungsträdgården** (Map p400), where locals gather in all weather. The park is home to an outdoor stage, winter ice-skating rink and restaurants, cafes and kiosks. Vasastan is the somewhat quieter, more residential area that extends to the north of Norrmalm.

Sweden's largest art museum, the excellent **Nationalmuseum** (Map p400; ☎ 51 95 44 10; www.nationalmuseum.se; Södra Blasieholmshamnen; adult/under 19yr Skr100/free; ☺ 11am-5pm Wed-Sun, to 8pm Tue Jun-Aug, 11am-5pm Wed-Sun, to 8pm Tue & Thu Sep-May) houses the national collection of painting, sculpture, drawings, decorative arts and graphics, from the Middle Ages to the present.

The main national historical collection is at the enthralling **Historiska Museet** (Museum of National Antiquities; Map pp396-7; ☎ 51 95 56 00; www.historiska.se; Narvavägen 13; adult/under 19yr Skr60/free; ☺ 11am-5pm, 11am-8pm Thu Oct-Apr, 10am-5pm May-Sep).

Displays cover prehistoric, Viking and medieval archaeology and culture; don't miss the incredible Gold Room with its rare treasures, including a seven-ringed gold collar.

The giant, boxy **Kulturhuset** (Map p400; ☎ 5083 1508; Sergels Torg) houses temporary exhibitions (often with entry fee), a theatre, bookshop, design store, reading room, several cafes, a comics library and bar. It's open daily, although some sections are closed on Monday.

Skeppsholmen

Across the bridge by the Nationalmuseum are more museums, including the sleek, impressive **Moderna Museet** (Map pp396-7; ☎ 51 95 52 00; www.modernamuseet.se; Exercisplan 4; adult/under 19yr Skr80/free; ☺ 10am-8pm Tue, 10am-6pm Wed-Sun), which boasts a world-class collection of modern art, sculpture, photography and installations, temporary exhibitions and an outdoor sculpture garden. The adjacent **Arkitekturmuseet** (Museum of Architecture; ☎ 58 72 70 02; www.arkitekturmuseet.se; Exercisplan 4; adult/under 19yr Skr50/free, free 4-6pm Fri; ☺ 10am-8pm Tue, 10am-6pm Wed-Sun), housed in a converted navy drill hall, focuses on the built environment, with a permanent exhibition spanning 1000 years of Swedish architecture and an archive of 2.5 million documents, photographs, plans, drawings and models.

Kungsholmen

The main visitor sight here is the landmark **Stadshuset** (City Hall; Map p400; ☎ 50 82 90 58; Hantverkargatan 1; admission by tour only, adult/child Skr60/30; tours in English ☺ 10am, 11am, noon, 2pm, 3pm & 4pm Jun-Aug, 10am, noon & 2pm rest of year), resembling a large church, with two internal courtyards. Inside are the mosaic-lined Gyllene Salen (Golden Hall), Prins Eugen's own fresco re-creation of the lake view from the gallery, and the Blå Hallen (Blue Hall), where the annual Nobel Prize banquet is held. You can walk down the staircase just like the Nobel laureates do, only without putting in all that hard work. The **tower** (adult/child Skr20/free; ☺ 9am-5pm Jun-Aug, 9am-4pm May & Sep) offers stellar views and a great thigh workout.

Södermalm

Once-working-class 'Söder' is Stockholm's coolest neighbourhood, jammed with up-and-coming boutiques and galleries, hip cafes and bars and a fistful of decent museums. SoFo (the area south of Folkungagatan) is the trendiest district, while Hornstull (at the

SWEDEN

SWEDEN

FREE THRILLS

The heady days of multiple free-admission museums in Stockholm are past, but with a little manoeuvring of your schedule and adjustment of plans, you can still score freebies.

- **Stockholms Stadsmuseum** (below) The city museum is always free.
- **Kulturhuset** (p403) It's free to go in and explore the offerings of this cultural centre, although some special exhibitions will charge admission.
- **Kungliga Mynttkabinettet** (p402) The royal coin cabinet has free admission on Mondays.
- **Nordiska Museet** (p402) Free admission on Wednesday from 4pm to 8pm September to May.
- **Arkitekturmuseet** (p403) Free admission 4pm to 6pm Friday.
- **Tekniska Museet** (below) Free admission 5pm to 8pm Wednesday.
- **Skogskyrkogården** (below) Visiting the impressive, Unesco World Heritage cemetery is always free.
- **Parks** in Stockholm never charge admission.

---

island's western edge) melds indie cool with old-school Söder shab.

The best place to start is at the top of **Katarinahissen** (Map p400; ☎ 743 13 95; Slussen; adult/7-15yr Skr10/5; ⏰ 8am-10pm mid-May–Aug, 10am-6pm rest of yr), a lift dating from the 1930s that takes you up 38m to the heights of Slussen. If you prefer, zigzagging wooden stairs also lead up the cliffs to the balcony. At the top is one of the city's best restaurants, Gondolen (p409).

Stockholms Stadsmuseum (City Museum; Map p400; ☎ 50 83 16 59; Slussen; admission free; ⏰ 11am-5pm Tue-Sun, 11am-8pm Thu) covers Stockholm's development via fortified port to modern metropolis via plague, fire and good old-fashioned scandal. The temporary exhibitions are often fresh and eclectic.

Ladugårdsgärdet

The vast parkland of Ladugårdsgärdet is part of the 27-sq-km **Ekoparken** (www.ekoparken.com), the world's first national park within a city. An impressive 14km long, its combo of forest and open fields stretches far into the capital's northern suburbs. This section of it, reached by bus 69 from Centralstationen or Sergels Torg, boasts three fine museums and one of Stockholm's loftiest views.

The very good **Etnografiska Museet** (Museum of Ethnography; Map pp396-7; ☎ 51 95 50 00; Djurgårdsbrunnsvägen 34; adult/under 20yr Skr60/free; ⏰ 10am-5pm Tue-Fri, 10am-8pm Wed, 11am-5pm Sat & Sun) brings the entire world under one roof. **Sjöhistoriska Museet** (National Maritime Museum; Map pp396-7; ☎ 51 95 49 00; Djurgårdsbrunnsvägen 24; adult/under 18yr Skr50/free; ⏰ 10am-5pm Tue-Sun, to 8.30pm Tue spring & autumn, also open 10am-5pm Mon Jun-Aug)

exhibits extensive maritime memorabilia. **Tekniska Museet** (Museum of Science & Technology; Map pp396-7; ☎ 450 56 00; Museivägen 7; adult/6-19yr Skr70/40, admission free from 5pm Wed; ⏰ 10am-5pm Mon-Fri, to 8pm Wed, 11am-5pm Sat & Sun) contains exhaustive exhibits on Swedish inventions and their applications.

The 155m-high TV tower, **Kaknästornet** (Map pp396-7; ☎ 667 21 80; adult/child Skr35/15; ⏰ 9am-10pm Jun-Aug, 10am-9pm Sep-Dec, 10am-9pm Mon-Sat, 10am-6pm Sun Jan-May), has an observation deck from which you can enjoy stunning 360-degree views.

Southern Suburbs

One of Stockholm's more unusual attractions, **Skogskyrkogården** (Map p416; Söckenvagen; admission free; T-Skogskyrkogården) is an arrestingly beautiful cemetery set in soothing pine woodland. Designed by the great Erik Gunnar Asplund and Sigurd Lewerentz, it's on the Unesco World Heritage list and famed for its functionalist buildings. Famous residents include Stockholm screen goddess Greta Garbo.

ACTIVITIES

Summer sees locals and visitors taking advantage of the fine weather; many head for the coast and the islands of the archipelago (with good swimming spots) or organise picnics in the parks. Winter also sees some outdoor activity, including ice-skating on a rink set up in Kungsträdgården.

Eriksdalsbadet (Map pp396-7; ☎ 50 84 02 58; Hammarby slussväg 8; adult/4-19yr Skr75/35) has indoor and open-air swimming pools in the far south of Södermalm, plus gym, aerobics and other activities. For more atmospheric splashing there's Art Nouveau **Centralbadet** (Map p400; ☎ 54 52 13 15; www.centralbadet.se; Drottninggatan 88; adult Skr120, Fri & Sat after 3pm Skr170; ⊙ 6am-9pm Mon-Fri, 8am-9pm Sat, 8am-6pm Sun), where entry includes pool, sauna and gym access. Treatments, including massage, facials and body wraps, are available for an additional fee and are best booked two weeks ahead.

From Djurgårdsbrons **Sjöcafe** (Map pp396-7; ☎ 660 57 57; canoes per hr/day Skr75/300; ⊙ 9am-9pm Apr-Sep), next to the bridge leading to Djurgården, you can rent bikes, in-line skates, kayaks, canoes, rowboats and pedalboats. Opposite, floating resto-bar **Strandbryggan** (Map pp396-7; ☎ 660 37 14; www.strandbryggan.se, in Swedish; Strandvägskajen 27) rents out sailing and motorboats from April to September. Sailing boats cost around Skr495 per hour, and all boats can be rented for a day, weekend or week.

Stockholm City Bikes (☎ 077-444 24 24; www.stockholmcitybikes.se) has 67 self-service bicycle hire stands across the city. To use, purchase a bike card (three days/season card Skr125/250) from the tourist office.

TOURS

Stockholm Sightseeing (Map p400; ☎ 12 00 40 00; www.stockholmsightseeing.com) operates frequent cruises from early April to mid-December around the central bridges and canals from Strömkajen (near the Grand Hotel), Nybroplan or Stadshusbron; you'll find ticket booths at these departure points. Some of the one-hour tours are free for Stockholm Card holders, but the two-hour tour, Under the Bridges of Stockholm (Skr180), covers more territory and passes under 15 bridges and through two locks, with a recorded commentary in several languages to fill in the history of the areas you pass by.

SLEEPING

Whether you slumber in youth hostels, B&Bs, boutique digs or big-name chains, you can expect high-quality accommodation in Stockholm. The trade-off is that it can be an expensive city to sleep in, but deals do exist! Major hotel chains are invariably cheaper if booked online and in advance, and most hotels offer discounted rates on weekends (Friday, Saturday and often Sunday night) and in summer (from midsummer to mid-August), sometimes up to 50% off the listed price. Unless otherwise noted, we list standard

prices for peak season here, but for most accommodation, the price you'll pay will depend on several variables, including demand at time of booking.

A number of agencies, including **Bed & Breakfast Service** (☎ 660 55 65; info@bedbreakfast.se; www.bedbreakfast.se) and **Bed & Breakfast Agency** (☎ 643 80 28; info@bba.nu; www.bba.nu), can arrange apartment or B&B accommodation from around Skr400 per person per night.

Stockholm has HI-affiliated STF hostels, as well as SVIF and independent hostels (no membership cards required). Many have options for single, double or family rooms. Many hostels have breakfast available, usually for an additional Skr50 to Skr70.

Budget

This category includes sub-Skr800-per-night accommodations.

ourpick Vandrarhem af Chapman & Skeppsholmen (Map p400; ☎ 463 22 66; www.stfchapman.com; adult Skr185-230, child Skr110, 2-bed r from Skr530; ▯) The legendary af Chapman is a storied vessel that has done plenty of travelling of its own. It's now well anchored in a superb, quiet location, swaying gently off Skeppsholmen. Bunks in dorms below decks have a nautical ambience, unsurprisingly. Staff members are friendly and knowledgeable about the city and surrounding areas. Apart from showers and toilets, all facilities are on dry land in the Skeppsholmen hostel, where you'll find a good kitchen with a laid-back common room and a separate TV lounge. Laundry facilities and 24-hour internet access are available.

Bredängs Vandrarhem (Map p416; ☎ 97 62 00; mail @bredangvandrarhem.se; Stora Sällskapsväg 51; camp sites Skr250, dm Skr200, 5-bed cabin Skr1450) A lakeside option 10km southwest of central Stockholm. It's well equipped, with a hostel and cabins. Take the metro to T-Bredäng, then walk 700m. If you're driving, it's well signposted from the E4/E20 motorway.

Långholmen Hotell & Vandrarhem (Map pp396-7; ☎ 668 05 10; www.langholmen.com; hostel dm adult/child Skr220/105, cells s/d Skr420/540, hotel s/d Skr1435/1740; ▯) Guests at this hotel/hostel, in a former prison on Långholmen island, sleep in bunks in a cell. The friendly, efficient staff members assure you they will not lock you in. The kitchen and laundry facilities are good, the restaurant serves meals all day, and Långholmen's popular summertime bathing spots are a towel flick away.

Zinkensdamm Hotell & Vandrarhem (Map pp396-7; ☎ 616 81 00; www.zinkensdamm.com; Zinkens väg 20; dm Skr220, r without/with bath Skr530/730; 🖳) With a foyer that looks like one of those old Main Street facade re-creations you find in cheesy museums, the Zinkensdamm STF is unabashedly fun. It's attractive and well equipped – complete with an ubersleek guest kitchen and personal lockers in each room – and caters for families with kids as well as pub-going backpackers, so it can be crowded and noisy, but that's the trade-off for an upbeat vibe. While the hostel breakfast buffet isn't spectacular, hostellers can buy the better hotel breakfast.

City Backpackers (Map p400; ☎ 20 69 20; www.citybackpackers.org; Upplandsgatan 2A; dm from Skr230; 🖳) The closest hostel to Centralstationen has clean rooms, friendly staff, free bike hire and excellent facilities, including sauna, laundry and a kitchen (with a free stash of pasta). City tours are also offered, from a free weekly neighbourhood walk to themed, payable options like 'Historic Horror'.

Den Röda Båten – Mälaren/Ran (Map p400; ☎ 644 43 85; www.theredboat.com; Söder Mälarstrand, Kajplats 6; dm Skr230-260, s/d with bathroom & breakfast Skr700/1200; 🖳) 'The Red Boat' is a hotel and hostel on two vessels, *Mälaren* and *Ran*. The hostel section is the cosiest of Stockholm's floating accommodations, thanks to lots of dark wood, nautical memorabilia and friendly staff. Hotel-standard rooms are also excellent.

Hostel Bed & Breakfast (Map pp396-7; ☎ 15 28 38; info@hostelbedandbreakfast.com; Rehnsgatan 21; dm from Skr270, s/d Skr490/740; 🖳) Near T-Rådmansgatan, north of the city centre, this pleasant, informal basement hostel comes complete with a kitchen and laundry.

STF Vandrarhem Gärdet (Map pp396-7; ☎ 463 22 99; gardet@stfturist.se; Sandhamnsgatan 59; dm Skr270, s/d from Skr540/680; 🖳) Located in quiet Gärdet, a quick metro ride from Östermalm, Stockholm's first 'designer hostel' ditches low-cost drab for smart, contemporary rooms featuring red pin chairs, fluffy sheepskins, textured rugs and designer flatscreen TVs. All have their own bathroom, some boast a small kitchenette, and towels and sheets are included in the price. Take bus 1 from Centralstationen to Östhammarsgatan bus stop.

Bed & Breakfast 4 Trappor (Map pp396-7; ☎ 642 3104, 0735-69 38 64; www.4trappor.se; Gotlandsgatan 78; apt s/d Skr650/800, with breakfast Skr700/900) For elegant slumming, it's hard to beat this sassy, urbane apartment, complete with cosy, floorboarded bedroom (maximum two guests), modern bathroom and well-equipped kitchen (espresso machine included!). Breakfast is served in the wonderful owners' next-door apartment, and the SoFo address means easy access to Stockholm's coolest shops and hangouts. There's a two-night minimum stay and a discounted rate for stays of more than five nights. It's a huge hit, so book months ahead.

Midrange

Finding midrange rooms (with a standard rate of Skr800 to Skr1600 per room) can seem like a bit of a struggle, but note that many of the top end choices fall into this category with the summer/flexi/early-booking discounts. See also the combined hotel/hostel options that are listed in the Budget section (p405).

Columbus Hotell (Map pp396-7; ☎ 50 31 12 00; www.columbus.se; Tjärhovsgatan 11; budget annex s/d/tr Skr725/925/1150, s/d Skr1295/1595; 🖳) Family owned and highly recommended, Columbus is nestled in a quiet part of Södermalm, near T-Medborgarplatsen, and set around a cobblestone courtyard by a pretty park. Accompanying the budget rooms (which have TV, telephone and shared bathroom facilities) are wonderfully homely hotel-standard rooms.

Mälardrottningen (Map p400; ☎ 54 51 87 80; www.malardrottningen.se; Riddarholmen; s/d cabins from Skr1180/1300) At one time the world's largest motor yacht, this stylish, cosy option features well-appointed cabins, each with en suite. Launched in 1924, was once owned by American heiress Barbara Hutton (a modest gift from her father for her 18th birthday). Upper-deck, sea-side rooms offer the best views, and three rooms come with queen-sized beds for spacious slumber.

Crystal Plaza Hotel (Map p400; ☎ 406 88 00; www.crystalplazahotel.se; Birger Jarlsgatan 35; standard s/d Skr1600/1800; 🖳) Flaunting an eight-storey tower and neoclassical columns, this friendly hotel, housed in an 1895 building, just squeezes into the midrange category thanks to routine early-booking discounts. Many of its wonderfully cosy (albeit smallish) rooms have been recently renovated.

Top End

There's no shortage of Stockholm hotels that fall into this category (above Skr1600 for a standard-price room). The listed price is rarely the lowest available – always ask about special deals and discounts when booking, and remember that even the poshest digs usually offer steep discounts at weekends and in summer. If you book online, look for discounted 'flexi' rates.

Rex Hotel (Map pp396-7; ☎ 16 00 40; www.rexhotel.se; Luntmakargatan 73; s/d Skr1890/2290; 🖳) While a little less luxe than its sibling Hotel Hellsten across the street, Rex's stylish, functional rooms deliver the same flatscreen TVs and svelte, Greek-stone bathrooms. Rooms in the brand new extension sport urbane concrete walls, walnut furniture and lush velvet textiles. Other positives include a fab glassed-in breakfast space and fascinating travel photography by the affable owner.

Lord Nelson Hotel (Map p400; ☎ 50 64 01 20; www.lordnelsonhotel.se; Västerlånggatan 22; s/d Skr1990/2390; 🖳) Yo-ho-ho, me scurvy barnacles! It's a tight squeeze but this pink-painted, glass-fronted building feels like a creaky old ship loaded with character. At just 5m wide, the 17th-century building is Sweden's narrowest hotel. Its nautical theme extends to brass and mahogany furnishings, antique sea-captain trappings and a model ship in each of the small rooms. Some are in need of a little TLC, but all are comfy and clean, and we adore the little rooftop sundeck.

ourpick Hotel Hellsten (Map pp396-7; ☎ 661 86 00; www.hellsten.se; Luntmakargatan 68; s/d Skr1990/2390; 🖳) Hip Hellsten is owned by anthropologist Per Hellsten and features objects from his travels and life, including Congan tribal masks and his grandmother's chandelier. Rooms are supremely comfortable and individually styled, with themes spanning rustic Swedish to Indian exotica; some even feature original tile stoves. The sleek bathrooms sport phones and hand-cut Greek slate. Hotel extras include a sauna and small fitness room, as well as live jazz in the ethno-chic lounge on Thursday evenings.

Rival Hotel (Map p400; ☎ 54 57 89 00; www.rival.se; Mariatorget 3; s/d Skr2290/2490; 🖳) Owned by ABBA's Benny Anderson and overlooking leafy Mariatorget, this ravishing design hotel is a chic retro gem, complete with vintage 1940s movie theatre and over-the-top Art Deco cocktail bar. The super-comfy rooms feature posters from great Swedish films and a teddy bear to make you feel at home. Both the smoking and nonsmoking rooms boast flatscreen TVs and good-sized bathrooms, and there's a scrumptious designer bakery/cafe beside the foyer.

Berns Hotel (Map p400; ☎ 56 63 22 00; www.berns.se; Näckströmsgatan 8; s/d from Skr2650/2950; 🖳) Popular with rock stars, the rooms at forever-hip Berns come equipped with CD players and styles ranging from 19th-century classical to contemporary sleek. Some rooms are more impressive than others (the balcony rooms get our vote); Room 431 was once a dressing room used by the likes of Marlene Dietrich and Ella Fitzgerald. Part of an historical entertainment complex, with buzzing restaurants, bars and live acts, it's a sparkly choice for the party crew.

EATING

Stockholmers like to think of themselves as consummate foodies. In a city with seven Michelin-starred restaurants, it's understandable. Admittedly, these epicurean highlights don't come cheap, although a few places offer more kronor-friendly lunch menus or lower-fuss bar grub.

If you're after a casual, filling lunch, your best bet is one of Stockholm's atmospheric cafes. Aside from the beloved Swedish ritual of coffee and cakes, these boltholes serve filling grub, from salads, focaccias and classic Swedish sandwiches (smörgåsar) to warming soups, quiche and pasta dishes.

For a comprehensive list of vegan restaurants around Stockholm, check www.veganstockholm.se.

Budget

Caffè Nero (Map pp396-7; ☎ 22 19 35; Roslagsgatan 4; coffee & pastries from Skr25; ⏱ 7am-10pm Mon-Fri, 8am-10pm Sat, 8am-6pm Sun) Architect Tadao Ando would approve of the brutal concrete interiors at this Vasastan hangout, where local hipsters down mighty caffè, grappa shots, salubrious panini and Italian home-cooking, from sublime veal meatballs to a naughty tiramisu.

ourpick Rosendals Trädgårdskafe (Map pp396-7; ☎ 54 58 12 70; Rosendalsterrassen 12; cakes Skr25-35, sandwiches Skr45-65; ⏱ 11am-5pm Mon-Fri, 11am-6pm Sat & Sun May-Sep, 11am-4pm Tue-Sun Oct-Dec, closed Jan; bus 47, 15min walk from Djurgårdsbron) Rosendals is an idyllic spot for heavenly carrot cake and an organic wine in summer or a warm cup of glögg (mulled wine) and a lussekatte (saffron bun) in winter. Much of the produce is biodynamic and grown onsite.

SWEDEN

Vetekatten (Map p400; ☎ 21 84 54; Kungsgatan 55; tea, coffee & snacks from Skr25; ⊗ 7.30am-8pm Mon-Fri, 9.30am-5pm Sat, noon-5pm Sun) A cardamom-scented labyrinth of cosy nooks, antique furnishings and oil paintings, Vetekatten is not so much a cafe as an institution. Wish back the old days over filling sandwiches, heavenly scrolls and warming cups of tea.

Vurma (Map pp396-7; ☎ 650 93 50; Polhemsgatan 15; sandwiches Skr27-69, salads Skr73, ⊗ 10am-6pm) Squeeze in among the chattering punters, fluff up the cushions and eavesdrop over a vegan latte at this kitsch-hip cafe/bakery. The scrumptious sandwiches and salads are utterly inspired; try the chevre cheese, marinated chicken, tomato, cucumber, walnuts, apple and mustard salad. You'll find other branches in Vasastan (Gästrikegatan 2) and Södermalm (Bergsunds Strand 31).

Chokladkoppen (Map p400; ☎ 20 31 70; Stortorget; cakes & snacks Skr30-70) Arguably Stockholm's best-loved cafe, hole-in-the-wall Chokladkoppen sits slap bang on the Old Town's enchanting main square. It's a gay-friendly spot, with cute, gym-fit waiters, a look-at-me summer terrace and yummy grub like broccoli and blue cheese pie and scrumptious cakes.

Nystekt Strömming (Map p400; Södermalmstorg; combo plates Skr30-50; ⊗ generally 10am-6pm Mon-Fri, 11am-4pm Sat & Sun) Pick up some authentically Swedish fast food – fried *(stekt)* herring – at this humble cart outside the metro station at Slussen.

Midrange

Pelikan (Map pp396-7; ☎ 55 60 90 90; Blekingegatan 40; mains Skr75-185; ⊗ dinner daily & lunch Sat & Sun) Lofty ceilings, wood panelling and no-nonsense waiters in waistcoats set the scene for classic *husmanskost* at this century-old beer hall. The herring options are particularly good and there's usually a vegetarian special to boot. There's a minimum age of 23.

Örtagården (Map p400; ☎ 662 17 28; Nybrogatan 31, 1st fl of Östermalms Saluhall Bldg; lunch buffet Skr85, dinner buffet Skr135; ⊗ 10.30am-9.30pm Mon-Fri, 11am-9pm Sat & Sun) Perched above Östermalms Saluhall, this popular, casual restaurant spoils punters with its extensive vegetarian lunch and dinner buffet, which includes fresh fruit and diet-defying sweet treats.

Tranan (Map pp396-7; ☎ 52 72 81 00; Karlbergsvägen 14; starters Skr55-125, mains Skr95-295; ⊗ 11.30am-midnight Mon-Thu, 11.30-1am Fri, 5pm-1am Sat, 5-11pm Sun, 6pm-midnight Mon-Sun late-Jun–Aug) Stockholmers

swear by this bistro-style eatery, with Technicolour brushstrokes pimping up the walls. Food combines Swedish *husmanskost* with savvy Gallic touches. On weekends, DJs hit the decks in the pumping, 30-something basement bar (except in summer, when the bar is closed).

Östgöta Källaren (Map pp396-7; ☎ 643 22 40; Östgötagatan 41; lunch Skr68-98, mains Skr115-189; ⊗ until 1am, kitchen closes 11.30pm) The regulars at this soulful pub-cum-restaurant span multi-pierced rockers to blue-rinse grandmas, all smitten with the dimly lit romantic atmosphere, amiable vibe, and hearty Swedish, Eastern European and French-Med grub.

Lao Wai (Map pp396-7; ☎ 673 78 00; Luntmakargatan 74; lunch Skr80, mains Skr125-185; ⊗ lunch Mon-Fri, dinner Tue-Sat) Tiny, herbivorous Lao Wai does sinfully good things to tofu and vegetable combos, hence the faithful regulars. Nosh virtuously on dishes like Sichuan-style smoked tofu with shitake, chillies, garlic shoots, snowpeas and black beans.

Bakfickan (Map p400; ☎ 676 58 08; mains Skr135-275; ⊗ 11.30am-11pm Mon-Fri, noon-10pm Sat) Calling the Opera House home, the 'back pocket' of fine-dining darling Operakällaren is crammed with opera photographs and Deco-style lampshades. Dexterous old-school waiters serve comforting Swedish *husmanskost* and the counter seats make it a perfect spot for solo supping. Come late at night and you just might stumble across a bitching soprano.

Sturehof (Map p400; ☎ 440 57 30; Stureplan 2; mains Skr155-545; ⊗ 11-2am Mon-Fri, noon-2am Sat, 1pm-2am Sun) Superb for late-night sipping and supping, this buzzing, convivial brasserie sparkles with gracious staff, celebrity regulars, and fabulous seafood-centric dishes (the bouillabaisse is brilliant). Both the front and back bars are a hit with the eye-candy brigade and perfect for a post-meal flirt.

Top End

Den Gyldene Freden (Map p400; ☎ 24 97 60; Österlånggatan 51; lunch mains Skr165-265, dinner mains Skr175-425; ⊗ closed Sun) Simmering since 1722, this venerable barrel-vaulted restaurant is run by the Swedish Academy, where (rumour has it) its members meet to decide the winners of the Nobel prize. Personally, we think it should go to the chefs, whose sublime offerings include civilised *husmanskost* dishes like quail stuffed with duck liver, celeriac purée, Gotland truffles and *rôti jus*.

Brasserie Elverket (Map pp396-7; ☎ 661 25 62; Linnégatan 69; lunch Skr79-145, dinner mains Skr185-285, 2-course theatre menu Skr265; 11am-1am Tue-Sat) In an old electricity plant reborn as an experimental theatre, this slick, dimly-lit resto-bar peddles bold, adventurous grub like melon and vanilla consommé served with cardamom pannacotta and a pineapple-sage salsa. Starters are a pick-and-mix tapas-style affair, and the weekend brunch buffet (Skr189) is one of Stockholm's best. Fed, kick back in the slinky lounge with an Absinthe-laced Belgian Bastard.

Kungsholmen (Map pp396-7; ☎ 50 52 44 50; Norr Mälarstrand, Kajplats 464; soup Skr95-230, sushi 140-325, grill Skr215-325; 5pm-1am Mon-Sun) Owned by celebrity chef Melker Andersson, this hip, sexed-up 'food court' features six open kitchens cooking up different specialities, including soups, sushi, bistro grub, bread and ice cream. Add a sleek, cocktail-savvy bar, weekend DJ sessions and a waterside location, and you'll understand why it's best to book.

Grill (Map p400; ☎ 31 45 30; Drottninggatan 89; starters Skr125-230, mains Skr175-310; 11.15am-2pm & 5pm-1am Mon-Fri, 11.15am-2pm & 4pm-1am Sat, 3-10pm Sun, closed early Jul-early Aug) Kick-started by culinary stars Melker Andersson and Danyel Couet, this outrageous restaurant/bar features differently themed spaces, from Miami Art Deco to AstroTurf garden party. The menu is a global affair, innovatively arranged by grill type. Vegetarians aren't overlooked, service is casual and accommodating, and there's a popular Sunday grill buffet (Skr295).

Gondolen (Map p400; ☎ 641 70 90; Stadsgården 6; mains Skr130-320, 3-course menu Skr490, degustation menu Skr750; lunch Mon-Fri, dinner Mon-Sat) Perched atop the iconic Katarinahissen (the vintage Slussen elevator), Gondolen combines killer city views with contemporary Nordic brilliance from chef Erik Lallerstedt. Play 'spot the landmark' while carving into gems like thyme-roasted halibut with lobster sauce and root vegetable cake.

Bergamott (Map pp396-7; ☎ 650 30 34; Hantverkargatan 35; mains Skr180-350; lunch Mon-Fri, dinner Tue-Sat) The trés-cool French chefs in the kitchen don't simply whip up to-die-for French-Italian dishes, they'll probably deliver them to your table, talk you through the produce and suggest the perfect drop. It's never short of a convivial crowd, so book ahead, especially when jazz musicians drop by for a soulful evening jam.

ourpick Mathias Dahlgren (Map p400; ☎ 679 35 84; Grand Hôtel Stockholm, Södra Blasieholmshamnen 6; matbaren mains Skr245-395, matsalen mains Skr325-455, 6-course tasting menu Skr1300; matbaren noon-1.30pm & 6pm-midnight, matsalen one-sitting only 7pm-midnight) Chef Matthias Dahlgren is hot property and his namesake newcomer has foodies in a flutter. Set in the Grand Hôtel, it's divided into three spaces: a luxe bar, Matbaren (Food Bar) for casual noshing, and the more formal Matsalen (Dining Room). The latter is where Dahlgren really delivers his tour-de-force: think organic foie gras terrine with mango black sesame and black pepper, or fried apple with goat's milk ice cream, vanilla cream and rye bread bowling over the critics. Book ahead.

Self-Catering

The handiest central supermarket is **Hemköp** (Map p400; Klarabergsgatan 50; 7am-9pm Mon-Fri, 10am-9pm Sat & Sun), in the Åhléns department store. More fun are Stockholm's market halls, prime spots to dig into local and global treats:

Östermalms Saluhall (Map p400; Östermalmstorg; 9.30am-6pm Mon-Thu, until 6.30pm Fri & 4pm Sat; T-Östermalmstorg) Stockholm's historic, blue-ribbon market spoils tastebuds with fresh fish, seafood and meat, as well as fruits, vegetables and hard-to-find cheeses. The building itself is a Stockholm landmark, designed as a Romanesque cathedral of food in 1885.

Hötorgshallen (Map p400; Hötorget; 10am-6pm Mon-Thu, 10am-6.30pm Fri, 10am-4pm Sat, 10am-6pm Mon-Fri, 10am-3pm Sat Jun & Jul; T-Hötorget) Below Filmstaden cinema, multicultural Hötorgshallen sells everything from fresh Nordic seafood to fluffy hummus and fragrant teas. Squeeze into galley-themed dining nook Kajsas Fiskrestaurang for soulful *fisksoppa* (fish stew) with mussels and aioli (Skr80).

Söderhallarna (Map pp396-7; Medborgarplatsen 3; 10am-6pm Mon-Wed, 10am-7pm Thu & Fri, 10am-4pm Sat; T-Medborgarplatsen) This more modern food hall peddles everything from cheese to vegetarian grub.

DRINKING

From grit-chic factory conversions to raucous vintage beer halls, you're bound to find a spot worth a toast. Many of the city's hottest restaurants have bars attached. For beautiful crowds and a glammy vibe, your best bet is Östermalm, although the undisputed bar scene heavyweight is Söder-malm, where options span old-school pubs to alt-cool bar/gallery hybrids.

Marie Laveau (Map p400; ☎ 668 85 00; www.marie laveau.se, in Swedish; Hornsgatan 66; ☼ 5pm-midnight Tue & Wed, 5pm-3am Thu-Sat) In an old sausage factory, this kicking Söder playpen draws a boho-chic crowd. The designer-grunge bar (think chequered floor and subway-style tiled columns) serves killer cocktails and contemporary nosh (Skr84 to Skr199), while the sweaty basement hosts thumping club night Bangers 'n' Mash on Saturdays.

Pet Sounds Bar (Map pp396-7; ☎ 643 82 25; www .petsoundsbar.se, in Swedish; Skånegatan 80; ☼ from 5pm Mon-Sat) A SoFo favourite, this jamming bar pulls in music journos, indie culture vultures and the odd Goth rocker. While the restaurant serves decent Italo-French grub, the real fun happens in the basement. Head down for a mixed bag of live bands, release parties and DJ sets.

Soldaten Svejk (Map pp396-7; ☎ 641 33 66; Östgötagatan 35) In this crowded, amber-windowed, wooden-floored pub, decorated with heraldic shields, punters pine for Prague with great Czech beer, including the massively popular Staropramen, on tap. Line your stomach with simple, solid Czech meals (Skr97 to Skr125); the smoked cheese is sublime. Head in early or prepare to queue for a table.

Berns Salonger (Map p400; ☎ 56 63 22 22; www .berns.se; Berzelii Park; ☼ bistro 11.30am-midnight Mon-Fri, noon-midnight Sat, 1-11pm Sun, 2.35:1 bar/nightclub 11pm-4am Thu-Sat, also Wed & Sun occasionally, midnight-5am Thu-Sat) A Stockholm institution since 1862, this glitzy entertainment palace remains one of Stockholm's hottest party spots. While the gorgeous ballroom hosts some brilliant live music gigs, the best of Berns' bars is the intimate basement bar/club 2.35:1, packed with cool creative types, top-notch DJs and projected arthouse images.

Allmänna Galleriet 925 (Map pp396-7; ☎ 41 06 81 00; www.ag925.se; Kronobergsgatan 37; ☼ from 5pm Tue-Sat, closed mid-Jun–Jul) AG925 has all the 'It kid' prerequisites: obscure urban location (ex-silver factory and anonymous facade), post-industrial fit-out (steel-plate floors, white-tiled walls, Tom Dixon lights), edgy art slung on the walls. While the bistro-style restaurant is a hit-and-miss affair, the grit-chic bar never fails to impress with its well-priced, well-mixed liquids.

Le Rouge (Map p400; ☎ 50 52 44 30; Österlånggatan 17; ☼ 11.30am-2pm & 5pm-1am Mon-Thu, 11.30am-2pm & 4pm-1am Fri, 5pm-1am Sat) Fin-de-siecle Paris is the inspiration for Gamla Stan's latest sip'n'sup darling, a decadent melange of rich red velvet, tasselled lampshades, inspired cocktails and French bistro grub. Operated by two of Stockholm's hottest chefs (Danyel Couet and Melker Andersson), the adjoining restaurant prepares luxe French and Italian dishes in period-glam surrounds. DJs hit the decks and will get you dancing from Thursday to Saturday.

ENTERTAINMENT

Scan the local papers for up-to-date listings of entertainment events, particularly the Friday *På Stan* section of *Dagens Nyheter* newspaper. The monthly *What's On Stockholm* brochure, available free from the tourist office, is another guide.

Nightclubs

Spy Bar (Map p400; ☎ 54 50 37 01; www.thespybar .com, in Swedish; Birger Jarlsgatan 20; admission Skr160; ☼ 10pm-5am Wed-Sat) Set in a turn-of-the-century flat (spot the tiled stoves), this party stalwart pulls in a 20- and 30-something media crowd, as well as the odd American heiress (yes, Paris partied here). Expect three bars, electro, rock and hip-hop beats and no entry after 2am (unless you're well connected, darling).

Grodan (Map p400; ☎ 679 61 00; www.grodan nattklubb.se, in Swedish; Grev Turegatan 16; admission Skr120; ☼ 10pm-3am Fri & Sat) At street level it's a packed bar and mock-baroque restaurant serving great mod-nosh. Down in the cellar, A-list DJ talent from Stockholm, London and beyond (think Axwell, Özgur Can, Ben Watt) spin the vinyl, pumping out house and electro tracks for all the sweat-soaked clubbers.

Café Opera (Map p400; ☎ 676 58 07; www.cafeopera .se; Operahuset, Karl XXI:s Torg; admission Skr180; ☼ 10pm-3am Wed-Sun) Rock stars and wannabe playboys need a suitably excessive place to schmooze, booze and groove, one with bulbous chandeliers, haughty ceiling frescoes and a jet-set vibe. This bar/club combo fits the bill. The adjoining Veranden bar is a crisp white creation by architect trio Claesson Koivisto Rune and a choice hangout for bartenders, meaning a mediocre martini is strictly out of the question.

Live Music

Debaser (Map p400; ☎ 462 98 60; www.debaser.se, in Swedish; Karl Johanstorg 1, Slussen; ☒ 7pm-1am, to 3am club nights Sun-Thu, 8pm-3am Fri & Sat; T-Slussen) The king of rock clubs hides away under the Slussen interchange. Emerging or bigger-name acts play most nights, while the killer club nights span anything from rock-steady to punk and electronica. One metro stop further south, **Debaser Medis** (Map pp396-7; Medborgarplatsen 8; T-Medborgarplatsen) is its sprawling sister venue, with three floors rocking to live acts and DJ-spun tunes.

Mosebacke Etablissement (Map p400; ☎ 55 60 98 90; www.mosebacke.se, in Swedish; Mosebacketorg 3; ☒ to 11pm Mon & Tue, to 1am Wed & Sun, to 2am Thu-Sat; tickets free-Skr250; T-Slussen, bus 3, 53, 76) Eclectic theatre and club nights aside, this historic culture palace hosts a mixed line-up of live music. Tunes span anything from homegrown pop to antipodean rock. The outdoor terrace combines dazzling city views with a thumping summertime bar.

Glenn Miller Café (Map p400; ☎ 10 03 22; Brunnsgatan 21A; ☒ 5pm-1am Mon-Thu, 5pm-2am Fri & Sat; T-Hötorget, bus 1, 43, 56) Loaded with character, this tiny jazz and blues bar draws a faithful, fun-loving crowd. It also serves excellent, affordable French-style classics like mussels with white wine sauce.

Concerts, Theatre & Dance

Konserthuset (Map p400; ☎ 50 66 77 88; www.konserthuset .se; Hötorget; tickets Skr80-325) Head here for classical concerts and other musical marvels, including the Royal Philharmonic Orchestra.

Operan (Map p400; ☎ 791 44 00; www.operan.se; Operahuset, Gustav Adolfs Torg; tickets Skr135-460) The Royal Opera is the place to go for thunderous tenors, sparkling sopranos and classical ballet. It also has some bargain tickets in seats with poor views for as little as Skr40, and occasional lunchtime concerts for Skr180 (including light lunch).

Folkoperan (Map p400; ☎ 616 07 50; www.folkoperan .se; Hornsgatan 72; tickets Skr260-420) Folkoperan gives opera a thoroughly modern overhaul with its intimate, cutting-edge and sometimes controversial productions. The under-26 enjoy half-price tickets.

Dramaten (Map p400; ☎ 667 06 80; www.dramaten .se; Nybroplan; tickets Skr190-320) The Royal Theatre stages a range of plays in a sublime Art Nouveau environment. Dramaten's experimental stage Elverket (Map pp396-7;

Linnégatan 69, same contact details) pushes all the boundaries with some edgier offerings that are performed within a converted power station.

Sport

Bandy matches, a uniquely Scandinavian phenomenon, take place all winter at Stockholm's ice arenas. Catch a game at **Zinkensdamms Idrottsplats** (Map pp396-7; ☎ 668 93 31; Ringvägen 16; ☒ Nov-Feb 8am-2pm Tue-Thu, 8am-11pm Sat, 1-4pm Sun; T-Zinkensdamm). The sport, a precursor to ice hockey but with more players (11 to a side) and less fighting, has grown massively popular since the late-1990s rise of the Hammarby team. The season lasts from November to March, so make sure you bring your own thermos of *kaffekask* – a warming mix of coffee and booze.

For the ultimate Scandi sport experience, head to an ice hockey game at **Globen** (☎ 50 83 53 00; www.globen.se; Arenavägen, Johanneshov; tickets Skr150-200; T-Globen); matches take place here up to three times a week from October to April.

SHOPPING

A progressive design and fashion hub, Stockholm is bliss for retail revellers. Good local buys include edgy streetwear, designer objects and edible treats like cloudberry jam, pickled herring and bottles of Yule-time Blossa *glögg* (spiced wine). Södermalm's SoFo district (the streets south of Folkungagatan) is your best bet for new-school, home-grown fashion.

PUB (Map p400; ☎ 402 16 11; Drottninggatan 72-6; ☒ 10am-7pm Mon-Fri, 10am-6pm Sat, 11am-5pm Sun) Until recently, historic department store PUB was best known as the former workplace of Great Garbo. A major revamp has since turned it into Stockholm's hottest new fashion and lifestyle hub.

Ekovaruhuset (Map p400; ☎ 22 98 45; Österlånggatan 28) With a sister shop in Manhattan, this enlightened concept store stocks fair-trade, organic products, from cosmetics and chocolates to trendy threads and too-cute babywear. Expect anything from Edun T-shirts from Peru to in-the-know labels like Zion and Misericordia.

Chokladfabriken (Map pp396-7; ☎ 640 05 68; Renstiernas Gata 12; ☒ closed Sun) For an edible souvenir, head straight to this chocolate

GAY & LESBIAN STOCKHOLM

Still glowing from EuroPride 2008, Stockholm is a dazzling spot for queer travellers. Sweden's legendary open-mindedness makes homophobic attitudes rare and party-goers of all persuasions are welcome in any bar or club. As a result, Stockholm doesn't do a 'gay ghetto', although you'll find most of the queer-centric venues in Södermalm and Gamla Stan. For club listings and events, pick up a free copy of street-press magazine *QX*, found at many clubs, stores and cafes around town. Its website (www.qx.se) is more frequently updated. *QX* also produces a free, handy Gay Stockholm Map.

RFSL (Map pp396-7; ☎ 50 16 29 50; www.rfsl.se/stockholm in Swedish; Sveavägen 57), the national organisation for gay and lesbian rights, is a good source of information, with a library and cafe to boot.

Torget (Map p400; ☎ 20 55 60; www.torgetbaren.com; Mälartorget 13) in Gamla Stan is Stockholm's premier gay bar-cum-restaurant, with eye-candy staff, mock-baroque touches and a civilised salon vibe.

Roxy (Map pp396-7; ☎ 640 96 55; www.roxysofo.se; Nytorget 6; ☺ closed Mon) in Södermalm is a chic resto-bar popular with lipstick lesbians, publishing types and SoFo's creative set, all of whom nibble on brilliant mod-Med nosh to sultry tango tunes.

Lino Club Sthlm (Map p400; ☎ 411 69 76; www.linoclub.se; Södra Riddarholmshamnen 19; ☺ Sat) is Stockholm's hottest Saturday night gay club, with four bars, three dance floors and mingle-friendly outdoor terrace.

Lady Patricia (Map p400; ☎ 743 05 70; Stadsgårdskajen 152; ☺ Sun), is the perennial Sunday night favourite with its superb seafood restaurant, two crowded dancefloors, drag shows and Schlager-loving crowd. It's all aboard a docked old royal yacht.

Side Track (Map p400; ☎ 641 16 88; www.sidetrack.nu; Wollmar Yxkullsgatan 7; ☺ Wed-Sat) is a particular hit with down-to-earth guys, with a low-key, pub-like ambience and decent grub for peckish punters on the prowl.

peddler, where seasonal Nordic ingredients are used to make some amazingly heavenly cocoa treats. There's a cafe for an on-the-spot fix, and smaller branches in Norrmalm (Regeringsgatan 58) and Östermalm (Grevgatan 37).

DesignTorget Götgatan (Map p400; ☎ 462 35 20; Götgatan 31, Södermalm); Sergels Torg (Map p400; ☎ 50 83 15 20; Basement, Kulturhuset, Sergels Torg B) If you love good design but don't own a Gold Amex, head to this chain, which sells the work of emerging designers alongside established denizens.

Tjallamalla (Map pp396-7; ☎ 640 78 47; www.tjallamalla.com; Bondegatan 46; ☺ noon-6pm Mon-Fri, noon-4pm Sat) Raid the racks at this fashion icon for rookie designers like Hot Sissy, Papagaio, and organic Malmö streetwear label Kärleksgatan. Graduates from Stockholm's prestigious Beckmans College of Design School sometimes sell their collections here on commission.

For all-in-one retail therapy, scour department store giant **Åhléns** (Map p400; ☎ 676 60 00; Klarabergsgatan 50) or its upmarket rival **NK** (Map p400; ☎ 762 80 00; Hamngatan 12-18).

GETTING THERE & AWAY
Air
Stockholm's main airport, **Stockholm Arlanda** (☎ 797 60 00; www.arlanda.se, www.lfv.se), 45km north of the city centre, reached from central Stockholm by bus and express train.

Bromma airport (☎ 797 68 00) is 8km west of Stockholm and is used for some domestic flights. **Skavsta airport** (☎ 0155-28 04 00), 100km south of Stockholm, near Nyköping, is mostly used by low-cost carriers like Ryanair.

The **SAS** (☎ 0770-72 77 27; www.sas.se) network serves 28 Swedish destinations from Arlanda, and has international services to Copenhagen, Oslo, Helsinki and a host of other European cities including Amsterdam, Barcelona, Brussels, Berlin, Dublin, Frankfurt, Geneva, Hamburg, London, Manchester, Milan, Moscow, Paris, Rome, St Petersburg and Zagreb. It also flies direct to Chicago, New York, Bangkok and Beijing.

Finnair (☎ 0771-78 11 00; www.finnair.com) flies several times daily to Helsinki. **Blue1** (☎ 0900-102 58 31; www.blue1.com) has direct flights to Helsinki, as well as to Tampere, Turku/Åbo and Vaasa.

Boat

Both **Silja Line** (☎ 22 21 40; www.silja.com) and **Viking Line** (☎ 452 40 00; www.vikingline.fi) run ferries to Turku and Helsinki. **Tallink** (☎ 22 21 40; www.tallink.ee) ferries head to Tallinn (Estonia) and Riga (Latvia).

Bus

Most long-distance buses arrive and depart from **Cityterminalen** (Map p400; www.cityterminalen.com), which is connected to Centralstationen. The main counter (open 7am to 6pm) sells tickets for several bus companies, including Flygbussarna (airport coaches), Swebus Express, Svenska Buss, Eurolines and Y-Buss.

Swebus Express (☎ 0771-21 82 18; www.swebusexpress.com; 2nd level, Cityterminalen) runs daily to Malmö (9¼ hours), Göteborg (seven hours), Norrköping (two hours), Kalmar (six hours), Mora (4¼ hours), Örebro (three hours) and Oslo (eight hours). There are also direct runs to Gävle (2½ hours), Uppsala (one hour) and Västerås (1¾ hours).

Ybuss (☎ 020 033 44 44; www.ybuss.se, in Swedish; Cityterminalen) runs services to the northern towns of Sundsvall, Östersund and Umeå (see relevant sections for details). You'll also find a number of companies running buses from many provincial towns directly to Stockholm.

Car & Motorcycle

The E4 motorway passes through the city, just west of the centre, on its way from Helsingborg to Haparanda. The E20 motorway from Stockholm to Göteborg via Örebro, follows the E4 as far as Södertälje. The E18 from Kapellskär to Oslo runs from east to west and passes just north of central Stockholm.

For car hire close to Centralstationen head to **Avis** (Map p400; ☎ 20 20 60; Vasagatan 10B) or **Hertz** (Map p400; ☎ 454 62 50; Vasagatan 26).

Train

Stockholm is the hub for national train services run by **Sveriges Järnväg** (SJ; ☎ 0771-75 75 75; www.sj.se). and **Tågkompaniet** (☎ 0771-44 41 11; www.tagkompaniet.se, in Swedish).

Centralstationen (Stockholm C; ☯ 5am-midnight) is the central train station. In the main hall you'll find the SJ **ticket office** (Map p400; ☯ domestic tickets 7.30am-7.45pm Mon-Fri, 8.30am-6pm Sat, 9.30am-7pm Sun, international tickets 10am-6pm Mon-Fri, general customer service 6am-11pm Mon-Fri, 6.30am-11pm Sat, 7am-11pm Sun). You'll also find automated ticket machines (☯ 5am-11.50pm Mon-Sun).

Direct SJ trains to/from Copenhagen, Oslo and Storlien (for Trondheim) arrive and depart from Centralstationen, as do the overnight services from Göteborg (via Stockholm and Boden) to Kiruna and Narvik; the Arlanda Express; and the SL *pendeltåg* commuter services that run to/from Nynäshamn, Södertälje and Märsta. Other SL local rail lines (Roslagsbanan and Saltsjöbanan) run from Stockholm Östra (T-Tekniska Högskolan) and Slussen, respectively.

In the basement at Centralstationen, you'll find lockers costing Skr40 to Skr90 (depending on size) for 24 hours, toilets for Skr5, and showers (next to the toilets) for Skr30. These facilities are open 5am to 12.30am daily. There's also a left-luggage office, open daily, and a **lost property office** (☎ 50 12 55 90; sj.lostproperty@bagport.se; ☯ 9am-7pm Mon-Fri); look for the 'Hittegods' sign.

Follow the signs to find your way to the local metro (T-bana) network; the underground station here is called T-Centralen.

GETTING AROUND
To/From the Airports

The **Arlanda Express** (Map p400; ☎ 020-22 22 24; tickets from Skr220) train from Centralstationen takes 20 minutes to reach Arlanda; trains run every 10 to 15 minutes from about 5am to 12.30am. The same trip in a taxi costs around Skr495.

The cheaper option is the **Flygbuss** service between Arlanda airport and Cityterminalen. Buses leave every 10 or 15 minutes (Skr110, 40 minutes). Tickets can be purchased on arrival at the Flygbuss counter at Arlanda airport's main terminal.

Bicycle

Stockholm boasts a wide network of bicycle paths and in summer you won't regret bringing a bicycle with you or hiring one to get around. The tourist offices have maps for sale, but they're not usually necessary if you have a basic city map.

Trails and bike lanes are clearly marked with traffic signs. Some long-distance routes are marked all the way from central Stockholm: Nynäsleden to Nynäshamn joins Sommarleden near Västerhaninge and swings west to Södertälje. Roslagsleden leads to Norrtälje (linking Blåleden and Vaxholm). Upplandsleden leads to Märsta north of Stockholm, and you can ride to Uppsala via Sigtuna. Sörmlandsleden leads to Södertälje.

Bicycles can be carried free on SL local trains, except during peak hour (6am to 9am and 3pm to 6pm weekdays). They're not allowed in Centralstationen or on the metro, although you'll occasionally see some daring souls.

Boat

Djurgårdsfärjan city ferry services connect Gröna Lund Tivoli on Djurgården with Nybroplan and Slussen as frequently as every 10 minutes in summer (less frequently in the low season); a single trip costs Skr30 (free with the SL transport passes).

Car & Motorcycle

Driving in central Stockholm is not recommended. Skinny one-way streets, congested bridges and limited parking all present problems; note that Djurgårdsvägen is closed near Skansen at night, on summer weekends and some holidays. Don't attempt driving through the narrow streets of Gamla Stan.

Parking is a major problem, but there are *P-hus* (parking stations) throughout the city; they charge up to Skr60 per hour, though the fixed evening rate is usually lower. If you do have a car, one of the best options is to stay on the outskirts of town and catch public transport into the centre.

Public Transport

Storstockholms Lokaltrafik (SL; www.sl.se) runs all tunnelbana (T or T-bana) metro trains, local trains and buses within the entire Stockholm county. There is an SL information office in the basement concourse at **Centralstationen** (6.30am-11.15pm Mon-Sat, 7am-11.15pm Sun) and another near the Sergels Torg entrance (open until 6.30pm weekdays, 5pm weekends), which issues timetables and sells the SL Tourist Card and Stockholm Card. You can also call ☎ 600 10 00 for schedule and travel information.

The Stockholm Card (see p398) covers travel on all SL trains and buses in greater Stockholm. The 24-hour (Skr100) and 72-hour (Skr200) SL Tourist Cards are primarily for transport and give free entry to only a few attractions. The 72-hour SL Tourist Card (Skr260) is good value, especially if you use the third afternoon for transport to either end of the county – you can reach the ferry terminals in Grisslehamn, Kapellskär or Nynäshamn, as well as all of the archipelago harbours. If you want to explore the county in more detail, bring a passport photo and get yourself a 30-day SL pass (Skr690, or Skr420 for children age seven to 18 and seniors).

On Stockholm's public transport system the minimum fare costs two coupons, and each additional zone costs another coupon (up to five coupons for four or five zones). Coupons cost Skr20 each (Skr15 from ticket machines at Tunnelbana stations), but it's much better to buy strips of tickets for Skr180. Coupons are stamped at the start of a journey. Travelling without a valid ticket can lead to a fine of Skr600 or more. Coupons, tickets and passes can be bought at metro stations, Pressbyrån kiosks, SL railway stations and SL information offices. Tickets cannot be bought on buses.

International rail passes (eg Scanrail, Interrail) aren't valid on SL trains.

BUS

While the bus timetables and route maps are complicated, they're worth studying as there are some useful connections to suburban attractions. Ask **SL** (☎ 600 10 00) or any tourist office for the handy inner-city route map *Innerstadsbussar*.

Inner-city buses radiate from Sergels Torg, Odenplan, Fridhemsplan (on Kungsholmen) and Slussen. Bus 47 runs from Sergels Torg to Djurgården, and bus 69 runs from Centralstationen and Sergels Torg to the Ladugårdsgärdet museums and Kaknästornet. Useful buses for hostellers include bus 65, which goes from Centralstationen to Skeppsholmen, and bus 43, which runs from Regeringsgatan to Södermalm.

Inner-city night buses run from 1am to 5pm on a few routes. Most leave from Centralstationen, Sergels Torg, Slussen, Odenplan and Fridhemsplan to the suburbs.

TRAIN

Local *pendeltåg* trains are useful for connections to Nynäshamn (for ferries to Gotland), to Märsta (for buses to Sigtuna and the short hop to Arlanda Airport) and Södertälje. SL coupons and SL travel passes are valid on these trains, and should be bought before boarding.

TRAM

The historic **No 7 tram** (☎ 660 77 00) runs between Norrmalmstorg and Skansen, passing most attractions on Djurgården. Both the Stockholm Card and SL Tourist Card are valid onboard.

METRO

The most useful mode of transport in Stockholm is the tunnelbana, run by SL. Its lines converge on T-Centralen, connected by an underground walkway to Centralstationen. There are three main lines with branches.

Taxi

Taxis are readily available but expensive, so check for a meter or arrange the fare first. The flag fall is Skr38, then about Skr13 per kilometre. Reputable firms include **Taxi Stockholm** (☎ 15 00 00), **Taxi 020** (☎ 020 93 93 93) and **Taxi Kurir** (☎ 30 00 00).

AROUND STOCKHOLM

Most locals will tell you that the one thing not to miss about Stockholm is leaving it – whether for a journey into the lovely rock-strewn archipelago or an excursion into the surrounding countryside. Within easy reach of the capital are idyllic islands, Viking gravesites, cute fishing villages and sturdy palaces.

NORTHERN SUBURBS

One of Stockholm's loveliest attractions is **Millesgården** (Map p416; ☎ 446 75 94; Carl Milles väg 2, Lidingö island; adult/child Skr80/free, ☉ 11am-5pm mid-May–Sep, noon-5pm Tue-Sun Oct–mid-May), a superb sculpture park and museum of works by Carl Milles and others. It's on Lidingö island with great views to the mainland; take the metro to T-Ropsten then bus No 207.

The extensive **Naturhistoriska Riksmuseet** (Map p416; ☎ 51 95 40 40; www.nrm.se; Frescativägen 40; T-Universitetet; adult/under 19yr Skr70/free; ☉ 10am-7pm Tue, Wed & Fri, 10am-8pm Thu, 11am-7pm Sat & Sun) was founded by Carl von Linné in 1739. There are hands-on displays about nature and the human body, as well as whole forests' worth of taxidermied wildlife, dinosaurs, marine life and the hardy fauna of the polar regions. The adjoining **Cosmonova** (Map p416; ☎ 51 95 51 30; adult/5-18yr Skr85/50, no children under 5) is a combined planetarium and Imax theatre.

Haga Park (Map p416) is also pleasant for walks and bicycle tours with attractions including the royal **Gustav III's Pavilion**, **Butterfly House** and colourful **Copper Tent**. To reach the park, take bus 515 from Odenplan to Haga Norra.

FJÄDERHOLMARNA

Located on the eastern side of Djurgården, these tiny, delightful islands ('Feather Islands') offer an easy escape from the city. They're just 25 minutes away by boat and a favourite swimming spot for locals. **Boats** (adult/child return Skr95/45) to the islands depart hourly from either Nybroplan or Slussen between May and early September. There are a couple of craft shops and restaurants here, though the main activity is low-key chilling. The last boats leave the islands at around midnight, making them a perfect spot to soak up the long daylight hours.

FERRY PORTS

Nynäshamn, 50km south of Stockholm, is the main gateway to Gotland; there are also regular ferries to Gdańsk (Poland). Regular local (SL) trains run from Stockholm to Nynäshamn; you can use SL passes, but international rail passes are not valid. There are also direct bus services from Stockholm's Cityterminalen to connect with the Gotland ferries (Skr85), leaving 1¾ hours before ferry departure times.

Ferries sail between tiny **Kapellskär** (90km northeast of Stockholm) and Turku (Finland) via the Åland islands. The ferry companies offer a direct bus from Stockholm Cityterminalen to meet the ferries (Skr55), but SL pass holders can take bus 640 from T-Tekniska Högskolan to Norrtälje and change there to 631, which runs every two hours or so (infrequent at weekends).

For more information on reaching the Åland islands, check www.visitaland.com or contact the main companies operating between Sweden and Åland. Of these, **Viking Line** (www.vikingline.aland.fi) and **Silja Line** (www.silja.com) continue on to Finland, while **Eckerö Linjen** (www.eckerolinjen.fi), **Ånedin Linjen** (www.anedinlinjen.com) and **Birka Cruises** (www.birkacruises.com) operate only between the islands and Sweden. Once on the islands, you can

SWEDEN

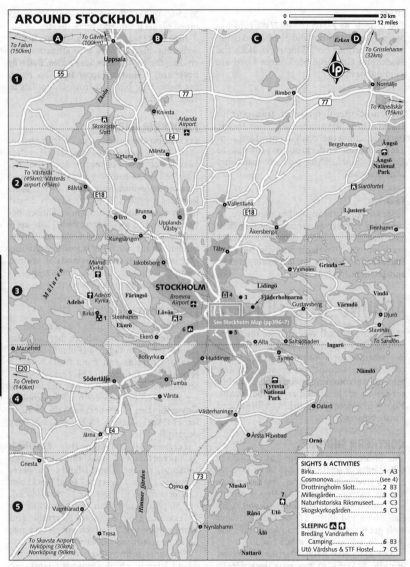

AROUND STOCKHOLM

SIGHTS & ACTIVITIES
Birka.................................**1** A3
Cosmonova...................(see 4)
Drottningholm Slott.......**2** B3
Millesgården...................**3** C3
Naturhistoriska Riksmuseet....**4** C3
Skogskyrkogården...........**5** C3

SLEEPING
Bredäng Vandrarhem & Camping..................**6** B3
Utö Värdshus & STF Hostel.....**7** C5

happily pedal almost anywhere thanks to the bridges and handy network ferries.

VAXHOLM
☎ 08 / pop 9500

Vaxholm, located about 35km northeast of the city, is the gateway to the central and northern reaches of Stockholm's archipel-ago and it positively swarms with tourists in summer. It has a collection of quaint summerhouses that were fashionable in the 19th century. The oldest buildings are in the Norrhamn area, a few minutes' walk north of the town hall, but there's also in-teresting architecture along Hamngatan (the main street).

Bus 670 from the metro station T-Tekniska Högskolan runs regularly to the town. **Waxholmsbolaget** (Map p400; ☎ 679 58 30; www.waxholmsbolaget.se) boats sail frequently between Vaxholm and Strömkajen in Stockholm (about 40 minutes). **Strömma Kanalbolaget** (Map p400; ☎ 12 00 40 00; www.strommakanalbolaget.com) sails between Strandvägen and Vaxholm three times daily from mid-June to mid-August (one way/return Skr125/200) and infrequently the rest of the year.

STOCKHOLM ARCHIPELAGO
☎ 08

The archipelago is the favourite time-off destination for Stockholm's locals, and summer cottages on rocky islets are popular among the well-to-do. Depending on whom you ask, the archipelago has between 14,000 and 100,000 islands (the consensus is 24,000).

Visit Skärgården (Map p400; ☎ 10 02 22; www.visitskargarden.se, in Swedish; Kajplats 18, Strandvägen; ☻ 9am-5pm Mon-Fri, 10am-4pm Sat, 11am-4pm Sun), a new, waterside information centre, can advise on (and book) accommodation and tours.

The biggest boat operator is **Waxholmsbolaget** (☎ 679 5830; www.waxholmsbolaget.se). Timetables and information are available from its offices outside the Grand Hotel on Strömkajen in Stockholm, at the harbour in Vaxholm, and online. It divides the archipelago into three areas: *Norra Skärgården* is the northern section (north from Ljusterö to Arholma); *Mellersta Skärgården* is the middle section, taking in Vaxholm, Ingmarsö, Stora Kalholmen, Finnhamn, Möja and Sandhamn; and *Södra Skärgården* is the southern section, with boats south to Nämdö, Ornö and Utö. The Båtluffarkortet pass (Skr350 for five days) gives you unlimited boat rides plus a handy map with suggested itineraries.

If time is short, consider taking the Thousand Island Cruise offered by **Stromma Kanabolaget** (Map p400; ☎ 12 00 40 00; www.strommakanalbolaget.com; Nybrokajen), running daily between late June and early August. The full-day tour departs from Stockholm's Nybrokajen at 9.30am and returns at 8.30pm; the cost of Skr995 includes lunch, dinner, drinks and guided tours ashore. The tour includes three island stops and swimming opportunities.

Sandhamn village on Sandön is popular with sailors and day-trippers. The historic **Sandhamns Värdshus** (☎ 57 15 30 51; s/d from Skr740/990) serves a lip-smacking fish and shellfish casserole (mains Skr100 to Skr223).

The 900m-long **Finnhamn**, northeast of Stockholm, combines lush woods and meadows with sheltered coves, rocky cliffs and visiting eagle owls. While it's a popular summertime spot, there are enough quiet corners to indulge your inner hermit. **Vandrarhem Finnhamn** (☎ 54 24 62 12; info@finnhamn.nu; dm Skr260; ☻ all year; 🖴) is an STF hostel in a large wooden villa, with boat hire available. It's the largest hostel in the archipelago; advance booking is essential.

A cycling paradise in the southern archipelago, **Utö** has it all: sublime sandy beaches, lush fairytale forests, sleepy farms and abundant birdlife. Reception for the **STF hostel** (☻ Sep-May) is at the nearby **Utö Värdshus** (Map p416; ☎ 50 42 03 00; receptionen@utovardshus.se; 2-person chalets incl breakfast per person from Skr995), whose **restaurant** (lunch Skr89-119, mains around Skr200; ☻ closed Jan) is ranked among the best in the archipelago.

EKERÖ DISTRICT
☎ 08 / pop 22,600

The pastoral Ekerö district, 20km west of Stockholm, is home to the romantic Drottningholm castle as well as several large islands in Mälaren lake, a dozen medieval churches and the Unesco World Heritage site at Birka.

Drottningholm

Still the royal family pad for part of the year, the Renaissance-inspired **Drottningholm Slott** (☎ 402 62 80; www.royalcourt.se; adult/child Skr70/35, combined ticket Skr110/55 includes Chinese Pavilion; ☻ 10am-4.30pm May-Aug, noon-3.30pm Sep, noon-3.30pm Sat & Sun Oct-Apr, closed mid-Dec–early Jan), with its geometric baroque gardens, was designed by architectural great Nicodemius Tessin the Elder and begun in 1662, about the same time as Versailles. You can walk around the wings open to the public on your own, but we recommend the one-hour guided tour (no additional charge; English tours at 10am, noon, 2pm and 4pm daily from June to August, reduced schedule rest of the year).

The unique **Drottningholms Slottsteater** (☎ 759 04 06; www.dtm.se; admission by tour adult/child Skr60/40; tours ☻ hourly noon-4pm May, 11am-4pm Jun-Aug, 1pm-3pm Sep) is the original 18th-century court theatre and is well worth a tour, especially the backstage sound-effects department;

SWEDEN

ask about opera, ballet and musical performances here in summer.

At the far end of the gardens is the 18th-century **Kina Slott** (☎ 402 62 70; adult/child Skr60/30, combined ticket incl royal palace Skr110/55; ⏰ 11am-4.30pm May-Aug, noon-3.30pm Sep), a lavishly decorated 'Chinese pavilion' that was built as a gift to Queen Lovisa Ulrika. Admission includes an entertaining guided tour.

Given the separate admission charges for each attraction, it's a good idea to use the Stockholm Card. If you're not short of time, you could cycle out here, otherwise take the metro to T-Brommaplan and change to bus 301 or 323. The most pleasant way to get to Drottningholm is by boat: **Strömma Kanalbolaget** (Map p400; ☎ 1200 40 00; www.strommakanalbolaget .com) will take you there. Frequent services depart from Stadshusbron (Stockholm) daily between May and mid-September, with less frequent daily departures mid- to late September, and weekend-only services in October (one way/return Skr105/140). A *kombibiljett* (combined ticket, Skr270) includes return travel and admission to the palace and Chinese Pavilion.

Birka

At the fascinating Viking trading centre of **Birka** (Map p416; ☎ 12 00 40 00; www.vikingastaden.se; ⏰ 11am-6.30pm late Jun–mid-Aug, 11am-3pm May–late Jun & mid-Aug–early Sep), a Unesco World Heritage Site on Björkö in Mälaren lake, archaeologists have excavated the ancient settlement's cemetery, harbour and fortress. Daily cruises to Birka run from early May to early September; the round-trip on Strömma Kanalbolaget's *Victoria* from Stadshusbron, Stockholm, is a full day's outing (Skr270). The cruise price includes a visit to the museum and a guided tour in English of the settlement's burial mounds and fortifications. Call ☎ 12 00 40 00 for details; boats leave around 9.30am. Ferries do not run during the midsummer holidays.

SIGTUNA
☎ 08 / pop 6500

About 40km northwest of Stockholm is the picturesque lakeside town of Sigtuna, the oldest surviving town in Sweden. It was founded in about 980; the first Swedish coins were struck here in 995. There's a popular **Medieval Festival** in July and good holiday markets throughout December. The friendly **tourist office** (☎ 59 48 06 50; Storagatan 33; ⏰ 10am-6pm

Mon-Sat, 11am-5pm Sun) inhabits an 18th-century wooden house.

Ten runestones still stand in various places around Sigtuna, and 150 more dot the surrounding landscape. Storagatan is probably Sweden's oldest main street, and there are ruins of 12th-century churches around town. The mid-13th-century **Mariakyrkan**, Sigtuna's most arresting sight, contains restored medieval paintings. The friendly **Sigtuna Museum** (☎ 59 12 66 70; Storagatan 55; adult/under 20yr Skr20/free; ⏰ noon-4pm Tue-Sun Sep-May, noon-4pm Jun-Aug) displays finds from excavations of the area.

There's little budget accommodation in town. Those with their own wheels should look for signs advertising *stugor* (cabins) at local farmhouses (usually Skr200 to Skr300) or ask at the tourist office. **Sigtuna Stadshotell** (☎ 59 25 01 00; info@sigtunastadshotell.se; Stora Nygatan 3; s/d Skr2090/2490; 🖵) features pale, uberstylish interiors, spa treatments and a restaurant hailed as a rising star.

There are a number of good cafes and restaurants to choose from, plus supermarkets for picnic supplies (and tables by the lake, among the ducks). Don't miss the delightful **Tant Brun Kaffestuga** (☎ 5925 0934; Laurentii gränd 3; snacks Skr20-40), a 17th-century cafe with a worryingly saggy roof and pretty courtyard just off Stora gatan.

Travel connections are easy from Stockholm. Take a local train to Märsta, from where there are frequent buses to Sigtuna (570 or 575).

SVEALAND

This area, the birthplace of Sweden, offers evidence of the region's long history, including rune stones so plentiful you might stumble over them. Pre-Viking burial mounds in Gamla Uppsala light the imaginations of myth-builders and history buffs. There's also the old mine in Falun, which accidentally provided the red paint for all those little cottages dotting the landscape. And in Mora, the definitive Swedish king's path toward the crown is still retraced today, by thousands of skiers each year in the Vasaloppet.

UPPSALA
☎ 018 / pop 182,000

Drenched in history but not stifled by the past, Uppsala has the party vibe of a university town to balance out its important

SWEDEN

buildings and atmosphere of weighty cultural significance. It's a good combination, one that makes the town both fun and functional, not to mention rewarding to the interested visitor.

On the edge of the city is Gamla (Old) Uppsala, the original site of the town, once a flourishing 6th-century religious centre.

Information

Forex (☎ 10 30 00; Fyristorg 8; ⏱ 9am-7pm Mon-Fri, 9am-3pm Sat) Currency exchange next to the tourist office.

Tourist office (☎ 727 48 00; www.uppsalatourism.se; Fyristorg 8; ⏱ 10am-6pm Mon-Fri, 10am-3pm Sat, also noon-4pm Sun mid-Jun–mid-Aug) Pick up the *Walking Tour of Uppsala* leaflet, and *What's On Uppsala* for event listings.

Sights

GAMLA UPPSALA

A great excursion for imaginative history buffs, especially in nice weather, is Gamla Uppsala – the city's beginnings, consisting of three great **grave mounds** 4km north of the modern city are well signposted (take bus 2 from Stora Torget). The mounds are said to be the graves of legendary pre-Viking kings (although recent evidence suggests that at least one of the occupants is a woman) and lie in a field including about 300 smaller mounds and a great heathen temple. Even more fascinating is all the myth-making that has grown up around the grave mounds. A 17th-century professor, Olof Rudbeck, argued that Gamla Uppsala was actually the ancient sunken city of Atlantis, for example.

For more myths, rumours and some of the actual science surrounding the site, visit **Gamla Uppsala Museum** (☎ 23 93 00; www.raa.se/gamlauppsala; adult/child Skr50/30, under 6yr free; ⏱ 11am-5pm May-Aug, noon-3pm Wed, Sat & Sun Sep–mid-Dec & Jan-Apr). The museum has exhibits of ancient artefacts excavated from Gamla Uppsala and the nearby archaeological sites. Guided tours will help you get more out of your visit – these are held at 3pm daily from May to August and are included in the entry price of the museum.

Christianity arrived in the 11th century and with it the bishops and other church officials. From 1164 the archbishop had his seat in a cathedral on the site of the present **church**, which, by the 15th century, was enlarged and painted with frescoes.

UPPSALA SLOTT

Originally constructed by Gustav Vasa in the mid-16th century, **Uppsala Slott** (☎ 54 48 11; www.uppsalaslott.se; admission by guided tour only, adult/child Skr70/20; ⏱ in English at 1pm & 3pm Tue-Sun Jun-Aug) features the state hall where kings were enthroned and a queen abdicated. Midsummer and other holidays are frequently marked by ringing the nearby, freestanding **Gunilla klockan**. The **Botanic Gardens** (☎ 471 28 38; www.botan.uu.se; Villavägen 6-8; admission free; ⏱ 7am-9pm May-Sep, 7am-7pm Oct-Apr) below the castle hill, show off more than 10,000 different species and are pleasant to wander through.

OTHER SIGHTS

The Gothic **Domkyrka** (☎ 18 72 01; www.uppsaladomkyrka.se; admission free; ⏱ 8am-6pm May-Sep, 10am-6pm Sat Oct-Apr) dominates the city, just as some of those buried there dominated their country, including St Erik, Gustav Vasa, Johan III and Carl von Linné. Gustav's funerary sword, silver crown and shiny golden buttons are kept in the **treasury** (☎ 18 72 01; adult/child Skr30/free; ⏱ 10am-5pm Mon-Sat & 12.30-5pm Sun May-Sep, limited hr Oct-Apr) in the north tower.

Museum Gustavianum (☎ 471 75 71; www.gustavianum.uu.se; Akademigatan 3; adult/under 12yr Skr40/free; ⏱ 11am-4pm Tue-Sun) rewards appreciation of the weird and well-organised. The shelves in the pleasantly musty building hold case after case of obsolete tools and preserved oddities; there's also a cleverly tucked-away anatomical theatre in the dome. **Upplandsmuseet** (☎ 16 91 00; www.upplandsmuseet.se, in Swedish; Sankt Eriks Torg 10; admission free; ⏱ noon-5pm Tue-Sun), in an 18th-century mill, houses county collections from the Middle Ages.

Carolina Rediviva (☎ 471 39 00; Dag Hammarskjölds väg 1; adult/under 12yr Skr20/free; ⏱ 9am-5pm Mon-Fri, 10am-5pm Sat, 11am-4pm Sun mid-Jun–mid-Aug, 9am-8pm Mon-Fri & 10am-5pm Sat mid-Aug–mid-Jun) is the old

---

UPPSALA KORTET

This handy little three-day discount card (Skr125) gives free or discounted admission to many of the town's attractions, plus free local bus travel and parking. There are also discounts at participating hotels, restaurants and shops. The card is valid from June to August, and can be bought from the tourist office. It covers one adult and up to two children.

SWEDEN

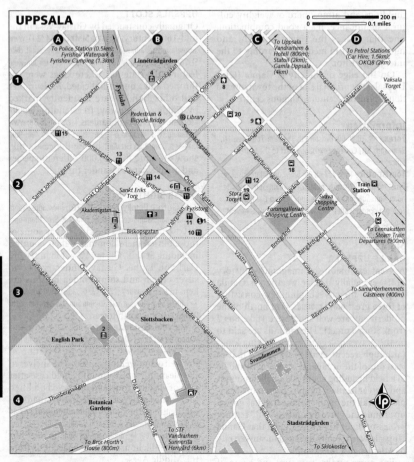

university library and has a display hall with maps and historical and scientific literature, the pride of which is the 6th-century *Codex Argentus* (aka 'Silver Bible').

The **Linnémuseet** (☎ 13 65 40; www.linnaeus.se; Svartbäcksgatan 27; adult/under 16yr Skr50/free; ✆ 11am-5pm Tue-Sun May-Sep) exhibits memorabilia of von Linné's work in Uppsala, and its **gardens** (☎ 471 25 76; admission free with Linnémuseet ticket; ✆ shop & exhibit 11am-5pm, park 11am-8pm Tue-Sun May-Sep), with more than 1000 herbs, were designed according to an 18th-century plan.

Sleeping

Fyrishov Camping (☎ 727 49 60; stugby@fyrishov.se; Idrottsgatan 2; camp sites Skr130, 4-bed cabins from Skr695; ✆ year-round; bus 1 from Dragarbrunnsgatan) This camp-

ing ground, 2km north of the city, is great for families with waterbabies: it's attached to one of Sweden's largest waterparks, with discounted swim-and-stay packages (cabins from Skr795).

STF Vandrarhem Sunnersta Herrgård (☎ 32 42 20; www.sunnerstaherrgard.se; Sunnerstavägen 24; dm Skr200, s/d from Skr340/380; ✆ Jan–mid-Dec; bus 20; 🖳 🛜) This hostel in a historic manor house about 6km south of the city centre has a parklike setting at water's edge and a good restaurant onsite. You can rent bikes (per day/week Skr50/200) or borrow a boat. There's free wi-fi. Hotel-standard rooms are also available (single/double Skr605/710).

Uppsala Vandrarhem City (☎ 10 00 08; www .uppsalavandrarhem.se; Sankt Persgatan 16; dm/s/d from

Skr220/400/500; year-round;) Vandrarhem City is recommended for its sheer convenience – you really can't stay anywhere more central for these prices. Rooms, all named after famous Uppsala landmarks, are small but decent (although dorms suffer from traffic and level-crossing noise). No breakfast is served, but a kitchen is available.

Hotel Uppsala (480 50 00; hoteluppsala@pro filhotels.se; Kungsgatan 27; s/d from Skr1350/1550;) Uppsala's largest hotel, and one of its nicest, Hotel Uppsala has all the standard business-hotel amenities plus Hästens beds, birchwood floors, and microwaves and fridges in many rooms. There's also a new Scottish-style pub attached to the hotel.

Eating

Ofvandahls (13 42 04; Sysslomansgatan 3-5; cakes & snacks around Skr40) Something of an Uppsala in-stitution, this classy *konditori* dates back to the 19th century and is a cut above your aver-age coffee-and-bun shop. It's endorsed by no less a personage than the king, and radiates old-world charm; somehow those faded red-striped awnings just get cuter every year.

Eko Caféet (12 18 45; Drottninggatan 5; snacks Skr50-70) This funky little place with retro and mismatched furniture serves some of the best coffee in town. It does Italian-style whole-food, turns into a tapas bar on Wednesday to Saturday evenings, and frequently hosts live jazz/folk, as well as changing art exhibits and general studenty goings-on. Things quiet down somewhat in the summer, when it just opens for lunch Monday to Friday.

Svenssons Taverna (10 09 08; Sysslomansgatan 14; mains Skr80-185) Pottery Barn meets the Ancient Mariner in the decorating scheme of this up-scale eatery, with a nice outdoor patio and a menu of gourmet Swedish staples.

Hambergs Fisk (71 00 50; Fyristorg 8; lunch from Skr80, mains Skr150-240; Tue-Sat) No need to ask at the tourist office about where to eat: if you're there, you'll be close enough to smell the aro-mas of dill and seafood tempting you into this excellent fish restaurant. Self-caterers should check out the fresh fish counter inside.

More casual options can be found inside **Saluhallen** (Sankt Eriks Torg; Mon-Sat), an indoor market between the cathedral and the river. Find groceries at the central **Hemköp super-market** (Stora Torget; to 10pm).

Getting There & Away

The **Flygbuss** (bus 801) departs at least twice an hour around the clock for nearby Arlanda airport (45 minutes, adult/child Skr100/ 60); it leaves from outside the Uppsala Central Station.

Swebus Express (0200-218 218; www.swe busexpress.se) runs regular direct services to Stockholm (Skr54, one hour, at least hourly), Gävle (Skr82, 1½ hours, two daily), Västerås (Skr157, 3½ hours, six daily), Örebro (Skr220, 4½ hours, four to seven daily) and Falun (Skr296, 5½ hours, one daily).

There are frequent SJ trains to/from Stockholm (Skr39 to Skr69, 40 minutes). SJ trains to/from Gävle (Skr135, 50 minutes, at least seven daily), Östersund (Skr764, five hours, at least two daily) and Mora (Skr224 to Skr572, 3¼ hours, two daily) also stop in Uppsala.

For car hire, contact **Statoil** (20 91 00; Gamla Uppsalagatan 48), next to the Scandic Uppsala Nord. There are also three pet-rol stations with car hire, 1.5km along Vaksalagatan: **OKQ8** (29 04 96; Årstagatan 5-7) often has good deals.

Getting Around

Upplands Lokaltrafik (0771-14 14 14; www.ul.se, in Swedish) runs traffic within the city and county.

SWEDEN

City buses leave from Stora Torget and the surrounding streets. Tickets for unlimited travel for 90 minutes cost from Skr20.

ÖREBRO

☎ 019 / pop 126,990

A substantial, culturally rich city, Örebro buzzes around its central feature, the huge and romantic castle surrounded by a moat filled with waterlilies. The city originally grew as a product of the textile industry, but it's now decidedly a university town – students on bicycles fill the streets, and relaxed-looking people gather on the restaurant patios and in parks.

The **tourist office** (☎ 21 21 21; www.orebro.se/turism; ⊙ 10am-6pm Mon-Fri, 10am-2pm Sat & Sun Sep-May, 10am-6pm Mon-Fri, 10am-4pm Sat & Sun Jun-Aug) is inside the castle.

Sights

The magnificent **Slottet** (☎ 21 21 21; guided tours adult/6-15yr Skr65/25; ⊙ Jun-Aug) now serves as the county governor's headquarters. Parts of the interior are open for exhibits, but to really explore you'll need to take a tour – there's a historical one at 4.30pm (in Swedish or English, depending on numbers), or a 'Secrets of the Vasa Fortress' option at 2.30pm (in English). The northwest tower holds a small **history exhibition** (admission free; ⊙ noon-4pm Tue-Sun Sep-Apr, 10am-5pm daily May-Aug). Tickets can be purchased from the tourist office.

Outside the castle is the **Länsmuseum & Konsthall** (☎ 602 87 00; info@orebrolansmuseum.se; Engelbrektsgatan 3; admission free; ⊙ 11am-5pm Tue & Thu-Sun, 11am-9pm Wed), the combined regional and art museums.

A pleasant stroll east of the castle along the river will take you through Stadsparken. Bikes are available to rent from May to September from the **kiosk** (Hamnplan) on the river's edge.

In Stadsparken, the **Stadsträdgården** greenhouse precinct has a great cafe, and further east, there's the excellent **Wadköping** museum village, which has craft workshops, a bakery and period buildings. There are guided tours at 1pm and 3pm June to August (Skr20).

The commercial centre and some grand buildings are around Stortorget, including the 13th-century **St Nikolai kyrka** (⊙ 10am-5pm Mon-Fri, 11am-3pm Sat), where Jean Baptiste Bernadotte (Napoleon's marshal) was chosen to take the Swedish throne.

Sleeping & Eating

Gustavsvik Camping (☎ 19 69 50; www.gustavsvik.se; Sommarrovägen; camp sites from Skr150, cabins from Skr575; ⊙ mid-Apr–early Nov; bus 11; 🏊) This camping facility is 2km south of the city centre. It's huge and family-oriented, with pools, minigolf, a cafe, gym, restaurant, and bike rental (Skr60 per day).

STF Vandrarhem Örebro/Grenadjären (☎ 31 02 40; www.grenadjaren.se; Kaptensgatan 1; dm from Skr160, s/d Skr330/360, with bath dm/s/d Skr220/370/460, flatlets from Skr550; bus 16 or 31) This large hostel in a former military building 1.6km northeast of the train station has bright, sunny rooms, a spacious kitchen and good, modern facilities. There are also well-equipped flats for up to four people in the apartment complex next door. Bicycle hire is available and encouraged (per day/week Skr70/300).

Behrn Hotell (☎ 12 00 95; www.behrnhotell.se; Stortorget 12; s/d Skr1095/1395; 🖥 💻) Excellently situated on the main square, the Behrn Hotell goes the extra mile, with homey rooms each individually decorated, ranging from strictly business to farmhouse to edgy modern Scandinavian. Do it right and get a room with a balcony, or a suite with old wooden beams, chandeliers and Jacuzzi. There's also a spa, and a restaurant which does dinner Tuesday to Friday.

Hälls Konditori Stallbacken (☎ 611 07 66; Engelbrektsgatan 12; Skr35-65) One of two locations of this bakery-cafe (the other's in Järntorget), Hälls is a classic old-style *konditori*. Sensible light meals (salads, quiche, sandwiches) are available, plus there's teetering piles of lurid-coloured creamy cakes and patisseries.

Farbror Melkers (☎ 611 81 99; Stortorget 6; meals around Skr60) If you're the modern sort, head for this stylish place, with good coffee, light meals (sandwiches, baked potatoes) and a large picture window so you can stare out onto the square.

Bredbar (☎ 31 50 20; Kungsgatan 1; salads from Skr60; ⊙ 10am-8pm Mon-Thu, 10am-7pm Fri, 11am-5pm Sat-Sun) In summer, Bredbar is an ultrapopular place for lunch, thanks to its outdoor seats in a courtyard suntrap. A constant dance of customers swirls in and out for ciabattas, huge bowls of salad and pasta, or hotplate dishes (mostly pasta-based).

Njuta (☎ 10 19 00; Kungsgatan 4; lunch from Skr69, mains Skr130-170; ⊙ 11am-10pm Mon-Thu, 11am-1am Fri & Sat, noon-midnight Sun) Formerly the ubertrendy

---

DETOURS: SIGURDSRISTNINGEN

The vivid, 3m-long Viking Age rock carving **Sigurdsristningen** (admission free; ☉ 24hr) illustrates the story of Sigurd the Dragon Slayer, a hero whose adventures are described in *Beowulf* and the Icelandic sagas. The story inspired Wagner's *Ring Cycle*, and *The Hobbit* and *Lord of the Rings* also borrow from it.

Carved into the bedrock around AD 1000, the carving shows Sigurd roasting the heart of the dragon Fafnir over a fire. Sigurd's step-father Regin has persuaded him to kill Fafnir for the dragon's golden treasure. Sigurd touches the heart to see if it's cooked, then sucks his finger, and voila – he suddenly understands the language of birds. They warn him that Regin is plotting to kill him and keep the treasure, so Sigurd attacks first, chopping off his step-father's head; the unfortunate fellow is shown in the left corner of the carving, among his scattered tools.

The carving is situated near Sundbyholms Slott and Mälaren lake, 12km northeast of Eskilstuna; take bus 225. Get more details at the **Eskilstuna tourist office** (☎ 710 23 75; www.eskilstuna.se; Nygatan 15; ☉ 10am-6pm Mon-Fri, 10am-2pm Sat, plus 10am-2pm Sun May-Aug).

Babar, this sleek hangout is still fashionable with young, hip student types; the menu gets more attention these days and includes tapas and Asian fusion dishes.

Getting There & Away

Long-distance buses, which leave from opposite the train station, operate pretty much everywhere in southern Sweden. From here, **Swebus Express** (☎ 0200-21 82 18; www.swebusexpress.se) has connections to Norrköping, Karlstad and Oslo, Mariestad and Göteborg, Västerås and Uppsala, and Eskilstuna and Stockholm.

Train connections are also good. Direct SJ trains run to/from Stockholm (Skr209, two hours) every hour, some via Västerås (Skr98, one hour); and Göteborg (Skr256, 2¾ hours). Other trains run daily to Gävle (Skr286, three to four hours) and Borlänge (Skr182, 2¼ hours), where you can change for Falun and Mora.

FALUN

☎ 023 / pop 55,000

An unlikely combination of industrial and adorable, Falun is home to the region's most important mine and, as a consequence, the source of the deep red paint that renders Swedish country houses so uniformly cute. It's the main city of Dalarna, putting it within easy striking distance of some of Sweden's best attractions – including the home of painter Carl Larsson, a work of art in itself.

The **tourist office** (☎ 830 50; www.visitfalun.se; Trotzgatan 10-12; ☉ 9am-7pm Mon-Fri, 9am-5pm Sat, 11am-4pm Sun) can help with information.

Sights & Activities

The **Kopparberget copper mine** (☎ 78 20 30; www.kopparberget.com; ☉ daily) was the world's most important by the 17th century and only closed in 1992 (it's now on Unesco's World Heritage List). As a by-product, the mine also provided the red coating that became the characteristic house paint of the age and is still in popular use today. The **mine museum** (adult/under 15yr Skr50/free; ☉ 10am-6pm) contains everything you could possibly want to know about the history, administration, engineering, geology and copper production of the mine. The complex is west of town at the top end of Gruvgatan (take bus 709). One-hour tours (adult/child Skr150/50) explore the bowels of the disused mine (bring warm clothing); call in advance to find out the times of English-language tours. On weekdays from October to April tours must be booked in advance.

Carl Larsson-gården (☎ 600 53; www.carllarsson.se; Sundborn; admission by guided tour only adult/child Skr100/50; ☉ 10am-5pm May-Sep, 11am Mon-Fri Oct-Apr) is the beautiful early-20th-century home of the artist Carl Larsson and his wife Karin in the pretty village of Sundborn (13km from Falun; bus 64). It's a bright, lively house with superb colour schemes, decoration and furniture. Tapestries and embroidery woven by Karin Larsson reveal she was as skilled an artist as her husband. Admission is by 45-minute guided tour only; call in advance for times of English tours.

There's more folk culture at **Dalarnas Museum** (☎ 76 55 00; www.dalarnasmuseum.se; Stigaregatan 2-4; admission free; ☉ 10am-5pm Tue-Fri, noon-5pm Sat & Sun), along with some cutting-edge temporary exhibits of Swedish artists.

Falun's oldest building is the late-14th-century **Stora Kopparbergs Kyrka** (☎ 546 00; Kyrkbacksvägen 8; ☒ 10am-6pm Mon-Fri, 10am-6pm Sat, 9am-6pm Sun), with brick vaulting and folk-art flowers running round the walls.

Hopptornen (☎ 835 61; ☒ 10am-6pm Sun-Thu, 10am-11pm Fri & Sat mid-May–mid-Aug), the tower and ski jump in the hills behind the town, has great views; you can either walk or take a lift to the top (Skr20).

Sleeping & Eating

Falu Fängelse Vandrarhem (☎ 79 55 75; info@falufangelse .se; Villavägen 17; dm/s Skr210/300; ☒) The SVIF hostel really feels like what it is – a former prison. Dorm beds are in cells, with heavy iron doors and thick walls, concrete floors, steel lockers for closets etc. The place is extremely friendly, and common areas are spacious and full of well-worn, den-like furniture. The shower/toilet facilities are somewhat limited, so it's worth asking for a room with bathroom if available.

Hotel Falun (☎ 291 80; Trotzgatan 16; s Skr520-620, d Skr620-720; ☒) There are some good hotel choices right by the tourist office, including this place which has comfortable modern rooms (cheaper rooms have private toilet and shared shower).

Kopparhattan Café & Restaurang (☎ 191 69; Stigaregatan 2-4; lunch buffet Skr80; mains Skr75-150) An excellent choice is this funky, arty cafe-restaurant, attached to Dalarnas Museum. Choose from sandwiches, soup or a good vegetarian buffet for lunch, and light veggie, fish and meat evening mains. There's an outside terrace overlooking the river, and live music on Friday nights in summer.

As ever, kebab shops and pizza joints abound. For self-caterers, there's a centrally located **ICA supermarket** (Falugatan 1) and a **Systembolaget** (Åsgatan 19).

Getting There & Away

Falun isn't on the main train lines – change at Borlänge when coming from Stockholm or Mora – but there are direct trains to and from Gävle (Skr129, 1¼ hours, roughly every two hours), or regional buses (Skr97, two hours) equally often.

Swebus Express (☎ 0200-21 82 18; www.swebusex press.se) has buses on the Göteborg–Karlstad–Falun–Gävle route, and connections to buses on the Stockholm–Borlänge–Mora route.

Regional transport is run by **Dalatrafik** (☎ 0771-95 95 95; www.dalatrafik.se, in Swedish), which covers all corners of the county of Dalarna.

Tickets cost Skr20 for trips within a zone, and Skr15 extra for each new zone. A 31-day *länskort* costs Skr1000 and allows you to travel throughout the county; cards in smaller increments are also available. Regional bus 70 goes approximately hourly to Rättvik (Skr50, one hour) and Mora (Skr80, 1¾ hours).

LAKE SILJAN REGION

This pretty, traditional area in the county of Dalarna is a popular summer- and winter-sports destination, with reasonable-sized towns offering good facilities and attractions. The area is a very popular summer destination, with numerous outdoor festivals and attractions. Maps of Siljansleden, an excellent network of walking and cycling paths extending for more than 300km around Lake Siljan, are available from tourist offices for Skr20. Another way to enjoy the lake is by boat: in summer, **M/S Gustaf Wasa** (☎ 070-542 10 25; www .wasanet.nu; cruises Skr80-275) runs a complex range of lunch, dinner and sightseeing cruises from the towns of Mora, Rättvik and Leksand. Ask at any tourist office or go online for a schedule.

Leksand

☎ 0247 / pop 15,500

Leksand's claim to fame is its Midsummer Festival, the most popular in Sweden, in which around 20,000 spectators fill the bowl-shaped green park on the first Friday evening after 21 June to sing songs and watch costumed dancers circle the maypole. The **tourist office** (☎ 79 61 30; leksand@siljan.se; Norsgatan 40; ☒ 9am-7pm Mon-Fri, 10am-5pm Sat & Sun mid-Jun–mid-Aug, 10am-5pm Mon-Fri rest of yr), is on the main drag.

Leksands Kyrka (☎ 807 00; Kyrkallén), with its distinctive onion dome, dates from the early 13th century. Nearby is **Leksands Konstmuseum** (☎ 79 79 74; Kyrkallén 8; adult/child Skr50/free; ☒ 11am-4pm May-Aug), which is fairly small but hosts strong collections of work by both young and well-established regional artists.

There are a couple of direct intercity trains every day running from Stockholm to Leksand (Skr240, three hours). Bus 58 regularly connects Leksand with Tällberg (Skr35, 20 minutes), and bus 258 goes to Rättvik (Skr50, 20 to 50 minutes).

Rättvik & Around

☎ 0248 / pop 10,900

Laidback Rättvik has sandy lakeside beaches for summer and ski slopes for winter. Don't miss the longest wooden pier in Sweden, the 625m **Långbryggan**. Views from surrounding hills are excellent. The **tourist office** (☎ 79 72 10; rattvik@siljan.se; Riksvägen 40; ◷ 10am-7pm Mon-Fri, 10am-5pm Sat & Sun mid-Jun–mid-Aug, 10am-5pm Mon-Fri rest of yr) is at the train station.

By the lake northwest of the train station, the 13th-century **church**, rebuilt in 1793, has 87 well-preserved **church stables**, the oldest dating from 1470.

Inviting all sorts of bad puns about rocking out, **Dalhalla** (☎ 79 79 50; www.dalhalla.se) is an old limestone quarry 7km north of Rättvik used as an open-air theatre and concert venue in summer; the acoustics are incredible and the setting is stunning.

Tiny **Tällberg**, midway between Rättvik and Leksand, is a pretty village of wooden buildings scattered like a handful of rubies along a hillside, and it's nearly as expensive if you want to stay the night. It has a population of around 200 and eight upmarket hotels. But it's a lovely place to enjoy lunch and have a wander. The **Tällberg** (www.infotallberg.nu, in Swedish) website has links to all the hotels. Bus 58 between Rättvik and Leksand stops in the village regularly, and it's worth going just for the scenic landscape along the route.

On the lakeshore near the train station is **Siljansbadets Camping** (☎ 516 91; www.siljansbadet .com; camp sites low/high season Skr130/200, 4-bed cabins from Skr350/450; ◷ May-Oct). **Rättviksparken** (☎ 561 10; rattviksparken@rattviksparken.fh.se; Furudalsvägen 1; camp sites low/high season Skr130/170, cabins from Skr425) is by the river off Centralgatan (1km from the train station).

By Rättviksparken camping ground is the highly rated hostel **STF Vandrarhem Rättvik** (☎ 105 66; Centralgatan; dm Skr150; ◷ reception 8-10am & 5-6pm; ℗ 🖳), in a charming complex of old wooden buildings.

The picturesque, church-run **Stiftsgården Rättvik** (☎ 510 20; www.stiftsgarden.org; Kyrkvägen 2; s with shared bathroom Skr380, s with/without shower Skr640/525, d with/without shower Skr1020/760) is by the lake, away from the hustle and bustle of town but within easy walking distance and near footpaths and outdoor activities. Rooms are simple but pleasant; breakfast is included, and lunch/dinner is available for Skr80/95. Canoes and cycles can be hired.

The cheapest eateries are opposite the train station, and Storgatan is home to a few supermarkets. **Restaurang Anna** (☎ 126 81; Vasagatan 3; dishes Skr75-100; ◷ noon-9pm Tue-Sun, to 10pm Fri &

Sat) has Thai and Chinese fixed-price menus (Skr100 to Skr110) and takeaway.

Buses depart from outside the train station. Dalatrafik's bus 70 runs regularly between Falun, Rättvik and Mora. A couple of direct intercity trains per day from Stockholm (Skr263, 3½ hours) stop at Rättvik (otherwise you have to change at Borlänge). Local trains run often between Rättvik and Mora (Skr53, 25 minutes).

Mora
☎ 0250 / pop 20,100

Legend has it that in 1520 Gustav Vasa arrived here, in a last-ditch attempt to start a rebellion against the Danish regime. The people of Mora weren't interested, and Gustav was forced to put on his skis and flee for the border. After he left, the town reconsidered and two yeomen, Engelbrekt and Lars, volunteered to follow Gustav's tracks, finally overtaking him in Sälen and changing Swedish history.

Today the world's biggest cross-country ski race **Vasaloppet**, which ends in Mora, commemorates this epic chase. Around 15,000 people take part on the first Sunday in March. In summer, you can walk the route on the 90km **Vasaloppsleden**.

The **tourist office** (☎ 59 20 20; mora@siljan.se; ◷ 10am-5pm Mon-Fri, 10am-2pm Sat; closed Mon mid-Sep–mid-Nov) is at the train station.

Even if you have no interest in skiing, you may be pleasantly surprised by the excellent **Vasaloppsmuseet** (☎ 392 25; www.vasaloppet.se; Vasagatan; adult/child Skr30/10; ◷ 10am-5pm mid-Jun–mid-Sep, 10am-5pm Mon-Fri mid-Sep–mid-Jun), which really communicates the passion behind the world's largest cross-country skiing event.

Mora's other big draw is the **Zornmuseet** (☎ 59 23 10; www.zorn.se; Vasagatan 36; adult/up to 15yr Skr50/free; ◷ 9am-5pm Mon-Sat, 11am-5pm Sun mid-May–mid-Sep, noon-5pm Mon-Sat, 1-5pm Sun rest of yr), which displays many of the best-loved portraits and characteristic nudes of the Mora painter Anders Zorn (1860–1920), one of Sweden's most renowned artists. Next door, the Zorn family house **Zorngården** (☎ 59 23 10; Vasagatan 36; admission & tour adult/7-15yr Skr60/20; ◷ 10am-4pm Mon-Sat, 11am-4pm Sun mid-May–mid-Sep, noon-3pm Mon-Sat, 1-4pm Sun rest of yr) reflects Zorn's National Romantic aspirations (check out the Viking-influenced hall and entryway). Access is by guided tour (every 15 minutes in summer; phone ahead for English tours).

SWEDEN

Traditional wooden Dala horses are painted in bright, cheerful colours, and to many they represent the original, genuine symbol of Sweden. The most reputable are made by **Nils Olsson Hemslöjd** (☎ 372 00; www.nohemslojd.se; ☺ 8am-6pm Mon-Fri, 9am-5pm Sat & Sun mid-Jun–mid-Aug, 8am-5pm Mon-Fri, 10am-2pm Sat rest of yr) at Nusnäs, 10km southeast of Mora (bus 108, three per day Monday to Friday).

Outside the town of Orsa (16km north of Mora) is **Grönklitt Björnpark** (☎ 462 00; www.orsa gronklitt.se; family/adult/6-15yr Skr380/140/100; ☺ 10am-6pm mid-Jun–Aug, 10am-3pm rest of yr), where you can see bears, wolves and lynxes in fairly natural surrounds. The bears are usually fed around noon, when you'll get a great view of them. Bus 118 runs from Mora to Grönklitt, via Orsa (twice daily weekdays, once on Sunday).

SLEEPING & EATING

There are a few old-style cafes on Kyrkogatan, plus fast-food joints and supermarkets. All the hotels also have pub-restaurants.

Målkull Ann's Restaurang, B&B & Vandrarhem (☎ 381 96; www.maalkullann.se; Vasagatan 19; dm/s/d Skr170/320/500, B&B s/d from Skr550/880, with bathroom Skr600/960, pensionat r from Skr720; 🖳) Housed in a series of variously rustic buildings is this hostel/B&B near the Vasaloppet museum. The STF hostel (at Fredsgatan 6) is part of the same complex. Call ahead, as reception hours vary a lot depending on the season.

Mora Parken (☎ 276 00; moraparken@mora.se; tent & car Skr160, 2-/4-bed cabins from Skr270/400, hotel s/d Skr995/1295; 🖳) This campsite and hotel are combined in a great waterside spot, 400m northwest of the church, and both have solid facilities.

Mora Hotell & Spa (☎ 59 26 50; www.morahotell.se; Strandgatan 12; s/d from Skr1170/1350; 🖳 🛋) There's been a hotel here since 1830, although the current version is as modern as it gets, with all the facilities you'd expect from a big chain plus personality. Rooms combine clean lines, wooden floors and earthtones with bright folk-art accents. Head to the spa for steam rooms, Jacuzzis, massage and body treatments.

Claras Restaurang (☎ 158 98; Vasagatan 38; lunch Skr75, mains Skr110-190) In the picturesque old town, near the Zorn museum, you'll find convivial Claras, with excellent service and a menu of filling staples. Try the wonderful dessert of deep-fried camembert with warm cloudberries.

GETTING THERE & AWAY

All Dalatrafik buses use the bus station at Moragatan 23. Bus runs to Rättvik and Falun, and buses 103, 104, 105 and 245 run to Orsa. Once or twice daily, bus 170 goes to Älvdalen, Särna, Idre and Grövelsjön, near the Norwegian border.

Mora is an **SJ** (☎ 0771-75 75 75; www.sj.se) train terminus and the southern terminus of Inlandsbanan (Inland Railway), which runs north to Gällivare (mid-June to mid-August). The main train station is about 1km east of town. The more central Mora Strand is a platform station in town, but not all trains stop there, so check the timetable. When travelling to Östersund, you can choose between Inlandsbanan (Skr395, 6¼ hours, one daily, June to August only) or bus 45 (Skr250, 5¼ hours, four daily).

SKÅNE

Artists adore southern Sweden. Down here, the light is softer, the foliage brighter, and the shoreline more dazzling and white. Sweden's southernmost county, Skåne (Scania) was Danish property until 1658 and still flaunts its differences. You can detect them in the strong dialect (skånska), in the half-timbered houses, and in Skåne's hybrid flag: a Swedish yellow cross on a red Danish background.

MALMÖ

☎ 040 / pop 280,801

Once dismissed as crime-prone and tatty, Sweden's third-largest city has rebranded itself as progressive and downright cool. Malmö's second wind blew in with the opening of the Öresund bridge and tunnel in 2000, connecting the city to bigger, cooler Copenhagen and creating a dynamic new urban conglomeration. Such a cosmopolitan outcome seems only natural for what is Sweden's most multicultural metropolis; 150 nationalities make up Malmö's headcount. Here, Nordic reserve is countered by hot cars with doof-doof stereos and exotic Middle Eastern street stalls.

Information

Forex (Centralstationen; ☺ 7am-9pm) Currency exchange; several branches around town.

Malmö Card The discount card covers free bus transport, street parking, entry to several museums and discounts at other attractions and on sightseeing tours; Skr130/160/190 for one/two/three days – the price includes one adult and up to two children under 16. Buy it at the tourist office.

Skånegården (☎ 040-20 96 00; www.skane.com; Stortorget 9, SE-21122 Malmö; ⓨ 9am-8pm Mon-Fri, 9am-4pm Sat & Sun mid-Jun–mid-Aug, 9am-6pm Mon-Fri, 9am-4pm Sat & Sun early–mid-Jun & mid–late Aug, 9am-5pm Mon-Fri, 10am-3pm Sat & Sun Sep, 9am-5pm Mon-Fri, 10am-3pm Sat rest of year) Tourist office, on the E20, 800m from the Öresund bridge tollgate. Designed for motorists entering from Denmark.

Tourist office (☎ 34 12 00; www.malmo.se; ⓨ 9am-7pm Mon-Fri, 10am-4pm Sat & Sun mid-Jun–early Sep, 9am-6pm Mon-Fri & 10am-3pm Sat & Sun late May–mid-Jun, 9am-5pm Mon-Fri, 10am-3pm Sat rest of year) Inside Centralstationen (train station); has free internet hotel-booking service. Bookings made at the tourist office incur a Skr70 booking fee.

Sights & Activities

The cobbled streets and interesting buildings around **Lilla Torg** are restored parts of the late-medieval town – the oldest of the half-timbered houses here was built in 1597. Houses are now occupied by galleries, boutiques and restaurants.

Various museums in and around **Malmöhus Slott** (castle) make up the **Malmö Museer** (☎ 34 44 37; www.malmo.se/museer; Malmöhusvägen; combined admission adult/7-15yr Skr40/10, free with Malmökortet; ⓨ 10am-4pm Jun-Aug, noon-4pm Sep-May). There are cafe-restaurants inside all the museums.

You can walk through the royal apartments, see the **Stadsmuseum** with its Malmö collection, and see works by important Swedish artists such as John Bauer and Sigrid Hjerten at the **Konstmuseum**.

Malmö Konsthall (☎ 34 12 94; www.konsthall .malmo.se; St Johansgatan 7; admission free; ⓨ 11am-5pm, to 9pm Wed during exhibitions only), south of central Malmö, is one of Europe's largest contemporary art spaces, with exhibitions spanning both Swedish and foreign talent.

Form/Design Center (☎ 664 51 50; Lilla Torg 9; admission free; ⓨ 11am-5pm Tue, Wed & Fri, 11am-6pm Thu, 11am-4pm Sat & Sun) showcases cutting-edge design, architecture and art. The surrounding cobbled streets are restored pockets of the late-medieval town; the half-timbered houses now housing **galleries** and **boutiques** selling some brilliant arts and crafts.

The northwest harbour redevelopment is home to the **Turning Torso**, a striking skyscraper that twists through 90 degrees from bottom to top. Designed by Spaniard Santiago Calatrava and inaugurated in 2005, it's now Sweden's tallest building (190m).

To scoot round Malmö's canals in a pedal boat, head to **City Boats Malmö** (☎ 0704-71 00 67; www.cityboats.se; Amiralsbron, Södra Promenaden; per 30/60min Skr80/130; ⓨ daily May-Aug, Sat & Sun Sep), just east of Gustav Adolfs Torg.

Sleeping

Private rooms or apartments from about Skr375 per person are available through **City Room** (☎ 795 94; www.cityroom.se); bedsheets and towels cost an additional Skr100 per set. The agency has no office address but is staffed on weekdays from 9am to noon. Otherwise, contact the tourist office.

STF Vandrarhem Malmö (☎ 822 20; www.mal mohostel.com; Backavägen 18; dm Skr150-190, s/d from Skr315/410; Ⓟ 🖳) Well-equipped, if rather large and impersonal, the STF hostel sits 3.5km south of the city centre, overlooking the E6 (take bus 2 from Centralstationen).

Bosses Gästvåningar (☎ 32 62 50; info@bosses.nu; Södra Förstadsgatan 110B; s/d/tr/q from Skr350/495/595/750; 🖳) The quiet, clean rooms in this central SVIF hostel are like those of a budget hotel, with proper beds, TVs and shared bathrooms. Service is helpful and it's close to Möllevångstorget and opposite the town hospital (follow the signs for 'Sjukhuset' if arriving by car).

Hotel Duxiana (☎ 607 70 00; bokning@malmo.hotel duxiana.com; Mäster Johansgatan 1; s/d/ste Skr1190/2090/2590; 🖳) Close to Centralstationen, ubersleek Hotel Duxiana is one for the style crew. In a palate of white, black and gunmetal grey, design features include Bruno Mattheson sofas and the same heavenly beds supplied to the world's first seven-star hotel in Dubai. Single rooms are small but comfy, while the decadent junior suites feature a clawed bathtub facing the bed.

Mäster Johan Hotel (☎ 664 64 00; reservation @masterjohan.se; Mäster Johansgatan 13; s/d Skr2375/2625; Ⓟ 🖳) Just off Lilla Torg is one of Malmös finest slumber spots, with spacious, elegantly understated rooms featuring beautiful oak floors and snowy-white fabrics. Bathrooms flaunt Paloma Picasso–designed tiles, there's a sauna and gym, and the immaculate breakfast buffet is served in a glass-roofed courtyard.

SWEDEN

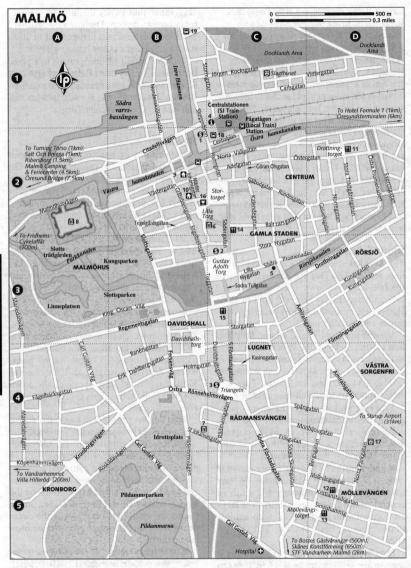

MALMÖ

Eating & Drinking

Malmö isn't short on dining experiences, whether its vegan grub chowed down in a grungy left-wing hangout or designer supping on contemporary Nordic flavours. For sheer atmosphere, head to the restaurant-bars on Lilla Torg: **Victors** (☎ 12 76 70), **Moosehead** (☎ 12 04 23) and **Mello Yello** (☎ 30 45 25) are all

great spots with affable service and alfresco summer seating (you may have to wait for a table).

Dolce Sicilia (☎ 611 31 10; Drottningtorget 6; gelato from Skr25; ☑ 11am-9pm May-Aug, 11am-7pm Mar, Apr & Sep) Run by certified Sicilians. Head here for fresh, organic Italian-style gelato (the chilli chocolate and fig flavours are divine).

Savoury edibles include ciabatta (Skr55) and salads (Skr65).

Solde (☎ 692 80 87; Regementsgatan 3; panini Skr40; ☒ closed Sun) Malmö's coolest cafe is a grit-chic combo of concrete bar, white-tiled walls, art exhibitions and indie-hip regulars. The owner is an award-winning barista; watch him in action over lip-smacking Italian panini, biscotti and *cornetti* (croissants).

Glassfabriken (☎ 23 81 01; Kristianstadsgatan 16; meals around Skr50; ☒ closed Mon) Easy to miss, this grungy, alcohol-free cafe/cultural bolthole cranks out cheap, salubrious grub like vegan salads, ciabatta, and freshly-baked cakes. Play boardgames over mango milkshakes, check out the local art on display or catch the occasional music or theatre gig.

Krua Thai (☎ 12 22 87; Möllevångstorget 14; mains Skr79-95; ☒ 11am-3pm Mon, 11am-3pm & 5-10pm Tue-Fri, 1-10pm Sat, 2-10pm Sun) Down the southern end of town is this authentic, long-standing Thai joint. The family also run a central takeaway (Södergatan 22) for spicy meals on the move.

Salt och Brygga (☎ 611 59 40; Sundspromenaden 7, Västra Hamnen; mains Skr195-250; ☒ lunch & dinner, closed Sat & Sun autumn & winter) Overlooking the Öresund bridge, this stylish, contemporary Slow Food restaurant serves contemporary Swedish cuisine with a clear conscience. Everything is organic (including the staff's uniforms), waste is turned into Biogas, and the interior is allergy-free. Flavours are clean and strictly seasonal – think rhubarb soup with lemon verbena, Tahitian vanilla ice cream and Tonka beans. Book ahead.

Entertainment

Debaser (☎ 23 98 80; Norra Parkgatan 2; ☒ 7pm-3am Wed-Sun) Stockholm's music club heavyweight has opened shop in Malmö, with live gigs and club nights spanning anything from indie, pop and hip-hop to soul, electronica and rock. There's a buzzing outdoor bar/lounge overlooking Folkets Park and decent grub till 10pm for a pre-party feed.

Getting There & Away

Sturup airport (☎ 613 10 00; www.malmoairport.se) is situated 33km southeast of Malmö. **SAS** (☎ 0770-72 77 27; www.sas.se) has up to 11 non-stop flights to Stockholm Arlanda daily. **Malmö Aviation** (☎ 0771-55 00 10; www.malmoaviation.se) flies several times daily to Stockholm Bromma airport. International destinations include Antalya, Budapest, Gran Canaria and Heraklon.

Trains run directly from Malmö to Copenhagen's main airport (Skr95, 35 minutes, every 20 minutes), which has a much wider flight selection.

Flygbuss (☎ 0771-77 77 77; www.flygbussarna.com) runs from Centralstationen to Sturup airport (adult/16 to 25/under 16 accompanied by adult Skr99/79/free, 40 minutes) roughly every 40 minutes on weekdays, with six services on Saturday and seven on Sunday; a taxi shouldn't cost more than Skr400.

There are two bus terminals with daily departures to Swedish and European destinations. **Travelshop** (Malmö Buss & Resecenter; ☎ 33 05 70; www.travelshop.se; Skeppsbron 10), north of the train station by the harbour, services (and sells tickets for) several companies, including **Swebus Express** (☎ 0771-21 82 18; www.swebusexpress.com), which runs two to four times daily to Stockholm (Skr400 to Skr600, 8½ hours), four times to Jönköping (Skr293, 4½ hours) and up to 10 times daily to Göteborg (Skr270, three

SWEDEN

to four hours); five continue to Oslo (Skr442, eight hours).

The second long-distance bus terminal, **Öresundsterminalen** (☎ 59 09 00; Terminalgatan 10) is reached via bus 35 from Centralstationen to Arlöv (Skr16; 30 minutes). From here, **Svenska Buss** (☎ 0771-67 67 67; www.svenskabuss.se) runs a service to Stockholm (Skr400, 11 hours) via Karlskrona, four times weekly.

Säfflebussen (☎ 0771-15 15 15; www.safflebus sen.se) has six buses on the Copenhagen–Malmö–Göteborg route per day, with a couple originating from Berlin and continuing on to Oslo.

Pågatågen (local trains) run regularly to Helsingborg (Skr94, one hour), Landskrona (Skr81, 40 minutes), Lund (Skr44, 15 minutes), Simrishamn (Skr84, 1½ hours), Ystad (Skr72, 50 minutes), and other destinations in Skåne (bicycles are half-fare, but not allowed during peak times, except during mid-June to mid-August). The platform is at the end of Centralstationen and you buy tickets from the machine. International rail passes are accepted.

The integrated Öresundregionen transport system operates trains from Helsingborg via Malmö and Copenhagen to Helsingør. The Malmö to Copenhagen Kastrup airport or Copenhagen central station trips take 20 and 35 minutes, respectively (both journeys Skr95); trains leave every 20 minutes.

X2000 (Skr281, 2½ hours) and regional (Skr294, 3¼ hours) trains run several times daily to/from Göteborg. X2000 (Skr422 to Skr1000, 4½ hours, hourly) and Intercity (Skr642, 6½ hours, infrequent) trains run between Stockholm and Malmö.

Getting Around

The customer service desks in Centralstationen, at Gustav Adolfs Torg and at Värnhemstorget (at the eastern end of Kungsgatan) provide bus information and tickets. Local tickets cost Skr16 for one hour's travel. The bus hubs are Centralplan (in front of Centralstationen), Gustav Adolfs Torg, Värnhemstorget and Triangeln. *Malmökortet* includes city bus travel.

LUND
☎ 046 / pop 105,286
Centred around a striking cathedral (complete with a giant in the crypt and a magical clock), learned Lund is a soulful blend of leafy parks, medieval abodes, and coffee-sipping bookworms. Like most university hubs, however, it loses some of its buzz during the summer, when students head home for the holidays.

The **tourist office** (☎ 35 50 40; www.lund.se; Kyrkogatan 11; ☯ 10am-7pm Mon-Fri, 10am-3pm Sat, 11am-3pm Sun mid-Jun–Aug, 10am-5pm Mon-Fri, 10am-3pm Sat May–mid-Jun & Sep, 10am-5pm Mon-Fri Oct-Apr) is opposite the cathedral.

Sights & Activities

The spectacular **Kulturen** (☎ 35 04 00; www.kulturen .com; Tegnerplatsen; adult/child Skr70/free; ☯ 11am-5pm mid-Apr–Sep, noon-4pm Tue-Sun Oct–mid-Apr) opened in 1892, is a huge open-air museum filling two whole blocks. Its 30-odd buildings include everything from the meanest birch-bark hovel to grand 17th-century houses. The popular outdoor cafe flanks several **rune stones**.

The magnificence of Lund's Romanesque **domkyrkan** (cathedral) is well publicised, but for a surprise, visit at noon or 3pm (1pm and 3pm Sunday and holidays) when the astronomical clock strikes up.

Behind the cathedral, **Historiska Museet** (☎ 222 79 44; Kraftstorg; adult/under 18yr Skr30/free; ☯ 11am-4pm Tue-Fri, noon-4pm Sun) has a large collection of pre-Viking Age finds, including a 7000-year-old skeleton. It's joined with **Domkyrkomuseet**, which explores the history of the church in the area; the rooms filled with countless statues of the crucified Christ are supremely creepy.

Sleeping & Eating

The tourist office can book private rooms from Skr300 per person plus a Skr50 fee.

STF Vandrarhem Lund Tåget (☎ 14 28 20; www .trainhostel.com; Vävaregatan 22; dm Skr150) This quirky hostel is based in old railway carriages in parkland behind the station. The triple bunks and tiny rooms are okay if you're cosying up with loved ones, but a little claustrophobic with strangers. Less novel are the hot water vending machines in the showers (have a few Skr1 coins handy).

Hotel Ahlström (☎ 211 01 74; info@hotellahlstrom.se; Skomakaregatan 3; s/d with shared bathroom Skr729/895, r with bathroom Skr1100) Lund's oldest hotel is friendly and affordable, and on a quiet, central street. Rooms have parquet floors, cool white walls and washbasins (most bathrooms are shared). Breakfast is brought to your door.

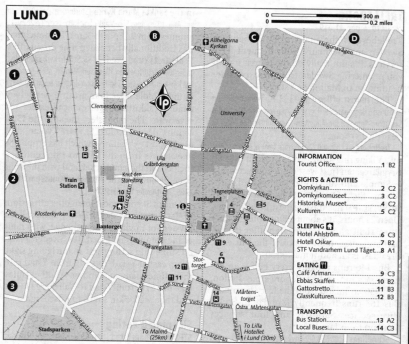

LUND

SWEDEN

Hotell Oskar (☎ 18 80 85; www.hotelloskar.com; Bytaregatan 3; s/d Skr1395/1595; ▣) This dinky place in a 19th-century townhouse has smashing rooms filled with sleek Scandi design. It's also well equipped, with DVD players, kettles and stereos. Breakfast is served in lovely Ebbas Skafferi next door.

Café Ariman (☎ 13 12 63; Kungsgatan 2B; snacks around Skr40; ☺ 11am-midnight Mon, 11-1am Tue-Thu, 11-3am Fri & Sat, 3-11pm Sun, closed Sun in summer) Head to this hip, grungy hangout for cathedral views, strong coffee and a fine cafe fare like ciabatta, salads and burritos. It's popular with leftwing students: think nose-rings, dreads and leisurely chess games. From September to May, DJs hit the decks on Friday and Saturday nights.

Gattostretto (☎ 32 07 77; Kattesund 6A; salads Skr59, mains Skr170-210; ☺ 9am-11pm Mon-Sat) Located over medieval ruins and co-run by an affable Roman chef, this breezy cafe/restaurant serves a tasty slice of *dolce vita*. Guzzle down proper Italian espresso, a slice of *torta rustica*, or long for Rome over hearty ragú, zesty artichoke salad or a hearty *pollo alla cacciatore*.

Ebbas Skafferi (☎ 13 41 56; Bytaregatan 5; lunch Skr65; ☺ 9am-7pm Mon-Fri, to 6pm Sat & Sun) Ebbas is

the perfect cafe: think warm wooden tables, green plants and flowers, odd bits of artwork, a laidback courtyard, and scrumptious coffee, teas, and tasty grub like hearty risotto and moreish cheesecake.

GlassKulturen (Stortorget) The locals will stand in line all afternoon to get a sample of the frozen delights this little ice-cream nook churns out; 50,000 Lund-ites can't be wrong, right?

Getting There & Away

Flygbuss (☎ 0771-77 77 77) runs regularly to Malmö's Sturup airport (Skr99).

It's 15 minutes from Lund to Malmö by train, with frequent local Pågatågen departures (Skr39). Some trains continue to Copenhagen (Skr125, one hour). Other direct services run from Malmö to Kristianstad and Karlskrona via Lund. All long-distance trains from Stockholm or Göteborg to Malmö stop in Lund.

Long-distance buses leave from outside the train station. Most buses to/from Malmö (except buses to Trelleborg and Falsterbo) run via Lund.

TRELLEBORG

☎ 0410 / pop 41,019

Trelleborg is the main gateway between Sweden and Germany, with frequent ferry services. It's not really on the tourist trail: if you're entering Sweden from here, consider heading on to Malmö or Ystad.

The **tourist office** (☎ 73 33 20; www.trelleborg.se/turism; Hamngatan 9; ☒ 9am-7pm Mon-Fri, 10am-6pm Sat, 10am-5pm Sun Jun-Aug, 9am-5pm Mon-Fri Sep-May) is near the harbour.

Trelleborgen (☎ 460 77; admission free) is a 9th-century Viking ring fortress, discovered in 1988 off Bryggaregatan (just west of the town centre).

Simple and functional with shared bathrooms, **Night Stop** (☎ 410 70; Östergatan 59; s/d Skr250/350; ℗) has the cheapest beds in town. Open 24 hours, it's about 500m from the ferry (turn right along Hamngatan after disembarking), diagonally opposite the museum. Breakfast is an additional Skr50.

Bus 146 runs roughly every half-hour between Malmö and Trelleborg's bus station, some 500m inland from the ferry terminals. Bus 165 runs frequently Monday to Friday (five services Saturday and four services Sunday) from Lund.

Scandlines (☎ 650 00; www.scandlines.se) ferries connect Trelleborg to Sassnitz (five daily) and Rostock (two or three daily). **TT-Line** (☎ 562 00; www.ttline.com) ferries shuttle between Trelleborg and Travemünde three to five times daily, and between Trelleborg and Rostock up to three times daily. Buy tickets inside the building housing the tourist office (Hamngatan 9).

YSTAD

☎ 0411 / pop 27,719

Half-timbered houses, rambling cobbled streets and the haunting sound of a night-watchman's horn give this medieval market town an intoxicating lure. Fans of writer Henning Mankell know it as the setting for his best-selling Inspector Wallander crime thrillers, while fans of drums and uniforms head in for the spectacular three-day **Military Tattoo** in August. Ystad is a terminal for ferries to Bornholm and Poland.

The **tourist office** (☎ 57 76 81; www.ystad.se; St Knuts Torg; ☒ 9am-7pm Mon-Fri, 10am-6pm Sat & Sun mid-Jun–mid-Aug, 9am-5pm Mon-Fri rest of yr, plus 11am-2pm Sat mid-May–mid-Jun & late Aug–late Sep) is opposite the train station.

Ever since 1250, a nightwatchman has blown his horn through the little window in the **Sankta Maria Kyrka** (Stortorget; ☒ 10am-6pm Jun-Aug, 10am-4pm Sep-May) clock-tower (every 15 minutes from 9.15pm to 3am). The watchman was traditionally beheaded if he dozed off!

Klostret i Ystad (☎ 57 72 86; St Petri Kyrkoplan; adult/under 16yr Skr50/free; ☒ 10am-5pm Mon-Fri, noon-4pm Sat & Sun Jun-Aug, noon-5pm Tue-Fri, noon-4pm Sat & Sun Sep-May), in the Middle Ages Franciscan monastery of Gråbrödraklostret, features local textiles and silverware. The monastery includes the 13th-century deconsecrated St Petri Kyrkan, now used for art exhibitions, which has around 80 gravestones from the 14th to 18th centuries. Included in the same ticket, and with the same opening hours, is the **Ystads Konstmuseum** (☎ 57 72 85; adult/under 16yr Skr50/free).

One of Skåne's most intriguing attractions is **Ales Stenar** (adult/child Skr20/10) – it has all the mystery of England's Stonehenge, with none of the commercial greed. It's Sweden's largest stone ship setting and an intriguing sight, 19km east of Ystad. Bus 322 from Ystad runs three times daily in summer. At other times, take bus 570 from Ystad to Valleberga kyrka, and then walk 5km south to Kåseberga.

Sleeping & Eating

STF Vandrarhem Ystad (☎ 665 66; kantarellen@turistlogi.se; Fritidsvägen 9; dm Skr170) In a charming sky-blue building is this beachside hostel with good facilities, including bike rental for covering the 2km into the town centre.

Vandrarhemmet Stationen (☎ 0708-57 79 95; ystad.stationen@home.se; dm from Skr200) More convenient is the central SVIF hostel, in the renovated railway building at Ystad train station. Bring cash as credit cards aren't accepted.

There are some lovely eating options among the historic buildings.

Book Café (☎ 134 03; Gåsegränd; ☒ closed Sun & Mon) For soup and sandwiches, seek out the charming Book Café – inside there's a room full of mismatched furniture and books; outside is a leafy courtyard.

Bryggeriet (☎ 699 99; Långgatan 20; mains Skr79-186) Unique and relaxed, this meat-leaning restaurant/pub is in an old brewery. The courtyard is an excellent spot to linger over a well-cooked meal and Ystad Färsköl, a beer brewed on the premises.

Getting There & Away

BOAT

Unity Line (☎ 55 69 00; www.unityline.se) and **Polferries** (☎ 040-12 17 00; www.polferries.se) operate daily crossings between Ystad and Swinoujscie. Ystad's ferry terminal is within walking distance of the train station (drivers follow a more circuitous route).

Bornholmstrafikken (☎ 55 87 00; www.bornholm strafikken.dk) runs frequent ferries and catamarans between Ystad and Rønne, on the Danish island of Bornholm. Catamarans operate from a terminal directly behind the train station.

BUS

Buses depart from outside Ystad train station. Bus 190 runs from Ystad to Trelleborg (Skr63, one hour) via Smygehuk 12 times daily on weekdays, six times on Saturday and twice on Sunday. The direct bus to Simrishamn (Skr45, one hour) via Löderup runs three to nine times daily.

SkåneExpressen bus 6 runs to Lund (Skr81, 1¼ hours, hourly on weekdays, infrequently on weekends) and bus 4 runs three to nine times daily to Kristianstad (Skr63, 1¾ hours). Local train is the only way to get to Malmö.

TRAIN

Pågatågen trains run roughly every hour (fewer on weekends) to/from Malmö (Skr75, 50 minutes). Other local trains run up to 12 times daily to Simrishamn (Skr39, 40 minutes).

HELSINGBORG

☎ 042 / pop 124,986

At its heart, Helsingborg is a sparkly showcase of rejuvenated waterfront, metro-glam restaurants, lively cobbled streets and lofty castle ruins. With Denmark looking on from a mere 4km across the Öresund, its flouncy, turreted buildings feel like a brazen statement.

The **tourist office** (☎ 10 43 50; www.helsingborg.se; Rådhuset, Stortorget; ⏰ 9am-8pm Mon-Fri, 9am-5pm Sat & 10am-3pm Sun mid-Jun–Aug, 10am-6pm Mon-Fri, 10am-2pm Sat Sep–mid-Jun) can help with inquiries.

First Stop Sweden (☎ 10 41 30; www.firststopswe den.com; Bredgatan 2; ⏰ 9am-8pm Mon-Fri, 9am-5pm Sat & Sun late Jun–mid-Aug, 9am-6pm Mon-Fri, 9am-4pm Sat, 9am-2pm Sun late May–late Jun & rest of Aug, 8am-5pm Mon-Fri rest of yr), near the car-ferry ticket booths, dispenses tourist information on the whole country and has an X-Change currency exchange counter.

Sights & Activities

Just north of the transport terminals, the crisp-n'-white **Dunkers Kulturhus** (☎ 10 74 00;

www.dunkerskulturhus.se; Kungsgatan 11; exhibitions adult/ under 18yr Skr70/free; ⏰ 10am-5pm Tue-Sun, to 8pm Thu) houses an interesting town museum and temporary art exhibitions (admission includes entry to both). The building's creator, Danish architect Kim Utzon, is the son of Sydney Opera House architect Jørn Utzon.

From here, saunter along **Norra Hamnen** (the North Harbour), where sleek apartments, restaurants and bars meet docked yachts and preened locals in one rather successful harbour-redevelopment project.

Dramatic steps and archways lead up from Stortorget to the square tower **Kärnan** (☎ 10 59 91; adult/under 16yr Skr20/10; ⏰ 10am-6pm Jun-Aug, closed Mon rest of yr), all that remains of the medieval castle.

Just 2km northeast of the centre, the Fredriksdal area is well worth a visit. Take bus 1 or 7 to the Zoégas bus stop. One of Sweden's best open-air museums, **Fredriksdals Friluftsmuseum** (☎ 10 45 00; www.fredriksdal.helsing borg.se; off Hävertgatan; adult/under 18yr Skr70/free May-Sep, Skr30/free Apr & Oct, admission free Nov-Mar; ⏰ 10am-7pm Jun-Aug, 10am-5pm May & Sep, 11am-4pm Oct-Apr) is based around an 18th-century manor house, with a street of old houses, children's farm, graphics museum, and blissfully leafy grounds.

Sleeping

Helsingborgs Vandrarhem (☎ 14 58 50; info@hbgtur ist.com; Järnvägsgatan 39; dm from Skr195) Despite the somewhat anonymous vibe, Helsingborg's only central hostel offers clean, comfortable rooms located about 200m from Knutpunkten. Reception is open between 3pm and 6pm.

Villa Thalassa (☎ 38 06 60; www.villathalassa.com; Dag Hammarskjöldsväg; dm from Skr200, 2-/4-bed r Skr600/800) This SVIF option is a lovely early 20th-century villa situated in beautiful gardens. Hostel accommodation is in huts, but the hotel-standard rooms (with or without private bathroom) are a cut above if your budget will stretch. The villa lies 3km north of central Helsingborg in the Pålsjö area. Bus 219 stops 500m short, at the Pålsjöbaden bus stop.

Hotel Maria (☎ 24 99 40; www.hotelmaria.se; Mariagatan 8A; s/d from Skr950/1250; ▣) Tucked away behind Olsons Skafferi, Hotel Maria is utterly inspired, with each room flaunting a different historical style. Themes include National Romantic, Art Deco and 1970s disco. Beds are divinely comfy, the staff are friendly, and there's a tapas bar downstairs.

SWEDEN

HELSINGBORG

INFORMATION
First Stop Sweden......................**1** C3
Tourist Office..............................**2** C2

SIGHTS & ACTIVITIES
Dunkers Kulturhus....................**3** B1
Kärnan..**4** C1

SLEEPING
Helsingborgs Vandrarhem........**5** D3
Hotel Maria...............................(see 8)

EATING
Ebbas Fik...................................**6** C2
Koppi..**7** C1
Olsons Skafferi..........................**8** C2
Vegeriet......................................**9** C2

TRANSPORT
ACE Link Ticket Booth & Ferry
   Terminal.................................**10** C2
Bus Station................................**11** C2
HH-Ferries Ticket Booth & Ferry
   Terminal.................................**12** C3
Scandlines Car Ferry Ticket
   Booths...................................**13** C3
Scandlines Foot Passenger Ticket
   Office & Ferry Terminal........**14** C2

Eating & Drinking

Koppi (☎ 13 30 33; Norra Storgatan 16; sandwiches Skr58, salads Skr68 closed Sun) This hip cafe/microroastery is your best bet for top-notch coffee. The savvy young owners sell their own roasted beans, alongside scrumptious edibles like fresh salads and gourmet ciabatta.

Ebbas Fik (☎ 28 14 40; Bruksgatan 20; 9am-6pm Mon-Fri, 9am-4pm Sat) It's still 1955 at this kitschtastic retro cafe, complete with jukebox, retro petrol pump and hamburgers made to Elvis's recipe. The extensive cafe menu also includes (huge) sandwiches, baked potatoes and crazy cakes and buns.

Vegeriet (☎ 24 03 03; Järnvägsgatan 25; lunch around Skr75; closed Sun) Vegetarians adore this appealing cafe-restaurant for tasty, flesh-free versions of quiche, lasagne, tortilla and stir-fries. Vegans aren't forgotten, although the place usually shuts for a month in summer.

Olsons Skafferi (☎ 14 07 80; Mariagatan 6; lunch Skr75-90, dinner mains Skr129-235; lunch & dinner Mon-Sat) Olsons is a super little spot, with alfresco seating on the pedestrian square right in front of Mariakyrkan. It doubles as an Italian deli and cafe, with rustic good looks, span-

gly chandeliers and pasta that would make Bologna proud. The dinner menu offers more elaborate Mediterranean flavours.

Getting There & Away

BOAT

Knutpunkten is the terminal for the frequent **Scandlines** (☎ 18 61 00; www.scandlines.se) car ferry to Helsingør (one way Skr28, car plus nine people Skr335, free with rail passes). Across the inner harbour, **ACE Link** (☎ 38 58 80) has a terminal with a passenger-only ferry to Helsingør every 20 minutes in summer and every 30 minutes the rest of the year (one way Skr44, free with rail passes). There's also a frequent **HH-Ferries** (☎ 19 80 00; www.hhferries .se) service to Helsingør (adult Skr24, car plus nine people Skr300, rail passes not valid).

BUS

The bus terminal is at ground level in Knutpunkten. Regional Skånetrafiken buses dominate (see respective destinations for details), but long-distance services are offered by **Swebus Express** (☎ 0771-21 82 18; www .swebusexpress.com), **Svenska Buss** (☎ 0771-67 67 67;

www.svenskabuss.se) and **Säfflebussen** (☎ 0771-15 15 15; www.safflebussen.se).

All three companies run north to Göteborg (Swebus Express and Säfflebussen services continue to Oslo), and south to Malmö. Swebus Express and Säfflebussen also operate services northeast to Stockholm via Karlstad. Fares to Stockholm cost around Skr500 (7½ hours), to Göteborg Skr250 (three hours), and to Oslo Skr300 (seven hours).

TRAIN

Underground platforms in Knutpunkten serve SJ, Pågatågen and Öresundståg trains, which depart daily for Stockholm (Skr630, five to seven hours), Göteborg (Skr230, 2½ to three hours), nearby towns including Lund (Skr75), Malmö (Skr87), Kristianstad (Skr87) and Halmstad (Skr107) as well as Copenhagen and Oslo.

GÖTALAND

This region has a rich history and plenty to offer the visitor. For one, it's home to Sweden's second city, Göteborg (also known as Gothenburg), with an amusement park for the kids and a huge range of grown-up entertainment. Norrköping, an urban-restoration achievement, has turned its workmanlike heart into a lovely showpiece. Linköping's medieval cathedral is one of Sweden's largest, and in Vadstena there's the abbey established by the country's most important saint, Birgitta. There's also the overwhelming natural beauty of the Bohuslän coast.

VARBERG

☎ 0340 / pop 56,114

A town built for sunsets, Varberg has plenty of hang-out space along the waterfront and some gorgeous views from the **medieval fortress** (☎ 828 30; adult/under 20yr Skr50/free; ♥ 10am-5pm mid-Jun–mid-Aug, 10am-4pm Mon-Fri, noon-4pm Sat & Sun rest of year), which has guided tours and excellent museums. You might also want to brave the brisk Nordic weather and swim at **Kallhusbadet** (☎ 173 96; adult/under 15yr Skr55/30; ♥ 1-8pm Wed mid-Jun–mid-Aug, 9am-5pm Sat & Sun rest of year), a striking bathing house built in Moorish style on stilts above the sea.

The **tourist office** (☎ 868 00; www.turist.varberg .se; Brunnsparken; ♥ 9.30am-7pm Mon-Sat, 1-6pm Sun late

Jun–early Aug, 10am-6pm Mon-Fri, 10am-3pm Sat Apr–late Jun & early Aug–Sep, 10am-5pm Mon-Fri rest of year) is in the centre of town.

Fästningens Vandrarhem (☎ 868 28; vandrar hem@turist.varberg.se; dm/s/d from Skr220/330/515) is within the fortress and offers single rooms in old prison cells or larger rooms in other buildings. Call ahead, as reception hours are very limited. Most dining options are along the pedestrianised Kungsgatan, but the fortress cafe offers the best sea views in town.

Buses depart from outside the train station; local buses run to Falkenberg, but regular trains are your best bet for Halmstad, Göteborg and Malmö. Stena Line ferries operate between Varberg and the Danish town of Grenå; the ferry dock is next to the town centre.

GÖTEBORG

☎ 031 / pop 493,502

Often caught in Stockholm's shadow, gregarious Göteborg (Gothenburg in English) socks a mighty good punch of its own. Some of the country's finest talent hails from its streets, including music icons José González and Soundtrack of Our Lives. Ornate architecture lines its tram-rattled streets and cafes hum with bonhomie. East of Kungsportsavenyn (dubbed the 'Champs Élysées' in brochures and a 'tourist trap' by locals), the Haga and Linné districts buzz with creativity. Fashionistas design fair-trade threads while artists collaborate over mean espressos. Stockholm may represent the 'big time', but many of the best and brightest ideas originate in this grassroots town.

Orientation

Both Centralstationen and the Nordstan shopping centre sit at the northern end of central Göteborg. From here, shop-lined Östra Hamngatan leads southeast through town. Upon crossing one of the city's few-remaining 17th-century canals, it becomes Kungsportsavenyn (known simply as 'Avenyn'). Directly west is the Vasastan district, with a cooler selection of shops, bars and eateries. Further west is the picture-perfect Haga District, followed by the boho-grunge of the Linné district, west of Jarntorget.

SWEDEN

Information

DISCOUNT CARDS & PACKAGES

The brilliant Göteborg Pass discount card is well worth bagging, even if all you're planning to do is park in Göteborg (home to Sweden's priciest street parking and most dedicated traffic wardens). Other perks include free or reduced admission to a bundle of attractions (including Liseberg and the museums), plus free city sightseeing tours, and travel by public transport within the region. The card costs Skr225/160 per adult/child for 24 hours, Skr310/225 for 48 hours. It's available at tourist offices, hotels, Pressbyrån newsagencies and online at www.goteborg.com.

Göteborgspaketet is an accommodation package offered at various hotels with prices starting at Skr475 per person per night. It includes the Göteborg Pass for the number of nights you stay. You can book the package in advance over the internet or telephone the tourist office on ☎ 61 25 00. More expensive packages include theatre or concert tickets, casino passes, spa visits etc.

INTERNET ACCESS

Sidewalk Express (www.sidewalkexpress.se; per hr Skr19) For internet access, at Centralstationen and the 7-Eleven shop on Vasaplatsen.

MEDICAL SERVICES

Apotek Vasan (☎ 0771-45 04 50; Nordstan complex; ⏰ 8am-10pm) Late-night pharmacy.

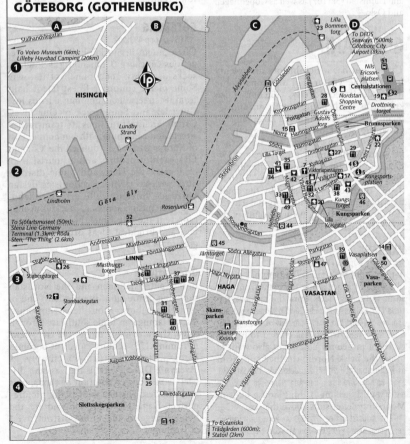

GÖTEBORG (GOTHENBURG)

Östra Sjukhuset (☎ 343 40 00) Major hospital about 5km northeast of central Göteborg, near the terminus at the end of tramline 1.

MONEY

Forex (☎ 0200-22 22 20; www.forex.se) Centralstationen (🕒 7am-9pm Mon-Sun); Kungsportsavenyn 22 (🕒 9am-7pm Mon-Fri, 10am-4pm Sat); Kungsportsplatsen (🕒 9am-7pm Mon-Fri, 10am-4pm Sat); Landvetter airport (🕒 5am-9pm Mon-Fri, 5am-8pm Sat, 5am-7pm Sun); Norstan Complex (🕒 9am-7pm Mon-Fri, 10am-6pm Sat, 11am-5pm Sun) Foreign-exchange office with numerous branches.

TOURIST OFFICES

Branch tourist office (Nordstan complex; 🕒 10am-6pm Mon-Fri, 10am-6pm Sat, noon-5pm Sun)

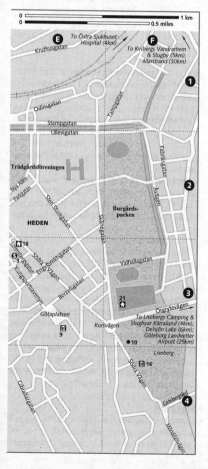

Main tourist office (☎ 61 25 00; www.goteborg.com; Kungsportsplatsen 2; 🕒 9.30am-8pm mid-Jun—mid-Aug, 9am-5pm Mon-Fri, 10am-2pm Sat Sep-Apr, 9.30am-6pm Mon-Fri, 10am-2pm Sat & Sun May—mid-Jun & end Aug) Central and busy, it has a good selection of free brochures and maps.

Sights

LISEBERG

Scream yourself silly at this mighty **theme park** (☎ 40 01 00; www.liseberg.se; adult/under 7yr Skr70/ free; 🕒 to 10pm or 11pm most days May-Aug, to 9pm or 10pm during Christmas period), southeast of the city centre. Sweden's largest, it draws more than three million visitors every year (and sometimes it feels as though they're all visiting at once!). Blockbuster rides include the 90km/h wooden rollercoaster Balder and the stomach-churning Kanonen, where you're blasted from 0 to 75km/h in less than two seconds. For views of the city without losing your lunch, the ride to the top of the Liseberg Tower, 83m above the ground, climaxes in a slow spinning dance with a breathtaking panorama.

Each ride costs between one and four coupons (Skr20 each) per go, but it probably makes sense to buy a pass (one/two days Skr290/380). Opening hours are complex – check the website. To get there, take tram 4 or 5, and enter from Örgrytevägen or Getebergsled.

MUSEUMS

After Liseberg the museums are Göteborg's strongest attractions. If several take your fancy, purchase the Göteborg Pass.

The striking **Universeum** (☎ 335 64 50; www .universeum.se; Södra Vägen 50; low season adult/4-16yr/family Skr145/95/440, high season Skr165/135/540; 🕒 10am-7pm late Jun–Aug, 10am-6pm Sep–late Jun) is a huge and impressive 'science discovery centre' featuring everything from rainforests to a shark tank.

The **Stadsmuseum** (☎ 61 27 70; Östindiska huset, Norra Hamngatan 12; adult/under 25yr Skr40/free; 🕒 10am-5pm May-Aug, 10am-5pm Tue-Sun, to 8pm Wed rest of year) has archaeological, local and historical collections, including Sweden's only original Viking ship.

Konstmuseet (☎ 61 29 80; www.konstmuseum .goteborg.se; Götaplatsen; adult/under 25yr Skr40/free, during special exhibitions adult Skr60; 🕒 11am-6pm Tue & Thu, 11am-9pm Wed, 11am-5pm Fri-Sun) boasts works by the French impressionists, Rubens, Van Gogh, Rembrandt, Picasso, as well as Scandinavian masters like Bruno Liljefors, Edvard Munch,

SWEDEN

Anders Zorn and Carl Larsson, plus the Hasselblad photo collection.

The excellent **Röhsska Museet** (☎ 61 38 50; www.designmuseum.se; Vasagatan 37; adult/under 20yr Skr40/free; Ⓥ noon-8pm Tue, noon-5pm Wed-Fri, 11am-5pm Sat & Sun) covers modern Scandinavian design and decorative arts, but also contains classical and Oriental items, and a design store and popular cafe.

Göteborg's **Maritiman** (☎ 10 59 50; Packhuskajen; adult/7-15yr Skr80/40; Ⓥ 10am-6pm Jun-Sep, 10am-4pm Apr, May & Oct, 10am-4pm Fri-Sun Mar & Nov) consists of 20 historical crafts, including fishing boats, a light vessel and a firefighter, linked by walkways.

The main museum of maritime history, **Sjöfartsmuseet** (☎ 368 35 50; www.sjofartsmuseum .goteborg.se; Karl Johansgatan 1-3; adult/under 25yr Skr40/free; Ⓥ 10am-5pm Tue-Sun, to 8pm Wed), is near Stigbergstorget about 2km west of the city centre. There's an interesting aquarium attached. Take tram 3, 9 or 11.

Naturhistoriska Museet (Natural History Museum; ☎ 775 24 00; www.gnm.se; Slottsskogen Park; adult/under 25yr Skr40/free; Ⓥ 11am-5pm Tue-Sun) contains the world's only stuffed blue whale. In the lead-up to Christmas, visitors are occasionally allowed to step inside its mouth for that Moby Dick feeling.

OTHER SIGHTS

The classical **domkyrkan** (Gustavi Cathedral; Västra Hamngatan; Ⓥ 9am-6pm Mon-Fri, 11am-5pm Sat, 10am-3pm Sun Jun-Aug, 8am-6pm Mon-Fri, 9am-4pm Sat, 10am-3pm Sun rest of yr) was consecrated in 1815 – two previous cathedrals were destroyed by town fires. One of the most impressive buildings in Göteborg, **Masthuggskyrkan** (Storebackegatan; Ⓥ 9am-6pm summer, 11am-4pm rest of yr) was completed in 1914, and its interior is like an upturned boat. The church is also a great viewpoint for the western half of the city.

Feskekörka (☎ 711 35 09; Rosenlundsgatan; Ⓥ 9am-5pm Tue-Fri, 9am-6pm Fri, 10am-2pm Sat), or 'Fish Church', isn't a church at all – it's a fish and seafood market, and a perfect stop for lunch or a snack.

The **Haga district**, south of the canal, is Göteborg's oldest suburb, dating back to 1648. In the 1980s and '90s, the area was thoroughly renovated and now includes shops and restaurants.

There are some lovely green oases in the city, including **Trädgårdsföreningen** (Nya Allén; adult/child mid-Apr–mid-Sep Skr15/free, other times free), laid out in 1842 and home to a couple of pretty cafes, a rosarium and a **palm house**. In Göteborg's southwest is **Slottsskogsparken**, the 'lungs' of the city; the **Botanic Gardens** – the largest in Sweden – are nearby.

Sleeping

Göteborg has several high-quality hostels near the city centre. Most hotels offer decent discounts at weekends and in summer.

For Skr60, the tourist office can arrange your accommodation for you.

BUDGET

STF Vandrarhem Stigbergssliden (☎ 24 16 20; www.hostel-gothenburg.com; Stigbergssliden 10; dm/d from Skr150/350; 🖳) In a renovated seaman's institute (tram 3, 9 or 11 to Stigbergstorget), this hostel has history. Staff are helpful, and there's a big kitchen, laundry, TV room, and perks include a sheltered garden and bike rental (per day Skr50).

STF Vandrarhem Slottsskogen (☎ 42 65 20; www.sov.nu; Vegagatan 21; dm Skr185-210; s/d Skr345/490; 🖳) Unlike many Swedish hostels, big, friendly Slottsskogen is a cracking place for meeting other travellers. For a small extra payment there's access to a laundry, sauna and sun bed, and the buffet breakfast (Skr55) is brilliant. Parking spaces can be booked for a fee and reception is closed between noon and 2pm. Take tram 1 or 6 to Olivedalsgatan.

Masthuggsterrassens Vandrarhem (☎ 42 48 20; www.mastenvandrarhem.com; Masthuggsterrassen 10H; dm/d Skr190/480; 🖳) If you're after a good night's sleep, try this clean, quiet, well-run place. Fine facilities include three lounges, three kitchens and a little library (mostly Swedish books), and it's handy if you're catching an early ferry to Denmark. Take tram 3, 9 or 11 to Masthuggstorget and follow the signs.

Kvibergs Vandrarhem & Stugby (☎ 43 50 55; www.vandrarhem.com; Kvibergsvägen 5; low season s/d/tr/q Skr270/360/460/560, high season tr/q Skr550/690; 🖳 📶) This sterling SVIF hostel, a few kilometres northeast of the city centre (tram 6, 7 or 11), boasts super amenities, including flatscreen TVs, sauna, sun beds, laundry, table tennis, two kitchens and two lounges. There are no dorms; you rent out the entire room. Hotel-style rooms and cabins are also available.

City Hotel Vid Avenyn (☎ 708 40 00; www.cityhotelgbg.se; Lorensbergsgatan 6; s/d without bathroom from Skr495/595) The City represents excellent value for such a central hotel (within yards of Sweden's 'Champs Elysées'). Staff are friendly, rooms are comfy and for about Skr200 extra you can have a private bathroom. A continental breakfast is brought to your door, or for Skr25 more you can opt for the breakfast buffet at the new in-house restaurant-pub (which boasts 60 varieties of beer).

MIDRANGE

Vanilj Hotel, Kafé & Bar (☎ 711 62 20; www.vaniljhotel.entersol.se; Kyrkogatan 38; s/d from Skr995/1145; 🅿 🖳)

On a quiet, central street, this petite slumber spot is cosy, homelike and adorable. There are individually decorated rooms and breakfast is served in the buzzing cafe downstairs. Get there early to grab one of the five parking spaces.

Hotel Flora (☎ 13 86 16; www.hotelflora.se; Grönsakstorget 2; s/d Skr1195/1495; 🖳) An extreme makeover has turned Flora from frumpy to fabulous, its uberslick rooms now flaunting black-and-white interiors, designer chairs, flatscreen TVs and sparkling bathrooms. Top-floor rooms have air-conditioning, several rooms offer river views and the chic split-level courtyard is perfect for sophisticated chilling.

Hotel Royal (☎ 700 11 70; www.hotelroyal.nu; Drottninggatan 67; s/d from Skr1295/1495; 🖳) Göteborg's oldest hotel (1852) has aged enviably. The grand entrance has been retained, complete with painted glass ceiling and sweeping staircase, and the elegant, airy rooms make necessary 21st-century concessions like flatscreen TVs and renovated bathrooms. There's also homemade cake for guests.

TOP END

Hotel Eggers (☎ 333 44 40; www.hoteleggers.se; Drottningtorget; s/d from Skr1495/1835; 🅿 🖳) Elegant Eggers would make a great set for a period drama. Founded as a railway hotel in 1859, its rooms are a Regency-style treat. A good few have private balconies overlooking the bustling square and nearby parking spots (per 24 hours Sk120) can be booked at reception.

Hotell Barken Viking (☎ 63 58 00; barken.viking@liseberg.se; Gullbergskajen; s/d Skr1495/2050; 🖳) Freshly revamped, *Barken Viking* is an elegant four-masted sailing ship, converted into a stylish hotel and restaurant and moored near Lilla Bommen harbour. Rooms are smart and suitably nautical, with handsome blue carpet, Hamptons-style linen and warm wood panelling. The discounted May to September rate includes entry to Liseberg.

Hotel Gothia Towers (☎ 750 88 10; hotelreservations@gothiatowers.com; Mässans Gata 24; s/d from Skr1645/1895; 🅿 🖳) Sweden's largest hotel is the 23-storey Gothia Towers (take tram 5). Its 704 rooms ooze Nordic cool, especially the 'Design' options: all sharp, clean lines and bathroom windows for a vista-friendly soak. More bird's-eye views await at Sky bar and restaurant Heaven 23, a hit with nonguests too and home to Göteborg's best shrimp sandwich.

Avalon (☎ 751 02 00; www.avalonhotel.se; Kungstorget 9; s/d from Skr1890/2190; 🖳 🖭) The new, design-conscious Avalon is steps away from the main tourist office. Rooms are sleek and uncluttered, with flatscreen TVs and heavenly pillows. Some rooms feature a mini spa (three even have their own gym equipment), and the hip resto-bar is an after-work hotspot. The ultimate highlight is the rooftop pool (open May to September), which leans out over the edge for a dizzying dip. Check the website for packages.

Eating

Stray off Kungsportsavenyn for anything from retro panino bars to champagne-and-lobster dining rooms. Cool cafes, cheap ethnic gems and foodie favourites abound around the Vasastan, Haga and Linné districts, often with lower prices than their tourist-trap Avenyn rivals. Many places are closed on Sundays.

CAFES

Bar Centro (☎ 711 00 27; Kyrkogatan 31; focaccia Skr30-60; 🕑 6am-6pm Mon-Fri, 7am-5pm Sat, 8am-5pm Sun) Fans of this iconic, retro espresso bar spill out onto the street, downing smooth espresso and tasty focaccias. The few window seats are perfect for urban voyeurs.

Bar Italia (Prinsgatan 7; panini Skr30-40; 🕑 7.30am-6pm) In the Linné district, this is another cultish espresso bar, complete with Italian baristi and suspended Vespa. In warm weather, watch the hip brigade squeeze onto the pavement banquette for perfect caffeine, *cornetti*, gourmet calzoni and gossip.

Bar Doppio (☎ 42 56 66; Linnégata; soup Skr40, brunch Skr70; 🕑 8am-6pm Mon-Fri, 9am-5pm Sat & Sun, from 7am Mon-Fri mid-Aug–May) More class-A caffeine awaits at this Scandi-cool cafe, where regulars keep track of their tabs on a giant blackboard. Run by two young Antipodeans, it's a laid-back hangout with a great neighbourhood vibe and fresh grub like homemade muesli, soup, focaccia and biscotti.

Da Matteo (☎ 13 06 09; Vallgatan 5; pizzas Skr75-89, salads Skr79-95; 🕑 9am-7pm Mon-Fri, 10am-5pm Sat, 11am-4pm Sun) A mecca for coffee snobs, head here for some wickedly-fine espresso, moreish mini *sfogliatelle* (Neapolitan pastries) and savouries such as real-deal pizzas, panini and salads. There's a sun-soaked courtyard to be enjoyed. A second branch is on Viktoriapassagen.

RESTAURANTS

Publik (☎ 14 65 20; Andra Långgatan 20; lunch Skr65, mains Skr100-130; 🕑 11.30-1am Mon-Sat) Arguably Göteborg's coolest hangout (think grit-chic interiors, local art exhibitions, DJ-spun tunes and creative indie crowds), this cafe/bar hybrid also serves brilliant, great-value grub like goat cheese-stuffed aubergines with red pesto potatoes. The well-priced house wine is perfectly drinkable and there's a backyard courtyard for fine-weather lounging.

Andrum (☎ 13 85 04; Östra Hamngatan 19; large plate Skr69; 🕑 11am-9pm Mon-Fri, noon-8pm Sat & Sun) Vegetarians love this casual, meat-free spot with its value for money, all-day lunch buffet. It's simple, tasty, wholesome stuff, and cheerfully recommended.

Smaka (☎ 13 22 47; Vasaplatsen 3; mains Skr120-205; 🕑 5pm-2am Mon-Thu & Sun, 5pm-3am Fri & Sat) This lively, down-to-earth restaurant/bar cooks up brilliant, old-school Swedish *husmanskost* (home cooking) like the speciality meatballs with mashed potato and lingonberries. Mod-Swedish options might include a goat's cheese soup with roasted beetroot and asparagus.

Tranquilo (☎ 13 45 55; Kungstorget 14; meals Skr140-235; 🕑 11.30am-late Mon-Sat, from 9pm Sun) Complete with glowing pink-and-blue bar and a giant Rio-style Jesus on the ceiling, this hip, bombastic resto-bar peddles grilled meats and tropic-flavoured brilliance like grilled mango and goat's cheese burger with grilled corn and rhubarb chutney. Done, order a pineapple mojito and flirt to a bossa nova beat.

Magnus & Magnus (☎ 13 30 00; Magasinsgatan 8; 2-/3-/4-/6-course tasting menus Skr445/555/555/785; 🕑 from 6pm) A hit with VIPs, this ever-fashionable restaurant serves inspired Euro-fusion flavours. The summer courtyard – complete with bar, DJs and different club nights from Wednesday to Monday – draws an ubercool crowd.

QUICK EATS

For something quick, the Nordstan shopping complex has loads of fast-food outlets.

Alexandras (☎ 711 23 81; Kungstorget) Located in the central Saluhallen, this famous bolthole dishes out excellent hearty soups and stews (around Skr40), particularly welcoming on a chilly day.

Super + Sushi (☎ 12 20 90; Prinsgatan 4; 🕑 to 9pm) Close to several of the hostels, head here for excellent Japanese lunch deals, including miso soup, green tea and 10 pieces of sushi for Skr65.

SELF-CATERING

Saluhallen (Kungstorget; ⏰ 9am-6pm Mon-Fri, 9am-3pm Sat) Göteborg's main central market is jammed with tasty budget eateries and food stalls, and the perfect place to stock up that picnic basket.

Saluhall Briggen (Nordhemsgatan 28; ⏰ 9am-6pm Mon-Fri, 9am-2pm Sat) It might lack Saluhallen's size and buzz, but this covered market (in an old fire-station) will have you drooling over its bounty of fresh bread, cheeses, quiches, seafood and ethnic treats. It's particularly handy for the hostel district.

Ekostore (☎ 13 60 23; Ekelundsgatan 4; ⏰ 10am-7pm Mon-Fri, 10am-2pm Sat Jul & Aug, 10am-8pm Mon-Fri, 10am-4pm Sat rest of year) An eco-chic grocery store selling organic and fair-trade products.

Drinking

Kungsportsavenyn brims with beer-downing tourists; try the following instead.

Lokal (☎ 13 32 00; Kyrkogatan 11; ⏰ 4pm-1am Mon-Sat) Awarded best bar in Göteborg and run by the team from Publik, this cool hangout pulls everyone from artists and media types to the odd punk rocker. The drinks are inspired (think kiwi and ginger daiquiri), the pick-and-mix menu brims with fusion flavours, and music spans soul, jazz and electro. Best of all, staff donate 10% of their tips to a Cambodian orphanage.

Club Social (☎ 13 87 55; Magasinsgatan 3; ⏰ 4pm-2am Tue-Sat) A svelte black-and-white leather bar demands classic cocktails, which is just what this glam-cool newbie delivers. Join in-the-know locals for smooth Bellinis, a tapas-fuelled catch-up session or the petite selection of savvy mains which change daily according to what looks best at the morning market.

Bliss (☎ 13 85 55; Magasinsgatan 3; ⏰ 11.30am-2.30pm Mon-Fri, 6pm-1am or 2am Tue-Thu & Sat, 5pm-1am or 2am Fri) Bliss boasts one of the hippest interiors in Göteborg, with low designer seats and slick contemporary tones. It's a long-standing nocturnal favourite: if you're not up to a main meal (lunch Skr79, dinner mains around Skr200; they're usually delicious), you can nibble on tapas-style snacks and groove to live DJs until late.

Ölhallen 7:an (☎ 13 60 79; Kungstorget 7) For low-fuss, old-school soul, don't miss this well-worn Swedish beerhall that hasn't changed in about 100 years. There's no food, wine or pretension, just beer, and plenty of choices.

Entertainment

Clubs have varying minimum-age limits, ranging from 18 to 25, and many may charge admission depending on the night.

Nefertiti (☎ 711 15 33; Hvitfeldtsplatsen 6; admission Skr90-320) A Göteborg institution, this effortlessly cool venue is famous for its smooth live jazz, blues and world music, usually followed by kicking club nights spanning from techno, deep house and soul to hip hop and funk. Times vary, so check the website.

Storan (☎ 60 45 00; Kungsparken 1) Another local icon, this old opera house now pumps out everything from live indie tunes to weekly club nights. The frozen margaritas at the in-house resto-bar, Grill El Mundo, enjoy cult status. Check the website for upcoming gigs.

Pustervik (☎ 368 32 77; Järntorgsgatan 12) Culture vultures and party people pack into this hybrid venue, with its heaving downstairs bar and upstairs club and stage. Gigs range from independent theatre and live music gigs (anything from emerging singer-songwriters to Neneh Cherry) to regular club nights spanning hip hop, soul and rock.

Röda Sten (☎ 12 08 16; www.rodasten.com; Röda Sten 1; ⏰ Fri & Sat) Paging Berlin with its post-industrial look, this power station-turned-art gallery cranks up the party vibe with live bands on Friday nights and club nights on Saturdays. Expect indie pop the first Saturday of the month, followed by '80s tunes (complete with retro-clad punters), reggae, and techno each subsequent Saturday.

Shopping

DesignTorget (☎ 774 00 17; Vallgatan 14) has cool, affordable design objects from both established and up-and-coming Scandi talent.

Prickig Katt (☎ 13 33 50; Magasinsgatan 17; ⏰ closed Sun) meaning 'Spotted Cat', sports retro-clad staff, idiosyncratic fashion from Dutch, Danish and home-grown labels, as well as kitschy wares and out-there handmade millinery and bling.

Nearby, **Prickig Katt Boudoir** (☎ 13 90 50; Magasinsgatan 19; ⏰ closed Sun), panders to trend-setting guys, who come for non-conformist labels like Denmark's Humor and Göteborg's Gissy. Sharing the same address, local label **Velour** (☎ 775 38 00; closed Sun) and Stockholm legend **Acne Jeans** (☎ 13 85 80) stock slick, stylish streetwear for guys and girls.

DEM Collective (☎ 12 38 84; Storgatan 11; ⏰ closed Sun) Head to this bite-size boutique for Scandi cool, fair-trade threads. Completely organic, designs are minimalist, street-smart and supremely comfortable.

Getting There & Away

AIR

About 25km east of the city, **Landvetter airport** (☎ 94 10 00; www.landvetter.lfv.se) has up to 22 direct daily flights to/from Stockholm Arlanda and Stockholm Bromma airports (with SAS and Malmö Aviation), as well as daily services to Umeå and several weekly services to Borlänge, Luleå and Sundsvall.

Direct European routes include Amsterdam (KLM), Brussels (Brussels Airlines), Copenhagen (SAS), Frankfurt (Lufthansa and SAS), Helsinki (Finnair and Blue1), London (SAS), Manchester (City Airline), Munich (Lufthansa), Oslo (Wideroe) and Paris (Air France).

Göteborg City Airport (☎ 92 60 60; www.goteborgairport.se), some 15km north of the city at Säve, is used for budget Ryanair flights to destinations including London Stansted, Glasgow and Frankfurt.

BOAT

Göteborg is a major entry point for ferries, with several car/passenger services to Denmark, Germany and Norway.

Nearest to central Göteborg, the **Stena Line** (☎ 704 00 00; www.stenaline.se) Denmark terminal near Masthuggstorget (tram 3, 9 or 11) has around eight daily departures for Frederikshavn in peak season, with a 20% discount for railpass holders.

Further west is the Stena Line terminal for the daily car ferry to Kiel (Germany). Take tram 3 or 9 to Chapmans Torg.

BUS

The bus station, Nils Ericson Terminalen, is next to the train station. There's a **Västtrafik information booth** (☎ 0771-41 43 00; ☼ 6am-10pm Mon-Fri, 9am-10pm Sat, 9am-7pm Sun) here, providing information and selling tickets for all city and regional public transport within the Göteborg, Bohuslän and Västergötland area.

Eurolines (☎ 10 02 40; www.eurolines.com; Nils Ericsonplatsen 17) has its main Swedish office at the bus station in central Göteborg.

Swebus Express (☎ 0771-21 82 18; www.swebus express.com) has an office located at the bus terminal and operates frequent buses to most of the major towns. Services to Stockholm (Skr420, seven hours) run five to seven times daily. Other direct destinations include Copenhagen (Skr300, four to five hours), Halmstad (Skr108, 1¾ hours), Helsingborg (Skr200, three hours), Jönköping (Skr140, 1¾ hours), Oslo (Skr220, four hours), Malmö (Skr281, three hours), and Örebro (Skr250, four hours).

Svenska Buss (☎ 0771-67 67 67; www.svenska buss.se) has daily departures for Stockholm (Skr410, 7½ hours) via Jönköping (Skr130, 2¼ hours).

Prices can be considerably lower than those quoted here for advanced bookings, especially for Swebus Express and Säfflebussen.

CAR & MOTORCYCLE

The E6 motorway runs north–south from Oslo to Malmö just east of the city centre and there's also a complex junction where the E20 motorway diverges east for Stockholm.

International car-hire companies Avis, Europcar and Hertz have desks at Landvetter and Göteborg City airports. For car hire in town, contact one of the petrol stations, for example **Statoil** (☎ 41 11 62; Marklandsgatan 2), in southwestern Göteborg.

TRAIN

Centralstationen is Sweden's oldest railway station in Sweden and now a listed building. It serves SJ and regional trains, with direct trains to Copenhagen (Skr387, four hours) and Malmö (Skr329, 3¼ hours), as well as numerous other destinations in the southern half of Sweden.

Intercity trains to Stockholm depart approximately every one to two hours (Skr490, five hours), with quicker but more expensive X2000 trains (Skr1110, three hours) also approximately every one to two hours.

Getting Around

Buses, trams and ferries run by **Västtrafik** (☎ 0771-41 43 00; www.vasttrafik.se) make up the city's public transport system; there are Västtrafik information booths selling tickets and giving out timetables inside **Nils Ericson Terminalen** (☼ 6am-10pm Mon-Fri, 9am-10pm Sat, 9am-7pm Sun), in front of the train station on **Drottningtorget** (☼ 6am-8pm Mon-Fri, 8am-8pm Sat & Sun), and at **Brunnsparken** (☼ 7am-7pm Mon-Fri, 9am-6pm Sat).

Holders of the Göteborg Pass travel free, including on late-night transport. Otherwise a city transport ticket costs adult/child Skr25/12 (Skr40 on late-night transport). Easy-to-use Maxirabatt 100 'value cards' cost Skr100 (from Västtrafik information booths or Pressbyrån newsagencies) and work out much cheaper than buying tickets each time you travel. A 24-hour Dagkort (day pass) for the whole city area costs Skr65.

The easiest way to cover lengthy distances in Göteborg is by tram. Lines, numbered 1 to 13, converge near Brunnsparken (a block from the train station).

Västtrafik has regional passes for 24 hours/30 days (Skr240/1350, under 26 Skr240/1150) that give unlimited travel on all *länstrafik* buses, trains and boats within Göteborg, Bohuslän and the Västergötland area.

Cykelkungen (☎ 184300; Chalmersgatan 19) offers bike rental for Skr120/500 per day/week.

MARSTRAND
☎ 0303 / pop 1300

Pretty **Marstrand** (www.marstrand.nu), with its wooden buildings, island setting and relaxed air, conveys the essence of the Bohuslän fishing villages that dot the coast from Göteborg to the Norwegian border, and provides an idyllic area for sailing, cycling or driving. Car traffic is banned on the island itself, so those with their own wheels should take the frequent passenger ferry from Koön, 150m to the east.

The 17th-century **Carlstens Fästning** (☎ 602 65; www.carlsten.se; adult/7-15yr Skr70/25; ❤ 11am-6pm early Jun–mid-Aug, 11am-4pm rest of Aug, 11am-4pm Sat & Sat rest of year) fortress reflects the town's martial and penal history; entry price includes a guided tour.

Marstrands Varmbadhus Båtellet (☎ 600 10; marstrandsvarmbadhus@telia.com; Kungsplan; d/tr/q from Skr675/885/1180; ❏ ❧) offers simple hostel accommodation. Turn right after disembarking from the ferry and follow the waterfront for 400m. Only dorm accommodation is available in the summer.

There are numerous eating options along the harbour, including fast-food stalls (one sells fresh fish and chips for about Skr50), cafes and upmarket restaurants.

From Göteborg you can take bus 312 to Arvidsvik (on Koön) then cross to Marstrand by frequent passenger-only ferry. The complete journey takes about an hour. Buy a Maxirabbat 100 carnet (Skr100) from the Västtrafik information booth at Nils Ericson Terminalen in Göteborg and validate it on the bus.

STRÖMSTAD
☎ 0526 / pop 11,558

A resort, fishing harbour and spa town, Strömstad is laced with ornate wooden buildings echoing nearby Norway. Indeed, Norwegians head in en masse in summer to take advantage of Sweden's cheaper prices, lending a particularly lively air to the town's picturesque streets and bars. One of Sweden's largest, most magnificent **stone ship settings** (admission free; ❤ 24hr) lies 6km northeast of Strömstad; ask for details at the tourist office.

The **tourist office** (☎ 623 30; www.stromstad tourist.se; Gamla Tullhuset, Norra hamnen, Ångbåtskajen 2; ❤ 9am-8pm Mon-Sat, 10am-7pm Sun Jun-Aug, shorter hours Sep-May), between the two harbours on the main square, also offers internet access (per 15 minutes Skr20).

No, **Cruselleska Hemmet** (☎ 101 93; info@crusell ska.com; Norra Kyrkogatan 12; dm/s/d Skr180/320/440; ❤ Mar–early Dec; ❏ ❏) is not a Disney villain; it's an exceptional STF hostel. Drifting white curtains, pale decor and wicker lounges lend the place a boutique vibe. The kitchen is seriously spacious, and there's a peaceful garden for alfresco contemplation, as well as a range of pampering spa treatments. Make sure you book ahead.

Try the fresh local *räkor* (shrimp) and delicious seafood in the many restaurants, or purchase from local fishmongers. Next to the tourist office is **Laholmens Fisk** (☎ 102 40; Torget), selling seafood baguettes (from Skr40), along with fish fresh off the boats. You'll find it just off the main square, next door to Restaurang Bryggan – also a cosy harbour restaurant.

Buses and trains both use the train station near the southern harbour. The **Swebus Express** (☎ 0771-21 82 18; www.swebusexpress.com) service from Göteborg to Oslo calls here up to two times daily and Västtrafik operates buses to Göteborg (Skr200) up to five times daily. Strömstad is the northern terminus of the Bohuståg train system, with around six trains every day to/from Göteborg (Skr200).

NORRKÖPING

☎ 011 / pop 126,680

The envy of industrial have-beens across Europe, Norrköping has managed to cleverly regenerate its defunct mills and canals into a posse of cultural and gastronomic hangouts fringing waterfalls and locks. Retro trams rattle down streets that are lined with eclectic architecture, while some 30km to the northeast, the animal park at Kolmården swaps urban regeneration for majestic Siberian tigers.

The well-stocked **tourist office** (☎ 15 50 00; www.destination.norrkoping.se; Dalsgatan 16; ☯ 10am-5pm Mon-Fri, 10am-2pm Sat & Sun Jul–mid-Aug, shorter hours rest of the year) has free internet access.

Sights

KOLMÅRDEN

Kolmården zoo (☎ 24 90 00; www.kolmarden.com; ☯ 10am-6pm Jul–mid-Aug, 10am-5pm May, Jun & rest of Aug, Sat & Sun Sep–early Oct) is Scandinavia's largest, with around 750 residents from all climates and continents. It's divided into two areas: the main **Djurparken** (zoo; adult/3-12yr Skr240/130) with a dolphin show and **Safariparken** (adult/3-12yr Skr140/100), complete with a safari park **bus tour** (adult/3-12yr Skr30/15) for the carless. A combined ticket for both the zoo and safari park will set you back Skr290/170. The cable car (Skr80/40) that goes around the park gives a far better view of the forest than of the animals.

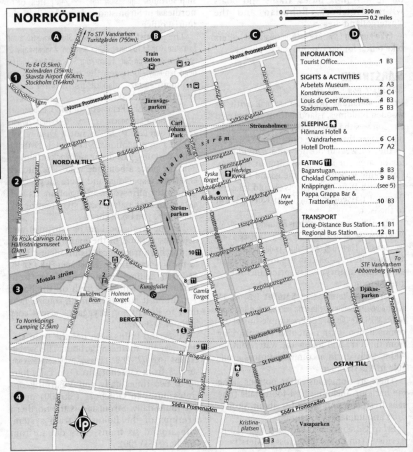

NORRKÖPING

0 — 300 m
0 — 0.2 miles

INFORMATION
Tourist Office...................................1 B3

SIGHTS & ACTIVITIES
Arbetets Museum.............................2 A3
Konstmuseum...................................3 C4
Louis de Geer Konserthus.............4 B3
Stadsmuseum...................................5 B3

SLEEPING 🏠
Hörnans Hotell &
  Vandrarhem..................................6 C4
Hotell Drott......................................7 A2

EATING 🍴
Bagarstugan.....................................8 B3
Choklad Companiet........................9 B4
Knäppingen..............................(see 5)
Pappa Grappa Bar &
  Trattorian....................................10 B3

TRANSPORT
Long-Distance Bus Station......11 B1
Regional Bus Station............12 B1

Kolmården lies 35km north of Norrköping, on the north shore of Bråviken (regular bus 432 or 433 from Norrköping; Skr60, 40 minutes).

OTHER SIGHTS

The industrial past is exhibited at the city museum, **Stadsmuseum** (☎ 15 26 20; Holmbrogränd; admission free; ☻ 10am-5pm Tue, Wed & Fri, to 4pm Jun-Aug, 10am-8pm Thu, 11am-4pm Sat & Sun). Sweden's only museum of work, the excellent **Arbetets Museum** (☎ 18 98 00; Laxholmen; admission free; ☻ 11am-5pm), is just across the bridge from the Stadsmuseum in a 1917 building designed to mirror the island it sits on; named Strykjärnet (flatiron), it has seven sides, seven floors and a total of 7000 sq metres of floor space.

A modern addition to the riverside scenery is the extraordinary 1300-seat **Louis de Geer Konserthus** (☎ 15 50 30; www.louisdegeer.com; Dalsgatan 15), in a former paper mill. Still containing the original balconies, it's a superb setting for orchestral, jazz and pop concerts.

The **Konstmuseum** (☎ 15 26 00; Kristinaplatsen; admission free; ☻ noon-4pm Tue & Thu-Sun, noon-8pm Wed Jun-Aug, 11am-5pm Wed & Fri-Sun, 11am-8pm Tue & Thu Sep-May) boasts important early 20th-century works as well as Carl Larsson's dreamy *Frukost i det gröna*.

Summer-only attractions include short guided tours on vintage trams; inquire at the tourist office.

Sleeping

Norrköpings Camping (☎ 17 11 90; info@norrkopings camping.com; Campingvägen; camp sites Skr120, 2-/4-bed cabins Skr400/550) This little camping ground sits on the south bank of Motala ström, approximately 2.5km from the city. It's short on bells and whistles, but there's a small cafe on site. Public transport is nonexistent.

STF Vandrarhem Abborreberg (☎ 31 93 44; abborre berg@telia.com; dm Skr220; ☻ Apr–mid-Oct) Stunningly situated in a coastal pine wood 6km east of town, this sterling hostel offers accommodation in huts scattered through the surrounding park. The associated ice-cream parlour is a hit with gluttons. Take bus 116 to Lindö.

Hörnans Hotell & Vandrarhem (☎ 16 58 90; www .hotellhornan.com; cnr Hörngatan & Sankt Persgatan; dm/s/d Skr270/405/740) The only central budget option, with comfy rooms above a busy pub and restaurant. All come with cable TV.

Hotell Drott (☎ 18 00 60; info@hotelldrott.com; Tunnbindaregatan 19; s/d Skr710/860; ☐) Peaceful Hotell Drott serves up old-fashioned but comfy rooms, as well as a kitchen for self-caterers. Breakfast includes meatballs and light evening meals are an option.

Eating & Drinking

There are plenty of eateries in the shopping district along Drottninggatan, and also in the student quarter around Kungsgatan. This is also where you'll find supermarkets.

Bagarstugan (☎ 470 20 20; Skolgatan 1A; sandwiches Skr40-49, salads Skr59-65; ☻ 10am-6pm Mon-Fri, 10am-4pm Sat, noon-4pm Sun) This stylish, floor-boarded bakery-cafe peddles freshly baked cookies, cinnamon buns, muffins and scones, as well as salubrious salads, sandwiches and take-away homemade marmalades. There's a courtyard for alfresco noshing.

Choklad Companiet (☎ 12 61 61; Prästgatan 3; ☻ closed Sun) Head to this chocolate shop-cum-cafe for exquisite homemade gelato (try a white chocolate, lime and chilli combo), desserts, pralines and truffles. As for the real-deal espresso, it could make an Italian barista weep.

Knäppingen (☎ 10 74 45; Västgötegatan 21; lunch Skr89; ☻ closed Mon) The Stadsmuseum's cafe makes a refreshing change, offering focaccias, tacos, crepes and better veggie options than boring pasta. In summer, you can munch away in a sunny courtyard tucked between stately old mills.

Pappa Grappa Bar & Trattorian (☎ 18 00 14; Gamla Rådstugugatan 26-28; mains Skr120-255; ☻ 6pm-late Mon-Sat, pizzeria also open Sun) Gobble up a brilliant wood-fired pizza in the pizzeria, or slip into the vaulted restaurant for scrumptious antipasto and meat and fish mains. Established by an Italian ballroom dancing champion, there's also an on-site deli for take-home treats.

Getting There & Around

Sweden's third-largest airport (Nyköping Skavsta) is 60km away. To get there take the train to Nyköping, then catch a local bus. **Norrköping airport** (www.norrkopingflygplats.se) has direct flights from Copenhagen, Munich and Helsinki.

The regional bus station is next to the train station, and long-distance buses leave from a terminal across the road. **Swebus Express** (☎ 0771-21 82 18; www.swebusexpress.com) has very frequent services to Stockholm (Skr170, 2¼ hours) and Jönköping (Skr215, 2½ hours), and several services daily to Göteborg (Skr330, five hours) and Kalmar (Skr265,

SWEDEN

four hours). **Svenska Buss** (☎ 0771-67 67 67; www .svenskabuss.se, in Swedish) runs similar, though less frequent, routes.

Norrköping is on the main north–south railway line, and SJ trains depart every one to two hours for Stockholm (Skr95 to Skr400, 1½ hours) and Malmö (Skr554 to Skr906, 3¼ hours). Trains run roughly every hour north to Nyköping (Skr60 to Skr72, one hour) and every 20 minutes south to Linköping (Skr80, 25 minutes).

LINKÖPING

☎ 013 / pop 140,367

Most famous for its mighty medieval cathedral, Linköping fancies itself as Norrköping's more upmarket rival. Its most infamous claim to fame is the 'bloodbath of Linköping'. Following the Battle of Stångebro (1598), many of King Sigismund's defeated Catholic army were executed in the town, leaving Duke Karl and his Protestant forces in full control of Sweden.

The **tourist office** (☎ 20 68 35; www.linkoping.se; Östgötagatan 5) is inside the **library** (Östgötagatan 5), not far from the cathedral; there's also free internet access here.

Sights & Activities

The enormous, copper-roofed **domkyrkan** (cathedral; ⌚ 9am-6pm) with its 107m spire is the landmark of Linköping and one of Sweden's oldest and largest churches. Learn more about its history and architecture at the museum inside the castle just across the way, the **Slotts & Domkyrkomuseum** (Castle & Cathedral Museum; ☎ 12 23 80; adult/under 7yr Skr40/free; ⌚ 11am-4pm Tue-Fri, noon-4pm Sat & Sun Apr-Sep, noon-4pm Tue-Sun Oct-Mar).

Just north of the cathedral, **Östergötlands Länsmuseum** (County Museum; ☎ 23 03 00; Vasavägen; adult/child Skr20/10; ⌚ 10am-4pm Tue-Sun, to 8pm Tue & Thu Sep–mid-Dec & mid-Jan–May) houses an extensive collection of art by a variety of European painters, including Cranach's view of Eden, *Original Sin*.

Some 2km west of the city is **Gamla Linköping** (☎ 12 11 10; admission free; bus 202 or 214), one of the biggest living-museum villages in Sweden. Among the 90 quaint houses are about a dozen theme museums, many handicraft shops, a small chocolate factory, a restaurant and a cafe. You can wander among the 19th-century buildings at will – the village and most museums are open daily. Just 300m through the forest behind the old village is the **Valla**

Fritidsområde (admission Skr20), a recreation area with domestic animals, gardens, a children's playground, minigolf, a few small museums and old houses.

Upstaged by the Göta Canal, Linköping boasts its own canal system, the 90km **Kinda Canal**. Opened in 1871, it has 15 locks, including Sweden's deepest. Cruises include evening sailings, musical outings and wine tasting trips. For a simple day excursion, from late June to early August the **M/S Kind** (☎ 0141-23 33 70) leaves Tullbron dock at 10am on Tuesday, Thursday and Saturday, and travels to Rimforsa (adult/child Skr370/110, return by bus or train included).

Sleeping

Linköping STF Vandrarhem & Hotell (☎ 35 90 00; www .lvh.se; Klostergatan 52A; dm from Skr210, s/d hotel rooms Skr765/840; 🖳) A swish central hostel with hotel-style accommodation too, mostly with kitchenettes. All rooms have private bathrooms and TVs. Book ahead.

Hotell Östergyllen (☎ 10 20 75; www.hotellostergyl len.se; Hamngatan 2B; s/d from Skr425/620) Despite the forlorn ambience (lino floors and anonymous corridors), this budget hotel offers cheap, comfy-enough rooms not far from the train station. You can pay up to Skr200 extra for a private bathroom.

Park Hotel (☎ 12 90 05; www.fawltytowers.se; Järnvägsgatan 6; s/d Skr890/1090; 🅿 🖳) Disturbingly billed as Sweden's 'Fawlty Towers', this hotel resembles that madhouse in appearance only (yes, there's a moose head at reception). A smart family-run establishment close to the train station, it's peppered with chandeliers, oil paintings and clean, parquet-floored rooms.

Eating & Drinking

Most places to eat and drink are on the main square or nearby streets, especially along buzzing Ågatan.

Barista (☎ 10 10 90; Tanneforsgatan 11; sandwiches Skr56-72; ⌚ 9am-8pm Mon-Fri, 10am-5pm Sat, 11am-4pm Sun) This hip cafe chain (attached to the equally hip store DesignTorget) peddles decent fair-trade coffee and other trendy perishables like chai tea, organic focaccias and pick-me-up chocolate bars under fashionable low-slung lamps.

Stångs Magasin (☎ 31 21 00; Södra Stånggatan 1; lunch around Skr90, mains Skr245-295; ⌚ lunch Mon-Fri, from 6pm Mon-Fri & from 4pm Sat Sep-Jun, from 2.30pm Tue-Sat Jul & Aug) In a 200-year-old warehouse

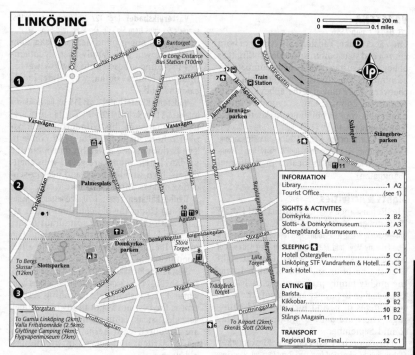

LINKÖPING

INFORMATION
Library....................................	1 A2
Tourist Office..........................	(see 1)

SIGHTS & ACTIVITIES
Domkyrka..............................	2 B2
Slotts- & Domkyrkomuseum...	3 A3
Östergötlands Länsmuseum...	4 A2

SLEEPING
Hotell Östergyllen..................	5 C2
Linköping STF Vandrarhem & Hotell...	6 C3
Park Hotel..............................	7 C1

EATING
Barista....................................	8 B3
Kikkobar................................	9 B2
Riva.......................................	10 B2
Stångs Magasin......................	11 D2

TRANSPORT
Regional Bus Terminal............	12 C1

down near the Kinda Canal docks, this elegant award winner fuses classic Swedish cuisine with continental influences – think glazed duck breast with almond potato puree and artichoke ragout in a wine balsamic sauce. The lunch buffet is good value.

Kikkobar (☎ 13 13 10; Klostergatan 26; mains Skr135-280) Head here for Zen designer details with Japanese classics like tempura, spicier southeast Asian numbers like tom yum soup, and the odd western staple.

Riva (☎ 12 95 15; Ågatan 43; mains Skr149-256; ☑ from 5pm Tue-Fri, from 6pm Sat) Trendy Riva serves Italian-with-a-twist bistro grub like buttered *taglierini* pasta, chilli-sautéed scampi, prawns, mussels, shallots, white wine, cherry- and sundried tomatoes.

Getting There & Away

The **airport** (☎ 18 10 30) is only 2km east of town. **Skyways** (☎ 0771-95 95 00; www.skyways.se) flies direct to Stockholm Arlanda on weekdays. **KLM** (☎ 08-58 79 97 57; www.klm.com) flies daily to Amsterdam. There's no airport bus, but taxi company **Taxibil** (☎ 14 60 00) charges around Skr150 for the ride.

Regional and local buses, run by **ÖstgötaTrafiken** (☎ 0771-21 10 10; www.ostgotatrafiken.se), leave from the terminal next to the train station; route maps and timetables are available at the information office. Journeys cost from Skr20; the 24-hour *dygnskort* (adult/under 26 Skr110/75) is valid on all buses and local trains within the region. Tickets can be purchased at Pressbyrån outlets or at the train station. Tickets purchased onboard cost an extra Skr20.

Up to five express buses per day go to Vadstena otherwise change at Motala.

Long-distance buses depart from a terminal 200m northwest of the train station. Swebus Express runs 10 to 12 times daily to Jönköping (Skr158, 1½ hours) and seven to eight times daily to Göteborg (Skr269, four hours), and north to Norrköping (Skr67, 45 minutes) and Stockholm (Skr231, three hours).

Linköping is on the main north–south railway line. Regional and express trains run to Stockholm roughly every hour; express trains go to Malmö. Frequent regional trains run north to Norrköping (Skr80, 25 minutes). Kustpilen SJ trains run every few hours to Norrköping, Nyköping and Kalmar.

SWEDEN

VADSTENA

☎ 0143 / pop 7536

On Vättern lake, Vadstena is a legacy of both church and state power, and today St Birgitta's abbey and Gustav Vasa's castle compete for admiration. The atmosphere in the old town (between Storgatan and the abbey), with its wonderful cobbled lanes, evocative street names and wooden buildings, makes the place a satisfying pitstop.

The **tourist office** (☎ 315 70; www.vadstena.com; ◷ 10am-6pm Jul, 10am-6pm Jun & early Aug, 10am-2pm Mon-Fri rest of year) is located in Rödtornet (Sånggatan).

Sights & Activities

The Renaissance castle, **Vadstena Slott** (☎ 315 70; Slottsvägen; adult/7-15yr Skr55/10; ◷ 10am-6pm Jun–mid-Aug & late Nov, 10am-5pm rest of Aug, 10am-3pm Mon-Fri early May–mid-May & Sep, 10am-4pm daily rest of May, 10am-2pm Mon-Fri Oct & Dec-Apr), looks straight over the harbour and lake beyond. It was the mighty family project of the early Vasa kings and in the upper apartments there are some items of period furniture and paintings. There are daily tours from mid-May to mid-September.

The superb 15th-century **Klosterkyrkan** (abbey church; admission free; ◷ 9am-8pm Jul, 9am-7pm Jun & Aug, 9am-5pm May & Sep), consecrated in 1430, has a combination of Gothic and some Renaissance features. Inside are the accumulated relics of St Birgitta and medieval sculptures. Near the church is the **Sankta Birgitta Klostermuseum** (☎ 100 31; Lasarettsgatan; adult/8-18yr Sk50/20; ◷ 10.30am-5pm Jul–early Aug, 11am-4pm Jun & rest of Aug, 11am-4pm Sat & Sun May, Sep & Oct), the old convent founded by St Birgitta.

The area around Vadstena is full of history and deserves a closer look. Cycling is an option as the scenic flatlands around Vättern lend themselves to the pedal. A series of ancient legends is connected with **Rökstenen**, Sweden's most famous rune stone, by the church at Rök, just off the E4 on the road to Heda and Alvastra.

Sleeping & Eating

STF Vandrarhem Vadstena (☎ 103 02; Skänningegatan 20; dm Skr180; P) A short walk from the town centre sits this big hostel, with affable staff, sunny dorms and a large underground kitchen decorated with cheery Dala horses. Book ahead from late August to early June.

Vätterviksbadet (☎ 127 30; camp sites Skr195, simple r & cabins from Skr350; ◷ May–mid-Sep; ✉) A quality camping ground near the lake, 2km north of town, with family friendly amenities including a beach with shallow waters, minigolf, boules, sauna, waterslide, kiosk, cafe and pub.

Vadstena Klosterhotel (☎ 315 30; hotel@klosterhotel.se; s/d from Skr1095/1395; P 💻) History and luxury merge at this wonderfully atmospheric hotel in St Birgitta's old convent. The bathrooms are a wee bit dated, but the medieval-style rooms are great, with chandeliers, high wooden beds, and heaven-sent coffee-makers. Most boast lake views.

Rådhuskällaren (☎ 121 70; Rådhustorget; mains Skr119-195) Under the old courthouse, this affable 15th-century cellar restaurant dishes out simple but filling burger, pasta and fish meals. Its outdoor area is a favourite afternoon drinking spot in summer.

Restaurant Munkklostret (☎ 130 00; lunch Skr85, mains Skr200-324; ◷ from noon in summer, shorter hours winter) The Klosterhotel's ravishing restaurant is the best nosh spot in town. Seasonal, succulent steak, lamb, game and fish dishes are flavoured with herbs from the monastery garden, and served in the monks' old dorms.

Getting There & Around

See Linköping (p447) for regional transport information. Only buses run to Vadstena – take bus 610 to Motala (for trains to Örebro), or bus 661 to Mjölby (for trains to Linköping and Stockholm). Swebus Express runs on Fridays and Sundays to/from Stockholm (Skr277, 4¼ hours). **Blåklints Buss** (☎ 0142-121 50; www.blaklintsbuss.se, in Swedish) runs one to three services daily from the Viking Line Terminal (Map pp396–7) in Stockholm to Vadstena (Skr170).

SMÅLAND

The region of Småland is one of dense forests, glinting lakes and bare marshlands. Historically it served as buffer zone between the Swedes and Danes; the eastern and southern coasts in particular witnessed territorial tussles. Today it's better known for the Glasriket (Kingdom of Crystal) in the central southeast.

SWEDEN

VÄXJÖ

☎ 0470 / pop 79,562

A venerable old market town, Växjö (pronounced *vak*-choo, with the 'ch' sound as in the Scottish 'loch'), in Kronobergs län, is an important stop for Americans seeking their Swedish roots. In mid-August, **Karl Oscar Days** commemorates the mass 19th-century emigration from the area, and the Swedish-American of the year is chosen.

The **tourist office** (☎ 414 10; www.turism.vaxjo.se; Västra Esplanaden 7; ⏰ 9.30am-6pm Mon-Fri, 10am-2pm Sat Jun-Aug, 9.30am-4.30pm Mon-Fri rest of year) shares a building with the library, which offers free internet access.

Utvandrarnas Hus (Emigrant House; ☎ 201 20; www .utvandrarnashus.se; Vilhelm Mobergs gata 4; adult/under 19yr Skr40/free; ⏰ 9am-5pm Tue-Fri, 11am-4pm Sat & Sun May-Aug, 9am-4pm Tue-Fri, 11am-4pm Sat Sep-Apr) has archives, information and historical exhibitions on the beckoning USA. It's just behind the train-and-bus station, close to **Smålands Museum** (☎ 70 42 00; www.smalandsmuseum.se; Södra Järnvägsgatan 2; adult/under 19yr Skr40/free; ⏰ 10am-5pm Mon-Fri, 11am-5pm Sat & Sun Jun-Aug, closed Mon Sep-May), with an absorbing exhibition of glass from Glasriket.

At Evedal, **Växjö Vandrarhem** (☎ 630 70; www .vaxjovandrarhem.nu; dm from Skr200; [P] [🖥]), a former spa hotel, dates from the late 18th century. All rooms have washbasins; there's a big kitchen, laundry, and a wonderful lounge in the attic. It's well-loved, so book early. Take bus 1C from town.

First Hotel Cardinal (☎ 72 28 00; cardinal@firsthotels .se; Bäckgatan 10; s Skr956-1296, d Skr396-1696; [P] [🖥]) is a jump up in quality, with stylish rooms, Persian rugs and the odd antique touch. There's a small fitness centre, bar and a restaurant serving modern Nordic nosh.

For sustenance, head to Storgatan or try **Café Momento** (☎ 391 29; meals around Skr70), Smålands Museum's cafe, serving gourmet sandwiches, pies, salads, soup, spuds and cakes. In summer, nibble blissfully in the cute courtyard.

Getting There & Away

Småland airport (☎ 75 85 00; www.smalandairport .se) is 9km northwest of Växjö. **SAS** (☎ 0770-72 77 27; www.flysas.com) has direct flights to Stockholm Arlanda, **Fly Smaland** (☎ 0771-71 72 00; www.flysmaland.com) to Stockholm Bromma, Berlin and Vilnius, and **Ryanair** (☎ 0900-20 20 240; www.ryanair.com) to Düsseldorf Weeze. An airport bus (Flygbussen) con-

nects with flights (Skr20), otherwise take a **taxi** (☎ 135 00).

Länstrafiken Kronoberg (☎ 0771-76 70 76; www .lanstrafikenkron.se, in Swedish) runs the regional bus network, with daily buses to Halmstad, Jönköping and Kosta. Long-distance buses depart beside the train station. Svenska Buss runs one or two services daily to Eksjö (Skr210, 1½ hours), Linköping (Skr290, 3¼ hours) and Stockholm (Skr390, 6½ hours).

Växjö is served by SJ trains running roughly hourly between Alvesta (on the main north–south line; Skr37 to Skr55, 15 minutes) and Kalmar (Skr118, 1¼ hours). A few trains run daily directly to Karlskrona (Skr118, 1½ hours), Malmö (Skr214, two hours) and Göteborg (Skr240, 3¼ hours).

GLASRIKET

One of the most impressive things to see in Sweden is traditional glass-blowing, and there's no better place to see it than here, in its birthplace, the so-called 'Kingdom of Crystal'. The rest of the scenery's not bad either – dense forests, quaint red houses and intricately winding roads. It's no surprise that the area known as **Glasriket** (www.glasriket.se) is the most visited area of Sweden outside of Stockholm and Göteborg. There are at least 11 glass factories (look for *glasbruk* signs), most with long histories: Kosta, for example, was founded in 1742.

The glassworks have similar opening hours, usually 10am to 6pm Monday to Friday, 10am to 4pm Saturday and noon to 4pm Sunday. Expert glass designers produce some extraordinary avant-garde pieces, often with a good dollop of Swedish wit involved. Factory outlets have substantial discounts on seconds (around 30% to 40% off), and larger places can arrange shipping to your home country.

Nybro

☎ 0481 / pop 19,643

The biggest town in Glasriket, Nybro makes a good base for exploration. It was once an important centre for hand-blown light bulbs(!), and still has two glassworks on its doorstep. Nybro's **tourist office** (☎ 450 85; www.nybro.se, in Swedish; Stadshusplan; ⏰ 10am-6pm Mon-Fri, 10am-4pm Sat mid-Jun–Aug, 10am-5pm Mon-Fri Sep–mid-Jun) is inside the town hall.

Of the two glassworks, 130-year-old **Pukeberg** (☎ 800 29; www.pukeberg.se; Pukebergarnas väg), just southeast of the centre, is perhaps more interesting for its quaint setting. **Nybro** (☎ 428 81; Herkulesgatan; www.nybro-glasbruk.se) is smaller and laced with quirky items (think Elvis Presley glass platters).

There's a superior homestead museum, **Madesjö Hembygdsgård** (☎ 179 35; adult/child Skr30/10; ⏱ 10am-5pm Mon-Fri, 11am-5pm Sat & Sun mid-May–mid-Sep), about 2.5km west of town. Housed inside the 200m-long *kyrkstallarna* (former church stables), it contains an admirable collection, with cannonballs, clothing, coffins, carpenters' tools, a classroom, and a fantastic (ice-) cycle – and they're just the things beginning with 'C'.

Nybro Lågprishotell & Vandrarhem (☎ 109 32; Vasagatan 22; dm Skr225, hotel s/d Skr490/790; (P)) The local STF hostel, near Pukeberg, is clean and comfortable, with a kitchen on each floor as well as a sauna. More expensive 'hotel' rooms have cable TV, nonbunk beds and private showers and toilets. You can also rent bicycles.

SJ trains between Alvesta and Kalmar stop here every hour or two. Regional bus 131 runs to/from Kalmar.

Kosta, Boda & Orrefors

These three tiny Småland villages are home to the three biggest names in Swedish glass production. Each namesake company is open daily and each factory complex has an outlet store, museum or gallery, glass-blowing demonstrations and tourist information for the area.

The **Kosta Boda** (☎ 503 00; www.kostaboda.se) complex pulls in coach loads of visitors, who raid the vast discount outlets (there's even discounted designer threads these days). Funnily, Sweden even manages to make its tourist traps pleasant places. The exhibition gallery (Skr30) contain some inspired creations, and there are plenty of glass-blowing demos in the old factory quarters.

Orrefors (☎ 341 95; www.orrefors.se; ⏱ year-round) was founded in 1898. The factory complex is impressive (make sure you check out the gallery) and there's a good hostel nearby.

The friendly, well-equipped **Vandrarhem Orrefors** (☎ 300 20; Silversparregatan 14; dm/s/d from Skr170/320/390; ⏱ May-Sep) is located conveniently near the factory. Quaint red houses surround a grassy garden, and the peaceful rooms have proper beds. Breakfast is available on request.

If you're here from June to August, ask about *hyttsill* parties at the glass factories,

where traditional meals are prepared using the furnaces and cooling ovens. The menu includes herring, smoked sausage, bacon and baked potatoes, as well as the regional speciality *ostkaka* (cheesecake). The cost starts at around Skr325 per person including drinks. Contact the regional tourist offices or the glassworks for more information.

Getting There & Around

Apart from the main routes, bus services around the area are practically nonexistent. The easiest way to explore is with your own transport (beware of elk). Bicycle tours on the unsurfaced country roads are excellent; there are plenty of hostels, and you can camp almost anywhere except near the military area on the Kosta-Orrefors road.

Kalmar Länstrafik's bus 139 runs from mid-June to mid-August only and calls at a few of the glass factories. The service operates four times per day on weekdays, once on Saturday, and runs from Nybro to Orrefors and Målerås. Year-round bus services connect Nybro and Orrefors (up to nine weekdays), and Kosta is served by regular bus 218 from Växjö (two or three daily).

OSKARSHAMN

☎ 0491 / pop 26,294

Oskarshamn is useful mostly for its regular boat connections with Gotland. The **tourist office** (☎ 881 88; www.oskarshamn.se; Hantverksgatan 18; ⏱ 9am-6pm Mon-Fri, 10am-3pm Sat & Sun Jun-late Aug, 9.30am-4.30pm Mon-Fri late Aug-May) is in Kulturhuset, along with the **library**, which has free internet access.

The well-run **STF Vandrarhem Oskarshamn** (☎ 158 00; info@forumoskarshamn.com; Södra Långgatan 15-17; hostel dm/s/d Skr205/305/410, hotel s/d Skr780/1050, discounted to Skr650/800; (P) (🛏)) is a brilliant budget option. Rooms have TV, fans and private bathrooms – only the kitchen for self-caterers gives it away as a hostel.

Oskarshamn airport (☎ 332 00) is 12km north of town and **Skyways** (☎ 0771-95 95 00; www.skyways.se) flies direct to Stockholm Arlanda three times daily Monday to Wednesday and twice daily Thursday and Friday. An extra flight each weekday flies to Stockholm Arlanda via Linköping.

Long-distance bus services stop at the very central bus station. Regional bus services run up to six times daily from Oskarshamn to Kalmar (Skr75, 1½ hours) and Västervik (Skr67, one hour).

Swebus Express has three daily buses between Stockholm and Kalmar calling in at Oskarshamn. The closest train station is in Berga, 25km west of town. Here, regional trains run from Linköping and Nässjö. Local buses connect Berga and Oskarshamn.

Boats to Visby depart from the ferry terminal near the now-disused train station, daily in winter and twice daily in summer. Boats to Öland depart from the ferry terminal off Skeppsbron.

KALMAR
☎ 0480 / pop 61,533

Not only is Kalmar dashing, it also claims one of Sweden's most spectacular castles, where the crowns of Sweden, Denmark and Norway agreed to the short-lived Kalmar Union of 1397. Other local assets include Sweden's largest gold hoard, from the 17th-century ship *Kronan* and the storybook cobbled streets of Gamla Stan (Old Town) to the west of Slottshotellet.

Information

The **tourist office** (☎ 41 77 00; www.kalmar .se/turism; Ölandskajen 9; ☺ 9am-9pm Mon-Fri, 10am-5pm Sat & Sun late Jun–mid-Aug, shorter hours other times) is handy.

Sights & Activities

The once-powerful Renaissance **Kalmar Slott** (☎ 45 14 90; adult/5-16yr Skr80/20; ☺ 10am-6pm Jul, 10am-5pm Aug, 10am-4pm May, Jun & Sep, 11am-3.30pm

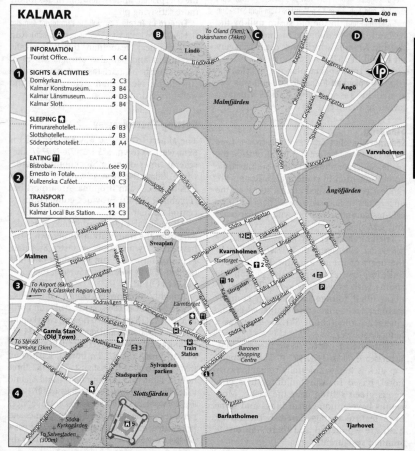

KALMAR

0 — 400 m
0 — 0.2 miles

INFORMATION
Tourist Office..................1 C4

SIGHTS & ACTIVITIES
Domkyrkan.....................2 C3
Kalmar Konstmuseum.......3 B4
Kalmar Länsmuseum.........4 D3
Kalmar Slott...................5 B4

SLEEPING 🏠
Frimurarehotellet.............6 B3
Slottshotellet.................7 B3
Söderportshotellet...........8 A4

EATING 🍴
Bistrobar.....................(see 9)
Ernesto in Totale.............9 B3
Kullzenska Caféet............10 C3

TRANSPORT
Bus Station...................11 B3
Kalmar Local Bus Station....12 C3

To Öland (7km);
Oskarshamn (74km)

Lindö

Lindövägen

Malmfjärden

Ängö

Varvsholmen

Ängöfjärden

Rappegatan
Bælgensgatan
Ölandsbron
Gröngatan
Bjelkegatan
Sparregatan
Ängöleden
Varvsgatan

Fabriksgatan

Sveaplan

Malmen
Lindégatan
Esplanaden
Norra Vägen
Unionsgatan
Tullgatan

Södravägen
Olof Palmesgatan
Järnvägsgatan
Bremergatan
Fredjagatan

Gamla Stan
(Old Town)

To Stenso
Camping (3km)

To Airport (6km);
Nybro & Glasriket Region (30km)

Kungsgatan
Slottsvägen
Molinsgatan
Vasallundsgatan

Sylvanderparken

Stadsparken

Slottsfjärden

Södra
Kyrkogården

To Salvestaden
(300m)

Söderportsgatan

Wernsköldsgatan
Stranggatan
Trädgårdsgatan

Södra Kanalgatan

Strömgatan

Kvarnholmen
Stortorget
Norra
Larmtorget

Södra Vallgatan

Södra Långgatan
Kaggensgatan
Storgatan
Olandsgatan
Skeppsbrogatan
Proviantgatan
Ö Vallgatan
Larmgatan
Östra Sjögatan
Fiskaregatan
Linnegatan
Ängbåtsbronsgatan

Larmgatan

Train
Station

Baronen
Shopping
Centre

Ölandskajen

Barlastgatan

Barlastholmen

Tjärhovsgatan

Tjärhovet

Sat & Sun Apr & Oct, 11am-3.30pm 2nd weekend of month Nov-Mar), located in a magnificent setting by the sea south of the railway, was the key to Sweden before the lands to the south were claimed from Denmark. The panelled King Erik chamber is the highlight of the castle's interior. **Guided tours** (in English at 2.30pm late Jun, plus 11.30am & 1.30pm Jul–mid-Aug, 11.30am only mid-Aug–early Sep) are included.

For art lovers the nearby **Kalmar Konstmuseum** (☎ 42 62 82; www.kalmarkonstmuseum.se; Stadsparken; adult/under 20yr Skr40/free; ◷ 11am-5pm, to 8pm Wed) is worth a look, while the pretty streets of the **Gamla Stan** area to the northeast of the castle are lovely for wandering.

The highlight of **Kalmar Länsmuseum** (County Museum; ☎ 45 13 00; www.kalmarlansmuseum.se; Skeppsbrogatan; adult/under 18yr Skr50/free; ◷ 10am-6pm mid-Jun–mid-Aug, 10am-4pm Mon-Fri, 11am-4pm Sat & Sun mid-Aug–mid-Jun), in the old steam mill by the harbour, is the exhibition of finds from the flagship *Kronan*, which sank controversially off Öland in 1676.

Home to a spectacular pulpit, the baroque **Domkyrkan** (Cathedral; Stortorget) was designed by Tessin, King Karl X Gustav's favourite architect.

Sleeping

Söderportshotellet (☎ 125 01; Slottsvägen 1; s/d Skr550/735; ◷ mid-Jun–mid-Aug) Right outside the castle, Söderportshotellet offers summertime accommodation in student digs. Rooms are modest yellow-washed affairs; some on the upper floor have castle views. There's a super cafe-restaurant downstairs with regular blues and jazz gigs.

Frimurarehotellet (☎ 152 30; www.frimurare hotellet.com; Larmtorget 2; s/d Skr1240/1460; ▯) In the heart of the action, this 19th-century building contains spacious, personable rooms with polished wooden floors. The plant-filled lounge comes with complimentary tea, coffee and biscuits, while one cheaper room (about Skr200 less) has a hallway shower.

Slottshotellet (☎ 882 60; www.slottshotellet.se; Slottsvägen 7; s/d Skr1390/1790; ▣ ▯) Kalmar's top pick is this wonderfully romantic, cosy hotel, based in four buildings in a gorgeous green setting near the castle. Most rooms have antique furnishings and some even feature vintage Swedish tile stoves. Staff are wonderful and there's an onsite summer restaurant.

Eating

A good area for upmarket dining is the harbour; the view of huge timber yards and cranes is industrial, but you don't want showy sailing boats *all* the time…

Kullzenska Caféet (☎ 288 82; 1st fl, Kaggensgatan 26; snacks from Skr30) The pick of the town's cafes is this gorgeous maze of genteel 19th-century rooms, with original tiled stoves and furniture. There's a range of sandwiches and cakes (try the yummy fruit crumbles).

Bistrobar (☎ 200 50; Larmtorget 4; pizzas Skr94-99, mains Skr169-189) The glam new kid in town, this restaurant/bar combo has an enviable location on a fountain-studded square. While the chocolate wikka lounges and Café del Mar tunes make for a perfect vino session, ditch the overpriced, underwhelming mains for the more satisfying pizzas.

Ernesto in Totale (☎ 200 50; Larmtorget 4; mains Skr148-248; ◷ lunch Sat & Sun, dinner Mon-Sun) Run by a real-deal Neapolitan, this Italian cafe, restaurant and bar also attracts scores of people with its baristas, extensive menu (including Neapolitan-style pizzas), and well-mixed drinks.

Getting There & Away

The **airport** (☎ 45 90 00; www.kalmarairport.se) is 6km west of town. **SAS** (☎ 0770-72 77 27) flies several times daily to Stockholm Arlanda, while **Kalmarflyg** (www.kalmarflyg.se, in Swedish) flies to Stockholm Bromma. An airport bus (Flygbuss; Skr40) provides connections to central Kalmar.

All regional and long-distance buses depart from the train station; local town buses have their own station on Östra Sjögatan. Regional buses are run by **Kalmar Länstrafik** (☎ 0491-76 12 00; www.klt.se, in Swedish), including buses to Öland.

Roughly three **Swebus Express** (☎ 0771-21 82 18; www.swebusexpress.com) services daily run north to Västervik (Skr130, two hours), Norrköping (Skr224, four hours) and Stockholm (Skr224, 6½ hours); and one to three services daily run south to Karlskrona (Skr82, 1¼ hours), Karlshamn (Skr110, two hours), Kristianstad (Skr182, three hours), Lund (Skr247, four hours) and Malmö (Skr247, 4½ hours). **Svenska Buss** (☎ 0771-67 67 67; www.svenskabuss.se, in Swedish) has four services per week on the same route; journey times and prices are similar. **Silverlinjen** (☎ 0485 261 11; www .silverlinjen.se, in Swedish) runs one to three daily direct buses from Öland to Stockholm (Skr280), calling at Kalmar; reservations are essential.

SJ trains run every hour or two between Kalmar and Alvesta (Skr151 to Skr164, 1¼ hours), where you can connect with the main Stockholm–Malmö line and with trains to Göteborg. Trains run to Linköping up to nine times daily (Skr238, three hours), also with connections to Stockholm.

ÖLAND
☎ 0485 / pop 25,000

Like a deranged vision of Don Quixote's, Öland is *covered* in old wooden windmills. Symbols of power and wealth in the mid-18th-century, they were a must-have for every aspiring man-about-town and the death knell for many of Öland's oak forests. Today, 400 or so remain, many lovingly restored by local windmill associations.

South of Färjestade the entire island is a Unesco World Heritage site, lauded for its unique agricultural landscape, in continuous use from the Stone Age to today, and peppered with runic stones and ancient burial cairns.

The bridge from Kalmar lands you on the island just north of Färjestaden, where there's a well-stocked **tourist office** (☎ 56 06 00; www .olandsturist.se) at the Träffpunkt Öland centre. Staff can book island accommodation (for a Skr195 booking fee). There are few hotels, but more than 25 camping grounds and at least a dozen hostels (book ahead). Camping between midsummer and mid-August can cost up to Skr300 per site.

Silverlinjen (☎ 0485-261 11; www.silverlinjen.se, in Swedish) runs one to two daily direct buses from Öland to Stockholm (Skr280, 6½ hours), calling at Kalmar – reservations are essential.

INFORMATION	
Tourist Office	1 A4
Tourist Office (Borgholm)	(see 3)

SIGHTS & ACTIVITIES	
Borgholms Slott	2 A4
Solliden Palace	(see 2)

SLEEPING	
Ebbas Vandrarhem & Trädgårdscafe	3 A3
Guntorps Herrgård	4 B3
Nya Conditoriet	(see 3)

EATING	
Pubben	(see 3)

TRANSPORT	
Bus Station	(see 3)

ÖLAND

SWEDEN

Borgholm & Around

Öland's 'capital' and busiest town, Borgholm seeps a vaguely tacky air with its discount shops and summer hordes of teens on the pull. The most dramatic (and satisfying) sight is the enormous ruined castle on its outskirts. The **tourist office** (☎ 890 00; Sandgatan 25) is at the bus station.

Northern Europe's largest ruined castle, **Borgholms Slott** (☎ 123 33; www.borgholmsslott.se; adult/12-17yr Skr50/20; ☺ 10am-6pm May-Aug, 10am-4pm Apr & Sep), looms just south of town. This epic limestone structure was burnt and abandoned early in the 18th century, after life as a dye works. There's a terrific museum inside and a nature reserve nearby, as well as summer concerts and children's activities.

Sweden's most famous 'summer house', **Solliden Palace** (☎ 153 55; adult/7-17yr Skr65/35; ☺ 11am-6pm mid-May–mid-Sep), 2.5km south of the town centre, is used by the Swedish royals. Its exceptional gardens are open to the public and well worth a wander.

SLEEPING & EATING

The tourist offices in Borgholm and Färjestaden can help you find inexpensive private rooms in the area.

Ebbas Vandrarhem & Trädgårdscafé (☎ 103 73; rum@ebbas.se; Storgatan 12; s/d Skr325/580; ☺ May-Sep) Right in the thick of things, Ebbas cafe has a small STF hostel above it. Five of the cosy lemon-yellow rooms overlook the gorgeous rose-laced garden, and four the bustling pedestrianised main street. There's a kitchen for self-caterers...or just pop downstairs for decent hot and cold grub (lunch Skr85), served until 9pm in the summer (earlier at other times). Book ahead in summer.

Guntorps Herrgård (☎ 130 00; www.guntorpsherrgard.se; Guntorpsgatan; s/d from Skr995/1195) This is a delightful old farmhouse east of town. The accommodation is excellent and unintentionally camp, with peachy tones and chandeliers above the beds. There's the added drawcard of a huge smörgåsbord (Skr195 per person; open from 6pm daily, summer) offering superb samples of local dishes.

Pubben (☎ 124 15; Storgatan 18) There are snacks and light meals here, but punters mainly come to this English-style pub for the beer and hefty selection of whiskeys.

KARLSKRONA

☎ 0455 / pop 62,338

If you like your Swedes in uniform, you'll appreciate Karlskrona. Marine cadets pepper the streets of what has always been an A-league naval base. In 1998 the entire town was added to the Unesco World Heritage List for its impressive collection of 17th- and 18th-century naval architecture. The **tourist office** (☎ 30 34 90; www.karlskrona.se/tourism; Stortorget 2; ☺ 9am-8pm Jun-Aug, 9am-6pm Mon-Fri, 10am-4pm Sat Sep-May) has internet access.

Sights & Activities

Karlskrona's star is the extraordinary offshore **Kungsholms Fort**, with its curious circular harbour, established in 1680 to defend the town. Four-hour **boat tours** (adult/12-18yr Skr180/80; ☺ 10am mid-Jun–Aug), including a tour, depart from Fisktorget; book at the tourist office or Marinmuseum (bring ID).

Bristling with cannons, the tower **Drottningskärs kastell** on the island of Aspö was described by Admiral Nelson of the British Royal Navy as 'impregnable'. You can visit it on a **Skärgårdstrafiken boat** (return adult Skr40-130, child Skr20-70; ☺ Jun-Aug), departing from Fisktorget.

The striking **Marinmuseum** (☎ 359 30 02; Stumholmen; adult/under 19yr Skr60/free; ☺ 10am-6pm Jun-Aug, 11am-5pm Tue-Sun Sep-May) is the national naval museum and has interesting ship and historical displays.

The evocative **Blekinge Museum** (☎ 30 49 60; Fisktorget 2; admission free; ☺ 10am-6pm Jun-Aug, 11am-5pm Tue-Sun, to 7pm Wed Sep-May) explores the local fishing, boat-building and quarrying trades.

Pick a sunny summer afternoon for a tour around Karlskrona's **archipelago**, made up of almost 1000 islands. A three-hour tour costs Skr130/70 per adult/child; contact the Skärgårdstrafiken office at Fisktorget or check www.affarsverken.se for timetables and information.

Sleeping & Eating

STF Vandrarhem Trossö Karlskrona (☎ 100 20; www.karlskronavandrarhem.se; Drottninggatan 39; dm/s/d from Skr140/245/320) Modern, clean and friendly, this hostel has a laundry, TV room and backyard for kids to play in; parking on the opposite side of the street is free.

Dragsö Camping (☎ 153 54; info@dragsocamping.nu; Dragsövägen; camp sites from Skr190, 2-bed cabins Skr750-850, d Skr320; (✷ Apr–mid-Oct) This large, good-looking camping ground, 2.5km northwest of town, is situated on a scenic bay. Facilities include boat and bicycle hire, as well as a Karlskrona-themed minigolf course. Bus 7 stops about 1km short of the camping ground.

First Hotel Ja (☎ 555 60; www.firsthotels.se; Borgmästaregatan 13; s/d Skr1398/1598; **P** ☐) Karlskrona's top slumber spot boasts slick, hip, recently renovated rooms in white and charcoal hues, with blissful beds and flatscreen TVs. Hotel perks include a sauna, bar/restaurant and a great breakfast buffet.

Glassiärens Glassbar (☎ 170 05; Stortorget 4; (✷ May–Sep) The queues at this legendary ice cream peddler are matched by the mammoth serves. Piled high in a heavenly waffle cone, the two-flavour option (Skr30) is a virtual meal.

Montmartre (☎ 31 18 33; Ronnebygatan 18; pizza Skr65-80, mains Skr80-189) Next door to the Museum Leonardo da Vinci Ideale, atmospheric Montmartre evokes a French bistro with its wine-red drapes, tasselled lampshades, and oil paintings. The menu is a more worldly affair, with pizzas, Swedish favourites and zestier fusion numbers like grilled tuna with wasabi, lime and chilli.

Getting There & Away

Ronneby airport (☎ 0457-255 90) is 33km west of Karlskrona; the Flygbuss leaves from Stortorget (Skr80). SAS flies to Stockholm Arlanda daily, and Blekingeflyg flies to Stockholm Bromma Sunday to Friday.

The bus and train stations are just north of central Karlskrona. **BlekingeTrafiken** (☎ 0455-569 00; www.blekingetrafiken.se) operates regional buses.

Svenska Buss runs four times a week from Malmö to Stockholm, calling at Kristianstad, Karlshamn and Karlskrona. Swebus Express service 834 runs once to twice daily from Malmö to Kalmar, calling at Kristianstad, Karlshamn and Karlskrona.

Kustbussen runs six times daily on weekdays (twice daily on weekends) each way between Karlskrona and Kalmar (around Skr150; 1½ hours).

Direct trains run at least 13 times daily to Karlshamn (Skr70, one hour) and Kristianstad (Skr117, two hours), at least seven times daily to Emmaboda (Skr54, 40 minutes), and 10 times to Lund (Skr177, 2¾ hours) and Malmo (Skr177, three hours).

Trains also run at least a couple of times to Göteborg (Skr382, five hours). Change at Emmaboda for Kalmar.

Stena Line ferries to Gdynia (Poland) depart from Verkö, 10km east of Karlskrona (take bus 6).

GOTLAND

Gorgeous Gotland has much to brag about: a Unesco-lauded capital, truffle-sprinkled woods, A-list dining hotspots, talented artisans, and more hours of sunshine than anywhere else in Sweden. It's also one of the country's richest historical regions, with around 100 medieval churches and countless prehistoric sites.

The island is situated nearly halfway between Sweden and Latvia, in the middle of the Baltic Sea. Just off its northeast tip you'll find the island of Fårö, most famous as the home of Sweden's great director, the late Ingmar Bergman. The island national park of Gotska Sandön is located 38km further north, while the petite islets of Stora Karlsö and Lilla Karlsö sit just off the western coast.

Information on the island abounds; www.gotland.net and www.guteinfo.com (in Swedish) are good places to start.

VISBY

☎ 0498 / pop 22,236

The port town of Visby is medieval eye candy and enough to warrant a trip to Gotland all by itself. Inside its thick city walls await twisting cobbled streets, fairytale wooden cottages, evocative ruins and steep hills with impromptu Baltic views. The city wall, with its 40-plus towers and the spectacular church ruins within, attest to the town's former Hanseatic glories.

Information

Gotland City (☎ 08-406 15 00; www.gotlandcity.se, in Swedish; Kungsgatan 57) A central travel agency in Stockholm, that is useful if you're planning your trip from the capital.

Library (Cramergatan, ☎ 29 90 00; (✷ 10am-7pm Mon-Fri, noon-4pm Sat & Sun) Free internet access (Skr20 mid-Jun–mid-Aug)

Tourist Information Centre (☎ 20 17 00; www.gotland.info; Skeppsbron 4-6; (✷ 8am-7pm in summer, shorter hours rest of year) At the harbour.

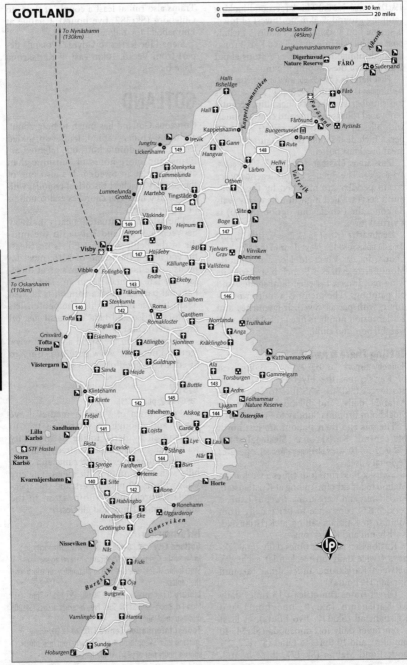

Sights

The town is a noble sight, with its 13th-century wall of 40 towers – savour a few hours walking around the perimeter (3.5km). Ask at the tourist office about guided walking tours, conducted in English a few times a week in summer (Skr85), or buy a copy of *Visby on Your Own* (Skr35) for a self-guided tour.

The **ruins** of 10 medieval churches are all within the town walls, contrasting with the stoic **Sankta Maria kykra** (Cathedral of St Maria; ☼ 8am-9pm Sun-Fri, to 7pm Sat late Jun–early Aug, 8am-7pm early to late Jun & early Aug–late Sep, 8am-5pm Mon-Wed & Fri, 8am-6pm Sat, 9am-8pm Sun late Sep–early Jun), built in the late 12th- and early 13th-centuries and heavily touched-up over the centuries.

Gotlands Fornsal (☎ 29 27 00; www.lansmuseet gotland.se; Strandgatan 14; adult/under 19yr Skr75/free; ☼ 10am-6pm Fri-Wed, to 7pm Thu Jun–mid-Sep, noon-4pm Tue-Sun mid-Sep–May) is one of the mightiest regional museums in Sweden. Highlights include amazing 8th-century pre-Viking picture stones, human skeletons from chambered tombs and medieval wooden sculptures, but the star is the legendary Spillings hoard. At 70kg, it's the world's largest booty of preserved silver treasure.

Sleeping

Moderately priced accommodation in and around Visby is in demand; we recommend booking well in advance if possible. Gotland's hotel prices work opposite to most hotel rates in Sweden: prices increase on summer weekends and in the peak tourist months.

Fängelse Vandrarhem (☎ 20 60 50; Skeppsbron 1; dm/d from Skr180/240) As hard to get into as it once was to get out of, this hostel offers beds year-round in the small converted cells of an old prison. It's in a handy location, between the ferry dock and the harbour restaurants, and there's a cute terrace bar in summer. Reserve well in advance and call ahead before arriving to ensure someone can let you in.

Gotlands Resor (☎ 20 12 60; info@gotlandsresor.se; Färjeleden 3; cottages from Skr670) This travel agency, in Hamnhotellet, books stylish, fully-equipped cottages in eastern and northern Gotland. Bookings for the summer should be made around six months in advance. The agency also organises bike hire and rents camping equipment.

Värdshuset Lindgården (☎ 21 87 00; lindgarden .vardshuset@telia.com; Strandgatan 26; s/d mid-May–Sep Skr1195/1395, Oct–mid-May Skr750/950; 💻) A sound

central option, with rooms set facing a soothing garden beside a popular restaurant. Dine outdoors and listen to music in the romantic courtyard in summer.

Hotel Villa Borgen (☎ 20 33 00; www.gtsab.se; Adelsgatan 11; s/d Skr1095/1395; 💻) This place has satisfying rooms set around a pretty, quiet courtyard and an intimate breakfast room with French doors and stained glass for that boutique feeling.

Clarion Hotel Wisby (☎ 25 75 00; cl.wisby@choice.se; Strandgatan 6; s/d Skr1795/2190; 💻) Top of the heap in Visby is the luxurious, landmark Wisby. Medieval vaulted ceilings and look-at-me candelabra contrast with funky contemporary furnishings. The gorgeous pool – complete with medieval pillar – occupies a converted merchant warehouse.

Eating & Drinking

There are more restaurants per capita in Visby than in any other Swedish city. Most are clustered around the Old Town squares, on Adelsgatan or at the harbour. Wherever you choose, do not pass up a chance to try the island's speciality – a saffron pancake (saffranspankaka) with berries and cream.

Skafferiet (☎ 21 45 97; Adelsgatan 38; sandwiches from Skr35) Shamelessly charming, this casual lunch spot offers salubrious sandwiches and lip-smacking cakes and pastries.

Vinäger (☎ 21 11 60; Hästgatan 3; sandwiches Skr49-68, salads Skr85-95) Sporting a slick, ethno-chic interior, this hip cafe/bar puts the emphasis on fresh food, whether it's a fetta and hummus wrap, lingonberry and cardamom muffins or sinfully good carrot cake. Directly across the street, Vinäger's outdoor resto-bar (summer only) cranks up the x-factor with a glam alfresco lounge, smooth cocktails and a dinner menu featuring Gotland's only sushi option.

Bakfickan (☎ 27 18 07; Stora Torget; mains Skr128-258; ☼ lunch & dinner) White tiled walls, merrily strung lights and boisterous crowds define this foodie-loved bolthole, where enlightened seafood gems might include pollock with lobster risotto and wild garlic.

Bolaget (☎ 21 50 80; Stora Torget 16; mains Skr179-205; ☼ to 2am, closed Mon winter) Take a defunct Systembolaget shop, chip the 'System' off the signage, and reinvent the space as a buzzing, bistro-inspired hotspot. Top-notch seasonal flavours shine through in French-inspired dishes like duck with cherry sauce, cocoa beans and walnut-roasted potatoes.

SWEDEN

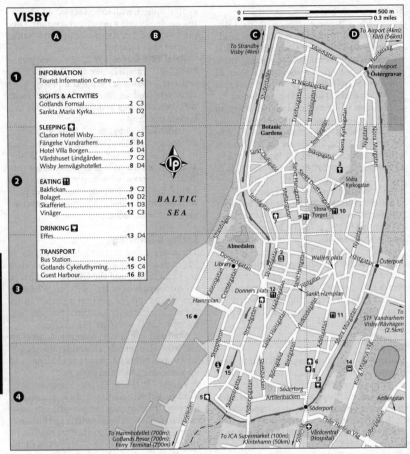

VISBY

Effes (☎ 21 06 22) Check out this pub/bar, just off Adelsgatan. Gloriously grungy and packed with characters (rockers and Goths love the place), Effes is built into the town wall and is a good place for a meal (snacks and meals Skr70 to Skr145) or drink. There's an outdoor courtyard, pool tables and live music in summer.

AROUND THE ISLAND

Renting a bicycle and following the well-marked **Gotlandsleden cycle path** is one of the best ways to spend time on the island. It loops all around the island, sometimes joining the roadways but more often winding through quiet fields and forests. You can hire cycles at several locations in Visby. There's an ex-cellent hostel network along the cycle route, with particularly good facilities in Bunge, Lummelunda, Lärbro and the small northern islet of Fårö.

GETTING THERE & AWAY
AIR

There are regular **Skyways** (☎ 0771-95 95 00; www.skyways.se) flights between Visby and Stockholm's Arlanda and Bromma airports (up to 10 times a day for each airport). Flights between Stockholm and Visby generally cost Skr517 and up; click on the 'Low fare calendar' link on the website to check for the best prices.

The cheaper local airline is **Gotlands Flyg** (☎ 22 22 22; www.gotlandsflyg.se), with regular flights between Visby and Stockholm Bromma (one to 10 times daily). Prices start at Skr321 one way; book early for discounts, and inquire after stand-by fares (adult/under 26 Skr621/321). Popular summer-only routes include Göteborg, Hamburg, Oslo and Helsingfors.

The island's **airport** (☎ 26 31 00) is 4km northeast of Visby. No buses serve the airport directly; your best bet is to catch a taxi into/from town (around Skr145).

BOAT
Year-round car ferries between Visby and both Nynäshamn and Oskarshamn are operated by **Destination Gotland** (☎ 0771-22 33 00; www.destinationgotland.se). There are departures from Nynäshamn one to five times daily (about three hours). From Oskarshamn, there are one or two daily departures in either direction (three to four hours).

Regular one-way adult tickets for the ferry cost from Skr180, but from mid-June to mid-August there is a far more complicated fare system; some overnight, evening and early-morning sailings in the middle of the week have cheaper fares.

Transporting a bicycle costs Skr45; a car usually costs from Skr298, although again in the peak summer season a tiered price system operates. Booking a nonrefundable ticket, three weeks in advance, will save you money. If you're thinking of taking a car on the ferry between mid-June and mid-August, make sure you reserve a place well in advance.

GETTING AROUND
Many travel agents and bike-rental places on the island also rent out camping equipment. In Visby, hire bikes from Skr75 per 24 hours at **Gotlands Cykeluthyrning** (☎ 21 41 33), behind the tourist office (on the harbour).

Kollektiv Trafiken (☎ 21 41 12) runs buses via most villages to all corners of the island. The most useful routes, that have connections up to seven times daily, operate between Visby and Burgsvik in the far south, Visby and Fårösund in the north (also with bus connections on Fårö), and Visby and Klintehamn. A one-way ticket will not cost you more than Skr68 (although if you take a bike on board it will cost an additional

Skr40), but enthusiasts will find a monthly ticket good value at Skr675.

NORRLAND

Norrland, the northern half of Sweden, is remote enough that travellers here aren't likely to see the tour-bus crowd – or, for that matter, much of anyone else. The population is sparse – reindeer outnumber cars on the roads, and much of the landscape consists of deep green forest. It's a paradise for nature lovers who enjoy hiking, skiing and other outdoor activities. The north is home to the Sami people, and several villages have well-preserved open-air museums that demonstrate traditional Sami lifestyles.

Norrland also rewards quirk-seekers: it boasts a rarely glimpsed monster lurking in a lake, a disappearing hotel made of ice, and a golf course that flits between Sweden and Finland. Inlandsbanan, the historic railway line from Mora to Gällivare via Östersund, Storuman, Arvidsjaur and Jokkmokk, is a fun if not particularly fast way to see the north.

SUNDSVALL
☎ 060 / pop 93,300
When Sundsvall burned to the ground in 1888, civic leaders made a decision that left behind the city's small-town feel and gave it a new sense of weight and significance: on the sites of the old wooden houses, they rebuilt the town in stone. This forced poorer residents to the city's outskirts while wealth and power collected in the centre, but it also meant that modern Sundsvall, which might have been just another architecturally bland coastal city, is today not only historically significant but also quite pretty.

The **tourist office** (☎ 61 04 50; www.sundsvalltur ism.com; Stora Torget; ⏰ 10am-5pm Mon-Fri, also 10am-3pm Sat Jul & Aug) has information on activities including summer boat tours.

Kulturmagasinet, on Sjögatan down near the harbour, is a magnificent restoration of some old warehouses. The buildings now contain the library and **Sundsvall Museum** (☎ 19 18 03; adult/child Skr20/free; ⏰ 10am-7pm Mon-Thu, 10am-6pm Fri, 11am-4pm Sat & Sun), which has exhibits of local art, natural history, Iron Age archaeology and geology. The tiny **cafe** (⏰ 10am-4pm) serves a buffet lunch (Skr65).

Sleeping & Eating

STF Vandrarhem Sundsvall (☎ 61 21 19; www.gaffel byn.se; Gaffelbyvägen; dm Skr160-220, s/d from Skr275/320) The STF hostel is above the town on Norra Stadsberget, and has both older rooms and more expensive modern rooms with private bathroom. The 20-minute walk to the hostel from the city centre is pleasant, but not much fun with heavy bags – a bus runs up here in summer from the train and bus stations.

Lilla Hotellet (☎ 61 35 87; Rådhusgatan 15; s/d Skr595/795) In a stone building designated a historical monument, this small family run hotel has a great location and a friendly vibe. Rooms have interesting architectural details, many including ceramic tile stoves.

Tant Anci & Fröcken Sara (☎ 785 57 00; Trädgårdsgatan 14; soup skr65, sandwiches Skr50; ☺ 11am-6pm Sat, 10am-9pm Mon-Fri, noon-9pm Sun) Humongous bowls of soup or salad are the speciality at this adorable organic cafe, where you can also get hearty sandwiches, giant bowls of pasta and pastries. There are only a few tables, but take-away is available; part of the space is devoted to a small health-food shop for organic tea and coffee, chocolate, snacks and cooking supplies.

Cafe Piccolo (☎ 12 10 84; Rådhusgatan 37; mains Skr65-75, ice-cream buffet Skr50; ☺ 10am-7pm Mon-Thu, 10am-midnight Fri, Sun in winter) This bright and spacious cafe/coffeeshop has a massive, tempting lunch buffet, plus an ice-cream buffet.

Getting There & Away

Midlanda airport (☎ 19 76 00) is 22km north of Sundsvall; buses run from the bus station three to nine times daily (Skr80) to connect with SAS and Skyways flights to Göteborg, Luleå and Stockholm.

Buses depart from the Sundsvall bus station, near Kulturmagasinet. Ybuss runs daily to Östersund (Skr190, 2½ hours, twice daily), Gävle (Skr240, 3½ hours, four daily) and Stockholm (Skr275, six hours, four to five daily). Länstrafiken Västerbotten bus 100 runs several times daily to Umeå (Skr285, 3¾ hours), Luleå (Skr423, eight hours) and most other coastal towns.

Trains run west to Östersund and south to Söderhamn, Gävle and Stockholm. The station is just east of the town centre, on Köpmangatan.

HÖGA KUSTEN
☎ 0613

Some of the most dramatic scenery on the Swedish coastline is found here, on the Höga Kusten ('High Coast'). The secret to its spectacular beauty is elevation; nowhere else on the coast do you find such a mountainous landscape, with sheer rocky cliffs plunging straight down to the sea, as well as lakes, fjords and islands. The region was recently recognised as geographically unique and listed as a Unesco World Heritage site.

The regional **tourist office** (☎ 504 80; www .hogakusten.com) can help you with information on exploring the region by bus, car or on an organised tour; it's located inside Hotell Höga Kusten, just north of **Höga Kustenbron**, the spectacular E4 suspension bridge over Storfjärden. Unfortunately, there's little by way of public transport (buses cruise along the E4 highway but don't make it into the region's villages). Hence, this area is virtually impossible to explore without having your own set of wheels.

In addition to the striking landscapes, the other major attractions around the region are the many well-preserved **fishing villages** – with the pick of them being Barsta, Bönhamn and Norrfällsviken – and the delightful offshore **islands**, especially Högbonden and Ulvön.

Norrfällsviken is a picture-perfect halfcircle of red-and-white fishing huts around a narrow inlet. There's a hilltop chapel from 1649 (the key is kept next to the door), and the friendly **Fiskar Fänget** (☎ 0613-211 42; fish plates Skr70-120; ☺ late Apr–mid-Sep) sells smoked fish to take away, as well as more substantial meals in its cosy wood-panelled restaurant-pub. Next door is a tiny **fishing museum** (☺ 11am-4pm) where you can learn the history of *surströmming*, the fermented herring that's famously an acquired taste, including how (and more to the point *why*) it's made.

Skuleberget Naturum (☎ 401 71; admission free; ☺ 9am-7pm May-Sep, 10am-5pm Wed-Sun Oct-Apr), by the E4 north of Docksta, has exhibitions and lots of information on hiking routes on and around **Skuleberget** (285m), the looming mountain.

Sleeping & Eating

STF Vandrarhem Docksta (☎ 130 64; dm Skr130-200, s/d from Skr170/260; ☒) is an attractive and busy hostel 3km south of Docksta at

Skoved, right along the Höga Kustenleden (High Coast Trail). Facilities include a restaurant and an outdoor stage for summer concerts. Camp sites (Skr130) are available; reservations recommended.

Kustgårdens Vandrarhem (☎ 212 55; dm Skr160), in Norrfällsviken, operated by the nearby **Brittas Restaurang** (☎ 212 55; d/family r from Skr695/1095; 🍴), is a popular summer complex consisting of a restaurant and pub, hotel and hostel, plus activities like mini-golf and fishing.

Vandrarhem Högbonden (☎ 230 05, 420 49; dm from Skr200; 🕑 May-Oct) is a relaxing getaway on the little island of Högbonden. There's a kitchen here, and a cafe opens in summer. Book well in advance.

Getting There & Around

Bus 217 runs one to six times daily between Nordingrå, the bridge and Kramfors. Länstrafiken Västerbotten bus 100 runs along the E4.

Ferries to Högbonden (☎ 0613-230 05, winter 231 00; adult/child return Skr150/50) go from Barsta only mid-May to mid-June and mid-August to October (noon Friday to Sunday), and from both Barsta and Bönhamn in peak summer (mid-June to mid-August). During this period boats leave from Barsta at 9.30am, 11.30am, 2.30pm and 5.30pm, and from Bönhamn at 10am, noon, 3pm and 6pm.

Ferries to Ulvön (☎ 070-651 92 65; adult/child return Skr150/50; 🕑 Jun-Aug) leave year-round from Köpmanholmen (Skr70 one way, twice daily) and mid-June to August from Ullånger (9.30am) and Docksta (10.15am), from Skr125.

ÖSTERSUND

☎ 063 / pop 58,400

This pleasant town by Lake Storsjön, in whose chilly waters is said to lurk a rarely sighted monster, has good budget accommodation and is a relaxed and scenic place and an excellent gateway town for further explorations of Norrland. The **tourist office** (☎ 1440 01; www.turist.ostersund.se; Rådhusgatan 44; 🕑 9am-5pm Mon-Thu, 10am-3pm Fri-Sun) is opposite the town hall; it has free internet access.

Sights & Activities

Don't miss **Jamtli** (☎ 15 01 00; www.jamtli.com; adult/child mid-Jun-Aug Skr110/free, rest of year Skr60/free; 🕑 11am-5pm Jun-Aug, closed Mon rest of yr), 1km north of the town centre. It combines an open-air museum park (a la Skansen in Stockholm)

with a first-rate regional culture museum. In the outdoor section, guides wearing period costumes explain the traditions of the area. Indoors, the regional museum exhibits the **Överhogdal tapestry**, a Viking relic from around 1100 that's perhaps the oldest of its kind in Europe.

An offshoot of Färgfabriken in Stockholm, the newly opened **Färgfabriken Norr** (☎ 390 00 00; www.fargfabriken.se; Byggnad 33, Infanterigatan 30; admission free; 🕑 noon-5pm Thu-Fri, noon-4pm Sat-Sun; bus 14 or 8) is a huge new art space across E14 from Jamtli. It's a cavernous room with an ambitious curatorial scope.

Several attractions lie on the adjacent island of Frösön, reached by road or footbridge from the middle of Östersund. These include **Frösöns Djurpark** (☎ 51 47 43; www.frosozoo.se; adult/child/family Skr180/90/500; 🕑 10am-4pm mid–late Jun & Aug, 10am-6pm Jul; bus 5). There are slalom and nordic ski runs on the island at Östberget, plus a **viewing tower** (adult/child Skr10/5; 🕑 11am-6pm mid-May–mid-Sep, 9am-6pm mid-Jun–mid-Aug) and cafe.

Ask at the tourist office about monster-spotting **lake cruises** (Skr65-95; 🕑 Jun-Sep). Bring your binoculars.

Sleeping & Eating

Frösötornets Vandrarhem (☎ 51 57 67; www.frosotornet.se; Utsiktsvägen 10; dm adult/child Skr150/75) This quiet hostel in the trees next to the Frösön viewing tower has dorm beds in small, cabin-like grass-roofed huts.

STF Vandrarhem Jamtli (☎ 12 20 60; vandrarhemmet@jamtli.com; Museiplan; s/d from Skr235/280, dm Skr140-160; bus 2) Right inside the gates of Jamtli museum park is this comfortable hostel, housed in a low, barnlike wooden building with a huge kitchen. Dorms are in two- to five-bed rooms, and facilities are all top-notch. Reservations are recommended.

Hotel Emma (☎ 51 78 40; www.hotelemma.com; Prästgatan 31; s/d from Skr895/995; 🖥 Ⓟ) Emma couldn't be better located: it's on the main pedestrian shopping street, right above a whiskey bar. The hotel has all the comforts of a fancy chain but with personality: its rooms are nestled into crooked hallways on two floors, with homey touches like squishy armchairs and imposing ceramic stoves; some rooms have french doors facing the courtyard and buttery wood floors. Parking costs Skr35.

News (☎ 10 11 31; Samuel Permansgata 9; lunch buffet Skr70) You can't miss this buzzing hangout on a busy corner, with its deck full of fashionable diners. The menu was recently revamped and now includes a vast Lebanese lunch buffet from 11am to 2pm weekdays. The restaurant gradually shifts toward nightclub as the evening progresses.

Brunkullans (☎ 10 14 54; Postgränd 5; mains Skr115-149; ☻ 11am-2pm Mon-Fri, from 5pm Tue-Sat, from 4pm Fri) A local favourite for its outdoor patio, Brunkullans also has a wonderfully atmospheric, candlelit 19th-century interior space. The menu features Swedish classics and upscale versions of basic bar food.

Getting There & Away

The **airport** (☎ 19 30 00) is on Frösön, 11km west of the town centre, and the airport bus leaves regularly from the bus terminal (adult/child Skr70/20). SAS flies several times daily to Stockholm; Fly Nordic and Nordic Regional serve Luleå and Umeå.

The train station is a short walk south from the town centre, but the main regional bus station is central on Gustav III Torg; local buses usually run to both. Local buses 1, 3, 4, 5 and 9 go to Frösön (Skr20). Most city buses stop in front of the tourist office.

Länstrafiken Bus 45 runs to Mora (5½ hours, two to four daily). Bus 155 runs west to Åre (1½ hours); bus 63 runs northeast to Umeå (six hours, two to four daily).

SJ trains run from Stockholm (Skr923, six hours) via Gävle, and some continue to Storlien (from where you can catch trains to Trondheim, Norway). You can also catch a train east to Sundsvall (Skr164, 2½ hours). In summer the Inlandsbanan train runs once daily, to Gällivare (Skr795) or Mora (Skr395).

ÅRE & AROUND
☎ 0647 / pop 9700

A fun, outdoorsy place to hang out in the off season, Åre is beautifully situated in a mountain valley, but it gets crowded in winter, thanks to its famed ski area (www.skistar.com/are). The place has 45 ski lifts, 100 pistes and 1000 vertical metres of skiable slopes, including a 6.5km downhill run. The skiing season is from November to mid-May, but conditions are best from February, when daylight hours increase.

The **tourist office** (☎ 177 20; www.visitare.se) is above the train station and has free internet access. The same building contains luggage lockers (small/large Skr30/70

per day), a sporting-goods store and an ICA supermarket.

Sleeping & Eating

Note that accommodations fill up quickly in winter, so plan well ahead. Not all hotels stay open in summer, but those that do offer bargains.

STF Vandrarhem Åre (☎ 301 38; www.brattlandsgarden.se; dm Skr140, s/d from Skr180/280) A lovely spot on an old farmstead with dorm rooms tucked into red wooden buildings and a huge living room–dining area. The place is 8km east of Åre, in Brattland; once-daily buses connect it to town, although service is spotty.

Fjällgården (☎ 145 00; www.fjallgarden.se; s/d from Skr495/990) Up on the hillside, this is as much an activity centre as a hotel. It offers fishing, mountain biking, golf, horse riding, paddling, and a chance to try the 'zipline', which lets you fly across the valley on a tiny string. Rooms are large and decorated in faux-rustic, apres-ski style.

ourpick Åre Bageri (☎ 523 20; Årevägen 55; sandwiches Skr50-60; ☻ 7am-3.30pm) A sprawling organic cafe and stone-oven bakery with a comfy, shabby-chic atmosphere, this place lends itself to lingering. In addition to great coffee, pastries and huge sandwiches, it does a fairly epic all-you-can-eat breakfast spread (Skr79).

Werséns (☎ 505 05; lunch Skr85, pizzas from Skr99, mains Skr139-269; ☻ 3-10pm Sun-Fri & noon-11pm Sat Jun-Aug, from noon daily rest of year) This white-tablecloth brasserie and pizzeria has take-away options and half-portions available. There's a bar and, in good weather, outside tables.

Getting There & Away

Regional bus 157 runs from Östersund and connects Åre to the nearby winter-sports centre of Duved (Skr20, 15 minutes, several daily). Bus 571 connects Duved to Storlien (Skr80, one hour). Regular trains between Stockholm and Storlien, via Östersund, stop at Åre (Skr724, seven hours).

UMEÅ
☎ 090 / pop 112,000

With the vibrant feel of a college town (it has around 30,000 students), Umeå is a welcome outpost of urbanity in the barren north. It's one of the fastest-growing towns in Sweden and an agreeable place to hang out, wind down or stock up for an outdoor adventure.

The **tourist office** (☎ 16 16 16; www.visitumea.se; Renmarkstorget 15) is central.

Sights & Activities

Gammlia (☎ 17 18 00; admission free; ☯ 10am-5pm mid-Jun–mid-Aug, 10am-4pm Tue-Fri, noon-4pm Sat, noon-5pm Sun rest of year), a cluster of museums 1km east of the town centre, includes the cultural/historical exhibits and Sami collections of the regional **Västerbottens Museum**; the modern art museum, **Bildmuseet**; and the **Maritime Museum**. These are surrounded by **Friluftsmuseet**, an open-air historic village where staff wear period clothes and describe traditional homestead life.

There are interesting offshore islands plus a number of activities in the surrounding area, including fishing, white-water rafting, jet-boating and canoeing in or on the local rivers, horse riding and a variety of walking trails. The tourist office can help organise these.

Sleeping & Eating

Royal Hotel (☎ 10 07 30; www.royalhotelumea.com; Skolgatan 62; s/d Skr1240/1440; ⬜) The Royal Hotel has its own cinema, a fancy sauna, and a popular restaurant, Greta's, right in the heart of town. Staff will serve you breakfast (on request) in your spacious, clean-lined, Scandi-chic room.

STF Vandrarhem Umeå (☎ 77 16 50; info@umeavandrarhem.com; Västra Esplanaden 10; dm Skr140, s/d from Skr240/280; ⬜) Rooms are tiny but comfortable at this busy and efficient youth hostel, one of the few in the region that's actually occupied by youth. It's in a great location, a residential neighbourhood at the edge of the town centre.

Hotel Pilen (☎ 14 14 60; Pilgatan 5; s Skr650-750, d Skr850) This smallish boutique hotel has comfortable, unfussy rooms located in a quiet area some 600m from the town centre and close to the river. There's a good restaurant attached.

Rost Mat & Kaffe (☎ 135 800; Rådhusesplanaden 4B; soup Skr65; ☯ 11am-6pm Mon-Fri, 11am-4pm Sat) This teeny industrial-chic coffeeshop is covered in tiles and doles out good espresso and light meals.

Getting There & Away

The **airport** (☎ 71 61 00) is 4km south of the city centre. SAS and Malmö Aviation each fly to Stockholm up to seven times daily; there are also direct flights to Luleå, Göteborg and Örebro.

RG Line (www.rgline.com) operates ferries between Umeå and Vaasa (Finland) once or twice daily (Sunday to Friday). A bus to the port leaves from near the tourist office an hour before RG Line's departures.

The long-distance bus station is directly opposite the train station. Ybuss runs services south up to three times daily to Gävle (Skr375, seven hours) and Stockholm (Skr415, nine hours), via the coastal towns of Örnsköldsvik, Härnösand, Sundsvall, Hudiksvall and Söderhamn.

Umeå is the main centre for **Länstrafiken i Västerbotten** (☎ 020-91 00 19; www.ltnbd.se), the regional bus network. Direct buses to Mo i Rana (Norway) run once daily (bus 300, eight hours), but buses going as far as Tärnaby (Skr233, 5½ hours) run up to four times a day. Other destinations include Östersund (Skr326, 6½ hours, three daily), Skellefteå (Skr148, two hours, several daily) and Luleå (Skr285, 4¾ hours, several daily).

Tågkompaniet trains leave daily from Umeå, to connect at Vännäs with the north–south trains between Stockholm (Skr831, 7½ hours, four daily) and Luleå (Skr262, 5½ hours, once daily); northbound trains stop in Boden, from where there are connections to Kiruna (Skr498, nine hours, twice daily) and Narvik (Norway).

LULEÅ

☎ 0920 / pop 45,050

Luleå is a pretty town with several parks and a sparkling bay surrounded by a marina. It's the capital of Norrbotten, chartered in 1621; the town centre moved to its present location in 1649 because of the falling sea level (9mm per year), due to postglacial uplift of the land. An extensive offshore archipelago contains some 1700 large and small islands.

The **tourist office** (☎ 45 70 00; www.lulea.se; Kulturens Hus; ☯ 10am-7pm Mon-Fri, 10am-4pm Sat & Sun) is inside Kulturens Hus.

Boat tours of the archipelago depart from Södra Hamn daily between June and August; typical prices are around Skr300 to Skr400 for adults, Skr150 for children. Evening cruises are also popular; pick up a brochure at the tourist office.

Unesco World Heritage-listed **Gammelstad** (☎ 45 70 10; www.lulea.se/gammelstad; admission free;

(☽ 24hr), or 'Old Town', contains row after zigzaggy row of cute little red-and-white cottages. This was the medieval centre of northern Sweden. The stone church (from 1492), 424 wooden houses (where the pioneers stayed overnight on their weekend pilgrimages) and six church stables remain. Many of the buildings are still in use, but some are open to the public, and the site is lovely to walk around.

Guided tours (Skr30) leave from the Gammelstad **tourist office** (☎ 25 43 10; worldheritage.gammelstad@lulea.se; ☽ 9am–6pm mid-Jun–mid-Aug, 10am-4pm Tue-Thu rest of year) every hour on the hour between 10am and 4pm, mid-June to mid-August. (Tours are given in the language of whoever booked first, so you may have to wait an hour for one in English.) Bus 32 runs hourly from Luleå.

Norrbottens Museum (☎ 24 35 02; Storgatan 2; admission free; ☽ 10am-4pm Tue-Fri, noon-4pm Sat-Sun) is worth a visit if only for the Sami section, but there are also exhibits about the Swedish settlers, plus there are films and musical performances, an outdoor maze and a kids' playground. In summer it's also open on Monday.

Sleeping & Eating
SVIF Vandrarhem Kronan/Luleå (☎ 43 40 50; www .vandrarhemmetkronan.se, in Swedish; Kronan H7; dm/s Skr170/250; 🖳) About 3km from the centre, this year-round hostel is the best budget option in the area, with good facilities set in a forested location. To get here, take any bus heading toward Kronanområdet.

Amber Hotel (☎ 102 00; www.amberhotell.nu; Stationsgatan 67; s/d Skr790/980) The pick of the city-centre hotels is this small wooden guesthouse; its spacious rooms have all the modern touches, flat-screen TVs etc, but still feel homey. It's just a few steps from the train station.

Cafe Mat & Prat (☎ 28 11 90; Storgatan 51; mains Skr56-71; ☽ 10am-6pm Mon-Fri, 10am-4pm Sat) Sure, it's inside a shopping mall, but this is a pleasant, homey cafe serving real espresso as well as pastas, focaccia, sandwiches, salads and a good Thai curry.

Getting There & Around
The **airport** (☎ 24 49 00) is 9km southwest of the town centre. SAS, Direktflyg and Nordic Airways fly regularly to Stockholm, Sundsvall and Umeå. Other airlines serve smaller destinations, including Pajala. Take the **airport bus** (☎ 122 00; Skr45) from outside the Comfort Hotel on Storgatan.

Bus 100 operates between Haparanda, Luleå, Skellefteå, Umeå and Sundsvall at least four times daily. Buses run frequently to Boden (Skr49, one hour), Arvidsjaur (Skr162, three hours, via Boden and Älvsbyn), and Jokkmokk (Skr179, three hours) and on to Gällivare (via Boden and Vuollerim).

Direct Tågkompaniet trains from Stockholm and Göteborg operate during nighttime only. Most trains from Narvik and Kiruna via Boden terminate at Luleå.

HAPARANDA
☎ 0922 / pop 10,500
Bargain-hunter's alert! Haparanda has become a full-scale shopper's paradise, thanks to a decision taken in 2005 to build an Ikea store in this tiny town nestled up against Finland. The furniture giant's arrival rescued the town's economy and encouraged other businesses (mainly big-box retail stores) to invest as well.

The main **tourist office** (☎ 120 10; www. haparandatornio.com; Green Line; ☽ 8am-8pm Mon-Fri, 10am-6pm Sat & Sun) in Haparanda is shared with the office in Tornio (in Finland) on the 'green line'.

Haparanda's primary attraction, other than shopping, is its **Green Zone Golf Course** (☎ 106 60), on the border with Finland. During a full round of golf the border is crossed four times. Around midsummer you can play under the midnight sun; book in advance.

The tourist office can arrange **white-water rafting** trips on the scenic Kukkolaforsen rapids. There's a small tourist village here, which includes a **camping ground and cabins** (☎ 310 00; camp sites Skr190, 4-bed cabins from Skr590), plus there is a restaurant, a cafe, fish smokehouse, saunas and a museum.

The waterfront **Vandrarhem Haparanda** (☎ 611 71; info@haparandavandrarhem.com; Strandgatan 26; dm/s/d from Skr180/250/470 from Skr180; ☽ year-round, reception 4-7pm) is at the edge of a park close to the town centre.

Tapanis Buss (☎ 129 55; www.tapanis.se) runs express coaches from Stockholm to Haparanda two to three times a week (Skr600, 15 hours). Regional buses reach Luleå (Skr134, 2½ hours, three daily) and towns further south.

ARVIDSJAUR

☎ 0960 / pop 6948

The small settlement of Arvidsjaur, on Inlandsbanan, was established as a Sami marketplace, but it's most famous now as a testing ground for fast machines. Local companies specialize in setting up test tracks on the frozen lakes in the area, then putting vehicles through their paces.

The **tourist office** (☎ 175 00; www.arvidsjaur .se/turism/; Östra Skolgatan 18C; ☼ 9.30am-6pm Mon-Fri, noon-4.30pm Sat & Sun Jun-Aug, 8.30am-4.30pm Mon-Fri rest of year) is just off Storgatan.

The first church was built in Arvidsjaur in 1607, in hopes of introducing the Sami to Christianity. Church attendance laws imposed a certain amount of pew time upon the nomadic Sami, so to make their church visits more manageable they built small cottages, or *gåhties*, for overnighting. Some 80 of these are preserved now in **Lappstaden** (admission free, tours Skr30; ☼ 10am-7pm, tours 5pm Jun-Aug), just across Storgatan from the modern church. The buildings are owned by the forest Sami and are still in use.

Friendly accommodation can be found at **Lappugglans Turistviste** (☎ 124 13; lappugglan@hem .utfors.se; Västra Skolgatan 9; per person Skr130-145, child Skr65; P), a hostel with a likeable hippie vibe, or at **Lapland Lodge** (☎ 13 720, 0768-47 57 17; www .laplandlodge.eu; Östra Kyrkogatan 18; s/d Skr550/700, family Skr750-1050, incl linen & breakfast; P), a new B&B next to the church.

Länstrafiken Norrbotten bus 45 goes daily between Gällivare and Östersund, stopping at the bus station on Storgatan. Bus 200 runs daily between Skellefteå and Bodø (Norway) via Arvidsjaur. In summer the Inlandsbanan train can take you north to Gällivare (Skr336) via Jokkmokk, or south to Mora via Östersund (Skr582).

JOKKMOKK

☎ 0971 / pop 5600

An important town in Sami culture, Jokkmokk has not only the definitive Sami museum but is also the site of an enormous annual market gathering. Just north of the Arctic Circle, it's a quiet little town that makes a nice base for visitors to Laponia World Heritage site; ask for information about the area at the tourist office.

The **tourist office** (☎ 121 40; www.turism.jokkmokk .se; Stortorget 4; ☼ 9am-7pm Mon-Fri, 10am-6pm Sat & Sun

mid-Jun–Aug, 8.30am-noon & 1-4pm Mon-Fri rest of year) has internet access.

The illuminating **Ájtte Museum** (☎ 170 70; Kyrkogatan 3; adult/child Skr50/free; ☼ 9am-6pm mid-Jun–mid-Aug, 10am-4pm Mon-Fri rest of year) gives a thorough introduction to Sami culture, including traditional costume, silverware and some 400-year-old magical painted shamans' drums. Look for replicas of sacrificial sites and a diagram explaining the uses and significance of various reindeer entrails. One section details the widespread practice of harnessing the rivers in Lappland for hydroelectric power and the consequences this has had for the Sami people and their territory. There are extensive notes in English.

Sleeping & Eating

STF Vandrarhem Åsgård (☎ 559 77; asgard @jokkmokkhostel.com; Åsgatan 20; dm Skr125-160; ☼ reception 8-10am & 5-8pm; 🖳) The STF hostel has a lovely setting among green lawns and trees, right near the tourist office; it's a comfortable place with numerous bunkbeds, kitchen, TV lounge and showers in the basement.

Hotell Gästis (☎ 100 12; www.hotell-gastis.com; Herrevägen 1; s/d from Skr850/1095; P) This place has pleasant rooms in a small grey building. There's also a good restaurant here, with lunch specials and a la carte dinners.

Café Glasskas (Porjusvägen 7; mains Skr35-75) A coffeeshop, bar and internet cafe, Glasskas has a great, wide patio for warm-weather dining, casual but filling meals (salads, quiches, sandwiches etc) and friendly service.

our pick Ájtte museum restaurant (mains Skr75-90; ☼ noon-4pm) At the museum cafe, it's possible to enhance what you've learned about the local wildlife by sampling some of them as a lunch special.

Getting There & Away

Buses arrive and leave from the bus station on Klockarvägen. Buses 44 and 45 run twice daily to and from Gällivare (Skr107, one to three hours), and bus 45 goes to and from Arvidsjaur once a day (Skr162, two to three hours). Bus 94 runs to Kvikkjokk (Skr134, two hours) twice daily.

In summer, Inlandsbanan trains stop in Jokkmokk. For main-line trains, take bus 94 to Murjek via Vuollerim (Skr68, one hour, up to six times daily) or bus 44 bus to Boden and Luleå (Skr163, two to three hours).

SWEDEN

GÄLLIVARE & MALMBERGET
☎ 0970 / pop 19,500

Gällivare and its northern twin, Malmberget, are surrounded by forest and dwarfed by the bald Dundret hill. After Kiruna, Malmberget ('Ore Mountain') is the second-largest iron-ore mine in Sweden; the town belongs to government-owned mining company LKAB. And like Kiruna, the area's sustaining industry is simultaneously threatening the town with collapse: all that digging around below the surface has weakened the foundations beneath Malmberget, so buildings are gradually being shifted to sturdier ground. The populace seems unfazed.

The **tourist office** (☎ 166 60; turistinfo@gellivare.se; Centralplan 3; ☺ 8am-6pm daily mid-Jun–mid-Aug, Mon-Fri rest of year) is near the train station.

Dundret (821m) is a nature reserve with excellent views, and you can see the midnight sun here from 2 June to 12 July. In winter there are four nordic courses and 10 ski runs of varying difficulty, and the mountaintop resort rents out gear and organises numerous activities. If you have your own car, it's a rather hair-raising drive to the top.

In Malmberget, 5km north of Gällivare, **Kåkstan** (admission free) is a historical 'shanty town' museum village, dating from the 1888 iron-ore rush. Contact the Gällivare tourist office for details of the **LKAB iron-ore mine tour** (Skr250; 9.30am-1pm mid-Jun–mid-Aug, by appointment in winter), which takes you down on a bus. And if you like that, you'll love the **Gruvmuseum** (Puoitakvägen; adult/child Skr40/free; ☺ 2-6pm Tue-Thu mid-Jul–late Aug, by appointment otherwise), covering 250 years of mining. Bus 1 to Malmberget departs from directly opposite the Gällivare church; outside of summer hours, contact the Gällivare tourist office to arrange a visit.

Grand Hotel Lapland (☎ 77 22 90; www.grandho tellapland.com; Lasarettsgatan 1; s/d Skr1295/1675) is a modern hotel opposite the train station and has comfortable rooms. Its 2nd-floor dining room is apparently *the* place to meet for dagens lunch (Skr78). The ground-level pub is dark and cosy, with covered outdoor seating for summer.

Restaurang Husmans (☎ 170 30; Malmbergsvägen 1; mains from Skr55; ☺ 9am-9pm Mon-Fri, 11am-8pm Sat-Sun), close to the tourist office and behind Hotel Lapland, serves kebabs and salads and in the evenings has a small dining nook where you can get Arabic food.

Getting There & Away

Regional buses depart from the train station. Bus 45 runs daily to Östersund (Skr465, 11 hours) via Jokkmokk and Arvidsjaur; bus 93 serves Ritsem (Skr204, three hours) and Kungsleden in Stora Sjöfallet National Park (mid-June to mid-September only); buses 10 and 52 go to Kiruna (Skr134, two hours); and bus 44 runs to Jokkmokk and Luleå (Skr234, three hours).

Tågkompaniet (☎ 0771-44 41 11; www.tagkom paniet.se, in Swedish) trains come from Luleå and Stockholm (sometimes changing at Boden), and from Narvik in Norway. More exotic is the **Inlandsbanan** (☎ 0771-53 53 53; www.inlandsbanan .se), which terminates at Gällivare.

KIRUNA
☎ 0980 / pop 23,407

Kiruna's citizens live up to their nickname – 'the no-problem people' – by remaining unperturbed at the news that their city is on the verge of collapsing into a mine pit. A few years back, it became clear that years of iron-ore extraction was sucking the stability out of the bedrock underneath the town. In 2007 the town voted to shift itself a couple of miles northwest; plans are to move the railway and about 450 homes by 2013, with the rest of the town centre to follow gradually.

The **tourist office** (☎ 188 80; www.lappland.se; Lars Janssonsgatan 17, in Folkets Hus; ☺ 8.30am-9pm Mon-Fri, 8.30am-6pm Sat & Sun Jun-Aug, Mon-Sat rest of year), on the main square, has computers for internet access and can book mine tours and accommodation as well as various activities, including rafting, dogsledding and snow scooter trips. There's a cafe upstairs.

A visit to the depths of the **LKAB iron-ore mine**, 540m underground, is recommended – some of the stats you'll hear on a tour are mind-blowing. Tours leave daily from the tourist office, more frequently from mid-June to mid-August (adult/student/child Skr280/180/50). Tours in English happen only a few times a week; make bookings through the tourist office.

Every winter at Jukkasjärvi, 18km east of Kiruna, the amazing **Ice Hotel** (www.icehotel .com) is built from hundreds of tonnes of ice from the frozen local river. This custom-built 'igloo' has a chapel and a bar – you can drink from a glass made of ice – and ice-sculpture exhibitions. It also has 50 'hotel rooms' outfitted with reindeer skins and sleeping

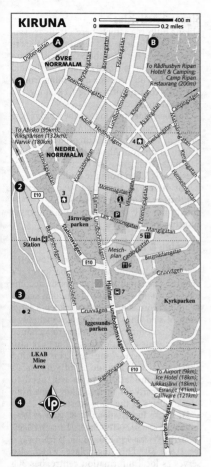

dition to its caravan and camp sites. Ask about the organised walk to Samegården, the museum of Sami culture (Skr450, 1pm Fridays), and other activities.

SVIF Yellow House (☎ 137 50; www.yellowhouse.nu; Hantverkaregatan 25; dm/s/d Skr150/300/400) The SVIF hostel also has budget hotel rooms; the excellent facilities include a sauna, kitchen and laundry, a TV in each room, and a nice, quiet enclosed garden.

Hotel Vinterpalatset (☎ 677 70; www.vinterpalat set.se; Järnvägsgatan 18; s/d from Skr720/930; 🖥) Inside this dark-brown wooden building near the train station are pretty, spacious B&B rooms, each with a TV and modern bathroom, plus an upstairs lounge and a breakfast room almost flowery enough to make you think you're in the Cotswolds. The decadent breakfast includes cured salmon and roast game.

Café Safari (☎ 174 60; Geologsgatan 4; meals Skr35-65) This is the nicest cafe in town, a long skinny room with good coffee, cakes and light meals such as sandwiches, quiche and baked potatoes.

Brända Tomten (☎ 101 09; Föreningsgatan 6; meals Skr35-65) In the city centre, this casual cafe and fast-food joint serves surprisingly good coffee and filling lunch items – layered sandwiches, salads, pies and so on. Big windows make for fun people-watching.

Getting There & Away
The small **airport** (☎ 680 00), 7km east of the town, has two to three daily nonstop flights to Stockholm with SAS, and to Umeå (weekdays only) with Skyways. The **airport bus** (☎ 156 90) operates during peak summer season.

Regional buses to and from the **bus station** (Hjalmar Lundbohmsvägen), opposite the Stadshus, serve all major settlements around Norrbotten. Bus 10 runs twice daily to

bags guaranteed to keep you warm despite the -5°C temperatures (and in winter that's nothing; outside the hotel it can be as low as -30°C).

Also in Jukkasjärvi is **Gárdi** (adult/child Skr60/30; ☿ tours 10am-6pm mid-Jun–mid-Aug), a reindeer yard that you can tour with a Sami guide to learn about reindeer farming and Sami culture. Regular bus 501 runs between Kiruna and Jukkasjärvi (Skr29, 30 minutes, several daily).

Sleeping & Eating
Rådhusbyn Ripan Hotell & Camping (☎ 630 00; www .ripan.se; Campingvägen 5; camp sites/s/d Skr125/1200/1535, cabins from Skr995; 🚲 🖥) In the northern part of town, this is a large and well-equipped camping ground with hotel-standard chalets in ad-

SWEDEN

Gällivare (Skr134) and Luleå (Skr293), and 92 goes two to four times daily to Nikkaluokta (Skr79) for the Kebnekaise trailhead. To reach Karesuando and Finland, take bus 50 (Skr179, not Saturday).

Trains between Kiruna and Narvik have earned a reputation as unreliable and often late, so you'll want to plan around a flexible schedule. SJ connects Kiruna with Luleå (Skr269, four hours), Stockholm (Skr854, overnight) and Narvik, Norway (Skr207, three hours). Trains to Narvik call at Abisko (Skr91, 1½ hours) and Riksgränsen.

ABISKO
☎ 0980

Spectacular scenery, friendly people, a long tradition of Sami culture and extremely easy access to all of the above make Abisko one of the highlights of any trip to Lappland. The 75-sq-km **Abisko National Park** spreads out from the southern shore of scenic Lake Torneträsk. It's framed by the striking profile of Lapporten, a 'gate' formed by neighbouring hills that serves as the legendary gate to Lappland.

Abisko is less rugged than either Sarek or Padjelanta, and easier to get to by trains, buses and the scenic mountain motorway between Kiruna and Narvik. This is also the driest part of Sweden, giving the area a completely distinct landscape – it's wide-open and arid, and consequently has a relatively long (for northern Sweden) hiking season.

Abisko has two train stops: Östra station puts you in the centre of the tiny, tiny village, while Abisko Turiststation is across the highway from the STF lodge.

The **STF Turiststation/Abisko Mountain Lodge** (☎ 402 00; www.abisko.nu) provides information on local hikes; **guides** (☼ 8-9am and 7-8pm) are available for consultation, and several **tours** (per person Skr290-640, Sami camp tours Skr150, 8.30pm Thu & Sun; ☼ 8.40am-5pm) leave from here. There's a small shop with supplies, snacks and **equipment rentals** (☼ 8am-8pm Jun, 8am-10pm Jul & Aug), as well as a restaurant and hostel (see right).

Naturum (☎ 401 77; ☼ 10am-6pm mid-Jun–Sep, to 9pm Wed & Fri) has an office and exhibition space next to STF Abisko Turiststation; staff can suggest hikes and answer questions about where to hike and what to bring. Various guided tours are available (per person Skr50 to Skr75), and a simple map offers suggestions based on available time ('if you have two hours...' etc).

Sights & Activities

Hiking is the big activity here – trails are varied in both distance and terrain, and they're easy to reach. Between the STF Turiststation and Naturum, you'll find all the expertise and equipment you need for everything from a day hike to a months-long trek along the popular Kungsleden.

The **Kungsleden** trail follows the Abiskojåkka valley, and day trips of 10km to 20km are no problem from Abisko. Kungsleden extends 450km south from Abisko to Hemavan, with STF huts serving most of the trail; the hut at Alesjaure is 15km from the trailhead.

For hikes in this area, use the map *Fjällkartan BD6* (Skr110 to Skr120), available at the STF lodge, Naturum and most sporting-goods stores.

Sleeping & Eating

Abisko Fjällturer (☎ 401 03; www.abisko.net; dm Skr175) Just behind the town, this is a backpacker's delight. The small hostel has basic accommodation and a wonderful wooden sauna. Brothers Tomas and Andreas keep a large team of sled dogs; one package includes a night's accommodation plus the chance to drive your own dogsled. There are also very popular week-long sled trips (around Skr8000), which include all of your meals and accommodation – you will need to book very early for these. Follow signs from Abisko Östra to the 'Dog Hostel'.

STF Abisko Turiststation (☎ 402 00; www.abisko .nu; hotel s/d from Skr690/1190, hostel s/d from Skr450/680, dm Skr210; ☼ 8am-9pm 22 Dec–3 Jan, 15 Feb–4 May, 6 Jun–21 Sep; ☐) This huge place, which also serves as local information centre, has 300 beds in various configurations, kept to the usual high STF standards. In winter, when the lake freezes, the Turiststation opens its new Abisko Ark Hotel, which consists of fishing hut-style cabins and a sauna built directly on the ice. Breakfast/lunch/dinner are available for Skr80/80/290 (lunch is noon to 2pm, dinner 6pm to 8pm, a la carte 8pm to 9pm).

Self-service **STF huts** (bed Skr215-260, nonmembers additional Skr50-100) along Kungsleden are spread at 10km to 20km intervals between Abisko and Kvikkjokk; you'll need a sleeping bag. Campers are charged Skr40.

Lapporten Stormarknad (☼ 9am-8pm Mon-Fri, shorter hr Sat & Sun), in Abisko village, is a grocery store that also carries a range of outdoor supplies, such as batteries, candles, bug spray and basic camping gear.

Getting There & Away
In addition to trains (stations at Abisko Östra and Abisko Turiststation) between Luleå and Narvik, bus 91 runs from Kiruna to Abisko (Skr107, 1¼ hours).

SWEDEN DIRECTORY

ACCOMMODATION
Most hotels in Sweden offer steep discounts (up to 50%) on Friday and Saturday nights and from mid-May through August. Many hotels have also started using 'flexi' prices, discounts for rooms booked online ahead of time. In this chapter we list the standard price; what you'll actually pay may vary significantly. For the best deals, book early and online. Our Sleeping entries are listed by budget, with least expensive options appearing first. 'budget' options cost under Skr800, 'midrange' options from Skr800 to Skr1600, and 'top end' places more than Skr1600.

Cabins & Chalets
Daily rates for *stugor* (cabins and chalets, often found at camping grounds or in the countryside) offer good value for small groups and families, and range in both quality and price (Skr350 to Skr800). Some are simple, with bunk beds and little else (you share the bathroom and kitchen facilities with campers); others are fully equipped with their own kitchen, bathroom and living room. Local and regional tourist offices have listings of cabins and cottages that may be rented by the week; these are often in idyllic forest, lakeside or coastal locations. See the **Stuga** (www.stuga.nu) website for more.

Camping
Sweden has hundreds of camping grounds; a free English-language guide with maps is available from tourist offices. Some are open year-round, but the best time for camping is from May to August. Prices vary with facilities, from Skr150 for a basic site to Skr250 for the highest standards. Most camping grounds have kitchens and laundry facilities, and many have the works – swimming pool, minigolf, bike and canoe rental, restaurant, store etc.

You must have a Camping Card Scandinavia to stay at most Swedish camping grounds. Apply for one in advance by writing to **Sveriges Camping & Stugföretagares Riksorganisation** (fax 0522-64 24 30; info@scr.se; Box 255, SE-45117 Uddevalla) or fill in the form on the website www.camping.se; otherwise pick up a temporary card at any Swedish campsite. The card costs Skr125 a year. One card covers the whole family.

Visit www.camping.se for lots of useful information.

Hostels
Sweden has well over 450 hostels *(van-drarhem)*, usually with excellent facilities. Outside major cities, hostels aren't backpacker hangouts but are used as holiday accommodation by Swedish families, couples or retired people. A related oddity is the frequent absence of dormitories, meaning you often have to rent out a room rather than a bed. Some hostels also have singles and doubles with en suite bathrooms that are almost of hotel quality, for very reasonable rates. About 50% of hostels open year-round; many others open from May to September, while some open only from mid-June to mid-August.

Be warned, Swedish hostels are virtually impossible to enter outside reception opening times, and these hours are frustratingly short (except in Stockholm and Göteborg): generally between 5pm and 7pm, occasionally also between 8am and 10am. The secret is to prebook by telephone – reservations are highly recommended in any case, as hostels fill up fast.

Some 315 hostels are affiliated with **Svenska Turistföreningen** (STF; ☎ 08-463 21 00; www.svenskaturistforeningen.se), part of Hostelling International (HI). Holders of HI membership cards pay the same rates as STF members. Nonmembers can pay Skr50 extra (Skr100 at some mountain lodges), or join up at hostels. In this book we quote prices at STF hostels for members. Children under 16 pay about half the adult price.

Around 190 hostels belong to STF's 'rival', **Sveriges Vandrarhem i Förening** (SVIF; ☎ 0413-55 34 50; www.svif.se). No membership is required and rates are similar to those of STF hostels. Most SVIF hostels have kitchens, but you sometimes need your own utensils. Pick up the free guide at tourist offices or SVIF hostels.

SWEDEN

Hotels

Sweden is unusual in that hotel prices tend to *fall* at weekends and in summer, sometimes by as much as 40% or 50%. In this book, we list standard rates unless noted. Many hotel chains are now also offering flex rates, which let you change your reservation details until the last minute, and lower rates for early booking online. Hotel prices include a breakfast buffet unless noted in individual reviews. Ask at tourist offices for the free booklet *Hotels in Sweden* or visit the website www.hotelsinsweden.net.

ACTIVITIES

Canoeing & Kayaking

Sweden is a real paradise for canoeists and kayakers (canoes are more common). The national canoeing body is **Svenska Kanotförbundet** (Swedish Canoe Federation; ☎ 0155-20 90 80; www.kanot.com; Rosvalla, SE-61162 Nyköping). It provides general advice and produces *Kanotvåg*, a free, annual brochure listing 75 approved canoe centres that hire out canoes (for around Skr300/1500 per day/week).

Hiking

Swedes love hiking, and there are thousands of kilometres of marked trails. European Long Distance Footpaths Numbers One and Six run from Varberg to Grövelsjön (1200km) and from Malmö to Norrtälje (1400km), respectively.

Nordkalottleden runs for 450km from Sulitjelma to Kautokeino (both in Norway), but passes through Sweden for most of its route. Finnskogleden is a 240km-long route along the border between Norway and the Värmland region in Sweden. The Arctic Trail (800km) is a joint development of Sweden, Norway and Finland and is entirely above the Arctic Circle; it begins near Kautokeino in Norway and ends in Abisko, Sweden. The most popular route is Kungsleden, in Lappland. Overnight huts and lodges are maintained by Svenska Turistföreningen (STF).

The best hiking time is between late June and mid-September, when trails are mostly snow-free. After early August the mosquitoes have gone.

Mountain trails in Sweden are marked with cairns, wooden signposts or paint on rocks and trees. Marked trails have bridges across all but the smallest streams, and wet or fragile areas are crossed on duckboards. Avoid following winter routes (marked by poles with red crosses) since they often cross lakes or marshes.

Skiing

Large ski resorts cater mainly to downhill (alpine and telemark) skiing and snowboarding, but there's also cross-country. For resort reviews in English, visit www.goski.com and www.thealps.com. **SkiStar** (www.skistar.com) manages two of the largest places, Sälen and Åre, and has good information on its website.

Cross-country (nordic) skiing opportunities vary, but the northwest usually has plenty of snow from December to April (but not much daylight in December and January). Kungsleden and other long-distance tracks provide great skiing. Practically all town areas (except those in the far south) have marked and often illuminated skiing tracks.

BUSINESS HOURS

General opening hours are listed here, but there are variations (particularly in the largest cities where opening hours may be longer). Hours are listed in individual reviews where they differ substantially from these.

Banks 9.30am to 3pm Monday to Friday; some city branches open 9am to 5pm or 6pm.

Department stores 10am to 7pm Monday to Saturday (sometimes later), noon to 4pm Sunday.

Government offices 9am to 5pm Monday to Friday.

Museums Generally museums have short opening hours, even in July and August; see individual destinations for more details.

Restaurants Lunch from 11.30am to 2pm, and dinner between 6pm and 10pm; often closed on Sundays and/or Mondays.

Shops 9am to 6pm Monday to Friday, 9am to 1pm Saturday.

Supermarkets 8am or 9am to 7pm or 9pm.

Systembolaget (state-owned alcohol stores) 10am to 6pm Monday to Friday, 10am to 2pm (often to 5pm) Saturday, sometimes with extended hours on Thursday and Friday evenings.

Tourist offices Usually open daily Midsummer to mid-August, 9am to 5pm Monday to Friday mid-August to Midsummer; see individual destinations for specific hours.

CUSTOMS

Duty-free goods can only be brought into Sweden from non-EU countries and Åland.

Tobacco products and alcoholic drinks can only be brought into Sweden duty-free by those over 18 and 20, respectively.

Duty-free alcohol allowances for travellers from outside the EU are 1L of spirits, 2L of fortified wine, 2L of wine and a quantity of beer that must be included within the Skr1700 limit. The tobacco allowance is 200 cigarettes, 50 cigars or 250g of smoking tobacco.

The limits on goods brought into Sweden with 'tax paid for personal use' from within the EU are more generous: 10L of spirits, 20L of fortified wine, 90L of wine (but no more than 60L of sparkling wine) and 110L of beer. The tobacco allowance is 800 cigarettes, 400 cheroots, 200 cigars or 1kg of tobacco.

Going through customs rarely involves any hassles, but rules on illegal drugs are strictly enforced; you may be searched on arrival, especially if you're travelling from Denmark. Live plants and animal products (meat, dairy etc) from outside the EU, and all animals, syringes and weapons must be declared to customs on arrival. For the latest regulations, contact **Swedish Customs** (☎ 0771-23 23 23; www.tullverket.se).

DISCOUNT CARDS

Göteborg, Malmö, Stockholm and Uppsala have worthwhile tourist cards that get you into their major attractions and offer parking, travel on public transport and discounts at participating hotels, restaurants and shops; see the individual city chapters for details.

A Hostelling International (HI) card means cheaper accommodation in STF hostels, mountain stations and mountain cabins. You can join the STF at hostels and many tourist offices while in Sweden (membership costs Skr295 for adults, Skr125 for those aged 16 to 25, Skr25 for six- to 15-year-olds and Skr430 for families).

The most useful student card is the International Student Identity Card (ISIC), which provides discounts on many forms of transport (including some airlines, international ferries and local public transport) and on admission to museums, sights, theatres and cinemas.

Seniors normally get discounts on entry to museums and other sights, cinema and theatre tickets, air tickets and other transport. No special card is required, but show your passport if asked for proof of age (the minimum qualifying age is generally 60 or 65).

EMBASSIES & CONSULATES

A list of Swedish diplomatic missions abroad (and links) is available at **Sweden Abroad** (www.swedenabroad.com).

The diplomatic missions listed below are in Stockholm, although some neighbouring countries also have consulates in Göteborg, Malmö and Helsingborg:

Australia (Map p400; ☎ 08-613 29 00; www.sweden .embassy.gov.au; 11th fl, Sergels Torg 12)

Canada (Map p400; ☎ 08-453 30 00; www.canadaemb .se; Tegelbacken 4)

Denmark (Map p400; ☎ 08-406 75 00; www.ambstock holm.um.dk, in Danish; Jakobs Torg 1)

Finland (Map pp396-7; ☎ 08-676 67 00; www.finland .se/fi, in Finnish & Swedish; Gärdesgatan 9-11)

France (Map p400; ☎ 08-459 53 00; www.ambafrance-se.org, in French & Swedish; Kommendörsgatan 13)

Germany (Map pp396-7; ☎ 08-670 15 00; www.stock holm.diplo.de, in German & Swedish; Skarpögatan 9)

Ireland (Map pp396-7; ☎ 08-661 80 05; irish.embassy @swipnet.se; Östermalmsgatan 97)

Netherlands (Map p400; ☎ 08-556 933 00; www .netherlands-embassy.se; Götgatan 16A)

Norway (Map pp396-7; ☎ 08-665 63 40; emb.stockholm @mfa.no; Skarpögatan 4)

UK (Map pp396-7; ☎ 08-671 30 00; www.british embassy.se; Skarpögatan 6-8)

USA (Map pp396-7; ☎ 08-783 53 00; http://stockholm .usembassy.gov; Dag Hammarskjöldsväg 31)

FESTIVALS & EVENTS

The biggest events celebrated throughout the country are Midsummer, Walpurgis Night, Lucia Day, Christmas and New Year's Eve. If you're in Stockholm for any of these, a great place to participate is Skansen (p402) open-air museum in Stockholm. Just don't plan on doing much on the days surrounding these holidays, as they are often claimed as 'squeeze days' and are effectively additional holidays.

Many Swedish towns host a summer festival between May and September. You can find more information on music festivals (opera, choir, folk, jazz and chamber music) online at **Svenka Musikfestivaler** (www.musikfestivaler.se).

Some highlights of the Swedish festival calendar:

Kiruna Snow Festival (last week of January; www .kiruna.com/snowfestival) Based around a snow-sculpting competition, this annual fest began in 1985 to celebrate a rocket launch and now draws artists from all over to carve ever more elaborate and beautiful shapes out of the snow.

Vasaloppet (first Sunday in March; www.vasaloppet.se) This huge annual ski race between Sälen and Mora, started in 1922, commemorates Gustav Vasa's history-making flight on skis in 1521; it has grown into a week-long ski fest and celebration with several different races, short, gruelling or just-for-fun.

Valborgsmässoafton (Walpurgis Night) (30 April) This public holiday, a pagan holdover that's partly to celebrate the arrival of spring, involves lighting huge bonfires, singing songs and forming parades; parties are biggest in student towns.

Swedish National Day (6 June) Known merely as 'Swedish flag day' until 1983, this public holiday commemorates the crowning in 1523 of King Gustav Vasa and Sweden's independence from the Danish-led Kalmar Union.

Smaka På Stockholm (first week of June) Taste samples from some of Stockholm's top kitchens in manageable, affordable quantities and watch cooking duels at this weeklong annual fest in Kungsträdgården (www.smaka pastockholm.se).

Midsummer's Eve & Midsummer Day (first Friday and Saturday after 21 June) Arguably the most important Swedish holiday, Midsummer starts on Friday afternoon/evening with the raising of the maypole, followed by lots of singing and dancing, drinking, and massive consumption of pickled herring with potatoes and sour cream.

Stockholm Jazz Festival (19 to 23 July; www.stock holmjazz.com) Held on the island of Skeppsholmen, this internationally known jazz fest brings artists from all over, including big names like Van Morrison and Mary J Blige; evening jam sessions at famed Stockholm jazz club Fasching are a highlight.

Music vid Siljan (early July; www.musikvidsiljan.se) This midsummer music festival takes place in the towns around Lake Siljan; local tourist offices will have up-to-date schedules.

Medieval Week, Visby (early August; www.medel tidsveckan.se) Find yourself an actual knight in shining armour at this immensely popular annual fest, which puts Gotland's medieval city to great use with a market, games, costumes, and a huge banquet.

Stockholm pride (late July to early August; www .stockholmpride.org/en/) This annual parade and festival is dedicated to creating an atmosphere of freedom and support for gay, lesbian, bisexual and transgender people.

Göteborg International Book Fair (late September; www.bok-bibliotek.se) Scandinavia's biggest book fair, this event brings together authors, readers, publishers, agents, teachers, librarians and the media.

Stockholm International Film Festival (mid- to late November; www.stockholmfilmfestival.se) Screenings of new international and independent films, director talks, and discussion panels draw cinephiles to this important annual festival; tickets go quickly, so book early if you're interested.

Luciadagen (St Lucia Day) (13 December) Wearing a crown of lighted candles, Lucia leads a white-clad choir in traditional singing in a celebration that seems to merge the folk tradition of the longest night and the story of St Lucia of Syracuse.

Julafton (Christmas Eve) (24 December) The night of the smörgåsbord and the arrival of *jultomten*, the Christmas gnome, carrying a sack of gifts. This is the biggest celebration at Christmas time.

GAY & LESBIAN TRAVELLERS

Sweden recognises civil unions or 'registered partnerships' that grant general marriage rights to gay and lesbian couples. The national organisation for gay and lesbian rights is **Riksförbundet för Sexuellt Likaberättigande** (RFSL; ☎ 08-457 13 00; Sveavägen 59, Box 350, SE-10126 Stockholm), with an affiliated bookshop, restaurant and nightclub. Gay bars and nightclubs in the big cities are mentioned in this book, but ask local RFSL societies or your home organisation for up-to-date information.

Another good source of local information is the free monthly magazine *QX*. You can pick it up at many clubs, stores and restaurants in Stockholm, Göteborg, Malmö and Copenhagen. The magazine's website www .qx.se has excellent information and recommendations in English.

HOLIDAYS

Many businesses close early the day before and all day after official public holidays, including the following:

Nyårsdag (New Year's Day) 1 January
Trettondedag Jul (Epiphany) 6 January
Långfredag, Påsk, Annandag Påsk (Good Friday, Easter Sunday & Monday) March/April
Första Maj (Labour Day) 1 May
Kristi Himmelsfärds dag (Ascension Day) May/June
Pingst, Annandag Pingst (Whit Sunday & Monday) Late May or early June
Midsommardag (Midsummer's Day) First Saturday after 21 June
Alla Helgons dag (All Saints' Day) Saturday, late October or early November
Juldag (Christmas Day) 25 December
Annandag Jul (Boxing Day) 26 December

INTERNET ACCESS

Most hotels have wireless LAN connections, and some even have laptops you can borrow. Hostels and tourist offices frequently have at least one internet-enabled computer available for use, occasionally with a fee of Skr10 to Skr25 per hour.

Nearly all public libraries offer free internet access, but often the timeslots are booked for days in advance by locals.

Internet cafes typically charge around Skr1 per online minute, or Skr50 per hour. Wireless internet at coffeeshops, train stations and hotels is on the increase, although in many cases you have to pay a fee for access.

INTERNET RESOURCES

The following websites are useful for planning:

An introduction to the Sami people (www.itv.se/boreale/samieng.htm) A good place to start learning about the indigenous people of northern Sweden and the issues they face, which include racism and habitat destruction.

Smorgasbord (www.sverigeturism.se/smorgasbord/index.html) A comprehensive website devoted to Swedish culture, industry, history, sports, tourism, environment and more, produced by the nonprofit FÖRST Föreningen Sverigeturism (Swedish Tourism Trade Association).

Sweden.se (www.sweden.se) All kinds of useful information about the country, in a variety of languages.

Swedish Institute (www.si.se) The Swedish Institute publishes the best academic information on Sweden in English and offers scholarships for study in Sweden.

Visit Sweden (www.visitsweden.com) The official website for tourism in Sweden.

MONEY

You should encounter few problems if you carry cash in any convertible currency or internationally recognised travellers cheques. The national ATM networks accept international Visa, Plus, EC, Eurocard, MasterCard or Cirrus cards.

Forex (☎ 0200-22 22 20; www.forex.se) is the biggest foreign money exchange company in Sweden, with good rates and branches in major airports, ferry terminals and town and city centres; these are noted in destination sections. It charges a service fee of Skr15 per travellers cheque exchanged. (Banks charge up to Skr60.)

Currency

The Swedish krona (plural: kronor), usually called 'crown' by Swedes speaking English, is denoted Skr and divided into 100 öre (prices are rounded to the nearest 50 öre). Coins are 50 öre and one, five and 10 kronor, and notes are 20, 50, 100, 500 and 1000 kronor.

Taxes & Refunds

At shops that display the 'Tax Free Shopping' sign, non-EU citizens making single purchases of goods exceeding Skr200 are eligible for a VAT refund of up to 17.5% of the purchase price. Show your passport and ask the shop for a 'Global Refund Cheque', which should be presented along with your unopened purchases (within three months) at your departure point from the country (before you check in), to get export validation. You can then cash your cheque at any of the refund points, which are found at international airports and harbours. The *Tax Free Shopping Guide to Sweden* is available from tourist offices free of charge, or call ☎ 020-74 17 41 for more information.

Tipping

Service charges and tips are usually included in restaurant bills; a common practice is to round up a restaurant bill to the nearest Skr10. There's certainly no problem if you want to reward good service with an extra tip. It's also customary to round up the taxi fare, particularly if there's luggage.

POST

In 2001–02, the Swedish postal service **Posten** (☎ 020-23 22 21; www.posten.se) closed its regular post offices and instead opened up a network of around 3000 counter services in shops, petrol stations and supermarkets across the country. Look for the yellow post symbol on a pale blue background, which indicates that postal facilities are offered.

Mailing letters or postcards weighing up to 20g within Sweden costs Skr5.50; it's Skr11 to elsewhere in Europe and beyond. The *ekonomibrev* (economy post) option for within Sweden takes longer to reach its destination and costs marginally less (Skr5). Air mail will take a week to reach most parts of North America, perhaps a little longer to Australia and New Zealand.

At the time of writing, a package weighing 2kg cost Skr282.50 by airmail within Europe, and Skr305 outside Europe.

RESPONSIBLE TRAVEL

Sweden makes it easy to be a responsible traveller: recycling, for example, is practically effortless, as bins and sorting instructions are everywhere, from inside hotel rooms to near highway rest stops. There's a high level of general environmental consciousness in the country. Two organisations that set standards for labelling products as ecologically sound are the food-focused **KRAV** (www.krav.se), a member of the International Federation of Organic Agriculture Movements, and **Swan** (www.svanen.nu), which has a wider scope and certifies entire hotels and hostels.

Aside from environmental concerns, one of Sweden's biggest challenges is protecting the cultural heritage of the Sami people. The two issues are closely linked: the harnessing of rivers for hydroelectric power can have massive (negative) impact on what has historically been Sami territory, whether by flooding reindeer feeding grounds or by diverting water and drying up river valleys. In general, the mining, forestry and space industries have wreaked havoc on Sami homelands. Travellers interested in learning more and experiencing Sami culture are encouraged to look for the 'Naturens Bäst' logo, which indicates that an excursion or organisation has been approved by **Svenska Ekoturismföreningen** (www.ekoturism .org, in Swedish), the country's first ecotourism regulating body.

TELEPHONE

Travellers may notice a lack of public telephones in Sweden; most of the population owns a mobile phone, so the number of public phones has dwindled in recent years. There are scarcely any coin phones; all public telephones take Telia phonecards (Skr50 or Skr120 for 50 or 120 units), available at most Pressbyrå shops.

It's worth considering bringing your mobile phone from your home country and buying a Swedish SIM card, which gives you a Swedish mobile number. Vodafone, for example, sells a local SIM card for Skr95, which you then need to load with at least Skr100 worth of credit. You can then purchase top-ups at many stores, including petrol stations and Pressbyrå shops. Your mobile may be locked onto your local network in your home country, so ask your home network for advice before going abroad.

For directory assistance dial ☎ 118118 (for numbers within Sweden) or ☎ 118119 (international), but note that these services aren't free.

Calls to Sweden from abroad require a country code (☎ 46) followed by the area code and telephone number (omitting the first zero in the area code). For international calls dial ☎ 00 followed by the country code and the local area code.

Swedish phone numbers have area codes followed by varying numbers of digits. You must use the area code when dialling from outside that area. Numbers beginning ☎ 020 or ☎ 0200 are free (but not from public phones or mobiles). Numbers beginning ☎ 077 are roughly the same price as a local call. Mobile phone numbers usually begin with ☎ 070.

TOILETS

Public toilets in parks, shopping malls, libraries and bus or train stations are rarely free in Sweden. Except at the larger train stations (where an attendant is on duty), pay toilets are coin operated, and usually cost Skr5 (so keep a Skr5 coin handy). The exception is museums, where toilets usually are free and well-maintained.

TOURIST INFORMATION

The official website for the **Swedish Travel Tourism Council** (www.visit-sweden.com) contains useful information in many languages.

Sweden has about 350 local tourist information offices. Most are open long hours in summer and short hours (or not at all) during winter. The offices in large towns stock brochures from all around Sweden. The **FörTur** (www.turism.se) website lists Sweden's tourist information offices and their contact details.

TRAVELLERS WITH DISABILITIES

Sweden is one of the easiest countries to travel around in a wheelchair. People with disabilities will find transport services with adapted facilities, ranging from trains to taxis, but contact the operator in advance for the best service. Public toilets and some hotel rooms have facilities for disabled people; **Hotels in Sweden** (www.hotelsinsweden.net) indicates whether hotels have adapted rooms.

For further information about Sweden, contact the national association for the disabled, **De Handikappades Riksförbund** (☎ 08-685 80 00; www.dhr.se; Katrinebergsvägen 6, Box 47305, SE-10074 Stockholm).

VISAS

Citizens of EU countries can enter Sweden with a passport or a national identification card (passports are recommended) and stay up to three months. Nationals of Nordic countries (Denmark, Norway, Finland and

Iceland) can stay and work indefinitely, but nationals of other countries require residence permits (uppehållstillstånd) for stays of between three months and five years; there is no fee for this permit for EU citizens.

Citizens of Australia, New Zealand, Canada and the USA can enter and stay in Sweden without a visa for up to three months. Australian and New Zealand passport holders aged 18 to 30 can qualify for a one-year working-holiday visa.

Citizens of South Africa and many other African, Asian and some Eastern European countries require tourist visas for entry. These are only available in advance from Swedish embassies (allow two months); there's a nonrefundable application fee of Skr550 for most applicants.

Residence permits must be applied for before entering Sweden. Allow up to eight months. Foreign students are granted residence permits if they can prove acceptance by a Swedish educational institution and are able to guarantee that they can support themselves financially.

Migrationsverket (☎ 011-15 60 00; www.migrations verket.se; SE-60170 Norrköping) is the Swedish migration board and it handles all applications for visas and work or residency permits.

TRANSPORT IN SWEDEN

GETTING THERE & AWAY
Air
The main airport is Stockholm Arlanda, which links Sweden with major European and North American cities. Göteborg Landvetter is Sweden's second-biggest international airport. Stockholm Skavsta (actually 100km south of Stockholm, near Nyköping) and Göteborg City both act as airports for the budget airline Ryanair. For travelling between international airports and city centres, see the Getting Around sections in the relevant sections.

Göteborg Landvetter (airline code GOT; ☎ 031-94 10 00; www.lfv.se)

Göteborg City (GSE; ☎ 031-92 60 60; www.goteborg cityairport.se)

Stockholm Arlanda (ARN; ☎ 08-797 60 00; www .lfv.se)

Stockholm Skavsta (NYO; ☎ 0155-28 04 00; www .skavsta-air.se)

AIRLINES FLYING TO & FROM SWEDEN
Scandinavian Airlines System (SAS) is the regional carrier and has a good safety record. Most of the usual airlines fly into Sweden including the following:

Air France (airline code AF; ☎ 08-5199 9990; www .airfrance.com; hub Charles de Gaulle, Paris, France)

Blue1 (KF; ☎ 0900-102 5831; www.blue1.com; hub Helsinki-Vantaa, Finland)

British Airways (BA; ☎ 0200-770098; www.britishair ways.com; hub Heathrow Airport, London, UK)

Lufthansa (LH; ☎ 08-611 5930; www.lufthansa.com; hub Frankfurt, Germany)

Ryanair (FR; ☎ 0900-202 0240; www.ryanair.com; hub Dublin, Ireland)

SAS (SK; ☎ 0770-72 77 27; www.scandinavian.net; hub Stockholm Arlanda)

Land
Direct access to Sweden by land is possible from Norway, Finland and Denmark (from Denmark via the remarkable Öresund toll bridge). Border-crossing formalities are nonexistent.

Train and bus journeys are also possible between Sweden and the continent – these vehicles go directly to ferries. Include ferry fares (or Öresund tolls) in your budget if you're driving from continental Europe.

Eurolines (☎ 031-100240; www.eurolines.com), the long-distance bus operator, has an office inside the bus terminals in Sweden's three largest cities: Stockholm, Göteborg and Malmö. Full schedules and fares are listed on the website.

CONTINENTAL EUROPE
Eurolines services run between Sweden and several European cities. The Stockholm to London service (Skr1250, 30 hours, one to four times weekly) goes via Malmö, Copenhagen, Hamburg and Amsterdam or Brussels. There are also services from Göteborg to Berlin (Skr710, 17 hours, three weekly).

DENMARK
Eurolines runs buses between Stockholm and Copenhagen (Dkr280, nine hours, at least three per week), and between Göteborg and Copenhagen (Dkr200, 4½ hours, daily). **Swebus Express** (☎ 0200-218218; www.swebusexpress.se) and **Säfflebussen** (☎ 0771-151515; www.safflebussen.se) both run regular buses on the same routes, and have discount fares for travel from Monday to Thursday. All companies offer student, youth (under 26) and senior discounts.

SWEDEN

Öresund trains operated by **Skånetrafiken** (www.skanetrafiken.se) run every 20 minutes from 6am to midnight (and once an hour thereafter) between Copenhagen and Malmö (round trip Skr140, 35 minutes each way) via the bridge. The trains usually stop at Copenhagen Airport.

From Copenhagen, it's necessary to change in Malmö for Stockholm trains. Six or seven services operate directly between Copenhagen and Göteborg (Skr327, four hours). Trains every hour or two connect Copenhagen, Kristianstad and Karlskrona. X2000 high-speed trains are more expensive.

You can drive from Copenhagen to Malmö across the Öresund bridge on the E20 motorway. Tolls are paid at Lernacken, on the Swedish side, in either Danish (single crossing per car Dkr260) or Swedish (Skr325) currency, or by credit or debit card.

FINLAND

Frequent bus services run from Haparanda to Tornio (Skr10, 10 minutes). **Tapanis Buss** (☎ 0922-129 55; www.tapanis.se, in Swedish) runs express coaches from Stockholm to Tornio via Haparanda twice a week (Skr570, 15 hours).

Länstrafiken i Norrbotten (☎ 020 47 00 47; www.ltnbd.se) operates buses as far as Karesuando, from where it's only a few minutes' walk across the bridge to Kaaresuvanto (Finland). There are also regular regional services from Haparanda to Övertorneå (some continue to Pello, Pajala and Kiruna) – you can walk across the border at Övertorneå or Pello and pick up a Finnish bus to Muonio, with onward connections from there to Kaaresuvanto and Tromsø (Norway).

NORWAY

Säfflebussen runs from Stockholm to Oslo (Skr425, 7½ hours, fives times daily) via Karlstad, and from Göteborg to Oslo (Skr265, four hours, seven daily). Swebus Express has the same routes with similar prices.

In the north, buses run once daily from Umeå to Mo i Rana (eight hours) and from Skellefteå to Bodø (nine hours, daily except Saturday); for details, contact **Länstrafiken i Västerbotten** (☎ 0771-10 01 10; www.tabussen.nu) and **Länstrafiken i Norrbotten** (☎ 0771-10 01 10; www.ltnbd.se), respectively.

The main rail links run from Stockholm to Oslo, from Göteborg to Oslo, from Stockholm to Östersund and Storlien (Norwegian trains continue to Trondheim), and from Luleå to Kiruna and Narvik.

Trains run daily between Stockholm and Oslo (Skr500 to Skr706, six to seven hours), and there's a night train from Stockholm to Narvik (Skr811, about 20 hours). You can also travel from Helsingborg to Oslo (Skr750, seven hours), via Göteborg. X2000 high-speed trains are more expensive.

Sea

Ferry connections between Sweden and its neighbours are frequent and straightforward. Most lines offer substantial discounts for seniors, students and children, and many rail-pass holders also get reduced fares. Most prices quoted in this section are for single journeys at peak times (weekend travel, overnight crossings, mid-June to mid-August); at other times, fares may be up to 30% lower.

DENMARK

Helsingør–Helsingborg

This is the quickest route and has frequent ferries (crossing time around 20 minutes).

ACE Link (☎ 042-38 58 80; www.acelink.se, in Swedish) Regular passenger-only ferries to Helsingør from around 7am to 8pm daily. Pedestrian/bicycle Skr48/16.

HH-Ferries (☎ 042-19 80 00; www.hhferries.se) 24-hour service. Pedestrian/car and up to nine passengers Skr24/300.

Scandlines (☎ 042-18 63 00; www.scandlines.se) Similar service and prices to HH-Ferries.

Göteborg–Fredrikshavn

Stena Line (☎ 031-704 00 00; www.stenaline.se) Three-hour crossing. Up to six ferries daily. Pedestrian/car and five passengers/bicycle Skr185/1525/225.

Stena Line (Express) Two-hour crossing. Up to three ferries daily. Pedestrian/car and five passengers/bicycle Skr285/1795/275.

Varberg–Grenå

Stena Line (☎ 031-704 00 00; www.stenaline.se) Four-hour crossing. Three or four daily. Pedestrian/car and five passengers/bicycle Skr285/1595/280.

Ystad–Rønne

BornholmsTrafikken (☎ 0411-55 87 00; www.bornholmstrafikken.dk) Conventional (1½ hours) and fast (80 minutes) services, two to nine times daily. Pedestrian/car and five passengers/bicycle from €23/133/25.

EASTERN EUROPE

To/from Estonia, **Tallink** (☎ 08-666 6001; www .tallink.ee in Estonian) runs the routes Stockholm–Tallinn and Kapellskär–Paldiski.

Scandlines (☎ 08-5206 02 90; www.scandlines.dk) operates Ventspils–Nynäshamn ferries around five times per week.

To/from Lithuania, **Lisco Line** (☎ 0454-33680; www.lisco.lt) operates daily between Karlshamn–Klaipėda.

To/from Poland, **Polferries** (☎ 040-121700; www.polferries.se) and **Unity Line** (☎ 0411-556900; www.unityline.pl) have daily Ystad–Swinoujscie crossings. Polferries also runs Nynäshamn–Gdańsk. **Stena Line** (☎ 031-704 0000; www.stenaline .se) sails Karlskrona–Gdynia.

FINLAND

Helsinki is called Helsingfors in Swedish, and Turku is Åbo.

Stockholm–Helsinki and Stockholm–Turku ferries run daily throughout the year via the Åland islands (exempt from the abolition of duty-free within the EU, making them a popular outing for Swedes). These ferries have minimum age limits; check before you travel.

Stockholm–Helsinki

Silja Line (☎ 08-22 21 40; www.silja.com) Around 15 hours. Ticket and cabin berth from €122.
Viking Line (☎ 08-452 40 00; www.vikingline.fi) Operates the same routes with slightly cheaper prices.

Stockholm–Turku

RG Line (☎ 090-18 52 00; www.rgline.com) Runs the routes Umeå–Vaasa and Sundsvall–Vaasa.
Silja Line (☎ 08-22 21 40; www.silja.com) 11 hours. Deck place €11, cabins from €49; prices are higher for evening trips. From September to early May, ferries also depart from Kapellskär (90km northeast of Stockholm); connecting buses operated by Silja Line are included in the full-price fare.
Viking Line (☎ 08-452 40 00; www.vikingline.fi) Operates the same routes with slightly cheaper prices. In high season it offers passage from both Stockholm and Kapellskär.

Stockholm–Åland Islands (Mariehamn)

Besides the Silja Line and Viking Line routes above, two companies offer foot passenger-only overnight cruises. Prices quoted are for return trips.

Ånedin-Linjen (☎ 08-456 22 00; www.anedinlinjen .com, in Swedish) Six hours, daily. Couchette Skr75, berth from Skr250.

Birka Cruises (☎ 08-702 72 00; www.birkacruises .com) A 22-hour round-trip. One or two daily. Berth from Skr350. Prices include supper and breakfast.
Eckerö Linjen (☎ 0175-258 00; www.eckerolinjen.fi) Runs to the Åland Islands from Grisslehamn.

GERMANY

Trelleborg–Sassnitz

Scandlines (☎ 042-18 61 00; www.scandlines.se) A 3¾-hour trip. Two to five times daily. Pedestrian/car and up to nine passengers/passenger with bicycle Skr125/925/195. A fuel surcharge of Skr50 to Skr80 may be added.

Trelleborg–Rostock

Scandlines (☎ 042-18 61 00; www.scandlines.se) Six hours (night crossing 7½ hours). Two or three daily. Pedestrian/car and up to nine passengers/passenger with bicycle Skr195/1025/225. A fuel surcharge of Skr50 to Skr80 may be added.
TT-Line (☎ 0410-562 00; www.ttline.com) Operates the same as Scandlines, with similar prices.

Trelleborg–Travemünde

TT-Line (☎ 0410-562 00; www.ttline.com) Seven hours. Two to five daily. Pedestrian/car and up to five passengers/passenger with bicycle from Skr290/1045/390. Berths are compulsory on night crossings.

Göteborg–Kiel

Stena Line (☎ 031-704 00 00; www.stenaline.se) 14 hours. One crossing nightly. Pedestrian/car and up to five passengers from Skr495/1760. Rates are flexible depending on how early you book and which cabin level you choose.

NORWAY

There's a daily overnight **DFDS Seaways** (☎ 031-65 06 80; www.dfdsseaways.com) ferry between Copenhagen and Oslo, via Helsingborg. Passenger fares between Helsingborg and Oslo (14 hours) cost from Skr1100, and cars Skr475, but the journey can't be booked online; you'll need to call. DFDS also sails from Göteborg to Kristiansand (Norway), three days a week (from seven hours); contact them for prices.

A **Color Line** (☎ 0526-620 00; www.colorline .com) ferry between Strömstad (Sweden) and Sandefjord (Norway) sails two to six times daily (2½ hours) year-round. Tickets cost from Nkr175 (rail passes get 50% discount).

SWEDEN

UK
DFDS Seaways (www.dfdsseaways.com) Göteborg
(☎ 031-65 06 50); UK (☎ 08705-33 30 00) There are two
crossings per week between Göteborg and Newcastle via
Kristiansand (Norway). The trip takes 25 hours. Fares start
from around £35 per person including economy berth; cars
cost £75 and bicycles are free. Again, though, booking these
trips online is somewhat maddening; it's best to call instead.

GETTING AROUND
Air
Domestic airlines in Sweden tend to use
Stockholm Arlanda (airline code ARN; ☎ 08-797 60 00;
www.lfv.se) as a hub, but there are 30-odd regional airports. Flying domestic is expensive
on full-price tickets (usually between Skr1000
and Skr3000 for a single ticket), but substantial discounts are available on internet bookings, student and youth fares, off-peak travel,
return tickets booked at least seven days in advance or low-price tickets for accompanying
family members and seniors. It's worthwhile
asking about stand-by fares.

The following is a selection of Sweden's
internal flight operators and the destinations
they cover. Skyways has the best deals.
Malmö Aviation (TF; ☎ 040-660 29 00; www
.malmoaviation.se; hub Stockholm Bromma) Göteborg,
Stockholm and Umeå.
Scandinavian Airlines System (SAS; airline code SK;
☎ 0770-72 77 27; www.flysas.com; hub Stockholm Ar-
landa) Arvidsjaur, Borlänge, Gällivare, Göteborg, Halmstad,
Ängelholm-Helsingborg, Hemavan, Hultsfred, Jönköping,
Kalmar, Karlstad, Kiruna, Kramfors, Kristianstad, Linköping,
Luleå, Lycksele, Norrköping, Malmö, Mora, Örnsköldsvik,
Oskarshamn, Oskersund, Skellefteå, Stockholm, Storuman,
Sundsvall, Sveg, Torsby, Trollhättan, Umeå, Vilhelmina,
Visby, Västerås and Örebro.
Skyways (JZ; ☎ 0771 95 95 00; www.skyways.se;
hub Stockholm Arlanda) Arvidsjaur, Borlänge, Göteborg,
Halmstad, Hemavan, Jönköping, Karlstad, Kramfors, Kris-
tianstad, Linköping, Lycksele, Norrköping, Mora, Skellefteå,
Stockholm, Storuman, Sundsvall, Trollhättan, Vilhelmina,
Visby and Örebro.

Boat
CANAL BOAT
The canals provide cross-country routes linking the main lakes. The longest cruises, on
the Göta Canal from Söderköping (south of
Stockholm) to Göteborg, run from mid-May
to mid-September, take at least four days and
include the lakes between.

Rederiaktiebolaget Göta Kanal (☎ 031-15 83
11; www.gotacanal.se) operates three ships over

the whole distance at fares from Skr9425 to
Skr17,825 for a four-day cruise, including full
board and guided excursions. For shorter,
cheaper trips on the canal, contact tourist
offices in the area.

Ferry
An extensive boat network and the 16-day
Båtluffarkortet boat passes (Skr340, plus a Skr40
supplement for first-time buyers) open up the
attractive Stockholm archipelago. Gotland is
served by regular ferries from Nynäshamn and
Oskarshamn, and the quaint fishing villages off
the west coast can normally be reached by boat
with a regional transport pass – enquire at the
Göteborg tourist offices.

Bus
Swebus Express (☎ 0200 21 82 18; www.swebusexpress
.se) has the largest network of express buses,
but they only serve the southern half of the
country (as far north as Mora in Dalarna).
Svenska Buss (☎ 0771-67 67 67; www.svenskabuss
.se, in Swedish) and **Säfflebussen** (☎ 0771-15 15 15;
www.safflebussen.se, in Swedish, Danish & Norwegian)
also connect many southern towns and cities with Stockholm; prices are often slightly
cheaper than Swebus Express, but services
are less frequent.

North of Gävle, regular connections with
Stockholm are provided by several smaller
operators, including **Ybuss** (☎ 0771-33 44 44;
www.ybuss.se, in Swedish), which has services to
Sundsvall, Östersund and Umeå.

You don't have to reserve a seat on Swebus
Express services. Generally, tickets for travel
between Monday and Thursday are cheaper,
or if they're purchased over the internet,
or more than 24 hours before departure. If
you're a student or senior, it's worth asking about fare discounts; however, most bus
companies will only give student prices to
holders of Swedish student cards (the exception is Swebus Express, where you can get an
ISIC discount).

REGIONAL NETWORKS
The *länstrafik* bus networks are well integrated with the regional train system, with
one ticket valid on any local or regional
bus or train. Rules vary but transfers are
usually free if used within one to four
hours. Fares on local buses and trains are
often identical.

BUS PASSES

Good-value daily or weekly passes are usually available from local and regional transport offices, and many regions have 30-day passes for longer stays, or a special card for peak-season summer travel.

Car & Motorcycle

Sweden has good-standard roads, and the excellent E-class motorways rarely have traffic jams.

AUTOMOBILE ASSOCIATIONS

The Swedish national motoring association is **Motormännens Riksförbund** (☎ 020-21 11 11; www.motormannen.se).

BRING YOUR OWN VEHICLE

If bringing your own car, you'll need your vehicle registration documents, unlimited third-party liability insurance and a valid driving licence. A right-hand drive vehicle brought from the UK or Ireland should have deflectors fitted to the headlights to avoid dazzling oncoming traffic. You must carry a reflective warning breakdown triangle.

DRIVING LICENCE

An international driving permit isn't necessary; your domestic licence will do.

HIRE

To hire a car you have to be at least 20 (sometimes 25) years of age, with a recognised licence and a credit card.

Fly-drive packages may save you money. International rental chains (such as Avis, Hertz and Europcar) are more expensive but convenient; all have desks at Stockholm Arlanda and Göteborg Landvetter airports and offices in most major cities. The best car hire rates are generally from larger petrol stations (like Statoil and OK-Q8) – look out for signs saying *biluthyrning* or *hyrbilar*.

Avis (☎ 0770-82 00 82; www.avisworld.com)

Europcar (☎ 020-78 11 80; www.europcar.com)

Hertz (☎ 0771 211 212; www.hertz-europe.com)

Mabi Hyrbilar (☎ 08-612 60 90; www.mabirent.se) National company with competitive rates.

OK-Q8 (☎ 020-85 08 50; www.okq8.se, in Swedish) Click on *hyrbilar* in the website menu to see car-hire pages.

Statoil (☎ 08-429 63 00; www.statoil.se/biluthyrning, in Swedish) Click on *uthyrningsstationer* to see branches with car hire, and on *priser* for prices.

ROAD HAZARDS

In the northern part of Sweden, privately owned reindeer and wild elk are serious road hazards, particularly around dawn and dusk. Look out for black plastic bags tied to roadside trees or poles – this is a sign from local Sami that they have reindeer herds grazing in the area. Report all incidents to police – failure to do so is an offence. Sandboxes on many roads may be helpful in mud or snow. Also, if driving in Göteborg and Norrköping watch out for trams.

ROAD RULES

The basic rules of the road conform to EU standards. In Sweden, you drive on and give way to the right. Headlights should always be dipped, but must be on at all times when driving. Seat belt use is obligatory for the driver and all passengers. The maximum blood-alcohol limit is a stringent 0.02%, and random breath tests are not uncommon. The speed limit on motorways and remote highways is usually 110km/h. Police often use hand-held radar equipment and cameras to detect speeding, and will impose on-the-spot fines.

On many highways you will see broken lines defining wide-paved edges. The vehicle being overtaken is expected to move into this area to allow faster traffic to pass by safely.

Local Transport

In Sweden, local transport is always linked with regional transport (*länstrafik*). Regional passes are valid both in the city and on the rural routes. Town and city bus fares are around Skr20, but it usually works out cheaper to get a day card or other travel pass.

Swedish and Danish trains and buses around the Öresund area form an integrated transport system, so buying tickets to Copenhagen from any station in the region is as easy as buying tickets for Swedish journeys.

Stockholm has an extensive underground metro system, and Göteborg and Norrköping run tram networks. Göteborg also has a city ferry service.

Train

Sweden has an extensive and reliable railway network, and trains are certainly faster than buses. Many destinations in the northern half of the country, however, cannot be reached by train alone.

SWEDEN

SWEDEN

TRAIN OPERATORS

Sveriges Järnväg (SJ; ☎ 0771-75 75 75; www.sj.se) National network covering most main lines, especially in the southern part of the country. Its X2000 fast trains run at speeds of up to 200km/h.

Tågkompaniet (☎ 0771-44 41 11; www.tagkom paniet.se, in Swedish) Operates excellent overnight trains from Göteborg and Stockholm north to Boden, Kiruna, Luleå and Narvik, and the lines north of Härnösand.

In summer, various tourist trains offer special rail experiences. The most notable is **Inlandsbanan** (☎ 0771-53 53 53; www.inlandsbanan .se), a slow and scenic 1300km route from Kristinehamn to Gällivare, one of the great rail journeys in Scandinavia. Several southern sections have to be travelled by bus, but the all-train route starts at Mora. It takes seven hours from Mora to Östersund (Skr395) and 15 hours from Östersund to Gällivare (Skr918). A pass allows two weeks' unlimited travel for Skr1450.

COSTS

Travel on the super-fast X2000 services is much pricier than on 'normal' trains. Full-price 2nd-class tickets for longer journeys are expensive (around twice the price of equivalent bus trips), but there are various discounts available, especially for booking a week or so in advance (*förköpsbiljet*), or at the last minute (for youth and pensioner fares). Students (with a Swedish CSN or SFS student card if aged over 26), and people aged under 26, get a 30% discount on the standard adult fare.

X2000 tickets include a seat reservation. All SJ ticket prices are reduced in summer, from late June to mid-August. Most SJ trains don't allow bicycles to be taken onto trains (they have to be sent as freight), but those in southern Sweden (especially Skåne) do; check when you book your ticket.

TRAIN PASSES

ScanRail no longer exists, but several other options provide similar benefits. The Sweden Rail Pass, Eurodomino tickets and international passes, such as Inter-Rail and Eurail, are accepted on SJ services and most regional trains.

The **Eurail Scandinavia Pass** (www.eurail.com) entitles you to unlimited rail travel in Denmark, Finland, Norway and Sweden; it is valid in 2nd class only and is available for four, five, six, eight or 10 days of travel within a two-month period (prices start from youth/adult US$255/335). It also provides free travel on Scandlines' Helsingør to Helsingborg route, and 20% to 50% discounts on the following ship routes:

Route	Operator
Frederikshavn-Göteborg	Stena Line
Grenå-Varberg	Stena Line
Stockholm-Helsinki	Viking or Silja Line
Stockholm-Turku	Viking or Silja Line

Regional Directory

CONTENTS

This chapter gives a general overview of the entire Scandinavian Europe region. For information relevant to one particular country, see the Directory section at the end of each country chapter.

Some subjects are covered in *both* places (eg general accommodation options are discussed following, but price ranges plus contact details for useful accommodation organisations appear in each country Directory). We've added cross references where appropriate.

ACCOMMODATION

Throughout this book, accommodation is divided into budget, midrange and top-end categories. Our choices are listed in order of price, with the cheapest first (although in Budget sections, camp sites are at the top of each list, no matter what). See the individual country Directories for an overview of

> **BOOK ACCOMMODATION ONLINE**
>
> For more accommodation reviews and recommendations by Lonely Planet authors, check out the online booking service at www.lonelyplanet.com. You'll find the true, insider lowdown on the best places to stay. Reviews are thorough and independent. Best of all, you can book online.

local options, and a rundown of prices and useful associations.

Cheap hotels are virtually unknown in far-northern Europe, but guesthouses, pensions, private rooms, farm accommodation and B&Bs can be good value. Self-catering flats and cottages are worth considering if you're travelling with a group, especially if you're staying in one place for a while.

If you arrive in a country by train, there's often a hotel-booking desk at the station. Tourist offices tend to have extensive accommodation lists and the more helpful ones will go out of their way to find you somewhere to stay. There's usually a small fee for this service, but it can save a lot of running around. Agencies offering private rooms can be good value; you may lack privacy, but staying with a local family brings you closer to the spirit of the country.

B&Bs, Guesthouses & Hotels

There's a huge range of accommodation above the hostel level. B&Bs, where you get a room and breakfast in a private home, can often be real bargains. Pensions and guesthouses are similar, but usually slightly more upmarket.

Above this level are hotels, which are always much more expensive than B&Bs and guesthouses; in cities, luxury five-star hotels have five-star prices. Categorisation varies from country to country.

Check your hotel room and the bathroom before you agree to take it, and make sure you know what it's going to cost – discounts are often available at certain times (eg at weekends in Finland, Norway and Sweden) and for longer stays. Also ask about breakfast –

it's usually included in the price of the room, but sometimes it's compulsory and you must pay extra for it (which can be a real rip-off).

If you think a hotel is too expensive, ask if they have a cheaper room. If you're with a group or are planning to stay for any length of time, it's always worth trying to negotiate a special rate.

Camping

Scandinavians love their tents! Camping is cheap and immensely popular throughout the region. There's usually a charge per tent or site, per vehicle and per person. National tourist offices have booklets or brochures listing camping grounds all over their country. See p487 for information on the Camping Card International and the Camping Card Scandinavia, both of which offer benefits and discounts.

In most larger towns and cities, camping grounds are some distance from the centre. If you're on foot, the money you save by camping can quickly be outweighed by the money spent commuting in and out of town.

Some camping grounds rent small cabins or chalets (common except in Iceland and the Faroes); otherwise you'll need a tent, sleeping bag and cooking equipment.

Camping other than in designated camping grounds is not always straightforward. In Denmark and the Faroes, it's illegal without permission from the local authorities (the police or local council office) or from landowners (don't be shy about asking!). As always, take care to keep toilet activities away from all surface water and use biodegradable soaps for washing up.

There's a concept in Sweden, Norway, Finland, and to a more limited extent, Iceland, of a right of public access to forests and wilderness areas. In these countries, within the framework of the regulations, camping for one night is legal; but there are important restrictions. See the Right of Common Access (p484) information, and the Directories of the relevant country chapters for additional information. Tourist offices usually stock official publications in English explaining your rights and responsibilities.

Hostels

Hostels offer the cheapest roof over your head in Scandinavia, and you don't have to be young to use them. Most hostels are part of national YHAs (Youth Hostel Associations), known collectively throughout the world as **Hostelling International** (HI; www.hihostels.com). Some Scandinavian hostels are operated privately, although the majority are affiliated with HI.

Technically you're supposed to be a YHA or HI member to use affiliated hostels (indicated by a blue triangle symbol) but in practice most are open to anyone. You may have to pay a bit extra without an HI card but this can be offset against future membership. Stay for six nights as a nonmember and you automatically become a member. Prices given throughout this book are member prices. To join HI, ask at any hostel, contact your local or national hostelling office, or register over the internet.

In Scandinavian countries, hostels are geared for budget travellers of all ages, including families with kids, and most have dorms and private rooms. Specially adapted rooms for disabled visitors are becoming more common, but check with the hostel first.

You must use a sleeping sheet and pillowcase or linen in most Scandinavian countries – simply using your own sleeping bag is not permitted – but you can often hire or buy these on the spot. Many hostels (exceptions include most hostels in Iceland and the Faroes) serve breakfast, and almost all have communal kitchens where you can prepare meals.

Some hostels accept reservations by phone or fax but not usually during peak periods; they'll often book the next hostel you're headed to for a small fee. The HI website has a booking form, where you can reserve a bed in advance – however, not all hostels are on the network. Popular hostels in capital cities can be heavily booked in summer and limits may be placed on how many nights you can stay.

Many hostel guides are available, including HI's annually updated *Official International Youth Hostels Guide*. For further information on Scandinavian hostels, including price ranges, see the Directory section in the individual country chapters.

University Accommodation

Some universities and colleges rent out their students' rooms to tourists from June to mid-August. These will often be single or double

---

WORLD HERITAGE LIST

Scandinavia is rich in sites that have made the Unesco list of 'cultural and national treasures of the world's heritage'. Sites mentioned in this book are as follows.

Denmark

Jelling Kirke (p87)

Kronborg Slot (p55)

Roskilde Domkirke (p59)

Finland

Fortress of Suomenlinna (p148)

Vanha Rauma (Old Rauma; p172)

Iceland

Þingvellir National Park (p250)

Norway

Bryggen (p333)

Røros (p352)

Alta's rock art (p373)

Urnes' stave church (p345)

West Norwegian Fjords – Geirangerfjorden (p347) and Nærøyfjorden (p331)

Sweden

Agricultural landscape of southern Öland (p453)

Birka and Hovgården (p418)

Church village of Gammelstad, Luleå (p463)

Falun mining area (p423)

Visby (p455)

Höga Kusten (High Coast; p460)

Karlskrona (p454)

Royal Domain of Drottningholm (p417)

---

rooms and cooking facilities may be available. Enquire directly at the college or university, at student information services or at local tourist offices.

ACTIVITIES

A love of the outdoors seems hard-wired into the Scandinavian brain. With such amazingly varied geography and vast wilderness areas, it's not really surprising. Outdoor activities include bird-watching, windsurfing, skiing, snowmobiling, skating, climbing, dogsledding, fishing, hiking, horse riding, mountaineering, kayaking, white-water rafting, cycling, whale-watching, and way-out white-knuckle sports like snowkiting.

For more information, see the relevant country chapters.

Bird-Watching

Scandinavia's large, unspoilt areas are fantastic places to spot huge varieties and numbers of birds. In coastal areas, kittiwakes, fulmars and puffins are common. Rarer species include golden eagles and sea eagles. Even reluctant twitchers will be wowed by the Vestmanna (p123) and Látrabjarg (p256) bird cliffs, in the Faroes and Iceland, respectively. Other good areas include the Danish islands Møn (p62), Falster (p63) and Lolland (p64); the Norwegian islands Runde (p351), Værøy and Røst (p368); and Oulanka National Park (p195) in Finland.

Boating

The Vikings' trade and communication routes – the lakes, rivers and meandering coastlines of Scandinavia – present a variety of boating options unmatched anywhere in the world. You can ride the rapids in a Finnish canoe (p205); take a trip on an Arctic icebreaker (p199); kayak around the feet of Icelandic mountains (p252); chug round peaceful lake Mjøsa in Norway (p329) on the world's oldest paddle steamer; or cruise from Helsinki to Stockholm (p210) – manifold possibilities! Country chapters contain more details.

Cycling

Along with hiking, cycling is the best way to get into the scenery and chat to the locals. It's also a fantastic way to whiz around cities without getting throbbing feet or stuck in traffic. The region offers some good country and courses for the hair raising sport of downhill mountain biking.

Popular cycling areas include much of Denmark, which sets the world standard for cycling infrastructure; greater Oslo; the islands of Gotland in Sweden; and Åland in Finland. Cycling in certain areas of Iceland can be tough, with blasting sandstorms or endless fjords. In western Norway – as beautiful as it is – there are tunnels galore which prohibit cyclists, the snaking roads to/from mountain passes are killers and, unless you want to pedal an extra 50km around a fjord, you'll have to add on ferry costs. The Faroes also have their fair share of hazardous, nonventilated tunnels and tortuous inclines.

Many long-distance routes (see individual country chapters for details) can be linked together to form an epic Scandinavia-wide cycle tour. A popular route is to start from Kiel in Germany, then make your way through Denmark, north along the west coast of Sweden and into Norway. (Note that bikes are banned on the Øresund toll bridge between Denmark and Sweden.)

If you come from outside Europe, you can often bring your bicycle along on the plane for a surprisingly reasonable fee – check out any restrictions with your carrier. Alternatively, this book lists places where you can rent one (the minimum rental period is usually half a day).

See p504 and the individual country chapters for more information on bicycle touring and tips on places to visit.

Dogsledding

Hurtling over the snow, pulled by a team of near-wolves, has to be one of life's most exhilarating experiences. Dogsledding is particularly popular in northern Finland, around Rovaniemi (p196), Muonio (p203) and Levi (p203) and various towns in Finnmark and Svalbard in northern Norway, and in the far north of Sweden and in Iceland.

Hiking

Keen walkers could spend several lifetimes exploring the region's hundreds of trails – there are enough national parks and nature reserves to make it a veritable paradise. Routes are usually well marked, and accommodation is available along the way. As always, be sure to bring enough food, appropriate clothing and equipment with you, and consult local weather forecasts before setting off.

The Right of Common Access law in effect in Sweden, Norway, Finland and to a lesser extent Iceland allows anyone to walk virtually anywhere, while respecting homeowners' and commercial premises' privacy. Most tourist offices in the first three countries have leaflets outlining what rights and responsibilities you have.

Huge national routes such as Kungsleden in Sweden (p468) and the UKK trekking route (p190) in Finland are popular, as are provincial or regional routes (spanning hundreds of kilometres) and extensive tracks through national parks. Local and regional tourist offices distribute free maps for shorter routes and sell excellent trekking maps for the national parks.

Horse Riding

Another way to see the breathtaking Scandinavian countryside is from the back of a horse. Most stables offer short rides for beginners, with longer treks for experienced riders. Iceland has its own breed of horse, the Icelandic pony, and a great equine tradition. On the Faroes, you can trek between Torhavn and Kirkjabour on Icelandic ponies (p122).

Skiing

A long snow season makes winter sports, particularly skiing, popular Scandinavian pastimes. The longest downhill (alpine) slopes are in Sweden and Norway, although it's quite an expensive activity (compared to skiing at other European resorts), once the costs of ski lifts, accommodation and evening drinking sessions have been factored in. Cross-country (nordic) skiing has a bigger following, and there are many world-class trails in the region.

Åre in Sweden (p462) is probably the single best area for alpine skiing. Lillehammer (p329) is a top resort where telemark skiing, a form of free-heel downhill skiing, is also popular. Finnish ski areas are fairly well equipped – the emphasis is on cross-country skiing – with Ylläs (p203) being one of the best resorts. Several towns in Iceland have lifts and trails.

Renting equipment for downhill skiing is easily organised. However, for cross-country skiing, travellers will normally have to rely on friendly locals to lend them equipment – or plan on buying their own skis, poles and boots. (Flea markets are the probably the cheapest and most likely places to look.)

Skiing – especially cross country – should only be attempted after studying trails and routes (wilderness trails are identified by colour codes on maps and signposts). Practically all towns and villages illuminate some skiing tracks. Wear appropriate clothing and carry food, extra clothing and emergency supplies, such as matches and something to burn. Skiers should be extra careful about darkness. In Scandinavia, days are very short in winter and, during the winter months of December and January, there's no daylight at all in the extreme north.

The skiing season generally lasts from early December to April. Snow conditions can vary greatly from one year to the next and from region to region, but January and February, as well as the Easter holiday period, tend to be the best (and busiest) months. Snow cannons for producing artificial snow are common.

Snowboarding & Snowkiting

The biggest downhill ski resorts (see above) usually make provisions for snowboarders. It's possible to try out the new sport snowkiting in Luleå (Sweden; p463) and Geilo (Norway; p331) – see the website www.snowkiting.com for more details.

Snowmobiling

If zipping through the untouched snowy wilderness on a deafening, bone-shaking, 190km/h machine sounds like fun, there are many places in Scandinavia where you can indulge in two-stroke pleasure. Snowmobile outfits are particularly prevalent in the far north of Finland, Norway and Sweden, with the season generally running from November to April; you can ride on Icelandic glaciers year-round. There's usually no minimum age for passengers, but if you want to drive, you'll need your driving licence.

Whale-Watching

Norway, Iceland and the Faroes are often severely criticised for their policies on hunting whales, so it's perhaps an encouraging sign that whale-watching tours are on the increase, in Norway and Iceland at least (pilot whales in the Faroes that come too close to shore are killed). For information on whaling in all three countries, see p113 (Faroes), p235 (Iceland) and p295 (Norway).

All three countries offer spotting trips from around May to October, with a wonderfully high chance of seeing cetaceans. Common species are minke, sperm and killer whales, white-beaked dolphins and the ubiquitous harbour porpoise. Humpback whales appear in certain seasons, and blue whales surface from time to time. In Iceland, Húsavík (p260) is the acknowledged hotspot; in Norway, you're practically guaranteed to see sperm whales on trips around the Vesterålen islands (p368).

Windsurfing & Kitesurfing

The beaches of Denmark, particularly on the West Jutland coast, attract crowds of windsurfers and kitesurfers in summer. Wetsuits enable keener surfers to continue their sport throughout the colder months. Sailboards can be rented in some tourist centres, and courses are sometimes on offer for beginners.

CHILDREN

Most of Scandinavia is very child-friendly, with domestic tourism largely dictated by children's needs. Iceland and the Faroes are exceptions: children are liked and have lots of freedom, but they're treated as mini-adults and there aren't many attractions tailored

REGIONAL DIRECTORY

particularly for them. In Denmark, Finland, Norway and Sweden, you'll find excellent theme parks, water parks and holiday activities. Many museums have a dedicated children's section with toys, games and dressing-up clothes.

Car-rental firms hire out children's safety seats at a nominal cost, but advance bookings are essential. Similarly, highchairs and cots (cribs) are standard in many restaurants and hotels, but numbers may be limited. The choice of baby food, infant formulas, soy and cow's milk, disposable nappies (diapers) etc is wide in most Scandinavian supermarkets.

In the Faroes and more rugged areas of Scandinavia, a baby carrier rather than a pram is crucial.

CLIMATE CHARTS

Generalisations about the weather over an area of approximately 2,500,000 sq km are something of an impossibility! Temperatures

range from -50°C in the Arctic Circle in winter to summer temperatures of more than 30°C in some parts of Sweden. Large chunks of Scandinavia lie within the Arctic Circle, yet the presence of the Gulf Stream makes coastal areas much warmer than you might expect at such northerly latitudes. See the climate charts, and tune in to local weather reports for conditions once you're on the road.

DANGERS & ANNOYANCES

Drugs

Always treat drugs with a great deal of caution. There's a fair amount of dope available in Scandinavia, sometimes quite openly, but that doesn't mean it's legal: a bit of hash can cause a lot of bother. Don't try to bring drugs home with you – energetic customs officials could well decide to take a closer look at your luggage.

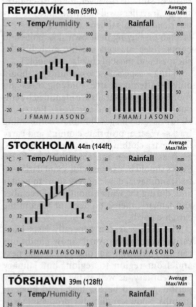

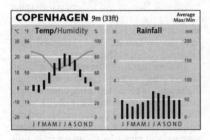

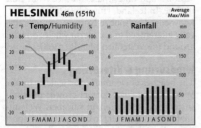

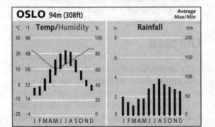

Remote Areas

In remote rural areas, hypothermia, injury and getting lost are serious hazards. Never underestimate the wilderness; always take proper equipment and seek local knowledge. People living in isolated places may be suspicious of outsiders, and winter darkness can lead to unpredictable behaviour and alcohol abuse.

Theft

Crime is rare and common sense should keep you safe. Guard your passport, other important documents, tickets and money – in that order. It's always best to carry these next to your skin or in a sturdy leather pouch on your belt.

Train-station lockers or luggage-storage counters are useful places to stash your bags (not valuables). Carry your own padlock for hostel lockers. Parked cars, especially those with foreign number plates and/or rental-agency stickers, are prime targets for petty criminals. Don't ever leave valuables in the car, and remove all luggage overnight.

In case of theft or loss, always report the incident to the police and ask for a statement, or your travel insurance won't pay up.

Wildlife

Wild animals pose a small risk. Polar bears and wolves roam the arctic archipelago of Svalbard (Norway). Arctic terns in coastal regions defend their nests aggressively – hold a stick up above your head, as they dive-bomb the highest part of you.

Clouds of mosquitoes, midges and black-flies can be a real annoyance in some parts of Scandinavia. You might look a fool, but a mosquito head-net (often found for sale in petrol stations) will save you from a faceful of flies.

DISCOUNT CARDS
Camping Card International

The **Camping Card International** (www.campingcardin ternational.com) is basically an ID card you can leave behind a camping ground's reception desk instead of your passport. It incorporates third-party insurance for any damage you may cause, and you may also get small discounts at some amusement parks, museums and camping grounds. They're obligatory in Denmark (you can also use the Camping Card Scandinavia) and at some Swedish camping grounds (others are affili-

ated with the Camping Card Scandinavia), valid in Finland and Norway, but not commonly recognised in Iceland or the Faroes.

You can buy one before you leave home from any organisation affiliated with the Fédération Internationale de Camping et de Caravanning (FICC), Fédération Internationale de l'Automobile (FIA) or Alliance Internationale de Tourisme (AIT) – these are usually your country's major automobile associations and/or camping and caravanning groups. The cards are valid for one year and cover up to 11 people.

Camping Card Scandinavia

Similar to the Camping Card International, **Camping Card Scandinavia** (www.camping.se) acts as an ID card, offers discounts at certain camping grounds and attractions, and has built-in third-party insurance.

It's valid in Denmark, Norway and Finland and at most Swedish camping grounds, and in some other European countries. One card covers you whether you're an individual, a couple or a family with children under 18.

Order the card through the website before you leave home, or pick up a temporary card directly from camping grounds in Scandinavia. The card is 'free' but you have to pay a small fee for a validity sticker, which means your card is valid for one year.

Hostel Card

While not mandatory in Scandinavia, a **Hostelling International** (HI; www.hihostels.com) card gives a sizable discount every time you check in to an affiliated hostel. It's best to buy the card from your national hostelling association before you set off, although in Scandinavia some hostels will issue one on the spot or after six stays (generally more expensive than getting one at home). See p482 for more details on hostelling in the region.

Senior Cards

Museums and other sights, public swimming pools, spas and transport companies frequently offer discounts to retirees, pensioners and to those over 60 (sometimes slightly younger for women; and over 65 in Sweden). Make sure you bring proof of age; the ever-proper and always polite Scandinavian ticket-collector is not going to admit that you look a day over 39.

If you're going to be travelling by train, those aged over 60 are entitled to discounted travel.

Student & Youth Cards

The most useful of these cards is the **International Student Identity Card** (ISIC), a plastic ID-style photocard, which provides discounts on numerous forms of transport (including airlines, international ferries and local public transport), reduced or free admission to museums and sights, and cheap meals in some student restaurants – a good way of cutting costs in expensive Scandinavia. Full-time students from the age of 12 upwards are eligible. If you're under 26 but not a student, you can apply for an **International Youth Travel Card** (IYTC), with similar benefits. Both are available through student unions, hostelling organisations or youth-oriented travel agencies: see the website of the **International Student Travel Confederation** (www.istc.org) for further details.

Also available to anyone aged under 26 is the **Euro26 card** (www.eyca.org), which goes by various names in different countries – see the website for more information.

These cards don't automatically entitle you to discounts and some companies and institutions don't recognise them – but you won't find out until you try.

DVD SYSTEMS

If you're thinking of buying DVDs, remember that Scandinavia uses Region 2 coding (covering Europe, the UK, Japan, the Middle East, South Africa) and so may not be compatible with your DVD player at home. Even if your DVD player is Region 2, discs bought in Scandinavia still may not be playable because of NTSC/PAL incompatibility (eg Region 2 Scandinavian discs will not play on Region 2 Japanese DVD players).

ELECTRICITY

Most of the region runs on 220V, 50Hz AC. Check the voltage and cycle (usually 50Hz) used in your home country. Most appliances that are set up for 220V will handle 240V quite happily without modifications (and vice versa); the same goes for 110V and 125V combinations.

It's always preferable to adjust your appliance to the exact voltage if you can (some modern battery chargers and radios will do this automatically). Just don't combine 110/125V

and 220/240V without a transformer (which will be built into an adjustable appliance).

Several countries outside Europe (eg the USA and Canada) run on 60Hz AC, which will affect the speed of electric motors even after the voltage has been adjusted to European values, so CD and tape players (where motor speed is all-important) will be useless. However, appliances such as electric razors, hair dryers, irons and radios will be fine.

The standard plug is the so-called 'europlug' with two round pins, although some plugs in the Faroes have three pins and some in Iceland have two slanted prongs. Adaptors are available from most supermarkets in Scandinavia. Many europlugs and some sockets don't have provision for earth since most local home appliances are double insulated; when provided, earth usually consists of two contact points along the edge.

EMBASSIES & CONSULATES

See the individual country Directory sections for specific embassy and consulate addresses.

It's important to realise the things your own embassy can and can't do to help you. Generally speaking, it won't be much help in emergencies if the trouble you're in is your own fault in any way. Remember that you are bound by the laws of the country you are in. Your embassy will not be sympathetic if you end up in jail after committing a crime locally, even if such actions are legal in your own country.

In genuine emergencies you might get some assistance, but only if other channels have been exhausted. For example, if you need to get home urgently, a free ticket is exceedingly unlikely – the embassy would expect you to have insurance. If you have all your money and documents stolen, it might assist with getting a new passport, but a loan for onward travel is out of the question.

GAY & LESBIAN TRAVELLERS

This book lists contact addresses and gay and lesbian venues in the individual country chapters, and your national gay and lesbian organisation should be able to give you more information before you travel.

Denmark, Iceland, Norway and Sweden allow gay and lesbian couples to form 'registered partnerships', which grant every right of matrimony except access to church weddings, adoption and artificial insemination. Finland, too, is tolerant of homosexual couples. However, public displays of affection are uncommon in Norway, and it's a good idea to be discreet in the Faroes, where a conservative society and strongly held religious beliefs may cause problems for gay and lesbian couples.

HOLIDAYS

Midsummer's Eve (the longest day of the year) is celebrated in late June across Scandinavia, generally with fervour and large bonfires! For holidays particular to each country, see the Directory sections at the end of each country chapter.

INSURANCE
Private Travel Insurance

A travel insurance policy to cover theft, personal liability, loss and medical problems is strongly recommended. There's a variety of policies available and travel agencies will have recommendations. International travel policies handled by STA Travel and other student travel organisations are usually good value. Check the small print; some policies specifically exclude 'dangerous activities' such as skiing, motorcycling, mountaineering or even hiking.

Travel insurance also covers cancellation or delays in travel arrangements, for example, if you fall seriously ill two days before departure. The cover will depend on your insurance so ask your insurer to explain where you stand. Ticket loss is also covered by travel insurance.

Buy insurance as early as possible. If you buy it the week before you are due to fly, you may find that you're not covered for delays to your flight caused by strikes or other industrial actions that may have been in force before you took out the insurance.

Paying for your airline ticket with a credit card often provides limited travel accident insurance, and you may be able to reclaim the payment if the operator doesn't deliver. In the UK, for instance, institutions issuing credit cards are required by law to reimburse consumers if a company goes into liquidation and the amount involved is more than £100. Ask your credit-card company what it is prepared to cover.

An insurance policy that pays doctors or hospitals directly may be preferable to one where you have to pay on the spot and claim back later. If you have to claim later, make sure the foreign health centre or hospital gives you all the necessary documentation you'll need for insurance purposes. Some policies ask you to call back (reverse charges) to a centre in your home country where an immediate assessment of your problem can be made. Check if the policy covers ambulances and an emergency flight home.

Worldwide cover to travellers from more than 44 countries is available online at www .lonelyplanet.com/bookings/insurance.do.

Reciprocal Medical Insurance Agreements

For further information about health insurance, see p511.

Car Insurance

See p507.

INTERNET ACCESS

If you're bringing your own laptop, make sure you've got a universal AC adaptor (which will stop the computer's innards frying if the power supply voltage varies) and a plug adaptor for each country you visit (cheaper if bought at home).

For more information on travelling with a laptop, see the World Wide Phone Guide on the internet at **TeleAdapt** (www.teleadapt.com).

Internet Cafes

You'll find internet cafes throughout Scandinavia: many are listed in the country chapters in this book. In general, libraries provide a free or very cheap internet service, although there may be a waiting list and locals may have priority. You can also find public internet access in some post offices, tourist offices, hostels, hotels and universities.

Wireless Hotspots

Scandinavia is rife with wireless (wi-fi) hotspots. An astonishing number of cafes, bars, hostels and hotels, particularly in cities, offer the service for free. Most modern laptops have built-in wireless LAN, which means you don't require a modem, jacks or other fiddly bits and pieces. If you set up your computer within a hotspot, it should automatically pick up a signal (you may need a password) and you'll be able

REGIONAL DIRECTORY

to surf the internet. Even if your laptop is an older model without built-in wireless, you can buy a wireless adaptor which plugs into a USB port on your laptop and does the job perfectly. As with most things in the region, wireless USB adaptors are relatively expensive, so it's better to pick one up at home.

MAPS

Good maps are easy to come by in Scandinavian Europe, but you might want to buy a few beforehand, especially if you're driving, cycling or have some hefty treks planned. The maps in this book are a useful first reference when you arrive in a city.

Michelin does a general road map of Scandinavia. Some people prefer the meticulous larger-scale Freytag & Berndt, Kümmerly + Frey or Hallwag maps, which have been recommended for Scandinavian countries. Falk Plan city maps are very usable and detailed, and the Falk map of Scandinavia is particularly good.

In Scandinavia, tourist offices are an excellent source for free and up-to-date maps, often in English-language versions. Local automobile associations also provide detailed, free maps to their members.

The following shops sell Scandinavian maps, including motoring maps and topographic maps for hikers, by mail order:

Map Land (☎ 03- 9557 8555; 408 Centre Rd, Bentleigh, Melbourne, Victoria 3204 Melbourne, VIC 3000, Australia)

Map Shop (☎ 0800 085 4080, 01684-593146; www .themapshop.co.uk; 15 High St, Upton-upon-Severn, Worcestershire, WR8 0HJ, UK)

Omni Resources (☎ 336-227 8300; www.omnimap .com; 1004 S Mebane St, PO Box 2096, Burlington, NC 27216-2096, USA)

MONEY

All Scandinavian currencies are fully convertible. Most foreign currencies can be easily exchanged but US dollars, pounds sterling

---

SCANDINAVIA & THE EU

Country	EU member	Currency
Denmark	yes	Danish krone (Dkr)
Faroe Islands	no	Faroese króna (Fkr) & Danish krone (Dkr)
Finland	yes	euro (€)
Iceland	no	Icelandic króna (Ikr)
Norway	no	Norwegian krone (Nkr)
Sweden	yes	Swedish krona (Skr)

---

and euros are the best to carry. You may well decide, however, that other currencies suit your purposes better. You lose out through commissions and customer exchange rates every time you change money, so if you only visit Sweden, for example, you may be better off buying some kronor before you leave home. See the relevant country Directory sections for further details.

ATMs

Credit and cash cards (eg Visa, Cirrus, Plus, Eurocard) are accepted widely throughout Scandinavian Europe; always make sure you know which ATMs abroad will accept your particular card by checking first with your bank at home. Remember that ATMs aren't completely fail-safe. If one swallows your card it can be a major headache. Note that many ATMs in Europe will not accept PINs of more than four digits.

Withdrawals may incur a 'loading fee' (conversion fee) of around 2.75%, plus a transaction fee (usually a flat rate of about $US2 to $US5, or a percentage of at least 2%) – check charge rates with your card provider. It's often more economical if you make fewer but larger withdrawals. If you travel abroad a lot, look into opening an account with a bank that *doesn't* charge rip-off fees!

Charge cards such as American Express and Diners Club may also be hooked up to ATM networks.

Cash

It's a good idea to bring some local currency in cash, if only to tide you over until you get to an exchange facility or find an ATM. Some extra cash in an easily exchanged currency (eg US dollars or pounds sterling) is also a good idea. Remember that banks will always accept foreign-currency paper money but very rarely

---

CREDIT & DEBIT CARD TIP

Let your bank know when you'll be going abroad. Unusual spending patterns, for example, a large cash withdrawal in Norway instead of your usual £20-per-week in Northampton, may lead to the bank freezing your card.

coins, so you might want to spend (or donate) local coins before you cross a border.

Credit Cards

A credit card can be an ideal travelling companion. Make sure you know what to do in case of theft (usually you need to call a telephone hotline).

Credit and debit cards are very popular in Scandinavia; Visa is the most common, followed by MasterCard. They are more widely accepted than charge cards (such as American Express and Diners Club) because they charge merchants lower commissions. Their major drawback is that they have a credit limit based on your regular income, and this limit can stop you in your tracks if you're charging major expenses such as long-term car rental or long-distance airline tickets and travelling extensively. You can avoid this by depositing money into your card account before you begin your travels.

Other drawbacks are that many banks slap a 'loading fee' of around 2.75% onto each transaction that you make abroad, which can really add up. Also, interest is charged on outstanding accounts, either immediately or after a set period (always immediately on cash advances), and the card can be very difficult to replace if lost abroad in remote areas.

Fraud is rare but to be safe try not to let the card out of your sight, and always check your statements carefully.

Moneychangers

Travellers should avoid banks in Scandinavian countries (except in the Faroes and Iceland, where banks are often a better option) in favour of *bureaux de change* (eg Forex) or post offices, which tend to offer better rates and charge lower fees or commissions than banks. They generally have longer opening hours than banks, which are closed at weekends and on public holidays (see the Directory sections in the individual country chapters for lists). However, most airports, central train stations, some fancy hotels and many border crossings have banking facilities outside working hours. If you're visiting several countries, buy a cheap pocket calculator, cut out the list of exchange rates from a newspaper, and stick it to the back of the calculator for easy reference.

Tipping

For the most part, tipping isn't required in Scandinavia, although if you round up the bill or leave a little something in recognition of good service, it won't be refused.

Travellers Cheques

The main advantage of travellers cheques, or the newer cash-cards (much like debit or credit cards but which are loaded with a set amount or money) over cash is the protection they offer against theft. American Express, Visa and Thomas Cook cheques are widely accepted and have efficient replacement policies for lost and stolen cheques.

It's vital to keep a record of your cheque numbers and which ones you have used, in case of theft. Keep your list separate from the cheques themselves.

Cheques denominated in US dollars, euros and pounds sterling are the easiest to cash. When you change them, don't just look at the exchange rate; ask about fees and commissions as well. There may be a per-cheque service fee, a flat transaction fee, or a percentage of the total amount irrespective of the number of cheques. In most European countries the exchange rate for travellers cheques is slightly better than the exchange rate for cash.

PHOTOGRAPHY & VIDEO

Scandinavia is extremely photogenic, but the local climate and when/where you travel will dictate how easy it is for you to get good results and for lovers of old-school film cameras, and what type you should take. In autumn, when the sky can often be overcast, photographers should use high-speed film (rated 200 or 400 ASA). In bright conditions, eg

---

TAXES & REFUNDS

A kind of sales tax called value-added tax (VAT) applies to most goods and services throughout Scandinavia. International visitors can usually claim back the VAT on purchases (above a set minimum amount) that are being taken out of the country. Remember, though, that travellers who reside in an EU country are not entitled to a refund on VAT paid on goods bought in another EU country (eg a Briton returning home with goods from Finland, Sweden or Denmark). The procedure for making the claim is usually pretty straightforward. For guidance, see the relevant country chapters.

in sunny weather or if there's lots of settled snow, slower film (with an ASA of 50 to 100) is the answer.

It's worth noting that if you're taking pictures in reflective conditions, eg of icebergs, water or snow, you need to overexpose your shots; otherwise automatic cameras think it's brighter than it really is, resulting in dark photos. Batteries tend to run out quickly in cold conditions, so carry a spare set. Try to avoid exposing your camera and films to extremes of temperature.

If you're using a digital camera, check that you have enough memory to store your snaps. If you do run out of memory space your best bet is to burn your photos onto a CD. Increasing numbers of processing labs now offer this service. To download your pics at an internet cafe you'll need a USB cable and a card reader. Some places provide a USB on request, but be warned that many of the bigger chain cafes don't let you plug your gear into their computers, meaning that it's back to plan A – the good old CD.

For more pointers, check out Lonely Planet's *Travel Photography,* by internationally renowned travel photographer Richard I'Anson. It's a full-colour guide designed to be taken on the road.

Still and video film and camera equipment is available throughout Scandinavia, but it would be advisable to bring as much as possible with you, as prices can be exorbitant. Print processing is generally available in towns and cities.

POST

Airmail typically takes about a week to reach North American or Australasian destinations. Postage costs vary from country to country. Postal services are very efficient in Scandinavia.

You can collect mail from post office poste restante sections. Ask people writing to you to print your name clearly on the envelope, underline your surname and use capital letters. When collecting mail, bring along your passport for identification. If an expected letter is not waiting for you, ask post office staff to check under your first name as letters are sometimes misfiled. Unless the sender specifies otherwise, mail will always be sent to the main post office of any city.

SOLO TRAVELLERS

Scandinavia is well developed and one of the safest places to travel in Europe, so travelling alone should pose no problems. Inhabitants of Scandinavia are often thought to be pleasant but not particularly gregarious, so you may have to brush up your social skills if you want to make friends locally.

Hostels and camping grounds are good places to meet other travellers.

TELEPHONE & FAX

You can call abroad from almost any phone box in Scandinavia. Reverse-charge (collect) calls are usually possible, and communicating with the local operator in English should not be much of a problem. In some countries you can avoid the local operator, and dial direct to your home operator.

You can send faxes and telegrams from most of the larger post offices and from some hotels.

Mobile Phones

Most populated parts of Scandinavia use GSM 900/1800, which is compatible with the rest of Europe and Australasia, but not with the North American GSM 1900 or the totally different system in Japan (although some North American GSM 1900/900 may work here). If you have a GSM phone, check with your service provider about using it in Scandinavia, and beware of calls being routed internationally (very expensive for a 'local' call). Local telephone companies and national tourist offices can advise on coverage.

Rental of mobile phones is possible everywhere except Norway, and is particularly easy in mobile-centric Finland. Another option is to buy a local SIM card with a rechargeable account – this is particularly good value in Sweden, Iceland and Finland.

Phone Codes

To call abroad you simply dial the international access code (IAC) for the country you are calling from (most commonly 00 in Europe), the country code (CC) for the country you are calling, the local area code (usually dropping the leading zero if there is one) and then the number. If, for example, you are in Norway (which has an international access code of 00) and want to make a call to Sweden (country code 46) in the Stockholm

TELEPHONE CODES

Country	☎ CC	☎ IAC	☎ IO
Denmark	45	00	141
Faroe Islands	298	00	808080
Finland	358	00, 990	020208 94, 999
Iceland	354	00	1811
Norway	47	00	1882
Sweden	46	00	118119

CC – country code (to call into that country)
IAC – international access code (to call abroad from that country)
IO – international operator (to make inquiries)

area (area code 08), number ☎ 123 4567, then dial ☎ 00-46-8-123 4567.

Phonecards

Public telephones accepting stored-value phonecards are the norm and, in some places, coin-operated phones are almost impossible to find. Phonecards are readily available from post offices, telephone centres, news stands or retail outlets. These cards solve the problem of having the correct coins for calls. More and more public telephone kiosks are giving callers the opportunity to pay by credit card. Beware of public telephones in bars and restaurants – most will eat up your money at an incredible rate.

TIME

Scandinavian Europe sprawls across six time zones. See the individual country Directory sections for details.

TOURIST INFORMATION

Tourist information offices in Scandinavia tend to be located at train stations or centrally (often in the town hall or central square) in most towns. They tend to be open for longer hours over the summer and reduced hours over the winter; smaller offices may only be open during the peak months of summer.

Facilities are generally excellent, with piles of regional and national brochures, helpful free maps and friendly employees. Staff are often multilingual, speaking several tongues including Scandinavian languages, English, German and French. They will book hotel and transport reservations and tours; a small charge may apply.

TRAVELLERS WITH DISABILITIES

Scandinavia leads the world in terms of facilities for wheelchair users, but getting around can still be awkward. By law, for example, every new restaurant in Finland must have a wheelchair-accessible toilet; however, that leaves plenty of older restaurants to contend with. There are ramps to practically all public buildings, most department stores, shopping centres and many private shops. Some train carriages are fitted with special lifts for wheelchairs. Iceland and the Faroes are a little further behind the rest of the region – check access issues before you travel.

If you have a physical disability, get in touch with your national support organisation (preferably the 'travel officer' if there is one) and ask about the countries you plan to visit. They often have complete libraries devoted to travel, and they can put you in touch with travel agents who specialise in tours for the disabled. Scandinavian tourist office websites (see 'Tourist Information' in the individual country directories) generally contain good information on disabled access.

VISAS

There's a wide variety of visas available, including tourist, transit, business and study visas. Transit visas are usually cheaper than tourist or business visas, but they only allow a very short stay (one or two days) and can be difficult to extend. Often you can get the visa at the border or at the airport on arrival; check first with the embassies or consulates of the countries you plan to visit.

It's important to remember that visas have a use-by date, and you'll be refused entry after that period has elapsed. Visa requirements do change, and you should always check with the individual embassies or consulates or a reputable travel agency before leaving home. If you wish to apply for a visa while still at home, make sure you do it at least three months in advance of your planned arrival. If you plan to get your visas as you go along rather than arranging them all beforehand, carry spare passport photos.

Citizens of the UK, the USA, Canada, Ireland, Australia and New Zealand don't require visas if visiting a Scandinavian country for less than three months; South Africans, on the other hand, need a visa to enter all Scandinavian countries. With a valid passport most travellers will be able to visit Scandinavian countries for up to three (sometimes even six) months, provided they have some sort of onward or return ticket and/or 'sufficient means of support' (money). Except at international airports, it's unlikely that immigration officials will give you and your passport more than a cursory glance.

Many EU countries have abolished passport controls between their borders and an identity card should be sufficient, but it's always safest to carry your passport.

For more specific visa information, refer to the individual Directory sections in the country chapters.

WEIGHTS & MEASURES

The metric system is used in Scandinavia. Decimals are indicated by commas and thousands are indicated by points.

WOMEN TRAVELLERS

Scandinavia is one of the safest places to travel in all of Europe and women travellers should experience little trouble; however, use common sense when dealing with potentially dangerous situations such as hitching or walking alone at night.

WORK

Officially, a citizen of the EU is allowed to work in other EU countries, although the paperwork isn't always straightforward for longer-term employment. Other country/nationality combinations require special work permits that are almost impossible to arrange, especially for temporary work. However, Australian and New Zealand passport holders aged between 18 and 30 can qualify for a one-year working holiday visa in some Scandinavian countries: see the individual country Directory sections for details.

That doesn't prevent enterprising travellers from topping up their funds occasionally, and not always illegally. Your national student-exchange organisation may be able to arrange temporary work permits to several countries through special programmes.

If you do find a temporary job, the pay may be less than that offered to locals, although this is not always the case in Scandinavia. Teaching English can pay well, but such work is hard to come by. Other typical tourist jobs (such as working in a restaurant, hotel or fish-processing plant) may come with board and lodging, and pay that's little more than pocket money, but it can be a good way to meet and party with other travellers.

Work Your Way Around the World by Susan Griffith gives good, practical advice on a wide range of issues. Selling goods on the street is generally frowned upon and can be tantamount to vagrancy, apart from at flea markets.

If you play an instrument or have other artistic talents, you could try busking (street entertainment). It's fairly common in many major cities. In Sweden, you'll need to get a busking permit, which is available from the police, although not everybody actually has the permit. In Copenhagen, acoustic music is allowed without a permit in pedestrian streets and squares between 4pm and 8pm on weekdays and noon to 5am at the weekend. Most other Scandinavian countries require municipal permits that can be hard to obtain. Talk to other buskers first.

Transport in Scandinavia

CONTENTS

GETTING THERE & AWAY

ENTERING THE REGION

Citizens of the UK, the USA, Canada, Ireland, Australia and New Zealand do not need to apply for a visa if they are visiting a Scandinavian country for less than three months. With a valid passport, most travellers will be able to visit the region for up to three (sometimes even six) months, provided they have some sort of onward or return ticket and/or 'sufficient means of support' (ie money) for the length of their stay.

Many EU countries have abolished passport controls between their borders, requiring only an identity card, but it's always safest to carry your passport. If it's about to expire, renew it before you go – some countries insist that it's valid for a specified minimum period (usually three months but sometimes up to six) after your visit.

Flights, tours and rail tickets can be booked online at www.lonelyplanet.com /travel_services.

Air

Increased competition among airlines is great news for travellers. There are plenty of cheap tickets from 'no-frills' airlines which sell budget tickets direct to customers.

London is one of the best centres for purchasing inexpensive, restricted-validity tickets through discount operators (see p498). Various classes of cheap air tickets and passes are also available on routes within Scandinavian countries (see p503), subject to restrictions. European 'gateway' cities include Amsterdam, Athens, Berlin, Copenhagen, Frankfurt, London, Oslo, Stockholm and Vienna.

Before booking a flight, wheelchair travellers should check the airline's lifting policy, whether it's possible to take a wheelchair with spillable battery on board, and whether the airline requires a 'fit to travel certificate'.

Bicycles are generally accepted as luggage if they're in a bike bag – check conditions with your airline.

Airports & Airlines

Major hubs in Scandinavia include Denmark's **Kastrup International Airport** (☎ 45 32 31 32 31; www .cph.dk), Finland's **Helsinki-Vantaa Airport** (☎ 358-2001 4636; www.helsinki-vantaa.fi), Iceland's **Keflavík Airport** (☎ 354-425-6000; www.keflavikairport.com), Norway's **Oslo Airport** (☎ 47 64 81 20 00, passenger services 47 06 400; www.osl.no) and Sweden's **Arlanda Airport** (☎ 46 879 76 000, 46 11 19 20 00; www.lfv.se).

The main international airlines flying into and out of Scandinavia and continental Europe are given on p496. Telephone numbers are for help desks and booking offices in the hub country; for an airline's representatives in other countries, check its website.

THINGS CHANGE...

The information in this chapter is particularly vulnerable to change. Check directly with the airline or a travel agent to make sure you understand how a fare (and ticket you may buy) works and be aware of the security requirements for international travel. Shop carefully. The details given in this chapter should be regarded as pointers and are not a substitute for your own careful, up-to-date research.

TRANSPORT IN SCANDINAVIA

CLIMATE CHANGE & TRAVEL

Climate change is a serious threat to the ecosystems that humans rely upon, and air travel is the fastest-growing contributor to the problem. Lonely Planet regards travel, overall, as a global benefit, but believes we all have a responsibility to limit our personal impact on global warming.

Flying & Climate Change

Pretty much every form of motor travel generates carbon dioxide (the main cause of human-induced climate change) but planes are far and away the worst offenders, not just because of the sheer distances they allow us to travel, but because they release greenhouse gases high into the atmosphere. The statistics are frightening: two people taking a return flight between Europe and the US will contribute as much to climate change as an average household's gas and electricity consumption over a whole year.

Carbon Offset Schemes

Climatecare.org and other websites use 'carbon calculators' that allow jetsetters to offset the greenhouse gases they are responsible for with contributions to energy-saving projects and other climate-friendly initiatives in the developing world – including projects in India, Honduras, Kazakhstan and Uganda.

Lonely Planet, together with Rough Guides and other concerned partners in the travel industry, supports the carbon offset scheme run by climatecare.org. Lonely Planet offsets all of its staff and author travel.

For more information check out our website: www.lonelyplanet.com.

Air Canada (airline code AC; ☎ 1-888-247-2262; www.aircanada.com) Hub: Toronto, Canada

Air France (AF; www.airfrance.com) France (☎ 08 20 32 08 20) Australia (☎ 1300 390 190 Hub: Charles de Gaulle, Paris, France)

Atlantic Airways (RC; ☎ 341000; www.atlantic.fo) Hub: Vágar, Faroes

Austrian Airlines (OS; ☎ 051789; www.aua.com) Hub: Vienna, Austria

Blue1 (RF; ☎ 20 585 6000; www.blue1.com) Hub: Helsinki-Vantaa, Finland

British Airways (BA; ☎ 0844 493 0787; www.britishairways.com) Hub: Heathrow, London, UK

Cathay Pacific (CX; ☎ 2747 1888; www.cathaypacific.com) Hub: Hong Kong

City Airline (CF; ☎ 0200 250 500; www.cityairline.com) Hub: Göteborg, Sweden

EasyJet (U2; ☎ 0905 821 0905; www.easyjet.com) Hub: Luton, London, UK

Finnair (AY; ☎ 600 140 140; www.finnair.com) Hub: Helsinki-Vantaa, Finland

Icelandair (FI; ☎ 505 0100; www.icelandair.is) Hub: Keflavík, Iceland

Iceland Express (FHE; ☎ 550 0600; www.icelandexpress.com) Hub: Keflavík, Iceland

KLM (KL; ☎ 20 474 7747; www.klm.com) Hub: Schipol, Amsterdam, Netherlands

Lufthansa (LO; ☎ 1805 83 84 26; www.lufthansa.com) Hub: Frankfurt, Germany

Norwegian Air Shuttle (DY; ☎ Norway 815 21 815, outside Norway 47 21 49 00 15; www.norwegian.no) Hub: Oslo, Norway

Qantas (QF; ☎ 13 13 13; www.qantas.com.au) Hub: Sydney, Australia

Ryanair (FR; ☎ 0818 30 30 30; www.ryanair.com) Hub: Dublin, Ireland

SAS (Scandinavian Airlines; SK; ☎ 70 10 20 00; www.flysas.com) Hub: Kastrup, Denmark

Swiss (SR; ☎ 0848 700 700; www.swiss.com) Hub: Zurich, Switzerland

Thai Airways (TG; ☎ 66 23 56 11 11; www.thaiairways.com) Hub: Bangkok, Thailand

Tickets

For 'full-service' airlines, it's usually cheaper to buy tickets from a travel agency rather than direct. For peace of mind, use a bonded agency, like one covered by the Air Transport Operators Licence (ATOL) scheme in the UK. Firms like STA Travel, with offices worldwide, are not going to disappear overnight and offer good prices to most destinations.

For budget airlines, turn to the internet, which has made booking cheap tickets a breeze. Usually the low-cost carriers' websites offer one-way tickets that are exactly half the cost of the return fare, so you can easily fly into one place and leave from another.

Flights to Scandinavia are most expensive in July and August and at Christmas.

Asia

Singapore and Bangkok are the discount plane-ticket capitals of Asia. Not all agencies are reliable: ask for advice from other travellers before buying tickets.

Finnair has direct daily flights from Helsinki to Bangkok (around €1700, 10 hours), Beijing (€1100, eight hours), Shanghai (€1500, nine hours); and several flights per week to Tokyo (€1300, 9½ hours). Finnair also flies Helsinki–Singapore (€1800, 13 hours) and Oslo–Singapore (Nkr20,000, 13 hours) with a stopover in Bangkok.

Thai Airways flies from Bangkok to Stockholm (Skr11,300, 10½ hours) and to Copenhagen (Dkr31,500, 11 hours).

SAS has flights from Tokyo to Copenhagen (Dkr17,500, 11½ hours).

Aeroflot offers inexpensive deals from India to Europe.

Recommended agencies:

Four Seas Tours (☎ 2200 7777; www.fourseastravel .com/english; Hong Kong)

No 1 Travel (☎ 03 3205 6073; www.no1-travel.com; Japan)

STA Travel (www.statravel.com); Bangkok (☎ 2236 0262; www.statravel.co.th); Hong Kong (☎ 2722 7378; www.statravel.hk); Japan (☎ 03 5391 2922; www .statravel.co.jp in Japanese); Singapore (☎ 6737 7188; www.statravel.com.sg)

STIC Travels (www.stictravel.com); Delhi (☎ 11 237 37 135); Mumbai (☎ 22 221 81 431)

Australia

Flights to Scandinavian capitals require stopovers, usually in Singapore or Bangkok and a European city. Return fares cost around A$3000, and take 24 hours.

Some travel agencies, particularly smaller ones, advertise cheap fares in the travel sections of the weekend newspapers. Well-known travel agencies with offices throughout Australia:

Flight Centre (☎ 133 133; www.flightcentre.com.au)

STA Travel (☎ 134 782; www.statravel.com.au)

Canada

Airlines flying to Scandinavia include Air Canada, Finnair, British Airways, Northwest Airlines and SAS. Flights leave from all major cities including Montreal, Ottawa, Toronto and Vancouver, and take between nine and 14 hours, with one change in Frankfurt, London or New York. Shop around as prices vary hugely, although an average of around C$2000 plus tax is a good benchmark.

Travel Cuts (☎ 1 866 246 9762; www.travelcuts.com) is Canada's national student travel agency, with offices in major cities.

For online bookings try www.expedia.ca and www.travelocity.ca.

Continental Europe

Several European cities, most particularly Amsterdam, Athens and Berlin, offer bargain flights. Scandinavian budget airline Blue1 (a subsidiary of SAS) flies from Helsinki; Norwegian Air Shuttle, another budget carrier, flies from Oslo to destinations throughout Europe.

Icelandair serves the USA via Reykjavík from numerous European cities. Budget airline Iceland Express has year-round flights between Copenhagen and Reykjavík and summer flights between Akureyri and Copenhagen; it also makes seasonal flights to Reykjavík from Alicante, Berlin and Frankfurt, for around €400 to €500 including taxes.

Atlantic Airways fly to the Faroes from Denmark (two hours) and Iceland (one hour) in the summer. Flights cost around €300.

Across Europe many travel agencies have ties with STA Travel. Agencies in important transport hubs:

FRANCE

Anyway (☎ 08 92 302 301; www.anyway.fr in French)

Lastminute (☎ 04 66 92 30 29; www.lastminute.fr in French)

Nouvelles Frontières (☎ 01 49 20 65 87; www .nouvelles-frontieres.fr in French)

OTU Voyages (☎ 01 55 82 32 32) Specialises in student and youth travel.

Voyageurs du Monde (☎ 08 92 23 56 56; www.vdm .com in French)

GERMANY

Expedia (☎ 01805 007 146; www.expedia.de in German)

Just Travel (☎ 089 747 3330; www.justtravel.de)

Lastminute (☎ 01805 284 366; www.lastminute.de in German)

STA Travel (☎ 069 743 032 92; www.statravel.de in German) For travellers under the age of 26.

ITALY

CTS Viaggi (☎ 06 44 111 66; www.cts.it in Italian) Specialises in student and youth travel.

TRANSPORT IN SCANDINAVIA

NETHERLANDS
Airfair (☎ 0900 771 7717; www.airfair.nl in Dutch)

SPAIN
Barcelo Viajes (☎ 902 200 400; www.barceloviajes .com in Spanish)

New Zealand

British Airways, KLM, Qantas and Swiss are some of the airlines flying to Scandinavia, usually with stopovers in southeast Asia and/or Europe. Return fares cost around NZ$3500 and take 26 hours.

It's easiest and cheapest to book flights via an agency such as:

Flight Centre (☎ 0800 243 544; www.flightcentre.co.nz)
STA Travel (☎ 0800 474 400; www.statravel.co.nz)

UK & Ireland

NO-FRILLS AIRLINES

Currently, three no-frills airlines offer cheap flights to major entry points in Scandinavia.

Ryanair flies from London Stansted to nine airports in Denmark, Norway, Sweden and Finland; from Glasgow Prestwick to Oslo and Stockholm; from Liverpool to Oslo and Tampere; and from Newcastle to Oslo. Some promotional fares cost from as little as £30, including taxes, although most are around £120 in peak season.

EasyJet flies from London Stansted to Copenhagen for around £100 return, less the further you book ahead.

Iceland Express flies from London Stansted to Reykjavík from UK£69 return, although most peak-season prices are around £200.

From Ireland, the cheapest way to Scandinavia is to catch a flight with Ryanair to London Stansted, then pick up one of the above no-frills flights.

FULL-SERVICE AIRLINES

SAS offers some good deals, including peak-season return flights from London to airports in Denmark, Finland, Norway and Sweden (from around £100 return).

City Airline flies from Birmingham and Manchester to Göteborg; internet offers start from £130 return, including tax.

DISCOUNT TRAVEL AGENCIES

Discount air travel is big business in London. Agencies advertise in the travel pages of the weekend papers, *Time Out*, the *Evening Standard* and the free magazine *TNT*.

Recommended travel agencies:
ebookers (☎ 0871 223 5000; www.ebookers.com)
Flight Centre (☎ 0870 499 0040; www.flightcentre .co.uk)
North-South Travel (☎ 01245 608 291; www .northsouthtravel.co.uk) Donates a portion of its profits to projects in the developing world.
Quest Travel (☎ 0845 263 6963; www.questtravel.com)
STA Travel (☎ 0871 230 0040; www.statravel.co.uk) For travellers under the age of 26.
Trailfinders (☎ 0845 058 5858; www.trailfinders.com)
Travel Bag (☎ 0800 804 8911; www.travelbag.co.uk)

USA

There are myriad flight options from the USA to Europe. To start with, check out weekly travel sections in larger newspapers, where you'll find travel agencies' advertisements. You should be able to fly return from New York and/or Boston to Copenhagen, Helsinki, Oslo or Stockholm for around US$2000 in high season, although there are frequent offers of up to two-thirds lower than this. The journey takes around 10 hours. Open-jaw tickets allow you to land in one city and return from another at no extra cost.

Icelandair flies from New York, Boston, Baltimore/Washington, Minneapolis, Orlando, and San Francisco (summer only), via Keflavík in Iceland to many European destinations including Glasgow, London, Oslo, Stockholm and Copenhagen. It has some of the best deals and also allows a free stopover of up to seven days in Reykjavík on transatlantic flights.

If you're planning to fly within Scandinavian Europe, SAS sells various internal air passes (see p503) if you travel across the pond with it. It departs from Chicago, New York, Seattle and Washington, DC, to Copenhagen and Stockholm.

Airhitch (www.airhitch.org) specialises in internet purchases of standby tickets to Europe from the east coast/west coast for around US$500/650 return. Destinations are by region (not a specific city or country), so you'll need to be flexible.

DISCOUNT TRAVEL AGENCIES

Discount travel agencies are known as consolidators in the USA, and San Francisco is the consolidator king. Other good deals can be found in Los Angeles, New York and other big cities. Track down consolidators through the *Yellow Pages* or the major daily newspapers.

Travel agencies recommended for online bookings:

Cheap Tickets (☎ 1 888 922 8849; www.cheaptickets .com)

Expedia (☎ 1 800 397 3342; www.expedia.com)

Lowestfare.com (☎ 1 800 678 0998; www.lowestfare .com) Website-based.

Orbitz (☎ 1 888 656 4546; www.orbitz.com)

STA Travel (☎ 1 800 781 4040; www.statravel.com)

Travelocity (☎ 1 888 872 8356; www.travelocity.com)

LAND
Bus
Without a rail pass, it's generally cheapest to get from Europe to Scandinavia by bus. Some coaches are quite luxurious with stewards, air-conditioning, toilet and snack bar. Small bargain-price bus companies regularly appear and disappear – ask student and discount travel agencies for the latest companies.

Eurolines (www.eurolines.com), a conglomeration of 32 coach companies, is the biggest and best-established express-bus network, and connects Scandinavia with the rest of Europe. Most buses operate daily in summer and between two and five days per week in winter; advance ticket purchases are usually necessary. Eurolines' representatives in Europe:

Bohemia Euroexpress International (☎ 245 005 245; www.bei.cz in Czech; Křižíkova 4-6, 18600 Prague 8, Czech Republic)

Bus Éireann (☎ 01-836 6111; www.eurolines.ie; Bus Éireann Travel Centre, Busáras Bus Station, Store St, Dublin 1)

Deutsche Touring (☎ 06 97 90 35 01; www.eurolines .de; Am Römerhof 17, 60486 Frankfurt am Main)

Eurolines Austria (☎ 01-798 29 00; www.eurolines.at; Busstation Wien-Mitte, Erdbergstrasse 202, 1030 Vienna, Austria)

Eurolines France (☎ 08 92 89 90 91; www.eurolines .fr in French; Gare Routiére Internationale, Boite 313, 28 ave du Général de Gaulle, F-93541 Bagnolet, Paris, France)

Eurolines Italy SRL (☎ 39 055 32 89 939; www .eurolines.it in Italian; Via GS Mercadente 2b, 50144 Firenze, Italy)

Eurolines Nederland (☎ 020-560 8788; www .eurolines.nl; Amstel Station, Julianaplein 5, 1097 DN Amsterdam, Netherlands)

Eurolines Scandinavia Denmark (☎ 33 88 70 00; www.eurolines.dk; Vesterbrogade 20, 4th 1620 Copenhagen) Norway (☎ 87 62 59 60; www.eurolines.no; Bussterminalen, Schweigaardsgate 6, 0185 Oslo); Sweden (☎ 031 100 240; www.eurolines.se; Busstop, Cityterminalen, Klarabergsviadukten 72, SE-11164 Stockholm, Sweden)

Eurolines Spain (☎ 902 40 50 40; www.eurolines.es in Spanish; Estación Sur de Autobuses, c/Méndez Alvaro, Madrid, Spain)

Eurolines UK Ltd (☎ 08717 818181; www.national express.com/eurolines; 52 Grosvenor Gardens, London, SW1W 0AG, UK)

Sample Eurolines fares: London to Copenhagen (from £116 return) and Frankfurt to Copenhagen (€220 return). There's a 10% discount for those under 26 or over 60 years.

The Eurolines Pass allows unlimited travel to 40 cities across Europe; the Scandinavian cities included are Copenhagen, Göteborg, Oslo and Stockholm. Between late June and mid-September, a 15-/30-day pass costs €329/439 (€279/359 for those under 26 years and over 60; cheaper at other times).

From St Petersburg in Russia, daily express buses run to Helsinki (see p209 for details). A Russian visa is required.

Car & Motorcycle
Driving to Scandinavia usually means taking a car ferry (p500). The only land borders in the region are between Finland/Norway and Russia, or between Denmark and Germany. It is possible to drive through Denmark into Sweden using bridges and tunnels.

If you're driving from the UK, you can put your car on a direct ferry to Scandinavia (p503); or get to mainland Europe using the Channel Tunnel car-carrying train, **Eurotunnel** (☎ 0870 535 3535, 321 002 061; www.eurotunnel.com), then from mainland Europe drive northwards.

See p506 for more information about required paperwork.

Hitching & Car-Ride Services
For local hitching conditions and laws, see the individual country chapters.

After hitching, the cheapest way to head further north in Europe is as a paying passenger in a private car. Car-sharing is particularly well organised in Germany. After paying a reservation fee to a city-based **Mitfahrzentrale agency** (www.mitfahrzentrale.de in German), you're then linked up with people driving in your direction (petrol money is also due to the driver). Local tourist information offices can help you locate agencies, or in larger German cities, dial the city area code and ☎ 19444.

A list of European car-ride agencies can be found at www.allostop.com under the section 'Carpooling in Europe'.

Train

The monthly *Thomas Cook European Timetable* is the train traveller's bible. It's available from Thomas Cook outlets in the UK (£13.99), or you can subscribe to the service updated monthly from www.thomascookpublishing.com.

The **Man in Seat 61** (www.seat61.com) is a slow-travel hero with a wonderfully helpful website about rail journeys.

For further information about rail passes, see p509.

ASIA

Travelling across Asia by train costs about the same as flying – but it's a real adventure. Three routes cross Siberia: the Vladivostok–Moscow Trans-Siberian route (packages around US$700, seven days); the Beijing–Moscow Trans-Manchurian route (packages around US$700, seven days); and the popular Beijing–Moscow Trans-Mongolian route (six days), where a 2nd-class sleeper in a four-berth compartment costs around US$585 excluding visas and meals. Trains then run daily from Moscow to Helsinki (p209), usually requiring a change at St Petersburg.

Prices vary enormously, depending on where you buy the ticket and what's included – prices quoted here are only a rough indication. **Monkey Business** (☎ 8610 6591 6519; www.monkeyshrine.com) in Beijing organises all-inclusive packages and visas for trips starting in Beijing; for the Hong Kong office call ☎ 2723 1376. More-expensive packages can be bought in Europe; one well-known UK operator is **Regent Holidays** (☎ 0845 277 3317; www.regent-holidays.co.uk).

Lonely Planet's *Trans-Siberian Railway* is a comprehensive guide to the route; also see www.seat61.com.

CENTRAL EUROPE

Hamburg is the main European gateway for Scandinavia but direct trains also run from Berlin. There are several direct trains daily to Copenhagen from Hamburg (2nd class from €85, five hours); the hour-long ferry trip is included in the ticket price.

In Germany, the Sparpreis fare structures are a good deal: use them to cheapen the rail journey to northern Germany. Sparpreis 25 and Sparpreis 50 give 25% and 50% respectively off long-distance return fares if booked at least three days in advance, with certain restrictions on times of travel and point of departure/return.

In Poland, take a train to Gdynia or Świnoujście for a ferry to Sweden (see p477). For Polish timetables and prices, see www.intercity.com.pl.

A useful website for planning European train journeys is www.europeanrail.com.

UK

Going by train to Scandinavia is more expensive and takes longer than flying, but it's more of an experience. The Channel Tunnel makes land travel possible between Britain and continental Europe. **Eurostar** (☎ 0870 518 6186, 01233 617575; www.eurostar.com) passenger services connect London with Calais, Paris, Lille and Brussels. From Brussels connect to Hamburg, which is the main gateway to Scandinavia.

From London, a 2nd-class return ticket costs from £170 to Copenhagen (via Cologne or Hamburg), and from around £390 return to Oslo and Stockholm (via Copenhagen). Contact **Deutsche Bahn UK** (☎ 08718 808066; www.bahn.co.uk) for details of frequent special offers, and for reservations and tickets.

For more information on international rail travel (including Eurostar services), contact the **Rail Europe Travel Centre** (☎ 08448 484 064; www.raileurope.co.uk; 178 Piccadilly, London W1).

SEA

Prices given in this section are sample starting prices, based on a foot-passenger travelling one way in high season, using the cheapest-available sleeping option (usually a reclining seat or couchette – see p509 for a definition). Booking a cabin, travelling on weekends or night boats, or taking a vehicle will obviously up the cost; travelling outside June to August will lower it. Book as early as possible to take advantage of limited cheaper tickets.

See the transport sections of the country chapters for information about boat-train links within Scandinavian Europe. See also p509 for rail passes and their validity on ferries.

Ferry Companies

The following details cover the larger ferry companies operating to Scandinavia.

COLOR LINE

The Norwegian company **Color Line** (www.color line.com) has year-round routes from Norway to Denmark (all €56) and Germany.

From Hirtshals in Denmark you can get to two Norwegian towns: Kristiansand (4½ hours) and Larvik (6½ hours). Boats also run to Oslo from Kiel in Germany (from €200, 20 hours).

It's possible to take a car on these ferry services (around €100 one way); if you have a full car, packages (around €450 for vehicle and five people) are more economical. Booking agencies:

Denmark (☎ 99 56 19 77)
Germany (☎ 0431-7300 300)
Norway (☎ 47 22 94 44 00)

DFDS SEAWAYS

DFDS Seaways (www.dfdsseaways.com) operates year-round routes between Denmark, Norway, Sweden and the UK. Prices here are per person, based on four people sharing the cheapest cabin. Cars cost from £95.

Boats run from Oslo to Copenhagen (from Nkr370, 16 hours), via Helsingborg in Sweden (14 hours); from Harwich in the UK to Esbjerg in Denmark (from £49, 19 hours); and from Newcastle in the UK to Göteborg in Sweden (from £69, 26 hours), via Kristiansand in Norway (19 hours). Booking agencies:

Denmark (☎ 33 42 30 82; Sundkrogsgade 11, DK-2100 Copenhagen Ø)
Germany (☎ 01805-8901 051; Högerdamm 41, D-20097 Hamburg)
Norway (☎ 21 62 13 40; Postboks 365 Sentrum, N-0102 Oslo)
Sweden (☎ 031-650650; Kajskjul 107, Frihamnen)
UK (☎ 0871 522 9955; Scandinavia House, Refinery Rd Parkeston, Essex, CO12 4QG)

FJORD LINE

Fjord Line (www.fjordline.com) sails from Denmark and the UK to western Norway.

Ferries run at least four times per week from Hirtshals in Denmark to Stavanger and Bergen (€46 with reclining seat, seven hours).

Prices are up to 50% lower for children, students and seniors. Booking agencies:

Denmark (☎ 97 96 30 00; Coastergade 10, DK-7730 Hanstholm)
Germany (☎ 82 17 09 7210; Kleine Johannisstrasse 10, D-20457 Hamburg)
Norway (☎ 815 33 500; Skoltegrunnskaien, Postboks 7250, N-5003 Bergen)

UK (☎ 0870 420 1267; Norway House, Royal Quays, North Shields, Tyne & Wear, NE29 6EG)

SILJA LINE

Silja Line (☎ 0600 174552; www.silja.com; Keilaranta 9, Espoo, 02060 Silja) runs ferry routes between Sweden, Finland, Latvia and Estonia.

SMYRIL LINE

Smyril Line (www.smyril-line.com) operates between Hanstholm or Esbjerg (Denmark), Tórshavn (Faroe Islands) and Seyðisfjörður (eastern Iceland). Fares are highest between mid-June and mid-August, when a one-way adult fare (including a rather claustrophobic couchette) from Hanstholm to Seyðisfjörður costs €265. If your budget will stretch a little further, we recommend the very pleasant cabins: prices start at €350. Bringing a vehicle is not much more expensive than paying for two foot passengers. There's a small charge for bicycles, and there are discounts available for seniors, students, disabled travellers and children. Booking agencies:

Denmark (☎ 96 55 03 60; www.smyril-line.dk; KaiLindbergs Gade 200, DK-7730 Hanstholm)
Faroe Islands (☎ 345900; www.smyril-line.com; J Broncksgøta 37, PO Box 370, FO-110 Tórshavn)
Iceland (☎ 570 8600; www.smyril-line.is; Sætúni 8, 105 Reykjavík)
Norway (☎ 55 59 65 20; www.smyril-line.no; Bontelabo 2, Postboks 4135, Dreggen, N-5835 Bergen)
UK (☎ 020 7554 3530; www.smyril-line.com; Scantours, 73 Mornington St, London NW1 7QE)

STENA LINE

Stena Line (www.stenaline.com) runs daily ferry services between Denmark and Sweden, Denmark and Norway, Germany and Sweden and, Poland and Sweden. Some boats sail overnight, with prices around double those quoted here for day sailings.

From Frederikshavn (Denmark), you can sail to Oslo in Norway (from Dkr240, 6½ hours) and Göteborg in Sweden (Dkr210, 3¼ hours). Express ferries (Dkr295, two hours) also run the latter route in summer. From Grenå (Denmark), there are twice-daily ferries to Varberg in Sweden (Dkr210, four hours).

From Kiel (Germany), there are daily ferries to Göteborg in Sweden (€79, 13½ hours).

From Gdynia (Poland) there are one or two ferries per day to Karlskrona in Sweden (Skr830, 10½ hours).

Booking agencies:

Denmark (☎ 96 20 02 00; www.stenaline.dk in Danish; Trafikhavnen, DK-9900 Frederikshavn)

Germany (☎ 01805-91 66 66; www.stenaline.de in German; Schwedenkai 1, D-24103 Kiel)

Norway (☎ 02010; www.stenaline.no in Norwegian; Postboks 764, Sentrum, N-0106 Oslo)

Poland (☎ 058-660 92 00; www.stenaline.pl in Polish; Kwiatkowskiego 60, PL-81-156 Gdynia)

Sweden (☎ 031-704 0000; www.stenaline.se in Swedish; Box 94, SE-43222 Varberg)

UK (☎ 0870 570 7070; www.stenaline.co.uk; Stena House, Station Approach, Holyhead, Anglesey LL65 1DQ)

Baltic Countries

There are regular sailings from Estonia, Latvia and Lithuania across the Baltic Sea to Sweden and Finland. In addition to the information here, see the Sweden (p477) and Finland (p210) transport sections.

ESTONIA

Silja Line sails two to six times daily from Tallinn to Helsinki (€48, 3½ hours).

Tallink (Estonia ☎ 640 9808; www.tallink.ee; Finland ☎ 010 804 123; www.tallink.fi; Sweden ☎ 08 22 21 40; www.tallink.se) sails several times daily from Tallinn to Helsinki (€25, 3½ hours); once daily in summer via Mariehamn to Stockholm (from €59 per person based on four people sharing, 16 hours); and from Paldiski in Estonia to Kapellskär (from €31 per person based on four people sharing, 10 hours), north of Stockholm.

LATVIA

Scandlines (www.scandlines.se; ☎ 04-218 6100) runs three services per week between Ventspils and Karlshamn in Sweden (from €89 per person based on four people sharing, 17 hours) and five per week between Ventspils and Nynäshamn (from €75 for reclining seat, 11 hours), also in Sweden. Prices include two meals.

Tallink sails between Stockholm and Riga three times weekly (Skr365 based on four people sharing, 18 hours).

LITHUANIA

DFDS Tor Line (in Sweden ☎ 46 31 65 08 00; in Lithuania 46 39 50 49; www.dfdstorline.com) shuttles daily between Klaipėda (Lithuania) and Karlshamn in Sweden (from Skr660, 16 hours).

Germany

The **Scandlines** (☎ 04-218 6100; www.scandlines.se) train, car and passenger ferry from Putt-

garden to Rødbyhavn in Denmark (the quickest way to Copenhagen) runs every half-hour around the clock and takes 45 minutes (€7). Frequent Scandlines ferries also run from Rostock to Gedser (€10, two hours) in Denmark.

From Kiel, there are daily Stena Line ferries to Göteborg in Sweden (€80, 13½ hours) and Color Line ferries to Oslo in Norway (from €220 for two-berth cabin, 20 hours).

Four large Scandlines ferries run in each direction daily between Sassnitz (eastern Germany) and Trelleborg (Dkr130, four hours), south of Malmö in Sweden. Three ferries run from Rostock to Trelleborg in Sweden (Dkr199, six hours).

Finnlines (☎ in Finland 358 10 343 4500, in Germany 49 450 280 532; www.finnlines.fi) has a daily service from Travemünde to Helsinki (berth or cabin from €200 per person based on four people sharing, 34 hours); and to Malmö (berth/cabin from €40/85, nine hours) – for these ferries, ☎ 04-5028 0520 in Germany, ☎ 04-017 6800 in Sweden.

TT Line (☎ in Sweden 0410-56200; www.ttline.com) has daily ferries to Sweden (mostly overnight) between Travemünde and Trelleborg (from €95 for car plus four people, seven hours); and between Rostock and Trelleborg (€30, 5½ hours).

See also the relevant Transport sections in the individual country chapters.

Poland

Regular ferries cross the Baltic Sea between Poland and Sweden. Stena Line has one or two ferries daily from Gdynia to Karlskrona (Skr670, 10½ hours).

Unity Line (☎ in Sweden 0411-556900, in Poland 091-359 5600; www.unityline.pl; Pl Rodla 8, 70-419 Szczecin) has a daily ferry (Skr510, eight hours) between Świnoujście and Ystad in Sweden.

Polferries (☎ in Sweden 48 91 32 26 140, in Poland 0801 003 171; www.polferries.pl; ul Dworcowa 1, 72-600 Świnoujście) links Gdansk with Nynäshamn in Sweden (from Skr640, 18 hours) three times per week. It has one night boat, which operates daily from Świnoujście to Ystad in Sweden (Skr550, seven hours).

It also has four departures per week from Świnoujście to Copenhagen (Skr460, 10½ hours), and one on Saturday to Rønne in Denmark (Skr290, 5¼ hours).

The UK

DFDS Seaways has ferries from Harwich to Esbjerg in Denmark (from £49, 19 hours) and from Newcastle to Kristiansand (from £69, 19 hours) and Göteborg (from £69, 27 hours, twice weekly).

See the relevant Transport sections in the individual country chapters for more details.

TOURS

For special-interest trips (canoeing, bird-watching, cycling), see the country chapters in this book, contact your local activity club, check out classified ads in hobby mags, or consult the national tourist offices of the country you're headed for. In the UK, the Cyclists' Touring Club (see p504) runs occasional cycling tours in Scandinavia.

If your time is limited, consider using one of the following tour operators:

Australia

Bentours (☎ 02-9241 1353; www.bentours.com .au; Level 7, 189 Kent St, Sydney 2000) With 25 years experience covering the highlights of Denmark, Norway, Sweden, Finland and Iceland/Greenland, with fjord cruises and trips to St Petersburg and Moscow.

France

Grand Nord Grand Large (☎ 01 40 46 05 14; www .gngl.com in French; 15 Rue du Cardinal Lemoine, 75005 Paris) A 'polar voyage' specialist, with trips to northern Finland, Norway (including Svalbard), Sweden, the Faroes and Iceland.

Germany

Norden Tours (☎ 040-37 69 30; www.nordentours.de in German; Kleine Johannisstrasse 10, D-20457 Hamburg) Wide range of Scandinavian tours, including cruises.

Nordwind Reisen (☎ 08331-87073; www.nordwin dreisen.de in German; Maximilianstrasse 17, D-87700 Memmingen, Nordwind) Specialist tours to Iceland, Greenland and Spitzbergen; some winter tours to Sweden and Finland.

Norway

Brand Cruises (☎ 47 91 30 21 50 Postbox 23, Vedavaa-gen, Norway) Norwegian cruises, including Svalbard.

UK

Arctic Experience: Discover the World (☎ 01737-218800; www.arctic-experience.co.uk; Arctic House, 8 Bolters Lane, Banstead, Surrey, SM7 2AR) Summer and winter wilderness, wildlife and activity holidays in the Faroes, Iceland, Sweden and arctic Norway.

Dick Phillips (☎ 01434-381440; www.icelandic-travel .com; Whitehall House, Nenthead, Alston, Cumbria, CA9 3PS) Mr Phillips has decades of experience leading rigorous, wild hiking and skiing trips in Iceland.

USA

Scantours (☎ 1 800 223 7226; www.scantours.com) Comfortable, hotel-based excursions and cruises throughout Scandinavia, with trips to St Petersburg.

Travcoa (☎ 1 866 591 0070; www.travcoa.com; 4340 Von Karman Ave, Suite 400, Newport Beach, CA 92660) Hotel-based tours visiting the highlights of Scandinavia.

GETTING AROUND

Getting around the populated areas of Scandinavia is generally a breeze, with efficient public transport systems and snappy connections. Remote regions usually have trustworthy but infrequent services.

AIR

Domestic networks in Scandinavia are safe and reliable. Internal flights can be expensive, but they're often cheaper than land-based alternatives for longer journeys, and of course can save days of travelling time. Companies running internal airline routes offer reduced rates for internet bookings. For domestic carriers, see the country Transport sections.

Travelling between airports and city centres isn't a problem in Scandinavia thanks to good bus and train networks.

Air Passes

Visitors flying **SAS** (☎ in North America 1 800 221 2350, in the UK 0871 521 2772; www.scandinavian.net) on a return ticket to Norway, Sweden or Finland from outside Europe can buy Visit Scandinavia/Europe Airpass coupons (starting at US$72 each), as can US travellers flying with United Airlines.

Visitors (but not residents of Denmark, Finland, Norway or Sweden) flying SAS return to Scandinavia from inside Europe can buy similar Visit Scandinavia Airpass coupons (starting at €69 each).

The passes allow one-way travel on direct flights between any two Scandinavian cities serviced by SAS, Blue1, Skyways, **Widerøe**

(☎ 47 75 11 11 11; www.wideroe.no) and other operators, with stopovers limited to one in each city. You can buy up to eight tickets which are valid for three months. Children fly for around 70% of the adult price. Tickets can be purchased after arriving in Scandinavia if you have a return SAS international ticket.

BICYCLE

A tour of northern Europe by bike is an exciting prospect, giving you the chance to see vast areas of wilderness under your own steam. One organisation that can help you gear up in the UK is the wonderful **Cyclists' Touring Club** (CTC; ☎ 0870 873 0060; www.ctc.org.uk; Parklands, Railton Rd, Guildford, Surrey, GU2 9JX, UK). It can help members with cycling conditions, routes, itineraries, maps and specialised insurance. It also organises occasional tours (www.cyclingholidays.org) to Denmark and the Norwegian fjords.

English-language books about cycling in Scandinavia are virtually nonexistent. *Europe by Bike*, by Karen and Terry Whitehill, is a little out of date but its descriptions of 18 cycling tours include two for Scandinavia (from Kiel across Denmark to Sweden and from southern Sweden to Stockholm via the Åland islands). *The Essential Touring Cyclist* by Richard A Lovett is full of useful general advice.

The North Sea Cycle Route covers parts of Denmark, Sweden, Norway and the Shetland Islands: see www.northsea-cycle.com for information.

Make sure you take sufficient tools and spare parts, as replacements may be pricey and hard to find. Panniers are essential, and of course a bike helmet is always a good idea. Take a decent lock and use it when you leave your bike unattended; theft is not uncommon in places like Helsinki and Copenhagen.

It's easy to hire bikes throughout Scandinavia, sometimes from train station bike-rental counters, and in some cases it's possible to return them to another outlet so you don't have to double back. On slower trains and local buses in Scandinavia, bikes can usually be transported as luggage, either free or for a small fee. Fast trains and long-distance buses rarely take bikes. Cycling across the Øresund bridge between Denmark and Sweden is prohibited.

For an overview of cycling in Scandinavian Europe, see p484 and the individual country chapters.

BOAT
Ferry

You can't really get around Scandinavia without using ferries extensively. The shortest routes from Denmark (Jutland) to Norway and from southern Sweden to Finland are ferry routes. Denmark is now well connected to mainland Europe and Sweden by bridges.

Ferry tickets are cheap on competitive routes, although transporting cars can be costly. Bicycles are usually carried free. On some routes, train-pass holders are entitled to free or discounted travel (p509).

Weekend ferries, especially on Friday night, are significantly more expensive. Teenage travellers are banned from travelling on some Friday night ferries due to problems with drunkenness.

For further information about the many ferry options available between the destinations in this book, see the Transport sections of the individual country chapters. Also see p500 for ferry companies running services between Scandinavian countries.

Steamer

Scandinavia's main lakes and rivers are served by both diesel-powered boats and steamers during the summer. Treat these extended boat trips as relaxing, scenic miniholidays; if you view them merely as a way to get from A to B, they can seem quite expensive.

Sweden has the largest fleets in Scandinavia. Most leave from Stockholm and sail east to the Stockholm archipelago (p417) – a maze of 24,000 islands and islets – and west to historic Lake Mälaren (p417) – home base of the Swedish Vikings a millennium ago. You can also cruise the Göta Canal (p478), the longest water route in Sweden.

The legendary Hurtigruten (p385) provides a link between Norway's coastal fishing villages. In Finland, steamships ply Lake Saimaa (p176) and its canal; there are also diesel-engine boats.

BUS

Buses provide a viable alternative to the rail network in Scandinavian countries, and are the only option in Iceland and the Faroes. Compared to trains, they're usually cheaper (Finland is the exception) and slightly slower. Connections with train services (where they exist) are good.

RAILWAYS & FERRIES

Bus travel tends to be perfect for getting around cities and for short hops, and is sometimes your only choice in remote rural areas (particularly northern Sweden).

Bus Passes

Eurolines offers a variety of city 'loops' and the Eurolines Pass – see p499 for more details.

See the Transport section in the country chapters for details of internal bus passes, or contact one of the main long-distance bus operators listed here.

DENMARK
Søndergaards Busser (☎ 70 10 00 33; www.sonder gaards-busser.dk)
Thinggaard Expressbusser (☎ 98 11 66 00; www .thinggaardbus.dkm in Danish)

FAROE ISLANDS
Strandfaraskip Landsins (☎ 343030; www.ssl.fo)

FINLAND
Oy Matkahuolto Ab (☎ 0200 4000; www.matka huolto.fi)

ICELAND
BSÍ (Bifreiðastöð Íslands; ☎ 562 1011; www.bsi.is)

NORWAY
Nor-Way Bussekspress (☎ 815 44 444; www .nor-way.no)

SWEDEN
Säfflebussen (☎ 0771-151515; www.safflebussen.se in Swedish)
Svenska Buss (☎ 0771-676767; www.svenskabuss .se in Swedish)
Swebus Express (☎ 0771-218218; www.swebusex press.se)
Ybuss (☎ 0771-334444; www.ybuss.se in Swedish)

Reservations

Advance reservations are rarely necessary. However, you do need to prepurchase your ticket before you board many city buses, and then validate your ticket on board. See the individual country chapters for specific details.

CAR & MOTORCYCLE

Travelling with your own vehicle is the best way to get to remote places and gives you independence and flexibility. Drawbacks include being isolated in your own little car-bubble, and stressful city-centre driving.

Scandinavia is excellent for motorcycle touring, with good-quality winding roads, stunning scenery and an active motorcycling scene – just make sure your wet-weather gear is up to scratch. The best time for touring is May to September. On ferries, motorcyclists rarely have to book ahead as they can generally be squeezed in. Anyone considering Scandinavia on two wheels should read *The Adventure Motorbiking Handbook*, by Chris Scott, which gives sound advice on motorcycle touring worldwide.

Bringing Your Own Vehicle

Proof of ownership of a private vehicle should always be carried (this is the Vehicle Registration Document for British-registered cars) when touring Europe. You may also need a *carnet de passage en douane*, which is effectively a passport for the vehicle and acts as a temporary waiver of import duty. The *carnet* may also need to specify any expensive spare parts that you're planning to carry with you, such as a gearbox. Contact your local automobile association for further information.

Vehicles crossing an international border should display a sticker showing their country of registration. (The exception is cars with Euro-plates being taken into another EU country). It's compulsory to carry a warning triangle in most places, to be used in the event of breakdown. You must also use headlamp beam reflectors/convertors on right-hand-drive cars.

Driving Licence

An EU driving licence is acceptable for driving throughout Scandinavia, as are North American and Australian licences (in general). If you have any other type of licence, you should obtain an International Driving Permit (IDP) from your motoring organisation before you leave home.

If you're thinking of going snowmobiling, you'll need to bring your driving licence with you.

Fuel & Spare Parts

Fuel is heavily taxed and very expensive in Scandinavia. Most types of petrol, including unleaded 95 and 98 octane, are widely available; leaded petrol is no longer sold. Diesel is significantly cheaper than petrol in most countries. Always check the type of fuel being supplied – usually pumps with green markings and the word *Blyfri* on them deliver unleaded fuel, and black pumps supply diesel.

Recommended accessories are a first-aid kit, a spare bulb kit and a fire extinguisher. In Iceland, it's wise to carry general spare parts, including a fan belt and clutch cable, and learn how to make basic repairs; garages and passing motorists can be few and far between. Contact your automobile association or, in the UK, contact the **AA** (☎ 0870 600 0371, 0161 495 8945; www.theaa.com) or the **RAC** (☎ 0870 572 2722; www.rac.co.uk) for more information.

Hire

Renting a car is more expensive in Scandinavia than in other European countries, and the variety of deals, terms and conditions can be mind-boggling. However, there are a few pointers that can help you through the morass. The big international firms – Hertz, Avis, Eurodollar, Budget, and Europe's largest rental agency, Europcar – will give you reliable service, a good standard of vehicle, and the (usually chargeable) option of returning the car to a different outlet when you've finished with it.

Try to prebook your vehicle, which always works out cheaper. If you've left it too late, look for national or local firms, which can often undercut the international companies substantially. It's generally more expensive to hire cars from airport-rental stands than to pick one up in town.

Fly/drive combinations are worth looking into; for example, SAS and Icelandair often offer cheaper car rentals to their international passengers. The ScanRail 'n' Drive package gives you a five-day rail pass and a car for two days to be used within 15 days in Denmark, Norway and/or Sweden. Prices start at US$473 for an adult on 2nd-class trains and an economy car (US$838 for two adults), with an option of retaining the car for US$51 per day.

Holiday Autos International (www.holidayautos .com) usually has good rates for rental, but you need to prebook. It has offices around Europe, including Denmark, Norway and Sweden. Ask in advance if you can drive a rented car across borders.

If you fancy chancing a banger, the US firm **Rent-a-Wreck** (www.rent-a-wreck.com) has franchises in Denmark, Finland, Iceland and Sweden.

Be sure you understand what's included in the price (unlimited or paid kilometres, injury insurance, tax, collision damage waiver etc) and what your liabilities are. Always take the collision damage waiver, although you can probably skip the injury insurance if you and your passengers have decent travel insurance.

The minimum rental age is usually 21, sometimes even 23, and you'll probably need a credit card (or a mountain of cash) for the deposit.

Motorcycle and moped rental isn't particularly common in Scandinavian countries, but it's possible in major cities.

Insurance

Third-party motor insurance is a minimum requirement in most of Europe. Most UK car-insurance policies automatically provide third-party cover for EU and some other countries. Ask your insurer for a Green Card – an internationally recognised proof of insurance (there may be a charge) – and check that it lists all the countries you intend to visit. You'll need this in the event of an accident outside the country in which the vehicle is insured. Also ask your insurer for a European Accident Statement form, which can simplify things if worse comes to worst. Never sign statements you can't read or understand – insist on a written translation and only sign it if it's acceptable.

A European breakdown-assistance policy, such as those provided by the AA or the RAC, is a good investment: expect to pay about £60 for 14 days' cover. It's also worth asking your motoring organisation for details of reciprocal services offered by affiliated organisations around Europe.

Road Conditions & Hazards

Conditions and types of roads vary widely across Scandinavia, but it's possible to make some generalisations. The fastest routes are four- or six-lane dual carriageways, which tend to skirt cities and plough through the countryside in straight lines, often avoiding the most scenic areas. Motorways and other primary routes, with the exception of some roads in Iceland, are universally in good condition.

Road surfaces on minor routes are not so reliable, although normally adequate. These roads are narrower and progress is slower, but in compensation, you'll pass through more scenic places along the way.

Norway has some particularly hair-raising roads; serpentine examples climb from sea level to 1000m in what seems no distance at all on a map. These rollercoasters will use plenty of petrol and strain the car's engine and brakes, not to mention your nerves! Driving a campervan on these kinds of routes is not recommended.

In Norway, there are tolls for some tunnels, bridges, roads and entry into larger towns, and for practically all ferries crossing fjords. Roads, tunnels, bridges and car ferries in Finland and Sweden are usually free, although there's a hefty toll of €38 (Dkr275) per car on the Øresund bridge between Denmark and Sweden.

During winter in Scandinavia, snow tyres are compulsory. The tyre chains common in the Alps are allowed in Norway, but are illegal elsewhere.

Suicidal stock, including sheep, elk, horses and reindeer, is a potential hazard. If you are involved in an animal incident, by law you must report it to the police.

Road Rules

You drive on the right-hand side of the road in all Scandinavian countries. Seat-belt use is compulsory for all passengers and headlights must be switched on at all times (except in built-up areas in Finland). Vehicles from the UK and Ireland need their headlights adjusted to avoid blinding oncoming traffic (a simple solution on older headlight lenses is to cover up the triangular section of the lens with a headlight deflector, available from motoring accessory shops). Priority is usually given to traffic approaching from the right.

It's compulsory for motorcyclists and their passengers to wear helmets. Check first if you're thinking of parking motorcycles on pavements (sidewalks). This is illegal in some countries, although the police usually turn a blind eye as long as pedestrians aren't obstructed.

Take care with speed limits, which vary from country to country. Many driving infringements are subject to on-the-spot fines in Scandinavian countries. If you receive a fine for any driving offence, make sure to get a receipt.

Drink-driving regulations are strict: one drink can put you over the limit. The maximum blood-alcohol concentration (BAC) is 0.01% in Norway (the strictest in Europe), 0.02% in Sweden and 0.05% in the rest of Scandinavia.

Your national motoring organisation may distribute free booklets summarising Scandinavian motoring regulations.

HITCHING

Hitching is never entirely safe in any country in the world, and we don't recommend it. Travellers, particularly women, who decide to hitch are taking a small but potentially serious risk – even in 'safe' Scandinavia. People who do choose to hitch will be safer if they travel in pairs and let someone know where they're planning to go.

Hitching is neither popular nor particularly rewarding in most of the region. That said, with a bit of luck, hitchers can end up making good time in some areas, but obviously your plans need to be flexible in case you suddenly become invisible to passing motorists. Don't try to hitch from city centres; take public transport to suburban exit routes. Hitching is usually illegal on motorways – stand on the entrance ramps.

It's sometimes possible to arrange a lift privately: scan student notice boards in colleges or contact car-sharing agencies (see p499).

TOURS

See the individual country chapters for details of recommended, locally organised tours.

TRAIN

Trains in Scandinavia are comfortable, frequent and punctual. As with most things in the region, prices are relatively expensive, although European train passes can make travel affordable. Finland has the cheapest rail service. There are no trains in Iceland or the Faroes, nor in most of far-northern Norway.

If you plan to travel extensively by train, get the *Thomas Cook European Timetable* (see p500), which gives a complete listing of train schedules and indicates where supplements apply or where reservations are necessary.

Express Trains

Fast trains in Europe, or ones that make few stops, are usually identified by the symbols EC (Eurocity) or IC (Intercity). There are national variations: in Norway, some expresses are called Signatur trains; in Finland they're Pendolino express trains; and in Sweden they're known as X2000. Supplements usually apply on fast trains and it's wise (sometimes obligatory) to make reservations at peak times and on certain lines.

Overnight Trains

If you don't fancy sitting upright all night with a stranger dribbling on your shoulder, overnight trains usually offer couchettes or sleepers. Again, reservations are advisable, particularly as sleeping options are generally allocated on a first-come, first-served basis.

Couchettes are basic bunkbeds numbering four (1st class) or six (2nd class) per compartment and are comfortable enough, if lacking a little privacy. In Scandinavia, a bunk costs around US$30 to US$45 for most international trains, irrespective of the length of the journey.

Sleepers are the most comfortable option, offering beds for one or two passengers in 1st class and two or three passengers in 2nd class. In Norway, when individual travellers book a bed for one they'll be booked into a compartment with two other people of the same sex. Denmark has six-person compartments, as well as single and double cabins; charges vary, but these tend to be significantly more expensive than couchettes.

Most long-distance trains have a dining car or snack trolley – bring your own nibbles to keep costs down.

Costs

Full-price tickets can be expensive, but there are generally lots of discounts, particularly if you book ahead. European rail passes are worth buying if you plan to do a reasonable amount of inter-country travelling within a short space of time.

Seniors and travellers under 26 years of age are eligible for discounted tickets, which can cut international fares by between 15% and 40%.

Reservations

It's a good idea (and sometimes obligatory) to make reservations at peak times and on certain train lines, especially long-distance trains. Check the individual country chapters for particulars.

Train Passes

There are a variety of passes available, for students, people under 26, seniors and those who intend to do a lot of train travel. Numerous agencies issue youth tickets in Europe, including **STA Travel** (www.statravel.com) and **Wasteels Rejser** (☎ 33 14 46 33; www.wasteels.dk in Danish; Skoubogade 6, DK-1158 Copenhagen K, Denmark).

Supplements (eg for high-speed services) and reservation costs are not covered by passes, and terms and conditions change – check carefully before buying. Pass-holders must always carry their passport on the train for identification purposes.

EURAIL

Eurail (www.eurail.com) passes offer great value for those prepared to carefully plan rail travel around Europe, including most of Scandinavia. It's always wise to buy a pass before you leave home: you *can* buy them inside Europe, but they're 20% more expensive and there are very few sales outlets. You can buy passes online; the website also has a list of sales agents. The passes can only be bought by *residents of non-European countries* (residents of Algeria, Morocco, Tunisia, Turkey and Russian Federation countries are ineligible to buy passes).

Eurail passes are valid for unlimited travel on national railways and some private lines in Austria, Belgium, Denmark, Finland, France (including Monaco), Germany, Greece, Hungary, Ireland, Italy, Luxembourg, the Netherlands, Norway, Portugal, Spain, Sweden and Switzerland (including Liechtenstein). The passes do *not* cover the UK.

Eurail also offers free or heavily discounted travel (of between 20% and 50%) on ferries on most Baltic routes. See the Eurail website for full details.

In addition to the passes listed here, there's a Eurail Regional Pass, offering unlimited rail travel in two countries, and valid for three to 10 days within a two-month period. Eurail has also created a new Eurail One Country Pass, providing unlimited rail travel in a single country, valid for between three and eight days within a one-month period depending on the country – versions of this pass exist for Denmark, Finland, Norway and Sweden. For both these types of pass, you can choose to travel 1st or 2nd class; Saver and Youth versions are also available.

On most Eurail passes, children aged between four and 11 get a 50% discount on the full adult fare.

The travel options are almost limitless but the classic Eurail passes include the following:

Eurail Scandinavia Pass A 4/5/6/8/10 days' rail travel within two months costs €177/197/224/248/276 for those aged under 26. It's €235/262/298/331/367 for those aged over 25.

Eurailpass A 15-/21-day pass costs US$698/895 while a one-/two-/three-month pass is US$1109/1569/1935. For those aged over 26; valid for unlimited 1st-class travel.

Eurailpass – Saver A 15-/21-day pass costs US$585/759 and a one-/two-/three-month pass is US$939/1329/1649. It's for two to five people travelling together; valid for unlimited 1st-class travel.

Eurailpass Youth A 10-/15-day pass is US$465/611. It's for those aged under 26 and is valid for 10 or 15 days' 2nd-class travel within a two-month period.

INTER RAIL

Inter Rail (www.interrailnet.com) passes are valid for unlimited 2nd-class travel in 30 countries in Europe and North Africa (including Denmark, Finland, Norway and Sweden), and are available to European residents of at least six months' standing – passport identification is required. Terms and conditions vary slightly from country to country, but in the country of origin there's only a discount of around 50% on normal fares, rather than free travel.

Prices range from €159/249 for adult/youth for passes permitting five days' travel within 10 days allowing 22 days up to €399/599 for youth/adult one month's travel.

Health

CONTENTS

Travel in Scandinavia presents very few health problems. The standard of health care is extremely high and English is widely spoken by doctors and medical clinic staff, tap water is safe to drink, the level of hygiene is high and there are no endemic diseases. The main health issues to be aware of are extreme climates (with the potential for such nasties like hypothermia, frostbite or viral infections such as influenza) and biting insects such as mosquitoes, though they're more of an annoyance than a real health risk.

BEFORE YOU GO

Prevention is the key to staying healthy while abroad. A little time spent planning before departure, particularly if you have pre-existing illnesses, will save trouble later: see your dentist before a long trip; carry a spare pair of contact lenses and glasses, and take your optical prescription with you. Bring your medications in their original, clearly labelled containers. A signed and dated letter from your physician describing your medical conditions and necessary medications, including their generic names, is also a good idea.

Specific travel vaccinations are not required for visitors to Scandinavia but you should be up to date with all normal childhood vaccinations.

INSURANCE

Citizens of the European Economic Area (EEA) are covered for emergency medical treatment in other EEA countries (including Denmark, Finland, Iceland, Norway and Sweden) on presentation of a European Health Insurance Card (EHIC), which replaced the old E111 form. Enquire about EHICs at your health centre, travel agency or (in some countries) post office well in advance of travel. Citizens from other countries should find out if there is a reciprocal arrangement for free medical care between their country and the country visited. Health insurance is still recommended, especially if you intend to go hiking or skiing. Make sure you get a policy that covers you for the worst possible scenario, such as an accident requiring an emergency flight home. Find out in advance if your insurance plan will make payments directly to providers or reimburse you later for overseas health expenditures.

ONLINE RESOURCES

The WHO's publication *International Travel and Health* is revised annually and is available online at www.who.int/ith/. Other useful websites include www.mdtravelhealth.com (travel-health recommendations for every country; updated daily), and www.mariestopes.org.uk (information on women's health and contraception).

FURTHER READING

Health Advice for Travellers (called the 'T7.1' leaflet) is an annually updated leaflet by the Department of Health in the UK that's available free from post offices. It contains some general information, legally required and recommended vaccines for different countries, reciprocal health agreements and information on how to apply for an EHIC. Other recommended references include *Traveller's Health* by Dr Richard Dawood and *The Traveller's Good Health Guide* by Ted Lankester.

IN TRANSIT

DEEP VEIN THROMBOSIS (DVT)

Blood clots may form in the legs during plane flights, chiefly because of prolonged immobility. The longer the flight, the greater the risk. The chief symptom of DVT is swelling or pain in the foot, ankle or calf, usually but not always on just one side. When a blood clot travels to the lungs, it may cause chest pain and breathing difficulties. Travellers with any of these symptoms should immediately seek medical attention.

To prevent the development of DVT on long flights you should walk about the cabin, contract the leg muscles while sitting, drink plenty of fluids and avoid alcohol and tobacco.

JET LAG & MOTION SICKNESS

To avoid jet lag (common when crossing more than five time zones) try drinking plenty of nonalcoholic fluids and eating light meals. Upon arrival, get exposure to natural sunlight and readjust your schedule (for meals, sleep and so on) as soon as possible.

Antihistamines such as dimenhydrinate (Dramamine) and meclizine (Antivert, Bonine) are usually the first choice for treating motion sickness. A herbal alternative is ginger.

IN SCANDINAVIA

AVAILABILITY & COST OF HEALTHCARE

Good healthcare is readily available and for minor self-limiting illnesses pharmacists can give valuable advice and sell over-the-counter medication. Major cities in Scandinavia have a 24-hour pharmacy. The staff can advise when more specialised help is required and point you in the right direction to find it. The standard of dental care is good, but it is sensible to have a dental check-up before a long trip.

TRAVELLER'S DIARRHOEA

Tap water and food is generally safe throughout Scandinavia, but a change in diet can sometimes cause diarrhoea.

If you develop diarrhoea, drink plenty of fluids, preferably an oral rehydration solution such as Dioralyte. A few loose stools don't require treatment, but if you have more than four or five stools a day you should start taking an antibiotic (usually a quinolone drug) and an antidiarrhoeal agent (such as loperamide).

ENVIRONMENTAL HAZARDS
Hypothermia

Proper preparation will reduce the risks of getting hypothermia. Even on a hot day in the mountains, the weather can change rapidly. Hikers should carry waterproof clothing, wear warm layers and inform others of the route taken.

Acute hypothermia follows a sudden drop of temperature over a short time. Chronic hypothermia is caused by a gradual loss of temperature over hours.

Hypothermia starts with shivering, loss of judgment and clumsiness. Unless rewarming occurs, the sufferer deteriorates into apathy, confusion and coma. Prevent further heat loss by providing shelter, warm dry clothing, hot sweet drinks and shared body warmth.

Frostbite is caused by freezing and subsequent damage to bodily extremities. It is dependent on wind chill, temperature and length of exposure. Frostbite starts as frostnip (white numb areas of skin) from which complete recovery is expected with rewarming. As frostbite develops, the skin blisters and then becomes black. The loss of damaged tissue eventually occurs. Adequate clothing, staying dry, keeping well hydrated and ensuring adequate calorie intake is the best way to prevent frostbite. Treatment involves rapid rewarming. Avoid refreezing and rubbing the affected areas.

Insect Bites & Stings

Mosquitoes are found in most parts of Scandinavia, particularly in Lapland during summer and around lake areas such as eastern Finland. Malaria is not a problem but irritation and infected bites are possible. Use a DEET-based insect repellent.

In northern Iceland, midges and blackflies can be a real annoyance in summer.

HEALTH

Bees and wasps only cause real problems to those with a severe allergy (anaphylaxis). If you have a severe allergy to bee or wasp stings, carry an 'epipen' or similar adrenalin injection.

Bed bugs lead to very itchy lumpy bites, but Scandinavian hotels and hostels are generally immaculate. Spraying the mattress with crawling-insect killer after changing bedding will get rid of them.

Scabies are tiny parasitic mites that live in the skin, particularly between the fingers. They cause an intensely itchy rash. Scabies are easily treated with lotion from a pharmacy.

WOMEN'S HEALTH

Emotional stress, exhaustion and travelling through different time zones can all contribute to an upset in the menstrual pattern. If using oral contraceptives, remember some antibiotics, diarrhoea and vomiting can stop the pill from working and lead to the risk of pregnancy. Tampons and similar products are available in Scandinavia.

Travelling during pregnancy is usually possible but always seek a medical check-up before planning your trip. The most risky times for travel are during the first 12 weeks of pregnancy and after 30 weeks.

Language

CONTENTS

This language guide contains pronunciation guidelines and basic vocabulary to help you during your travels in Scandinavian Europe. For a more detailed guide to the languages in this region, pick up a copy of Lonely Planet's *Scandinavian* phrasebook.

DANISH

While the majority of Danes speak English, any effort to learn a few basic words and phrases will be greatly appreciated by the people you meet.

Danish has a polite form of address, using the personal pronouns *De* and *Dem*. The Danish translations in this book mostly use the informal pronouns *du* and *dig*, except where it's appropriate and/or wise to use the polite form. In general, you should use the polite form when speaking to senior citizens and officials, and the informal rest of the time.

Nouns in Danish have two genders: masculine and neuter. In the singular, the definite article ('the' in English) is suffixed to the noun: *-en* (masculine) and *-et* (neuter). In the plural *-ne* is used for the indefinite ('some' in English) and *-ene* for the definite, regardless of gender.

PRONUNCIATION

You may find Danish pronunciation difficult. Consonants are drawled, swallowed and even omitted completely, creating, in conjunction with vowels, the peculiarity of the glottal stop or *stød*. Its sound is rather as a Cockney would say the 'tt' in 'bottle'. Stress is usually placed on the first syllable or on the first letter of the word. In general though, the best advice is to listen and learn. Good luck!

Vowels

a	as in 'father'
a, æ	as in 'act'
å, o &	
u(n)	a long rounded 'a' as in 'walk'
e(g)	as the sound of 'eye'
e, i	as the 'e' in 'bet'
i	as the 'e' in 'theme'
ø	as the 'er' in 'fern'
o, u	as the 'oo' in 'cool'
o	as in 'pot'
o(v)	as the 'ou' in 'out'
o(r)	as the 'or' in for' with less emphasis on the 'r'
u	as in 'pull'
y	say 'ee' while pursing your lips

Consonants

sj	as in 'ship'
ch	a sharper sound than the 'ch' in 'cheque'
c	as in 'cell'
(o)d	a flat 'dh' sound, like the 'th' in 'these'
ng	as in 'sing'
g	a hard 'g' as in 'get', if followed by a vowel
h	as in 'horse'
k	as the 'c' in 'cat'
r	a rolling 'r' abruptly cut short
w	similar to the 'wh' in 'what'
j	as the 'y' in 'yet'

ACCOMMODATION

hotel	*hotel*
guesthouse	*gæstgiveri*
hostel	*vandrerhjem*
camping ground	*campingplads*

Do you have any rooms available?	*Har I ledige værelser?*
How much is it per night/ per person?	*Hvor meget koster det per nat/ per person?*
Does it include breakfast?	*Er morgenmad inkluderet?*

I'd like ...   *Jeg ønsker ...*
  a single room   *et enkeltværelse*
  a double room   *et dobbeltværelse*

one day/two days   *en nat/to nætter*

CONVERSATION & ESSENTIALS

Hello.	*Hallo/Hej.* (informal)
Goodbye.	*Farvel.*
Yes.	*Ja.*
No.	*Nej.*
Please.	*Må jeg bede/Værsgo.*
Thank you.	*Tak.*
That's fine/You're welcome.	*Det er i orden/Selv tak*
Excuse me/Sorry.	*Undskyld.*
Do you speak English?	*Taler De engelsk?*
How much is it?	*Hvor meget koster det?*
What's your name?	*Hvad hedder du?*
My name is ...	*Mit navn er ...*

EMERGENCIES – DANISH

Help!	*Hjælp!*
Call a doctor!	*Ring efter en læge!*
Call the police!	*Ring efter politiet!*
Go away!	*Forsvind!*
I'm lost.	*Jeg har gået vild.*

SHOPPING & SERVICES

a bank	*en bank*
a chemist/pharmacy	*et apotek*
the ... embassy	*den ... ambassade*
my hotel	*mit hotel*
the market	*markedet*
a newsagent	*en aviskiosk*
the post office	*postkontoret*
the tourist office	*turistinformationen*

What time does it open/close?   *Hvornår åbner/lukker det?*

TIME, DAYS & NUMBERS

What time is it?	*Hvad er klokken?*
today	*i dag*
tomorrow	*i morgen*
morning	*morgenen*
afternoon	*eftermiddagen*
Monday	*mandag*
Tuesday	*tirsdag*
Wednesday	*onsdag*
Thursday	*torsdag*
Friday	*fredag*
Saturday	*lørdag*
Sunday	*søndag*

SIGNS – DANISH

Indgang	Entrance
Udgang	Exit
Åben	Open
Lukket	Closed
Forbudt	Prohibited
Information	Information
Politistation	Police Station
Toiletter	Toilets
Herrer	Men
Damer	Women

0	*nul*
1	*en*
2	*to*
3	*tre*
4	*fire*
5	*fem*
6	*seks*
7	*syv*
8	*otte*
9	*ni*
10	*ti*
100	*hundrede*
1000	*tusind*

TRANSPORT

What time does ... leave/arrive?   *Hvornår går/ ankommer ...?*
  the boat   *båden*
  the bus (city)   *bussen*
  the bus (intercity) *rutebilen*
  the tram   *sporvognen*
  the train   *toget*

Where can I hire a car/bicycle?   *Hvor kan jeg leje en bil/cykel?*

I'd like ...   *Jeg vil gerne have ...*
  a one-way ticket   *en enkeltbillet*
  a return ticket   *en tur-retur billet*

1st class	*første klasse*
2nd class	*anden klasse*
left luggage office	*reisegodsoppbevar ingen*
timetable	*køreplan*
bus stop	*bus holdeplads*
tram stop	*sporvogn holdeplads*
train station	*jernbanestation (banegård)*

LANGUAGE

Directions

Where is ...?	*Hvor er ...?*
Go straight ahead.	*Gå ligefrem.*
Turn left/right.	*Drej til venstre/højre.*
near/far	*nær/fjern*

FAROESE

Faroese is a Germanic language derived from old Norse, closely related to Icelandic and some Norwegian and Swedish dialects. In 1890, a standard written version of Faroese, *Føroyskt*, was made official and given equal status with Danish in public and government affairs.

All Faroese speak Danish, can handle Norwegian and Swedish, and some speak English. Nearly every Faroese learns Danish at school (and many also learn English and German), but foreign languages have had little impact on everyday life.

PRONUNCIATION

In most cases, Faroese words are stressed on the first syllable. Grammar is very similar to that of Icelandic, but pronunciation is quite different due to a mix of Icelandic, Danish, and even Gaelic influences, eg the name of Eiði village is inexplicably pronounced 'oy-yeh'; the nearby village of Gjógv is referred to as 'Jagv'; the capital, Tórshavn, gets the more or less Danish pronunciation, 'torsh-hown'.

Vowels & Diphthongs

a, æ	short, as the 'u' in 'cut'; long, as the 'ai' in 'hair'
á	short, as the 'o' in 'hot'; long, as the 'oi' in French moi
e	as in 'get'
i, y	short, as the 'i' in 'hit'; long, as the 'i' in 'marine'
í, ý	as the 'ui' in Spanish muy
o	as in 'hot'
ó	short, as the 'a' in 'ago'; long, as the 'o' in 'note'
ø	as the 'a' in 'ago'
u	as in 'pull'
ú	short, as a sharp 'u' – purse your lips and say 'ee'; long, as the 'ou' in 'you'
ei	as the 'i' in 'dive'
ey	short, as the 'e' in 'get'; long, as the 'ay' in 'day'
oy	as the 'oy' in 'boy'

Consonants

ð	silent in final position, otherwise taking on the value of surrounding vowels
ðr	as the 'gr' in 'grab'
dj	as the 'j' in 'jaw'
ft	as the 'tt' in 'bitter'
g	silent in final position, otherwise taking on the value of surrounding vowels
ggj	as the 'j' in 'jaw'
hv	as 'kv'
hj	as the 'y' in 'yellow'
ll	as the 'dl' in 'saddle'

ACCOMMODATION

hotel	*hotell*
guesthouse	*gistingarhús*
youth hostel	*vallarheim*
campground	*tjáldplass*

Do you have any rooms available?	*Eru nøkur leys kømur?*
How much is it (per person/per night)?	*Hvussu nógv kostar tað (fyri hvønn/eina natt)?*
Does it include breakfast?	*Er morgunmatur innifalinn?*

I'd like (a) ...	*Eg vil fegin hava ...*
single room	*eitt einkultkamar*
double room	*eitt dupultkamar*

CONVERSATION & ESSENTIALS

Hello.	*Hey/Halló/Góðan dag.*
Goodbye.	*Farvæl.*
Yes.	*Ja.*
No.	*Nei.*
Please.	*Gerið so væl.*
Thank you.	*Takk fyri.*
Excuse me/Sorry.	*Orsaka.*
Do you speak English?	*Tosar tú eingilskt?*
How much is it?	*Hvussu nógv kostar tað?*
What's your name?	*Hvussu eita tygum?*
My name is ...	*Eg eiti ...*

SHOPPING & SERVICES

bank	*banka*
chemist	*apotekið*
the ... embassy	*... ambassaduni*
market	*handilsgøtuni*
the post office	*posthúsinum*
a public toilet	*almennum vesi*
the tourist office	*ferðaskrivstovuni/ turistkontórinum*

EMERGENCIES – FAROESE

Help!	Hjálp!
Call a doctor!	Ringið eftir lækna!
Call the police!	Ringið eftir løgregluni!
Go away!	Far burtur!
I'm lost.	Eg eri vilst/vilstur. (m/f)

TIME, DAYS & NUMBERS

What time is it?	Hvat er klokkan?
today	í dag
tomorrow	í morgin
morning	morgun
afternoon	seinnapartur
night	nátt

Monday	mánadagur
Tuesday	týsdagur
Wednesday	mikudagur
Thursday	hósdagur
Friday	fríggjadagur
Saturday	leygardagur
Sunday	sunnudagur

1	eitt
2	tvey
3	trý
4	fíra
5	fimm
6	seks
7	sjey
8	átta
9	níggju
10	tíggju
20	tjúgu
100	hundrað
1000	túsund

TRANSPORT

boat	bátur
bus	bussur
map	kort
road	vegur
street	gøta
village	bygd

I'd like a ...	Kundi eg fingið ...
one-way ticket	einvegis ferðaseðil
return ticket	ferðaseðil aftur og fram

SIGNS – FAROESE

Atgongd	Entrance
Útgongd	Exit
Neyðútgongd	Emergency Exit
Bannað	Prohibited
Upplýsingar	Information
Løgregla	Police

FINNISH

Finnish is a Uralic language spoken by just six million people, the vast majority of whom live in Scandinavia and in Russian Karelia. The most widely spoken of the Finno-Ugric family is Hungarian, but its similarities with Finnish are few. Suomi refers to both the Finnish-speaking part Finland and its language.

Staff at hotels, hostels and tourist offices generally speak fluent English. Bus drivers or restaurant and shop staff outside the cities may not, but they'll always fetch a colleague or bystander who does. You can certainly get by with English in Finland, but don't assume that everyone speaks it.

Swedish is spoken on Åland, as well as on the west ('Swedish') coast and around Helsinki and Turku, and all Finns learn Swedish at school.

PRONUNCIATION

Finnish pronunciation is more or less consistent – there is a one to one relationship between letters and sounds. There are nine vowels: **a**, **e**, **i**, **o**, **u**, **y**, **ä**, **å** and **ö** (the **å** has been adopted from the Norwegian and Swedish alphabets). The final letters of the alphabet are **å**, **ä** and **ö** (important to know when looking for something in a telephone directory).

Vowels

y	as the 'u' in 'pull' but with the lips stretched back (like the German 'ü')
å	as the 'oo' in 'poor'
ä	as the 'a' in 'act'
ö	as the 'a' in 'ago'

Consonants

z	pronounced (and sometimes written) as 'ts'
v/w	as the 'v' in 'vain'

LANGUAGE

h	a weak sound, except at the end of a syllable, when it is almost as strong as 'ch' in German *ich*
j	as the 'y' in 'yellow'
r	a rolled 'r'

Double consonants like **kk** in *viikko* or **mm** in *summa* are held longer.

ACCOMMODATION

hotel	*hotelli*
guesthouse	*matkustajakoti*
youth hostel	*retkeilymaja*
camping ground	*leirintäalue*
Do you have any rooms available?	*Onko teillä vapaata huonetta?*
How much is it per night/per person?	*Paljonko se on yöltä/hengeltä?*
Does it include breakfast?	*Kuuluko aamiainen hintaan?*
I'd like ...	*Haluaisin ...*
a single room	*yhden hengen huoneen*
a double room	*kahden hengen huoneen*
one day	*yhden päivän*
two days	*kaksi päivää*

CONVERSATION & ESSENTIALS

Hello.	*Hei/Terve.*
Moi. (informal)	
Goodbye.	*Näkemiin.*
Moi. (informal)	
Yes.	*Kyllä/Joo.*
No.	*Ei.* (pronounced 'ay')
Please.	*Kiitos.*
Thank you.	*Kiitos.*
That's fine/You're welcome.	*Ole hyvä.*
	Eipä kestä. (informal)
Excuse me/Sorry.	*Anteeksi.*
Do you speak English?	*Puhutko englantia?*
How much is it?	*Paljonko se makasaa?*
What's your name?	*Mikä teidän nimenne on?*
My name is ...	*Minun nimeni on ...*

SHOPPING & SERVICES

bank	*pankkia*
chemist/pharmacy	*apteekki*
... embassy	*...-n suurlähetystöä*
market	*toria*
newsagent	*lehtikioski*
post office	*postia*
stationer	*paperikauppa*

tourist office	*matkailutoimistoa/ matkailutoimisto*
What time does it open/close?	*Milloin se aukeaan/ sul jetaan?*

EMERGENCIES – FINNISH

Help!	*Apua!*
Call a doctor!	*Kutsukaa lääkäri!*
Call the police!	*Soittakaa poliisi!*
Go away!	*Mene pois! (Häivy!)*
I'm lost.	*Minä olen eksynyt.*

TIME, DAYS & NUMBERS

What time is it?	*Paljonko kello on?*
today	*tänään*
tomorrow	*huomenna*
morning	*aamulla*
afternoon	*iltapäivällä*
night	*yö*
Monday	*maanantai*
Tuesday	*tiistai*
Wednesday	*keskiviikko*
Thursday	*torstai*
Friday	*perjantai*
Saturday	*lauantai*
Sunday	*sunnuntai*
0	*nolla*
1	*yksi*
2	*kaksi*
3	*kolme*
4	*neljä*
5	*viisi*
6	*kuusi*
7	*seitsemän*
8	*kahdeksan*
9	*yhdeksän*
10	*kymmenen*
100	*sata*
1000	*tuhat*

TRANSPORT

What time does ... leave/arrive?	*Mihin aikaan ... lähtee/saapuu?*
the boat	*laiva*
the bus (city/intercity)	*bussi/linja-auto*
the tram	*raitiovaunu/raitikka*
the train	*juna*
I'd like a one way/ return ticket.	*Saanko menolipun/ menopaluulipun.*

LANGUAGE

SIGNS – FINNISH	
Sisään	Entrance
Ulos	Exit
Avoinna	Open
Suljettu	Closed
Kielletty	Prohibited
Opastus	Information
Poliisiasema	Police Station
WC	Toilets
Miehet	Men
Naiset	Women

Where can I hire a car?	*Mistä mina voisin vuokrata auton?*
Where can I hire a bicycle?	*Mistä mina voin vuokrata polkupyörän?*
1st class	*ensimmäinen luokka*
2nd class	*toinen luokka*
left luggage	*säilytys*
timetable	*aikataulu*
bus/tram stop	*pysäkki*
train station	*rautatieasema*
ferry terminal	*satamaterminaali*

Directions
Where is ...?	*Missä on ...?*
Go straight ahead.	*Kulje suoraan.*
Turn left.	*Käänny vasempaan.*
Turn right.	*Käänny oikeaan.*
near/far	*lähellä/kaukana*

ICELANDIC

Icelandic belongs to the Germanic language family that includes German, Dutch and all the Nordic languages except Finnish. Its closest 'living relative' is Faroese. Both Icelandic and Faroese are derived from Old Norse and they've changed little since the time of the Vikings.

Icelandic grammar is very complicated; the suffixes which are added to nouns and place names to indicate case may render a place name quite unrecognisable. This can lead to a great deal of confusion, especially when you're trying to read bus timetables and find names of towns spelt several different ways. For example, the sign that welcomes visitors to the town of Höfn reads *Velkomin til Hafnar. Hafnar* is the dative of Höfn.

Fortunately, it's not essential for foreigners to speak Icelandic. The second language of most young people is English, then Danish (and therefore Swedish and Norwegian to some degree) and German. Some people also learn French, Italian or Spanish. Other Icelanders will normally know enough English and German to exchange pleasantries.

PRONUNCIATION
Stress generally falls on the first syllable of a word. Double consonants are given a long pronunciation.

Vowels & Diphthongs
a	long, as in 'father' or short, as in 'at'
á	as the 'ou' in 'out'
au	as the word 'furry' without 'f' or 'rr'
e	long, as in 'fear' or short, as in 'bet'
é	as the 'y' in 'yet'
ei, ey	as the 'ay' in 'day'
i, y	as the 'i' in 'hit'
í, ý	as the 'i' in 'marine'
o	as in 'pot'
ó	as the word 'owe'
u	a bit like the 'u' in 'purr'
ú	as the 'o' in 'moon', or as the 'o' in 'woman'
ö	as the 'er' in 'fern', but without a trace of 'r'
æ	as the word 'eye'

Consonants
ð	as the 'th' in 'lather'
f	as in 'far'. When between vowels or at the end of a word it's pronounced as 'v'. When followed by **l** or **n** it's pronounced as 'b'.
g	as in 'go'. When between vowels or before **r** or **ð** it has a guttural sound as the 'ch' in Scottish loch.
h	as in 'he', except when followed by **v**, when it's pronounced as 'k'
j	as the 'y' in 'yellow'
l	as in 'let'; when doubled it's pronounced as 'dl'
n	as in 'no'; when doubled or word-final it's pronounced as 'dn' (unless **nn** forms part of the definite article *hinn*)
p	as in 'hip', except when followed by **s** or **t**, when it's pronounced as 'f'
r	always rolled
þ	as the 'th' in 'thin' or 'three'

LANGUAGE

ACCOMMODATION

hotel	hótel
guesthouse	gistiheimili
youth hostel	farfuglaheimili
camping ground	tjaldsvæði

Do you have any rooms available?	Eru herbergi laus?
How much is each night per person?	Hvað kostar nóttin fyrir manninn?
Does it include breakfast?	Er morgunmatur innifalinn?

I'd like ...	Gæti ég fengið ...
a single room	einstaklingsherbergi
a double room	tveggjamannaherbergi

one day	einn dag
two days	tvo daga

CONVERSATION & ESSENTIALS

Hello.	Halló.
Goodbye.	Bless.
Yes.	Já.
No.	Nei.
Please.	Gjörðu svo vel.
Thank you.	Takk fyrir.
That's fine.	Allt í lagi.
You're welcome.	Ekkert að þakka.
Excuse me/Sorry.	Afsakið.
Do you speak English?	Talar þú ensku?
How much is it?	Hvað kostar það?
What's your name?	Hvað heitir þú?
My name is ...	Ég heiti ...

SHOPPING & SERVICES

bank	banka
chemist/pharmacy	apótek
... embassy	... sendiráðinu
market	markaðnum
newsagent/stationer	blaðasala/bókabúð
post office	pósthúsinu
tourist office	upplýsingaþjónustu fyrir ferðafólk

TIME, DAYS & NUMBERS

What time is it?	Hvað er klukkan?
today	í dag
tomorrow	á morgun
in the morning	að morgni
in the afternoon	eftir hádegi

Monday	mánudagur
Tuesday	þriðjudagur
Wednesday	miðvikudagur
Thursday	fimmtudagur
Friday	föstudagur
Saturday	laugardagur
Sunday	sunnudagur

0	núll
1	einn
2	tveir
3	þrír
4	fjórir
5	fimm
6	sex
7	sjö
8	átta
9	níu
10	tíu
20	tuttugu
100	eitt hundrað
1000	eitt þúsund

TRANSPORT

What time does ... leave/arrive?	Hvenær fer/kemur ...?
the boat	báturinn
the bus (city)	vagninn
the tram	sporvagninn

I'd like ...	Gæti ég fengið ...
a one-way ticket	miða/aðra leiðina
a return ticket	miða/báðar leiðir
bus stop	biðstöð

ferry terminal	*ferjuhöfn*
timetable	*tímaðætlun*

I'd like to hire a car/bicycle.	*Ég vil leigia bíl/reiðhjól.*

Directions

Where is ...?	*Hvar er ...?*
Go straight ahead.	*Farðu beint af áfram.*
Turn left.	*Beygðu til vinstri.*
Turn right.	*Beygðu til hægri.*
near/far	*nálægt/langt í burtu*

NORWEGIAN

Norway has two official languages – Bokmål and Nynorsk – but the differences between the two languages are effectively very minor. In this language guide we have used Bokmål – it's by far the most common language travellers to Norway will encounter.

English is widely understood and spoken, especially in the urban areas and in most tourist destinations. In the rural areas (where Nynorsk predominates) you may come across people who speak very little English. If you show an effort to speak Norwegian, it will help a great deal in connecting with the Norwegians you meet.

PRONUNCIATION
Vowels & Diphthongs

a	long, as in 'father'; short, as in 'cut'
å	as the 'aw' in 'paw'
æ	as the 'a' in 'act'
e	long as in 'where'; short, as in 'bet'; when unstressed, as the 'a' in 'ago'
i	long, as the 'ee' in 'seethe'; short, as in 'hit'
o	long, as the 'oo' in 'cool'; short, as in 'pot'
ø	long, as the 'er' in 'fern'; short, as the 'a' in 'ago'
u, y	say 'ee' while pursing your lips
ai	as the word 'eye'
ei	as the 'ay' in 'day'
au	as the 'o' in 'note'
øy	as the 'oy' in 'toy'

Consonants & Semivowels

d	at the end of a word, or between two vowels, it's often silent

g	as the 'g' in 'get'; as the 'y' in 'yard' before **ei, i, j, øy, y**
h	as in 'her'; silent before **v** and **j**
j	as the 'y' in 'yard'
k	as in 'kin'; as the 'ch' in 'chin' before **ei, i, j, øy** and **y**
ng	as in 'sing'
r	a trilled 'r'. The combination rs is pronounced as the 'sh' in 'fish'.
s	as in 'so' (never as in 'treasure'); as the 'sh' in 'she' before **ei, i, j, øy** and **y**

ACCOMMODATION

hotel	*hotell*
guesthouse	*gjestgiveri/pensionat*
youth hostel	*vandrerhjem*
camping ground	*kamping/leirplass*

Do you have any rooms available?	*Har du ledige rom?*
How much is it per night/person?	*Hvor mye er det pr dag/person?*
Does it include breakfast?	*Inklusive frokosten?*

I'd like ...	*Jeg vil gjerne ha ...*
a single room	*et enkeltrom*
a double room	*et dobbeltrom*

one day	*en dag*
two days	*to dager*

EMERGENCIES – NORWEGIAN

Help!	*Hjelp!*
Call a doctor!	*Ring en lege!*
Call the police!	*Ring politiet!*
Go away!	*Forsvinn!*
I'm lost.	*Jeg har gått meg vill.*

CONVERSATION & ESSENTIALS

Hello.	*Goddag.*
Goodbye.	*Ha det.*
Yes.	*Ja.*
No.	*Nei.*
Please.	*Vær så snill.*
Thank you.	*Takk.*
You're welcome.	*Ingen årsak.*
Excuse me/Sorry.	*Unnskyld.*
Do you speak English?	*Snakker du engelsk?*
How much is it?	*Hvor mye koster det?*
What's your name?	*Hva heter du?*
My name is ...	*Jeg heter ...*

SHOPPING & SERVICES

bank	banken
chemist/pharmacy	apotek
... embassy	... ambassade
market	torget
newsagent	kiosk
post office	postkontoret
tourist office	turistinformasjon

TIME, DAYS & NUMBERS

What time is it?	Hva er klokka?
today	i dag
tomorrow	i morgen
in the morning	om formiddagen
in the afternoon	om ettermiddagen
Monday	mandag
Tuesday	tirsdag
Wednesday	onsdag
Thursday	torsdag
Friday	fredag
Saturday	lørdag
Sunday	søndag
0	null
1	en
2	to
3	tre
4	fire
5	fem
6	seks
7	sju
8	åtte
9	ni
10	ti
100	hundre
1000	tusen

TRANSPORT

What time does ... leave/arrive?	Når går/kommer ...?
the boat	båten
the (city) bus	(by)bussen
the intercity bus	linjebussen
the train	toget
the tram	trikken
I'd like ...	Jeg vil gjerne ha ...
a one-way ticket	enkeltbillett
a return ticket	tur-retur
1st class	første klasse
2nd class	annen klasse

left luggage	reisegods
timetable	ruteplan
bus stop	bussholdeplass
tram stop	trikkholdeplass
train station	jernbanestasjon
ferry terminal	ferjeleiet
Where can I rent a car/bicycle?	Hvor kan jeg leie en bil/sykkel?

SIGNS – NORWEGIAN

Inngang	Entrance
Utgang	Exit
Åpen	Open
Stengt	Closed
Forbudt	Prohibited
Opplysninger	Information
Politistasjon	Police Station
Toaletter	Toilets
Herrer	Men
Damer	Women

Directions

Where is ...?	Hvor er ...?
Go straight ahead.	Det er rett fram.
Turn left.	Ta til venstre.
Turn right.	Ta til høyre.
near/far	nær/langt

SWEDISH

Swedish belongs to the Nordic branch of the Germanic language family and is spoken throughout Sweden and in parts of Finland. Swedes, Danes and Norwegians can understand each others' languages. Most Swedes speak English as a second language.

Definite articles in Swedish ('the' in English) are determined by the ending of a noun: -en and -et for singular nouns and -na and -n for plural.

If you learn a few common phrases, your attempts will be greatly appreciated by Swedes, who aren't used to foreigners speaking Swedish.

Sami dialects, which fit into three main groups, belong to the Uralic language family, and are ancestrally related to Finnish, not Swedish.

EMERGENCIES – SWEDISH

Help!	Hjälp!
Call a doctor!	Ring efter en doktor!
Call the police!	Ring polisen!
Go away!	Försvinn!
I'm lost.	Jag har gått vilse.

PRONUNCIATION
Vowels
The vowels are pronounced as short sounds if there's a double consonant afterwards, otherwise they are long sounds. Sometimes Swedish **o** sounds like the **å**, and **e** similar to the **ä**. There are, however, not as many exceptions to the rules of pronunciation as there are in English.

a	long, as in 'father'; short, as the 'u' in 'cut'
o, u	long, as the 'oo' in 'cool'; short, as in 'pot'
i	long, as the 'ee' in 'seethe'; short, as in 'pit'
e	long, as the 'ea' in 'fear'; short, as in 'bet'
å	long, as the word 'awe'; short as the 'o' in 'pot'
ä	as the 'a' in 'act'
ö	as the 'er' in 'fern', but without the 'r' sound
y	try saying 'ee' while pursing your lips

Consonants
The consonants are pronounced almost the same as in English. The following letter combinations and sounds are specific to Swedish:

c	as the 's' in 'sit'
ck	as a double 'k'; shortens the preceding vowel
tj/rs	as the 'sh' in 'ship'
sj/ch	similar to the 'ch' in Scottish loch
g	as in 'get'; sometimes as the 'y' in 'yet'
lj	as the 'y' in 'yet'

ACCOMMODATION
hotel	hotell
guesthouse	gästhus
youth hostel	vandrarhem
camping ground	campingplats

Do you have any rooms available?	Finns det några lediga rum?
Does it include breakfast?	Inkluderas frukost?
How much is it per night/person?	Hur mycket kostar det per natt/person?
I'd like ...	Jag skulle vilja ha ...
a single room	ett enkelrum
a double room	ett dubbelrum
for one/two nights	i en natt/två nätter

CONVERSATION & ESSENTIALS
Hello.	Hej.
Goodbye.	Adjö/Hej då.
Yes.	Ja.
No.	Nej.
Please.	Snälla/Vänligen.
Thank you.	Tack.
You're welcome.	Det är bra/Varsågod.
Excuse me/Sorry.	Ursäkta mig/Förlåt.
Do you speak English?	Talar dũ engelska?
How much is it?	Hur mycket kostar den?
What's your name?	Vad heter du?
My name is ...	Jag heter ...

SHOPPING & SERVICES
bank	bank
chemist/pharmacy	apotek
... embassy	... ambassaden
market	marknaden
newsagent/stationer	nyhetsbyrå/pappers handel
post office	postkontoret
a public telephone	en offentlig telefon
tourist office	turistinformation
What time does it open/close?	När öppnar/stänger de?

TIME, DAYS & NUMBERS
What time is it?	Vad är klockan?
today	idag
tomorrow	imorgon
morning	morgonen
afternoon	efter middagen
Monday	måndag
Tuesday	tisdag
Wednesday	onsdag
Thursday	torsdag
Friday	fredag
Saturday	lördag
Sunday	söndag

LANGUAGE

0	noll
1	ett
2	två
3	tre
4	fyra
5	fem
6	sex
7	sju
8	åtta
9	nio
10	tio
100	ett hundra
1000	ett tusen

TRANSPORT

What time does ... leave/arrive?	När avgår/kommer ...?
the boat	båten
the city bus	stadsbussen
the intercity bus	landsortsbussen
the train	tåget
the tram	spårvagnen

I'd like ...	Jag skulle vilja ha ...
a one-way ticket	en enkelbiljett
a return ticket	en returbiljett
1st class	första klass
2nd class	andra klass

left luggage	effektförvaring
timetable	tidtabell
bus stop	busshållplats
train station	tågstation

| Where can I hire a car/bicycle? | Var kan jag hyra en bil/cykel? |

SIGNS – SWEDISH

Ingång	Entrance
Utgång	Exit
Öppet	Open
Stängt	Closed
Förbjudet	Prohibited
Information	Information
Polisstation	Police Station
Toalett	Toilets
Herrar	Men
Damer	Women

Directions

Where is ...?	Var är ...?
Go straight ahead.	Gå rakt fram.
Turn left.	Sväng till vänster.
Turn right.	Sväng till höger.
near/far	nära/långt

Scandinavian

Also available from Lonely Planet:
Scandinavian phrasebook

LANGUAGE

The Authors

ANDREW STONE
Coordinating author; Denmark

Andrew has been a regular visitor to Scandinavia, and Denmark in particular, since the mid-1990s as a traveller and journalist. He has written for previous editions of this title as well as editions of Lonely Planet's *Denmark*.

TOM MASTERS
Faroe Islands

Tom has long been a fan of the far north, travelling widely in Arctic Russia, Greenland and Norway. This assignment to the Faroes in mid-summer was one of the most enjoyable Lonely Planet jobs he's ever taken on, and it was refreshing to find out just how spectacular and foreign this group of islands a short distance north of his native Britain really were, whether from the window seat of an Atlantic Airways helicopter or on a long hike across the spectacular cliffscapes of Mykines. Tom lives in London and can be found at www.mastersmafia.com.

BECKY OHLSEN
Sweden

Becky grew up with a thick book of Swedish fairy tales illustrated by John Bauer, so the deep, black forests of Norrland hold particular fascination. Hiking through them, she's alert for tomtes and trolls (which, to the untrained eye, look just like big rocks). Though raised in Colorado, Becky has been an explorer of Sweden since childhood, while visiting her grandparents in Stockholm and her great-aunt in Härnösand. She loves the extremes of light up north, its round-the-clock summer glare and near-total absence in winter. She loves herring and gravlax, Swedish potatoes and aquavit. But mostly she loves getting lost in those forests, among the trolls and tomtes.

LONELY PLANET AUTHORS

Why is our travel information the best in the world? It's simple: our authors are passionate, dedicated travellers. They don't take freebies in exchange for positive coverage so you can be sure the advice you're given is impartial. They travel widely to all the popular spots, and off the beaten track. They don't research using just the internet or phone. They discover new places not included in any other guidebook. They personally visit thousands of hotels, restaurants, palaces, trails, galleries, temples and more. They speak with dozens of locals every day to make sure you get the kind of insider knowledge only a local could tell you. They take pride in getting all the details right, and in telling it how it is. Think you can do it? Find out how at **lonelyplanet.com**.

FRAN PARNELL
Iceland

Fran's passion for the country was born while studying for a masters degree in Anglo-Saxon, Norse and Celtic, and has just kept on growing like a monstrous cuckoo baby. Choosing a favourite place is nigh-on impossible, although she has a particular love of isolation, islands and seacliffs, putting the Westfjords, Grímsey and the Vestmannaeyjar high on the list. On this research trip, she went wild for outdoor activities, and was lucky enough to fit in scuba diving, white-water rafting, horse riding, glacier walking, hiking and kayaking – all of which she heartily recommends. Fran has also worked on Lonely Planet's guides to *Sweden*, *Iceland* and *Reykjavík*.

JOHN SPELMAN
Norway

John frequently travels to Norway to be overwhelmed by the world's most stunning landscape. He's embarked upon Arctic Circle dogsled rides, countless trips amid the Western Fjords and has licked several glaciers. Otherwise, find him in Oslo slowly wandering from cafe to cafe. When Lonely Planet isn't footing the bill, John is a PhD student researching architectural and urban histories, some of them Norwegian. He currently lives in New England. This is the sixth time he has covered Norway for a Lonely Planet title.

ANDY SYMINGTON
Finland

Andy first visited Finland many years ago more or less by accident, and walking on frozen lakes with the midday sun low in the sky made a quick and deep impression on him, even as fingers froze in the -30°C temperatures. Since then they can't keep him away, fuelled as he is by a love of huskies, saunas, Finnish mustard, moody Suomi rock and metal, but above all of Finnish people and their beautiful country.

CONTRIBUTING AUTHORS

Carolyn Bain Melbourne-based Carolyn has investigated great pockets of Europe in the name of work, including Sweden, Denmark and the Baltic countries. For this book she ventured north to Estonia, a country that combines the best of Eastern Europe and Scandinavia and delivers something heart-warmingly unique. Carolyn wrote the Tallinn chapter.

Simon Richmond An award-winning writer and photographer, Simon has been travelling to Russia for over 15 years. He's the co-author of the first and subsequent editions of Lonely Planet's *Trans-Siberian Railway* as well as *Russia*. He's also written about the country for several other publications including the Russian edition of *Newsweek*. Catch him online at www.simonrichmond.com. Simon wrote the St Petersburg chapter.

THE AUTHORS

Behind the Scenes

THIS BOOK

Scandinavian Europe is part of Lonely Planet's Europe series, which includes *Eastern Europe*, *Western Europe*, *Mediterranean Europe*, *Central Europe* and *Europe on a Shoestring*. Lonely Planet also publishes phrasebooks to these regions. This guidebook was commissioned in Lonely Planet's London office, and produced by the following:

Commissioning Editor Joanne Potts
Coordinating Editor Justin Flynn
Coordinating Cartographer Jolyon Philcox
Coordinating Layout Designer Margaret Jung
Managing Editor Sasha Baskett
Managing Cartographers Herman So, Mark Griffiths
Managing Layout Designer Indra Kilfoyle
Assisting Editors Victoria Harrison, Simon Williamson, Rowan McKinnon
Assisting Cartographers Valentina Kremenchutskaya, James Bird
Cover Designer Katy Murenu
Colour Designer Vicki Beale
Project Manager Glenn van der Knijff

Thanks to Helen Christinis, Jessica Crouch, Melanie Dankel, Sally Darmody, Aomi Hongo, Carol Jackson, Laura Jane, Lisa Knights, Wayne Murphy, Trent Paton, Sarah Sloane, Lyahna Spencer, Gerard Walker

THANKS
ANDREW STONE

I'm grateful to the many experts who spared their time and their expertise on Denmark's cultural quirks, environmental issues and everyday tips and fact checking. They include Erik Rimmer, Mads Flarup Christensen and Birgitta Capetillo. Thanks also to Linda Lerdorff, Anne Marie Barsøe and everyone at the Danish Tourist Board for all their help with my many questions. Once more I owe Denmark expert Michael Booth and Lissen, his wonderful wife, a great debt for all their help and hospitality on this trip and all the other ones before it.

TOM MASTERS

Big thanks to Mark Elliot for his hard work on the previous edition and advice to me for this one. Thanks also to Ella O'Donnell and Fiona Buchan at Lonely Planet for sending me to the Faroes. On the ground, thanks to Katrina of Kristianhús on Mykines, Niels at A Giljanes, Friðtor at Sandoyar Kunningarstova, Pøla at Tvøroyri's Tourist Office and Birna at rentacar.fo in Tórshavn.

BECKY OHLSEN

Thanks to Cristian Bonetto, who co-authored the Sweden guidebook with me; all the Scandinavian

---

THE LONELY PLANET STORY

Fresh from an epic journey across Europe, Asia and Australia in 1972, Tony and Maureen Wheeler sat at their kitchen table stapling together notes. The first Lonely Planet guidebook, *Across Asia on the Cheap,* was born.

Travellers snapped up the guides. Inspired by their success, the Wheelers began publishing books to Southeast Asia, India and beyond. Demand was prodigious, and the Wheelers expanded the business rapidly to keep up. Over the years, Lonely Planet extended its coverage to every country and into the virtual world via lonelyplanet.com and the Thorn Tree message board.

As Lonely Planet became a globally loved brand, Tony and Maureen received several offers for the company. But it wasn't until 2007 that they found a partner whom they trusted to remain true to the company's principles of travelling widely, treading lightly and giving sustainably. In October of that year, BBC Worldwide acquired a 75% share in the company, pledging to uphold Lonely Planet's commitment to independent travel, trustworthy advice and editorial independence.

Today, Lonely Planet has offices in Melbourne, London and Oakland, with over 500 staff members and 300 authors. Tony and Maureen are still actively involved with Lonely Planet. They're travelling more often than ever, and they're devoting their spare time to charitable projects. And the company is still driven by the philosophy of *Across Asia on the Cheap*: 'All you've got to do is decide to go and the hardest part is over. So go!'

Europe co-authors; LP commissioning editors Emma Gilmour, Fiona Buchan and Jo Potts; my frequent co-explorers Joel and Christina Ohlsen and Karl, Natalie and Clara Ohlsen; my would-be co-explorer RSE; Mormor Elisabeth Odeen, Moster Kristina Björholm and Captain Joe 'The Singing Sailor' Eriksson; Matt and Lindy in Tärnaby; Jannike Åhlund in Fårö; the awesome librarians in Rättvik; the commander of the paintball war in Härnösand who rescued us from certain discomfort; the bartender in Gävle who let me watch the MotoGP race on TV; and the cyclist who shared his breakfast at Björkvatten youth hostel.

FRAN PARNELL

Huge thanks to everyone who helped during research and writing of the Iceland chapter: all the tourist office staff, particularly Solrún at Húsavík and Surekha at Nonni Travel; to Kári Bjarnason at Heimaey Library; to Tobias at Dive.is for an unforgettable scuba-diving trip, and Hlynur Oddsson for being such good kayaking company and singing so nicely; to the wonderful Ella and Julia for their cheery hospitality; to Guðni and his brother for putting up with me after the Björk/Sígurrós gig!; and to Jón Trausti Sigurðarson at Grapevine for keeping me in the Reykjavík loop. Thanks too to other travellers for sharing their advice and enthusiasm (especially Dave Rayner and Marnix Koets; and Catherine Anderson and her mum for taking me horse-riding); and to all the LP readers who wrote in with tips and comments. And of course, praise and gratitude to the lovely Lonely Planet in-house crew: Mark Griffiths, Fi Buchan and Jo Potts. Last but not least, I'm so pleased my Mum and Dad finally made it to Iceland! Thanks for a super five days: and now you know why I love it so much xx.

JOHN SPELMAN

Thanks to Alv Gustavsen, Anja Lyngsmark and Therese Rustad for ceaseless hospitality and excellent guidance; to Solveig and Christian; to the depravity of M Gibson; to Jannicke Risjord, her friends and their observations; to Black Metal specialist Megan Knight; and to Ariel Acosta's friendship and generosity. Thanks also to my comrades at LP – Jo Potts, Andrew Stone, Becky Ohlsen and Mark Griffiths – you make my life more interesting and my manuscripts less humiliating.

ANDY SYMINGTON

Many thanks to George Dunford for joint research on this project and to Jo Potts, Fiona Buchan and Ella O'Donnell for running it from the LP end. Big thanks for proofreading and Finnish support go to Riika Åkerlind, and to my family for their encour-agement. Thanks to Jorma Hynninen for answering my questions; I'm also indebted to numerous helpful people that I met on the way, particularly in tourist offices, and owe thanks to many Finnish friends for kindnesses and hospitality.

OUR READERS

Many thanks to the travellers who used the last edition and wrote to us with helpful hints, useful advice and interesting anecdotes:

Wasyl Abrat, Bahman Ahmadbehbahani, Marije and Tijs Boks, Annett Borchardt, Erica Brennen, David Conway, Joy De Los Santos, Ida Doksaeter, Sue Dyet, Karin Ekman, Chris Feierabend, John Foulger, Ezra Johnson, Sanna Juopperi, Belinda Kendall-White, Michael Kleindienst, Victoria Machado, Ruth Mair, Mick Nishikawa, Taru Öster, Kristen Pace, Birgit Pearson, Cecilie Pedersen, Spencer Plaitin, Barbara Reinhartz, Erin Riches, Jasmin Riedi, Laurie Sanders, Johannes Schmid, Theo Schmitz, Kathrin Schnoeller, Ann Stoughton, Bill Stoughton, Alison Tuckett, Vincent Van Beusekom, Duncan Watson, Jesse Weil, Ralph Weinmann, Antonio Wong, Eva Zichova

ACKNOWLEDGMENTS

Many thanks to the following for the use of their content:

Globe on title page ©Mountain High Maps 1993 Digital Wisdom, Inc.

Internal photographs p302 (#1) Icelandic Photo Agency/Alamy; p302 (#2) Yadid Levy/Alamy; p307 (#4) Peter de Clercq/Alamy. All other images by

---

SEND US YOUR FEEDBACK

We love to hear from travellers – your comments keep us on our toes and help make our books better. Our well-travelled team reads every word on what you loved or loathed about this book. Although we cannot reply individually to postal submissions, we always guarantee that your feedback goes straight to the appropriate authors, in time for the next edition. Each person who sends us information is thanked in the next edition – and the most useful submissions are rewarded with a free book.

To send us your updates – and find out about Lonely Planet events, newsletters and travel news – visit our award-winning website: **lonelyplanet.com/contact.**

Note: we may edit, reproduce and incorporate your comments in Lonely Planet products such as guidebooks, websites and digital products, so let us know if you don't want your comments reproduced or your name acknowledged. For a copy of our privacy policy visit lonelyplanet.com/privacy.

Index